MATCHING MAJOR STAGES OF PRODUCT AND PROCESS LIFE CYCLES

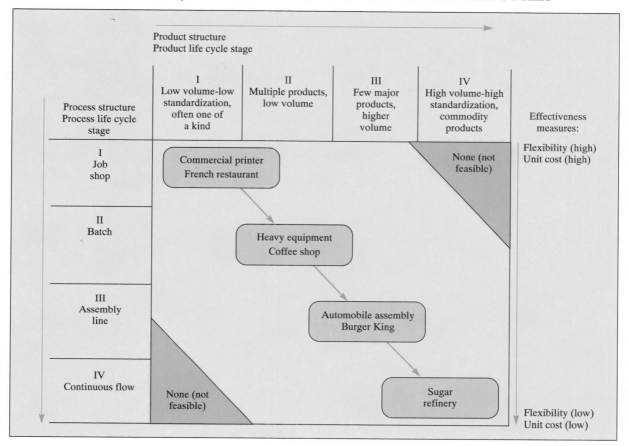

SERVICE SYSTEM DESIGN MATRIX

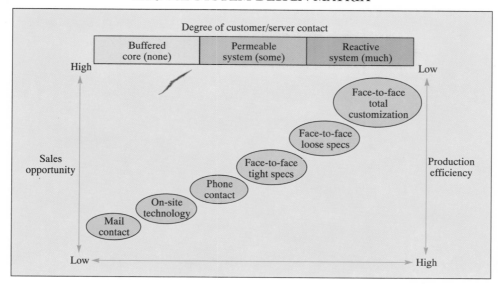

Production and Operations Management
Manufacturing and Services

Eighth Edition

Richard B. Chase
University of Southern California

Nicholas J. Aquilano
University of Arizona

F. Robert Jacobs
Indiana University

Boston   Burr Ridge, IL   Dubuque, IA   Madison, WI   New York   San Francisco   St. Louis
Bangkok   Bogotá   Caracas   Lisbon   London   Madrid
Mexico City   Milan   New Delhi   Seoul   Singapore   Sydney   Taipei   Toronto

Note to Instructors

First, thank you for using our book in the past and considering this new edition for the future. We are delighted to introduce our new coauthor to this edition, Bob Jacobs of Indiana University, who after a diligent search has proven to be a perfect collaborator on the text.

Operations management is a dynamic discipline, with new concepts appearing frequently. A critical priority is making this material available quickly. The challenge for a textbook is not only to capture these concepts but to anchor them to the existing body of knowledge in an understandable way. It goes without saying that the basics must be covered effectively as well.

We take pride in our reputation established in the previous seven editions as being the first textbook to introduce and make teachable the latest (and now standard) topics in the field.

We have continued to innovate in this edition. The major revisions to be found are:

- Virtually all of the chapters now have references to Internet Web sites corresponding to companies, commercial software vendors, and key professional organizations. These Web sites contain interesting and relevant information to augment the material in the book.
- Additional cases, classroom exercises, test questions, and updates are available on a Web site supported by the authors of the book. This Web site address is *http://www.pom.edu.*
- Many chapter updates have been made in the book including current examples in all of the chapters. Some of the most significant changes are the following:
  - Chapter 1: An interesting new Web-based exercise using the Purchasing Managers Index has been added.
  - Chapter 2: The operations strategy material has been updated to better cover Terry Hill's "order winners" and "qualifiers" paradigm.
  - Chapter 3: Project management has been moved earlier in the book. This allows adopters who cover the topics in the order presented in the book to cover this important topic earlier in the course. A new case titled "The Campus Wedding" has been added to the chapter.
  - Chapter 4: Product Design and Process Selection—Manufacturing has been updated extensively and now includes Geoffrey Boothroyd and Peter Dewhurst's design for manufacturing and assembly material. The coverage of production design has been expanded and now includes quality function deployment and concurrent engineering.
  - Chapter 6: Quality Management has been streamlined with a better focus on the Baldrige Quality Award and ISO 9000 registration. An interesting comparison of past and current Baldrige criteria has been added to the discussion questions. The Chapter 6 Supplement on Statistical Quality Control has been revised to better explain process capability and the capability index.

- Chapter 7: Strategic Capacity Management has been updated and now includes present value calculations in the decision tree analysis. The Supplement on Linear Programming includes examples using the Solver option in Microsoft Excel®.

- Chapter 11: The learning curves material has been moved to the Supplement. This allows this material to be either included or not, depending on the preferences of the instructor.

- Section Four: Now titled Supply Chain Management, this section has been organized as a comprehensive module covering this major topic. Chapter 12 is a new chapter that covers the basics of supplier management, outsourcing, and purchasing within the context of supply chain management.

- Chapter 14: The examples in Aggregate Planning now use the more conventional accounting format (dates in the columns) so students can easily see the similarity of these calculations to the MRP calculations. Spreadsheets are now available for the examples in this chapter and for the MRP examples in Chapter 16.

- Supplement to Chapter 16, SAP/R3: This supplement is new and includes an overview of this important new software product.

- Chapter 18: In the final section of the book, Operations Consulting is new. Since so many business students go to work for consulting firms we felt it was very important to give an overview of how consulting companies work and which OM tools they are likely to use on consulting projects. We are very excited about this chapter, which we believe is the first of its kind in any OM text.

In this edition of the book we have continued our emphasis on showing both a manufacturing and services perspective on all of the topics. In addition, we have stressed a global perspective and where appropriate shown how the concepts apply in a global context. A final emphasis of the book has been to show the importance of cross-functional integration of the topics. Special icons are used in the book to highlight services, global, and cross-functional material.

Opening vignettes set the stage for the material in each chapter. Most of these vignettes have been updated with current examples. We believe we have found some real grabbers that can be used as interesting discussion items. Also included within each chapter are operations "Breakthroughs" which provide examples or extensions of the concepts we are presenting.

The book includes 30 interesting cases (8 of which are new this edition), solved problems at the end of chapters, formula summaries, new and revised problems, and updated bibliographies. The four-color design and extensive use of color photos speak for themselves.

Because spreadsheets have become more important as a tool in operations management, we include a Student CD-ROM with each copy of the book that contains templates and data sets from problems and cases. A list of these files can be found on the back endpaper of the text, along with a description of other resources on the CD.

We have included in the Instructor's Edition annotations to help teach the course. Text and figures that are included in the PowerPoint Presentation are indicated by an icon. Titles of video segments from the Irwin Operations Management Video series are noted where they can enhance the text topic. Check answers are placed in the margin next to end-of-chapter problems. Disk icons next to problems indicate that the problem can be solved using Irwin/McGraw-Hill's software DECISION SUPPORT SYSTEMS FOR OPERATIONS MANAGEMENT AND MANAGEMENT SCIENCE by Lotfi & Pegels. The pages that follow provide more detail on pedagogical features in the book.

The support package for Production and Operations Management includes:

Student CD-ROM, prepared by the authors, contains Excel templates and data sets, PowerPoint slides, sample practice exams, Web links to text references, a video glossary, and industry applications such as *OPTIMA!, SURETRAK PROJECT MANAGER, EXPERT CHOICE PROFESSIONAL DECISION SUPPORT SOFTWARE,* and *TREEAGE DECISION ANALYSIS.*

Instructor's Solutions Manual, prepared by Ross Fink of Bradley University, includes answers to discussion questions and solutions to text problems with grids indicating which problems correspond to specific topics in the chapters.

Instructor's Resource Manual, prepared by the authors, contains sample course syllabi; ideas for innovative class sessions; some additional cases and classroom exercises; and teaching notes for all the cases.

Presentation CD-ROM, an interactive lecture aid, puts video clips, PowerPoint slides, photos, and print supplements at your fingertips. You can use this to customize your lecture notes and your visual presentation.

Test Bank, prepared by Joseph Moore of Indiana University, provides true/false, multiple-choice, and narrative problems for each chapter. It indicates whether questions are quantitative or nonquantitative. Along with the manual, a separate computerized testing package is available from the publisher that allows you to generate, add, and edit questions; save and reload tests; and select questions based on type or difficulty.

The Irwin Operations Management Video Series consists of 18 segments on four volumes covering quality, inventory, lean production, computer-integrated manufacturing, production processes, and services. They show students chapter concepts at work and how critical operations management is to organizations such as Motorola, Toyota, Hewlett-Packard, and Microsoft.

100 Four-Color Teaching Acetates contain exhibits from the text, as well as additional material not in the text that add variety to class lectures.

PowerPoint Presentation and Transparency Masters, prepared by William Youngdahl of Thunderbird School of International Business, give you lecture outlines plus graphic material from the text to complement your lectures. These can be customized to fit your classroom needs. Transparency masters of these slides are also provided in the PowerPoint Transparency Master supplement.

Study Guide, prepared by Marilyn Helms of the University of Tennessee at Chattanooga, provides students with a summary of each chapter and includes a terminology section that highlights key terms, along with solved and unsolved quantitative problems that parallel text problems.

Packages available with the text include:

HOM OPERATIONS MANAGEMENT SOFTWARE FOR WINDOWS by Moses, Seshadri, and Yakirevich offers powerful Windows-based programs for solving real world operating problems such as forecasting, process analysis, waiting line design and analysis, project management, MRP and inventory, and capacity planning. HOM imports and exports files to and from Excel®, and each module has a detailed step-by-step "how to solve" dialogue box for quick reference for beginning students.

PROSIM III FOR WINDOWS: A Production Management Simulation, 3/e, by Chu, Hottenstein and Greenlaw.

DECISION SUPPORT SYSTEMS FOR OPERATIONS MANAGEMENT AND MANAGEMENT SCIENCE, 3/e, by Lotfi & Pegels.

ESSENTIALS OF BUSINESS: A MULTIMEDIA LIBRARY and **MULTIME-DIA BUSINESS LIBRARY: COMPREHENSIVE EDITION** These CD-ROMs contain either 8 (Essentials version) or 10 (Comprehensive edition) best-selling text-books from accounting, finance, marketing, etc., and include everything—text, graphics, etc.—except end-of-chapter problems. These texts have cross-book links embedded within the hypertext so students can easily see how various business functions relate to each other. Eight self-contained tutorials including operations management, the Internet, business communication, and management information systems are included incorporating animation, Web links, photos, charts, and maps.

We have written the book to make it more teachable for you with help from reviewers, colleagues, and focus group attendees who are gratefully acknowledged in the preface of the book.

Finally, we have done our best to make the book interesting reading. We hope you and your students enjoy it.

Dick Chase
Nick Aquilano
Bob Jacobs

Text Features

The following section highlights the key features developed to provide you with the best overall teaching text available. We hope these features give you maximum support while allowing you to tailor your course to fit the needs of your students.

■ FOR THE STUDENT

Chapter Outlines, Key Terms, and Web Links
These prepare the student by providing an overview of the chapter material and highlighting key terms and Internet Web sites that will be introduced.

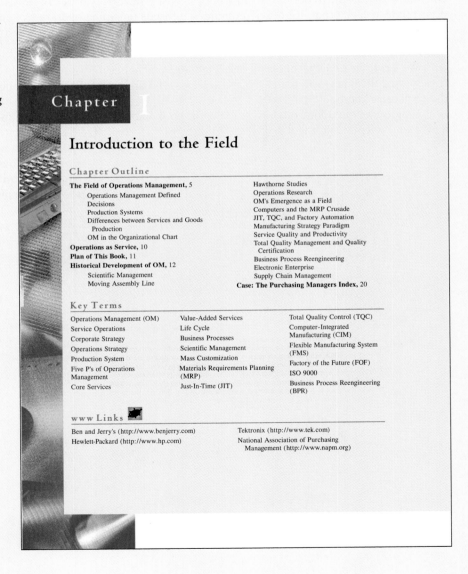

Chapter I

Introduction to the Field

Chapter Outline

The Field of Operations Management, 5
  Operations Management Defined
  Decisions
  Production Systems
  Differences between Services and Goods
    Production
  OM in the Organizational Chart
Operations as Service, 10
Plan of This Book, 11
Historical Development of OM, 12
  Scientific Management
  Moving Assembly Line

  Hawthorne Studies
  Operations Research
  OM's Emergence as a Field
  Computers and the MRP Crusade
  JIT, TQC, and Factory Automation
  Manufacturing Strategy Paradigm
  Service Quality and Productivity
  Total Quality Management and Quality
    Certification
  Business Process Reengineering
  Electronic Enterprise
  Supply Chain Management
Case: The Purchasing Managers Index, 20

Key Terms

Operations Management (OM)
Service Operations
Corporate Strategy
Operations Strategy
Production System
Five P's of Operations Management
Core Services

Value-Added Services
Life Cycle
Business Processes
Scientific Management
Mass Customization
Materials Requirements Planning (MRP)
Just-In-Time (JIT)

Total Quality Control (TQC)
Computer-Integrated Manufacturing (CIM)
Flexible Manufacturing System (FMS)
Factory of the Future (FOF)
ISO 9000
Business Process Reengineering (BPR)

www Links

Ben and Jerry's (http://www.benjerry.com)
Hewlett-Packard (http://www.hp.com)

Tektronix (http://www.tek.com)
National Association of Purchasing Management (http://www.napm.org)

 WHAT THE CUSTOMER WANTS:

I want a car that's built right.

I want dealer service that is fair, reliable, and pleasant.

I want some career skills that I can sell so I can afford to buy a car!

Building a quality car and having it serviced well are the essence of operations management (OM). Providing you with OM concepts that can help you in your career is the essence of this book.

American industry has entered this decade with a dramatically changed view of manufacturing and service operations' role in attaining competitive advantage. In the 70s and 80s, many domestic companies saw their market share decline due to their inability to compete with foreign firms in terms of product design, cost, or quality. Theories to explain this development span cultural differences, government macroeconomic policies, merger mania, neglect of human resources, insufficient investment in technology and R&D, and an excess of lawyers and/or MBAs. Whatever the cause, most experts now agree that world-class performance by operations in delivering high-quality, cost-competitive products and services is essential to survival in today's global economy. ●

3

Opening Vignettes

Each chapter opens with a short vignette to set the stage and help pique students' interest in the material about to be studied. A few examples include

· Rubbermaid—A New Product Machine (Chapter 4)

· General Electric and Quality "Black Belts" (Chapter 5)

· The New Workplace: Walls Are Falling (Chapter 10)

Breakthrough Boxes

The Breakthroughs provide examples or expansions of the topics presented by highlighting leading companies practicing new, breakthrough ways to run their operations: Breakthroughs include

· Motorola Pagers: To Each His Own (Supplement to Chapter 4)

· Quality One on One at Hewlett-Packard (Chapter 6)

· Untapped Savings Abound—Logistics Management at Microsoft (Chapter 12)

BREAKTHROUGH

Project Management Information System in Everyday Use

The 1990s have seen an explosion of interest in the techniques and concepts of project management with a parallel increase in project management software offerings. A few years ago, there were but a handful of microcomputer-based project management software packages. Now, there are over 100 such project management information systems—and the use of these tools is proliferating exponentially. Within our own MBA-level project management classes, about half of the students now enter having had some exposure to such software; all leave knowing at least one package and having been exposed to several others (Microsoft Project for Windows, Primavera Project Planner, Time Line, Project Scheduler, Milestone, Schedule Publisher, Texim Project). As recently as the early 1990s, perhaps one student per class would have prior experience with a PMIS, and our only in-class software was incapable of managing costs, leveling resources, or even displaying a PERT or Gantt chart. Here are examples of three PMISs leading this operations breakthrough.

The Microsoft Project program comes with an excellent on-line tutorial, which is one reason for its overwhelming popularity with project managers tracking midsized projects. This package aids in scheduling, allocating, and leveling resources, as well as in controlling costs and producing presentation-quality graphics and reports. Exhibit 3.12 shows a Microsoft Project sample output.

If the focus is primarily in scheduling, Kidasa's Milestones, Etc. program, produces Gantt charts that can even show dependencies among activities. As the project unfolds and schedules need updating, a Gantt chart's activity start and end dates can easily be modified.

Finally, for managing very large projects or programs having several projects, Primavera Project Plan-

ner is often the choice. Primavera Project Planner was selected to track the multihundred-million–dollar rebuilding of the World Trade Center after the terrorist bombing of February 26, 1993 (described in the opening vignette of the chapter). Primavera's Monte Carlo risk analysis program was also used to determine how much time and money were risked under different assumptions.

You will find it interesting to check out Primava Systems, Inc.'s Web site at http://www.primavera.com for the latest information on their software products.

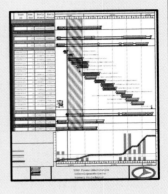

On December 20, 1991, Toys "R" Us–the world's largest toy retailer–opened its first retail store in Japan. What may now sound like an American success story in Japan traveled a difficult road for two years. The retailer had established locations in Canada, the United Kingdom, Germany, France, Singapore, Hong Kong, Malaysia, and Taiwan well before it attempted to enter the Japanese market.

In January 1990, Toys "R" Us formally applied to open its first (large) toy store in Niigata, Japan. This caused local toy retailers to proclaim their opposition by invoking provisions contained in the Large-Scale Retail Store Act. Then they organized a lobbying group to mobilize support against the American firm. Toys "R" Us appealed for help directly through the U.S. trade representative and other channels. Sustained American political pressure and widespread publicity finally forced MITI to confront the local lobby

and limit to 18 months the application process under the restrictive retail law. It was April 1990, and Toys "R" Us had overcome its first major hurdle.

But there was another hurdle to cross. Toys "R" Us succeeds in large part by selling below suggested retail price. It accomplishes this mainly through exploiting economies it obtains through volume purchases. Anticipating the threat posed by that strategy to their own profit margins, Japanese toy manufacturers banded together and vowed not to sell their wares to Toys "R" Us. But Nintendo depends heavily on Toys "R" Us for the distribution of its products in the United States and other major markets. Nintendo's defection triggered an ultimate end to this boycott.

Private sector countermeasures consciously adopted by numerous major Japanese corporations are replacing the falling barriers to entry of public sector regulation.

Toys "R" Us in Japan

(http://www.tru.com)

Toys "R" Us has successfully entered the Japanese toy market through private sector help–in this case, with the help of Nintendo.

Source: Mark Mason, ™United States Direct Investment in Japan: Trends and Prospects, *California Management Review*, Fall 1992, pp. 98±115. © 1992, by The Regents of the University of California. Reprinted from the California Management Review, vol. 35, No. 1. By permission of The Regents.

Box Inserts

Insight into some of the best current operations management practices are provided here. The inserts come from a variety of newspapers, journals, and business magazines. Examples include

· Red, White, & Boom: U.S. Economy Shines (Chapter 2)

· The Quality Business Base in Europe (Chapter 9)

· Characteristics of a Well-Designed Service System (Chapter 5)

Service Icons

Icons appear next to service discussions and examples. These emphasize that operations management encompasses services as well as manufacturing, and that both are important to the operations function.

■ OPERATIONS STRATEGY IN SERVICES

Operations strategy in service firms is generally inseparable from the corporate strategy. For most services, the service delivery system is the business, and hence, any strategic decision must include operations considerations. However, operations executives do not always have a voice equal to other functions of the firm. A marketing decision to add a new route for an airline or to add new in-flight services may be made despite operations' protests about feasibility (just as in manufacturing).

Although we will discuss service strategy in Chapter 5, we should note that many of the strategy concepts discussed relative to manufacturing also apply to services. For example, service firms may use the plant-within-a-plant (PWP) structure to achieve focus. Hospitals using the PWP focus may have separate units for distinct patient services such as cardiac units, oncology units, labor and delivery units, and

Globe Icons

International examples and text discussions are identified by globe icons in the margin. In addition, many photos reflect international companies.

For many years, few companies regarded the operating processes of a firm as a source of competitive advantage. The goals of the firm relating to operations were cost reduction and improved labor utilization. Decisions were made on narrow, tactical grounds. This was the domain of the technically oriented engineering specialists. Little attention was paid to how the processes, which deliver the goods and services of the firm, fit with its strategy.

In the 1970s and 1980s, a new perspective emerged. As global competitors (mainly from Japan) began to dominate major industries such as automobiles, motorcyles, domestic appliances, and virtually all consumer electronics, managers looked for the reasons that these companies were so successful. What emerged were stories of highly efficient operations quickly producing high-quality products. These companies were able not only to produce great products but also to bring new products to market quicker, while avoiding the start-up problems so typical of existing producers. These new world-class companies established new benchmarks in the areas of quality and productivity. Operations emerged as the key competitive weapon required for global success.

Cross-Functional Icons

These icons highlight areas where operations management concepts "link" and integrate with other business functions such as accounting, marketing, finance, and management information systems.

The general process is that customer-based new-product or current-product requirements give rise to performance priorities that then become the required priorities for operations. Exhibit 2.2 shows these priorities linking into an enterprise capabilities "barrel," because operations cannot satisfy customer needs without the involvement of R&D and distribution and without the direct or indirect support of financial management, human resource management, and information management. Given its performance requirements, an operations division uses its capabilities (as well as those of its suppliers) to achieve those requirements–that is, to win orders. These capabilities include technology, systems, and people. CIM (computer-integrated manufacturing), JIT (just-in-time), and TQM (total quality management) represent fundamental concepts and tools used in each of the three areas. We have shown suppliers in the operations capabilities barrel to reflect the fact that suppliers do not become suppliers unless their capabilities in technology, systems, and people management pass certification tests. In addition, virtually every operations capability is now subjected to a "make-or-buy" decision. It is current practice among world-class manufacturers to subject each part of a manufacturing operation to the question, if we are not among the best in the world at, say, metal forming, should we be doing this at all, or should we subcontract to someone who is the best? In the computer industry, for example, the majority of manufacturers outsource the fabrication of component parts, leaving just assembly and testing to be done in-house (or, as is becoming quite common, at the customer's facility, since that is where the product must function properly).

FINANCE
HUMAN RESOURCES
MIS

S

■ example S5.1   *Customers in Line*   Western National Bank is considering opening a drive-through window for customer service. Management estimates that customers will arrive at the rate of 15 per hour. The teller who will staff the window can service customers at the rate of one every three minutes.

Part 1   Assuming Poisson arrivals and exponential service, find

1. Utilization of the teller.
2. Average number in the waiting line.
3. Average number in the system.
4. Average waiting time in line.
5. Average waiting time in the system, including service.

solution–*Part 1*

1. The average utilization of the teller is

$$\rho = \frac{\lambda}{\mu} = \frac{15}{20} = 75 \text{ percent}$$

2. The average number in the waiting line is

$$\overline{n}_l = \frac{\lambda^2}{\mu(\mu - \lambda)} = \frac{(15)^2}{20(20 - 15)} = 2.25 \text{ customers}$$

3. The average number in the system is

$$\overline{n}_s = \frac{\lambda}{\mu - \lambda} = \frac{15}{20 - 15} = 3 \text{ customers}$$

Examples with Solutions
Examples follow quantitative topics and demonstrate specific procedures and techniques. Clearly set off from the text, they help students understand the computations.

Exhibit S7.12   Microsoft Excel Solver Screen

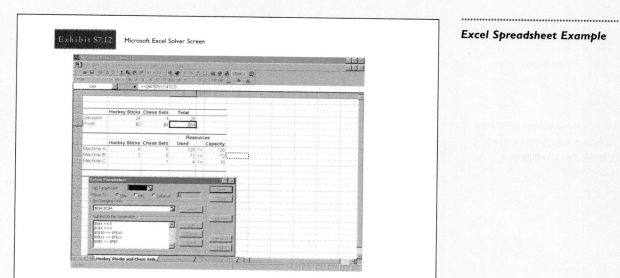

Excel Spreadsheet Example

Photos and Exhibits

The Eighth Edition includes photos and exhibits to enhance the visual appeal of the text and clarify textual discussions. Similar text figures, for example, are treated the same from chapter to chapter to reinforce student understanding.

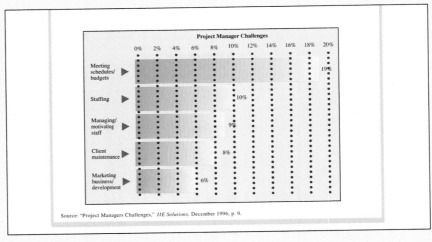

Source: "Project Managers Challenges," *IIE Solutions*, December 1996, p. 9.

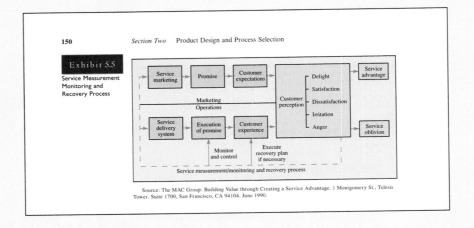

Chapter 4 Product Design and Process Selection–Manufacturing   **97**

The Miller Brewing Company uses a continuous production process. Beer is brewed, bottled, packaged, and shipped on one long production line with specialized automated equipment.

Kawasaki Motors Manufacturing uses an assembly production line with a fixed sequence of assembly tasks and workers checking quality at each step.

150   *Section Two* Product Design and Process Selection

Exhibit 5.5

Service Measurement Monitoring and Recovery Process

Source: The MAC Group: Building Value through Creating a Service Advantage. 1 Montgomery St., Telesis Tower. Suite 1700, San Francisco, CA 94104. June 1990.

FORMULA REVIEW

Expected time

$$ET = \frac{a + 4m + b}{6}$$ (3.1)

Variance (σ^2) of the activity times

$$\sigma^2 = \left(\frac{b - a}{6}\right)^2$$ (3.2)

Z transformation formula

$$Z = \frac{D - T_E}{\sqrt{\Sigma\, \sigma_{cp}^2}}$$ (3.3)

Formula Reviews
These lists at the end of chapters summarize formulas in one spot for easy student access and review.

SOLVED PROBLEMS

SOLVED PROBLEM 1

Quick Lube Inc. operates a fast lube and oil change garage. On a typical day, customers arrive at the rate of three per hour, and lube jobs are performed at an average rate of one every 15 minutes. The mechanics operate as a team on one car at a time.

Assuming Poisson arrivals and exponential service, find

a. Utilization of the lube team.
b. The average number of cars in line.
c. The average time a car waits before it is lubed.
d. The total time it takes to go through the system (i.e., waiting in line plus lube time).

Solution

$\lambda = 3,\ \mu = 4$

a.   Utilization $\rho = \dfrac{\lambda}{\mu} = \dfrac{3}{4} = 75\%$.

b. $\bar{n}_l = \dfrac{\lambda^2}{\mu(\mu - \lambda)} = \dfrac{3^2}{4(4 - 3)} = \dfrac{9}{4} = 2.25$ cars in line.

c. $\bar{t}_l = \dfrac{\lambda}{\mu(\mu - \lambda)} = \dfrac{3}{4(4 - 3)} = \dfrac{3}{4} = 45$ minutes in line.

d. $\bar{t}_s = \dfrac{1}{\mu - \lambda} = \dfrac{1}{1} = 1$ hour (waiting + lube).

SOLVED PROBLEM 2

American Vending Inc. (AVI) supplies vended food to a large university. Because students kick the machines at every opportunity out of anger and frustration, management has a constant repair problem. The machines break down on an average of three per hour, and the breakdowns are distributed in a Poisson manner. Downtime costs the company $25/hour per machine, and each maintenance worker gets $4 per hour. One worker can service machines at an average rate of five per hour, distributed exponentially; two workers working together can service seven per hour, distributed exponentially; and a team of three workers can do eight per hour, distributed exponentially.

What is the optimum maintenance crew size for servicing the machines?

Solved Problems
Representative example problems are placed at the end of appropriate chapters. Each includes a detailed, worked-out solution and provides another level of support for students before they try problems on their own.

Review and Discussion Questions

These questions let students review the chapter concepts before attempting the problems and provide a basis for classroom discussion. Suggested responses are included in the Instructor's Solutions Manual for your convenience.

REVIEW AND DISCUSSION QUESTIONS

1. Can a factory be fast, dependable, flexible, produce high-quality products, and still provide poor service from a customer's perspective?
2. Why should a service organization worry about being world class if it does not compete outside its own national border?
3. What are the major priorities associated with operations strategy? How has their relationship to each other changed over the years?
4. For each of the different priorities describe the unique characteristics of the market niche with which it is most compatible.
5. During 1988, for example, the dollar showed relative weakness with respect to foreign currencies such as the yen, mark, and pound. This stimulated exports. Why would long-term reliance on a lower-valued dollar be at best a short-term solution to the competitiveness problem?
6. In your opinion, do business schools have competitive priorities?
7. Why does the "proper" operations strategy keep changing for companies that are world-class competitors?
8. What is meant by the expressions order winners and order qualifiers? What was the order winner(s) for your last major purchase of a product or service?
9. What do we mean when we say productivity is a "relative" measure?
10. What are the typical performance measures for quality, speed of delivery, and flexibility?
11. What should be the criteria for management to adopt a particular performance measure?

Cases

Located at the end of most chapters, cases allow students to think critically about issues discussed in the chapter. Cases include:

- Operations Strategy at Compaq Computer (Chapter 2)

- Product Development in Japan (Chapter 4)

- Shouldice Hospital—A Cut Above (Chapter 7)

Chapter 3   Project Management   **79**

Case

Project Management at CPAone

The auditing division at CPAone (one of the "Big Six" accounting firms) generates financial statements to meet generally accepted accounting principles. In larger audits, the size of the task and the range of problems require the involvement of several people. In the audit of a national corporation, for example, numerous auditors with diverse specialties are required to investigate all aspects of the operation in various geographic areas. Given the number of people and the variety in skills, expertise, and personalities involved, a project manager is needed to oversee and conduct the audit efficiently. Thus, every audit begins by assigning the client to a partner, usually someone who is familiar with the client's business. The partner becomes the "project director" of the audit and is responsible for writing proposals, staffing the audit, delegating tasks, scheduling, and budgeting.

The project director begins by studying the client's income statement, balance sheet, and other financial statements. If the client has a bad financial reputation, the project director can make the decision for CPAone to refuse to do the audit. If the client is accepted, the director prepares a proposal outlining the general approach for conducting the audit, the completion date, and the cost estimate.

In determining the general approach for conducting the audit, the project director considers the size of the company and the number of departments. Auditors are then assigned on a department by department basis. The audit team is a pure project team, created anew for every audit with people having the skills best suited to the needs of the audit. Generally, each audit has one or two staff accountants, one or two senior accounts, and the project director. Before the proposal is even accepted, the director specifies who will be performing each task and the completion dates. Cost estimates are based on estimated labor hours.

During the audit the project director must ensure that all work strictly adheres to the Book of Auditing Standards and is completed on schedule. Each week the client and project director meet to review progress. When problems cannot be solved immediately, the director may call in people from CPAone's tax or consulting divisions. When the team has trouble interpreting financial statements, the project director may request that the client's own personnel be involved. Follow-up service is provided after the audit is completed. The project director sees to it that the client is represented if the IRS requests an examination.

Questions

1. What are the major milestones associated with this project? What additional information would you need to develop a PERT chart?

2. What are the project director's managerial responsibilities?

Source: *Managing Business and Engineering Projects,* by Nicholas, © 1990. Reprinted by permission of Prentice Hall, Inc., Upper Saddle River, NJ.

■ FOR THE INSTRUCTOR

The following elements are contained only in the instructor's edition of the text:

■ COMPUTER-INTEGRATED MANUFACTURING (CIM)

All of these automation technologies are brought together under **Computer-integrated manufacturing (CIM).** CIM is the automated version of the manufacturing process, where the three major manufacturing functions–product and process design, planning and control, and the manufacturing process itself–are replaced by the automated technologies just described. Further, the traditional integration mechanisms of oral and written communication are replaced by computer technology. Such highly automated and integrated manufacturing also goes under other names:

Vol. I, "Computer-Integrated Manufacturing"

Computer-Integrated Manufacturing (CIM)

---

4. Sharp Discounts Wholesale Club is considering consolidating its two service desks (see Problem 3) into one location, staffed by two clerks. The clerks will continue to work at the same individual speed of four minutes per customer.
   a. What is the probability of waiting in line?
   b. How many customers, on average, are waiting in line?
   c. How much time does a customer spend at the service desk (waiting plus service time)?
   d. Do you think the Sharp Discounts Wholesale Club should consolidate the service desks?

4. *a.* 55%.
   b. 1.1 customers.
   c. .12 hours or 7.2 minutes.
   d. Yes.

✓ 5. Burrito King (a new fast food franchise opening up nationwide) has successfully automated burrito production for its drive-up fast food establishments. The Burro-Master 9000 requires a constant 45 seconds to produce a batch of burritos. It has been estimated that customers will arrive at the drive-up window according to a Poisson distribution at an average of one every 50 seconds. To help determine the amount of space needed for the line at the drive-up window, Burrito King would like to know the expected average time in the system, the average line length (in cars), and the average number of cars in the system (both in line and at the window).

5. $\bar{T}_s$ = 4.125 minutes.
   $\bar{n}_l$ = 4.05 cars.
   $\bar{n}_s$ = 4.95 cars.

6. The Bijou Theater in Hermosa Beach, California, shows vintage movies. Customers arrive at the theater line at the rate of 100 per hour. The ticket seller averages 30 seconds per customer, which includes placing parking validation stamps on customers' parking lot receipts and punching holes in their frequent watcher cards. (Because of these added services, many customers don't get in until after the feature has started.)
   a. What is the average customer waiting time in the system?

6. *a.* 3-minutes.
   b. 45 seconds.
   c. Yes, about 36 seconds.

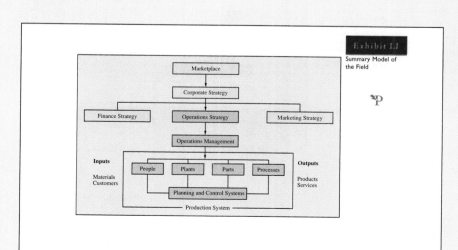

Exhibit 1.1

Summary Model of the Field

℗

Video Icons
These margin icons include the title of a segment in the Irwin/McGraw-Hill Operations Management Video Series that enhances the text discussion.

Disk Icons
These identify problems that can be solved using DECISION SUPPORT SYSTEMS FOR Operations and Management Science software by Lotfi & Pegels, which is available as a package with the text.

Check Answers
These answers provide instructors with a quick reference in class.

Checkmark
A checkmark is placed before problems that have answers provided to the student in Appendix H.

PowerPoint Icons
The PowerPoint icon appears when text or exhibits are found in the PowerPoint Presentation done for this book. They are also included as a transparency master in the PowerPoint Transparency Master supplement.

HOM Operations Management Software for Windows, by Moses, Seshadri, and Yakirevich

This new software package developed at NYU offers powerful Windows-based programs for solving real world type operating problems, such as forecasting, process analysis, waiting line design and analysis, project management, MRP and inventory management, and capacity planning and management. All programs include standard edit, file, and help icons and constant "run," "results," and "plot" options. HOM imports and exports files to and from Excel and each module has detailed, step-by-step "how to solve" dialog boxes for quick reference or for beginning students.

The HOM package also includes data sets drawn from classic Operations cases as well as two integrative cases which utilize all the modules, one from a service company (United Branch Bank) and one from a manufacturer (Ice Queen).

HOM is available as an independent text/software package or at a discount, shrinkwrapped with the text.

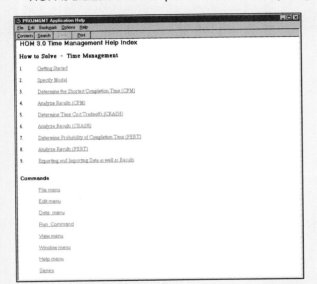

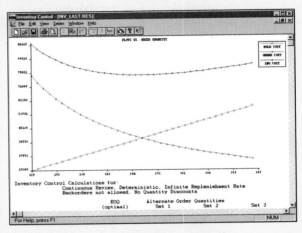

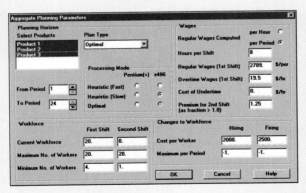

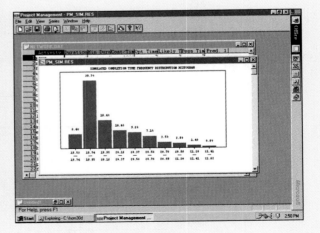

Production and Operations Management
Manufacturing and Services

THE IRWIN/MCGRAW-HILL SERIES
Operations and Decision Sciences

OPERATIONS MANAGEMENT

Aquilano, Chase, and Davis
Fundamentals of Operations Management
Second Edition

Chase, Aquilano, and Jacobs
Production and Operations Management: Manufacturing and Services
Eighth Edition

Chu, Hottenstein, and Greenlaw
PROSIM for Windows
Third Edition

Cohen and Apte
Manufacturing Automation
First Edition

Dilworth
Operations Management
Second Edition

Flaherty
Global Operations Management
First Edition

Fitzsimmons and Fitzsimmons
Service Management: Operations, Strategy, Information Technology
Second Edition

Hill
Manufacturing Strategy: Text & Cases
Second Edition

Hopp and Spearman
Factory Physics
First Edition

Lambert and Stock
Strategic Logistics Management
Third Edition

Leenders and Fearon
Purchasing and Materials Management
Eleventh Edition

Lotfi and Pegels
Decision Support Systems for Operations & Management Science
Third Edition

Melnyk and Denzler
Operations Management: A Value-Driven Approach
First Edition

Moses and Seshadri
HOM Operations Management Software for Windows
First Edition

Nahmias
Production and Operations Analysis
Third Edition

Nicholas
Competitive Manufacturing Management
First Edition

Niebel
Motion and Time Study
Ninth Edition

Noori and Radford
Production and Operations Management
First Edition

Sanderson and Uzumeri
Managing Product Families
First Edition

Schroeder
Operations Management: Decision Making in the Operations Function
Fourth Edition

Schonberger and Knod
Operations Management: Customer-Focused Principles
Sixth Edition

Stevenson
Production/Operations Management
Fifth Edition

Vollmann, Berry, and Whybark
Manufacturing Planning & Control Systems
Fourth Edition

Zipkin
Foundations of Inventory Management
First Edition

QUANTITATIVE METHODS AND MANAGEMENT SCIENCE

Bodily, Carraway, Frey, Pfeifer
Quantitative Business Analysis: Casebook
First Edition

Text and Cases
First Edition

Bonini, Hausman, and Bierman
Quantitative Analysis for Business Decisions
Ninth Edition

Hesse
Managerial Spreadsheet Modeling and Analysis
First Edition

Lotfi and Pegels
Decision Support Systems for Operations and Management Science
Third Edition

Stevenson
Introduction to Management Science
Second Edition

Turban and Meredith
Fundamentals of Management Science
Sixth Edition

Production and Operations Management
Manufacturing and Services

Eighth Edition

Richard B. Chase
University of Southern California

Nicholas J. Aquilano
University of Arizona

F. Robert Jacobs
Indiana University

Boston   Burr Ridge, IL   Dubuque, IA   Madison, WI   New York   San Francisco   St. Louis
Bangkok   Bogotá   Caracas   Lisbon   London   Madrid
Mexico City   Milan   New Delhi   Seoul   Singapore   Sydney   Taipei   Toronto

Irwin/McGraw-Hill

*A Division of The **McGraw·Hill** Companies*

PRODUCTION AND OPERATIONS MANAGEMENT: MANUFACTURING AND SERVICES

Photo credits appear on page 869.

This book is printed on acid-free paper.

1 2 3 4 5 6 7 8 9 0 VNH/VNH 9 0 9 8 7 (U.S. edition)
1 2 3 4 5 6 7 8 9 0 VNH/VNH 9 0 9 8 7 (International edition)

ISBN 0-256-22556-7 (student's edition)   ISBN 0-07-561278-X (student edition package)
ISBN 0-256-26921-1 (instructor's edition)   ISBN 0-07-561277-1 (instructor's edition package)
ISBN 0-07-289881-X (*Business Week* edition)   ISBN 0-07-561710-2 (*Business Week* edition package)

Publisher: *Jeffrey J. Shelstad*   Cover illustration: *Carlos Alejandro*
Executive editor: *Richard T. Hercher, Jr.*   Cover and interior design: *Kay Fulton, Fulton Design*
Senior developmental editor: *Gail Korosa*   Senior photo research coordinator: *Keri Johnson*
Senior marketing manager: *Colleen J. Suljic*   Photo research: *Charlotte Goldman*
Senior project manager: *Susan Trentacosti*   Compositor: *Interactive Composition Corporation*
Production supervisor: *Heather D. Burbridge*   Typeface: *10/12 Times Roman*
Designer: *Larry J. Cope*   Printer: *Von Hoffmann Press, Inc.*

SAP is a registered trademark of SAP Aktiengesellschaft, Systems, Applications and Products in Data Processing, Neurottstrasse 16, 69190 Walldorf, Germany. The publisher gratefully acknowledges SAP's kind permission to use its trademark in this publication. SAP AG is not the publisher of this book and is not responsible for it under any aspect of press law.

Citibank logo on cover: Courtesy of Citicorp.

Library of Congress Cataloging-in-Publication-Data

Chase, Richard B.
    Production and operations management: manufacturing and services
/Richard B. Chase, Nicholas J. Aquilano, F. Robert Jacobs. —8th
ed.
        p.   cm.
    Includes indexes.
        ISBN 0-256-22556-7 (students ed.). —ISBN 0-256-26921-1
(instructors ed.)
        1. Production management.   I. Aquilano, Nicholas J.   II. Jacobs,
F. Robert.   III. Title.
TS155.C424   1998
658.5—dc21   97-36919

INTERNATIONAL EDITION
Copyright © 1998. Exclusive rights by The McGraw-Hill Companies, Inc. for manufacture and export. This book cannot be re-exported from the country to which it is consigned by McGraw-Hill. The International edition is not available in North America.

When ordering the title, use ISBN 0-07-115222-9.

http://www.mhhe.com

To our wives
Harriet, Nina, and Jeanne
and to our children
Laurie, Andy, Glenn, and Rob
Don, Kara, and Mark
Jennifer and Suzy

Preface

Operations Management (OM) has seen many innovations in recent years, becoming a topic of critical importance in business today. Demands for business reengineering, quality, time-based competition, value-adding processes, and a global view have demonstrated that superior management of the operations function is vital to the survival of the firm. An understanding of OM strategy and its function is a necessary part of any good business education.

Operations Management should appeal to individuals who want to be directly involved in making products or providing services. The entry-level operations specialist is the person who determines how best to design, supply, and run the processes. Senior operations managers are responsible for setting the strategic direction of the company from an operations standpoint, deciding what technologies should be used, where facilities should be located, and managing the facilities that make the products or provide the services. Operations Management is an interesting mix of managing people and applying sophisticated technology. The goal is to efficiently create wealth by supplying quality goods and services.

The field of operations management ranges from high-tech manufacturing to high-touch services, so we have tried to balance the treatment of the manufacturing and service aspects. Operations management now requires a global perspective for many of the topics. Operations management is best done with significant cross-functional integration. Accounting, finance, marketing, human resources management, purchasing, logistics, and engineering impact how firms are run operationally. To highlight our emphasis on services, globalization, and cross-functional integration, we've used the logos you see here in the text margin next to these discussions. In addition, many references to World Wide Web sites are indicated with this special Internet logo.

Features to aid in your understanding the material include the following:

- Solved problems at the end of chapters to serve as models that can be reviewed prior to attempting problems.
- Checkmarks next to problems that have answers in Appendix H.
- Breakthrough Boxes to demonstrate leading-edge companies or practices that are innovative and trailblazing.
- Excel® spreadsheet templates and data sets, which are included on the CD-ROM packaged at the back of each text.

Our aim is to cover the latest and the most important issues facing OM managers, as well as the basic tools and techniques. We supply many examples of leading-edge companies and practices. We have done our best to make the book interesting reading. We hope you enjoy it.

■ ACKNOWLEDGMENTS

It is with a great deal of pleasure that we welcome Bob Jacobs to the authorship team. After seven editions over 25 years you don't make such decisions lightly. We had our own "Star Search" involving discussions with colleagues around the country seeking out the best of potential co-authors. Our criteria were tough. He or she needed to be on top of developments in the field, be a leader in the discipline, and enjoy writing and teaching. Bob filled these criteria to a T. In addition, he has significant business and international experience and teaches at a top-notch university, with a large and highly successful program in operations management. We are confident that his work on this 8th edition will enhance your learning of this fascinating and important subject.

Several very talented scholars have made major contributions to specific chapters in the book. We are pleased to thank the following individuals:

Dan Heiser and Doug Blocher for their help with Quality Management.

Jack Muth for his ideas on Strategic Capacity Management.

Morgan Swink and Vince Mabert for their help with Supply Chain Management.

Joe Moore for his ideas for Aggregate Planning and Operations Strategy.

Chris Albright for the AHP spreadsheet in Chapter 12 on Supply Chain Management.

Ash Sony for the references to SAP R/3.

Jim Patterson for his ideas on Project Management.

Ravi Behara of George Mason University for assistance with Business Process Reengineering, Facility Location, and Strategic Capacity Planning.

Louis R. Chase, editor extraordinaire and Shakespeare expert for ideas on several chapters.

Marilyn Helms of the University of Tennessee at Chattanooga for her help with Operations Strategy and Competitiveness, and Just-in-Time Systems.

Michael J. Maggard of Northeastern University, for his ideas on Service Design.

David O'Donnell of the University of Southern California for his assistance with Project Management.

"Raj" Rajagopalan of the University of Southern California for his input on Operations Consulting.

Alex Zhang of the University of Southern California for his help with Simulation.

Special thanks to Joseph Moore of Indiana University and Phillip Fry of Boise State University who solved all of the examples and problems and checked our answers for accuracy. Special thanks also go out to colleagues at USC: Sriram Dasu, Richard D. McBride, K. Ravi Kumar, Bob Schmidt, Jon Yormark, and Constantin Vaitsos.

Joseph Moore also prepared the Test Bank, and Ross L. Fink of Bradley University prepared the Instructor's Solutions Manual. Marilyn Helms of the University of Tennessee at Chattanooga revised the Study Guide. William Youngdahl of Thunderbird American Graduate School of International Management prepared the Power-Point slides. These supplements are a great deal of work to write, and we appreciate their efforts, which make teaching the course easier for everyone who uses the text.

We also thank the following reviewers for their many thoughtful suggestions for this edition: D. Leblanc, *Vanderbilt University*; Gary Scudder, *Vanderbilt University*; David Cabell, *McNeese State University*; Kannan Sethuraman, *University of Michigan*; Dilip Chhajed, *University of Illinois*; S. D. Deshumukh, *Northwestern University*; Dennis Krumwiede, *Kansas State University*; Harry Boer, *University of Twent–Netherlands*; Ashok Rao, *Babson College*; James Lawson, *Mississippi State University*; Constantin Vaitsos, *University of Southern California*; Y. L. Helio Yang, *San Diego State University*; Keah-Choon Tan, *Mesa State University*; Emre Veral, *Baruch College*; Peter Kelle, *Louisiana State University*; Joseph Moore, *Indiana University*; Bruce Hartman, *University of Arizona*; and Ross Fink, *Bradley University*.

Participants in two focus groups shared their in-depth ideas about ways to improve teaching the course and what we could do to improve the text. We want to thank: Ann Marucheck, *University of North Carolina at Chapel Hill*; Richard Metters, *Vanderbilt University*; Arthur Smith, *University of Toledo*; Louis A. LeBlanc, *University of Arkansas at Little Rock*; Powell Robinson, *Texas A&M University*; John Wacker, *Iowa State University*; Morgan Swink, *Indiana University*; Ravi Behara, *George Mason University*; M. Zarrugh, *James Madison University*; Diane Parente, *University of Mississippi—Tupelo*; Susan A. Slotnick, *State of New York University at Stony Brook*; Drew Rosen, *University of North Carolina at Wilmington*; Robert J. Vokurka, *Texas A&M University*; and Kenneth Murphy, *Florida International University*. Thanks also to John Bradford of Miami University.

We once again thank those individuals whose input over past editions has helped the book evolve to its present form: Joseph Blackburn, *Vanderbilt University*; James Blocher, *Indiana University*; Jim Browne, *New York University*; Farzaneh Fazel, *Illinois State University*; Lissa Galbraith, *Florida State University*; Dennis Geyer, *Golden Gate University*; Stephen Huxley, *University of San Francisco*; Yunus Kathawala, *Eastern Illinois University*; Doan Modianos, *Bradley University*; Winter Nie, *Colorado State University*; Roderick Reasor, *Virginia Polytechnic Institute and State University*; Powell Robinson, *Texas A&M University*; Jerry Wei, *University of Notre Dame*; Wayne Cunningham, *University of Scranton*; Edward Gillenwater, *University of Mississippi*; Satish Mehra, *Memphis State University*; Graham Morbey, *University of Massachusetts at Amherst*; R. Natarajan, *Tennessee Technological University*; Fred Raafat, *San Diego State University*; Edward Rosenthal, *Temple University*; David Booth, *Kent State University*; Thomas Cywood, *University of Chicago*; Mike Martin, *Dalhousie University*; James Perry, *George Washington University*; Dan Rinks, *Louisiana State University*; Raj Srivastavo, *Marquette University*; Robert Trend, *University of Virginia*; Everette Adam, *University of Missouri–Columbia*; Lawrence Bennigson, *Harvard University*; Amiya K. Chakravarty, *Tulane University*; Joel Corman, *Suffolk University*; Willima A. Fischer, *University of North Carolina*; Dale R. Flowers, *Case Western University*; Carter Franklin III, *Houston Baptist University*; Oliver Galbraith III, *California State University–San Diego*; Stanley J. Garstka, *University of Chicago*; Michael Hottenstein, *Penn State University*; Gordon Johnson, *California State University–Northridge*; Frank L. Kaufman, *California State University–Sacramento*; Lee Krajewski, *University of Notre Dame*; Hugh V. Leach, *Washburn University*; John D. Longhill, *East Carolina University*; John R. Matthews, *University of Wisconsin*; Brooke Saladin, *Wake Forest University*; Ted Stafford, *University of Alabama–Huntsville*; Trevor Sainsbury, *University of Pittsburgh*; Chuck Baron Shook, *University of Hawaii at Manoa*; John E. Stevens, *Lehigh University*; Jesse S. Tarleton, *College of William and Mary,* and Larry Ritzman of Boston College.

We also want to thank former doctoral students who have contributed to the book over the years, including, most recently, Douglas Stewart (*Michigan State University*) and Andreas Soteriou (*University of Cyprus*), and, earlier on, Arvinder Loomba (*University of Northern Iowa*), Deborah Kellogg (*University of Colorado—Denver*), Blair Berkeley (*California State University—Los Angeles*) and the now grizzled veteran Bill Youngdahl (*Thunderbird American Graduate School of International Management*).

Much thanks to Danie Mann, program manager at the center for Service Excellence for her help. Also thanks to Heidi English at Indiana University for her help with the book.

We indeed appreciate the enthusiastic support and innovativeness of Dick Hercher, our long-time editor at Irwin/McGraw-Hill, whose help in coordinating all of the resources behind the scenes has been terrific. And to Gail Korosa (our developmental editor) what can we say? Your dedication (obsession?) to helping us make this our best edition ever cannot be overstated.

Thanks to the Irwin/McGraw-Hill team who make it all possible—Colleen Suljic, marketing manager; Susan Trentacosti, project supervisor; Larry Cope, designer; Heather Burbridge, production supervisor; and Keri Johnson, photo research coordinator.

Last, but certainly not least, we thank our families, who for the eighth time let the life cycle of the book disrupt theirs. And for the new kid on the block, for the first time.

Richard B. Chase
Nicholas J. Aquilano
F. Robert Jacobs

Contents in Brief

Section One

Nature and Context of Operations Management *1*

1 Introduction to the Field *2*
2 Operations Strategy and Competitiveness *22*
3 Project Management *46*

Section Two

Product Design and Process Selection *81*

4 Product Design and Process Selection—Manufacturing *82*
Supplement 4 Operations Technology *119*
5 Product Design and Process Selection—Services *140*
Supplement 5 Waiting Line Management *168*
6 Quality Management *198*
Supplement 6 Statistical Quality Control Methods *235*

Section Three

Design of Facilities and Jobs *261*

7 Strategic Capacity Management *262*
Supplement 7 Linear Programming *291*
8 Just-in-Time Production Systems *322*
9 Facility Location *350*
10 Facility Layout *374*
11 Job Design and Work Measurement *412*
Supplement 11 Learning Curves *445*

Section Four

Managing the Supply Chain *463*

12 Supply Chain Management *464*
13 Forecasting *496*
14 Aggregate Planning *550*
15 Inventory Systems for Independent Demand *580*
16 Inventory Systems for Dependent Demand: MRP-Type Systems *624*
Supplement 16 SAP R/3 *669*
17 Operations Scheduling *678*
Supplement 17 Simulation *713*

Section Five

Revising the System *741*

18 Operations Consulting *742*
19 Business Process Reengineering *764*
20 Synchronous Manufacturing and Theory of Constraints *788*

Appendixes *833*
A. Financial Analysis of Operations *834*
B. Uniformly Distributed Random Digits *855*
C. Normally Distributed Random Digits *856*
D. Areas of the Standard Normal Distribution *857*
E. Areas of the Cumulative Standard Normal Distribution *858*
F. Negative Exponential Distribution: Values of e^{-x} *860*
G. Interest Tables *862*
H. Answers to Selected Problems *866*
Photo Credits *869*
Name Index *871*
Subject Index *876*

xi

Contents

Section One

Nature and Context of Operations Management 1

1 Introduction to the Field 2
- ■ The Field of Operations Management 5
- Operations Management Defined 5
- Decisions 5
- Production Systems 7
- Differences between Services and Goods Production 8
- OM in the Organizational Chart 9
- ■ Operations as Service 10
- ■ Plan of This Book 11
- ■ Historical Development of OM 12
- Scientific Management 13
- Moving Assembly Line 14
- Hawthorne Studies 15
- Operations Research 15
- OM's Emergence as a Field 15
- Computers and the MRP Crusade 15
- JIT, TQC, and Factory Automation 16
- Manufacturing Strategy Paradigm 17
- Service Quality and Productivity 17
- Total Quality Management and Quality Certification 18
- Business Process Reengineering 18
- Electronic Enterprise 18
- Supply Chain Management 18
- ■ Conclusion 19
- ■ Review and Discussion Questions 20
- ■ Case: The Purchasing Managers Index (PMI) 20
- ■ Selected Bibliography 21

2 Operations Strategy and Competitiveness 22
- ■ Operations Strategy 24
- What Is Operations Strategy? 24
- ■ Priorities 25
- Operations Priorities 25
- The Notion of Trade-offs 27
- Priorities Determined by the Marketplace 28
- Changing Competitive Priorities 28
- Order Winners and Qualifiers: The Marketing/Operations Link 29
- ■ A Framework for Operations Strategy in Manufacturing 30
- Developing a Manufacturing Strategy 31
- ■ Operations Strategy in Services 33
- ■ Meeting the Competitive Challenge 36
- Some Causes of America's Improved Competitiveness 37
- Productivity Measurement 39
- ■ Conclusion 40
- ■ Solved Problem 41
- ■ Review and Discussion Questions 42
- ■ Problems 42
- ■ Case: Operations Strategy at Compaq Computer 43
- ■ Case: Los Angeles Toy Company 44
- ■ Selected Bibliography 45

3 Project Management 46
- ■ Definition of Project Management 48
- Work Breakdown Structure 49
- ■ Project Control 50
- Reporting Mechanisms 50
- ■ Organizational Structures 52
- Pure Project 53
- Functional Project 53
- Matrix Project 54
- ■ Critical Path Scheduling 54
- ■ Time-Oriented Techniques 55
- CPM with a Single Time Estimate 56
- CPM with Three Activity Time Estimates 59
- Maintaining Ongoing Project Schedules 63
- ■ Time-Cost Models 63
- Minimum-Cost Scheduling (Time-Cost Trade-off) 63
- ■ Managing Resources 66
- ■ Tracking Progress 66
- ■ Cautions on PERT and CPM 66
- ■ Conclusion 69
- ■ Formula Review 69
- ■ Solved Problems 70
- ■ Review and Discussion Questions 72
- ■ Problems 72

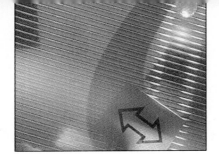

- Case: The Campus Wedding (A) 77
- Case: The Campus Wedding (B) 78
- Case: Project Management at CPAone 79
- Selected Bibliography 79

Section Two

Product Design and Process Selection 81

4 Product Design and Process Selection—
Manufacturing 82
- The Product Design Process 85
- Designing for the Customer 89
  Quality Function Deployment 90
  Value Analysis/Value Engineering 92
- Designing Products for Manufacture and
  Assembly 92
  How Does Design for Manufacturing and Assembly
  (DFMA) Work? 93
- Process Selection 96
  Process Selection Contrasted with Process Planning 96
  Types of Processes 96
  Process Flow Structures 97
  Product-Process Matrix 99
  The Virtual Factory 100
  Specific Equipment Selection 100
  Choosing among Alternative Processes and
  Equipment 100
- Process Flow Design 102
- Process Analysis 105
  An Example of Process Analysis 105
- Global Product Design and Manufacturing 108
  The Global Joint Venture 108
  Global Product Design Strategy 109
- Measuring Product Development Performance 109
- Conclusion 110
- Solved Problem 111
- Review and Discussion Questions 111
- Problems 112
- Plant Tour: Dell Computer: Mr. Cozzette Buys a
  Computer 114
- Case: The Best Engineered Part Is No Part 116

- Case: Product Development in Japan 117
- Selected Bibliography 117

Supplement 4   Operations Technology 119
- Technologies in Manufacturing 123
  Hardware Systems 124
  Software Systems 128
- Computer-Integrated Manufacturing (CIM) 129
- Technologies in Services 129
  Office Automation 129
  Image Processing Systems 130
  Electronic Data Interchange 131
  Decision Support Systems and Expert Systems 132
  Networked Computer Systems 132
- Evaluation of Technology Investments 132
  Cost Reductions 133
  Other Benefits 134
  Risks in Adopting New Technologies 135
- Conclusion 137
- Review and Discussion Questions 138
- Case: The Post-Information Age: Beyond
  Demographics 138
- Selected Bibliography 139

5 Product Design and Process Selection—
Services 140
- The Nature of Services 142
  Service Businesses and Internal Services 143
  A Contemporary View of Service Management 143
- Operational Classification of Services 144
- Designing Service Organizations 146
  Service Strategy: Focus and Advantage 147
- Structuring the Service Encounter: Service-System
  Design Matrix 151
  Strategic Uses of the Matrix 153
- Service Blueprinting and Fail-Safing 154
- Three Contrasting Service Designs 156
  The Production Line Approach 157
  The Self-Service Approach 158
  The Personal Attention Approach 158
- Service Guarantees as Design Drivers 161
- Conclusion 162
- Review and Discussion Questions 163
- Problems 163
- Case: Kinko's Copier Stores 164
- Case: AOL's Move to Flat-Rate Pricing 166
- Selected Bibliography 167

Supplement 5   Waiting Line Management 168
- Economics of the Waiting Line Problem 169
  Cost Effectiveness Balance 169
  The Practical View of Waiting Lines 169

■ **The Queuing System** 170
Customer Arrivals 172
The Queuing System 175
Exit 179
■ **Waiting Line Models** 180
■ **Computer Simulation of Waiting Lines** 189
■ **Conclusion** 190
■ **Formula Review** 190
■ **Solved Problems** 191
■ **Review and Discussion Questions** 192
■ **Problems** 193
■ **Selected Bibliography** 197

6 **Quality Management** *198*
■ **Quality Management and the Malcolm Baldrige National Quality Award** 200
Eligibility for the Baldrige Award 203
Description of the 1997 Baldrige Award Criteria 203
The Baldrige Award and the Quality Gurus 207
■ **Quality Specifications and Quality Costs** 208
Developing Quality Specifications 209
Cost of Quality 209
Generic Tools and Tools of the QC Department 211
■ **Continuous Improvement (CI)** 212
Tools and Procedures of CI 213
Benchmarking for CI 213
■ **The Shingo System: Fail-Safe Design** 216
■ **ISO 9000** 219
The ISO 9000 Series 220
ISO 9000 Certification 221
ISO 9000: An Everyday Example 223
ISO 9000 versus the Baldrige Criteria 225
■ **Conclusion** 225
■ **Review and Discussion Questions** 226
■ **Problems** 229
■ **Case: Hank Kolb, Director of Quality Assurance** 229
■ **Case: Shortening Customers' Telephone Waiting Time** 231
■ **Selected Bibliography** 234

Supplement 6 **Statistical Quality Control Methods** *235*
■ **Acceptance Sampling** 236
Design of a Single Sampling Plan for Attributes 236
Operating Characteristic Curves 238
Shaping the OC Curve 239
The Effects of Lot Size 240
■ **Process Control Procedures** 240
Process Control with Attribute Measurements: Using p Charts 240
Process Control with Variable Measurements: Using $\overline{X}$ and R Charts 241

How to Construct $\overline{X}$ and R Charts 242
Process Capability 245
Capability Index (Cpk) 246
Taguchi Methods 248
Is an Out-of-Spec Product Really Out of Spec? 248
■ **Conclusion** 251
■ **Formula Review** 252
■ **Solved Problems** 252
■ **Review and Discussion Questions** 254
■ **Problems** 254
■ **Selected Bibliography** 259

Section Three

Design of Facilities and Jobs   *261*

7 **Strategic Capacity Planning** *262*
■ **Capacity Management in Operations** 264
■ **Capacity Planning Concepts** 267
Economies and Diseconomies of Scale 268
The Experience Curve 269
Where Economies of Scale Meet the Experience Curve 270
Capacity Focus 270
Capacity Flexibility 271
■ **Capacity Planning** 272
Considerations in Adding Capacity 272
Determining Capacity Requirements 274
Using Decision Trees to Evaluate Capacity Alternatives 276
■ **Planning Service Capacity** 279
Capacity Planning in Service versus Manufacturing 279
Capacity Utilizations and Service Quality 280
■ **Adding Capacity through Multisite Service Growth** 281
Entrepreneurial Stage 281
Multisite Rationalization Stage 282
Growth Stage 284
Maturity Stage 284
■ **Conclusion** 285
■ **Solved Problem** 285
■ **Review and Discussion Questions** 286
■ **Problems** 286
■ **Case: Shouldice Hospital—A Cut Above** 288
■ **Selected Bibliography** 290

Supplement 7 **Linear Programming** *291*
■ **The Linear Programming Model** 294
■ **Graphical Linear Programming** 294
■ **The Simplex Method** 297

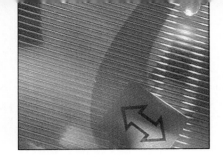

The Six-Step Solution Procedure 297
Search Path Followed by the Simplex Method 303
Shadow Prices, Ranging, and Sensitivity 304
Linear Programming Using Microsoft Excel 305
■ Transportation Method 307
Step 1: Set Up Transportation Matrix 308
Step 2: Make Initial Allocations 309
Step 3: Develop Optimal Solution 312
■ Conclusion 315
■ Solved Problems 316
■ Review and Discussion Questions 317
■ Problems 317
■ Selected Bibliography 321

8 Just-in-Time Production Systems 322
■ JIT Logic 324
■ The Japanese Approach to Productivity 325
Eliminiation of Waste 325
Respect for People 332
■ North American Modifications of JIT 333
■ JIT Implementation Requirements 334
JIT Layouts and Design Flows 335
JIT Applications for Line Flows 336
JIT Applications for Job Shops 337
TQC (Total Quality Control) 338
A Stable Schedule 338
Work with Suppliers 339
■ JIT in Services 340
■ Conclusion 344
■ Review and Discussion Questions 344
■ Problems 345
■ Case: Quick Response Apparel 345
■ Case: Toyota Work Contracts 346
■ Case: Quality Parts Company 347
■ Reading: Just-in-Time: Is It Really Good for the
Automobile Industry? 348
■ Selected Bibliography 349

9 Facility Location 350
■ Issues in Facility Location 352
■ Plant Location Methods 356
Factor-Rating Systems 356
Linear Programming 358

Center of Gravity Method 358
Analytic Delphi Model 360
■ Locating Service Facilities 361
■ Conclusion 367
■ Formula Review 367
■ Solved Problem 368
■ Review and Discussion Questions 368
■ Problems 369
■ Case: Is It Russian Roulette? 370
■ Case: The Plant Location Puzzle 371
■ Selected Bibliography 373

10 Facility Layout 374
■ Basic Production Layout Formats 376
■ Process Layout 377
Computerized Layout Techniques—CRAFT 380
Applying CRAFT to the Toy Factory 380
Systematic Layout Planning 381
■ Product Layout 383
Assembly Lines 383
Assembly-Line Balancing 385
Splitting Tasks 387
Flexible Line Layouts 389
Computerized Line Balancing 389
Mixed-Model Line Balancing 389
Current Thoughts on Assembly Lines 392
■ Group Technology (Cellular) Layout 392
Developing A GT Layout 392
Virtual GT Cell 395
■ Fixed-Position Layout 395
■ Retail Service Layout 397
Servicescapes 397
Ambient Conditions 397
Spatial Layout and Functionality 398
Signs, Symbols, and Artifacts 399
■ Office Layout 400
■ Conclusion 400
■ Solved Problems 401
■ Review and Discussion Questions 403
■ Problems 404
■ Case: Soteriou's Souvlaki 408
■ Case: State Automobile License Renewals 410
■ Selected Bibliography 410

11 Job Design and Work Measurement 412
■ Job Design Decisions 414
■ Behavioral Considerations in Job Design 415
Degree of Labor Specialization 415
Job Enrichment 416
Sociotechnical Systems 417

■ Physical Considerations in Job Design   418
■ Work Methods   418
A Production Process   419
Worker at a Fixed Workplace   422
Worker Interacting with Equipment   422
Workers Interacting with Other Workers   423
■ Work Measurement and Standards   424
Work Measurement Techniques   425
■ Financial Incentive Plans   435
Basic Compensation Systems   435
Individual and Small-Group Incentive Plans   436
Organizationwide Plans   436 Pay-for-Performance   437
■ Conclusion   439
■ Formula Review   439
■ Solved Problems   439
■ Review and Discussion Questions   440
■ Problems   441
■ Case: Teamwork at Volvo   443
■ Selected Bibliography   444

Supplement 11   Learning Curves   *445*
■ Application of Learning Curves   446
■ Plotting Learning Curves   447
Logarithmic Analysis   448
Learning Curve Tables   449
Estimating the Learning Percentage   452
How Long Does Learning Go On?   453
■ General Guidelines for Learning   453
Individual Learning   453
■ Organizational Learning   454
■ Learning Curves Applied to Heart Transplant Mortality   455
■ Formula Review   457
■ Solved Problem   457
■ Review and Discussion Questions   457
■ Problems   458
■ Selected Bibliography   461

Section Four
Managing the Supply Chain   *463*

12   Supply-Chain Management   *464*
■ Supply-Chain Management   466
Make or Buy   467
Outsourcing   469
Value Density (Value per Unit of Weight)   471
■ Purchasing   472
The Purchasing Organization   473
The Firm as a Supplier   474
Partnership Relationships: Buyer–Supplier   476

Supplier Selection Using the Analytic Hierarchy Process   476
■ Just-in-Time Purchasing   479
Multiple Suppliers versus Few Suppliers   480
■ Global Sourcing   482
Purchasing in the International Marketplace   483
International Distribution   484
■ Electronic Information Flow   486
Quick Response (QR)   488
Efficient Consumer Response (ECR)   488
Wal-Mart's Information System   489
■ Conclusion   489
■ Review and Discussion Questions   490
■ Problems   490
■ Case: Thomas Manufacturing Company   492
■ Case: Ohio Tool Company (Vendor Selection)   493
■ Selected Bibliography   495

13   Forecasting   *496*
■ Demand Management   498
■ Types of Forecasting   500
■ Components of Demand   500
■ Qualitative Techniques in Forecasting   503
Grass Roots   503
Market Research   503
Panel Consensus   503
Historical Analogy   504
Delphi Method   504
■ Time Series Analysis   505
Simple Moving Average   506
Weighted Moving Average   507
Exponential Smoothing   509
Forecast Errors   512
Sources of Error   513
Measurement of Error   513
Linear Regression Analysis   516
Decomposition of a Time Series   520
■ Casual Relationship Forecasting   526
Multiple Regression Analysis   528
■ Choosing a Forecasting Method   529
■ Focus Forecasting   530
Methodology of Focus Forecasting   530
Developing a Focus Forecasting System   530
■ Computer Programs   533
■ Conclusion   533
■ Formula Review   536
■ Solved Problems   537
■ Review and Discussion Questions   541
■ Problems   542
■ Selected Bibliography   549

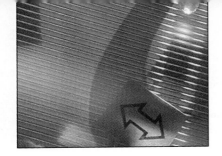

14 Aggregate Planning *550*
- Overview of Operations Planning Activities **552**
- Hierarchical Production Planning **554**
- Aggregate Production Planning **555**
Production Planning Environment **556**
Relevant Costs **558**
- Aggregate Planning Techniques **559**
A Cut-and-Try Example: The CA&J Company **559**
Aggregate Planning Applied to Services: Tucson Parks and Recreation Department **564**
Level Scheduling **568**
Mathematical Techniques **569**
- Conclusion **572**
- Solved Problem **573**
- Review and Discussion Questions **573**
- Problems **574**
- Case: XYZ Brokerage Firm **578**
- Selected Bibliography **579**

15 Inventory Systems for Independent Demand *580*
- Definition of Inventory **582**
- Purposes of Inventory **583**
- Inventory Costs **584**
- Independent versus Dependent Demand **585**
- Inventory Systems **585**
Classifying Models **586**
- Fixed-Order Quantity Models **587**
Fixed-Order Quantity Model with Usage During Production Time **590**
Establishing Safety Stock Levels **591**
Fixed-Order Quantity Model with Specified Service Level **595**
- Fixed-Time Period Models **599**
Fixed-Time Period Model with Specified Service Level **599**
- Special-Purpose Models **601**
- Miscellaneous Systems and Issues **605**
Three Simple Inventory Systems **605**
ABC Inventory Planning **606**
Inventory Accuracy and Cycle Counting **608**
Inventory Control in Services **611**
- Conclusion **613**

- Formula Review **613**
- Solved Problems **614**
- Review and Discussion Questions **614**
- Problems **615**
- Selected Bibliography **623**

16 Inventory Systems for Dependent Demand MRP-Type Systems *624*
- Where MRP Can Be Used **627**
- A Simple MRP Example **627**
- Master Production Schedule **629**
Time Fences **630**
- Material Requirements Planning (MRP) Systems **631**
Purposes of MRP **631**
Advantages of MRP **632**
Disadvantages of MRP **633**
- Material Requirements Planning System Structure **633**
Demand for Products **634**
Bill of Materials File **635**
Inventory Records File **636**
MRP Computer Program **637**
Output Reports **638**
Net Change Systems **639**
- An Example Using MRP **639**
Forecasting Demand **639**
Developing a Master Production Schedule **639**
Bill of Materials (Product Structure) File **640**
Inventory Records (Item Master) File **641**
Running the MRP Program **641**
- Improvements in the MRP System **644**
Computing Work Center Load **644**
Closed-Loop MRP **645**
MRP II (Manufacturing Resource Planning) **646**
- Embedding JIT into MRP **647**
- Lot Sizing in MRP Systems **648**
Lot-for-Lot **650**
Economic Order Quantity **650**
Least Total Cost **651**
Least Unit Cost **652**
Lot Size Choice **653**
Choosing the Best Lot Size **653**
- Advanced MRP-Type Systems **653**
SAP AG's R/3 **654**
- Conclusion **655**
- Solved Problems **655**
- Review and Discussion Questions **657**
- Problems **658**
- Case: Nichols Company **665**
- Selected Bibliography **668**

Supplement 16   SAP R/3   669
■ R/3 History   670
R/3 before 1994   670
R/3 in 1995   670
R/3 in 1996   672
R/3 in 1997   672
R/3 beyond 1997   672
■ Details of the Functional Components   672
Financial Accounting   673
Human Resources (HR)   673
Manufacturing and Logistics   674
Sales and Distribution (SD)   674
■ Implementing SAP R/3   676
■ Review and Discussion Questions   677
■ Selected Bibliography   677

17   Operations Scheduling   678
■ The Nature and Importance of Work Centers   680
Typical Scheduling and Control Functions   682
Objectives of Work-Center Scheduling   683
Job Sequencing   684
■ Priority Rules and Techniques   684
Scheduling *n* Jobs on One Machine   684
Comparison of Priority Rules   687
Scheduling *n* Jobs on Two Machines   688
Scheduling a Set Number of Jobs on the Same Number of Machines   689
Scheduling *n* Jobs on *m* Machines   691
■ Shop-Floor Control   692
Gantt Charts   693
Tools of Shop-Floor Control   693
Input/Output Control   693
Data Integrity   695
■ Example of a Shop Floor-Control System   696
Principles of Work-Center Scheduling   696
■ Improving Shop Performance   697
■ Personnel Scheduling in Services   698
Scheduling Consecutive Days Off   698
Scheduling Daily Work Times   700
Scheduling Hourly Work Times   701
■ Conclusion   702
■ Solved Problem   702
■ Review and Discussion Questions   703
■ Problems   704
■ Case: Keep Patients Waiting? Not in My Office   708
■ Case: McCall Diesel Motor Works   710
■ Selected Bibliography   712

Supplement 17   Simulation   713
■ Definition of Simulation   715
■ Simulation Methodology   715

Problem Definition   716
Constructing a Simulation Model   716
Specifing Values of Variables and Parameters   718
Evaluating Results   719
Validation   719
Proposing a New Experiment   720
Computerization   720
■ Simulating Waiting Lines   721
Example: A Two-Stage Assembly Line   721
■ Spreadsheet Simulation   725
■ Simulation Programs and Languages   726
Desirable Features of Simulation Software   728
■ Advantages and Disadvantages of Simulation   730
■ Conclusion   730
■ Solved Problems   731
■ Review and Discussion Questions   732
■ Problems   733
■ Selected Bibliography   740

Section Five
Revising the System   *741*

18   Operations Consulting   742
■ What Is Operations Consulting?   744
■ The Nature of the Management Consulting Industry   745
■ Economics of Consulting Firms   747
■ When Operations Consulting Is Needed   748
When Are Operations Consultants Needed?   749
■ The Operations Consulting Process   750
■ Operations Consulting Tool Kit   752
Problem Definition Tools   753
Data Gathering   755
Data Analysis and Solution Development   756
Cost Impact and Payoff Analysis   758
Implementation   759
■ Conclusion: Example of a Consulting Project— "Creating a Service Advantage at a Cellular Telephone Service Provider"   759
■ Review and Discussion Questions   765
■ Problems   765
■ Selected Bibliography   765

19   Business Process Reengineering   766
■ The Nature of Business Process Reengineering (BPR)   768
■ Principles of Reengineering   768
■ The Reengineering Process   771
State a Case for Action   772
Identify the Process   772

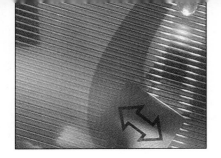

Evaluate Enablers   773

Understand the Current Process   774

Create a New Process Design   775

Implement the Reengineered Process   775

■ Process Redesign Techniques and Tools   776

■ Reengineering and Total Quality Management   779

■ Integrating Reengineering and Process Improvement   780

■ Conclusion   781

■ Review and Discussion Questions   781

■ Case: A California Auto Club Reengineers Customer Service   782

■ Case: Deborah Phelps of Showtime   784

■ Selected Bibliography   786

20   Synchronous Manufacturing and Theory of Constraints   788

■ Hockey-Stick Phenomenon   792

■ Goal of the Firm   793

■ Performance Measurements   793

Financial Measurements   794

Operational Measurements   794

Productivity   795

■ Unbalanced Capacity   795

Dependent Events and Statistical Fluctuations   796

■ Bottlenecks and Capacity-Constrained Resources   798

■ Basic Manufacturing Building Blocks   799

■ Methods for Control   800

Time Components   801

Finding the Bottleneck   801

Saving Time   802

Avoid Changing a Nonbottleneck into a Bottleneck   802

Drum, Buffer, Rope   803

Importance of Quality   805

Batch Sizes   806

How to Treat Inventory   809

■ Comparing Synchronous Manufacturing to MRP and JIT   810

■ VAT Classification of Firms   810

"V" Plant   811

"A" Plant   812

"T" Plant   814

■ Relationship with Other Functional Areas   815

■ Accounting's Influence   815

■ Marketing and Production   816

■ Conclusion   824

■ Solved Problem   824

■ Review and Discussion Questions   826

■ Problems   827

■ Selected Bibliography   830

Appendixes

A.   *Financial Analysis of Operations*   834

B.   *Uniformly Distributed Random Digits*   855

C.   *Normally Distributed Random Digits*   856

D.   *Areas of the Standard Normal Distribution*   857

E.   *Areas of the Cumulative Standard Normal Distribution*   858

F.   *Negative Exponential Distribution: Values of e^{-x}*   860

G.   *Interest Tables*   862

H.   *Answers to Selected Problems*   866

Photo Credits   869

Name Index   871

Subject Index   876

Production and Operations Management
Manufacturing and Services

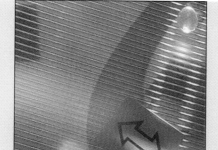

Nature and Context of Operations Management

1 Introduction to the Field

2 Operations Strategy and
   Competitiveness

3 Project Management

H OW WE MANAGE PRODUCTIVE RESOURCES IS CRITICAL to strategic growth and competitiveness. Operations management is the managing of these productive resources. It entails the design and control of systems responsible for the productive use of raw materials, human resources, equipment, and facilities in the development of a product or service. This section addresses the issues of operations strategy and competitiveness and how the field of operations management can provide direction in gaining and maintaining competitive advantage.

Chapter 1

Introduction to the Field

Chapter Outline

The Field of Operations Management, 5

    Operations Management Defined

    Decisions

    Production Systems

    Differences between Services and Goods
      Production

    OM in the Organizational Chart

Operations as Service, 10

Plan of This Book, 11

Historical Development of OM, 12

    Scientific Management

    Moving Assembly Line

    Hawthorne Studies

    Operations Research

    OM's Emergence as a Field

    Computers and the MRP Crusade

    JIT, TQC, and Factory Automation

    Manufacturing Strategy Paradigm

    Service Quality and Productivity

    Total Quality Management and Quality
      Certification

    Business Process Reengineering

    Electronic Enterprise

    Supply Chain Management

Case: The Purchasing Managers Index, 20

Key Terms

Operations Management (OM)

Service Operations

Corporate Strategy

Operations Strategy

Production System

Five P's of Operations
Management

Core Services

Value-Added Services

Life Cycle

Business Processes

Scientific Management

Mass Customization

Materials Requirements Planning
(MRP)

Just-In-Time (JIT)

Total Quality Control (TQC)

Computer-Integrated
Manufacturing (CIM)

Flexible Manufacturing System
(FMS)

Factory of the Future (FOF)

ISO 9000

Business Process Reengineering
(BPR)

www Links

Ben and Jerry's (http://www.benjerry.com)

Hewlett-Packard (http://www.hp.com)

Tektronix (http://www.tek.com)

National Association of Purchasing
Management (http://www.napm.org)

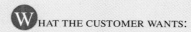

WHAT THE CUSTOMER WANTS:

I want a car that's built right.

I want dealer service that is fair, reliable, and pleasant.

I want some career skills that I can sell so I can afford to buy a car!

Building a quality car and having it serviced well are the essence of operations management (OM). Providing you with OM concepts that can help you in your career is the essence of this book.

American industry has entered this decade with a dramatically changed view of manufacturing and service operations' role in attaining competitive advantage. In the 70s and 80s, many domestic companies saw their market share decline due to their inability to compete with foreign firms in terms of product design, cost, or quality. Theories to explain this development span cultural differences, government macroeconomic policies, merger mania, neglect of human resources, insufficient investment in technology and R&D, and an excess of lawyers and/or MBAs. Whatever the cause, most experts now agree that world-class performance by operations in delivering high-quality, cost-competitive products and services is essential to survival in today's global economy. ●

Helping students understand the fundamental concepts and techniques necessary for attaining world-class performance in manufacturing and service operations is the main objective of this book. Besides its importance to corporate competitiveness, reasons for studying this field are

1. *A business education is incomplete without an understanding of modern approaches to managing operations.* Every organization produces some product or service so students must be exposed to modern approaches for doing this effectively. Moreover, hiring organizations now expect business graduates to speak knowledgeably about many issues in the field. While this has long been true in manufacturing, it is becoming equally important in services, both public and private. For example, "reinventing government" initiatives draw heavily on total quality management, business process reengineering, and just-in-time delivery—concepts that fall under the OM umbrella.

2. *Operations management provides a systematic way of looking at organizational processes.* OM uses analytical thinking to deal with real-world problems. It sharpens our understanding of the world around us, whether we are talking about how to compete with Japan or how many lines to have at the bank teller's window.

3. *Operations management presents interesting career opportunities.* These can be in direct supervision of operations or in staff positions in OM specialties such as supply chain management and quality assurance. In addition, consulting firms regularly recruit individuals with strong OM capabilities to work in such areas as process reengineering and computer-based inventory systems.

ACCOUNTING
FINANCE
MARKETING
MIS

4. *The concepts and tools of OM are widely used in managing other functions of a business.* All managers have to plan work, control quality, and ensure productivity of individuals under their supervision. Other employees must know how operations work to effectively perform their jobs. (See insert, "OM and Other Business Specialities.")

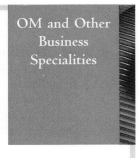

OM and Other Business Specialties

Accountants need to understand the basics of inventory management, capacity utilization, and labor standards to develop accurate cost data, perform audits, and prepare financial reports. Cost accountants in particular must be aware of how just-in-time (JIT) and computer-integrated manufacturing (CIM) work.

Financial managers can use inventory and capacity concepts to judge the need for capital investments, to forecast cash flow, and to manage current assets. Further, there is a mutual concern between OM and finance in specific decisions such as make-or-buy and plant expansion and/or relocation.

Marketing specialists need to understand what operations can do relative to meeting customer due dates, product customization, and new product introduction.

In service industries, marketing and production often take place simultaneously, so marketing and OM have overlapping interests.

Personnel specialists must know how jobs are designed, the relationship between standards and incentive plans, and the types of production skills required of the direct workforce.

MIS specialists often install operations information systems that they themselves design or that are developed as off-the-shelf software by computer companies. A major business application of computers is in production control.

Entrepreneurs often fail because they run out of working capital due to poor production planning and inventory management.

■ THE FIELD OF OPERATIONS MANAGEMENT

Operations Management Defined

Operations management may be defined as the design, operation, and improvement of the production systems that create the firm's primary products or services. Like marketing and finance, OM is a functional field of business with clear line management responsibilities. This point is important because operations management is frequently confused with operations research and management science (OR/MS) and industrial engineering (IE). The essential difference is that OM is a field of management, while OR/MS is the application of quantitative methods to decision-making in all fields, and IE is an engineering discipline. Thus, while operations managers use the decision-making tools of OR/MS (such as critical path scheduling) and are concerned with many of the same issues as IE (such as factory automation), OM's distinct management role distinguishes it from these other disciplines.

Operations Management

Decisions

Operations decisions are made in the context of the firm as a whole. Starting at the top of Exhibit 1.1, the marketplace (the firm's customers for its products or services) shapes the firm's **corporate strategy.** This strategy is based on the corporate mission, and in essence, it reflects how the firm plans to use all its resources and functions (marketing, finance, and operations) to gain competitive advantage. The **operations strategy** specifies how the firm will employ its production capabilities to support its corporate strategy. (Similarly, the marketing strategy addresses how the firm will sell and distribute its goods and services, and the finance strategy identifies how best to utilize the firm's financial resources.)

Corporate Strategy

Operations Strategy

Summary Model of the Field

```
                    ┌─────────────────┐
                    │   Marketplace   │
                    └────────┬────────┘
                             │
                    ┌────────▼────────┐
                    │ Corporate Strategy │
                    └────────┬────────┘
         ┌───────────────────┼───────────────────┐
 ┌───────▼───────┐  ┌────────▼────────┐  ┌───────▼────────┐
 │ Finance Strategy │  │ Operations Strategy │  │ Marketing Strategy │
 └───────────────┘  └────────┬────────┘  └────────────────┘
                    ┌────────▼────────┐
                    │ Operations Management │
                    └────────┬────────┘
```

Inputs

Materials
Customers

People   Plants   Parts   Processes

Planning and Control Systems

Outputs

Products
Services

— Production System —

Ben and Jerry's mission statement impacts decisions such as where to locate, and how to make the product. The company believes its social mission is to improve the quality of life in its local, national, and international communities. Its success, however, is based upon producing a great ice cream (with large chunks of chocolate in each quart of Cherry Garcia).

(http://www.benjerry.com)

Within the operations function, management decisions can be divided into three broad areas:

Strategic (long-term) decisions.
Tactical (intermediate-term) decisions.
Operational planning and control (short-term) decisions.

The strategic issues are usually very broad in nature, addressing such questions as: How will we make the product? Where do we locate the facility or facilities? How much capacity do we need? When should we add more capacity? Thus, by necessity, the time frame for strategic decisions is typically very long—usually several years or more, depending on the specific industry. (Chapter 2 discusses operations strategy in depth.)

Operations management decisions at the strategic level impact the company's long-range effectiveness in terms of how it can address its customers' needs. Thus, for the firm to succeed, these decisions must be in alignment with the corporate strategy. Decisions made at the strategic level become the fixed conditions or operating constraints under which the firm must operate in both the intermediate and short term.

At the next level in the decision-making process, tactical planning primarily addresses how to efficiently schedule material and labor within the constraints of previously made strategic decisions. Issues on which OM concentrates on this level are: How many workers do we need? When do we need them? Should we work overtime or put on a second shift? When should we have material delivered? Should we have a finished goods inventory? These tactical decisions, in turn, become the operating constraints under which operational planning and control decisions are made.

Management decisions with respect to operational planning and control are narrow and short-term by comparison. Issues at this level include: What jobs do we work on today or this week? Who do we assign to what tasks? What jobs have priority?

Production Systems

The heart of OM is the management of production systems. A **production system** uses operations resources to transform inputs into some desired output. An input may be a raw material, a customer, or a finished product from another system. As indicated in the bottom of Exhibit 1.1, operations resources consist of what we term the **five P's of operations management:** people, plants, parts, processes, and planning and control systems. *People* are the direct and indirect workforce. *Plants* include the factories or service branches where production is carried out. *Parts* include the materials (or, in the case of services, the supplies) that go through the system. *Processes* include the equipment and steps by which production is accomplished. *Planning and control systems* are the procedures and information management uses to operate the system. Transformations that take place include

Physical, as in manufacturing.

Location, as in transportation.

Exchange, as in retailing.

Storage, as in warehousing.

Physiological, as in health care.

Informational, as in telecommunications.

These transformations, of course, are not mutually exclusive. For example, a department store can (1) allow shoppers to compare prices and quality (informational), (2) hold items in inventory until needed (storage), and (3) sell goods (exchange). Exhibit 1.2 presents sample input–transformation–output relationships for a variety of systems. Note that only the direct resources are listed. A more complete system description would also include managerial and support functions.

Production System

Five P's of Operations Management

System	Primary Inputs	Resources	Primary Transformation Function(s)	Typical Desired Output
Hospital	Patients	MDs, nurses, medical supplies, equipment	Health care (physiological)	Healthy individuals
Restaurant	Hungry customers	Food, chef, wait-staff, environment	Well-prepared, well-served food; agreeable environment (physical and exchange)	Satisfied customers
Automobile factory	Sheet steel, engine parts	Tools, equipment, workers	Fabrication and assembly of cars (physical)	High-quality cars
College or university	High school graduates	Teachers, books, classrooms	Imparting knowledge and skills (informational)	Educated individuals
Department store	Shoppers	Displays, stocks of goods, sales clerks	Attract shoppers, promote products, fill orders (exchange)	Sales to satisfied customers
Distribution center	Stockkeeping units (SKUs)	Storage bins, stockpickers	Storage and redistribution	Fast delivery, availability of SKUs

Exhibit 1.2

Input–Transformation–Output Relationships for Typical Systems

Differences between Services and Goods Production

She essential difference between the two is that service is an intangible process, while a good is the physical output of a process. To put it another way, a service is something that "if you drop it on your foot it won't hurt you." Other differences are that in services, location of the service facility and direct customer involvement in creating the output are often essential factors; in goods production, they usually are not. There are many shades of gray here. Manufacturers provide many services as part of their product, and many services often manufacture the physical products that they deliver to their customers or consume goods in creating the service. McDonald's manufactures a tangible product, but because it is designed to have some contact with the customer to complete the service production process, the firm is in the service category.

Vol. I
"Services"

Also, from an operations perspective, customers are on the "shop floor" when consuming many services. The shop floor may be called the front office, dining area, operating room, or passenger cabin, depending on the industry. There are also many behind-the-scenes activities with tangible inputs and outputs. For example, major airlines, banks, and insurance companies have large back offices that support customer contact operations. As Chapter 5 on service process design relates, such back-office operations process things and information (e.g., tickets, checks, and claims) and so can be run much like a factory.

Exhibit I.3   OM in the Organization Chart

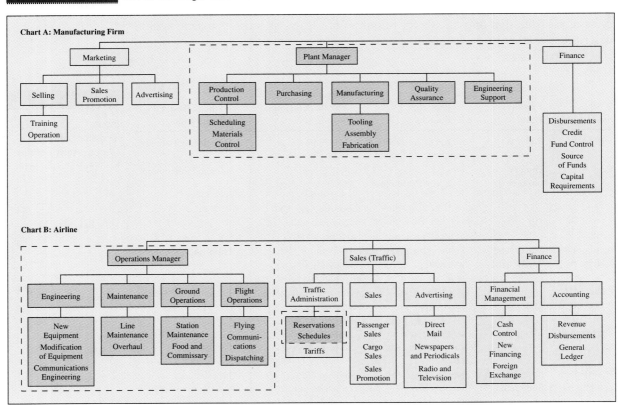

OM in the Organizational Chart

Exhibit 1.3 locates operations activities within a manufacturing organization and a service organization. Aside from differences in terminology, the service organization also differs from the manufacturing firm in structure. The manufacturing company typically groups operations activities to produce its products in one department. Service firms scatter operations activities throughout the organization. For example, reservations scheduling in an airline is part of the production process for airline travel, even though it is carried out by a non-operations department. This is seen even more clearly in banking, where there is often a retail operations department and a check processing operations department. Note that in manufacturing, the plant manager's position is used to administer the various support activities required for production. Note also that in both types of organizations, it is typical for operations activities to account for the lion's share of capital investment and workforce. Exhibit 1.4 lists some line and staff jobs that are frequently viewed as relating to the operations function.

Organizational Level	Manufacturing Industries	Service Industries
Upper	Vice president of manufacturing Regional manager of manufacturing	Vice president of operations (airline) Chief administrator (hospital)
Middle	Plant manager Program manager	Store manager (department store) Facilities manager (wholesale distributor)
Lower	Department supervisor Shift supervisor Crew chief	Branch manager (bank) Department supervisor (insurance company) Assistant manager (hotel)
Staff	Production controller Materials manager Quality manager Purchasing agent Work methods analyst Process engineer	Systems and procedures analyst Purchasing agent Inspector Dietician (hospital) Customer service manager

Exhibit 1.4

Line and Staff Jobs in Operations Management

Tektronix, a manufacturer of electronic equipment, has pioneered direct communication between customers and shop-floor employees. Into the shipping carton of every oscilloscope it sells, the company inserts a postcard listing the names of the workers who built the scope, along with an "800" number to a phone on the shop floor. Every day the factory gets several calls from customers; the six people working in the repair area who answer them have all received telephone training.

Customers call for various reasons: to ask questions about the use of their oscilloscopes, to request information about other Tektronix products, and to see if "they can really talk to the person who made their product." Workers and managers meet daily to discuss these calls; if necessary, further conversations with the customer follow up the meetings. In some cases, workers will call customers six months after delivery to find out how well their products are performing. (*http://www.tek.com*)

Linking the Shop-Floor Worker to the Customer

Source: R. B. Chase and D. A. Garvin, "The Service Factory," *Harward Business Review,* July–August 1989, pp. 65–66.

■ OPERATIONS AS SERVICE

The emerging model in industry is that every organization is in the service business. This is true whether the organization makes big planes or Big Macs. From this we must recognize that manufacturing operations, as well as every other part of the organization, are also in the service business even if the customer is an internal one. In manufacturing, such services can be divided into core and value-added services that are provided to internal and external customers of the factory.

Core Services

The **core services** customers want are products that are made correctly, are customized to their needs, are delivered on time, and are priced competitively. These are commonly summarized as the classic performance objectives of the operations function: *quality, flexibility, speed,* and *price* (or cost of production). Achieving these services is the focus of this book and is discussed in detail in Chapter 2.

Value-Added Services

Value-added services are services that simply make the external customer's life easier or, in the case of internal customers, help them to better carry out their particular function. Value-added factory services can be classified into four broad categories: information, problem solving, sales support, and field support.

1. *Information* is the ability to furnish critical data on product performance, process parameters, and cost to internal groups (such as R&D) and to external customers, who then use the data to improve their own operations or products. For example, Hewlett-Packard's Fort Collins quality department provides quality data sheets and videotapes documenting actual product testing and field quality performance to field sales and service personnel. (*http://www.hp.com*)

2. *Problem solving* is the ability to help internal and external groups solve problems, especially in quality. For example, Raritan Corporation, a metal rod fabricator, sends factory workers out with salespeople to troubleshoot quality problems. Those factory workers then return to the factory and join with shop-floor personnel on remedial efforts.

3. *Sales support* is the ability to enhance sales and marketing efforts by demonstrating the technology, equipment, or production systems the company is trying to sell. In part, Digital Equipment Corporation sells its CIM (computer-integrated manufacturing) system by showcasing it on its own factory floor. Sometimes sales are enhanced by the factory showing off its workforce's skills. For example, to demonstrate its products' quality, Sara Lee has visitors observe the artistic skills of its "meringue fluffers" on its pie line.

4. *Field support* is the ability to replace defective parts quickly (for example, Caterpillar promises to make repair parts available anywhere in the world within 48 hours) or to replenish stocks quickly to avoid downtime or stockouts (for example, The Limited, a retail chain, is linked to its Hong Kong textile mills via a sophisticated computer system that signals factories to begin producing fast-selling items as soon as weekly sales figures are collected).

Value-added services provided to external customers yield two benefits. First, they differentiate the organization from the competition. Indeed, in many cases it is easier to copy a firm's product than it is to create the value-added service infrastructure to support it. Second, these services build relationships that bind customers to the organization in a positive way.

■ PLAN OF THIS BOOK

This book is organized around the stages that a production system goes through in its birth-to-maturity **life cycle.** This life cycle approach is summarized in Exhibit 1.5. We have chosen this structure because it mirrors system development in a changing real world. The text starts by analyzing the competitive strategy under which the system is to operate. The fact that this strategy will change over time, as the firm grows, is developed in this section. Making changes in an organization usually involves a project of some sort. Much of the success of projects, particularly complex ones requiring many people from diverse areas, depends on proper organization. Project management covers this important topic.

Life Cycle

The book then looks at product design and process choices that set the foundation for the production system. The importance of quality as a fundamental building block around which systems are designed is included in this section. Next, the text considers the design of the various parts of the production system—getting the five P's of OM into alignment to achieve efficient production.

The text then continues with extensive coverage of the tools required to manage day-to-day supply chain operations. This is the "block and tackle" of operations management, and it involves methods for working with suppliers, forecasting demand and planning short-term capacity requirements, designing inventory control systems, and scheduling.

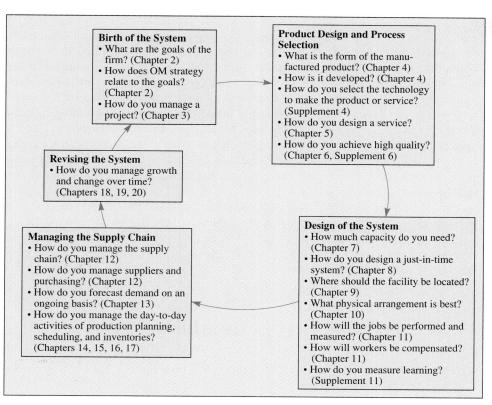

Exhibit 1.5

Key Issues in the Life of Production System

Birth of the System
• What are the goals of the firm? (Chapter 2)
• How does OM strategy relate to the goals? (Chapter 2)
• How do you manage a project? (Chapter 3)

Revising the System
• How do you manage growth and change over time? (Chapters 18, 19, 20)

Managing the Supply Chain
• How do you manage the supply chain? (Chapter 12)
• How do you manage suppliers and purchasing? (Chapter 12)
• How do you forecast demand on an ongoing basis? (Chapter 13)
• How do you manage the day-to-day activities of production planning, scheduling, and inventories? (Chapters 14, 15, 16, 17)

Product Design and Process Selection
• What is the form of the manufactured product? (Chapter 4)
• How is it developed? (Chapter 4)
• How do you select the technology to make the product or service? (Supplement 4)
• How do you design a service? (Chapter 5)
• How do you achieve high quality? (Chapter 6, Supplement 6)

Design of the System
• How much capacity do you need? (Chapter 7)
• How do you design a just-in-time system? (Chapter 8)
• Where should the facility be located? (Chapter 9)
• What physical arrangement is best? (Chapter 10)
• How will the jobs be performed and measured? (Chapter 11)
• How will workers be compensated? (Chapter 11)
• How do you measure learning? (Supplement 11)

The text concludes with a section focused on revising the system. All organizations must change over time. This change is driven largely by the progress of technology and by changing customer expectations. Consultants often play an important role in the change. Chapter 18 on the subject gives an overview of how the largest consulting companies are leading the charge to improve operations. Chapter 19, "Business Process Reengineering," and Chapter 20, "Synchronous Manufacturing," contain current thinking on how change should be implemented. You will see that the topics covered in these last two chapters strongly relate to our introductory section, particularly Chapter 2, "Operations Strategy and Competitiveness," and so the cycle of change progresses.

Note that the text is not built around the life cycle of any one system. On the contrary, we have intentionally chosen examples from a variety of manufacturing and service operations to emphasize that good operations management is essential in such diverse systems as hospitals, banks, universities, and factories.

Business Processes

Much of the emphasis today in operations management is concerned with the management of **business processes.** A business process is some activity that a business must perform in order to meet the needs of its customers. Business processes can be divided into those that are operationally oriented (essentially, those related to the product and customer) and those that are management oriented (those that deal with obtaining and coordinating resources). Each chapter of the book provides information that is important to the design and operation of these business processes. Essentially, this is what this book and the course you are taking are all about.

One of the more difficult things to explain is how all the topics of this book fit together. Actually, the various topics, concepts, and techniques can be mixed and matched to all types of situations. Take, for example, Chapter 15, "Inventory Systems for Independent Demand." The ideas in that chapter can be applied to managing inventory in grocery stores, department stores, and automobile parts stores. But they can also be applied to the drug pharmacy in a hospital, to a gas station, to inventory in a beer distribution center, to salt in a highway department preparing for the winter, to supplies for a space shuttle mission, and to food for the local high school cafeteria. Similarly, the information provided in Chapter 3, "Project Management," can be applied to virtually any kind of project. Whether we want to build a house, install a new machine, build a manufacturing plant, build an airplane, implement a new marketing plan, or install a new cost accounting system, the techniques covered in this chapter will be relevant and applicable.

Part of the trick to getting the most out of this book and the course you are taking is figuring out exactly how you can apply the lessons you are learning to a particular situation. Part of being a great manager is learning how to take a proven concept from one context and apply it to another. We give you all kinds of examples in this book, but we are only scratching the surface. We show you proven ways to approach many problems, and we hope that you are innovative in how you apply these ideas.

■ HISTORICAL DEVELOPMENT OF OM

Exhibit 1.6 gives a timeline of OM's history. We now highlight some of its major concepts and their developers.[1]

---

[1] See Victor Sower, Jaideep Motwani, and Michael Savoie, *Classic Readings in Operations Management* (Fort Worth: The Dryden Press, 1995) for additional details.

Historical Summary of OM

Exhibit 1.6

Year	Concept	Tool	Originator
1910s	Principles of scientific management	Formalized time-study and work-study concepts	Frederick W. Taylor (United States)
	Industrial psychology	Motion study	Frank and Lillian Gilbreth (United States)
	Moving assembly line	Activity scheduling chart	Henry Ford and Henry L. Gantt (United States)
	Economic lot size	EOQ applied to inventory control	F. W. Harris (United States)
1930s	Quality control	Sampling inspection and statistical tables for quality control	Walter Shewhart, H. F. Dodge, and H. G. Romig (United States)
	Hawthorne studies of worker motivation	Activity sampling for work analysis	Elton Mayo (United States) and L. H. C. Tippett (England)
1940s	Multidisciplinary team approaches to complex system problems	Simplex method of linear programming	Operations research groups (England) and George B. Dantzig (United States)
1950s–60s	Extensive development of operations research tools	Simulation, waiting-line theory, decision theory, mathematical programming, project scheduling techniques of PERT and CPM	Many researchers in the United States and Western Europe
1970s	Widespread use of computers in business	Shop scheduling, inventory control, forecasting, project management, MRP	Led by computer manufacturers, in particular, IBM; Joseph Orlicky and Oliver Wight were the major MRP innovators (United States)
	Service quality and productivity	Mass production in the service sector	McDonald's restaurants
1980s	Manufacturing strategy paradigm	Manufacturing as a competitive weapon	Harvard Business School faculty (United States)
	JIT, TQC, and factory automation	KANBAN, Poka-yokes, CIM, FMS, CAD/CAM, robots, etc.	Tai-Ichi Ohno of Toyota Motors (Japan), W. E. Deming and J. M. Juran (United States), and engineering disciplines (United States, Germany, and Japan)
	Synchronous manufacturing	Bottleneck analysis, OPT, theory of constraints	Eliyahu M. Goldratt (Israel)
1990s	Total quality management	Baldrige quality award, ISO 9000 registration, quality function deployment, value and concurrent engineering, continuous improvement paradigm	National Institute of Standards and Technology, American Society of Quality Control (United States), and International Organization for Standardization (Europe)
	Business process reengineering	Radical change paradigm	Michael Hammer and major consulting firms (United States)
	Electronic enterprise	Internet, World Wide Web	U.S. government, Netscape Communications Corporation, and Microsoft Corporation
	Supply chain management	SAP/R3, client/server software	SAP (Germany), Oracle (United States)

Scientific Management

Although operations management has existed since people started to produce, the advent of **scientific management** around the turn of the century is probably the major historical landmark for the field. This concept was developed by Frederick W. Taylor, an imaginative engineer and insightful observer of organizational activities.

Scientific
Management

The essence of Taylor's philosophy was that (1) scentific laws govern how much a worker can produce per day, (2) it is the function of management to discover and use these laws in the operation of productive systems, and (3) it is the function of the worker to carry out management's wishes without question. Taylor's philosophy was not greeted with approval by all of his contemporaries. On the contrary, some unions resented or feared scientific management—with some justification. In too many instances, managers of the day were quick to embrace the mechanisms of Taylor's philosophy—time-study, incentive plans, and so forth—but ignored their responsibility to organize and standardize the work to be done. Hence, there were numerous cases of rate cutting (reducing the payment per piece if the production rate was deemed too high), overwork of labor, and poorly designed work methods. The overreaction to such abuses led to the introduction of a bill in Congress in 1913 to prohibit the use of time-study and incentive plans in federal government operations. The unions advocating the legislation claimed that Taylor's subject in several of his time-study experiments, a steelworker called Schmidt, had died from overwork as a result of following Taylor's methods. (As evidence, they even distributed pictures of Schmidt's "grave.") It was later discovered that Schmidt (whose real name was Henry Nolle) was alive and well and working as a teamster.[2] Ultimately, the bill was defeated.

Note that Taylor's ideas were widely accepted in contemporary Japan. A Japanese translation of Taylor's book, *Principles of Scientific Management* (titled *The Secret of Saving Lost Motion*), sold more than 2 million copies. To this day, there is a strong legacy of Taylorism in Japanese approaches to manufacturing management.[3]

Notable coworkers of Taylor were Frank and Lillian Gilbreth and Henry L. Gantt. Their work is well known to management scholars. It is probably not well known that Taylor, a devout Quaker, requested "cussing lessons" from an earthy foreman to help him communicate with workers; that Frank Gilbreth defeated champion bricklayers in bricklaying contests by using his own principles of motion economy; or that Gantt won a presidential citation for his application of the Gantt chart to shipbuilding during World War I.

Moving Assembly Line

The year 1913 saw the introduction of one of the machine age's greatest technological innovations—the moving assembly line for the manufacture of Ford cars.[4] Before the line was introduced, in August of that year, each auto chassis was assembled by one worker in about $12\frac{1}{2}$ hours. Eight months later, when the line was in its final form, with each worker performing a small unit of work and the chassis being moved mechanically, the average labor time per chassis was 93 minutes. This technological break-through, coupled with concepts of scientific management, represents the classic application of labor specialization and is still common today.

---

[2] Milton J. Nadworny, "Schmidt and Stakhanov: Work Heroes in Two Systems," *California Management Review* 6, no. 4 (Summer 1964), pp. 69–76.

[3] Charles J. McMillan, "Production Planning in Japan," *Journal of General Management* 8, no. 4, pp. 44–71.

[4] Ford is said to have gotten the idea for an assembly line from observing a Swiss watch manufacturer's use of the technology. Incidentally, all Model-T Fords were painted black. Why? Because black paint dried fastest.

Hawthorne Studies

Mathematical and statistical developments dominated the evolution of operations management from Taylor's time up to around the 1940s. An exception was the Hawthorne studies, conducted in the 1930s by a research team from the Harvard Graduate School of Business Administration and supervised by sociologist Elton Mayo. These experiments were designed to study the effects of certain environmental changes on assembly workers' output at the Western Electric plant in Hawthorne, Illinois. The unexpected findings, reported in *Management and the Worker* (1939) by F. J. Roethlisberger and W. J. Dickson, intrigued sociologists and students of "traditional" scientific management alike. To the surprise of the researchers, changing the level of illumination, for example, had much less effect on output than did the way in which the changes were introduced to the workers. That is, reductions in illumination in some instances led to increased output because workers felt an obligation to their group to keep output high. Discoveries such as these had tremendous implications for work design and motivation and ultimately led many organizations to establish personnel management and human relations departments.

Operations Research

World War II, with its complex problems of logistics control and weapons systems design, provided the impetus for the development of the interdisciplinary, mathematically oriented field of operations research. Operations research (OR) brings together practitioners in such diverse fields as mathematics, psychology, and economics. Specialists in these disciplines form a team to structure and analyze a problem in quantitative terms so they can obtain a mathematically optimal solution. As mentioned earlier, operations research, or its approximate synonym *management science,* now provides many of the quantitative tools used in operations management as well as other business disciplines.

OM's Emergence as a Field

In the late 1950s and early 1960s, scholars began to deal specifically with operations management as opposed to industrial engineering or operations research. Writers such as Edward Bowman and Robert Fetter (*Analysis for Production and Operations Management* [1957]) and Elwood S. Buffa (*Modern Production Management* [1961]) noted the commonality of problems faced by all productive systems and emphasized the importance of viewing production operations as a system. They also stressed the useful applications of waiting-line theory, simulation, and linear programming, which are now standard topics in the field. In 1973, Chase and Aquilano's first edition of this book stressed the need "to put the management back into operations management" and suggested the life cycle as a means of organizing the subject.

Computers and the MRP Crusade

The major development of the 1970s was the broad use of computers in operations problems. For manufacturers, the big breakthrough was the application of **materials requirements planning (MRP)** to production control. This approach ties together in a computer program all the parts that go into complicated products. This program then enables production planners to quickly adjust production schedules and inventory

Materials Requirements Planning

Japan's Personalized Bike Production

Does your bike fit you to a "T"? Would you like one that does? If you are willing to pay 20 to 30 percent more than you would pay for a mass-produced bike, you can get a Panasonic bike manufactured to exactly match your size, weight, and color preference. You can even get your bike within three weeks of your order (only two weeks if you visit Japan). This is accomplished via a process called the Panasonic Individual Customer System (PICS), which skillfully employs computers, robots, and a small factory workforce to make one-of-a-kind models at the National Bicycle Industrial Company factory in Kokubu, Japan.

The National Bicycle Industrial Company (NBIC), a subsidiary of electronics giant Matsushita, began making the bikes under the Panasonic brand in 1987. With the introduction of its personalized order system (POS) for the Japanese market (PICS was developed for overseas sales), the firm gained international attention as a classic example of **mass customization**—producing products to order in lot sizes of one.

The factory itself has 21 employees and a computer-aided design system, and is capable of producing any of 8 million variations on 18 models of racing, road, and mountain bikes in 199 color patterns for virtually any size person.

The PIC system works in the following way. A customer visits a local Panasonic bicycle store and is measured on a special frame. The storeowner then faxes the specifications to the master control room at the factory. There, an operator punches the specs into a minicomputer, which automatically creates a unique blueprint and produces a bar code. (The CAD blueprint takes about three minutes as opposed to three hours required by company draftspeople prior to computerization.) The bar code is then attached to metal tubes and gears that ultimately become the customer's personal bike. At various stages in the process, line workers access the customer's requirement using the bar code label and a scanner. This information, displayed on a CRT terminal at each station, is fed directly to the computer-controlled machines that are part of a local area computer network. At each step of production, a computer reading the code knows that each part belongs to a specific bike, and it tells a robot where to weld or tells a painter which pattern to follow.

Despite the use of computers and robots, the process is not highly automated. Gears are hand-wired, assembly is manual, and the customer's name is silk-screened by hand with the touch of an artisan. The entire manufacturing and assembly time required to

purchases to meet changing demands for final products. Clearly, the massive data manipulation required for changing schedules on products with thousands of parts would be impossible without such programs and the computer capacity to run them. The promotion of this approach (pioneered by Joseph Orlicky of IBM and consultant Oliver Wight) by the American Production and Inventory Control Society (APICS) has been termed *the MRP Crusade.*

JIT, TQC, and Factory Automation

Just-in-Time

The 1980s saw a revolution in the management philosophies and the technologies by which production is carried out. **Just-in-time (JIT)** production is the major breakthrough in manufacturing philosophy. Pioneered by the Japanese, JIT is an integrated set of activities designed to achieve high-volume production using minimal inventories of parts that arrive at the workstation just in time. This philosophy—coupled with **total quality control (TQC),** which aggressively seeks to eliminate causes of production defects—is now a cornerstone in many manufacturers' production practices.

Total Quality Control

As profound as JIT's impact has been, factory automation in its various forms promises to have even greater impact on operations management in coming decades. Such terms as **computer-integrated manufacturing (CIM), flexible manufacturing systems (FMS),** and **factory of the future (FOF)** are already familiar to many readers of this book and are becoming everyday concepts to OM practitioners.

CIM
FMS
FOF

complete a single bike is 150 minutes, and the factory can make about 60 a day. NBIC's mass-production factory (which makes 90 percent of its annual production) can make a standard model in 90 minutes. One might ask why a customer must wait up to three weeks given that it takes less than three hours to make a custom model. According to the general manager of sales, "We could have made the time shorter, but we want people to feel excited about waiting for something special."

To provide a more personal touch to mass customization, the factory is given the responsibility to communicate directly with the customer. Immediately after the factory receives the customer's order, a personalized computer-generated drawing of the bicycle is mailed with a note thanking the customer for choosing the bike. This is followed up with a second personal note, three months later, inquiring about the customer's satisfaction with the bicycle. Finally, a "bicycle birthday card" is sent to commemorate the first anniversary of the bicycle.

NBIC is now contemplating extending the Panasonic system to all of its bicycle production, while Matsushita is considering applying the concept to industrial machinery.

Customers are custom fitted in the retail store with options for 11,231,862 possible variations of the bicycle.

Source: Surech Kotha, "The National Bicycle Industrial Company: Implementing a Strategy of Mass-Customization," case study from the International University of Japan, 1993; and Susan Moffat, "Japan's New Personalized Production," *Fortune,* October 22, 1990, pp. 132–35.

Manufacturing Strategy Paradigm

The late 1970s and early 1980s saw the development of the Manufacturing Strategy Paradigm by researchers at the Harvard Business School. This work by professors William Abernathy, Kim Clark, Robert Hayes, and Steven Wheelwright (built on earlier efforts by Wickham Skinner) emphasized how manufacturing executives could use their factories' capabilities as strategic competitive weapons. The paradigm itself identified how what we call the five P's of production management can be analyzed as strategic and tactical decision variables. Central to their thinking was the notion of factory focus and manufacturing trade-offs. They argued that because a factory cannot excel on all performance measures, its management must derive a focused strategy, creating a focused factory that does a limited set of tasks extremely well. This raised the need for making trade-offs among such performance measures as low cost, high quality, and high flexibility in designing and managing factories.

Service Quality and Productivity

The great diversity of service industries—ranging from airlines to zoos, with about 2,000 different types in between—precludes identifying any single pioneer or developer that has made a major impact across the board in these areas. However, one service company's—McDonald's—unique approach to quality and productivity has been so successful that it stands as a reference point in thinking about how to deliver high-volume standardized services. In fact, McDonald's operating system is so successful that the president of Chaparral Steel used it as a model in planning the company's highly efficient minimills.

Total Quality Management and Quality Certification

The unquestioned major development in the field of operations management, as well as in management practice in general, is total quality management (TQM). Though practiced by many companies in the 1980s, TQM became truly pervasive in the 1990s. All operations executives are aware of the quality message put forth by the so-called quality gurus—W. Edwards Deming, Joseph M. Juran, and Philip Crosby. Helping the quality movement along is the Baldrige National Quality Award, which was started in 1986 under the direction of the American Society of Quality Control and the National Institute of Standards and Technology. The Baldrige Award recognizes up to five companies a year for outstanding quality management systems.

 **ISO 9000**

The **ISO 9000** certification standards put forth by the International Organization for Standardization now play a major role in setting quality standards for global manufacturers in particular. Many European companies require that their vendors meet these standards as a condition for obtaining contracts.

Business Process Reengineering

Business Process Reengineering

The need to become lean to remain competitive in the global economic recession in the 1990s pushed companies to seek major innovations in the processes by which they run their operations. The flavor of **business process reengineering (BPR)** is conveyed in the title of Michael Hammer's influential article "Reengineering Work: Don't Automate, Obliterate." The approach seeks to make revolutionary changes as opposed to evolutionary changes (which are commonly advocated in TQM). It does this by taking a fresh look at what the organization is trying to do in all its business processes, and then eliminating nonvalue-added steps and computerizing the remaining ones to achieve the desired outcome.

Electronic Enterprise

The recent quick adoption of the Internet and the World Wide Web during the late 1990s is amazing. Electronic enterprise refers to the use of the Internet as an essential element of business activity. The Internet is an outgrowth of a government network called the ARPANET, which was created in 1969 by the Defense Department of the United States government. The use of Web pages, forms, and interactive search engines is changing the way people collect information, shop, and communicate. Even today, connections to the Internet are relatively inexpensive, and Microsoft and Netscape have led the way by making the "Web browsing" software virtually free.

Supply Chain Management

The idea is to apply a total system approach to managing the flow of information, materials, and services from raw material suppliers through factories and warehouses to the end customer. Recent trends such as outsourcing and mass customization are forcing companies to find flexible ways to meet customer demand. The focus is on optimizing those core activities to maximize the speed of response to changes in customer expectations.

■ CONCLUSION

We conclude our introductory chapter with a summary of current issues facing OM executives. These interrelated issues will be addressed as we move through the system life cycle.

Vol.1 "Lean Production"

1. Speeding up the time it takes to get new products into production   This calls for coordination between product designers, process engineers, and production. To be effective, such specialties must work as a team to avoid the common "silo effect," in which each group worries only about its particular function. Completing activities "concurrently" rather than sequentially is an important ingredient to reducing the time it takes to deliver new products.

ENGINEERING
MARKETING

2. Developing flexible production systems to enable mass customization of products and services   In virtually every industry, there is a broadening of product lines to provide the variety of choices that customers want (or at least, that marketers say they want). This is seen in cars, where Buick has a suspension system that lets a driver choose between a soft or a sport ride; in computers, where Toshiba alone produces more than 30 varieties of laptop computers; and even in diapers, where Procter & Gamble's Pampers line has 13 different product designs (not just sizes) that reflect changes in infants as they grow to toddlers.[5]

3. Managing global production networks   This issue has three aspects. One is assuring that components produced outside of the United States meet design and quality requirements. This entails careful selection of suppliers and anticipating local labor and government actions. The second is managing the logistics of shipping and receiving parts. The third is developing the information system to track and monitor the first two.

4. Developing and integrating new process technologies into existing production systems   Technology is abundant, but applying it effectively is often difficult. Sometimes the problem lies in the complexity of linking computer-based systems. Other times it involves cost accounting measures that force high utilization of expensive equipment, even if some less-expensive machine could perform the task just as well. (A common example here is dedicating expensive flexible manufacturing machinery to making long runs of a single product model rather than using cheaper inflexible equipment.)

5. Achieving high quality quickly and keeping it up in the face of restructuring   TQM is here to stay, but companies do not have the luxury of the long development periods to achieve quality parity with the competition. Likewise, it is hard to maintain workforce enthusiasm for quality when their jobs are at risk.

6. Managing a diverse workforce   Multiple languages and multiple cultures are common on U.S. shop floors as well as in other developed countries. For example, 26 different cultures are represented among the 420 workers at Toyota Autobody of California's truck bed assembly plant in Long Beach. (Only four of these workers are Japanese, and they are staff advisers on assignment from Japan.)

7. Conforming to environmental constraints, ethical standards, and government regulations   Issues of social responsibility affect all parts of the organization, but operations is often the focal point because it is the prime user of physical resources that may lead to pollution and other safety hazards. Companies are now developing so-called *green* strategies as part of their corporate planning.[6]

---

[5] These examples are taken from B. Joseph Pine II, *Mass Customization: The New Frontier in Business Competition* (Boston: Harvard Business School Press, 1993), pp. 33–39.

[6] See Michael Porter and Claas Vander Linde, "Green and Competitive: Ending the Stalemate," *Harvard Business Review,* September–October 1995, pp. 120–37.

REVIEW AND DISCUSSION QUESTIONS

1. What is the difference between OM and OR/MS? Between OM and IE?

2. How would you distinguish OM from management and organizational behavior as taught at your university?

3. Look at the want ads in *The Wall Street Journal* and evaluate the opportunities for an OM major with several years of experience.

4. What factors account for the resurgence of interest in OM today?

5. Using Exhibit 1.2 as a model, describe the input–transformation–output relationships in the following systems:
   a. An airline.
   b. A state penitentiary.
   c. A branch bank.
   d. The home office of a major banking firm.

6. Sketch the production-delivery system used by the National Bicycle Industrial Company in providing the Panasonic bicycle. How do the five P's work together to satisfy the "sixth P," the purchaser? Could this approach be applied to other consumer goods? Give examples.

7. What is the life cycle approach to production/operations management? Does it make sense to you? Could it be applied to any other fields you are studying?

8. What are the implications for marketing of Tektronix's "hot-line" to the shop-floor worker?

9. Suppose that *Variety*, the Hollywood trade paper noted for its colorful jargon, presented the following headlines relating to OM. To what particular historical events or individuals would they refer?

FRED RISKS X-RATING TO GET ACROSS PRINCIPLES

HAWTHORNE WORKERS DO IT FASTER IN THE DARK

STEEL KING VISITS GOLDEN ARCHES

MATERIALS MANAGEMENT MAVENS GET WITH THE PROGRAM

INVENTORY—OH NO!

FRANKY BURIES YOUNG STUDS AT BRICKOFF

CLOCKWISE HENRY BECOMES MARVEL OF MOTOWN

P.S.M. TOPS CHARTS IN GINZA

HERO MEDAL FOR HANK AS BOAT BIZ BOOMS

CRIMSON GANG SEEKS COMPROMISE ON SHOP FLOOR

EXECS FOLLOW GURU'S RECIPE FOR BIG Q STEW

Case

The Purchasing Managers Index (PMI)

During the first week of every month, headlines on the front page of *The Wall Street Journal* announce the current reading of the Purchasing Managers Index (PMI). What is the PMI? Why is it so important to economists? How does it relate to the study of operations management?

The National Association of Purchasing Management (NAPM) has been calculating this index since 1931. The index is like the Dow Jones Industrial Average, but instead of measuring the rise and fall of a set of stocks, the PMI measures the rise and fall of manufacturing in the United States. The index is calculated using a set of measures of new manufacturing orders, production volume, supplier deliveries, inventory levels, and employment. The data is collected from a monthly survey conducted by NAPM.

The PMI is a leading indicator of economic activity. A PMI over 44.5 percent, over a period of time, indicates that the overall economy, or gross domestic product (GDP) is generally expanding; a PMI below 44.5 percent indicates that the GDP is generally declining. The distance from 44.5 percent is indicative of the strength of the expansion or decline.

The indicator is calculated from the activity levels for functions we study in operations management. We will study how manufacturing orders are processed, how decisions related to the volume that can be processed through a process are made, the coordination of supplier deliveries, the management of inventory, and the scheduling of employees.

Log into the NAPM World Wide Web page at http://www.napm.org, and answer the following questions that relate to Operations Management functions:

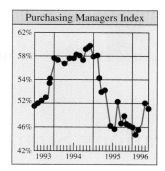

1. How have employment levels in manufacturing companies in the United States changed over the past three years? A spreadsheet containing the current PMI data is available at http://www.pom.edu.

2. Have manufacturing companies been successful in reducing inventories?

3. How do inventory levels fluctuate with new orders (sales)?

SELECTED BIBLIOGRAPHY

Apte, Uday. "Operations Management Course Notes." Southern Methodist University, 1997.

Chase, Richard B., and David A. Garvin. "The Service Factory." *Harvard Business Review* 67, no. 4 (July–August 1989), pp. 61–69.

Chase, Richard B., and Eric L. Prentis. "Operations Management: A Field Rediscovered." *Journal of Management* 13, no. 2 (October 1987), pp. 351–66.

Cole, Robert E. "The Quality Revolution." *Production and Operations Management* 1, no. 1 (Winter 1992).

Davidow, W. H., and M. S. Malone. *The Virtual Corporation.* New York: HarperCollins, 1993.

Deming, W. Edwards. *Out of the Crisis.* Cambridge, MA: Massachusetts Institute of Technology, Center for Advanced Engineering Study, 1986.

Drucker, Peter F. "The Emerging Theory of Manufacturing." *Harvard Business Review,* May–June 1990, pp. 94–102.

Gates, William H. *The Road Ahead.* New York: Penguin Books, 1996.

Giffi, Craig, Aleda V. Roth, and Gregory M. Seal, eds. *Competing in World-Class Manufacturing: National Center for Manufacturing Sciences.* Homewood, IL: Business One Irwin, 1990.

Hammer, Michael, "Reengineering Work: Don't Automate, Obliterate." *Harvard Business Review,* July–August 1990, pp. 104–12.

Hayes, Robert H., Steven C. Wheelwright, and Kim B. Clark. *Dynamic Manufacturing.* New York: Free Press, 1988.

Kotha, Surech. "The National Bicycle Industrial Company: Implementing a Strategy of Mass-Customization," Case study from the International University of Japan, 1993.

McMillan, Charles J. "Production Planning in Japan," *Journal of General Management* 8, no. 4, pp. 44–71.

Moffat, Susan. "Japan's New Personalized Production," *Fortune,* October 22, 1990, pp. 132–35.

Nadworny, Milton J. "Schmidt and Stakhanov: Work Heros in Two Systems." *California Management Review* 6, no. 4 (Summer 1964), pp. 69–76.

Osborn, D. *Reinventing Government.* New York: Plume, 1993.

Pine II, B. Joseph. *Mass Customization: The New Frontier in Business Competition.* Boston: Harvard Business School Press, 1993.

Porter, Micheal, and Claas Vander Linde. "Green and Competitive: Ending the Stalemate." *Harvard Business Review,* September–October 1995, pp. 120–37.

Quinn, James Brian. *Intelligent Enterprise.* New York: Free Press, 1992.

Schonberger, Richard J. *World Class Manufacturing: The Lessons of Simplicity Applied.* New York: Free Press, 1986.

Sower, Victor E., Jaideep Motwani, and Michael J. Savoie. *Classic Readings in Operations Management.* Fort Worth: The Dryden Press, 1995.

Stalk, Jr., George, and Thomas M. Hout. *Competing against Time.* New York: Free Press, 1990.

Vargas, Gustavo A., and Thomas W. Johnson. "An Analysis of Operational Experience in the US/Mexico Production Sharing (Maquiladora) Program." *Journal of Operations Management* 11 (1993), pp. 17–34.

Womak, James P., Daniel T. Jones, and Daniel Roos. *The Machine That Changed the World.* New York: Rawson Associates, 1990.

Chapter 2

Operations Strategy and Competitiveness

Chapter Outline

Operations Strategy, 24

    What Is Operations Strategy?

Priorities, 25

    Operations Priorities

    The Notion of Trade-offs

    Priorities Determined by the Marketplace

    Changing Competitive Priorities

    Order Winners and Qualifiers: The
      Marketing/Operations Link

**A Framework for Operations Strategy in
Manufacturing,** 30

    Developing a Manufacturing Strategy

Operations Strategy in Services, 33

Meeting the Competitive Challenge, 36

    Some Causes of America's Improved
      Competitiveness

Productivity Measurement, 39

**Case: Operations Strategy at Compaq
Computer,** 43

Case: Los Angeles Toy Company, 44

Key Terms

Operations Strategy

Corporate Strategy

Operations Priorities
   Cost
   Product Quality
   Process Quality
   Delivery Speed
   Delivery Reliability
   Changes in Demand
   Flexibility

Plant-Within-a-Plant (PWP)

World-Class Manufacturers

Value

Order Winners

Order Qualifiers

Core Enterprise

Operations Capabilities

Core Capabilities

Keiretsu

Productivity

www Links

Federal Express (http://www.fedex.com)

Citicorp (http://www.citicorp.com)

Compaq Computer (http://www.compaq.com)

O PERATIONS, PARTICULARLY IN MANUFACTURING, has been the Rodney Dangerfield of business functions—it's gotten no respect.

For many years, few companies regarded the operating processes of a firm as a source of competitive advantage. The goals of the firm relating to operations were cost reduction and improved labor utilization. Decisions were made on narrow, tactical grounds. This was the domain of the technically oriented engineering specialists. Little attention was paid to how the processes, which deliver the goods and services of the firm, fit with its strategy.

In the 1970s and 1980s, a new perspective emerged. As global competitors (mainly from Japan) began to dominate major industries such as automobiles, motorcycles, domestic appliances, and virtually all consumer electronics, managers looked for the reasons that these companies were so successful. What emerged were stories of highly efficient operations quickly producing high-quality products. These companies were able not only to produce great products but also to bring new products to market quicker, while avoiding the start-up problems so typical of existing producers. These new world-class companies established new benchmarks in the areas of quality and productivity. Operations emerged as the key competitive weapon required for global success.

To regain a competitive position, Western managers realized that major change was required. Operations had to become an integral part of the corporate strategy. This corporate strategy had to be responsive to the needs of the firm's customers. Companies learned how different customers had different priorities. The old idea that cost minimization was always the goal was shattered. A new field called operations strategy emerged.

Operations strategy offers a new perspective about operations problems, as well as a new set of concepts and techniques. The new perspective relates to the context within which decisions are made. This context considers the needs of the customer together with the overall strategy of the firm. New concepts and tools such as total quality management, lean manufacturing, and process reengineering have emerged to support this new perspective.

In the 1990s, the companies that are now the market leaders have succeeded in making the transformation. Certainly, marketing skills and the financial environment have helped, but operations has become a dominant competitive weapon. ●

A company that is considered to be world class recognizes that its ability to compete in the marketplace depends on developing an operations strategy that is properly aligned with its mission of serving the customer. A company's competitiveness refers to its relative position in comparision to other firms in the local or global marketplace. In this chapter, we first define what operations strategy is and how it relates to competitive priorities. In our discussion of priorities we explain how priorities change over time for a company. We then address operations strategy in manufacturing and services, how the United States is faring in industrial competitiveness, and how operations performance is measured.

▧ OPERATIONS STRATEGY

Operations Strategy

Corporate Strategy

What Is Operations Strategy?

Operations strategy is concerned with setting broad policies and plans for using the resources of the firm to best support the firm's long-term competitive strategy. A firm's operations strategy is comprehensive through its integration with **corporate strategy**. The strategy involves a long-term process that must foster inevitable change. In discussing operations strategy, we are referring mainly to manufacturing operations. Service operations strategy bears many similarities, especially when the service company uses materials as part of its service offerings.

An operations strategy involves decisions that relate to the design of a process and the infrastructure needed to support the process. Process design includes the selection of appropriate technology, sizing the process over time, the role of inventory in the process, and locating the process. The infrastructure decisions involve the logic associated with the planning and control systems, quality assurance and control approaches, work payment structures, and the organization of the operations function.

Operations strategy can be viewed as part of a planning process that coordinates operational goals with those of the larger organization. Since the goals of the larger organization change over time, the operations strategy must be designed to anticipate future needs. The operations capabilities of a firm can be viewed as a portfolio best suited to adapt to the changing product and/or service needs of the firm's customers.

Looking at operations strategy from a historical perspective, U.S. companies, for example in the post–World War II era experienced tremendous consumer demand, which had been pent-up during the war. As a result, manufacturing in the U.S. emphasized turning out high volumes of products to statisfy this demand. In contrast, during the same time period, Japanese manufacturing companies focused on the quality of their products. Priorities needed to remain competitive were different for companies in the different countries. Keys to success in operations strategy lie in identifying what the priority choices are, in understanding the consequences of each choice, and in the trade-offs involved.

■ PRIORITIES

Operations Priorities

From the early work of C. Wickham Skinner at the Harvard Business School and the more recent work of Terry Hill at the London Business School, a few basic operations priorities have been identified. These priorities include **cost, product quality and reliability, delivery speed, delivery reliability,** ability to cope with **changes in demand, flexibility and new product introduction speed,** and **other criteria** particular to a given product.[1]

Vol. IV
"Value-Driven Production at Trek"

Cost   Within every industry, there is usually a segment of the market that buys strictly on the basis of low cost. To successfully compete in this niche, a firm must be the low-cost producer, but even doing this does not always guarantee profitability and success.

Cost

Products sold strictly on the basis of cost are typically commodity-like in nature. In other words, customers cannot distinguish the products of one firm from those of another, As a result, customers use cost as the primary determinant for making a purchase.

However, this segment of the market is frequently very large, and many companies are lured by the potential for significant profits, which they associate with the large unit volumes of product. As a consequence, competition in this segment is fierce—and so is the failure rate. After all, there can only be one low-cost producer, which usually establishes the selling price in the market.

Product Quality and Reliability   Quality can be divided into two categories: **product quality** and **process quality.** The level of quality in a product's design will vary with the market segment to which it is aimed. Obviously, a child's first two-wheeled bicycle is of significantly different quality than the bicycle of a world-class cyclist. The use of special aluminum alloys and special lightweight sprockets and chains are important to the performance needs of the cyclist. These two types of bicycle are designed for different customers' needs. The higher-quality cyclist product commands a higher price in the marketplace due to its special features.

Product Quality

Process Quality

The goal in establishing the proper level of product quality is to focus on the requirements of the customer. Over-designed products with too much quality will be viewed as being prohibitively expensive. Under-designed products, on the other hand, will lose customers to products that cost a little more but are perceived by the customers as offering greater benefits.

Process quality is critical as it relates directly to the reliability of the product. Regardless of whether the product is a child's first two-wheeler or a bicycle for an international cyclist, customers want products without defects. Thus, the goal of process quality is to produce error-free products. Product specifications, given in dimensional tolerances, precisely define how the product is to be made. Adherence to these tolerances is essential to ensure the reliability of the product as defined by its intended use.

Delivery Speed   In some markets, a company's ability to deliver more quickly than its competitors may be critical. Take, for example, a company that offers a repair

Delivery Speed

---

[1] Terry Hill, *Manufacturing Strategy—Text and Cases,* 2nd ed. (Burr Ridge, IL: Richard D. Irwin, 1994), pp. 43–76.

At Federal Express's hub in Memphis, Tennessee, more than 650,000 packages are sorted and dispatched each night for delivery. Seeing a need for speedy, reliable overnight delivery, Federal Express became a $7.7 billion company and the world's largest expedited delivery service.

(http://www.fedex.com)

service for computer-networking equipment. A company that can offer on-site repair in only 1 or 2 hours has a significant advantage over a competing firm that only guarantees service within 24 hours.

Delivery Reliability

Delivery Reliability   This priority relates to the ability of the firm to supply the product or service on or before a promised delivery due date. For an automobile manufacturer, it is very important that their supplier of tires provide the needed quantity and types for each day's car production. If the tires needed for a particular car are not available on the assembly line when the car reaches the point where the tires are installed, the whole assembly line may have to be shut down until they arrive. The focus during the 1980s and 1990s on reducing stocks of inventory to reduce cost has placed increasing emphasis on delivery reliability as a criterion for evaluating alternative vendors.

Changes in Demand

Coping with Changes in Demand   In many markets, a company's ability to respond to increases and decreases in demand is an important factor in their ability to complete. It is well known that a company with increasing demand can do little wrong. When demand is strong and increasing, costs are continuously reduced due to economies of scale, and investments in new technologies can be easily justified. Scaling back when demand decreases may require many difficult decisions relating to laying off employees and related reductions in assets. The ability to effectively deal with dynamic market demand over the long term is an essential element of operations strategy.

Flexibility

Flexibility and New Product Introduction Speed   Flexibility, from a strategic perspective, refers to the ability of a company to offer a wide variety of products to its customers. An important element of this ability to offer different products is the time required for a company to develop a new product and to convert its processes to offer the new product.

Other Product-Specific Criteria   The priorities described above are certainly the most common. However, there are often other priorities that relate to specific products or situations. Notice that most of the priorities given below are primarily service in nature. Often, special services are provided to augment the sales of manufactured products.

Technical liaison and support. A supplier may be expected to provide technical assistance for product development particularly during the early stages of design and manufacturing.

Meeting a launch date. A firm may be required to coordinate with other firms on a complex project. In such cases, manufacturing may take place while development work is still being completed. Coordinating work between firms and working simultaneously on a project will reduce the total time required to complete the project.

Supplier after-sale support. An important priority may be the ability of the firm to support the product after the sale. This involves the availability of replacement parts and, possibly, the modification of older, existing products to new performance levels. Speed of response to these after-sale needs is often important as well.

Other priorities. These typically include such factors as colors available, size, weight, location of the fabrication site, customization available, and product mix options.

The Notion of Trade-offs

Central to the concept of operations strategy during the late 1960s and 1970s was the notion of operations focus and trade-offs. The underlying logic was that an operation could not excel simultaneously on all performance measures. Consequently, management had to decide which parameters of performance were critical to the firm's success, and then concentrate or focus the resources of the firm on those particular characteristics.

For example, if a company wanted to focus on speed of delivery, then it could not be very flexible in terms of its ability to offer a wide range of products. Similarly, a low-cost strategy was not compatible with either speed of delivery or flexibility. High quality was also viewed as a trade-off to low cost. For those firms with large existing manufacturing facilities, Skinner even suggested the creation of a **plant-within-a-plant (PWP)** concept, in which different locations within the facility would be allocated to different product lines, each with their own operations strategy. Under the PWP concept, even the workers would be separated to minimize the confusion associated with shifting from one type of strategy to another.[2]

Plant-within-a-Plant

The concepts of factory focus and PWPs are still widely employed today. However, as is discussed next, the notion of trade-offs has given way to the need to do everything well, and the issue has instead become one of determining priorities.

[2] C. Wickham Skinner, "The Focused Factory, " *Harvard Business Review* 52, no. 3 (May–June 1974), pp. 113–22.

Priorities Determined by Marketplace

As a one-world economy (or global village) evolves, there has emerged a group of companies that have adopted an international perspective toward both operations and marketing. Within this global arena, competition is significantly more intense due to both the greater number of "players" and the tremendous opportunities that exist.

World-Class Manufacturers

Those product-producing companies that have excelled on the international level have often been called **world-class manufacturers.** Events in the world marketplace during the 1970s and 1980s—specifically, the growing intensity in competition—forced these companies to reexamine the concept of operations strategy, especially in terms of the so-called necessary trade-offs.

Managers began to realize that they did not really have to make trade-offs between these different strategies. What emerged instead was a realization of the need to establish priorities as dictated by the marketplace. Further, it was recognized that these priorities will change over time.

Changing Competitive Priorities

A group at Boston University has worked to track the changing competitive priorities at 212 U.S. manufacturing companies over approximately the past 10 years. This work is called the Manufacturing Futures Survey. The work has shown that as manufacturing firms continue to improve their performance, the requirements for being competitive also change.[3]

Since the inception of the survey, respondents have been asked to indicate how important each of 16 competitive capabilities is in achieving the goals of their business units in the next five years. The results of the last four surveys are presented in Exhibit 2.1.

Over the years, the top three priorities have included conformance quality (this relates to the ability to build a product to design specifications), product reliability, and delivery dependability. It appears that these basic requirements do not change, and if a firm cannot deliver these basics, it cannot stay in business.

Exhibit 2.1	1990	1992	1994	1996
Top Five Competitive Priorities	1. Conformance quality	1. Conformance quality	1. Conformance quality	1. Conformance quality
	2. On-time delivery	2. Product reliability	2. On-time delivery	2. Product reliability
	3. Product reliability	3. On-time delivery	3. Product reliability	3. On-time delivery
	4. Performance quality	4. Performance quality	**4. Low price**	**4. Low price**
	5. Low price	**5. Low price**	5. Fast delivery	5. Fast delivery
			6. Speedy NPI*	6. Performance quality
				7. Speedy NPI*
		8. Speedy NPI*		
	9. Speedy NPI*			

* NPI: New product introduction.

[3] J. S. Kim, "Search for a New Manufacturing Paradigm," *Research Report Series* (Boston University School of Management), October 1996.

Moving beyond the top three, we see that the competitive priorities have changed. The data indicates that low price and new-product introduction speed are becoming increasingly important in the 1990s. The low-price capability in particular has moved up, becoming the fourth most important priority for the respondents. It appears that quality alone does not satisfy customers any longer. The customer is looking for the combination of quality and related criteria (conformance quality, delivery speed, and product reliability) at a low price.

A currently used term for this combination of customer requirements is **value.** Value to the customer means buying a product with the most important attributes (in this case conformance quality, delivery speed and reliability) at the lowest price possible. To improve value, we must either improve on those criteria that are most important to the customer, reduce cost to the customer, or do both.

The firms also appear to be aware of the increasing importance of introducing new products into the market quickly. Since 1990, when this priority was first included in the survey, its importance has consistently risen.

Value

Order Winners and Qualifiers: The Marketing/Operations Link

MARKETING

Order Winners

Order Qualifiers

An interface between marketing and operations is necessary to provide a business with an understanding of its markets from both perspectives. Terry Hill has coined the terms **order winners** and **order qualifiers** to describe marketing-oriented priorities that are key to competitive success. An order-winner is a criterion that differentiates the products or services of one firm from another. Depending on the situation, the order-winning criterion may be the cost of the product (price), product quality and reliability, or any of the other priorities developed earlier. An order qualifier is a screening criterion that permits a firm's products to even be considered as possible candidates for purchase. Professor Hill relates a firm must requalify the order qualifiers every day it is in business.

From the Manufacturing Futures Survey data cited in the previous section, it would appear that in general, conformance quality, on-time delivery, and product reliability are now order qualifiers for most large manufacturers. Low price is emerging as the order winner. The survey data is general, however, and the individual product detail is lost. In developing an operations strategy, the identification of relevant order winners for specific products is a key step.

It is important to remember that the order-winning and order-qualifying criteria may change over time. For example, when Japanese companies entered the world automobile markets in the 1970s, they changed the way in which these products won orders, from predominantly price to product quality and reliability. American automobile producers were losing orders through quality to the Japanese companies. By the late 1980s, product quality was raised by Ford, General Motors, and Chrysler so that they are now "qualified" to be in the market. Consumer groups continually monitor the quality and reliability criteria, thus requalifying the top-performing companies. Today the order winners for automobiles vary greatly depending on the model. Customers know the set of features they want (such as reliability, design features, and gas mileage) and they want to purchase a particular combination at the lowest price, thus maximizing value.

■ A FRAMEWORK FOR OPERATIONS STRATEGY IN MANUFACTURING

Vol. IV
"Vision Light"

Core Enterprise

Operations Capabilities

Core Capabilities

Operations strategy cannot be done in a vacuum. It must be linked vertically to the customer and horizontally to other parts of the enterprise. Exhibit 2.2 shows these linkages between customer needs, their performance priorities and requirements for manufacturing operations, and the operations and related enterprise resource capabilities to satisfy those needs. Overlying this framework is senior management's strategic vision of the firm. The vision identifies, in general terms, the target market, the firm's product line, and its **core enterprise** and **operations capabilities.**

The choice of a target market can be difficult, but it must be made. Indeed, it may lead to turning away business—ruling out a customer segment that would simply be unprofitable or too hard to serve given the firm's capabilities. Examples here are U.S. car companies not producing right-hand drive cars for the Japanese and British markets, as well as clothing manufacturers not making half-sizes in their dress lines. **Core capabilities** (or competencies) are those skills that differentiate the manufacturing (or service firm) from its competitors.

Exhibit 2.2

Operations Strategy Framework: From Customer Needs to Order Fulfillment

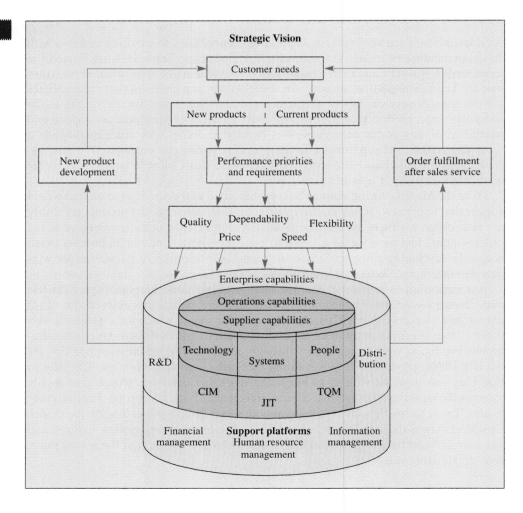

The general process is that customer-based new-product or current-product require-ments give rise to performance priorities that then become the required priorities for operations. Exhibit 2.2 shows these priorities linking into an enterprise capabilities "barrel," because operations cannot satisfy customer needs without the involvement of R&D and distribution and without the direct or indirect support of financial manage-ment, human resource management, and information management. Given its perfor-mance requirements, an operations division uses its capabilities (as well as those of its suppliers) to achieve those requirements—that is, to win orders. These capabilities include technology, systems, and people. CIM (computer-integrated manufacturing), JIT (just-in-time), and TQM (total quality management) represent fundamental con-cepts and tools used in each of the three areas. We have shown suppliers in the operations capabilities barrel to reflect the fact that suppliers do not become suppliers unless their capabilities in technology, systems, and people management pass certification tests. In addition, virtually every operations capability is now subjected to a "make-or-buy" decision. It is current practice among world-class manufacturers to subject each part of a manufacturing operation to the question, if we are not among the best in the world at, say, metal forming, should we be doing this at all, or should we subcontract to someone who is the best? In the computer industry, for example, the majority of manufacturers outsource the fabrication of component parts, leaving just assembly and testing to be done in-house (or, as is becoming quite common, at the customer's facility, since that is where the product must function properly).

Possibly the most difficult thing for a firm to do is part with tradition. Wickham Skinner in a recent article argues that managers are often too comfortable with just tinkering with the current system.[4] All the new advanced technologies present them-selves as quick fixes. It is easy to patch these technologies into the current system with great enthusiasm. While doing this may be exciting to managers and engineers work-ing for the firm, they may not be creating a distinctive core competence—a compe-tence that wins future customers. Skinner argues that what companies need in this new world of intense global competition is not more techniques, but a way to structure a whole new product realization system differently and better than any competitor. In the next section we give guidelines for how that is done.

Developing a Manufacturing Strategy

The main objectives of manufacturing strategy development are (*a*) to translate re-quired priorities (typically obtained from marketing) into specific performance requirements for operations, and (*b*) to make the necessary plans to assure that operations (and enterprise) capabilities are sufficient to accomplish them. The steps for developing priorities are

1. Segment the market according to the product group.
2. Identify the product requirements, demand patterns, and profit margins of each group.
3. Determine the order winners and order qualifiers for each group.
4. Convert order winners into specific performance requirements.

An example of this process, along with a discussion of focus, is presented in "Manufacturing Strategy and Focus."

---

[4] Wickham Skinner, "Three Yards and a Cloud of Dust: Industrial Management at Century End," *Produc-tion and Operations Management* 5, no. 1, Spring 1996, pp. 15–41.

The process of achieving a satisfactory manufacturing segmentation that maintains focus is often a matter of deciding which products or product groups fit together in the sense that they have similar market performance characteristics and/or they place similar demands on the manufacturing system. For example, the accompanying table shows how two product groups manufactured by one instrument manufacturer differ in their manufacturing requirements. The first product group is a range of standard electronic medical equipment that was sold "off the shelf" direct to hospitals and clinics. The second product group is a wider range of measuring devices that were sold to original equipment manufacturers and often had to be customized to individual customer requirements. The analysis of the two product groups in the table shows that they have very different market competitive characteristics. Therefore, very different external performance objectives are required from the manufacturing operation. Each product group also has different priorities for its internal performance objectives. Product group 1 needs to concentrate on cost and quality performance. All other internal performance objectives should be bent to achieving this. Product group 2 needs the flexibility to cope with a wide product range and with considerable design turbulence.

Such very different competitive needs will almost certainly require two separate focused units, each devoted to providing the things that are important in their separate markets.

Manufacturing Strategy and Focus

Manufacturing Requirements Differences	Product Group 1	Product Group 2
Products	Standard medical equipment	Electronic measuring devices
Customers	Hospitals/clinics	Medical and other OEMs
Product specs	Not high-tech, but periodic updates	Varies; some high specs and others less so
Product range	Narrow—4 variants	Wide; many types and variants; some customization
Design changes	Infrequent	Continuous process
Delivery	Customer lead-time important— ship directly from stock on hand	On-time delivery important
Quality	Conformance/reliability	Performance/conformance
Demand variation	Financial year related but predictable	Lumpy and unpredictable
Volume/line	High	Medium to low
Margins	Low	Low to very high
External Performance Priorities	↓	↓
Order winners	Price Product reliability	Product specification Product range
Qualifiers	Delivery lead-time Product specification Quality conformance	Delivery dependability Delivery lead-time Price
	↓	↓
Main Internal Performance Requirements	Cost Quality	New product flexibility Range flexibility Dependability

Source: Nigel Slack, *The Manufacturing Advantage,* (London: Management Books 2000 Ltd., 1992), pp. 14–15.

OPERATIONS STRATEGY IN SERVICES

Operations strategy in service firms is generally inseparable from the corporate strategy. For most services, the service delivery system is the business, and hence, any strategic decision must include operations considerations. However, operations executives do not always have a voice equal to other functions of the firm. A marketing decision to add a new route for an airline or to add new in-flight services may be made despite operations' protests about feasibility (just as in manufacturing).

Although we will discuss service strategy in Chapter 5, we should note that many of the strategy concepts discussed relative to manufacturing also apply to services. For example, service firms may use the plant-within-a-plant (PWP) structure to achieve focus. Hospitals using the PWP focus may have separate units for distinct patient services such as cardiac units, oncology units, labor and delivery units, and rehabilitation units. Major department stores group products and services into separate units or "departments," each with a separate customer focus, ordering, product arrangement, flow, and strategy. Each department—women's sportswear, customer service, children's apparel, housewares, and men's clothing—focuses on specific customer niches with unique needs, particularly if the organization serves a variety of customers and markets with distinct needs. Likewise, order winners and qualifiers have service applications. For a bank, qualifiers might be a good location, availability of tellers and loan officers, and ATMs. Order winners might be relationship banking and customer-oriented banking hours.

(http://www.citicorp.com)

The nature of operations' role in achieving corporate-wide competitiveness in services is shown in the four-stage model in Exhibit 2.3. The first column of the exhibit lists four proposed stages of service-firm competitiveness. Across the top are the major service dimensions that operations executives must address in strategy development. The entries in the table reflect our interpretation of the views held by senior management of companies that fit into each stage.

Here are some additional comments about the framework: First, the stage attained by any given firm is a composite. Every service-delivery system embodies a unique set of choices about service quality, workforce policies, and so forth. A company may be at a different stage for a given dimension, or have service units that are further or less advanced than others. Second, a firm can be very competitive (Stage III or even Stage IV) even if it is not outstanding on all dimensions. This could happen when it is doing an exceptional job on its critical success factors. Third, it is difficult or impossible to skip a stage in moving up the ladder. A company obviously must achieve journeyman performance before distinctive competence, and it must attain distinctive competence before becoming world class. (However, a firm can move through the stages relatively rapidly. For example, Scandinavian Airlines System (SAS) instituted some 120 service improvements that moved it from Stage I to Stage III within a year and a half.

Exhibit 2.3 Four Stages of Service Firm Competitiveness

		Important Performance Dimensions			
Stage	Characteristics	Service Quality	New Technology	Workforce	First-Line Management
I. Available for service	Customers patronize service firm for reasons other than performance. Operations is reactive at best.	Subsidiary to cost; highly variable.	When necessary for survival, under duress.	Negative constraint.	Controls workers.
II. Journeyman	Customers neither seek out nor avoid the firm. Operations functions in a mediocre, uninspired fashion.	Meets some customer expectations; consistent on one or two key dimensions.	When justified by cost savings.	An efficient resource; disciplined; follows procedures.	Controls the process.
III. Distinctive competence achieved	Customers seek out the firm based on its sustained reputation for meeting customer expectations. Operations continually excels, reinforced by personnel management and systems that support an intense customer focus.	Exceeds customer expectations; consistent on multiple dimensions.	When it promises to enhance service.	Permitted to elect among alternative procedures.	Listens to customers; coaches and facilitates workers.
IV. World-class service delivery	The name of the company is synonymous with service excellence. Its service does not just satisfy customers, it delights them, and it thereby expands customer expectations to levels its competitors cannot fill. Operations is a quick learner and fast innovator; it masters every step of the service-delivery process and provides capabilities that are superior to competitors' capabilities.	Raises customer expectations; seeks challenges; improves continuously.	Source of first-mover advantages, creating ability to do things competitors cannot do.	Innovative; creates procedures.	Is listened to by top management as a source of new ideas. Mentors workers to enhance their career growth.

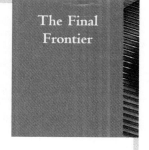

The Final Frontier

The industrial economies should be re-named the service economies: They employ twice as many workers in services as in industry. The growth of services is nothing new. As early as 1900 America and Britain both had more jobs in services than in industry. By 1950 services employed half of all American workers. Last year the figure hit 76 percent.

America has by far the biggest service sector, accounting for 72 percent of its GDP. At the rich world's other extreme, Germany's still provides only 57 percent of its GDP, thanks partly to a multitude of restrictive practices which have choked expansion.

Meanwhile, the share of manufacturing has fallen in all the big economies. It now accounts for only 23 percent of America's GDP (and an even smaller 18 percent of jobs). In Britain and Canada manufacturing has tumbled to less than 20 percent of total output. Even in Japan and Germany, the strongholds of industry, manufacturing is now no more than 30 percent of GDP.

Services are also the fastest-growing part of international trade, accounting for 20 percent of total world trade and 30 percent of American exports. This excludes those services that are not traded, but are delivered by subsidiaries set up in foreign markets. Services account for about 40 percent of the stock of foreign direct investment by the five big "industrial economies."

Sales of services by the foreign affiliates of American companies were worth $119 billion in 1990 (the latest figures available), not far behind America's $138 billion-worth of cross-border sales of private services. These sales do not contribute directly to output or jobs in America, but the economy does benefit when the profits from American company operations abroad are brought home. As governments open their borders to foreign companies, the scope for future expansion of trade and foreign direct investment in services is huge.

Policemen and prostitutes, bankers and butchers are all lumped together in the ser-vice sector, but not all have grown at the same rate. Top of the league are legal and business services, which grew by 106 percent and 67 percent, respectively, followed closely by health (59 percent) and recreation (53 percent). Jobs in older services grew more slowly. Employment in transport and communication, for instance, grew by only 13 percent.

Some economists argue that the boom in services is caused mainly by firms contracting out jobs they used to do for themselves, such as catering, advertising, and data-processing. But studies in American and Britain suggest that this explains only a fraction of the increase.

If anything, official figures may understate the true importance of services in both output and jobs, as many activities in manufacturing firms are really services. Government number-crunchers stick *The Economist,* along with all newspapers, in the manufacturing sector, even though few employees actually make anything. The work of a freelance journalist, by contrast, is counted in the service sector. The division between services and manufacturing is becoming steadily less useful.

As a 1992 OECD report* points out, services and manufacturing have become increasingly interconnected, as manufacturers buy more inputs from service firms and vice versa. Higher spending on advertising, financial management, and a speedier delivery system mean that more service value is added to each unit of manufacturing output.

Take General Motors, the archetypal manufacturer. Its biggest single supplier is not a steel or glass firm, but a health care provider, Blue Cross–Blue Shield. In terms of output, one of GM's biggest "products" is financial and insurance services, which together with EDS, its computing-services arm, account for a fifth of total revenue.

But few manufacturers will admit how much they rely on services. Sony's chairman, Akio Morita, proclaimed in a speech at this year's meeting of the World Economic Forum in Davos that "an increased

---

* "Structural Shifts in Major OECD Countries," *Industrial Policy in OECD Countries: Annual Review, 1992,* published by the OECD.

focus on manufacturing will help us to re-lay the foundation of our economy. Only manufacturing can provide employment opportunities of quality, scope and number . . . The Service sector can only survive if there is a productive manufacturing sector to serve." Yet look closer at Sony: as much as one-fifth of its revenues now come from its film and music businesses. Add in design, marketing, finance, and after-sales support, and service activities probably account for at least half of Sony's business.

Those who call for an industrial policy to help manufacturing are missing the point. If services account for half of the sales price of goods, then improving efficiency there may be a better way to trim the cost of the final product, and thus to become more competitive, than tinkering with the production process.

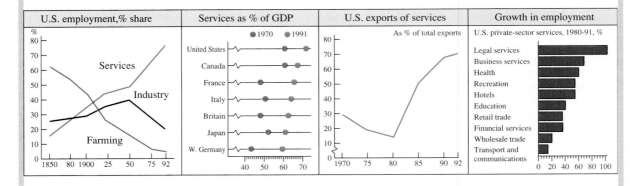

Source: "The Final Frontier," *The Economist*, February 20, 1993 © 1993 The Economist Newspaper Group. Inc. Reprinted with permission.

■ MEETING THE COMPETITIVE CHALLENGE

In 1985, the MIT Commission on Industrial Productivity recommended the following actions:

1. Place less emphasis on short-term financial payoffs and invest more in R&D.
2. Revise corporate strategies to include responses to foreign competition. This, in turn, calls for greater investment in people and equipment to improve manufacturing capability.
3. Knock down communication barriers within organizations and recognize mutuality of interests with other companies and suppliers (the former relative to international competition, in particular).
4. Recognize that the labor force is a resource to be nurtured, not just a cost to be avoided.
5. Get back to basics in managing production operations. Build in quality at the design stage. Place more emphasis on process innovations rather than focusing sole attention on product innovations.

How are we doing now? Have we taken these suggestions to heart? Apparently so, as evidenced in the box "Red, White, and Boom: U.S. Economy Shines."

A 3 percent economic growth rate, a gain of 2 million new jobs in the past year and an inflation rate reminiscent of the 1960s make the United States the envy of the industrialized world. The amount the average U.S. worker can produce, already the highest in the world, is growing faster than in other wealthy countries, including Japan.

The United States has become the world's low-cost provider of many sophisticated products and services, from plastics to software to financial services. And after years of decline, the nation's share of the world export market has been rising.

For the most part, these advantages will continue even after countries such as Japan and Germany snap out of their recessions. It is the United States, not Japan, that is the master of the next generation of commercially important computer and communications technologies as well as leading-edge services from medicine to movie making.

And U.S. managers are not only investing heavily in new equipment, they are also much farther along than those in Europe and Japan in streamlining and re-engineering their companies to make them more competitive.

That's one reason that U.S. industries that recently were losers—such as makers of automobiles, machine tools, steel and computer chips—are back with a vengeance.

The turnaround reflects more than 10 years of sometimes innovative and often wrenching change driven by recession, deregulation, tougher foreign competition, the threat of takeovers, and, not least, new technology.

Red, White and Boom: U.S. Economy Shines

Foreign leaders and executives who once lectured Americans on their shortcomings now speak enviously of this country's cleverness in churning out everything from jobs to Jeeps.

While such sentiments may seem more common abroad than at home, there are signs that America's self-esteem is recovering. Some polls show that Americans once again see the United States as an economic giant.

Some of the evidence of America's impressive economic performance has been around for years but ignored. Most of it is fairly new.

Start with the most basic yardstick of economic health, the growth of productivity, or output per worker. Productivity determines how fast living standards can rise.

The American worker is already the most productive in the world by far, producing on average $49,600 in goods and services in 1990—$5,000 more than German workers and $10,000 more than their Japanese counterparts.

Moreover, while productivity was growing more quickly abroad than in the United States for most of the 20th century, America has lately been gaining more quickly, as companies here figure out how to provide more and better products and services with new technologies and fewer workers.

Since the start of the economic recovery nearly three years ago, U.S. productivity has been growing at an annual rate of 2.5 percent, more than twice as fast as the average from 1970 to 1990 and markedly better than elsewhere in the world.

Source: Sylvia Nasar, "The American Economy, Back on Top," *The New York Times*, February 27, 1994. Copyright © 1994 by The New York Times Company. Reprinted by permission.

Some Causes of America's Improved Competitiveness

James P. Womack, principal research scientist of the MIT Japan Program, offers some intriguing observations on the specific underlying causes behind the recent improvement in U.S. competitiveness.[5] His thesis is that it is *not* the fact that U.S. firms are

---

[5] James P. Womack, "Book Reviews" section, *Sloan Management Review*, Winter 1994, p. 107.

better innovators than most foreign competitors. This capability has existed since long before the United States encountered its competitiveness problems. Rather, it is the fact that "we're proving to be very effective copiers. We've spent a decade examining the advantages of our rivals in product development, production operations, supply chain management and corporate governance (spurred, in many cases, by the demonstration effect of Japanese direct investment) and are putting in place 'functional equivalents' that 'incrementally improve' on their best techniques." Womack cites four examples of where and how this is occurring:

1.   New approaches to product development team structure and management that get products to market faster, with better designs and manufacturability. ("Chrysler has been a striking leader in this area with a new product development system initially copied from Honda but then 'improved' into something quite different and now apparently superior. Xerox and Boeing are two more examples of creative adaptation.")

2.   Improving performance of manufacturing facilities through dramatic reductions of work-in-process, space, tool costs, and human effort, while improving quality and flexibility. (Womack calls this "focusing on the value stream," which owes much of its philosophy to Japanese JIT concepts.)

Keiretsu

3.   Adopting new methods of customer–supplier cooperation that borrow from the Japanese **keiretsu** (large holding companies) practices of close linkages, but maintain the independence of the organizations desired by U.S. companies.

4.   Better leadership through strong, independent boards of directors that will dismiss managers who are not doing their jobs effectively. (This has achieved results that are comparable to or better than the oversight systems used by the Japanese keiretsu and German banks.)

There are many specific examples of U.S. firms that have risen to the competitive challenge. Monroe Auto Equipment, for example, has succeeded at producing such high-quality shock absorbers that one of its customers, Toyota of Japan, recently gave an appraisal of "defects—zero" in a shipment of 60,000 shocks. Exhibit 2.4 shows how a number of companies are improving the time they take to get their new products to market.

Exhibit 2.4

Shortening Product Cycle Times

Company/Product	Product Cycle Time Reduction	Company/Product	Product Cycle Time Reduction
General Motors		Honeywell	
New Buick model	60 to 40 months	Thermostat	48 to 12 months
Hewlett-Packard		Ingersoll Rand	
Computer printer	52 to 24 months	Air grinder	42 to 12 months
IBM		Warner Electric	
Personal computer	48 to 13 months	Clutch brake	36 to 10 months

Source: Data from Donald Relnersen and Preston Smith, *Developing Products in Half the Time.* (New York: Van Nostrand Reinhold, 1990), reported in *Boardroom Reports,* June 15, 1991, p.7.

PRODUCTIVITY MEASUREMENT

Productivity is a common measure of how well a country, industry, or business unit is using its resources (or factors of production). In its broadest sense, productivity is defined as

Productivity

$$\text{Productivity} = \frac{\text{Outputs}}{\text{Inputs}}$$

To increase productivity, we want to make this ratio of outputs to inputs as large as practical.

Productivity is what we call a *relative measure*. In other words, to be meaningful, it needs to be compared with something else. For example, what can we learn from the fact that we operate a restaurant, and that its productivity last week was 8.4 customers per labor hour? Nothing!

Productivity comparisons can be made in two ways. First, a company can compare itself with similar operations within its industry, or it can use industry data when such data are available (i.e., comparing productivity among the different stores in a franchise).

Another approach is to measure productivity over time within the same operation. Here we would compare our productivity in one time period with that of the next.

As Exhibit 2.5 shows, productivity may be expressed as partial measures, multifactor measures, or total measures. If we are concerned with the ratio of output to a single input, we have a *partial productivity measure*. If we want to look at the ratio of output to a group of inputs (but not all inputs), we have a *multifactor productivity measure*. If we want to express the ratio of all outputs to all inputs, we have a *total factor measure of productivity* that might be used to describe the productivity of an entire organization or even a nation.

A numerical example of productivity appears in Exhibit 2.6. The data reflect quantitative measures of input and output associated with the production of a certain product. Notice that for the multifactor and partial measures it is not necessary to use total output as the numerator. Often, it is desirable to create measures that represent productivity as it relates to some particular output of interest. For example, as in Exhibit 2.6, total units might be the output of interest to a production control manager, whereas total output may be of key interest to the plant manager. This process of

Partial measure	$\dfrac{\text{Output}}{\text{Labor}}$ or $\dfrac{\text{Output}}{\text{Capital}}$ or $\dfrac{\text{Output}}{\text{Materials}}$ or $\dfrac{\text{Output}}{\text{Energy}}$
Multifactor measure	$\dfrac{\text{Output}}{\text{Labor} + \text{Capital} + \text{Energy}}$ or $\dfrac{\text{Output}}{\text{Labor} + \text{Capital} + \text{Materials}}$
Total measure	$\dfrac{\text{Output}}{\text{Inputs}}$ or $\dfrac{\text{Goods and services produced}}{\text{All resources used}}$

Exhibit 2.5

Examples of Productivity Measures

Source: David J. Sumanth and Kitty Tang, "A Review of Some Approaches to the Management of Total Productivity in a Company/Organization," *Institute of Industrial Engineering Conference Proceedings,* Fall 1984, p. 305. Copyright Institute of Industrial Engineers, 25 Technology Park/Atlanta, Norcross, Georgia 30092.

Exhibit 2.6

Numerical Example of
Productivity Measures

Input and Output Production Data ($)		Productivity Measure Examples
Output		Total measure:
1. Finished units	$10,000	$\dfrac{\text{Total output}}{\text{Total input}} = \dfrac{13,500}{15,193} = .89$
2. Work in process	2,500	
3. Dividends	1,000	Multifactor measures:
4. Bonds		$\dfrac{\text{Total output}}{\text{Human + Material}} = \dfrac{13,500}{3,153} = 4.28$
5. Other income	———	
Total output	$13,500	$\dfrac{\text{Finished units}}{\text{Human + Material}} = \dfrac{10,000}{3,153} = 3.17$
Input		
1. Human	$ 3,000	Partial measures:
2. Material	153	$\dfrac{\text{Total output}}{\text{Energy}} = \dfrac{13,500}{540} = 25$
3. Capital	10,000	
4. Energy	540	$\dfrac{\text{Finished units}}{\text{Energy}} = \dfrac{10,000}{540} = 18.52$
5. Other expenses	1,500	
Total input	$15,193	

Source: David J. Sumanth and Kitty Tang, "A Review of Some Approaches to the Management of Total Productivity in a Company/Orgnization," *Institute of Industrial Engineering Conference Proceedings,* Fall 1984, p. 305. Copyright Institute of Industrial Engineers, 25 Technology Park/Atlanta, Norcross, Georgia 30092.

Exhibit 2.7

Partial Measures of
Productivity

Business	Productivity Measure
Restaurant	Customers (meals) per labor hour
Retail store	Sales per square foot
Chicken farm	Lb. of meat per lb. of feed
Utility plant	Kilowatts per ton of coal
Paper mill	Tons of paper per cord of wood

aggregation and disaggregation of productivity measures provides a means of shifting the level of the analysis to suit a variety of productivity measurement and improvement needs.

Exhibit 2.6 shows all units in dollars. Often, however, management can better understand how the company is performing when units other than dollars are used. In these cases, only partial measures of productivity can be used, as we cannot combine dissimilar units such as labor hours and pounds of material. Some commonly used partial measures of productivity are presented as examples in Exhibit 2.7. Such partial measures of productivity give managers information in familiar units, allowing them to easily relate these measures to the actual operations.

■ CONCLUSION

Professor Aleda Roth of the University of North Carolina at Chapel Hill proposes a "strategic map" that outlines her view of the strategic direction of manufacturing.[6] This view ties into our discussion of competitive priorities, the importance of adding

---

[6] Aleda V. Roth, "Neo-Operations Strategy," *Handbook of Technology Management*, ed. G. H. Gaynor (New York: McGraw-Hill, 1996), pp. 38.1–38.44.

Evolving Management Perspectives: Neo-operations View of Capabilities

Exhibit 2.8

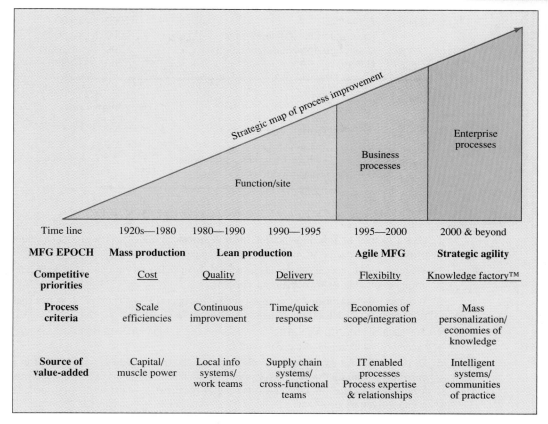

Time line	1920s—1980	1980—1990	1990—1995	1995—2000	2000 & beyond
MFG EPOCH	**Mass production**	**Lean production**		**Agile MFG**	**Strategic agility**
Competitive priorities	Cost	Quality	Delivery	Flexibilty	Knowledge factory™
Process criteria	Scale efficiencies	Continuous improvement	Time/quick response	Economies of scope/integration	Mass personalization/ economies of knowledge
Source of value-added	Capital/ muscle power	Local info systems/ work teams	Supply chain systems/ cross-functional teams	IT enabled processes Process expertise & relationships	Intelligent systems/ communities of practice

value, and performance evaluation criteria. Exhibit 2.8 shows this map from a historical perspective and into the future. Roth argues that there have been major *strategic epochs* over time (indicated by the vertical lines in Exhibit 2.8). These *epochs* are strategic moments in time where top management perspectives of what competitive capabilities are required to compete, dramatically shift.[7]

MARKETING
FINANCE
MIS

Operations strategy and competitiveness, particularly as they pertain to manufacturing, are often viewed by non-operations students as not being especially relevant to their specialty areas. We hope that this chapter conveys the important link between operations and the other functional areas, particularly marketing. The concepts of order winners and qualifiers, priorities, and capabilities apply to almost any marketing, finance, or personnel decision. Productivity measures are useful for comparisons and for measuring improvement. These are important terms that make up the new language of operations strategy—and the language of business.

SOLVED PROBLEM

SOLVED PROBLEM 1

A furniture manufacturing company has provided the following data. Compare the labor, raw materials and supplies, and total productivity of 1996 and 1997.

---

[7] In Exhibit 2.8, a "knowledge factory" is a manufacturing organization that creates knowledge and learning in parallel with its product creation. Other terms used in this exhibit are defined in later chapters.

		1996	**1997**
Output:	Sales value of production	$22,000	$35,000
Input:	Labor	10,000	15,000
	Raw materials and supplies	8,000	12,500
	Capital equipment depreciation	700	1,200
	Other	2,200	4,800

Solution

	1996	**1997**
Partial productivities		
Labor	2.20	2.33
Raw materials and supplies	2.75	2.80
Total productivity	1.05	1.04

REVIEW AND DISCUSSION QUESTIONS

1. Can a factory be fast, dependable, flexible, produce high-quality products, and still provide poor service from a customer's perspective?

2. Why should a service organization worry about being world class if it does not compete outside its own national border?

3. What are the major priorities associated with operations strategy? How has their relationship to each other changed over the years?

4. For each of the different priorities describe the unique characteristics of the market niche with which it is most compatible.

5. During 1988, for example, the dollar showed relative weakness with respect to foreign currencies such as the yen, mark, and pound. This stimulated exports. Why would long-term reliance on a lower-valued dollar be at best a short-term solution to the competitiveness problem?

6. In your opinion, do business schools have competitive priorities?

7. Why does the "proper" operations strategy keep changing for companies that are world-class competitors?

8. What is meant by the expressions order winners and order qualifiers? What was the order winner(s) for your last major purchase of a product or service?

9. What do we mean when we say productivity is a "relative" measure?

10. What are the typical performance measures for quality, speed of delivery, and flexibility?

11. What should be the criteria for management to adopt a particular performance measure?

PROBLEMS

1. Productivity (hours) ✓
   Deluxe car 0.20
   Limited car 0.20
   Productivity (dollars)
   Deluxe car 133.33
   Limited car 135.71

1. Two types of cars (Deluxe and Limited) were produced by a car manufacturer in 1997. Quantities sold, price per unit, and labor hours follow. What is the labor productivity for each car? Explain the problem(s) associated with the labor productivity.

	Quantity	**$/Unit**
Deluxe car	4,000 units sold	$8,000/car
Limited car	6,000 units sold	$9,500/car
Labor, Deluxe	20,000 hours	$12/hour
Labor, Limited	30,000 hours	$14/hour

2. A U.S. manufacturing company operating a subsidiary in an LDC (less-developed country) shows the following results:

	U.S.	**LDC**
Sales (units)	100,000	20,000
Labor (hours)	20,000	15,000
Raw materials (currency)	$ 20,000	FC 20,000
Capital equipment (hours)	60,000	5,000

a. Calculate partial labor and capital productivity figures for the parent and subsidiary. Do the results seem misleading?

b. Now compute multifactor labor and capital productivity figures. Are the results better?

c. Finally, calculate raw material productivity figures (units/$ where $1 = FC 10). Explain why these figures might be greater in the subsidiary.

3. Various financial data for 1997 and 1998 follow. Calculate the total productivity measure, and the partial measures for labor, capital, and raw materials for this company for both years. What do these measures tell you about this company?

		1997	**1998**
Output:	Sales	$200,000	$220,000
Input:	Labor	30,000	40,000
	Raw materials	35,000	45,000
	Energy	5,000	6,000
	Capital	50,000	50,000
	Other	2,000	3,000

Answers in margin:

2. *a.* Yes:

U.S.	LDC
5.00	1.33
1.67	4.00

b. Yes:

U.S.	LDC
1.25	1.00

c.

U.S.	LDC
5	10

3.

	1997	1998
Total productivity	1.64	1.53
Partial labor	6.67	5.50
Partial raw materials	5.71	4.89
Partial capital	4.00	4.40

Case

Operations Strategy at Compaq Computer *(http://www. compaq.com)*

Swaying from the ceiling at its Houston factory is a white banner that reads:

WE AT COMPAQ COMPUTER ARE ABSOLUTELY COMMITTED TO PROVIDE DEFECT FREE PRODUCTS AND SERVICES TO OUR CUSTOMERS.

The message jibes with what one sees below: a sparkling assembly line, surrounded by potted ficus trees and ferns, washed with light from vast skylight, that looks more like an expensive health club than a factory. Founded in 1982, the company has its ideal inscribed in its name, an amalgam of the words *computer, compact,* and *quality.*

A maker of IBM-compatible PCs as well as ultrafast computers that manage data on office networks, Compaq has grown into an 11,800-employee business that in 1990 earned $455 million on $3.6 billion in sales. It commands 20 percent of the world PC market, compared with 25 percent each of IBM and Apple Computer, and has almost no foreign rivals, except in the fast-growing field of laptop PCs. Still, competition is ferocious—fighting for sales, Compaq cut prices on its computers this spring as much as 34 percent and warned that second-quarter earnings would drop 80 percent.

Part of Compaq's success derives from its speed at offering the latest processor chips, disk drives, and display screens in its products. Yes, even faster than IBM. A major challenge, says CEO and co-founder Rod Canion, is to keep a breakneck pace of innovation across burgeoning product lines—nine new ones last year alone.

When the company was small, speeding products to market seemed a breeze. Today Compaq tries to maintain its entrepreneurial edge through small product-development teams that include marketers, designers, engineers, and manufacturing experts. Rather than moving a new computer step by step from drawing board to the factory, explains Canion, "The secret is to do all things in parallel."

Compaq's greatest advantage, Canion believes, is that it buys most components rather than making them itself: "Vertical integration is the old way of doing things. The way to succeed in the 1990s is to be open to technology from anywhere in the world." (Japanese competitors, such as Toshiba, continue to make nearly all their components.)

When Compaq needed a hard disk drive for is first laptop in 1986, it considered building one itself. Instead, it helped finance Conner Peripherals, a Silicon Valley startup with a disk drive already under way. "We worked so closely with Conner that they were literally an extension of our design team," says Canion. "We got all the benefits but weren't tied down. If another company had come along with a better drive, we'd have bought from them as well."

In March [1991], Compaq began a nervy foray beyond the realm of PCs into the $7.5-billion-a-year market for powerful desktop workstations used primarily by scientists and engineering. Rather than attacking market leaders Sun Micro-systems and Hewlett-Packard head-on, Compaq assembled more than a dozen hardware and software companies, including Microsoft and Digital Equipment Corp., in an alliance. The group aims to win by defining a new technical standard for high-speed desktop computing, much like the IBM standard in PCs. Any workstation designed in accordance with the standard would work with any other. That would free customers to buy the latest, fastest machine without fear of being wedded to a single manufacturer.

Industry experts think rivalry among participants may tear the alliance apart. Observes Dick Shaffer, editor of *Computer Letter:* "All the participants are entrepreneurial companies with big egos." The group's prospects may not become clear until late next year, when Compaq and other members are due to roll out the new computers and software. If the products all work together, Compaq's workstation would be a winner. If not, says Stewart Alsop, publisher of *PC Letter,* Compaq may have to lower its sights: "As a $3.6 billion company, Compaq can't keep up a high rate of growth anymore just by building PCs."

Questions

1. Relate the elements of Compaq's strategy to the operations strategy framework shown in Exhibit 2.2. Specifically identify what appear to be the key performance priorities of Compaq's strategy and the required enterprise and support platform capabilities that must be effectively employed for Compaq's strategy to succeed.

2. What are the risks Compaq runs by outsourcing so much of its production?

Source: "The New American Century," *Fortune,* special issue, Spring/Summer 1991, p. 27 © 1991 Time, Inc. All rights reserved.

Case

Los Angeles Toy Company

The Los Angeles Toy Company (LATC) views its primary task as making for stock a standardized line of high-quality, unique toys that "last from pablum to puberty." As a rule, LATC introduces one or two new toys a year. In August 1997 the owner and manufacturing manager, Dwight Smith-Daniels, has been informed by his toy inventors that they have designed a Jerry Seinfeld doll. This doll will stand two feet high and is capable of telling jokes via an electronic voice synthesizer. One of the company's three manufacturing staff departments, design engineering, states that the product can be made primarily from molded plastic using the firm's new all-purpose molders (now used for making small attachments to the firm's wooden toys). LATC, in its previous initial production of new toys, has relied heavily on its skilled workforce to "debug" the product design as they make the product and to perform quality inspections on the finished product. Production runs have been short runs to fill customer orders.

If the Jerry Seinfeld doll is to go into production, however, the production run size will have to be large and assembly and testing procedures will have to be more refined. Currently, each toymaker performs almost all of the processing steps at his or her workbench. The production engineering department believes that the assembly of the new toy is well within the skill levels of the current workforce but that the voice synthesizer and battery-operated movement mechanism will have to be subcontracted. LATC has always had good relations with subcontractors, primarily because the firm has placed its orders with sufficient lead time so that its vendors could optimally sequence LATC's orders with those of some larger toy producers in Los Angeles. Dwight Smith-Daniels has always favored long-range production planning so that he can keep his 50 toymakers busy all year. (One of the reasons he set up the factory in Los Angeles was so that he could draw upon the large population of "hip" toymakers who lived there.) Smith-Daniels believes the supervisors of the firm's three production departments—castles, puppets, and novelties—are favorable to the new product. The novelty department supervisor, Fred Avide, has stated, "My workers can make any toy—you give us an output incentive, and we'll produce around the clock."

The marketing department has forecast a demand of 50,000 Jerry Seinfeld dolls for the Christmas rush. The dolls should sell at retail for $29.50. A preliminary cost analysis from the process engineering department is that they will cost no more than $7 each to manufacture. The company is currently operating at 70 percent capacity. Financing is available and there is no problem with cash flow. Dwight Smith-Daniels is wondering if he should go into production of Jerry Seinfeld dolls.

Questions

1. How consistent is the Jerry Seinfeld doll order with the current capabilities and focus of LATC?

2. Should LATC (*a*) manufacture the doll itself, (*b*) subcontract the work to a Tijuana, Mexico, manufacturing plant that specializes in high-volume production (at a cost of $8 per doll to LATC), or (*c*) look for another product more in line with its capabilities? The agency that holds the license to Jerry Seinfeld products wants a decision right away, as does the Mexican supplier.

SELECTED BIBLIOGRAPHY

Bernstein, A. "Quality Is Becoming Job One in the Office, Too." *Business Week,* April 29, 1991.

_____."The Good Life Isn't Only in America." *Business Week,* November 2, 1992, p. 34.

Blackburn, Joseph D. *Time-Based Competition: The Next Battleground in American Manufacturing.* Homewood, IL: Business One Irwin, 1991.

Bremmer, B., and M. Ivey. "Tough Times, Tough Bosses, Corporate America Calls in New, Cold-Eyed Breed of CEOs." *Business Week,* November 25, 1991, pp. 174–79.

Chase, Richard B., and David A. Garvin. "The Service Factory." *Harvard Business Review* 67, no. 4 (July–August 1989), pp. 61–69.

Cohen, Stephen S., and John Zysman. *Why Manufacturing Matters: The Myth of the Post-Industrial Society.* New York: Basic Books, 1987.

Giffi, Craig A., and Aleda V. Roth. "Winning in Global Markets: Survey of U.S. and Japanese Manufacturing." Paper presented at the 1992 ORSA/TIMS Meeting, San Francisco, November 1–3, 1992.

Hart, Christopher W. L., James L. Heskett, and W. Earl Sassar, Jr. *Service Breakthroughs: Changing the Rules of the Game.* New York: Free Press, 1990.

Hayes, Robert H., and Gary P. Pisano. "Beyond World Class: The New Manufacturing Strategy." *Harvard Business Review* 72, no. 1 (January–February 1994), pp. 77–86.

Hayes, Robert H., Steven Wheelwright, and Kim B. Clark. *Dynamic Manufacturing Creating the Learning Organization.* New York: Free Press, 1988.

Hill, T. J. *Manufacturing Strategy—Text and Cases,* Burr Ridge IL: Richard D. Irwin, Inc., 1994. Gawin, David A. *Operations Strategy—Text and Cases,* Englewood Cliffs. NJ: Prentice Hall, 1992.

Hopp, Wallace, and Mark Spearman. *Factory Physics: A New Approach to Manufacturing Management.* Burr Ridge IL: Richard D. Irwin, 1996.

Malhotra, M. K., D. C. Steel, and V. Grover. "Important Strategic and Tactical Manufacturing Issues in the 1990s." *Decision Sciences* 25, no. 2 (March–April 1994), pp. 189–214.

Marucheck, A., R. Pannesi, and C. Anderson. "An Exploratory Study of the Manufacturing Strategy Process in Practice." *Journal of Operations Management* 9, no. 1 (January 1990), pp. 109–18.

Roth, Aleda V. "Neo-Operations Strategy." *Handbook of Technology Management,* ed. G. H. Gaynor. New York: McGraw-Hill, 1996, pp. 38.1–38.44.

Skinner, C. Wickham. *Manufacturing: The Formidable Competitive Weapon.* New York: John Wiley & Sons, 1985.

_____. "Manufacturing—The Missing Link in Corporate Strategy." *Harvard Business Review* 47, no. 3 (May–June 1969), pp. 136–45.

_____. "The Focused Factory." *Harvard Business Review* 52, no. 3 (May–June 1974), pp. 113–22.

_____. "The Productivity Paradox." *Harvard Business Review* 64, no. 4 (July–August 1986), pp. 55–59.

_____. "Three Yards and a Cloud of Dust: Industrial Management at Century End." *Production and Operations Management* 5, no. 1 (Spring 1996), pp. 15–41.

Skinner, Wickham (ed.). "Special Issue on Manufacturing Strategy," *Production and Operations Management* 5, no. 1 (Spring 1996).

Slack, Nigel. *The Manufacturing Advantage.* London: Management Books 2000 Ltd., 1991.

Solo, S. "Stop Whining and Get Back to Work." *Fortune,* March 12, 1991, pp. 49–50.

Stalk, G., Jr. "Time—The Next Source of Competitive Advantage." *Harvard Business Review,* July–August 1988.

Starr, Martin K. *Global Competitiveness: Getting the U.S. Back on Track.* New York: W. W. Norton, 1988.

_____."Global Production and Operations Strategy." *Columbia Journal of World Business* 19, no. 4 (Winter 1984), pp. 17–32.

Swaim, Jeffery C., and D. Scott Sink. "Current Developments in Firm or Corporate Level Productivity Measurements and Evaluation." *Issues in White Collar Productivity.* Atlanta, GA: Institute of Industrial Engineering, 1984, pp. 8–17.

Thomas, D. R. "Strategy Is Different in a Service Business." *Harvard Business Review,* July–August 1978, pp. 158–65.

Wheelwright, Steven C., and Robert H. Hayes. "Competing through Manufacturing." *Harvard Business Review,* January-February 1985.

Womack, James R., and Daniel T. Jones, *Lean Thinking: Banish Waste and Create Wealth in Your Corporation.* New York: Simon and Shuster, 1996.

Womack, James R.; Daniel T. Jones; and David Ross. *The Machine That Changed the World.* New York: Rawson Associates, 1990.

Chapter 3

Project Management

Chapter Outline

Definition of Project Management, 48
Work Breakdown Structure
Project Control, 50
Reporting Mechanisms
Organizational Structures, 52
Pure Project
Functional Project
Matrix Project
Critical Path Scheduling, 54
Time-Oriented Techniques, 55
CPM with a Single Time Estimate
CPM with Three Activity Time
Estimates
Maintaining Ongoing Project
Schedules

Time-Cost Models, 63
Minimum-Cost Scheduling (Time–Cost
Trade-off)
Managing Resources, 66
Tracking Progress, 66
Cautions on PERT and CPM, 66
Case: The Campus Wedding (A and B), 77
Case: Project Management at CPAone, 78

Key Terms

Project

Project Management

Milestone

Work Breakdown Structure

Gantt Chart

Pure Project

Functional Project

Matrix

PERT

CPM

Early Start/Late Start Schedules

Time–Cost Model

www Links

Primavera Systems, Inc. (http://www.primavera.com)

IT LOOKS LIKE AN ORGANIZATIONAL CHART FOR A multinational conglomerate, laid on its side. It is the map used to steer the small army of engineers, electricians, carpenters, plumbers, and laborers that is pressing to put the World Trade Center back together after the tragic terrorist bombing of the building on February 26, 1993. These workers hope to fix the building in three and a half weeks.

The chart is part of an intricate management technique that is guiding the enormous repair job, a process called the "critical path method." Several times a day, a personal computer spawns a fresh map, which Port Authority managers and their contractors use not only to figure out where they stand but also to determine what to do next, where to expect roadblocks, and where to concentrate their efforts. "We're getting our arms around the problem," said Robert DiCiara, assistant director of the World Trade department of the Port Authority of New York and New Jersey.

Aided by Computers

Displaced from his office by the bomb, Mr. DiCiara, who is in charge of coordinating the repairs of the Trade Center, is now working from a corner of a former restaurant on the concourse. He can get along without his office, but not without the organizing system. As he began describing the critical path method that directs his decisions, Mr. DiCiara had one desktop computer and six laptops running the management operation. While he was talking, a weary-looking man with a shopping cart wheeled in an eighth computer.

Mr. DiCiara is directing thousands, if not millions, of tasks—from bracing girders to installing emergency lighting—that affect one another in innumerable ways, some obvious and some hidden. Some jobs must be completed before others can begin; others can proceed all at once.

The challenge for critical path management is not only to find the order in which clusters of tasks must be undertaken, it is also to pinpoint the chain of tasks that will take the longest, thereby showing where it is most essential to avoid delays.

47

Thus, if two bottlenecks emerge, the one on the critical path must be tackled at once, before it causes a ripple of delays that pushes back the project's completion. For the time being, the other bottleneck, not part of the crucial chain, can safely wait. "I wonder what would have happened if we didn't have all the computer systems and software," Mr. DiCiara mused. One wonders how the pyramids were built.

The approach followed in rebuilding the World Trade Center—developing a highly motivated project team and supporting it with advanced project management software—is now standard in many organizations. On an everyday basis, planning and execution of projects using project management tools are common responsibilities of managers in both the public and private sectors. From an organizational perspective, companies ranging from Andersen Consulting to Xerox organize major parts of their businesses by project or programs. ●

Source: Matthew L. Wald, "The Twin Towers: How to Fix Them," *The New York Times,* March 9, 1993. © 1993 by the New York Times Co. Reprinted by permission.

S

While most of the material in this chapter is focused on the technical aspects of project management: structuring project networks and calculating the critical path, the management aspects are certainly equally as important. Success in projects is very much a group activity. Paul B. Williams, a teacher of project management for the J. C. Penney Company, stresses how success in working on projects, particularly during the early years, is an important promotion criterion.

With reference to the top ten list to understanding why project management is important, Mr. Williams points out that if you find yourself working or leading a team, you may be leading or participating in a project and not even recognize it. He argues that the only difference between leading a team and leading a project is that the team focuses on the activity and relationships while the project focuses more on the outcome. Success in leading a team is the quick path to promotion.

▇ DEFINITION OF PROJECT MANAGEMENT

Project

Project Management

A **project** may be defined as a series of related jobs usually directed toward some major output and requiring a significant period of time to perform. **Project management** can be defined as planning, directing, and controlling resources (people, equipment, material) to meet the technical, cost, and time constraints of the project.

While projects are often thought to be one-time occurrences, the fact is that many projects can be repeated or transferred to other settings or products. The result will be another project output. A contractor building houses or a firm producing low-volume products such as supercomputers, locomotives, or linear accelerators can effectively consider these as projects.

A project starts out as a *statement of work* (SOW). The SOW may be a written description of the objectives to be achieved, with a brief statement of the work to be done and a proposed schedule specifying the start and completion dates. It could also contain performance measures in terms of budget and completion steps (milestones) and the written reports to be supplied.

A *task* is a further subdivision of a project. It is usually not longer than several months in duration and is performed by one group or organization. A *subtask* may be used if needed to further subdivide the project into more meaningful pieces.

A *work package* is a group of activities combined to be assignable to a single organizational unit. It still falls into the format of all project management; the package

BREAKTHROUGH

Top Ten Reasons Why Project Management Is Important

10. Organizations that are willing to allow hastily planned, poorly led projects weaken themselves and endanger employees by wasting precious resources.

9. Organizations that are flattening (e.g., through reengineering, downsizing, or rightsizing) will depend on projects and project leaders to get work done that was once handled by departments.

8. With rare exceptions, project prime movers believe that project meltdowns are the result of weak project leadership.

7. More than one lumpy project leadership performance can give you a reputation that will repel future project participants.

6. Project work is often disguised by the use of the word *team;* if you find yourself on or leading teams, you're probably working with others to complete a project.

5. The abilities that are required to organize and carry out successful projects will enhance other aspects of your job.

4. Leading successful projects is the best way to prove your promotability to the people who make those decisions.

3. The best way to promote effective project leadership is to set examples that are so powerful and positive that others wouldn't dare do less.

2. Project leaders seldom get better until they know how to do it right.

1. If you're not getting better, you're getting worse as you get older.

Source: Paul B. Williams, *Getting a Project Done on Time: Managing People, Time, and Results,* (New York: The American Management Association, 1996), p. ix.

provides a description of what is to be done, when it is to be started and completed, the budget, measures of performance, and specific events to be reached at points in time (called **milestones**). Typical milestones might be the completion of the design, the production of a prototype, the completed testing of the prototype, and the approval of a pilot run.

Milestones

Work Breakdown Structure

The **work breakdown structure** (WBDS) defines the hierachy of project tasks, subtasks, and work packages. Completion of one or more work packages results in the completion of a subtask; completion of one or more subtasks results in the completion of a task; and finally the completion of all tasks is required to complete the project. A representation of this structure is shown in the indented diagram below.

Work Breakdown Structure

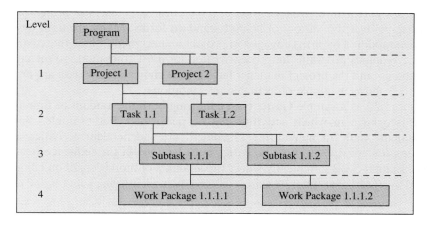

Exhibit 3.1

Work Breakdown Structure, Large Optical Scanner Design

Level 1	Level 2	Level 3	Level 4		
x				1	Optical simulator design
	x			1.1	Optical design
		x		1.1.1	Telescope design/fab
		x		1.1.2	Telescope/simulator optical interface
		x		1.1.3	Simulator zoom system design
		x		1.1.4	Ancillary simulator optical component specification
	x			1.2	System performance analysis
		x		1.2.1	Overall system firmware and software control
			x	1.2.1.1	Logic flow diagram generation and analysis
			x	1.2.1.2	Basic control algorithm design
		x		1.2.2	Far beam analyzer
		x		1.2.3	System inter- and intra-alignment method design
		x		1.2.4	Data recording and reduction requirements
	x			1.3	System integration
	x			1.4	Cost analysis
		x		1.4.1	Cost/system schedule analysis
		x		1.4.2	Cost/system performance analysis
	x			1.5	Management
		x		1.5.1	System design/engineering management
		x		1.5.2	Program management
	x			1.6	Long lead item procurement
		x		1.6.1	Large optics
		x		1.6.2	Target components
		x		1.6.3	Detectors

Exhibit 3.1 shows the work breakdown structure for a project. Note the ease in identifying activities through the level numbers. For example, telescope design (the third item down) is identified as 1.1.1 (the first item in level 1, the first item in level 2, and the first item in level 3). Data recording (the 13th item down) is 1.2.4.

The keys to a good work breakdown structure are

- Allow the elements to be worked on independently.
- Make them manageable in size.
- Give authority to carry out the program.
- Monitor and measure the program.
- Provide the required resources.

■ PROJECT CONTROL

Reporting Mechanisms

The U.S. Department of Defense (one of the earliest large users of project management) has published a variety of helpful standard forms. Many are used directly or have been modified by firms engaged in project management. Since those early days, however, graphics programs have been written for most computers, so management, the customer, and the project manager have a wide choice of how data are presented. Exhibit 3.2 shows a sample of available presentations.

Gantt Chart

Exhibit 3.2A is a sample **Gantt chart** showing both the amount of time involved and the sequence in which activities can be performed. For example, "long lead procurement" and "manufacturing schedules" are independent activities and can occur simultaneously. All other activities must be done in the sequence from top to bottom. Exhibit 3.2B graphically shows the amounts of money spent on labor, material, and overhead over time. Its value is its clarity in identifying sources and amounts of cost.

A Sample of Graphic Project Reports

Exhibit 3.2

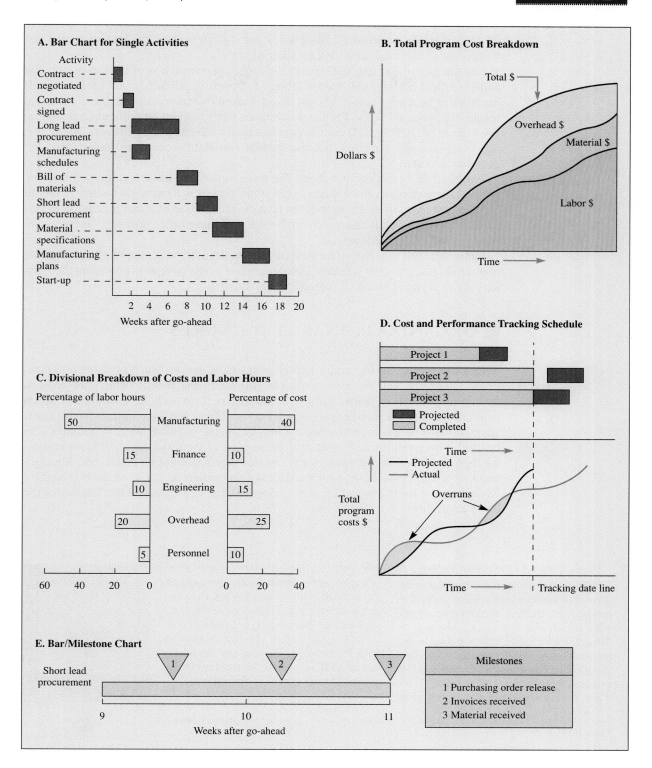

A. Bar Chart for Single Activities

Activity

Contract negotiated
Contract signed
Long lead procurement
Manufacturing schedules
Bill of materials
Short lead procurement
Material specifications
Manufacturing plans
Start-up

Weeks after go-ahead

B. Total Program Cost Breakdown

Dollars $

Total $
Overhead $
Material $
Labor $

Time

C. Divisional Breakdown of Costs and Labor Hours

Percentage of labor hours   Percentage of cost

50	Manufacturing	40
15	Finance	10
10	Engineering	15
20	Overhead	25
5	Personnel	10

60   40   20   0   0   20   40

D. Cost and Performance Tracking Schedule

Project 1
Project 2
Project 3

Projected
Completed

Time

Total program costs $

Projected
Actual

Overruns

Time   Tracking date line

E. Bar/Milestone Chart

Short lead procurement

1   2   3

9   10   11

Weeks after go-ahead

Milestones

1 Purchasing order release
2 Invoices received
3 Material received

Exhibit 3.2C shows the percentage of the project's labor hours that come from the various areas of manufacturing, finance, and so on. These labor hours are related to the proportion of the project's total labor cost. For example, manufacturing is responsible for 50 percent of the project's labor hours, but this 50 percent has been allocated just 40 percent of the total labor dollars charged.

The top half of Exhibit 3.2D shows the degree of completion of these projects. The dotted vertical line signifies today. Project 1, therefore, is already late because it still has work to be done. Project 2 is not being worked on temporarily, so there is a space before the projected work. Project 3 continues to be worked on without interruption. The bottom of Exhibit 3.2D compares actual total costs and projected costs. As we see, two cost overruns occurred, but the current cumulative costs are under projected cumulative costs.

Exhibit 3.2E is a milestone chart. The three milestones mark specific points in the project where checks can be made to see if the project is on time and where it should be. The best place to locate milestones is at the completion of a major activity. In this exhibit, the major activities completed were "purchase order release," "invoices received," and "material received."

Other standard reports can be used for a more detailed presentation comparing cost to progress (such as cost schedule status report—CSSR) or reports providing the basis for partial payment (such as "earned value" report).

■ ORGANIZATIONAL STRUCTURES

Before the project starts, senior management must decide which of three organizational structures will be used to tie the project to the parent firm: pure project, functional project, or matrix project. If the matrix form is chosen, different projects (rows of the matrix) borrow resources from functional areas (columns). Senior management must then decide whether a weak, balanced, or strong form of a matrix is to be used. This establishes whether project managers have little, equal, or more authority than the functional managers with whom they negotiate for resources. Management must also consider the characteristics of the project leader. (See the box entitled "Selecting the Right Project Leader.") Here are the strengths and weaknesses of the three main forms.

Selecting the Right Project Leader

Senior management must exercise judgment and initiative in finding, selecting, hiring, and training the specific people who will fulfill a project's charter. At Toyota, for example, senior managers explicitly choose a project leader whose personality is consistent with the type of product they intend to introduce. Thus, when it was a sporty car targeted to a young, aggressive customer, they looked for a "fighter-pilot" type. When the project was to develop a luxurious sedan, they selected an "executive" type. The aim is to select project leaders who, by identifying with both the project and the customer, can internalize much of what counts in the product's total system performance.

Source: Steven C. Wheelwright and Kim B. Clark, *Leading Product Development* (New York: The Free Press, 1995), p. 91.

Pure Project

Tom Peters predicts that "most of the world's work will be 'brainwork,' done in semipermanent networks of small project oriented teams, each one an autonomous, entrepreneurial center of opportunity; where the necessity for speed and flexibility dooms to the dodo's fate the hierarchical management structures we and our ancestors grew up with."[1] Thus, out of the three basic project organizational structures, Peters favors the **pure project** (nicknamed skunk works), where a self-contained team works full time on the project.

Pure Project

Advantages

- The project manager has full authority over the project.
- Team members report to one boss. They do not have to worry about dividing loyalty with a functional-area manager.
- Lines of communication are shortened. Decisions are made quickly.
- Team pride, motivation, and commitment are high.

Disadvantages

- Duplication of resources. Equipment and people are not shared across projects.
- Organizational goals and policies are ignored, as team members are often both physically and psychologically removed from headquarters.
- The organization falls behind in its knowledge of new technology due to weakened functional divisions.
- Since team members have no functional area "home," they worry about life-after-project, and project termination is delayed.

Functional Project

At the other end of the project organization spectrum is the **functional project,** housing the project within a functional division.

Functional Project

Advantages

- A team member can work on several projects.
- Technical expertise is maintained within the functional area even if individuals leave the project or organization.
- The functional area is a "home" after the project is completed. Functional specialists can advance vertically.
- A critical mass of specialized functional-area experts creates synergystic solutions to a project's technical problems.

```
                    President
        ┌──────────────┼──────────────┐
   Research        Engineering     Manufacturing
     and
  Development
  ┌──┬──┐          ┌──┬──┐         ┌──┬──┐
Project Project Project  Project Project Project  Project Project Project
  A    B    C         A    B    C          A    B    C
```

Disadvantages

- Aspects of the project that are not directly related to the functional area get short-changed.
- Motivation of team members is often weak.
- Needs of the client are secondary and are responded to slowly.

---

[1] Tom Peters, *Liberation Management* (New York: Alfred A. Knopf, 1992), p. 5 and cover flyleaf.

Matrix Project

The classic specialized organizational form—the **matrix**—attempts to blend properties of functional and pure project structures. Each project utilizes people from different functional areas. The project manager (PM) decides what tasks and when they will be performed, but the functional managers control which people and technologies are used.

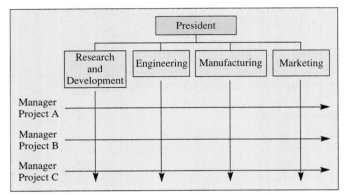

Advantages

- Communication between functional divisions is enhanced.
- A project manager is held responsible for successful completion of the project.
- Duplication of resources is minimized.
- Team members have a functional "home" after project completion, so they are less worried about "life-after-project" than if they were a pure project organization.
- Policies of the parent organization are followed. This increases support for the project.

Disadvantages

- There are two bosses. Often the functional manager will be listened to before the project manager. After all, who can promote you or give you a raise?
- It is doomed to failure unless the PM has strong negotiating skills.
- Suboptimization is a danger, as PMs hoard resources for their own project, thus harming other projects.

Note that regardless of which of the three major organizational forms is used, the project manager is the primary contact point with the customer. Communication and flexibility are greatly enhanced, as one person is responsible for successful completion of the project.

■ CRITICAL PATH SCHEDULING

Critical path scheduling refers to a set of graphic techniques used in planning and controlling projects. In any given project, the three factors of concern are time, cost, and resource availability. Critical path techniques have been developed to deal with each of these, individually and in combination. Following a brief history of how the terminology developed, the rest of this chapter focuses on time-based models, time–cost models, and limited-resource models.

PERT (*program evaluation and review technique*) and **CPM** (*critical path method*), the two best-known critical path scheduling techniques, were both developed in the late 1950s. PERT was developed under the sponsorship of the U.S. Navy Special Projects Office in 1958 as a management tool for scheduling and controlling the Polaris missile project. CPM was developed in 1957 by J. E. Kelly of Remington-Rand and M. R. Walker of Du Pont to aid in scheduling maintenance shutdowns of chemical processing plants.

Critical path scheduling techniques display a project in graphic form and relate its component tasks in a way that focuses attention on those crucial to the project's

At Boeing, effective project management techniques were essential both in setting up the 777 assembly system and in its scheduling and manufacturing. Twenty percent of the 777 is built in Japan, along with manufacturing help from Australia (rudder), Northern Ireland and Singapore (nose gear), Korean Air (wingtip), Brazil (fin and wingtip assembly), and Italy (outboard wing flaps).

completion. For critical path scheduling techniques to be most applicable, a project must have the following characteristics:

1. It must have well-defined jobs or tasks whose completion marks the end of the project.
2. The jobs or tasks are independent; they may be started, stopped, and conducted separately within a given sequence.
3. The jobs or tasks are ordered; they must follow each other in a given sequence.

Construction, airplane manufacture, and shipbuilding industries commonly meet these criteria, and critical path techniques find wide application within them. We also previously noted that applications of project management and critical path techniques are becoming much more common within firms in rapidly changing industries.

◼ TIME-ORIENTED TECHNIQUES

The basic forms of PERT and CPM focus on finding the longest time-consuming path through a network of tasks as a basis for planning and controlling a project. Both PERT and CPM use nodes and arrows for display. Originally, the basic differences between PERT and CPM were that PERT used the arrow to represent an activity and CPM used the node. The other original difference was that PERT used three estimates—optimistic, pessimistic, and best—of an activity's required time, whereas CPM used just the best estimate. This distinction reflects PERT's origin in scheduling advanced projects that are characterized by uncertainty and CPM's origin in the scheduling of the fairly routine activity of plant maintenance. As years passed, these two features no longer distinguished PERT from CPM. This is because CPM users started to use three time estimates and PERT users often placed activities on the nodes.

We believe the activity on the node is much easier to follow logically than the activity on the arrow. The three time estimates are used to measure the probability.

the probability of completion times. Therefore, in this book we use the activity on the node and either a single estimate for activity time or three time estimates, depending on our objective. We use the terms *CPM* and *PERT* interchangeably and mean the same thing, although we tend to use *CPM* more frequently.

In a sense, both techniques owe their development to their widely used predecessor, the Gantt chart. While the Gantt chart is able to relate activities to time in a usable fashion for very small projects, the interrelationship of activities, when displayed in this form, becomes extremely difficult to visualize and to work with for projects with more than 25 or 30 activities. Also, the Gantt chart provides no direct procedure for determining the critical path, which, despite its theoretical shortcomings, is of great practical value.

CPM with a Single Time Estimate

Here is an example of a project that we will develop in a normal project scheduling manner. Note that, the times for each activity have been given as a single best estimate (rather than three estimates, which we discuss in a later example).

■ **example 3.1**   *Single Time Estimate*   Many firms that have tried to enter the notebook computer market have failed. Suppose your firm believes that there is a big demand in this market because existing products have not been designed correctly. They are either too heavy, too large, or too small to have standard-size keyboards. Your intended computer will be small enough to carry inside a jacket pocket if need be. The ideal size will be no larger than 5 inches $\times$ 9½ inches $\times$ 1 inch with a folding keyboard. It should weigh no more than 15 ounces, have an LCD display, have a micro disk drive, and an ethernet port. This should appeal to traveling businesspeople, but it could have a much wider market including students. It should be priced to sell in the $175–$200 range.

The project, then, is to design, develop, and produce a prototype of this small computer. In the rapidly changing computer industry, it is crucial to hit the market with a product of this sort in less than a year. Therefore, the project team has been allowed approximately eight months (35 weeks) to produce the prototype.

solution   The first charge of the project team is to develop a project network chart and estimate the likelihood of completing the prototype computer within the 35 weeks. Let's follow the steps in the development of the network.

1. Activity identification.   The project team decides that the following activities are the major components of the project: design of the computer, prototype construction, prototype testing, methods specification (summarized in a report), evaluation studies of automatic assembly equipment, an assembly equipment study report, and a final report summarizing all aspects of the design, equipment, and methods.

2. Activity sequencing and network construction.   On the basis of discussion with his staff, the project manager develops the precedence table and sequence network shown in Exhibit 3.3. Activities are indicated as nodes, and arrows show the sequence in which the activities must be completed.

When constructing a network, take care to ensure that the activities are in the proper order and that the logic of their relationships is maintained. For example, it would be illogical to have a situation where Event A precedes Event B, B precedes C, and C precedes A.

Exhibit 3.3

CPM Network for
Computer Design
Project

CPM Activity Designations and Time Estimates

Activity	Designation	Immediate Predecessors	Time in Weeks
Design	A	–	21
Build prototype	B	A	5
Evaluate equipment	C	A	7
Test prototype	D	B	2
Write equipment report	E	C, D	5
Write methods report	F	C, D	8
Write final report	G	E, F	2

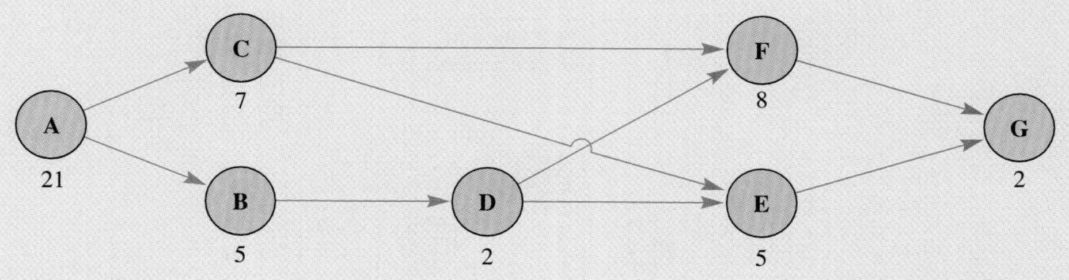

3. Determine the critical path.

The critical path is the longest sequence of connected activities through the network and is defined as the path with zero slack time. (The times are consecutive.) *Slack time,* in turn, is calculated for each activity; it is the difference between the latest and the earliest expected completion time for an event. Slack may be thought of as the amount of time the start of a given activity may be delayed without delaying the completion of the project. To arrive at slack time, we must calculate four time values for each activity:

· *Early start time* (ES), the earliest possible time that the activity can begin.
· *Early finish time* (EF), the early start time plus the time needed to complete the activity.
· *Late finish time* (LF), the latest time an activity can end without delaying the project.
· *Late start time* (LS), the late finish time minus the time needed to complete the activity.

The procedure for arriving at these values and for determining slack and the critical path can best be explained by reference to the simple network shown in Exhibit 3.4. The letters denote the activities; the numbers denote the activity times.

a. Find ES time. Take 0 as the start of the project and set this equal to ES for activity A. To find ES for B, we add the duration of A (which is 2) to 0 and obtain 2. Likewise, ES for C would be $0 + 2 = 2$. To find ES for D, we take the larger ES and duration time for the preceding activities. Since $B = 2 + 5 = 7$ and $C = 2 + 4 = 6$, ES for $D = 7$. These values are entered on the diagram (Exhibit 3.4, Step a). The largest value is selected since activity D cannot begin until the longest time-consuming activity preceding it is completed.

b. Find EF times. The EF for A is its ES time, 0, plus its duration of 2. B's EF is its ES of 2 plus its duration of 5, or 7. C's is $2 + 4$, or 6, and D's is $7 + 3$, or 10

Exhibit 3.4

Steps to Develop and
Solve a CPM Network

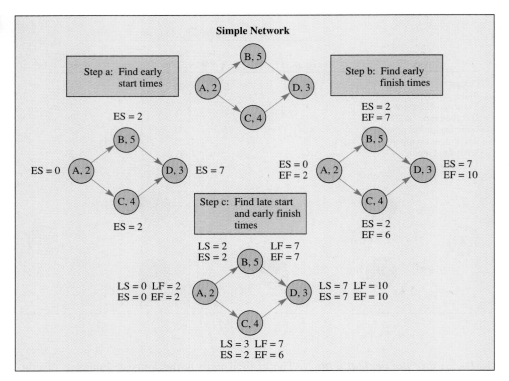

(Exhibit 3.4, Step b). In practice, one computes ES and EF together while proceeding through the network. Since ES plus activity time equals EF, the EF becomes the ES of the following event, and so forth.

c. Find late start and late finish times. While the procedure for making these calculations can be presented in mathematical form, the concept is much easier to explain and understand if it is presented in an intuitive way. The basic approach is to start at the end of the project with some desired or assumed completion time. Working back toward the beginning, one activity at a time, we determine how long the starting of this activity may be delayed without affecting the start of the one that follows it.

In reference to the sample network in Exhibit 3.4, Step c, let us assume that the late finish time for the project is equal to the early finish time for activity D, that is, 10. If this is the case, the latest possible starting time for D is 10 − 3, or 7. The latest time C can finish without delaying the LS of D is 7, which means that C's LS is 7 − 4, or 3. The latest time B can finish without delaying the LS of D is also 7, which means that B's LS is 7 − 5, or 2. Since A precedes two activities, the choice of LS and LF values depends on which of those activities must be started first. Clearly, B determines the LF for A since its LS is 2, whereas C can be delayed one day without extending the project. Finally, since A must be finished by day 2, it cannot start any later than day 0, so its LS is 0.

d. Determine slack time for each activity. Slack for each activity is defined as either LS − ES or LF − EF. In this example, only activity C has slack (one day) so the critical path is A, B, D. ■

Early Start Schedule

Early Start and Late Start Schedules   An **early start schedule** is one that lists all of the activities by their early start times. For activities not on the critical path,

CPM Network for Computer Design Project

Exhibit 3.5

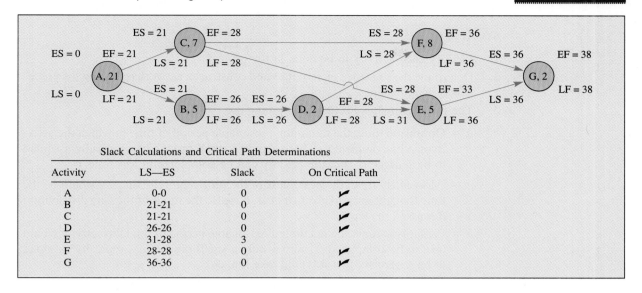

Slack Calculations and Critical Path Determinations

Activity	LS—ES	Slack	On Critical Path
A	0-0	0	✔
B	21-21	0	✔
C	21-21	0	✔
D	26-26	0	✔
E	31-28	3	
F	28-28	0	✔
G	36-36	0	✔

there is slack time between the activity completion and the start of the next activity that succeeds it. The early start schedule completes the project and all of its activities as soon as possible.

A **late start schedule** lists the activities to start as late as possible without delaying the completion date of the project. One motivation for using a late start schedule is that savings are realized by postponing purchases of materials, the use of labor, and other costs until necessary.

Late Start Schedule

Applying CPM to the Computer Design Project   Following through the steps just described, we find the critical path and early and late start times as shown in Exhibit 3.5. Note that in this case we have two critical paths through the network. This first path includes activities A, C, F, and G. The second path is A, B, D, F, and G. Only activity E is not on a critical path. This might be a fairly difficult project to complete in the minimum time.

CPM with Three Activity Time Estimates

If a single estimate of the time required to complete an activity is not reliable, the best procedure is to use three time estimates. These three times not only allow us to estimate the activity time but also let us obtain a probability estimate for completion time for the entire network. Briefly, the procedure is as follows: The estimated activity time is a weighted average, with more weight given to the best estimate and less to the maximum and minimum times. The ratio generally used is 4, 1, 1, as shown later. The estimated completion time of the network is computed using basic statistics, which states that the standard deviation of a sequence of events is the square root of the sum of the variances of each event. This is the logic of Z shown in step 7 below. Then, simply by locating Z (the number of standard deviations) in a probability table (as in Appendix D) we obtain the probability of completion.

■ example 3.2   *Three Time Estimates*   We use the same information as in Example 3.1 with the exception that activities have three time estimates.

solution

1. Identify each activity to be done in the project.
2. Determine the sequence of activities and construct a network reflecting the precedence relationships.
3. The three estimates for an activity time are

    a = Optimistic time: the minimum reasonable period of time in which the activity can be completed. (There is only a small probability, typically assumed to be 1 percent, that the activity can be completed in less time.)

    m = Most likely time: the best guess of the time required. Since m would be the time thought most likely to appear, it is also the mode of the beta distribution discussed in step 4.

    b = Pessimistic time: the maximum reasonable period of time the activity would take to be completed. (There is only a small probability, typically assumed to be 1 percent, that it would take longer.)

    Typically, this information is gathered from those people who are to perform the activity.

4. *Calculate the expected time (ET) for each activity.* The formula for this calculation is

    $$\text{ET} = \frac{a + 4m + b}{6} \qquad (3.1)$$

    This is based on the beta statistical distribution and weights the most likely time (m) four times more than either the optimistic time (a) or the pessimistic time (b). The beta distribution is extremely flexible; it can take on the variety of forms that typically arise, it has finite end points (which limit the possible activity times to the area between a and b) and, in the simplified version, permits straightforward computation of the activity mean and standard deviation.

5. *Determine the critical path.* Using the expected times, a critical path is calculated in the same way as the single time case.

6. *Calculate the variances (σ^2) of the activity times.* Specifically, this is the variance, σ^2, associated with each ET, and is computed as follows:

    $$\sigma^2 = \left(\frac{b - a}{6} \right)^2 \qquad (3.2)$$

    As you can see, the variance is the square of one-sixth the difference between the two extreme time estimates. Of course, the greater this difference, the larger the variance.

7. *Determine the probability of completing the project on a given date.* A valuable feature of using three time estimates is that it enables the analyst to assess the effect of uncertainty on project completion time. The mechanics of deriving this probability are as follows:
    a. Sum the variance values associated with each activity on the critical path. (For the case where there is more than one critical path, see the following example.)

b. Substitute this figure, along with the project due date and the project expected completion time, into the *Z* transformation formula. This formula is

$$Z = \frac{D - T_E}{\sqrt{\Sigma\ \sigma_{cp}^2}} \tag{3.3}$$

where

D = Desired completion date for project

T_E = Expected completion time for the project

$\Sigma\ \sigma_{cp}^2$ = Sum of the variances along the critical path

c. *Calculate the value of* Z, which is the number of standard deviations the project due date is from the expected completion time.

d. Using the value of Z, find the probability of meeting the project due date (using a table of normal probabilities such as Appendix E). The *expected completion time* is the starting time plus the sum of the activity times on the critical path.

Following the steps just outlined, we developed Exhibit 3.6 showing expected times and variances. The project network was created the same as we did previously. The only difference is that the activity times are weighted averages. We determine the critical path as before, using these values as if they were single numbers. The difference between the single time estimate and three times (optimistic, most likely, and pessimistic) is in computing probabilities of completion. Exhibit 3.7 shows the network and critical path.

Activity	Activity Designation	Time Estimates a m b	Expected Times (ET) $\dfrac{a + 4m + b}{6}$	Activity Variances (σ^2) $\left(\dfrac{b - a}{6}\right)^2$
Design	A	10 22 28	21	9
Build prototype	B	4 4 10	5	1
Evaluate equipment	C	4 6 14	7	2⅞
Test prototype	D	1 2 3	2	⅑
Write report	E	1 5 9	5	1⅞
Write methods report	F	7 8 9	8	⅑
Write final report	G	2 2 2	2	0

Exhibit 3.6

Activity Expected Times and Variances

Exhibit 3.7

Computer Design Project with Three Time Estimates

Since there are two critical paths in the network, we must decide which variances to use in arriving at the probability of meeting the project due date. A conservative approach dictates using the path with the largest total variance since this would focus management's attention on the activities most likely to exhibit broad variations. On this basis, the variances associated with activities A, C, F, and G would be used to find the probability of completion. Thus $\Sigma \sigma_{cp}^2 = 9 + 2\frac{7}{9} + \frac{1}{9} + 0 = 11.89$. Suppose

Project Managers, Challenges

Despite the fact that 84 percent of project managers are responsible for staying within a project budget, only 15 percent of the time are they faced with direct ramifications for not doing so. In fact, 16 percent of project managers don't always know the budget of their jobs, according to a survey of project managers conducted by Zweig White & Associates, of Natick, Massachusetts.

The survey showed that project managers consider meeting schedules/budgets to be the greatest challenge that they face (19 percent). This may be partially attributed to the areas they rated as their two top complaints—insufficient or inadequate staff support (10 percent) and responsibility without authority (9 percent).

Project managers cited several reasons for not performing their best. Seventeen percent said that all team members are rarely or never allowed to see their own portion of the scope of services for a project. Also, they do not receive much training. Just 26 percent of firms have mandatory formal training for project managers, while 40 percent have optional training, and 29 percent have no training. For the firms that do offer training, the level is inadequate. Less than half of project managers are trained to perform basic tasks such as opening a job number, charging time, and budgeting.

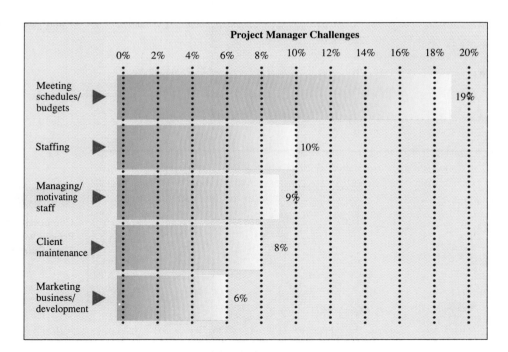

Source: "Project Managers Challenges," *IIE Solutions,* December 1996, p. 9.

management asks for the probability of completing the project in 35 weeks. D, then, is 35. The expected completion time was found to be 38. Substituting into the Z equation and solving, we obtain

$$Z = \frac{D - T_E}{\sqrt{\Sigma \, \sigma_{cp}^2}} = \frac{35 - 38}{\sqrt{11.89}} = -0.87$$

Looking at Appendix D we see that a Z value of -0.87 yields a probability of 0.19, which means that the project manager has only about a 19 percent chance of completing the project in 35 weeks. Note that this probability is really the probability of completing the critical path ACEG. Since there is another critical path and other paths that might become critical, the probability of completing the project in 35 weeks is actually less than .19. ■

Maintaining Ongoing Project Schedules

It is important to keep a project schedule accurate and current. The schedule tracks progress and identifies problems as they occur while corrective time may still be available. It also monitors the progress of cost and is often the basis for partial payments. Yet, schedules are often sloppily kept or even totally abandoned.

A recent study that surveyed project managers indicates that there are many potential roadblocks to success. See the box titled "Project Managers, Challenges."

■ TIME–COST MODELS

In practice, project managers are as much concerned with the cost to complete a project as with the time to complete the project. For this reason, **time–cost models** have been devised. These models—extensions of PERT and CPM—attempt to develop a minimum-cost schedule for an entire project and to control expenditures during the project.

Time–Cost Models

Minimum-Cost Scheduling (Time–Cost Trade-off)

The basic assumption in minimum-cost scheduling is that there is a relationship between activity completion time and the cost of a project. On one hand, it costs money to expedite an activity; on the other, it costs money to sustain (or lengthen) the project. The costs associated with expediting activities are termed *activity direct costs* and add to the project direct cost. Some may be worker-related, such as overtime work, hiring more workers, and transferring workers from other jobs; while others are resource-related, such as buying or leasing additional or more efficient equipment and drawing on additional support facilities.

The costs associated with sustaining the project are termed *project indirect costs:* overhead, facilities, and resource opportunity costs, and, under certain contractual situations, penalty costs or lost incentive payments. Since *activity direct costs* and *project indirect costs* are opposing costs dependent on time, the scheduling problem is essentially one of finding the project duration that minimizes their sum, or in other words, finding the optimum point in a time–cost trade-off.

The procedure for finding this point consists of the following five steps. It is explained by using the simple four-activity network that we expanded from Exhibit 3.4

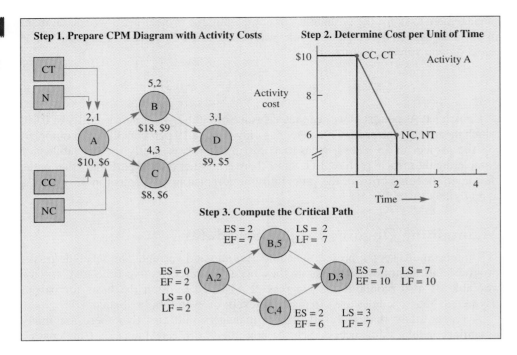

and is shown in Exhibit 3.8. Assume that the indirect costs remain constant for eight days and then increase at the rate of $5 per day.

1. Prepare a CPM-type network diagram.   For each activity this diagram should list

   a. Normal cost (NC): the lowest expected activity cost. (These are the lesser of the cost figures shown under each node in Exhibit 3.8.)
   b. Normal time (NT): the time associated with each normal cost.
   c. Crash time (CT): the shortest possible activity time.
   d. Crash cost (CC): the cost associated with each crash time.

2. Determine the cost per unit of time (assume days) to expedite each activity.   The relationship between activity time and cost may be shown graphically by plotting CC and CT coordinates and connecting them to the NC and NT coordinates by a concave, convex, or straight line—or some other form, depending on the actual cost structure of activity performance, as in Exhibit 3.8. For activity A, we assume a linear relationship between time and cost. This assumption is common in practice and helps us derive the cost per day to expedite since this value may be found directly by taking the slope of the line using the formula Slope = (CC − NC) ÷ (NT − CT). (When the assumption of linearity cannot be made, the cost of expediting must be determined graphically for each day the activity may be shortened.)

The calculations needed to obtain the cost of expediting the remaining activities are shown in Exhibit 3.9.

3. Compute the critical path.   For the simple network we have been using, this schedule would take 10 days. The critical path is A, B, D.

4. Shorten the critical path at the least cost.   The easiest way to proceed is to start with the normal schedule, find the critical path, and reduce the path time by one day

Activity	CC − NC	NT − CT	$\dfrac{CC - NC}{NT - CT}$	Cost per Day to Expedite	Number of Days Activity May Be Shortened
A	$10 − $6	2 − 1	$\dfrac{\$10 - \$6}{2 - 1}$	$4	1
B	$18 − $9	5 − 2	$\dfrac{\$18 - \$9}{5 - 2}$	$3	3
C	$ 8 − $6	4 − 3	$\dfrac{\$8 - \$6}{4 - 3}$	$2	1
D	$ 9 − $5	3 − 1	$\dfrac{\$9 - \$5}{3 - 1}$	$2	2

Exhibit 3.9

Calculation of Cost per Day to Expedite Each Activity

Current Critical Path	Remaining Number of Days Activity May Be Shortened	Cost per Day to Expedite Each Activity	Least Cost Activity to Expedite	Total Cost of All Activities in Network	Project Completion Time
ABD	All activity times and costs are normal.			$26	10
ABD	A–1, B–3, D–2	A–4, B–3, D–2	D	28	9
ABD	A–1, B–3, D–1	A–4, B–3, D–2	D	30	8
ABD	A–1, B–3	A–4, B–3	B	33	7
ABCD	A–1, B–2, C–1	A–4, B–3, C–2	A*	37	6
ABCD	B–2, C–1	B–3, C–2	B&C†	42	5
ABCD	B–1	B–3	B	45	5

Exhibit 3.10

Reducing the Project Completion Time One Day at a Time

*To reduce the critical path by one day, reduce either A alone, or B and C together at the same time (since either B or C by itself just modifies the critical path without shortening it).

†B&C must be crashed together to reduce the path by one day.

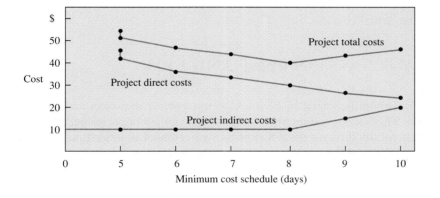

Exhibit 3.11

Plot of Costs and Minimum Cost Schedule

using the lowest-cost activity. Then recompute and find the new critical path and reduce it by one day also. Repeat this procedure until the time of completion is satisfactory, or until there can be no further reduction in the project completion time. Exhibit 3.10 shows the reduction of the network one day at a time.

5. *Plot project direct, indirect, and total-cost curves and find minimum-cost schedule.* Exhibit 3.11 shows the indirect cost plotted as a constant $10 per day for eight days and increasing $5 per day thereafter. The direct costs are plotted from Exhibit 3.10 and the total project cost is shown as the total of the two costs.

Summing the values for direct and indirect costs for each day yields the project total cost curve. As you can see, this curve is at its minimum with an eight-day schedule, which costs $40 ($30 direct + $10 indirect).

■ MANAGING RESOURCES

In addition to scheduling each task, we must assign resources. Modern software quickly highlights overallocations—situations in which allocations exceed resources.

To resolve overallocations manually, you can either add resources or reschedule. Moving a task within its slack can free up resources.

Mid- to high-level project management information systems software (PMIS) can resolve overallocations through a "leveling" feature. Several rules of thumb can be used. You can specify that low-priority tasks should be delayed until higher-priority ones are complete, or that the project end before or after the original deadline.

■ TRACKING PROGRESS

The real action starts after the project gets underway. Actual progress will differ from your original, or baseline, planned progress. Software can hold several different baseline plans, so you can compare monthly snapshots.

A *tracking Gantt chart* superimposes the current schedule onto a baseline plan so deviations are easily noticed. If you prefer, a spreadsheet view of the same information could be output. Deviations between planned start/finish and newly scheduled start/finish also appear, and a "slipping filter" can be applied to highlight or output only those tasks that are scheduled to finish at a later date than the planned baseline.

Management by exception can also be applied to find deviations between budgeted costs and actual costs.

■ CAUTIONS ON PERT AND CPM

Several assumptions need to be made to use project networks and CPM or PERT analysis. This section summarizes some significant assumptions and their criticisms. One particularly difficult point for operating personnel is understanding the statistics when three time estimates are used. The beta distribution of activity times, the three time estimates, the activity variances, and the use of the normal distribution to arrive at project completion probabilities are all potential sources of misunderstandings, and with misunderstanding comes distrust and obstruction. Thus, management must be sure that the people charged with monitoring and controlling activity performance understand the statistics.

1. *Assumption:* Project activities can be identified as entities. (There is a clear beginning and ending point for each activity.)
   Criticism: Projects, especially complex ones, change in content over time so a network made at the beginning may be highly inaccurate later on. Also, the very fact that activities are specified and a network is formalized tends to limit the flexibility that is required to handle changing situations as the project progresses.

BREAKTHROUGH

Project Management Information System in Everyday Use

The 1990s have seen an explosion of interest in the techniques and concepts of project management with a parallel increase in project management software offerings. A few years ago, there were but a handful of microcomputer-based project management software packages. Now, there are over 100 such project management information systems—and the use of these tools is proliferating exponentially. Within our own MBA-level project management classes, about half of the students now enter having had some exposure to such software; all leave knowing at least one package and having been exposed to several others (Microsoft Project for Windows, Primavera Project Planner, Time Line, Project Scheduler, Milestone, Schedule Publisher, Texim Project). As recently as the early 1990s, perhaps one student per class would have prior experience with a PMIS, and our only in-class software was incapable of managing costs, leveling resources, or even displaying a PERT or Gantt chart. Here are examples of three PMISs leading this operations breakthrough.

The Microsoft Project program comes with an excellent on-line tutorial, which is one reason for its overwhelming popularity with project managers tracking midsized projects. This package aids in scheduling, allocating, and leveling resources, as well as in controlling costs and producing presentation-quality graphics and reports. Exhibit 3.12 shows a Microsoft Project sample output.

If the focus is primarily in scheduling, Kidasa's Milestones, Etc. program, produces Gantt charts that can even show dependencies among activities. As the project unfolds and schedules need updating, a Gantt chart's activity start and end dates can easily be modified.

Finally, for managing very large projects or programs having several projects, Primavera Project Plan-

ner is often the choice. Primavera Project Planner was selected to track the multihundred-million–dollar rebuilding of the World Trade Center after the terrorist bombing of February 26, 1993 (described in the opening vignette of the chapter). Primavera's Monte Carlo risk analysis program was also used to determine how much time and money were risked under different assumptions.

You will find it interesting to check out Primava Systems, Inc.'s Web site at http://www. primavera.com for the latest information on their software products.

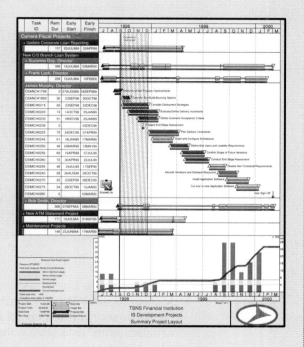

2. *Assumption:* Project activity sequence relationships can be specified and networked.

   Criticism: Sequence relationships cannot always be specified beforehand. In some projects, in fact, ordering certain activities is conditional on previous activities. (PERT and CPM, in their basic form, have no provision for treating this problem although some other techniques have been proposed that allow the project manager several contingency paths, given different outcomes from each activity.)

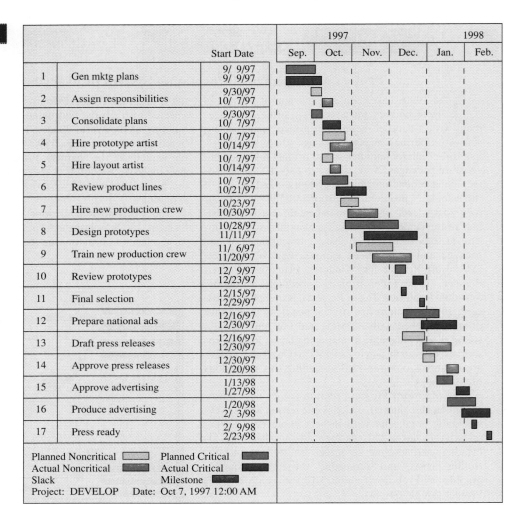

			1997				1998	
		Start Date	Sep.	Oct.	Nov.	Dec.	Jan.	Feb.
1	Gen mktg plans	9/ 9/97 9/ 9/97						
2	Assign responsibilities	9/30/97 10/ 7/97						
3	Consolidate plans	9/30/97 10/ 7/97						
4	Hire prototype artist	10/ 7/97 10/14/97						
5	Hire layout artist	10/ 7/97 10/14/97						
6	Review product lines	10/ 7/97 10/21/97						
7	Hire new production crew	10/23/97 10/30/97						
8	Design prototypes	10/28/97 11/11/97						
9	Train new production crew	11/ 6/97 11/20/97						
10	Review prototypes	12/ 9/97 12/23/97						
11	Final selection	12/15/97 12/29/97						
12	Prepare national ads	12/16/97 12/30/97						
13	Draft press releases	12/16/97 12/30/97						
14	Approve press releases	12/30/97 1/20/98						
15	Approve advertising	1/13/98 1/27/98						
16	Produce advertising	1/20/98 2/ 3/98						
17	Press ready	2/ 9/98 2/23/98						

Planned Noncritical   Planned Critical
Actual Noncritical   Actual Critical
Slack   Milestone
Project: DEVELOP   Date: Oct 7, 1997 12:00 AM

3.   *Assumption:* Project control should focus on the critical path.

Criticism: It is not necessarily true that the longest time-consuming path (or the path with zero slack) obtained from summing activity expected time values ultimately determines project completion time. What often happens as the project progresses is that some activity not on the critical path becomes delayed to such a degree that it extends the entire project. For this reason it has been suggested that a "critical activity" concept replace the critical path concept as focus of managerial control. Under this approach, attention would center on those activities that have a high potential variation and lie on a "near-critical path." A near-critical path is one that does not share any activities with the critical path and, though it has slack, could become critical if one or a few activities along it become delayed. Obviously, the more parallelism in a network, the more likely that one or more near-critical paths exist. Conversely, the more a network approximates a single series of activities, the less likely it is to have near-critical paths.

4. *Assumption:* The activity times in PERT follow the beta distribution, with the variance of the project assumed to equal the sum of the variances along the critical path.

Criticism: Although originally the beta distribution was selected for a variety of good reasons, each component of the statistical treatment has been brought into question. First, the formulas are in reality a modification of the beta distribution mean and variance, which, when compared to the basic formulas, could be expected to lead to absolute errors on the order of 10 percent for ET and 5 percent for the individual variances. Second, given that the activity-time distributions have the properties of unimodality, continuity, and finite positive end points, other distributions with the same properties would yield different means and variances. Third, obtaining three "valid" time estimates to put into the formulas presents operational problems; it is often difficult to arrive at one activity time estimate, let alone three, and the subjective definitions of a and b do not help the matter.

Finally, the cost of applying critical path methods to a project is sometimes used as a basis for criticism. However, the cost of applying PERT or CPM rarely exceeds 2 percent of total project cost. When used with added features of a work breakdown structure and various reports, it is more expensive but rarely exceeds 5 percent of total project costs. Thus, this added cost is generally outweighed by the saving from improved scheduling and reduced project time.

◼ CONCLUSION

Although much of this chapter has dealt with networking techniques, we would like to again emphasize the importance of teamwork. Effective project management involves much more than simply setting up a CPM or PERT schedule; it also requires clearly identified project responsibilities, a simple and timely progress reporting system, and good people-management practices.

Projects fail for a number of reasons. The most important reason is insufficient effort in the planning phase. In addition, the implementation of a project will fail unless the team has the commitment of top management and has a talented project manager.

FORMULA REVIEW

Expected time

$$ET = \frac{a + 4m + b}{6} \tag{3.1}$$

Variance (σ^2) of the activity times

$$\sigma^2 = \left(\frac{b - a}{6}\right)^2 \tag{3.2}$$

Z transformation formula

$$Z = \frac{D - T_E}{\sqrt{\Sigma \, \sigma_{cp}^2}} \tag{3.3}$$

SOLVED PROBLEMS

SOLVED PROBLEM 1

A project has been defined to contain the following list of activities, along with their required times for completion:

Activity	Time (Days)	Immediate Predecessors
A	1	—
B	4	A
C	3	A
D	7	A
E	6	B
F	2	C, D
G	7	E, F
H	9	D
I	4	G, H

a. Draw the critical path diagram.
b. Show the early start and early finish times.
c. Show the critical path.
d. What would happen if activity F was revised to take four days instead of two?

Solution
The answers to *a*, *b*, and *c* are shown in the following diagram.

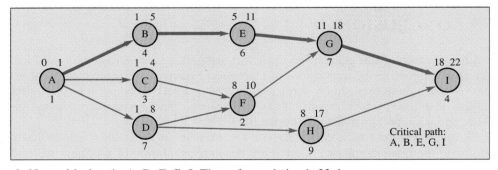

d. New critical path: A, D, F, G, I. Time of completion is 23 days.

SOLVED PROBLEM 2

Here are the precedence requirements, normal and crash activity times, and normal and crash costs for a construction project.

Activity	Preceding Activities	Required Time (Weeks) Normal	Crash	Cost Normal	Crash
A	—	4	2	$10,000	$11,000
B	A	3	2	6,000	9,000
C	A	2	1	4,000	6,000
D	B	5	3	14,000	18,000
E	B, C	1	1	9,000	9,000
F	C	3	2	7,000	8,000
G	E, F	4	2	13,000	25,000
H	D, E	4	1	11,000	18,000
I	H, G	6	5	20,000	29,000

a. What is the critical path and the estimated completion time?
b. To shorten the project by three weeks, which tasks would be shortened and what would the final total project cost be?

Solution

Construction project network is shown below.

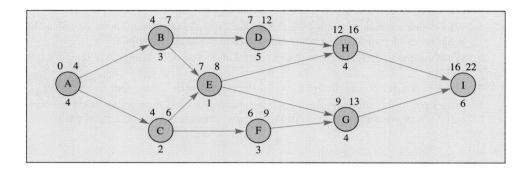

a. Critical path A, B, D, H, I.
   Normal completion time is 22 weeks.
b.

Activity	Crash Cost	Normal Cost	Normal Time	Crash Time	Cost per Week	Weeks
A	$11,000	$10,000	4	2	$ 500	2
B	9,000	6,000	3	2	3,000	1
C	6,000	4,000	2	1	2,000	1
D	18,000	14,000	5	3	2,000	2
E	9,000	9,000	1	1		0
F	8,000	7,000	3	2	1,000	1
G	25,000	13,000	4	2	6,000	2
H	18,000	11,000	4	1	2,333	3
I	29,000	20,000	6	5	9,000	1

1. 1st week: CP = A B D H I. Cheapest is A at $500. Critical path stays the same.
2. 2d week: A is still the cheapest at $500. Critical path stays the same.
3. 3d week: Since A is no longer available, the choices are B (at $3,000), D (at $2,000), H (at $2,333), or I (at $9,000).

   Therefore, choose D at $2,000.
   Total project cost shortened three weeks is

A	$ 11,000
B	6,000
C	4,000
D	16,000
E	9,000
F	7,000
G	13,000
H	11,000
I	20,000
	$ 97,000

REVIEW AND DISCUSSION QUESTIONS

1. Define project management.
2. Describe or define work breakdown structure, program, project, task, subtask, and work package.
3. What are some reasons project scheduling is not done well?
4. Discuss the graphic presentations in Exhibit 3.2. Are there any other graphic outputs you would like to see if you were project manager?
5. Which characteristics must a project have for critical path scheduling to be applicable? What types of projects have been subjected to critical path analysis?
6. What are the underlying assumptions of minimum-cost scheduling? Are they equally realistic?
7. "Project control should always focus on the critical path." Comment.
8. Why would subcontractors for a government project want their activities on the critical path? Under what conditions would they try to avoid being on the critical path?

PROBLEMS

1. *a.* See SM.
  b. A–C–D–E–G.
  c. 26 weeks.
  d. Six weeks (15 − 9).

1. The following activities are part of a project to be scheduled using CPM:

Activity	Intermediate Predecessor	Time (Weeks)
A	—	6
B	A	3
C	A	7
D	C	2
E	B, D	4
F	D	3
G	E, F	7

a. Draw the network.
b. What is the critical path?
c. How many weeks will it take to complete the project?
d. How much slack does activity B have?

2. *a.* See SM.
  b. A–B–D–E–H.
  c. 15 weeks.
  d. C, 3 weeks; F, 1 week;
      G, 1 week.

2. Schedule the following activities using CPM:

Activity	Immediate Predecessor	Time (Weeks)
A	—	1
B	A	4
C	A	3
D	B	2
E	C, D	5
F	D	2
G	F	2
H	E, G	3

a. Draw the network.
b. What is the critical path?
c. How many weeks will it take to complete the project?
d. Which activities have slack, and how much?

✓ **3.** The R&D Department is planning to bid on a large project for the development of a new communication system for commercial planes. The accompanying table shows the activities, times, and sequences required.

Activity	Immediate Predecessor	Time (Weeks)
A	—	3
B	A	2
C	A	4
D	A	4
E	B	6
F	C, D	6
G	D, F	2
H	D	3
I	E, G, H	3

a. Draw the network diagram.
b. What is the critical path?
c. Suppose you want to shorten the completion time as much as possible, and have the option of shortening any or all of B, C, D, and G each two weeks. Which would you shorten?
d. What is the new critical path and earliest completion time?

4. A construction project is broken down into the following 10 activities:

Activity	Immediate Predecessor	Time (Weeks)
1	—	4
2	1	2
3	1	4
4	1	3
5	2, 3	5
6	3	6
7	4	2
8	5	3
9	6, 7	5
10	8, 9	7

a. Draw the network diagram.
b. Find the critical path.
c. If activities 1 and 10 cannot be shortened, but activities 2 through 9 can be shortened to a minimum of one week each at a cost of $10,000 per week, which activities would you shorten to cut the project by four weeks?

5. The following represents a project that should be scheduled using PERT:

Activity	Immediate Predecessors	Times (Days) a	m	b
A	—	1	3	5
B	—	1	2	3
C	A	1	2	3
D	A	2	3	4
E	B	3	4	11
F	C, D	3	4	5
G	D, E	1	4	6
H	F, G	2	4	5

3. *a.* See SM.
b. A–C–F–G–I,
+ A–D–F–G–I.
c. C: 2 weeks;
D: 2 weeks;
G: 2 weeks.
d. Three paths:
A–B–E–I; A–C–F–G–I; and
A–D–F–G–I. 14weeks.

4. *a.* See SM.
b. 1–3–6–9–10.
c. See SM.

5. *a.* See SM.
b. B–E–G–H.
c. 14.67 days.
d. P(< 16) = .7852.

a. Draw the network.
b. What is the critical path?
c. What is the expected project completion time?
d. What is the probability of completing this project within 16 days?

6. Here is a CPM network with activity times in weeks:

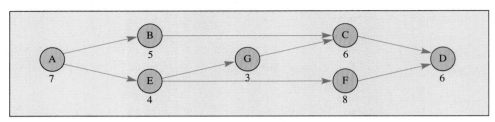

a. Determine the critical path.
b. How many weeks will the project take to complete?
c. Suppose F could be shortened by two weeks and B by one week. How would this affect the completion date?

7. The following table represents a plan for a project:

Job No.	Predecessor Job(s)	*a*	*m*	*b*
1	—	2	3	4
2	1	1	2	3
3	1	4	5	12
4	1	3	4	11
5	2	1	3	5
6	3	1	2	3
7	4	1	8	9
8	5, 6	2	4	6
9	8	2	4	12
10	7	3	4	5
11	9, 10	5	7	8

a. Construct the appropriate network diagram.
b. Indicate the critical path.
c. What is the expected completion time for the project?
d. You can accomplish any one of the following at an additional cost of $1,500:
   (1) Reduce job 5 by two days.
   (2) Reduce job 3 by two days.
   (3) Reduce job 7 by two days.
   If you will save $1,000 for each day that the earliest completion time is reduced, which action, if any, would you choose?
e. What is the probability that the project will take more than 30 days to complete?

8. Here is a network with the activity times shown under the nodes in days:

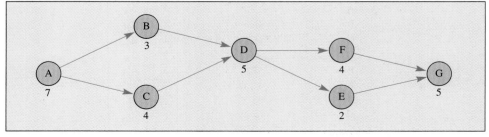

a. Find the critical path.

b. The following table shows the normal times and the crash times, along with the associated costs for each activity.

Activity	Normal Time	Crash Time	Normal Cost	Crash Cost
A	7	6	$7,000	$ 8,000
B	3	2	5,000	7,000
C	4	3	9,000	10,200
D	5	4	3,000	4,500
E	2	1	2,000	3,000
F	4	2	4,000	7,000
G	5	4	5,000	8,000

If the project is to be shortened by four days, show which activities, in order of reduction, would be shortened and the resulting cost.

9. The home office billing department of a chain of department stores prepares monthly inventory reports for use by the stores' purchasing agents. Given the following information, use the critical path method to determine

a. How long the total process will take.

b. Which jobs can be delayed without delaying the early start of any subsequent activity.

9. *a.* 100 hours.
b. Those not on the critical path (i.e., b and d).

	Job and Description	Immediate Predecessors	Time (Hours)
a	Start	—	0
b	Get computer printouts of customer purchases	a	10
c	Get stock records for the month	a	20
d	Reconcile purchase printouts and stock records	b, c	30
e	Total stock records by department	b, c	20
f	Determine reorder quantities for coming period	e	40
g	Prepare stock reports for purchasing agents	d, f	20
h	Finish	g	0

10. For the network shown:

10. *a.* A–B–D–G, 25 weeks.
b. D by 1 week, G by 1 week, and A by 1 week.

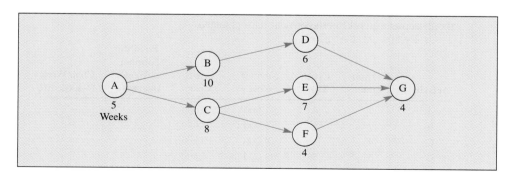

a. Determine the critical path and the early completion time for the project.

b. For the data shown, reduce the project completion time by 3 weeks. Assume a linear cost per day shortened, and show, step by step, how you arrived at your schedule.

Activity	Normal Time	Normal Cost	Crash Time	Crash Cost
A	5	$ 7,000	3	$13,000
B	10	12,000	7	18,000
C	8	5,000	7	7,000
D	6	4,000	5	5,000
E	7	3,000	6	6,000
F	4	6,000	3	7,000
G	4	7,000	3	9,000

11. *a.* A–C–D–F–G.
   b. 25 weeks.
   c. E, 2 weeks;
      B, 2 weeks.
   d. Shorten A by one
      week at a cost of
      $1,000.
      Shorten C by one
      week at a cost of
      $1,200.
      Total cost for two
      weeks is $2,200.
      Critical path is still
      the same.

11. The following CPM network has estimates of the *normal time* listed for the activities:

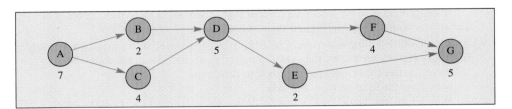

Activity	Time (Weeks)
A	7
B	2
C	4
D	5
E	2
F	4
G	5

   a. Identify the critical path.
   b. What is the length of time to complete the project?
   c. Which activities have slack, and how much?
   d. Here is a table of normal and crash times and costs. Which activities would you shorten to cut two weeks from the schedule in a rational fashion? What would be the incremental cost? Is the critical path changed?

Activity	Normal Time	Crash Time	Normal Cost	Crash Cost	Possible Number of Weeks Decrease	Cost/Week to Expedite
A	7	6	$7,000	$ 8,000		
B	2	1	5,000	7,000		
C	4	3	9,000	10,200		
D	5	4	3,000	4,500		
E	2	1	2,000	3,000		
F	4	2	4,000	7,000		
G	5	4	5,000	8,000		

Case

The Campus Wedding (A)

On March 31 of last year, Mary Jackson burst into the family living room and announced that she and Larry Adams (her college boyfriend) were going to be married. After recovering from the shock, her mother hugged her and asked, "When?" The following conversation resulted:

Mary: April 22.

Mother: What!

Father: The Adams–Jackson wedding will be the social hit of the year. Why so soon?

Mary: Because on April 22 the cherry blossoms on campus are always in full bloom! The wedding pictures will be beautiful.

Mother: But honey, we can't possibly finish all the things that need to be done by then. Remember all the details that were involved in your sister's wedding? Even if we start tomorrow, it takes a day to reserve the church and reception hall, and they need at least 17 days notice. That has to be done before we can start decorating the church, which takes three days. An extra $100 contribution on Sunday would probably cut that 17-day notice to 10 days, though.

Father: Ugh!

Mary: I want Jane Summers to be my maid of honor.

Father: But she's in the Peace Corps, in Guatemala, isn't she? It would take her 10 days to get ready and drive up here.

Mary: But we could fly her up in two days, and it would only cost $500. She would have to be here in time to have her dress fitted.

Father: Ugh!

Mother: And catering! It takes two days to choose the cake and table decorations, and Jack's Catering wants at least 10 day's notice prior to the rehearsal dinner (the night before the wedding).

Mary: Can I wear your wedding dress, Mom?

Mother: Well, we'd have to replace some lace, but you could wear it, yes. We could order the lace from New York when we order the material for the bridesmaids' dresses. It takes eight days to order and receive the material. The pattern needs to be chosen first, and that would take three days.

Father: We could get the material here in five days if we paid an extra $25 to air freight it.

Mary: I want Mrs. Watson to work on the dresses.

Father: But she charges $120 a day!

Mother: If we did all the sewing, we could finish the dresses in 11 days. If Mrs. Watson helped, we could cut that down to 6 days, at a cost of $120 for each day less than 11 days.

Mary: I don't want anyone but her.

Mother: It would take another two days to do the final fitting. It normally takes two days to clean and press the dresses, but that new cleaners downtown could do them in one day if we pay the $30 charge for express service.

Father: Everything should be completed by rehearsal night, and that's only 21 days from now.

Mother: We've forgotten something. The invitations.

Father: We should order the invitations from Bob's Printing Shop, and that usually takes 12 days. I'll bet he would do it in 5 days if we slipped him an extra $35.

Mother: It would take us three days to choose the invitation style before we could order them, and we want the envelopes printed with our return address.

Mary: Oh! That will be elegant.

Mother: The invitations should go out at least 10 days before the wedding. If we let them go any later, some of the relatives would get theirs too late to come and that would make them mad. I'll bet that if we didn't get them out until eight days before the wedding, Aunt Ethel couldn't make it, and she would reduce her wedding gift by $200.

Father: Ugh!

Mother: We'll have to take them to the Post Office to mail them, and that takes a day. Addressing would take four days unless we hired some part-time help, and we can't start until the printer is finished. If we hired someone, we could probably save two days by spending $25 for each day saved.

Mary: We need to get gifts to give to the bridesmaids at the rehearsal dinner. I can spend a day and do that.

Mother: Before we can even start to write out those invitations, we need a guest list. Heavens, that will take four days to get in order, and only I can understand our address file.

Mary: Oh, Mother, I'm so excited. We can start each of the relatives on a different job.

Mother: Honey, I don't see how we can do it. Why, we've got to choose the invitations and patterns and reserve the church and . . . .

Father: Why don't you just take $1500 and elope. Yours sister's wedding cost me $1200, and she didn't have to fly people up from Guatemala, hire extra people, use air freight, or anything like that.

Questions

1. Given the activities and precedence relationships described in the (A) case, develop a network diagram for the wedding plans.
2. Identify the paths. Which are critical?
3. What is the minimum cost plan that meets the April 22 date?

Case

The Campus Wedding (B)

Several complications arose during the course of trying to meet the deadline of April 21 for the Adams–Jackson wedding rehearsal. Since Mary Jackson was adamant on having the wedding on April 22 (as was Larry Adams, because he wanted her to be happy), the implications of each of these complications had to be assessed.

1. On April 1 the Chairman of the Vestry Committee at the church was left unimpressed by the added donation and said he wouldn't reduce the notice period from 17 to 10 days.
2. A call to Guatemala revealed that the potential bridesmaid had several commitments and could not possibly leave the country until April 10.
3. Mother comes down with the four-day flu just as she started on the guest list.
4. The lace and dress materials were lost in transit. Notice of the loss was delivered to the Jackson home early on April 10.
5. There was a small fire at the caterer's shop on April 8. It was estimated that the shop would be closed two or three days for repairs.

Mary Jackson's father, in particular, was concerned about expense and kept offering $1500 to Mary and Larry for them to elope.

Questions

1. Given your answers to the (A) case, describe the effects on the wedding plans of each incident noted in the (B) case.

Source: Adapted from a case originally written by Professor D. Clay Whybark, University of North Carolina, Chapel Hill, North Carolina.

Case

Project Management at CPAone

The auditing division at CPAone (one of the "Big Six" accounting firms) generates financial statements to meet generally accepted accounting principles. In larger audits, the size of the task and the range of problems require the involvement of several people. In the audit of a national corporation, for example, numerous auditors with diverse specialties are required to investigate all aspects of the operation in various geographic areas. Given the number of people and the variety in skills, expertise, and personalities involved, a project manager is needed to oversee and conduct the audit efficiently. Thus, every audit begins by assigning the client to a partner, usually someone who is familiar with the client's business. The partner becomes the "project director" of the audit and is responsible for writing proposals, staffing the audit, delegating tasks, scheduling, and budgeting.

The project director begins by studying the client's income statement, balance sheet, and other financial statements. If the client has a bad financial reputation, the project director can make the decision for CPAone to refuse to do the audit. If the client is accepted, the director prepares a proposal outlining the general approach for conducting the audit, the completion date, and the cost estimate.

In determining the general approach for conducting the audit, the project director considers the size of the company and the number of departments. Auditors are then assigned on a department by department basis. The audit team is a pure project team, created anew for every audit with people having the skills best suited to the needs of the audit. Generally, each audit has one or two staff accountants, one or two senior accounts, and the project director. Before the proposal is even accepted, the director specifies who will be performing each task and the completion dates. Cost estimates are based on estimated labor hours.

During the audit the project director must ensure that all work strictly adheres to the Book of Auditing Standards and is completed on schedule. Each week the client and project director meet to review progress. When problems cannot be solved immediately, the director may call in people from CPAone's tax or consulting divisions. When the team has trouble interpreting financial statements, the project director may request that the client's own personnel be involved. Follow-up service is provided after the audit is completed. The project director sees to it that the client is represented if the IRS requests an examination.

Questions

1. What are the major milestones associated with this project? What additional information would you need to develop a PERT chart?

2. What are the project director's managerial responsibilities?

Source: *Managing Business and Engineering Projects,* by Nicholas, © 1990. Reprinted by permission of Prentice Hall, Inc., Upper Saddle River, NJ.

SELECTED BIBLIOGRAPHY

Cleland, David I., and William R. King. *Project Management Handbook.* New York: Van Nostrand Reinhold, 1983.

Kerzner, Harold. *Project Management for Executives.* New York: Van Nostrand Reinhold, 1984.

Peterson, P., "Project Management Software Survey." *PMNETwork* 8, no. 5 (May 1994), pp. 33–41.

Rogers, Tom. "Project Management: Emerging as a Requisite for Success." *Industrial Engineering.* June 1993, pp. 42–43.

Smith-Daniels, Dwight E., and Nicholas J. Aquilano. "Constrained Resource Project Scheduling." *Journal of Operations Management* 4, no. 4 (1984), pp. 369–87.

Smith-Daniels, Dwight E., and Vicki Smith-Daniels. "Optimal Project Scheduling with Materials Ordering." *IIE Transactions* 19, no. 2 (June 1987), pp. 122–29.

Williams, Paul B. *Getting a Project Done on Time: Managing People, Time, and Results.* New York: The American Management Association, 1996.

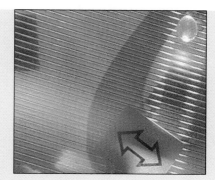

Section two

Product Design and Process Selection

4 Product Design and Process Selection—Manufacturing

Supplement 4 *Operations Technology*

5 Product Design and Process Selection—Services

Supplement 5 *Waiting Line Management*

6 Quality Management

Supplement 6 *Statistical Quality Control Methods*

THE FIRST DECISION IN CREATING A PRODUCTION SYSTEM is selecting or designing the product or service to be produced. The second decision is defining the process technology and supporting organization by which production is to be carried out. The third decision is developing a quality philosophy and integrating it into the operations of the firm. Section Two considers these subjects in the two main categories of industry—manufacturing and services.

Chapter 4

Product Design and Process Selection—Manufacturing

Chapter Outline

The Product Design Process, 85

Designing for the Customer, 89

    Quality Function Deployment

    Value Analysis/Value Engineering

Designing Products for Manufacture and Assembly, 92

    How Does Design for Manufacturing and Assembly (DFMA) Work?

Process Selection, 96

    Process Selection Contrasted with Process Planning

    Types of Processes

    Process Flow Structures

    Product-Process Matrix

    The Virtual Factory

    Specific Equipment Selection

    Choosing Among Alternative Processes and Equipment

Process Flow Design, 102

Process Analysis, 105

    An Example of Process Analysis

Global Product Design and Manufacturing, 108

    The Global Joint Venture

    Global Product Design Strategy

Measuring Product Development Performance, 109

Plant Tour: Dell Computer: Mr. Cozzette Buys a Computer, 114

Case: The Best Engineered Part Is No Part, 116

Case: Product Development in Japan, 117

Key Terms

Concurrent Engineering

Industrial Design

Quality Function Deployment

House of Quality

Value Analysis/Value Engineering

Conversion Processes

Fabrication Processes

Assembly Processes

Testing Processes

Process Flow Structure

Job Shop

Batch

Assembly Line

Continuous Flow

Product-Process Matrix

Virtual Factory

Break-Even Analysis

Process Flow Diagram

Joint Venture

Strategic Suppliers

www Links

Rubbermaid (http://www.rubbermaid.com)

Hewlett Packard (http://www.hp.com)

Boeing (http://www.boeing.com)

MARKETING
FINANCE
MANUFACTURING
SALES

RUBBERMAID IS KNOWN AS A NEW-PRODUCT MACHINE. It churns out new products at the rate of one a day. Developing this many new products year after year requires an aggressive product management effort. Recently, the company put together a $150 million restructuring plan to eliminate 9 percent of its workforce and streamline manufacturing. As part of this process, Rubbermaid has cut nearly 45 percent of its total product offerings that had accounted for just 5 percent of company sales. Don't worry, Rubbermaid is not going out of business soon; they still produce over 4,000 different products, which are available in over 100 countries.

Most ideas for products flow from a single source: teams. Twenty teams, each made up of four to seven people (taken from marketing, manufacturing, R&D, finance, sales, and other departments), focus on specific product lines, such as bathroom accessories. So successful has been the team approach to innovation that the head of product development fears to contemplate a world without it. "If we weren't organized that way," he says, a look of concern spreading over his face, "who would be thinking about johnny mops?" Hey, you little trays and johnny mops—rest easy. Rubbermaid has got you covered. Covered, too, are birdhouses (the company makes 25 models, one with a Spanish tile roof) and dustpans. The company's original rubber dustpan is protected, behind glass, at headquarters.

So what new product does the company have on the horizon? They have targeted the trash-bag market, a business that is growing at a healthy 7 percent each year. The new Rubbermaid Roughneck is expected to have twice the strength of other leading brands in its resistance to punctures and tears. The trash bag's strength comes from the use of an advanced polyethylene resin, for which Rubbermaid has a supply agreement with a resin maker, in combination with a proprietary manufacturing process. Rubbermaid isn't expected to charge a premium for the bags. Its internal plan calls for the Rubbermaid brand to be the best-selling trash bags in two key retail segments, mass merchandisers and home-products stores.

From a quick look at this new product, we can see the keys to Rubbermaid's great new-product success over the years. These keys are the use of the latest technology (the new polythylene resin), a great manufacturing process, competitive prices, and gigantic retail markets. Of course, those teams of dedicated employees are needed to generate all the new ideas. (http://www.rubbermaid.com) ●

Source: Adapted from the following sources: Alan Farnham, *Fortune,* February 7, 1994, p. 52; and Raju Narisetti, *The Wall Street Journal,* August 12, 1996, p. A3.

Designing new products and getting them to market quickly is the challenge facing manufacturers in industries as diverse as computer chips and potato chips. Customers of computer chip manufacturers, such as computer companies, need ever more powerful semiconductors for their evolving product lines. Food producers need to provide their grocery store customers the new taste sensation to sustain or enlarge their retail market share.

MARKETING
MANUFACTURING

How manufactured products are designed and how the process to produce them is selected are the focuses of this chapter. As shown below, three major functions are involved in these activities: marketing, product development, and manufacturing. Marketing has the responsibility for suggesting ideas for new products and for providing product specifications for existing product lines. Product development has the responsibility for moving the technical concept for the product to its final design. Manufacturing has the responsibility for selecting and/or configuring the processes by which the product is to be manufactured.

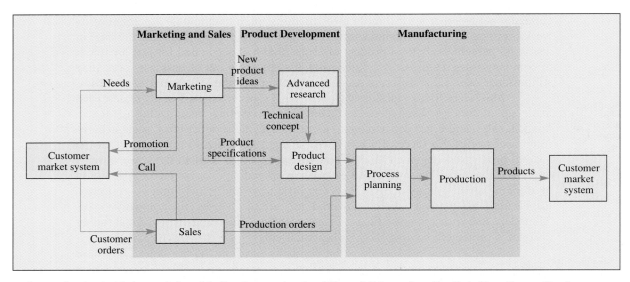

Source: Reprinted with the permission of the Free Press, an imprint of Simon & Schuster from *Fast Cycle Time: How to Align Purpose, Strategy, and Structure for Speed* by Christopher Meyer. Copyright © 1993 by Christopher Meyer.

The product development activity provides the link between the customer needs and expectations and the activities required to manufacture the product. We will learn about the modern requirement for a speedy development process. Further, the process must be responsive to changing customer expectations and dynamic technological innovations. Finally, the process must cater to diverse local preferences in a global marketplace.

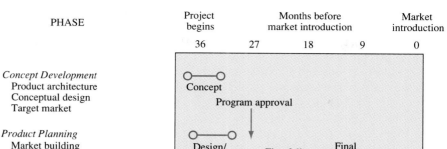

TIME SCHEDULE

Exhibit 4.1

Typical Phases of
Product Development

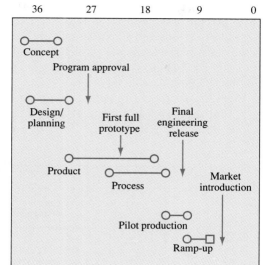

PHASE	Project begins	Months before market introduction	Market introduction
	36	27 18 9	0

Concept Development
  Product architecture
  Conceptual design
  Target market

Product Planning
  Market building
  Small-scale testing
  Investment/financial

Product/Process Engineering
  Detailed design of product
    and tools/equipment
  Building/testing prototypes

Pilot Production/Ramp-Up
  Volume production prove out
  Factory start-up
  Volume increases to commercial
    targets

Concept

Program approval

Design/
planning

First full
prototype

Final
engineering
release

Product

Process

Market
introduction

Pilot production

Ramp-up

Source: Reprinted with the permission of The Free Press, a Division of Simon & Schuster from *Revolutionizing Product Development: Quantum Leaps in Speed, Efficiency, and Quality* by Steven C. Wheelwright and Kim B. Clark. Copyright © 1992 by Steven C. Wheelwright and Kim B. Clark.

◼ THE PRODUCT DESIGN PROCESS

MARKETING
FINANCE
MANUFACTURING
ENGINEERING

While the potential opportunities to be realized in developing new products are exciting, making them happen is a demanding challenge. New product development entails a complex set of activities that cuts across most functions in a business. Exhibit 4.1 lays out the phases of a typical development project.[1] In the first two phases, concept development and product planning, information about market opportunities, competitive moves, technical possibilities, and production requirements must be combined to define the architecture of the new product. This includes its conceptual design, target market, desired level of performance, investment requirements, and financial impact. Before a new product development program is approved, firms also attempt to prove out the concept through small-scale testing. This test may involve the construction of models and discussions with potential customers.

Once approved, a new-product project moves into detailed engineering. The primary activity in this phase is the design and construction of working prototypes and the development of tools and equipment to be used in commercial production. At the heart of detailed product engineering is the "design-build-test" cycle. Both the products and the processes needed are defined in concept, captured in a working model (which may exist on a computer or in physical form), and then subjected to tests that simulate product use. If the model fails to deliver the desired performance characteristics, engineers search for design changes that will close the gap, and the design-build-test cycle is repeated. The conclusion of the detailed engineering phase of development is marked by an engineering "release" or "sign-off" that signifies that the final design meets requirements.

---

[1] Steven C. Wheelwright and Kim B. Clark, *Revolutionizing Product Development* (New York: The Free Press, 1992), pp. 6–8.

At this time, the firm typically moves development into a pilot manufacturing phase, during which the individual components, built and tested on production equipment, are assembled and tested as a system in the factory. During pilot production, units of the product are produced and the ability of the new or modified manufacturing process to execute at a commercial rate is tested. At this stage all tooling and equipment should be in place and all parts suppliers should be ready for volume production. This is the point in development at which the total system—design, detailed engineering, tools and equipment, parts, assembly sequences, production supervisors, operators, and technicians—come together.

The final phase of development is ramp-up. The process has been refined and debugged, but it has yet to operate at a sustained level of production. In ramp-up, production starts at a relatively low level of volume; as the organization develops

Exhibit 4.2

Functional Activities Under Cross-Functional Integration

Functional activities	Phases of Development	
	Concept Development	Product Planning
Product Development	Propose new technologies: develop product ideas; build models conduct simulations	Choose components and interact with suppliers; build early system prototypes; define product architecture
Marketing	Provide market-based input; propose and investigate product concepts	Define target customer's parameters; develop estimates of sales and margins; conduct early interaction with customers
Manufacturing	Propose and investigate process concepts	Develop cost estimates; define process architecture; conduct process simulation; validate suppliers

Key Milestones	• Concept for product and process defined	• Establish product and process architecture • Define program parameters
Key Decisions	Concept approval	Program approval

confidence in its (and its suppliers') abilities to execute production consistently and marketing's abilities to sell the product, the volume increases.

An individual development project is usually not done in isolation. It interacts with other projects and must fit with the operating organization to be effective. Projects may share critical components and use the same support groups. Additionally, new products may require compatibility in design and function with existing products.

To speed the product development process, many companies have begun using **concurrent engineering** (CE) approaches to organizing the project. Rather than a simple serial approach in which we proceed from one phase to another, CE emphasizes cross-functional integration and concurrent development of product and its associated processes (see Exhibit 4.2).[2]

Concurrent
Engineering

Phases of Development			
Detailed Product/Process Engineering		Pilot Production/ Ramp-Up	Market Introduction
Phase I	Phase II		
Do detailed design of product and interact with process; build full-scale prototypes conduct prototype testing	Refine details of product design; participate in building second-phase prototypes	Evaluate and test pilot units; solve problems	Evaluate field experience with product
Conduct customer tests of prototypes participate in prototyping evaluation	Conduct second phase customer tests; evaluate prototypes; plan marketing rollout; establish distribution plan	Prepare for market rollout; train sales force and field service personnel; prepare order entry/process system	Fill distribution channels; sell and promote; interact with key customers
Do detailed design of process; design and develop tooling and equipment; participate in building full-scale prototypes	Test and try out tooling and equipment; build second-phase prototypes; install equipment and bring up new procedures	Build pilot units in commercial process; refine process based on pilot experience; train personnel and verify supply channel	Ramp up plant to volume targets; meet targets for quality, yield, and cost
• Build and test complete prototype •Verify product design	• Build and refine 2nd phase prototype •Verify process tools and design	• Produce pilot units •Operate and test complete commercial system	• Ramp up to volume production •Meet initial commercial objectives
Detailed design approval	Joint product and process approval	Approval for first commercial sales	Full commercial approval

[2] Morgan L. Swink, V. A. Mabert, and J. C. Sandvig describe this approach in "Customizing Concurrent Engineering Processes: Five Case Studies," *Journal of Product Innovation Management* 13 (1996), pp. 229–44.

BREAKTHROUGH

777 Sets Boeing on New Course

When Boeing Co. unveiled the first model of its 777 twin-engine jet, it marked more than a milestone in its most ambitious project since the 747 jumbo jet.

The ceremonial rollout, attended by 100,000 Boeing employees, subcontractors, customers and guests, produced the first tangible evidence of an effort by one of the nation's biggest manufacturers to re-engineer itself for the 21st century.

"There is a different culture at Boeing—a kind of workout ethic that gets you a lot closer to higher productivity," said Nicholas Heymann of County Natwest Securities.

The 777, the world's largest twin engine jet, is Boeing's first all-new model in more than a decade. It represents other firsts as well.

It is Boeing's first "fly-by-wire" jet, in which moving parts are controlled electronically with no cable connections, and it is the first "paperless" plane, designed entirely on computer.

Boeing officials say the process has resulted in more accurate fittings and fewer adjustments on the floor of its huge assembly plant in Everett, Washington, 30 miles north of Seattle.

And industry analysts and executives say the 777 marks the first time customers and Boeing employees at every level have been so fully involved in the design process.

"In past programs, we didn't really have any contact with Boeing in the design process. This time we sat in from our first day on their basic design teams," said Gordon McKinzie, 777 project manager for Elk Grove Township–based United Airlines.

United has ordered 34 of the jets and is the launch customer for the new plane, which went into commercial service in May 1995.

Boeing has been forced to change the way it does business in large part to meet growing competition from Europe's Airbus Industrie, which has jets that compete with all Boeing's models except the 747.

"In the past if you wanted a Boeing, you'd have to stand in line," said McKinzie.

But times have changed. While Boeing still dominates the market for new planes with more than 60 percent of new orders, airlines have cut back drastically and Boeing has had to cut its workforce 25 percent since 1989.

Analysts and company officials saw the market bottoming out in late 1995, but Boeing still faces a selfimposed challenge of cutting manufacturing expenses by reducing the average time it takes to build an aircraft to 6 months from the current 12.

J. A. Donoghue, editor of the trade magazine *Air Transport World*, said airlines, faced with continuing excess capacity in the world market, have become increasingly tightfisted and won't buy new models unless they see operating cost savings.

"If you can't show an advantage over what's currently out there, airlines are getting very reluctant to spend that kind of money," Donoghue said, referring to the 777's price of $116 million to $140 million.

 (http://www.boeing.com)

Source: Adapted from *Chicago Tribune,* April 4, 1994, Reprinted by permission of Reuters.

Teams provide the primary integration mechanism in CE programs. Three types of teams frequently appear: a program management team, a technical team, and numerous design-build teams. Depending on the project's complexity, an integration team may be needed to consolidate the efforts of the various design-build teams. Task forces may be formed to address specific problems, such as investigating an emerging technology.

The benefits of the CE approach comes mainly from the reduced time to complete a project. The concurrency involves the parallel completion of project phases—for example, simultaneously developing market concepts, product design, manufacturing processes, and product support structure. Frequent information sharing using electronic mail or face-to-face meetings, together with shared integrated design databases, are important elements to CE success. Hewlett-Packard uses an integral set of technology focused teams operating in parallel as part of their strategy. Each team works on a key technology essential to the development of their products (see Exhibit 4.3).

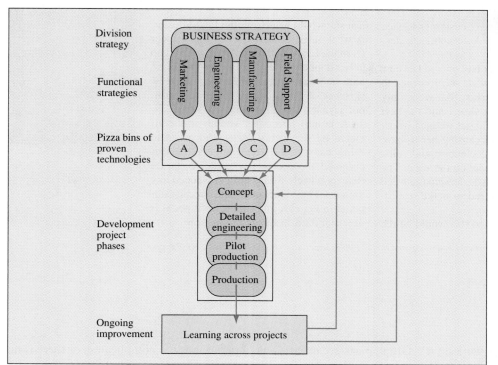

Exhibit 4.3

Hewlett Packard
Product Development
Strategy*

(http://www.hp.com)

* Hewlett Packard conceives of the business and functional strategies as key drivers in assessing which technological opportunities hold the greatest promise for a business. Advanced development projects around those technologies then prove technical feasibility *prior* to their application in specific development projects. (Note that HP uses a standard four-phase process in development, followed by efforts to consolidate learning across the set of projects.)

Source: Steven C. Wheelwright and Kim B. Clark, *Revolutionizing Product Development* (New York: Free Press, 1992), p.40.

The time saving that results from performing activities in parallel rather than in series can be significant. The saving can come from not only the time overlap but also from the reduction in errors that might be made in one phase, but not caught until a later stage. We analyzed projects with structures like the product development ones in Chapter 3, "Project Management."

◾ DESIGNING FOR THE CUSTOMER

Before we detail the hows and whys of designing and producing products, it is useful to reflect (or, perhaps more accurately, to editorialize) on the issue of product design from the user's standpoint. In recent years, companies have been so caught up with technological efforts and advances—especially in the field of electronics—that somewhere along the line, consumers were forgotten. (See the box entitled "Lexus Product Design Improvement—A Continuous Process.")

Designing for aesthetics and for the user is generally termed **industrial design.** Industrial design is probably the most abused area by manufacturers. When frustrated with products—setting the VCR, working on the car, adjusting a computerized furnace thermostat, or operating a credit card telephone at the airport—most of us have said to ourselves, "The blankety-blank person who designed this should be made to

Industrial Design

The following example of customer service happened at a Lexus Automobile dealership in Louisiana.

A female customer had owned her new Lexus about a week when she returned to the dealership in distress. She wore only one brand of designer shoes, and the heel of the right shoe would get wedged below the accelerator pedal, causing her to have difficulty with the accelerator and, ultimately, to break the heel on the shoe. The service manager at the dealership recorded the problem and offered to make restitution for the shoes.

The woman assumed this would be the last she would hear from the Lexus dealer. A week later, however, a design engineer from the Lexus factory in Japan showed up at her doorstep. He asked to see the shoes, and he made measurements and drew sketches of them. The engineer left without saying a word.

A month later, the woman was contacted by the Lexus dealer and asked to bring her car in. The engineer had redesigned the accelerator pedal to ensure that shoe heels would not get wedged any longer. They replaced the accelerator pedal in her car, and that retrofit pedal is now standard in Lexus production.

Lexus Product Design Improvement—A Continuous Process

Source: Tom Taormina, *Virtual Leadership and the ISO 9000 Imperative* (Englewood Cliffs, NJ: Prentice Hall, 1996), p. 158.

work on it!" Often, parts are inaccessible, operation is too complicated, or there is no logic to setting or controlling the unit. Sometimes, even worse conditions exist: metal edges are sharp and consumers cut their hands trying to reach for adjustment or repairs.

Many products have too many technological features—far more than necessary. The fact is that most purchasers of electronic products cannot fully operate them and only use a small number of the available features. This has occurred because computer chips are inexpensive and adding more controls has negligible cost. Including an alarm clock or a calculator on a microwave oven involves little added cost. But do you need it? What happens when you lose the operator's manual to any of these complex devices?

Quality Function Deployment

Quality Function Deployment (QFD)

One approach to getting the voice of the customer into the design specification of a product is **quality function deployment (QFD)**.[3] This approach, which uses interfunctional teams from marketing, design engineering, and manufacturing, has been credited by Toyota Motor Corporation for reducing costs on its cars by more than 60 percent by significantly shortening design times.

The QFD process begins with studying and listening to customers to determine the characteristics of a superior product. Through market research, the consumers' product needs and preferences are defined and broken down into categories called *customer requirements*. One example is an auto manufacturer that would like to improve the design of a car door. Through customer surveys and interviews, it determines that two important customer requirements in a car door are that it "stays open on a hill" and is "easy to close from the outside." After the customer requirements are

---

[3] The term *quality* is actually a mistranslation of the Japanese word for *qualities*, because QFD is widely used in the context of quality management.

Exhibit 4.4

Completed House of
Quality Matrix for a
Car Door

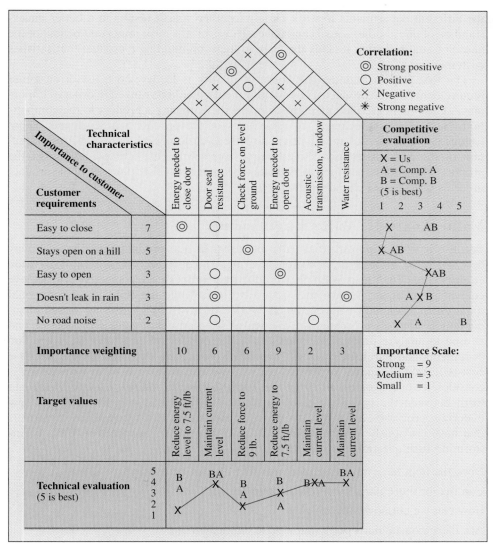

Source: Based on John R. Hauser and Don Clausing. "The House of Quality," *Harvard Business Review,*
May–June 1988, pp. 62–73.

defined, they are weighted based on their relative importance to the customer. Next,
the consumer is asked to compare and rate the company's products with the products
of competitors. This process helps the company determine the product characteristics
that are important to the consumer and to evaluate its product in relation to others.
The end result is a better understanding and focus on product characteristics that
require improvement.

Customer requirement information forms the basis for a matrix called the **house of
quality** (see Exhibit 4.4). By building a house-of-quality matrix, the cross-functional
QFD team can use customer feedback to make engineering, marketing, and design
decisions. The matrix helps the team to translate customer requirements into concrete
operating or engineering goals. The important product characteristics and goals for
improvement are jointly agreed on and detailed in the house. This process encourages

House of Quality

the different departments to work closely together, and it results in a better understanding of one another's goals and issues. However, the most important benefit of the house of quality is that it helps the team to focus on building a product that satisfies customers.

The first step in building the house of quality is to develop a list of customer requirements for the product. These requirements should be ranked in order of importance. Customers are then asked to compare the company's product to the competition. Next, a set of technical characteristics of the product are developed. These technical characteristics should relate directly to customer requirements. An evaluation of these characteristics should support or refute customer perception of the product. This data is then used to evaluate the strengths and weaknesses of the product in terms of technical characteristics.

Value Analysis/Value Engineering

Value Analysis Value Engineering (VA/VE)

Because it is so important that value be designed into products, we should briefly describe value analysis and value engineering. The purpose of **value analysis/value engineering (VA/VE)** is to simplify products and processes. Its objective is to achieve equivalent or better performance at a lower cost while maintaining all functional requirements defined by the customer. VA/VE does this by identifying and eliminating unnecessary cost. Technically, VA deals with products already in production and is used to analyze product specifications and requirements as shown in production documents and purchase requests. Typically, purchasing departments use VA as a cost-reduction technique. Performed before the production stage, value engineering is considered a cost-avoidance method. In practice, however, there is a looping back and forth between the two for a given product. This occurs due to the fact that new materials, processes, and so forth require the application of VA techniques to products that have previously undergone VE. The VA/VE analysis approach involves brainstorming such questions as

Does the item have any design features that are not necessary?

Can two or more parts be combined into one?

How can we cut down the weight?

Are there nonstandard parts that can be eliminated?

In the following section, we describe a more formal approach that is often used to guide the process of designing and improving the design of products.

▓ DESIGNING PRODUCTS FOR MANUFACTURE AND ASSEMBLY

Vol. III
"Reengineering at Caterpillar"

The word "design" has many different meanings. To some it means the aesthetic design of a product, such as the external shape of a car or the color, texture, and shape of the casing of a can opener. In another sense, design can mean establishing the basic parameters of a system. For example, before considering any details, the design of a power plant might mean establishing the characteristics of the various units such as generators, pumps, boilers, connecting pipes, and so forth.

Yet another interpretation of the word design is the detailing of the materials, shapes, and tolerance of the individual parts of a product. This is the concern of this section. It is an activity that starts with sketches of parts and assemblies and then progresses to the computer-aided design (CAD) workstation (described in the supplement to this chapter), where assembly drawings and detailed part drawings are produced. Traditionally, these drawings are then passed to the manufacturing and assembly engineers, whose job it is to optimize the processes used to produce the final product. Frequently, it is at this stage that manufacturing and assembly problems are encountered and that requests are made for design changes. Often these design changes are major and result in considerable additional expense and delays in the final product release.

Traditionally, the attitude of designers has been "We design it, you build it." This has now been termed the "over-the-wall approach," where the designer is sitting on one side of the wall and throwing the design over the wall to the manufacturing engineers. These manufacturing engineers then have to deal with the problems that arise because they were not involved in the design effort. One way to overcome this problem is to consult the manufacturing engineers during the design stage. The resulting teamwork avoids many of the problems that will arise. These concurrent engineering teams require analysis tools to help them study proposed designs and evaluate them from the point of view of manufacturing difficulty and cost.

How Does Design for Manufacturing and Assembly (DFMA) Work?

Let's follow an example from the conceptual design stage.[4] Exhibit 4.5 represents a motor drive assembly that is required to sense and control its position on two steel guide rails. This might be the motor that controls a power window in a drive-through window at McDonald's, for example. The motor must be fully enclosed and have a removable cover for access to adjust the position sensor. A major requirement is a

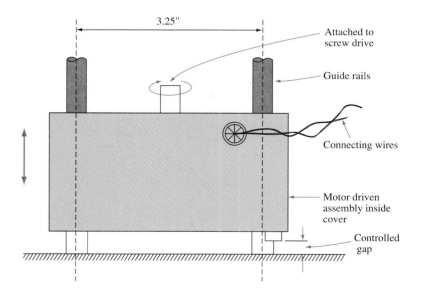

Exhibit 4.5

Configuration of Required Motor Drive Assembly

---

[4] Example adapted from Geoffrey Boothroyd, Peter Dewhurst, and Winston Knight, *Product Design for Manufacture and Assembly* (New York: Marcel Dekker, Inc., 1994), pp. 5–10.

rigid base designed to slide up and down the guide rails, which will both support the motor and locate the sensor. The motor and sensor have wires connecting to a power supply and control unit.

A proposed solution is shown in Exhibit 4.6. The base has two bushing inserts so that the holes will not wear out. The motor is secured to the base with two screws and a hole accepts the cylindrical sensor, which is held in place with a set screw. To provide the required covers, an end plate is screwed to two stand-offs, which are screwed into the base. To keep the wires from shorting out on the metal cover, should they become worn, a plastic bushing is fitted to the end plate, through which the wires pass. Finally, a box-shaped cover slides over the whole assembly from below the base and is held in place by four screws, two passing into the base and two passing into the end cover.

The current design has 19 parts that must be assembled to make the motor drive. These parts consist of the two subassemblies—the motor and the sensor—an additional eight main parts (cover, base, two bushings, two stand-offs, a plastic bushing, and the end plate), and nine screws.

The greatest improvements related to DFMA arise from simplification of the product by reducing the number of separate parts. In order to give guidance to the designer in reducing the part count, the methodology provides three criteria against which each part must be examined as it is added to the product during assembly:

1. During the operation of the product, does the part move relative to all other parts already assembled?

2. Must the part be of a different material than or be isolated from other parts already assembled?

3. Must the part be separate from all other parts to allow the disassembly of the product for adjustment or maintenance?

Exhibit 4.6   Proposed Motor Drive Design

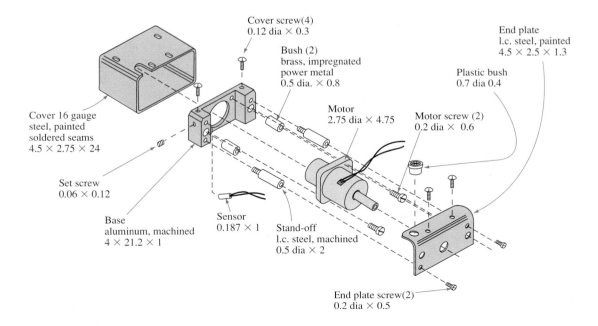

Application of these criteria to the proposed design would proceed as follows:

1. Base—Since this is the first part to be assembled, there are no other parts with which to combine, so it is theoretically a necessary part.
2. Bushings (2)—These do not satisfy the second criterion. Theoretically, the base and bushings could be of the same material.
3. Motor—The motor is a subassembly purchased from a supplier. The criteria do not apply.
4. Motor screws (2)—In most cases, separate fasteners are not needed, because a fastening arrangement integral to the design (for example, snapping the part into place) is usually possible.
5. Sensor—This is another standard subassembly.
6. Set screw—Similar to 4, this should not be necessary.
7. Standoffs (2)—These do not meet the second criterion, they could be incorporated into the base.
8. End plate—This must be separate to allow disassembly (apply criterion three).
9. End plate screws (2)—These should not be necessary.
10. Plastic bushing—Could be of the same material, and therefore combined with, the end plate.
11. Cover—Could be combined with the end plate.
12. Cover screws (4)—Not necessary.

From this analysis, it can be seen that if the motor and sensor subassemblies could be arranged to snap or screw into the base, and if a plastic cover could be designed to snap on, there would be only 4 separate items needed instead of 19. These four items represent the theoretical minimum number needed to satisfy the constraints of the product design.

At this point, it is up to the design team to justify why the parts above the minimum should be included. Justification may be due to practical, technical, or economic considerations. In this example, it could be argued that two screws are needed to secure the motor and that one set screw is needed to hold the sensor, because any alternatives would be impractical for a low-volume product such as this. However, the design of these screws could be improved by providing them with pilot points to facilitate assembly.

Exhibit 4.7 is a drawing of a redesigned motor drive assembly that uses only seven separate parts. Notice how the parts have been eliminated. The new plastic cover is

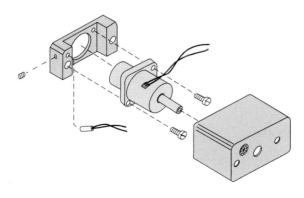

Exhibit 4.7

Redesign of Motor Drive Assembly Following Design for Assembly (DFA) Analysis designed to snap onto the base plate. This new product is much simpler to assemble. In addition, it should be much less expensive due to the reduced number of parts.

■ PROCESS SELECTION

Process Selection Contrasted with Process Planning

Process engineering as used in Exhibit 4.1 refers to the tactical planning activities that regularly occur in manufacturing. Process selection, in contrast, refers to the strategic decision of selecting which kind of production processes to have in the plant. For example, in the case of our motor drive, if the volume is very low we might just have a worker sit at a table and produce a small batch of these assemblies. On the other hand, if the volume is very high, setting up an assembly line might be appropriate.

Types of Processes

At the most basic level, the types of processes can be categorized as follows:

Conversion Processes

Conversion processes. Examples are changing iron ore into steel sheets, or making all the ingredients listed on the box of toothpaste into toothpaste.

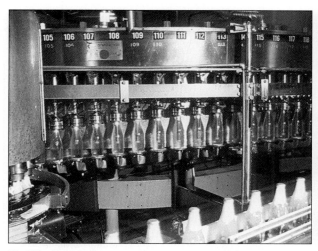

The Miller Brewing Company uses a continuous production process. Beer is brewed, bottled, packaged, and shipped on one long production line with specialized automated equipment.

Kawasaki Motors Manufacturing uses an assembly production line with a fixed sequence of assembly tasks and workers checking quality at each step.

Fabrication processes. Examples are changing raw materials into some specific form (for example, making sheet metal into a car fender or forming gold into a crown for a tooth).

Fabrication
Processes

Assembly processes. Examples are assembling a fender to a car, putting toothpaste tubes into a box, or fastening a dental crown in somebody's mouth.

Assembly Processes

Testing processes. This is not, strictly speaking, a fundamental process, but it is so widely mentioned as a stand-alone major activity that it is included here for completeness.

Testing Processes

Process Flow Structures

A **process flow structure** refers to how a factory organizes material flow using one or more of the process technologies just listed.

Process Flow
Structure
Vol. I "The Manufacturing
Process"

Hayes and Wheelwright have identified four major process flow structures:

Job shop. Production of small batches of a large number of different products, most of which require a different set or sequence of processing steps. Commercial printing firms, airplane manufacturers, machine tool shops, and plants that make custom-designed printed circuit boards are examples of this type of structure.

Job Shop
Vol. III "Washburn Guitars"

Batch. Essentially, a somewhat standardized job shop. Such a structure is generally employed when a business has a relatively stable line of products, each of which is produced in periodic batches, either to customer order or for inventory. Most of these items follow the same flow pattern through the plant. Examples include heavy equipment, electronic devices, and specialty chemicals.

Batch

Assembly line. Production of discrete parts moving from workstation to workstation at a controlled rate, following the sequence needed to build the product. Examples include manual assembly of toys and appliances, and automatic assembly (called insertion) of components on a printed circuit board. When other processes are

Assembly Line

Exhibit 4.8 *How to Make a Car* The production process in a modern car plant includes lots of checks on quality and extensive treatment to prevent corrosion.

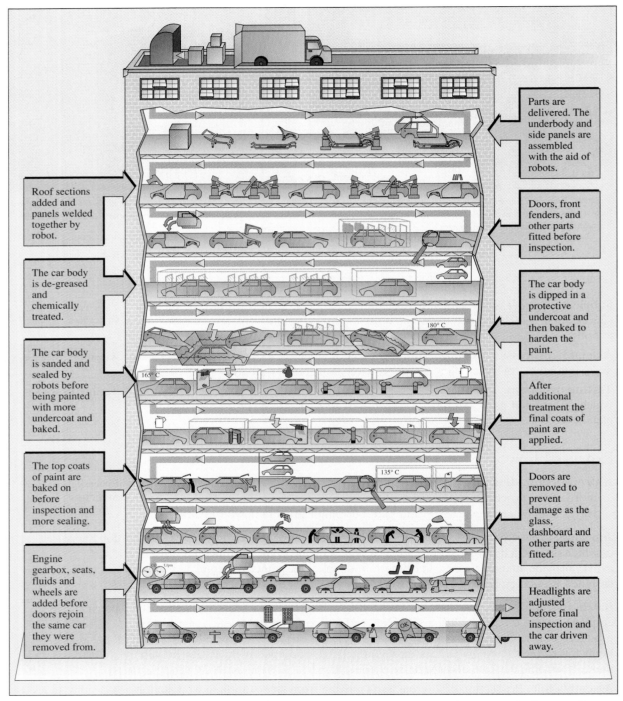

Parts are delivered. The underbody and side panels are assembled with the aid of robots.

Doors, front fenders, and other parts fitted before inspection.

The car body is dipped in a protective undercoat and then baked to harden the paint.

After additional treatment the final coats of paint are applied.

Doors are removed to prevent damage as the glass, dashboard and other parts are fitted.

Headlights are adjusted before final inspection and the car driven away.

Roof sections added and panels welded together by robot.

The car body is de-greased and chemically treated.

The car body is sanded and sealed by robots before being painted with more undercoat and baked.

The top coats of paint are baked on before inspection and more sealing.

Engine gearbox, seats, fluids and wheels are added before doors rejoin the same car they were removed from.

Source: General Motor's Opal plant at Eisenach, Germany, *The Economist*. October 17, 1992. © 1992 The Economist Newspaper Group. Inc. Reprinted with permission.

employed in a line fashion along with assembly, it is commonly referred to as a *production line.* (See Exhibit 4.8.)

Continuous flow. Conversion or further processing of undifferentiated materials such as petroleum, chemicals, or beer, as the photo on page 97 shows. As on assembly lines, production follows a predetermined sequence of steps, but the flow is continuous rather than discrete. Such structures are usually highly automated and, in effect, constitute one integrated "machine" that must be operated 24 hours a day to avoid expensive shutdowns and start-ups.

Continuous Flow

The choice of which flow structure to select, with the exception of continuous flow structures, is generally a function of the volume requirements for each product.

Product-Process Matrix

MARKETING

The relationship between process structures and volume requirements is often depicted on a **product-process matrix** (Exhibit 4.9). The way to interpret this matrix is that as volume increases and the product line (the horizontal dimension) narrows,

Product-Process Matrix

Matching Major Stages of Product and Process Life Cycles

Exhibit 4.9

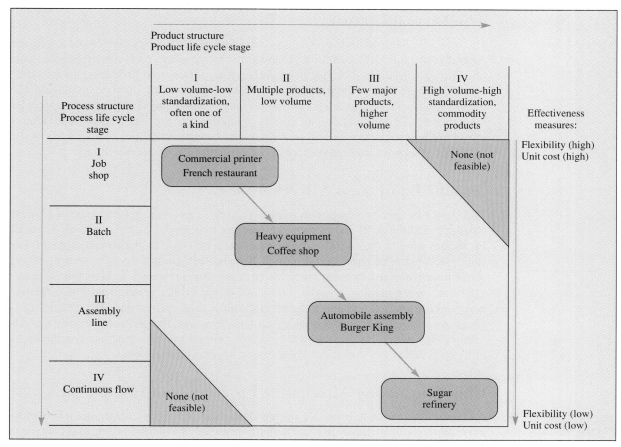

Source: Modified from Robert Hayes and Steven Wheelwright, *Restoring Our Competitive Edge: Competing through Manufacturing* (New York: John Wiley & Sons. 1984), p. 209.

specialized equipment and standardized material flows (the vertical dimension) become economically feasible. Since this evolution in process structure is frequently related to the product's life cycle stage (introduction, growth, and maturity), it is very useful in linking marketing and manufacturing strategies.

The industries listed within the matrix are presented as ideal types that have found their structural niche. (Sample foodservice systems are included to help readers get a gut feel for the dimensions.) It is certainly possible for an industry member to choose another position on the matrix, however. For example, Volvo made cars on movable pallets rather than an assembly line at their Uddevalla, Sweden, plant. Thus, on the matrix, it would be at the intersection of process stages II and III. Volvo's production rate was lower than its competitors because it was giving up speed and efficiency of the line. On the other hand, the Volvo system had more flexibility because it used multiskilled workers who were not paced by a mechanical assembly line. The plant was closed in 1996.

A major issue in today's manufacturing strategy is to seek benefits of flexibility found in stage I job shop structures along with the cost advantages that go with assembly line or even continuous flow structures of stages III and IV. At the present time, however, this is only feasible when a production system is under complete computer control, using the flexible manufacturing systems (FMS) technology described in the supplement to this chapter.

Virtual Factory

The Virtual Factory

The new term **virtual factory** refers to manufacturing activities carried out not in one central plant, but rather, in multiple locations by suppliers and partner firms as part of a strategic alliance. The role of manufacturing for an auto producer, for example, will shift from solely monitoring activities at one central plant to managing the integration of all steps in the process—no matter where physical production actually takes place. The implications for process planning are profound: The manufacturer must have a deep understanding of the manufacturing capabilities of all parties in the production network and must excel at the difficult task of coordination.

Specific Equipment Selection

The choice of specific equipment follows the selection of the general type of process structure. Exhibit 4.10 shows some key factors to consider in the selection decision. Firms may have both general-purpose equipment and special-purpose equipment. For example, a machine shop would have lathes and drill presses (general-purpose) and could have transfer machines (special-purpose). An electronics firm may have a single-function test module to perform only one test at a time (general-purpose) and may have a multifunction test unit to perform multiple tests at the same time (special-purpose). As computer-based technology evolves, however, the general-purpose/special-purpose distinction becomes blurred, since a general-purpose machine has the capability to produce just as efficiently as many special-purpose ones.

Choosing among Alternative Processes and Equipment

Break-Even Analysis

A standard approach to choosing among alternative processes or equipment is **break-even analysis.** A break-even chart visually presents alternative profits and losses due to the number of units produced or sold. The choice obviously depends on anticipated

Decision Variable	Factors to Consider
Initial investment	Price
	Manufacturer
	Availability of used models
	Space requirements
	Need for feeder/support equipment
Output rate	Actual versus rated capacity
Output quality	Consistency in meeting specs
	Scrap rate
Operating requirements	Ease of use
	Safety
	Human factors impact
Labor requirements	Direct to indirect ratio
	Skills and training
Flexibility	General-purpose versus special-purpose equipment
	Special tooling
Setup requirements	Complexity
	Changeover speed
Maintenance	Complexity
	Frequency
	Availability of parts
Obsolescence	State of the art
	Modification for use in other situations
In-process inventory	Timing and need for supporting buffer stocks
Systemwide impacts	Tie-in with existing or planned systems
	Control activities
	Fit with manufacturing strategy

Exhibit 4.10

Major Decision Variables in Equipment Selection

demand. The method is most suitable when processes or equipment entails a large initial investment and fixed cost, and when variable costs are reasonably proportional to the number of units produced. By way of example, suppose a manufacturer has identified the following options for obtaining a machined part: It can buy the part at $200 per unit (including materials), it can make the part on a numerically controlled semiautomatic lathe at $75 per unit (including materials), or it can make the part on a machining center at $15 per unit (including materials). There is negligible fixed cost if the item is purchased: a semiautomatic lathe costs $80,000, and a machining center costs $200,000.

The total cost for each option is

$$\text{Purchase cost} = \$200 \times \text{Demand}$$

$$\text{Produce using lathe cost} = \$80,000 + \$75 \times \text{Demand}$$

$$\text{Produce using machining center cost} = \$200,000 + \$15 \times \text{Demand}$$

Whether we approach the solution to this problem as cost minimization or profit maximization really makes no difference as long as the relationships remain linear; that is, variable costs and revenue are the same for each incremental unit. Exhibit 4.11 shows the break-even points for each of the processes. If demand is expected to be more than 2,000 units (point A), the machine center is the best choice since this would result in the lowest total cost. If demand is between 640 (point B) and 2,000 units, the NC lathe is the cheapest. If demand is less than 640 (between 0 and point B), the most economical course is to buy the product.

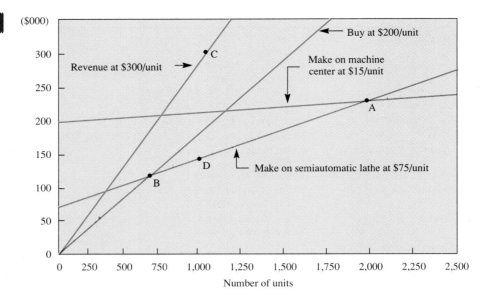

The break-even point A calculation is

$$\$80,000 + \$75 \times \text{Demand} = \$200,000 + \$15 \times \text{Demand}$$
$$\text{Demand (point A)} = 120,000/60 = 2,000 \text{ units}$$

The break-even point B calculation is

$$\$200 \times \text{Demand} = \$80,000 + \$75 \times \text{Demand}$$
$$\text{Demand (point B)} = 80,000/125 = 640 \text{ units}$$

Consider the effect of revenue, assuming the part sells for $300 each. As Exhibit 4.11 shows, profit (or loss) is the distance between the revenue line and the alternative process cost. At 1,000 units, for example, maximum profit is the difference between the $300,000 revenue (point C) and the semiautomatic lathe cost of $160,000 (point D). For this quantity the semiautomatic lathe is the cheapest alternative available. The optimal choices for both minimizing cost and maximizing profit are the lowest segments of lines: origin to B, to A, and to the right side of Exhibit 4.11 as shown in red.

■ PROCESS FLOW DESIGN

Process flow design focuses on the specific processes that raw materials, parts, and subassemblies follow as they move through the plant. The most common production management tools used in planning the process flow are assembly drawings, assembly charts, route sheets, and flow process charts. Each of these charts is a useful diagnostic tool and can be used to improve operations during the steady state of the productive system. Indeed, the standard first step in analyzing any production system is to map the flows and operations using one or more of these techniques. These are the "organization charts" of the manufacturing system.

An *assembly drawing* (Exhibit 4.12) is simply an exploded view of the product showing its component parts. An *assembly chart* (Exhibit 4.13) uses the information

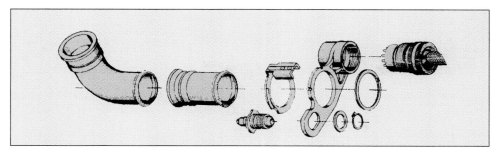

Exhibit 4.12

Plug Assembly
Drawing

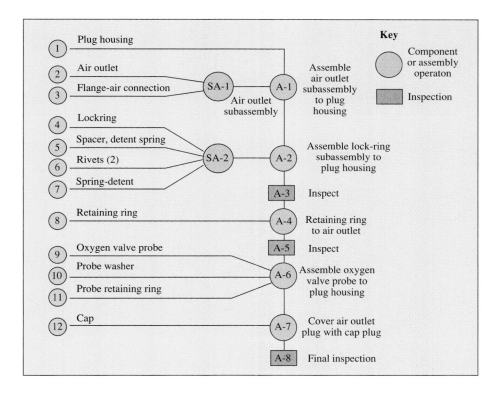

Exhibit 4.13

Assembly (or Gozinto)
Chart for Plug
Assembly

presented in the assembly drawing and defines (among other things) how parts go together, their order of assembly, and often the overall material flow pattern.[5] An *operation and route sheet* (Exhibit 4.14), as its name implies, specifies operations and process routing for a particular part. It conveys such information as the type of equipment, tooling, and operations required to complete the part.

A flow process chart such as Exhibit 4.15 typically uses standard American Society of Mechanical Engineers (ASME) symbols to denote what happens to the product as it progresses through the productive facility. The symbols for the various processes are explained at the side of the chart. As a rule, the fewer the delays and storages in the process, the better the flow.

---

[5] Also called a *Gozinto chart,* named, so the legend goes, after the famous Italian mathematician Zepartzat Gozinto.

Operation and Route
Sheet for Plug
Assembly

Material Specs _____		Part Name _____ Plug Housing		Part No. _____ TA 1274		
Purchased Stock Size _____		Usage _____ Plug Assembly		Date Issued _____		
Pcs. Per Pur Size _____		Assy. No. _____ TA 1279		Date Supplied _____		
Weight _____		Sub.Assy. No. _____		Issued By _____		

Oper. No.	Operation Description	Dept.	Machine.	Set Up Hr.	Rate Pc. Hr.	Tools
20	Drill hole .32 $^{+.015}_{-.005}$	Drill	Mach. 513 Drill	1.5	254	Drill Fixture L-76 Jig # 10393
30	Deburr .312 $^{+.015}_{-.005}$ Dia. Hole	Drill	Mach. 510 Drill	.1	424	Multi tooth burring Tool
40	Chamfer .009/875. Bore .878/.875 dia (2 Passes). Bore .7600/7625 (1 Pass)	Lathe	Mach. D 109 Lathe	1.0	44	Ramet-1, TPG 221, Chamfer tool
50	Tap hole as designated 1/4 Min. Full Thread	Tap	Mach. 517 Drill Tap	2.0	180	Fixture #CR-353 Tap. 4 Flute Sp.
60	Bore hole 1.33 to 1.138 Dia.	Lathe	H&H E107	3.0	158	L44 Turrent Fixture Hartford
						Superspacer, pl. #45 Holder #L46
						FDTW-100, Inser #21 Chk. Fixture
70	Deburr .005 to.010 Both Sides, Hand Feed to Hard Stop	Lathe	E162 Lathe	..3	175	Collect CR #179 1327 RPM
80	Broach Keyway to Remove Thread Burrs	Drill	Mach. 507 Drill	.4	91	B87 Fixture, L59 Broach Tap. .875120 G-H6
90	Hone thread I.D. .822/ .828	Grind	Grinder	1.5	120	
95	Hone .7600/ .7625	Grind	Grinder	1.5	120	

Flow Process Chart of
Plug Housing from
Plug Assembly

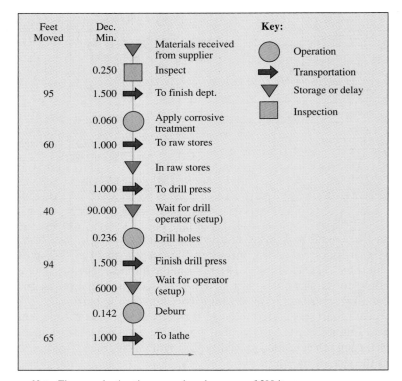

Note: These production times were based on a run of 500 items.
Source: Arizona Gear & Manufacturing Company.

▓ PROCESS ANALYSIS

Detailed process plannning entails planning the steps of the process itself. In Chapter 1 we introduced the term *process,* which can be described as a set of tasks that transform inputs into useful outputs. A process usually consists of (1) a set of *tasks,* (2) a *flow* of material and information that connect the set of tasks, and (3) *storage* of material and information.

1. *Task:* Each task in a process accomplishes, to a certain degree, the transformation of input into the desired output.
2. *Flow:* The flow in a process consists of flow of material as well as flow of information. The flow of material involves the transfer of a product from one task to its next task. The flow of information helps in determining how much of the transformation has been done in the previous task and what exactly remains to be completed in the present task.
3. *Storage:* When neither a task is being performed nor a part is being transferred, the part has to be stored. Goods in storage, waiting to be processed by the next task, are often called work-in-process inventory.

An Example of Process Analysis

Process analysis involves adjusting the capacities and balance among different parts of the process to maximize output or minimize the costs with available resources. Our company supplies a component to several large auto manufacturers.[6] This component is assembled in a shop by 15 workers working an eight-hour shift on an assembly line that moves at the rate of 150 components per hour. The workers receive their pay in the form of a group incentive amounting to 30 cents per completed good part. This wage is distributed equally among the workers. Management believes that it can hire 15 more workers for a second shift if necessary.

Parts for the final assembly come from two sources. The molding department makes one very critical part and the rest come from outside suppliers. There are 11 machines capable of molding the one part done in-house; but historically, one machine is being overhauled or repaired at any given time. Each machine requires a full-time operator. The machines could each produce 25 parts per hour, and the workers are paid on an individual piece rate of 20 cents per good part. The workers will work overtime at a 50 percent increase in rate, or for 30 cents per good part. The workforce for molding is flexible; currently, only six workers are on this job. Four more are available from a labor pool within the company. The raw materials for each part molded cost 10 cents per part; a detailed analysis by the accounting department has concluded that 2 cents of electricity is used in making each part. The parts purchased from the outside cost 30 cents for each final component produced.

This entire operation is located in a rented building costing $100 per week. Supervision, maintenance, and clerical employees receive $1,000 per week. The accounting department charges depreciation for equipment against this operation at $50 per week.

---

[6] This section is modified from Paul W. Marshall et al., *Operations Management: Text and Cases* (Homewood, IL: Richard D. Irwin, 1975), pp. 12–16.

The accompanying process flow diagram describes the process. The tasks have been shown as rectangles and the storage of goods (inventories) as triangles.

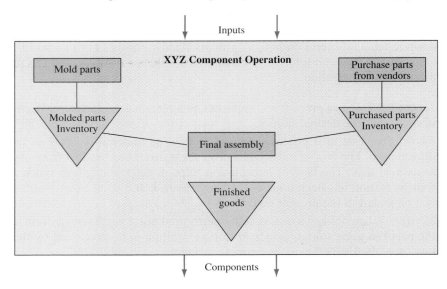

a. Determine the capacity (number of components produced per week) of the entire process. Are the capacities of all the processes balanced?

Capacity of the molding process:

Only six workers are employed for the molding process, each working as a full-time operator for one machine. Thus, only 6 of the 11 machines are operational at present.

$$\frac{\text{Molding}}{\text{capacity}} = \frac{\text{6 machines} \times \text{25 parts per hour per machine} \times \text{8 hours per}}{\text{day} \times \text{5 days per week} = \text{6,000 parts per week}}$$

Capacity of the assembly process:

$$\frac{\text{Assembly}}{\text{capacity}} = \frac{\text{150 components per hour} \times \text{8 hours per day} \times \text{5 days per}}{\text{week} = \text{6,000 components per week}}$$

Since capacity of both the tasks is 6,000 units per week, they are balanced.

b. If the molding process were to use 10 machines instead of 6, and no changes were to be made in the final assembly task, what is the capacity of the entire process?

Molding capacity with 10 machines:

$$\frac{\text{Molding}}{\text{capacity}} = \frac{\text{10 machines} \times \text{25 parts per hour per machine} \times \text{8 hours per}}{\text{day} \times \text{5 days per week} = \text{10,000 parts per week}}$$

Since no change has been made in the final assembly task, the capacity of the assembly process remains 6,000 components per week. Thus, even though the molding capacity is 10,000 per week, the capacity of the entire process is only 6,000 per week because in the long run the overall capacity cannot exceed the slowest task.

c. If our company went to a second shift of eight more hours on the assembly task, what would be the new capacity?

A second shift on the assembly task:

As calculated in the previous section, the molding capacity is 10,000.

$$\frac{\text{Assembly}}{\text{capacity}} = \frac{150 \text{ components per hour} \times 16 \text{ hours per day} \times 5 \text{ days}}{\text{per week}} = 12,000 \text{ components per week}$$

Here, even though the assembly capacity is 12,000 per week, the capacity of the entire process remains at 10,000 per week because now the slowest task is the molding process, which has a capacity of 10,000 per week. Thus, we can note here that capacity of a process is not a constant factor; it depends on the availability of inputs and the sequence of tasks. In fact, it depends on several other factors not covered here.

d. Determine the cost per unit output when the capacity is (1) 6,000 per week or (2) 10,000 per week.

(1) Cost per unit when output per week = 6,000

First, we calculate the cost of producing all the 6,000 parts per week:

Item	Calculation	Cost
Raw material for molding	$0.10 per part × 6,000 =	$ 600
Parts purchased from outside	$0.30 per component × 6,000 =	1,800
Electricity	$0.02 per part × 6,000 =	120
Molding labor	$0.20 per part × 6,000 =	1,200
Assembly labor	$0.30 per part × 6,000 =	1,800
Rent	$100 per week	100
Supervision	$1,000 per week	1,000
Depreciation	$50 per week	50
Total cost		$6,670

$$\text{Cost per unit} = \frac{\text{Total cost per week}}{\text{Number of units produced per week}} = \frac{\$6,670}{6,000} = \$1.11$$

(2) Cost per unit when output per week = 10,000

Next, we calculate the cost of producing all the 10,000 parts per week:

Item	Calculation	Cost
Raw material for molding	$0.10 per part × 10,000 =	$ 1,000
Parts purchased from outside	$0.30 per component × 10,000 =	3,000
Electricity	$0.02 per part × 10,000 =	200
Molding labor	$0.20 per part × 10,000 =	2,000
Assembly labor	$0.30 per part × 10,000 =	3,000
Rent	$100 per week	100
Supervision	$1,000 per week	1,000
Depreciation	$50 per week	50
Total cost		$10,350

$$\text{Cost per unit} = \frac{\text{Total cost per week}}{\text{Number of units produced per week}} = \frac{\$10,350}{10,000} = \$1.04$$

As you can see, our cost per unit has been reduced by spreading the fixed cost over a greater number of units.

Such process analysis calculations are required for many production decisions discussed throughout this book.

■ GLOBAL PRODUCT DESIGN AND MANUFACTURING

The globalization of product markets presents a unique challenge to companies today. Globalization relates to the ability to develop and produce products for regions of the world different from their home country. The objective when a company "goes global" is to leverage its size and knowledge to produce additional sales in the new markets. Often, due to the cost of supplying distant locations with product, the company is forced to manufacture locally in the new market area, rather than in its home country.

Joint Venture

Typically, it is difficult for a company to globalize on its own. Companies often team up in a joint venture arrangement to facilitate the process. A **joint venture** is an arrangement where two companies form a third independent company to carry out business. The two companies provide assets and other expertise to the third company, and share in its profits.

The Global Joint Venture

Often interesting arrangements are made between companies to facilitate the globalization effort. The players would typically involve a parent company, a joint venture partner located in the foreign country, and one or more suppliers working in the foreign country. The parent company actually controls the product. For example, Whirlpool with their "world washer" is known globally for their comprehensive line of home appliances. Whirlpool's excellent design and marketing expertise is an important factor in the successful offering of washers in China. Due to the size of the product, though, it is not economical for Whirlpool to produce the "world washer" in the United States and sell it in China.

Using a joint venture partner with manufacturing expertise in a particular country, Whirlpool is able to produce and deliver the product to the foreign market. The partner is responsible for local customization of the product and for all local production of the product. In identifying a partner, a company such as Whirlpool may seek the low cost producer of a similar product in the region. In addition to the production capability, the ideal partner might also have a gap in their current product line that is filled by the parent company's product. The parent company can then apply its expertise in product and process design, together with its marketing clout, to augment the current capability of the partner. This can often result in a winning arrangement for both companies.

Strategic Suppliers

Just as in the home country, suppliers are important to the foreign arrangement. The ideal supplier would be one that already has operations in the foreign country. Suppliers with operations that match up with the parent company's foreign operations are referred to as **strategic suppliers.** Suppliers provide not only the materials needed to produce the product but also the equipment used in the manufacturing processes. Suppliers often follow the parent company to the foreign country during the globalization effort.

More and more, the supplier is in the position to drive change, particularly technological, in the product or the process. Over the past 10 years, there has been a major shift to more extensive use of suppliers. Often, the supplier takes ownership of the process of supplying major groups of items to the joint venture. Supplier choice is based on capability rather than cost.

Global Product Design Strategy

Typically, a moderately complex product is structured as a series of modules. The focus is on developing a set of standard modules common to all units sold globally.

Standard CAD databases, tolerances, and other design elements are established for these modules. As global requirements, and particularly things like emission standards, become common to the world, more of the product can be standardized.

For these standard modules, common converting processes, which can be easily copied, can be developed. Investment in these common processes can be justified due to the higher volumes. Global sourcing of the equipment for these processes may be an important consideration in selecting suppliers.

The basis for the customization of the product to local needs is through a second set of modules. Unique country characteristics, such as language requirement, styling or design preference, packaging norms, electric power and fuel availability, and local taste preferences are accommodated in these modules. For example, Whirlpool refrigerators, like these sold in Bangkok, come in bright colors because they often are put in living rooms. Often there may be import restrictions or duties that constrain the amount of content not locally produced.

■ MEASURING PRODUCT DEVELOPMENT PERFORMANCE

There is some evidence that generating a steady stream of new products to market may be extremely important to ongoing profitability. To succeed, firms must be responsive to changing customer needs and the moves of their competitors. The ability to identify opportunities, mount the development effort, and bring to market new products and processes quickly is critical. Firms also must bring new products and

	Performance Dimension	Measures	Impact on Competitiveness
Exhibit 4.16 Performance Measures for Development Projects	Time-to-market	Frequency of new product introductions Time from initial concept to market introduction Number started and number completed Actual versus plan Percent of sales coming from new products	Responsiveness to customers/competitors Quality of design—close to market Frequency of projects—model life
	Productivity	Engineering hours per project Cost of materials and tooling per project Actual versus plan	Number of projects—freshness and breadth of line Frequency of projects—economics of development
	Quality	Conformance—reliability in use Design—performance and customer satisfaction Yield—factory and field	Reputation—customer loyalty Relative attractiveness to customers—market share Profitability—cost of ongoing service

Source: Steven C. Wheelwright and Kim B. Clark, *Revolutionizing Product Development* (New York: The Free Press, 1992), pp. 6–8.

processes to market efficiently. Because the number of new products and new process technologies has increased while model lives and life cycles have shrunk, firms must mount more development projects than previously, and these projects must use substantially fewer resources per project.

In the U.S. automobile market, for example, the growth of models and market segments over the last 25 years has meant that an auto firm must initiate close to four times as many development projects simply to maintain its market share position. But smaller volumes per model and shorter design lives mean resource requirements must drop dramatically. Remaining competitive requires efficient engineering, design, and development activities.

Measures of product development success can be categorized into those that relate to the speed and frequency of bringing new products on line, to the productivity of the actual development process, and to the quality of the actual products introduced (see Exhibit 4.16). Taken together, time, quality, and productivity define the performance of development, and in combination with other activities—sales, manufacturing, advertising, and customer service—determine the market impact of the project and its profitability.

■ CONCLUSION

Designing a customer-pleasing product is an art. Building the product is a science. Moving the product from design to the customer is management. World-class manufacturers excel at the speedy and flexible integration of these processes. A key to this is teamwork, not only on the part of marketing, product development, manufacturing, and distribution, but on the part of the supplier and customer as well.

Vol. IV "Quality Product & Process Design at Detroit Diesel"

Effective process planning requires clear understanding of what the factory can and cannot do relative to process structures. Many plants use a combination of the structures identified in this chapter—job shops for some parts, batch or assembly operations for others. Frequently a choice exists as to when demand seems likely to favor a switch from one to the other. Making such decisions also requires understanding the nuances of each production process to determine if the process really fits new product specifications. On a day-to-day basis, it requires the ability to systematically analyze capacity capabilities of each processing step, as was done in this chapter.

Finally, there is the issue of technology. While the details of manufacturing processes constitute the world of the engineer, awareness of modern technologies—particularly computer-integrated manufacturing—is now seen as an essential part of a business education. CIM, along with other operations technologies, is discussed in this chapter's supplement.

SOLVED PROBLEM

SOLVED PROBLEM 1

A company is considering adding a new feature that will increase unit sales by 6 percent and product cost by 10 percent. Profit is expected to increase by 16 percent of the increased sales. Initially the product cost incurred by the company was 63 percent of the sales price. Should the new feature be added?

Solution
Let the sales be $100 M.

Sales increase by 6% = $100 M $\times$ 6% = $6 M.

   Benefits: Profits increase by 16% of the increased sales = $6 M $\times$ 16% = $0.96 M.

   Cost: Increase product cost by 10% = ($100 M $\times$ 63%) $\times$ 10% = $6.3 M.

Since costs exceed benefits, the new feature should not be added.

REVIEW AND DISCUSSION QUESTIONS

1. Discuss the product design philosophy behind industrial design and design for manufacture and assembly. Which one do you think is more important in a customer-focused product development?

2. Discuss design-based incrementalism, which is frequent product redesign throughout the product's life. What are the pros and cons of this idea?

3. What is the primary production document derived from the product design process? What other types of documents does one need to make a product?

4. What factors must be traded off by product development before introducing a new product?

5. How does the QFD approach help? What are some limitations of the QFD approach?

6. What does the product-process matrix tell us? Where would you place a Chinese restaurant on the matrix?

7. It has been noted that during World War II Germany made a critical mistake by having its formidable Tiger tanks produced by locomotive manufacturers, while the less formidable U.S. Sherman tank was produced by American car manufacturers. Use the product-process matrix to explain that mistake and its likely result.

8. What impact does the concept and design stage have on the product's overall cost?
9. Discuss concurrent engineering and how it can benefit a production system.
10. How does the production volume affect break-even analysis?
11. What is meant by a process? Describe its important features.

PROBLEMS

1. See SM.

1. Pick a product and make a list of issues that need to be considered in its design and manufacture. The product can be something like a stereo, telephone, desk, or kitchen appliance. Consider the functional and aesthetic aspects of design as well as the important concerns for manufacturing.

2. See SM.

2. Consider the construction of a simple 8″ × 10″ wood picture frame. The picture frame consists of four wood pieces that are cut from the wood molding, four staples to hold the frame together, a piece of glass, a backing board made of cardboard, six points to hold the glass and backing board to the frame, and a clip for hanging the picture frame from the wall.
    a. Construct an assembly chart for the picture frame.
    b. Construct a flow process chart for the entire process from receiving materials to final inspection.

3. See SM.

3. The following is a partial house of quality for a golf club. Provide an importance weighting from your perspective (or that of a golfing friend) in the unshaded areas. If you can, using the QFD approach, compare it to a club where you or your friends play.

WHATs versus HOWs Strong Relationship: ● Medium Relationship: ○ Weak Relationship: △	Physical Aspects	Course location	Ground maintainance	Landscaping	Pin placement	Course tuning	Tee placement	Service Facilities	Customer-trained attendants	Top quality food	Highly rated chefs	Attractive restaurant	Tournament Activities	Calloway handicapping	Exciting door prizes	Perception Issues	Invitation only	Types of guests	Income level	Celebrity
Physical Aspects																				
Manicured grounds																				
Easy access																				
Challenging																				
Service Facilities																				
Restaurant facilities																				
Good food																				
Good service																				
Good layout																				
Plush locker room																				
Helpful service attendants																				
Tournament Facilities																				
Good tournament prize																				
Types of players																				
Fair handicapping system																				
Perception Issues																				
Prestigious																				

4. The purpose of this system design exercise is to gain experience in setting up a manufacturing process. (We suggest that this be done as a team project.) Assignment:

a. Get one Ping-Pong paddle.

b. Specify the type of equipment and raw materials you would need to manufacture that paddle, from the receipt of seasoned wood to packaging for shipment.

c. Assume that one unit of each type of equipment is available to you. Further assume that you have a stock of seasoned wood and other materials needed to produce and box 100 paddles. Making reasonable assumptions about times and distances where necessary.

   (1) Develop an assembly drawing for the paddle.
   (2) Prepare an assembly chart for the paddle.
   (3) Develop a flow process chart for the paddle.
   (4) Develop a route sheet for the paddle.

5. The Goodparts Company produces a component that is subsequently used in the aerospace industry. The component consists of three parts (A, B, and C) that are purchased from outside and cost 40, 35, and 15 cents per piece, respectively. Parts A and B are assembled first on assembly line 1, which produces 140 components per hour. Part C undergoes a drilling operation before being finally assembled with the output from assembly line 1. There are in total six drilling machines, but at present only three of them are operational. Each drilling machine drills part C at a rate of 50 parts per hour. In the final assembly, the output from assembly line 1 is assembled with the drilled part C. The final assembly line produces at a rate of 160 components per hour. At present, components are produced on a basis of eight hours a day and five days a week. Management believes that if need arises, it can go for a second shift of eight hours for the assembly lines.

The cost of assembly labor is 30 cents per part for each of the assembly lines; the cost of drilling labor is 15 cents per part. For drilling, the cost of electricity is 1 cent per part. The total overhead cost has been calculated as $1,200 per week. The depreciation cost for equipment has been calculated as $30 per week.

a. Draw a process flow diagram and determine the process capacity (number of components produced per week) of the entire process.

b. Suppose a second shift of eight hours is run for the assembly line 1 and the same is done for the final assembly line. In addition, four of the six drilling machines are made operational. The drilling machines, however, operate for just eight hours a day. What is the new process capacity (number of components produced per week)? Which of the three operations limits the capacity?

c. Management decides to run a second shift of eight hours for assembly line 1 plus a second shift of only four hours for the final assembly line. Five of the six drilling machines operate for eight hours a day. What is the new capacity? Which of the three operations limits the capacity?

d. Determine the cost per unit output for questions *b* and *c*.

e. The product is sold at $4.00 per unit. Assuming that the cost of a drilling machine (fixed cost) is $30,000 and the company produces 8,000 units per week, perform a break-even analysis. Assume that four drilling machines are used for production. If the company had an option to buy the same part at $3.00 per unit, what would be the break-even analysis?

4. See SM.

5. a. See SM for diagram; 5,600 components.
   b. 8,000; drilling operation
   c. 9,600; final assembly operation.
   d. $1.81, $1.79
   e. See SM.

Plant Tour

Dell Computer:
Mr. Cozzette Buys a Computer

It's every consumer's dream. You want to make a major purchase, like a car or a computer. You're after high quality at a reasonable price, and you know exactly the features you want. So you call a manufacturer and place an order. Instantly, a modern factory sets to work and custom builds your machine for delivery to your door within a week. (Roll over, Henry Ford!)

You can get it today from Dell Computer, the number one direct marketer of PCs. The build-to-order system isn't just a recent addition meant to help the company, based in Austin, Texas, compete in the please-the-consumer Nineties. Dell has specialized in custom PCs since 1984, when founder Michael Dell got his start assembling machines in his college dorm room.

Its Burger King assembly lines for desktop machines are the envy of the industry. Compaq Computer, Dell's archrival in Houston, is restructuring its entire logistics operation in hopes of achieving similar manufacturing flexibility by 1996.

Dell hasn't forgotten Henry Ford completely. Lately it has expanded into the retail arena, where merchants typically order hundreds of the same model PC. So Dell has jiggered some assembly lines to handle bulk orders. John Varol, director of manufacturing operations, says, "We call it mass customization, and it's a lot easier than sending hundreds of orders down the line." PCs built to order account for over 90 percent of Dell's $2.9 billion in annual sales. *Fortune* followed one machine from the moment a customer ordered it until Dell delivered it 46 hours, 42 minutes later.

Wednesday, 10:49 AM (Central Time)

Dave Cozzette, an accountant at Rothfos Corp., calls in his order for a Dell Dimension PC. At Dell's order center, a sales rep promises the PC will arrive within five business days. (She estimates it will arrive sooner, but sales reps are trained to keep customer expectations low.)

12:50 PM

Dell's financial services unit verifies the charge with Cozzette's credit card company, and the details of his $2,700.22 order print out on the production floor across the street at Dell's factory. An information sheet—called a traveler—lists the 60 items that Cozzette's computer must include, from cables to software. The order is branded with a serial number that will identify the PC for its lifetime.

1:00 PM

The assembly process starts with the installation of an Intel Pentium chip—the brains of Cozzette's computer—onto the machine's main circuit board, known as the motherboard. A worker across the room is readying the floppy drives and hard disk for installation later.

1:55 PM

An employee applies a sticker bearing the nascent PC's serial number to the chassis and then lays in the motherboard, fastening it with screws.

2:01 PM

A fax modem, a device that can send documents created on the PC to fax machines or other computers via telephone lines, is inserted.

2:10 PM

Someone installs the floppy drive that was prepared earlier, along with a tape backup unit. It will let Cozzette make up-to-date duplicates of his hard disk files in the event his machine has a breakdown.

2:20 PM

The power supply, a transformer that converts electrical current for use in the PC, goes into the unit, and the PC's faceplate is attached with the Dell logo subtly displayed.

2:26 PM

A worker scans the computer's bar code to update Dell's inventory. The components that have been installed in Cozzette's PC are now listed as removed from the company's storage facility in another area of the plant.

2:27 PM

The PC gets its first quality inspection. An employee checks the traveler to make sure co-workers have installed every component the computer should have. Then a test diskette is created that will keep track of which software Cozzette has ordered and which components need to be tested.

2:28 PM

The PC powers up for the first time during a "quick test" that checks memory, video circuits, and floppy and hard disk functions. If the test diskette finds a bad sector on the hard disk, a crewmember will install a new hard disk. The test diskette sets the computer's clock to Central Time.

2:45 PM–7:45 PM

Cozzette's computer sits on a rack for an extended test called "burn in." For five hours the diskette runs the PC's components through grueling tests that simulate heavy use. An indicator light hooked to the back of the PC changes color to help workers monitor the testing. Only 2 percent of the PCs fail. Finally, the test diskette uses the network to download the programs Cozzette has ordered, such as Microsoft Windows, and installs them on the hard disk.

8:20 PM

An employee shoots a 25,000-volt charge into the PC's power supply. If the PC handles the jolt without going haywire, it earns a Federal Communications Commission Class B certification that it is safe to use in homes and offices.

8:32 PM

During the PC's final test, the system is hooked up to a monitor and keyboard and operated without its test diskette, just as Cozzette will use it.

8:37 PM

Cozzette's computer is put in a box with its keyboard, manuals, and warranty papers.

9:25 PM

An Airborne Express worker loads the PC onto a truck. If Cozzette had called Dell a few hours earlier, his PC would have made it onto the truck before the 7 PM deadline for next-day delivery. Instead, he'll get it on Friday.

Friday, 10:31 AM (Eastern Time)

Airborne drops off the package at Cozzette's office. He plugs in his PC, and Dell's greeting software offers its congratulations. It's up to Cozzette to reset the computer's clock to Eastern Time.

Case

The Best Engineered Part Is No Part

Putting together NCR Corp.'s new 2760 electronic cash register is a snap. In fact, William R. Sprague can do it in less than two minutes—blindfolded. To get that kind of easy assembly, Sprague, a senior manufacturing engineer at NCR, insisted that the point-of-sale terminal be designed so that its parts fit together with no screws or bolts.

The entire terminal consists of just 15 vendor-produced components. That's 85 percent fewer parts, from 65 percent fewer suppliers, than in the company's previous low-end model, the 2160. And the terminal takes only 25 percent as much time to assemble. Installation and maintenance are also a breeze, says Sprague. "The simplicity flows through to all of the downstream activities, including field service."

The new NCR product is one of the best examples to date of the payoffs possible from a new engineering approach called "design for manufacturability," mercifully shortened to DFM. Other DFM enthusiasts include Ford, General Motors, IBM, Motorola, Perkin-Elmer, and Whirlpool. Since 1981, General Electric Co. has used DFM in more than 100 development programs, from major appliances to gearboxes for jet engines. GE figures that the concept has netted $200 million in benefits, either from cost savings or from increased market shares.

Nuts to Screws

One U.S. champion of DFM is Geoffrey Boothroyd, a professor of industrial and manufacturing engineering at the University of Rhode Island and the co-founder of Boothroyd Dewhurst Inc. This tiny Wakefield (R.I.) company has developed several computer programs that analyze designs for ease of manufacturing.

The biggest gains, notes Boothroyd, come from eliminating screws and other fasteners. On a supplier's invoice, screws and bolts may run mere pennies apiece, and collectively they account for only about 5 percent of a typical product's bill of materials. But tack on all of the associated costs, such as the time needed to align components while screws are inserted and tightened, and the price of using those mundane parts can pile up to 75 percent of total assembly costs. "Fasteners should be the first thing to design out of a product," he says.

Had screws been included in the design of NCR's 2760, calculates Sprague, the total cost over the lifetime of the model would have been $12,500—per screw. "The huge impact of little things like screws, primarily on overhead costs, just gets lost," he says. That's understandable, he admits, because for new-product development projects "the overriding factor is hitting the market window. It's better to be on time and over budget than on budget but late."

But NCR got its simplified terminal to market in record time without overlooking the little details. The product was formally introduced last January, just 24 months after development began. Design was a paperless, interdepartmental effort from the very start. The product remained a computer model until all members of the team—from design engineering, manufacturing, purchasing, customer service, and key supplier—were satisfied.

That way, the printed circuit boards, the molds for its plastic housing, and other elements could all be developed simultaneously. This eliminated the usual lag after designers throw a new product "over the wall" to manufacturing, who then must figure out how to make it. "Breaking down the walls between design and manufacturing to facilitate simultaneous engineering," Sprague declares, "was the real breakthrough."

The design process began with a mechanical computer-aided engineering program that allowed the team to fashion three-dimensional models of each part on a computer screen. The software also analyzed the overall product and its various elements for performance and durability. Then the simulated components were assembled on a computer workstation's screen to assure that they would fit together properly. As the design evolved, it was checked periodically with Boothroyd Dewhurst's DFM software. This prompted several changes that trimmed the parts count from an initial 28 to the final 15.

No Mock-Up

After everyone on the team gave their thumbs-up, the data for the parts were electronically transferred directly into computer-aided manufacturing systems at the various suppliers. The NCR designers were so confident everything would work as intended that they didn't bother making a mock-up.

DFM can be a powerful weapon against foreign competition. Several years ago, IBM used Boothroyd Dewhurst's software to analyze dot-matrix printers it was sourcing from Japan—and found it could do substantially better. Its Proprinter has 65 percent fewer parts and slashed assembly time by 90 percent. "Almost anything made in Japan," insists Professor Boothroyd, "can be improved upon with DFM—often impressively."

Question

What development problems has the NCR approach overcome?

Source: Otis Port, "The Best-Engineered Part Is No Part at All," *Business Week,* May 8, 1989, p. 150. Reprinted with permission.

Case

Product Development in Japan

Like the wizard of Oz, Japan's giant industrial combines are not what they appear to be. They do not develop all of their own product line, nor do they manufacture it. In reality, these huge businesses are more like "trading companies." That is, rather than design and manufacture their own goods, they actually coordinate a complex design and manufacturing process that involves thousands of smaller companies. The goods you buy with a famous maker's name inscribed on the case are seldom the product of that company's factory—and often not even the product of its own research. Someone else designed it, someone else put it together, someone stuck it in a box with the famous maker's name on it and then shipped it to its distributors.

Does this operation sound unnecessarily complex? Obviously, these huge corporations have their own factories and workers. So why don't they employ their own resources to produce the goods they sell?

They do, of course—but only partially. For instance, it would make very little sense for an electronics giant like Matsushita to farm out the design, manufacture, and assembly of a refrigerator or microwave oven. These products are ideally suited to mass production in the kind of large, highly automated factories that the giant companies can afford. Their factories produce hundreds of thousands of these units every year.

But what about products that companies must continually redesign to compete for public acceptance— like headphone stereos, small compact disc players, or personal computers? Redesigning means retooling a production line. It means sourcing new parts and lots of other things. For a typical product, a company might expect to sell 30,000 units in a few months, retool, sell another 50,000 units, redesign some basic components, retool again, see what the competition brings out, retool again, and on and on, throughout the life cycle of the entire product line. Although some of the giant makers are now employing the newest flexible manufacturing systems (FMS) to allow them more freedom in production, this retooling process is something many big companies want to eliminate.

Thus, they farm out much of this business to subcontractors—smaller companies they can depend on. These companies in turn, faced with redesigning and producing a product three or four times a year, will subcontract the design or manufacture of a dozen key components to still smaller companies.

How extensive is this subcontracting pyramid? Would you guess a few dozen companies? A few hundred? Think again. One electronics company I know has well over 6,000 subcontractors in its industrial group, most of them tiny shops that exist just to fill a few little orders for the companies above them.

Welcome to the real world of Japanese manufacturing.

Question

What are the strengths and weaknesses of the Japanese approach to product development?

Source: Kuniyasu Sakai, "The Feudal World of Japanese Manufacturing," *Harvard Business Review,* November–December 1990, pp. 38–49.

SELECTED BIBLIOGRAPHY

Adler, Paul S., Avi Mandelbaum, Viên Nguyen, and Elizabeth Schwerer. "Getting the Most out of Your Product Development Process." *Harvard Business Review,* March–April 1996, pp. 134–152.

Adler, Paul, S., Henry E. Riggs, and Steven C. Wheelwright. "Product Development Know-How: Trading Tactics for Strategy." *Sloan Management Review,* Fall 1989, pp. 7–17.

Boothroyd, Geoffrey, Peter Dewhurt, and Winston Knight. *Product Design for Manufacture and Assembly.* New York: Marcel Dekker, Inc., 1994.

Drucker, Peter F. "The Emerging Theory of Manufacturing." *Harvard Business Review,* May–June 1990, pp. 94–102.

Edmondson, Harold E., and Steven C. Wheelwright. "Outstanding Manufacturing in the Coming Decade." *California Management Review,* Summer 1989, pp. 70–90.

Hammer, Michael. "Reengineering Work: Don't Automate, Obliterate." *Harvard Business Review,* July–August 1990, pp. 104–12.

Hayes, Robert H., and Steven C. Wheelwright. *Restoring Our Competitive Age.* New York: John Wiley & Sons, 1984.

Hill, Terry. *Manufacturing Strategy.* 2nd ed. Burr Ridge IL.: Richard D. Irwin, 1994.

Huthwaite, Bart. *Design for Competitiveness: A Concurrent Engineering Handbook.* Institute for Competitive Design, 530 N. Pine, Rochester, Michigan, 1991.

Meyer, Christopher. *Fast Cycle Time.* New York: Free Press, 1993.

Petroski, Henry. *Invention by Design: How Engineers Get from Thought to Thing.* Boston, MA: Harvard University Press, 1996.

Roehm, Harper A., Donald Klein, and Joseph F. Castellano. "Springing to World-Class Manufacturing." *Management Accounting,* March 1991, pp. 40–44.

Sakai, Kuniyasu. "The Feudal World of Japanese Manufacturing." *Harvard Business Review,* November–December 1990, pp. 38–49.

Shunk, Dan L. *Integrated Process Design and Development.* Homewood, Ill.: Business One Irwin, 1992.

Wheelwright, Steven C., and Kim B. Clark. *Revolutionizing Product Development.* New York: The Free Press, 1992.

———. *Leading Product Development.* New York: The Free Press, 1995.

Ziemke, M. Carl, and Mary S. Spann. "Warning: Don't Be Half-Hearted in Your Efforts to Employ Concurrent Engineering." *Industrial Engineering,* February 1991, pp. 45–49.

Operations Technology

Supplement Outline

Technologies in Manufacturing, 123

    Hardware Systems

    Software Systems

Computer-Integrated Manufacturing (CIM), 129

Technologies in Services, 129

    Office Automation

    Image Processing Systems

    Electronic Data Interchange

    Decision Support Systems and Expert
      Systems

    Networked Computer Systems

Evaluation of Technology Investments, 132

    Cost Reductions

    Other Benefits

    Risks in Adopting New Technologies

Case: The Post-Information Age: Beyond Demographics, 138

Key Terms

Numerically Controlled (NC) Machine

Machining Centers

Industrial Robots

Automated Materials Handling (AMH) Systems

Manufacturing Cells

Flexible Manufacturing Systems (FMS)

Computer-Aided Design (CAD)

Automated Manufacturing Planning and Control Systems (MP&CS)

Computer-Integrated Manufacturing (CIM)

Office Automation

Image Processing Systems

Electronic Data Interchange (EDI)

Decision Support and Expert Systems

Client/Server Systems

www Links

McDonald's Corporation
(http://www.mcdonalds.com)

Motorola Corporation (http://www.mot.com)

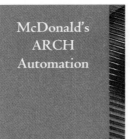

At first glance, the fry station at the McDonald's restaurant in Mishakawa, Indiana, looks like any other fry station—same size, same silver color. Closer scrutiny, however, reveals that it is no run-of-the-mill spud fryer. Most notably, it has no human attendant. Instead, it weighs, cooks, times, shakes, and dumps fries by itself, without help from crew members.

The fry station, part of a McDonald's program known as ARCH (Automated Restaurant Crew Helper), is one of the country's highest-profile examples of food-service automation. It is also part of a growing trend that is slowly moving the industrial robot into the service sector. "When you look at an automotive assembly line, you realize that it's not much of a stretch to apply automation to fast food or any number of other applications," notes Gay Engelberger, chairman of the International Service Robot Association in Ann Arbor, Michigan.

McDonald's fry-maker is only one prong of a corporate program that has begun to automate the firm's food preparation. The company also has introduced ARCH drink, an automated drink machine that eliminates the need for crew members to grab cups, shovel ice, and operate drink valves. ARCH robots are now employed at 5.5 percent of the company's 9,000 domestic stores. The company's grand plan is to remove as much labor as possible from the kitchen area and move it to the service counter. Robots significantly reduce the time it takes to fill an order, thereby reducing the time a customer waits after placing an order.

The fry-maker automatically drops fries into baskets, lowering the baskets into the cooking oil, shaking them intermittently to remove clumps, and then dumping finished fries for bagging.

Because they were custom-designed to blend with existing cooking equipment, both robots look remarkably unrobotic. They are neither as big nor as complex as the robots often seen on factory floors. Designed for use by people who have never before seen a real robot, let alone worked with one, they have been endowed with special safety features—among them, a shutdown mechanism that is activated when the robot arm encounters human resistance.

McDonald's ARCH program is not limited to robots or just automating food production. An automated ARCH production system helps a store manager in sales forecasting and production planning. The system, for example, tells the manager how many hamburgers, cheeseburgers, or fries he or she can expect to sell over the

The ARCH drink-maker enables crew members to push a button and pick up finished drinks seconds later. It is particularly effective in the busiest McDonald's restaurants, which often have a crew member handling only drink production.

next 10 minutes. It indicates how many packages of tartar or Big Mac sauce the manager should have on hand for the day depending on recent sales patterns. Based on the demand patterns in a day, the sys-

tem could also help the manager decide how many employees are needed at different time slots and thus assist in staff planning.

(http://www.mcdonalds.com)

Source: Condensed from an article by Chuck Murray, "Robots Roll from Plant to Kitchen," in the *Chicago Tribune,* October 17, 1993.

Technology is a resource of profound importance not only to operations but also to corporate profitability and growth. It has been said that technology drives change in the world. Technology affects the competitive capabilities of both individual companies and national economies. Technology is critical to the global success of firms such as Hewlett-Packard, McDonald's, Ford, and General Motors. (See the box on the previous page "McDonald's ARCH Automation.") It is interesting that the future success of Intel and Microsoft, two companies that have fueled the information technology frenzy, is most dependent on international growth.

Firms that have made technology a competitive weapon have effectively integrated the company's technology strategy and business strategy. As these companies invent and develop new technologies, they offer new products and services. These companies operate in an environment where obsolescence means six months old and product life cycle is measured in months.

Information technology has changed significantly with the wide adoption of the Internet and Web-based information systems. The cost of providing information, collecting information, and communicating electronically has dropped quickly. This trend will continue at a feverish rate. Further, the move toward information integration—that is, everyone working from the same information source, be it sales data, cost data, inventory data, or factory schedules—is dramatically changing the way companies do business. We live in an exciting world for those that embrace technology, and a scary world for those that fight technological change.

Michael Hammer, the noted reengineering author, observes "The new operating principle is, 'If I can tell you precisely what to do, then I don't need you to do it. I can tell a machine to do it, and the machine is cheaper and doesn't need vacations.' The only work left for humans to do is work that truly requires human capabilities."[1] While Mr. Hammer's claim may be exaggerated, it certainly is interesting to think about.

Technology is not limited to computer technology. New types of materials, methods for making things, and scientific discoveries (such as those involving genetic engineering) drive change as well. For example, the prospect of a car that never needs an oil change is a direct result of the development of new synthetic oils, combined with new materials and improved methods for machining engine parts. Certainly, one of the areas of greatest impact will be in the recycling of products. Parts of many products, especially those made of plastic, will be recycled as part of government-mandated life-cycle programs, which make companies responsible for the disposal of their products after their useful life. Materials technology will play a key role in the development of these programs.

---

[1] Michael Hammer, *Beyond Reengineering* (New York: HarperBusiness, 1996), p. 40.

GPS Technology Can Micromanage Fields Right Down to the Thistle Patch

Arlen Ruestman's business card lists his name, telephone number, and the precise geographical coordinates of his Toluca, Ill., corn and soybean farm—41 degrees 2.066 minutes north latitude and 89 degrees 7.528 minutes west longitude.

It is Mr. Ruestman's way of touting a satellite-cultivation technique that many experts say will transform U.S. farming. Using global-positioning-satellite technology, or GPS, he and other farmers are striving to control costs and boost crop yields.

With GPS, farmers map and analyze their fields for characteristics such as acidity and soil type, feed the data into computers, and pick up signals from space that calibrate their actions as they drive over their fields. So instead of covering a large tract with a uniform amount of seeds, fertilizer or herbicides, for example, they can spread just the right amount needed on each square yard.

Spurred by the pressure to boost profits and control chemical use, interest in GPS is exploding, from the wheat fields of Kansas to the cornfields of Illinois. "It's probably the biggest thing to hit in years," says Jerry Read, a farm-equipment dealer in Henry, Ill. Of the 14 combines he has sold so far this season, 11 were equipped with satellite receivers, and he expects to retrofit older models all summer.

Downloading the Yield

At harvest, farmers can use the geographic fixes along with a new computerized counter to record how much grain is being harvested, bushel-by-bushel, meter-by-meter and second-by-second, as the combine chugs through the field. (The old way meant eyeballing the grain coming on board, and weighing it afterwards to get a per-field average). Later, farmers can download the yield information onto a home PC to produce contour maps that show variations of 60 bushels-an-acre or more, variations that surprise even seasoned farmers like Mr. Ruestman.

By cross-referencing such information with other variables, including soil acidity or drainage conditions, farmers can analyze more precisely why some land is less productive. After rendering a diagnosis, they can then use GPS to program farm equipment to fix the problem. For example, they can direct the herbicide sprayer to hit only a patch of thistles that's at a certain geographical fix 300-feet down the field.

Other precision-farming products are also popping up. They include infrared soil sensors that can be mounted on tractors and used with GPS information to detect organic material, as well as cameras that can "see" weeds and record their location for later spraying. There is even an experimental robotic harvestor, guided by GPS, that cuts hay by itself.

Farmers Begin Harvesting Satellite Data to Boost Yields

More fertilizer? Pest alert? Examples of how satellites provide data to farmers.

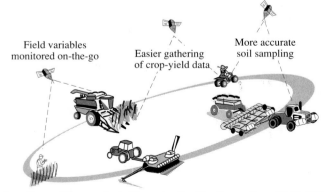

Field variables monitored on-the-go

Easier gathering of crop-yield data

More accurate soil sampling

Source: Barbara Carton, "Farmers Begin Harvesting Satellite Data to Boost Yields," *The Wall Street Journal*, July 12, 1996. Reprinted by permission of The Wall Street Journal, © 1996 Dow Jones & Company, Inc. All rights reserved worldwide.

For you city slickers, it should be noted that in no single industry has technology had a more dramatic impact than in farming. The box on the previous page about Global Positioning Satellite (GPS) data describes what possibly marks another new era in farming. We see similar shifts in the move toward cellular phone technology, and the new digital, high-definition television standards. It is difficult to isolate oneself from change driven by technology.

Vol. IV "Quality Product and Process Design at Detroit Diesel"

TECHNOLOGIES IN MANUFACTURING

While technological changes have occurred in almost every industry, many may be unique to an industry. For instance, a prestressed concrete block is a technological advance unique to the construction industry. Major developments in the design of automobiles will result in cars that are made from recyclable parts. (See Exhibit S4.1 for a description of the materials and process technologies that are being developed.)

Some technological advances in recent decades have had a significant, widespread impact on manufacturing firms in many industries. These advances, which are the

Automobile Recycling   **Exhibit S4.1**

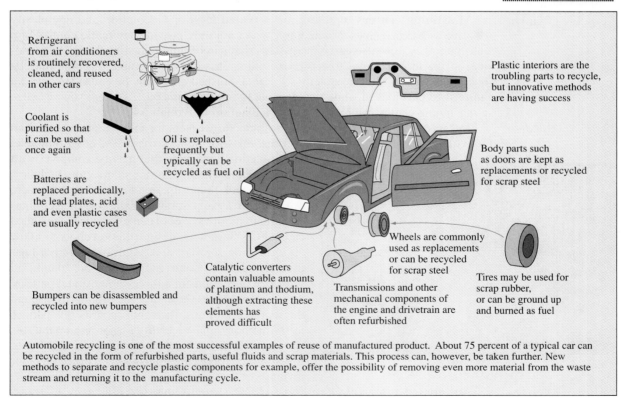

Refrigerant from air conditioners is routinely recovered, cleaned, and reused in other cars

Coolant is purified so that it can be used once again

Oil is replaced frequently but typically can be recycled as fuel oil

Batteries are replaced periodically, the lead plates, acid and even plastic cases are usually recycled

Bumpers can be disassembled and recycled into new bumpers

Catalytic converters contain valuable amounts of platinum and thodium, although extracting these elements has proved difficult

Transmissions and other mechanical components of the engine and drivetrain are often refurbished

Plastic interiors are the troubling parts to recycle, but innovative methods are having success

Body parts such as doors are kept as replacements or recycled for scrap steel

Wheels are commonly used as replacements or can be recycled for scrap steel

Tires may be used for scrap rubber, or can be ground up and burned as fuel

Automobile recycling is one of the most successful examples of reuse of manufactured product. About 75 percent of a typical car can be recycled in the form of refurbished parts, useful fluids and scrap materials. This process can, however, be taken further. New methods to separate and recycle plastic components for example, offer the possibility of removing even more material from the waste stream and returning it to the manufacturing cycle.

Source: Robert A. Frosch, "The Industrial Ecology," *Scientific American*, September 1995, p. 18.

topic of this section, can be categorized in two ways: hardware systems and software systems.

Hardware technologies have generally resulted in greater automation of processes; they perform labor intensive tasks originally performed by humans. Examples of these major types of hardware technologies are numerically controlled machine tools, machining centers, industrial robots, automated material handling systems, and flexible manufacturing systems. These are all computer-controlled devices that can be used in the manufacturing of products. Software-based technologies aid in the design of manufactured products and in the analysis and planning of manufacturing activities. These technologies include computer-aided design and automated manufacturing planning and control systems. Each of these technologies will be described in greater detail in the following sections.

Hardware Systems

Numerically Controlled (NC) Machines

Numerically controlled (NC) machines are comprised of (1) a typical machine tool used to turn, drill, or grind different types of parts; and (2) a computer that controls the sequence of processes performed by the machine. NC machines were first adopted by U.S. aerospace firms in the 1960s, and they have since proliferated to many other industries. In more recent models, feedback control loops determine the position of the machine tooling during the work, constantly compare the actual location with the programmed location, and correct as needed. This is often called adaptive control.

Machining Centers

Machining centers represent an increased level of automation and complexity relative to NC machines. Machining centers not only provide automatic control of a machine, they may also carry many tools that can be automatically changed depending on the tool required for each operation. In addition, a single machine may be equipped with a shuttle system so that a finished part can be unloaded and an unfinished part loaded while the machine is working on a part. To help you visualize a machining center, we have included a diagram in Exhibit S4.2.

Industrial Robots

Industrial robots are used as substitutes for workers for many repetitive manual activities, and tasks that are dangerous, dirty, or dull. A robot is a programmable,

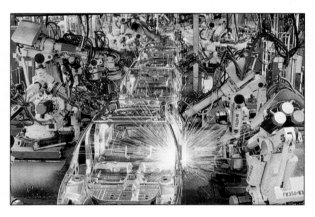

multifunctional machine that may be equipped with an end effector. Examples of end effectors include a gripper to pick things up, or a tool such as a wrench, a welder, or a paint sprayer. Exhibit S4.3 examines the human motions a robot can reproduce. Advanced capabilities have been designed into robots to allow vision, tactile sensing, and hand-to-hand coordination. In addition, some models can be "taught" a sequence of motions in a three-dimensional pattern. As a worker moves the end of the robot arm through the required motions, the robot records this pattern in its memory and repeats them on command. As shown in the box "Formula for Evaluating a Robot Investment," robots are often justified based on labor savings.

Automated Materials Handling (AMH) Systems

Automated materials handing (AMH) systems improve efficiency of transportation, storage, and retrieval of materials. Examples are computerized conveyors, and automated storage and retrieval systems (AS/RS) in which computers direct automatic loaders to pick and place items. Automated guided vehicle (AGV) systems

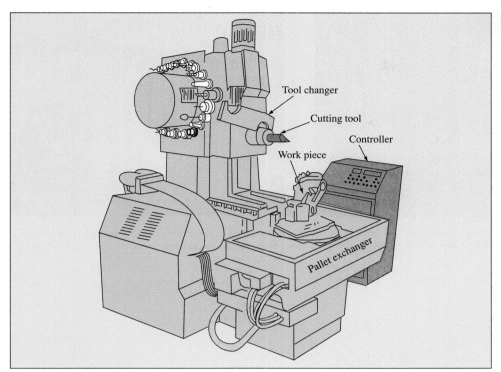

Source: J. T. Black, *The Design of the Factory with a Future*, New York: McGraw-Hill, 1991, p. 39, with permission of The McGraw-Hill Companies.

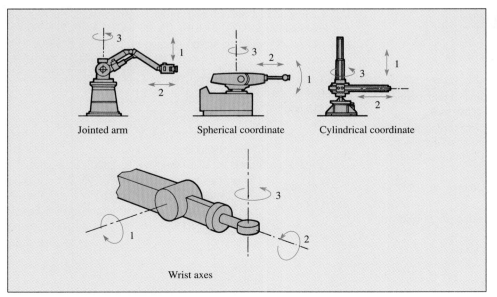

Source: L. V. Ottinger, "Robotics for the IE: Terminology, Types of Robots," *Industrial Engineering*, November 1981, p. 30.

Exhibit S4.2

The CNC Machining

Exhibit S4.3

Typical Robot Axes of Motion

These automated guided vehicles at Xerox are routed by wires in the floor to move around the production floor delivering materials and picking and placing inventory.

One of the three large machining centers (see Exhibit S4.4) that are part of the flexible manufacturing systems at Cincinnati Milicron's Mt. Orab, Ohio, plant.

Formula for Evaluating a Robot Investment

Many companies use the following modification of the basic payback formula in deciding if a robot should be purchased:

$$P = \frac{I}{L - E + q(L + Z)}$$

Where

P = Payback period in years

I = Total capital investment required in robot and accessories

L = Annual labor costs replaced by the robot (wage and benefit costs per worker times the number of shifts per day)

E = Annual maintenance cost for the robot

q = Fractional speedup (or slowdown) factor

Z = Annual depreciation

Example:

I = \$50,000

L = \$60,000 (two workers $\times$ \$20, 000 each working one of two shifts; overhead is \$10,000 each)

E = \$9,600 (\$2/hour $\times$ 4,800 hours/year)

q = 1.5 (robot works 150 percent as fast as a worker)

Z = \$10,000

then

$$P = \frac{\$50,000}{\$60,000 - \$9,600 + 1.5(\$60,000 + \$10,000)}$$

$$= 1/3 \text{ year}$$

use embedded floor wires to direct driverless vehicles to various locations in the plant. Benefits of AMH systems include quicker material movement, lower inventories and storage space, reduced product damage, and higher labor productivity.

These individual pieces of automation can be combined to form **manufacturing cells** or even a complete **flexible manufacturing systems (FMS).** A manufacturing cell might consist of a robot and a machining center. The robot could be programmed to automatically insert and remove parts from the machining center, thus allowing unattended operation. An FMS is a totally automated manufacturing system that consists of machining centers with automated loading and unloading of parts, an automated guided vehicle system for moving parts between machines, and other automated elements to allow unattended production of parts. In an FMS, a comprehensive computer control system is used to run the entire system.

A good example of an FMS is the Cincinnati Milacron facility in Mt. Orab, Ohio, which has been in operation for over 10 years. Exhibit S4.4 is a layout of this FMS. In this system, parts are loaded onto standardized fixtures (these are called "risers"), which are mounted on pallets that can be moved by the AGVs. Workers load and

Manufacturing Cells

Flexible Manufacturing System (FMS)

The Cincinnati Milacron Flexible Manufacturing System

Exhibit S4.4

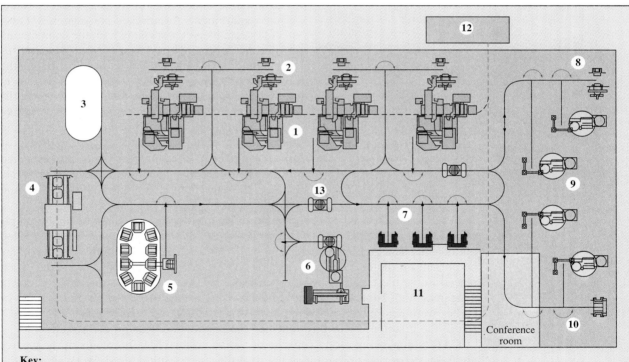

Key:

1 Four Milacron T-30 CNC Machining Centers.
2 Four tool interchange stations, one per machine, for tool storage chain delivery via computer-controlled cart.
3 Cart maintenance station. Coolant monitoring and maintenance area.
4 Parts wash station, automatic handling.

5 Automatic Workchanger (10 pallets) for online pallet queue.
6 One inspection module—horizontal type coordinate measuring machine.
7 Three queue stations for tool delivery chains.
8 Tool delivery chain load/unload stations.
9 Four part load/unload stations.
10 Pallet/fixture build station.

11 Control center, computer room (elevated).
12 Centralized chip/coolant collection/recovery system (----flume path).
13 Three computer-controlled carts, with wire-guided path.
⌒ Cart turnaround station (up to 360° around its own axis)

Source: Tour brochure from the plant.

unload tools and parts onto the standardized fixtures at the workstations shown on the right side of the diagram. Most of this loading and unloading is done during a single shift. The system can operate virtually unattended for the other two shifts each day.

Within the system there are areas for the storage of tools (area 7) and for parts (area 5). This system is designed to machine large castings used in the production of the machine tools made by Cincinnati Milacron. The machining is done by the four CNC machining centers (area 1). When the machining has been completed on a part, it is sent to the parts washing station (area 4), where it is cleaned. The part is then sent to the automated inspection station (area 6) for a quality check. The system is capable of producing hundreds of different parts. We will study the design of manufacturing systems in depth in Section Three of this book, "Design of Facilities and Jobs."

Software Systems

Computer-Aided Design (CAD)

Computer-aided design (CAD) is an approach to product and process design that utilizes the power of the computer. CAD covers several automated technologies, such as *computer graphics* to examine the visual characteristics of a product, and *computer-aided engineering* (CAE) to evaluate its engineering characteristics. Rubbermaid used

CAD to refine dimensions of its ToteWheels to meet airline requirements for checked baggage. CAD also includes technologies associated with the manufacturing process design, referred to as *computer-aided process planning* (CAPP). CAPP is used to design the computer part programs that serve as instructions to computer-controlled machine tools, and to design the programs used to sequence parts through the machine centers and other processes (such as the washing and inspection) needed to complete the part. These programs are referred to as process plans. Sophisticated CAD systems are also able to do on-screen tests, replacing the early phases of prototype testing and modification.

CAD has been used to design everything from computer chips to potato chips. Frito-Lay, for example, used CAD to design its O'Grady's double-density, ruffled potato chip. The problem in designing such a chip is that if it is cut improperly, it may be burned on the outside and soggy on the inside, be too brittle (and shatter when placed in the bag), or display other characteristics that make it unworthy for, say, a guacamole dip. However, through the use of CAD, the proper angle and number of ruffles were determined mathematically, and the O'Grady's model passed its stress test in the infamous Frito-Lay "crusher" and is now on your grocer's shelf.

CAD is now being used to custom design swimsuits. Measurements of the wearer are fed into the CAD program, along with the style of suit desired. Working with the customer, the designer modifies the suit design as it appears on a human-form drawing on the computer screen. Once the design is decided upon, the computer prints out a pattern, and the suit is cut and sewn on the spot.

Automated Manufacturing Planning and Control Systems (MP&CS)

Automated manufacturing planning and control systems (MP&CS) are simply computer-based information systems that help plan, schedule, and monitor a manufacturing operation. They obtain information from the factory floor continuously about work status, material arrivals, and so on, and they release production and purchase orders. Sophisticated manufacturing and planning control systems include order-entry processing, shop-floor control, purchasing, and cost accounting. We will cover the details of how these systems work later in this book in Section Four titled, "Managing the Supply Chain."

▣ COMPUTER-INTEGRATED MANUFACTURING (CIM)

Vol. I, "Computer-Integrated Manufacturing"

Computer-Integrated Manufacturing (CIM)

All of these automation technologies are brought together under **Computer-integrated manufacturing (CIM).** CIM is the automated version of the manufacturing process, where the three major manufacturing functions—product and process design, planning and control, and the manufacturing process itself—are replaced by the automated technologies just described. Further, the traditional integration mechanisms of oral and written communication are replaced by computer technology. Such highly automated and integrated manufacturing also goes under other names: *total factory automation* and the *factory of the future*. The breakthrough box on page 130 titled "Custom Manufacturing" describes what manufacturing might be like in the future.

All of the CIM technologies are tied together using a network and integrated database. For instance, data integration allows CAD systems to be linked to **computer-aided manufacturing (CAM),** numerical-control parts programs, and the manufacturing planning and control system can be linked to the AMH systems to facilitate parts pick list generation. Thus, in a fully integrated system, the areas of design, testing, fabrication, assembly, inspection, and material handling are not only automated but also integrated with each other and with the manufacturing planning and scheduling function.

MIS

Computer-Aided Manufacturing (CAM)

▣ TECHNOLOGIES IN SERVICES

A key element in improving the cost, quality, and speed of service operations is the ability to effectively manage the flow and processing of information.[2] While the nineteenth century gave birth to the Industrial Revolution, the twentieth century has spawned the Information Revolution. The Information Revolution refers to the development of technologies that permit quicker and cheaper transmission, processing, storage, and retrieval of information. Rapid advances in electronics have resulted in a number of new information technologies adopted extensively by the service sector in the past few decades, as we discuss next.

Office Automation

Office automation is achieved by integrating many new office technologies with improved office processes to improve the efficiency and effectiveness of office workers. Office automation is frequently associated with technologies such as personal

Office Automation

---

[2] Many examples cited in this section are from Blair J. Berkley and A. Gupta, "Improving Service Quality with Information Technology," Working Paper 9-93-9 (Madison: University of Wisconsin, 1993).

BREAKTHROUGH

Custom Manufacturing

Where can a cross-country bicyclist find a spare derailleur gear for an Italian bicycle when it breaks down in a small town in Nevada? Ten years or so from now, the answer may reside on the floppy disk carried in the rider's backpack. In coming decades, a spare part for a bicycle, automobile, or an array of other consumer goods may be simply "printed" from a computer design file at the corner factory, the futuristic equivalent of the all-night copy shop.

In the case of the gear, a machine tool might receive from a file on the disk a geometric description of the broken part. The program could then tell the tool how to deposit a thin layer of structural material by spraying droplets of liquid metal or by directing the energy of a laser onto a bed of metal powder. Subsequent layers deposited in this manner would fuse together, gradually building up a complete derailleur gear.

This approach to manufacturing has its beginnings in a suite of technologies collectively known as rapid prototyping. Today, stereolithography, shape deposition, laser sintering, and other related technologies can construct full-scale models for testing designs, and they can help build a tool for making a part. In years to come, improvements to such processes—and an expected decline in equipment costs—may allow them to be used to manufacture finished parts directly.

As they mature, these techniques may also introduce an unprecedented degree of product customization—a machine that could make a bicycle gear one day might make an automobile carburetor the next. This ability to reduce information about an individual's needs to a series of printable computer files is part of a bigger shift away from mass production of a standardized product, an approach pioneered by auto magnate Henry Ford. Postindustrial manufacturing is evolving toward an era of mass customization: production of substantial quantities of personalized goods.

computers, word processing, spreadsheets, electronic mail, teleconferencing, voice mail, and fax. John Naisbitt wrote in his best-seller *Megatrends,* "We are drowning in information but starved for knowledge and intelligence." Office automation tools help to create knowledge out of the data and transfer that knowledge efficiently.

Word processing and spreadsheets are two of many office systems that help transform ideas and data into intelligence in a form that everyone can easily share. Word processing systems boost productivity by reducing the time it takes to draft, revise, proof, copy, print, and file text material. Spreadsheets reduce the time required to organize, analyze, and interpret large amounts of data. Electronic mail and fax machines help in quickly and efficiently moving and distributing information to others and in storing it for later access by a user. Voice mail is similar to electronic mail in its purpose, except that it is meant for communicating, storing, and retrieving verbal rather than nonverbal information. While the tools just described allow information to be communicated easily, teleconferencing technology allows *interactive* communication of information and images on a real-time basis. It is therefore an alternative to in-person meetings, thus reducing travel expenses while allowing fast responses to problems at geographically dispersed sites.

Image Processing Systems

Image Processing
Systems

Image processing systems use modern digital and optical technology to scan, capture, store, and reproduce images of any complexity. Banks use image processing equipment extensively in their credit card and check processing operations. In its credit card operations, American Express uses an image processing camera to convert the charge slips (pieces of paper) into digital images. An optical character reader then

Customized fabrication, however, would require more than a trip to the corner factory. Manufacturers need to make more than just the odd bicycle gear. For large-scale fabrication, communications networks may link suppliers to an automobile or blue-jeans maker so that they can fill orders speedily. Networks may also connect customers and factories more closely. A postmillennial Gap store might be equipped with optical scanners that take waist, hip, length, and other measurements; send them over a network; and have the custom-tailored pants delivered with a matter of days. Clothing stores have begun to experiment with such tailoring.

Source: Editors, "Custom Manufacturing," *Scientific American,* September 1995, pp. 160–61. Reprinted with permission. Copyright © 1995 by Scientific American. All rights reserved.

This oil pump model was built with stereolithography, a technique for building up structures layer by layer with a laser.

scans the digital image for the account and invoice number (with 99 percent accuracy). Charge amounts are entered by computer operators using the digital image rather than the paper slip. In addition to improving billing accuracy, the system permits customer service operators to find image records of customer transactions within seconds rather than days (as finding microfilm records sometimes requires).

Barcoding and scanning technologies have helped supermarkets and discount stores reduce inventories and track sales patterns. Wal-Mart has used these technologies, together with electronic data interchange, to increase sales per square foot and improve coordination with suppliers.

Electronic Data Interchange

Electronic data interchange (EDI) is the process by which the output of one firm's information system (for example, in purchasing) is transmitted electronically for direct input to another firm's information system (in sales) without the delay associated with regular mail or the need for data entry in either firm. The Limited clothing store chain has linked all its stores with its textile mills in Hong Kong via an EDI system. The system gathers and processes sales information from the stores and sends it to the factories to initiate production of items that are selling well. Wells Fargo Bank allows its commercial customers to manage their own cash accounts by tapping directly into Wells Fargo's computer account via EDI. Use of EDI is extensive in both service and manufacturing sectors. Overall, it provides an efficient means of transmitting information quickly between suppliers of a product or service and their customers.

Electronic Data Interchange (EDI)

Decision Support Systems and Expert Systems

Many technologies we have discussed so far improve the efficiency of information transfer, storage, retrieval, and processing. **Decision support systems** and **expert systems** go one step further by supporting and even supplanting decision making. They are useful in developing decision alternatives, gathering and analyzing the information required for evaluating the decision alternatives, and identifying either the best decision or a set of good decision alternatives. These systems are also useful in assessing the cost or other impacts of a decision alternative proposed by a manager. For instance, Chemical Bank has developed a personal computer-based retail banking expert system, Genesys, that serves each employee group having direct contact with customers. One element of Genesys is the capability to make personal loan decisions through automated credit evaluation, where the expert system analyzes information on the client in many different databases and makes decisions using standard rules set by experienced credit agents.

Networked Computer Systems

It is rare to find an organization now that has a solitary mainframe computer performing all the computing functions. From the smallest microcomputer to the largest mainframe, computers are being interconnected or networked with each other and with printers, copiers, facsimile machines, and so forth by telecommunication links. This distribution of computing power throughout the organization is also referred to as distributed processing. This is often achieved by using a client/server approach, with networks of end-user microcomputers (clients) tied together with microcomputers or mainframes or even powerful microcomputers that act as servers or superservers.

Jon Yormark, Professor of Information Systems at the University of Southern California, describes its benefits nicely: **"Client/server** systems provide a division of labor between computers—mainframes and powerful minis do what they do best, crunch massive amounts of data, and client PCs do what they do best, analyze and present data in the way the user wants it." A leading computer system using this technology is SAP R/3, which is the topic of the Supplement to Chapter 16.

Networked computer systems allow end-users to communicate electronically and share the use of hardware, software, data, and other resources. For instance, end-users in an office local area network (LAN) of microcomputers can share the use of software packages and large databases that reside on the server and may be connected to a high-quality, expensive laser color printer. The declining cost and the increasing capabilities of microcomputers and telecommunication links in the past two decades have enabled the widespread adoption of such client/server networks in recent years, and this is likely to be the dominant trend in the future.

■ EVALUATION OF TECHNOLOGY INVESTMENTS

Modern technologies such as flexible manufacturing systems or computerized order processing systems represent large capital investments. Hence, a firm has to carefully assess its financial and strategic benefits from a technology before acquiring it. Evaluating such investments is especially hard since the purpose of acquiring new technologies is not just to reduce labor costs but also to increase product quality and variety, to shorten production lead times, and to increase the flexibility of an operation. Since some of these benefits are intangible relative to labor cost reduction, justification becomes difficult. Further, rapid technological change renders new equipment obsolete in just a few years, making the cost-benefit evaluation more complex.

But never assume that new automation technologies are always cost-effective. Even when there is no uncertainty about the benefits of automation, it may not be worthwhile to adopt it. For instance, many analysts predicted that integrated CAD/CAM systems would be the answer to all manufacturing problems. But a number of companies investing in such systems lost money in the process. The idea was to take a lot of skilled labor out of the process of tooling up for new or redesigned products and to speed up the process.[3] However, it can take less time to mill complex, low-volume parts than to program the milling machine, and programmer time is more expensive than the milling operator time. Also, it may not always be easy to transfer all the expert knowledge and experience that a milling operator has gained over the years into a computer program. Only recently has CAD/CAM integration software become available that can be cost-effective even in high-variety, low-volume manufacturing environments.

Next, we describe some typical benefits from adopting new technologies, both tangible and intangible, that can be used to develop financial and strategic justifications for their purchase. The tangible benefits can be used in traditional modes of financial analysis, such as discounted cash flow, to justify the investments. A manager can then use the results of the traditional financial analysis, together with the intangible benefits, to make sound investment decisions.

Cost Reductions

Labor Costs   Traditionally, automation helps reduce labor costs by decreasing labor requirements. For instance, an industrial robot may replace a person performing spot welding or painting operations, saving labor costs. Modern steel mills require almost no direct labor at all. In some instances, one person may be required to operate older equipment or a new machine, but the new equipment may have a greater output rate per unit time, thus requiring less labor time per unit of output. A fast copier requires one person to operate it, as does a slow one, but makes more copies per minute. In this case, labor time and labor cost per copy are lower. Do not assume that new technologies always reduce labor costs. They may actually increase labor costs but still have other benefits. While a sophisticated machine may require a more skilled person with higher wages to operate it, it may improve product quality or permit greater product variety.

Material Costs   A new technology may allow the use of alternative materials that are cheaper or can generate greater output. For instance, a major recent technological advance in the telecommunications industry is the replacement of copper cables with fiberoptic cables, which can carry much more information. This has drastically

---

[3] From the article "Automating the Automators," *Forbes*, February 14, 1994.

lowered unit information transmission costs. In the textile and paper industries, new optimization techniques embedded in computer software have reduced material waste (and costs) when cutting out patterns from large rolls of cloth or paper.

Inventory Costs   In many manufacturing companies, some of the greatest benefits of new technologies may come through reduced inventory holding costs. Automated order processing systems, better scheduling systems, and flexible manufacturing equipment with low setup times can reduce inventories dramatically. But in some cases, firms purchase high-speed machines with high setup times, which actually increase inventory carrying costs. The high setup times force the firm to have long product runs, resulting in high inventories. The reduction in inventories also reduces space requirements.

Transportation or Distribution Costs   Historically, the arrival of the railroad and then the automobile decreased transportation costs substantially, cutting transportation times in the process. Subsequent technological improvements in air, surface, and ocean-going transportation modes have again reduced costs, while major changes in information technologies in recent decades have tremendously reduced costs and improved the speed of information transfer. This has had a particularly significant impact in service operations, where transfer of information dominates the transfer of goods. Even in the manufacturing sector, these technologies have allowed firms to better integrate with their suppliers and customers and reduce their purchase, distribution, and other transaction costs.

Quality Costs   The adoption of automated process equipment leads to more uniform production and, often, to an order-of-magnitude decline in defects. Many firms have seen 5- to 10-fold reductions in waste, scrap, and rework when manual operations were replaced with automated equipment. Also, as defect rates decrease and process control improves, fewer inspection stations and inspectors are required. These benefits are easy to quantify. These capabilities lead, in turn, to significant reductions in warranty expenditures. The warranty benefits may be more difficult to estimate accurately, but they should not be ignored.

Other Costs   Over the years, maintenance costs, energy costs, and so on have also decreased as a result of new technologies. Newer machines, especially in electronics, require little maintenance and repair. Also, the development of new materials and technologies in the construction industry have lowered energy costs in offices.

Other Benefits

Other benefits obtained by adopting new technologies are described next. Some benefits may be intangible and harder to estimate than the cost reductions mentioned earlier.

Increased Product Variety   In the 1920s, consumers flocked to Henry Ford's cars even though they were all black. But this would be unlikely in today's intensely competitive environment. New technologies allow firms to give the customer significant product variety. For instance, flexible manufacturing systems offer the potential for low-cost production of high-variety, low-volume goods, which is generally called economies of scope. Firms introduce new products frequently. For instance, Sony has introduced over 300 versions of its basic Walkman since the product's inception.

Improved Product Features and Quality   New technologies may allow a firm to significantly improve its product features, the quality of the product or service offerings, and its consistency in quality over time. For instance, new chip-making technologies and machines have allowed firms like Intel to produce more sophisticated and capable microprocessors for use in computers, and auto manufacturers have used new painting technologies and robots to improve finishes on their cars.

Shorter Cycle Times   Another benefit frequently cited by firms adopting new technologies like flexible or computer-integrated manufacturing systems is the decrease in manufacturing cycle times or delivery lead times. Generally, reductions in inventories are also accompanied by shorter cycle times. While some benefits of reduced cycle times have been incorporated via inventory savings, the marketing advantages of reduced cycle times have to be recognized. Shorter cycle times have twin benefits: they allow the firm to quote shorter delivery times (which can be an important competitive advantage) and also permit the firm to respond quickly to changes in market demand.

Increased product variety, improved product features and quality, or shorter cycle times normally allow a firm to increase its sales volume or charge a premium price. But these benefits are hard to accurately estimate or predict because they depend so much on competitors' actions, which are not easy to forecast. Despite the difficulty in quantifying such benefits, they should not be ignored, as they are strategic in nature and critical to the long-term success of a company. Kaplan says, "Rather than attempt to put a dollar tag on benefits that by their nature are difficult to quantify, managers should reverse the process and estimate first how large these benefits must be in order to justify the proposed investment."[4]

Risks in Adopting New Technologies

While there may be many benefits in acquiring new technologies, several types of risk accompany the acquisition of new technologies. These risks have to be evaluated and traded off against the benefits before they are adopted. Some of these risks are described as follows.

Technological Risks   An early adopter of a new technology has the benefit of being ahead of the competition, but he also runs the risk of acquiring an untested technology whose problems could disrupt the firm's operations. There is also the risk of obsolescence, especially with electronics-based technologies where change is rapid and when the fixed cost of acquiring new technologies or the cost of upgrades is high. Also, alternative technologies may become more cost-effective in the future, negating the benefits of a technology today.

---

[4] Robert Kaplan, "Must CIM Be Justified by Faith Alone?" *Harvard Business Review,* March–April 1986, pp. 87–97.

BREAKTHROUGH

Motorola Pagers: To Each His Own

In the early 1980s, the electronic pager industry in America was stormed by Japanese competitors selling high-quality pagers for $100, half the price charged by the half-dozen American manufacturers. By 1985, most domestic producers were out of the business. Motorola realized that, even if it streamlined its traditional production system, it could not hope for more than a 20 percent increase in productivity. A drastic transformation of the production process was necessary, but it had to be done quickly. Motorola therefore decided to develop a fully automated production process using the best off-the-shelf technology in the world to be sure it worked. The idea was not only to reduce production costs drastically and achieve very high quality, but also to gain the flexibility to make different pager models faster than its competitors.

Motorola used many concepts and technologies discussed here to achieve its ambitious goal of *mass customization*. It developed a completely automated, computer-integrated manufacturing process and assembly line to produce its Bravo line of pagers. The pager was designed to have only 134 parts assembled robotically. The electronic devices in the pager provided the customization necessary to allow 29 million possible variations.

The goal was not to transform just the manufacturing line, but rather to transform the entire order-to-delivery process. Instead of taking a month or so to process orders, Motorola now transmits orders for customized pagers by computer to its plant at Boynton Beach, Florida, where pagers can be manufactured, tested, and ready for delivery in less than two hours. A salesperson obtains pager specifications from the customer and transmits them to the plant. Computers in the plant use the order information to determine the exact production schedule plus the machines and robots that will produce the pager. The plant is a showcase facility with automated, minimal setup time and flexible, build-to-order manufacturing operations. The technology is so flexible that Motorola has been able to dismantle and use some of the equipment in other pager lines. This is an example of a firm that has used technology with ingenuity to dramatically improve all four strategic dimensions: cost, quality, speed of delivery, and flexibility.

 (http://www.mot.com)

Effective Use of Information Technology at 7-Eleven (Japan)

7-Eleven—Japan's largest food retailer—is distinct from the U.S. convenience store chain of the same name. There are about 3,900 7-Eleven convenience stores in Japan, most owned by franchise holders.

Operational Risks   There could also be risks in applying a new technology to a firm's operations. Installation of a new technology generally results in significant disruptions, at least in the short run, in the form of plantwide reorganization, retraining, and so on. Further risks are due to the delays and errors introduced in the production process and the uncertain and sudden demands on various resources.

Organizational Risks   Firms may lack the organizational culture and top management commitment required to absorb the short-term disruptions and uncertainties associated with adopting a new technology. In such organizations, there is a risk that the firm's employees or managers may quickly abandon the technology when there are short-term failures or that they will avoid major changes by simply automating the firm's old, inefficient process and therefore not obtain the benefits of the new technology.

Environmental or Market Risks   In many cases, a firm may invest in a particular technology only to discover a few years later that changes in some environmental or

7-Eleven is a very profitable operation, with its return on equity being the highest among Japanese retailers.

On average, a 7-Eleven has only about 1,000 square feet of shelf space to stock over 3,500 items. Given the limited space and the large variety of products, the mix of products on the shelves is varied according to the time of day. The store owner needs to know what products to sell and when to maximize sales. Electronic point-of-sale terminals at each 7-Eleven are connected by a sophisticated computer network. The POS terminals, which look like simple cash registers, are owned by 7-Eleven to control technical standards across the network. When an item is purchased, the terminal stores information about the sale, such as brand name, manufacturer, and price of the item plus the age and sex of the buyer. The store owner can later obtain information from the machine (in the form of charts) about sales of an item during different hours of the day, days of the week, and so on. Sales patterns can be analyzed and used to change the mix of products stored on the shelves at different times.

Store owners can send orders directly from the terminal to suppliers. This saves on paperwork and time—the only paper they see is the delivery note. They can also check whether a particular supplier has a certain item in stock before placing an order. Inventory is constantly checked by the computer, and orders placed are based on current inventory status.

With one or more deliveries per day, the time between order placement and delivery can be as little as eight hours. This enables store owners to carry little inventory and replenish it frequently. This reduces inventory carrying costs and also allows them to carry a greater variety of items on the shelves, maximizing effectiveness.

7-Eleven, the parent company, can obtain aggregate statistics about sales patterns from many stores and sell manufacturers purchase information relating to their own products. 7-Eleven also gathers data about regional or national sales patterns and changes in consumer tastes or spending patterns and provides it to store owners, thereby binding them into the organization. 7-Eleven sells about 8,000 different products in a given year. Its sophisticated information system allows it to weed out products selling poorly and replace them with new ones. Thus, the system has proved beneficial in carrying out tactical operations such as order transmission and also for more strategic purposes such as determining who is shopping for which product and when, and how consumer tastes and spending patterns are changing.

Source: Motorola adapted from "The Economist," December 5, 1992, p. 71; 7-Eleven adapted from the Survey on Telecommunications in *The Economist*, March 10, 1990.

market factors make the investment worthless. For instance, in environmental issues auto firms have been reluctant to invest in technology for making electric cars because they are uncertain about future emission standards of state and federal governments, the potential for decreasing emissions from gasoline-based cars, and the potential for significant improvements in battery technology. Typical examples of market risks are fluctuations in currency exchange rates and interest rates.

■ CONCLUSION

Technology has played the dominant role in the productivity growth of most nations and has provided the competitive edge to firms that have adopted it early and implemented it successfully. While each of the manufacturing and information technologies described here is a powerful tool by itself and can be adopted separately, their benefits grow exponentially when they are integrated with each other. This is particularly the case with CIM technologies.

With more modern technologies, the benefits are not entirely tangible and many benefits may be realized only on a long-term basis. Thus, typical cost accounting methods and standard financial analysis may not adequately capture all the potential benefits of technologies such as CIM. Hence, we must take into account the strategic benefits in evaluating such investments. Further, since capital costs for many modern technologies are substantial, the various risks associated with such investments have to be carefully assessed.

Implementing flexible manufacturing systems or complex decision support systems requires a significant commitment for most firms. Such investments may even be beyond the reach of small to medium-sized firms. However, as technologies continue to improve and are adopted more widely, their costs may decline and place them within the reach of smaller firms. Given the complex, integrative nature of these technologies, the total commitment of top management and all employees is critical for the successful implementation of these technologies.

REVIEW AND DISCUSSION QUESTIONS

1. Give three examples each of companies that have acquired new technologies to achieve the following:
   a. Reduced cost.
   b. Reduced lead time.
   c. Improved quality.
   d. Increased customizing ability.
2. Give two examples each of recent process and product technology innovations.
3. It is generally believed that the impact of new technologies on service operations is difficult to measure. Why may this be true?
4. What could be the benefits of introducing a computerized registration system at a university? Are these benefits quantifiable?
5. In the McDonald's case at the beginning of this supplement, what are the tangible and intangible benefits?
6. What is the difference between an NC machine and a machining center?
7. How would The Limited apparel chain benefit by using EDI in its operations?
8. The major auto companies are planning to invest millions of dollars on developing new product and process technologies required to make electric cars. Describe briefly why they are investing in these technologies. Discuss the potential benefits and risks involved in these investments.

Case

The Post-Information Age: Beyond Demographics

The transformation from an industrial age to a post-industrial or information age has been discussed so much and for so long that we may not have noticed that we are passing into a post-information age. The industrial age, very much an age of atoms, gave us the concept of mass production, with the economies that come from manufacturing with uniform and repetitious methods in any one given space and time. The information age, the age of computers, showed us the same economies of scale but with less regard for space and time. The manufacturing of bits could happen anywhere, at any time, and, for example, move among the stock markets of New York, London, and Tokyo as if they were three adjacent machine tools.

In the information age, mass media got bigger and smaller at the same time. New forms of broadcast, like

CNN and *USA Today,* reached larger audiences and made broadcast broader. Niche magazines, video-cassette sales, and cable services were examples of narrowcasting, catering to small demographic groups. Mass media got bigger and smaller at the same time.

In the post-information age, we often have an audience the size of one. Everything is made to order, and information is extremely personalized. A widely held assumption is that individualization is the extrapolation of narrowcasting—you go from a large, to a small, to a smaller group, and ultimately to the individual. By the time you have my address, my marital status, my age, my income, my car brand, my purchases, my drinking habits, and my taxes, you have me—a demographic unit of one.

This line of reasoning completely misses the fundamental difference between narrowcasting and being digital. In being digital I am me, not a statistical subset. Me includes information and events that have no demographic or statistical meaning. Where my mother-in-law lives, whom I had dinner with last night, and what time my flight departs for Richmond this afternoon have absolutely no correlation or statistical basis from which to derive suitable narrowcast services.

But that unique information about me determines news services I might want to receive about a small obscure town, a not so famous person, and (for today) the anticipated weather conditions in Virginia. Classic demographics do not scale down to the digital individual. Thinking of the post-information age as infinitesimal demographics or ultrafocused narrowcasting is about as personalized as Burger King's, "Have It Your Way."

True personalization is now upon us. It's not just a matter of selecting relish over mustard once. The post-information age is about acquaintance over time: machines' understanding individuals with the same degree of subtlety (or more than) we can expect from other human beings, including idiosyncrasies (like always wearing a blue-striped shirt) and totally random events, good and bad, in the unfolding narrative of our lives.

For example, having heard from the liquor store's agent, a machine could call to your attention a sale on a particular Chardonnay or beer that it knows the guests you have coming to dinner tomorrow night liked last time. It could remind you to drop the car off at a garage near where you are going, because the car told it that it needs new tires. It could clip a review of a new restaurant because you are going to that city in 10 days and, in the past, you seemed to agree with that reviewer. All of these are based on a model of you as an individual, not as part of a group who might buy a certain brand of soapsuds or toothpaste.

Questions

1. Negroponte's views of the future are controversial to many. There are complex issues associated with privacy that need to be addressed in the near future. What are your feelings about the kinds of information described in the article being available in a public database?

2. Do you think Mom and Pop would feel the same way as you do about this issue?

3. How will personalization affect the operations of suppliers of the beverages used for dinner or dropping off your car for new tires?

4. What kind of new service businesses will be developed to take advantage of this information?

Source: Nicholas Negroponte, *Being Digital* (New York: First Vantage Books edition, 1995), pp. 163–65. © 1995 by Nicholas Negroponte. Reprinted by permission of Alfred A. Knopf Inc.

SELECTED BIBLIOGRAPHY

Avishai, Bernard. "A CEO's Common Sense of CIM: An Interview with J. Tracy O'Rourke." *Harvard Business Review,* January–February 1989, pp. 110–17.

Black, J. T. *The Design of the Factory with a Future.* New York: McGraw-Hill, 1991.

Busby, J. S. *The Value of Advanced Manufacturing Technology.* Oxford, England: Butterworth-Heinemann, 1992.

Flaig, L. Scott. *Integrative Manufacturing: Transforming the Organization through People, Process, and Technology.* Burr Ridge, IL: Irwin Professional Publishing, 1993.

Gaynor, Gerard H. *Achieving the Competitive Edge through Integrated Technology Management.* New York: McGraw-Hill, 1991.

Melnyk, Steven A., and Ram Narasimhan. *Computer Integrated Manufacturing.* Burr Ridge, IL: Irwin Professional Publishing, 1992.

Negroponte, Nicholas. *Being Digital.* New York: Vantage Books, 1995.

Noori, Hamid, and Russell W. Radford. *Reading and Cases in the Management of New Technology: An Operations Perspective.* Englewood Cliffs, NJ: Prentice Hall, 1990.

Tidd, Joseph. *Flexible Manufacturing Technologies and International Competitiveness.* London: Pinter, 1991.

Chapter 5

Product Design and Process Selection—Services

Chapter Outline

The Nature of Services, 142

    Service Businesses and Internal Services

    A Contemporary View of Service
    Management

An Operational Classification of Services, 144

Designing Service Organizations, 146

    Service Strategy: Focus and Advantage

**Structuring the Service Encounter:
Service-System Design Matrix,** 151

    Strategic Uses of the Matrix

Service Blueprinting and Fail-Safing, 154

Three Contrasting Service Designs, 156

    The Production Line Approach

    The Self-Service Approach

    The Personal Attention Approach

Service Guarantees as Design Drivers, 161

Case: Kinko's Copier Stores, 164

Case: AOL's Move to Flat-Rate Pricing, 166

Key Terms

Service Package

Facilities-Based Services

Field-Based Services

Customer

High and Low Degrees of
    Customer Contact

Service Focus

Service-System Design Matrix

Service Blueprint

Poka-Yoke

Service Guarantees

www Links

Nordstrom Department Stores
(http://www.nordstrom-pta.com)

Marriott International, Inc.
(http://www.marriott.com)

I F YOU'VE EVER LANGUISHED ON HOLD, ENDURING Muzak, wondering why you do business with some company that has transferred you six times and still hasn't answered your question, here's a newsflash: Customer phone service stinks.

Management expert Tom Peters, co-author of *In Search of Excellence,* called 13 firms to pose a basic question or file a complaint. His research turned up everything from great service (Nordstrom) to being cut off (General Motors). "Many of the problems we called [about] weren't all that big," he says. "But we were abused by [some] companies." Peters' staff targeted organizations from Procter & Gamble to the White House. The results appear in the June issue of his newsletter, *On Achieving Excellence.* Some examples:

Nordstrom. The caller called the switchboard and asked to speak to the CEO about a problem in the shoe department. One transfer later, CEO Bruce Nordstrom was on the line. He listened patiently and promised to call his store and fix the matter.

IBM. Request: an annual report and information regarding IBM's annual meeting. Call was transferred to stockholder relations. "An enthusiastic operator gave way to a disinterested automaton," says Peters' report. Date of request for annual report: March 28. Date it arrived: May 5—two weeks after the annual meeting. IBM's explanation: Unless the caller requests first-class mail, annual reports go bulk mail.

Yoplait. The caller wanted to know the yogurt-maker's position on bovine growth hormone, an additive that boosts milk production in cows. The operator refused to transfer the call. At **Ben & Jerry's,** the same question brought a swift transfer to the public relations department and an eight-minute discussion on why B&J shuns the hormone.

General Motors. Why is it taking automakers so long to develop electric cars, the caller asked. Request to speak to CEO Jack Smith was denied. Transferred to library, then to non-working number and cut off. A GM spokesman says the caller should have been sent to the electric car department, where an official would have answered the question.

Peters admits his survey isn't scientific. In fairness, he called his own circulation department. Service was mediocre. "Could have been worse, but their performance didn't make my day," Peters says. Some companies—even big ones like Nordstrom—are thrilling their customers with prompt service, while others are blowing it, Peters says. "The people answering the phones are major competitive assets—or liabilities." ●

Source: Ellen Neuborne, "Customer Service Flops on the Phone," *Chicago Sun-Times,* May 10, 1994, p. 4. Copyright 1994, Gannett Co., Inc. Reprinted with permission.

It's not just phone service where customers experience problems at the "moment of truth"[1]—the encounter with a service organization; it is at the bank, the restaurant, and the airline as well. While the front-line service workers are often the focal point of criticism (or praise), they are only one part of the often complicated process of service delivery.

In this chapter, after some preliminary comments about services, we address the issue of service delivery system design, starting with the notion of customer contact as a way of classifying service operations. Next, we discuss service organization design, service strategy, and service focus, and describe how marketing and operations interrelate to achieve (or fail to achieve) competitive advantage. We also look at a service-system design matrix that can define the broad features of a service process, and at service blueprints as a way of designing the precise steps of a process. In the latter part of the chapter, we present three service designs used in service industries and discuss how service guarantees can be used as "design drivers." The chapter ends with two case studies of service organizations familiar to many readers of this book—Kinko's Copier Stores and America Online (AOL).

■ THE NATURE OF SERVICES

Our study of the nature of services leads to seven generalizations:

1. **Everyone is an expert on services.** We all think we know what we want from a service organization and, by the very process of living, we have a good deal of experience with the service creation process.
2. **Services are idiosyncratic**—what works well in providing one kind of service may prove disastrous in another. For example, consuming a restaurant meal in less than half an hour may be exactly what you want at Jack-in-the-Box but be totally unacceptable at an expensive French restaurant.
3. **Quality of work is not quality of service.** An auto dealership may do good work on your car, but it may take a week to get the job done.

[1] The term *moment of truth* was coined by Jan Carlzon, former president of Scandinavian Airlines System. See in Karl Albrecht and Ron Zemke, *Service America! Doing Business in the New Economy* (Burr Ridge, IL: Irwin Professional Publishing, 1985), p. 19.

4. Most services contain a mix of tangible and intangible attributes that constitute a **service package.** This package requires different approaches to design and management than the production of goods.

5. High-contact services (described later) are *experienced,* whereas goods are *consumed.*

6. Effective management of services requires an understanding of marketing and personnel, as well as operations.

7. Services often take the form of cycles of encounters involving face-to-face, phone, electromechanical, and/or mail interactions. (The term *encounter,* by the way, is defined as "meeting in conflict or battle" and hence is often apt as we make our way through the service economy.)

Service Package

Service Businesses and Internal Services

Service operations management issues exist in two broad organizational contexts:

1. Service business is the management of organizations whose primary business requires interaction with the customer to produce the service. These include such familiar services as banks, airlines, hospitals, law firms, retail stores, and restaurants. Within this category, we can make a further major distinction: **facilities-based services,** where the customer must go to the service facility, and **field-based services,** where production and consumption of the service take place in the customer's environment (e.g., cleaning and home repair services).

Facilities-Based Services

Field-Based Services

Technology has allowed for the transfer of many facility-based services to field-based services. Dental vans bring the dentist to your home; some auto repair services have repair-mobiles; and telemarketing brings the shopping center to your TV screen.

2. Internal services is the management of services required to support the activities of the larger organization. These services include such functions as data processing, accounting, engineering, and maintenance. Their customers are the various departments within the organization that require such services. Incidentally, it is not uncommon for an internal service to start marketing its services outside the parent organization and become a service business itself.

Our emphasis in this chapter is on service businesses, but most of the ideas apply equally well to internal services.

A Contemporary View of Service Management

A glance at the management book section in your local bookstore gives ample evidence of the concern for service among practitioners. The way we now view service parallels the way we view quality: The **customer** is (or should be) the focal point of all decisions and actions of the service organization. This philosophy is captured nicely in the service triangle in Exhibit 5.1. Here, the customer is the center of things— the service strategy, the systems, and the people who serve him or her. From this view, the organization exists to serve the customer, and the systems and the people exist to facilitate the process of service. Some suggest that the service organization also exists to serve the workforce because they generally determine how the service is perceived by the customers. Relative to the latter point, the customer gets the kind of service that management deserves; in other words, how management treats the worker is how the worker will treat the public. If the workforce is well trained and well motivated by management, they will do good jobs for their customers.

Customer

Exhibit 5.1

The Service Triangle

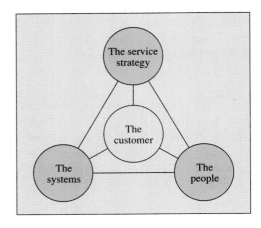

Source: Karl Albrecht and Ron Zemke, *Service America! Doing Business in the New Economy* (Burr Ridge, IL: Irwin Professional Publishing, 1985), p. 41.

The role of operations in the triangle is a major one. Operations is responsible for service systems (procedures, equipment, and facilities) and is responsible for managing the work of the service workforce, who typically comprise the majority of employees in large service organizations. But before we discuss this role in depth, it is useful to classify services to show how the customer affects the operations function.

■ AN OPERATIONAL CLASSIFICATION OF SERVICES

Service organizations are generally classified according to the service they provide (financial services, health services, transportation services, and so on). These groupings, though useful in presenting aggregate economic data, are not particularly appropriate for OM purposes because they tell us little about the process. In manufacturing, by contrast, there are fairly evocative terms to classify production activities (such as *intermittent* and *continuous production*); when applied to a manufacturing setting, they readily convey the essence of the process. While it is possible to describe services in these same terms, we need one additional item of information to reflect the fact that the customer is involved in the production system. That item, which we believe operationally distinguishes one service system from another in its production function, is the extent of customer contact in the creation of the service.

Customer contact refers to the physical presence of the customer in the system, and *creation of the service* refers to the work process involved in providing the service itself. *Extent of contact* here may be roughly defined as the percentage of time the customer must be in the system relative to the total time it takes to perform the customer service. Generally speaking, the greater the percentage of contact time between the service system and the customer, the greater the degree of interaction between the two during the production process.

Design Decision	High-Contact System (A Branch Office)	Low-Contact System (A Check Processing Center)
Facility location	Operations must be near the customer.	Operations may be placed near supply, transport, or labor.
Facility layout	Facility should accommodate the customer's physical and psychological needs and expectations.	Facility should focus on production efficiency.
Product design	Environment as well as the physical product define the nature of the service.	Customer is not in the service environment so the product can be defined by fewer attributes.
Process design	Stages of production process have a direct, immediate effect on the customer.	Customer is not involved in majority of processing steps.
Scheduling	Customer is in the production schedule and must be accommodated.	Customer is concerned mainly with completion dates.
Production planning	Orders cannot be stored, so smoothing production flow will result in loss of business.	Both backlogging and production smoothing are possible.
Worker skills	Direct workforce constitutes a major part of the service product and so must be able to interact well with the public.	Direct workforce need only have technical skills.
Quality control	Quality standards are often in the eye of the beholder and, thus, are variable.	Quality standards are generally measurable and, thus, fixed.
Time standards	Service time depends on customer needs so time standards are inherently loose.	Work is performed on customer surrogates (e.g., forms) so time standards can be tight.
Wage payment	Variable output requires time-based wage systems.	"Fixable" output permits output-based wage systems.
Capacity planning	To avoid lost sales, capacity must be set to match peak demand.	Storable output permits capacity at some average demand level.

From this conceputalization, it follows that service systems with a **high degree of customer contact** are more difficult to control and more difficult to rationalize than those with a **low degree of customer contact.** In high-contact systems, the customer can affect the time of demand, the exact nature of the service, and the quality, or perceived quality, of service since the customer is involved in the process.

Exhibit 5.2 describes the implications of this distinction. Here we see that each design decision is impacted by whether the customer is present during service delivery. We also see that when work is done behind the scenes (in this case in a bank's processing center), it is performed on customer surrogates—reports, databases, and invoices. We can thus design it according to the same principles we would use in designing a factory—to maximize the amount of items processed during the production day.

There can be tremendous diversity of customer influence and, hence, system variability within high-contact service systems. For example, a bank branch offers both simple services such as cash withdrawals that take just a minute or so, and complicated services such as loan application preparation that can take in excess of an hour.

High and Low Degree of Customer Contact

Moreover, these activities many range from being self-service through an ATM, to coproduction where bank personnel and the customer work as a team to develop the loan application. Subsequent sections of this chapter say more on ways to configure service activities.

◼ DESIGNING SERVICE ORGANIZATIONS

In designing service organizations we must remember one distinctive characteristic of services—we cannot inventory services. Unlike manufacturing, where we can build up inventory during slack periods for peak demand and thus maintain a relatively stable level of employment and production planning, in services we must (with a few exceptions) meet demand as it arises. Consequently, in services *capacity* becomes a dominant issue. Think about the many service situations you find yourself in—for example, eating in a restaurant or going to a Saturday night movie. Generally speaking, if the restaurant or the theater is full, you will decide to go someplace else. So, an important design parameter in services is "What capacity should we aim for?" Too much capacity generates excessive costs. Insufficient capacity leads to lost customers. In these situations, of course, we seek the assistance of marketing. This is one reason we have discount airfares, hotel specials on weekends, and so on. This is also a good illustration of why it is difficult to separate the operations management functions from marketing in services.

Waiting-line models, which are discussed in the supplement to this chapter, provide a powerful mathematical tool for analyzing many common service situations. Questions such as how many tellers we should have in a bank or how many phone lines we need in a mail-order operation can be analyzed with these models. These models can be easily implemented using spreadsheets.

Credit card issuer MBNA sets up scoreboards to keep employees posted on how quickly they are servicing customers. The company rates performance according to 15 standards that are posted daily.

Designing a service organization involves four elements of what James Heskett calls the "Strategic Service Vision."[2] The first element is identification of the target market (Who is our customer?); the second is the service concept (How do we differentiate our service in the market?); the third is the service strategy (What is our service package and the operating focus of our service?); and the fourth is the service delivery system (What are the actual processes, staff, and facilities by which the service is created?).

Choosing a target market and developing the service package are top management decisions setting the stage for the direct operating decisions of service strategy and delivery system design.

Several major factors distinguish service design and development from typical manufactured product development. First, the process and the product must be developed simultaneously; indeed, in services, the process is the product. (We say this with the general recognition that many manufacturers are using such concepts as concurrent engineering and DFM [design for manufacture] as approaches to more closely link product design and process design.)

Second, although equipment and software that support a service can be protected by patents and copyrights, a service operation itself lacks the legal protection commonly available to goods production. Third, the service package, rather than a definable good, constitutes the major output of the development process. Fourth, many parts of the service package are often defined by the training individuals receive before they become part of the service organization. In particular, in professional service organizations (PSOs) such as law firms and hospitals, prior certification is necessary for hiring. Fifth, many service organizations can change their service offerings virtually overnight. Routine service organizations (RSOs) such as barbershops, retail stores, and restaurants have this flexibility.

Service Strategy: Focus and Advantage

Service strategy begins by selecting the operating focus—those performance priorities—by which the service firm will compete. These include

1. Treatment of the customer in terms of friendliness and helpfulness.
2. Speed and convenience of service delivery.
3. Price of the service.
4. Variety of services (essentially a one-stop shopping philosophy).
5. Quality of the tangible goods that are central to or accompany the service. Examples include a "world-class" corned-beef sandwich, eyeglasses made while you wait, or an understandable insurance policy.
6. Unique skills that constitute the service offering, such as hair styling, brain surgery, or piano lessons.

---

[2] James Heskett, "Lessons from the Service Sector," *Harvard Business Review,* March–April 1987, pp. 118–26.

Service Focus

Exhibit 5.3 presents what we view as the operating **service focus** choices of a number of well-known companies. If our interpretation is correct, it shows that most companies choose to compete on relatively few dimensions—that trade-offs have been made. What best practices are being emphasized by service executives? While most people often think that service quality or service consistency might lead the list, a 1997 survey of executives at 181 service firms showed that accessibility to the service provider was number one. The list on the next page suggests that accessibility (defined in the study as the ability to get in touch with a service provider, any time, by multiple communication channels) is the "location, location, location" of service industries.

Exhibit 5.3

Operations Focus of Selected Service Firms

	Treatment	Speed/ Convenience	Price	Variety	Unique Skills/ Tangibles
Nordstrom Department Stores	X				
Federal Express Corporation	X	X			
Merrill Lynch & Company (Cash Management Account)		X		X[a]	
Crown Books			X		
Wal-Mart Stores	X		X[b]	X	
Price Club			X[c]		
Disneyland	X				X
American Express Company	X	X			
McDonald's Corporation		X	X		
Domino's Pizza		X[d]	X		
Marriott Corporation	X				
Club Med Resorts	X[e]		X		
American Airlines		X[f]		X	
Singapore Airlines	X				
Southwest Airlines			X[g]		
Riverside Methodist Hospital (Columbus, Ohio)	X[h]				
H & R Block		X	X		
American Automobile Association		X[i]			

---

[a] A cash management account includes checkbook, credit card, money market fund, and other services in one account.

[b] Wal-Mart controls cost of inventory by driving tough bargains with suppliers.

[c] Price Club converts shoppers into warehouse order pickers in exchange for low-priced volume purchases.

[d] First to use the automated pizza maker where an attendant puts a raw pie in one side and pulls out a cooked pie on the other.

[e] All-inclusive, low-cost resorts where staff known as *Gentils Organisateurs* (GOs) coproduce a fun vacation with the guests, *Gentils Membres* (GMs).

[f] Sabre reservation system makes it easy for travel agents to book seats and for the company to instantaneously change prices to counter competitors' rates.

[g] No-frills service (i.e., no computerized reservation system, no assigned seating, and no meals) allows lowest prices in the industry.

[h] Riverside Hospital treats patients and their families like customers—give adult heart patients teddy bears to hold and colorful smocks with hearts imprinted on them. Holding a teddy bear feels good and helps the healing process.

[i] AAA phone/computer network uses the number of the phone a customer is calling from anywhere in the United States to pinpoint the nearest AAA garage.

Items "Most" Emphasized	Item Mean*
Accessibility	4.02
Openness to employees	3.91
Leadership	3.87
Listening to the customer	3.82
Service tangibles	3.79
Employee handling of service failures	3.79
Competitive positioning	3.72
Quality values	3.68
Consistently meeting customers' needs	3.68
Customer orientation	3.66
Management involvement in quality	3.66

Scale: 1 = Little emphasis, 3 = Moderate emphasis, 5 = High emphasis.

*Top 10 most emphasized practices out of 55 best practice items listed in the survey.

Source: Aleda V. Roth, Richard B. Chase, and Chris Voss, "Service in the U.S.: A Study of Service Practice and Performance in the United States," supported by Severn Trent Plc, U.K. Government's Department of Trade and Industry, Department of National Heritage, 1997.

Integrating Marketing and Operations to Achieve Competitive Advantage

Achieving competitive advantage in services requires integration of service marketing with service delivery to meet or exceed customer expectations. This holds true no matter which competitive dimensions are emphasized. Companies that do extremely well (or extremely poorly) in this process create legends and nightmares (Exhibit 5.4).

MARKETING

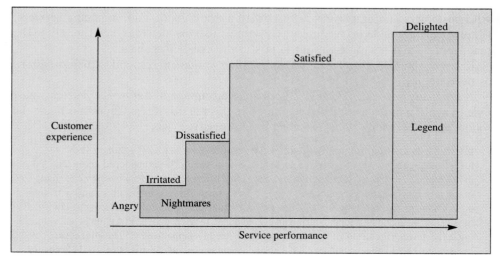

Exhibit 5.4

Levels of Satisfaction Achieved Due to Service Performance

Source: The MAC Group: Building Value through Creating a Service Advantage. 1 Montgomery St., Telesis Tower. Suite 1700, San Francisco, CA 94104, June 1990.

Exhibit 5.5

Service Measurement
Monitoring and
Recovery Process

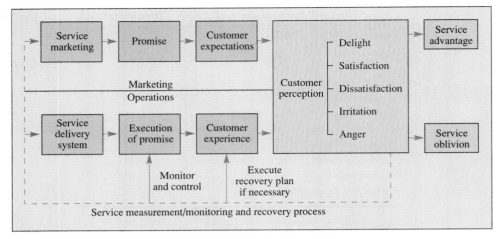

Source: The MAC Group: Building Value through Creating a Service Advantage. 1 Montgomery St., Telesis Tower. Suite 1700, San Francisco, CA 94104, June 1990.

Exhibit 5.5 gives an overview of the elements leading to service advantage and service oblivion. As it shows, marketing typically has responsibility for communicating the service promise to the customer and thereby creating customer expectations about service outcomes. Operations is responsible for the actions executing the promise and managing the customer experience. The feedback loop indicates that if outcomes are not satisfactory or do not create service advantage, management may alter either the service marketing strategy or the delivery system. The need to monitor and control the execution phase and have a recovery plan to diffuse negative reactions before the customer leaves the system is also indicated.

Monitoring and controlling involve the standard managerial actions of reassigning workers to deal with short-run demand variations (e.g., Lucky Supermarkets opening up another checkout stand when there are more than three people in line); checking with customers and employees as to how things are going; and, for many services, simply being available to customers. (Customers like the idea that they can talk to the manager . . . and few people want to talk to the assistant manager.)

Recovery planning involves training frontline workers to respond to such situations as overbooking, lost luggage, or a bad meal.

A company that can't achieve competitive advantage in its service delivery must at least achieve parity with its competitors. In this regard, Kevin Coyne has made the following observations about investing in improved service:

> Investments to reach minimum standards cannot be "traded off" against other investments; they are a cost of doing business and should be considered required investments. However, achieving effective parity often requires less investment than managers might expect, for three reasons: First, most service encounters and attributes do not matter to customers except in extreme situations. Second, most customers are indifferent to a fairly wide variation in the level of service provided for most encounters, once the lower threshold of service is reached. Finally, customers have imprecise impressions as to the actual level of service being provided, and it is often difficult for customers to compare one provider's service offerings to those of competitors. Thus,

Marriott rewards employees who provide superior customer service and gives employees decision-making authority. The company mails out one million questionnaries a year to keep informed about customer satisfaction and service gaps.

(http://www.marriott.com)

two providers may offer significantly different levels of service in a particular encounter, yet be at effective parity.[3]

One approach to measuring the economic value of customer satisfaction is to survey your customers. Ask them to rate each of a list of service and quality dimension items on two scales: importance and satisfaction. The point is to focus your attention on factors that are most important to your customers. In particular, focus on factors where their satisfaction rating is below their importance rating.

■ STRUCTURING THE SERVICE ENCOUNTER: SERVICE-SYSTEM DESIGN MATRIX

Service encounters can be configured in a number of different ways. The **service-system design matrix** in Exhibt 5.6 identifies six common alternatives.

The top of the matrix shows the degree of customer/server contact: the *buffered core,* which is physically separated from the customer; the *permeable system,* which is penetrable by the customer via phone or face-to-face contact; and the *reactive*

Service-System Design Matrix

Vol. I "Service"

Vol. II "Service System Design Matrix"

---

[3] Kevin Coyne, "Beyond Service Fads—Meaningful Strategies for the Real World." *Sloan Management Review,* Summer 1989, p. 74.

Exhibit 5.6

Service-System Design
Matrix

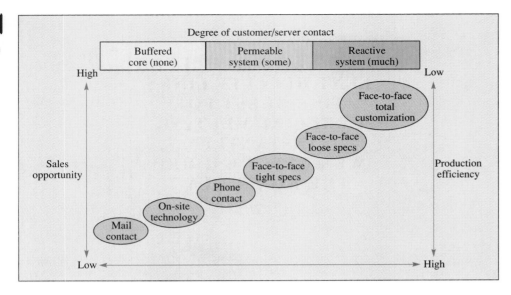

system, which is both penetrable and reactive to the customer's requirements. The left side of the matrix shows what we believe to be a logical marketing proposition, namely, that the greater the amount of contact, the greater the sales opportunity; the right side shows the impact on production efficiency as the customer exerts more influence on the operation.

The entries within the matrix list the ways in which service can be delivered. At one extreme, service contact is by mail; customers have little interaction with the system. At the other extreme, customers "have it their way" through face-to-face contact. The remaining four entries in the exhibit contain varying degrees of interaction.

As one would guess, production efficiency decreases as the customer has more contact (and therefore more influence) on the system. To offset this, the face-to-face contact provides high sales opportunity to sell additional products. Conversely, low contact, such as mail, allows the system to work more efficiently because the customer is unable to significantly affect (or disrupt) the system. However, there is relatively little sales opportunity for additional product sales.

There can be some shifting in the positioning of each entry. Consider the Exhibit 5.6 entry "face-to-face tight specs." This refers to those situations where there is little variation in the service process—neither customer nor server has much discretion in creating the service. Fast-food restaurants and Disneyland come to mind. Face-to-face loose specs refers to situations where the service process is generally understood but there are options in how it will be performed or in the physical goods that are part of it. A full-service restaurant or a car sales agency are examples. Face-to-face total customization refers to service encounters whose specifications must be developed through some interaction between the customer and server. Legal and medical services are of this type, and the degree to which the resources of the system are mustered for the service determines whether the system is reactive or merely permeable. Examples would be the mobilization of an advertising firm's resources in preparation for an

Characteristics of Workers, Operations, and Innovations Relative to the Degree of Customer/Service Contact

Exhibit 5.7

Degree of customer/server contact

Low ⟵————————————————————————⟶ High

Worker requirements	Clerical skills	Helping skills	Verbal skills	Procedural skills	Trade skills	Diagnostic skills
Focus of operations	Paper handling	Demand management	Scripting calls	Flow control	Capacity management	Client mix
Technological innovations	Office automation	Routing methods	Computer databases	Electronic aids	Self-serve	Client/worker teams

office visit by a major client, or an operating team scrambling to prepare for emergency surgery.

Exhibit 5.7 extends the design matrix. It shows the changes in workers, operations, and types of technical innovations as the degree of customer/service system contact changes. For worker requirements, the relationships between mail contact and clerical skills, on-site technology and helping skills, and phone contact and verbal skills are self-evident. Face-to-face tight specs require procedural skills in particular, because the worker must follow the routine in conducting a generally standardized, high-volume process. Face-to-face loose specs frequently call for trade skills (shoemaker, draftsperson, maitre d', dental hygienist) to finalize the design for the service. Face-to-face total customization tends to call for diagnostic skills of the professional to ascertain the needs or desires of the client.

Strategic Uses of the Matrix

The matrix in Exhibit 5.6, along with Exhibit 5.7, has both operational and strategic uses. Their operational uses are reflected in their identification of worker requirements, focus of operations, and innovations previously discussed. The strategic uses include

1. Enabling systematic integration of operations and marketing strategy. Trade-offs become more clear-cut, and more important, at least some of the major design variables are crystalized for analysis purposes. For example, the matrix indicates that it would make little sense relative to sales for a service firm to invest in high-skilled workers if it plans to operate using tight specs.

2. Clarifying exactly which combination of service delivery the firm is in fact providing. As the company incorporates the delivery options listed on the diagonal, it is becoming diversified in its production process.

3. Permitting comparison with how other firms deliver specific services. This helps to pinpoint a firm's competitive advantage.

4. Indicating evolutionary or life cycle changes that might be in order as the firm grows. Unlike the product-process matrix for manufacturing, however, where natural growth moves in one direction (from the job shop to assembly line as volume increases), evolution of service delivery can move in either direction along the diagonal as a function of a sales-efficiency trade-off.

■ SERVICE BLUEPRINTING AND FAIL-SAFING

Service Blueprint

Just as is the case with manufacturing process design, the standard tool for service process design is the flowchart. Recently, the service gurus have begun calling the flowchart a **service blueprint** to emphasize the importance of process design. A unique feature of the service blueprint is the distinction made between the high customer contact aspects of the service (i.e., that part of the process that the customer sees) and those activities that the customer does not see. This distinction is made through a "Line of Visibility" on the flowchart.

Exhibit 5.8 is a blueprint of a typical automobile service operation. Each activity that makes up a typical service encounter is mapped into the flowchart. To better show

Exhibit 5.8   Fail-Safing a Typical Automotive Service Operation

Failure: Customer forgets the need for service.
Poka-Yoke: Send automatic reminders with a 5 percent discount.

Failure: Customer cannot find service area, or does not follow proper flow.
Poka-Yoke: Clear and informative signage directing customers.

Failure: Customer has difficulty communicating problem.
Poka-Yoke: Joint inspection— service advisor repeats his/her understanding of the problem for confirmation or elaboration by the customer.

Failure: Customer does not understand the necessary service.
Poka-Yoke: Preprinted material for most services, detailing work, reasons, and possibly a graphic representation.

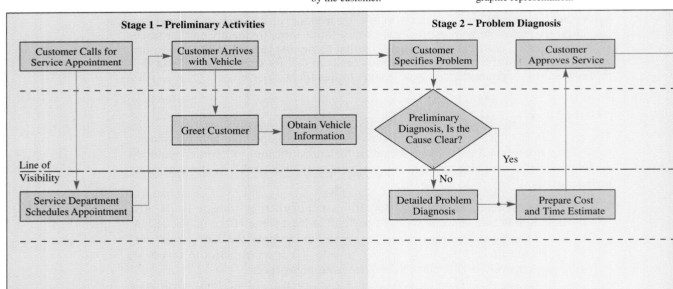

Failure: Customer arrival unnoticed.
Poka-Yoke: Use a bell chain to signal arrivals.

Failure: Customers not served in order of arrival.
Poka-Yoke: Place numbered markers on cars as they arrive.
Failure: Vehicle information incorrect and process is time consuming.
Poka-Yoke: Maintain customer database and print forms with historical information.

Failure: Incorrect diagnosis of the problem.
Poka-Yoke: High-tech check-lists, such as expert systems and diagnostic equipment.

Failure: Incorrect estimate.
Poka-Yoke: Checklists itemizing costs by common repair types.

the entity who controls the activities, levels are shown in the flowchart. The top level are those activities that are under the control of the customer. Next are those activities performed by the service manager in handling the customer. The third level are the repair activities performed in the garage; the lowest level is the internal accounting activity.

Basic blueprinting describes the features of the service design but does not provide any direct guidance for how to make the process conform to that design. A developing approach to this problem is the application of **poka-yokes**—procedures that block the inevitable mistake from becoming a service defect.[4] Poka-yokes (roughly translated from the Japanese as "avoid mistakes") are common in factories (see Chapter 6 "Quality Management," for examples) and consist of such things as fixtures to ensure

Poka-Yokes

Failure: Customer not located.
Poka-Yoke: Issue beepers to customers who wish to leave facility.

Failure: Bill is illegible.
Poka-Yoke: Top copy to customer, or plain paper bill.

Failure: Feedback not obtained.
Poka-Yoke: Customer satisfaction postcard given to customer with keys to vehicle.

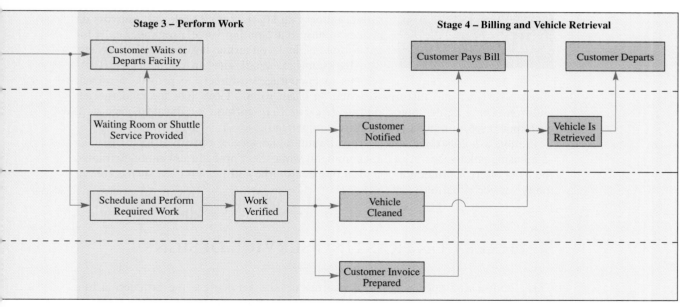

Failure: Service shuttle is inconvenient.
Poka-Yoke: Seating in available shuttles is allocated when scheduling appointments. Lack of free spaces indicates that customers needing shuttle service should be scheduled for another time.
Failure: Parts are not in stock.
Poka-Yoke: Limit switches activate signal lamps when part level falls below order point.

Failure: Vehicle not cleaned correctly.
Poka-Yoke: Person retrieving vehicle inspects, orders a touch-up if necessary, and removes floor mat in presence of customer.

Failure: Vehicle takes too long to arrive.
Poka-Yoke: When cashier enters customer's name in order to print the bill, information is electronically sent to runners who retrieve vehicle while the customer is paying.

---

[4] Richard B. Chase and Douglas M. Stewart, "Make Your Service Fail-Safe," *Sloan Management Review*, Spring 1994, pp. 35–44.

that parts can only be attached in the right way, electronic switches that automatically shut off equipment if a mistake is made, kitting of parts prior to assembly to make sure the right quantities are used, and checklists to ensure that the right sequence of steps is followed. The Toyota plant in Japan, for example, has an average of 12 poka-yoke devices per machine.[5]

There are many applications of poka-yokes to services as well. These can be classified into warning methods, physical or visual contact methods, and by what we call the **Three T's**—the Task to be done (Was the car fixed right?); the Treatment

accorded to the customer (Was the service manager courteous?); and the Tangible or environmental features of the service facility (Was the waiting area clean and comfortable?). Finally (unlike in manufacturing), service poka-yokes often must be applied to fail-safing the actions of the customer as well as the producer (i.e., the service worker).

Poka-yoke examples include height bars at amusement parks, indented trays used by surgeons to ensure that no instruments are left in the patient; chains to configure waiting lines; take-a-number systems; turnstiles; beepers on ATMs to warn people to take their card out of the machine; beepers at restaurants to make sure customers do not miss their table call; mirrors on phones to ensure a "smiling voice"; reminder calls for appointments; locks on airline lavatory doors that activate lights inside; small gifts in comment card envelopes to encourage customers to provide feedback about a service; and pictures of what "a clean room" looks like for kindergarten children. On a lighter note, look at *The Far Side* cartoon on the next page as a customer resolution poka-yoke (not recommended).

Exhibit 5.8 illustrates how a typical automobile service operation might be fail-safed using poka-yokes. As a final comment, while these procedures cannot guarantee the level of error protection found in the factory, they still can reduce such errors in many service situations.

▋ THREE CONTRASTING SERVICE DESIGNS

Three contrasting approaches to delivering on-site service are the production line approach, made famous by McDonald's Corporation; the self-service approach, made famous by ATMs and gas stations; and the personal attention approach, made famous by Nordstrom department stores and the Ritz-Carlton Hotel Company.

---

[5] See Alan Robinson and Dean Schroeder, "The Limited Role of Statistical Quality Control in Zero Defect Environment," *Production and Inventory Management Journal,* Third Quarter 1990, pp. 60–65.

THE FAR SIDE © 1992 FarWorks, Inc. Dist. by Universal Press
Syndicate. Reprinted with permission. All rights reserved.

The Production Line Approach

The production line approach pioneered by McDonald's refers to more than just the
steps required to assemble a Big Mac. Rather, as Theodore Levitt notes, it is treating
the delivery of fast food as a manufacturing process rather than a service process.[6] The
value of this philosophy is that it overcomes many problems inherent in the concept
of service itself. That is, service implies subordination or subjugation of the server to
the served; manufacturing, on the other hand, avoids this connotation because it
focuses on things rather than people. Thus in manufacturing and at McDonald's, "the
orientation is toward the efficient production of results not on the attendance on
others." Levitt notes that besides McDonald's marketing and financial skills, the
company carefully controls "the execution of each outlet's central function—the
rapid delivery of a uniform, high-quality mix of prepared foods in an environment
of obvious cleanliness, order, and cheerful courtesy. The systematic substitution of
equipment for people, combined with the carefully planned use and positioning of
technology, enables McDonald's to attract and hold patronage in proportions no
predecessor or imitator has managed to duplicate."

---

[6] Theodore Levitt, "Production-Line Approach to Service," *Harvard Business Review* 50, no. 5
(September–October 1972), pp. 41–52.

Levitt cites several aspects of McDonald's operations to illustrate the concepts. Note the extensive use of what we term poka-yokes.

· The McDonald's french fryer allows cooking of the optimum number of french fries at one time.
· A wide-mouthed scoop is used to pick up the precise amount of french fries for each order size. (The employee never touches the product.)
· Storage space is expressly designed for a predetermined mix of prepackaged and premeasured products.
· Cleanliness is pursued by providing ample trash cans in and outside each facility. (Larger outlets have motorized sweepers for the parking area.)
· Hamburgers are wrapped in color-coded paper.
· Through painstaking attention to total design and facilities planning, everything is built integrally into the (McDonald's) machine itself—into the technology of the system. The only choice available to the attendant is to operate it exactly as the designers intended. Using our service-system design matrix (Exhibit 5.6), we would categorize this as a face-to-face tight spec service.

The Self-Service Approach

In contrast to the production line approach, C. H. Lovelock and R. F. Young propose that the service process can be enhanced by having the customer take a greater role in the production of the service.[7] Automatic teller machines, self-service gas stations, salad bars, and in-room coffee-making equipment in motels are approaches that shift the service burden to the consumer. Based on our service-system design matrix, these are great examples of the use of on-site technology. Many customers like self-service because it puts them in control. For others, this philosophy requires some selling on the part of the service organization to convince customers that it helps them. To this end, Lovelock and Young propose a number of steps, including developing customer trust; promoting the benefits of cost, speed, and convenience; and following up to make sure that the procedures are being effectively used. In essence, this turns customers into "partial employees" who must be trained in what to do and, as noted earlier, be "fail-safed" in case of mistake.

It is often most profitable to provide both full service and self-service at the same facility. As Globerson and Maggard report, "Analysis of gasoline sales after decontrol of the U.S. gasoline market in 1981 shows that cutting prices for self-service gasoline while increasing prices for full service increased dealer profits, in spite of the fact that self-service gas sales increased by from about 22 percent in 1978 to 41 percent in 1984."[8]

The Personal Attention Approach

An interesting contrast in the way personal attention is provided can be seen in Nordstrom Department Stores and the Ritz-Carlton Hotel Company.

---

[7] C. H. Lovelock and R. F. Young, "Look to Customers to Increase Productivity," *Harvard Business Review* 57, no. 2, pp. 168–78.
[8] S. Globerson and M. J. Maggard, "A Conceptual Model of Self-Service," *International Journal of Production and Operations Management* 11, no. 4 (1991) pp. 33–43.

At Nordstrom, a rather loose, unstructured process relies on developing a relationship between the individual salesperson and the customer (this is a face-to-face with total customization service). At the Ritz-Carlton, the process is virtually scripted, and the information system rather than the employee keeps track of the guest's (customer's) personal preferences (this is a face-to-face loose spec example). Tom Peters describes Nordstrom's approach here:

> After several visits to a store's men's clothing department, a customer's suit still did not fit. He wrote the company president, who sent a tailor to the customer's office with a new suit for fitting. When the alterations were completed, the suit was delivered to the customer—free of charge.
>
> This incident involved the $1.3 billion, Seattle-based Nordstrom, a specialty clothing retailer. Its sales per square foot are about five times that of a typical department store. Who received the customer's letter and urged the extreme (by others' standards) response? Co-chairman John Nordstrom.
>
> The frontline providers of this good service are well paid. Nordstrom's salespersons earn a couple of bucks an hour more than competitors, plus a 6.75 percent commission. Its top salesperson moves over $1 million a year in merchandise. Nordstrom lives for its customers and salespeople. Its only official organization chart puts the customer at the top, followed by sales and sales support people. Next come department managers, then store managers, and the board of directors at the very bottom.
>
> Salespersons religiously carry a "personal book," where they record voluminous information about each of their customers; senior, successful salespeople often have three or four bulging books, which they carry everywhere, according to Betsy Sanders, the vice president who orchestrated the firm's wildly successful penetration of the tough southern California market. "My objective is to get one new personal customer a day," says a budding Nordstrom star. The system helps him do just that. He has a virtually unlimited budget to send cards, flowers, and thank-you notes to customers. He also is encouraged to shepherd his customer to any department in the store to assist in a successful shopping trip.
>
> He also is abetted by what may be the most liberal returns policy in this or any other business: Return *anything,* no questions asked. Sanders says that "trusting customers," or "our bosses" as she repeatedly calls them, is vital to the Nordstrom philosophy. President Jim Nordstrom told the *Los Angeles Times,* "I don't care if they roll a Goodyear tire into the store. If they say they paid $200, give them $200 (in cash) for it." Sanders acknowledges that a few customers rip the store off—"rent hose from us," to use a common insider's line. But this is more than offset by goodwill from the 99 percent-plus who benefit from the "No Problem at Nordstrom" logo that the company lives up to with unmatched zeal.
>
> No bureaucracy gets in the way of serving the customer. Policy? Sanders explains to a dumbfounded group of Silicon Valley executives, "I know this drives the lawyers nuts, but our whole 'policy manual' is just one sentence, 'Use your own best judgment at all times'." One store manager offers a translation, "Don't chew gum. Don't steal from us."[9]

The Ritz-Carlton approach is described in the following excerpts from the company's Baldrige Award Application Summary and discussions with Scott Long of Ritz-Carlton's Huntington Hotel in Pasadena, California. Exhibit 5.9 shows the formalized service procedure (the Three Steps of Service). Exhibit 5.10 displays the information system used to capture data about guests ("The Ritz-Carlton Repeat Guest History Program"). Note that the three steps of service are integrated into the guest history information system.

---

[9] Tom Peters, *Quality!* (Palo Alto, CA: TPC Communications. 1986), pp. 10–12.

The Ritz-Carlton
Hotel Company
(Three Steps of
Service)

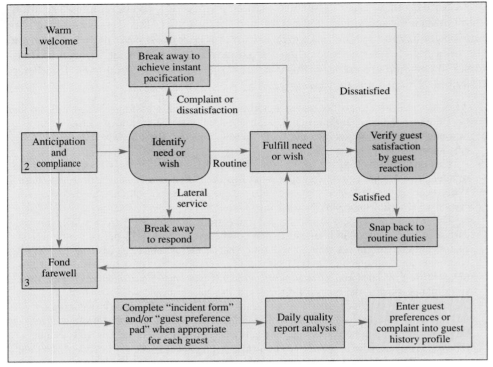

Source: *Ritz-Carlton Malcolm Baldrige National Quality Award Application Summary,* 1993, p. 11.

The Ritz-Carlton Repeat Guest History Program (An Aid to Highly Personalized Service
Delivery)

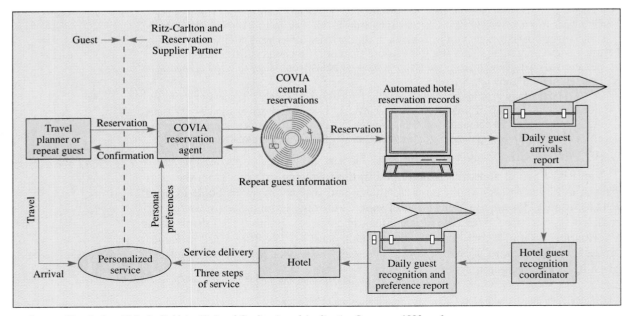

Source: *Ritz-Carlton Malcolm Baldrige National Quality Award Application Summary,* 1993, p. 6.

Systems for the collection and utilization of customer reaction and satisfaction are widely deployed and extensively used throughout the organization. Our efforts are centered on various customer segments and product lines.

Our approach is the use of systems which allow every employee to collect and utilize quality-related data on a daily basis. These systems provide critical, responsive data which includes:

(1) On-line guest preference information;
(2) Quantity of error free products and services;
(3) Opportunities for quality improvement.

Our automated property management systems enable the on-line access and utilization of guest preference information at the individual customer level. All employees collect and input this data, and use the data as part of their service delivery with individual guests.

Our quality production reporting system is a method of aggregating hotel level data from nearly two dozen sources into a summary format. It serves as an early warning system and facilitates analysis. The processes employees use to identify quality opportunities for improvement are standardized in a textbook, and available throughout our organization.[10]

No matter what approach is taken to design a service, the need for the service characteristics shown in the box titled "Seven Characteristics of a Well-Designed Service System" should be evident.

■ SERVICE GUARANTEES AS DESIGN DRIVERS

The phrase "Positively, absolutely, overnight" is an example of a service guarantee most of us know by heart. Hiding behind such marketing promises of service satisfaction are a set of actions that must be taken by the operations organization to fulfill these promises.

Thousands of companies have launched **service guarantees** as a marketing tool designed to provide peace of mind for customers unsure about trying their service. From an operations perspective, a service guarantee can be used not only as an improvement tool but also at the design stage to focus the firm's delivery system squarely on the things it must do so well to satisfy the customer.

Even professional service firms such as Rath and Strong Consulting have service guarantees. (Theirs allows the client to choose from a menu of payouts if they do not, for example, cut lead time by *x* percent. Menu options include refunds and no charge for overtime work to get the job done.)

The elements of a good service guarantee are that it is:[11]

Unconditional (no small print).

Meaningful to the customer (the payoff fully covers the customer's dissatisfaction).

Easy to understand and communicate (for employees as well as customers).

Painless to invoke (given proactively).

Service Guarantees

---

[10] *Ritz-Carlton Malcolm Baldrige National Quality Award Application Summary.* 1993, p. 6.

[11] Christopher W. L. Hart, "The Power of Unconditional Service Guarantee," *Harvard Business Review* 56, no. 4 (July–August 1988), p. 55.

Seven
Characteristics
of a
Well-Designed
Service System

1. *Each element of the service system is consistent with the operating focus of the firm.* For example, when the focus is on speed of delivery, each step in the process should help to foster speed.

2. *It is user-friendly.* This means that the customer can interact with it easily—that is, it has good signage, understandable forms, logical steps in the process, and service workers available to answer questions.

3. *It is robust.* That is, it can cope effectively with variations in demand and resource availability. For example, if the computer goes down, effective backup systems are in place to permit service to continue.

4. *It is structured so that consistent performance by its people and systems is easily maintained.* This means the tasks required of the workers are doable, and the supporting technologies are truly supportive and reliable.

5. *It provides effective links between the back office and the front office so that nothing falls between the cracks.* In football parlance, there should be "no fumbled handoffs."

6. *It manages the evidence of service quality in such a way that customers see the value of the service provided.* Many services do a great job behind the scenes but fail to make this visible to the customer. This is particularly true where a service improvement is made. Unless customers are made aware of the improvement through explicit communication about it, the improved performance is unlikely to gain maximum impact.

7. *It is cost-effective.* There is minimum waste of time and resources in delivering the service. Even if the service outcome is satisfactory, customers are often put off by a service company that appears inefficient.

An issue of growing importance in service relates to the ethical and possibly legal responsibility of a company to actually provide the service that is promised. For example, is an airline responsible for transporting a passenger with a guaranteed reservation, even though the flight has been overbooked? Or consider the Internet service provider's responsibility to provide enough phone lines so that customers do not receive busy signals when they try to connect to the service (see the case entitled, "AOL's Move to Flat-Rate Pricing"). These are difficult issues, because having excess capacity is expensive. Demand can be nearly impossible to predict with great accuracy, thus making the estimates of needed capacity difficult.

A very powerful tool, though, is available to help better understand the relationships between the factors that drive a service system. These factors include the average number of customers that arrive over a period of time, the average time that it takes to serve each customer, the number of servers, and information about the size of the customer population. Waiting line models have been developed that allow the estimation of expected waiting time and expected resource utilization. This is the topic of the supplement to this chapter.

■ CONCLUSION

In this chapter, we have shown how service businesses are in many ways very similar to manufacturing businesses. Likewise is the need for tradeoffs in developing a focus. Focus, for example, is important to success, just as it was with the design of manufacturing systems.

The service-system design matrix is in many ways similar to the product-process matrix we used to categorize manufacturing operations. Further, the tools of flow diagrams and capacity analysis are similar as well.

Services are, however, very different compared to manufacturing when we consider the high degree of personalization often required, the speed of delivery needed, the direct customer contact, and the inherent variability of the service encounter. The buffering and scheduling mechanisms that we have available to smooth the demand placed on a manufacturing operation are often not available to the service operation. Services generally require much higher levels of capacity relative to demand. In addition, it places a greater need for flexibility on the part of the workers involved in providing the service.

REVIEW AND DISCUSSION QUESTIONS

1. Who is the "customer" in a jail? A cemetery? A summer camp for children?

2. How have price and variety competition changed McDonald's basic formula for success?

3. Could a service firm use a production line approach or self-serve design and still keep a high customer focus (personal attention)? Explain and support your answer with examples.

4. Why should a manager of a bank home office be evaluated differently than a manager of a bank branch?

5. Identify the high-contact and low-contact operations of the following services:
   a. A dental office.
   b. An airline.
   c. An accounting office.
   d. An automobile agency.

6. Some suggest that customer expectation is the key to service success. Give an example from your own experience to support or refute this assertion.

7. Where would you place a drive-in church, a campus food vending machine, and a bar's automatic mixed drink machine on the service-system design matrix?

8. Can a manufacturer have a service guarantee in addition to a product guarantee?

9. Suppose you were the manager of a restaurant and you were told honestly that a couple eating dinner had just seen a mouse. What would you say to them? How would you recover from this service crisis?

PROBLEMS

1. Place the following functions of a department store on the service-system design matrix: mail order (i.e., catalog), phone order, hardware, stationery, apparel, cosmetics, customer service (i.e., complaints).

   1. See SM.

2. Do the same as in the previous problem for a hospital with the following activities and relationships: physician/patient, nurse/patient, billing, medical records, lab tests, admissions, diagnostic tests (e.g., X-rays).

   2. See SM.

3. Perform a quick service audit the next time you go shopping at a department store. Evaluate the three T's of service: the Task, the Treatment and the Tangible features of the service on a 1 (poor), 3 (average), and 5 (excellent). Remember that the tangible features include the environment, layout, and appearance of the store, not the goods you purchased.

   3. See SM.

4. See SM.

4. SYSTEM DESCRIPTION EXERCISE

The beginning step in studying a productive system is to develop a description of that system. Once a system is described, we can better determine why the system works well or poorly and recommend production-related improvements. Since we are all familiar with fast-food restaurants, try your hand at describing the production system employed at, say, a McDonald's. In doing so, answer the following questions:

a. What are the important aspects of the service package?

b. Which skills and attitudes are needed by the service personnel?

c. How can customer demand be altered?

d. Provide a rough-cut blueprint of the delivery system. (It is not necessary to provide execution times. Just diagram the basic flow through the system.) Critique the blueprint. Are there any unnecessary steps or can fail points be eliminated?

e. Can the customer/provider interface be changed to include more technology? More self-serve?

f. Which measures are being used to evaluate and measure the service? Which could be used?

g. How does it measure up on the seven characteristics of a well-designed service?

Case

Kinko's Copier Stores

"We're not your average printer," says Annie Odell, Kinko's regional manager for Louisiana. She's right. She may have the only printshops in town where customers come as much for the company as for the copies. It's a free-wheeling, hitech operation that marches to the beat of a different drum machine. It looks chaotic; it is chaotic. Yet it produces profit as well as fun.

Odell's copy shop empire has grown from one to seven in six years, including five in the greater New Orleans area.

Kinko's keeps its sales figures a secret, but Odell estimates her New Orleans stores make about 40 million copies a year. At the firm's advertised 4½ cents-per-copy price, that would mean around $1.8 millon a year in sales, or an average of over $300,000 per shop. The New Orleans operations rank among Kinko's top 25 percent nationally, reports Becky Barieau of Kinko's of Georgia.

Sales in New Orleans have climbed even while the marketplace has been sinking. At the Carrollton store, revenues increased 10 percent over last year, an excellent showing considering the 4½ cents-per-copy rate has not budged since 1980.

"Depression seems to generate more need for copies," says Wallis Windsor, manager of the Carrollton store, "There are bankruptcies, legal documents and resumes—hundreds of people who want 50 copies of their resumes on specialty paper."

Printers Sneer

Kinko's is unique. For one thing, it doesn't do a lick of offset printing. It makes copies, copies, and almost nothing but copies. On the side it binds, folds, staples, collates, makes pads, and takes passport photos.

Kinko's is also unique among quick printing chains in that it doesn't franchise. All 300 or so Kinko's stores are divided among a few closely held corporations, and founder Paul Orfalea holds a piece of virtually all of them. Odell explains that the company avoids franchising to ensure tight control over quality at its outlets.

Others attribute the structure to a desire to avoid the legal restrictions and paperwork demanded by setting up franchises in different states. How it's been kept together is a management feat in itself.

Even the name sticks out. The Yellow Pages list dozens of quick printers with some reference to speed in their names, often intentionally misspelled. "Kinko's" denotes a place that's . . . well, a little kinky. For the record, Orfalea, who plugged in his first photocopier when he was in college, was nicknamed by classmates as "Kinko" for his curly head of hair.

Broadway and Benihana

Kinko's management style draws on both the restaurant business and the stage. Fast copies are like fast food, say the managers. It's not just that every Big Mac is a copy of every other one. Images of eating come up again and again as they try to explain what keeps their customers coming back.

"Making copies is addictive," says Windsor, and points to her clientele of "regulars," who "have made this their office. They will spend four or five hours here although they don't spend more than $5 or $6. People have suggested we open a bar in here."

"Instant gratification is what Kinko's is offering," says another manager.

The last time managers from around the country huddled in Santa Barbara for the company "picnic," they studied looseleaf binders crammed full of floor plans for McDonald's and Benihana of Tokyo—a variation on the acclaimed art of Japanese management.

"You'd find it hard to believe," says Odell, "but Benihana is a lot like Kinko's. They're masters of efficiency. We'll try to set up the floor to get one person operating two copiers, just like Benihana puts one cook between two tables. Our paper is centrally located, just as they have all the chopping prepared ahead of time. Then there's the floater, who floats around and pops in wherever he's needed."

Both Kinko's and Benihana's use theater to attract clients, charging their employees with putting on a good show as well as putting out good service. At the Japanese restaurant, the show is the cook, who sizzles a sukiyaki right in front of your table. At Kinko's it's the clatter of copy machines and the Charlie Chaplin-like spectacle of operators running back and forth between them.

"They do it right in front of you and you get instant quality control," says Odell, "There's no way you're going to drop that document with the customer watching you."

She deliberately displays all her machines and personnel in one big room. "We work out with the public. That's why it's fun," says Odell, "The other guys are behind closed doors."

Windsor enjoys working in a fishbowl. "My personality changes," she says. "I'll be a little more dramatic and louder than I would be in a closed group. I walk quickly. I'll wad up and throw papers a lot."

She believes customers unconsciously get into the act. "Some of the mildest-mannered people get aggressive in here. I've seen a little old lady elbow her way in ahead of people, where if she were in a bank she'd stand in line neatly."

Kinko's does no broadcast and little print advertising, counting on price and word-of-mouth to draw customers, and ambience doesn't hurt. Each Kinko's has its "regulars," who get friendly with particular operators and who favor particular machines. The area in front of the counter is strewn with computers, lettering machines and light tables, all the better to hook people into making themselves comfortable and coming back.

A recent addition to that melange is the customer comment form. The customer mails the postage-paid form straight to headquarters in Santa Barbara, where senior management review it and send a thank-you note to the author before routing it back to the shop manager for action. Odell has several inches of forms on file, along with notes on the follow-up calls she made to the customers.

"We don't choose our market so much as our market chooses us," she says. Each shop keeps a different mix of machines, depending on the needs of its patrons. An operator learns quickly that the Xerox 1000 series picks up blue but not yellow, while the 9000 series picks up yellow and black but not blue. Thus, the store adjoining the Tulane campus does not have a 9000 because students tend to bring in notes and books highlighted with yellow markers.

Another adaptation to the market is "Professor Publishing," a service which lets professors excerpt chapters from several books and print them up together as a single textbook. During the first two weeks of every semester, the Broadway office works virtually around-the-clock on this specialty.

Odell maintains that her managers clear all material with publishers before printing a professor's anthology. Indeed, Kinko's says it is one of the most scrupulous of the copy chains about observing copyright laws.

Printing in a Fishbowl

If working at the Kinko's shops in New Orleans is like working in a fishbowl, it's a two-way fishbowl where the fish are always peering back at their audience. The crazy-quilt mix of customers provides endless entertainment and a fund of oddball stories to exchange over beers. A sampling:

- One woman insisted that the manager throw away the ribbon on the self-service typewriter she'd just used, fearing that someone might try to use it to recreate her document. Another customer wanted several confidential pages typed, and asked, "Can you get me a typist who won't read them?"

- Some artists enjoy using the photocopiers for the oddest things. One woman brings in stuffed dead birds for reproduction. Another brought in a box of pecans purported to be from the backyard of a house where Tennessee Williams once lived.

- A tipsy woman, about 25 years of age, meandered in from a Mardi Gras parade, curled up next to a window, and fell asleep. There she remained for four hours, while the copiers and binding machines pounded and rattled. Manager Raynell Murphy called the home office. "What should I do?" She asked. "Get a picture," came the word from California, "We can use it as a promotion, you know, to show what a relaxed atmosphere we have at Kinko's."

- Finally, a hulking woman who had just bought some copies walked over to the sleeper, kicked her a couple of times, and asked, "Are you ready yet?" The sleeper arose and groggily headed out the door.

Questions

1. Can general operational standards be developed and implemented in all or a majority of Kinko's shops?

2. Discuss the idea of grouping copiers in machine centers so that certain copiers are available for specific tasks.

3. How do the different services offered (private copying versus copying services provided) present separate types of problems for management?

Source: Mark Ballard, "Working in a Fishbowl," *Quick Printing,* May 1987, pp. 30–32. Reprinted by permission.

Case

AOL's Move to Flat-Rate Pricing

This case traces the mess that America Online got itself in when they moved to flat-rate pricing in late 1996. The number of people who signed up for AOL's flat-rate service exceeded all expectations. In January 1997, *The Wall Street Journal* article by Thomas Petzinger blasts AOL for not anticipating the customer response. In a second article, about a week later, we see that the government has gotten involved and is forcing AOL to make amends to their customers.

"Gunning for Growth," AOL's Steve Case Shot Himself in the Foot[1]

To some people, the customer-service crisis at America Online is a technology issue. Others see it as a management issue. Predictably, a few opportunistic lawyers are trying to turn it into a legal issue.

But I think one thing's for sure: The service breakdown at AOL is an ethical issue. Today's topsy-turvy business world does not excuse a company from offering a product it knows it cannot reliably deliver.

Here's the gist of the morality play: Eager for market share as competition heats up in the on-line world, AOL offered a deep price cut, publicly admitting it would have trouble meeting the added demand. In fact, the strain on the system had exceeded the company's worst fears. AOL is now hitting many of its eight million customers—me, for instance—with an unremitting busy

signal instead of the instant communication services it assured them they could count on.

Compounding the problem, millions of business people have come to depend on the service to some degree, meaning that AOL's failings reach its customers' customers. It gets worse. Although AOL says it has severely cut back on marketing, at the very moment I was listening to AOL's busy signal the other day my kids were watching the company's pitch for new customers over the Nickelodeon network, complete with a toll-free number. You can get through to sign up, but not to log in.

AOL to Pay Refunds to Its Customers[2]

America Online Inc., bowing to pressure from attorneys general in 36 states, reached a preliminary settlement yesterday that will require it to pay refunds of up to $40 per customer to compensate frustrated subscribers who have been unable to gain unlimited access to the crowded on-line service for the past two months.

The tentative settlement announced yesterday requires AOL to provide customers who used the service less than two hours each month in December and January with a refund of $39.90—twice the monthly fee for unlimited access. AOL also must cease advertising during the month of February, and any advertising after that must disclose that users might encounter problems getting on-line. The on-line service also must make it easier for customers to cancel their subscriptions,

---

[1] Adapted from Thomas Petzinger, Jr., "The Front Lines," *The Wall Street Journal,* January 24, 1997, p. B1.

[2] Adapted from Jared Sandberg, "AOL to Pay Refunds to Its Customers," *The Wall Street Journal,* January 30, 1997, p. A3. © 1997 Dow Jones & Company, Inc. All rights reserved worldwide.

providing fax numbers and postal addresses to do so, and will have to provide written reports to the state officials updating them on the progress of the refunds.

Questions

1. Should AOL be held accountable for its inability to provide immediate access to its network?

2. Compare the case of AOL with that of airline companies who regularly oversell their seats.

3. Suggest a policy that AOL should use that relates the capacity of their system to the number of potential users.

4. Should the government get involved in this?

SELECTED BIBLIOGRAPHY

Bitran, Gabriel R., and Johannes Hoech. "The Humanization of Service: Respect at the Moment of Truth." *Sloan Management Review,* Winter 1990, pp. 89–96.

Chase, R. B. "The Mall Is My Factory: Reflections of a Service Junkie." *Production and Operations Management,* Winter 1996, pp. 298–308.

_____. "The Customer Contact Approach to Services: Theoretical Bases and Practical Extensions." *Operations Research* 21, no. 4 (1981), pp. 698–705.

_____. and D. M. Stewart. "Make Your Service Fail-Safe," *Sloan Management Review,* Spring 1994, pp. 35–44.

_____. *Mistake-Proofing: How to Design Errors Out.* Cambridge, MA: Productivity Press, 1994.

Cohen, Morris A., and Hau L. Lee. "Out of Touch with Customer Needs?" *Sloan Management Review,* Winter 1990, pp. 55–56.

Colley, John L. *Case Studies in Service Operations.* Duxbury Press: Wadsworth Publishing Company, 1996.

Collier, D. A. *The Service/Quality Solution.* Burr Ridge, IL: Irwin Professional Publishing, 1993.

Farsad, Behshid, and Ahmad K. Elshennawy. "Defining Service Quality Is Difficult for Service and Manufacturing Firms." *Industrial Engineering,* March 1989, pp. 17–20.

Finsthal, Timothy W. "My Employees Are My Service Guarantee." *Harvard Business Review,* July–August 1989, pp. 28–33.

Fitzsimmons, J. A., and R. S. Sullivan. *Service Operations Management.* New York: McGraw-Hill, 1983.

Flint, Jerry, and William Heuslein. "An Urge to Service." *Forbes,* September 18, 1989, pp. 172–74.

Hackett, Gregory P. "Investment in Technology: The Service Sector Sinkhole?" *Sloan Management Review,* Winter 1990, pp. 97–103.

Hart, Christopher W. L. "The Power of Unconditional Service Guarantees." *Harvard Business Review,* July–August 1988, pp. 54–62.

Heskett, J. L. *Managing in the Service Economy.* Cambridge, MA: Harvard University Press, 1986.

Heskett, James L.; W. Earl Sasser, Jr; and Christopher L. Hart. *Service Breakthroughs: Changing the Rules of the Game.* New York: Free Press, 1990.

Pyzdek, Thomas. "Toward Service Systems Engineering." *Quality Management Journal,* April 1986, pp. 26–42.

Roth, Aleda V., Richard B. Chase; and Chris Voss. "Service in the U.S.: A Study of Service Practice and Performance in the United States," supported by Severn Trent Plc, U.K. Government's Department of Trade and Industry, Department of National Heritage, 1997.

Shapiro, Benson P., V. Kasturi Rangan, Rowland T. Moriarty, and Elliot B. Ross. "Manage Customers for Profits, Not Just Sales." *Harvard Business Review,* September–October 1987, pp. 101–8.

Sonnenberg, Frank K. "Service Quality: Forethought, Not Afterthought." *Journal of Business Strategy,* September–October 1989, pp. 54–57.

Waiting Line Management

Supplement Outline

Economics of the Waiting Line Problem, 169
    Cost Effectiveness Balance
    The Practical View of Waiting Lines

The Queuing System, 170
    Customer Arrivals
    The Queuing System
    Exit

Waiting Line Models, 180

Computer Simulation of Waiting Lines 189

Key Terms

Queue

Queuing System

Arrival Rate

Exponential Distribution

Poisson Distribution

Service Rate

Single Channel, Single Phase

Multichannel, Multiphase

Finite Queue

www Links

Disney Enterprises, Inc. (http://www.disney.com)

Understanding waiting lines or **queues** and learning how to manage them is one of the most important areas in operations management. It is basic to creating schedules, job design, inventory levels, and so on. In our service economy we wait in line every day, from driving to work to checking out at the supermarket. We also encounter waiting lines at factories—jobs wait in lines to be worked on at different machines, and machines themselves wait their turn to be overhauled. In short, waiting lines are pervasive.

Queues

In this supplement we discuss the basic elements of waiting line problems and provide standard steady-state formulas for solving them. These formulas, arrived at through queuing theory, enable planners to analyze service requirements and establish service facilities appropriate to stated conditions. Queuing theory is broad enough to cover such dissimilar delays as those encountered by customers in a shopping mall or aircraft in a holding pattern awaiting landing slots. Recently, Internet access providers have had problems providing enough modem telephone lines for subscribers dialing into the Internet. This problem can be analyzed by queuing models.

■ ECONOMICS OF THE WAITING LINE PROBLEM

The central problem in virtually every waiting line situation is a trade-off decision. The manager must weigh the added cost of providing more rapid service (more traffic lanes, additional landing strips, more checkout stands) against the inherent cost of waiting.

Frequently, the cost trade-off decision is straightforward. For example, if we find that the total time our employees spend in the line waiting to use a copying machine would otherwise be spent in productive activities, we could compare the cost of installing one additional machine to the value of employee time saved. The decision could then be reduced to dollar terms and the choice easily made.

On the other hand, suppose that our waiting line problem centers on demand for beds in a hospital. We can compute the cost of additional beds by summing the costs for building construction, additional equipment required, and increased maintenance. But what is on the other side of the scale? Here we are confronted with the problem of trying to place a dollar figure on a patient's need for a hospital bed that is unavailable. While we can estimate lost hospital income, what about the human cost arising from this lack of adequate hospital care?

Cost Effectiveness Balance

Exhibit S5.1 shows the essential trade-off relationship under typical (steady-state) customer traffic conditions. Initially, with minimal service capacity, the waiting line cost is at a maximum. As service capacity is increased, there is a reduction in the number of customers in the line and in their waiting times, which decreases waiting line cost. The variation in this function is often represented by the negative exponential curve. The cost of installing service capacity is shown simplistically as a linear rather than step function. The aggregate or total cost is shown as a U-shaped curve, a common approximation in such equilibrium problems. The idealized optimal cost is found at the crossover point between the service capacity and waiting line curves.

The Practical View of Waiting Lines

Before we proceed with a technical presentation of waiting line theory, it is useful to look at the intuitive side of the issue to see what it means. Exhibit S5.2 shows arrivals

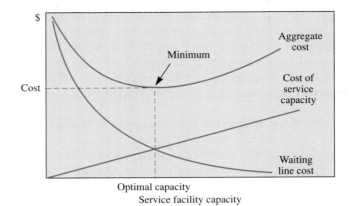

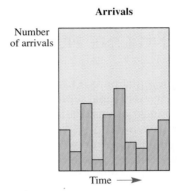 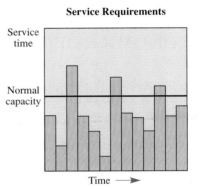

at a service facility (e.g., a bank) and service requirements at that facility (e.g., tellers, loan officer). One important variable is the number of arrivals over the course of the hours that the service system is open. From the service delivery viewpoint, customers demand varying amounts of service, often exceeding normal capacity. We can have some control over arrivals in a variety of ways. For example, we can have a short line (such as a drive-in at a fast food restaurant with only several spaces), we can establish specific hours for specific customers, or we can run specials. For the server, we can affect service time by using faster or slower servers, faster or slower machines, different tooling, different material, different layout, faster setup time, and so on.

The essential point is waiting lines are *not* a fixed condition of a productive system but are to a very large extent within the control of the system management and design. Professor Richard Larson (the famous "wait-watcher") and his colleagues offer useful suggestions for managing queues based on their research in the banking industry. (See the box, "Suggestions for Managing Queues.")

■ THE QUEUING SYSTEM

Queuing
System

The **queuing system** consists essentially of three major components: (1) the source population and the way customers arrive at the system, (2) the servicing system, and (3) the condition of the customer exiting the system (back to source population or not?), as seen in Exhibit S5.3. The following sections discuss each of these areas.

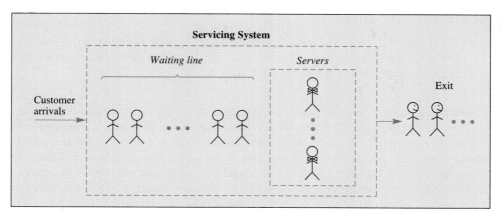

Servicing System

Waiting line   *Servers*

Customer arrivals   Exit

Components of a Queuing System

The following are some useful suggestions for managing queues that go beyond the quantitative waiting line models.

1. *Determine an acceptable waiting time for your customers.* How long do your customers expect to wait? Set operational objectives based on what is acceptable.

2. *Try to divert your customer's attention when waiting.* Providing music, a video, or some other form of entertainment may help to distract the customers from the fact they are waiting.

3. *Inform your customers of what to expect.* This is especially important when the waiting time will be longer than normal. Tell them why the waiting time is longer than normal and what you are doing to alleviate the queue.

4. *Keep employees not serving the customers out of sight.* Nothing is more frustrating to someone waiting in line than to see employees who potentially could be serving those in line, working on other activities.

5. *Segment customers.* If a group of customers needs something that can be done very quickly, give them a special line so they do not have to wait for the slower customers.

6. *Train your servers to be friendly.* Greeting the customer by name, or providing some other special attention, can go a long way toward overcoming the negative feeling of a long wait. (Hint: Rather than telling servers to just "be friendly," psychologists suggest that workers be told when to invoke specific friendly actions such as smiling—when greeting customers, when taking orders, and when giving change (in a convenience store). Tests using such specific behavioral actions have shown significant increases in perceived friendliness of the servers in the eyes of the customer.)

7. *Encourage customers to come during the slack periods.* Inform customers of times when they usually would not have to wait; also, tell them when the peak periods are—this may help to smooth the load.

8. *Take a long term perspective toward getting rid of the queues.* Develop plans for alternative ways to serve your customers. Where appropriate, develop plans for automating or speeding up the process in some manner. This is not to say you want to eliminate personal attention; some customers expect this.

Suggestions for Managing Queues

Source: Based on K. Katz, B. M. Larson, and R. C. Larson, "Prescription for the Waiting-in-Line Blues," *Sloan Management Review,* Winter 1991, pp. 51–52.

Customer Arrivals

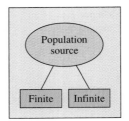

Arrivals at a service system may be drawn from a *finite* or an *infinite* population. The distinction is important because the analyses are based on different premises and require different equations for their solution.

Finite Population   A *finite population* refers to the limited-size customer pool that will use the service and, at times, form a line. The reason this finite classification is important is because when a customer leaves its position as a member for the population (a machine breaking down and requiring service, for example), the size of the user group is reduced by one, which reduces the probability of the next occurrence. Conversely, when a customer is serviced and returns to the user group, the population increases and the probability of a user requiring service also increases. This finite class of problems requires a separate set of formulas from that of the infinite population case.

As an example, consider a group of six machines maintained by one repairperson. When one machine breaks down, the source population is reduced to five, and the chances of one of the remaining five breaking down and needing repair is certainly less than when six machines were operating. If two machines are down with only four operating, the probability of another breakdown is again changed. Conversely, when a machine is repaired and returned to service, the machine population increases, thus raising the probability of the next breakdown. A finite population model with one server that can be used in such cases is presented in Exhibits S5.7 and S5.9.

Infinite Population   An *infinite population* is one large enough in relation to the service system so that the population size caused by subtractions or additions to the population (a customer needing service or a serviced customer returning to the population) does not significantly affect the system probabilities. If, in the preceding finite explanation, there were 100 machines instead of six, then if one or two machines broke down, the probabilities for the next breakdowns would not be very different and the assumption could be made without a great deal of error that the population (for all practical purposes) was infinite. Nor would the formulas for "infinite" queuing problems cause much error if applied to a physician with 1,000 patients or a department store with 10,000 customers.

Arrival Rate

Distribution of Arrivals   When describing a waiting system, we need to define the manner in which customers or the waiting units are arranged for service.

Waiting line formulas generally require an **arrival rate,** or the number of units per period (such as an average of one every six minutes). A *constant* arrival distribution is periodic, with exactly the same time period between successive arrivals. In productive systems, about the only arrivals that truly approach a constant interval period are those that are subject to machine control. Much more common are *variable* (random) arrival distributions.

In observing arrivals at a service facility, we can look at them from two viewpoints: First, we can analyze the time between successive arrivals to see if the times follow some statistical distribution. Usually, we assume that the time between arrivals is exponentially distributed. Second, we can set some time length (T) and try to determine how many arrivals might enter the system within T. We typically assume that the number of arrivals per time unit is Poisson distributed.

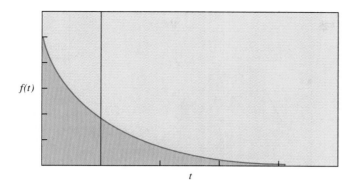

Exponential Distribution   In the first case, when arrivals at a service facility occur in a purely random fashion, a plot of the interarrival times yields an **exponential distribution** such as that shown in Exhibit S5.4. The probability function is

Exponential
Distribution

$$f(t) = \lambda e^{-\lambda t} \qquad (S5.1)$$

where λ is the mean number of arrivals per time period.

The cumulative area beneath the curve in Exhibit S5.4 is the summation of Equation S5.1 over its positive range, which is $e^{-\lambda t}$. This integral allows us to compute the probabilities of arrivals within a specified time. For example, for the case of single arrivals to a waiting line ($\lambda = 1$), the following table can be derived either by solving $e^{-\lambda t}$ or by using Appendix F. Column 2 shows the probability that it will be more than t minutes until the next arrival. Column 3 shows the probability of the next arrival within t minutes (computed as 1 minus column 2)

(1) t (Minutes)	(2) Probability That the Next Arrival Will Occur in t Minutes or More (from Appendix F or Solving e^{-t})	(3) Probability That the Next Arrival Will Occur in t Minutes or Less [1 − Column (2)]
0	1.00	0
0.5	0.61	0.39
1.0	0.37	0.63
1.5	0.22	0.78
2.0	0.14	0.86

Poisson Distribution   In the second case, where one is interested in the number of arrivals during some time period T, the distribution appears as in Exhibit S5.5 and is obtained by finding the probability of exactly n arrivals during T. If the arrival process is random, the distribution is the **Poisson,** and the formula is

Poisson
Distribution

$$P_T(n) = \frac{(\lambda T)^n e^{-\lambda T}}{n!} \qquad (S5.2)$$

Equation S5.2 shows the probability of exactly n arrivals in time T.[1] For example, if the mean arrival rate of units into a system is three per minute ($\lambda = 3$) and we want

---
[1] $n!$ is defined as $n(n-1)(n-2)\ldots(2)(1)$.

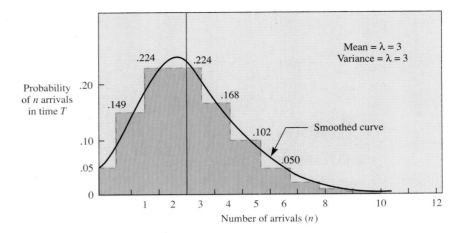

Exhibit S5.5

Poisson Distribution
for $\lambda T = 3$

to find the probability that exactly five units will arrive within a one-minute period ($n = 5$, $T = 1$), we have

$$P_1(5) = \frac{(3 \times 1)^5 e^{-3 \times 1}}{5!} = \frac{3^5 e^{-3}}{120} = 2.025 e^{-3} = 0.101$$

That is, there is a 10.1 percent chance that there will be five arrivals in any one-minute interval.

Although often shown as a smoothed curve, as in Exhibit S5.5, the Poisson is a discrete distribution. (The curve becomes smoother as n becomes large.) The distribution is discrete because n refers, in our example, to the number of arrivals in a system, and this must be an integer. (For example, there cannot be 1.5 arrivals.)

Also note that the exponential and Poisson distributions can be derived from one another. The mean and variance of the Poisson are equal and denoted by λ. The mean of the exponential is $1/\lambda$ and its variance is $1/\lambda^2$. (Remember that the time between arrivals is exponentially distributed and the number of arrivals per unit of time is Poisson distributed.)

Other Arrival Characteristics   Other arrival characteristics include arrival patterns, size of arrival units, and degree of patience. (See Exhibit S5.6.)

Arrival patterns The arrivals at a system are far more *controllable* than is generally recognized. Barbers may decrease their Saturday arrival rate (and supposedly shift it to other days of the week) by charging an extra $1 for adult haircuts or charging adult prices for children's haircuts. Department stores run sales during the off-season or hold one-day-only sales in part for purposes of control. Airlines offer excursion and off-season rates for similar reasons. The simplest of all arrival-control devices is the posting of business hours.

Some service demands are clearly *uncontrollable*, such as emergency medical demands on a city's hospital facilities. But even in these situations, arrivals at emergency rooms in specific hospitals are controllable to some extent by, say, keeping ambulance drivers in the service region informed of the status of their respective host hospitals.

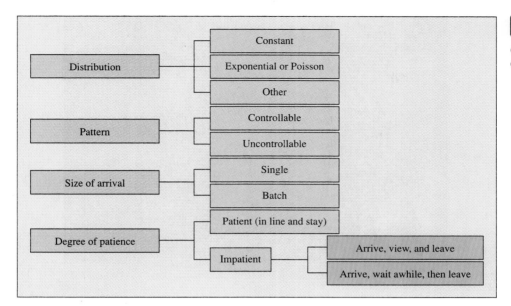

Size of arrival units A *single arrival* may be thought of as one unit. (A unit is the smallest number handled.) A single arrival on the floor of the New York Stock Exchange (NYSE) is 100 shares of stock; a single arrival at an egg-processing plant might be a dozen eggs or a flat of 2 ½ dozen; a single arrival at a restaurant is a single person.

A *batch arrival* is some multiple of the unit, such as a block of 1,000 shares on the NSYE, a case of eggs at the processing plant, or a party of five at a restaurant.

Degree of patience A *patient* arrival is one who waits as long as necessary until the service facility is ready to serve him or her. (Even if arrivals grumble and behave impatiently, the fact that they wait is sufficient to label them as patient arrivals for purposes of waiting line theory.)

There are two classes of *impatient* arrivals. Members of the first class arrive, survey both the service facility and the length of the line, and then decide to leave. Those in the second class arrive, view the situation, join the waiting line, and then, after some period of time, depart. The behavior of the first type is termed *balking,* while the second is termed *reneging.*

The Queuing System

The queuing system consists primarily of the waiting line(s) and the available number of servers. Here we discuss issues pertaining to waiting line characteristics and management, line structure, and service rate.

The Waiting Line Factors to consider with waiting lines include the line length, number of lines, and queue discipline.

Length In a practical sense, an infinite line is simply one that is very long in terms of the capacity of the service system. Examples of *infinite potential length* are a line

of vehicles backed up for miles at a bridge crossing and customers who must form a line around the block as they wait to purchase tickets at a theater.

Gas stations, loading docks, and parking lots have *limited line capacity* caused by legal restrictions or physical space characteristics. This complicates the waiting line problem not only in service system utilization and waiting line computations but also in the shape of the actual arrival distribution. The arrival denied entry into the line because of lack of space may rejoin the population for a later try or may seek service elsewhere. Either action makes an obvious difference in the finite population case.

Number of lines   A *single line* or single file is, of course, one line only. The term *multiple lines* refers to the single lines that form in front of two or more servers or to single lines that converge at some central redistribution point. The disadvantage of multiple lines in a busy facility is that arrivals often shift lines if several previous services have been of short duration or if those customers currently in other lines appear to require a short service time.

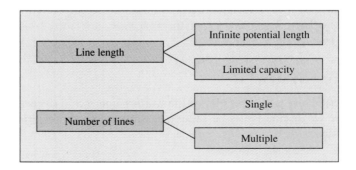

Queue discipline   A queue discipline is a priority rule or set of rules for determining the order of service to customers in a waiting line. The rules selected can have a dramatic effect on the system's overall performance. The number of customers in line, the average waiting time, the range of variability in waiting time, and the efficiency of the service facility are just a few of the factors affected by the choice of priority rules.

Probably the most common priority rule is *first come, first served* (FCFS). This rule states that customers in line are served on the basis of their chronological arrival; no other characteristics have any bearing on the selection process. This is popularly accepted as the fairest rule although in practice, it discriminates against the arrival requiring a short service time.

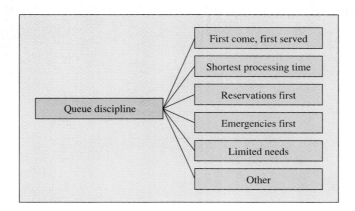

Reservations first, emergencies first, highest-profit customer first, largest orders first, best customers first, longest waiting time in line, and *soonest promised date* are other examples of priority rules. There are two major practical problems in using any rule: One is ensuring that customers know and follow the rule. The other is ensuring that a system exists to enable the employees to manage the line (e.g., take-a-number systems).

Service Time Distribution   Another important feature of the waiting structure is the time the customer or unit spends with the server once the service has started. Waiting line formulas generally specify **service rate** as the capacity of the server in number of units per time period (such as 12 completions per hour) and *not* as service time, which might average five minutes each. A *constant* service time rule states that each service takes exactly the same time. As in constant arrivals, this characteristic is generally limited to machine-controlled operations.

Service Rate

When service times are random, a good approximation of them can be given by the exponential distribution. When using the exponential distribution as an approximation of the service times, we will refer to μ as the average number of units or customers that can be served per time period.

Line Structures   As the figure on page 178 shows, the flow of items to be serviced may go through a single line, multiple lines, or some mixtures of the two. The choice of format depends partly on the volume of customers served and partly on the restrictions imposed by sequential requirements governing the order in which service must be performed.

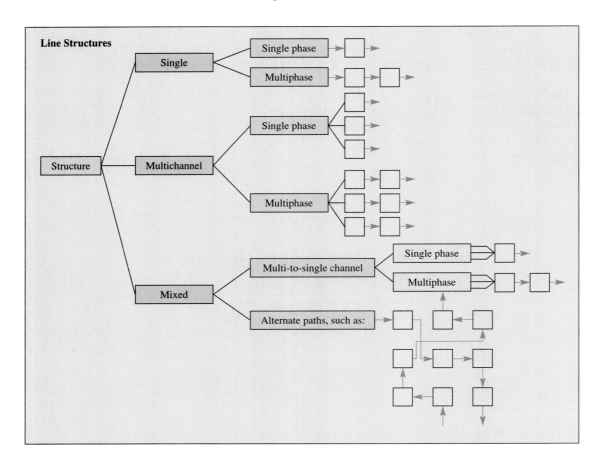

Single channel, single phase This is the simplest type of waiting line structure, and straightforward formulas are available to solve the problem for standard distribution patterns of arrival and service. When the distributions are nonstandard, the problem is easily solved by computer simulation. A typical example of a single-channel, single-phase situation is the one-person barbershop.

Single channel, multiphase A car wash is an illustration since a series of services (vacuuming, wetting, washing, rinsing, drying, window cleaning, and parking) is performed in a fairly uniform sequence. A critical factor in the single-channel case with service in series is the amount of buildup of items allowed in front of each service, which in turn constitutes separate waiting lines.

Multichannel, single phase Tellers' windows in a bank and checkout counters in high-volume department stores exemplify this type of structure. The difficulty with this format is that the uneven service time given each customer results in unequal speed or flow among the lines. This results in some customers being served before others who arrived earlier, as well as in some degree of line shifting. Varying this structure to ensure the servicing of arrivals in chronological order would require forming a single line, from which, as a server becomes available, the next customer in the queue is assigned.

The major problem of this structure is that it requires rigid control of the line to maintain order and to direct customers to available servers. In some instances, assigning numbers to customers in order of their arrival helps alleviate this problem.

Multichannel, multiphase This case is similar to the preceding one except that two or more services are performed in sequence. The admission of patients in a hospital follows this pattern because a specific sequence of steps is usually followed: initial contact at the admissions desk, filling out forms, making identification tags, obtaining a room assignment, escorting the patient to the room, and so forth. Since several servers are usually available for this procedure, more than one patient at a time may be processed.

Mixed Under this general heading we consider two subcategories (1) *multiple-to-single channel structures* and (2) *alternate path structures*. Under (1), we find either lines that merge into one for single-phase service, as at a bridge crossing where two lanes merge into one, or lines that merge into one for multiphase service, such as subassembly lines feeding into a main line. Under (2), we encounter two structures that differ in directional flow requirements. The first is similar to the multichannel–multiphase case, except that (1) there may be switching from one channel to the next after the first service has been rendered, and (2) the number of channels and phases may vary—again—after performance of the first service.

Exit

Once a customer is served, two exit fates are possible: (1) The customer may return to the source population and immediately become a competing candidate for service again; or (2) there may be a low probability of reservice. The first case can be illustrated by a machine that has been routinely repaired and returned to duty but may break down again; the second can be illustrated by a machine that has been overhauled or modified and has a low probability of reservice over the near future. In a lighter vein, we might refer to the first as the "recurring-common-cold case" and to the second as the "appendectomy-only-once case."

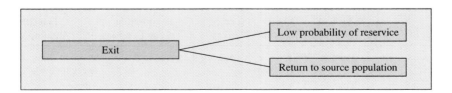

It should be apparent that when the population source is finite, any change in the service performed on customers who return to the population modifies the arrival rate at the service facility. This, of course, alters the characteristics of the waiting line under study and necessitates reanalysis of the problem.

WAITING LINE MODELS

In this section we present four sample waiting line problems followed by their solutions. Each has a slightly different structure (see Exhibit S5.7) and solution equation (see Exhibit S5.9). There are more types of models than these four, but the formulas and solutions become quite complicated, and those problems are generally solved using computer simulation (see Supplement to Chapter 17). Also, in using these formulas, keep in mind that they are steady-state formulas derived on the assumption that the process under study is ongoing. Thus, they may provide inaccurate results when applied to processes where the arrival rates and/or service rates change over time.

Here is a quick preview of our four problems to illustrate each of the four waiting line models in Exhibits S5.7 and S5.9. Exhibit S5.8 defines the notations used in Exhibit S5.9.

Problem 1: Customers in line. A bank wants to know how many customers are waiting for a drive-in teller, how long they have to wait, the utilization of the teller, and what the service rate would have to be so that 95 percent of the time there will not be more than three cars in the system at any time.

Problem 2: Equipment selection. A franchise for Robot Car Wash must decide which equipment to purchase out of a choice of three. Larger units cost more, but wash cars faster. To make the decision, costs are related to revenue.

Problem 3: Determining the number of servers. An auto agency parts department must decide how many clerks to employ at the counter. More clerks cost more money, but there is a savings because mechanics wait less time.

Problem 4: Finite population source. Whereas the previous models assume a large population, finite queuing employs a separate set of equations for those cases where the calling customer population is small. In this last problem, there are just four weaving machines that mechanics must service to keep them operating. Based on the costs associated with machines being idle and the costs of mechanics to service them, the problem is to decide how many mechanics to use.

example S5.1 *Customers in Line* Western National Bank is considering opening a drive-through window for customer service. Management estimates that customers will arrive at the rate of 15 per hour. The teller who will staff the window can service customers at the rate of one every three minutes.

Exhibit S5.7 Properties of Some Specific Waiting Line Models

Model	Layout	Service Phase	Source Population	Arrival Pattern	Queue Discipline	Service Pattern	Permissible Queue Length	Typical Example
1	Single channel	Single	Infinite	Poisson	FCFS	Exponential	Unlimited	Drive-in teller at bank; one-lane toll bridge
2	Single channel	Single	Infinite	Poisson	FCFS	Constant	Unlimited	Automatic car wash; roller coaster rides in amusement park
3	Multichannel	Single	Infinite	Poisson	FCFS	Exponential	Unlimited	Parts counter in auto agency
4	Single channel	Single	Finite	Poisson	FCFS	Exponential	Unlimited	Machine breakdown and repair in a factory

Exhibit S5.8 Notations for Equations (Exhibit S5.9)

Infinite Queuing Notation: Models 1–3	**Finite Queuing Notation: Model 4**

Infinite Queuing Notation: Models 1–3

λ = Arrival rate

μ = Service rate

$\dfrac{1}{\mu}$ = Average service time

$\dfrac{1}{\lambda}$ = Average time between arrivals

ρ = Ratio of total arrival rate to service rate for a single server $\left(\dfrac{\lambda}{\mu}\right)^{*}$

$\overline{n}_l$ = Average number waiting in line

$\overline{n}_s$ = Average number in system (including any being served)

$\overline{t}_l$ = Average time waiting in line

$\overline{t}_s$ = Average total time in system (including time to be served)

n = Number of units in the system

M = Number of identical service channels

P_n = Probability of exactly n units in system

P_w = Probability of waiting in line

Finite Queuing Notation: Model 4

D = Probability that an arrival must wait in line

F = Efficiency factor, a measure of the effect of having to wait in line

H = Average number of units being serviced

J = Population source less those in queuing system $(N - n)$

L = Average number of units in line

M = Number of service channels

n = Average number of units in queuing system (including the one being served)

N = Number of units in population source

P_n = Probability of exactly n units in queuing system

T = Average time to perform the service

U = Average time between customer service requirements

W = Average waiting time in line

X = Service factor, or proportion of service time required

* For single server queues this is equivalent to utilization.

Exhibit S5.9 Equations for Solving Four Model Problems

Model 1

$$\overline{n}_l = \frac{\lambda^2}{\mu(\mu - \lambda)} \qquad \overline{t}_l = \frac{\lambda}{\mu(\mu - \lambda)} \qquad P_n = \left(1 - \frac{\lambda}{\mu}\right)\left(\frac{\lambda}{\mu}\right)^n \qquad P_o = \left(1 - \frac{\lambda}{\mu}\right)$$

$$\overline{n}_s = \frac{\lambda}{\mu - \lambda} \qquad \overline{t}_s = \frac{1}{\mu - \lambda} \qquad \rho = \frac{\lambda}{\mu}$$

(S5.3)

Model 2

$$\overline{n}_l = \frac{\lambda^2}{2\mu(\mu - \lambda)} \qquad \overline{t}_l = \frac{\lambda}{2\mu(\mu - \lambda)}$$

$$\overline{n}_s = \overline{n}_l + \frac{\lambda}{\mu} \qquad \overline{t}_s = \overline{t}_l + \frac{1}{\mu}$$

(S5.4)

(Exhibit S5.10 provides the value of $\overline{n}_l$ given $\rho = \lambda/\mu$ and the number of servers M.)

Model 3

$$\overline{n}_s = \overline{n}_l + \lambda/\mu \qquad \overline{t}_s = \overline{n}_l/\lambda + 1/\mu$$

$$\overline{t}_l = \overline{n}_l/\lambda \qquad P_w = \overline{n}_l (M - \rho)/\rho$$

(S5.5)

Model 4 is a finite queuing situation that is most easily solved by using finite tables. These tables, in turn, require the manipulation of specific terms.

Model 4

$$X = \frac{T}{T + U} \qquad\qquad H = FNX \qquad\qquad L = N(1 - F) \qquad\qquad n = L + H$$

$$P_n = \frac{N!}{(N - n)!}X^n P_0 \qquad\qquad J = NF(1 - X)$$

$$W = \frac{L(T - U)}{N - L} = \frac{LT}{H} \qquad\qquad F = \frac{T + U}{T + U + W}$$

(S5.6)

Part 1   Assuming Poisson arrivals and exponential service, find

1.   Utilization of the teller.
2.   Average number in the waiting line.
3.   Average number in the system.
4.   Average waiting time in line.
5.   Average waiting time in the system, including service.

solution—*Part 1*

1.   The average utilization of the teller is

$$\rho = \frac{\lambda}{\mu} = \frac{15}{20} = 75 \text{ percent}$$

2.   The average number in the waiting line is

$$\overline{n}_l = \frac{\lambda^2}{\mu(\mu - \lambda)} = \frac{(15)^2}{20(20 - 15)} = 2.25 \text{ customers}$$

3.   The average number in the system is

$$\overline{n}_s = \frac{\lambda}{\mu - \lambda} = \frac{15}{20 - 15} = 3 \text{ customers}$$

4.   Average waiting time in line is

$$\overline{t}_l = \frac{\lambda}{\mu(\mu - \lambda)} = \frac{15}{20(20 - 15)} = 0.15 \text{ hour, or 9 minutes}$$

5.   Average waiting time in the system is

$$\overline{t}_s = \frac{1}{\mu - \lambda} = \frac{1}{20 - 15} = 0.2 \text{ hour, or 12 minutes}$$

Part 2   Because of limited space availability and a desire to provide an acceptable level of service, the bank manager would like to ensure, with 95 percent confidence, that not more than three cars will be in the system at any one time. What is the present level of service for the three-car limit? What level of teller use must be attained and what must be the service rate of the teller to ensure the 95 percent level of service?

solution—*Part 2*   The present level of service for three cars or less is the probability that there are 0, 1, 2, or 3 cars in the system. From Model 1, Exhibit S5.9,

$$P_n = \left(1 - \frac{\lambda}{\mu}\right)\left(\frac{\lambda}{\mu}\right)^n$$

at $n = 0$, $P_0 = (1 - 15/20)$ $(15/20)^0 = 0.250$
at $n = 1$, $P_1 = (1/4)$ $(15/20)^1 = 0.188$
at $n = 2$, $P_2 = (1/4)$ $(15/20)^2 = 0.141$
at $n = 3$, $P_3 = (1/4)$ $(15/20)^3 = \underline{0.106}$
$\hphantom{at n = 3, P_3 = (1/4)   (15/20)^3 = }0.685$ or   68.5 percent

The probability of having more than three cars in the system is 1.0 minus the probability of three cars or fewer ($1.0 - 0.685 = 31.5$ percent).

For a 95 percent service level of three cars or fewer, this states that $P_0 + P_1 + P_2 + P_3 = 95$ percent.

$$0.95 = \left(1 - \frac{\lambda}{\mu}\right)\left(\frac{\lambda}{\mu}\right)^0 + \left(1 - \frac{\lambda}{\mu}\right)\left(\frac{\lambda}{\mu}\right)^1 + \left(1 - \frac{\lambda}{\mu}\right)\left(\frac{\lambda}{\mu}\right)^2 + \left(1 - \frac{\lambda}{\mu}\right)\left(\frac{\lambda}{\mu}\right)^3$$

$$0.95 = \left(1 - \frac{\lambda}{\mu}\right)\left[1 + \frac{\lambda}{\mu} + \left(\frac{\lambda}{\mu}\right)^2 + \left(\frac{\lambda}{\mu}\right)^3\right]$$

We can solve this by trial and error for values of λ/μ. If $\lambda/\mu = 0.50$,

     $0.95 \stackrel{?}{=} 0.5(1 + 0.5 + 0.25 + 0.125)$
     $0.95 \neq 0.9375$

With $\lambda/\mu = 0.45$,

     $0.95 \stackrel{?}{=} (1 - 0.45)(1 + 0.45 + 0.203 + 0.091)$
     $0.95 \neq 0.96$

With $\lambda/\mu = 0.47$,

     $0.95 \stackrel{?}{=} (1 - 0.47)(1 + 0.47 + 0.221 + 0.104) = 0.9512$
     $0.95 \approx 0.95135$

Therefore, with the utilization $\rho = \lambda/\mu$ of 47 percent, the probability of three cars or fewer in the system is 95 percent.

To find the rate of service required to attain this 95 percent service level, we simply solve the equation $\lambda/\mu = 0.47$, where $\lambda =$ number of arrivals per hour. This gives $\mu = 32$ per hour.

That is, the teller must serve approximately 32 people per hour (a 60 percent increase over the original 20-per-hour capability) for 95 percent confidence that not more than three cars will be in the system. Perhaps service may be speeded up by modifying the method of service, adding another teller, or limiting the types of transactions available at the drive-through window. Note that with the condition of 95 percent confidence that three or fewer cars will be in the system, the teller will be idle 53 percent of the time. ∎

■ **example S5.2**   *Equipment Selection*   The Robot Company franchises combination gas and car wash stations throughout the United States. Robot gives a free car wash for a gasoline fill-up or, for a wash alone, charges $0.50. Past experience shows that the number of customers that have car washes following fill-ups is about the same as for a wash alone. The average profit on a gasoline fill-up is about $0.70, and the cost of the car wash to Robot is $0.10. Robot stays open 14 hours per day.

Robot has three power units and drive assemblies, and a franchisee must select the unit preferred. Unit I can wash cars at the rate of one every five minutes and is leased for $12 per day. Unit II, a larger unit, can wash cars at the rate of one every four minutes but costs $16 per day. Unit III, the largest, costs $22 per day and can wash a car in three minutes.

The franchisee estimates that customers will not wait in line more than five minutes for a car wash. A longer time will cause Robot to lose the gasoline sales as well as the car wash sale.

If the estimate of customer arrivals resulting in washes is 10 per hour, which wash unit should be selected?

solution   Using unit I, calculate the average waiting time of customers in the wash line (μ for unit I $= 12$ per hour). From the Model 2 equations (Exhibit S5.9),

$$\bar{t}_l = \frac{\lambda}{2\mu(\mu - \lambda)} = \frac{10}{2(12)(12 - 10)} = 0.208 \text{ hour, or } 12 \tfrac{1}{2} \text{ minutes}$$

For unit II at 15 per hour,

$$\bar{t}_l = \frac{10}{2(15)(15 - 10)} = 0.067 \text{ hour, or } 4 \text{ minutes}$$

If waiting time is the only criterion, unit II should be purchased. But before we make the final decision, we must look at the profit differential between both units.

With unit I, some customers would balk and renege because of the 12 ½-minute wait. And, although this greatly complicates the mathematical analysis, we can gain some estimate of lost sales with unit I by increasing $\bar{t}_l = 5$ minutes or $\frac{1}{12}$ hour (the average length of time customers will wait) and solving for λ. This would be the effective arrival rate of customers:

$$\bar{t}_l = \frac{\lambda}{2\mu(\mu - \lambda)}$$

$$\lambda = \frac{2\bar{t}_l\lambda^2}{1 + 2\bar{t}_l\,\mu}$$

$$\lambda = \frac{2(\frac{1}{12})(12)^2}{1 + 2(\frac{1}{12})(12)} = 8 \text{ per hour}$$

Therefore, since the original estimate of λ was 10 per hour, an estimated 2 customers per hour will be lost. Lost profit of 2 customers per hour $\times$ 14 hours $\times$ ½ ($0.70 fill-up profit + $0.40 wash profit) = $15.40 per day.

Because the additional cost of unit II over unit I is only $4 per day, the loss of $15.40 profit obviously warrants installing unit II.

The original five-minute maximum wait constraint is satisfied by unit II. Therefore unit III is not considered unless the arrival rate is expected to increase. ∎

■ example S5.3   *Determining the Number of Servers*   In the service department of the Glenn-Mark Auto Agency, mechanics requiring parts for auto repair or service present their request forms at the parts department counter. The parts clerk fills a request while the mechanic waits. Mechanics arrive in a random (Poisson) fashion at the rate of 40 per hour, and a clerk can fill requests at the rate of 20 per hour (exponential). If the cost for a parts clerk is $6 per hour and the cost for a mechanic is $12 per hour, determine the optimum number of clerks to staff the counter. (Because of the high arrival rate, an infinite source may be assumed.)

solution   First, assume that three clerks will be used because having only one or two clerks would create infinitely long lines (since $\lambda = 40$ and $\mu = 20$). The equations for Model 3 from Exhibit S5.9 will be used here. But first we need to obtain the average number in line using the table of Exhibit S5.10. Using the table and values $\lambda/\mu = 2$ and $M = 3$, we obtain $\bar{n}_l = 0.8888$ mechanic.

At this point, we see that we have an average of 0.8888 mechanic waiting all day. For an eight-hour day at $12 per hour, there is a loss of mechanic's time worth 0.8888 mechanic $\times$ $12 per hour $\times$ 8 hours = $85.32.

Our next step is to reobtain the waiting time if we add another parts clerk. We then compare the added cost of the additional employee with the time saved by the mechanics. Again, using the table of Exhibit S5.10 but with $M = 4$, we obtain

$\bar{n}_l = 0.1730$ mechanic in line

$0.1730 \times \$12 \times 8$ hours $= \$16.61$ cost of a mechanic waiting is line

Value of mechanics' time saved is $\$85.32 - \$16.61 \qquad = \$68.71$

Cost of an additional parts clerk is 8 hours $\times \$6$/hour $= \underline{48.00}$

Cost of reduction by adding fourth clerk $\qquad\qquad = \$20.71$

This problem could be expanded to consider the addition of runners to deliver parts to mechanics; the problem then would be to determine the optimal number of runners. This, however, would have to include the added cost of lost time caused by errors in parts receipts. For example, a mechanic would recognize a wrong part at the counter and obtain immediate correction, whereas the parts runner might not. ∎

■ **example S5.4** *Finite Population Source* Studies of a bank of four weaving machines at the Loose Knit textile mill have shown that, on average, each machine needs adjusting every hour and that the current serviceperson averages 7½ minutes per adjustment. Assuming Poisson arrivals, exponential service, and a machine idle time cost of $40 per hour, determine if a second serviceperson (who also averages 7½ minutes per adjustment) should be hired at a rate of $7 per hour.

solution This is a finite queuing problem that can be solved by using finite queuing tables. (See Exhibit S5.11.) The approach in this problem is to compare the cost of machine downtime (either waiting in line or being serviced) and of one repairperson, to the cost of machine downtime and two repairpeople. We do this by finding the average number of machines that are in the service system and multiply this number by the downtime cost per hour. To this we add the repairpeople's cost.

Before we proceed, we first define some terms:

$N = $ Number of machines in the population
$M = $ Number of repairpeople
$T = $ Time required to service a machine
$U = $ Average time a machine runs before requiring service
$X = $ Service factor, or proportion of service time required for each machine
    ($X = T/(T + U)$)
$L = $ Average number of machines waiting in line to be serviced
$H = $ Average number of machines being serviced

The values to be determined from the finite tables are

$D = $ Probablity that a machine needing service will have to wait
$F = $ Efficiency factor, which is a measure of the effect of having to wait in line to be serviced

The tables are arranged according to three variables: N, population size; X, service factor; and M, the number of service channels (repairpeople in this problem). To look up a value, first find the table for the correct N size, then search the first column for the appropriate X, and finally find the line for M. Then read off D and F. (In addition to these values, other characteristics about a finite queuing system can be found by using the finite formulas.)

Exhibit S5.10 Expected Number of People Waiting in Line (n_l) for Various Values of M and λ/μ

Number of Service Channels, M

λ/μ	1	2	3	4	5	6	7	8	9	10	11	12	13	14	15
0.10	0.0111														
0.15	0.0264	0.0006													
0.20	0.0500	0.0020													
0.25	0.0833	0.0039													
0.30	0.1285	0.0069													
0.35	0.1884	0.0110													
0.40	0.2666	0.0166													
0.45	0.3681	0.0239	0.0019												
0.50	0.5000	0.0333	0.0030												
0.55	0.6722	0.0149	0.0043												
0.60	0.9090	0.0593	0.0061												
0.65	1.2071	0.0767	0.0084												
0.70	1.6333	0.0976	0.0112												
0.75	2.2500	0.1227	0.0147												
0.80	3.2000	0.1523	0.0189												
0.85	4.8165	0.1873	0.0239	0.0031											
0.90	8.1000	0.2285	0.0300	0.0041											
0.95	18.0500	0.2767	0.0371	0.0053											
1.0		0.3333	0.0454	0.0067											
1.2		0.6748	0.0940	0.0158											
1.4		1.3449	0.1778	0.0324	0.0059										
1.6		2.8441	0.3128	0.0604	0.0121										
1.8		7.6731	0.5320	0.1051	0.0227										
2.0			0.8888	0.1730	0.0390	0.0047									
2.2			1.4907	0.2770	0.0059	0.0090									
2.4			2.1261	0.4205	0.1047	0.0158	0.0065								
2.6			4.9322	0.6581	0.1609	0.0266	0.0110								
2.8			12.2724	1.0000	0.2411	0.0425	0.0180								
3.0				1.5282	0.3541	0.0659	0.0282	0.0077							
3.2				2.3855	0.5128	0.0991	0.0427	0.0122							
3.4				3.9060	0.7365	0.1452	0.0631	0.0189							
3.6				7.0893	1.0550	0.2085	0.0912	0.0283	0.0084						
3.8				16.9366	1.5181	0.2947	0.1292	0.0412	0.0127						

x											
4.0	2.2164	0.5694	0.1801	0.0590	0.0189						
4.2	3.3269	0.7837	0.2475	0.0827	0.0273	0.0087					
4.4	5.2675	1.0777	0.3364	0.1142	0.0389	0.0128					
4.6	9.2885	1.4857	0.4532	0.1555	0.0541	0.0184					
4.8	21.6384	2.0708	0.6071	0.2092	0.0742	0.0260					
5.0		2.9375	0.8102	0.2785	0.1006	0.0361	0.0125				
5.2		4.3004	1.0804	0.3680	0.1345	0.0492	0.0175				
5.4		6.6609	1.4441	0.5871	0.1779	0.0663	0.0243	0.0085			
5.6		11.5178	1.9436	0.6313	0.2330	0.0683	0.0330	0.0119			
5.8		26.3726	2.6481	0.8225	0.3032	0.1164	0.0443	0.0164			
6.0			3.6878	1.0707	0.3918	0.1518	0.0590	0.0224			
6.2			5.2979	1.3967	0.5037	0.1964	0.0775	0.0300	0.0113		
6.4			8.0768	1.8040	0.6454	0.2524	0.1008	0.0398	0.0153		
6.6			13.7992	2.4198	0.8247	0.3222	0.1302	0.0523	0.0205		
6.8			31.1270	3.2441	1.0533	0.4090	0.1666	0.0679	0.0271	0.0105	
7.0				4.4471	1.3471	0.5172	0.2119	0.0876	0.0357	0.0141	
7.2				6.3133	1.7288	0.6521	0.2677	0.1119	0.0463	0.0187	
7.4				9.5102	2.2324	0.8202	0.3364	0.1420	0.0595	0.0245	0.0097
7.6				16.0379	2.9113	1.0310	0.4211	0.1789	0.0761	0.0318	0.0129
7.8				35.8956	3.8558	1.2972	0.5250	0.2243	0.0966	0.0410	0.0168
8.0					5.2264	1.6364	0.6530	0.2796	0.1214	0.0522	0.0220
8.2					7.3441	2.0736	0.8109	0.3469	0.1520	0.0663	0.0283
8.4					10.9592	2.6470	1.0060	0.4288	0.1891	0.0834	0.0361
8.6					18.3223	3.4160	1.2484	0.5236	0.2341	0.1043	0.0459
8.8					40.6824	4.4805	1.5524	0.6501	0.2885	0.1208	0.0577
9.0						6.0183	1.9366	0.7980	0.3543	0.1603	0.0723
9.2						8.3869	2.4293	0.9788	0.4333	0.1974	0.0899
9.4						12.4183	3.0732	1.2010	0.5267	0.2419	0.1111
9.6						20.6160	3.9318	1.4752	0.5437	0.2952	0.1367
9.8						45.4769	5.1156	1.8165	0.7827	0.3699	0.1673
10							6.8210	2.2465	0.9506	0.4352	0.2040

Exhibit S5.II

Finite Queuing Tables

Population 4

X	M	D	F	X	M	D	F	X	M	D	F
.015	1	.045	.999		1	.479	.899	.400	3	.064	.992
.022	1	.066	.998	.180	2	.088	.991		2	.372	.915
.030	1	.090	.997		1	.503	.887		1	.866	.595
.034	1	.102	.996	.190	2	.098	.990	.420	3	.074	.990
.038	1	.114	.995		1	.526	.874		2	.403	.903
.042	1	.126	.994	.200	3	.008	.999		1	.884	.572
.046	1	.137	.993		2	.108	.988	.440	3	.085	.986
.048	1	.143	.992	.200	1	.549	.862		2	.435	.891
.052	1	.155	.991	.210	3	.009	.999		1	.900	.551
.054	1	.161	.990		2	.118	.986	.460	3	.097	.985
.058	1	.173	.989		1	.572	.849		2	.466	.878
.060	1	.179	.988	.220	3	.011	.999		1	.914	.530
.062	1	.184	.987		2	.129	.984	.480	3	.111	.983
.064	1	.190	.986		1	.593	.835		2	.498	.864
.066	1	.196	.985	.230	3	.012	.999	.480	1	.926	.511
.070	2	.014	.999		2	.140	.982	.500	3	.125	.980
	1	.208	.984		1	.614	.822		2	.529	.850
.075	2	.016	.999	.240	3	.014	.999		1	.937	.492
	1	.222	.981		2	.151	.980	.520	3	.141	.976
.080	2	.018	.999		1	.634	.808		2	.561	.835
	1	.237	.978	.250	3	.016	.999		1	.947	.475
.085	2	.021	.999		2	.163	.977	.540	3	.157	.972
	1	.251	.975		1	.654	.794		2	.592	.820
.090	2	.023	.999	.260	3	.018	.998		1	.956	.459
	1	.265	.972		2	.175	.975	.560	3	.176	.968
.095	2	.026	.999		1	.673	.780		2	.623	.805
	1	.280	.969	.270	3	.020	.998		1	.963	.443
.100	2	.028	.999		2	.187	.972	.580	3	.195	.964
	1	.294	.965		1	.691	.766		2	.653	.789
.105	2	.031	.998	.280	3	.022	.998		1	.969	.429
	1	.308	.962		2	.200	.968	.600	3	.216	.959
.110	2	.034	.998		1	.708	.752		2	.682	.774
	1	.321	.958	.290	3	.024	.998		1	.975	.415
.115	2	.037	.998		2	.213	.965	.650	3	.275	.944
	1	.335	.954		1	.725	.738		2	.752	.734
.120	2	.041	.997	.300	3	.027	.997		1	.985	.384
	1	.349	.950		2	.226	.962	.700	3	.343	.926
.125	2	.044	.997		1	.741	.724		2	.816	.695
	1	.362	.945	.310	3	.030	.997		1	.991	.357
.130	2	.047	.997		2	.240	.958	.750	3	.422	.905
	1	.376	.941		1	.756	.710		2	.871	.657
.135	2	.051	.996	.320	3	.033	.997		1	.996	.333
	1	.389	.936		2	.254	.954	.800	3	.512	.880
.140	2	.055	.996		1	.771	.696		2	.917	.621
	1	.402	.931	.330	3	.036	.996		1	.998	.312
.145	2	.058	.995		2	.268	.950	.850	3	.614	.852
	1	.415	.926		1	.785	.683		2	.954	.587
.150	2	.062	.995	.340	3	.039	.996		1	.999	.294
	1	.428	.921		2	.282	.945	.900	3	.729	.821
.155	2	.066	.994		1	.798	.670		2	.979	.555
	1	.441	.916	.360	3	.047	.994	.950	3	.857	.786
.160	2	.071	.994		2	.312	.936		2	.995	.526
	1	.454	.910		1	.823	.644				
.165	2	.075	.993	.380	3	.055	.993				
	1	.466	.904		2	.342	.926				
.170	2	.079	.993		1	.846	.619				

Number of Repairpeople	Number of Machines Down ($H + L$)	Cost per Hour for Machines Down [($H + L$) × \$40/Hour]	Cost of Repairpeople (\$7/Hour Each)	Total Cost per Hour
1	0.597	\$23.88	\$ 7.00	\$30.88
2	0.451	18.04	14.00	32.04

A Comparison of Downtime Costs for Service and Repair of Four Machines

To solve the problem, consider Case I with one repairperson and Case II with two repairpeople.

Case I: One repairperson. From the problem statement,

$N = 4$
$M = 1$
$T = 7½$ minutes
$U = 60$ minutes

$$X = \frac{T}{T + U} = \frac{7.5}{7.5 + 60} = 0.111$$

From Exhibit S5.11, which displays the table for $N = 4$, F is interpolated as being approximately 0.957 at $X = 0.111$ and $M = 1$.

The number of machines waiting in line to be serviced is L, where

$$L = N(1 - F) = 4(1 - 0.957) = 0.172 \text{ machines}$$

The number of machines being serviced is H, where

$$H = FNX = 0.957(4)(0.111) = 0.425 \text{ machines}$$

Exhibit S5.12 shows the cost resulting from unproductive machine time and the cost of the repairperson.

Case II: Two repairpeople. From Exhibit S5.11, at $X = 0.111$ and $M = 2$, $F = 0.998$.

The number of machines waiting in line, L, is

$$L = N(1 - F) = 4(1 - 0.998) = 0.008 \text{ machines}$$

The number of machines being serviced, H, is

$$H = FNX = 0.998(4)(0.111) = 0.443 \text{ machines}$$

The costs for the machines being idle and for the two repairpeople are shown in Exhibit S5.12. The final column of that exhibit shows that retaining just one repairperson is the best choice. ■

■ COMPUTER SIMULATION OF WAITING LINES

Some waiting line problems that seem very simple on first impression turn out to be extremely difficult or impossible to solve. Throughout this supplement we have been treating waiting line situations that are independent; that is, either the entire system consists of a single phase, or else each service that is performed in a series is independent. (This could happen if the output of one service location is allowed to build up in front of the next one so that this, in essence, becomes a calling population for the next service.) When a series of services is performed in sequence where the output rate of one becomes the input rate of the next, we can no longer use the simple formulas. This is also true for any problem where conditions do not meet the conditions of the equations, as specified in Exhibit S5.8. The technique best suited to solving this type of problem is computer simulation. We treat the topic of modeling and simulation in the Supplement to Chapter 17.

■ CONCLUSION

Waiting line problems both challenge and frustrate those who try to solve them. The basic objective is to balance the cost of waiting with the cost of adding more resources. For a service system this means that the utilization of a server may be quite low to provide a short waiting time to the customer. One main concern in dealing with waiting line problems is which procedure or priority rule to use in selecting the next product or customer to be served.

Many queuing problems appear simple until an attempt is made to solve them. This supplement has dealt with the simpler problems. When the situation becomes more complex, when there are multiple phases or where services are performed only in a particular sequence, computer simulation is necessary to obtain the optimal solution.

FORMULA REVIEW

Exponential distribution

$$f(t) = \lambda e^{-\lambda t} \tag{S5.1}$$

Poisson distribution

$$P_T(n) = \frac{(\lambda T)^n e^{-\lambda T}}{n!} \tag{S5.2}$$

Model 1 (See Exhibit S5.7.)

$$\bar{n}_l = \frac{\lambda^2}{\mu(\mu - \lambda)} \qquad \bar{t}_l = \frac{\lambda}{\mu(\mu - \lambda)} \qquad P_n = \left(1 - \frac{\lambda}{\mu}\right)\left(\frac{\lambda}{\mu}\right)^n \qquad P_o = \left(1 - \frac{\lambda}{\mu}\right) \tag{S5.3}$$

$$\bar{n}_s = \frac{\lambda}{\mu - \lambda} \qquad \bar{t}_s = \frac{1}{\mu - \lambda} \qquad \rho = \frac{\lambda}{\mu}$$

Model 2

$$\bar{n}_l = \frac{\lambda^2}{2\mu(\mu - \lambda)} \qquad \bar{t}_l = \frac{\lambda}{2\mu(\mu - \lambda)} \tag{S5.4}$$

$$\bar{n}_s = \bar{n}_l + \frac{\lambda}{\mu} \qquad \bar{t}_s = \bar{t}_l + \frac{1}{\mu}$$

Model 3

$$\bar{n}_s = \bar{n}_l + \lambda/\mu \qquad (S5.5)$$
$$\bar{t}_l = \bar{n}_l/\lambda$$
$$\bar{t}_s = \bar{n}_l/\lambda + 1/\mu$$
$$P_w = \bar{n}_l(M - \rho)/\rho$$

Model 4

$$X = \frac{T}{T + U} \qquad H = FNX \qquad L = N(1 - F) \qquad n = L + H \qquad (S5.6)$$

$$P_n = \frac{N!}{(N - n)!}X^n P_0 \qquad\qquad J = NF(1 - X)$$

$$W = \frac{L(T + U)}{N - L} = \frac{LT}{H} \qquad\qquad F = \frac{T + U}{T + U + W}$$

SOLVED PROBLEMS

SOLVED PROBLEM 1

Quick Lube Inc. operates a fast lube and oil change garage. On a typical day, customers arrive at the rate of three per hour, and lube jobs are performed at an average rate of one every 15 minutes. The mechanics operate as a team on one car at a time.

Assuming Poisson arrivals and exponential service, find

  a. Utilization of the lube team.
  b. The average number of cars in line.
  c. The average time a car waits before it is lubed.
  d. The total time it takes to go through the system (i.e., waiting in line plus lube time).

Solution

$$\lambda = 3, \mu = 4$$

a. Utilization $\rho = \dfrac{\lambda}{\mu} = \dfrac{3}{4} = 75\%$.

b. $\bar{n}_l = \dfrac{\lambda^2}{\mu(\mu - \lambda)} = \dfrac{3^2}{4(4 - 3)} = \dfrac{9}{4} = 2.25$ cars in line.

c. $\bar{t}_l = \dfrac{\lambda}{\mu(\mu - \lambda)} = \dfrac{3}{4(4 - 3)} = \dfrac{3}{4} = 45$ minutes in line.

d. $\bar{t}_s = \dfrac{1}{\mu - \lambda} = \dfrac{1}{1} = 1$ hour (waiting + lube).

SOLVED PROBLEM 2

American Vending Inc. (AVI) supplies vended food to a large university. Because students kick the machines at every opportunity out of anger and frustration, management has a constant repair problem. The machines break down on an average of three per hour, and the breakdowns are distributed in a Poisson manner. Downtime costs the company $25/hour per machine, and each maintenance worker gets $4 per hour. One worker can service machines at an average rate of five per hour, distributed exponentially; two workers working together can service seven per hour, distributed exponentially; and a team of three workers can do eight per hour, distributed exponentially.

What is the optimum maintenance crew size for servicing the machines?

Solution

Case I: One worker:

   $\lambda = 3$/hour Poisson, $\mu = 5$/hour exponential

There is an average number of machines in the system of:

$$\bar{n}_s = \frac{\lambda}{\mu - \lambda} = \frac{3}{5 - 3} = \frac{3}{2} = 1\frac{1}{2} \text{ machines}$$

Downtime cost is $\$25 \times 1.5 = \$37.50$ per hour; repair cost is $\$4.00$ per hour; and total cost per hour for 1 worker is $\$37.50 + \$4.00 = \$41.50$.

   Downtime $(1.5 \times \$25) = \$37.50$
   Labor $(1 \text{ worker} \times \$4) = \underline{\quad 4.00}$
                              $\$41.50$

Case II: Two workers:

   $\lambda = 3, \mu = 7$

$$\bar{n}_s = \frac{\lambda}{\mu - \lambda} = \frac{3}{7 - 3} = .75 \text{ machines}$$

   Downtime $(.75 \times \$25)\quad = \$18.75$
   Labor $(2 \text{ workers} \times \$4.00) = \underline{\quad 8.00}$
                              $\$26.75$

Case III: Three workers:
   $\lambda = 3, \mu = 8$

$$\bar{n}_s = \frac{\lambda}{\mu - \lambda} = \frac{3}{8 - 3} = \frac{3}{5} = .60 \text{ machines}$$

   Downtime $(.60 \times \$25)\quad = \$15.75$
   Labor $(3 \text{ workers} \times \$4) = \underline{\quad 12.00}$
                              $\$27.00$

Comparing the costs for one, two, or three workers, we see that Case II with two workers is the optimal decision.

REVIEW AND DISCUSSION QUESTIONS

   1. How many waiting lines did you encounter during your last airline flight?
   2. Distinguish between a *channel* and a *phase*.
   3. What is the major cost trade-off that must be made in managing waiting line situations?
   4. Which assumptions are necessary to employ the formulas given for Model 1?
   5. In what way might the first-come, first-served rule be unfair to the customer waiting for service in a bank or hospital?
   6. Define, in a practical sense, what is meant by an *exponential service time*.
   7. Would you expect the exponential distribution to be a good approximation of service times for
      a. Buying an airline ticket at the airport?
      b. Riding a merry-go-round at a carnival?
      c. Checking out of a hotel?
      d. Completing a midterm exam in your OM class?
   8. Would you expect the Poisson distribution to be a good approximation of
      a. Runners crossing the finish line in the Boston Marathon?
      b. Arrival times of the students in your OM class?
      c. Arrival times of the bus to your stop at school?

PROBLEMS

1. Students arrive at the Administrative Services Office at an average of one every fifteen minutes and their requests take on average ten minutes to be processed. At the present time the service counter is staffed only by one clerk, Judy Gumshoes, who works eight hours per day. Assume Poisson arrivals and exponential service times.
   a. What percentage of time is Judy idle?
   b. How much time, on average, does a student spend waiting in line?
   c. How long is the (waiting) line on average?
   d. What is the probability that an arriving student (just before entering the Administrative Services Office) will find at least one other student waiting in line?

2. The management of the Administrative Services Office estimate that the time a student spends waiting in line costs them (due to goodwill loss, etc.) $10 per hour. To reduce the time a student spends waiting, they know that they need to improve Judy's processing time (see Problem 1). They are currently considering the following two options:
   a. Install a computer system, with which Judy expects, after it becomes operational, to be able to complete a student request 40% faster.
   b. Hire another temporary clerk, who will work at the same rate as Judy.
   If the computer costs $99.50 to operate per day, while the temporary clerk gets paid $75 per day, is Judy right to prefer the hired help? Assume Poisson arrivals and exponential service times.

3. Sharp Discounts Wholesale Club has two service desks, one at each entrance of the store. Customers arrive at each service desk at an average of one every six minutes. The service rate at each service desk is four minutes per customer.
   a. How often (what percentage of time) is each service desk idle?
   b. What is the probability that both service clerks are busy?
   c. What is the probability that both service clerks are idle?
   d. How many customers, on average, are waiting in line in front of each service desk?
   e. How much time does a customer spend at the service desk (waiting plus service time)?

4. Sharp Discounts Wholesale Club is considering consolidating its two service desks (see Problem 3) into one location, staffed by two clerks. The clerks will continue to work at the same individual speed of four minutes per customer.
   a. What is the probability of waiting in line?
   b. How many customers, on average, are waiting in line?
   c. How much time does a customer spend at the service desk (waiting plus service time)?
   d. Do you think the Sharp Discounts Wholesale Club should consolidate the service desks?

✓ **5.** Burrito King (a new fast food franchise opening up nationwide) has successfully automated burrito production for its drive-up fast food establishments. The Burro-Master 9000 requires a constant 45 seconds to produce a batch of burritos. It has been estimated that customers will arrive at the drive-up window according to a Poisson distribution at an average of one every 50 seconds. To help determine the amount of space needed for the line at the drive-up window, Burrito King would like to know the expected average time in the system, the average line length (in cars), and the average number of cars in the system (both in line and at the window).

6. The Bijou Theater in Hermosa Beach, California, shows vintage movies. Customers arrive at the theater line at the rate of 100 per hour. The ticket seller averages 30 seconds per customer, which includes placing parking validation stamps on customers' parking lot receipts and punching holes in their frequent watcher cards. (Because of these added services, many customers don't get in until after the feature has started.)
   a. What is the average customer waiting time in the system?

b. What would be the effect on system waiting time of having a second ticket taker doing nothing but validations and card punching, thereby cutting the average service time to 20 seconds?

c. Would system waiting time be less than you found in *b* if a second window was opened with each server doing all three tasks?

7. *a.* $2^1/_{12}$ people.
   b. $2^{11}/_{12}$ people.
   c. 0.208 hour.
   d. 0.291 hour.
   e. Infinity

7. To support National Heart Week, the Heart Association plans to install a free blood pressure testing booth in El Con Mall for the week. Previous experience indicates that, on the average, 10 persons per hour request a test. Assume arrivals are Poisson from an infinite population. Blood pressure measurements can be made at a constant time of five minutes each. Assume the queue length can be infinite with FCFS discipline.

a. What average number in line can be expected?
b. What average number of persons can be expected to be in the system?
c. What is the average amount of time that a person can expect to spend in line?
d. On the average, how much time will it take to measure a person's blood pressure, including waiting time?
e. On weekends, the arrival rate can be expected to increase to nearly 12 per hour. What effect will this have on the number in the waiting line?

8. *a.* 3 people.
   b. 1 minute.
   c. 75%.
   d. .4219.
   Time reduced by 22.5 seconds; avg. no. of people reduced by 1.125.

8. A cafeteria serving line has a coffee urn from which customers serve themselves. Arrivals at the urn follow a Poission distribution at the rate of three per minute. In serving themselves, customers take about 15 seconds, exponentially distributed.

a. How many customers would you expect to see on the average at the coffee urn?
b. How long would you expect it to take to get a cup of coffee?
c. What percentage of time is the urn being used?
d. What is the probability that three or more people are in the cafeteria?
   If the cafeteria installs an automatic vendor that dispenses a cup of coffee at a constant time of 15 seconds, how does this change your answers to *a* and *b*?

9. *a.* L = 4(.055) = .22 ✓
   waiting.
   b. W = .466 hours.
   c. D = .362.

9. An engineering firm retains a technical specialist to assist four design engineers working on a project. The help that the specialist gives engineers ranges widely in time consumption. The specialist has some answers available in memory, others require computation, and still others require significant search time. On the average, each request for assistance takes the specialist one hour.

The engineers require help from the specialist on the average of once each day. Since each assistance takes about an hour, each engineer can work for seven hours, on the average, without assistance. One further point: Engineers needing help do not interrupt if the specialist is already involved with another problem.

Treat this as a finite queuing problem and answer the following questions:

a. How many engineers, on the average, are waiting for the technical specialist for help?
b. What is the average time that an engineer has to wait for the specialist?
c. What is the probability that an engineer will have to wait in line for the specialist?

10. *a.* 2 people.   ✓
    b. 6 minutes.
    c. .2964.
    d. 67%.
    e. 0.03375 hour.

10. L. Winston Martin (an allergist in Tucson) has an excellent system for handling his regular patients who come in just for allergy injections. Patients arrive for an injection and fill out a name slip, which is then placed in an open slot that passes into another room staffed by one or two nurses. The specific injections for a patient are prepared and the patient is called through a speaker system into the room to receive the injection. At certain times during the day, patient load drops and only one nurse is needed to administer the injections.

Let's focus on the simpler case of the two—namely, when there is one nurse. Also assume that patients arrive in a Poisson fashion and the service rate of the nurse is exponentially distributed. During this slower period, patients arrive with an interarrival time of approximately three minutes. It takes the nurse an average of two minutes to prepare the patients' serum and administer the injection.

a. What is the average number you would expect to see in Dr. Martin's facilities?
b. How long would it take for a patient to arrive, get an injection, and leave?

    c. What is the probability that there will be three or more patients on the premises?

    d. What is the utilization of the nurse?

    e. Assume three nurses are available. Each takes an average of two minutes to prepare the patients' serum and administer the injection. What is the average total time of a patient in the system?

11. The Judy Gray Income Tax Service is analyzing its customer service operations during the month prior to the April filing deadline. On the basis of past data it has been estimated that customers arrive according to a Poisson process with an average interarrival time of 12 minutes. The time to complete a return for a customer is exponentially distributed with a mean of 10 minutes. Based on this information, answer the following questions:

    a. If you went to Judy, how much time would you allow for getting your return done?

    b. On average, how much room should be allowed for the waiting area?

    c. If Judy stayed in the office 12 hours per day, how many hours on average, per day, would she be busy?

    d. What is the probability that the system is idle?

    e. If the arrival rate remained unchanged but the average time in system must be 45 minutes or less, what would need to be changed?

12. A graphics reproduction firm has four units of equipment that are automatic but occasionally become inoperative because of the need for supplies, maintenance, or repair. Each unit requires service roughly twice each hour or, more precisely, each unit of equipment runs an average of 30 minutes before needing service. Service times vary widely, ranging from a simple service (such as hitting a restart switch or repositioning paper) to more involved equipment disassembly. The average service time, however, is five minutes.

    Equipment downtime results in a loss of $20 per hour. The one equipment attendant is paid $6 per hour.

    Using finite queuing analysis, answer the following questions:

    a. What is the average number of units in line?

    b. What is the average number of units still in operation?

    c. What is the average number of units being serviced?

    d. The firm is considering adding another attendant at the same $6 rate. Should the firm do it?

13. Benny the Barber owns a one-chair shop. At barber college, they told Benny that his customers would exhibit a Poisson arrival distribution and that he would provide an exponential service distribution. His market survey data indicate that customers arrive at a rate of two per hour. It will take Benny an average of 20 minutes to give a haircut. Based on these figures, find the following:

    a. The average number of customers waiting.

    b. The average time a customer waits.

    c. The average time a customer is in the shop.

    d. The average utilization of Benny's time.

14. Benny the Barber (see Problem 13) is considering the addition of a second chair. Customers would be selected for a haircut on a FCFS basis from those waiting. Benny has assumed that both barbers would take an average of 20 minutes to give a haircut, and that business would remain unchanged with customers arriving at a rate of 2 per hour. Find the following information to help Benny decide if a second chair should be added:

    a. The average number of customers waiting.

    b. The average time a customer waits.

    c. The average time a customer is in the shop.

15. Customers enter the camera department of a department store at the average rate of six per hour. The department is staffed by one employee, who takes an average of six minutes to serve each arrival. Assume this is a simple Poisson arrival exponentially distributed service time situation.

a. As a casual observer, how many people would you expect to see in the camera department (excluding the clerk)? How long would a customer expect to spend in the camera department (total time)?

b. What is the utilization of the clerk?

c. What is the probability that there are *more than* two people in the camera department (excluding the clerk)?

d. Another clerk has been hired for the camera department who also takes an average of six minutes to serve each arrival. How long would a customer expect to spend in the department now?

16. Kenny Livingston, bartender at the Tucson Racquet Club, can serve drinks at the rate of one every 50 seconds. During a hot evening recently, the bar was particulary busy and every 55 seconds someone was at the bar asking for a drink.

a. Assuming that everyone in the bar drank at the same rate and that Kenny served people on a first-come, first-served basis, how long would you expect to have to wait for a drink?

b. How many people would you expect to be waiting for drinks?

c. What is the probability that three or more people are waiting for drinks?

d. What is the utilization of the bartender (how busy is he)?

e. If the bartender is replaced with an automatic drink dispensing machine, how would this change your answer in part *a*?

17. An office employs several clerks who originate documents and one operator who enters the document information in a word processor. The group originates documents at a rate of 25 per hour. The operator can enter the information with average exponentially distributed time of two minutes. Assume the population is infinite, arrivals are Poisson, and queue length is infinite with FCFS discipline.

a. Calculate the percent of utilization of the operator.

b. Calculate the average number of documents in the system.

c. Calculate the average time in the system.

d. Calculate the probability of four or more documents being in the system.

e. If another clerk were added, the document origination rate would increase to 30 per hour. What would this do to the word processor workload? Show why.

18. A study-aid desk manned by a graduate student has been established to answer students' questions and help in working problems in your OM course. The desk is staffed eight hours per day. The dean wants to know how the facility is working. Statistics show that students arrive at a rate of four per hour, and the distribution is approximately Poisson. Assistance time averages 10 minutes, distributed exponentially. Assume population and line length can be infinite and queue discipline is FCFS.

a. Calculate the percent of utilization of the graduate student.

b. Calculate the average number of students in the system.

c. Calculate the average time in the system.

d. Calculate the probability of four or more students being in line or being served.

e. Before a test, the arrival of students increases to six per hour on the average. What does this do to the average length of the line?

19. At the California border inspection station, vehicles arrive at the rate of 10 per minute in a Poisson distribution. For simplicity in this problem, assume that there is only one lane and one inspector, who can inspect vehicles at the rate of 12 per minute in an exponentially distributed fashion.

a. What is the average length of the waiting line?

b. What is the average time that a vehicle must wait to get through the system?

c. What is the utilization of the inspector?

d. What is the probability that when you arrive there will be three or more vehicles ahead of you?

20. The California border inspection station (see Problem 19) is considering the addition of a second inspector. The vehicles would wait in one lane and then be directed to the first available inspector. Arrival rates would remain the same (10 per minute) and the new inspector would process vehicles at the same rate as the first inspector (12 per minute).

    a. What would be the average length of the waiting line?

    b. What would be the average time that a vehicle must wait to get through the system? If a second lane was added (one lane for each inspector):

    c. What would be the average length of the waiting line?

    d. What would be the average time that a vehicle must wait to get through the system?

20. *a.* .175.
    b. .101 minutes or 6.06 seconds.
    c. .596.
    d. .143 minutes or 8.58 seconds.

21. During the campus Spring Fling, the bumper car amusement attraction has a problem of cars becoming disabled and in need of repair. Repair personnel can be hired at the rate of $20 per hour, but they only work as one team. Thus, if one person is hired, he or she works alone; two or three people only work together on the same repair.

    One repairperson can repair cars in an average time of 30 minutes. Two repairpeople take 20 minutes, and three take 15 minutes. While these cars are down, lost income is $40 per hour. Cars tend to break down at the rate of two per hour.

    How many repairpeople should be hired?

21. 1 repairman $∞/hr,
    2 repairmen $120/hr.
    3 repairmen $100/hr.

22. A toll tunnel has decided to experiment with the use of a debit card for the collection of their tolls. Initially, only one lane will be used. Cars are estimated to arrive at this experimental lane at the rate of 750 per hour. It will take exactly 4 seconds to verify the debit card.

    a. How much time would you expect the customer to wait in line, pay with the debit card, and leave?

    b. How many cars would you expect to see in the system?

22. *a.* 14 seconds.
    b. 2.92 cars.

SELECTED BIBLIOGRAPHY

Chase, R. B. "The Mall Is My Factory: Reflections of a Service Junkie." *Productions and Operations Management,* Winter 1996, pp. 298–308.

Cooper, Robert B. *Introduction to Queuing Theory.* 2nd ed. New York: Elsevier–North Holland, 1980.

Davis, Mark M., and M. J. Maggard, "An Analysis of Customer Satisfaction with Waiting Times in a Two-Stage Service Process." *Journal of Operations Management* 9, no. 3 (August 1990), pp. 324–34.

Fitzsimmons, James A., and M. J. Fitzsimmons, *Service Management.* Burr Ridge, IL: Irwin/McGraw-Hill, 1997, pp. 318–39.

Hillier, Frederick S., et al. *Queuing Tables and Graphs.* New York: Elsevier–North Holland, 1981.

Katz, K. L.; B. M. Larson; and R. C. Larson. "Prescription for the Waiting-in-Line Blues: Entertain, Enlighten, and Engage." *Sloan Management Review* 32, no. 2 (Winter 1991), pp. 44–53.

Winston, Wayne L., and S. Christian Albright. *Practical Management Science: Spreadsheet Modeling and Application.* New York: Duxbury, 1997, pp. 537–79.

Chapter 6

Quality Management

Chapter Outline

Quality Management and the Malcolm Baldrige National Quality Award, 200

  Eligibility for the Baldrige Award
  Description of the 1997 Baldrige Award
    Criteria
  The Baldrige Award and the Quality Gurus

Quality Specifications and Quality Costs, 207

  Developing Quality Specifications
  Cost of Quality
  Generic Tools and Tools of the QC
    Department

Continuous Improvement (CI), 212

  Tools and Procedures of CI
  Benchmarking for CI

The Shingo System: Fail-Safe Design, 216

ISO 9000, 217

  The ISO 9000 Series
  ISO 9000 Certification
  ISO 9000: An Everyday Example
  ISO 9000 versus the Baldrige Criteria

Case: Hank Kolb, Director of Quality Assurance, 229

Case: Shortening Customers' Telephone Waiting Time, 231

Key Terms

Total Quality Management
(TQM)

Malcolm Baldrige National
Quality Award

Deming Prize

Benchmarking

Design Quality

Conformance Quality

Quality at the Source

Zero Defects

Dimensions of Quality

Cost of Quality (COQ)

Continuous Improvement (CI)
(Kaizen)

PDCA Cycle

Fail-Safe Procedures (Poka-Yoke)

ISO 9000

www Links

Baldrige Award (http://www.quality.nist.gov)

ISO 9000 (http://www.iso.ch)

Deming Institute (http://www.deming.org)

Joнn F. Welch, chairman of General Electric Co., in describing how he is driving a new quality program into GE's far-flung plants, says, "You can't behave in a calm, rational manner. You've got to be out there on the lunatic fringe." Slicing his hands down to his desk, Mr. Welch says: "You have to tell your people that quality is critical to survival, you have to demand everybody gets trained, you have to cheerlead, you have to have incentive bonuses, you have to say, "'We must do this.'"

The quality-control program, Mr. Welch says, is "a mammoth undertaking; I mean, I can't even begin to describe the size of this undertaking." A sure sign of top management's determination: 40 percent of GE executive bonuses, which run as high as $1 million, now will depend on implementation of the program. Previously, bonuses were based only on profit and cash flow.

GE's quality program, which was borrowed from Motorola, Inc., involves training "black belts" for four months in statistical and other quality-enhancing measures. The black belts then spend full time roaming GE plants and setting up quality-improvement projects. Mr. Welch has told young managers that they haven't much of a future at GE unless they are selected to become black belts. The company has already trained 2,000 black belts and it plans to increase that number to 4,000 by year's end and to 10,000 by the year 2000. In all, GE is investing hundreds of millions of dollars in training, in specific projects, and in computer systems to analyze and run the quality-control program.

The program is producing a variety of benefits, Mr. Welch says. "Your customers are happy with you, you are not firefighting, you are not running a reactive mode." GE hopes the program, by preventing costly snafus, will save $7–$10 billion over the next decade and thus bolster profits. ●

Vol. I "Quality"

**Total Quality
Management**

GE's black-belt program is typical of the intense effort that world-class companies are directing to quality management. The effort is a worldwide phenomenon. Companies realize that producing high-quality products is essential to success in the global marketplace. It is interesting to observe how the ideas in this chapter and in the supplement to this chapter have developed.

The quality movement started in Japan. The Deming Prize, first awarded in 1951, marked the beginning of an effort that has accelerated over the past 15 years. In the late 1950s, the U.S. Department of Defense adopted a series of quality standards that were later adopted by the British Standards Institute and have now evolved into the International Organization for Standardization (ISO) 9000 standards. The first awarding of the Malcolm Baldrige National Quality Award in the United States took place in 1987.

The quality movement is more than just a series of awards and quality standards, the movement involves a total rethinking of how a business should be run. The term **total quality management (TQM)** has been coined to describe a philosophy that makes quality values the driving force behind leadership, design, planning, and improvement initiatives. The belief is that for long term financial success, quality is essential. The first part of the Chapter develops this TQM philosophy.

Meeting global quality standards is difficult due to the differences in operating practices in different countries. In one country, a tolerance may be measured in centimeters, while in another, the measurement may be tenths of an inch. The International Organization for Standardization (ISO) defined how things should be measured. Their specifications go beyond just measurement, and define how processes should be documented and what processes are essential to ensuring quality. Using the ISO standards, a company producing a part in China can be compared to a company producing the same part in the United States. The second half of this chapter is about these ISO 9000 standards and how companies can register their ISO 9000 compliance.

Returning to our Karate analogy, in becoming a black belt you need to know the moves and leveraging techniques for overcoming your opponent. The same is true in quality. In quality, statistics is used for leveraging, and our moves include statistical process control, sampling plans, and process capability analysis. The details of these "moves" are the topics of the supplement to this chapter. Now, let's break some bricks!

■ QUALITY MANAGEMENT AND THE MALCOLM BALDRIGE NATIONAL QUALITY AWARD

Exhibit 6.1 presents a framework summarizing the important elements of TQM discussed in the chapter and supplement.

We define TQM as "managing the entire organization so that it excels on all dimensions of products and services that are important to the customer." This definition is more applicable than another commonly used one—"conformance to specifications." Though valid for goods production, the second definition is problematic for many services. Precise specifications for service quality are hard to define and measure. It is possible, however, to find out what's important to the customer, and then create the kind of organizational culture that motivates and enables the worker to do what is necessary to deliver a quality service.

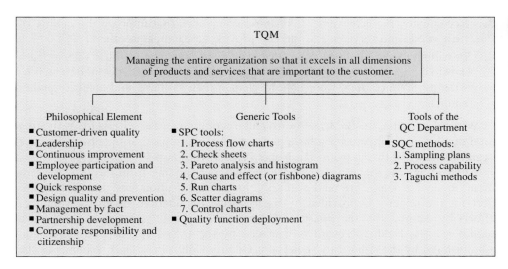

Exhibit 6.1

Elements of Total
Quality Management

TQM

Managing the entire organization so that it excels in all dimensions
of products and services that are important to the customer.

Philosophical Element
- Customer-driven quality
- Leadership
- Continuous improvement
- Employee participation and
  development
- Quick response
- Design quality and prevention
- Management by fact
- Partnership development
- Corporate responsibility and
  citizenship

Generic Tools
- SPC tools:
  1. Process flow charts
  2. Check sheets
  3. Pareto analysis and histogram
  4. Cause and effect (or fishbone) diagrams
  5. Run charts
  6. Scatter diagrams
  7. Control charts
- Quality function deployment

**Tools of the
QC Department**
- SQC methods:
  1. Sampling plans
  2. Process capability
  3. Taguchi methods

The philosophical elements of TQM stress the operation of the firm using quality as the integrating element. The generic tools consist of various statistical process control (SPC) methods that are used for problem solving and continuous improvement by quality teams; and quality function deployment that is typically used by managers to drive the voice of the customer into the organization. (See Chapter 4 for a discussion of QFD.) Tools of the QC department consist of statistical quality control (SQC) methods that are used by the quality professionals working in this department.

On August 20, 1987, President Ronald Reagan affixed his signature to Public Law 100–107. This groundbreaking legislation, known commonly as the Malcolm Baldrige National Quality Improvement Act, established the nation's annual award to recognize total quality management in American industry. The **Malcolm Baldrige National Quality Award** represents the United States government's endorsement of quality as an essential part of successful business strategy.

As an instrument of government, the Baldrige Award seeks to improve quality and productivity by

1. Helping to stimulate American companies to improve quality and productivity for the pride of recognition while obtaining a competitive edge through decreased costs and increased profits.

2. Establishing guidelines and criteria that can be used by business, industrial, governmental, and other organizations in evaluating their quality improvement efforts.

**Malcolm Baldrige
National Quality
Award**

*(http://www.quality.nist.
gov)*

3. Recognizing the achievements of those companies that improve the quality of their goods and services and thereby provide an example to others.

4. Providing specific guidance for other American organizations that wish to learn how to manage for high quality by making available detailed information on how winning organizations were able to change their cultures and achieve quality eminence.

Without question, the Baldrige Award and its comprehensive criteria for evaluating total quality in an organization have had considerable impact. Some observers have begun referring to the award as the Nobel Prize for business.

Applications for the award are reviewed without funding from the U.S. government. Review expenses are paid primarily through application fees, and partial support for the reviews is provided by the Baldrige Foundation. Extensive volunteer efforts by members of the Board of Examiners keep application review fees to a minimum. The Baldrige Award is managed by the U.S. Dept. of Commerce and administered by the American Society for Quality Control (ASQC). Winners of the award are announced annually by the President of the United States during a special ceremony held at the White House.

While applications for the Baldrige have declined in 1996 to around 25, quality standards are being reborn in various state-sponsored quality awards. The Baldrige organization sends out over 200,000 criteria packets per year. The Baldrige is clearly meeting its goals of awareness and use of its template.

Japan also has an award for outstanding business accomplishment. For over 40 years, Japan has recognized its corporate quality leaders by bestowing on them the prestigious **Deming Prize** (see Exhibit 6.2), named after American statistician Dr. W. Edwards Deming, whose quality concepts provided the road map for Japanese success

Deming Prize

Exhibit 6.2

Comparison of the Deming Prize and Baldrige Award

Japan's highly coveted Deming Prize recognizes successful efforts in instituting companywide quality control (CWQC) principles. The Deming Prize is awarded to all companies that meet a standard based on the evaluation process. For those that do not qualify, the examination process is automatically extended (up to two times over three years). Although both the Deming Prize and the Baldrige Award are designed to recognize outstanding business accomplishments, some notable differences follow:

Topic	Baldrige Award	Deming Prize
Primary focus	Performance excellence and competitiveness improvement	Statistical quality control
Grading criteria	Leadership strategic planning Customer and market focus Information and analysis Human resource development and management Process management Business results	Policy and objectives Organization and operation Education and extension Data gathering/reporting Analysis Standardization Control Quality assurance Effects Future plans
Winners	Maximum of two per category	All firms meeting standard
Scope	Firms with U.S. operations	Firms from any country
First award	1987	1951
Sponsor	National Institute of Standards and Technology	Union of Japanese Scientists and Engineers

in quality after World War II. The Deming Prize has become so esteemed in Japan that each year, much like America's Academy Awards, millions of Japanese watch the Deming Prize ceremony aired live on television.

Eligibility for the Baldrige Award

There are three categories for the Baldrige Award:

1. Manufacturing companies or subsidiaries that (1) produce and sell manufactured products or manufacturing processes or (2) produce agricultural, mining, or construction products.
2. Service companies or subsidiaries that sell service. Whether a company is classified as manufacturing or service is determined by the larger percentage of sales.
3. Small businesses, which are defined as those that have fewer than 500 employees and that operate independently of any other firm that may have equity ownership.

Up to two awards can be given in each of the three categories. Winners are expected to make themselves available to other firms and openly discuss what they did to achieve quality success. Exhibit 6.3 lists winners through 1996.

Description of the 1997 Baldrige Award Criteria[1]

Exhibit 6.4 shows a framework for the award criteria. Note how the Baldrige Award mirrors the broad spectrum of issues necessary for a total quality management system. Scoring for the award falls into the seven categories shown in Exhibit 6.5. Note that the greatest scoring weight is on business results.

Baldrige Award Winners

 Exhibit 6.3

ADAC Laboratories (1996)

Ames Rubber Corporation (1993)

Armstrong World Industries Building Products Operations (1995)

AT&T Consumer Communications Services (1994)

AT&T Network Systems Group (1992)

AT&T Universal Card Services (1992)

Cadillac Motor Car Company (1990)

Corning Telecommunications Products Division (1995)

Custom Research, Inc. (1996)

Dana Commerical Credit Corporation (1996)

Eastman Chemical Company (1993)

Federal Express Corporation (1990)

Globe Metallurgical Inc. (1988)

Granite Rock Company (1992)

GTE Directories Corporation (1994)

IBM Rochester (1990)

Marlow Industries (1991)

Milliken & Company (1989)

Motorola Inc. (1988)

The Ritz-Carlton Hotel Company (1992)

Solectron Corporation (1991)

Texas Instruments Incorporated—Defense Systems & Electronics Group (1992)

Trident Precision Manufacturing, Inc. (1996)

Wainwright Industries, Inc. (1994)

Wallace Co., Inc. (1990)

Westinghouse Electric Corporation—Commerical Nuclear Fuel Division (1988)

Xerox Corporation—Business Products & Systems (1989)

Zytec Corporation (1991)

[1] Extracted from the Malcolm Baldrige National Quality Award 1997 award criteria.

Exhibit 6.4

Baldrige Award
Criteria Framework:
A Systems Perspective

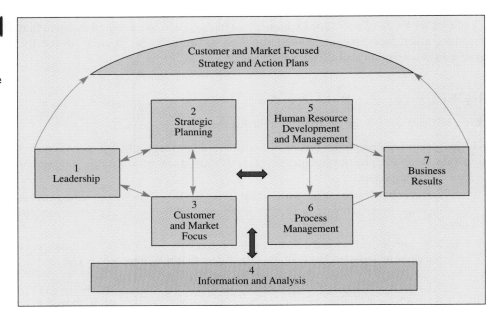

Exhibit 6.5

1997 Award Criteria—
Item Listing

1997 Categories/Items	Point Values
1 Leadership	**110**
1.1 Leadership System	80
1.2 Company Responsibility and Citizenship	30
2 Strategic Planning	**80**
2.1 Strategy Development Process	40
2.2 Company Strategy	40
3 Customer and Market Focus	**80**
3.1 Customer and Market Knowledge	40
3.2 Customer Satisfaction and Relationship Enhancement	40
4 Information and Analysis	**80**
4.1 Selection and Use of Information and Data	25
4.2 Selection and Use of Comparative Information and Data	15
4.3 Analysis and Review of Company Performance	40
5 Human Resource Development and Management	**100**
5.1 Work Systems	40
5.2 Employee Education, Training, and Development	30
5.3 Employee Well-Being and Satisfaction	30
6 Process Management	**100**
6.1 Management of Product and Service Processes	60
6.2 Management of Support Processes	20
6.3 Management of Supplier and Partnering Processes	20
7 Business Results	**450**
7.1 Customer Satisfaction Results	130
7.2 Financial and Market Results	130
7.3 Human Resource Results	35
7.4 Supplier and Partner Results	25
7.5 Company-Specific Results	130
TOTAL POINTS	**1000**

Benchmarking and Baldrige   Measuring an organization's performance against its own historical performance is central to the Baldrige criteria. Tracking performance encourages continuous improvement. Part of the reasoning for emphasizing quality results is the experience that "if it doesn't get measured, it doesn't improve."

To truly create improvement, a firm must continually compare its performance on critical criteria against the best in the business. This is **benchmarking.** Baldrige is a starting point to understand each part of the organization, and it forces self-evaluation. A company can then adjust its goals and set strategies based on these benchmarks.

Benchmarking

Baldrige Award Winners' Successes   The following are a few of the claims by companies that have won the Baldrige Award. These statements may be biased, but we have no doubt that most winners showed significant benefits.

- At Globe Metallurgical, exports have grown from 2 percent to 20 percent of sales from 1988 to 1992, while overall sales grew by 24 percent.
- IBM Rochester had a 25 percent growth in market share from 1988 to 1992, with new installations in 1992 at twice the rate of 1988.
- The Ritz-Carlton Hotel Company has been honored by the travel industry with 121 quality awards since 1991.
- Texas Instruments Defense Systems & Electronics Group had a 21 percent reduction in production cycle time in 1992, with a 56 percent reduction in stock-to-production time.
- At Federal Express, staff Quality Action Teams (QATs) have generated significant savings: $27 million in the Personnel Division since 1986; $1.5 million in recovered revenue by a computer automation QAT; and $462,000 in saved overtime payments in six months by a payroll QAT.
- The Westinghouse Commerical Nuclear Fuel Division's product reliability has continuously improved over the past 10 years, resulting in the industry's best fuel performance and a doubling of orders, compared to eight years ago.
- Motorola's employee productivity has improved 100 percent over the past six years (an annual compounded rate of 12.2 percent) through robust design, continuous improvement in defect reduction, and employee education and empowerment. It claims to save $125 million per year through quality improvements.
- Dana Commercial Credit Corporation has reduced the time it takes to approve a transaction from about seven hours in 1992 to an hour or less in 1996.
- The AT&T Universal Card program opened its 1 millionth account 78 days after program launch, and a month later, it was one of the top 10 credit card programs in the nation.
- AT&T Transmission Systems Business Unit reduced time to market by 50 percent in three years.
- Solectron, by focusing on customer satisfaction, has seen average yearly revenue growth of 46.8 percent, and by focusing on process quality, it has seen average yearly net income growth of 57.3 percent over the past five years.

According to a study conducted by the National Institute of Standards and Technology, companies that have won the Baldrige Award have performed very well as a stock market investment (see the box, "Study Finds 'Quality Stocks' Yield Big Payoff").

 What Are the Characteristics of a Baldrige Award Winner?[2]   So far, no one single approach to achieving high quality appears common. Nor does there seem to be one recipe for firms to follow to ensure success. Some firms send employees to school, some hire consultants, and some do it themselves internally. However, there were four common elements for all Baldrige winners:

1. The companies formulated a vision of what they thought quality was and how they would achieve it.
2. Senior management was actively involved.
3. Companies carefully planned and organized their quality effort to be sure it would be effectively initiated.
4. They vigorously controlled the overall process.

For each of the winners, the quality drive became more than a program. It penetrated every aspect of corporate life: performance appraisals and incentive pay supported quality objectives, hiring practices, team training, job posting systems, and so on. The quality of human resources was as important as productivity measures such as cycle time reduction and vendor quality assurance.

Baldrige winners carry their commitment to customer satisfaction to extremes. Motorola managers wear pagers so that customers can reach them at any time and any place. Globe responds to all customer questions within 24 hours. Westinghouse's Commercial Nuclear Fuel Division spends $18 million per year on training specifically devoted to quality improvement processes, principles, technology, and objectives.

The Baldrige Award is not without its shortcomings, especially for professional service firms. A major consulting firm applied for the Baldrige in 1994, but could not

---

[2] This section is based on Richard M. Hodges, *Blueprint for Continuous Improvement: Lessons from the Baldrige Winners* (New York: American Management Association, 1993).

The Quality Gurus Compared

Exhibit 6.6

	Crosby	Deming	Juran
Definition of quality	Conformance to requirements	A predictable degree of uniformity and dependability at low cost and suited to the market	Fitness for use (satisfies customer's needs)
Degree of senior management responsibility	Responsible for quality	Responsible for 94% of quality problems	Less than 20% of quality problems are due to workers
Performance standard/ motivation	Zero defects	Quality has many "scales"; use statistics to measure performance in all areas; critical of zero defects	Avoid campaigns to do perfect work
General approach	Prevention, not inspection	Reduce variability by continuous improvement; cease mass inspection	General management approach to quality, especially human elements
Structure	14 steps to quality improvement	14 points for management	10 steps to quality improvement
Statistical process control (SPC)	Rejects statistically acceptable levels of quality [wants 100% perfect quality]	Statistical methods of quality control must be used	Recommends SPC but warns that it can lead to tool-driven approach
Improvement basis	A process, not a program; improvement goals	Continuous to reduce variation; eliminate goals without methods	Project-by-project team approach; set goals
Teamwork	Quality improvement teams; quality councils	Employee participation in decision making; break down barriers between departments	Team and quality circle approach
Costs of quality	Cost of nonconformance; quality is free	No optimum; continuous improvement	Quality is not free; there is not an optimum
Purchasing and goods received	State requirements; supplier is extension of business; most faults due to purchasers themselves	Inspection too late; sampling allows defects to enter system; statistical evidence and control charts required	Problems are complex; carry out formal surveys
Vendor rating	Yes and buyers; quality audits useless	No, critical of most systems	Yes, but help supplier improve

make its best case since the award process prohibits evaluators from talking to clients. Also, the concept of a university as a supplier of a firm's resources—business school graduates—is not a common view of manufacturing-oriented evaluators.

The Baldrige Award and the Quality Gurus

One of the intentions of the Baldrige designers was to develop an award that captured the ideas of the leading quality philosophers (or gurus)—Philip Crosby, W. Edwards Deming, and Joseph M. Juran—while at the same time being "nondenominational" with respect to advocating one particular quality view. (See the box, on page 208, "W. Edwards Deming," for more information about this quality guru.) While there are differences in many areas among the three philosophies compared in Exhibit 6.6, it is fair to say that this goal was achieved. The reason lies in the nonprescriptive nature of the Baldrige criteria, the fact that the gurus all advocate generally the same thing, and, in our opinion, that they all emphasize top management leadership in the quality effort. The proof is in the pudding as well—different Baldrige winners have been adherents to Deming, Crosby, or Juran approaches.

The 14 points.

1. Create constancy of purpose toward improvement of product and service, with the aim to become competitive and to stay in business, and to provide jobs.

2. Adopt the new philosophy. We are in a new economic age. Western management must awaken to the challenge, must learn their responsibilities, and take on leadership for change.

3. Cease dependence on inspection to achieve quality. Eliminate the need for inspection on a mass basis by building quality into the product in the first place.

4. End the practice of awarding business on the basis of price tag. Instead, minimize total cost. Move toward a single supplier for any one item, on a long-term relationship of loyalty and trust.

5. Improve constantly and forever the system of production and service, to improve quality and productivity, and thus constantly decrease costs.

6. Institute training on the job.

7. Institute leadership. The aim of supervision should be to help people and machines and gadgets to do a better job. Supervision of management is in need of overhaul, as well as supervision of production workers.

8. Drive out fear, so that everyone may work effectively for the company.

9. Break down barriers between departments. People in research, design, sales, and production must work as a team, to foresee problems of production and in use that may be encountered with the product or service.

10. Eliminate slogans, exhortations, and targets for the work force which ask for zero defects and new levels of productivity. Such exhortations only create adversarial relationships, since the bulk of the causes of low quality and low productivity belong to the system and thus lie beyond the power of the work force.
    - Eliminate work standards (quotas) on the factory floor. Substitute leadership.
    - Eliminate management by objectives. Eliminate management by numbers, numerical goals. Substitute leadership.

11. Remove barriers that rob the hourly worker of his right to pride of workmanship. The responsibility of supervisors must be changed from sheer numbers to quality.

12. Remove barriers that rob people in management and in engineering of their right to pride of workmanship. This means, for example, abolishment of annual or merit rating and of management by objectives.

13. Institute a vigorous program of education and self-improvement.

14. Put everybody in the company to work to accomplish the transformation. The transformation is everyone's job.

Source: Deming Institute.
(http://www.deming.org)

W. Edwards Deming, 1900–1993

■ QUALITY SPECIFICATION AND QUALITY COSTS

Fundamental to any quality program is the determination of quality specifications and the costs of achieving (or *not* achieving) those specifications.

Dimension	Meaning
Performance	Primary product or service characteristics
Features	Added touches, bells and whistles, secondary characteristics
Reliability	Consistency of performance over time, probability of failing
Durability	Useful life
Serviceability	Ease of repair
Response	Characteristics of the human-to-human interface (speed, courtesy, competence)
Aesthetics	Sensory characteristics (sound, feel, look, etc.)
Reputation	Past performance and other intangibles (perceived quality)

Exhibit 6.7

The Dimensions of
Design Quality

Developing Quality Specifications

The quality specification of a product or service derive from decisions and actions made relative to the quality of its design and the quality of its conformance to that design. **Design quality** refers to the inherent value of the product in the marketplace and is thus a strategic decision for the firm. The common dimensions of design quality are listed in Exhibit 6.7.

Design Quality

Conformance quality refers to the degree to which the product or service design specifications are met. Execution of the activities involved in achieving conformance are of a tactical day-to-day nature. It should be evident that a product or service can have high design quality but low conformance quality, and vice versa.

Conformance Quality

Quality at the source is frequently discussed in the context of conformance quality. This means that the person who is doing the production takes responsibility for making sure that his/her output meets specification. If this can be accomplished, then in theory, the ultimate goal of **zero defects** throughout the process is achievable. (Zero defects had been frequently used as the rallying cry for a companywide quality effort. The term has fallen into disrepute because it was often just a slogan, unsupported by quality training and real quality commitment by management.)

Quality at the Source

Zero Defects

Where a product is involved, achieving the quality specifications is typically the responsibility of manufacturing management; in a service industry, it is usually the responsibility of the branch operations management. Exhibit 6.8 shows two examples of the **dimensions of quality.** One is a stereo amplifier that meets the signal-to-noise ratio standard; the second is a checking account transaction in a bank.

Dimensions of Quality

Both quality of design and quality of conformance should provide products that meet the customer's objectives for those products. This is often termed the product's *fitness for use,* and it entails identifying the dimensions of the product (or service) that the customer wants (i.e., the voice of the customer) and developing a quality control program to ensure these dimensions are met.

Cost of Quality

While few can quarrel with the notion of prevention, management often needs hard numbers to determine how much prevention activities will cost. This issue was recognized by Joseph Juran, who wrote about it in 1951 in his *Quality Control Handbook.* Today, **cost of quality (COQ)** analyses are common in industry and constitute one of the primary functions of QC departments.

Cost of Quality

Exhibit 6.8

Examples of
Dimensions of Quality

| | Measures | |
Dimension	Product Example: Stereo Amplifier	Service Example: Checking Account at a Bank
Performance	Signal-to-noise ratio, power	Time to process customer requests
Features	Remote control	Automatic bill paying
Reliability	Mean time to failure	Variability of time to process requests
Durability	Useful life (with repair)	Keeping pace with industry trends
Serviceability	Modular design	On-line reports
Response	Courtesy of dealer	Courtesy of teller
Aesthetics	Oak-finished cabinet	Appearance of bank lobby
Reputation	Market leader for 20 years	Endorsed by community leaders

There are a number of definitions and interpretations of the term *cost of quality.* From the purist's point of view, it means all of the costs attributable to the production of quality that is not 100 percent perfect. A less stringent definition considers only those costs that are the difference between what can be expected from excellent performance and the current costs that exist.

How significant is the cost of quality? It has been estimated at between 15 and 20 percent of every sales dollar—the cost of reworking, scrapping, repeated service, inspections, tests, warranties, and other quality-related items. Philip Crosby states that the correct cost for a well-run quality management program should be under 2.5 percent.[3]

Three basic assumptions justify an analysis of the costs of quality: (1) that failures are caused, (2) that prevention is cheaper, and (3) that performance can be measured.

The *costs of quality* are generally classified into four types:

1. *Appraisal costs:* the costs of the inspection, testing, and other tasks to ensure that the product or process is acceptable.

2. *Prevention costs:* the sum of all the costs to prevent defects, such as the costs to identify the *cause* of the defect, to implement corrective action to eliminate the cause, to train personnel, to redesign the product or system, and for new equipment or modifications.

3. *Internal failure costs:* The costs for defects incurred within the system: scrap, rework, repair.

4. *External failure costs:* The costs for defects that pass through the system: customer warranty replacements, loss of customer or goodwill, handling complaints, and product repair.

Exhibit 6.9 illustrates the type of report that might be submitted to show the various costs by categories.

Prevention is the most important influence. The rule of thumb says that for every dollar you spend in prevention, you can save $10 in failure and appraisal costs.

---

[3] Philip B. Crosby, *Quality Is Free* (New York: New American Library, 1979), p. 15.

Exhibit 6.9

Quality Cost Report

	Current Month's Cost	Percent of Total
Prevention costs		
Quality training	$ 2,000	1.3%
Reliability consulting	10,000	6.5
Pilot production runs	5,000	3.3
Systems development	8,000	5.2
Total prevention	25,000	16.3
Appraisal costs		
Materials inspection	6,000	3.9
Supplies inspection	3,000	2.0
Reliability testing	5,000	3.3
Laboratory testing	25,000	16.3
Total appraisal	39,000	25.5
Internal failure costs		
Scrap	15,000	9.8
Repair	18,000	11.8
Rework	12,000	7.8
Downtime	6,000	3.9
Total internal failure	51,000	33.3
External failure costs		
Warranty costs	14,000	9.2
Out-of-warranty repairs and replacement	6,000	3.9
Customer complaints	3,000	2.0
Product liability	10,000	6.5
Transportation losses	5,000	3.3
Total external failure	38,000	24.9
Total quality costs	$153,000	100.0

Often, increases in productivity occur as a by-product of efforts to reduce the cost of quality. A bank, for example, set out to improve quality and reduce the cost of quality and found that it had also boosted productivity. The bank developed this productivity measure for the loan processing area: the number of tickets processed divided by the resources required (labor cost, computer time, ticket forms). Before the quality improvement program, the productivity index was 0.2660 [2,080/($11.23 × 640 hours + $0.05 × 2,600 forms + $500 for systems costs)]. After the quality improvement project was completed, labor time fell to 546 hours and the number of forms fell to 2,100, for a change in the index to 0.3088, an increase in productivity of 16 percent.

Generic Tools and Tools of the QC Department

The generic tools of TQM are those developed for statistical process control (SPC), which we include later in this chapter under "Tools and Procedures of CI" and in the supplement to this chapter.

The typical manufacturing QC department has a variety of functions to perform. These include testing designs for their reliability in the lab and the field; gathering performance data on products in the field and resolving quality problems in the field; planning and budgeting the QC program in the plant; and, finally, designing and overseeing quality control systems and inspection procedures, and actually carrying out inspection activities requiring special technical knowledge to accomplish. The tools of the QC department fall under the heading of statistical quality control (SQC) and consist of two main sections: acceptance sampling and process control. These topics are covered in the supplement to this chapter.

**Continuous
Improvement**

Vol. II
"Improving Operations
Methods"

■ CONTINUOUS IMPROVEMENT (CI)

Continuous improvement (CI) is a management philosophy that approaches the challenge of product and process improvement as a never-ending process of achieving small wins. It is an integral part of a total quality management system. Specifically, **continuous improvement** seeks *continual improvement of machinery, materials, labor utilization, and production methods through application of suggestions and ideas of team members*. Though pioneered by U.S. firms, this philosophy has become the cornerstone of the Japanese approach to operations and is often contrasted with the traditional Western approach of relying on major technological or theoretical innovations to achieve "big win" improvements. In a survey of 872 North American manufacturing executives, the majority of world-class manufacturers favored continuous improvement over 11 other management enhancement programs. Clearly, continuous improvement is a subject that warrants a careful look.

In this section, we discuss the key managerial elements of continuous improvement and apply some of the basic tools associated with the CI process. We also discuss its impact on quality improvement.

Although management in both Japan and the West historically have implemented CI in manufacturing plants, it has become quite common in services as well. Consider the following *Fortune* excerpt about Federal Express:

By rethinking product design, members of this "bullet train" team at Yokogawa's Kofu factory cut the cost of making industrial recordings, like those shown on the table, by 45%. General Electric is now copying its techniques.

At lunch with one team [of back-office employees], this reporter sat impressed as entry-level workers, most with only high school educations, ate their chicken and dropped sophisticated management terms like **kaizen,** the Japanese art of continuous improvement, and *pareto,* a form of problem solving that requires workers to take a logical step-by-step approach. The team described how one day during a weekly meeting, a clerk from quality control pointed out a billing problem. The bigger a package, he explained, the more Fedex charges to deliver it. But the company's wildly busy delivery people sometimes forgot to check whether customers had properly marked the weight of packages on the air bill. That meant that Fedex, whose policy in such cases is to charge customers the lowest rate, was losing money. The team switched on its turbochargers. An employee in billing services found out which field offices in Fedex's labyrinthine 30,000-person courier network were forgetting to check the packages, and then explained the problem to the delivery people. Another worker in billing set up a system to examine the invoices and made sure the solution was working. Last year alone the team's ideas saved the company $2.1 million.[4]

Kaizen

Tools and Procedures of CI

The approaches companies take to CI as a process range from very structured programs utilizing statistical process control (SPC) tools to simple suggestion systems relying on brainstorming and "back-of-an-envelope" analyses. Exhibit 6.10 shows some common SPC tools used for problem solving and continuous improvement.

Another tool is the **PDCA** (*plan-do-check-act*) **cycle,** often called the Deming Wheel (see Exhibit 6.11), which conveys the sequential and continual nature of the CI process. The *plan* phase of the cycle is where an improvement area (sometimes called a *theme*) and a specific problem with it are identified. It is also where the analysis is done, Exhibit 6.12 is a CI example using the 5W2H method. (5W2H stands for *w*hat, *w*hy, *w*here, *w*hen, *w*ho, *h*ow, and *h*ow much.)

PDCA Cycle

The *do* phase of the PDCA cycle deals with implementing the change. Experts usually recommend that the plan be done on a small scale first, and that any changes in the plan be documented. (Check sheets are useful here, too.) The *check* phase deals with evaluating data collected during the implementation. The objective is to see if there is a good fit between the original goal and the actual results. During the *act* phase, the improvement is codified as the new standard procedure and replicated in similar processes throughout the organization.

The group-level CI process is frequently represented as if we were developing a storyboard for a movie. Exhibit 6.13, for example, summarizes the steps just discussed as the "QI (quality improvement) Story."

Benchmarking for CI

The CI approaches described so far are more or less inward looking: They seek to make improvements by analyzing in detail the current practices of the company itself. Benchmarking, however, goes outside the organization to examine what industry competitors and excellent performers outside the industry are doing. Its basic objective is simple: Find the best practices that lead to superior performance and see how you can use them. The practice of benchmarking is a hallmark of Malcolm Baldrige

---

[4] Brian Dumaine, "Who Needs a Boss?" *Fortune,* May 7, 1990, p. 54.

These tools do not substitute for judgment and process knowledge. They help deal with complexity and turn raw data into information that can be used to take action.

Process Flow Chart

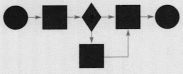

A picture which describes the main steps, branches and eventual outputs of a process.

Pareto Analysis

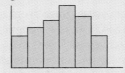

A coordinated approach for identifying, ranking, and working to permanently eliminate defects. Focuses on important error sources. 80/20 rule: 80 percent of the problems are due to 20 percent of the causes.

Run Chart

A time sequence chart showing plotted values of a characteristic.

Data Collection

Always have an agreed upon and clear reason for any data you collect. Prepare in advance your strategy for both collecting and analyzing the data. Questions that might be asked of data collection: Why? What? Where? How much? When? How? Who? How long?

Histogram

A distribution showing the frequency of occurrences between the high and low range of data.

Scatter Diagram

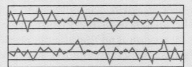

Also known as a correlation chart. A graph of the value of one characteristic versus another characteristic.

Checksheet

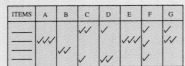

An organized method for recording data.

Causes and Effect Diagram

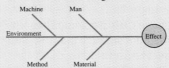

A tool that uses a graphical description of the process elements to analyze potential sources of process variation.

Control Charts

A time sequence chart showing plotted values of a statistic, including a central line and one or more statistically derived control limits.

Exhibit 6.11

PDCA Cycle
(Deming Wheel)

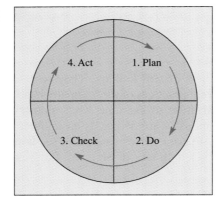

Type	5W2H	Description	Countermeasure
Subject matter	What?	What is being done? Can this task be eliminated?	Eliminate unnecessary tasks.
Purpose	Why?	Why is this task necessary? Clarify the purpose.	
Location	Where?	Where is it being done? Does it have to be done there?	Change the sequence or combination.
Sequence	When?	When is the best time to do it? Does it have to be done then?	
People	Who?	Who is doing it? Should someone else do it? Why am I doing it?	
Method	How?	How is it being done? Is this the best method? Is there some other way?	Simplify the task.
Cost	How much?	How much does it cost now? What will the cost be after improvement?	Select an improvement method.

Exhibit 6.12

The 5W2H Method

A number of simple guidelines have been developed to help people or groups generate new ideas. In general, these guidelines urge you to question everything, from every conceivable angle. The figure outlines the 5W2H method. The five "W's" are what, why, where, when, and who; the two "H's" are how and how much.

National Quality Award winners and is widely used throughout industry in general. Benchmarking typically involves the following steps:

1. *Identify those processes needing improvement.* This is equivalent to selecting a theme in CI.

2. *Identify a firm that is the world leader in performing the process.* For many processes, this may be a company that is not in the same industry. Examples include Xerox using L. L. Bean as the benchmark in evaluating its order entry system, or ICL (a major British computer maker) benchmarking Marks and Spenser (a large U.K. clothing retailer) to improve its distribution system. A McKinsey study cited a firm that measured pit stops on a motor racing circuit as a benchmark for worker changes on its assembly line.[5]

3. *Contact the managers of that company and make a personal visit to interview managers and workers.* Many companies select a team of workers from that process to be on a benchmarking team as part of a CI program.

4. *Analyze data.* This entails looking at gaps between what your company is doing and what the benchmark company is doing. There are two aspects of the study: one is comparing the actual processes; the other is comparing the performance of those processes according to some set of measures. The processes are often described using flow charts or written descriptions. (In some cases, companies permit videotaping, although there is a tendency now for benchmarked companies to keep things under wraps in fear of giving away process secrets.)

Typical performance measures for process comparisons are breakouts of cost, quality, and service, such as cost per order, percent defectives, and service response time.

---

[5] Steven Walleck, David O'Halloran, and Charles Leader, "Benchmarking World-Class Performance," *McKinsey Quarterly,* 1991, no. 1, p. 7.

| | Exhibit 6.13 | The QI Story | | |

	QI Story Step	Function	Tools
	1. Select theme.	· Decide theme for improvement. · Make clear why the theme is selected.	"Next processes are our customers." · Standardization · Education · Immediate remedy versus recurrence prevention
	2. Grasp the current situation.	· Collect data. · Find the key characteristics of the theme. · Narrow down the problem area. · Establish priorities: serious problems first.	· Check sheet · Histogram · Pareto

Plan	3. Conduct analysis.	· List all the possible causes of the
		  most serious problem.
		· Study the relations between possible
		  causes and between
		  causes and problem.
		· Select some causes and establish
		  hypotheses about possible relations.
		· Collect data and study
		  cause-and-effect relation.
			· Fishbone
			· Check sheet
			· Scatter diagram
			· Stratification

	4. Devise countermeasures.	· Devise countermeasures to eliminate the cause(s) of a problem.	· Intrinsic technology · Experience
Do		· Implement countermeasures. (Experiment.)	
Check	5. Confirm the effect of countermeasures.	· Collect data on the effects of the countermeasures. · Do before-after comparison.	· All seven tools

Act	6. Standardize the countermeasures.	· Amend the existing standards
		  according to the countermeasures
		  whose effects are confirmed.	

	7. Identify the remaining problems and evaluate the whole procedure.		

Source: Paul Lillrank and Noriak Kano, *Continuous Improvement: Quality Control Circles in Japanese Industry* (Ann Arbor: University of Michigan, Center for Japanese Studies, 1989), p. 27.

■ THE SHINGO SYSTEM: FAIL-SAFE DESIGN

The Shingo system developed in parallel and in many ways in conflict with the statistically based approach to quality control. As we discussed in Chapter 5 relating to service applications, this system—or, to be more precise, philosophy of production management—is named after the codeveloper of the Toyota just-in-time system, Shigeo Shingo. Although famous in Japan where he was known as Mr. Improvement, Shingo's work is now recognized in the West. Two aspects of the Shingo system in particular have received great attention. One is how to accomplish drastic cuts in equipment setup times by single minute exchange of die (SMED) procedures. The other, the focus of this section, is the use of source inspection and the poka-yoke system to achieve zero defects.

Exhibit 6.14

Poka-Yoke Example
(Placing labels on
parts coming down a
conveyor)

Before Improvement

The operation depended on the
worker's vigilance.

After Improvement

Device to ensure attachment of
labels

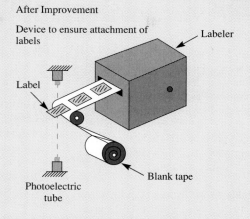

Label

Labeler

Blank tape

Photoelectric
tube

The tape fed out by the labeler turns sharply so that the
labels detach and project out from the tape. This is
detected by a photoelectric tube and, if the label is not
removed and applied to the product within the tact time
of 20 seconds, a buzzer sounds and the conveyor stops.

Effect: Label application failures were eliminated.
Cost: ¥ 15,000 ($75)

Shingo has argued that SQC methods do not prevent defects. Although they provide information to tell us probabilistically when a defect will occur, they are after the fact. The way to prevent defects from coming out at the end of a process is to introduce controls within the process. Central to Shingo's approach is the difference between errors and defects. Defects arise because people make errors. Even though errors are inevitable, defects can be prevented if feedback leading to corrective action takes place immediately after the errors are made. Such feedback and action require inspection, which should be done on 100 percent of the items produced. This inspection can be one of three types: successive check, self check, and source inspection. *Successive check* inspection is performed by the next person in the process or by an objective evaluator such as a group leader. Information on defects is immediate feedback for the worker who produced the product, who then makes the repair. *Self-check* is done by the individual worker and is appropriate by itself on all but items that require sensory judgment (e.g., existence or severity of scratches, or correct matching of shades of paint). These require successive checks. *Source inspection* is also performed by the individual worker, except instead of checking for defects, the worker checks for the errors that will cause defects. This prevents the defects from ever occurring and, hence, requiring rework. All three types of inspection rely on controls consisting of ***fail-safe procedures*** or devices (called **poka-yoke**). Poka-yoke includes such things as checklists or special tooling that (1) prevents the worker from making an error that leads to a defect before starting a process or (2) gives rapid feedback of abnormalities in the process to the worker in time to correct it.

Fail-Safe Procedures

Poka-Yoke

There is a wide variety of poka-yokes, ranging from kitting parts from a bin (to ensure that the right number is used in assembly) to sophisticated detection and electronic signaling devices. An example taken from the writings of Shingo is shown in Exhibit 6.14.

BREAKTHROUGH

Quality 1 on 1   **S**

Even though the Hewlett-Packard Company (HP) has enjoyed financial success and industry kudos, it has not been immune to increasing pressures in today's business world. Pressures such as rising customer expectations, emerging high-growth markets, an increasing dependence on suppliers and other third parties, and accelerating product life cycles have led HP to introduce a new quality campaign: Quality 1 on 1.

"Quality 1 on 1 heralds a shift from quality as a set of beliefs and practices to quality as a purposeful game plan," stated Richard LeVitt, director of HP quality, in an internal company document. "Quality 1 on 1, means knowing quality as a customer does and systematically acting on that knowledge to grow a business."

The phrase "Knowing quality as a customer does" means:

- Having more awareness of how customers feel about their experiences when they do business with HP.
- Understanding their problems and goals when possible and collaborating on solutions.
- Knowing how customers sum up their experiences and decide whether to do more business with HP.

The phrase "Acting on that knowledge" means more than just fixing problems. It means:

- Seeing HP employees and operations as a customer does.
- Creating customer-centered quality systems that span entire value chains.
- Influencing not only an entity's performance, but also the performance of partners, suppliers, and channels that affect the customer experience. Part of the Quality 1 on 1 process asks employees to not only look at their work from a producer's view, but also from a consumer's view.

The Producer's View

Employees are accustomed to taking the producer's view of quality—a view that is rational and objective. The producer's view of quality has changed over the years at HP, according to LeVitt. "Many ideas have come to represent quality as a *goal* and quality as a *strategy.*" The goals have included conforming to requirements, ensuring fitness for use, meeting customer expectations, and providing superior value. The strategies have included tests and inspections, process improvement, and total quality management.

Although these goals and strategies still have an important role in HP today, they don't necessarily lead to customer loyalty. To achieve customer loyalty, the consumer's view is also needed.

The Consumer's View

Consumers don't usually think of quality in terms of conformance to requirements or fitness for use, rather, they have impressions of quality and goals that they hope to fulfill by using a product or service. "Their impressions and goals influence their choices," said LeVitt. "As something is chosen, each consumer begins a sequence of experiences over a span of time. These experiences lead to emotional states, such as satisfaction, delight, anger, or dismay, which influence future choices. Attention to their impressions, goals, experiences, and emotional states can help producers create mutually beneficial relationships with their customers. These relationships are the foundation of Quality 1 on 1."

There are certain events surrounding the purchase and use of a product or service that become

---

There is a good deal more to say about the work of Shingo. Blasting industry's preoccupation with control charts, Shingo states they are nothing but a mirror reflecting current conditions. When a chemical plant QC manager proudly stated that it had 200 charts in a plant of 150 people, Shingo asked him if "they had a control chart for control charts?"[6] In addition to his insights into the quality area, his work on SMED is must reading for manufacturing executives.

---

[6] Alan, Robinson. *Modern Approaches to Manufacturing Improvement: The Shingo System* (Cambridge, MA: Productivity Press, 1990), p. 234.

part of a consumer's experience. These events can either increase the person's confidence in the company's product or service or increase the likelihood that he or she will make the next purchase elsewhere.

Although each product or service has its own consumer-experience life cycle, customers generally go through these stages:

1. *Clarifying a purpose and selecting a solution.* The customer becomes aware of his or her needs and selects a product or service that will meet those needs.

2. *Ordering what is chosen at an agreed-on price.* The customer actually buys (or places an order to buy) the product or service. This could be as quick and simple as buying a toothbrush or as time-consuming and complex as buying a new car.

3. *Becoming ready to use the selection.* The customer prepares to use the product or service (e.g., setting up a new computer or taking the plastic wrapper off of a new compact disc). Problems and frustrations at this step commonly cause customer dissatisfaction.

4. *Becoming proficient.* The customer learns how to use the product or service. This stage is often more time-consuming with high-technology products, such as computers and videocassette recorders. At this point, a customer discovers whether the product or service meets his or her expectations, so first impressions are important.

5. *Receiving the intended benefits.* The customer receives the anticipated benefits. When no problems arise and the customer's purpose for buying the product or service is met, the customer feels gratified by the good choice he or she made. When problems occur the customer begins to wonder if he or she should have chosen another product.

6. *Keeping everything going.* If something goes wrong with a product or service, the customer will be at a peak of emotional engagement with the product. The responsiveness of the company at this time is critical. If a situation is not handled well, the customer can develop long-lasting feelings of anger. Conversely, when a situation is effectively handled with an attitude of personal caring and concern, the customer's emotional response can be strongly positive.

7. *Letting go and moving on.* The customer decides to discontinue use of the product or service because it no longer meets his or her needs. By reflecting on his or her interactions with the product or service and the company that sold it, the customer forms a lasting impression that guides future decisions. These reflections can influence brand loyalty, so attention to the customer relationship at this late stage in the life cycle is also important.

Two Views Are Better Than One

Quality 1 on 1 helps employees make a conscious effort to account for the customer's entire experience with the product or service. This is important, said LeVitt, because, "Quality isn't just something producers do for consumers. It is a result of the producer's creation of a product and the customer's experience with a product." Thus, taking both the producer's and consumer's view is necessary in today's marketplace.

Source: Richard LeVitt, "Quality 1 on 1: Becoming Customer Centered," Quality Progress, October 1996, p. 33. © 1996 American Society for Quality Control. Reprinted with permission.

ISO 9000

ISO 9000 is a series of standards agreed upon by the International Organization for Standardization (ISO) and adopted in 1987. More than 100 countries now recognize the 9000 series for quality standards and certification for international trade. ISO 9000 evolved in Europe and in the European Common Market (ECM) alone, almost 50,000 companies have been certified as complying with these standards. The United

ISO 9000

(http://www.iso.ch)

States has been slower to respond, but several thousand U.S. companies have adopted ISO 9000. (Most of these companies have multiple plants and locations.) Certainly, all companies that intend to engage in international trade will have to adopt these standards eventually.

Historians claim that ISO 9000 originated from the quality standards of the U.S. Dept. of Defense (MIL-Q9858) in the late 1950s. The British Standards Institution adopted these standards and expanded them to include the entire business process in 1979 and called them the British Standard 5750. The International Organization for Standardization adopted the British Standard 5750 in 1987 and called it the ISO 9000 series.

The ISO 9000 Series

ISO 9000 consists of five primary parts numbered as 9000 through 9004 (Exhibit 6.15). If we were to display them on a continuum of an operating firm, the series would range from design and development through procurement, production, installation, and servicing (Exhibit 6.16). While ISO 9000 and 9004 only establish guidelines for operation, ISO 9001, 9002, and 9003 are well-defined standards.

Quite a bit of work and expense may be needed to be accredited at the highest level, which is 9001. Furthermore, some firms may not need ISO 9001 accreditation. For example, note that in Exhibit 6.16, ISO 9003 covers quality in production's final

---

Exhibit 6.15

ISO 9000 Series Systems and Guidelines for Use

Quality System

9001: Model for Quality Assurance in Design, Production Installation, and Servicing. (To be used when conformance to specified requirements is to be assured by the supplier during several stages which *may* include design/development, production, installation, and servicing)

9002: Model for Quality Assurance in Production and Installation. (To be used when conformance to specified requirements is to be assured by the supplier during production and installation)

9003: Model for Quality Assurance in Final Inspection Test. (To be used when conformance to specified requirements is to be assured by the supplier solely at final inspection and test)

Guidelines for Use

9000: Quality Management and Quality Assurance Standards—Guidelines for Selection and Use.

9004: Quality Management and Quality System Elements—Guidelines.

Exhibit 6.16

ISO 9000 Standards and Their Areas of Application in Production Flow

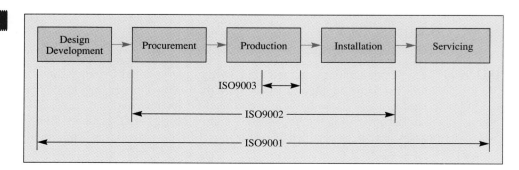

inspection and testing. A firm can be accredited at this level of final production only. This would essentially guarantee the firm's quality of final output and be attractive to customers. A broader accreditation would be 9002, which extends from purchasing and production through installation.

There are 20 elements in the ISO 9000 standards that relate to how the system operates and how well it is performing. These are contained in section 4 of the ISO 9000 Guidelines (Exhibit 6.17). Each of these elements applies in varying degrees to the three standards 9001, 9002, and 9003. (ISO 9001 contains all of them.)

ISO 9000 is somewhat intentionally vague. A *firm* interprets the requirements as they relate to *its* business. From a practical and useful standpoint for businesses, ISO 9000 is valuable to firms because it provides a framework so they can assess where they are and where they would like to be. In its simplest terms, it is sometimes stated that ISO 9000 directs you to "document what you do and then do as you documented." While to some extent this is true, ISO 9000 is much more than that since it promotes awareness and continuous improvement. The International Organization for Standardization intended the 9000 series to be more than a standard, reflecting a well-organized operation with trained, motivated people. It is proposed as the new challenge, with firms that move quickly enjoying the benefits of being a leader, while those that delay lose business. In reviewing the parts of ISO 9000 that we show in the exhibits, note that they are commonsense principles that have existed for many years.

ISO 9000 Certification

Why is it important to become ISO 9000 certified? For one reason, it is essential from a purely competitive standpoint. Consider the situation where you need to purchase parts for your firm, and several suppliers offer similar parts at similar prices. Assume that one of these firms has been ISO 9000 certified and the others have not. From whom would you purchase? There is no doubt that the ISO 9000–certified company would have the inside track in your decision making. Why? Because ISO 9000 specifies the way the supplier firm operates as well as its quality standards, delivery times, service levels, and so on.

There are three forms of certification:

1. First party: A firm audits itself against ISO 9000 standards.
2. Second party: A customer audits its supplier.
3. Third party: A "qualified" national or international standards or certifying agency serves as auditor.

The best certification of a firm is through a third party. Once passed by the third-party audit, a firm is certified and may be registered and recorded as having achieved ISO 9000 status, and it becomes part of a registry of certified companies. This third-party certification also has legal advantages in the European Community. For example, a manufacturer is liable for injury to a user of the product. The firm, however, can free itself from any liability by showing that it has used the appropriate standards in its production process and carefully selected its suppliers as part of its purchasing requirement. For this reason, there is strong motivation to choose ISO 9000–certified suppliers.

If a manufacturer wants to purchase from a noncertified supplier, the manufacturer should visit the supplier and examine its processes, past performances, workers' credentials, and so on to verify that the supplier can meet the required quality levels

Exhibit 6.17   The 20 Elements to Be Addressed in an ISO 9000 Quality System

1. Management Responsibility
  a. The quality policy shall be defined, documented, understood, implemented, and maintained.
  b. Responsibilities and authorities for all personnel specifying, achieving, and monitoring quality shall be defined. In-house verification resources shall be defined, trained, and funded. A designated management person sees that the Q91 program is implemented and maintained.

2. Quality System
  a. Procedures shall be prepared.
  b. Procedures shall be implemented.

3. Contract Review
  a. Incoming contracts (and purchase orders) shall be reviewed to see whether the requirements are adequately defined, agree with the bid, and can be implemented.

4. Design Control
  a. The design project shall be planned.
  b. Design input parameters shall be defined.
  c. Design output, including crucial product characteristics, shall be documented.
  d. Design output shall be verified to meet input requirements.
  e. Design changes shall be controlled.

5. Document Control
  a. Generation of documents shall be controlled.
  b. Distribution of documents shall be controlled.
  c. Changes to documents shall be controlled.

6. Purchasing
  a. Potential subcontractors and subsuppliers shall be evaluated for their ability to provide stated requirements.
  b. Requirements shall be clearly defined in contracting data.
  c. Effectiveness of the subcontractor's quality assurance system shall be assessed.

7. Customer-Supplied Material
  a. Any customer-supplied material shall be protected against loss or damage.

8. Product Identification and Traceability
  a. The product shall be identified and traceable by item, batch, or lot during all stages of production, delivery, and installation.

9. Process Control
  a. Production (and installation) processes shall be defined and planned.
  b. Production shall be carried out under controlled conditions: documented instructions, in-process controls, approval of processes and equipment, and criteria for workmanship.
  c. Special processes that cannot be verified after the fact shall be monitored and controlled throughout the processes.

10. Inspection and Testing
  a. Incoming materials shall be inspected or verified before use.
  b. In-process inspection and testing shall be performed.
  c. Final inspection and testing shall be performed prior to release of finished product.
  d. Records of inspection and test shall be kept.

11. Inspection, Measuring, and Test Equipment
  a. Equipment used to demonstrate conformance shall be controlled, calibrated, and maintained:
   · Identify measurements to be made.
   · Identify affected instruments.
   · Calibrate instruments (procedures and status indicators).
   · Periodically check calibration.
   · Assess measurement validity if found out of calibration.
   · Control environmental conditions in metrology lab.
  b. Measurement uncertainty and equipment capability shall be known.
  c. Where test hardware or software is used, it shall be checked before use and rechecked during use.

12. Inspection and Test Status
  a. Status of inspections and tests shall be maintained for items as they progress through various processing steps.
  b. Records shall show who released conforming product.

13. Control of Nonconforming Product
  a. Nonconforming product shall be controlled to prevent inadvertent use or installation.
  b. Review and disposition of nonconforming product shall be accomplished in a formal manner.

14. Corrective Action
  a. Problem causes shall be identified.
  b. Specific problems and their causes shall be corrected.
  c. Effectiveness of corrective actions shall be assessed.

15. Handling, Storage, Packaging, and Delivery
  a. Procedures for handling, storage, packaging, and delivery shall be developed and maintained.
  b. Handling controls shall prevent damage and deterioration.
  c. Secure storage shall be provided. Product in stock shall be checked for deterioration.
  d. Packing, preservation, and marking processes shall be controlled.
  e. Quality of the product after final inspection shall be maintained. This might include delivery controls.

16. Quality Records
  a. Quality records shall be identified, collected, indexed, filed, stored, maintained, and dispositioned.

17. Internal Quality Audits
  a. Audits shall be planned and performed.
  b. Results of audits shall be communicated to management.
  c. Any deficiencies found shall be corrected.

18. Training
  a. Training needs shall be identified.
  b. Training shall be provided.
  c. Selected tasks might require qualified individuals.
  d. Records of training shall be maintained.

19. Servicing
  a. Servicing activities shall be performed to written procedures.
  b. Servicing activities shall meet requirements.

20. Statistical Techniques
  a. Statistical techniques shall be identified.
  b. Statistical techniques shall be used to verify acceptability of process capability and product characteristics.

Source: Dennis R. Arter, "Demystifying the ISO 9000/290 Series Standards," *Quality Progress*, November 1992, p. 66. © 1992 American Society for Quality Control. Reprinted with permission.

and performance schedule. Of course, it is easier, cheaper, quicker, and legally safer to select an already certified supplier.

Certification can take as little as three to six months (if a firm is currently using military standards) or as long as two years (if top management is not fully committed). Certification involves getting the proper documents, initiating the required procedures and practices, and conducting internal audits. This can be followed by a second- or third-party audit as desired.

ISO 9000: An Everyday Example

One example that demonstrates how ISO 9000 applies to an everyday situation is having the brakes of your car worked on at the local garage.[7] You remember a local garage's ad for a special on brake repairs; in addition, you recall a neighbor speaking highly of the place.

As you approach the front counter of the shop, your journey through ISO 9000 begins. The clerk listens to your experience with the brakes and details about your car. He informs you that your car will require metallic brake pads that will cost extra. You agree to go ahead with the job, and the clerk promises your car will be ready in one hour.

As you wait, you mull over your main concerns: Will the car stop properly? Will the repair cost more than was stated? Will they complete the work in an hour? This is what ISO 9000 is all about—confidence that the task will be done *as promised*. The ISO 9000 standard encompasses many details that would easily be taken for granted. As illustrated in the rest of this example, the standard requires that attention be paid to every aspect of the brake job.

You realize that when you picked up the advertisement there was a management structure that made sure the business ran well and that quality methods and practices are used, which gave the garage a good reputation. You want to be confident that the mechanic knows where to get the work order papers for your car, and actually gets *your* car. Hopefully the mechanic has been trained to drive your car onto the ramp properly, disassemble the brakes, and inspect them to ensure nothing else is wrong. Also, you hope the mechanic goes to the proper documents and determines which brake pads are right for your car and retrieves the parts from a bin with the pads correctly identified. You would expect that if a mechanic tried to use some parts that ended up not fitting, he would have removed them from stock rather than putting them back in and passing the problem on to you. You hope that this person can assemble and adjust the brakes to the proper specifications and finally test them by driving your car around the block. You expect to be provided with a check sheet of the items tested and that your car was parked in a safe place. This example covers many of the 20 ISO 9000 elements.

1. *Management responsibility*—Someone is in control ensuring that the organization is selling products and services in the fashion it claims to.

2. *Quality system*—The owners of the operation have a quality system in place to ensure their business operates as indicated. When you approached the counter, the clerk created a contract with you. This person was knowledgeable about the

---

[7] This section is from John T. Rabbitt and Peter A. Bergh, *The ISO 9000 Book* (White Plains, NY: Quality Resources, 1993), pp. 17–20.

product and communicated with the shop to know approximately how long it would be. The clerk had the training and documents to know that your car required metallic pads, where you should leave your car, and what to do when you returned to pick it up. This person was also willing and able to address your further questions and concerns.

3. *Contract review*—Ensures that the work performed by the mechanic was what you had agreed to with the clerk.

4. *Design control*—Ensures that the brakes placed on your car were properly designed, tested, and documented so as to perform the job as specified.

5. *Document control*—Ensures that the documents and reference books were available to the mechanic for the proper selection of materials and the appropriate testing.

6. *Purchasing*—Ensures that the mechanic had the correct parts available.

7. *Customer-supplied material*—(In this case, no material was supplied by the customer.)

8. *Product identification and traceability*—Ensures that the brake linings retrieved from the stock bin were marked properly.

9. *Process control*—There were established procedures for the mechanic to do the job, fill out the paperwork, find information on the materials, and access usable assembly instructions.

10. *Inspection and testing*—The mechanic did some form of inspection and test to ensure that your new brakes were acting properly.

11. *Inspection, measuring, and test equipment*—Ensures that the testing and measurement-setting devices are calibrated to the correct torques and that the right tools are being used to do it.

12. *Inspection and test status*—Ensures that the check-off sheet is a working document and that tests were performed.

13. *Control of nonconforming product*—Ensures that the mechanic knows what to do if a possible problem is detected with the material and how it should be treated and identified to prevent it from ending up on the other side of your car.

14. *Corrective action*—Ensures that the mechanic and his management have a procedure for fixing known problems.

15. *Handling, storage, packaging, and delivery*—The mechanic must know how to handle the brake pads before installation and ensure that they have been stored in a protected area. In addition, the mechanic must know where to put your car, keys, and paperwork when completed.

16. *Quality records*—The mechanic fills out a standard checklist, makes additional notes on the procedure being performed, and perhaps even has a place to record related issues for you to consider and for the shop to note.

17. *Internal quality audits*—The supervisor should be regularly observing the areas to ensure that the mechanic has all the correct materials and documents and is performing tasks correctly.

18. *Training*—This ensures that the mechanic had the proper training before working on your car and that the supervisor went over the task and verified that the mechanic was successful in all aspects of the job.

19. *Servicing*—Ensures that the mechanic knows what to do if something doesn't work correctly with the new brakes.

20. *Statistical techniques*—This ensures that metrics are kept regarding the quality of the service provided at the garage and are reviewed to ensure that the processes remain in control and that problem areas are quickly identified.

You notice an hour has passed. You go to the front desk. The clerk says, "Your car is coming out right now and we noticed that your driver's side windshield wiper was worn, so we replaced it free of charge, as our management believes your safety is paramount. Here are your keys and an itemized check sheet of all the tasks completed. This will also act as your warranty. Please note our toll-free number should you have any problems or wish to make an appointment for any of your other vehicles. Thank you for your patronage and please drive carefully."

This is a simple tale about brakes being fixed and a very happy customer in the end. It illustrated an ISO 9000–compliant organization taking care of the customer in a way that met the customer's expectations.

ISO 9000 versus the Baldrige Criteria

Rabbitt and Bergh nicely answer three questions relating ISO 9000 and the Baldrige award as follows:[8]

1. Should we go for the Baldrige Award or ISO 9000 certification first?   Go for ISO 9000 compliance first. Achieving certification will help you prepare for the Baldrige. Since 1992 applications for the Baldrige Award have dropped. The feeling of the Baldrige committee that this is in response to companies going for ISO 9000 certification first.

2. What's the difference between ISO 9000 and the Baldrige Award?   ISO focuses very closely on internal processes, especially manufacturing, sales, administration, and technical support and services. The Baldrige places more emphasis on customer satisfaction and business results.

3. Do you have to be certified to ISO 9000 before going for the Baldrige?   The Baldrige assumes you have your processes under control and therefore awards relatively few points in this area. The Baldrige addresses the issues of customer satisfaction, business results, and the competitive aspects of gaining increased sales and profitability. ISO 9000 virtually ignores competitive positioning.

ISO is at the beginning of the quality evolution. ISO 9000 provides stability in the system and the minimum requirements for market survival. Once this is in place, it is easier to build to higher levels as Exhibit 6.18 shows.

■ CONCLUSION

This chapter contains a great deal of material that likely will form the basis by which many companies will operate in the future. The idea of a total quality environment including vendors and customers as well as all personnel and operations in the firm itself will probably not be a competitive weapon—it will be a requirement! A TQM environment with defect-free production will be an entry credential even to begin to

---

[8] Ibid., p. 22.

Exhibit 6.18   ISO 9000—the Basic End of the Quality Evolution

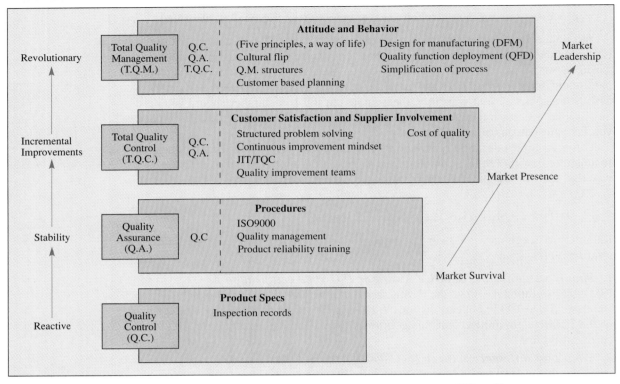

Source: John T. Rabbitt and Peter A. Bergh, *The ISO 9000 Book* (White Plains, NY: Quality Resources, 1993), p. 23.

play the competitive game. Quality guru Phil Crosby, in his recent book, stresses the need for continued emphasis on these ideas (see the Breakthrough box on page 227 "Quality Is Still Free").

ISO 9000 has provided international standards for certification and entry into foreign markets. It develops language for dealing with suppliers and customers, and its international adoption will continue at a rapid rate.

The Baldrige Award has greatly helped industry to become aware of problems we have had with quality. It has spilled over to the general public in their sensitivity and concern for quality. Further, its current widespread use in the U.S. government will cause significant change in the future. Baldrige criteria seem to be the best guidelines so far to develop a total quality management system. Firms are using the application forms for this purpose.

What is next after TQM? We can only speculate, but one thing is certain: It will be based on the presumption that a total quality system is a given.

REVIEW AND DISCUSSION QUESTIONS

1. What are the commonalities among companies winning the Baldrige Award?

2. How could you apply the Baldrige Award criteria to your university?

BREAKTHROUGH

Quality Is Still Free!

In his popular book *Quality Is Free*, published in 1978, Phil Crosby declared that quality is free. In his latest book *Quality Is Still Free* (McGraw-Hill, 1996), Mr. Crosby is still claiming that it is free. The first book stressed prevention and cooperation rather than detection and discipline as the keys to quality management. It showed that the result of quality lay in the hands of management, not in the quality control department. Crosby developed the idea that poor quality actually costs a company and that excellent quality led to profit improvement. He is credited with proposing the performance standard of zero defects back in 1961.

In his latest book, Crosby says that we now find ourselves faced again by systems (ISO 9000 is one; the Baldridge Award criteria is another) that can be installed in a company with the idea that it will take over the job of managing quality. Crosby says: "This situation is like my days in aerospace during the 1950s and 1960s. All companies and their suppliers were certified to Mil-Q-9858A, which the Department of Defense monitored closely. We all had books of procedures to show how we conformed. Yet in all the years I worked in that environment, I have no memory of anyone ever using "9858" or its procedures to do anything about running the company. In fact, it always

was hard to find a copy to use when the Department of Defense came by for an audit. What we were actually doing was much more than this specification contained. It was not enough, just as the ISO documents are not enough. No system can be installed to make management happen in any function."

Many who doubt the value of ISO 9000 and the Baldrige Award have argued that these guidelines have become too prescriptive. They claim that the implementers are only interested in receiving the "points" associated with a criteria. Crosby argues that the success of the early 1990s has brought about a relaxing of the need for zero defects in the minds of those who manage quality. He argues ". . . the nonconformance situation semiconductor suppliers found recently emerged from embracing the standard of "six sigma." This permits 3.4 defects per million components. Why anyone would want to do that is beyond me. But they are now paying the price. When even ordinary chips contain a million or more components, such a standard means that they are all defective."

Phil Crosby's ideas are thought provoking. What do you think about ISO 9000 and the Baldrige Award? Does the idea of zero defects make sense?

3. "Baldrige criteria are more appropriate for evaluating manufacturing firms than service firms." Comment.

4. How is the Baldrige Award process beneficial to companies that do not win?

5. "If line employees are required to assume the quality control function, their productivity will decrease." Discuss this.

6. "You don't inspect quality into a product; you have to build it in." Discuss the implications of this statement.

7. "Before you build quality in, you must think it in." How do the implications of this statement differ from those of Question 6?

8. Business writer Tom Peters has suggested that in making process changes, we should "Try it, test it, and get on with it." How does this philosophy square with the continuous improvement philosophy?

9. Shingo told a story of a poka-yoke he developed to make sure that operators avoided the mistake of putting less than the required four springs in a push button device. The existing method involved assemblers taking individual springs from a box containing several hundred, and then placing two of them behind an ON button and two more behind an OFF button. What was the poka-yoke Shingo created?

10. The typical computerized word processing package is loaded with poka-yokes. List three. Are there any others you wish the packages had?

11. Malcolm Baldrige Award Criteria: 1994 versus 1997—A Shift in Focus? The following are the award criteria, as listed in the 1994 and 1997 Award Criteria booklet published by the National Institute of Standards and Technology.

1994 Examination Categories/Items	Point Values
1 **Leadership**	**95**
1.1 Senior Executive Leadership	45
1.2 Management for Quality	25
1.3 Public Responsibility and Corporate Citizenship	25
2 **Information and Analysis**	**75**
2.1 Scope and Management of Quality and Performance Data and Information	15
2.2 Competitive Comparisons and Benchmarking	20
2.3 Analysis and Uses of Company-Level Data	40
3 **Strategic Quality Planning**	**60**
3.1 Strategic Quality and Company Performance Planning Process	35
3.2 Quality and Performance Plans	25
4 **Human Resource Development and Management**	**150**
4.1 Human Resource Planning and Management	20
4.2 Employee Involvement	40
4.3 Employee Education and Training	40
4.4 Employee Performance and Recognition	25
4.5 Employee Well-Being and Satisfaction	25
5 **Management of Process Quality**	**140**
5.1 Design and Introduction of Quality Products and Services	40
5.2 Process Management: Product and Service Production and Delivery Processes	35
5.3 Process Management: Business and Support Service Processes	30
5.4 Supplier Quality	20
5.5 Quality Assessment	15
6 **Quality and Operational Results**	**180**
6.1 Product and Service Quality Results	70
6.2 Company Operational Results	50
6.3 Business and Support Service Results	25
6.4 Supplier Quality Results	35
7 **Customer Focus and Satisfaction**	**300**
7.1 Customer Expectations: Current and Future	35
7.2 Customer Relationship Management	65
7.3 Commitment to Customers	15
7.4 Customer Satisfaction Determination	30
7.5 Customer Satisfaction Results	85
7.6 Customer Satisfaction Comparison	70
TOTAL POINTS	**1000**

1997 Categories/Items	Point Values
1 **Leadership**	**110**
1.1 Leadership System	80
1.2 Company Responsibility and Citizenship	30
2 **Strategic Planning**	**80**
2.1 Strategy Development Process	40
2.2 Company Strategy	40
3 **Customer and Market Focus**	**80**
3.1 Customer and Market Knowledge	40
3.2 Customer Satisfaction and Relationship Enhancement	40
4 **Information and Analysis**	**80**
4.1 Selection and Use of Information and Data	25
4.2 Selection and Use of Comparative Information and Data	15
4.3 Analysis and Review of Company Performance	40
5 **Human Resource Development and Management**	**100**
5.1 Work Systems	40
5.2 Employee Education, Training, and Development	30
5.3 Employee Well-Being and Satisfaction	30
6 **Process Management**	**100**
6.1 Management of Product and Service Processes	60
6.2 Management of Support Processes	20
6.3 Management of Supplier and Partnering Processes	20
7 **Business Results**	**450**
7.1 Customer Satisfaction Results	130
7.2 Financial and Market Results	130
7.3 Human Resource Results	35
7.4 Supplier and Partner Results	25
7.5 Company Specific Results	130
TOTAL POINTS	**1000**

a. Evaluate the two lists in terms of the actual criteria wording and also the criteria weights.

b. Has the focus of the award changed over time? How has the focus changed with respect to quality?

c. What is the new focus of the award?

PROBLEMS

1. Professor Chase is frustrated by his inability to make a good cup of coffee in the morning. Show how you would use a fishbone diagram to analyze the process he uses to make a cup of his evil brew.

1. See SM.

2. Use the benchmarking process and as many CI tools as you can to improve your performance in your weakest course in school.

2. See SM.

Case

Hank Kolb, Director Quality Assurance

Hank Kolb was whistling as he walked toward his office, still feeling a bit like a stranger since he had been hired four weeks before as director, quality assurance. All that week he had been away from the plant at an interesting seminar, entitled "Quality in the 90s," given for quality managers of manufacturing plants by the corporate training department. He was now looking forward to digging into the quality problems at this industrial products plant employing 1,200 people.

Kolb poked his head into Mark Hamler's office, his immediate subordinate as the quality control manager, and asked him how things had gone during the past week. Hamler's muted smile and an "Oh, fine," stopped Kolb in his tracks. He didn't know Hamler very well and was unsure about pursuing this reply any further. Kolb was still uncertain of how to start building a relationship with him since Hamler had been passed over for the promotion to Kolb's job—Hamler's evaluation form had stated "superb technical knowledge; managerial skills lacking." Kolb decided to inquire a little further and asked Hamler what had happened; he replied: "Oh, just another typical quality snafu. We had a little problem on the Greasex line last week [a specialized degreasing solvent packed in a spray can for the high technology sector]. A little high pressure was found in some cans on the second shift, but a supervisor vented them so that we could ship them out. We met our delivery schedule! Since Kolb was still relatively unfamiliar with the plant and its products, he asked Hamler to elaborate; painfully, Hamler continued:

> We've been having some trouble with the new filling equipment and some of the cans were pressurized beyond our AQL [acceptable quality level] on a psi rating scale.

The production rate is still 50 percent of standard, about 14 cases per shift, and we caught it halfway into the shift. Mac Evans [the inspector for that line] picked it up, tagged the cases, "hold," and went on about his duties. When he returned at the end of the shift to write up the rejects, Wayne Simmons, first-line supervisor, was by a pallet of finished goods finishing sealing up a carton of the rejected Greasex; the reject "hold" tags had been removed. He told Mac that he had heard about the high pressure from another inspector at coffee break, had come back, taken off the tags, individually turned the cans upside down and vented every one of them in the eight rejected cartons. He told Mac that production planning was really pushing for the stuff and they couldn't delay by having it sent through the rework area. He told Mac that he would get on the operator to run the equipment right next time. Mac didn't write it up but came in about three days ago to tell me about it. Oh, it happens every once in a while and I told him to make sure to check with maintenance to make sure the filling machine was adjusted; and I saw Wayne in the hall and told him that he ought to send the stuff through rework next time.

Kolb was a bit dumbfound at this and didn't say much—he didn't know if this was a big deal or not. When he got to his office he thought again what Morganthal, general manager, had said when he had hired him. He warned Kolb about the "lack of quality attitude" in the plant, and said that Kolb "should try and do something about this." Morganthal further emphasized the quality problems in the plant: "We have to improve our quality, it's costing us a lot of money, I'm sure of it, but I can't prove it! Hank, you have my full support in this matter; you're in charge of these quality problems. This downward quality-productivity-turnover spiral has to end!"

The incident had happened a week before; the goods were probably out in the customer's hands by now, and everyone had forgotten about it (or wanted to). There seemed to be more pressing problems than this for Kolb to spend his time on, but this continued to nag him. He felt that the quality department was being treated as a joke, and he also felt that this was a personal slap from manufacturing. He didn't want to start a war with the production people, but what could he do? Kolb was troubled enough to cancel his appointments and spend the morning talking to a few people. After a long and very tactful morning, he learned the following information:

1. *From personnel.* The operator for the filling equipment had just been transferred from shipping two weeks ago. He had no formal training in this job but was being trained by Wayne, on the job, to run the equipment. When Mac had tested the high-pressure cans the operator was nowhere to be found and had only learned of the rejected material from Wayne after the shift was over.

2. *From plant maintenance.* This particular piece of automated filling equipment had been purchased two years ago for use on another product. It had been switched to the Greasex line six months ago and maintenance had had 12 work orders during the last month for repairs or adjustments on it. The equipment had been adapted by plant maintenance for handling the lower viscosity of Greasex, which it had not originally been designed for. This included designing a special filling head. There was no scheduled preventive maintenance for this equipment and the parts for the sensitive filling head, replaced three times in the last six months, had to be made at a nearby machine shop. Nonstandard downtime was running at 15 percent of actual running time.

3. *From purchasing.* The plastic nozzle heads for the Greasex can, designed by a vendor for this new product on a rush order, were often found with slight burrs on the inside rim, and this caused some trouble in fitting the top to the can. An increase in application pressure at the filling head by maintenance adjustment had solved the burr application problem or had at least forced the nozzle heads on despite burrs. Purchasing agents said that they were going to talk to the sales representative of the nozzle head supplier about this the next time he came in.

4. *From product design and packaging.* The can, designed especially for Greasex, had been contoured to allow better gripping by the user. This change, instigated by marketing research, set Greasex apart from the appearance of its competitors and was seen as significant by the designers. There had been no test of the effects of the contoured can on filling speed or filling hydrodynamics from a high-pressured filling head. Kolb had a hunch that the new design was acting as a venturi (carrier creating suction) when being filled, but the packaging designer thought that was unlikely.

5. *From manufacturing manager.* He had heard about the problem; in fact, Simmons had made a joke about it, bragging about how he beat his production quota to the other foremen and shift supervisors. The manufacturing manager thought Simmons was one of the "best foremen we have . . . he always got his production out." His promotion papers were actually on the manufacturing manager's desk when Kolb dropped by. Simmons was being strongly considered for promotion to shift supervisor. The manufacturing manager, under pressure from Morganthal for cost improvements and reduced delivery times, sympathized with Kolb but said that the rework area would have vented with their pressure gauges what Wayne had done by hand. "But, I'll speak with Wayne about the incident," he said.

6. *From marketing.* The introduction of Greasex had been rushed to market to beat competitors and a major promotional-advertising campaign was underway to increase consumer awareness. A deluge of orders was swamping the order-taking department and putting Greasex high on the back-order list. Production had to turn the stuff out; even being a little off spec was tolerable because "it would be better to have it on the shelf than not there at all. Who cares if the label is a little crooked or the stuff comes out with a little too much pressure? We need market share now in that high-tech segment."

What bothered Kolb most was the safety issue of the high pressure in the cans. He had no way of knowing how much of a hazard the high pressure was or if Simmons had vented them enough to effectively reduce the hazard. The data from the can manufacturer, which Hamler had showed him, indicated that the high pressure found by the inspector was not in the danger area. But, again, the inspector had only used a sample testing procedure to reject the eight cases. Even if he could morally accept that there was no product safety hazard, could Kolb make sure that this would never happen again?

Skipping lunch, Kolb sat in his office and thought about the morning's events. The past week's seminar had talked about the role of quality, productivity and quality, creating a new attitude, and the quality challenge, but where had they told him what to do when this happened? He had left a very good job to come here because he thought the company was serious about the importance of quality, and he wanted a challenge. Kolb had demanded and received a salary equal to the manufacturing, marketing, and R&D directors, and he was one of the direct reports to the general manager. Yet he still didn't know exactly what he should or shouldn't do, or even what he could or couldn't do under these circumstances.

Questions

1. What are the causes of the quality problems on the Greasex line? Display your answer on a fishbone diagram.

2. What general steps should Hank follow in setting up a continuous improvement program for the company? What problems will he have to overcome to make it work?

Source: Copyright 1981 by President and Fellows of Harvard College, Harvard Business School. Case 681.083. This case was prepared by Frank S. Leonard as the basis for class discussion rather than to illustrate either effective or ineffective handling of an administrative situation. Reprinted by permission of the Harvard Business School.

Case

Shortening Customers' Telephone Waiting Time

This case illustrates how a bank applied some of the basic seven SPC tools shown in Exhibit 6.10 and storyboard concepts to improve customer service. It is the story of a quality circle (QC) program implemented in the main office of a large bank. An average of 500 customers call this office every day. Surveys indicated that callers tended to become irritated if the phone rang more than five times before it was answered, and often would not call the company again. In contrast, a prompt answer after just two rings reassured the customers and made them feel more comfortable doing business by phone.

Selection of a Theme

Telephone reception was chosen as a QC theme for the following reasons: (1) Telephone reception is the first impression a customer receives from the company, (2) this theme coincided with the company's telephone reception slogan, "Don't make customers wait, and avoid needless switching from extension to extension," and (3) it also coincided with a companywide campaign being promoted at that time that advocated being friendly to everyone one met.

First, the staff discussed why the present method of answering calls made callers wait. Case Exhibit C6.1

illustrates a frequent situation, where a call from customer B comes in while the operator is talking with customer A. Let's see why the customer has to wait.

At (1), the operator receives a call from the customer but, due to lack of experience, does not know where to connect the call. At (2), the receiving party cannot answer the phone quickly, perhaps because he or she is unavailable, and no one else can take the call. The result is that the operator must transfer the call to another extension while apologizing for the delay.

Cause-and-Effect Diagram and Situation Analysis

To fully understand the situation, the quality circle members decided to conduct a survey regarding callers who waited for more than five rings. Circle members itemized factors at a brainstorming discussion and arranged them in a cause-and-effect diagram. (See Exhibit C6.2.) Operators then kept check sheets on several points to tally the results spanning 12 days from June 4 to 16. (See Exhibit C6.3A.)

Results of the Check Sheet Situation Analysis

The data recorded on the check sheets unexpectedly revealed that "one operator (partner out of the office)" topped the list by a big margin, occurring a total of 172

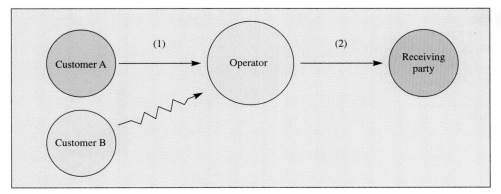

Exhibit C6.1

Why Customers Had to Wait

Exhibit C6.2   Cause-and-Effect Diagram

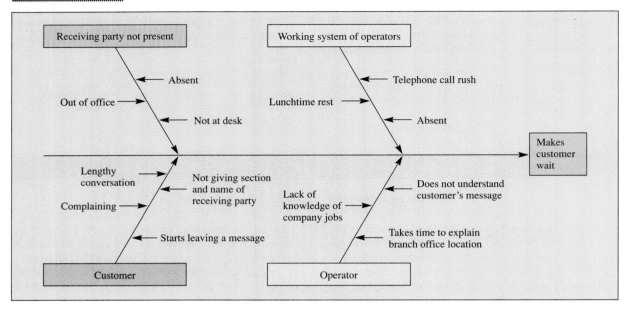

Exhibit C6.3   Causes of Callers' Waits

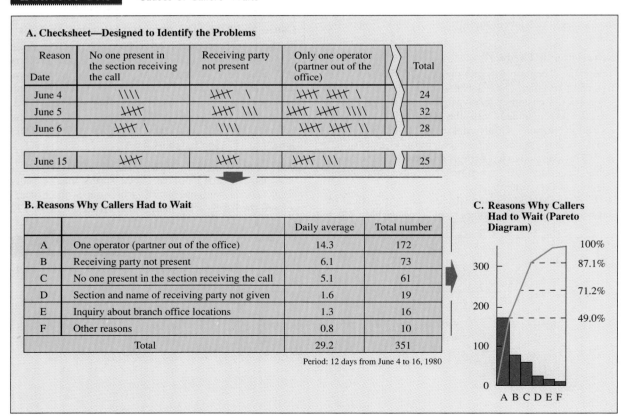

A. Checksheet—Designed to Identify the Problems

Reason Date	No one present in the section receiving the call	Receiving party not present	Only one operator (partner out of the office)		Total
June 4	\\\\	✝✝✝ \	✝✝✝ ✝✝✝ \		24
June 5	✝✝✝	✝✝✝ \\\	✝✝✝ ✝✝✝ \\\\		32
June 6	✝✝✝ \	\\\\	✝✝✝ ✝✝✝ \\		28
June 15	✝✝✝	✝✝✝	✝✝✝ \\\		25

B. Reasons Why Callers Had to Wait

		Daily average	Total number
A	One operator (partner out of the office)	14.3	172
B	Receiving party not present	6.1	73
C	No one present in the section receiving the call	5.1	61
D	Section and name of receiving party not given	1.6	19
E	Inquiry about branch office locations	1.3	16
F	Other reasons	0.8	10
	Total	29.2	351

Period: 12 days from June 4 to 16, 1980

C. Reasons Why Callers Had to Wait (Pareto Diagram)

times. In this case, the operator on duty had to deal with large numbers of calls when the phones were busy. Customers who had to wait a long time averaged 29.2 daily, which accounted for 6 percent of the calls received every day. (See Exhibits C6.3B and C6.3C.)

Setting the Target

After an intense but productive discussion, the staff decided to set a QC program goal of reducing the number of waiting callers to zero. That is to say that all incoming calls would be handled promptly, without inconveniencing the customer.

Measures and Execution

(a) Taking Lunches on Three Different Shifts, Leaving at Least Two Operators on the Job at All Times: Up until this resolution was made, a two-shift lunch system had been employed, leaving only one operator on the job while the other was taking a lunch break. However, since the survey revealed that this was a major cause of customers waiting on the line, the company brought in a helper operator from the clerical section.

(b) Asking All Employees to Leave Messages When Leaving Their Desks: The objective of this rule was to simplify the operator's chores when the receiving party was not at his desk. The new program was explained at the employees' regular morning meetings, and companywide support was requested. To help implement this practice, posters were placed around the office to publicize the new measures.

(c) Compiling a Directory Listing the Personnel and Their Respective Jobs: The notebook was specially designed to aid the operators, who could not be expected to know the details of every employee's job. The notebook would help properly route calls.

Confirming the Results

Although the waiting calls could not be reduced to zero, all items presented showed a marked improvement as shown in Exhibits C6.4A and C6.4B. The major cause of delays, "one operator (partner out of the office)," plummeted from 172 incidents during the control period to 15 in the follow-up survey.

Source: From "The Quest for Higher Quality—the Deming Prize and Quality Control," Ricoh Company, Ltd., in Masaaki Imai, *Kaizen: The Key to Japan's Competitive Success* (New York: Random House, 1986), pp. 54–58.

Exhibit C6.4

Effects of QC

A. Effects of QC (Comparison of before and after QC)

	Reasons why callers had to wait	Total Number Before	Total Number After	Daily Average Before	Daily Average After
A	One operator (partner out of the office)	172	15	14.5	1.2
B	Receiving party not present	73	17	6.1	1.4
C	No one present in the section receiving the call	61	20	5.1	1.7
D	Section and name of receiving party not given	19	4	1.6	0.3
E	Inquiry about branch office locations	16	3	1.3	0.2
F	Others	10	0	0.8	0
	Total	351	59	29.2	4.8

Period: 12 days from Aug. 17 to 30.

Problems are classified according to cause and presented in order of the amount of time consumed. They are illustrated in a bar graph. 100% indicates the total number of time-consuming

B. Effects of QC (Pareto Diagram)

SELECTED BIBLIOGRAPHY

Chowdhury, Subir, and Ken Zimmer. *QS-9000 Pioneers—Registered Companies Share Their Strategies for Success.* Burr Ridge, IL: Richard D. Irwin, 1996.

Creech, Bill. *The Five Pillars of TQM: How to Make Total Quality Managment Work for You.* New York: Truman Talley Books/Dutton, 1994.

Crosby, Philip B. *Quality Is Free.* New York: McGraw-Hill, 1979.

_____. *Quality without Tears.* New York: McGraw-Hill, 1984.

_____. *Running Things.* New York: McGraw-Hill, 1986.

_____. *Quality Is Still Free.* New York: McGraw-Hill, 1996.

Deming, Walter E. *Quality, Productivity, and Competitive Position.* Cambridge, MA: MIT Center for Advanced Engineering Study, 1982.

_____. *Out of the Crisis.* Cambridge, MA: MIT Center for Advanced Engineering Study, 1986.

Durand, Ian G.; Donald W. Marquardt; Robert W. Peach; and James C. Pyle. "Updating the ISO 9000 Quality Standards: Responding to Marketplace Needs." *Quality Progress,* July 1993, pp 23–28.

Ernst & Young Quality Improvement Consulting Group. *Total Quality: An Executive's Guide for the 1990s.* Homewood, IL: Business One Irwin, 1990.

Feigenbaum, A. V. *Total Quality Control.* New York: McGraw-Hill, 1991.

Gitlow, Howard S., and Shelly J. Gitlow. *The Deming Guide to Quality and Competitive Position.* Englewood Cliffs, NJ: Prentice Hall, 1987.

Giffi, Craig, Aleda V. Roth, and Gregory M. Seal. *Competing in World-Class Manufacturing: America's 21st-Century Challenge.* Homewood, IL: Richard D. Irwin, 1990.

Hendricks, Kevin B., and Vinod R. Singhal. "Quality Awards and the Market Value of the Firm: An Empirical Investigation." *Management Science* 42, no. 3 (March 1996), pp. 415–36.

Hodges, Richard M. *Blueprints for Continuous Improvement: Lessons from the Baldrige Winners.* New York: American Management Association, 1993.

Hoffherr, Glen D., and Gerald Nadler. *Breakthrough Thinking in Total Quality Management.* Englewood Cliffs, NJ: Prentice Hall, 1993.

Ishikawa, Kaoru (translated by David J. Lu). *What Is Total Quality Control?—the Japanese Way.* Englewood Cliffs, NJ: Prentice Hall, 1985.

Johnson, Richard S. *TQM: Leadership for the Quality Transformation,* vols. 1–4. Milwaukee: ASQC Quality Press, 1993.

Juran, Joseph M. *Quality Control Handbook.* 3rd ed. New York: McGraw-Hill, 1979.

Juran, Joseph M., and F. M. Gryna. *Quality Planning and Analysis.* 2nd ed. New York: McGraw-Hill, 1980.

Lampercht, James L. *Implementing the ISO 9000 Series.* New York: Marcel Dekker, 1993.

Lawler, Edward E., and Susan Albers Mohrman. *Employee Involvement and Total Quality Management: Practices and Results in Fortune 1000 Companies.* San Francisco: Jossey-Bass, 1992.

Mahoney, Francis X., and Carl G. Thor. *The TQM Trilogy: Using ISO 9000, the Deming Prize, and the Baldrige Award to Establish a System for Total Quality Management.* New York: American Management Association, 1994.

The Malcolm Baldrige National Quality Award. Managed by: U.S. Dept. of Commerce, Technology Administration, National Institute of Standards and Technology, Route 270 and Quince Orchard Road, Administration Building, Room A537, Gaithersburg, MD 20899–0001. Administered by: American Society for Quality Control, P.O. Box 3005, Milwaukee, WI 53201–3005.

Rabbitt, John T., and Peter A. Bergh. *The ISO 9000 Book.* White Plains, NY: Quality Resources, 1993.

Robinson, Alan. *Moderate Approaches to Manufacturing Improvement: The Shingo System.* Cambridge, MA: Productivity Press, 1990.

Rothery, Brian. *ISO 9000.* 2nd ed. Brookfield, VT: Gower, 1993.

Shiba, Shoji, Alan Graham, and David Waldman. *The New American TQM: Four Pratical Revolutions in Management.* Cambridge, MA: Productivity Press, 1993.

Shingo, Shiego. *Zero Quality Control: Source Inspection and the Poka-Yoke System.* Stamford, CT: Productivity Press, 1986.

Taguchi, G. *On-Line Quality Control during Production.* Tokyo: Japanese Standards Association, 1987.

Taormina, Tom. *Virtual Leadership and the ISO 9000 Imperative.* Englewood Cliffs, NJ: Prentice Hall, 1996.

Weimershirch, Arnold, and Stephen George. *Total Quality Management: Strategies and Techniques Proven at Today's Most Successful Companies.* New York: John Wiley & Sons, 1994.

1997 *Malcolm Baldrige National Quality Award: Criteria and Application Instructions.* Washington, DC: National Institute of Standards and Technology, 1997.

Statistical Quality Control Methods

Supplement Outline

Acceptance Sampling, 236

    Design of a Single Sampling Plan for
      Attributes
    Operating Characteristic Curves
    Shaping the OC Curve
    The Effects of Lot Size

Process Control Procedures, 240

    Process Control with Attribute
      Measurements: Using p Charts

Process Control with Variable
    Measurements: Using $\bar{X}$ and R Charts
How to Construct $\bar{X}$ and R Charts
Process Capability
Capability Index (C_{pk})

Taguchi Methods, 248

    Is an Out of Spec Product Really Out of
      Spec?

Key Terms

Statistical Quality Control (SQC)

Acceptance Sampling

Statistical Process Control (SPC)

Acceptance Quality Level (AQL)

Lot Tolerence Percent Defective (LTPD)

Operating Characteristic (OC) Curves

Six-Sigma Quality

Upper and Lower Tolerence Limits

Capability Index (C_{pk})

Taguchi Methods

www Links

ASQC (http://www.asqc.org)

Statistical Quality
Control (SQC)

Acceptance
Sampling

Statistical Process
Control (SPC)

Vol I "Quality"

The subject of **statistical quality control (SQC)** can be divided into *acceptance sampling* and *process control*. **Acceptance sampling** involves testing a random sample of existing goods and deciding whether to accept an entire lot based on the quality of the random sample. **Statistical process control (SPC)** involves testing a random sample of output from a process to determine whether the process is producing items within a preselected range. When the tested output exceeds that range, it is a signal to adjust the production process to force the output back into the acceptable range. This is accomplished by adjusting the process itself. Acceptance sampling is frequently used in a purchasing or receiving situation, while process control is used in a production situation of any type.

Quality control for both acceptance sampling and process control measures either attributes or variables. Goods or services may be observed to be either good or bad, or functioning or malfunctioning. For example, a lawnmower either runs or it doesn't; it attains a certain level of torque and horsepower or it doesn't. This type of measurement is known as sampling by attributes. Alternatively, a lawnmower's torque and horsepower can be measured as an amount of deviation from a set standard. This type of measurement is known as sampling by variables. The following sections describe some standard approaches to developing acceptance sampling plans and process control procedures.

◾ ACCEPTANCE SAMPLING

Design of a Single Sampling Plan for Attributes

Acceptance sampling is performed on goods that already exist to determine what percentage of products conform to specifications. These products may be items received from another company and evaluated by the receiving department or they may be components that have passed through a processing step and are evaluated by

An employee inspects the manufacture of Reese's Peanut Butter Cups. This is the last stage of full quality control where defective cups are removed.

company personnel either in production or later in the warehousing function. Whether inspection should be done at all is addressed in the following example.

Acceptance sampling is executed through a sampling plan. In this section, we illustrate the planning procedures for a single sampling plan—that is, a plan in which the quality is determined from the evaluation of one sample. (Other plans may be developed using two or more samples. See J. M. Juran and F. M. Gryna's *Quality Planning and Analysis* for a discussion of these plans.)

■ **example** S6.1   *Costs to Justify Inspection*   Total (100 percent) inspection is justified when the cost of a loss incurred by not inspecting is greater than the cost of inspection. For example, suppose a faulty item results in a $10 loss. If the average percentage of defective items in a lot is 3 percent, the expected cost of faulty items is $0.03 \times \$10$, or $0.30 each. Therefore, if the cost of inspecting each item is less than $0.30, the economic decision is to perform 100 percent inspection. Not all defective items will be removed, however, since inspectors will pass some bad items and reject some good ones.

The purposes of a sampling plan are to test the lot to either (1) find its quality or (2) ensure that the quality is what it is supposed to be. Thus, if a quality control supervisor already knows the quality (such as the 0.03 given in the example), he or she does not sample for defects. Either all of them must be inspected to remove the defects or none of them should be inspected, and the rejects pass into the process. The choice simply depends on the cost to inspect and the cost incurred by passing a reject. ■

A single sampling plan is defined by n and c, where n is the number of units in the sample and c is the acceptance number. The size of n may vary from one up to all the items in the lot (usually denoted as N) from which it is drawn. The acceptance number c denotes the maximum number of defective items that can be found in the sample before the lot is rejected. Values for n and c are determined by the interaction of four factors (AQL, α, LTPD, and β) that quantify the objectives of the product's producer and its consumer. The objective of the producer is to ensure that the sampling plan has a low probability of rejecting good lots. Lots are defined as high quality if they contain no more than a specified level of defectives, termed the **acceptable quality level (AQL)**.[1] The objective of the consumer is to ensure that the sampling plan has a low probability of accepting bad lots. Lots are defined as low quality if the percentage of defectives is greater than a specified amount, termed **lot tolerance percent defective (LTPD)**. The probability associated with rejecting a high quality lot is denoted by the Greek letter alpha (α) and is termed the *producer's risk*. The probability associated with accepting a low quality lot is denoted by the letter beta (β) and is termed the *consumer's risk*. The selection of particular values for AQL, α, LTPD, and β is an economic decision based on a cost trade-off or, more typically, on company policy or contractual requirements.

There is a humorous story supposedly about Hewlett-Packard during its first dealings with Japanese vendors, who place great emphasis on high-quality production. HP

Acceptable Quality Level (AQL)

Lot Tolerance Percent Defective (LTPD)

---

[1] There is some controversy surrounding AQLs. This is based on the argument that specifying some acceptable percent of defectives is inconsistent with the philosophical goal of zero defects. In practice, even in the best QC companies, there is an acceptable quality level. The difference is that it may be stated in parts per million rather than in parts per hundred. This is the case in Motorola's six-sigma quality standard, which holds that no more than 3.4 defects per million parts are acceptable.

c	LTPD ÷ AQL	n · AQL	c	LTPD ÷ AQL	n · AQL
0	44.890	0.052	5	3.549	2.613
1	10.946	0.355	6	3.206	3.286
2	6.509	0.818	7	2.957	3.981
3	4.890	1.366	8	2.768	4.695
4	4.057	1.970	9	2.618	5.426

Exhibit S6.1

Excerpt from a Sampling Plan Table for $\alpha = 0.05$, $\beta = 0.10$

had insisted on 2 percent AQL in a purchase of 100 cables. During the purchase agreement, some heated discussion took place wherein the Japanese vendor did not want this AQL specification; HP insisted that they would not budge from the 2 percent AQL. The Japanese vendor finally agreed. Later, when the box arrived, there were two packages inside. One contained 100 good cables. The other package had 2 cables with a note stating: "We have sent you 100 good cables. Since you insisted on 2 percent AQL, we have enclosed 2 defective cables in this package, though we do not understand why you want them."

The following example, using an excerpt from a standard acceptance sampling table, illustrates how the four parameters—AQL, α, LTPD, and β—are used in developing a sampling plan.

■ **example S6.2**   *Values of n and c*   Hi-Tech Industries manufactures Z-Band radar scanners used to detect speed traps. The printed circuit boards in the scanners are purchased from an outside vendor. The vendor produces the boards to an AQL of 2 percent defectives and is willing to run a 5 percent risk (α) of having lots of this level or fewer defectives rejected. Hi-Tech considers lots of 8 percent or more defectives (LTPD) unacceptable and wants to ensure that it will accept such poor-quality lots no more than 10 percent of the time (β). A large shipment has just been delivered. What values of n and c should be selected to determine the quality of this lot?

solution   The parameters of the problem are AQL = 0.02, α = 0.05, LTPD = 0.08, and β = 0.10. We can use Exhibit S6.1 to find c and n.

First, divide LTPD by AQL (0.08 ÷ 0.02 = 4). Then, find the ratio in column 2 that is equal to or just greater than that amount (i.e., 4). This value is 4.057, which is associated with $c = 4$.

Finally, find the value in column 3 that is in the same row as $c = 4$, and divide that quantity by AQL to obtain n (1.970 ÷ 0.02 = 98.5).

The appropriate sampling plan is $c = 4$, $n = 99$. ■

Operating Characteristic Curves

While a sampling plan such as the one just described meets our requirements for the extreme values of good and bad quality, we cannot readily determine how well the plan discriminates between good and bad lots at intermediate values. For this reason, sampling plans are generally displayed graphically through the use of **operating characteristic (OC) curves.** These curves, which are unique for each combination of n and c, simply illustrate the probability of accepting lots with varying percent defectives. The procedure we have followed in developing the plan, in fact, specifies two points on an OC curve—one point defined by AQL and $1 - \alpha$, and the other

Operating Characteristics (OC) Curves

Operating Characteristic Curve for AQL = 0.02, α = 0.05, LTPD = 0.08, β = 0.10   **Exhibit S6.2**

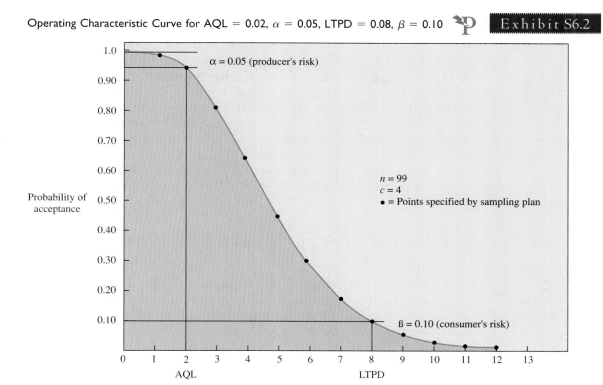

point defined by LTPD and β. Curves for common values of n and c can be computed or obtained from available tables.[2]

Shaping the OC Curve

A sampling plan discriminating perfectly between good and bad lots has an infinite slope (vertical) at the selected value of AQL. In Exhibit S6.2, any percent defective to the left of 2 percent would always be accepted, and those to the right, always rejected. However, such a curve is possible only with complete inspection of all units and thus is not a possibility with a true sampling plan.

An OC curve should be steep in the region of most interest (between the AQL and the LTPD), which is accomplished by varying n and c. If c remains constant, increasing the sample size n causes the OC curve to the more vertical. While holding n constant, decreasing c (the maximum number of defective units) also makes the slope more vertical, moving closer to the origin.

[2] See, for example, H. F. Dodge and H. G. Romig, *Sampling Inspection Tables—Single and Double Sampling* (New York: John Wiley & Sons, 1959); and *Military Standard Sampling Procedures and Tables for Inspection by Attributes* (MIL-STD-105D) (Washington, DC: U.S. Government Printing Office, 1983).

The Effects of Lot Size

The size of the lot that the sample is taken from has relatively little effect on the quality of protection. Consider, for example, that samples—all of the same size of 20 units—are taken from different lots ranging from a lot size of 200 units to a lot size of infinity. If each lot is known to have 5 percent defectives, the probability of accepting the lot based on the sample of 20 units ranges from about 0.34 to about 0.36. This means that so long as the lot size is several times the sample size, it makes little difference how large the lot is. It seems a bit difficult to accept, but statistically (on the average in the long run) whether we have a carload or box full, we'll get about the same answer. It just seems that a carload should have a larger sample size. Of course, this assumes that the lot is randomly chosen and that defects are randomly spread through the lot.

◼ PROCESS CONTROL PROCEDURES

Process control is concerned with monitoring quality *while the product or service is being produced*. Typical objectives of process control plans are to provide timely information on whether currently produced items are meeting design specifications and to detect shifts in the process that signal that future products may not meet specifications. The actual control phase of process control occurs when corrective action is taken, such as a worn part replaced, a machine overhauled, or a new supplier found. Process control concepts, especially statistically based control charts, are being used in services as well as in manufacturing.

Process Control with Attribute Measurements: Using *p* Charts

Measurement by attributes means taking samples and using a single decision—the item is good, or it is bad. Because it is a yes or no decision, we can use simple statistics to create a *p* chart with an upper control limit (UCL) and a lower control limit (LCL). We can draw these control limits on a graph and then plot the fraction defective of each individual sample tested. The process is assumed to be working correctly when the samples, which are taken periodically during the day, continue to stay between the control limits.

$$\overline{p} = \frac{\text{Total number of defects from all samples}}{\text{Number of samples} \times \text{Sample size}} \tag{S6.1}$$

$$s_p = \sqrt{\frac{\overline{p}(1 - \overline{p})}{n}} \tag{S6.2}$$

$$\text{UCL} = \overline{p} + zs_p \tag{S6.3}$$

$$\text{LCL} = \overline{p} - zs_p \tag{S6.4}$$

where $\overline{p}$ is the fraction defective, s_p is the standard deviation, n is the sample size and z is the number of standard deviations for a specific confidence. Typically, $z = 3$ (99.7 percent confidence) or $z = 2.58$ (99 percent confidence) are used.

Exhibit S6.3 shows information that can be gained from control charts. We will not give an example of attribute process control but will demonstrate $\overline{X}$ and R charts instead.

Control Chart Evidence for Investigation (Using Attributes)   Exhibit S6.3

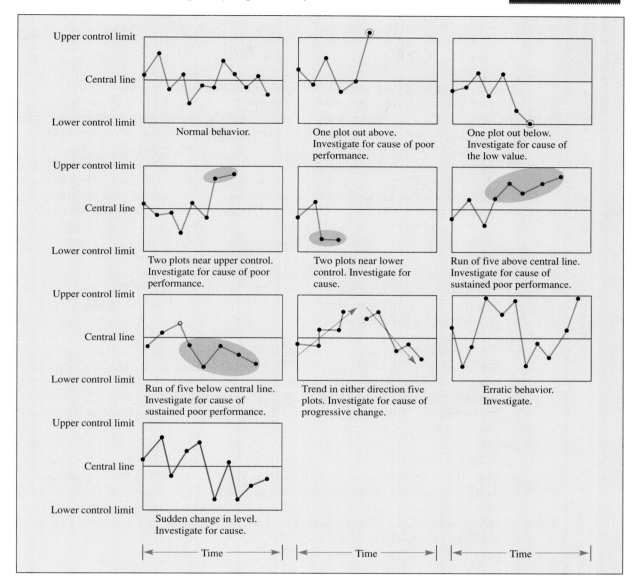

Process Control with Variable Measurements: Using $\overline{X}$ and R Charts

$\overline{X}$ and R (range) charts are widely used in statistical process control.

In attributes sampling, we determine whether something is good or bad, fit or didn't fit—it is a go/no-go situation. In variables sampling, however, we measure the actual weight, volume, number of inches, or other variable measurements, and we develop control charts to determine the acceptability or rejection of the process based on those measurements. For example, we might have a decision in attribute sampling that if something is over 10 pounds to reject it and under 10 pounds to accept it. In variable sampling we measure a sample and may record weights of 9.8 pounds or 10.2 pounds. These values are used to create or modify control charts and to see whether or not they fall within the acceptable limits.

There are four main issues to address in creating a control chart: the size of the samples, number of samples, frequency of samples, and control limits.

Size of Samples   For industrial applications in process control, it is preferable to keep the sample size small. There are two main reasons. First, the sample needs to be taken within a reasonable length of time; otherwise, the process might change while the samples are taken. Second, the larger the sample, the more it costs to take.

Sample sizes of four or five units seem to be the preferred numbers. The *means* of samples of this size have an approximately normal distribution, no matter what the distribution of the parent population looks like. Sample sizes greater than five give narrower control limits and thus more sensitivity. For detecting finer variations of a process, it may be necessary, in fact, to use larger sample sizes. However, when sample sizes exceed 15 or so, it would be better to use $\overline{X}$ charts with standard deviation σ rather than $\overline{X}$ charts with the range R.

Number of Samples   Once the chart has been set up, each sample taken can be compared to the chart and a decision can be made about whether the process is acceptable. To set up the charts, however, prudence (and statistics) suggests that 25 or so samples be taken.

Frequency of Samples   How often to take a sample is a trade-off between the cost of sampling (along with the cost of the unit if it is destroyed as part of the test) and the benefit of adjusting the system. Usually, it is best to start off with frequent sampling of a process and taper off as confidence in the process builds. For example, one might start with a sample of five units every half-hour and end up feeling that one sample per day is adequate.

Control Limits   Standard practice in statistical process control for variables is to set control limits three standard deviations above the mean and three standard deviations below. This means that 99.7 percent of the sample means are expected to fall within these control limits (that is, within a 99.7 percent confidence interval). Thus, if one sample mean falls outside this obviously wide band, we have strong evidence that the process is out of control.

How to Construct $\overline{X}$ and R Charts

If the standard deviation of the process distribution is known, the $\overline{X}$ chart may be defined

$$\text{UCL}_{\overline{X}} = \overline{\overline{X}} + zs_{\overline{X}} \quad \text{and} \quad \text{LCL}_{\overline{X}} = \overline{\overline{X}} - zs_{\overline{X}} \qquad (\text{S6.5})$$

where

$s_{\overline{X}} = s/\sqrt{n} =$ Standard deviation of sample means
$s \quad =$ Standard deviation of the process distribution
$n \quad =$ Sample size
$\overline{\overline{X}} \quad =$ Average of sample means or a target value set for the process
$z \quad =$ Number of standard deviations for a specific confidence (typically, $z = 3$)

An $\bar{X}$ chart is simply a plot of the means of the samples that were taken from a process. $\bar{\bar{X}}$ is the average of the means.

In practice, the standard deviation of the process is not known. For this reason, an approach that uses actual sample data is commonly used. This practical approach is described in the next section.

An R chart is a plot of the range within each sample. The range is the difference between the highest and the lowest numbers in that sample. R values provide an easily calculated measure of variation used like a standard deviation. An $\bar{R}$ chart is the average of the range of each sample. More specifically defined, these are

$$\bar{X} = \frac{\sum\limits_{i=1}^{n} X_i}{n} \tag{S6.6}$$

where

$\bar{X}$ = Mean of the sample
i = Item number
n = Total number of items in the sample

$$\bar{\bar{X}} = \frac{\sum\limits_{j=1}^{m} \bar{X}_j}{m} \tag{S6.7}$$

Number of Observations in Subgroup n	Factor for $\bar{X}$ Chart A_2	Factors for R Chart	
		Lower Control Limit D_3	Upper Control Limit D_4
2	1.88	0	3.27
3	1.02	0	2.57
4	0.73	0	2.28
5	0.58	0	2.11
6	0.48	0	2.00
7	0.42	0.08	1.92
8	0.37	0.14	1.86
9	0.34	0.18	1.82
10	0.31	0.22	1.78
11	0.29	0.26	1.74
12	0.27	0.28	1.72
13	0.25	0.31	1.69
14	0.24	0.33	1.67
15	0.22	0.35	1.65
16	0.21	0.36	1.64
17	0.20	0.38	1.62
18	0.19	0.39	1.60
19	0.19	0.40	1.61
20	0.18	0.41	1.59

Upper control limit for $\bar{X} = UCL_{\bar{X}} = \bar{\bar{X}} + A_2\bar{R}$
Lower control limit for $\bar{X} = LCL_{\bar{X}} = \bar{\bar{X}} - A_2\bar{R}$
Upper control limit for $R = UCL_R = D_4\bar{R}$
Lower control limit for $R = LCL_R = D_3\bar{R}$

Exhibit S6.4

Factors for Determining from $\bar{R}$ the Three-Sigma Control Limits for $\bar{X}$ and R Charts

Note: All factors are based on the normal distribution.

where

$\overline{\overline{X}}$ = The average of the means of the samples
j = Sample number
m = Total number of samples
R_j = Difference between the highest and lowest measurement in the sample
$\overline{R}$ = Average of the measurement differences R for all samples, or

$$\overline{R} = \frac{\sum\limits_{j=1}^{m} R_j}{m} \tag{S6.8}$$

E. L. Grant and R. Leavenworth computed a table that allows us to easily compute the upper and lower control limits for both the $\overline{X}$ chart and the R chart.[3] These are defined as

$$\text{Upper control limit for } \overline{X} = \overline{\overline{X}} + A_2 \overline{R} \tag{S6.9}$$

$$\text{Lower control limit for } \overline{X} = \overline{\overline{X}} - A_2 \overline{R} \tag{S6.10}$$

$$\text{Upper control limit for } R = D_4 \overline{R} \tag{S6.11}$$

$$\text{Lower control limit for } R = D_3 \overline{R} \tag{S6.12}$$

Sample Number	Each Unit in Sample					Average $\overline{X}$	Range R
1	10.60	10.40	10.30	9.90	10.20	10.28	.70
2	9.98	10.25	10.05	10.23	10.33	10.17	.35
3	9.85	9.90	10.20	10.25	10.15	10.07	.40
4	10.20	10.10	10.30	9.90	9.95	10.09	.40
5	10.30	10.20	10.24	10.50	10.30	10.31	.30
6	10.10	10.30	10.20	10.30	9.90	10.16	.40
7	9.98	9.90	10.20	10.40	10.10	10.12	.50
8	10.10	10.30	10.40	10.24	10.30	10.27	.30
9	10.30	10.20	10.60	10.50	10.10	10.34	.50
10	10.30	10.40	10.50	10.10	10.20	10.30	.40
11	9.90	9.50	10.20	10.30	10.35	10.05	.85
12	10.10	10.36	10.50	9.80	9.95	10.14	.70
13	10.20	10.50	10.70	10.10	9.90	10.28	.80
14	10.20	10.60	10.50	10.30	10.40	10.40	.40
15	10.54	10.30	10.40	10.55	10.00	10.36	.55
16	10.20	10.60	10.15	10.00	10.50	10.29	.60
17	10.20	10.40	10.60	10.80	10.10	10.42	.70
18	9.90	9.50	9.90	10.50	10.00	9.96	1.00
19	10.60	10.30	10.50	9.90	9.80	10.22	.80
20	10.60	10.40	10.30	10.40	10.20	10.38	.40
21	9.90	9.60	10.50	10.10	10.60	10.14	1.00
22	9.95	10.20	10.50	10.30	10.20	10.23	.55
23	10.20	9.50	9.60	9.80	10.30	9.88	.80
24	10.30	10.60	10.30	9.90	9.80	10.18	.80
25	9.90	10.30	10.60	9.90	10.10	10.16	.70

$$\overline{\overline{X}} = 10.21$$

$$\overline{R} = .60$$

Exhibit S6.5

Measurements in Samples of Five from a Process

---

[3] E. L. Grant and R. Leavenworth, *Statistical Quality Control* (New York: McGraw-Hill, 1964), p. 562.

■ **example** S6.3 $\overline{X}$ *and R Charts*   We would like to create $\overline{X}$ and R charts for a process. Exhibit S6.5 shows measurements for all 25 samples. The last two columns show the average of the sample $\overline{X}$ and the range R.

Values for A_2, D_3, and D_4 were obtained from Exhibit S6.4.

Upper control limit for $\overline{X} = \overline{\overline{X}} + A_2\overline{R} = 10.21 + .58(.60) = 10.56$

Lower control limit for $\overline{X} = \overline{\overline{X}} - A_2\overline{R} = 10.21 - .58(.60) = 9.86$

Upper control limit for $R = D_4\overline{R} = 2.11(.60) = 1.27$

Lower control limit for $R = D_3\overline{R} = 0(.60) = 0$

Exhibit S6.6 shows the $\overline{X}$ chart and R chart with a plot of all the sample means and ranges of the samples. All the points are well within the control limits, although sample 23 is close to the $\overline{X}$ lower control limit.

Process Capability

Six-Sigma

Upper and Lower Specification or Tolerance Limits

Motorola made process capability and product design famous by adopting its now well-known **six-sigma** limits. Six-sigma is a short cut for saying six standard deviations from the mean. When we design a part, we specify that certain dimensions should be within a range. These design limits are often referred to as the **upper and lower specification limits** or the **upper and lower tolerance limits.** Note that these are different from the upper and lower control limits that we specified for the process.

As a simple example, assume that we are designing a bearing for a rotating shaft— say an axle for the wheel of a car. There are many variables involved for both the bearing and the axle—for example, the width of the bearing, the size of the rollers, the size of the axle, the length of the axle, how it is supported, and so on. The designer specifies tolerances for each of these variables to ensure that the parts will fit properly. Suppose that initially a design is selected and the diameter of the bearing is set at 1.250 inches ± 0.005 inches. This means that acceptable parts may have a diameter that varies between 1.245 to 1.255 inches (which are the lower and upper tolerance limits).

Next, consider the process in which the bearing will be made. Let's say that by running some tests, we determine the machine output to have a variation of sigma equal to 0.002 inch. If we are using three-sigma control limits on our process, bearings will have a variation of ± 0.006 inch. Assuming that the process is centered at 1.250 inches, this means that we will produce parts that vary between 1.244 and 1.256

$\overline{X}$ Chart and R Chart

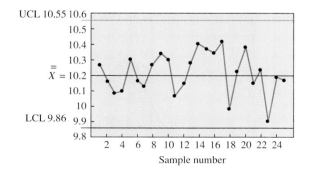

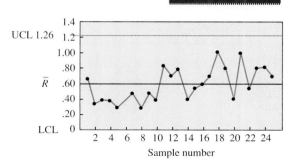

inches. As we can see, our process limits are greater than the tolerance limits specified by our designer. This is not good, because we will produce many parts that do not meet specification.

Motorola, with their six-sigma criterion, insists that a process making a part must be capable of operating so that the design tolerances are six standard deviations away from the process mean. For our bearing, this would mean that our process variation would need to be less than or equal to 0.00083 inches (remember our tolerance was ±0.005, which, when divided by 6, is 0.00083). To reduce the variation in the process, we would need to find some better method for controlling the formation of the bearing. Of course, another option would be to redesign the axle assembly so that such perfect bearings are not needed.

We can show the six-sigma limits using an exhibit. Assume that we have changed the process to produce with 0.00083 variation. Now, the design limits and the process limits are acceptable according to Motorola standards. Let's assume that the bearing diameter follows a bell-shaped normal distribution as in Exhibit S6.7. From our knowledge of the normal distribution, we know that 99.7 percent of the bell-shaped curve falls within ±3 sigma. We would only expect about three parts in 1,000 to fall outside of the 3 sigma limits. The tolerance limits are another 3 sigma out from these control limits! In this case, the actual number of parts we would expect to produce outside the tolerance limits is only two parts per *billion*!

Suppose the central value of the process output shifts away from the mean. Exhibit S6.8 shows the mean shifted one standard deviation closer to the upper specification limit. This causes a slightly higher number of expected defects, about 4 parts per million. This is still pretty good, by most people's standards. We use a calculation called the **capability index** to measure how well our process is capable of producing relative to the design tolerances. We describe how to calculate this index in the next section.

Capability Index (C_{pk})

Capability Index (c_{pk})

The **capability index** (C_{pk}) shows how well the parts being produced fit into the range specified by the design limits. If the design limits are larger than the three sigma allowed in the process, then the mean of the process can be allowed to drift off-center before readjusting, and a high percentage of good parts will still be produced.

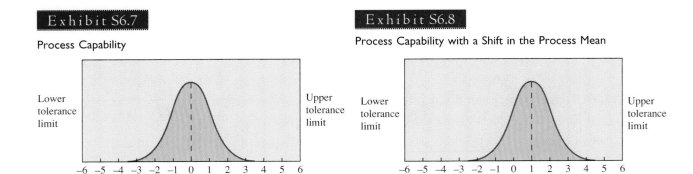

Exhibit S6.7

Process Capability

Lower tolerance limit / Upper tolerance limit

Standard deviation (σ)

Exhibit S6.8

Process Capability with a Shift in the Process Mean

Lower tolerance limit / Upper tolerance limit

Referring to Exhibits S6.7 and S6.8, the capability index (C_{pk}) is the position of the mean and tails of the process relative to design specifications. The more off-center, the greater the chance to produce defective parts.

Since the process mean can shift in either direction, the direction of shift and its distance from the design specification set the limit on the process capability. The direction of shift is toward the smaller number.

Formally stated, the capability index (C_{pk}) is calculated as the smaller number as follows:

$$C_{pk} = \min\left[\frac{\overline{X} - \text{LTL}}{3\sigma} \text{ or } \frac{\text{UTL} - \overline{X}}{3\sigma}\right] \qquad (S6.13)$$

For simplicity, let's assume our process mean is one inch and $\sigma = .001$. Further, the process mean is exactly in the center as in Exhibit S6.7. Then for $\overline{X} = 1.000$

$$C_{pk} = \min\left[\frac{1.000 - .994}{3(.001)} \text{ or } \frac{1.006 - 1.000}{3(.001)}\right] =$$

$$= \min\left[\frac{.006}{.003} = 2 \text{ or } \frac{.006}{.003} = 2\right]$$

Since the mean is in the center, the two calculations are the same and equal to 2. If the mean shifted to $+1.5\sigma$ or 1.0015, then for $\overline{X} = 1.0015$

$$C_{pk} = \min\left[\frac{1.0015 - .994}{3(.001)} \text{ or } \frac{1.006 - 1.0015}{3(.001)}\right] =$$

$$= \min[2.5 \text{ or } 1.5]$$

$C_{pk} = 1.5$, which is the smaller number

This tells us that the process mean has shifted to the right similar to Exhibit S6.8, but parts are still well within design limits.

Assuming that the process is producing within ± 3 sigma and the process is centered exactly between the design limits, as in Exhibit S6.7, Birch calculated the fraction of defective units that would fall outside various design limits as follows:[4]

Design Limit	Defective Parts	Fraction Defective
$\pm 1\sigma$	317 per thousand	.3173
$\pm 2\sigma$	45 per thousand	.0455
$\pm 3\sigma$	2 per thousand	.0027
$\pm 4\sigma$	63 per million	.000063
$\pm 5\sigma$	574 per billion	.000000574
$\pm 6\sigma$	2 per billion	.000000002
$\pm 7\sigma$	.3 per billion	.0000000000003
$\pm 8\sigma$	.001 per billion	.0000000000000001

Motorola's design limit of six sigma with a shift of the process off the mean by 1.5σ $(C_{pk} = 1.5)$ gives 3.4 defects per million. If the mean is exactly in the center $(C_{pk} = 2)$, then 2 defects per *billion* are expected, as the table above shows.

---

[4] David Birch, "The True Value of 6 Sigma," *Quality Progress,* April 1993, p. 6.

■ TAGUCHI METHODS

We have discussed quality control from the point of view of process adjustments. In what many have termed a revolution in quality thinking, Genichi Taguchi of Japan has suggested the following: Instead of constantly fiddling with production equipment to ensure consistent quality, design the product to be robust enough to achieve high quality despite fluctuations on the production line. This simple idea has been employed by such companies as Ford Motor Company, ITT, and IBM; they have saved millions of dollars in manufacturing costs as a result.

Taguchi Methods   **Taguchi methods** are basically statistical techniques for conducting experiments to determine the best combinations of product and process variables to make a product. *Best* means lowest cost with highest uniformity. This can be a complicated, time- consuming process. For example, in designing the process for a new product, one might find that a single processing step with only eight process variables (machine speed, cutting angle, and so on) could be combined in up to 5,000 different ways. Thus, finding the combination that makes the product with the highest uniformity at the lowest cost cannot be done by trial and error. Taguchi has found a way around this problem focusing on only a few combinations that represent the spectrum of product/process outcomes.

Taguchi is also known for the development of the concept of a quality loss function (QLF) to tie cost of quality directly to variation in a process. The following discussion from an article by Joseph Turner develops this concept in detail.[5]

Is an Out-of-Spec Product Really Out of Spec?

Variation around Us

It is generally accepted that, as variation is reduced, quality is improved. Sometimes that knowledge is intuitive. If a train is always on time, schedules can be planned more precisely. If clothing sizes are consistent, time can be saved by ordering from a catalog. But rarely are such things thought about in terms of the value of low variability. With engineers, the knowledge is better defined. Pistons must fit cylinders, doors must fit openings, electrical components must be compatible, and boxes of cereal must have the right amount of raisins—otherwise quality will be unacceptable and customers will be dissatisfied.

However, engineers also know that it is impossible to have zero variability. For this reason, designers establish specifications that define not only the target value of something but also acceptable limits about the target. For example, if the aim value of a dimension is 10 inches, the design specifications might then be 10.00 inches ±0.02 inch. This would tell the manufacturing department that, while it should aim for exactly 10 inches, anything between 9.98 and 10.02 inches is OK.

A traditional way of interpreting such a specification is that any part that falls within the allowed range is equally good, while any part falling outside the range is totally bad. This is illustrated in Exhibit S6.9. (Note that the cost is zero over the entire specification range, and then there is a quantum leap in cost once the limit is violated.)

---

[5] Adapted from Joseph Turner, "Is an Out-of-Spec Product Really Out of Spec?" *Quality Progress,* December 1990, pp. 57–59.

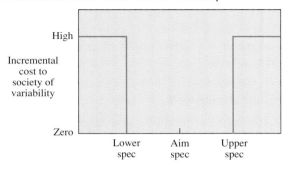

Exhibit S6.9

A Traditional View of the Cost of Variability

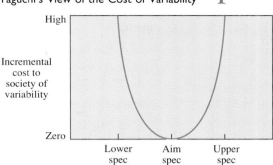

Exhibit S6.10

Taguchi's View of the Cost of Variability

Taguchi has pointed out that such a view is nonsense for two reasons:

1. From the customer's view, there is often practically no difference between a product just inside specifications and a product just outside. Conversely, there is a far greater difference in the quality of a product that is the target and the quality of one that is near a limit.

2. As customers get more demanding, there is pressure to reduce variability. However, Exhibit S6.9 does not reflect this logic.

Taguchi suggests that a more correct picture of the loss is shown in Exhibit S6.10. Notice that in this graph the cost is represented by a smooth curve. There are dozens of illustrations of this notion; the meshing of gears in a transmission, the speed of photographic film, the temperature in a workplace or department store. In nearly anything that can be measured, the customer sees not a sharp line, but a gradation of acceptability. Customers see the loss function as Exhibit S6.10 rather than Exhibit S6.9.

What are the elements of loss to society? While different authorities suggest different things, it seems reasonable to think of both internal and external costs. Internally, the more variable the manufacturing process, the more scrap generated and the more a company will have to spend on testing and inspecting for conformance. Externally, customers will find that the product does not last as long or work as well if it is not close to the target value. Perhaps, when used in adverse situations, the product will not perform at all, even though it meets specifications that were developed based on normal usage.

While the actual shape of the loss curve might vary considerably, a simple parabolic curve, as shown in Exhibit 6.10, has a lot of intuitive appeal, especially when specification limits are symmetrical about the target value. With a parabola, the loss is relatively small when we are close to aim and grows at an increasing rate the farther we move from the target.

Of course, if products are consistently scrapped when they are outside specifications, the loss curve flattens out in most cases at a value equivalent to scrap cost in the ranges outside specifications. This is because such products, theoretically at least, will never be sold so there is no external cost to society. However, in many practical situations, either the process is capable of producing a very high percentage of product within specifications and/or 100 percent checking is not done and/or out-of-spec products can be reworked to bring them within specs. In any of these situations, the parabolic loss function is usually a reasonable assumption.

In such cases, the following formula applies:

$$L = K(x - a)^2 \qquad (S6.14)$$

where

L = Loss to society associated with a unit of product produced at a value x
a = Aim or target; assume that at a, $L = 0$
K = A constant

Then, adding the following variables, and solving for K,

c = The loss associated with a unit of product produced at a specification limit, assuming that the loss for a unit at target is zero
d = Distance from the target to the spec limit

$$K = c/d^2 \qquad (S6.15)$$

With n units of product, the average loss per unit becomes

$$\bar{L} = K[\Sigma(x - a)^2/n] \qquad (S6.16)$$

While this formula assesses average loss, it is somewhat cumbersome because data are not usually collected in a way that makes the computation of $\Sigma(x - a)$ convenient. However, data are often available on the historical mean and standard deviation for the item of interest. When these are known, the average loss is closely approximated by

$$\bar{L} = K[\sigma^2 + (\bar{x} - a)^2] \qquad (S6.17)$$

where

$\bar{x}$ = Process average
σ = Process standard deviation

The only difficulty in applying the preceding formula to a practical situation is coming up with a valid estimate of c, the incremental loss to society associated with a unit of product produced at the limit, compared to the loss associated with a unit produced at target. While this is, at best, a guesstimate, it is possible for knowledgeable people to suggest a value that represents educated thinking. One group of engineers suggested the value should be one-tenth of the selling price of a particular item. This means that if a unit were right at the limit, there is a reasonable chance that, because of test variability, the unit might fail final inspection. Furthermore, there is a reasonable chance the customer would encounter greater problems with a unit at the limit than with a unit made at target, and this would result in loss to the customer and possible warranty returns. While this estimate was admittedly a bit arbitrary, it seemed a reasonable starting point as a minimum estimate and resulted in a surprisingly high estimated loss value.

The approach is illustrated in the following example: The specification for a key dimension on an automotive part is 8.5 inches ±0.05 inch. Historical data indicate that over the past several months, the mean value has been 8.492 inches and the standard deviation, 0.016 inch. The part sells for $20, and engineers have estimated the loss to society as $2 for a part that is exactly at the upper or lower limit. Production is 250,000 parts per year. The situation is pictured in Exhibit S6.11.

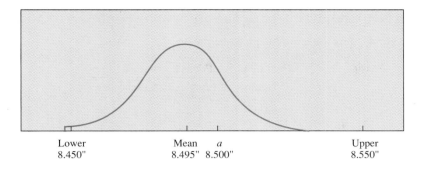

Example of
Automotive Part

Lower
8.450"

Mean   *a*
8.495" 8.500"

Upper
8.550"

Applying equation (4), the average loss per part is

$$\bar{L} = [2/(0.05)^2][(.016)^2 + (.008)^2] = 25.6 \text{ cents}$$

Applying this to the volume of 250,000 units produces a total annual loss of $64,000. If engineers want to reduce this loss, they can pursue three avenues:

1. Shift the mean value so it is on target (i.e., 8.5 inches).
2. Reduce the variability. (For example, make $\sigma = 0.01$ inch.)
3. Accomplish both 1 and 2.

Applying equation (4) to the three situations produces the following results:

1. By moving the mean value to aim, $\bar{L} = 20.5$ cents; total annual loss = $51,250.
2. By reducing the variability to $\sigma = 0.01$ inch, $\bar{L} = 13.1$ cents; total annual loss = $32,750.
3. By accomplishing both 1 and 2, $\bar{L} = 8$ cents; total annual loss = $20,000.

Note that if higher or lower estimates were used for c, the resulting numbers would be affected proportionately. Thus, it is possible to easily perform a sensitivity analysis assuming a range of values for c. For example, if c were estimated at $4 rather than $2, all of the results would be exactly double those shown.

■ CONCLUSION

Statistical quality control is a vital topic. We put it in this supplement rather than Chapter 6 not with the intention of giving it a second class status. Rather, quality has become so important that statistical quality procedures are *expected* to be part of successful firms. Sampling plans and statistical process control are taken as given with the emphasis shifting to broader aspects (such as eliminating dockside acceptance sampling because of reliable supplier quality, and employee empowerment transforming much of the process control). We're finding that world-class manufacturing companies are expecting people to understand the basic concepts of the materials presented in this supplement.

FORMULA REVIEW

Process control charts using attribute measurements

$$\bar{p} = \frac{\text{Total number of defects from all samples}}{\text{Number of samples} \times \text{Sample size}} \tag{S6.1}$$

$$s_p = \sqrt{\frac{\bar{p}(1 - \bar{p})}{n}} \tag{S6.2}$$

$$\text{UCL} = \bar{p} + zs_p \tag{S6.3}$$

$$\text{LCL} = \bar{p} + zs_p \tag{S6.4}$$

$$\text{UCL}_{\bar{x}} = \bar{\bar{X}} + zs_{\bar{x}} \quad \text{and} \quad \text{LCL}_{\bar{x}} = \bar{\bar{X}} - zs_{\bar{x}} \tag{S6.5}$$

Process control $\bar{X}$ and R charts

$$\bar{X} = \frac{\sum_{i=1}^{n} X_i}{n} \tag{S6.6}$$

$$\bar{\bar{X}} = \frac{\sum_{j=1}^{m} \bar{X}_j}{m} \tag{S6.7}$$

$$\bar{R} = \frac{\sum_{j=1}^{m} R_j}{m} \tag{S6.8}$$

$$\text{Upper control limit for } \bar{X} = \bar{\bar{X}} + A_2\bar{R} \tag{S6.9}$$

$$\text{Lower control limit for } \bar{X} = \bar{\bar{X}} - A_2\bar{R} \tag{S6.10}$$

$$\text{Upper control limit for } R = D_4\bar{R} \tag{S6.11}$$

$$\text{Lower control limit for } R = D_3\bar{R} \tag{S6.12}$$

Capability index

$$C_{pk} = \min\left[\frac{\bar{X} - \text{LTL}}{3\sigma}, \frac{\text{UTL} - \bar{X}}{3\sigma}\right] \tag{S6.13}$$

$$L = K(x - a)^2 \tag{S6.14}$$

$$K = c/d^2 \tag{S6.15}$$

$$\bar{L} = K[\Sigma(x - a)^2/n] \tag{S6.16}$$

$$\bar{L} = K[\sigma^2 + (\bar{x} - a)^2] \tag{S6.17}$$

SOLVED PROBLEMS

SOLVED PROBLEM 1

Completed forms from a particular department of an insurance company were sampled on a daily basis as a check against the quality of performance of that department. To establish a tentative norm for the department, one sample of 100 units was collected each day for 15 days, with these results:

Sample	Sample Size	Number of Forms with Errors	Sample	Sample Size	Number of Forms with Errors
1	100	4	9	100	4
2	100	3	10	100	2
3	100	5	11	100	7
4	100	0	12	100	2
5	100	2	13	100	1
6	100	8	14	100	3
7	100	1	15	100	1
8	100	3			

a. Develop a *p*-chart using a 95 percent confidence interval ($1.96\, s_p$).

b. Plot the 15 samples collected.

c. What comments can you make about the process?

Solution

a. $$\bar{p} = \frac{46}{15(100)} = .0307$$

$$s_p = \sqrt{\frac{\bar{p}(1 - \bar{p})}{n}} = \sqrt{\frac{.0307(1 - .0307)}{100}} = \sqrt{.0003} = .017$$

$$\text{UCL} = \bar{p} + 1.96 s_p = .031 + 1.96(.017) = .064$$

$$\text{LCL} = \bar{p} - 1.96 s_p = .031 - 1.96(.017) = -.003 \text{ or zero}$$

b. The defectives are plotted below.

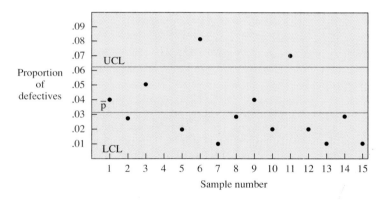

c. Of the 15 samples, 2 were out of the control limits. Since the control limits were established as 95 percent, or 1 out of 20, we would say that the process is out of control. It needs to be examined to find the cause of such widespread variation.

SOLVED PROBLEM 2

Management is trying to decide whether Part A, which is produced with a consistent 3 percent defective rate, should be inspected. If it is not inspected, the 3 percent defectives will go through a product assembly phase and have to be replaced later. If all Part A's are inspected, one-third of the defectives will be found, thus raising the quality to 2 percent defectives.

a. Should the inspection be done if the cost of inspecting is $0.01 per unit and the cost of replacing a defective in the final assembly is $4.00?

b. Suppose the cost of inspecting is $0.05 per unit rather than $0.01. Would this change your answer in *a*?

Solution
Should Part A be inspected?
.03 defective with no inspection.
.02 defective with inspection.

a. This problem can be solved simply by looking at the opportunity for 1 percent improvement.

Benefit $= .01(\$4.00) = \$0.04$
Cost of inspection $= \$0.01$

Therefore, inspect and save $0.03 per unit.

b. A cost of $0.05 per unit to inspect would be $0.01 greater than the savings so inspection should not be performed.

REVIEW AND DISCUSSION QUESTIONS

1. Discuss the trade-off between achieving a zero AQL (acceptable quantity level) and a positive AQL (e.g., an AQL of 2 percent).

2. The capability index allows for some drifting of the process mean. Discuss what this means in terms of product quality output.

3. Discuss the purposes and differences between p-charts and $\overline{X}$ and R charts.

4. In an agreement between a supplier and a customer, the supplier must ensure that all parts are within tolerance before shipment to the customer. What is the effect on the cost of quality to the customer?

5. In the situation described in Question 4, what would be the effect on the cost of quality to the supplier?

6. Discuss the logic of Taguchi methods.

PROBLEMS

1. *a.* Not inspecting   ✓
   cost $= \$20$/hr. Cost
   to inspect $= \$9$/hr.
   Therefore, inspect.
   b. $.18 each.
   c. $.22 per unit.

1. A company currently using an inspection process in its material receiving department is trying to install an overall cost reduction program. One possible reduction is the elimination of one of the inspection positions. This position tests material that has a defective content on the average of 0.04. By inspecting all items, the inspector is able to remove all defects. The inspector can inspect 50 units per hour. Hourly rate including fringe benefits for this position is $9. If the inspection position is eliminated, defects will go into product assembly and will have to be replaced later at a cost of $10 each when they are detected in final product testing.
   a. Should this inspection position be eliminated?
   b. What is the cost to inspect each unit?
   c. Is there benefit (or loss) from the current inspection process? How much?

2. *a.* $C_{pk} = .889$.
   b. The process is
   capable but needs to
   adjust the mean
   downward to achieve
   the best quality.

2. A metal fabricator produces connecting rods with an outer diameter that has a $1 \pm .01$ inch specification. A machine operator takes several sample measurements over time and determines the sample mean outer diameter to be 1.002 inches with a standard deviation of .003 inch.
   a. Calculate the process capability ratio for this example.
   b. What does this figure tell you about the process?

3. Ten samples of 15 parts each were taken from an ongoing process to establish a p-chart for control. The samples and the number of defectives in each are shown here.

Sample	n	Number of Defects in Sample	Sample	n	Number of Defects in Sample
1	15	3	6	15	2
2	15	1	7	15	0
3	15	0	8	15	3
4	15	0	9	15	1
5	15	0	10	15	0

3. *a.* $\bar{p}$ = .067.
  UCL = .194.
  LCL = 0.
b. Stop the process.
  Something wrong.
  There is wide
  variation and 2 are
  out of limits.

a. Develop a p-chart for 95 percent confidence (1.96 standard deviations).
b. Based on the plotted data points, what comments can you make?

4. Output from a process contains 0.02 defective units. Defective units that go undetected into final assemblies cost $25 each to replace. An inspection process, which would detect and remove all defectives, can be established to test these units. However, the inspector, who can test 20 units per hour, is paid a rate of $8 per hour, including fringe benefits. Should an inspection station be established to test all units?
a. What is the cost to inspect each unit?
b. What is the benefit (or loss) from the inspection process?

4. *a.* Cost to
  inspect = $.40/unit.
  Cost of defect =
  $.50/unit. Inspect.
b. Benefit is $.10/unit.

5. There is a 3 percent error rate at a specific point in a production process. If an inspector is placed at this point, all the errors can be detected and eliminated. However, the inspector is paid $8 per hour and can inspect units in the process at the rate of 30 per hour.

    If no inspector is used and defects are allowed to pass this point, there is a cost of $10 per unit to correct the defect later on.

    Should an inspector be hired?

5. Yes, inspecting is
  cheaper, Cost to inspect
  is $.267/unit. Cost of
  defect is $.30/unit.

✓ **6.** Resistors for electronic circuits are being manufactured on a high-speed automated machine. The machine is being set up to produce a large run of resistors of 1,000 ohms each.

    To set up the machine and to create a control chart to be used throughout the run, 15 samples were taken with four resistors in each sample. The complete list of samples and their measured values are as follows:

6. $\bar{\bar{X}}$ = 999.1;
  UCL = 1014.965;
  LCL = 983.235;
  $\bar{R}$ = 21.733;
  UCL = 49.551;
  LCL = 0.
  See SM for graph.

Sample Number	Readings (in ohms)			
1	1010	991	985	986
2	995	996	1009	994
3	990	1003	1015	1008
4	1015	1020	1009	998
5	1013	1019	1005	993
6	994	1001	994	1005
7	989	992	982	1020
8	1001	986	996	996
9	1006	989	1005	1007
10	992	1007	1006	979
11	996	1006	997	989
12	1019	996	991	1011
13	981	991	989	1003
14	999	993	988	984
15	1013	1002	1005	992

    Develop an $\bar{X}$ chart and an R chart and plot the values. From the charts, what comments can you make about the process? (Use three-sigma control limits as in Exhibit S6.4.)

7. *a.* 87.1 sample size.
   b. c = 5.

7. In the past, Alpha Corporation has not performed incoming quality control inspections but has taken the word of its vendors. However, Alpha has been having some unsatisfactory experience recently with the quality of purchased items and wants to set up sampling plans for the receiving department to use.

For a particular component, X, Alpha has a lot tolerance percent defective of 10 percent. Zenon Corporation, from whom Alpha purchases this component, has an acceptable quality level in its production facility of 3 percent for component X. Alpha has a consumer's risk of 10 percent and Zenon has a producer's risk of 5 percent.
   a. When a shipment of Product X is received from Zenon Corporation, what is the sample size that the receiving department should test?
   b. What is the allowable number of defects in order to accept the shipment?

8. *a.* $\bar{p}$ = .06;
   s_p = .0075;
   UCL = .075;
   LCL = .045.
   b. Quality is erratic and out of control

8. You are the newly appointed assistant administrator at a local hospital, and your first project is to investigate the quality of the patient meals put out by the food-service department. You conducted a 10-day survey by submitting a simple questionnaire to the 400 patients with each meal, asking that they simply check-off that the meal was either satisfactory or unsatisfactory. For simplicity in this problem, assume that the response was 1,000 returned questionnaires from the 1,200 meals each day. The results are

	Number of Unsatisfactory Meals	Sample Size
December 1	74	1,000
December 2	42	1,000
December 3	64	1,000
December 4	80	1,000
December 5	40	1,000
December 6	50	1,000
December 7	65	1,000
December 8	70	1,000
December 9	40	1,000
December 10	75	1,000
	600	10,000

   a. Construct a *p*-chart based on the questionnaire results, using a confidence interval of 95.5 percent, which is two standard deviations.
   b. What comments can you make about the results of the survey?

9. *a. n* = 31.3. (Round ✓ sample size *n* up).
   b. Random sample 32; reject if more than 8 are defective.

9. Large-scale integrated (LSI) circuit chips are made in one department of an electronics firm. These chips are incorporated into analog devices that are then encased in epoxy. The yield is not particularly good for LSI manufacture, so the AQL specified by that department is 0.15 while the LTPD acceptable by the assembly department is 0.40.
   a. Develop a sampling plan.
   b. Explain what the sampling plan means; that is, how would you tell someone to do the test?

10. $\bar{p}$ = .0083;
   s_p = .00287;
   UCL = .01396;
   LCL = .00270;
   Based on *p*-chart, crime rate has not increased.

10. The state and local police departments are trying to analyze areas' crime rates so they can shift their patrols from decreasing-rate areas to areas where rates are increasing. The city and county have been geographically segmented into areas containing 5,000 residences. The police recognize that all crimes and offenses are not reported; people either do not want to become involved, consider the offenses too small to report, are too embarrassed to make a police report, or do not take the time, among other reasons. Every month, because of this, the police are contacting by phone a random sample of 1,000 of the 5,000 residences for data on crime. (Respondents are guaranteed anonymity.) The data collected for the past 12 months for one area are

Month	Crime Incidence	Sample Size	Crime Rate
January	7	1,000	0.007
February	9	1,000	0.009
March	7	1,000	0.000
April	7	1,000	0.007
May	7	1,000	0.007
June	9	1,000	0.009
July	7	1,000	0.007
August	10	1,000	0.010
September	8	1,000	0.008
October	11	1,000	0.011
November	10	1,000	0.010
December	8	1,000	0.008

Construct a *p*-chart for 95 percent confidence (1.96) and plot each of the months. If the next three months show crime incidences in this area as

> January = 10 (out of 1,000 sampled)
> February = 12 (out of 1,000 sampled)
> March = 11 (out of 1,000 sampled)

what comments can you make regarding the crime rate?

11. Some citizens complained to city council members that there should be equal protection under the law against the occurrence of crimes. The citizens argued that this equal protection should be interpreted as indicating that high-crime areas should have more police protection than low-crime areas. Therefore, police patrols and other methods for preventing crime (such as street lighting or cleaning up abandoned areas and buildings) should be used proportionately to crime occurrence.

In a fashion similar to Problem 10, the city has been broken down into 20 geographic areas, each containing 5,000 residences. The 1,000 sampled from each area showed the following incidence of crime during the past month:

Area	Number of Crimes	Sample Size	Crime Rate
1	14	1,000	0.014
2	3	1,000	0.003
3	19	1,000	0.019
4	18	1,000	0.018
5	14	1,000	0.014
6	28	1,000	0.028
7	10	1,000	0.010
8	18	1,000	0.018
9	12	1,000	0.012
10	3	1,000	0.003
11	20	1,000	0.020
12	15	1,000	0.015
13	12	1,000	0.012
14	14	1,000	0.014
15	10	1,000	0.010
16	30	1,000	0.030
17	4	1,000	0.004
18	20	1,000	0.020
19	6	1,000	0.006
20	30	1,000	0.030
	300		

11. $\bar{p} = 0.015$;
$s_p = 0.00384$;
UCL = 0.0225;
LCL = 0.0075.
Three areas outside UCL warrant further investigation; four areas below LCL warrant investigation.

Suggest a reallocation of crime protection effort, if indicated, based on a *p*-chart analysis. To be reasonably certain in your recommendation, select a 95 percent confidence level (i.e., $Z = 1.96$).

12. Amalgo Tech engineers are trying to improve the design of a gear that has an outer diameter of 13 inches with a tolerance of $\pm.003$ inch. Available inspection data from the past year indicate that the mean value of the diameter has been 13.001 with standard deviation of .0025 inch. The gear sells for $125. The estimated loss to society is $20 for any gear that has a diameter at the upper or lower tolerance limit. Annual sales of the gear amount to 40,000 units.

a. Calculate the average loss per unit of production.

b. What is the expected loss per year?

c. What happens to the average loss per unit and the expected loss per year if the mean is shifted to the target value of 13 inches?

13. The operations manager of a small metal fabricating company is concerned about the variability of a milling process. Although the average width of a metal connector is identical to the target of .25 inch, the standard deviation of the process is .01 inch. The tolerance limits for the part are $\pm.008$ inch. The expected loss to society for any metal connector that is produced with widths at the limits of tolerance is $1.75 per unit. The specialized connectors sell for $18.00 each.

a. Calculate the average loss per unit of production.

b. If the average width shifts from the target value of .25 inch but stays within tolerance, what will happen to value of the average loss per unit of production?

c. What is the value of the average loss per unit if the standard deviation can be reduced from .01 to .0075?

14. The following table contains the measurements of the key length dimension from a fuel injector. These samples of size five were taken at one hour intervals.

Sample Number	Observations				
	1	**2**	**3**	**4**	**5**
1	.486	.499	.493	.511	.481
2	.499	.506	.516	.494	.529
3	.496	.500	.515	.488	.521
4	.495	.506	.483	.487	.489
5	.472	.502	.526	.469	.481
6	.473	.495	.507	.493	.506
7	.495	.512	.490	.471	.504
8	.525	.501	.498	.474	.485
9	.497	.501	.517	.506	.516
10	.495	.505	.516	.511	.497
11	.495	.482	.468	.492	.492
12	.483	.459	.526	.506	.522
13	.521	.512	.493	.525	.510
14	.487	.521	.507	.501	.500
15	.493	.516	.499	.511	.513
16	.473	.506	.479	.480	.523
17	.477	.485	.513	.484	.496
18	.515	.493	.493	.485	.475
19	.511	.536	.486	.497	.491
20	.509	.490	.470	.504	.512

Construct a 3-sigma *X*-bar and *R* chart (use Exhibit S6.4) for the length of the fuel injector. What can you say about this process?

12. *a.* $K = \dfrac{20}{(0.003)^2} =$

2,222,222.22;

$\bar{L} = \$16.11$ per unit.

b. $644,444.44.

c. $\bar{L} = \$13.89$ per unit;

$555,600

13. *a.* $K = \dfrac{1.75}{(.008)^2} =$ ✓

27,343.75;

$\bar{L} = 27,343.75(.01)^2$

$= \$2.73$ per unit.

b. Loss per unit will increase since $\bar{X} - a$ increases.

c. $\bar{L} = 27,343.74(.0075)^2$

$= \$1.54$ per unit.

14. $X = .500$

UCL $= .523$

LCL $= .477$

$R = .040$

UCL $= .084$

LCL $= .000$

15. C-Spec, Inc. is attempting to determine whether an existing machine is capable of milling an engine part that has a key specification of $4 \pm .003$ inches. After a trial run on this machine, C-Spec has determined that the machine has a sample mean of 4.001 inches with a standard deviation of .002 inches.

    a. Calculate the C_{pk} for this machine.

    b. Should C-Spec use this machine to produce this part? Why?

15. *a.* $C_{pk} = .333$
   b. No, the machine is not capable of producing this part.

SELECTED BIBLIOGRAPHY

Aslup, Fred, and Ricky M. Watson. *Practical Statistical Process Control: A Tool for Quality Manufacturing.* New York: Van Nostrand Reinhold, 1993.

Feigenbaum, A. V. *Total Quality Control.* New York: McGraw-Hill, 1991.

Hardesky, John L. *Productivity and Quality Improvement: A Practical Guide to Implementing Statistical Process Control.* New York: McGraw-Hill, 1988.

Juran, J. M., and F. M. Gryna. *Quality Planning and Analysis.* 2nd ed. New York: McGraw-Hill, 1980.

Small, Bonnie B. (with committee). *Statistical Quality Control Handbook.* Western Electric Co., Inc., 1956.

Taguchi, G. *On-Line Quality Control During Production.* Tokyo: Japanese Standards Association, 1987.

Thompson, James R., and Jacek Koronacki. *Statistical Process Control for Quality Improvement.* New York: Chapman & Hall, 1993.

Wetherill, G. Barrie, and Don W. Brown. *Statistical Process Control: Theory and Practice.* New York: Chapman & Hall, 1991.

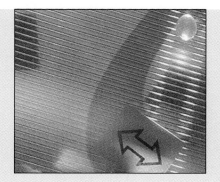

Design of Facilities and Jobs

7 Strategic Capacity Planning

Supplement 7 *Linear Programming*

8 Just-in-Time Production Systems

9 Facility Location

10 Facility Layout

11 Job Design and Work Measurement

Supplement 11 *Learning Curves*

ONCE A FIRM DECIDES WHAT TO MAKE AND HOW TO MAKE it, the focus shifts to putting production and distribution systems in place. This section addresses the design issues associated with this process. The question of how much capacity is needed and the implications of this decision on cost, is considered first. Companies around the world have embraced the use of just-in-time (JIT) systems and this is treated next. Discussion of the concepts essential to understanding JIT are given full coverage. In the last three chapters of this section we cover the details of how to locate facilities, the internal layout design of a facility, and the design of individual jobs. In addition to some quantitative techniques for solving specific OM problems, this section introduces two powerful analytical tools—decision trees and linear programming— that find application in virtually all areas of business administration.

Chapter 7

Strategic Capacity Planning

Chapter Outline

Capacity Management in Operations, 264

Capacity Planning Concepts, 267

    Economies and Diseconomies of Scale

    The Experience Curve

    Where Economies of Scale Meet the Experience Curve

    Capacity Focus

    Capacity Flexibility

Capacity Planning, 272

    Considerations in Adding Capacity

    Determining Capacity Requirements

    Using Decision Trees to Evaluate Capacity Alternatives

Planning Service Capacity, 279

    Capacity Planning in Service versus Manufacturing

    Capacity Utilization and Service Quality

Adding Capacity through Multisite Service Growth, 281

    Entrepreneurial Stage

    Multisite Rationalization Stage

    Growth Stage

    Maturity Stage

Case: Shouldice Hospital—A Cut Above (Revised), 288

Key Terms

Capacity

Strategic Capacity Planning

Best Operating Level

Capacity Utilization Rate

Capacity Focus

Capacity Flexibility

Economies of Scope

Capacity Cushion

Decision Tree

"Bermuda Triangle" of Operational Complexity

www Links

M&M Mars (http://m-ms.com)

TreeAge Software (http://www.treeage.com/)

Shouldice Hospital (http://www.shouldice.com)

ONCE UPON A TIME, IN A FARAWAY PARIS SUBURB, A Magic Kingdom was born. The natives were aghast! Minnie and Mickey wouldn't last, they cried! But people now come from far and wide, to stand in line for fantasy rides, and the little kingdom grew fast. This modern-day success story has all the makings of a fairy tale, with even the requisite happy ending. With its long lines, heftier profits, and higher hotel occupancy rates, Disneyland Paris seems likely to live happily ever after.

Five years after it opened to French insults and widespread skepticism, the American-style theme park 18 miles east of Paris has surpassed the Eiffel Tower and the Louvre as the No. 1 tourist draw in France, even among the French.

Disney's "kick-the-door-down" attitude in the planning, building, and financing of Euro Disney accounts for many of the huge problems that initially faced the resort. In 1994 Euro Disney was renamed Disneyland Paris and financially restructured. Essentially this restructuring delayed payments to Disney USA and some other financial backers until 1999. In addition to the financial changes, there were also changes in pricing and marketing, drastic cost cutting, and subtle adjustments to the park itself. The following are some of the operational errors related to capacity that contributed to the startup problems at the park.

1. Disney Paris planners assumed that a visitor's stay at the park would be similar to the four days typically spent at Florida's Disney. Florida's Disney has three theme parks, whereas Disney Paris only has one. Disney Paris is a two-day experience at the most. The excessive checking in and out that resulted required additional computer stations in the park's hotels.

2. Disney Paris has 5,200 hotel rooms—more than the entire French city of Cannes. Disney priced the rooms more to meet revenue targets than to meet demand. During the first two years, the hotels were just over half-full on average. Disney has now changed its approach and announced separate peak, average, and low season rates.

3. Disney thought that Monday would be a light day for visitors and Friday a heavy one so it allocated staff accordingly; the reality was the reverse. The problem is compounded by the fact that the number of visitors in the high season can be 10 times the number in the low season. Inflexible labor schedules in France also aggravate the problem.

4. Disney built expensive trams along a lake to take guests from the hotels to the park. But people prefer to walk.

5. "We were told that Europeans don't take breakfast, so we downsized the restaurants," recalls one executive. But crowds showed up for a full breakfast. Disney was trying to serve 2,500 breakfasts in 350-seat restaurants at some hotels. Lines were horrendous. Disney reacted quickly with prepackaged breakfast delivery services.

6. The parking space was too small for buses. Restrooms were built for 50 drivers, though there were 200 drivers on peak days.

These problems have now all been solved. Thanks to over 50 million visitors, who enjoy the new rides like Space Mountain, Disneyland Paris is now a great success. Mickey and Minnie, it turns out, are pretty much universal celebrities. ●

Sources: Peter Gumbel and Richard Turner, "Mouse Trap," *The Wall Street Journal,* March 10, 1994, p A1. Updated from the following articles: Staff Reporter, "The Kingdom Inside a Republic," *The Economist,* April 13, 1996, pp. 66–67; and an Associated Press release "Paris' Mickey Has Better Mousetrap," April 20, 1997.

How much should a plant be able to produce? How many customers should a service facility be able to serve? What kinds of problems arise as the production system expands? Whether we are talking about Euro Disney near Paris, France, or Clint's Machine Shop in Paris, Texas, such capacity questions are of major concern to their managers. In this chapter, we look at capacity from a strategic perspective—that is, how manufacturing and service firms plan capacity over the long run. We begin by discussing the nature of capacity from an OM perspective.

■ CAPACITY MANAGEMENT IN OPERATIONS

Capacity

A dictionary definition of **capacity** is "the ability to hold, receive, store, or accommodate." In a general business sense, it is most frequently viewed as the amount of output that a system is capable of achieving over a specific period of time. In a service setting, this might be the number of customers that can be handled between 12 o'clock and 1 o'clock in the afternoon. In manufacturing, this might be the number of automobiles that can be produced in a single shift.

When looking at capacity, operations managers need to look at both resource input *and* product outputs. The reason is that, for planning purposes, real (or effective) capacity is dependent on what is to be produced. For example, a firm that makes multiple products inevitably can produce more of one kind than of another with a given level of resource inputs. Thus, while the management of an automobile factory may state that their facility has 10,000 labor hours available per year, they are also thinking that these labor hours can be used to make either 50,000 two-door models or 40,000 four-door models (or some mix of the two- and four-door models). This reflects their knowledge of what their current technology and labor force inputs can produce and the product mix that is to be demanded from these resources.

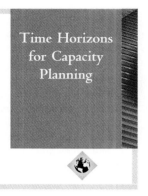

Capacity planning is generally viewed in three time durations:

Long range—greater than one year. Where productive resources take a long time to acquire or dispose of, such as buildings, equipment, or facilities. Long-range capacity planning requires top management participation and approval.

Intermediate range—monthly or quarterly plans for the next 6 to 18 months. Here, capacity may be varied by such alternatives as hiring, layoffs, new tools, minor equipment purchases, and subcontracting.

Short range—less than one month. This is tied into the daily or weekly scheduling process and involves making adjustments to eliminate the variance between planned output and actual output. This includes alternatives such as overtime, personnel transfers, and alternative production routings.

Time Horizons for Capacity Planning

An operations management view also emphasizes the time dimension of capacity. This is evidenced in the common distinction drawn between long-range, intermediate-range, and short-range capacity planning. (See the box "Time Horizons for Capacity Planning.") Capacity must also be stated relative to some period of time.

Finally, capacity planning itself has different meaning to individuals at different levels within the operations management hierarchy. The vice president of manufacturing is concerned with aggregate capacity of all factories within the firm. The vice president's concern relates mainly to the financial resources required to support these factories. You will study this process when you cover capital budgeting during your finance course.

FINANCE

The plant manager (PM) is concerned with the capacity of the individual plant. The PM must decide how best to use this capacity to meet the anticipated demand for products. Since short-term demand may greatly exceed short-term capacity during peak demand periods during the year, the PM must determine when and how much inventory to build in anticipation of these peaks. We will deal with this topic in depth when we cover aggregate planning in Chapter 14.

At a lower level, the first-level supervisor is concerned with capacity of the equipment and manpower mix at the department level. This person will work out detailed work schedules to accommodate the daily flow of work. We will study this scheduling process in Chapter 17.

While there is no one person with the job title "capacity manager," there are several managerial positions charged with the effective use of capacity. Capacity is a relative term, and in an operations management context, may be defined as *the amount of resource inputs available relative to output requirements over a particular period of time.* Note that this definition makes no distinction between efficient and inefficient use of capacity. In this respect, it is consistent with how the government Bureau of Economic Analysis defines "maximum practical capacity" used in its surveys: "That output attained within the normal operating schedule of shifts per day and days per week including the use of high cost inefficient facilities"[1]

---

[1] In gathering capacity statistics, the Bureau of Economic Analysis asks two questions of surveyed firms: (1) At what percentage of manufacturing capacity did your company operate in (month and year)? (2) At what percentage of (month and year) manufacturing capacity would your company have preferred to operate in order to achieve maximum profits or other objective? See "Survey of Current Business," an annual publication of the *U.S. Department of Commerce Journal*.

Why is productivity important? How does it relate to capacity?

Politicians and business leaders perpetually joust over which nation's workers are more productive. They pay far less attention to equally important questions about who uses capital most productively. By "capital" we mean both physical capital (machinery and buildings) and financial capital (stocks and bonds).

Bill Lewis of the McKinsey Global Institute in Washington, D.C., argues that the productive use of capital—along with labor—not only enhances a nation's material standard of living, it also determines the return that its citizens get on their savings. The higher the returns you earn, the less you need to save for the future and the more you can consume today. In the U.S., rates of return on both debt and equity capital averaged 9.1 percent between 1974 and 1993, compared to 7.4 percent for Germany and 7.1 percent for Japan. You might think about it in this way: If you invested $1,000 in the U.S. in 1974, by 1993 you would have $5,666, compared to $4,139 in Germany and $3,597 in Japan.

Why has the U.S. used its capital so well? The answer lies in the way American managers market their products and run their factories. High productivity comes from the clever and subtle trade-offs they make between giving customers what they want and operating efficiently.

For example, Japanese electric utilities—which trail their U.S. counterparts by better than 50 percent in capital productivity—keep massive generating capacity in reserve in order to meet the huge demand for power on the hottest summer days. Much of this capacity lies unused for the rest of the year. In the U.S., utilities reduce such peaks through clever pricing schemes and incentives for the consumers to cool their homes more efficiently.

In telecommunications, the U.S. leads both Germany and Japan in capital productivity by well over 50 percent. Innovations like 800 numbers, faxes, and cheap long-distance service mean that the U.S. phone wires are packed with calls. Higher use means a higher return on the billions of dollars invested in telephone networks.

So why do managers in Germany operate with this excess of capital and capacity? Mr. Lewis argues that it is not because they're less savvy or skilled;

The telecommunications system of AT&T provides interstate and intrastate long-distance calling, voice-messaging, and language translation services to 80 million U.S. consumers.

rather, it is because of the system in which they operate. In the U.S., low entry barriers, intense competition on price and value, and frequent startups and bankruptcies spur managers to use their capital well. In the McKinsey Institute study, data from case studies in food, auto, and retail industries indicate that the more competitive the product market, the better the productivity. Regulations ranging from zoning to trade protection were often the basic cause of poor performance in Germany and Japan, because they made it harder for competitors to enter and drive out inefficient management.

Mr. Lewis argues that it's the U.S.'s higher capital productivity that makes the difference. It leads to higher returns on savings, which allow Americans to create more new wealth while saving less and consuming more. Americans wind up wealthier because their money works harder. A neat trick if there ever was one.

Source: Adapted from an editorial by Bill Lewis, "The Wealth of Nations," *The Wall Street Journal*, June 7, 1996.

A recent report by the McKinsey Global Institute (see box titled "The Wealth of a Nation") indicates that how well a company, or a group of companies, manages long-term capacity, may impact the generation of wealth in a country. These findings tie together the notions of productivity, which were discussed in Chapter 2, with capacity management issues discussed in this chapter.

The objective of **strategic capacity planning** is to provide an approach for determining the overall capacity level of capital intensive resources—facilities, equipment, and overall labor force size—that best supports the company's long-range competitive strategy. The capacity level selected has a critical impact on the firm's response rate, its cost structure, its inventory policies, and its management and staff support requirements. If capacity is inadequate, a company may lose customers through slow service or by allowing competitors to enter the market. If capacity is excessive, a company may have to reduce prices to stimulate demand, or else underutilize its workforce, carry excess inventory, or seek additional, less profitable products to stay in business.

Strategic Capacity Planning

CAPACITY PLANNING CONCEPTS

The term *capacity* implies an attainable rate of output, for example 300 cars per day, but says nothing about how long that rate can be sustained. Thus, we do not know if this 300 cars per day is a one-day peak or a six-month average. To avoid this problem, the concept of **best operating level** is used. This is the level of capacity for which the process was designed and thus is the volume of output at which average unit cost is minimum. Determining this minimum is difficult because it involves a complex trade-off between the allocation of fixed overhead costs and the cost of overtime, equipment wear, defect rates, and other costs.

Best Operating Level

An important measure is the **capacity utilization rate,** which reveals how close a firm is to its best operating point (i.e., design capacity):

Capacity Utilization Rate

$$Capacity\ utilization\ rate = \frac{Capacity\ used}{Best\ operating\ level}$$

The capacity utilization rate is expressed as a percentage and requires that the numerator and denominator be measured in the same units and time periods (machine hour/day, barrels of oil/day, dollar of output/day).

Economies and Diseconomies of Scale

The basic notion of economies of scale is that as a plant gets larger and volume increases, the average cost per unit of output drops. This is partially due to operating and capital cost declines, because a piece of equipment with twice the capacity of another piece typically does not cost twice as much to purchase or operate. Plants also gain efficiencies when they become large enough to fully utilize dedicated resources for tasks such as material handling, computer equipment, and administrative support personnel.

In a study sponsored by the National Science Foundation, it was found that for companies that produce discrete parts defined as Standardized Industrial Code

Big versus Little Manufacturing Plants

It is well accepted that small manufacturing plants are vital to the United States economy. If we consider those industries that produce discrete products as opposed to commodity products, such as gasoline, sugar, chemicals, and the like, over 70 percent of these manufacturing plants are small, with less than 100 employees. Further, according to one estimate, "virtually all net jobs created since 1984" in the U.S. are attributable to small firms.

According to evidence obtained by a study completed by Paul Swamidass, the advantage of larger plants over small plants cannot be overstated. In his study of U.S. manufacturing plants in industries covered by Standardized Industrial Classifications (SIC) 34–38 (discrete parts manufacturers), small plants report a return on investment (ROI) of 11.5 percent, versus 14.7 percent for larger plants. Further, the data show that sales per employee for small plants is $114,000, versus $144,000 for larger plants. That is, on the average, an employee in a large plant generates $30,000 more in sales compared to an employee in small plants, a good justification for higher salaries for employees in large plants.

The notable findings of the study are as follows:

- Small plants are inferior to larger plants in return on investment and sales per employee.
- Small plants report shorter average lead time in weeks, perhaps because they make less complex products. They also report lower cost-of-goods-sold (COGS) as a percent of total costs, which may represent lower wages. Lower COGS for the smaller plants is not translated into superior profitability, perhaps due to offsetting higher marketing and overhead costs.
- Larger plants report a shorter time for investment recovery than smaller plants (27.7 months versus 32.5 months). This means that larger plants are *able* to recover the capital invested in equipment sooner than smaller plants, a definite advantage for larger plants when it comes to investing in capital intensive equipment.
- Small and larger plants are similar in inventory turns and the number of product lines produced.

Source: Adapted from Paul M. Swamidass, "Technology Base of Manufacturing Plants Explains Larger Plants' Advantage Over Small Plants," research report, January 23, 1995.

Classifications (SIC) 34–38, large plants do seem to have an advantage over small plants (see the box titled, "Big versus Little Manufacturing Plants"). The relationships are complex, however, and may change by industry.

At some point, the size of a plant becomes too large and diseconomies of scale become a problem. These diseconomies may surface in many different ways. For example, maintaining the demand required to keep the large facility busy may require significant discounting of the product. The U.S. automobile manufacturers face this problem on an ongoing basis. Another example, which is typical, involves using a few large-capacity pieces of equipment. Minimizing equipment downtime is essential in this type of operation. M&M Mars, for example, has highly automated and high-volume equipment to make M&Ms. A single packaging line moves 2.6 million M&Ms each hour. Even though direct labor to operate the equipment is very low, the labor required to maintain the equipment is high. If you would like to tour the M&M factory, check out *http://m-ms.com/tour*.

In many cases, the size of a plant may be influenced by factors other than the internal equipment, labor, and other capital expenditures. A major factor may be the cost to transport raw materials and finished product to and from the plant. A cement factory, for example, would have a difficult time serving customers more than a few hours from its plant. Analogously, automobile companies such as Ford, Honda, Nissan, and Toyota have found it advantageous to locate plants within specific international markets. The anticipated size of these intended markets will largely dictate the size of the plant. As is related in the box, "Risky Expansion in Korea," the Korean auto manufacturers seem to think they may be able to overcome these regional constraints. Their success or failure remains to be seen.

The Experience Curve

A well-known concept is the experience curve. As plants produce more products, they gain experience in the best production methods, which reduce their costs of production in a predictable manner. Every time a plant's cumulative production doubles, its production costs decline by a specific percentage depending on the nature of the business. Exhibit 7.1 demonstrates the effect of a 90 percent experience curve on the production costs of hamburgers. (Additional discussion of experience or learning curves is provided in the Supplement to Chapter 11.)

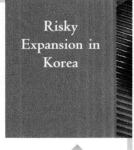

Risky Expansion in Korea

In an already crowded domestic market, South Korea's five car producers have earmarked about $10 billion to double production capacity by 2001. Local manufacturers say that their expansion plans mainly target exports. But industry analysts say that there is no guarantee that export sales will be robust enough to offset dwindling market share at home. This is supported by recent trends in the U.S. market, which is seeing an increasing rate of purchase of U.S.–made cars and light trucks, compounded by strong demand for light trucks that is outpacing demand for cars.

Source: *The Wall Street Journal,* March 10, 1994, p. B6; *Business Week,* March 7, 1994, p. 46; and *Business Week,* March 21, 1994, p. 32.

Exhibit 7.1   The Experience Curve

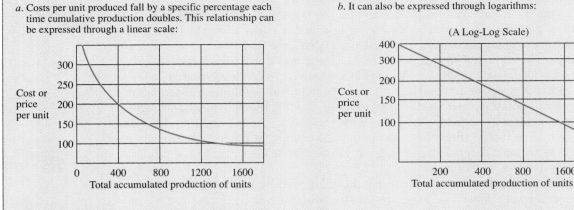

a. Costs per unit produced fall by a specific percentage each time cumulative production doubles. This relationship can be expressed through a linear scale:

b. It can also be expressed through logarithms:

The experience-curve percentage varies across industries.

To apply this concept to the restaurant industry, consider a hypothetical fast food chain that has produced five million hamburgers. Given a current variable cost of $0.55 per burger, what will the cost per burger be when cumulative production reaches ten million burgers? If the firm has a 90-percent experience curve, costs will fall to 90 percent of $0.55, or $0.495, when accumulated production reaches ten million.

Note that sales volume becomes an important issue in achieving cost savings. If firm A serves twice as many hamburgers daily as firm B, it will accumulate "experience" twice as fast.

Source: C. Hart, G. Spizizen, and D. Wyckoff, "Scale Economies and the Experience Curve: Is Bigger Better for Restaurant Companies?" *The Cornell HRA Quarterly,* May 1984, p. 96.

Where Economies of Scale Meet the Experience Curve

The astute reader will realize that larger plants can have a two-way cost advantage over their competitors. Not only does a larger plant gain from economies of scale but it will also produce more, giving it experience curve advantages as well. Companies often use this dual advantage as a competitive strategy by first building a large plant with substantial economies of scale, and then using its lower costs to price aggressively and increase sales volume. The increased volume moves them down the experience curve more quickly than their competitors, allowing the company to lower prices further, gaining still more volume. There are, however, two criteria that must be met for this strategy to be successful: (1) The product must fit customers' needs, and (2) the demand must be sufficiently large to support the volume. Consider the case of Chrysler. By the 1970s, economies of scale and experience had given Chrysler the lowest production costs of all of the U.S. auto manufacturers. Unfortunately, its cars no longer fit customers' needs, so Chrysler could not sell enough of them to operate its large plants at their design levels, driving their costs up to the highest level among the other U.S. producers in the United States at that time.

Capacity Focus

As noted in Chapter 2, the concept of the focused factory holds that a production facility works best when it focuses on a fairly limited set of production objectives.[2]

---

[2] Wickham Skinner, "The Focused Factory," *Harvard Business Review,* May–June 1974, pp. 113–21.

The Xerox focused factory creates a flexible and efficient work environment where teams of employees are responsible for the end-to-end manufacturing of specific products. The factory was designed with input from the industrial staff, working in tandem with engineers and management.

MANAGEMENT
ENGINEERING

This means, for example, that a firm should not expect to excel in every aspect of manufacturing performance: cost, quality, flexibility, new-product introductions, reliability, short lead times, and low investment. Rather, it should select a limited set of tasks that contribute the most to corporate objectives. However, given the breakthroughs in manufacturing technology, there is an evolution in factory objectives toward trying to do everything well. How do we deal with these apparent contradictions? One way is to say that if the firm does not have the technology to master multiple objectives, then a narrow focus is the logical choice. Another way is to recognize the practical reality that not all firms are in industries that require them to use their full range of capabilities to compete.

The **capacity focus** concept can also be operationalized through the mechanism of plants within plants—*PWPs* in Skinner's terms. A focused plant may have several PWPs, each of which may have separate suborganizations, equipment and process policies, workforce management policies, production control methods, and so forth for different products—even if they are made under the same roof. This, in effect, permits finding the best operating level for each department of the organization and thereby carries the focus concept down to the operating level.

Capacity Focus

Capacity Flexibility

Capacity flexibility means having the ability to rapidly increase or decrease production levels, or to shift production capacity quickly from one product or service to another. Such flexibility is achieved through flexible plants, processes, and workers, as well as through strategies that use the capacity of other organizations.

Capacity Flexibility

Flexible Plants   Perhaps the ultimate in plant flexibility is the *zero-changeover-time* plant. Using movable equipment, knockdown walls, and easily accessible and reroutable utilities, such a plant can adapt to change in real time. An analogy to a familiar service business captures the flavor quite well—a plant with equipment "that is easy to install and easy to tear down and move—like the Ringling Bros.–Barnum and Bailey Circus in the old tent-circus days."[3]

Flexible Processes   Flexible processes are epitomized by flexible manufacturing systems on the one hand and simple, easily set up equipment on the other. Both of these technological approaches permit rapid low-cost switching from one product line to another, enabling what is sometimes referred to as **economies of scope.** (By definition, economies of scope exist when multiple products can be produced at a lower cost in combination than they can separately.)

Economies of Scope

Flexible Workers   Flexible workers have multiple skills and the ability to switch easily from one kind of task to another. They require broader training than specialized workers and need managers and staff support to facilitate quick changes in their work assignments.

■ CAPACITY PLANNING

Considerations in Adding Capacity

Vol. IV "Scheduling Services—the United Solution"

Many issues must be considered when adding capacity. Three important ones are maintaining system balance, frequency of capacity additions, and the use of external capacity.

Maintaining System Balance   In a perfectly balanced plant, the output of stage 1 provides the exact input requirement for stage 2. Stage 2's output provides the exact input requirement for stage 3, and so on. In practice, however, achieving such a "perfect" design is usually both impossible and undesirable. One reason is that the best operating levels for each stage generally differ. For instance, department 1 may operate most efficiently over a range of 90 to 110 units per month, while department 2, the next stage in the process, is most efficient at 75 to 85 units per month, and department 3, the third stage, works best over a range of 150 to 200 units per month. Another reason is that variability in product demand and the processes themselves generally lead to imbalance except in automated production lines, which, in essence, are just one big machine.

There are various ways of dealing with imbalance. One is to add capacity to those stages that are the bottlenecks. This can be done by temporary measures such as scheduling overtime, leasing equipment, or going outside the system and purchasing additional capacity through subcontracting. A second way is through the use of buffer inventories in front of the bottleneck stage to ensure that it always has something to work on. (This is a central feature of the synchronous manufacturing approach detailed in Chapter 20.) A third approach involves duplicating the facilities of one department on which another is dependent.

Frequency of Capacity Additions   There are two types of costs to consider when adding capacity: the cost of upgrading too frequently and that of upgrading too

---

[3] See R. J. Schonberger, "The Rationalization of Production," *Proceedings of the 50th Anniversary of the Academy of Management* (Chicago: Academy of Management, 1986), pp. 64–70.

BREAKTHROUGH

Time-Share Manufacturing

With the support of the U.S. Dept. of Commerce (DOC) and other U.S. government agencies and universities, microfactories are now being built for use by consortiums of small and medium-sized U.S. businesses. The essential aspect of such a flexible computer-integrated factory is that its manufacturing facilities are shared. A company can buy time in a facility equipped to make thousands of products for different companies in different industries through the frequent reprogramming of software. The facility can make 1, 10, or 1,000 of a kind at essentially

the cost and economies of scale of a dedicated plant, but it also has the world-class operation. In addition, the high entry costs for new product manufacturing can be greatly reduced because a dedicated plant operating at partial capacity is no longer necessary. A flexible factory can also support new business development and test marketing. Time-shared manufacturing provides an alternative approach to capacity addition.

Source: Excepted from Shirley B. Dreifus (ed.), *Business International's Global Management Desk Reference* (New York: McGraw-Hill, 1992), pp. 242–43.

infrequently. Upgrading capacity too frequently is expensive. First there are direct costs, such as removing and replacing old equipment and training employees on the new equipment.

In addition, the new equipment must be purchased, often for considerably more than the selling price of the old. Finally, there is the opportunity cost of idling the plant or service site during the changeover period.

Conversely, upgrading capacity too infrequently is also expensive. Infrequent expansion means that capacity is purchased in larger chunks. Any excess capacity that is purchased must be carried as overhead until it is utilized. (Exhibit 7.2 illustrates frequent versus infrequent capacity expansion.)

External Sources of Capacity   In some cases, it may be less expensive to not add capacity at all, but rather to use some existing external source of capacity. Two common strategies used by organizations are subcontracting and sharing capacity. An

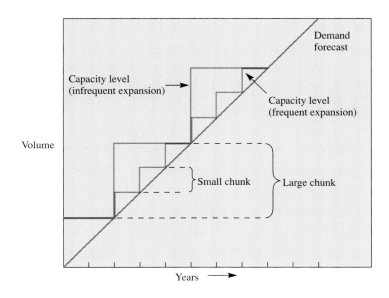

Exhibit 7.2

Frequent versus Infrequent Capacity Expansion

example of subcontracting is Japanese banks in California subcontracting check-clearing operations. An example of sharing capacity is two domestic airlines flying different routes with different seasonal demands exchanging aircraft (suitably re-painted) when one's routes are heavily used and the other's are not. A new twist is airlines sharing routes—using the same flight number even though the airline company may change through the course of the route. A new approach to sharing capacity involves consortiums' time-sharing flexible factories. (See the *Breakthrough* box on page 273 titled, "Time-Share Manufacturing.")

Determining Capacity Requirements

In determining capacity requirements, we must address the demands for individual product lines, individual plant capabilities, and allocation of production throughout the plant network. Typically this is done according to the following steps:

1. Use forecasting techniques (see Chapter 13) to forecast sales for individual products within each product line.
2. Calculate equipment and labor requirements to meet product line forecasts.
3. Project labor and equipment availabilities over the planning horizon.

Capacity Cushion

Often the firm then decides on some **capacity cushion** that will be maintained between the projected requirements and the actual capacity. A capacity cushion is an amount in excess of expected demand. For example, if the expected annual demand on a facility is $10 million in products per year and the design capacity is $12 million per year, it has a 20 percent capacity cushion. A 20 percent capacity cushion equates to an 83 percent utilization rate (100%/120%).

When a firm's design capacity is less than the capacity required to meet its demand, it is said to have a negative capacity cushion. If, for example, a firm has a demand of $12 million in products per year but can only produce $10 million per year, it has a negative capacity cushion of 20 percent.

We now apply these three steps to an example.

■ **example 7.1**   *Determining Capacity Requirements*   The Stewart Company produces two flavors of salad dressings: Paul's and Newman's. Each is available in bottles and single-serving plastic bags. Management would like to determine equipment and labor requirements for the next five years.

MARKETING

solution   *Step 1. Use forecasting techniques to forecast sales for individual products within each product line.* The marketing department, which is now running a promotional campaign for Newman's dressing, provided the following forecasted demand values (in thousands) for the next five years. The campaign is expected to continue for the next two years.

	Year				
	1	**2**	**3**	**4**	**5**
Paul's					
Bottles (000s)	60	100	150	200	250
Plastic bags (000s)	100	200	300	400	500
Newman's					
Bottles (000s)	75	85	95	97	98
Plastic bags (000s)	200	400	600	650	680

Step 2. Calculate equipment and labor requirements to meet product line forecasts. Currently, three machines that can package up to 150,000 bottles each per year are available. Each machine requires two operators and can produce bottles of both Newman's and Paul's dressings. Six bottle machine operators are available. Also, five machines that can package up to 250,000 plastic bags each per year are available. Three operators are required for each machine, which can produce plastic bags of both Newman's and Paul's dressings. Currently, 20 plastic-bag machine operators are available.

Total product line forecasts can be calculated from the preceding table by adding the yearly demand for bottles and plastic bags as follows:

			Year		
	1	**2**	**3**	**4**	**5**
Bottles	135	185	245	297	348
Plastic bags	300	600	900	1,050	1,180

We can now calculate equipment and labor requirements for the current year (year 1). Since the total available capacity for packaging bottles is 450,000/year (3 machines × 150,000 each), we will be using $135/450 = 0.3$ of the available capacity for the current year, or $0.3 \times 3 = 0.9$ machines. Similarly, we will need $300/1250 = 0.24$ of the available capacity for plastic bags for the current year, or $0.24 \times 5 = 1.2$ machines. The number of crew required to support our forecasted demand for the first year will consist of the crew required for the bottle and the plastic bag machines:

The labor requirement for year 1's bottle operation is

$$0.9 \text{ bottle machines} \times 2 \text{ operators} = 1.8 \text{ operators}$$

$$1.2 \text{ bag machines} \times 3 \text{ operators} = 3.6 \text{ operators}$$

Step 3. Project labor and equipment availabilities over the planning horizon. We repeat the preceding calculations for the remaining years:

			Year		
	1	**2**	**3**	**4**	**5**
Plastic Bag Operation					
Percent capacity utilized	24	48	72	84	94
Machine requirement	1.2	2.4	3.6	4.2	4.7
Labor requirement	3.6	7.2	10.8	12.6	14.1
Bottle Operation					
Percent capacity utilized	30	41	54	66	77
Machine requirement	.9	1.23	1.62	1.98	2.31
Labor requirement	1.8	2.46	3.24	3.96	4.62

A positive capacity cushion exists for all five years since the available capacity for both operations is always in excess of the expected demand. The Stewart Company can now begin to develop the intermediate range or aggregate plan for the two production lines. (See Chapter 14 for a discussion of aggregate planning.) ∎

Decision Tree

Using Decision Trees to Evaluate Capacity Alternatives

A convenient way to lay out the steps of a capacity problem is through the use of decision trees. The tree format helps not only in understanding the problem but also in finding a solution. A **decision tree** is a schematic model of the sequence of steps in a problem and the conditions and consequences of each step. In recent years, there have been a few commercial software packages developed to assist in the construction and analysis of decision trees. These packages make the process quick and easy.

Decision trees are composed of decision nodes with branches to and from them. Usually, squares represent decision points, and circles represent chance events. Branches from decision points show the choices available to the decision maker; branches from chance events show the probabilities for their occurrence.

In solving decision-tree problems, we work from the end of the tree backward to the start of the tree. As we work back, we calculate the expected values at each step. In calculating the expected value, the time value of money is important if the planning horizon is long.

Once the calculations are made, we prune the tree by eliminating from each decision point all branches except the one with the highest payoff. This process continues to the first decision point, and the decision problem is thereby solved.

We now demonstrate an application to capacity planning for Hackers Computer Store. The exhibits used to solve this problem were generated using a program called DATA by TreeAge Software. (A demonstration version of the software, capable of solving the problems given in this chapter, is available from the World-Wide-Web at *http://www.treeage.com.*)

■ **example** 7.2   *Decision Trees*   The owner of Hackers Computer Store is considering what to do with his business over the next five years. Sales growth over the past couple of years has been good, but sales could grow substantially if a major electronics firm is built in his area as proposed. Hackers' owner sees three options. The first is to enlarge his current store, the second is to locate at a new site, and the third is to simply wait and do nothing. The decision to expand or move would take little time, and, therefore, the store would not lose revenue. If nothing were done the first year and strong growth occurred, then the decision to expand would be reconsidered. Waiting longer than one year would allow competition to move in and would make expansion no longer feasible.

The assumption and conditions are as follows:

1. Strong growth as a result of the increased population of computer fanatics from the electronics new firm has a 55 percent probability.
2. Strong growth with a new site would give annual returns of $195,000 per year. Weak growth with a new site would mean annual returns of $115,000.
3. Strong growth with an expansion would give annual returns of $190,000 per year. Weak growth with an expansion would mean annual returns of $100,000.
4. At the existing store with no changes, there would be returns of $170,000 per year if there is strong growth and $105,000 per year if growth is weak.
5. Expansion at the current site would cost $87,000.
6. The move to the new site would cost $210,000.
7. If growth is strong and the existing site is enlarged during the second year, the cost would still be $87,000.
8. Operating costs for all options are equal.

solution We construct a decision tree to advise Hackers' owner on the best action. Exhibit 7.3 shows the decision tree for this problem. There are two decision points (shown with the square nodes) and three chance occurrences (round nodes).

The values of each alternative outcome shown on the right of the diagram in Exhibit 7.4 are calculated as follows:

Alternative	Revenue	Cost	Value
Move to new location, strong growth	\$195,000 × 5 yrs	\$210,000	\$765,000
Move to new location, weak growth	\$115,000 × 5 yrs	\$210,000	\$365,000
Expand store, strong growth	\$190,000 × 5 yrs	\$87,000	\$863,000
Expand store, weak growth	\$100,000 × 5 yrs	\$87,000	\$413,000
Do nothing now, strong growth, expand next year	\$170,000 × 1 yr + \$190,000 × 4 yrs	\$87,000	\$843,000
Do nothing now, strong growth, do not expand next year	\$170,000 × 5 yrs	\$0	\$850,000
Do nothing now, weak growth	\$105,000 × 5 yrs	\$0	\$525,000

Working from the right most alternatives, which are associated with the decision whether or not to expand, we see that the alternative of doing nothing has a higher value than the expand alternative. We, therefore, eliminate the expand in the second year alternatives. What this means is that if we do nothing in the first year and we experience strong growth, then in the second year it makes no sense to expand.

Now, we can calculate the expected values associated with our current decision alternatives. We simply multiply the value of the alternative by its probability, and sum the values. The expected value for the alternative of moving now is \$585,000. The expand alternative has an expected value of \$660,500, and doing nothing now has an expected value of \$703,750. Our analysis indicates that our best decision is to do nothing (both now and next year)! ■

Decision Tree for Hacker's Computer Store Problem

Exhibit 7.3

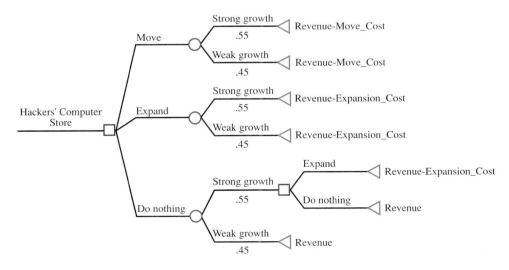

Exhibit 7.4

Decision Tree Analysis Using DATA (TreeAge Software, Inc.)

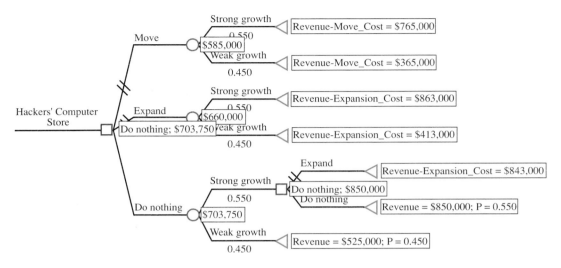

Exhibit 7.5

Decision Tree Analysis Using Net Present Value Calculations

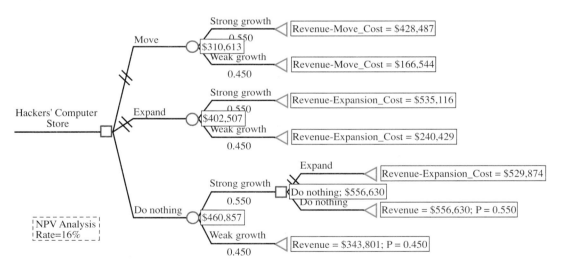

Due to the five year time horizon, it may be useful to consider the time value of the revenue and cost streams when solving this problem. Details concerning the calculation of the discounted monetary values are given in Appendix A ("Financial Analysis of Operations"). For example, if we assume a 16 percent interest rate, the first alternative outcome (move now, strong growth) has a discounted revenue valued at $428,487 (195,000 × 3.274293654) minus the $210,000 cost to move immediately. Exhibit 7.5 shows the analysis considering the discounted flows. Details of the calculations are given below. Present value table G.3 (in Appendix G) can be used to look up the discount factors. In order to make our calculations agree with those completed by the computer program, we have used discount factors that are calculated to 10 digits of precision (it is easy to do this with Excel). The only calculation that is a little tricky is the one for revenue when we do nothing now and we expand at the beginning of next year. In this case, we have a revenue stream of $170,000 the first year, followed by four years at $190,000. The first part of the calculation (170,000 × .862068966) discounts the first year revenue to present. The next part (190,000 × 2.798180638) discounts the next four years to the start of year two. We then discount this four year stream to present value. The computer program used to generate Exhibit 7.5 performed the calculations automatically.

Alternative	Revenue	Cost	Value
Move to new location, strong growth	$195,000 × 3.274293654	$210,000	$428,487
Move to new location, weak growth	$115,000 × 3.274293654	$210,000	$166,544
Expand store, strong growth	$190,000 × 3.274293654	$87,000	$535,116
Expand store, weak growth	$100,000 × 3.274203654	$87,000	$240,429
Do nothing now, strong growth, expand next year	$170,000 × .862068966 $190,000 × 2.798180638 × .862068966	$87,000 × .862068966	$529,874
Do nothing now, strong growth, do not expand next year	$170,000 × 3.274293654	$0	$556,630
Do nothing now, weak growth	$105,000 × 3.274293654	$0	$343,801

▪ PLANNING SERVICE CAPACITY

Capacity Planning in Service versus Manufacturing

Although capacity planning in services is subject to many of the same issues as manufacturing capacity planning, and facility sizing can be done in much the same way, there are several important differences. Service capacity is more time- and location-dependent, it is subject to more volatile demand fluctuations, and utilization directly impacts service quality.

Time   Unlike goods, services cannot be stored for later use. The capacity must be available to produce a service at the time when it is needed. For example, a customer cannot be given a seat that went unoccupied on a previous airline flight if the current flight is full. Nor could the customer purchase a seat on a particular day's flight and take it home to be used at some later date.

Location   The service capacity must be located near the customer. In manufacturing, production takes place, and then the goods are distributed to the customer. With services, however, the opposite is true. The capacity to deliver the service must first be distributed to the customer (either physically or through some communications media such as the telephone); then, the service can be produced. A hotel room or rental car that is available in another city is not much use to the customer—it must be where the customer is when that customer needs it.

Volatility of Demand   The volatility of demand on a service delivery system is much higher than that on a manufacturing production system for three reasons. First, as just mentioned, services cannot be stored. This means that inventory cannot be used to smooth the demand as in manufacturing. The second reason is that the customers interact directly with the production system—and each of these customers often has different needs, will have different levels of experience with the process, and may require different numbers of transactions. This contributes to greater variability in the processing time required for each customer and hence greater variability in the minimum capacity needed. The third reason for the greater volatility in service demand is that it is directly affected by consumer behavior. Influences on customer behavior ranging from the weather to a major event can directly affect demand for different services. Go to any restaurant near your campus during spring break and it will probably be almost empty. Or try to book a room at a local hotel during Homecoming weekend. This behavioral effect can be seen over even shorter time frames such as the lunch-hour rush at a bank's drive-through window or the sudden surge in pizza orders at Domino's during halftime on Superbowl Sunday. Because of this volatility, planning capacity in services is often done in increments as small as 10 to 30 minutes, as opposed to the one-week increments more common in manufacturing.

Capacity Utilization and Service Quality

Planning capacity levels for services must consider the day-to-day relationship between service utilization and service quality. Exhibit 7.6 shows a service situation cast in waiting line terms (arrival rates and service rates).[4] As noted by Haywood-Farmer and Nollet, the best operating point is near 70 percent of the maximum capacity. This is "enough to keep servers busy but allows enough time to serve customers individually and keep enough capacity in reserve so as not to create too many managerial headaches."[5] In the critical zone, customers are processed through the system, but service quality declines. Above the critical zone, the line builds up and it is likely that many customers may never be served.

Haywood-Farmer and Nollet also note that the optimal utilization rate is very context specific. Low rates are appropriate when both the degree of uncertainty and the stakes are high. For example, hospital emergency rooms and fire departments should aim for low utilization because of the high level of uncertainty and the life-or-death nature of their activities. Relatively predictable services such as commuter trains or service facilities without customer contact, such as postal sorting operations, can plan to operate much nearer 100 percent utilization. Interestingly, there is a third group for which high utilization is desirable. All sports teams like sellouts, not only because of the virtually 100 percent contribution margin of each customer, but be-

---

[4] Waiting lines are discussed in the supplement to Chapter 5.

[5] John Haywood-Farmer and Jean Nollet, *Services Plus: Effective Service Management* (Boucherville, Quebec, Canada: G. Morin Publisher Ltd., 1991), p. 58.

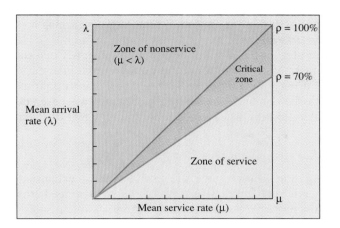

Exhibit 7.6

Relationship between the Rate of Service Utilization (ρ) and Service Quality

Source: John Haywood-Farmer and Jean Nollet, *Services Plus: Effective Service Management* (Boucherville, Quebec, Canada: G. Morin Publisher Ltd., 1991), p. 59.

cause a full house creates an atmosphere that pleases customers, motivates the home team to perform better, and boosts future ticket sales. Stage performances and bars share this phenomenon. On the other hand, many airline passengers feel that a flight is too crowded when the seat next to theirs is occupied. Airlines capitalize on this response to sell more business-class seats.[6]

ADDING CAPACITY THROUGH MULTISITE SERVICE GROWTH

Many services, particularly franchises, start with one unit and grow by adding similar units at different locations. Research by Sasser, Olsen, and Wyckoff indicated that this growth followed four life cycle stages: entrepreneurial, multisite rationalization, (rapid) growth, and maturity.[7]

Entrepreneurial Stage

Services are conceived in the entrepreneurial stage. Services generally offer a single service at a single location. Many services, such as small groceries, specialty stores, and restaurants, never grow out of this stage. Capacity expansion consists of the addition of equipment and personnel at the current site to meet a growing demand for the service. Planning issues revolve around (1) equipment cost and (2) how the addition of equipment and personnel into a normally already cramped facility will affect service delivery.

Two strategies are commonly used by a single-site firm to cope with the highly volatile demand typical of services. The first is cultivating the ability to shift resources from other tasks to where they are needed. Services will commonly cross-train personnel to fill in at other positions when they are needed, such as training a bank

[6] Ibid.

[7] W. E. Sasser, R. P. Olsen, and D. D. Wyckoff, *Management of Service Operations: Text, Cases, and Readings* (Boston: Allyn and Bacon, 1978), pp. 534–66.

clerk to fill in as a teller during the lunch-hour rush or teaching a salesperson to run a register whenever a line forms.

The second strategy is the use of customer coproduction. Coproduction takes place when the customer does some or all of the work required in a service transaction, as with self-serve drink fountains or self-bussing tables in restaurants. Coproduction tends to smooth the demands on the system because whenever demand increases, these additional customers also provide labor to help meet this demand.

Multisite Rationalization Stage

At the multisite rationalization stage, the service firm has exhausted the local market for its existing service and must make a decision about continued growth. The firm can duplicate its existing service in additional locations (which is often called cookie-cutter growth), it can add new services at its current location, or it can attempt to do both.

If a firm decides to grow by adding services to the existing site, it manages capacity expansion in much the same manner as firms at the entrepreneurial stage. Service firms that choose multiple sites have an additional option for managing the demand volatility—by shifting resources between sites to cover the peak demands. Car and truck rental firms will shift vehicles from slow locations to areas where the demand is currently highest. In fact, through the use of select discount fares on one-way rentals, these firms actually have the customers transport the vehicles to where they are most needed. Companies with multiple telephone-call-handling centers will often reroute the overload during peak hours to call centers in other time zones that peak earlier or later in the day. One engineering firm is able to handle rush jobs by electronically moving the work among sites around the globe. By passing work on at the end of one site's day to a new site where the day is just beginning, the company is able to work 24 hours a day on an important project, even though none of its offices actually keep those hours.

As shown in Exhibit 7.7, some firms (such as resorts, universities, and hospitals) manage to grow quite large without ever becoming multisite operations by adding more and more services at their existing site. Other firms (such as chain restaurants and hotels) replicate a more focused concept in a large number of different sites. Despite the success of a limited number of firms, those that try to expand in both directions most often fail. In some cases, this is because the complexity of managing

Exhibit 7.7

Service Growth Matrix

	Single-service	Multiservice
Multisite	Chain restaurants Hotels Car and truck rentals Airlines Specialty stores	Department stores Banks HMOs
Single-site	Dry cleaners Restaurants Mom and pop stores	Hospitals Resorts Universities

a large variety of services at multiple sites becomes overwhelming. In other cases, some or all components of a complex package of services that evolve to serve customers in one location may simply not be appropriate for customers in another.

Different types of economies apply, depending on how the service firm expands. As the capacity of a service at a given site increases, there will be economies of scale, just as in a manufacturing plant. Adding sites to a service firm, however, produces more limited economies of scale. Fixed costs are still distributed over a greater volume, but we do not expect to see the capital and operating cost reductions. This is because adding a site does not actually increase the "plant" size, it merely adds another small "plant." Diseconomies of scale are also evident as service firms acquire too many sites and the complexity becomes increasingly unmanageable. Exhibit 7.8 shows an empirical study of how the perceived quality of food services deteriorates as the number of sites grows very large. Multiservice firms often experience the other type of economy, economies of scope. In other words, offering related services at a single site can be less expensive than offering the services independently at separate sites. This is possible because some common resources such as databases or specific employee skills that have been developed and maintained to support a particular service can support additional related services at little or no additional cost. To take full advantage of economies of scope, therefore, it is important to focus on adding new services that can efficiently use existing resources.

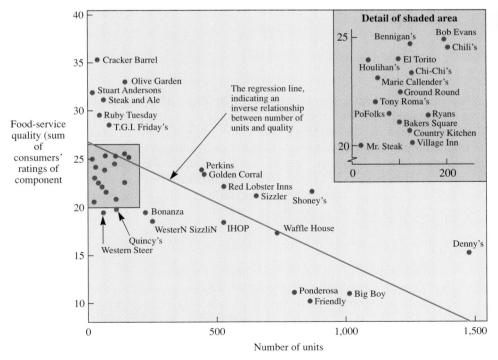

Exhibit 7.8

Food Service Quality Relative to Number of Units

Exhibit 7.9

Operational
Complexity

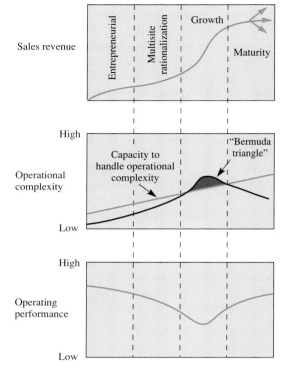

Source: W. E. Sasser, R. P. Olsen, and D. D. Wyckoff, *Management of Service Operations: Text, Cases, and Readings* (Boston: Allyn and Bacon, 1978), p. 561.

Growth Stage

When the service firm enters its rapid growth stage, its sales volume typically increases exponentially. Unfortunately, so does the operational complexity of running the firm. This is what Sasser, Olsen, and Wycoff refer to as the **"Bermuda triangle" of operational complexity,** where the difficulty in running the business outstrips the manager's ability to handle it. (See Exhibit 7.9.) Other new capacity planning challenges at this stage include (1) the need to incorporate fresh ideas into the existing facilities and (2) the need to upgrade older facilities that are nearing the end of their useful life or that require remodeling or expansion.

"Bermuda
Triangle" of
Operational
Complexity

Maturity Stage

By the mature stage, a service firm has tapped most of its potential market and may have lost much of its original uniqueness. At this stage, operational efficiencies become particularly important as the competition becomes largely price based. Because of the age of the facilities, capacity issues generally focus on remodeling and replacement. Sometimes, however, it is necessary to modify the service concept because it has become stale over time. If the concept is revitalized, capacity planning must address the complicated issue of duplicating any required changes across the entire existing system.

■ CONCLUSION

Strategic capacity planning involves an investment decision that must match resource capabilities to a long-term demand forecast. As discussed in this chapter, factors to be taken into account in selecting capacity additions for both manufacturing and services include

- The likely effects of economies of scale.
- The effects of experience curves.
- The impact of changing facility focus and balance among production stages.
- The degree of flexibility of facilities and the workforce.

For services in particular, key considerations include (1) the effect of capacity changes on the quality of the service offering and (2) the implications of increasing the number of services in parallel with increasing the number of service outlets. In the next chapter, we discuss the related issue of where to locate the firm's facilities by using them in the solution of some linear programming problems.

SOLVED PROBLEM

SOLVED PROBLEM 1

Calcom (a new hand-held calculator manufacturing company based in Los Angeles) has demand from both domestic and foreign markets. Currently Calcom has produced 100,000 calculators, and the unit production cost is $3.50. The company believes that an 85 percent experience curve is about right for its production capacity.

    a. What is Calcom's unit production cost if the cumulative production volume reaches 800,000?

    b. At approximately what cumulative production volume can Calcom reduce production cost to below $2.55?

Solution

    a. An 85 percent learning curve means that Calcom's production cost will fall 15 percent when the cumulative production doubles. We can tabulate the calculation as follows:

Cumulative Production Volume	Unit Production Cost
100,000	$3.5
200,000	$3.5 × 0.85 = $2.98
400,000	$2.98 × 0.85 = $2.53
800,000	$2.53 × 0.85 = $2.15

    Therefore, when Calcom's cumulative production volume reaches 800,000, the unit cost will be $2.15.

    b. As the preceding table shows, unit cost falls to $2.53 when cumulative production volume is 400,000. Hence unit production cost drops below $2.55 when cumulative volume approaches 400,000.

REVIEW AND DISCUSSION QUESTIONS

1. What were the capacity problems encountered at the opening of Euro Disney? What lessons are there for other service companies in planning capacity?

2. List some practical limits to economies of scale; that is, when should a plant stop growing?

3. Discuss the Korean auto manufacturers' decision to expand local production (page 269). What are the cost trade-offs associated with this decision?

4. What are some capacity balance problems faced by the following organizations or facilities?
   a. An airline terminal.
   b. A university computing center.
   c. A clothing manufacturer.

5. What is the cause of the "Bermuda triangle" phenomenon in multisite services? Does it exist in growing manufacturing firms?

6. What are some major capacity considerations in a hospital? How do they differ from those of a factory?

7. Management may choose to build up capacity in anticipation of demand or in response to developing demand. Cite the advantages and disadvantages of both approaches.

8. What is capacity balance? Why is it hard to achieve? What methods are used to deal with capacity imbalances?

9. What are some reasons for a plant to maintain a capacity cushion? How about a negative capacity cushion?

10. At first glance, the concepts of the focused factory and capacity flexibility may seem to contradict each other. Do they really?

PROBLEMS

1. See SM.

1. AlwaysRain Irrigation, Inc., would like to determine capacity requirements for the next four years. Currently two production lines are in place for bronze and plastic sprinklers. Three types of sprinklers are available in both bronze and plastic: 90-degree nozzle sprinklers, 180-degree nozzle sprinklers, and 360-degree nozzle sprinklers. Management has forecasted demand for the next four years as follows:

	Yearly Demand			
	1 (in 000s)	**2 (in 000s)**	**3 (in 000s)**	**4 (in 000s)**
Plastic 90	32	44	55	56
Plastic 180	15	16	17	18
Plastic 360	50	55	64	67
Bronze 90	7	8	9	10
Bronze 180	3	4	5	6
Bronze 360	11	12	15	18

Both production lines can produce all the different types of nozzles. Each bronze machine requires two operators to run and can produce up to 12,000 sprinklers. The plastic injection molding machine requires four operators to run and can produce up to 200,000 sprinklers. Three bronze machines and only one injection molding machine are available. What are the capacity requirements for the next four years?

2. Not enough capacity after second year.

2. Suppose that AlwaysRain Irrigation's marketing department will undertake an intense ad campaign for the bronze sprinklers, which are more expensive but also more

durable than the plastic ones. Forecasted demand for the next four years is

Yearly Demand

	1 (in 000s)	2 (in 000s)	3 (in 000s)	4 (in 000s)
Plastic 90	32	44	55	56
Plastic 180	15	16	17	18
Plastic 360	50	55	64	67
Bronze 90	11	15	18	23
Bronze 180	6	5	6	9
Bronze 360	15	16	17	20

What are the capacity implications of the marketing campaign?

✓ **3.** In anticipation of the ad campaign, AlwaysRain bought an additional bronze machine. Will this be enough to ensure that enough capacity is available?

4. Suppose that operators have enough training to operate both the bronze machines and the injection molding machine for the plastic sprinklers. Currently AlwaysRain has 10 such employees. In anticipation of the ad campaign described in Problem 2, management approved the purchase of two additional bronze machines. What are the labor requirement implications?

5. Expando, Inc. is considering the possibility of building an additional factory that would produce a new addition to their product line. They are currently considering two options. The first is a small facility that they could build at a cost of $6 million. If demand for their new products is low, they are expecting to receive $10 million in discounted revenues (present value of future revenues) with the small facility. On the other hand, if demand is high, they expect $12 million in discounted revenues using the small facility. The second option is to build a large factory at a cost of $9 million. Were demand to be low, they are expecting $10 million in discounted revenues with the large plant. If demand is high, they estimate that the discounted revenues would be $14 million. In either case, they have estimated the probability of demand being high at .40, and the probability of being low at .60. Not constructing a new factory would result in no additional revenue being generated as their current factories cannot produce these new products. Construct a decision tree to help Expando decide what is the best decision.

6. A builder has located a piece of property that he would like to buy and eventually build on. The land is currently zoned for four homes per acre, but he is planning to request new zoning. What he builds depends on approval of zoning requests and your analysis of this problem to advise him. With his input and your help, the decision process has been reduced to the following costs, alternatives, and probabilities:

Cost of land: $2 million.

Probability of rezoning: .60.

If the land is rezoned, there will be additional costs for new roads, lighting, and so on, of $1 million.

If the land is rezoned, the contractor must decide whether to build a shopping center or 1,500 apartments that the tentative plan shows would be possible. If he builds a shopping center, there is a 70 percent chance that he can sell the shopping center to a large department chain for $4 million over his construction cost, which excludes the land; and there is a 30 percent chance that he can sell it to an insurance company for $5 million over his construction cost (also excluding the land). If, instead of the shopping center, he decides to build the 1,500 apartments, he places probabilities on the profits as follows: There is a 60 percent chance that he can sell

3. No additional need after third year.

4. See SM.

5. Expected NPV—Small $4.8 million
Expected NPV—Large $2.6 million

6. See SM.
   Point one = $4.3 million.
   Point two = $3.9 million.
   Point three = $.4 million.
   Expected results:
   .60(1.3) + 0.40(.4) = $.94 million.

the apartments to a real estate investment corporation for $3,000 each over his construction cost; there is a 40 percent chance that he can get only $2,000 each over his construction cost. (Both exclude his land cost.)

If the land is not rezoned, he will comply with the existing zoning restrictions and simply build 600 homes on which he expects to make $4,000 over his construction cost on each one (excluding his cost of land).

Draw a decision tree of the problem and determine the best solution and the expected net profit.

Case

Vol. III "Shouldice Hospital"   **Shouldice Hospital—A Cut Above[8]**

"Shouldice Hospital, the house that hernias built, is a converted country estate which gives the hospital 'a country club' appeal."

A quote from *American Medical News*

Shouldice Hospital in Canada is widely known for one thing—hernia repair! In fact, that is the only operation it performs, and it performs a great many of them. Over the past two decades this small 90-bed hospital has averaged 7,000 operations annually. Last year, they had a record year and performed nearly 7,500 operations. Patients' ties to Shouldice do not end when they leave the hospital. Every year the gala Hernia Reunion dinner (with complimentary hernia inspection) draws in excess of 1,000 former patients, some of who have been attending the event for over 30 years.

A number of notable features in Shouldice's service delivery system contribute to its success. (1) Shouldice only accepts patients with the uncomplicated external hernias, and it uses a superior technique developed for this type of hernia by Dr. Shouldice during World War II. (2) Patients are subject to early ambulation, which promotes healing. (Patients literally walk off the operating table and engage in light exercise throughout their stay, which lasts only three days.) (3) Its country club atmosphere, gregarious nursing staff, and built-in socializing make a surprisingly pleasant experience out of an inherently unpleasant medical problem. Regular times are set aside for tea, cookies, and socializing. All patients are paired up with a roommate with similar background and interests.

The Production System

The medical facilities at Shouldice consist of five operating rooms, a patient recovery room, a laboratory, and six examination rooms. Shouldice performs, on average, 150 operations per week, with patients generally staying at the hospital for three days. Although operations are performed only five days a week, the remainder of the hospital is in operation continuously to attend to recovering patients.

An operation at Shouldice Hospital is performed by 1 of the 12 full-time surgeons assisted by one of 7 parttime assistant surgeons. Surgeons generally take about one hour to prepare for and perform each hernia operation, and they operate on four patients per day. The surgeons' day ends at 4 P.M., although they can expect to be on call every fourteenth night and every tenth weekend.

The Shouldice Experience

All patients undergo a screening exam prior to setting a date for their operation. Patients in the Toronto area are encouraged to walk in to have the diagnosis done. Examinations are done between 9 A.M. and 3:30 P.M. Monday through Friday, and between 10 AM. and 2 P.M. on Saturday. Out-of-town patients are mailed a medical information questionnaire (also available over the Internet), which is used for the diagnosis. A small percentage of the patients who are overweight or otherwise represent an undue medical risk are refused treatment. The remaining patients receive a confirmation card with the scheduled date for their operation. A patient's folder is transferred to the reception desk once an arrival date is confirmed.

Patients arrive at the clinic between 1 and 3 P.M. the day before their surgery. After a short wait, they receive a brief preoperative examination. They are then sent to see an admissions clerk to complete any necessary paperwork. Patients are next directed to one of the two nurses' stations for blood and urine tests and then are shown to their rooms. They spend the remaining time before orientation getting settled and aquainting themselves with their roommate.

Orientation begins at 5 P.M., followed by dinner in the common dining room. Later in the evening, at 9 P.M.,

---

[8] Shouldice Hospital is at *http://www.shouldice.com/*. The web site has much additional information concerning the history of the hospital and current hernia operation procedures.

patients gather in the lounge area for tea and cookies. Here, new patients can talk with patients who have already had their surgery. Bedtime is between 9:30 and 10 P.M.

On the day of the operation, patients with early operations are awakened at 5:30 A.M. for preoperative sedation. The first operations begin at 7:30 A.M. Shortly before an operation starts, the patient is administered a local anesthetic, leaving him alert and fully aware of the proceedings. At the conclusion of the operation, the patient is invited to walk from the operating table to a nearby wheelchair, which is waiting to return him to his room. After a brief period of rest, he is encouraged to get up and start exercising. By 9 P.M. that day, he is in the lounge having cookies and tea, and talking with new, incoming patients.

The skin clips holding the incision together are loosened, and some are removed the next day. The remainder are removed the following morning just before the patient is discharged.

When Shouldice Hospital started, the average hospital stay for hernia surgery was three weeks. Today, many institutions push "same day surgery" for a variety of reasons. Shouldice Hospital firmly believes that this is not in the best interests of patients, and is committed to their three day process. Shouldice's post-op rehabilitation program is designed to enable the patient to resume normal activities with minimal interruption and discomfort. Shouldice patients frequently return to work in a few days, the average total time off is eight days.

"It is interesting to note that approximately 1 out of every 100 Shouldice patients is a medical doctor."

Future Plans

The management of Shouldice is thinking of expanding the hospital's capacity to serve considerable unsatisfied demand. To this effect, the vice president is seriously considering two options. The first involves adding one more day of operations (Saturday) to the existing five-day schedule, which would increase capacity by 20 per-

cent. The second option is to add another floor of rooms to the hospital, increasing the number of beds by 50 percent. This would require more aggressive scheduling of the operating rooms.

The administrator of the hospital, however, is concerned about maintaining control over the quality of the service delivered. He thinks the facility is already getting very good utilization. The doctors and the staff are happy with their jobs and the patients are satisfied with the service. According to him, further expansion of capacity might make it hard to maintain the same kind of working relationships and attitudes.

Questions

Exhibit C7.1 is a room-occupancy table for the existing system. Each row in the table follows the patients that checked in on a given day. The columns indicate the number of patients in the hospital on a given day. For example, the first row of the table shows that 30 people checked in on Monday and were in the hospital for Monday, Tuesday, and Wednesday. By summing the columns of the table for Wednesday, we see that there are 90 patients staying in the hospital that day.

1. How well is the hospital currently utilizing its beds?

2. Develop a similar table to show the effects of adding operations on Saturday. (Assume that 30 operations would still be performed each day.) How would this affect the utilization of the bed capacity? Is this capacity sufficient for the additional patients?

3. Now look at the effect of increasing the number of beds by 50 percent. How many operations could the hospital perform per day before running out of bed capacity? (Assume operations are performed five days per week, with the same number performed on each day.) How well would the new resources be utilized relative to the current operation? Could the hospital really perform this many operations? Why? (Hint: Look at the capacity of the 12 surgeons and the 5 operating rooms.)

	Beds Required							Exhibit C7.1
Check-in day	**Monday**	**Tuesday**	**Wednesday**	**Thursday**	**Friday**	**Saturday**	**Sunday**	
Monday	30	30	30					Operations with 90 Beds (30 patients per day)
Tuesday		30	30	30				
Wednesday			30	30	30			
Thursday				30	30	30		
Friday								
Saturday								
Sunday	30	30					30	
Total	60	90	90	90	60	30	30	

4. Although financial data is sketchy, an estimate from a construction company indicates that adding bed capacity would cost about $100,000 per bed. In addition, the rate charged for the hernia surgery varies between about $900 to $2,000 (U.S. dollars), with an average rate of $1,300 per operation. The surgeons are paid a flat $600 per operation. Due to all the uncertainties in government health care legislation, Shouldice would like to justify any expansion within a five-year time period.

Source: This case is based on S. Oliver, "A Canadian Hospital Does Brisk Business in Rupture Repairs," *The Wall Street Journal,* February 7, 1978; James L. Heskitt, W. Earl Sasser, and Christopher W. L. Hart, *Service Breakthroughs* (New York: The Free Press, 1990); "Shouldice Hospital Limited," Harvard Business School Case 5-686-120 (Boston: Harvard Business School, 1986); and The Shouldice Hospital World Wide Web page (*http:// www.shouldice.com/*); August 1996.

SELECTED BIBLIOGRAPHY

Bakke, Nils Arne, and Ronald Hellberg. "The Challenges of Capacity Planning." *International Journal of Production Economics* 31–30 (1993), pp. 243–64.

Hammesfahr, R. D. Jack, James A. Pope, and Alireza Ardalan. "Strategic Planning for Production Capacity." *International Journal of Operations and Production Management* 13, no. 5 (1993), pp. 41–53.

Haywood-Farmer, John, and Jean Nollet. *Services Plus: Effective Services Management.* Boucherville, Quebec, Canada: G. Morin Publisher Ltd., 1991.

Johnston, Robert, Stuart Chambers, Christine Harland, Alan Harrison, and Nigel Slack. *Cases in Operations Management.* London, England: Pitman, 1993.

Martin, Hugh F. "Mass Customization at Personal Lines Insurance Center". Planning Review 21, no. 4 (July–August 1993), pp. 27, 56.

Meyer, Christopher. *Fast Cycle Time: How to Align Purpose, Strategy and Structure for Speed.* New York: Free Press, 1993.

Giffi, Craig, Aleda V. Roth, and Gregory M. Seals, eds. *Competing in World-Class Manufacturing: National Center for Manufacturing Sciences* Homewood, IL: Business One Irwin, 1990.

Pine II, B. Joseph, *Mass Customization: The New Frontier in Business Competition.* Boston: Harvard Business School Press, 1993.

Supplement 7

Linear Programming

Supplement Outline

The Linear Programming Model, 294
Graphical Linear Programming, 294
The Simplex Method, 297
    The Six-Step Solution Procedure
    Search Path Followed by the Simplex
      Method
    Shadow Prices, Ranging, and
      Sensitivity

    Linear Programming Using
      Microsoft Excel
Transportation Method 307
    Step 1: Set Up Transportation Matrix
    Step 2: Make Initial Allocations
    Step 3: Develop Optimal Solution

Key Terms

Linear Programming

Graphical Linear Programming

Objective Function

Constraint Equation

Slack Variable

Simplex Method

Pivot Method

Maximization

Minimization

Sensitivity Analysis

Shadow Price

Solver

Transportation Method

Degeneracy

www Links

Airlines Online (http://www.airlines.com)

Methods

Simplex Method

Aggregate production planning: Finding the minimum-cost production schedule, including production rate change costs, given constraints on size of workforce and inventory levels.

Service productivity analysis: Comparing how efficiently different service outlets are using their resources compared to the best performing unit. (This approach is called data envelopment analysis.)

Product planning: Finding the optimal product mix where several products have different costs and resource requirements (e.g., finding the optimal blend of constituents for gasolines, paints, human diets, animal feeds).

Product routing: Finding the optimal routing for a product that must be processed sequentially through several machine centers, with each machine in a center having its own cost and output characteristics.

Process control: Minimizing the amount of scrap material generated by cutting steel, leather, or fabric from a roll or sheet of stock material.

Inventory control: Finding the optimal combination of products to stock in a warehouse or store.

Transportation Method

Aggregate production planning: Finding the minimum-cost production schedule (excluding production rate change costs).

Distribution scheduling: Finding the optimal shipping schedule for distributing products between factories and warehouses or warehouses and retailers.

Plant location studies: Finding the optimal location of a new plant by evaluating shipping costs between alternative locations and supply and demand sources.

Materials handling: Finding the minimum-cost routings of material handling devices (e.g., forklift trucks) between departments in a plant and of hauling materials from a supply yard to work sites by trucks, with each truck having different capacity and performance capabilities.

Examples

American Red Cross Blood Collection and Distribution

The blood service of the American Red Cross (ARC) is divided into a number of regions. Each region has responsibility for blood collection, testing, and distribution. The mid-Atlantic region of the American Red Cross (ARC) has responsibility for most of Virginia and northeastern North Carolina. The ARC was concerned with the feasibility and effect of a proposed facility relocation of its permanent blood collection and distribution sites in the mid-Atlantic region. Linear programming models were used to quickly provide insights into its current scheduling of blood collections and distribution as well as the changes imposed by the proposed relocation. As a result of the analysis, ARC decided to postpone its facility relocation and to optimize the operations of its existing facilities.[†]

Typical Operations Management Applications of Linear Programming*

Vol. IV "Scheduling Services—the United Solution"

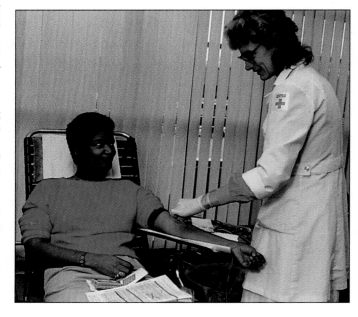

Red Cross blood collection.

* Grouped by the two primary methods covered in this supplement. (The graphical method is not included in this listing since it is limited to problems with two variables.)

† Source: Derya A. Jacobs, Murat N. Silan, and Barry A. Clemson, "An Analysis of Alternative Locations and Service Areas of American Red Cross Blood Facilities," *Interfaces,* May/June 1996, pp. 40–50.

Judging Performance Appraisal Consistency

Three researchers used linear programming to determine consistency of performance appraisals of major league baseball players. The model calculated weights for objective performance measures that best fit the subjective ranking assigned to each player. Comparison of the LP results with the appraisal ranking made comparisons within the league possible. Such an application of LP would be equally applicable to evaluating the consistency of business managers' performance appraisals of employees.[*]

Valuing Forest Resources

When the New Zealand government was privatizing the state-run forest plantations they needed to value the expected cash flows from the forests to determine a fair selling price. Using linear programming, a forest estate modeling system was developed that calculated renewable harvesting and log allocation of the 14 districts over a 40 to 70 year time horizon. The expected cash flows from these operations were used to help set reserve prices, and indicative valuations. The potential buyers also used the system to help develop their bidding strategies.[†]

[*] Christopher Zappe, William Webster, and Ira Horowitz, "Using Linear Programming to Determine Post-Facto Consistency in Performance Evaluations of Major League Baseball Players," *Interfaces,* November/December 1993, pp. 107–13.

[†] Bruce R. Manley and John A. Threadgill, "LP Used for Valuation and Planning of New Zealand Plantation Forests," *Interfaces,* November/December 1991, pp. 66–79.

Tool time! In this supplement we present the basics of one of the most powerful tools of management science—linear programming.

Linear Programming (LP)

Linear programming (or simply **LP**) refers to several related mathematical techniques that are used to allocate limited resources among competing demands in an optimal way. LP is the most popular of the approaches falling under the general heading of mathematical optimization techniques, and, as can be seen in the box, "Typical Operations Management Applications of Linear Programming," has been applied to a myriad of operations management problems. Our focus here is on the simplex method (which can solve any type of linear programming problem) and the graphical and transportation methods (which are useful in dealing with certain special cases). In addition to illustrating how linear programming methods lead to an optimum solution for a given problem, we will discuss shadow prices and other valuable "free information" provided by the simplex method.

There are five essential conditions in a problem situation for linear programming to pertain. First, there must be *limited resources* (e.g., a limited number of workers, equipment, finances, and material); otherwise there would be no problem. Second, there must be an *explicit objective* (such as maximize profit or minimize cost). Third, there must be *linearity* (two is twice as good as one; if it takes three hours to make a part, then two parts would take six hours, three parts would take nine hours). Fourth, there must be *homogeneity* (the products produced on a machine are identical, or all the hours available from a worker are equally productive). Fifth is *divisibility:* Normal linear programming assumes that products and resources can be subdivided into fractions. If this subdivision is not possible (such as flying half an airplane or hiring one-fourth of a person), a modification of linear programming, called *integer programming,* can be used.

When a single objective is to be maximized (e.g., profit) or minimized (e.g., costs), we can use *linear programming*. When multiple objectives exist, *goal programming* is used. If a problem is best solved in stages or time frames, this is *dynamic programming*. Other restrictions on the nature of the problem may require that it be solved by other variations of the technique, such as *nonlinear programming* or *quadratic programming*.

■ THE LINEAR PROGRAMMING MODEL

Stated formally, the linear programming problem entails an optimizing process in which nonnegative values for a set of decision variables $X_1, X_2, \ldots, X_n$ are selected so as to maximize (or minimize) an objective function in the form

$$\text{Maximize (minimize) } Z = C_1 X_1 + C_2 X_2 + \cdots + C_n X_n$$

subject to resource constraints in the form

$$A_{11} X_1 + A_{12} X_2 + \cdots + A_{1n} X_n \leq B_1$$
$$A_{21} X_1 + A_{22} X_2 + \cdots + A_{2n} X_n \leq B_2$$
$$\vdots$$
$$A_{m1} X_1 + A_{m2} X_2 + \cdots + A_{mn} X_n \leq B_m$$

where C_n, A_{mn}, and B_m are given constants.

Depending on the problem, the constraints may also be stated with equal-to signs ($=$) or greater-than-or-equal-to signs ($\geq$).

■ GRAPHICAL LINEAR PROGRAMMING

Graphical Linear Programming

Though limited in application to problems involving two decision variables (or three variables for three-dimensional graphing), **graphical linear programming** provides a quick insight into the nature of linear programming and illustrates what takes place in the general simplex method described later.

We describe the steps involved in the graphical method in the context of a sample problem, that of the Puck and Pawn Company, which manufactures hockey sticks and chess sets. Each hockey stick yields an incremental profit of $2, and each chess set, $4. A hockey stick requires four hours of processing at machine center A and two hours at machine center B. A chess set requires six hours at machine center A, six hours at machine center B, and one hour at machine center C. Machine center A has a maximum of 120 hours of available capacity per day, machine center B has 72 hours, and machine center C has 10 hours.

If the company wishes to maximize profit, how many hockey sticks and chess sets should be produced per day?

1. Formulate the Problem in Mathematical Terms   If H is the number of hockey sticks and C is the number of chess sets, to maximize profit the **objective function** may be stated as

Objective Function

$$\text{Maximize } Z = \$2H + \$4C$$

The maximization will be subject to the following constraints:

$$4H + 6C \leq 120 \text{ (machine center A constraint)}$$
$$2H + 6C \leq 72 \text{ (machine center B constraint)}$$
$$1C \leq 10 \text{ (machine center C constraint)}$$
$$H, C \geq 0$$

This formulation satisfies the five requirements for standard LP stated in the second paragraph of this supplement:

1. There are limited resources (a finite number of hours available at each machine center).
2. There is an explicit objective function (we know what each variable is worth and what the goal is in solving the problem).
3. The equations are linear (no exponents or cross products).
4. The resources are homogeneous (everything is in one unit of measure, machine hours).
5. The decision variables are divisible and non-negative (we can make a fractional part of a hockey stick or chess set; however, if this were deemed undesirable, we would have to use integer programming).

2. Plot Constraint Equations   The **constraint equations** are easily plotted by letting one variable equal zero and solving for the axis intercept of the other. (The inequality portions of the restrictions are disregarded for this step.) For the machine center A constraint equation when $H = 0$, $C = 20$, and when $C = 0$, $H = 30$. For the machine center B constraint equation, when $H = 0$, $C = 12$, and when $C = 0$, $H = 36$. For the machine center C constraint equation, $C = 10$ for all values of H. These lines are graphed in Exhibit S7.1.

Constraint Equations

3. Determine the Area of Feasibility   The direction of inequality signs in each constraint determines the area where a feasible solution is found. In this case, all inequalities are of the less-than-or-equal-to variety, which means that it would be impossible to produce any combination of products that would lie to the right of any constraint line on the graph. The region of feasible solutions is unshaded on the graph and forms a convex polygon. A convex polygon exists when a line drawn between any two points in the polygon stays within the boundaries of that polygon. If this condition of convexity does not exist, the problem is either incorrectly set up or is not amenable to linear programming.

4. Plot the Objective Function   The objective function may be plotted by assuming some arbitrary total profit figure and then solving for the axis coordinates, as was done for the constraint equations. Other terms for the objective function, when used in this context, are the *iso-profit* or *equal contribution line,* because it shows all possible production combinations for any given profit figure. For example, from the dotted line closest to the origin on the graph, we can determine all possible combinations of hockey sticks and chess sets that yield $32 by picking a point on the line and reading the number of each product that can be made at that point. The combination yielding $32 at point *a* would be 10 hockey sticks and three chess sets. This can be verified by substituting $H = 10$ and $C = 3$ in the objective function:

$$\$2(10) + \$4(3) = \$20 + \$12 = \$32$$

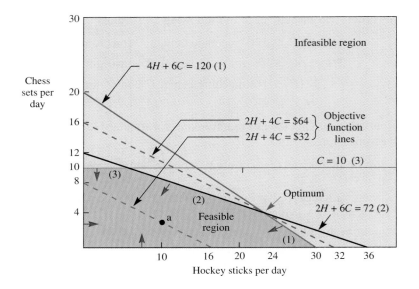

H	*C*	**Explanation**
0	120/6 = 20	Intersection of Constraint (1) and *C* axis
120/4 = 30	0	Intersection of Constraint (1) and *H* axis
0	72/6 = 12	Intersection of Constraint (2) and *C* axis
72/2 = 36	0	Intersection of Constraint (2) and *H* axis
0	10	Intersection of Constraint (3) and *C* axis
0	32/4 = 8	Intersection of $32 iso-point line (objective function) and *C* axis
32/2 = 16	0	Intersection of $32 iso-profit line and *H* axis
0	64/4 = 16	Intersection of $64 iso-profit line and *C* axis
64/2 = 32	0	Intersection of $64 iso-profit line and *H* axis

5. Find the Optimum Point   It can be shown mathematically that the optimal combination of decision variables is always found at an extreme point (corner point) of the convex polygon. In Exhibit S7.1 there are four corner points (excluding the origin), and we can determine which one is the optimum by either of two approaches. The first approach is to find the values of the various corner solutions algebraically. This entails simultaneously solving the equations of various pairs of intersecting lines and substituting the quantities of the resultant variables in the objective function. For example, the calculations for the intersection of $2H + 6C = 72$ and $C = 10$ are as follows:

Substituting $C = 10$ in $2H + 6C = 72$ gives $2H + 6(10) = 72$, $2H = 12$, or $H = 6$. Substituting $H = 6$ and $C = 10$ in the objective function, we get

$$\text{Profit} = \$2H + \$4C = \$2(6) + \$4(10)$$
$$= \$12 + \$40 = \$52$$

A variation of this approach is to read the *H* and *C* quantities directly from the graph and substitute these quantities into the objective function, as shown in the previous calculation. The drawback in this approach is that in problems with a large number of constraint equations, there will be many possible points to evaluate, and the procedure of testing each one mathematically is inefficient.

The second and generally preferred approach entails using the objective function or iso-profit line directly to find the optimum point. The procedure involves simply drawing a straight line *parallel* to any arbitrarily selected initial iso-profit line so that the iso-profit line is farthest from the origin of the graph. (In cost-minimization problems, the objective would be to draw the line through the point closest to the origin.) In Exhibit S7.1, the dashed line labeled $2H + $4C = $64 intersects the most extreme point. Note that the initial arbitrarily selected iso-profit line is necessary to display the slope of the objective function for the particular problem.[1] This is important since a different objective function (try profit = $3H + 3C$) might indicate that some other point is farthest from the origin. Given that $2H + $4C = $64 is optimal, the amount of each variable to produce can be read from the graph: 24 hockey sticks and four chess sets. No other combination of the products yields a greater profit.

◼ THE SIMPLEX METHOD

The **simplex method** is an algebraic procedure that, through a series of repetitive operations, progressively approaches an optimal solution.[2] Theoretically, the simplex method can solve a problem consisting of any number of variables and constraints, although for problems containing more than, say, four variables or four constraint equations, the actual calculations are best left to the computer. Still, to know how to construct equations that would be put into a program, and to be able to use the output from the computer program, it is well worth the effort to go through the simplex method manually.

Simplex Method

The Six-Step Solution Procedure

There are a number of technical steps in the simplex method, and each one is described in detail and summarized at the end the of the section. We use the hockey stick and chess set problem to demonstrate the procedure involved.

Step 1: Formulate the Problem   Recall that to maximize profit we had

$$\text{Maximize } Z = \$2H + \$4C$$

subject to

(1) $4H + 6C \leq 120$ (machine center A constraint)
(2) $2H + 6C \leq 72$ (machine center B constraint)
(3) $1C \leq 10$ (machine center C constraint)
      $H, C \geq 0$ (nonnegativity requirement)

Step 2: Set Up Initial Tableau with Slack Variables in Solution   To use the simplex method requires two major adjustments to the problem as stated: (1) the introduction of slack variables and (2) the establishment of a solution table or tableau.

---

[1] The slope of the objective function is -2. If P = profit, $P = \$2H + \$4C; \$2H = P - \$4C; H = p/2 - 2C$. Thus the slope is -2.

[2] Simplex does not mean "simple"; it is a term used in n-space geometry.

Slack Variable

Introduce slack variables. Each constraint equation is expanded to include a slack variable. A **slack variable,** which may be thought of as an idle resource in a practical sense, computationally represents the amount required to make one side of a constraint equation equal to the other—in other words, to convert the inequalities to equalities. For our problem, we need three slack variables: S_1 for the first constraint equation, S_2 for the second, and S_3 for the third.

The constraint equations are

$$4H + 6C + 1S_1 = 120$$
$$2H + 6C + 1S_2 = 72$$
$$1C + 1S_3 = 10$$

So that all variables are represented in each equation, each slack variable not originally associated with a constraint equation is given a zero coefficient and added to that equation. Adjusting the system of equations in this way gives

$$4H + 6C + 1S_1 + 0S_2 + 0S_3 = 120$$
$$2H + 6C + 0S_1 + 1S_2 + 0S_3 = 72$$
$$0H + 1C + 0S_1 + 0S_2 + 1S_3 = 10$$

Note that the variable H, with a zero coefficient, is entered in the third equation to ensure that it also will be represented in all equations. Likewise, the objective function reflects the addition of slack variables, but since they yield no profit, their coefficient is $0:

$$Z = \$2H + \$4C + \$0S_1 + \$0S_2 + \$0S_3$$

Construct initial tableau. A tableau (see Exhibit S7.2) is a convenient way of setting up the problem for simplex computation. A tableau tells us

1. The variables in the solution at that point.
2. The profit associated with the solution.
3. The variable (if any) that adds most to profit if brought into the solution.
4. The amount of reduction in the variables in the solution that results from introducing one unit of each variable. This amount is termed the *substitution rate.*
5. The worth of an additional unit (e.g., hour) of resource capacity. This is called a *shadow price.*

The first four features are discussed in reference to the first tableau; the last one is considered later.

Exhibit S7.2

Initial Tableau of the Hockey Stick and Chess Set Problem

C_j	C_j Row	$2	$4	$0	$0	$0		Machine
Column	Solution Mix	H	C	S_1	S_2	S_3	Quantity	Center
$0	S_1	4	6	1	0	0	120	A
$0	S_2	2	6	0	1	0	72	B
$0	S_3	0	1	0	0	1	10←	C
	Z_j	$0	$0	$0	$0	$0	$0	
	$C_j - Z_j$	$2	$4	$0	$0	$0		
			↑					

The top row of Exhibit S7.2 contains the C_j values (the contribution to total profit associated with the production of one unit of each alternative product). This row is a direct restatement of the coefficients of the variables in the objective function, and therefore remains the same for all subsequent tableaus. The first column, headed by C_j, merely lists, for convenience, the profit per unit of the variables included in the solution at any stage of the problem.

The variables chosen for the first tableau are listed under Solution Mix. As you can see, only slack variables are considered in the initial solution, and their profit coefficients are zero, which is indicated by the C_j column.

The constraint variables are listed to the right of Solution Mix, and under each one is the particular variable's coefficient in each constraint equation. That is, 4, 6, 1, 0, and 0 are the coefficients of the machine center A constraint; 2, 6, 0, 1, and 0 for machine center B; and 0, 1, 0, 0, and 1 for machine center C.

Substitution rates can be ascertained from the numbers as well. For example, consider 4, 2, and 0, listed under H in the third column. For every unit of product H introduced into the solution, four units of S_1, two units of S_2, and zero units of S_3 must be withdrawn from the quantities available. The entries in the Quantity column refer to how many units of each resource are available in each machine center. In the initial tableau, this is a restatement of the right side of each constraint equation. With the exception of the value in the quantity column, the Z_j values in the second row from the bottom refer to the amount of *gross* profit that is given up by introducing one unit of that variable into the solution. The subscript j refers to the specific variable being considered. The Z_j value under the quantity column is the total profit for the solution. In the initial solution of a simplex problem, all values of Z_j are zero because no real product is being produced (all machines are idle), and hence there is no gross profit to be lost if they are replaced.

The bottom row of the tableau contains the *net* profit per unit, obtained by introducing one unit of a given variable into the solution. This row is designated the $C_j - Z_j$ row. The procedure for calculating Z_j and each $C_j - Z_j$ appears in Exhibit S7.3.

The initial solution to the problem is read directly from Exhibit S7.2: The company produces 120 units of S_1, 72 units of S_2, and 10 units of S_3. Total profit from this solution is $0. Thus, no capacity has yet been allocated and no real product produced.

Step 3: Determine Which Variable to Bring into Solution   An improved solution is possible if there is a positive value in $C_j - Z_j$ row. Recall that this row provides the net profit obtained by adding one unit of its associated column variable in the

C_j H		C_j C		C_j S_1		C_j S_2		C_j S_3		C_j Quantity	
$0 \times 4 =$	0	$0 \times 6 =$	0	$0 \times 1 =$	0	$0 \times 0 =$	0	$0 \times 0 =$	0	$0 \times 120 =$	0
	+		+		+		+		+		+
$0 \times 2 =$	0	$0 \times 6 =$	0	$0 \times 0 =$	0	$0 \times 1 =$	0	$0 \times 0 =$	0	$0 \times 72 =$	0
	+		+		+		+		+		+
$0 \times 0 =$	0	$0 \times 1 =$	0	$0 \times 0 =$	0	$0 \times 0 =$	0	$0 \times 1 =$	0	$0 \times 10 =$	0
$Z_H = \overline{\$0}$		$Z_C = \overline{\$0}$		$Z_{S_1} = \overline{\$0}$		$Z_{S_2} = \overline{\$0}$		$Z_{S_3} = \overline{\$0}$		$Z_Q = \overline{\$0}$	

Exhibit S7.3

Calculations of Z_j and $C_j - Z_j$

$C_j - Z_j$ calculations:

$C_H - Z_H = \$2 - 0 = \$2$

$C_C - Z_C = \$4 - 0 = \$4$

$C_{S_1} - Z_{S_1} = \$0 - 0 = \$0$

$C_{S_2} - Z_{S_2} = \$0 - 0 = \$0$

$C_{S_3} - Z_{S_3} = \$0 - 0 = \$0$

solution. In this example, there are two positive values to choose from: $2, associated with H, and $4, associated with C. Since our objective is to maximize profit, the logical choice is to pick the variable with the largest payoff to enter the solution, so variable C will be introduced. The column associated with this variable is designated by the small arrow beneath column C in Exhibit S7.2. (Only one variable at a time can be added in developing each improved solution.)

Step 4: Determine Which Variable to Replace   Given that it is desirable to introduce C into the solution, the next question is to determine which variable it will replace. To make this determination, we divide each amount in the Quantity column by the amount in the comparable row of the C column and choose the variable associated with the smallest positive quotient as the one to be replaced:

For the S_1 row: $120/6 = 20$
For the S_2 row: $72/6 = 12$
For the S_3 row: $10/1 = 10$

Since the smallest quotient is 10, S_3 will be replaced, and its row is identified by the small arrow to the right of the tableau in Exhibit S7.2. This is the maximum amount of C that can be brought into the solution. That is, production of more than 10 units of C would exceed the available capacity of machine C. This can be verified mathematically by considering the constraint $C \leq 10$ and visually by examining the graphical representation of the problem in Exhibit S7.1. The graph also shows that the 20 and 12 are the C intercepts of the other two constraints, and if $C \leq 10$ were removed, the amount of C introduced could be increased by two units.

Step 5: Calculate New Row Values for Entering Variable   The introduction of C into the solution requires that the entire S_3 row be replaced. The values for C, the replacing row, are obtained by dividing each value presently in the S_3 row by the value in column C in the same row. This value is termed the *intersectional element* because it occurs at the intersection of a row and column. This intersectional relationship is abstracted from the rest of the tableau and the necessary divisions are shown in Exhibit S7.4.

Step 6: Revise Remaining Rows   The new third-row values (now associated with C) are 0, 1, 0, 0, 1, and 10, which in this case are identical to those of the old third row.

Introducing a new variable into the problem affects the values of the remaining variables, and a second set of calculations must be performed to update the tableau. Specifically, we want to determine the effect of introducing C on the S_1 and S_2 rows. These calculations can be carried out by using what is termed the **pivot method** or by algebraic substitution. The pivot method is a more mechanical procedure and is generally used in practice, while algebraic substitution is more useful in explaining the

Pivot Method

Exhibit S7.4

Calculation of New Row Values for Entering Variable

$$
\begin{array}{l}
\quad\quad C \\
\quad\quad 6 \\
\quad\quad 6 \\
S_3 \quad 0 \ \textcircled{1} \ 0 \ 0 \ 1 \ 10 \quad\quad 0/1 = 0,\ 1/1 = 1,\ 0/1 = 0,\ 0/1 = 0,\ 1/1 = 1,\ 10/1 = 10 \\
\quad\quad \$4
\end{array}
$$

logic of the updating process. The procedure using the pivot method to arrive at new values for S_1 and S_2 is shown in Exhibit S7.5. (In essence, the method subtracts six times row 3 from both the S_1 and S_2 rows.)

Updating by algebraic substitution entails substituting the entire equation for the entering row into each of the remaining rows and solving for the revised values for each row's variable. The procedure, summarized in Exhibit S7.6, illustrates the fact that linear programming via the simplex method is essentially the solving of a number of simultaneous equations.

Isolating the variable coefficients yields the same values for the new S_1 row as did the pivot method: 4, 0, 1, 0, −6, 60.

Pivot Method

Old S_1 Row	−	Inter-sectional Element of Old S_1 Row	×	Corre-sponding Element of New C Row	=	Updated S_1 Row	Old S_2 Row	−	Inter-sectional Element of Old S_2 Row	×	Corre-sponding Element of New C Row	=	Updated S_2 Row
4	−	(6	×	0)	=	4	2	−	(6	×	0)	=	2
6	−	(6	×	1)	=	0	6	−	(6	×	1)	=	0
1	−	(6	×	0)	=	1	0	−	(6	×	0)	=	0
0	−	(6	×	0)	=	0	1	−	(6	×	0)	=	1
0	−	(6	×	1)	=	−6	0	−	(6	×	1)	=	−6
120	−	(6	×	10)	=	60	72	−	(6	×	10)	=	12

To find new values for S_1,

Algebraic Substitution

1. Reconstruct old S_1 row as a constraint with slack variables added (from first tableau).

$$4H + 6C + 1S_1 + 0S_2 + 0S_3 = 120$$

2. Write entering row as a constraint with slack variables added. (These are the values computed in Exhibit S7.4.)

$$0H + C + 0S_1 + 0S_2 + 1S_3 = 10$$

3. Rearrange entering row in terms of C, the entering variable.

$$10 - S_3$$

4. Substitute $10 - S_3$ for C in the first equation (the old S_1 row) and solve for each variable coefficient.

$$4H + 6(10 - S_3) + 1S_1 = 120$$
$$4H + 60 - 6S_3 + 1S_1 = 120$$
$$4H + 1S_1 - 6S_3 = 120 - 60$$
$$4H + 1S_1 - 6S_3 = 60$$

or

$$4H + 0C + 1S_1 + 0S_2 - 6S_3 = 60$$

The results of the computations carried out in Steps 3 through 6, along with the calculations of Z_j and $C_j - Z_j$ are shown in the revised tableau, Exhibit S7.7. In mathematical programming terminology, we have completed one *iteration* of the problem.

In evaluating this solution, we note two things: The profit is $40, but, more important, further improvement is possible because there is a positive value in the $C_j - Z_j$ row.

Second iteration.   The entering variable is H because it has the largest $C_j - Z_j$ amount (2). The replaced variable is S_2 because it has the smallest quotient when the Quantity column values are divided by their comparable amounts in the H column:

$$S_1 = 60/4 = 15, \ S_2 = 12/2 = 6, \ C_3 = 10/0 = \infty$$

Values of entering (H) row are

$$2/2 = 1, \ 0/2 = 0, \ 0/2 = 0, \ 1/2 = 1/2, \ -6/2 = -3, \ 12/2 = 6$$

Updated S_1 row from Exhibit S7.8: 0, 0, 1, −2, 6, 36.

Updated C row from Exhibit S7.8: 0, 1, 0, 0, 1, 10.

Using the result from Exhibit S7.8, we obtain the third tableau, Exhibit S7.9.

Exhibit S7.7

Second Tableau of the Hockey Stick and Chess Problem

C_j			$2	$4	$0	$0	$0	
		Solution Mix	H	C	S_1	S_2	S_3	Quantity
$0	S_1		4	0	1	0	−6	60
$0	S_2		2	0	0	1	−6	12 ←
$4	C		0	1	0	0	1	10
	Z_j		$0	$4	$0	$0	$ 4	$40
	$C_j - Z_j$		$2	$0	$0	$0	$−4	
			↑					

Exhibit S7.8   Updating S_1 and C Rows

Old S_1 Row	−	Inter-sectional Element of Old S_1 Row	×	Corre-sponding Element of New H Row	=	New S_1 Row	Old C Row	−	Inter-sectional Element of Old C Row	×	Corre-sponding Element of New H Row	=	New C Row
4	−	(4	×	1)	=	0	0	−	(0	×	1)	=	0
0	−	(4	×	0)	=	0	1	−	(0	×	0)	=	1
1	−	(4	×	0)	=	1	0	−	(0	×	0)	=	0
0	−	(4	×	$1/2$)	=	−2	0	−	(0	×	$1/2$)	=	0
−6	−	(4	×	−3)	=	6	1	−	(0	×	−3)	=	1
60	−	(4	×	6)	=	36	10	−	(0	×	6)	=	10

Examining the third tableau, we see that further improvement is possible by introducing the maximum amount of S_3 that is technically feasible. From the computation at the bottom of Exhibit S7.9, the maximum amount of S_3 that can be brought into the solution is six units because of the limited supply of S_1. Replacing S_1 by S_3 and performing the updating operations yields the tableau in Exhibit S7.10. Since the $C_j - Z_j$ row contains only negative numbers, no further improvement is possible, and an optimal solution ($H = 24$, $C = 4$) has been achieved in three iterations. See the boxed insert for a summary of steps.

Minimization Problems   The Puck and Pawn example dealt with **maximization**. An identical procedure is followed for solving **minimization** problems. Since the objective is to minimize rather than maximize, a negative $C_j - Z_j$ value indicates potential improvement; therefore the variable associated with the largest negative $C_j - Z_j$ value would be brought into solution first. Additional variables must be brought in to set up such problems, however, since minimization problems include greater-than-or-equal-to constraints, which must be treated differently from less-than-or-equal-to constraints, which typify maximization problems. (See section dealing with greater-than-or-equal-to and equal-to constraints in the simplex method.)

Maximization
Minimization

Search Path Followed by the Simplex Method

As mentioned earlier, the optimal solution to linear programming problems is obtained by finding the extreme corner point. The simplex procedure starts with an

C_j		$2	$4	$0	$0	$0	
	Solution Mix	H	C	S_1	S_2	S_3	Quantity
$0	S_1	0	0	1	−2	6	36←
$2	H	1	0	0	$1/2$	−3	6
$4	C	0	1	0	0	1	10
	Z_j	$2	$4	$0	$ 1	$−2	$52
	$C_j - Z_j$	$0	$0	$0	$−1	$ 2	
						↑	

$$36/6 = 6 \qquad 6/-3 = -2 \text{ (negative)}* \qquad 10/1 = 10$$

* Because there are three constraint equations, there must be three variables with non-negative values in the solution. Therefore a negative amount cannot be considered for introduction into the solution.

Exhibit S7.9

Third Tableau of the Hockey Stick and Chess Set Problem

C_j		$2	$4	$0	$0	$0	
	Solution Mix	H	C	S_1	S_2	S_3	Quantity
$0	S_3	0	0	$1/6$	$−1/3$	1	6
$2	H	1	0	$1/2$	$−1/2$	0	24
$4	C	0	1	$−1/6$	$1/3$	0	4
	Z_j	$2	$4	$ $1/3$	$ $1/3$	$0	$64
	$C_j - Z_j$	$0	$0	$−1/3$	$−1/3$	$0	

Exhibit S7.10

Fourth Tableau of the Hockey Stick and Chess Set Problem (Optimal Solution)

1. Formulate problem in terms of an objective function and a set of constraints.
2. Set up initial tableau with slack variables in the solution mix and calculate the Z_j and $C_j - Z_j$ rows.
3. Determine which variable to bring into solution (largest $C_j - Z_j$ value).
4. Determine which variable to replace (smallest positive ratio of quantity column to its comparable value in the column selected in Step 3).
5. Calculate new row values for entering variable and insert into new tableau (row to be replaced plus intersectional element).
6. Update remaining rows and enter into new tableau; compute new Z_j and $C_j - Z_j$ rows (old row minus intersectional element of old row times corresponding element in new row). If no positive $C_j - Z_j$ value is found, solution is optimal. If there is a positive value of $C_j - Z_j$, repeat Steps 3 to 6.

Summary of Steps in the Simplex Method: Maximization Problems

initial solution, searches for the most profitable direction to follow, and hops from point to point of intersecting lines (or planes in multidimensional space). The evaluation of a corner point takes one iteration, and when the furthermost point is reached (in the case of profit-maximization problems as shown by the next point's decreasing profit), the solution is complete.

Consider the graph of the example problem shown in Exhibit S7.11, where the simplex method began at point *a* (profit = $0). In the first iteration, 10 units of *C* were introduced at point *b* (profit = $40). In the second iteration, six units of *H* were introduced at point *c* (profit = $52). The third iteration left the problem at point *d* (profit = $64), which is optimal. Note that the solution procedure did not calculate profit for all corners of this problem. It did, however, *look ahead*—by virtue of the $C_j - Z_j$ calculations—to see if further improvement was possible by moving to another point (point *e*), but no improvement was indicated by such a change. These two characteristics—evaluating corner points and looking ahead for improvements—are the essential features of the simplex method.

Another feature that is also characteristic of the basic simplex method is that it does not necessarily converge on the optimum point by the shortest route around the feasible area. Reference to the graph shows that if the solution procedure had proceeded along the path $a \rightarrow e \rightarrow d$, an optimum would have been reached in two iterations rather than three.

The reason why this route was not followed was that the profit per chess set was higher than profit per hockey stick so the simplex method indicated that *C*, rather than *H*, be introduced in the first iteration. This, in turn, set the pattern for subsequent iterations to points *c* and *d*. Note that since the solution space forms a convex polygon (as previously defined), profit cannot increase, decrease, and then again increase.

Shadow Prices, Ranging, and Sensitivity

By examining the final (optimal) simplex tableau, we can learn a great deal. Besides showing the solution, the final tableau provides valuable information about the resources used, the range where the optimal decision remains unchanged, and the range where the coefficients in the objective function do not change the optimal solution. Specifically, it enables us to answer such questions as: Would you like to buy any more

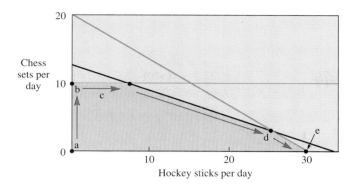

Exhibit S7.11

Graph of Hockey
Stick and Chess Set
Problem Showing
Successive Corner
Evaluations

of a resource? If so, what price should you pay? How many units should you buy at that price? Similar questions can be answered about selling resources; even though a resource may be currently used in making products, at some price it is worthwhile to forgo production and sell it. These considerations are of interest because they lead to decisions that can increase profit or reduce cost. These profit increases or cost decreases are *in addition* to the optimal solution calculated in the final tableau objective function.

Other questions are of the sort: If we change the profit per unit (by changing the coefficient in the objective function), will this change the optimal solution? This is **sensitivity analysis,** and refers to how much the solution changes for a small change in the objective function or, conversely, for a small change in the solution, the change that occurs in the objective function.   **Sensitivity Analysis**

Referring to Exhibit S7.10, the $C_j - Z_j$ values associated with the slack variables are termed **shadow prices,** *marginal values, incremental values,* or *break-even prices.* Note that the shadow prices for S_1 and S_2 were \$1/3 (or 33 cents) each, and the shadow price for S_3 was \$0. Above each price, management would be willing to sell resources, and below each price, it would be willing to buy. Let's take another look at this problem and all the information available in a computer printout.   **Shadow Prices**

Linear Programming Using Microsoft Excel

Spreadsheets can be used to solve linear programming problems. Most spreadsheets have built-in optimization routines that are very easy to use and understand. Microsoft Excel has an optimization tool called **Solver** that we will demonstrate by using it to solve the hockey stick and chess problem. We invoke the Solver from the Tools menu. A dialogue box requests information required by the program.   **Solver**

First, we define the problem by identifying a target cell (or objective function), the changing cells (or decision variables), and the constraints that we want in the analysis. Exhibit S7.12 shows a spreadsheet with the information required for the problem. Our "Target Cell" (cell D5) contains a formula that multiplies the quantities of hockey sticks and chess sets produced by their corresponding profit. The "Changing Cells" correspond to the decision variables for the problem. The "Subject to the Constraints" box contains cells that calculate the individual machine requirements for a solution. Note that we must indicate that our solution values must be greater than or equal to zero.

In Exhibit S7.12, we do not show the "Options" dialog box. If you click on this box, though, you will see a box that allows you to indicate this is a "linear problem." This

Exhibit S7.12   Microsoft Excel Solver Screen

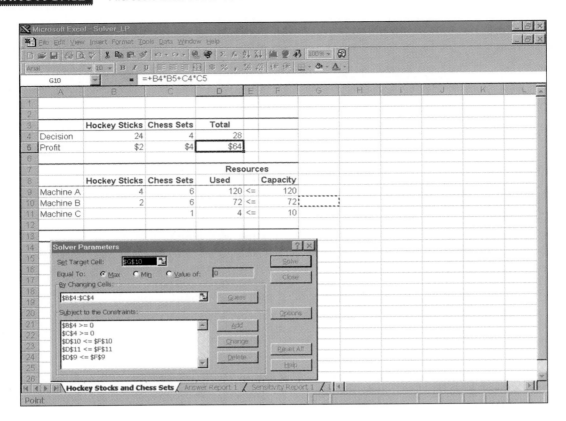

will speed the solution process for our problem. There are many other items that can be selected in the "Options" dialog box that control the solution search mechanism used by Solver. The program is capable of solving problems using search strategies different from the simplex approach.

After we input all of the information in the dialog boxes, we can press the solve button to resolve the problem. A number of different reports can be obtained. The most interesting reports for our problem are the "Answer Report" and the "Sensitivity Report," both of which are shown in Exhibit S7.13. The Answer Report shows the final answers for the total profit ($64) and the amounts produced (24 hockey sticks and 4 chess sets). In the constraints section of the answer report, the status of each resource is given. All of Machine A and Machine B are used, and there are six units of slack for Machine C.

The Sensitivity Report is divided into two parts. The first part titled "changing cells" corresponds to objective function coefficients. The profit per unit for the hockey sticks can be either up or down $.67 (between $2.67 and $1.33) without having an impact on the solution. Similarly, the profit of the chess sets could be between $6 and $3 without changing the solution. In the case of Machine A, the right-hand side could increase to 144 (120 + 24) or decrease to 84 with a resulting $.33 increase or decrease in the objective function. The right-hand side of Machine B can increase to 90 units or decrease to 60 units with the same $.33 change in the objective function.

Answer Report

Target Cell (Max)

Cell	Name	Original Value	Final Value
$D$5	Profit Total	$64	$64

Adjustable Cells

Cell	Name	Original Value	Final Value
$B$4	Decision Hockey Sticks	24	24
$C$4	Decision Chess Sets	4	4

Constraints

Cell	Name	Cell Value	Formula	Status	Slack
$D$9	Machine A Used	120	$D$9<=$F$9	Binding	0
$D$10	Machine B Used	72	$D$10<=$F$10	Binding	0
$D$11	Machine C Used	4	$D$11<=$F$11	Not Binding	6
$B$4	Decision Hockey Sticks	24	$B$4>=0	Not Binding	24
$C$4	Decision Chess Sets	4	$C$4>=0	Not Binding	4

Sensitivity Report

Changing Cells

Cell	Name	Final Value	Reduced Cost	Objective Coefficient	Allowable Increase	Allowable Decrease
$B$4	Decision Hockey Sticks	24	0	2	0.666666667	0.666666667
$C$4	Decision Chess Sets	4	0	4	2	1

Constraints

Cell	Name	Final Value	Shadow Price	Constraint R.H. Side	Allowable Increase	Allowable Decrease
$D$9	Machine A Used	120	0.333333333	120	24	36
$D$10	Machine B Used	72	0.333333333	72	18	12
$D$11	Machine C Used	4	0	10	1E+30	6

For Machine C, the right-hand side could increase to infinity (1E + 30 is scientific notation for a very large number) or decrease to 4 units, with no change in the objective function.

■ TRANSPORTATION METHOD

The **transportation method** is a simplified special case of the simplex method. It gets its name from its application to problems involving transporting products from several sources to several destinations. The two common objectives of such problems are

Transportation Method

Data for Chess Set
Transportation
Problem

				Shipping Costs per Case (in Dollars)				
Factory	**Supply**	**Warehouse**	**Demand**	**From**	**To E**	**To F**	**To G**	**To H**
A	15	E	10	A	$25	$35	$36	$60
B	6	F	12	B	55	30	45	38
C	14	G	15	C	40	50	26	65
D	11	H	9	D	60	40	66	27

Transportation Matrix
for Chess Set
Problem

From \ To	E	F	G	H	Factory supply
A	25	35	36	60	15
B	55	30	45	38	6
C	40	50	26	65	14
D	60	40	66	27	11
Destination requirements	10	12	15	9	46 / 46

either (1) minimize the cost of shipping *n* units to *m* destinations or (2) maximize the profit of shipping *n* units to *m* destinations. There are three general steps in solving transportation problems. We will now discuss each one in the context of a simple example.

Suppose the Puck and Pawn Company has four factories supplying four warehouses and its management wants to determine the minimum-cost shipping schedule for its monthly output of chess sets. Factory supply, warehouse demands, and shipping costs per case of chess sets are shown in Exhibit S7.14.

Step 1: Set Up Transportation Matrix

The transportation matrix for this example appears in Exhibit S7.15, where supply availability at each factory is shown in the far right column and the warehouse demands are shown in the bottom row. The unit shipping costs are shown in the small boxes within the cells. It is important at this step to make sure that the total supply availabilities and total demand requirements are equal. In this case they are both the same, 46 units, but often there is an excess supply or demand. In such situations, for the transportation method to work, a dummy warehouse or factory must be added. Procedurally, this involves inserting an extra row (for an additional factory) or an extra column (for an additional warehouse). The amount of supply or demand required by the dummy equals the difference between the row and column totals.

For example, the following problem might be restated to indicate a total demand of 36 cases, and therefore, a new column would be inserted with a demand of 10 cases to bring the total up to 46 cases. The cost figures in each cell of the dummy row would be set at zero so any units sent there would not incur a transportation cost. Theoretically, this adjustment is equivalent to the simplex procedure of inserting a slack

Solution of the Puck and Pawn Company Transportation Problem Using Microsoft Excel　

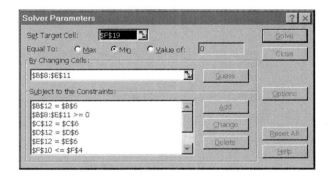

From/To	E	F	G	H	Factory Supply		
A	25	35	36	60	15		
B	55	30	45	38	6		
C	40	50	26	65	14		
D	60	40	66	27	11		
Destination Requirements	10	12	15	9	46		
A	10	4	1	0	15		
B	0	6	0	0	6		
C	0	0	14	0	14		
D	0	2	0	9	11		
	10	12	15	9	46	46	
Cost							
A	250	140	36	0			
B	0	180	0	0			
C	0	0	364	0			
D	0	80	0	243			
Total Cost					1293		

variable in a constraint inequality to convert it to an equation, and, as in the simplex, the cost of the dummy would be zero in the objective function.

This problem can be solved using Microsoft Excel. Exhibit S7.16 shows how the problem can be set up. Rows 1 through 6 are used to specify cost, factory supply, and destination requirements. The solution ("changing cells") are in the range B8 to E11. Costs are calculated in rows 15 through 19. Total cost is calculated in cell F19. In the following section, we continue with the explanation of the manual approach.

Step 2: Make Initial Allocations

Initial allocation entails assigning numbers to cells to satisfy supply and demand constraints. Next we will discuss several methods for doing this: the northwest-corner method, least-cost method, and Vogel's approximation method.

Exhibit S7.17

Northwest-Corner
Assignment

From \ To	E	F	G	H	Factory supply
A	25 10	35 5	36	60	15
B	55	30 6	45	38	6
C	40	50 1	26 13	65	14
D	60	40	66 2	27 9	11
Destination requirements	10	12	15	9	46 46

Total cost = 10($25) + 5($35) + 6($30) + 1($50) + 13($26) + 2($66) + 9($27) = $1,368

Northwest-Corner Method of Allocation   The northwest-corner method, as the name implies, begins allocation by starting at the northwest corner of the matrix and assigning as much as possible to each cell in the first row.[3] The procedure is then repeated for the second row, third row, and so on, until all row and column requirements are met. Exhibit S7.17 shows a northwest-corner assignment. (Cell *A-E* was assigned first, *A-F* second, *B-F* third, and so forth.)

Inspection of Exhibit S7.17 indicates some high-cost cells were assigned and some low-cost cells bypassed by using the northwest-corner method. Indeed, this is to be expected because this method ignores costs in favor of following an easily programmable allocation algorithm.

Least-Cost Method of Allocation   This method allocates as much as possible to the least-cost cell. Ties may be broken arbitrarily. Rows and columns that have been completely allocated are not considered, and the process of allocation is continued. The procedure is completed when all row and column requirements are addressed. Exhibit S7.18 shows a least-cost assignment. (Cell *A-E* was assigned first, *C-G* second, *D-H* third, *B-F* fourth, and so on.)

Vogel's Approximation Method of Allocation   This method also takes costs into account in allocation. Five steps are involved in applying this heuristic:

Step 1: Determine the difference between the lowest two cells in all rows and columns, including dummies.

Step 2: Identify the row or column with the largest difference. Ties may be broken arbitrarily.

Step 3: Allocate as much as possible to the lowest-cost cell in the row or column with the highest difference.

Step 4: Stop the process if all row and column requirements are met. If not, go to the next step.

Step 5: Recalculate the differences between the two lowest cells remaining in all rows and columns. Any row and column with zero supply or demand should not be used in calculating further differences. Then go to Step 2.

---

[3] Assign as many units as possible to each cell to meet the requirements of having no more than $m + n - 1$ filled cells, where m = number of rows and n = number of columns.

Least-Cost
Assignment

From \ To	E	F	G	H	Factory supply
A	25 \ 10	35 \ 5	36	60	15
B	55	30 \ 6	45	38	6
C	40	50	26 \ 14	65	14
D	60	40 \ 1	66 \ 1	27 \ 9	11
Destination requirements	10	12	15	9 / 46	46

Total cost = 10($25) + 14($26) + 9($27) + 6($30) + 5($35) + 1($40) + 1($66) = $1,318

Vogel's Approximation Method

From \ To	E	F	G	H	Factory supply
A	25 \ 10	35 \ 4	36 \ 1	60	15
B	55	30 \ 6	45	38	6
C	40	50	26 \ 14	65	14
D	60	40 \ 2	66	27 \ 9	11
Destination requirements	10	12	15	9 / 46	46

Difference Iterations

	1	2	3	4	5	6	7
A	10	1	1	1	1	(25)	–
B	8	8	8	8	8	8	8
C	14	(14)	–	–	–	–	–
D	13	13	(13)	(20)	–	–	–

Difference Iterations

	E	F	G	H
1	(15)	5	10	11
2		5	10	11
3		5	9	11
4		5	9	–
5		5	(9)	–
6		5	–	–
7		20	–	–

Total cost = 10($25) + 14($26) + 9($27) + 2($40) + 1($36) + 4($35) + 6($30) = $1,293

The Vogel's approximation method (VAM) usually produces an optimal or near-optimal starting solution. One study found that VAM yields an optimum solution in 80 percent of the sample problems tested. (Our students have observed that the remaining 20 percent of sample problems are found on examinations.) Exhibit S7.19 shows the VAM assignments for the chess set problem. (Cell *A-E* was assigned first, *C-G* second, *D-H* third, *D-F* fourth, and so on.) Note that this starting solution is the same as the optimal solution obtained after making all possible improvements to the starting solution obtained using the northwest-corner method. (See Exhibit S7.22.)

Step 3: Develop Optimal Solution

Developing an optimal solution in a transportation problem involves evaluating each unused cell to determine whether a shift into it is advantageous from a total-cost standpoint. If it is, the shift is made, and the process is repeated. When all cells have been evaluated and appropriate shifts made, the problem is solved.

Stepping Stone Method of Evaluation   One approach to making this evaluation is the stepping stone method. The term *stepping stone* appeared in early descriptions of the method, in which unused cells were referred to as "water" and used cells as "stones"—from the analogy of walking on a path of stones half-submerged in water. We now apply the method to the northwest-corner solution to the sample problem, as shown in Exhibit S7.18.

Step 1: Pick any empty cell identify the closed path leading to that cell. A closed path consists of horizontal and vertical lines leading from an empty cell back to itself.[4] In the closed path there can only be one empty cell that we are examining. The 90-degree turns must therefore occur at those places that meet this requirement. Two closed paths are identified in Exhibit S7.20. Closed path *a* is required to evaluate empty cell *B-E*; closed path *b* is required to evaluate empty cell *A-H*.

Step 2: Move one unit into the empty cell from a filled cell at a corner of the closed path and modifying the remaining filled cells at the other corners of the closed path to reflect this move.[5] Modifying entails adding to and subtracting from filled cells in such a way that supply and demand constraints are not violated. This requires that one unit always be subtracted in a given row or column for each unit added to that row or column. Thus, the following additions and subtractions would be required path *a*:

Add one unit to *B-E* (the empty cell).

Subtract one unit from *B-F*.

Add one unit to *A-F*.

Subtract one unit from *A-E*.

For the longer path *b*,

Add one unit to *A-H* (the empty cell).

Subtract one unit from *D-H*.

Add one unit to *D-G*.

Subtract one unit from *C-G*.

Add one unit to *C-F*.

Subtract one unit from *A-F*.

Step 3: Determine desirability of the move. This is easily done by (1) summing the cost values for the cell to which a unit has been added, (2) summing the cost values of the cells from which a unit has been subtracted, and (3) taking the difference between the two sums to determine if there is a cost reduction. If the cost is reduced by making the move, as many units as possible should be shifted out of the evaluated

---

[4] If assignments have been made correctly, the matrix has only one closed path for each empty cell.

[5] More than one unit could be used to test the desirability of a shift. However, since the problem is linear, if it is desirable to shift one unit, it is desirable to shift more than one, and vice versa.

From \ To	E	F	G	H	Factory supply
A	25	35	36	60	15
	10 *a* 5		*b*		
B	55	30	45	38	6
	6				
C	40	50	26	65	14
	1	13			
D	60	40	66	27	11
		2	9		
Destination requirements	10	12	15	9 / 46	46

filled cells into the empty cell. If the cost is increased, no move should be made and the empty cell should be crossed out or otherwise marked to show that it has been evaluated. (A large plus sign is typically used to denote a cell that has been evaluated and found undesirable in cost-minimizing problems. A large minus sign is used for this purpose in profit-maximizing problems.) For cell *B-E*, the pluses and minuses are

+	−
$55 (*B-E*)	$30 (*B-F*)
35 (*A-F*)	25 (*A-E*)
$90	$55

For cell *A-H* they are

+	−
$60 (*A-H*)	$27 (*D-H*)
66 (*D-G*)	26 (*C-G*)
50 (*C-F*)	35 (*A-F*)
$176	$88

Thus in both cases it is apparent that no move into either empty cell should be made.

Step 4: Repeat Steps 1 through 3 until all empty cells have been evaluated. To illustrate the mechanics of carrying out a move, consider cell *D-F* and the closed path leading to it, which is a short one: *C-F*, *C-G*, and *D-G*. The pluses and minuses are

+	−
$40 (*D-F*)	$50 (*C-F*)
26 (*C-G*)	66 (*D-G*)
$66	$116

Because there is a savings of $50 per unit from shipping via *D-F*, as many units as possible should be moved into this cell. In this case, however, the maximum amount that can be shifted is one unit—because the maximum amount added to any cell may not exceed the quantity found in the lowest-amount cell from which a subtraction is

From \ To	E	F	G	H	Factory supply
A	25 / 10	35 / 5	36	60 / +	15
B	55 / +	30 / 6	45	38	6
C	40	50 / +	26 / 14	65	14
D	60	40 / 1	66 / 1	27 / 9	11
Destination requirements	10	12	15	9 / 46	46

Total cost = 10($25) + 5($35) + 6($30) + 14($26) + 1($40) + 1($66) + 9($27) = $1,318

From \ To	E	F	G	H	Factory supply
A	25 / 10	35 / 5 − 1 = 4	36 / 0 + 1 = 1	60	15
B	55	30 / 6	45	38	6
C	40	50	26 / 14	65	14
D	60	40 / 1 + 1 = 2	66 / 1 − 1 = 0	27 / 9	11
Destination requirements	10	12	15	9 / 46	46

Total cost = 10($25) + 4($35) + 1($36) + 6($30) + 14($26) + 2($40) + 9($27) = $1,293

to be made. To do otherwise would violate the supply and demand constraints of the problem. Here we see that the limiting cell is *C-F* because it contains only one unit.

The revised matrix, showing the effects of this move and the previous evaluations, is presented in Exhibit S7.21. Applying the stepping stone method to the remaining unfilled cells and making shifts were indicated yields an optimal solution.

In particular, the empty cell *A-G* in Exhibit S7.21 has closed path *D-G*, *D-F*, and *A-F*. The pluses and minuses are

+		−	
36	(*A-G*)	35	(*A-F*)
40	(*D-F*)	66	(*D-G*)
76		101	

Because savings = 101 − 76 = $25, we shift one unit to *A-G*. Exhibit S7.22 shows the optimal matrix, with minimum transportation cost of $1,293.

To verify that we have the optimum, we should evaluate each empty cell to see if it is desirable to bring in that cell. If we did this, we would have a plus sign in each of these cells.

From \ To	W		X		Y		Factory supply	
T		8		6		4	11	
	3		8		θ			
U		9		8		0	9	
					9			
V		5		3		10	3	
	3							
Destination requirements	6		8		9		23	23

$m + n - 1 = 5$ filled cells

Actual allocation = 4 filled cells

Degeneracy   **Degeneracy** exists in a transportation problem when the number of filled cells is less than the number of rows plus the number of columns minus one (i.e., $m + n - 1$). Degeneracy may be observed during the initial allocation when the first entry in a row or column satisfies *both* the row and column requirements. Degeneracy requires some adjustment in the matrix to evaluate the solution achieved. The form of this adjustment involves inserting some value in an empty cell so a closed path can be developed to evaluate other empty cells. This value may be thought of as an infinitely small amount, having no direct bearing on the cost of the solution.

Procedurally, the value (often denoted by the Greek letter theta, θ) is used exactly the same manner as a real number except that it may initially be placed in any empty cell, even though row and column requirements have been met by real numbers. A degenerate transportation problem showing an optimal minimum cost allocation is presented in Exhibit S7.23, where we can see that if θ were not assigned to the matrix, it would be impossible to evaluate several cells (including the one where it is added). Once a θ has been inserted into the solution, it remains there until it is removed by subtraction or until a final solution is reached.

While the choice of where to put a θ is arbitrary, it saves time if it is placed where it may be used to evaluate as many cells as possible without being shifted. In this regard, verify for yourself that θ is optimally located in Exhibit S7.23.

Alternate Optimal Solutions   When the evaluation of an empty cell yields the same cost as the existing allocation, an alternate optimal solution exists.[6] In such cases, management has additional flexibility and can invoke nontransportation cost factors in deciding on a final shipping schedule. (A large zero is commonly placed in an empty cell that has been identified as an alternate optimal route.)

■ CONCLUSION

This supplement has dealt mainly with the mechanics of solution procedures for linear programming problems. It would be a rare instance when a linear programming problem would actually be solved by hand. There are too many computers around and

Degeneracy

---

[6] Assuming that all other cells are optimally assigned.

too many LP software programs to justify spending time for manual solution.[7] We firmly believe, though, that to truly understand the computer output, it is useful to take the time to solve some simple problems, as we have done here.

SOLVED PROBLEMS

SOLVED PROBLEM 1

Two products, X and Y, both require processing time on machines I and II. Machine I has 200 hours available, and machine II has 400 hours available. Product X requires one hour on machine I and four hours on machine II. Product Y requires one hour on machine I and one hour on machine II. Each unit of product X yields $10 profit and each unit of Y yields $5 profit. These statements reduce to the following set of equations:

$$X + Y \leq 200 \text{ (Machine I)}$$
$$4X + Y \leq 400 \text{ (Machine II)}$$

Maximize $10X + $5Y$

Solve the problem graphically showing the optimal utilization of machine time.

Solution
The optimal point, as shown on the graph, is $X = 67$ and $Y = 133$. Profit at this point would be $10(67) + $5(133) = $1,335$.

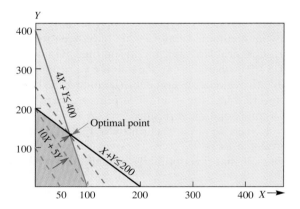

To plot the first isoprofit line, assume:

$$10X + 5Y = 500$$
$$@X = 0, Y = 100$$
$$@Y = 0, X = 50$$

Continue to move this isoprofit line outward until it reaches the furthest point in the feasible region (at approximately $X = 67$, $Y = 133$).

SOLVED PROBLEM 2

Solve Problem 1 using the simplex method.

Solution

The simplex solution to Problem 1 is

		$10	$5	0	0	
		X	Y	S_1	S_2	
	S_1	1	1	1	0	200
	S_2	4	1	0	1	400
		$10	$5	0	0	
First iteration	S_1	0	3/4	1	−1/4	100
	X	1	1/4	0	1/4	100
		0	2.50	0	−2.50	
Second iteration	Y	0	1	4/3	−1/3	133
	X	1	0	−1/3	1/3	67
				$−3.33	$−1.66	

With $X = 67$ and $Y = 133$, the value of the objective function would be $Z = \$10(67) + \$5(133) = \$1,335$.

REVIEW AND DISCUSSION QUESTIONS

1. What structural requirements of a problem are needed to solve it by linear programming?
2. What type of information is provided in a solved simplex tableau?
3. What type of information is provided by shadow prices?
4. What are slack variables? Why are they necessary in the simplex method? When are they used in the transportation method?
5. It has been stated in this supplement that an optional solution for a simplex problem always lies at a corner point. Under what conditions might an equally desirable solution be found anywhere along a constraint line?
6. What is a convex polygon? How is it identified?
7. How do you know if a transportation problem is degenerate? What must be done if a degenarate problem is to be tested for optimality?

PROBLEMS

1. Solve the following problem graphically.

$$12X + 14Y \le 84$$
$$3X + 2Y \le 18$$
$$Y \le 4$$

Maximize $3X + Y$

1. X = 6
Y = 0
Z = 18

✓ 2. Solve the following problem using the graphical method of linear programming.

$$4A + 6B \ge 120$$
$$2A + 6B \ge 72$$
$$B \ge 10$$

Minimize $2A + 4B$

2. See SM for graph.
Optimum combination is
$B = 10$ and $A = 15$.

3. Bindley Corporation has a one-year contract to supply motors for all washing machines produced by Rinso Ltd. Rinso manufactures the washers at four locations around the country: New York, Fort Worth, San Diego, and Minneapolis. Plans call for the following numbers of washing machines to be produced at each location:

New York	50,000
Fort Worth	70,000
San Diego	60,000
Minneapolis	80,000

Bindley has three plants that can produce the motors. The plants and production capacities are

Boulder	100,000
Macon	100,000
Gary	150,000

Due to varying production and transportation costs, the profit Bindley earns on each 1,000 units depends on where they were produced and where they were shipped. The following table gives the accounting department estimates of the dollar profit per unit. (Shipment will be made in lots of 1,000.)

	Shipped to			
Produced at	New York	Fort Worth	San Diego	Minneapolis
Boulder	7	11	8	13
Macon	20	17	12	10
Gary	8	18	13	16

Given profit *maximization* as a criterion, Bindley would like to determine how many motors should be produced at each plant and how many motors should be shipped from each plant to each destination.
a. Develop a transportation tableau for this problem
b. Find the optimal solution.

4. Solve the problem using the graphical method of linear programming.

$$16X + 10Y \leq 160$$
$$12X + 14Y \leq 168$$
$$Y \geq 2$$

Maximize $2X + 10Y$

5. A manufacturing firm has discontinued production of a certain unprofitable product line. Considerable excess production capacity was created as a result. Management is considering devoting this excess capacity to one or more of three products: X_1, X_2, and X_3.
Machine hours required per unit are

	Product		
Machine Type	X_1	X_2	X_3
Milling machine	8	2	3
Lathe	4	3	0
Grinder	2	0	1

The available time in machine hours per week is

	Machine Hours per Week
Milling machines	800
Lathes	480
Grinders	320

The salespeople estimate that they can sell all the units of X_1 and X_2 that can be made. But the sales potential of X_3 is 80 units per week maximum.

Unit profits for the three products are

	Unit Profits
X_1	$20
X_2	6
X_3	8

a. Set up the equations that can be solved to maximize the profit per week.

b. Solve these equations using the simplex method.

c. What is the optimal solution? How many of each product should be made and what should the resultant profit be?

d. What is this situation with respect to the machine groups? Would they work at capacity, or would there be unused available time? Will X_3 be at maximum sales capacity?

e. Suppose that an additional 200 hours per week can be obtained from the milling machines by working overtime. The incremental cost would be $1.50 per hour. Would you recommend doing this? Explain how you arrived at your answer.

✓ **6.** Rent'R Cars is a multi-site car rental company in the city. It is trying out a new "return the car to the location most convenient for you" policy to improve customer service. But this means that the company has to constantly move cars around the city to maintain required levels of vehicle availability. The supply and demand for economy cars, and the total cost of moving these vehicles between sites, are shown below.

From \ To	D	E	F	G	Supply
A	$9	$8	$6	$5	50
B	9	8	8	0	40
C	5	3	3	10	75
Demand	50	60	25	30	165 / 165

a. Find the solution that minimizes moving costs.

b. What would you have to do to the costs to assure that A always sends a car to D as part of the optimal solution?

7. A diet is being prepared for the University of Arizona dorms. The objective is to feed the students at the least cost, but the diet must have between 1,800 and 3,600 calories. No more than 1,400 calories can be starch, and no fewer than 400 can be protein. The varied diet is to be made of two foods: A and B. Food A costs $0.75 per pound and contains 600 calories, 400 of which are protein and 200 starch. No more than two pounds of food A can be used per resident. Food B costs $0.15 per pound and contains 900 calories, of which 700 are starch, 100 are protein, and 100 are fat.

a. Write out the equations representing this information.

b. Solve the problem graphically for the amounts of each food that should be used.

8. Cost per student:
$1.75A + 2.50 B =$
$1.75(.75) + 2.50(1.5) =$
$\$5.0625$

8. Do Problem 7 with the added constraint that not more than 150 calories shall be fat, and that the price of food has escalated to $1.75 per pound for food A and $2.50 per pound for food B.

9. Logan Manufacturing wants to mix two fuels (A and B) for its trucks to minimize cost. It needs no fewer than 3,000 gallons to run its trucks during the next month. It has a maximum fuel storage capacity of 4,000 gallons. There are 2,000 gallons of fuel A and 4,000 gallons of fuel B available. The mixed fuel must have an octane rating of no less than 80.

9. *a.* $A + B \geq 3,000$
$A + B \leq 4,000$
$A \leq 2,000$
$B \leq 4,000$
$90A + 75B \geq 80$
$(A + B)$, or
$2A \geq B$ Minimize
$1.20A + .90B$

b. Optimum:
$A = 1,000$:
$B = 2,000$.

When mixing fuels, the amount of fuel obtained is just equal to the sum of the amounts put in. The octane rating is the weighted average of the individual octanes, weighted in proportion to the respective volumes.

The following is known: Fuel A has an octane of 90 and costs $1.20 per gallon. Fuel B has an octane of 75 and costs $0.90 per gallon.

a. Write out the equations expressing this information.

b. Solve the problem graphically, giving the amount of each fuel to be used. State any assumptions necessary to solve the problem.

✓   **10.** Given the following solved simplex tableau,

10. *a.* $X = 60$, $Y = 0$,
$Z = 90$; $S_1 = 0$
$S_2 = 0$, $S_3 = 40$.

X	Y	Z	S_1	S_2	S_3	
0	5	0	−2	1	1	40
0	−3	1	3	−2	0	90
1	4	0	−4	3	0	60
0	−7	0	−2	−3	0	

a. What are the values of X, Y, Z, S_1, S_2, and S_3?

b.

	Would you buy?	At what price?	How many?
S_1	Yes	< 2	15
S_2	Yes	< 3	45
S_3	Yes	< 0	∞

	Would you sell?	At what price?	How many?
S_1	Yes	> 2	30
S_2	Yes	> 3	20
S_3	Yes	> 0	40

11. Food = $300
Shelter = $700
Entertainment = $300
Satisfaction value = $4,200

11. You are trying to create a budget to optimize the use of a portion of your disposable income. You have a maximum of $1,500 per month to be allocated to food, shelter, and entertainment. The amount spent on food and shelter combined must not exceed $1,000. The amount spent on shelter alone must not exceed $700. Entertainment cannot exceed $300 per month. Each dollar spent on food has a satisfaction value of 2, each dollar spent on shelter has a satisfaction value of 3, and each dollar spent on entertainment has a satisfaction value of 5.

Assuming a linear relationship, use the simplex method of linear programming to determine the optimal allocation of your funds.

12. Solve the following using the simplex method:

$$3X_1 + 2X_2 + 4X_3 \leq 32$$

$$X_1 + 3X_2 + 4X_3 \leq 36$$

$$X_1 + X_2 + \leq 13$$

Maximize $10X_1 + 12X_2 + 16X_3$.

12. $X_1 = 3$
    $X_2 = 10$
    $X_3 = .75$
    $Z = 162$

SELECTED BIBLIOGRAPHY

Eppen, G. D., and F. J. Gould. *Introductory Management Science.* 4th ed. Englewood Cliffs, NJ: Prentice Hall, 1993.

Greeberg, H. J. "How to Analyze the Results of Linear Programs—Part 2: Price Interpretation." *Interfaces* 23, no. 5, September—October 1993, pp. 97–114.

Llewellyn, John, and Ramesh Sharda. "Linear Programming Software for Personal Computers: 1990 Survey." *OR/MS Today,* October 1990, pp. 35–47.

Sharda, R. "Mathematical Programming on Microcomputers: Directions in Performance and User Interfaces." In *Mathematical Models for Decision Support,* ed. G.

Mitra. New York: Springer-Verlag, 1988, pp. 279–93.

————."Linear Programming Software for the Microcomputer: Recent Advance." In *Decision-Aiding Software and Decision Analysis,* ed. S. Nagel. Cambridge, England: Cambridge University Press, 1990.

Taha, Hamdy A. *Operations Research.* New York: Macmillan, 1992.

Winston, Wayne L., and S. Christian Albright. *Practical Management Science: Spreadsheet Modeling and Applications.* Belmont, CA: Duxbury Press, 1997.

Chapter 8

Just-in-Time Production Systems

Chapter Outline

JIT Logic, 324

The Japanese Approach to Productivity, 325

    Elimination of Waste

    Respect for People

North American Modifications of JIT, 333

JIT Implementation Requirements, 334

    JIT Layouts and Design Flows

    JIT Applications for Line Flows

    JIT Applications for Job Shops

    TQC (Total Quality Control)

    A Stable Schedule

    Work with Suppliers

JIT in Services, 340

Case: Quick Response Apparel, 345

Case: Toyota Work Contracts, 346

Case: Quality Parts Company, 347

Key Terms

JIT

Focused Factory Network

Group Technology

Quality at the Source

Autonomation

Automated Inspection

Uniform Plant Loading

Cycle Times

Kanban Pull System

Bottom-Round Management

Quality Circles

Preventive Maintenance

Total Quality Control (TQC)

Level Schedule

Freeze Window

Backflush

www Links

Arvin Automotive (http://www.arvin.com)

Saturn Corporation (http://www.saturncars.com)

LIKE CLOCKWORK. ACCORDING TO SATURN'S VP OF purchasing Alec Bedricky, Saturn "runs the tightest JIT system in the auto business." Certainly, no one at GM will argue the point. Indeed, one will find little buffer anywhere in the Saturn plant. For instance, the number of powertrains on the floor between the engine plant and vehicle assembly at any time will be less than 140, or barely enough to cover two hours of production, which is in sharp contrast to the two-week float that one likely will find at other GM plants. Elsewhere, it's the same story. Less than 95 body frames will be found in transit at any time between body fabrication and the start of trim operations.

"You can't build out-of-sequence here." says Bedricky. "If there is a hiccup in the powertrain plant, it will be felt immediately on the assembly line."

All material arrives at the Saturn plant directly from the supplier's dock without passing through a consolidation point, which is a typical practice at the Japanese transplants. Production parts are delivered daily, some more frequently (e.g., large items like radiators and front-end modules). Seats arrive in sequence from the seating supplier every 30 minutes. The scheduling of dock times and truck routes is all plotted by Saturn's logistics partner, namely Ryder, from its office inside the assembly plant. Ryder Systems worked with Saturn to design a state of the art JIT delivery system. Ryder picks up components for Saturn from over 200 suppliers and delivers directly to the assembly line as needed. Then Ryder transports finished cars to dealers across the country.

Suppliers are paid as the parts are consumed in production ("pay on production" or "POP"). While the supplier community at large generally has resisted such an idea, Saturn's suppliers have bought into the concept, says Curt Gibbs, director of material flow and logistics, because "the pipeline at Saturn is so short." ●

(*http://www. saturncars.com*)

Source: Ernest Raia, "Saturn: Rising Star," *Purchasing,* September 9, 1993, pp. 44–47. Copyright by Cahners Publishing Company.

The most significant production management approach of the post–World War II era is just-in-time (JIT) production. Developed by the Japanese, this approach integrates the five Ps of OM to streamline production of high-quality goods and services. Like TQM, virtually every modern manufacturing organization has used at least some JIT elements in its design. This chapter relates the logic of JIT. It also details approaches to JIT implementation and JIT's application in service organizations.

■ JIT LOGIC

JIT

JIT (just-in-time) is an integrated set of activities designed to achieve high-volume production using minimal inventories of raw materials, work in process, and finished goods. Parts arrive at the next workstation "just in time" and are completed and move through the operation quickly. Just-in-time is also based on the logic that nothing will be produced until it is needed. Exhibit 8.1 illustrates the process. Need is created by actual demand of the product. When an item is sold, in theory, the market pulls a replacement from the last position in the system—final assembly in this case. This triggers an order to the factory production line, where a worker then pulls another unit from an upstream station in the flow to replace the unit taken. This upstream station then pulls from the next station further upstream and so on back to the release of raw materials. To enable this pull process to work smoothly, JIT demands high levels of quality at each stage of the process, strong vendor relations, and a fairly predictable demand for the end product.

JIT can be viewed colloquially as "big JIT" and "little JIT." Big JIT (often termed lean production[1]) is the philosophy of operations management that seeks to eliminate waste in all aspects of a firm's production activities: human relations, vendor relations, technology, and the management of materials and inventories. Little JIT focuses more narrowly on scheduling goods inventories and providing service resources where and when needed. For example, companies such as Manpower Temporary Services

JIT gained worldwide prominence in the 1970s, but some of its philosophy can be traced to the early 1900s in the United States. Henry Ford used JIT concepts as he streamlined his moving assembly lines to make automobiles. For example, to eliminate waste, he used the bottom of the packing crates for car seats as the floor board of the car. Although elements of JIT were being used by Japanese industry as early as the 1930s, it was not fully refined until the 1970s, when Tai-ichi Ohno of Toyota Motors used JIT to take Toyota's cars to the forefront of delivery time and quality. Around the same time, quality experts Deming and Juran lectured on the need for American producers to adopt many JIT principles.

Historical Note

---

[1] James P. Womack, D. T. Jones, and D. Roos, *The Machine That Changed the World* (New York: R. A. Rawston Associates, 1990).

Pull System

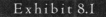

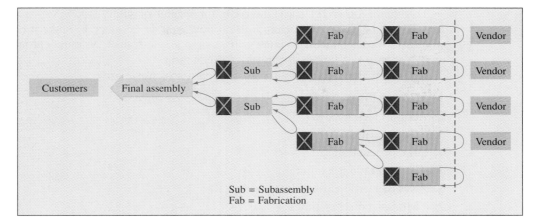

Sub = Subassembly
Fab = Fabrication

and Pizza Hut essentially use pull signals to fill openings for replacement workers or Big Foot pizzas, respectively. However, they do not necessarily integrate operations around other aspects of the JIT philosophy.

◼ THE JAPANESE APPROACH TO PRODUCTIVITY[2]

The Japanese have had a national goal of full employment through industrialization since World War II. The strategy for obtaining market dominance has been targeted to specific product areas. When choosing industries to target for improvement, the Japanese Ministry of International Trade and Industry (MITI) selected only industries with a competitive advantage.

To improve their country's competitive posture, they imported technology. Instead of inventing new technology, they avoided major R&D expenditures and corresponding risks by buying licensing agreements frequently from U.S. companies. To make these new products, they concentrated their efforts on the factory floor to achieve high productivity and lower unit costs. They directed their best engineering talent to the shop floor, not to product design activities. They also worked to improve product quality and reliability above what competitors could supply. Central to this effort were two philosophies: elimination of waste and respect for people.

Elimination of Waste

The Japanese are true believers in eliminating waste. Waste in Japan, as defined by Toyota's Fujio Cho, is "anything other than the minimum amount of equipment, materials, parts, and workers (working time) which are absolutely essential to production." [An expanded JIT definition advanced by Fujio Cho identifies seven prominent types of waste to be eliminated: (1) waste from overproduction, (2) waste of waiting

[2] Kenneth A. Wantuck, "The Japanese Approach to Productivity" (Southfield, MI: Bendix Corporation, 1983).

time, (3) transportation waste, (4) inventory waste, (5) processing waste, (6) waste of motion, and (7) waste from product defects.[3]]

This definition of JIT leaves no room for surplus or safety stock. No safety stocks are allowed because if you cannot use it now, you do not need to make it now. That would be waste. Hidden inventory in storage areas, transit systems, carousels, and conveyors are key targets for inventory reduction.

The seven elements that address elimination of waste are

1.   Focused factory networks.
2.   Group technology.
3.   Quality at the source.
4.   JIT production.
5.   Uniform plant loading.
6.   Kanban production control system.
7.   Minimized setup times.

Focused Factory Networks   The Japanese build small specialized plants rather than large vertically integrated manufacturing facilities. They find large operations and their bureaucracies difficult to manage and not in line with their management styles. Plants designed for one purpose can be constructed and operated more economically. The bulk of Japanese plants, some 60,000, have between 30 and 1,000 workers.

Group Technology

Group Technology   **Group technology,** while invented in the United States, was most successfully employed in Japan. Instead of transferring jobs from one department to another to specialized workers, the Japanese consider all operations required to make a part and group those machines together. Exhibit 8.2 illustrates the difference between the clusters of various machines grouped into work centers for parts versus departmental layouts. The group technology cells eliminate movement and queue (waiting) time between operations, reduce inventory, and reduce the number of employees required. Workers, however, must be flexible to run several machines and processes. Due to their advanced skill level, these workers have increased job security.

Quality at the Source

Quality at the Source   **Quality at the source** means do it right the first time and, when something goes wrong, stop the process or assembly line immediately. Factory workers become their own inspectors, personally responsible for the quality of their outputs. Workers concentrate on one part of the job at a time so quality problems are uncovered, such as these air bag crash sensors inspected at the TRW plant in Marshall, Illinois. If the pace is too fast, if the worker finds a quality problem, or if a safety issue is discovered, the worker is obligated to push a button to stop the

---

[3] Kiyoshi Suzaki, *The New Manufacturing Challenge: Techniques for Continuous Improvement* (New York: Free Press, 1987), pp. 7–25.

Group Technology versus Departmental Specialty

Exhibit 8.2

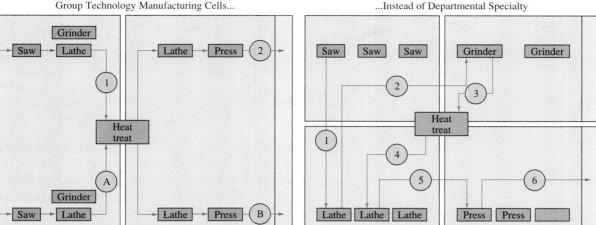

Exhibit 8.2 — Group Technology Manufacturing Cells... ...Instead of Departmental Specialty

WHAT IT IS	WHAT IT DOES
■ Management philosophy ■ "Pull" system through the plant	■ Attacks waste (time, inventory, scrap) ■ Exposes problems and bottlenecks ■ Achieves streamlined production

WHAT IT REQUIRES	WHAT IT ASSUMES
■ Employee participation ■ Industrial engineering/basics ■ Continuing improvement ■ Total quality control ■ Small lot sizes	■ Stable environment

Exhibit 8.3

"The What's of Just-in-Time"

line and turn on a visual signal. People from other areas respond to the alarm and the problem. Workers are empowered to do their own maintenance and housekeeping until the problem is fixed.

This quality at the source includes **autonomation** or **automated inspection.** Japanese prefer to have quality inspections performed by automation or robotics because it is faster, easier, repeatable, and suitable for jobs too redundant for a worker to perform.

Autonomation

Automated Inspection

JIT Production   JIT means producing what is needed when needed and no more. Anything over the minimum amount necessary is viewed as waste, because effort and material expended for something not needed now cannot be utilized now. This is in contrast to relying on extra material just in case something goes wrong. Exhibit 8.3 shows JIT requirements and assumptions.

JIT has been applied to repetitive manufacturing. Such applications do not require large volumes and are not limited to processes that produce the same parts over and over. JIT can be applied to any repetitive segments of a business regardless of where they appear. Under JIT the ideal lot size is one. A worker completes the task and passes it on to the next worker for processing. While workstations may be geographically dispersed, the Japanese minimize transit time and keep transfer quantities small—typically, one-tenth of a day's production is a lot size. Vendors even ship several times a day to their customers to keep lot sizes small and inventory low. When all queues are driven to zero, inventory investment is minimized, lead times are shortened, firms can react faster to demand changes, and quality problems are uncovered.

Exhibit 8.4 illustrates this idea. If the water in a pond represents inventory, the rocks represent problems that could occur in a firm. A high level of water hides the problems (rocks). Management assumes everything is fine, but as the water level drops in an economic downturn, problems are presented. If you force the water level down on purpose (particularly in good economic times), you can expose and correct problems before they cause worse problems. JIT manufacturing exposes problems otherwise hidden by excess inventories and staff.

Uniform Plant Loading

Cycle Times

Uniform Plant Loading   Smoothing the production flow to dampen the reaction waves that normally occur in response to schedule variations is called **uniform plant loading.** When a change is made in a final assembly, the changes are magnified throughout the line and the supply chain. The only way to eliminate the problem is to make adjustments as small as possible by setting a firm monthly production plan for which the output rate is frozen. (This is how a company addresses the need for a stable demand environment noted in Exhibit 8.3.)

The Japanese found they could do this by building the same mix of products every day in small quantities. Thus they always have a total mix available to respond to variations in demand. A Toyota example is shown in Exhibit 8.5. Monthly car style quantities are reduced to daily quantities (assuming a 20-day month) in order to compute **cycle times** (the time between two identical units completed on a line). The

Exhibit 8.4

Inventory Hides
Problems

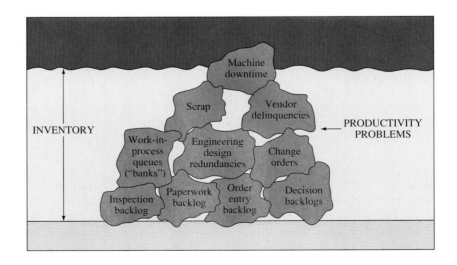

cycle time figure is used to adjust resources to produce the precise quantity needed. Speed of equipment or of the production line is not important. Producing only the needed quantity each day is important. JIT strives to produce on schedule, on cost, and on quality. [Additional discussion of mixed-model assembly is provided in Chapter 10.]

Kanban Production Control Systems   A kanban control system uses a signaling device to regulate JIT flows. **Kanban** means "sign" or "instruction card" in Japanese. In a paperless control system, containers can be used instead of cards. The cards or containers make up the **kanban pull system.** The authority to produce or supply additional parts comes from downstream operations. Consider Exhibit 8.6, where we have an assembly line that is supplied with parts by a machine center. The machine center makes two parts, A and B. These two parts are stored in containers that are located next to the assembly line and next to the machine center. Each container next to the assembly line has a withdrawal kanban, and each container next to the machine center has a production kanban. This is often referred to as a two-card kanban system.

When the assembly line takes the first part A from a full container, a worker takes the withdrawal kanban from the container, and takes the card to the machine center storage area. In the machine center area, the worker finds a container of part A, removes the production kanban, and replaces it with the withdrawal kanban. Placement of this card on the container authorizes the movement of the container to the assembly line. The freed production kanban is placed on a rack by the machine center, which authorizes the production of another lot of material. The cards on the rack become the dispatch list for the machine center. Cards are not the only way to signal the need for production of a part; other visual methods are possible, as shown in Exhibit 8.7.

Kanban

Kanban Pull System

Model	Monthly Quantity	Daily Quantity	Cycle Time (Minutes)
Sedan	5,000	250	2
Hardtop	2,500	125	4
Wagon	2,500	125	4

Sequence: Sedan, hardtop, sedan, wagon, sedan, hardtop, sedan, wagon, etc.

Exhibit 8.5

Toyota Example of Mixed-Model Production Cycle in a Japanese Assembly Plant

Exhibit 8.6

Flow of Two Kanbans

Production Kanban   Withdrawal Kanban

Machine center   A   Assembly line

                        B

Storage

Exhibit 8.7

Diagram of Outbound
Stockpoint with
Warning Signal
Marker

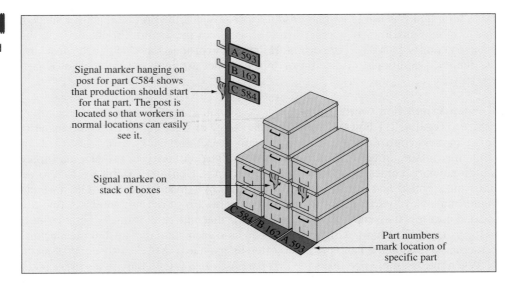

Signal marker hanging on
post for part C584 shows
that production should start
for that part. The post is
located so that workers in
normal locations can easily
see it.

Signal marker on
stack of boxes

Part numbers
mark location of
specific part

The following are some other possible approaches:

Container system. Sometimes the container itself can be used as a signal device. In this case, an empty container on the factory floor visually signals the need to fill it with a disk drive unit. The amount of inventory is adjusted by simply adding or removing containers.

Kanban squares. Some companies use marked spaces on the floor or on a table to identify where material should be stored. When the square is empty, like the one on the left, the supplying operations is authorized to produce; when the square is full, no parts are needed.

Colored golf balls. At a Kawasaki engine plant, when a part used in a subassembly is down to its queue limit, the assembler rolls a colored golf ball down a pipe to the replenishment machine center. This tells the operator which part to make next. Many variations have been developed on this approach.

The kanban pull approach can be used not only within a manufacturing facility but also between manufacturing facilities (pulling engines and transmission into an automobile assembly operation, for example), and also between manufacturers and external suppliers.

Determining the Number of Kanbans Needed   Setting up a kanban control system requires the determination of the number of kanban cards (or containers) needed. In the case of a two-card system, we are finding the number of sets of withdrawal and production cards. The kanban cards represent the number of containers of material that flow back and forth between the supplier and the user areas. Each container represents the minimum production lot size to be supplied. The number of containers, therefore, directly controls the amount of work-in-process inventory in the system.

An accurate estimate of the lead time needed to produce a container of parts is the key to determining the number of containers. This lead time is a function of the processing time for the container, any waiting time during the production process, and the time required to transport the material to the user. Enough kanbans are needed to cover the expected demand during this lead time plus some additional amount for safety stock. The number of kanban card sets is:

$$k = \frac{\text{Expected demand during lead time } + \text{ Safety stock}}{\text{Size of the container}}$$

$$= \frac{DL(1 + S)}{C}$$

where

  k = Number of kanban card sets
  D = Average number of units demanded over some time period
  L = Lead time to replenish an order (expressed in the same units as demand)
  S = Safety stock expressed as a percentage of demand during the lead time (This can be based on a service level and variance as shown in Chapter 15.)
  C = Container size

Observe that a kanban system does not produce zero inventory; rather it controls the amount of material that can be in process at a time—the number of containers of each item. The kanban system can be easily adjusted to fit the current way the system is operating, because card sets can be easily added or removed from the system. If the workers find that they are not able to consistently replenish the item on time, an additional container of material, with the accompanying kanban cards, can be added. If it is found that excess containers of material accumulate, card sets can be easily removed, thus reducing the amount of inventory.

■ **example 8.1** *Determining the Number of Kanban Card Sets*   Arvin Automotive, a company that makes muffler assemblies for the Big Three, is committed to the use of kanban to pull material through its manufacturing cells. Arvin has designed each cell to fabricate a specific family of muffler products. Fabricating a muffler assembly involves cutting and bending pieces of pipe that are welded to a muffler and a catalytic converter. The mufflers and catalytic converters are pulled into the cell based on current demand. In the case of the catalytic converters, these are made in a specialized cell designed for this purpose.

Catalytic converters are made in batches of 10 units and are moved in special hand carts to the fabrication cells. The catalytic converter cell is designed so that different types of catalytic converters can be made with virtually no setup loss. The cell has found that it can respond to an order for a batch of catalytic converters in approximately four hours. Since the catalytic converter cell is right next to the muffler assembly fabrication cell, transportation time is virtually zero.

The muffler assembly fabrication cell averages approximately eight assemblies per hour. Each assembly uses the same catalytic converter. Due to some variability in the process, management has decided to have safety stock equivalent to 10 percent of the needed inventory.

How many kanban sets are needed to manage the replenishment of the catalytic converters?

s o l u t i o n   In this case, the lead time for replenishment of the converters (L) is four hours. The demand (D) for the catalytic converters is 8 per hour. Safety stock (S) is 10 percent of the expected demand, and the container size (C) is 10 units.

$$k = \frac{8x4(1+.1)}{10} = \frac{35.2}{10} = 3.52$$

In this case, we would need four kanban card sets, and we would have four containers of converters in the system. In all cases, when we calculate k, we will round the number up, because we always need to work with full containers of parts. ■

Minimized Setup Times   Because small lot sizes are the norm, machine setups must be quickly accomplished to produce the mixed models on the line. In a widely cited example from the late 1970s, Toyota teams of press operators producing car hoods and fenders were able to change an 800-ton press in 10 minutes, compared with the average of six hours for U.S. workers and four hours for German workers. [Now, however, such speed is common in most U.S. auto plants. At the John Deere plant, punch press setup time was cut from one hour to one minute back in 1985.] To achieve such setup time reduction, setups are divided into internal and external activities. Internal setups must be done while a machine is stopped. External setups can be done while the machine is running. Other time-saving devices such as duplicate tool holders are also used to reduce setups. It is not unusual for a Japanese setup team to spend a full Saturday practicing changeovers.

Respect for People

Respect for people is a key to the Japanese improvements. They have traditionally stressed lifetime employment for permanent positions within major firms. Companies try to maintain level payrolls even when business conditions deteriorate. Permanent workers (about one-third of the total workforce) have job security and tend to be more flexible, remain with a company, and do all they can to help a firm achieve its goals. [The recent recession in Japan has caused many Japanese companies to move away from this ideal. See the "Toyota Work Contracts" case at the end of this chapter.]

Company unions in Japan exist to foster a cooperative relationship with management. All employees receive two bonuses a year in good times. Employees know that if the company performs well, they will get a bonus. This encourages workers to improve productivity. Management views workers as assets, not as human machines. Automation and robotics are used extensively to perform dull or routine jobs so employees are free to focus on important improvement tasks.

Subcontractor networks are very important in Japan. The specialized nature of Japanese factories features little vertical integration. More than 90 percent of all Japanese companies are part of the supplier network of small firms. Some suppliers are specialists in a narrow field serving multiple customers. The other, more prominent, type are sole-source suppliers that make a small variety of parts for a single customer. Firms have long-term partnerships with their suppliers and customers. Suppliers consider themselves part of a customer's family.

They use a **bottom-round management** style made up of consensus management by committees or teams. This decision process is slow but attempts to reach a consensus (not a compromise) by involving all parties, seeking information, and making a decision at the lowest level possible. Unlike in the United States, Japanese top management makes very few operating decisions, but concentrates on strategic planning. This system is effective in the smaller, focused factories of Japan.

Bottom-Round Management

Quality circles of volunteer employees meet weekly to discuss their jobs and problems. These small group improvement activities (SGIA) attempt to devise solutions to problems and share the solutions with management. They are led by a supervisor or production worker and typically include employees from a given production area. Others are multidiscipline teams led by a trained group leader or facilitator. Westinghouse Electric Corporation, for example, has 275 quality circles and 25 facilitators. These circles are part of the consensus, bottom-round management approach.

Quality Circles

■ NORTH AMERICAN MODIFICATIONS OF JIT

Some of these approaches are difficult to implement in North America. Lifetime employment, company unions, and subcontractor networks are not prevalent in the United States and Canada. Also, U.S. and Canadian companies traditionally use a top-down planning and management structure, which is counter to bottom-round management. In addition, U.S. and Canadian companies are vulnerable to labor strikes over union contracts. A recent General Motors labor strike resulted in over 20,000 layoffs in North America (see the reading "Just-in-Time: Is It Really Good for the Automobile Industry?" page 348).

What we can (and have) adopted in the United States and Canada is the Japanese general philosophy and approach to JIT. We have discovered that while the process may take many years to implement, reducing setup times, eliminating inventory, identifying problems, and utilizing the expertise of workers are important, practical guidelines for all organizations. Indeed, in a survey on the implementation of 1,035 U.S. manufacturers, 86.4 percent of the respondents agreed that JIT provided an overall net benefit for their organization. Less than 5 percent reported no overall benefit from their JIT implementation. Throughput time (the time it takes to make one product in a plant from start to finish) decreased an average of 59.4 percent. The study found that organizations with 500 or more employees typically implement JIT management practices more often than organizations with fewer than 500 employees. JIT was also practiced for a longer period of time for the larger organizations. Regardless of size or type of process employed, JIT manufacturing was seen as beneficial for U.S. manufacturers.[4] Arvin's Total Quality Production System (ATQPS) is a great example of how American companies have implemented JIT (see Plant Tour on page 334).

In Europe as well, many organizations have seen JIT benefits. In a study of 80 European plants, improvements included a 50 percent average reduction in inventory,

---

[4] Richard E. White, "An Empirical Assessment of JIT in U.S. Manufacturers," *Production and Inventory Management Journal* 34, no. 2 (second quarter 1993), pp. 38–42.

PLANT TOUR

Arvin North American Automotive (NAA)

Arvin Automotive was founded in 1919 and has been a supplier of complete exhaust systems for the original equipment market since 1929. Arvin has had great success achieving excellence with their Arvin Total Quality Production System (ATQPS). Their JIT production system is just a part of their team approach; NAA is involved early in the vehicle design with their customers.

Teams meet frequently to assess progress, solve problems, and make decisions. At Arvin, employees work in teams, learn in teams, and succeed in teams. Suggestions and ideas from teams and individuals are the fuel of continuous improvement.

Team Production

Each manufacturing cell is laid out to assure visual communications among operators, a smooth flow of materials, timely delivery of components, and responsive shipment of finished products.

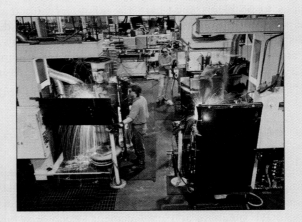

a 50 to 70 percent reduction in throughput time, a reduction in setup time by as much as 50 percent (without major plant and equipment investments), 20 to 50 percent productivity increases, and a payback for the JIT investment in less than nine months.[5]

■ JIT IMPLEMENTATION REQUIREMENTS

This section is structured around the model shown in Exhibit 8.8. It discusses ways to accomplish JIT production. These suggestions are geared to repetitive production systems—those that make the same products again and again. Also, bear in mind that these elements are linked: Any changes in part of the production system impact other features of the system.

---

[5] Amrik Sohal and Keith Howard, "Trends in Material Management," *International Journal of Production Distribution and Materials Management* 17, no. 5 (1987), pp. 3–41.

Team-devised color coding facilitates quick changeover, improving flexibility and quality and promoting production of small lots to meet customer needs precisely. Visual controls remove ambiguity and assure quality at the source.

. . . and to external customers, too.
ARVIN AUTOMOTIVE (*http://www.arvin.com*)

NAA's disciplined "pull system" utilizes production leveling and kanban signals to produce small, efficient lots delivered just-in-time to internal customers. . . .

JIT Layouts and Design Flows

JIT requires the plant layout to be designed to ensure balanced work flow with a minimum of work-in-process inventory. Each workstation is part of a production line, whether or not a physical line actually exists. Capacity balancing is done using the same logic for an assembly line, and operations are linked through a pull system. In addition, the system designer must have a vision of how all aspects of the internal and external logistics system tie to the layout.

Preventive maintenance is emphasized to ensure that flows are not interrupted by downtime or malfunctioning equipment. Operators perform much of the maintenance because they are most familiar with their machines and because machines are easier to repair, as JIT operations favor several simple machines rather than one large complex one.

The reductions in setup and changeover times previously discussed are necessary to achieve a smooth flow. Exhibit 8.9 shows the relationship between lot size and setup costs. Under a traditional approach, setup cost is treated as a constant, and the optimal

Preventive
Maintenance

Exhibit 8.8   How to Accomplish Just-in-Time Production

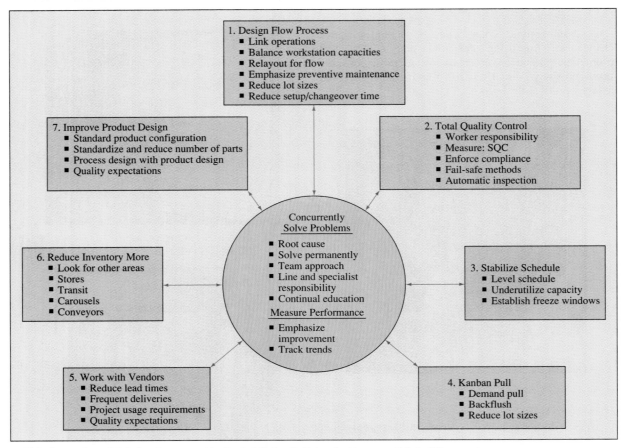

This diagram is modeled after the one used by Hewlett-Packard's Boise plant to accomplish its JIT program.

order quantity is shown as six. Under the kanban approach of JIT, setup cost is treated as a variable and the optimal order quantity is reduced. In the exhibit, the order quantity has been reduced from six to two under JIT by employing setup-time–saving procedures. This organization will ultimately strive for a lot size of one.

JIT Applications for Line Flows

Exhibit 8.10 illustrates a pull system in a simple line flow. In a pure JIT environment, no employee does any work until the product has been pulled from the end of the line by the market. The product could be a final product or a component used in later production. When a product is pulled, a replenishment unit is pulled from upstream operations. In the exhibit, an item of finished goods is pulled from F, the finished goods inventory. The inventory clerk then goes to processing station E and takes replacement product to fill the void. This pattern continues up the line to worker A, who pulls material from the raw material inventory. The rules of the flow layout require employees to keep completed units at their workstation, and if someone takes

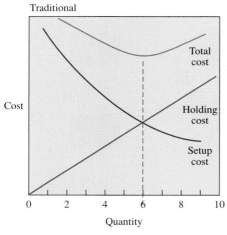

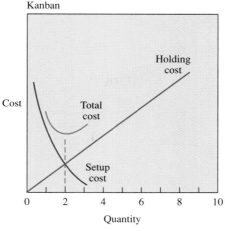

Exhibit 8.9

Relationship between Lot Size and Setup Cost

Definitions: *Holding cost* includes the costs of storing inventory and the cost of money tied up in inventory. *Setup cost* includes the wage costs attributable to workers making the setup, and various administrative and supplies costs. (These are defined in total in Chapter 15, "Inventory Systems for Independent Demand.")

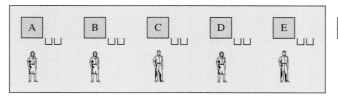

Exhibit 8.10

JIT in a Line Flow Layout

the completed work away, the employee must move upstream in the flow to get additional work to complete.

JIT Applications for Job Shops

JIT is traditionally applied to line flows, but job shop environments also offer JIT benefits. The focus of JIT is product flow. Though job shops are characterized by low volume and high variety, JIT can be used if demand can be stabilized to permit repetitive manufacture. Stabilizing demand is usually easier to accomplish when the demand is from a downstream production stage rather than an end customer. (The logic is that internal customers can smooth their input requirements far easier than a distributor or individual purchaser.)

Vol. II "Improving Operations Methods."

Factory machining centers, paint shops, and shirt making are examples of job-shop–type operations that process parts and components before they reach final production stages. By way of example, consider the production system in Exhibit 8.11. If a work center produces nine different parts used by several product varieties that are produced just in time, the work center keeps containers of completed output of all nine parts at the center to be picked up by users. Operators could make periodic rounds throughout the facility (hourly or more frequently) to pick up empty containers and drop them off at the corresponding upstream work center and to pick up full containers. In Exhibit 8.11, automatic guided vehicles pick up and deliver part numbers M5 and M8 to line two and line three for processing. These handling procedures

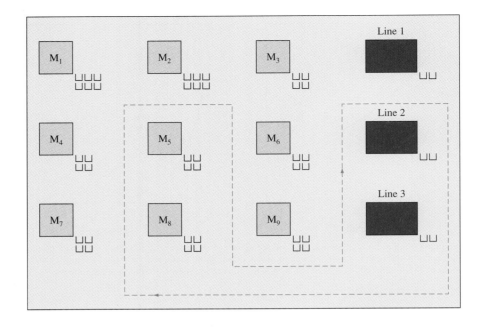

can be manual or automated, but either way, these periodic pickups and drop-offs allow the system to operate in a just-in-time mode.

TQC (Total Quality Control)

Total Quality
Control (TQC)

JIT and TQC have merged in theory and practice. **Total quality control (TQC)** is the practice of building quality into the process and not identifying quality by inspection. It also refers to the theory of employees assuming responsibility for the quality of their own work. When employees are responsible for quality, JIT works at its best because only good-quality products are pulled through the system. When all products are good, no "just-in-case" extra inventory is needed. Thus, organizations can achieve high quality and high productivity as shown in Exhibit 8.12. By using statistical quality control methods and training workers to maintain quality, inspections can be reduced to the first and last units produced. If they are perfect, we can assume the other units between these points are perfect as well.

A component of quality is improved product design. Standard product configurations, fewer parts, and standardized parts are important elements in JIT. These design modifications reduce variability in the end item or in the materials that go into the product. Besides improving the producibility of a product, product design activities can facilitate the processing of engineering changes.

A Stable Schedule

Level Schedule

As noted earlier, JIT firms require a stable schedule over a lengthy time horizon. This is accomplished by level scheduling, freeze windows, and underutilization of capacity. A **level schedule**

is one that requires material to be pulled into final assembly in a pattern uniform enough to allow the various elements of production to respond to pull signals. It does

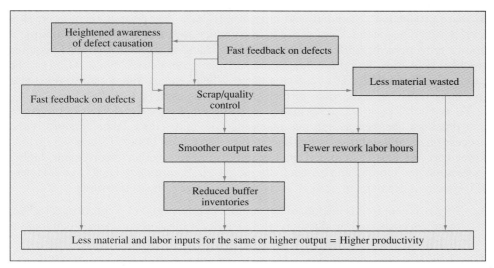

Exhibit 8.12

Relationship between JIT and Quality

Source: Richard J. Schonberger, "Some Observations on the Advantages and Implementation Issues of Just-in-Time Production Systems," *Journal of Operations Management* 3, no. 1 (November 1982), p. 5.

not necessarily mean that the usage of every part on an assembly line is identified hour by hour for days on end; it does mean that a given production system equipped with flexible setups and a fixed amount of material in the pipelines can respond.[6]

The term **freeze window** refers to that period of time during which the schedule is fixed and no further changes are possible. An added benefit of the stable schedule is seen in how parts and components are accounted for in a pull system. Here, the concept of **backflush** measurement is used to periodically explode an end item's bill of materials (the parts that go into each product) to calculate how many of each part went into the final product(s). This eliminates much of the shop-floor data collection activity, which is required if each part must be tracked and accounted for during production.

Freeze Window

Backflush

Underutilization of capacity is a controversial feature of JIT. Excess or underutilized capacity is realized when excess inventory buffers are removed from a system. The safety stocks and early deliveries were used as a hedge against production problems like poor quality, machine failures, and unanticipated bottlenecks in traditional manufacturing. Under JIT, excess labor and machines provide the hedge. The excess capacity in labor and equipment that results is much cheaper than carrying excess inventory. During idle periods personnel can be put to work on other activities such as special projects, work group activities, and workstation housekeeping.

Work with Suppliers

Just as customers and employees are key components of the JIT system, vendors are also important to the process. If a firm shares its projected usage requirements with its vendors, they have a long-run picture of the demands that will be placed on their production and distribution systems. Some vendors are linked on-line with a customer

Vol. II "Supplier Development Outreach Program"

---

[6] Robert H. Hall, *Zero Inventories* (Homewood, IL: Dow Jones-Irwin, 1983) p. 64.

to share production scheduling and input needs data. This permits them to develop level production systems. Confidence in the supplier or vendor's delivery commitment allows reductions of buffer inventories. Maintaining stock at a JIT level requires frequent deliveries during the day. Some suppliers even deliver to a location on the production line and not at a receiving dock. When vendors adopt quality practices, incoming receiving inspections of their products can even be bypassed.

To assess JIT progress, performance measures emphasize the number of processes and practices changed to improve materials flow and reduce labor content. If the process physically improves over time, lower costs follow. Other JIT benefits include lower carrying costs, scrap and quality improvements, worker involvement, higher motivation and morale, and productivity increases. According to Hall,[7] in a Japanese JIT system, a department head is likely to be evaluated on six measures:

1. Improvement trends, including the number of improvement projects undertaken, trends in costs, and productivity. Productivity is measured as department output divided by total number of direct and indirect employees.

2. Quality trends, reduction in defect rates, improvement in process capability, and improvement in quality procedures.

3. Running to a level schedule and providing parts when others need them.

4. Trends in department inventory levels (e.g., higher inventory turns).

5. Staying within budgets for expenses.

6. Developing workforce skills, versatility, participation in changes, and morale.

ACCOUNTING   While these quantitative and qualitative improvement measures are realistic and fit the system, many previous cost accounting measures no longer work in the JIT environment. These traditional systems, used since the U.S. Industrial Revolution, have focused on direct labor. Under JIT, overhead costs are as much as 20 times as high as direct labor costs. Also, as workers take on maintenance duties, direct and indirect labor distinctions are blurred and cost allocation measures must be changed. (See the box "JIT and Cost Accounting.")

■ JIT IN SERVICES

Many JIT techniques have been successfully applied by service firms. Just as in manufacturing, the suitability of each technique and the corresponding work steps depends on the characteristics of the firm's markets, production and equipment technology, skill sets, and corporate culture. Service firms are not different in this respect. Here are 10 of the more successful applications.[8]

Organize Problem-Solving Groups   Honeywell is extending its quality circles from manufacturing into its service operations. Other corporations as diverse as First Bank/Dallas, Standard Meat Company, and Miller Brewing Company are using similar approaches to improve service. British Airways used quality circles as a

[7] Ibid., pp. 254–55.

[8] Randall J. Benson. "JIT: Not Just For the Factory!" *APICS 29th Annual International Conference Proceedings* (1986), pp. 370–74.

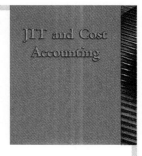

Cost accounting systems have focused on direct labor since the Industrial Revolution. However, under JIT (and computer-integrated manufacturing) overhead costs are dominant, often 20 times as high as direct labor. Moreover, with workers maintaining their own equipment, and other measures, the distinction between direct and indirect labor has become blurred for cost-allocation purposes.

Hewlett-Packard has recognized this and has eliminated the cost category of direct labor, now simply using "labor" instead.

It presently appears that the primary difference between traditional and JIT cost accounting is the application of overhead on the basis of product time in the system (cycle time) rather than direct labor or machine hours.

Source: Mohan V. Tatikonda, "Just-in-Time and Modern Manufacturing Environments: Implications for Cost Accounting," *Production and Inventory Management Journal* 28, no. 1 (1988), pp. 1–5.

fundamental part of its strategy to implement new service practices. (See "JIT in an Express Package Service" on page 342 for another example of team efforts in JIT.)

Upgrade Housekeeping   Good housekeeping means more than winning the clean broom award. It means that only the necessary items are kept in a work area, that there is a place for everything, and that everything is clean and in a constant state of readiness. The employees clean their own areas.

Service organizations such as McDonald's, Disneyland, and Speedi-Lube have recognized the critical nature of housekeeping. Their dedication to housekeeping has meant that service processes work better, the attitude of continuous improvement is easier to develop, and customers perceive that they are receiving better service.

Upgrade Quality   The only cost-effective way to improve quality is to develop reliable process capabilities. Process quality is quality at the source—it guarantees first-time production of consistent and uniform products and services.

McDonald's is famous for building quality into its service delivery process. It literally "industrialized" the service delivery system so that part-time, casual workers could provide the same eating experience anywhere in the world. Quality doesn't mean producing the best; it means consistently producing products and services that give the customers their money's worth.

Clarify Process Flows   Clarification of the flows, based on the JIT themes, can dramatically improve the process performance. Here are examples.

First, Federal Express Corporation changed air flight patterns from origin-to-destination to origin-to-hub, where the freight is transferred to an outbound plane heading for the destination. This revolutionized the air transport industry. Second, the order-entry department of a manufacturing firm converted from functional subdepartments to customer-centered work groups and reduced the order processing lead time from eight to two days. Third, a county government used the JIT approach to cut the time to record a deed transfer by 50 percent. Finally, Supermaids sends in a team of house cleaners, each with a specific responsibility, to clean each house quickly with parallel processes. Changes in process flows can literally revolutionize service industries.

BREAKTHROUGH

JIT in an Express Package Service

Company A, an overnight package delivery service, retains an inventory of supplies (shipping airbills, sorting bags, service guides, overnight envelopes, boxes, tubes, and employee uniforms). While utilizing a traditional inventory system, Company A saw their inventory investment swell from $16 million to $34 million.

Since Company A is a service industry, there is no real "conversion process." But being a service industry does not disqualify a firm from benefiting from a JIT program. After becoming aware of the potential benefits of JIT, Company A's CEO began a push to see it implemented at his firm.

After researching the issue further, Company A's management issued this statement

> The strategic objective of the JIT program at Company A is not to decrease inventory; it is to increase profit by providing a 99.9% service level to our customers in fulfilling their revenue document need. Inventory will fall, but as an effect of JIT, not as an achieved objective. Another important strategic objective is to further enhance company A's competitive position against other express package delivery companies.

This statement emphasizes the customer focus that underlies JIT implementation within a service industry. A JIT team (composed of members from all affected departments) met weekly to work out communication and coordination problems encountered by the JIT effort. All involved personnel were educated on all aspects of JIT and were made aware of the company's corresponding goals. All vendors were brought in for a formal presentation on delivery and quality expectations. Vendors were even encouraged to attend the weekly meetings of the JIT team to offer input and support. In order to facilitate a better vendor relationship, the length of vendor contracts was extended to a longer period than in the past. Through the education and coordination efforts of the JIT team, the JIT philosophy was implemented at Company A based on prerequisites of communication, quality and commitment.

By dividing the weekly number of items filled by the number of items requested, Company A was able to compute a service level ratio for gauging their service performance. Prior to JIT implementation, their service level ran a respectable 79%. After JIT, the service level increased to 99%, with the expectation of an eventual 99.9%.

In addition to an increased service level, Company A's JIT program yielded enhanced forecasts, reduced traffic time, a more proactive expediter function, enhanced buyer awareness, improved quality, a stronger focus on customer service, improved communication, price reductions, improved processing of paperwork, and a sense of team spirit.

Source: R. Anthony Inman and Satish Mehra, "JIT Applications for Service Environments," *Production and Inventory Management Journal*, third quarter 1991, pp. 16–20. Reprinted with permission of APICS—The Educational Society for Resource Management, Falls Church, VA.

Revise Equipment and Process Technologies   Revising technologies involves evaluation of the equipment and processes for their ability to meet the process requirements, to process consistently within tolerance, and to fit the scale and capacity of the work group.

Speedi-Lube converted the standard service station concept to a specialized lubrication and inspection center by changing the service bays from drive-in to drive-through and by eliminating the hoists and instead building pits under the cars where employees have full access to the lubrication areas on the vehicle.

A hospital reduced operating room setup time so that it had the flexibility to perform a wider range of operations without reducing the operation room availability.

Level the Facility Load   Service firms synchronize production with demand. They have developed unique approaches to leveling demand so they can avoid making customers wait for service. CompuServe sells time for less during the evening. McDonald's offers a special breakfast menu in the morning. Retail stores use take-a-number systems. The post office charges more for next-day delivery. These are all examples of the service approach for creating uniform facility loads.

BREAKTHROUGH

A New Type of Partnership

A partnership between customers and suppliers has evolved at companies such as Honeywell, Bose, and AT&T. This partnership was conceived by Lance Dixon, director of purchasing at Bose Corporation. His system, entitled JIT II, brings the vendor into the plant to participate in the customer's purchasing office on a full-time daily basis. Whereas the typical JIT process eliminated inventory and brought the customer and supplier closer, this system adds such benefits as eliminating the buyer and sales representative from the customer–supplier relationship. This vendor replaces the buyer and salesperson. He or she is directed to use the customer's purchase orders and to practice concurrent design and engineering. By being in-plant, this empowered employee, or facilitator, can raise the level of communication between the supplier and the customer company employees. Following JIT principles, the practices are customer-focused, cost-effective, quality-driven, and team-based.

Having vendor representatives work with Bose engineers on designs has led to substantial improvements in design quality and productivity for the component-quality high fidelity loudspeakers Bose manufactures. The major advantage is that the customer representative at the Bose location is empowered to use its system. Bose also applied these concepts to its transportation system and plans material in transit just like its inventory in the warehouse. AT&T and Honeywell have adopted JIT II and have been able to save money and improve productivity by combining the voice of the customer with that of the employee.

Source: Martin M. Stein, "The Ultimate Customer–Supplier Relationship at Bose, Honeywell, and AT&T," *National Productivity Review* 12, no. 4 (Autumn 1993), pp. 543–48; and Sherwin Greenblatt, "Continuous Improvement in Supply Chain Management," *Chief Executive* 86 (June 1993), pp. 40–43.

Eliminate Unnecessary Activities   A step that does not add value is a candidate for elimination. A step that does add value may be a candidate for reengineering to improve the process consistency or to reduce the time to perform the tasks.

A hospital discovered that significant time was spent during an operation waiting for an instrument that was not available when the operation began. It developed a checklist of instruments required for each category of operation. Speedi-Lube eliminated steps, but it also added steps that did not improve the lubrication process but did make customers feel more assured about the work being performed.

Reorganize Physical Configuration   Work area configurations frequently require reorganization during a JIT implementation. Often, manufacturers accomplish this by setting up manufacturing cells to produce items in small lots, synchronous to demand. These cells amount to "microfactories" inside the plant.

Most service firms are far behind manufacturers in the area. However, a few interesting examples do come out of the service sector. Some hospitals—instead of routing patients all over the building for tests, exams, X-rays, and injections—are reorganizing their services into work groups based on the type of problem. Teams that treat only trauma are common, but other work groups have been formed to treat less immediate conditions like hernias. These amount to microclinics within the hospital facility.

Introduce Demand-Pull Scheduling   Due to the nature of service production and consumption, demand-pull (customer-driven) scheduling is necessary for operating a service business. Moreover, many service firms are separating their operations into "back room" and "customer contact" facilities. This approach creates new problems in coordinating schedules between the facilities. The original Wendy's restaurants were set up so cooks could see cars enter the parking lot. They put a preestablished number of hamburger patties onto the grill for each car. This pull system was designed to have a fresh patty on the grill before the customer even placed an order.

Develop Supplier Networks   Supplier networks in the JIT context refer to the cooperative association of suppliers and customers working over the long term for mutual benefit. (See the Breakthrough box on the previous page titled "A New Type of Partnership.") Service firms have not emphasized supplier networks for materials because the service costs are often predominantly labor. Notable exceptions must include service organizations like McDonald's, one of the biggest food products purchasers in the world. A small manufacturer recognized that it needed cooperative relationships for temporary employees as well as for parts. It is considering a campaign to establish JIT-type relationships with a temporary employment service and a trade school to develop a reliable source of trained assemblers.

◼ CONCLUSION

JIT represents a powerful tool for reducing inventory and improving production and service operations. Its principles can result in many improvements, but users are cautioned that JIT applications are not universal. Like TQM, JIT implementation faces many problems led by a resistance to change shown by many employees. Education of top management is important. Visible initial pilot programs (rather than a plantwide implementation of JIT all at once) are a good beginning. Management should use care in choosing an implementation team who will be responsible for making the major changes on the plant floor. The team can include 5 to 15 individuals from quality control, engineering, manufacturing, traffic, purchasing, marketing, and other areas. Ongoing team education is important to help employees discard practices that block JIT progress. Again, like TQM, JIT is a series of small improvements that take time. It requires the patience of all involved parties.

JIT is an encompassing philosophy considering product design, process design, equipment, selection, material management, quality assurance, job design, and productivity improvements. The goal of synchronized, streamlined one-piece-at-a-time production is a world-class standard seldom achieved in practice. Because zero lead time and zero idle time are hard to accomplish, some JIT projects are put quickly in place and later forgotten. Management support, commitment, and training to continue JIT progress are needed.

REVIEW AND DISCUSSION QUESTIONS

1. What JIT principles are being used by Saturn Corporation (see opening vignette)? Use the categories in Exhibit 8.8 to develop your answer.
2. Is it possible to achieve zero inventories? Why or why not?
3. Stopping waste is a vital part of JIT. Identify some sources of waste and discuss how they may be eliminated.
4. Discuss JIT in a job-shop layout and in a line layout.

5. Why must JIT have a stable schedule?

6. Will JIT work in service environments? Why or why not?

7. Discuss ways to use JIT to improve one of the following: a pizza restaurant, a hospital, or an auto dealership.

8. Which objections might a marketing manager have against uniform plant loading?

9. What are the implications for cost accounting of JIT production?

10. What are the roles of suppliers and customers in a JIT system?

11. Explain how cards are used in a kanban system.

12. In which ways, if any, are the following systems analogous to kanban: returning empty bottles to the supermarket and picking up filled ones; running a hot dog stand at lunchtime; withdrawing money from a checking account; raking leaves into bags?

13. How is a U.S. JIT system different from a Japanese one?

14. Why is JIT hard to implement in practice?

15. Explain the relationship between quality and productivity under the JIT philosophy.

PROBLEMS

✓ 1. A supplier of instrument gauge clusters uses kanban system to control material flow. The gauge cluster housings are transported 5 at a time. A fabrication center produces approximately 10 gauges per hour. It takes approximately 2 hours for the housing to be replenished. Due to variations in processing times, management has decided to keep 20 percent of the needed inventory as safety stock. How many kanban card sets are needed?

1. 5 kanban card sets.

2. Transmissions are delivered to the fabrication line 4 at a time. It takes 1 hour for transmissions to be delivered. Approximately 4 vehicles are produced each hour, and management has decided that 50 percent of expected demand should be maintained as safety stock. How many kanban card sets are needed?

2. 2 kanban card sets.

Case

Quick Response Apparel

Imagine walking into a store and ordering clothing manufactured to your size and specifications. This phenomenon—called "apparel on demand"—is an extension of JIT linking retailers and manufacturers for a just-in-time responsiveness. With this quick response, retailers can send their point-of-sale information directly to the factory floor to minimize downtime. Clothing is delivered to the purchaser through normal retail channels. Custom Clothing Technology Corporation (CCTC) is making reasonably priced custom jeans for women. This apparel-on-demand concept could result in 30 percent production savings. It also reduces the need for inventory and markdowns. CCTC was launched by Sung Park, who feels women will pay the $48 price for a pair of jeans guaranteed to fit.

Women are electronically measured and select their jeans' style in stores contracting with CCTC's JIT service. The jeans are cut in Vermont, sewn in Texas, and shipped to the customer in less than two weeks. The current market for women's jeans is $2 billion, so Park feels this is a great market to test JIT jeans.

Questions

1. If you were a traditional retailer selling jeans, how worried would you be about this new trend?

2. Do you think customers will be willing to wait two weeks for product delivery?

3. How can CCTC compete on customer service if delivery takes two weeks?

4. Discuss what other strategic variables CCTC is competing on.

5. How can JIT concepts be used to improve customer service and flexibility in other industries? Choose one of the following industries and brainstorm creating JIT solutions: health care, grocery stores, physical fitness, or home repair and maintenance.

6. Another example of quick response clothing is Second Skin Swimwear in North Palm Beach, Florida. The firm custom manufactures 10,000 bathing suits annually using a body scanning system to eliminate embarrassment in bathing suit shopping. Delivery is in two to three weeks. Given these examples, what other clothing styles or types could benefit from just-in-time customization?

7. What other improvements can retailers experience with these new systems? Discuss end-of-season inventory, size of department store or retail floor space, and inventory record keeping and cycle counting.

8. How must other organizational functions change their strategies to support this manufacturing shift to JIT apparel?

Source: Martha E. Manglesdorf, "Quick-Response Apparel," *Inc.*, November 1993, p. 35.

Case

Toyota Work Contracts

While lifetime employment has been the norm for a portion of the workers in Japan, recessionary economic systems have made this trend difficult if not impossible for some corporations. In an effort to eliminate the costly lifetime-employment contracts while at the same time avoiding layoffs, organizations led by Toyota Motor Corporation have created a new category of temporary professional worker for its labor force in Japan.

These temporary workers will have a limited number of one-year contracts. Employees like automotive designers will not be offered the customary lifelong employment. The company will pay these employees a salary based on individual merit rather than the past pay practice of linking pay to seniority and overall company performance.

According to Toyota, "As the business conditions surrounding Japanese corporations underwent radical change . . . it was inevitable that the rigid organizational structure of the past would impose limits on corporate growth."

Toyota President Tatsuro Toyoda plans to gradually increase the number of white-collar contract workers in Japan. Other Japanese organizations may follow Toyota's trend. The number of white-collar contract employees is increasing, and this class of worker is easier to terminate than lifetime workers.

Contract workers in blue- and white-collar segments increased from 14 percent in 1989 to 19 percent in 1993. These temporary workers will be the safety valve during cyclical economic conditions. The practice will reduce the number of white-collar workers blamed for many corporate earnings declines. According to a leading Japanese business organization, executives agree Japan "must thoroughly revise the lifetime employment system."

Questions

1. Why do you think the Japanese are reversing their employment trend?

2. What are the advantages and disadvantages of this new employment practice?

3. Are the Japanese attempting to adopt an American-style employment and evaluation policy?

4. Would the former lifetime employment system work for U.S. companies? Why?

Source: Michael Williams, "Toyota Creates Work Contracts Challenging Lifetime-Job System," *The Wall Street Journal*, January 24, 1994, p. A8.

Case

Quality Parts Company

Quality Parts Company is a supplier of gizmos for a computer manufacturer located a few miles away. The company produces two different models of gizmos in production runs ranging from 100 to 300 units.

The production flow of models X and Y is shown in Exhibit C8.1. Model Z requires milling as its first step, but otherwise follows the same flow pattern as X and Y. Skids can hold up to 20 gizmos at a time. Approximate times per unit by operation number and equipment setup times are shown in Exhibit C8.2.

Demand for gizmos from the computer company ranges between 125 and 175 per month, equally divided among X, Y, and Z. Subassembly builds up inventory early in the month to make certain that a buffer stock is always available. Raw materials and purchased parts for subassemblies each constitute 40 percent of the manufacturing cost of a gizmo. Both categories of parts are multiple-sourced from about 80 vendors and are delivered at random times. (Gizmos have 40 different part numbers.)

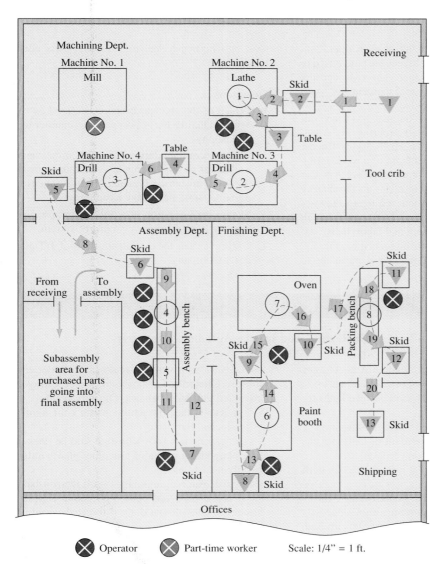

Exhibit C8.1

Gizmo Production Flow

Operator   Part-time worker   Scale: 1/4" = 1 ft.

Exhibit C8.2	Operation Number and Name	Operation Time (Minutes)	Setup Time (Minutes)
Operations and Setup Time	Milling for Model Z	20	60
	1 Lathe	50	30
	2 Mod. 14 drill	15	5
	3 Mod. 14 drill	40	5
	4 Assembly step 1	50	
	Assembly step 2	45	
	Assembly step 3	50	
	5 Inspection	30	
	6 Paint	30	20
	7 Oven	50	
	8 Packing	5	

Scrap rates are about 10 percent at each operation, inventory turns twice yearly, employees are paid on a day rate, employee turnover is 25 percent per year, and net profit from operations is steady at 5 percent per year. Maintenance is performed as needed.

The manager of Quality Parts Company has been contemplating installing an automated ordering system to help control inventories and to "keep the skids filled." (He feels that two days of work in front of a workstation motivates the worker to produce at top speed.) He is also planning to add three inspectors to clean up the quality problem. Further, he is thinking about setting up a rework line to speed repairs. While he is pleased with the high utilization of most of his equipment and labor, he is concerned about the idle time of his milling machine. Finally, he has asked his industrial engineering department to look into high-rise shelving to store parts coming off machine 4.

Questions

1. Which of the changes being considered by the manager of Quality Parts Company go counter to the JIT philosophy?
2. Make recommendations for JIT improvements in such areas as scheduling, layout, kanban, task groupings, and inventory. Use quantitative data as much as possible; state necessary assumptions.
3. Sketch the operation of a pull system for quality for Quality Parts Company's current system.
4. Outline a plan for the introduction of JIT at Quality Parts Company.

Reading

Just-in-Time: Is It Really Good for the Automobile Industry?

DETROIT—The effects of a Canadian Auto Workers strike against General Motors Corp. spread across the border Monday, as 1,850 workers were laid off at two U.S. parts plants.

"We knew sooner or later it was going to impact us," said Chuck Zurawski, president of United Auto Workers Local 735, representing workers at a Ypsilanti, Michigan, plant, "I'd just say it goes with the territory."

The U.S. workers were sent home because the parts they make for Canadian plants aren't needed. Zurawski's plant, Willow Run, west of Detroit, had 800 layoffs among its 4,000 workers. A GM Powertrain plant in Tonawanda, N.Y., which employs 5,500, had 1,050 layoffs.

The New York workers make six cylinder engines for Chevrolet Luminas and Monte Carlos assembled at GM's Oshawa, Ontario, plant. Willow Run makes transmissions for Canadian-built vehicles, Park said.

GM spokesman Tom Klipstine said he does not expect any effect at major assembly plants until possibly next week.

David J. Andrea, an analyst with Detroit-based Roney & Co. said GM could be making U.S. layoff announcements almost daily if the strike continues for many more days.

"It starts slowly and then it will escalate," he said. "The thing it does create is the awareness of how important the entire chain is."

The strike began Wednesday with 15,000 autoworkers in Oshawa, Ontario, and St. Therese, Quebec, and spread Sunday to a St. Catharines, Ontario, plant where about 5,300 CAW members walked out.

Source: The Associated Press, *The Herald-Times,* October 8, 1996.

Articles like this one are frequent given the wide-spread use of JIT techniques in the automobile industry. Who is the winner in these strikes? The Union? General Motors? The Consumers?

Prepare the following questions for our discussion of JIT concepts

1. Precisely describe why a strike in a Canadian plant would force the shutdown of the U.S. engine and transmission plants.

2. Why are the major assembly plants not expected to shut down until next week?

3. What other plants would you expect to shut down as a result of the strike?

4. What could be done to prevent massive shutdowns like described in the article?

SELECTED BIBLIOGRAPHY

Ansari, A., and B. Modarress. *Just in Time Purchasing.* New York: Free Press, 1990, pp. 105–6.

Blackburn, Joseph D. *Time-Based Competition.* Homewood, IL: Business One Irwin, 1991.

Fucini, Joseph J., and Suzy Fucini. *Working for the Japanese.* New York: Free Press, 1990.

Giunipero, Larry C. "Motivating and Monitoring JIT Supplier Performance." *Journal of Purchasing and Material Management,* Winter 1990, pp. 19–24.

Hall, Robert. *Attaining Manufacturing Excellence.* Homewood, IL: Dow Jones-Irwin, 1987.

————. *Zero Inventories.* Homewood, IL: Dow Jones-Irwin, 1983.

Monden, Yasuhiro. *Toyota Production System. Practical Approach to Production Management.* Atlanta, GA: Industrial Engineering and Management Press, 1983.

————. *The Toyota Management System: Linking the Seven Key Functional Areas.* Cambridge, MA.: Productivity Press, 1993.

Ohno, Taiichi. *Toyota Production System: Beyond Large-Scale Production.* Cambridge, MA: Productivity Press, 1988.

Ohno, Taiichi, and Setsuo Mito. *Just-in-Time for Today and Tomorrow.* Cambridge, MA: Productivity Press, 1988.

Schonberger, Richard J. *Building a Chain of Customers: Linking Business Functions to Create a World-Class Company.* New York: Free Press, 1989.

————. *Japanese Manufacturing Techniques.* New York: Free Press, 1982.

————. *World-Class Manufacturing: The Lessons of Simplicity Applied.* New York: Free Press, 1986.

Schonberger, Richard. *World Class Manufacturing: The Next Decade: Building Power, Strength, and Value.* New York: Free Press, 1996.

Sewell, G. "Management Information Systems for JIT Production." *Omega* 18, no. 5 (1990), pp. 481–503.

Shingo, Shigeo. *A Revolution in Manufacturing: The SMED System.* Tokyo: Japan Management Association, 1983.

————. *A Study of the Toyota Production System from an Industrial Engineering Viewpoint.* Cambridge, MA: Productivity Press, 1989.

Suzaki, Kiyoshi. *The New Manufacturing Challenge: Techniques for Continuous Improvement.* New York: Free Press, 1987.

Wantuck, Kenneth A. "The Japanese Approach to Productivity." Southfield, MI: Bendix Corporation, 1983.

White, Richard E. "An Empirical Assessment of JIT in U.S. Manufacturers." *Production and Inventory Management Journal* 34, no. 2 (second quarter 1993).

Womack, James P., D. T. Jones, and D. Roos. *The Machine That Changed the World.* New York: R. A. Rawston Associates, 1990.

Zipkin, Paul H. "Does Manufacturing Need a JIT Revolution?" *Harvard Business Review,* January–February 1991, pp. 40–50.

Chapter 9

Facility Location

Chapter Outline

Issues in Facility Location, 352
Plant Location Methods, 356
    Factor-Rating Systems
    Linear Programming
    Center of Gravity Method
    Analytic Delphi Model

Locating Service Facilities, 361
Case: Is It Russian Roulette? 370
Case: The Plant Location Puzzle, 371

Key Terms

Free Trade Zone

Trading Blocs

Factor-Rating Systems

Center of Gravity Method

Analytic Delphi Model

Regression Model

Ardalan Heuristic Method

www Links

Toyota (http://www.toyota.com)

Toys "R" Us (http://www.tru.com)

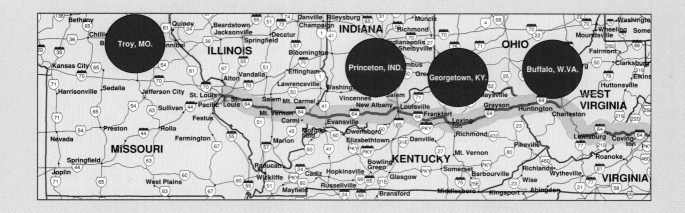

G EORGE TAYLOR FOUGHT THE EMPIRE OF JAPAN AS A U.S. Marine in World War II, and he still has bitter memories. But now, as mayor of Princeton, Indiana, he gladly put them aside last spring when Toyota unveiled plans to build a $700 million pickup-truck plant in this economically sagging town. "I've changed my mind a little bit," Taylor says. "The way I look at it, the Japanese are coming over here and giving American workers good jobs, while American companies are closing factories and taking work overseas for low wages." In a sign of appreciation, Taylor recently traded in his 1987 Chrysler Fifth Avenue for a new Camry sedan that Toyota built just down Highway I-64 at its plant in Georgetown, Kentucky.

Maybe I-64 should be renamed Toyota Road. Along the 500-mile stretch of interstate that winds past Georgetown and Princeton on its way from West Virginia to St. Louis, Missouri, the world's no. 3 automaker—after General Motors and Ford—has quietly become America's fastest growing automaker. Amid the rich corn, wheat, and soybean fields, Toyota is building a vast industrial empire in the center of America's heartland, with I-64 as the hub for some $8 billion of North American investments.

By the year 2000, Toyota hopes the public will view the company as the fourth member of the Big Three automotive family, though Detroit has no intention of extending a membership invitation.

Toyota is adding a new line of minivans to its $3.4 billion plant in George-town, where Camrys and Avalons are now produced, and tripling the output of its St. Louis-based Bodine Aluminum subsidiary, which makes engine components. Next will come a new $400 million engine plant in Buffalo, West Virginia, and the T100 pickup-truck plant in Princeton, Indiana. Toyota is expanding other facilities, like its Corolla factory in Cambridge, Ontario. There's a $310 million technical center building in Ann Arbor, Michigan, and Toyota recently opened the world's largest proving ground, a 12,000-acre property outside Phoenix, Arizona. ●

(http://www.toyota.com)

Source: John Greenwald, "Toyota Road USA," *Time*, October 7, 1996. © 1996 Time Inc. Reprinted by permission.

Where should a plant or service facility be located? This is a top question on the strategic agendas of contemporary manufacturing and service firms, particularly in this age of global markets and global production. Dramatic changes in trade agreements, both in North America and in Europe, have made the world truly a "global village," allowing companies greater flexibility in their location choices. In practice, however, the question of location is very much linked to two competitive imperatives:

1. The need to produce close to the customer due to time-based competition, trade agreements, and shipping costs.
2. The need to locate near the appropriate labor pool to take advantage of low wage costs and/or high technical skills.

This chapter discusses these and other issues in facility location decisions. Examples cover different industries with a global perspective. The chapter presents typical techniques involved in facility location analysis and two cases on global location decisions are at the end of the chapter.

■ ISSUES IN FACILITY LOCATION

The problem of facility location is common to new and existing businesses. This planning is critical to a company's eventual success. For instance, 3M has moved a significant part of its corporate activity, including R&D, to the more temperate climate of Austin, Texas. Toys "R" Us has opened a new location in Japan as a part of its global strategy. Disney chose Paris, France, for its Euro Disney theme park. Manufacturing and service companies' location decisions are guided by a variety of criteria defined by competitive imperatives. Criteria that influence manufacturing plant and warehouse location planning are discussed next.

Proximity to Customers A location close to the customer is important because of the ever-increasing need to be customer-responsive. This enables faster delivery of

Archer Daniels Midland (ADM) is a major processor of agricultural products. ADM's Eurooport plant in Rotterdam, the Netherlands, is the largest grain processing facility in the world where it can ship by land, rail, river, and sea.

goods to customers. In addition, it ensures that customers' needs are incorporated into the products being developed and built. Population characteristics provide a basis for decision making on these criteria.

Business Climate   A favorable business climate can include the presence of similar-sized businesses, the presence of companies in the same industry, and, in the case of international locations, the presence of other foreign companies. Probusiness

The Quality Business Base in Europe

Within the past 25 years Ireland has been transformed from a predominantly agricultural country into one of the most vibrant industrial economies in Europe. Today Ireland has a trade surplus in excess of IR£1.7 billion (equivalent to more than 7 percent of GNP), an overall balance of payment surplus of 2 percent of GNP, and an above average rate of GNP growth.

The consistency of government policies for industrial development has been a major contributor toward growth. Industrial policy consists of specific incentives and programs, infrastructure support, and wider economic measures. A corporate tax rate of 10 percent (guaranteed to the end of year 2010) is available to manufacturing and internationally traded service companies. The attractive climate for investment created by such measures has attracted a variety of companies from different sectors including information technology, engineering, health care and pharmaceutical products, consumer products, financial services, and telemarketing-based services. (See the following table.)

A strong, capable, competitive local supplier base in Ireland is also of great importance to the overseas firms. This involves not just the availability and quality of components, but also the physical proximity and ability to establish long-term partnership relationships. For instance, foreign companies operating locally spend about IR£1.3 billion annually on raw materials, components, and subassemblies sourced from local suppliers in the areas of electronics, engineering, food, and health care. A well-educated workforce is an additional advantage.

Ireland's membership in the European Economic Community (EEC) certainly has added value to locating in that country!

Some Overseas Companies in Ireland

From the United States	From the Far East	From Europe
Apple	Brother	Braun
Claris	Daiwa Bank	Cadbury-Schweppes
Chase Bank	Fujitsu	Deutsche Bank
Dell	Goldstar	Ericsson
Digital Equipment	Hitachi	Moulinex
Fruit of the Loom	Mitsubishi Trust	Nestlé
IBM	Mitsumi	Phillips
Intel	NEC	Sandoz
Merck	Saehan Media	Siemens
Microsoft	Sumitomo Bank	Unilever
Pratt & Whitney	Yamanouchi	
Thermoking		

Source: IDA Ireland advertisement, *Site Selection,* June 1993, p. 643.

government legislation and local government intervention to facilitate businesses locating in an area via subsidies, tax abatements, and other support are also factors. (See "The Quality Business Base in Europe" on the previous page.)

Total Costs   The objective is to select a site with the lowest total cost. This includes regional costs, inbound distribution costs, and outbound distribution costs. Land, construction, labor, taxes, and energy costs comprise the regional costs. In addition, there are hidden costs that are difficult to measure. These involve (1) excessive moving of preproduction material between locations before final delivery to the customers and (2) loss of customer responsiveness arising from locating away from the main customer base.

Infrastructure   Adequate road, rail, air, and sea transportation is vital. Energy and telecommunications requirements must also be met. In addition, the local government's willingness to invest in upgrading infrastructure to the levels required may be an incentive to select a specific location.

Quality of Labor   The educational and skill levels of the labor pool must match the company's needs. Even more important are the willingness and ability to learn.

Suppliers   A high-quality and competitive supplier base makes a given location suitable. The proximity of important suppliers' plants also supports lean production methods.

Other Facilities   The location of other plants or distribution centers of the same company may influence a new facility's location in the network. Issues of product mix and capacity are strongly interconnected to the location decision in this context.

Free Trade Zone

Free Trade Zones   A foreign trade zone or a **free trade zone** is typically a closed facility (under the supervision of the customs department) into which foreign goods can be brought without being subject to the necessary customs requirements. There are about 170 such free trade zones in the United States today. Such specialized locations also exist in other countries. Manufacturers in free trade zones can use imported components in the final product and delay payment of customs duties until the product is shipped into the host country.

Political Risk   The fast-changing geopolitical scenes in numerous nations present exciting, challenging opportunities. But the extended phase of transformation that many countries are undergoing makes the decision to locate in those areas extremely difficult. Political risks in both the country of location and the host country influence location decisions.

Government Barriers   Barriers to enter and locate in many countries are being removed today through legislation. Yet many nonlegislative and cultural barriers should be considered in location planning. (See "Toys 'R' Us in Japan.")

Trading Blocs

Trading Blocs   The world of **trading blocs** gained a new member with the ratification of the North American Free Trade Agreement (NAFTA). Such agreements influence location decisions, both within and outside trading bloc countries. Firms typically locate, or relocate, within a bloc to take advantage of new market

On December 20, 1991, Toys "R" Us—the world's largest toy retailer—opened its first retail store in Japan. What may now sound like an American success story in Japan traveled a difficult road for two years. The retailer had established locations in Canada, the United Kingdom, Germany, France, Singapore, Hong Kong, Malaysia, and Taiwan well before it attempted to enter the Japanese market.

In January 1990, Toys "R" Us formally applied to open its first (large) toy store in Niigata, Japan. This caused local toy retailers to proclaim their opposition by invoking provisions contained in the Large-Scale Retail Store Act. Then they organized a lobbying group to mobilize support against the American firm. Toys "R" Us appealed for help directly through the U.S. trade representative and other channels. Sustained American political pressure and widespread publicity finally forced MITI to confront the local lobby and limit to 18 months the application process under the restrictive retail law. It was April 1990, and Toys "R" Us had overcome its first major hurdle.

But there was another hurdle to cross. Toys "R" Us succeeds in large part by selling below suggested retail price. It accomplishes this mainly through exploiting economies it obtains through volume purchases. Anticipating the threat posed by that strategy to their own profit margins, Japanese toy manufacturers banded together and vowed not to sell their wares to Toys "R" Us. But Nintendo depends heavily on Toys "R" Us for the distribution of its products in the United States and other major markets. Nintendo's defection triggered an ultimate end to this boycott.

Private sector countermeasures consciously adopted by numerous major Japanese corporations are replacing the falling barriers to entry of public sector regulation.

Toys "R" Us in Japan

(http://www.tru.com)

Toys "R" Us has successfully entered the Japanese toy market through private sector help—in this case, with the help of Nintendo.

opportunities or lower total costs afforded by the trading agreement. Other companies (those outside the trading bloc countries) decide on locations within the bloc so as not to be disqualified from competing in the new market. Examples include the location of various Japanese auto manufacturing plants in Europe before 1992 as well as recent moves by many communications and financial services companies into Mexico in a post-NAFTA environment.

Environmental Regulation   The environmental regulations that impact a certain industry in a given location should be included in the location decision. Besides measurable cost implications, this influences the relationship with the local community.

Host Community   The host community's interest in having the plant in its midst is a necessary part of the evaluation process. Local educational facilities and the broader issue of quality of life are also important.

Competitive Advantage   An important decision for multinational companies is the nation in which to locate the home base for each distinct business. Porter suggests that a company can have different home bases for distinct businesses or segments. Competitive advantage is created at a home base where strategy is set, the core product and process technology are created, and a critical mass of production takes place. So a company should move its home base to a country that stimulates innovation and provides the best environment for global competitiveness.[1] This concept can also be applied to domestic companies seeking to gain sustainable competitive advantage. It partly explains the southeastern states' recent emergence as the preferred corporate destination within the United States (i.e., its business climate fosters innovation and low-cost production).

■ PLANT LOCATION METHODS

"If the boss likes Bakersfield, I like Bakersfield." Exhibit 9.1 summarizes the set of decisions that a company must make in choosing a plant location. While the exhibit implies a step-by-step process, virtually all activities listed take place simultaneously. As suggested by the preceding vote for Bakersfield, political decisions may occasionally override systematic analysis.

Evaluation of alternative regions, subregions, and communities is commonly termed *macro analysis*. Evaluation of specific sites in the selected community is termed *micro analysis*. Techniques used to support macro analyses include factor-rating systems, linear programming, and center of gravity. A detailed cost analysis would accompany each of these methods, and they must, of course, be related to business strategy. (See the box inserts on AM/PM stores on page 365 and Mercedes-Benz on page 366 for examples.)

Factor-Rating Systems

Factor-rating systems are perhaps the most widely used of the general location techniques because they provide a mechanism to combine diverse factors in an easy-to-understand format.

Factor-Rating Systems

---

[1] Michael E. Porter, "The Competitive Advantage of Nations," *Harvard Business Review*, March–April 1990, pp. 73–93.

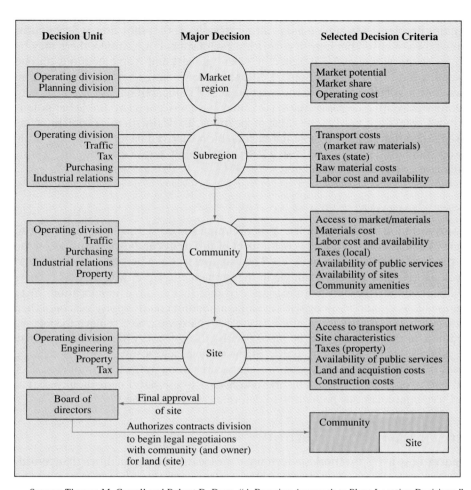

Exhibit 9.1

Plant Search:
Company XYZ

Source: Thomas M. Carroll and Robert D. Dean, "A Bayesian Approach to Plant-Location Decisions," *Decision Sciences* 11, no. 1 (January 1980), p. 87.

By way of example, a refinery assigned the following range of point values to major factors affecting a set of possible sites.

	Range
Fuels in region	0 to 330
Power availability and reliability	0 to 200
Labor climate	0 to 100
Living conditions	0 to 100
Transportation	0 to 50
Water supply	0 to 10
Climate	0 to 50
Supplies	0 to 60
Tax policies and laws	0 to 20

Each site was then rated against each factor, and a point value was selected from its assigned range. The sums of assigned points for each site were then compared. The site with the most points was selected.

A major problem with simple point-rating schemes is that they do not account for the wide range of costs that may occur within each factor. For example, there may be only a few hundred dollars' difference between the best and worst locations on one factor and several thousands of dollars' difference between the best and the worst on another. The first factor may have the most points available to it but provide little help in making the location decision; the second may have few points available but potentially show a real difference in the value of locations. To deal with this problem, it has been suggested that points possible for each factor be derived using a weighting scale based on standard deviations of costs rather than simply total cost amounts. In this way, relative costs can be considered.

Linear Programming

The transportation method of linear programming (discussed in the supplement to Chapter 7) can be used to test the cost impact of different candidate locations on the entire production-distribution network. The way it works can be seen by reference to the Puck and Pawn Company example in the supplement. Here, we might add a new row which contains the unit shipping costs from a factory in a new location, X, to warehouses E, F, G, and H, along with the total amount it could supply. We could then solve this particular matrix for minimum total cost. Next we would replace the factory located in X in the same row of the matrix with a factory at a different location, say Y, and again solve for minimum total cost. Assuming factories in X and Y would be identical in other important respects, the location resulting in the lowest total cost for the network would be selected. This method is easy to use but it does require that at least subregional locations be identified before a solution can be found.

Center of Gravity Method

Center of Gravity Method

The **center of gravity method** is a technique for locating single facilities that considers the existing facilities, the distances between them, and the volumes of goods to be shipped. The technique is often used to locate intermediate or distribution warehouses. In its simplest form, this method assumes that inbound and outbound transportation costs are equal, and it does not include special shipping costs for less than full loads.

The center of gravity method begins by placing the existing locations on a coordinate grid system. The choice of coordinate systems is entirely arbitrary. The purpose is to establish relative distances between locations. Using longitude and latitude coordinates might be helpful in international decisions. Exhibit 9.2 shows an example of a grid layout.

The center of gravity is found by calculating the X and Y coordinates that result in the minimal transportation cost. We use the formulas

$$C_x = \frac{\Sigma d_{ix} V_i}{\Sigma V_i} \tag{9.1}$$

$$C_y = \frac{\Sigma d_{iy} V_i}{\Sigma V_i}$$

where

C_x = X coordinate of the center of gravity
C_y = Y coordinate of the center of gravity
d_{ix} = X coordinate of the ith location

d_{iy} = Y coordinate of the *i*th location

V_i = Volume of goods moved to or from the *i*th location

■ **example 9.1**   *HiOctane Refining Company*   The HiOctane Refining Company needs to locate an intermediate holding facility between its refining plant in Long Beach and its major distributors. Exhibit 9.2 shows the coordinate map. The amount of gasoline shipped to or from the plant and distributors appears in Exhibit 9.3.

In this example, for the Long Beach location (the first location) d_{1x} = 325, d_{1y} = 75, and V_1 = 1,500.

solution   Using the information in Exhibits 9.2 and 9.3, we can calculate the coordinates of the center of gravity:

$$C_x = \frac{(325 \times 1,500) + (400 \times 250) + (450 \times 450) + (350 \times 350) + (25 \times 450)}{1,500 + 250 + 450 + 350 + 450}$$

$$= \frac{923,750}{3,000} = 307.9$$

$$C_y = \frac{(75 \times 1,500) + (150 \times 250) + (350 \times 450) + (400 \times 350) + (450 \times 450)}{1,500 + 250 + 450 + 350 + 450}$$

$$= \frac{650,000}{3,000} = 216.7$$

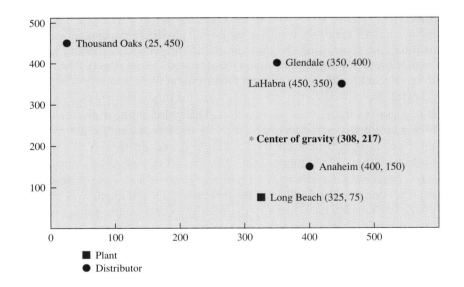

Exhibit 9.2

Grid Map for Center of Gravity Example

Locations	Gallons of Gasoline per Month (000,000)
Long Beach	1,500
Anaheim	250
LaHabra	450
Glendale	350
Thousand Oaks	450

Exhibit 9.3

Shipping Volumes, Center of Gravity Example

This gives management the *X* and *Y* coordinates of approximately 308 and 217, respectively and provides an initial starting point to search for a new site. By examining the location of the calculated center of gravity on the grid map, we can see that it might be more cost-efficient to ship directly between the Long Beach plant and the Anaheim distributor than to ship via a warehouse near the center of gravity. Before a location decision is made, management would probably recalculate the center of gravity, changing the data to reflect this (i.e., decrease the gallons shipped from Long Beach by the amount Anaheim needs and remove Anaheim from the formula). ■

Analytic Delphi Model

Typical location analyses consider single-facility locations and are based on criteria such as minimizing travel time or distance between demand and supply points, minimization of the cost function, or minimizing the average response time. But multiple facilities and varied objectives have subsequently been added to this problem scenario. Some decision criteria are based on intangible—even emotional—issues. One approach to address the more complex location decision is by using the **Analytic Delphi Model** that incorporates tangible and intangible factors into the decision-making process.[2] The Analytic Delphi Method involves using a combination of three teams: a coordinating team, the forecasting team, and a strategic team. Each of these teams take on different roles in the decision-making process. The following are the steps involved in executing the method.

Step I   *Form two Delphi panels.* An in-house or outside consultant team acts as coordinator to design questionnaires and conduct the Delphi inquiries. This team then selects two panels from within the organization to participate in two Delphi inquiries—one to forecast the trends in social and physical environments affecting the organization (the forecasting Delphi panel), and the second to identify the strategic goals and priorities of the organization (the strategic Delphi panel). This latter panel should be selected from among the top management of each division/department in the organization, as well as the managers from all functional areas.

Step II   *Identify threats and opportunities.* The coordinating team, through several rounds of questionnaires and feedback, asks for the forecasting Delphi panel to identify major trends, opportunities in the marketplace, and any threats against which the organization must guard. As much as possible, this process should obtain a consensus.

Step III   *Determine direction(s) and strategic goals of the organization.* The coordinating team conveys the findings of the forecasting Delphi inquiry (as above) to the strategic Delphi panel, which then uses them in the second Delphi inquiry to determine the organization's direction and strategic goals.

Step IV   *Develop alternative(s).* Once the strategic Delphi panel establishes the long-term goals, it should focus its attention on developing various alternatives. (The alternatives as applied to location selection should be expansion and/or contraction of the existing plant(s) facilities, and/or developing alternative locations for some parts or the entire organization).

Step V   *Prioritize the alternative(s).* The set of alternatives developed in Step IV should be presented to the participants of the strategic Delphi panel to obtain their

[2] Hossein Azani and Reza Khorramshahgol, *Engineering Costs & Production Economics* 20, no. 1 (July 1990), pp. 23–28.

subjective value judgments. If the value judgments are complex, it is possible to use the Analytic Hierarchy Process described in Chapter 12 to quantitatively evaluate the value judgments.

This systematic approach identifies trends, developments, and opportunities, while considering the organization's strengths and weaknesses. Additionally, the approach brings the firm's strategic goals and objectives into this important decision process. This approach is typical of the integrative, team-based approach that is being used by companies today.

LOCATING SERVICE FACILITIES

Because of the variety of service firms and the relatively low cost of establishing a service facility compared to one for manufacturing, new service facilities are far more common than new factories and warehouses. Indeed, there are few communities in which rapid population growth has not been paralleled by concurrent rapid growth in retail outlets, restaurants, municipal services, and entertainment facilities.

Services typically have multiple sites to maintain close contact with customers. The location decision is closely tied to the market selection decision. If the target market is college-age groups, locations in retirement communities—despite desirability in terms of cost, resource availability, and so forth—are not viable alternatives. Market needs also affect the number of sites to be built, the size, and the characteristics of the sites. Whereas manufacturing location decisions are often made by minimizing costs, many service location decision techniques maximize the profit potential of various sites. Below we present two examples of analytical approaches that can be used to help select good sites. The first employs regression modeling; the second involves a simple heuristic procedure.

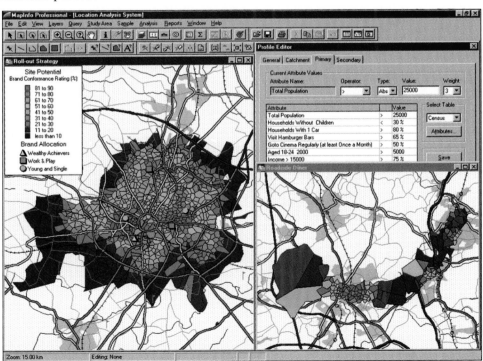

Geographic Information Systems (GIS), shown here from MapInfo, are used by retailers, financial services groups, and others in the site selection process. Mapping information on potential sites such as demographics, competitors, etc., allows information to be seen in a single, comprehensive view for more informed decision making.

■ **example** 9.2 *Screening Location Sites at La Quinta Motor Inns* Selecting good sites is crucial to a hotel chain's success. Of the four major marketing considerations (price, product, promotion, and location), location and product have been shown to be most important for multisite firms. As a result, hotel chain owners who can pick good sites quickly have a distinct competitive advantage.

Exhibit 9.4 shows the initial list of variables included in a study to help La Quinta Motor Inns screen potential locations for its new hotels.[3] Data were collected on 57 existing La Quinta Inns. Analysis of the data identified the variables that correlated with operating profit in 1983 and 1986. (See Exhibit 9.5.)

Exhibit 9.4 Independent Variables Collected for the Initial Model Building Stage

Category	Name	Description
Competitive	INNRATE	Inn price
	PRICE	Room rate for the inn
	RATE	Average competitive room rate
	RMS1	Hotel rooms within 1 mile
	RMSTOTAL	Hotel rooms within 3 miles
	ROOMSINN	Inn rooms
Demand generators	CIVILIAN	Civilian personnel on base
	COLLEGE	College enrollment
	HOSP1	Hospital beds within 1 mile
	HOSPTOTL	Hospital beds within 4 miles
	HVYIND	Heavy industrial employment
	LGTIND	Light industrial acreage
	MALLS	Shopping mall square footage
	MILBLKD	Military base blocked
	MILITARY	Military personnel
	MILTOT	MILITARY + CIVILIAN
	OFC1	Office space within 1 mile
	OFCTOTAL	Office space within 4 miles
	OFCCBD	Office space in Central Business District
	PASSENGR	Airport passengers enplaned
	RETAIL	Scale ranking of retail activity
	TOURISTS	Annual tourists
	TRAFFIC	Traffic count
	VAN	Airport van
Demographic	EMPLYPCT	Unemployment percentage
	INCOME	Average family income
	POPULACE	Residential population
Market awareness	AGE	Years inn has been open
	NEAREST	Distance to nearest inn
	STATE	State population per inn
	URBAN	Urban population per inn
Physical	ACCESS	Accessibility
	ARTERY	Major traffic artery
	DISTCBD	Distance to downtown
	SIGNVIS	Sign visibility

Exhibit 9.5 A Summary of the Variables That Correlated with Operating Margin in 1983 and 1986

Variable	1983	1986
ACCESS	.20	
AGE	.29	.49
COLLEGE		.25
DISTCBD		−.22
EMPLYPCT	−.22	−.22
INCOME		−.23
MILTOT		.22
NEAREST	−.51	
OFCCBD	.30	
POPULACE	.30	.35
PRICE	.38	.58
RATE		.27
STATE	−.32	−.33
SIGNVIS	.25	
TRAFFIC	.32	
URBAN	−.22	−.26

[3] Sheryl E. Kimes and James A. Fitzsimmons, "Selecting Profitable Hotel Sites at La Quinta Motor Inns," *Interfaces* 20 (March–April 1990), pp. 12–20.

solution   A **regression model** was constructed. Its final form was

$$\text{Profitability} = 39.05 - 5.41 \times \text{State population per inn } (1,000)$$
$$+ 5.86 \times \text{Price of the inn}$$
$$- 3.91 \times \text{Square root of the median income}$$
$$\text{of the area } (1,000)$$
$$+ 1.75 \times \text{College students within four miles}$$

The model shows that profitability is affected by market penetration, positively affected by price, negatively affected by higher incomes (the inns do better in lower-median-income areas), and positively affected by colleges nearby.

La Quinta implemented the model on a spreadsheet and routinely uses the spreadsheet to screen potential real estate acquisitions. The founder and president of La Quinta has accepted the model's validity and no longer feels obligated to personally select the sites.

This example shows that a specific model can be obtained from the requirements of service organizations and used to identify the most important features in site selection. ■

A common problem encountered by service-providing organizations is deciding how many service outlets to establish within a geographic area, and where. The problem is complicated by the many possible locations and several options in the absolute number of service centers. Thus, attempting to find a good solution, much less an optimal one, can be extremely time consuming even for a relatively small problem. For example, there would be 243 possible solutions for a problem involving choosing among one, two, or three retail outlets to serve four geographically dispersed customer populations, even where there are only three possible locations for the outlets. To illustrate one approach to searching for feasible solutions to such problems, we apply, to a sample problem, the **Ardalan heuristic method** described by Alireza Ardalan.[4]

■ example 9.3   *Locating Two Medical Clinics Using the Ardalan Heuristic*
Suppose that a medical consortium wishes to establish two clinics to provide medical care for people living in four communities in Off Tackle County, Ohio. Assume that the sites under study are in each community and that the population of each community is evenly distributed within the community's boundaries. Further, assume that the potential use of the clinics by members of the various communities has been determined and weighting factors reflecting the relative importance of serving members of the population of each community have been developed. (This information appears in Exhibit 9.6.) The objective of the problem is to find the two clinics that can serve all communities at the lowest weighted travel-distance cost.

From Community	Miles to Clinic				Population of Community (Thousands)	Relative Weighting of Population
	A	**B**	**C**	**D**		
A	0	11	8	12	10	1.1
B	11	0	10	7	8	1.4
C	8	10	0	9	20	0.7
D	9.5	7	9	0	12	1.0

Exhibit 9.6

Distances, Population, and Relative Weights

[4] Alireza Ardalan, "An Efficient Heuristic for Service Facility Location," *Proceedings, Northeast Decision Sciences Institute Conference,* 1984, pp. 181–82.

Weighted Population
Distances

From Community	To Clinic			
	A	**B**	**C**	**D**
A	0	121	88	132
B	123.2	0	112	78.4
C	112	140	0	126
D	114	84	108	0

solution   *Step 1.* Construct a weighted population-distance table from the initial data table, multiplying distance times the population times the relative weighting factor (Exhibit 9.7). For example, Community A to Clinic B is $11 \times 1.1 \times 10 = 121$.

Step 2. Add the amounts in each column. Choose the community with the lowest cost and locate a facility there (Community C in our example). (Recall that costs are expressed in weighted population-distance units.)

From Community	To Clinic Located in Community			
	A	**B**	**C**	**D**
A	0	121	88	132
B	123.2	0	112	78.4
C	112	140	0	126
D	114	84	108	0
	349.2	345	308	336.4

Step 3. For each row, compare the cost of each column entry to the community clinics already located. If the cost is less, do not change them. If the cost is greater, reduce the cost to the lowest of the sites already selected.

From Community	To Clinic Located in Community			
	A	**B**	**C**	**D**
A	0	88	88	88
B	112	0	112	78.4
C	0	0	0	0
D	108	84	108	0
	220	172	308	166.4

Step 4. If additional locations are desired, choose the community with the lowest cost from those not already selected (Community D in our example).

Step 5. Repeat Step 3, reducing each row entry that exceeds the entry in the column just selected.

From Community	To Clinic Located in Community		
	A	**B**	**D**
A	0	88	88
B	78.4	0	78.4
C	0	0	0
D	0	0	0
	78.4	88	166.4

AM/PM convenience stores are a subsidiary of the ARCO Corporation. These stores are usually connected with service stations. The goals of AM/PM International are to leverage the existing AM/PM program through brand licensing agreements in foreign countries and joint venture participation. Furthermore, ARCO wants to participate aggressively in emerging international markets and leverage its international presence. ARCO also wants to generate additional long-term profits.

To select a new potential country, AM/PM International looks at four main criteria:

1. The population should be over 1 million in a targeted city.
2. Annual per capita income should be over $2,000.
3. The political system should be fairly stable.
4. The host country should have minimal restrictions on hard currency repatriation.

Once AM/PM has selected a potential country for its business, it evaluates the country's

1. Stage of industrial development.

2. People/car ratio. (This is important because the AM/PM stores are located in service stations.)
3. Population density in rural and urban areas.
4. Availability and cost of labor.
5. Infrastructure (supply and distribution, equipment availability, real estate cost, and reliability of utilities).
6. Tax regulations.
7. Legal issues.

AM/PM International uses franchising as a rapid and convenient way to expand in the Pacific Rim, Europe, and North America. The company's prospect list for the next expansion includes Italy, France, Denmark, Mexico, Brazil, Malaysia, and Canada.

AM/PM's International expansion strategy is based on three points:

1. Use the existing service-station staff to run the convenience store.
2. For the first year an American-trained manager works closely with the new licensee.
3. Develop new stores in selected countries as quickly as possible.

Source: ARCO presentation to University of Southern California MBA Students, June 5, 1991.

Continue repeating Steps 4 and 5 until the desired number of locations is selected. If we wished to compute the complete list, it would be:

	To Clinic Located in Community	
From Community	**A**	**B**
A	0	0
B	78.4	0
C	0	0
D	0	0
	78.4	0

BREAKTHROUGH

Mercedes-Benz Parks in Vance, Alabama

Mercedes has always pursued automotive excellence with little regard to costs. But it now has a 30 percent cost disadvantage against Japanese and U.S. competitors, and has seen its share of the luxury market slip since the late 1980s. As a key element in reinventing itself, Mercedes decided to go ahead with its luxury sports-utility vehicle project. The Multi-Purpose Vehicle (MPV), as the vehicle is known, is aimed mainly at the United States because it is the world's largest market for this type of automobile. Andreas Renschler, the relatively new deputy to Chairman Helmut Werner, was named to head the project and was given a bold brief: Find a site outside Germany for the project. A worldwide selection process began in January 1993.

In April 1993, Mercedes announced that it would locate the MPV plant in the United States. Studies showed that combined costs of labor, shipping, and components would be lowest there. Mercedes considered more than 100 sites in 35 states before narrowing the search in August 1993 to Alabama, North Carolina, and South Carolina. One of the main criteria was transportation costs because Mercedes expects to export about half the vehicles produced. The U.S. site will be the only production facility for the MPV.

In September 1993, the Mercedes-Benz board approved the project team's selection of Vance, Alabama, for the $300 million, 1,500-employee, 65,000-vehicles-per-year manufacturing plant. Vance is located along Interstate 20/59 between Tuscaloosa and Birmingham, Alabama. State officials have even offered to rename a section of I-20/59 the Mercedes-Benz Autobahn.

According to Mercedes, the state's probusiness climate was significant to the site selection process. Other selection criteria included

- Access to interstate highways.
- Access to railroads and ports.
- Adequate available labor.
- A lucrative package of financial incentives and tax breaks. ■

The problem has now been solved for all four possible locations. Choose C first, then D, then A, then B.

The logic in this procedure is as follows:

1. We select the least total cost column since this column location represents the lowest travel cost of all communities traveling to that location.

2. Once a location is chosen, no rational member of a community would travel to any other community that was more costly. In Step 2, for example, Community A residents would certainly prefer going to a clinic located in Community C (88), which has already been decided on, than to B (121) or D (132). Therefore, the maximum number of weighted population-distance units that residents of A would be willing to pay is 88, and we can use this amount as our top limit. If a clinic is located in A, however, residents of A would patronize their own community clinic (at a cost of 0). Residents in Community B would prefer C (112) to A (123.2) but not to B (0) or D (78.4). Therefore, the cost 123.2 is reduced to 112, but 0 and 78.4 remain unchanged.

3. Once a community location is selected and the matrix costs are adjusted, that community can be dropped from the matrix because the column costs are no longer relevant. ■

- Proximity to schools and universities in Tuscaloosa and Birmingham.
- The quality of life.

Alabama's incentive package totaled about $253 million, more than twice what South Carolina gave BMW in 1992. Alabama's package included

- $92.2 million to buy and build the 966-acre site, create a foreign trade zone, and build an employee training center.
- $77.5 million to extend water, gas, and sewer lines to the site and provide other infrastructure.
- $60 million to train Mercedes employees, suppliers, and workers in related industries.
- $15 million from private business.
- $8.7 million in sales/use tax abatements on machinery, equipment, and construction material.

Studies show that this money is well spent. The plant's economic impact is estimated at $365 million for the first year and $7.3 billion over 20 years.

The three finalists in the site selection process were in a dead heat when it came to business climate, education levels, and transportation. Long-term operating costs at all three locations were approximately equal, despite slight differences in incentive packages. Right-to-work laws and low unionization were not factors in the decision-making process. The deciding factor was Alabama's dedication to the project. One final factor did not hurt: The wooded, rolling hills around the site reminded the Germans of the Swabian countryside near Stuttgart, home of their headquarters.

Construction of the facility began in spring 1994, with vehicle production to start in January 1997.

Sources: David Woodruff and John Templeman, "Why Mercedes Is Alabama Bound," *Business Week,* October 11, 1993, pp. 138–39; Tim Venable, "Mercedes-Benz Parks $300 Million Plant in Alabama," *Site Selection,* December 1993, p. 1292; Bill Vlasic, "In Alabama, the Soul of a New Mercedes?" *Business Week,* March 31, 1997, pp. 70–71.

■ CONCLUSION

Facility location decisions are a key element in any firm's overall strategic plan. Dramatic changes in the global geopolitical environment, coupled with rapid advances in technology, have provided decision makers with a variety of options and opportunities for locating their businesses. The criteria for selecting appropriate locations have also evolved beyond the singular focus of minimizing cost or distance. Today, a number of quantitative and qualitative issues impact location decisions. A company's long-term success depends on its managers' ability to make a comprehensive synthesis of the various dimensions of the multifaceted location problem.

FORMULA REVIEW

Center of gravity

$$C_x = \frac{\Sigma d_{ix} V_i}{\Sigma V_i}$$

$$C_y = \frac{\Sigma d_{iy} V_i}{\Sigma V_i}$$

$$(9.1)$$

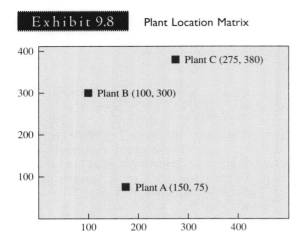

Exhibit 9.8   Plant Location Matrix

Plant C (275, 380)	
Plant B (100, 300)	
Plant A (150, 75)	

Exhibit 9.9   Quantity of Compressors Required by Each Plant

Plant	Compressors Required per Year
A	6,000
B	8,200
C	7,000

SOLVED PROBLEM

SOLVED PROBLEM 1

Cool Air, a manufacturer of automotive air conditioners, currently produces its XB-300 line at three different locations: Plant A, Plant B, and Plant C. Recently management decided to build all compressors, a major product component, in a separate dedicated facility, Plant D.

Using the center of gravity method and the information displayed in Exhibits 9.8 and 9.9, determine the best location for Plant D. Assume a linear relationship between volumes shipped and shipping costs (no premium charges).

Solution

$$d_{1x} = 150 \qquad d_{1y} = 75 \qquad V_1 = 6{,}000$$
$$d_{2x} = 100 \qquad d_{2y} = 300 \qquad V_2 = 8{,}200$$
$$d_{3x} = 275 \qquad d_{3y} = 380 \qquad V_3 = 7{,}000$$

$$C_x = \frac{\Sigma d_{ix} V_i}{\Sigma V_i} = \frac{(150 \times 6{,}000) + (100 \times 8{,}200) + (275 \times 7{,}000)}{6{,}000 + 8{,}200 + 7{,}000} = 172$$

$$C_y = \frac{\Sigma d_{iy} V_i}{\Sigma V_i} = \frac{(75 \times 6{,}000) + (300 \times 8{,}200) + (380 \times 7{,}000)}{21{,}200} = 262.7$$

Plant D$[C_x, C_y]$ = D[172, 263]

REVIEW AND DISCUSSION QUESTIONS

1. What motivations typically cause firms to initiate a facilities location or relocation project?
2. List five major reasons why a new electronic components manufacturing firm should move into your city or town.
3. How do facilities location decisions differ for service facilities and manufacturing plants?
4. What are the pros and cons of relocating a small or midsized manufacturing firm (that makes mature products) from the United States to Mexico in the post-NAFTA environment?
5. If you could locate your new software development company anywhere in the world, which place would you choose, and why?

PROBLEMS

✓   **1.** Refer to the information given in the Solved Problem. Suppose management decides to shift 2,000 units of production from Plant B to Plant A. Does this change the proposed location of Plant D, the compressor production facility? If so, where should Plant D be located?

✓   **2.** A drugstore chain plans to open four stores in a medium-sized city. However, funds are limited, so only two can be opened this year.
   a. Given the following matrix showing the weighted population distance costs for each of the four areas and four store sites, select the two to be opened up first.
   b. If additional funds become available, which store should be the third to open?

1. $C_x = 176.7$
   $C_y = 241.5$

2. *a.* Store #2 first, Store
      #3 second
   b. Store #4 third.

		\multicolumn{4}{c}{Store}
		1	2	3	4
Geographic Area	1	0	20	160	60
	2	80	0	40	80
	3	120	80	0	100
	4	80	100	60	0

3. A firm is considering four possible office locations within a particular city. The firm would like to have an office in each location eventually, but at present, its managers would like to open just one. They want to know the sequence in which they should open all four offices. The accompanying matrix shows costs for opening each office in each area. Determine the order in which they should be opened.

3. B, D, A, C.

		\multicolumn{4}{c}{Office}
		A	B	C	D
Geographic Area	A	0	34	40	30
	B	24	0	36	54
	C	60	20	0	36
	D	50	40	60	0

4. A small manufacturing facility is being planned that will feed parts to three heavy manufacturing facilities. The location of the current plants with their coordinates and volume requirements is given in the following table.

4. $C_x = 374$.
   $C_y = 357$.

Plant Location	Coordinates (X, Y)	Volume (Parts per Year)
Peoria	300, 320	4,000
Decatur	375, 470	6,000
Joliet	470, 180	3,000

Use the center of gravity method to determine the best location for this new facility.

Case

Is It Russian Roulette?

Dramatic changes in the former Soviet Union have turned business conditions there into a roller-coaster ride. The unstable situation has created a great deal of uncertainty for firms that look at this part of the world as a market for goods and services. Yet the size of the market and the potential for international expansion remain tempting. Russia, with all its uncertainties, remains the most popular destination among the Commonwealth of Independent States (CIS).

Exhibit C9.1 shows the risks of doing business in the former USSR based on responses to a 1992 survey of U.S.-based businesses.

"Only put in what you can afford to lose. Decide up front what you want—profits, market share, and the like," advises Erich Zarnfaller, senior international treasury analyst at EG&G, Inc., a Wellesley, Massachusetts–based provider of environmental management services and manufacturer of radiation and security devices. Adds Kathy Creculius, a vice president at BayBank in Boston, "The former USSR presents . . . great risks. However, for those with ethnic and linguistic ties to the CIS countries, with solid business experience and capital to invest—and risk—there are now opportunities." A recent survey of CFOs of leading companies also echoes such sentiments of risk.

Also, most firms view host governments as being neutral toward U.S. firms. Some firms even found them to be a barrier to doing business. The following incidents are reported by Intertech International Corporation, a Boston-based firm whose Austrian subsidiary was involved in a joint venture to install air-conditioning systems in new buildings in the Republic of Georgia. The Soviet embassy in Washington, DC, said a letter from the Soviet partner was not sufficient to provide work and travel visas. But the Soviet embassy in Vienna, home of Intertech's joint venture partner, did agree to provide visas based on the same letter. Furthermore, in an attempt to send cargo by air freight to the Black Sea via Moscow, Intertech lost six precious weeks waiting for bureaucrats in Moscow to "find" the shipment. In that time, the goods could have been delivered by ocean freight to Odessa or air freight to Vienna and trucked to the site. Such are the remnants of an incredibly complex web of bureaucracy left in the aftermath of decentralized control in the Soviet Union!

Yet the majority of firms surveyed—including manufacturing, service, and sales and distribution companies—plan to either maintain or expand current levels of investment in their existing activities.

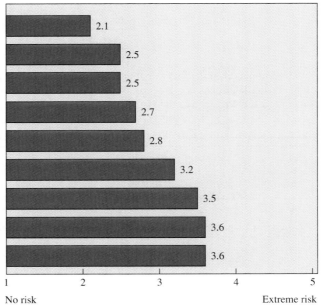

Exhibit C9.1

Risk Faced by Western Businesses

Risk	Rating
Corruption and bribery	2.1
Workforce issues	2.5
Difficulty repatriating profits	2.5
Lack of suitably experienced partners	2.7
Undeveloped financial markets and institutions	2.8
Difficulty obtaining supplies and raw materials	3.2
Lack of laws governing and protecting business interests	3.5
Lack of infrastructure	3.6
Political instability	3.6

Scale: 1 (No risk) to 5 (Extreme risk)

Questions

1. Discuss advantages and disadvantages of facility location analysis in the old Soviet Union with reference to the typical location selection criteria.
2. Discuss the issues involved in locating a specific company in Russia.

Source: Daniel J. McCarthy, Sheila M. Puffer, and Peter J. Simmonds, "Riding the Russian Roller Coaster: U.S. Firms' Recent Experience and Future Plans in the Former USSR," *California Management Review,* Fall 1993, pp. 99–115. © 1993 Regents of the University of California. Reprinted from the *California Management Review,* Vol. 36, No. 1. By permission of The Regents.

Case

The Plant Location Puzzle*

Ann Reardon made her way across the crowded tradeshow floor, deep in thought and oblivious to the noisy activity all around her. As CEO of the Eldora Company (EDC) for the previous 13 years, she had led her organization through a period of extraordinary success. While larger bicycle makers had moved their manufacturing operations overseas to take advantage of lower labor costs, Eldora had stuck with a domestic manufacturing strategy, keeping its plant on the same campus as its corporate offices in Boulder, Colorado. Ann felt that her strategy of keeping all the parts of the company in the same location, while unconventional, had contributed greatly to cooperation among various departments and, ultimately, to the company's growth: EDC had become the largest and most profitable bicycle company in the United States. Yet her manufacturing vice president, Sean Andrews, was now urging her to build a plant in China.

"Look at the number of companies here," he had said that morning, as they helped several other EDC staffers stack brochures on the exhibit table and position the company's latest models around the perimeter of their area. Manufacturing heads rarely attended trade shows; in fact, this was Sean's first, but he had wanted to attend, and Ann had supported his interest. "There are too many players in this market," he had said. "I've been saying this for two months now, and you know the forecasters' numbers back me up. But if they weren't enough to convince you, just look around. The industry is reaching the saturation point here in the States. We have to break into Asia."

"Leave it alone, Sean," Ann had replied. "I know this is something you're pushing; you've said so in the past. But let's set up a time to talk about it in detail later. This isn't the time or the place."

Now, three hours later, with the show in full swing, Ann understood why Sean had been compelled to speak up again. Having all their competitors in the same room at the same time was a powerful visual reminder of how the industry had changed. She thought about what Sean had said about the U.S. market. In 1992, EDC's sales and earnings had hit record levels. The company now produced almost 30% of the bicycles sold in the United States. U.S. mass-market bicycle sales were growing by only 2 percent per year, while the Asian market for those same bikes was nearly doubling on an annual basis. And Eldora could not competitively serve those markets from its U.S. manufacturing facility. Two of the largest bike manufacturers in the world, located in rapidly growing Asian markets, enjoyed a significant labor and distribution cost advantage.

She stopped at a mountain bike display set up by a fast-growing, young bike company. Mountain bikes with front suspension were the latest trend—the added support and cushion allowed riders to better absorb the shocks inherent in off-road riding without slowing down or losing balance. Most of these bikes were still prohibitively expensive. But Eldora, too, had an entry in this product category, retailing for about $190, and Ann was proud of it. For years, the company had concentrated its efforts on inexpensive bicycles, which retailed through mass merchandisers for between $100 and $200. Eldora's prices were slightly higher than other low-end competitors, but large retailers were willing to pay the premium because EDC had consistently been able to offer many state-of-the-art styles and features with quick, timely deliveries that competitors building overseas couldn't match.

One of the reasons the company had been so successful was that Boulder, Colorado, was a bicyclists' mecca. Eldora employees at all levels shared a genuine love of bicycling and eagerly pursued knowledge of the industry's latest trends and styles. Someone was always suggesting a better way to position the hand brakes, or a new toe grip that allowed for better traction and easier dismounts. And Eldora never had a shortage of people willing to test out the latest prototypes.

Another reason was that all marketing staff, engineers, designers, and manufacturing personnel worked on one campus, within a 10-minute walk of one another. Ann had bet big on that strategy, and it had paid

* This is a broad top-management–oriented strategy case designed to elicit debate.

off. Communication was easy, and changes in styles, production plans, and the like could be made quickly and efficiently. Mountain bikes, for example, had gone from 0 percent to more than 50 percent of the market volume since 1988, and Eldora had met the increased demand with ease. And when orders for cross-bikes—a mountain/road bike hybrid that had enjoyed a spurt of popularity—began to fall off, Eldora had been able to adjust its production run with minimal disruption.

EDC had also benefited from its foray into the high-end market (bicycles retailing for between $400 and $700) 12 years earlier. One of Ann's first moves as CEO had been to enter into a joint venture with Rinaldi, a high-end Italian bicycle manufacturer that at the time was specializing in racing models. As part of the agreement, EDC had begun importing Rinaldi bikes under the brand name Summit and selling them through specialty bike dealers. Similarly, Rinaldi had begun marketing EDC bikes in Europe. That arrangement had had lasting rewards: although racing bikes were no longer very popular, EDC's offerings had taken off. About 20 percent of EDC's sales were now made outside the United States (primarily in Europe and Canada) through this and other agreements.

The relationships with Rinaldi and the specialty bike shops also helped keep EDC management aware of the latest industry trends over the years. Most recently, those trends had included a move toward more exotic frame materials like aluminum and carbon fiber and more advanced components, including the new front-fork suspension systems. Ann examined another rival's brochure touting a soon-to-be-released high-end model with these advances. EDC engineers were clearly ahead of the curve.

Her satisfaction was quickly tempered with thoughts of foreign sales performance. Between 1987 and 1991, EDC's foreign sales had grown at an annual rate of over 80 percent. But during the previous two years they had been flat.

Sean appeared at Ann's side, jolting her out of her thoughts and into the reality of her surroundings. "Dale just finished up the first round of retailers' meetings," he said. "We'd like to get some lunch back over at the hotel and talk about our options." Dale Stewart was Eldora's marketing vice president. His views of what was best for the company often differed from Sean's, but the two had an amiable working relationship and enjoyed frequent spirited verbal sparring matches.

"You won't let this go, will you," Ann said, throwing up her hands in a gesture of surrender. "Fine, let's talk. But you know I won't make a decision until we've had a more formal round of discussions back in Boulder next month."

Over sandwiches, Sean made his case. "Our primary markets in North America and western Europe represent less than a quarter of the worldwide demand. Of the 200 million bicycles made in the world last year, 40 million were sold in China, 30 million in India, and 9 million in Japan. Historically, bikes sold in Asia's developing markets were low-end products used as primary modes of transportation. But the economic picture is changing fast. There's a growing middle class. Suddenly people have disposable income. Many consumers there are now seeking higher quality and trendier styles. Mountain bikes with suspension are in. And cross-bikes are still holding their own. In fact, the demand in these markets for the product categories we produce has been doubling annually, and the growth rates seem sustainable.

"If we're going to compete in Asia, though, we need a local plant. My staff has evaluated many locations there. We've looked at wage rates, proximity to markets, and materials costs, and we feel that China is our best bet. We'd like to open a plant there as soon as possible, and start building our position."

Dale jumped in. "Two of our largest competitors, one from China, one from Taiwan, have been filling the demand so far," he said. "In 1990, 97 percent of the volume produced by these companies was for export. In 1994, they are projecting that 45 percent of their production will be for local markets. We can't compete with them from here. About 20% of our product cost is labor, and the hourly wages of the manufacturing workforce in these countries are between 5 percent and 15 percent of ours. It also costs us an additional 20 percent in transportation and duties to get our bicycles to these markets."

He glanced at Sean quickly and continued. "But here's where I disagree with Sean. I think we need a short-term solution. These companies have a big lead on us, and the more I think about it, the more I believe we need to put a direct sales operation in Asia first."

"Dale, you're crazy," Sean said, pouring himself some ice water from the pitcher on the table. "What good would an Asian sales operation do without a manufacturing plant? I know we source components in Asia now, but we could save another 10 percent of those parts if we were located there. Then we would really be bringing Eldora to Asia. If we want to compete there, we have to play from our greatest strength—quality. If we did it your way, you wouldn't be selling Eldora bikes. You'd just be selling some product with our label on it. You wouldn't get the quality. You wouldn't build the same kind of reputation we have here. It wouldn't really be Eldora. Over the long term, it couldn't work."

"We're building bicycles, not rocket ships," Dale countered. "There are lots of companies in Asia that could provide us with a product very quickly if we gave them our designs and helped them with their production process. We could outsource production in the short term, until we made more permanent arrangements." He turned to Ann. "We could even outsource the product permanently, despite what Sean says. What do we know about building and running a plant in China? All I know is we're losing potential share even as we sit here. The trading companies aren't giving our products the attention they deserve, and they also aren't giving us the information we need on the features that consumers in these markets want. A sales operation would help us learn the market even as we're entering it. Setting up a plant first would take too long. We need to be over there now, and opening a sales operation is the quickest way."

Ann cut in. "Dale has a good point, Sean," she said. "We've been successful here in large part because our entire operation is in Boulder, on one site. We've had complete control over our own flexible manufacturing operation, and that's been a key factor in our ability to meet rapid change in the local market. How would we address the challenges inherent in manufacturing in a facility halfway around the world? Would you consider moving there? And for how long?

"Also, think about our other options. If the biggest issue keeping us out of these markets right now is cost, then both of you are ignoring a few obvious alternatives. Right now, only our frame-building operation is automated. We could cut labor costs significantly by automating more processes. And why are you so bent on China? Frankly, when I was there last month touring facilities, a lot of what I saw worried me. You know, that day I was supposed to tour a production facility, there was a power failure. Judging by the reactions of the personnel in the plant the next day, these outages are common. The roads to the facility are in very poor condition. And wastewater and cleaning solvents are regularly dumped untreated into the waterways. We could operate differently if we located there, but what impact would that have on costs?

"Taiwan has a better developed infrastructure than China. What about making that our Asian base? And I've heard that Singapore offers attractive tax arrangements to new manufacturing operations. Then there's Mexico. It's closer to home, and aside from

distribution costs, the wage rates are similar to Asia's and many of the other risks would be minimized. You both feel strongly about this, I know, but this isn't a decision we can make based on enthusiasm." Ann crumpled up her sandwich wrapper and drank the last of her soda. "Let's get back over to the exhibits. I'm attending the IT seminar at 1:30. We'll schedule a formal meeting on this subject soon. I was going to say next month, but how about bumping it up two weeks?"

Walking back to the convention center with Dale and Sean, Ann realized that she wasn't just frustrated because she didn't know which course EDC should pursue. She was concerned that she really didn't know which aspects of the decision were important and which were irrelevant. Should she establish a division in China? If so, which functions should she start with? Manufacturing? Marketing? And what about engineering? Or should she consider a different location? Would China's low labor costs offset problems caused by a poor infrastructure?

Growth had always been vitally important to Eldora, both in creating value to shareholders and in providing a work environment that could attract and retain the most talented people. Now it appeared that Ann would have to choose between continued growth and a domestic-only manufacturing strategy that had served her well. Ann knew the plant location decision she had made years earlier had been critical to the company's success, and she felt the company's next move would be just as crucial.

Questions

1. What is the competitive environment facing EDC?

2. What are EDC's strengths in manufacturing?

3. Should EDC establish a manufacturing division in Asia?

4. What plan of action would you recommend to Ann Reardon?

SELECTED BIBLIOGRAPHY

Ballou, Ronald H. *Business Logistics Management,* 3rd ed. Englewood Cliffs, NJ: Prentice-Hall, 1992.

Blackburn, Joseph, D. *Time-Based Competition: The Next Battleground in American Manufacturing.* Homewood, IL: Richard D. Irwin, 1991.

Coyle, John J. and Edward J. Bardi. *The Management of Logistics*, 2nd ed. St. Paul: West Publishing, 1980, pp. 294–98.

Drezner, Zvi. *Facility Location: A Survey of Applications and Methods.* New York: Springer, 1995.

Francis, R. L., and J. A. White. *Facilities Layout and Location: An Analytical Approach.* Englewood Cliffs, NJ: Prentice-Hall, 1992.

Heskett, J. L.; W. E. Sasser, Jr.; and C. W. L. Hart. *Service Breakthroughs: Changing the Rules of the Game.* New York: Free Press, 1990.

Shycon, Harvey N. "Site Location Analysis, Cost and Customer Service Consideration." *Proceedings of the Seventeenth Annual International Conference,* American Production and Inventory Control Society, 1974, pp. 335–47.

Skinner, Wickham. "The Focused Factory." *Harvard Business Review,* May–June 1974, pp. 113–21.

Sule, D. R. *Manufacturing Facilities: Location, Planning and Design.* Boston: PWS Publishing Company, 1994.

Tompkins, James A., and John A. White. *Facilities Planning.* New York: John Wiley & Sons, 1984.

Chapter 10

Facility Layout

Chapter Outline

Basic Production Layout Formats, 376

Process Layout, 377

    Computerized Layout Techniques—CRAFT

    Applying CRAFT to the Toy Factory

    Systematic Layout Planning

Product Layout, 383

    Assembly Lines

    Assembly-Line Balancing

    Splitting Tasks

    Flexible Line Layouts

    Computerized Line Balancing

    Mixed-Model Line Balancing

    Current Thoughts on Assembly Lines

Group Technology (Cellular) Layout, 392

    Developing a GT Layout

    "Virtual" GT Cell

Fixed-Position Layout, 395

Retail Service Layout, 397

    Servicescapes

    Ambient Conditions

    Spatial Layout and Functionality

    Signs, Symbols, and Artifacts

Office Layout, 400

Case: Soteriou's Souvlaki, 408

Case: State Automobile License Renewals, 410

Key Terms

Process Layout

Product Layout

Group Technology (Cellular) Layout

Fixed-Position Layout

CRAFT

Systematic Layout Planning

Cycle Time

Assembly-Line Balancing

Precedence Relationship

Retail Service Layout

Servicescape

Office Layout

www Links

Cimtechnologies Corporation (http://www.cimtech.com)

With its dimpled aluminum facade and TV-screen-shaped windows, Pittsburgh's Alcoa Building once exemplified the power and pizzazz of the classic corporate skyscraper. When it went up in the 1950s, 2,000 company employees streamed into the 31-story tower every morning, each to work in a private 12-by-15-foot office.

But go looking for Aluminum Company of America Chief Executive Paul H. O'Neil in his office these days, and you discover that he doesn't exactly have one. The executive suite has no permanent walls or doors. All of Alcoa's senior executives work in open cubicles and gather around a "communications center" with televisions, fax machines, newspapers, and tables to encourage impromptu meetings. O'Neil's own favorite hangout is the kitchen, where he and his staff nuke take-out food, huddle, and talk work. "It's like being at home in your own kitchen and sitting around the table."

This experiment has taken place only on Alcoa's top floor. But O'Neil will soon bring kitchenettes and open offices to the whole company. "We're going to have an opportunity to do things with the way people relate to each other. It will be freer and easier," O'Neil says. With escalators instead of elevators and plenty of meeting rooms, "there'll be a lot of places where people can gather."

Alcoa is eager to solve an increasingly urgent workplace problem: After having downsized, reengineered, customer-focused, shattered old hierarchical structures, and reorganized work around teams—all the things that were supposed to make companies more responsive and competitive—corporations such as Alcoa aren't getting the results they expected. They are, quite literally, running into walls, because the new work styles don't work in buildings designed for the old top-down corporation. "Companies feel work processes need to change, and physical environments can get in the way," says Karen Lalli, senior associate with the Hillier Group, an architectural firm based in Princeton, New Jersey. ●

Source: "The New Workplace: Walls Are Falling as the New 'Office of the Future' Finally Takes Shape," *Business Week*, April 29, 1996, pp. 106–17. Excerpted with permission from *Business Week* magazine.

The changes in Alcoa's corporate office building are indicative of the major changes that have occurred around the world in how facilities are designed. The emphasis is on flexibility and change. Organizing around teams of people working to complete a task requires a facility that is designed to accommodate the new way work is organized.

Layout decisions entail determining the placement of departments, workgroups within the departments, workstations, machines, and stock-holding points within a production facility. The objective is to arrange these elements in a way that ensures a smooth work flow (in a factory) or a particular traffic pattern (in a service organization). In general, the inputs to the layout decision are as follows:

1. Specification of the objectives and corresponding criteria to be used to evaluate the design. The amount of space required, and the distance that must be traveled between elements in the layout, are common basic criteria.
2. Estimates of product or service demand on the system.
3. Processing requirements in terms of number of operations and amount of flow between the elements in the layout.
4. Space requirements for the elements in the layout.
5. Space availability within the facility itself, or if this is a new facility, possible building configurations.

All of these inputs are, in fact, outputs of process selection and capacity planning, discussed in previous chapters. In our treatment of layout in this chapter, we examine how layouts are developed under various formats (or work-flow structures). Our emphasis is on quantitative techniques, but we also show examples of how qualitative factors are important in the design of the layout. Both manufacturing and service facilities are covered in the chapter.

■ BASIC PRODUCTION LAYOUT FORMATS

Vol. I "The Manufacturing Process"

The formats by which departments are arranged in a facility are defined by the general pattern of work flow; there are three basic types (process layout, product layout, and fixed-position layout) and one hybrid type (group technology or cellular layout).

Process Layout

A **process layout** (also called a *job-shop* or *functional layout*) is a format in which similar equipment or functions are grouped together, such as all lathes in one area and all stamping machines in another. A part being worked on then travels, according to the established sequence of operations, from area to area, where the proper machines are located for each operation. This type of layout is typical of hospitals, for example, where areas are dedicated to particular types of medical care, such as maternity wards and intensive care units.

Product Layout

A **product layout** (also called a *flow-shop layout*) is one in which equipment or work processes are arranged according to the progressive steps by which the product is made. The path for each part is, in effect, a straight line. Production lines for shoes, chemical plants, and car washes are all product layouts.

Group Technology (Cellular) Layout

A **group technology (cellular) layout** groups dissimilar machines into work centers (or cells) to work on products that have similar shapes and processing requirements. A group technology (GT) layout is similar to process layout in that cells are designed to perform a specific set of processes, and it is similar to product layout in that the cells are dedicated to a limited range of products. (*Group technology* also refers to the parts classification and coding system used to specify machine types that go into a cell.)

In a **fixed-position layout,** the product (by virtue of its bulk or weight) remains at one location. Manufacturing equipment is moved to the product rather than vice versa. Shipyards, construction sites, and movie lots are examples of this format.

Fixed-Position Layout

Many manufacturing facilities present a combination of two layout types. For example, a given floor may be laid out by process, while another floor may be laid out by product. It is also common to find an entire plant arranged according to product layout (fabrication, subassembly, and final assembly), with process layout within fabrication and product layout within the assembly department. Likewise, a group technology layout is frequently found within a department that itself is located according to a plantwide product-oriented layout.

■ PROCESS LAYOUT

The most common approach to developing a process layout is to arrange departments consisting of like processes in a way that optimizes their relative placement. For example, the departments in a low-volume toy factory might consist of the shipping and receiving department, the plastic molding and stamping department, the metal forming department, the sewing department, and the painting department. Parts for the toys are fabricated in these departments and then sent to assembly departments where they are put together. In many installations, optimal placement often means placing departments with large amounts of interdepartment traffic adjacent to one another.

Suppose that we want to arrange the eight departments of a toy factory to minimize the interdepartmental material handling cost. Initially, let us make the simplifying assumption that all departments have the same amount of space (say, 40 feet by 40 feet) and that the building is 80 feet wide and 160 feet long (and thus compatible with the department dimensions). The first things we would want to know are the nature of the flow between departments and how the material is transported. If the company has another factory that makes similar products, information about flow patterns might be abstracted from the records. On the other hand, if this is a new product line, such information would have to come from routing sheets or from estimates by knowledgeable personnel such as process or industrial engineers. Of course, these data, regardless or their source, will have to be modified to reflect the nature of future orders over the projected life of the proposed layout.

Let us assume that this information is available. We find that all material is transported in a standard-size crate by forklift truck, one crate to a truck (which constitutes one "load"). Now suppose that transportation costs are $1 to move a load between adjacent departments and $1 extra for each department in between. The expected loads between departments for the first year of operation are tabulated in Exhibit 10.1; available plant space is depicted in Exhibit 10.2. Note that in our example, diagonal moves are permitted so that department 2 and 3, and 3 and 6 are considered adjacent.

Given this information, our first step is to illustrate the interdepartmental flow by a model, such as Exhibit 10.3. This provides the basic layout pattern, which we will try to improve.

The second step is to determine the cost of this layout by multiplying the material handling cost by the number of loads moved between each pair of departments.

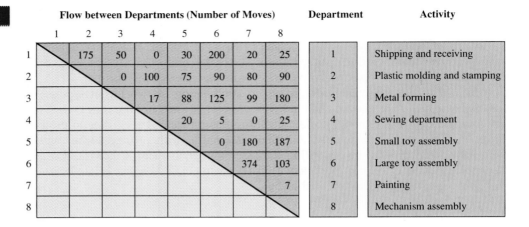

Exhibit 10.1

Interdepartmental
Flow

Flow between Departments (Number of Moves)

	1	2	3	4	5	6	7	8
1		175	50	0	30	200	20	25
2				0	100	75	90	80	90
3				17	88	125	99	180
4					20	5	0	25
5						0	180	187
6							374	103
7								7
8								

Department	Activity
1	Shipping and receiving
2	Plastic molding and stamping
3	Metal forming
4	Sewing department
5	Small toy assembly
6	Large toy assembly
7	Painting
8	Mechanism assembly

Exhibit 10.2

Building Dimensions
and Departments

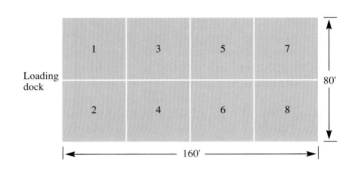

Exhibit 10.3

Interdepartmental
Flow Graph with
Number of Annual
Movements

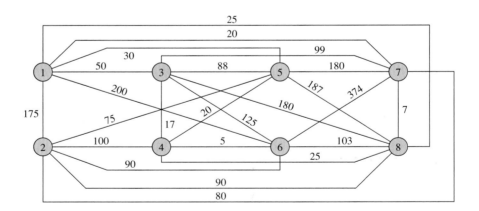

Exhibit 10.4 presents this information, which is derived as follows: The annual material handling cost between Departments 1 and 2 is \$175 (\$1 × 175 moves), \$60 between Departments 1 and 5 (\$2 × 30 moves), \$60 between Departments 1 and 7 (\$3 × 20 moves), \$240 between diagonal Departments 2 and 7 (\$3 × 80), and so forth. (The "distances" are taken from Exhibit 10.2 or 10.3, not Exhibit 10.1.)

The third step is a search for departmental changes that will reduce costs. On the basis of the graph and the cost matrix, it seems desirable to place Departments 1 and 6 closer together to reduce their high move-distance costs. However, this requires

Exhibit 10.4 Cost Matrix—First Solution

$	1	2	3	4	5	6	7	8
1		175	50	0	60	400	60	75
2			0	100	150	180	240	270
3				17	88	125	198	360
4					20	5	0	50
5						0	180	187
6							374	103
7								7
8								

Total cost: $3,474

Exhibit 10.5 Revised Interdepartmental Flow Chart (Only interdepartmental flow with effect on cost is depicted.)

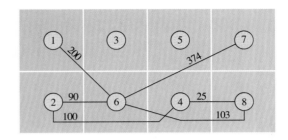

	1	2	3	4	5	6	7	8	Net cost change
1		175	50	0	60	(200)	60	75	–$200
2			0	(200)	150	(90)	240	270	+ 10
3				17	88	125	198	360	
4					20	5	0	(25)	– 25
5						0	180	187	
6							(748)	(206)	+ $374, + $103
7								7	
8									

+ $262
Total cost: $3,736

Exhibit 10.6

Cost Matrix—Second Solution

shifting several other departments, thereby affecting their move-distance costs and the total cost of the second solution. Exhibit 10.5 shows the revised layout resulting from relocating Department 6 and an adjacent department. (Department 4 is arbitrarily selected for this purpose.) The revised cost matrix for the exchange, showing the cost changes, is given in Exhibit 10.6. Note the total cost is $262 *greater* than in the initial solution. Clearly, doubling the distance between Departments 6 and 7 accounted for the major part of the cost increase. This points out the fact that, even in a small problem, it is rarely easy to decide the correct "obvious move" on the basis of casual inspection.

Thus far, we have shown only one exchange among a large number of potential exchanges; in fact, for an eight-department problem, there are 8! (or 40,320) possible arrangements. Therefore, the procedure we have employed would have only a remote possibility of achieving an optimal combination in a "reasonable" number of tries. Nor does our problem stop here.

Suppose that we *do* arrive at a good solution solely on the basis of material handling cost, such as that shown in Exhibit 10.7 (whose total cost is $3,244). We would note, first of all, that our shipping and receiving department is near the center of the

Exhibit 10.7

A Feasible Layout

Small toy assembly	Mechanism assembly	Shipping and receiving	Large toy assembly
5	8	1	6
Metal forming	Plastic molding and stamping	Sewing	Painting
3	2	4	7

factory—an arrangement that probably would not be acceptable. The sewing department is next to the painting department, introducing the hazard that lint, thread, and cloth particles might drift onto painted items. Further, small-toy assembly and large-toy assembly are located at opposite ends of the plant, which would increase travel time for assemblers (who very likely would be needed in both departments at various times of the day) and for supervisors (who might otherwise supervise both departments simultaneously). Often, factors other than material handling cost need to be considered in finalizing a layout.

Computerized Layout Techniques—CRAFT

CRAFT

A number of computerized layout programs have been developed since the 1970s to help devise good process layouts. Of these, the most widely applied is the Computerized Relative Allocation of Facilities Technique (**CRAFT**).[1]

The CRAFT method follows the same basic idea that we developed in the layout of the toy factory, but with some significant operational differences. Like the toy factory example, it requires a load matrix and a distance matrix as initial inputs, but in addition, it requires a cost-per-unit distance traveled, say $.10 per foot moved. (Remember, we made the simplifying assumption that cost doubled when material had to jump one department, tripled when it had to jump two departments, and so forth.) With these inputs and an initial layout in the program, CRAFT then tries to improve the relative placement of the departments as measured by total material handling cost for the layout. (Material handling cost between departments = Number of loads × Rectilinear distance between department centroids × Cost-per-unit distance.) It makes improvements by exchanging pairs of departments in an iterative manner until no further cost reductions are possible. That is, the program calculates the effect on total cost of exchanging departments; if this yields a reduction, the exchange is made, which constitutes an iteration. As we saw in the manual method, the departments are part of a material flow network, so even a simple pairwise exchange generally will affect flow patterns among many other departments.

Applying CRAFT to the Toy Factory

A CRAFT layout solution to the toy factory problem is shown in Exhibit 10.8. It provides a higher-cost layout than the manual one ($3,497 versus $3,244). Note, however, that these costs are not precisely comparable because CRAFT uses rectilin-

---

[1] For a discussion of CRAFT and other methods, see R. L. Francis and J. A. White, *Facility Layout and Location: An Analytical Approach* (Englewood Cliffs, NJ: Prentice-Hall, 1974).

Exhibit 10.8

CRAFT Solution to
Toy Factory Layout

Shipping and receiving	Large toy assembly	Painting	Metal forming
Sewing	Plastic molding and stamping	Small toy assembly	Mechanism assembly

Material handling cost   1 and 2 = \$2 × 175 = \$350
between departments   6 and 7 = \$1 × 374 = \$374

ear distances as opposed to Euclidean (straight-line) distances, and links centroids of departments instead of "entrances." Because we were not given cost-per-unit distances in this example, CRAFT simply broke the stated \$1-per-unit cost of movement between departments into 50¢ segments. Exhibit 10.8 shows two example calculations of the CRAFT movement costs. (Having square departments in the toy factory makes this calculation method a reasonable one for example purposes.) Also note that we fixed the location of the shipping and receiving department in the CRAFT solution so that it would be adjacent to the loading dock.

Distinguishing features of CRAFT and issues relating to it are

1. It is a heuristic program; it uses a simple rule of thumb in making evaluations: "Compare two departments at a time and exchange them if it reduces the total cost of the layout." This type of rule is obviously necessary to analyze even a modest-size layout.

2. It does not guarantee an optimal solution.

3. CRAFT is "biased" by its starting conditions: where you start (i.e., the initial layout) will determine the final layout.

4. Starting with a reasonably good solution is more likely to yield a lower-cost final solution, but it does not always. This means that a good strategy for using CRAFT is to generate a variety of different starting layouts to expose the program to different pairwise exchanges.

5. It can handle up to 40 departments and rarely exceeds 10 iterations in arriving at a solution.

6. CRAFT departments consist of combinations of square modules (typically representing floor areas 10 feet by 10 feet). This permits multiple departmental configurations, but often results in strange departmental shapes that have to be modified manually to obtain a realistic layout.

7. A modified version called SPACECRAFT has been developed to handle multi-story layout problems.[2]

8. CRAFT assumes the existence of variable path material handling equipment such as forklift trucks. Therefore, when computerized fixed-path equipment is employed, CRAFT's applicability is greatly reduced.

Systematic Layout Planning

In certain types of layout problems, numerical flow of items between departments either is impractical to obtain or does not reveal the qualitative factors that may be

---

[2] Roger Johnson, "Spacecraft for Multi-Floor Layout Planning," *Management Science* 28, no. 4 (April 1982), pp. 407–17.

Exhibit 10.9

Systematic Layout
Planning for a Floor of
a Department Store

A. Relationship Chart (Based upon Tables B and C)

From	To				Area (sq. ft.)
	2	3	4	5	
1. Credit department	I 6	U —	A 4	U —	100
2. Toy department		U —	I 1	A 1,6	400
3. Wine department			U —	X 1	300
4. Camera department				X 1	100
5. Candy department					100

Letter	Closeness rating
Number	Reason for rating

B.

Code	Reason*
1	Type of customer
2	Ease of supervision
3	Common personnel
4	Contact necessary
5	Share same space
6	Psychology

*Others may be used.

C.

Value	Closeness	Line code*	Numerical weights
A	Absolutely necessary		16
E	Especially important		8
I	Important		4
O	Ordinary closeness OK		2
U	Unimportant		0
X	Undesirable		80

*Used for example purposes only.

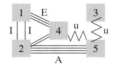

Initial relationship diagram
(based upon Tables A and C)

Initial layout based upon
relationship diagram
(ignoring space and
building constraints)

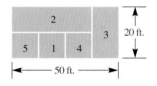

Final layout adjusted by square
footage and building size

Systematic Layout Planning

crucial to the placement decision. In these situations, the venerable technique known as **systematic layout planning** (SLP) can be used.[3] It involves developing a relationship chart showing the degree of importance of having each department located adjacent to every other department. From this chart, an activity relationship diagram similar to the flow graph used for illustrating material handling between departments, is developed. The activity relationship diagram is then adjusted by trial and error until a satisficing adjacency pattern is obtained. This pattern, in turn, is modified department by department to meet building space limitations. Exhibit 10.9 illustrates the technique with a simple five-department problem involving laying out a floor of a department store.

The SLP approach has been quantified for ease of evaluating alternative layouts. This entails assigning numerical weights to the closeness preferences and then trying different layout arrangements. The layout with the highest total closeness score is

---

[3] See Richard Muther and John D. Wheeler, "Simplified Systematic Layout Planning," *Factory* 120, nos. 8, 9, 10 (August, September, October 1962), pp. 68–77, 111–19, 101–13.

selected. For example, Lotfi and Pegels' educational software program[4] assigns weights of 16 for "A," 8 for "E," 4 for "I," 2 for "O," 0 for "U," and −80 for "X." The choice of this weight structure is rather ad hoc, but the logic is that the most undesirable preference weighting (−80 for "X") is five times worse than the most desirable weighting of 16 for "A." Applying this weighting scheme using the software gives a score of 40 to the final layout in Exhibit 10.9. (The score is the summation of the preference scores for each pair—in this case, 10 pairs. Exchanges may be made randomly, by user choice, or by pairs in this software program.)

Integrating Factory Layout Software with Layout Planning   The Breakthrough Box on "Improving a Manufacturing Process" on page 384 illustrates how layout planning is currently conducted using one of the many new software packages. This represents an interesting contrast to the 1980s attempts to model the preferences of layout planners through massive artificial intelligence systems.[5]

■ PRODUCT LAYOUT

The basic difference between product layout and process layout is the pattern of work-flow. As we have seen in process layout, the pattern can be highly variable, because material for any given job may have to be routed to the same processing department several times during its production cycle. In product layout, equipment or departments are dedicated to a particular product line, duplicate equipment is employed to avoid backtracking, and a straight-line flow of material movement is achievable. Adopting a product layout makes sense when the batch size of a given product or part is large relative to the number of different products or parts produced.

Vol. II "Layout Improvements and Equipment Strategies."

Assembly Lines

Assembly lines are a special case of product layout. In a general sense, the term *assembly line* refers to progressive assembly linked by some material handling device. The usual assumption is that some form of pacing is present and the allowable processing time is equivalent for all workstations. Within this broad definition, there are important differences among line types. A few of these are material handling devices (belt or roller conveyor, overhead crane); line configuration (U-shape, straight, branching); pacing (mechanical, human); product mix (one product or multiple products); workstation characteristics (workers may sit, stand, walk with the line, or ride the line); and length of the line (few or many workers).

The range of products partially or completely assembled on lines includes toys, appliances, autos, planes, guns, garden equipment, clothing, and a wide variety of electronic components. In fact, it is probably safe to say that virtually any product that has multiple parts and is produced in large volume uses assembly lines to some degree. Clearly, lines are an important technology; to really understand their managerial requirements, we should have some familiarity with how a line is balanced.

---

[4] Vahid Lotfi and C. Carl Pegels, *Decision Support Systems for Operations Management,* 2nd ed. (Homewood, IL: Richard D. Irwin, 1991), Chapter 8.

[5] See, for example, the discussion of Facilities Design Expert System (FADES) in Edward L. Fisher, "An AI Based Methodology for Factory Design," *AI Magazine,* Fall 1986, pp. 72–85.

BREAKTHROUGH

Improving a Manufacturing Process Using Planning Software

A challenge many facilities planners face today is finding a way to quickly and effectively evaluate proposed layout changes and material handling systems, so that the material handling costs and distances are minimized. This challenge was addressed during a three-day on-site software training session conducted at an appliance manufacturer. The facilities planners were learning the basics on using the FactoryFLOW software package, a computer-based facilities planning tool developed by Cimtechnologies Corp. The training group evaluated a current layout proposal of a console assembly area to see if any improvements could be made.

The FactoryFLOW software quantitatively evaluates facility layouts and material handling systems by showing the material flow paths and costs, both in output text reports and in a graphic overlay of an AutoCAD layout drawing. FactoryFLOW evaluates the material flow and material handling costs and distances using the following input information: an AutoCAD layout drawing, part routing data (i.e. part names, from/to locations, and move quantities), and material handling system characteristics (i.e., fixed and variable costs, load/unload times, and speeds).

The facilities planners had a drawing of the area and the industrial engineers supplied the part routing and material equipment information; therefore, data entry and analysis of the current layout took about one-half of a day. Output diagrams and reports showed material handling distances of over 407 million feet per year and material handling costs of just over $900,000 per year.

The second half of the day was used to come up with alternative layouts by analyzing the output text reports and the material flow lines. One alternative was to rotate a line of 16 plastic presses 90 degrees, so they fed right into the subassembly area, and to rotate the main console assembly lines 90 degrees, so they were closer to the same area. Since the primary material handling system was an overhead conveyor, minimizing the length of conveyor was a major concern. Factory-FLOW was used to evaluate the alternative layout and the output reports showed the material handling costs had been reduced by over $100,000 to $792,265 per year. Also, by decreasing the material travel distance, the length of overhead conveyor needed had been reduced from 3,600 feet to just over 700 feet.

The FactoryFLOW software made it possible to complete this project in a short amount of time and the facilities planners at this company now have a tool for further evaluation of facility layouts and material handling systems.

Source: "Factory Planning Software Cimtechnologies Corp. (Ames, IA)," *Industrial Engineering*, December 1993, p. SS3.

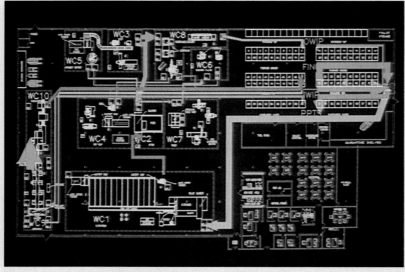

FactoryFLOW integrates material handling data and a layout drawing to compute material handling distances, costs, and equipment utilization.   (http://www.cimtech.com)

Assembly-Line Balancing

Though primarily a scheduling issue, assembly-line balancing often has implications for layout. This would occur when, for balance purposes, workstation size or the number used would have to be physically modified.

Cycle Time

The most common assembly line is a moving conveyor that passes a series of workstations in a uniform time interval called the **cycle time** (which is also the time between successive units coming off the end of the line). At each workstation, work is performed on a product either by adding parts or by completing assembly operations. The work performed at each station is made up of many bits of work, termed *tasks, elements,* and *work units.* Such tasks are described by motion-time analysis. Generally, they are groupings that cannot be subdivided on the assembly line without paying a penalty in extra motions.

The total work to be performed at a workstation is equal to the sum of the tasks assigned to that workstation. The **assembly-line balancing** problem is one of assigning all tasks to a series of workstations so that each workstation has no more than can be done in the cycle time, and so that the unassigned (i.e., idle) time across all workstations is minimized. The problem is complicated by the relationships among tasks imposed by product design and process technologies. This is called the **precedence relationship,** which specifies the order in which tasks must be performed in the assembly process.

Assembly-Line Balancing

Precedence Relationship

Steps in Assembly-Line Balancing   The steps in balancing an assembly line are straightforward:

1. Specify the sequential relationships among tasks using a precedence diagram. The diagram consists of circles and arrows. Circles represent individual tasks; arrows indicate the order of task performance.

2. Determine the required cycle time (C), using the formula

$$C = \frac{\text{Production time per day}}{\text{Required output per day (in units)}}$$

3. Determine the theoretical minimum number of workstations (N_t) required to satisfy the cycle time constraint using the formula (note that this must be rounded up to the next highest integer)

$$N_t = \frac{\text{Sum of task times } (T)}{\text{Cycle time } (C)}$$

4. Select a primary rule by which tasks are to be assigned to workstations, and a secondary rule to break ties.

5. Assign tasks, one at a time, to the first workstation until the sum of the task times is equal to the cycle time, or no other tasks are feasible because of time or sequence restrictions. Repeat the process for Workstation 2, Workstation 3, and so on, until all tasks are assigned.

6. Evaluate the efficiency of the balance derived using the formula

$$\text{Efficiency} = \frac{\text{Sum of task times } (T)}{\text{Actual number of workstations } (N_a) \times \text{Cycle time } (C)}$$

7. If efficiency is unsatisfactory, rebalance using a different decision rule.

■ **example** 10.1   *Assembly-Line Balancing*   The Model J Wagon is to be assembled on a conveyor belt. Five hundred wagons are required per day. Production time per day is 420 minutes, and the assembly steps and times for the wagon are given in Exhibit 10.10. Assignment: Find the balance that minimizes the number of workstations, subject to cycle time and precedence constraints.

solution

1. Draw a precedence diagram. Exhibit 10.11 illustrates the sequential relationships identified in Exhibit 10.10. (The length of the arrows has no meaning.)

2. Cycle-time determination. Here, we have to convert to seconds because our task times are in seconds.

$$C = \frac{\text{Production time per day}}{\text{Output per day}} = \frac{60 \text{ sec.} \times 420 \text{ min.}}{500 \text{ wagons}} = \frac{25,200}{500} = 50.4$$

	Task	**Task Time (in Seconds)**	**Description**	**Tasks That Must Precede**
Exhibit 10.10 Assembly Steps and Times for Model J Wagon	A	45	Position rear axle support and hand fasten four screws to nuts.	—
	B	11	Insert rear axle.	A
	C	9	Tighten rear axle support screws to nuts.	B
	D	50	Position front axle assembly and hand fasten with four screws to nuts.	—
	E	15	Tighten front axle assembly screws.	D
	F	12	Position rear wheel #1 and fasten hubcab.	C
	G	12	Position rear wheel #2 and fasten hubcab.	C
	H	12	Position front wheel #1 and fasten hubcap.	E
	I	12	Position front wheel #2 and fasten hubcap.	E
	J	8	Position wagon handle shaft on front axle assembly and hand fasten bolt and nut.	F, G, H, I
	K	9	Tighten bolt and nut.	
		195		

Exhibit 10.11

Precedence Graph for Model J Wagon

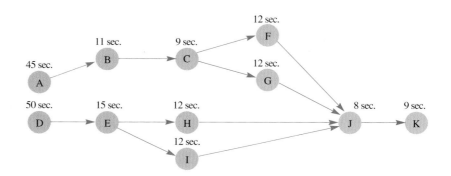

3. Theoretical minimum number of workstations required (the actual number may be greater):

$$N_t = \frac{T}{C} = \frac{195 \text{ seconds}}{50.4 \text{ seconds}} = 3.87 = 4 \text{ (rounded up)}$$

4. Select assignment rules. Research has demonstrated that some rules are better than others for certain problem structures. In general, the strategy is to use a rule assigning tasks that either have many followers or are of long duration since they effectively limit the balance achievable. In this case, we use as our primary rule:
   a. Assign tasks in order of the largest number of following tasks.

Task	Number of Following Tasks
A	6
B or D	5
C or E	4
F, G, H, or I	2
J	1
K	0

   Our secondary rule, to be invoked where ties exist from our primary rule, is
   b. Assign tasks in order of longest task time (shown in Exhibit 10.12).

5. Make task assignments to form Workstation 1, Workstation 2, and so forth until all tasks are assigned. The actual assignment is given in Exhibit 10.12A and is shown graphically in Exhibit 10.12B.

6. Do the efficiency calculation. This is shown in Exhibit 10.12C.

7. Evaluate solution. An efficiency of 77 percent indicates an imbalance or idle time of 23 percent $(1.0 - .77)$ across the entire line. From Exhibit 10.12A we can see that there are 57 total seconds of idle time, and the "choice" job is at Workstation 5.

Is a better balance possible? In this case, yes. Try balancing the line with rule *b* and breaking ties with rule *a*. (This will give you a feasible four-station balance.) ■

Splitting Tasks

Often the longest required task time forms the shortest cycle time for the production line. This task time is the lower time bound unless it is possible to split the task into two or more workstations.

Consider the following illustration: Suppose that an assembly line contains the following task times in seconds: 40, 30, 15, 25, 20, 18, 15. The line runs for 7½ hours per day and demand for output is 750 per day.

The cycle time required to produce 750 per day is 36 seconds ([7½ hours × 60 minutes × 60 seconds]/750). Our problem is that we have one task that takes 40 seconds. How do we deal with this task?

There are several ways that we may be able to accommodate the 40-second task in a 36-second cycle. Possibilities are

1. *Split the task.* Can we split the task so that complete units are processed in two workstations?

Exhibit 10.12

A. Balance Made According to Largest Number of Following Tasks Rule

	Task	Task Time (in Seconds)	Remaining Unassigned Time (in Seconds)	Feasible Remaining Tasks	Task with Most Followers	Task with Longest Operation Time
Station 1	A	45	5.4 idle	None		
Station 2	D	50	0.4 idle	None		
Station 3	B	11	39.4	C, E	C, E	E
	E	15	24.4	C, H, I	C	
	C	9	15.4	F, G, H, I	F, G, H, I	F, G, H, I
	F*	12	3.4 idle	None		
Station 4	G	12	38.4	H, I	H, I	H, I
	H*	12	26.4	I		
	I	12	14.4	J		
	J	8	6.4 idle	None		
Station 5	K	9	41.4 idle	None		

*Denotes task arbitrarily selected where there is a tie between longest operation times.

B. Precedence Graph for Model J Wagon

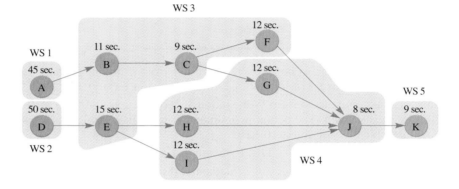

C. Efficiency Calculation

$$\text{Efficiency} = \frac{T}{N_a C} = \frac{195}{(5)(50.4)} = .77, \text{ or } 77\%$$

2. *Share the task.* Can the task somehow be shared so an adjacent workstation does part of the work? This differs from the split task in the first option because the adjacent station acts to assist, not to do some units containing the entire task.

3. *Use parallel workstations.* It may be necessary to assign the task to two workstations that would operate in parallel.

4. *Use a more skilled worker.* Because this task exceeds the cycle time by just 11 percent, a faster worker may be able to meet the 36-second time.

5. *Work overtime.* Producing at a rate of one every 40 seconds would produce 675 per day, 75 short of the needed 750. The amount of overtime required to do the additional 75 is 50 minutes (75 × 40 seconds/60 seconds).

6. *Redesign.* It may be possible to redesign the product to reduce the task time slightly.

Other possibilities to reduce the task time include equipment upgrading, a roaming helper to support the line, a change of materials, and multiskilled workers to operate the line as a team rather than as independent workers.

This assembly line at Hewlett-Packard allows technicians the flexibility to trade work elements, and allows management to add or subtract operators as necessary.

Flexible Line Layouts

As we saw in the preceding example, assembly line balances frequently result in unequal workstation times. Flexible line layouts such as shown in Exhibit 10.13 are a common way of dealing with this problem. In our toy company example, the U-shaped line with work sharing at the bottom of the figure could help resolve the imbalance.

Computerized Line Balancing

Companies engaged in assembly methods commonly employ a computer for line balancing. Most develop their own computer programs, but commercial package programs are also widely applied. One of these in General Electric Company's *Assembly-Line Configuration (ASYBL$),* which uses the "ranked positional weight" rule in selecting tasks for workstations. Specifically, this rule states that tasks are assigned according to their positional weights, which is the time for a given task plus the task times of all those that follow it. Thus, the task with the highest positional weight would be assigned to the first workstation (subject to time, precedence, and zoning constraints). As is typical with such software, the user has several options for how the problem is to be solved. Exhibit 10.14 illustrates a portion of program output when a target level of efficiency is used as a basis for deriving and comparing different balances for a 35-task assembly line. (The program can handle up to 450 tasks.) Note the trade-offs that take place as the number of workstations changes. In this case, the larger number of workstations allows for a better balance and, therefore, a higher efficiency.

Mixed-Model Line Balancing

This approach is used by JIT manufacturers such as Toyota. Its objective is to meet the demand for a variety of products and to avoid building high inventories. Mixed-

Flexible Line Layouts

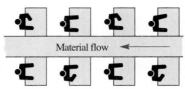

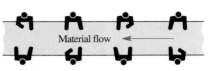

Bad: Operators caged. No chance
to trade elements of work
between them.
(subassembly line layout
common in American plants)

Better: Operators can trade elements of
work. Can add and subtract
operators. Trained ones can
nearly self-balance at different
output rates.

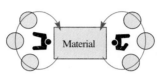

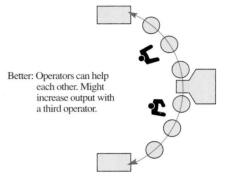

Bad: Operators birdcaged. No chance
to increase output with a
third operator

Better: Operators can help
each other. Might
increase output with
a third operator.

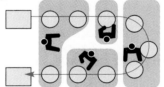

Bad: Straight line difficult to balance.

Better: One of several advantages
of U-Line is better operator
access. Here, five operators
were reduced to four.

Source: Robert W. Hall, *Attaining Manufacturing Excellence* (Homewood. IL: Dow Jones-Irwin, 1987), p. 125.

Sample Computer
Output

```
ENTER OPTION NUMBER? 3
ENTER TARGET EFFICIENCY? .85

TOTAL EFFICIENCY   = 82%
STANDARD DEVIATION =   0.0153
TARGET CYCLE TIME  =   0.347
MINIM. CYCLE TIME  =   0.343
NO. OF STATIONS =   19

TOTAL EFFICIENCY   = 80%
STANDARD DEVIATION =   0.0175
TARGET CYCLE TIME  =   0.368
MINIM. CYCLE TIME  =   0.368
NO. OF STATIONS  = 18

TOTAL EFFICIENCY   = 75%
STANDARD DEVIATION =   0.0214
TARGET CYCLE TIME  =   0.417
MINIM. CYCLE TIME  =   0.415
NO. OF STATIONS =   17
```

Source: General Electric Company, *Assembly-Line Configuration, ASYBL$ User's Guide,* Revised (1985), p. 17.

model line balancing involves scheduling several different models to be produced over a given day or week on the same line in a cyclical fashion.

■ **example** I0.2   *Mixed-Model Line Balancing*   To illustrate how this is done, suppose our toy company has a fabrication line to bore holes in its Model J wagon frame and its Model K wagon frame. The time required to bore the holes is different for each wagon type.

Assume that the final assembly line downstream requires equal numbers of Model J and Model K wagon frames. Assume also that we want to develop a cycle time for the fabrication line that is balanced for the production of equal numbers of J and K frames. Of course, we could produce Model J frames for several days and then produce Model K frames until an equal number of frames has been produced. However, this would build up unnecessary work in process inventory.

If we want to reduce the amount of in-process inventory, we could develop a cycle mix that greatly reduces inventory buildup while keeping within the restrictions of equal numbers of J and K wagon frames.

Process times: 6 minutes per J and 4 minutes per K.

The day consists of 480 minutes (8 hours $\times$ 60 minutes).

solution

$$6J + 4K = 480$$

Because equal numbers of J and K are to be produced (or J = K), produce 48J and 48K per day, or 6J and 6K per hour.

The following shows one balance of J and K frames.

Balanced Mixed-Model Sequence

Model sequence	J J	K K K	J J	J J	K K K	
Operation time	6 6	4 4 4	6 6	6 6	4 4 4	Repeats 8 times per day
Minicycle time	12	12	12	12	12	

Total cycle time   60

This line is balanced at 6 frames of each type per hour with a minicycle time of 12 minutes.

Another balance is J K K J K J, with times of 6, 4, 4, 6, 4, 6. This balance produces 3J and 3K every 30 minutes with a minicycle time of 10 minutes (JK, KJ, KJ). ■

The simplicity of mixed-model balancing (under conditions of a level production schedule) is seen in Yasuhiro Mondon's description of Toyota Motor Corporation's operations:

Final assembly lines of Toyota are mixed product lines. The production per day is averaged by taking the number of vehicles in the monthly production schedule classified by specifications, and dividing by the number of working days.

In regard to the production sequence during each day, the cycle time of each different specification vehicle is calculated. To have all specification vehicles appear at their own cycle time, different specification vehicles are ordered to follow each other.[6]

Current Thoughts on Assembly Lines

It is true that the widespread use of assembly-line methods in manufacturing has dramatically increased output rates. Historically, the focus has almost always been on full utilization of human labor; that is, to design assembly lines minimizing human idle time. Equipment and facility utilization stood in the background as much less important. Past research has tried to find optimal solutions as if the problem stood in a never-changing world.

Newer views of assembly lines take a broader perspective. The intentions are to incorporate greater flexibility in products produced on the line, more variability in workstations (such as size and number of workers), improved reliability (through routine preventive maintenance), and high-quality output (through improved tooling and training). The Breakthrough Box on Compaq Computer on page 394 describes how a combination of assembly lines and manufacturing cells (the topic of the next section) can be used when product demand changes quickly.

◼ GROUP TECHNOLOGY (CELLULAR) LAYOUT

Vol. IV
"The Vision Light System at Federal Signal"

Group technology (or cellular) layout allocates dissimilar machines into cells to work on products that have similar shapes and processing requirements. Group technology (GT) layouts are now widely used in metal fabricating, computer chip manufacture, and assembly work. The overall objective is to gain the benefits of product layout in job-shop kind of production. These benefits include

1. Better human relations. Cells consist of a few workers who form a small work team; a team turns out complete units of work.
2. Improved operator expertise. Workers see only a limited number of different parts in a finite production cycle, so repetition means quick learning.
3. Less in-process inventory and material handling. A cell combines several production stages, so fewer parts travel through the shop.
4. Faster production setup. Fewer jobs mean reduced tooling and hence faster tooling changes.

Developing a GT Layout

Shifting from process layout to a GT cellular layout entails three steps:

1. Grouping parts into families that follow a common sequence of steps. This step requires developing and maintaining a computerized parts classification and coding system. This is often a major expense with such systems, although many companies have developed short-cut procedures for identifying parts families.

---

[6] Yasuhiro Monden, *Toyota Production System: Practical Approach to Production Management* (Atlanta, GA: Industrial Engineering and Management Press, Institute of Industrial Engineers, 1983), p. 208.

2. Identifying dominant flow patterns of parts families as a basis for location or relocation of processes.

3. Physically grouping machines and processes into cells. Often there will be parts that cannot be associated with a family and specialized machinery that cannot be placed in any one cell because of its general use. These unattached parts and machinery are placed in a "remainder cell."

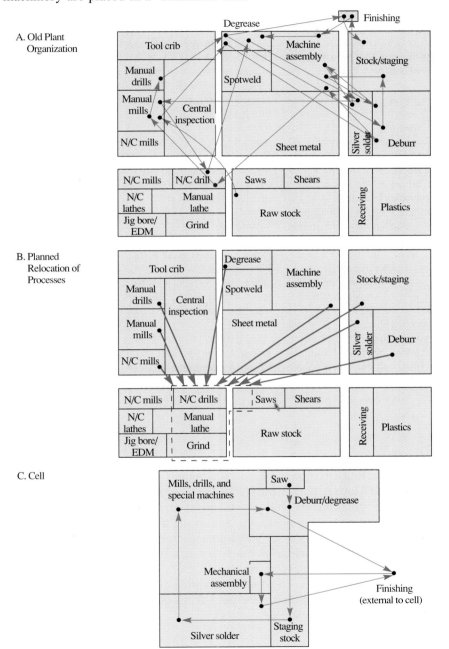

A. Old Plant Organization

B. Planned Relocation of Processes

C. Cell

Exhibit 10.15

Developing a Cell to Produce Wave-Guide Parts

Source: Reprinted with permission of The Free Press, an imprint of Simon and Schuster, from *World Class Manufacturing* by Richard J. Schonberger. Copyright © 1986 by Schonberger & Associates.

BREAKTHROUGH

Staying Loose in a Tense Tech Market

Last month, with great fanfare, Compaq introduced notebook computers that boasted the latest in design, speed, and power. Called the Armada, this vaunted new hardware replaced the company's Contura line, which was unveiled last year. Compaq has high expectations for the Armada, but regardless of how well the products perform, their shelf life could be limited.

With cutting-edge innovation advancing rapidly and Silicon Valley competition intensifying so quickly, technological turnover is speeding up today. This means that computer makers must reengineer their factories to have the flexibility to constantly build new and improved models. "You have to plan for the birth of a new product and for its burial at the same time," explains David Wu, a technology analyst for the Chicago Corp. "If you're not planning for both of those events, you're going to lose a lot of money and market share."

With nearly $15 billion in 1995 sales, Houston-based Compaq has invested heavily in its factories. The company has developed a system that enables it to respond nimbly to retailers and businesses rather than just supply them from inventory stockpiles, a crippling problem for technology enterprises. The key to this approach is "cell manufacturing," which is being used along with traditional assembly-line techniques for many Compaq models. Each cell has three people who operate a workstation, where computers are built,

tested, and shipped. Ironically, cell manufacturing is an old idea, based on the way groups of people built products in their homes before the Industrial Revolution.

One of the great advantages of cell manufacturing is that it allows an individual workstation to manufacture a different computer model each day, if that's what is needed. And with 48 cells replacing one traditional assembly line, it's easier for Compaq to produce the hundreds of different models it offers. "Cell manufacturing gives us the ability to make changes when we need to," says Compaq Senior Vice President Ross Cooley, "but it's not for every situation." The bottom line: Compaq has found that cell workstations increase employee output by 23 percent and product quality by 25 percent.

Costs

Despite these gains, cell manufacturing remains expensive. A typical assembly line at Compaq costs $2.5 million to outfit; "cellularizing" that same work space costs $10 million, because full sets of tools have to be deployed at each workstation and cell workers must be better trained and paid than assembly-line workers.

For now, Compaq is using a combination of assembly-line and cell manufacturing. The company's Presario computers were produced with traditional — and less costly — assembly-line methods in the

Exhibit 10.15 illustrates the cell development process followed by Rockwell's Telecommunication Division, maker of wave-guide parts. Part A shows the original process-oriented layout; part B, the planned relocation of process based on parts-family production requirements; and part C, an enlarged layout of the cell designed to perform all but the finishing operation. According to Schonberger, cellular organization was practical here because (1) distinct parts families existed; (2) there were several of each type of machine so taking a machine out of a cluster did not rob the cluster of all its capacity, leaving no way to produce other products; (3) the work centers were easily movable stand-alone machine tools—heavy, but anchored to the floor rather simply. He adds that these three features represent general guidelines for deciding where cells make sense.[7]

---

[7] Richard J. Schonberger, *World Class Manufacturing* (New York: Free Press, 1986), p. 112.

Cell workers are better trained and paid than assembly-line workers.

first few months of their shelf life, when demand was exceptionally strong. But when orders taper off, Compaq can switch over to cell manufacturing and gear up the assembly line for its next generation of products.

As it tries to become the world leader in all product categories—notebooks, servers, consumer and commercial desktops—Compaq faces stiff competition from companies that specialize in certain market segments. Gateway, for example, builds to order without retail sales. This puts even more pressure on production efficiency and inventory management. Compaq hopes that the old idea of cell manufacturing can help meet the demands of the new—and ever-changing—high-tech marketplace.

Source: Dan McGraw, "Staying Loose in a Tense Tech Market," *U.S. News & World Report,* July 8, 1996, p. 46. © U.S. News & World Report.

Virtual GT Cell

When equipment is not easily movable, many companies dedicate a given machine out of a set of identical machines in a process layout. A virtual GT cell for, say, a two-month production run for the job might consist of Drill 1 in the drills area, Mill 3 in the mill area, and Assembly Area 1 in the machine assembly area. To approximate a GT flow, all work on the particular part family would be done only on these specific machines.

■ FIXED-POSITION LAYOUT

Fixed-position layout is characterized by a relatively low number of production units in comparison with process and product layout formats. In developing a fixed-position layout, we may visualize the product as the hub of a wheel with materials and equipment arranged concentrically around the production point in their order of use and movement difficulty. Thus, in shipbuilding, for example, rivets that are used throughout construction would be placed close to or in the hull; heavy engine parts, which must travel to the hull only once, would be placed at a more distant location; and cranes would be set up close to the hull because of their constant use.

In fixed-position layout, a high degree of task ordering is common, and to the extent that this precedence determines production stages, a fixed-position layout might be developed by arranging materials according to their technological priority. This procedure would be expected in making a layout for a large machine tool, such as a stamping machine, where manufacture follows a rigid sequence; assembly is performed from the ground up, with parts being added to the base in almost a building-block fashion.

As far as quantitative layout techniques are concerned, there is little in the literature devoted to fixed-position formats, even though they have been utilized for thousands of years. In certain situations, however, it may be possible to specify objective criteria and develop a fixed-position layout through quantitative means. For instance, if the material handling cost is significant and the construction site permits more or less straight-line material movement, the CRAFT process layout technique might be advantageously employed.

Exhibit 10.16   Taco Bell Restaurant Floor Plans

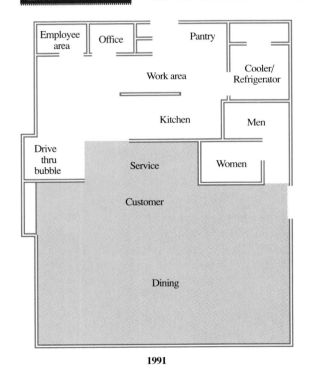

1991

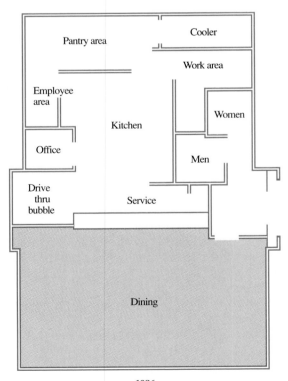

1986

Source: Courtesy of Taco Bell Corp., Los Angeles, CA.

RETAIL SERVICE LAYOUT

The objective of a **retail service layout** (as is found in stores, banks, and restaurants) is to maximize net profit per square foot of store space. A company that has been very successful in leveraging every inch of its layout space to achieve this objective is Taco Bell Restaurants. Exhibit 10.16 illustrates Taco Bell store layouts used in 1986 and from 1991 to the present. The nature of layout changes reflects actions required to support the company's value strategy of speed and low prices. Key operational modifications include elimination of many on-site food preparation steps, which simultaneously increased the speed of service while reducing the amount of working space needed. For example, the chopping and bagging of lettuce and the precooking and seasoning of meats, beans, and hard tortilla products are now done at central kitchens or by suppliers. The restaurant kitchens are now heating and assembly units only. In addition to such outsourcing, changes were made in queue structures, such as moving from a single line running parallel to the counter, to a double line running perpendicular to it. This improved product flow facilitated serving drive-through windows, increased capacity, and allowed customers to see assembly workers' faces (as opposed to just their backsides, as was the case before).

Retail Service Layout

Servicescapes

As previously noted, the broad objective of layout in retail services is generally to maximize net profit per square foot of floor space. Operationally, this goal is often translated into such criteria as "minimize handling cost" or "maximize product exposure." Although as Sommers and Kernan observed more than 30 years ago, employing these and similar criteria in service layout planning "results in stores that look like warehouses and requires shoppers to approach the task like order pickers or display case stockers."[8] There are other more humanistic aspects of the service that must also be considered in the layout.

Mary Jo Bitner coined the term **servicescape** to refer to the physical surroundings in which the service takes place, and how these surroundings affect customers and employees. An understanding of the servicescape is necessary to create a good layout for the service firm (or the service-related portions of the manufacturing firm). The servicescape has three elements that must be considered: the ambient conditions; the spatial layout and functionality; and the signs, symbols, and artifacts.[9]

Servicescape

Ambient Conditions

Ambient conditions refer to background characteristics such as the noise level, music, lighting, temperature, and scent that can affect employee performance and morale as well as customers' perceptions of the service, how long they stay, and how much money they spend. Although many of these characteristics are influenced primarily by the design of the building (e.g., the placement of light fixtures, acoustic tiles, and

---

[8] Montrose S. Sommers and Jerome B. Kernan, "A Behavioral Approach to Planning, Layout and Display," *Journal of Retailing*, Winter 1965–66, pp. 21–27.

[9] Mary Jo Bitner, "Servicescapes: The Impact of Physical Surroundings on Customers and Employees," *Journal of Marketing* 56 (April 1992), pp. 57–71.

exhaust fans), the layout within a building can also have an effect. Areas near food preparation will smell like food, lighting in a hallway outside a theater must be dim, tables near a stage will be noisy, and locations near an entrance will be drafty.

Spatial Layout and Functionality

Two aspects of the *spatial layout and functionality* are especially important: planning the circulation path of the customers, and grouping the merchandise. The goal of circulation planning is to provide a path for the customers that exposes them to as much of the merchandise as possible while placing any needed services along this path in the sequence they will be needed. For example, the above photo shows a bank reception area placed where the customer will encounter it immediately upon entering the bank. Aisle characteristics are of particular importance. Aside from determining the number of aisles to be provided, decisions must be made as to the width of the aisles because this is a direct function of expected or desired traffic. Aisle width can also affect the direction of flow through the service. Stu Leonard's Dairy Store in Norwalk, Connecticut, is designed so that it is virtually impossible to turn around a shopping cart once you have entered the shopping flow path. Focal points that catch the customers' attention in the layout can also be used to draw the customers in the desired direction. The famous blue light at Kmart is an example. Another is shown in the photo above.

To enhance shoppers' view of merchandise as they proceed down a main aisle, secondary and tertiary aisles may be set at an angle. Consider the two layouts in Exhibit 10.17. The rectangular layout would probably require less expensive fixtures and contain more display space. If storage considerations are important to the store management, this would be the more desirable layout. On the other hand, the angular layout provides the shopper with a much clearer view of the merchandise and, other things being equal, presents a more desirable selling environment.

Alternate Store Layouts

Exhibit 10.17

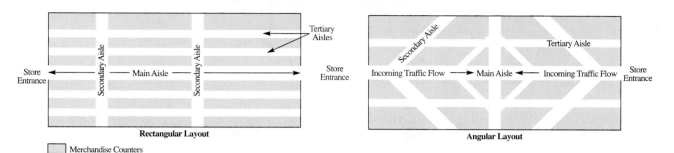

Merchandise Counters

It is common practice now to base merchandise groupings on the shopper's view of related items, as opposed to the physical characteristics of the products or shelf-space and servicing requirements. This grouping-by-association philosophy is seen in boutiques in department stores and gourmet sections in supermarkets.

Special mention is in order for a few guidelines derived from marketing research and relating to circulation planning and merchandise grouping.

1. People in supermarkets tend to follow a perimeter pattern in their shopping behavior. Placing high-profit items along the walls of a store will enhance their probability of purchase.

2. Sale merchandise placed at the end of an aisle in supermarkets almost always sells better than the same sale items placed in the interior portion of an aisle.

3. Credit and other nonselling departments that require customers to wait for the completion of their services should be placed either on upper floors or in "dead" areas.

4. In department stores, locations nearest the store entrances and adjacent to front-window displays are most valuable in terms of sales potential.

Signs, Symbols, and Artifacts

Signs, symbols, and artifacts refer to the parts of the service that have social significance. As with the ambiance, these are often a characteristic of the design of the building, although the orientation, location, and size of many objects and areas can carry special meaning. As examples,

- In the old days, bank loan officers were easily identified because their desks were located on a raised section of the bank floor called the platform.
- A person seated at the desk closest to the entrance is usually in charge of greeting customers and directing them to their destination.
- In a department store, the tiled areas indicate the aisles for travel, while carpeted areas indicate departments for browsing.
- Some car salespeople have blackboards installed in their offices because a person writing on a blackboard symbolizes someone who should be listened to and trusted (e.g., a teacher).

As you might have gathered from these examples, the influence of behavioral factors makes the development of hard and fast rules for servicescape layout rather difficult. Suffice it to say that making the layout choice is not simply a matter of choosing between display space and ease of operation.

OFFICE LAYOUT

Office Layout

The trend in **office layout** is toward more open offices, with personal work spaces separated only by low divider walls. Companies have removed fixed walls to foster greater communication and teamwork. Signs, symbols, and artifacts, as discussed in the section on service layout, are possibly even more important in office layout than in retailing. For instance, size and orientation of desks can indicate the importance or professionalism of the people behind them. (See, for example, the box "Office Layout in Japan" about the layout of a Japanese office.)

Central administration offices are often designed and laid out so as to convey the desired image of the company. For example, Scandinavian Airlines System's (SAS) administrative office complex outside of Stockholm is a two-story collection of glass-walled pods that provide the feeling of open communication and flat hierarchy (few levels of organization) that characterize the company's management philosophy.

Service-Master (the highly profitable janitorial management company) positions its "Know-How Room" at the center of its headquarters. This room contains all of the physical products, operations manuals, and pictorial displays of career paths and other symbols for the key knowledge essential to the business. "From this room, the rest of the company can be seen as a big apparatus to bring the knowledge of the marketplace to its employees and potential customers."[10]

CONCLUSION

Facility layout is where the rubber meets the road in the design and operation of a production system. A good factory (or office) layout can provide real competitive advantage by facilitating material and information flow processes. It can also enhance employees' work life. A good service layout can be an effective "stage" for playing out the service encounter. In conclusion, here are some marks of a good layout in these environments:

Marks of a Good Layout for Manufacturing and Back-Office Operations

1. Straight-line flow pattern (or adaptation).
2. Backtracking kept to a minimum.
3. Production time predictable.
4. Little interstage storage of materials.
5. Open plant floors so everyone can see what is happening.
6. Bottleneck operations under control.

---

[10] Richard Norman, *Service Management,* 2nd ed. (New York: John Wiley & Sons, 1991), p. 28.

The positioning of the desks in Japanese offices symbolizes the importance of those who sit behind them. The rank-and-file workers sit, facing each other, in a column of adjacent desks (as shown in the accompanying figure). The employee who sits closest to the door is lowest in the hierarchy and must get up to open the door and greet all visitors. At the top of this column of desks sits the head of the office, with the second and third in command at the desks to either side. Seats by the window, so coveted by western managers, are reserved for those who have been passed over for promotion and are now no longer on the career track. They will spend the remainder of their days at the company doing work of little consequence and looking out the window.

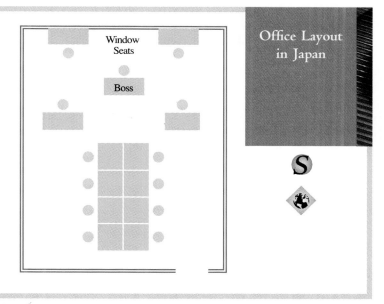

Office Layout in Japan

7. Workstations close together.
8. Orderly handling and storage of materials.
9. No unnecessary rehandling of materials.
10. Easily adjustable to changing conditions.

Marks of a Good Layout for Face-to-Face Services

1. Easily understood service flow pattern.
2. Adequate waiting facilities.
3. Easy communication with customers.
4. Easily maintained customer surveillance.
5. Clear exit and entry points with adequate checkout capabilities.
6. Departments and processes arranged so that customers see only what you want them to see.
7. Balance between waiting areas and service areas.
8. Minimum walking and material movement.
9. Lack of clutter.
10. High sales volume per square foot of facility.

SOLVED PROBLEMS

SOLVED PROBLEM 1

A university advising office has four rooms, each dedicated to specific problems: petitions (Room A), schedule advising (Room B), grade complaints (Room C), and student counseling (Room D). The office is 80 feet long and 20 feet wide. Each room is 20 feet by 20 feet. The present location of rooms is A, B, C, D; that is, a straight line. The load summary shows the number of contacts that each advisor in a room has with other advisors in the other rooms. Assume that all advisors are equal in this value.

Load summary: $AB = 10$, $AC = 20$, $AD = 30$,
$\qquad\qquad\quad BC = 15$, $BD = 10$, $CD = 20$.

    a. Evaluate this layout according to the material handling cost method.
    b. Improve the layout by exchanging functions within rooms. Show your amount of improvement using the same method as in (*a*).

Solution
    a.

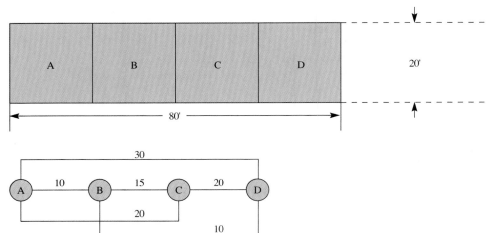

Using the material handling cost method shown in the toy company example we obtain the following costs, assuming that every nonadjacency doubles the initial cost/unit distance:

$AB = 10 \times 1 = 10$
$AC = 20 \times 2 = 40$
$AD = 30 \times 3 = 90$
$BC = 15 \times 1 = 15$
$BD = 10 \times 2 = 20$
$CD = 20 \times 1 = 20$
    Current cost $= 195$

    b. A better layout would be BCDA.

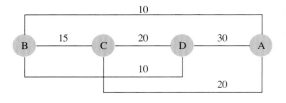

$AB = 10 \times 3 = 30$
$AC = 20 \times 2 = 40$
$AD = 30 \times 1 = 30$
$BC = 15 \times 1 = 15$
$BD = 10 \times 2 = 20$
$CD = 20 \times 1 = 20$
Improved cost $= 155$

SOLVED PROBLEM 2

The following tasks must be performed on an assembly line in the sequence and times specified.

Task	Task Time (Seconds)	Tasks That Must Precede
A	50	—
B	40	—
C	20	A
D	45	C
E	20	C
F	25	D
G	10	E
H	35	B, F, G

a. Draw the schematic diagram.
b. What is the theoretical minimum number of stations required to meet a forecasted demand of 400 units per 8-hour day?
c. Use the longest task time rule and balance the line in the minimum number of stations to produce 400 units per day.

Solution

a.

b. Theoretical minimum number of stations to meet D = 400 is

$$N_t = \frac{T}{C} = \frac{245 \text{ seconds}}{\left(\dfrac{60 \text{ seconds} \times 480 \text{ minutes}}{400 \text{ units}}\right)} = \frac{245}{72} = 3.4 \text{ stations}$$

c.

	Task	Task Time (Seconds)	Remaining Unassigned Time	Feasible Remaining Task
Station 1	A	50	22	C
	C	20	2	None
Station 2	D	45	27	E, F
	F	25	2	None
Station 3	B	40	32	E
	E	20	12	G
	G	10	2	None
Station 4	H	35	37	None

REVIEW AND DISCUSSION QUESTIONS

1. What kind of layout is used in a physical fitness center?
2. What is the key difference between SLP and CRAFT?

3. What is the objective of assembly-line balancing? How would you deal with the situation where one worker, although trying hard, is 20 percent slower than the other 10 people on a line?

4. How do you determine the idle-time percentage from a given assembly-line balance?

5. What information of particular importance do route sheets and process charts (discussed in Chapter 3) provide to the layout planner?

6. What is the essential requirement for mixed-model lines to be practical?

7. Why might it be difficult to develop a GT layout?

8. In what respects is facility layout a marketing problem in services? Give an example of a service system layout designed to maximize the amount of time the customer is in the system.

9. Consider a department store. Which departments probably should not be located near each other? Would any departments benefit from close proximity?

10. How would a flowchart help in planning the servicescape layout? What sorts of features would act as focal points or otherwise draw customers along certain paths through the service? In a supermarket, what departments should be located first along the customers' path? Which should be located last?

PROBLEMS

1. See SM.

1. The Cyprus Citrus Cooperative ships a high volume of individual orders for oranges to northern Europe. The paperwork for the shipping notices is done in the accompanying layout. Revise the layout to improve the flow and conserve space if possible.

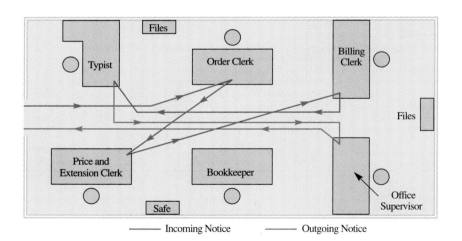

——— Incoming Notice   ——— Outgoing Notice

2. See SM. Output/day:
24B + 24D. Process times:
12 min./B and 8 min./D.
BB/DDD BB BB/DDD
repetitively

3. a. See SM.
 b. 120 seconds.
 c. See SM.
 d. 87.5%.

2. An assembly line makes two models of trucks: a Buster and a Duster. Busters take 12 minutes each, and Dusters take 8 minutes each. The daily output requirement is 24 of each per day. Develop a perfectly balanced mixed-model sequence to satisfy demand.

3. An assembly line is to operate 8 hours per day with a desired output of 240 units per day. The following table contains information on this product's task, task time, and precedence relationship.

Task	Task Time (Seconds)	Immediate Predecessor
A	60	—
B	80	A
C	20	A
D	50	A
E	90	B, C
F	30	C, D
G	30	E, F
H	60	G

a. Draw the precedence diagram.
b. What is the cycle time?
c. Balance this line using longest task time.
d. What is the efficiency of your line balance?

4. The desired daily output for an assembly line is 360 units. This assembly line will operate 450 minutes per day. The following table contains information on this product's task, task time and precedence relationship.

Task	Task Time (Seconds)	Immediate Predecessor
A	30	—
B	35	A
C	30	A
D	35	B
E	15	C
F	65	C
G	40	E, F
H	25	D, G

4. *a.* See SM.
 b. 75 seconds.
 c. See SM.
 d. 91.7%.

a. Draw the precedence diagram.
b. What is the cycle time?
c. Balance this line using largest number of following tasks. Use longest task time as a secondary criteria.
d. What is the efficiency of your line balance?

5. The following tasks and the order in which they must be performed according to their assembly requirements are shown in the following table. These are to be combined into workstations to create an assembly line. The assembly line operates $7^{1}/_{2}$ hours per day. The output requirement is 1,000 units per day.

5. *a.* 27 seconds.
 b. 6 stations
 c. 91.4%.
 d. Work 45 minutes per day overtime.

Task	Preceding Tasks	Time (Seconds)
A	—	15
B	A	24
C	A	6
D	B	12
E	B	18
F	C	7
G	C	11
H	D	9
I	E	14
J	F, G	7
K	H, I	15
L	J, K	10

a. What is the cycle time?

b. Balance the line using longest task time based on the 1,000 unit forecast, stating which tasks would be done in each workstation.

c. For *b* above, what is the efficiency of your line balance?

d. After production was started, Marketing realized that they understated demand and must increase output to 1,100 units. What action would you take? Be specific in quantitative terms, if appropriate.

6. $44,500.

6. An initial solution has been given to the following process layout problem. Given the flows described and a cost of $2.00 per unit per foot, compute the total cost for the layout. Each location is 100 feet long and 50 feet wide as shown on the following figure. Use the centers of departments for distances and measure distance using metropolitan-rectilinear distance.

	Department			
Department	**A**	**B**	**C**	**D**
A	0	10	25	55
B		0	10	5
C			0	15
D				0

```
       100'    100'    100'
     ┌──────┬──────┬──────┐
50'  │  A   │  B   │  C   │  50'
     └──────┴──────┼──────┤
                   │  D   │  50'
                   └──────┘
```

7. b. 90 seconds.
   c. 4.55.
   d. 5 stations.
   e. $\dfrac{410}{5 \times 90} = 91\%$.
   f. Reduce cycle time to 85 seconds and work 17.6 minutes overtime.

7. An assembly line to be designed to operate $7^1/_2$ hours per day and supply a steady demand of 300 units per day. Here are the tasks and their performance times.

Task	Preceding Tasks	Performance Time (Seconds)	Task	Preceding Tasks	Performance Time (Seconds)
a	—	70	g	d	60
b	—	40	h	e	50
c	—	45	i	f	15
d	a	10	j	g	25
e	b	30	k	h, i	20
f	c	20	l	j, k	25

a. Draw the precedence diagram.

b. What is the cycle time?

c. What is the theoretical minimum number of workstations?

d. Assign tasks to workstations using longest operating time.

e. What is the efficiency of your line balance?

f. Suppose demand increases by 10 percent. How would you react to this?

8. See SM for layouts.
Nonadjacency
3–2: 10
6–2: 8
6–5: 3
———
21
d. Doubtful. Station is not centrally located; nurses do a great deal of walking.

8. S. L. P. Craft would like your help in developing a layout for a new outpatient clinic to be built in California. Based on analysis of another recently built clinic, he obtains the data on page 407. This includes the number of trips made by patients between departments on a typical day (shown above the diagonal line) and the numbered weights (defined in Exhibit 10.9, page 382) between departments as specified by the new clinic's physicians (below the diagonal). The new building will be 60 feet by 20 feet.

a. Develop an interdepartmental flow graph that minimizes patient travel.

b. Develop a "good" relationship diagram using systematic layout planning.

c. Choose either of the layouts obtained in *a* or *b* and sketch the departments to scale within the building.

d. Will this layout be satisfactory to the nursing staff? Explain.

Departments	2	3	4	5	6	Area requirement (sq. ft.)
1 Reception	A / 2	O / 5	E / 200	U / 0	O / 10	100
2 X-ray		E / 10	I / 300	U / 0	O / 8	100
3 Surgery			I / 100	U / 0	A / 4	200
4 Examining rooms (5)				U / 0	I / 15	500
5 Lab					O / 3	100
6 Nurses' station						100

9. The following tasks are to be performed on an assembly line:

Task	Seconds	Tasks that Must Precede
A	20	—
B	7	A
C	20	B
D	22	B
E	15	C
F	10	D
G	16	E, F
H	8	G

The workday is seven hours long.
Demand for completed product is 750 per day.
a. Find the cycle time.
b. What is the theoretical number of workstations?
c. Draw the precedence diagram.
d. Balance the line using sequential restrictions and the longest operating time rule.
e. What is the efficiency of the line balanced as in *d*?
f. Suppose that demand rose from 750 to 800 units per day. What would you do? Show any amounts or calculations.
g. Suppose that demand rose from 750 to 1,000 units per day. What would you do? Show any amounts or calculations.

10. The Dorton University president has asked the OM department to assign eight biology professors (A, B, C, D, E, F, G, and H) to eight offices (numbered 1 to 8 in the diagram) in the new Biology Building.

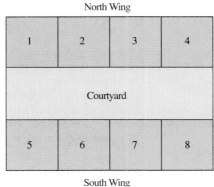

North Wing

| 1 | 2 | 3 | 4 |

Courtyard — New Biology Building

| 5 | 6 | 7 | 8 |

South Wing

The following distances and two-way flows are given:

Distances between Offices (Feet)										**Two-Way Flows (Units per Period)**							
	1	**2**	**3**	**4**	**5**	**6**	**7**	**8**		**A**	**B**	**C**	**D**	**E**	**F**	**G**	**H**
1	—	10	20	30	15	18	25	34	A	—	2	0	0	5	0	0	0
2		—	10	20	18	15	18	25	B		—	0	0	0	3	0	2
3			—	10	25	18	15	18	C			—	0	0	0	0	3
4				—	34	25	18	15	D				—	4	0	0	0
5					—	10	20	30	E					—	1	0	0
6						—	10	20	F						—	1	0
7							—	10	G							—	4
8								—	H								—

a. If there are no restrictions (constraints) on the assignment of professors to offices, how many alternative assignments are there to evaluate?

b. The biology department has sent the following information and requests to the OM department:

> Offices 1, 4, 5, and 8 are the only offices with windows.
> A must be assigned Office 1.
> D and E, the biology department co-chairpeople, must have windows.
> H must be directly across the courtyard from D.
> A, G, and H must be in the same wing.
> F must *not* be next to D or G or directly across from G.

Find the optimal assignment of professors to offices that meets all the requests of the biology department and minimizes total material handling cost. You may use the path flow list as a computational aid.

Path	Flow	Path	Flow	Path	Flow	Path	Flow	Path	Flow
A–B	2	B–C	0	C–D	0	D–E	4	E–F	1
A–C	0	B–D	0	C–E	0	D–F	0	E–G	0
A–D	0	B–E	0	C–F	0	D–G	0	E–H	0
A–E	5	B–F	3	C–G	0	D–H	0	F–G	1
A–F	0	B–G	0	C–H	3			F–H	0
A–G	0	B–H	2					G–H	4
A–H	0								

Case

Soteriou's Souvlaki

Mr. Soteriou looks up from cleaning the floor—the lights are on. This means that the power has finally been hooked up, and soon his restaurant will reopen here in its new location.

Soteriou's Souvlaki is typical of many of the small dining establishments scattered around the perimeter of the university. Specializing in Greek cuisine—souvlaki

(lamb kabobs), gyros, tiropita (cheese-filled pastries), and baklava (a honey and pistachio nut dessert)—the restaurant has been very popular with the student body.

The operations are similar to those of most fast-food restaurants. Customers enter and queue near the register to place their orders and pay. Food is prepared and given to the customer over the main counter. Drinks are self-serve, and the tables are bussed by the customers upon leaving. The kitchen is normally run by Mr. Soteriou with help from an assistant working the cash register.

Until recently, Soteriou's had been located in a local food court, but earthquake damage, space constraints, and deteriorating sanitary conditions prompted him to move the restaurant to these new quarters. The new facility is a small, free-standing building, formerly a hamburger joint. Although the previous owners have removed all equipment and tables, the large fixed service counter remains, physically marking out the kitchen and dining areas. (See the accompanying figure.)

Aware of students' growing health consciousness (and possibly a little heady with the extra floor space in the new building), Mr. Soteriou has decided to add a self-service salad bar to the new restaurant. The salad bar will be much like those in other restaurants, but with a more Mediterranean flair.

The new kitchen does not appear to be much larger than the old one, though it is narrower. To prepare his Greek specialties in this new kitchen, Mr. Soteriou will need a grill/oven, a storage refrigerator, a preparation table (with hot and cold bins for the condiments, side dishes, and pita bread), a vertical spit broiler for the gyros meat, and a display case to hold the tiropitas, baklava, and cups for the self-serve drink machines.

The new dining area will include smoking and nonsmoking seating, the salad bar, self-serve drink machines, and an area for the register queues. Of course, the location of the cash register will be important to both the kitchen and dining area layouts.

Leaning against the mop handle, Mr. Soteriou looks around the clean, empty floor. Eager to open the new location, he has already ordered all the necessary

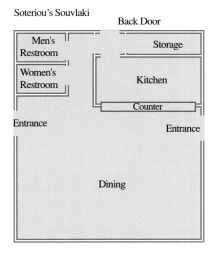

Soteriou's Souvlaki

equipment, but where will he put it? Unfortunately, the equipment will be arriving tomorrow morning. Once it is placed by the delivery crew, it will be hard for Mr. Soteriou and his assistant to rearrange it by themselves.

Question

The matrices in Exhibits C10.1 and C10.2 show the importance of proximity for the kitchen equipment and dining area features. Use systematic layout planning (with numerical reference weightings) to develop a floor layout for the kitchen and the dining area for Soteriou's Souvlaki.

Source: This case was prepared by Douglas Stewart. It is not intended to show proper or improper handling of food.

	Grill	Prep. Table	Refrig.	Vertical Broiler	Display Case	
Cash register	X	A	X	U	A	**The Kitchen**
Grill	—	A	A	U	E	
Prep. table	—	—	I	A	U	
Refrigerator	—	—	—	U	X	
Vertical broiler	—	—	—	—	U	
Display case	—	—	—	—	—	

	No Smoking	Smoking	Drinks	Salad Bar	Waiting Area	Exhibit C10.2
Cash register	U	U	I	I	A	**The Dining Area**
No smoking	—	X	E	E	U	
Smoking	—	—	I	I	U	
Drinks	—	—	—	U	U	
Salad bar	—	—	—	—	X	
Waiting area	—	—	—	—	—	

Case

State Automobile License Renewals

Henry Coupe, manager of a metropolitan branch office of the state department of motor vehicles, attempted to perform an analysis of the driver's license renewal operations. Several steps were to be performed in the process. After examining the license renewal process, he identified the steps and associated times required to perform each step as shown in Exhibit C10.3.

Coupe found that each step was assigned to a different person. Each application was a separate process in the sequence shown in the exhibit. Coupe determined that his office should be prepared to accommodate the maximum demand of processing 120 renewal applicants per hour.

He observed that the work was unevenly divided among the clerks, and that the clerk who was responsible for checking violations tended to shortcut her task to keep up with the other clerks. Long lines built up during the maximum demand periods.

Coupe also found that jobs 1, 2, 3, and 4 were handled by general clerks who were each paid $6.00 per hour. Job 5 was by a photographer paid $8 per hour. Job 6, the issuing of temporary licenses, was required by state policy to be handled by a uniformed motor vehicle officer. Officers were paid $9 per hour, but they could be assigned to any job except photography.

A review of the jobs indicated that job 1, reviewing the application for correctness, had to be performed

before any other step could be taken. Similarly, job 6, issuing the temporary license, could not be performed until all the other steps were completed. The branch offices were charged $10 per hour for each camera to perform photography.

Henry Coupe was under severe pressure to increase productivity and reduce costs, but he was also told by the regional director of the Department of Motor Vehicles that he had better accommodate the demand for renewals. Otherwise, "heads would roll."

Questions

1. What is the maximum number of applications per hour that can be handled by the present configuration of the process?

2. How many applications can be processed per hour if a second clerk is added to check for violations?

3. Assuming the addition of one more clerk, what is the maximum number of applications the process can handle?

4. How would you suggest modifying the process to accommodate 120 applications per hour?

Source: P. R. Olsen, W. E. Sasser, and D. D. Wyckoff, *Management of Service Operations: Text, Cases, and Readings,* pp. 95–96. © 1978. Reprinted by permission of Prentice Hall, Englewood Cliffs, New Jersey.

Exhibit C10.3	Job	Average Time to Perform (Seconds)
State Automobile License Renewals Process Times	**1.** Review renewal application for correctness	15
	2. Process and record payment	30
	3. Check file for violations and restrictions	60
	4. Conduct eye test	40
	5. Photograph applicant	20
	6. Issue temporary license	30

SELECTED BIBLIOGRAPHY

Bachman, Timothy A. "Information and Advice: Innovations and Product Delivery for Financial Service." *Design Management Journal* 3, no. 1 (Winter 1992), pp. 103–10.

Bitner, Mary Jo. "Servicescapes: The Impact of Physical Surroundings on Customers and Employees." *Journal of Marketing* 56 (April 1992), pp. 57–71.

Bonett, Douglas G., and Robert E. D. Woolsey. "Load-Distance Analysis with Variable Loads." *Production and Inventory Management Journal,* 1st quarter 1993, pp. 32–34.

Choobineh, F. "A Framework for the Design of Cellular Manufacturing Systems." *International Journal of Production Research* 26, no. 7 (1988), pp. 1161–72.

Francis, R. L., and J. A. White. *Facility Layout and Location: An Analytical Approach.* Englewood Cliffs, NJ: Prentice-Hall, 1992.

Ghosh, Soumen, and Roger Gagnon. "A Comprehensive Literature Review and Analysis of the Design, Balancing and Scheduling of Assembly Systems." *International Journal of Production Research* 27, no. 4 (1989), pp. 637–70.

Green, Timothy J., and Randall P. Sadowski. "A Review of Cellular Manufacturing Assumptions, Advantages and Design Techniques." *Journal of Operations Management* 4, no. 2 (February 1984), pp. 85–97.

Gunther, R. E., G. D. Johnson, and R. S. Peterson. "Currently Practiced Formulations for the Assembly Line Balance Problem." *Journal of Operations Management* 3, no. 4 (August 1983), pp. 209–21.

Heragu, Sunderesh. *Facilities Design.* Boston, MA: PWS Publishing Company, 1997.

Hyer, Nancy Lea. "The Potential of Group Technology for U.S. Manufacturing." *Journal of Operations Management* 4, no. 3 (May 1984), pp. 183–202.

Johnson, Roger. "Optimally Balancing Large Assembly Lines with FABLE." *Management Science* 34, no. 2 (February 1988), pp. 240–53.

Love, John F. *McDonald's: Behind the Arches:* New York: Bantam, 1986.

Monden, Yasuhiro. *Toyota Production System: Practical Approach to Production Management.* Atlanta: Industrial Engineering and Management Press, 1983.

Norman, Richard. *Service Management.* 2nd ed. New York: John Wiley & Sons, 1991.

Schonberger, Richard J. *Japanese Manufacturing Techniques.* New York: Free Press, 1982.

Sule, D. R. *Manufacturing Facilities: Location, Planning, and Design.* Boston: PWS Publishing Company, 1994.

Chapter 11

Job Design and Work Measurement

Chapter Outline

Job Design Decisions, 414
Behavioral Considerations in Job Design, 415
    Degree of Labor Specialization
    Job Enrichment
    Sociotechnical Systems
Physical Considerations in Job Design, 418
Work Methods, 418
    A Production Process
    Worker at a Fixed Workplace
    Worker Interacting with Equipment

Workers Interacting with Other
    Workers
Work Measurement and Standards, 424
    Work Measurement Techniques
Financial Incentive Plans, 435
    Basic Compensation Systems
    Individual and Small-Group Incentive Plans
    Organizationwide Plans
    Pay-for-Performance
Case: Teamwork at Volvo, 443

Key Terms

Job Design

Specialization of Labor

Job Enrichment

Sociotechnical Systems

Work Physiology

Ergonomics

Work Measurement

Time Study

Normal Time

Standard Time

Elemental Standard-Time Data

Predetermined Motion-Time Data
Systems

Methods Time Measurement

Most Work Measurement
Systems

Work Factor

Work Sampling

Financial Incentive Plans

Profit Sharing

Gain Sharing

www Links

The MTM Association (http://www.mtm.org)

J OB DESIGN THEN . . .

Frederick W. Taylor recounts his "motivation" of his trusty worker, Schmidt (in *Principles of Scientific Management,* 1910):

"Schmidt, are you a high-priced man?"

"Vell, I don't know vat you mean."

"Oh yes you do. What I want to know is whether you are a high-priced man or not. . . . What I want to find out is whether you want to earn $1.85 a day or whether you are satisfied with $1.15, just the same as all those cheap fellows are getting?"

"Vell, yes, I vas a high-priced man."

"Now come over here. You see that pile of pig iron?"

"Yes."

"You see that car?"

"Yes."

"Well, if you are a high-priced man, you will load that pig iron on that car tomorrow for $1.85."

"You see that man over there? . . . Well, if you are a high-priced man, you will do exactly as this man tells you tomorrow, from morning till night. When he tells you to pick up a pig and walk, you pick it up and you walk, and when he tells you to sit down and rest, you sit down and rest. You do that straight through the day. And what's more, no back talk."

AND NOW . . .

Researcher Paul S. Adler describes job design at New United Motor Manufacturing Inc.'s (NUMMI) Fremont, California, plant. NUMMI is a joint venture between General Motors and Toyota.

413

Team members hold the stopwatch and design their own jobs. Team members begin by timing one another, seeking the most efficient way to do each task at a sustainable pace. They pick the best performance, break it down into its component parts, and then look for ways of improving each element. The team then takes the resulting methods, compares them with those used by teams working on the other shift at the same workstation, and writes detailed specifications that become the standard work definition for everyone on both teams. ●

Source: Discussions with Paul S. Adler; Paul S. Adler, "Time and Motion Regained," *Harvard Business Review* 71, no. 1 (January–February 1993), pp. 97–110; and "Return of the Stopwatch," *The Economist*, January 23, 1993, p. 69.

The operations manager's job, by definition deals with managing the personnel that create the firm's products and services. To say that this is a challenging job in today's complex environment is an understatement. The diversity of the workforce's cultural and educational background, coupled with frequent organization restructuring, calls for a much higher level of people management skills than have been required in even the recent past.

The objective in managing personnel is to obtain the highest productivity possible without sacrificing quality, service, or responsiveness. The operations manager uses job design techniques to structure the work so that it will be conducive to both the physical and behavioral needs of the human worker. Work measurement methods are used to determine the most efficient means of performing a given task, as well as to set reasonable standards for performing it. People are motivated by many things, only one of which is financial reward. Operations managers can structure such rewards not only to motivate consistently high performance but also to reinforce the most important aspects of the job. A working knowledge of learning curves is also needed to allow the operations manager to anticipate the gains in efficiency that naturally arise as workers gain experience.

■ JOB DESIGN DECISIONS

Job Design

Job design may be defined as the function of specifying the work activities of an individual or group in an organizational setting. Its objective is to develop job structures that meet the requirements of the organization and its technology and that satisfy the jobholder's personal and individual requirements. Exhibit 11.1 summarizes the decisions involved. These decisions are being affected by the following trends:

1. *Quality control as part of the worker's job.* Now often referred to as "quality at the source" (see Chapter 6), quality control is linked with the concept of *empowerment.* Empowerment, in turn, refers to workers being given authority to stop a production line if there is a quality problem, or to give a customer an on-the-spot refund if service was not satisfactory.

2. *Cross-training workers to perform multiskilled jobs.* As companies engage in downsizing, the remaining workforce is expected to do more and different tasks.

3. *Employee involvement and team approaches to designing and organizing work.* This is a central feature in total quality management (TQM) and continuous

Job Design Decisions

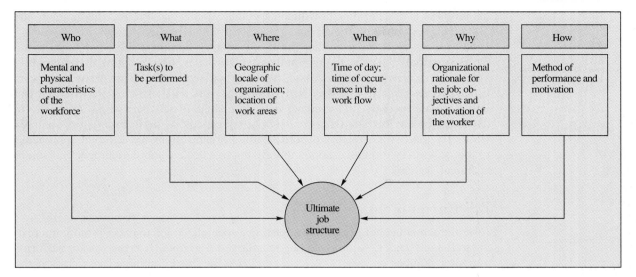

Who	What	Where	When	Why	How
Mental and physical characteristics of the workforce	Task(s) to be performed	Geographic locale of organization; location of work areas	Time of day; time of occurrence in the work flow	Organizational rationale for the job; objectives and motivation of the worker	Method of performance and motivation

Ultimate job structure

improvement efforts. In fact, it is safe to say that virtually all TQM programs are team based.

4. *"Informating" ordinary workers through telecommunication networks and computers, thereby expanding the nature of their work and their ability to do it.* In this context, informating is more than just automating work—it is revising work's fundamental structure. Northeast Utilities' computer system, for example, can pinpoint a problem in a service area before the customer-service representative answers the phone. The rep uses the computer to troubleshoot serious problems, to weigh probabilities that other customers in the area have been affected, and to dispatch repair crews before other calls are even received.

5. *Extensive use of temporary workers.* Manpower, a company specializing in providing temporary employees, is vying with McDonald's as the largest private employer in the United States with over 500,000 workers on its payroll.

6. *Automation of heavy manual work.* Examples abound in both services (one-person trash pickup trucks) and manufacturing (robot spray painting on auto lines). These changes are driven by safety regulations as well as economics and personnel reasons.

7. *Most important of all, organizational commitment to providing meaningful and rewarding jobs for all employers.* Hewlett-Packard's mission statement lists three "People related objectives: (1) Belief in our people; (2) Emphasis on working together and sharing rewards (teamwork and partnership); and (3) A superior working environment which other companies seek but few achieve."

■ BEHAVIORAL CONSIDERATIONS IN JOB DESIGN

Degree of Labor Specialization

Specialization of labor is the two-edged sword of job design. On one hand, specialization has made possible high-speed, low-cost production, and from a materialistic standpoint, it has greatly enhanced our standard of living. On the other hand, extreme

Specialization of Labor

specialization (as we see in mass-production industries) often has serious adverse effects on workers, which in turn are passed on to the production systems. In essence, the problem is to determine how much specialization is enough. At what point do the disadvantages outweigh the advantages? (See Exhibit 11.2.)

Recent research suggests that the disadvantages dominate the advantages much more commonly than was thought in the past. However, simply stating that, for purely humanitarian reasons, specialization should be avoided is risky. The reason, of course, is that people differ in what they want from their work and what they are willing to put into it. Some workers prefer not to make decisions about their work, some like to daydream on the job, and others are simply not capable of performing more complex work. To improve the quality of jobs, leading organizations try different approaches to job design. Two popular contemporary approaches are job enrichment and socio-technical systems.

Job Enrichment

Job enlargement generally entails adjusting a specialized job to make it more interesting to the job holder. A job is said to be enlarged *horizontally* if the worker performs a greater number or variety of tasks, and it is said to be enlarged *vertically* if the worker is involved in planning, organizing, and inspecting his own work. Horizontal job enlargement is intended to counteract oversimplification and to permit the worker to perform a "whole unit of work." Vertical enlargement (traditionally termed job enrichment) attempts to broaden workers' influence in the transformation process by giving them certain managerial powers over their own activities. Today, common practice is to apply both horizontal and vertical enlargement to a given job and refer to the total approach as **job enrichment.**

Job Enrichment

Exhibit 11.2	Advantages of Specialization	
Advantages and Disadvantages of Specialization of Labor	**To Management**	**To Labor**
	1. Rapid training of the workforce	1. Little or no education required to obtain work
	2. Ease in recruiting new workers	2. Ease in learning job
	3. High output due to simple and repetitive work	
	4. Low wages due to ease of substitutability of labor	
	5. Close control over work flow and workloads	

	Disadvantages of Specialization	
	To Management	**To Labor**
	1. Difficulty in controlling quality since no one person has responsibility for entire product	1. Boredom stemming from repetitive nature of work
	2. Worker dissatisfaction leading to hidden costs arising from turnover, absenteeism, tardiness, grievances, and intentional disruption of production process	2. Little gratification from work itself because of small contribution to each item
	3. Reduced likelihood of improving the process because of workers' limited perspective	3. Little or no control over the workpace, leading to frustration and fatigue (in assembly-line situations)
	4. Limited flexibility to change the production process to produce new or improved products	4. Little opportunity to progress to a better job since significant learning is rarely possible on fractionated work

The organizational benefits of job enrichment occur both in quality and productivity. Quality in particular improves dramatically because when individuals are responsible for their work output, they take ownership of it and simply do a better job. Also, because they have a broader understanding of the work process, they are more likely to catch errors and make corrections than if the job is narrowly focused. Productivity improvements also occur from job enrichment, but they are not as predictable or as large as the improvements in quality. The reason is that enriched work invariably contains a mix of tasks that (for manual labor) causes interruptions in rhythm and different motions when switching from one task to the next. Such is the not the case for specialized jobs.[1]

Sociotechnical Systems

Sociotechnical Systems

Consistent with the job enrichment philosophy but focusing more on the interaction between technology and the work group is the **sociotechnical systems** approach. This approach attempts to develop jobs that adjust the needs of the production process technology to the needs of the worker and work group. The term was developed from studies of weaving mills in India and of coal mines in England in the early 1950s. These studies revealed that work groups could effectively handle many production problems better than management if they were permitted to make their own decisions on scheduling, work allocation among members, bonus sharing, and so forth. This was particularly true when there were variations in the production process requiring quick reactions by the group or when one shift's work overlapped with other shifts' work.

Since those pioneering studies, the sociotechnical approach has been applied in many countries—often under the heading of "autonomous work groups," "Japanese-style work groups," or employee involvement (EI) teams. Most major American manufacturing companies have work teams as the basic building block in so-called high employee involvement plants. They are now becoming common in service organizations as well. The benefits of teams are similar to those of individual job enrichment: they provide higher quality and greater productivity (they often set higher production goals than general management), do their own support work and equipment maintenance, and have increased chances to make meaningful improvements.[2]

One major conclusion from these applications is that the individual or work group requires a logically integrated pattern of work activities that incorporates the following job design principles:

Task Variety   An attempt must be made to provide an optimal variety of tasks within each job. Too much variety can be inefficient for training and frustrating for the employee. Too little can lead to boredom and fatigue. The optimal level is one that allows the employee to take a rest from a high level of attention or effort while working on another task or, conversely, to stretch after periods of routine activity.

Skill Variety   Research suggests that employees derive satisfaction from using a number of skill levels.

---

[1] Edward E. Lawler III, *The Ultimate Advantage: Creating the High Involvement Organizations* (San Francisco: Jossey-Bass Publishers, 1992), pp. 85–86.
[2] Ibid., pp. 98–99.

Feedback   There should be some means for informing employees quickly when they have achieved their targets. Fast feedback aids the learning process. Ideally, employees should have some responsibility for setting their own standards of quantity and quality.

Task Identity   Sets of tasks should be separated from other sets of tasks by some clear boundary. Whenever possible, a group or individual employee should have responsibility for a set of tasks that is clearly defined, visible, and meaningful. In this way, work is seen as important by the group or individual undertaking it, and others understand and respect its significance.

Task Autonomy   Employees should be able to exercise some control over their work. Areas of discretion and decision making should be available to them.[3]

■ PHYSICAL CONSIDERATIONS IN JOB DESIGN

Beyond the behavioral components of job design, another aspect warrants consideration: the physical side. Indeed, while motivation and work group structure strongly influence job performance, they may be of secondary importance if the job is too demanding from a physical (or "human factors") standpoint. One approach to incorporating the physical costs of moderate to heavy work in job design is **work physiology.** Pioneered by Eastman Kodak in the 1960s, work physiology sets work-rest cycles according to the energy expended in various parts of the job. For example, if a job entails caloric expenditure above five calories per minute (the rough baseline for sustainable work), the required rest period must equal or exceed the time spent working. Obviously, the harder the work, the more frequent and longer the rest periods. (Exhibit 11.3 shows caloric requirements for various activities.)

Work Physiology

Ergonomics

    Ergonomics is the term used to describe the study of the physical arrangement of the work space together with the tools used to perform a task. In applying ergonomics, we strive to fit the work to the body rather than forcing the body to conform to the work. As logical as this may sound, it is actually a pretty recent point of view.

■ WORK METHODS

In contemporary industry, responsibility for developing work methods in large firms is typically assigned either to a staff department designated *methods analysis* or to an industrial engineering department. In small firms, this activity is often performed by consulting firms that specialize in work methods design.

    The principal approach to the study of work methods is the construction of charts, such as operations charts, worker-machine charts, simo (simultaneous motion) charts,

[3] This summary is taken from Enid Mumford and Mary Weir, *Computer Systems in Work Design—the ETHICS Method* (New York: Halstead, 1979), p. 42.

and activity charts, in conjuction with time study or standard time data. The choice of which charting method to use depends on the task's activity level; that is, whether the focus is on (1) a production process, (2) the worker at a fixed workplace, (3) a worker interacting with equipment, or (4) a worker interacting with other workers (see Exhibit 11.4). (Several of these charting techniques were introduced in Chapter 4, where they were used to aid in manufacturing process design. Chapter 5 introduced the service blueprint that accounts for customer interactions.)

A Production Process

The objective in studying a production process is to identify delays, transport distances, processes, and processing time requirements to simplify the entire operation.

Type of Activity	Typical Energy Cost in Calories per Minute*	Required Minutes of Rest for Each Minute of Work
Sitting at rest	1.7	—
Writing	2.0	—
Typing on a computer	2.0	—
Medium assembly work	2.9	—
Shoe repair	3.0	—
Machining	3.3	—
Ironing	4.4	—
Heavy assembly work	5.1	—
Chopping wood	7.5	1
Digging	8.9	2
Tending furnace	12.0	3
Walking upstairs	12.0	3

Exhibit 11.3

Calorie Requirements for Various Activities

* Five calories per minute is generally considered the maximum sustainable level throughout the workday.

Activity	Objective of Study	Study Techniques
Production process	Eliminate or combine steps; shorten transport distance; identify delays	Flow diagram, service blueprint, process chart
Worker at fixed workplace	Simplify method; minimize motions	Operations charts, simo charts; apply principles of motion economy
Worker's interaction with equipment	Minimize idle time; find number or combination of machines to balance cost of worker and machine idle time	Activity chart, worker-machine charts
Worker's interaction with other workers	Maximize productivity; minimize interference	Activity charts, gang process charts

Exhibit 11.4

Work Methods Design Aids

The underlying philosophy is to eliminate any step in the process that does not add value to the product. The approach is to flow chart the process and then ask the following questions:

What is done? Must it be done? What would happen if it were not done?

Where is the task done? Must it be done at that location or could it be done somewhere else?

When is the task done? Is it critical that it be done then or is there flexibility in time and sequence? Could it be done in combination with some other step in the process?

How is the task done? Why is it done this way? Is there another way?

Who does the task? Can someone else do it? Should the worker be of a higher or lower skill level?

These thought-provoking questions usually help to eliminate much unnecessary work and simplify the remaining work, by combining a number of processing steps and changing the order of performance.

The process chart is valuable in studying an overall system, though care must be taken to follow the same item throughout the process. The subject may be a product being manufactured, a service being created, or a person performing a sequence of activities. Exhibit 11.5 shows a process chart (and flow diagram) for a clerical operation. Exhibit 11.6 shows common notation in process charting. Can you suggest any ways to improve this process? (See problem 2.)

Exhibit 11.5

Flow Diagram and
Process Chart
of an Office
Procedure—Present
Method

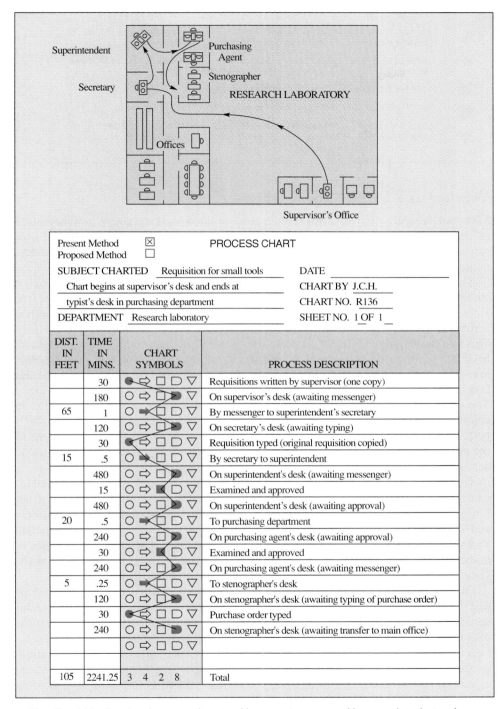

PROCESS CHART

Present Method ☒
Proposed Method ☐

SUBJECT CHARTED   Requisition for small tools   DATE _____

Chart begins at supervisor's desk and ends at   CHART BY J.C.H.

typist's desk in purchasing department   CHART NO. R136

DEPARTMENT   Research laboratory   SHEET NO. 1 OF 1

DIST. IN FEET	TIME IN MINS.	CHART SYMBOLS	PROCESS DESCRIPTION
	30		Requisitions written by supervisor (one copy)
	180		On supervisor's desk (awaiting messenger)
65	1		By messenger to superintendent's secretary
	120		On secretary's desk (awaiting typing)
	30		Requisition typed (original requisition copied)
15	.5		By secretary to superintendent
	480		On superintendent's desk (awaiting messenger)
	15		Examined and approved
	480		On superintendent's desk (awaiting approval)
20	.5		To purchasing department
	240		On purchasing agent's desk (awaiting approval)
	30		Examined and approved
	240		On purchasing agent's desk (awaiting messenger)
5	.25		To stenographer's desk
	120		On stenographer's desk (awaiting typing of purchase order)
	30		Purchase order typed
	240		On stenographer's desk (awaiting transfer to main office)
105	2241.25	3 4 2 8	Total

Note: Requisition is written by a supervisor, typed by a secretary, approved by a superintendent, and approved by a purchasing agent. Then a purchase order is prepared by a stenographer.

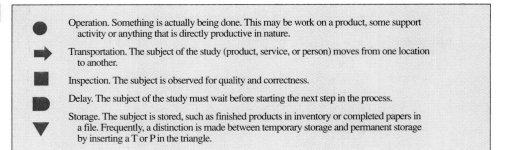

● Operation. Something is actually being done. This may be work on a product, some support activity or anything that is directly productive in nature.

➡ Transportation. The subject of the study (product, service, or person) moves from one location to another.

■ Inspection. The subject is observed for quality and correctness.

◗ Delay. The subject of the study must wait before starting the next step in the process.

▼ Storage. The subject is stored, such as finished products in inventory or completed papers in a file. Frequently, a distinction is made between temporary storage and permanent storage by inserting a T or P in the triangle.

Worker at a Fixed Workplace

Many jobs require the worker to remain at a specified workstation. When the nature of the work is primarily manual (such as sorting, inspecting, making entries, or assembly operations), the focus of work design is on simplifying the work method and making the required operator motions as few and as easy as possible.

There are two basic ways to determine the best method when a methods analyst studies a single worker performing an essentially manual task. The first is to search among the workers and find the one who performs the job best. That person's method is then accepted as the standard, and others are trained to perform it in the same way. This was basically F. W. Taylor's approach, though after determining the best method, he searched for "first-class men" to perform according to the method. (A first-class man possessed the natural ability to do much more productive work in a particular task than the average. Men who were not first class were transferred to other jobs.) The second way is to observe the performance of a number of workers, analyze in detail each step of their work, and pick out the superior features of each worker's performance. This results in a composite method that combines the best elements of the group studied. Frank Gilbreth, the father of motion study, used this procedure to determine the "one best way" to perform a work task.

Taylor observed actual performance to find the best method; Frank Gilbreth and his wife Lillian relied on movie film. Through micromotion analysis—observing the filmed work performance frame by frame—the Gilbreths studied work very closely and defined its basic elements, which were termed *therbligs* ("Gilbreth" spelled backward, with the *t* and *h* transposed). Their study led to the rules or principles of motion economy, such as "The hands should begin and complete the motions at the same time," and "Work should be arranged to permit natural rhythm."

Once the motions for performing the task have been identified, an *operations chart* may be made, listing the operations and their sequence of performance. For greater detail, a *simo* (simultaneous motion) *chart* may be constructed, listing not only the operations but also the times for both left and right hands. This chart may be assembled from the data collected with a stopwatch, from analysis of a film of the operation, or from predetermined motion-time data (discussed later in the chapter). Many aspects of poor design are immediately obvious: a hand being used as a holding device (rather than a jig or fixture), an idle hand, or an exceptionally long time for positioning.

Worker Interacting with Equipment

When a person and equipment operate together to perform the productive process, interest focuses on the efficient use of the person's time and equipment time. When

Worker-Machine Chart for a Gourmet Coffee Store

Exhibit 11.7

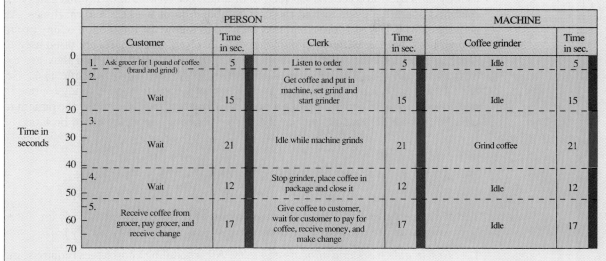

	PERSON				MACHINE	
	Customer	Time in sec.	Clerk	Time in sec.	Coffee grinder	Time in sec.
1.	Ask grocer for 1 pound of coffee (brand and grind)	5	Listen to order	5	Idle	5
2.	Wait	15	Get coffee and put in machine, set grind and start grinder	15	Idle	15
3.	Wait	21	Idle while machine grinds	21	Grind coffee	21
4.	Wait	12	Stop grinder, place coffee in package and close it	12	Idle	12
5.	Receive coffee from grocer, pay grocer, and receive change	17	Give coffee to customer, wait for customer to pay for coffee, receive money, and make change	17	Idle	17

Time in seconds (scale: 0 to 70)

Summary

	Customer	Clerk	Coffee grinder
Idle time	48 sec.	21 sec.	49 sec.
Working time	22	49	21
Total cycle time	70	70	70
Utilization in percent	Customer utilization = $\frac{22}{70} = 31\%$	Clerk utilization = $\frac{49}{70} = 70\%$	Machine utilization = $\frac{21}{70} = 30\%$

The customer, the clerk, and the coffee grinder (machine) are involved in this operation. It required 1 minute 10 seconds for the customer to purchase a pound of coffee in this store. During this time the customer spent 22 seconds, or 31 percent of the time, giving the clerk his order, receiving the ground coffee, and paying the clerk. He was idle the remaining 69 percent of the time. The clerk worked 49 seconds, or 70 percent of the time, and was idle 21 seconds, or 30 percent of the time. The coffee grinder was in operation 21 seconds, or 30 percent of the time, and was idle 70 percent of the time.

the operator's working time is less than the equipment run time, a worker-machine chart is a useful device in analysis. If the operator can operate several pieces of equipment, the problem is to find the most economical combination of operator and equipment, when the combined cost of the idle time of a particular combination of equipment and the idle time for the worker is at a minimum.

Worker-machine charts are always drawn to scale, the scale being time as measured by length. Exhibit 11.7 shows a worker-machine chart in a service setting. The question here is, whose use is most important?

Workers Interacting with Other Workers

A great amount of our productive output in manufacturing and service industries is performed by teams. The degree of interaction may be as simple as one operator handing a part to another, or as complex as a cardiovascular surgical team of doctors, nurses, anesthesiologist, operator of an artificial heart machine, X-ray technician, standby blood donors, and pathologist (and perhaps a minister to pray a little).

An activity or a gang process chart is useful in plotting each individual's activities on a time scale similar to that of the worker-machine chart. A gang process chart is usually employed to trace the interaction of a number of workers with machines of a specified operating cycle to find the best combination of workers and machines. An activity chart is less restrictive and may be used to follow the interaction of any group of operators, with or without equipment being involved. Such charts are often used to study and define each operation in an ongoing repetitive process, and they are extremely valuable in developing a standardized procedure for a specific task. Exhibit 11.8, for example, shows an activity chart for a hospital's emergency routine in performing a tracheotomy (opening a patient's throat surgically to allow the patient to breathe), where detailed activity analysis is critical and any delay could be fatal.

■ WORK MEASUREMENT AND STANDARDS

Work Measurement

The fundamental purpose of **work measurement** is to set time standards for a job. Such standards are necessary for four reasons:

1. *To schedule work and allocate capacity.* All scheduling approaches require some estimate of how much time it takes to do the work being scheduled.

Exhibit 11.8	Activity Chart of Emergency Tracheotomy

	Nurse	First doctor	Orderly	Second doctor	Nurse supervisor	Scrub nurse	
0							0
1	Detects problem Notifies doctor						1
2							2
3	Gets mobile cart	Makes diagnosis					3
4							4
5							5
6	Notifies nurse supervisor	Assists patient to breathe			Opens OR Calls scrub nurse		6
7	Notifies second doctor						7
8	Notifies orderly			Assures availability of laryngoscope and endotracheal tube			8
9	Moves patient to OR	Moves to OR	Moves patient to OR			Moves to OR Sets up equipment	9
10		Scrubs					10
11		Dons gown and gloves		Operates laryngoscope and inserts endotracheal tube			11
12				Calls for IPPB machine			12
13		Performs tracheotomy					13
14							14
15							15
16							16

Source: Data taken from Harold E. Smalley and John Freeman, *Hospital Industrial Engineering* (New York: Reinhold, 1966), p. 409.

2. *To provide an objective basis for motivating the workforce and measuring their performance.* Measured standards are particularly critical where output-based incentive plans are employed.

3. *To bid for new contracts and to evaluate performance on existing ones.* Questions such as "Can we do it?" and "How are we doing?" presume the existence of standards.

4. *To provide benchmarks for improvement.* In addition to internal evaluation, benchmarking teams regularly compare work standards in their company with those of similar jobs in other organizations.

Work measurement and its resulting work standards have been controversial since Taylor's time. Much of this criticism has come from unions, which argue that management often sets standards that cannot be achieved on a regular basis. (To counter this, in some contracts, the industrial engineer who sets the standard must demonstrate that he or she can do the job over a representative period of time at the rate which was set.) There is also the argument that workers who find a better way of doing the job get penalized by having a revised rate set. (This is commonly called rate cutting.)

With the widespread adoption of W. Edwards Deming's ideas, the subject has received renewed criticism. Deming argued that work standards and quotas inhibit process improvement and tend to focus the worker's efforts on speed rather than quality.

Despite these criticisms, work measurement and standards have proven to be effective. Much depends on sociotechnical aspects of the work. Where the job requires work groups to function as teams and create improvements, the NUMMI approach of worker-set standards discussed in the opening vignette makes sense. On the other hand, where the job really boils down to doing the work quickly, with little need for creativity (such as delivering packages for UPS as the box insert on page 426 relates), tightly engineered standards set by pros are appropriate.

Work Measurement Techniques

There are four basic techniques for measuring work: time study (stopwatch and filmed micromotion analysis), elemental standard time data, predetermined motion time data, and work sampling. The choice of techniques depends on the level of detail desired and the nature of the work itself. Highly detailed, repetitive work usually calls for time study and predetermined motion-time data analysis. When work is done in conjunction with fixed-processing-time equipment, elemental data are often used to reduce the need for direct observation. When work is infrequent or entails a long cycle time, work sampling is the tool of choice.

Time Study   A **time study** is generally made with a stopwatch, either on the spot or by analyzing a videotape of the job. The job or task to be studied is separated into measurable parts or elements, and each element is timed individually.

Time Study

Some general rules for breaking down the elements are

1. Define each work element to be short in duration but long enough so that it can be timed with a stopwatch and the time can be written down.

2. If the operator works with equipment that runs separately (meaning the operator performs a task and the equipment runs independently), separate the actions of the operator and of the equipment into different elements.

3. Define any delays by the operator or equipment into separate elements.

Grabbing a package under his arm, Joseph Polise, a driver for United Parcel Service (UPS), bounds from his brown delivery truck and toward on office building here. A few paces behind him, Marjorie Cusack, a UPS industrial engineer, clutches a digital timer.

Her eyes fixed on Mr. Polise, she counts his steps and times his contact with customers. Scribbling on a clipboard, Ms. Cusack records every second taken up by stoplights, traffic, detours, doorbells, walkways, stairways, and coffee breaks. "If he goes to the bathroom, we time him," she says.

Seventy-five thousand UPS drivers travel 1.8 billion miles per year and deliver more than 11 million packages a day. On average, UPS drivers move in and out of the truck 200 times a day. An unnecessary step or indirect travel path reduces the effectiveness of the driver and impacts service to the customer. One minute saved each day saves the company $5 million annually. For this reason, UPS spends millions each year to train its drivers in proper, efficient, and safe work methods.

Approximately 3,200 industrial engineers at UPS ensure efficient and reliable customer service by conducting time studies on drivers' routes to provide job method instruction. They have measured even the finest details of the drivers' job, including determining on which finger drivers should consistently carry their key rings to avoid losing them.

Loading efficiency is studied extensively by UPS resulting in UPS trucks that carry as much as 30 percent more packages than an average truck.

In addition to developing specific job methods, UPS provides drivers with custom-built package cars with features including:

- Domed seats that allow the driver to slide on and off easily at each delivery stop.
- A drop floor well located behind the rear wheel housing making the rear of the vehicle only a short step from the ground for easy entry.
- Bulkhead doors that allow easy access to the package compartment and save the driver steps in selecting parcels for delivery.

Source: Abstracted from Daniel Machalaba, "Up to Speed: United Parcel Service Gets Deliveries Done by Driving Its Workers," *The Wall Street Journal*, April 22, 1986, p. 1. Information provided by UPS, 1994.

After a number of repetitions, the collected times are averaged. (The standard deviation may be computed to give a measure of variance in the performance times.) The averaged times for each element are added, yielding the performance time for the operator. However, to make this operator's time usable for all workers, a measure of speed or *performance rating* must be included to "normalize" the job. The application of a rating factor gives what is called *normal time*. For example, if an operator performs a task in two minutes and the time-study analyst estimates him to be performing about 20 percent faster than normal, the normal time would be computed as 2 minutes + 0.20(2 minutes), or 2.4 minutes. In equation form,

Normal Time   **Normal time** = Observed performance time per unit $\times$ Performance rating

In this example, denoting normal time by *NT*,

$$NT = 2(1.2) = 2.4 \text{ minutes}$$

When an operator is observed for a period of time, the number of units produced during this time, along with the performance rating, gives

$$NT = \frac{\text{Time worked}}{\text{Number of units produced}} \times \text{Performance rating}$$

Standard time is derived by adding to normal time allowances for personal needs (e.g., washroom and coffee breaks), unavoidable work delays (e.g., equipment break-down, lack of materials), and worker fatigue (physical or mental). Two such equations are   Standard Time

$$\text{Standard time} = \text{Normal time} + (\text{Allowances} \times \text{Normal time})$$

or

$$ST = NT(1 + \text{Allowances}) \tag{11.1}$$

and

$$ST = \frac{NT}{1 - \text{Allowances}} \tag{11.2}$$

Equation (11.1) is most often used in practice. If one presumes that allowances should be applied to the total work period, then equation (11.2) is the correct one. To illustrate, suppose that the normal time to perform a task is 1 minute and that allowances for personal needs, delays, and fatigue total 15 percent; then by equation (11.1)

$$ST = 1(1 + 0.15) = 1.15 \text{ minutes}$$

In an eight-hour day, a worker would produce $8 \times 60/1.15$, or 417 units. This implies 417 minutes working and $480 - 417$ (or 63) minutes for allowances.

With equation (11.2),

$$ST = \frac{1}{1 - 0.15} = 1.18 \text{ minute}$$

In the same eight-hour day, $8 \times 60/1.18$ (or 408) units are produced with 408 working minutes and 72 minutes for allowances. Depending on which equation is used, there is a difference of 9 minutes in the daily allowance time.

Exhibit 11.9 shows a time study of 10 cycles of a four-element job. For each element, there is a space for the watch reading in 100ths of a minute (*R*) and each element subtracted time (*T*). The value for *T* is obtained after the time study observations are completed, because in this case, the watch is read continuously.[4] *PR* denotes the performance rating, and *T* is the average time for each element. The standard time, calculated according to equation (11.1), is given at the bottom of Exhibit 11.9.

How many observations are enough? Time study is really a sampling process; that is, we take relatively few observations as being representative of many subsequent

---

[4] Not surprisingly, this is called the *continuous method* of timing. When the watch is reset after each element is recorded, it is called the *snapback method*.

Exhibit II.9

Time-Study
Observation Sheet

Time Study Observation Sheet															
Identification of operation		*Assemble 24" x 36" chart blanks*											Date *10/9*		
Began timing: *9:26* Ended timing: *9:32*		Operator 109				Approval *BgR*						Observer *fDT*			
Element description and breakpoint		**Cycles**										**Summary**			
		1 0.00	2	3	4	5	6	7	8	9	10	ΣT	T̄	PR	NT
1	*Fold over end (grasp stapler)*	.07	.07	.05	.07	.09	.06	.05	.08	.08	.06	.68	.07	.90	.06
		.07	.61	.14	.67	.24	.78	.33	.88	.47	.09				
2	*Staple five times (drop stapler)*	.16	.14	.14	.15	.16	.16	.14	.17	.14	.15	1.51	.15	1.05	.16
		.23	.75	.28	.82	.40	.94	.47	.05	.61	.24				
3	*Bend and insert wire (drop pliers)*	.22	.25	.22	.25	.23	.23	.21	.26	.25	.24	2.36	.24	1.00	.24
		.45	.00	.50	.07	.63	.17	.68	.31	.86	.48				
4	*Dispose of finished chart (touch next sheet)*	.09	.09	.10	.08	.09	.11	.12	.08	.17	.08	1.01	.10	.90	.09
		.54	.09	.60	.15	.72	.28	.80	.39	.03	.56				
5												0.55 *normal minute for cycle*			
6															
10															

Normal cycle time *0.55* + Allowance *(0.55 ¥ 0.143) or 0.08* = Std. time *0.63 min./pc.*

cycles to be performed by the worker. Based on a great deal of analysis and experience, Benjamin Niebel's table shown in Exhibit 11.10 indicates that enough is a function of cycle length and number of repetitions of the job over a one-year planning period.

Elemental Standard-Time Data

Elemental Standard-Time Data   **Elemental standard-time data** are obtained from previous time studies and codified in tables in a handbook or computer data bank. Such data are used to develop time standards for new jobs or to make time adjustments to reflect changes in existing jobs. They are more correctly viewed as *normal-time data,* because tabled values have been modified by an average performance rating, and allowances must be added to obtain a standard time.

Calculating a time standard for a new job using elemental standard-time data tables entails four steps:

1. Break down the new job into its basic elements (such as shown in Exhibit 11.9's time-study sheet).
2. Match these elements to the time for similar elements in the table.
3. Adjust element times for special characteristics of the new job. (In metal cutting, for instance, this is often done by a formula that modifies the time required as a function of type of metal, size of the cutting tool, depth of the cut, and so forth.)
4. Add element times together and add delay and fatigue allowances as specified by company policy for the given class of work.

The obvious benefit of elemental standard data is cost savings. It eliminates the need for a new time study for each new job. This saves staff time and avoids disruption of the workforce. The main practical requirement of the approach is that elemental data must be kept up to date and easily accessible.

Predetermined Motion-Time Data Systems (PMTS)

Predetermined Motion-Time Data Systems   **Predetermined motion-time data systems (PMTS)** also use existing tabled data to artificially create a time standard. These systems differ from elemental standard data systems in several respects. First,

Exhibit 11.10

Guide to Number of
Cycles to Be
Observed in a Time
Study

When Time per Cycle Is More than	Minimum Number of Cycles of Study (Activity)		
	Over 10,000 per Year	**1,000–10,000**	**Under 1,000**
8 hours	2	1	1
3	3	2	1
2	4	2	1
1	5	3	2
48 minutes	6	3	2
30	8	4	3
20	10	5	4
12	12	6	5
8	15	8	6
5	20	10	8
3	25	12	10
2	30	15	12
1	40	20	15
.7	50	25	20
.5	60	30	25
.3	80	40	30
.2	100	50	40
.1	120	60	50
Under .1	140	80	60

Source: Benjamin W. Niebel, *Motion and Time Study,* 9th ed. (Homewood, IL: Richard D. Irwin, 1993), p. 390.

they provide times for basic motions rather than job-specific work elements. Second, they are generic to a wide range of manual work; elemental standard data are company or industry specific. Finally, because they typically require the use of many basic motions to describe even a short-duration job, they require far more analyst time to develop a standard. For this reason, the systems discussed next are being simplified as much as possible to facilitate their use, and new, faster versions with computer support are being marketed.

The three predetermined motion-time data systems that are most often used are **methods time measurement (MTM), most work measurement systems (MOST),** and **work factor.** Each was developed in the laboratory, and all are proprietary. MTM even has its own journal, user certification program, and an association of MTM organizations (the International MTM Directorate).

The sample MTM table in Exhibit 11.11 describes the movement designated as Reach, stipulating the different times allowed for varying conditions. (Other standard movement categories in the basic version of the system, MTM-1, are Grasp, Move, Position, and Release.) Note that times are measured in *time measurement units* (TMUs) of .0006 minute. To derive an MTM standard time for a job, you would list all the movements that go into it, find the appropriate TMU value for each, sum the times, and add allowances.

PMTS have been used successfully for more than 40 years. Among their advantages are

1. They enable development of standards before the job is started.
2. They have been tested extensively in the laboratory and field.

**Methods Time
Measurement
(MTM)**

**Most Work
Measurement
Systems (MOST)**

Work Factor

Exhibit II.II   MTM Predetermined Motion-Time Data for the Hand and Arm Movement "Reach"
(1 TMU = .0006 minute)

(http://www.mtm.org)

REACH—R

Distance moved (inches)	Time TMU				Hand in motion		CASE AND DESCRIPTION	
	A	B	C or D	E	A	B		
3/4 or less	2.0	2.0	2.0	2.0	1.6	1.6	A	Reach to object in fixed location, or to object in other hand or on which other hand rests.
1	2.5	2.5	3.6	2.4	2.3	2.3		
2	4.0	4.0	5.9	3.8	3.5	2.7		
3	5.3	5.3	7.3	5.3	4.5	3.6		
4	6.1	6.4	8.4	6.8	4.9	4.3	B	Reach to single object in location which may vary slightly from cycle to cycle.
5	6.5	7.8	9.4	7.4	5.3	5.0		
6	7.0	8.6	10.1	8.0	5.7	5.7		
7	7.4	9.3	10.8	8.7	6.1	6.5		
8	7.9	10.1	11.5	9.3	6.5	7.2	C	Reach to object jumbled with other objects in a group so that search and select occur.
9	8.3	10.8	12.2	9.9	6.9	7.9		
10	8.7	11.5	12.9	10.5	7.3	8.6		
12	9.6	12.9	14.2	11.8	8.1	10.1		
14	10.5	14.4	15.6	13.0	8.9	11.5		
16	11.4	15.8	17.0	14.2	9.7	12.9	D	Reach to a very small object or where accurate grasp is required.
18	12.3	17.2	18.4	15.5	10.5	14.4		
20	13.1	18.6	19.8	16.7	11.3	15.8		
22	14.0	20.1	21.2	18.0	12.1	17.3		
24	14.9	21.5	22.5	19.2	12.9	18.8	E	Reach to indefinite location to get hand in position for body balance or next motion or out of way.
26	15.8	22.9	23.9	20.4	13.7	20.2		
28	16.7	24.4	25.3	21.7	14.5	21.7		
30	17.5	25.8	26.7	22.9	15.3	23.2		

Source: Copyright by the MTM Association for Standards and Research. Reprinted with permission from the MTM Association, 1111 East Touhy Ave., Des Plaines, IL 60018.

3. They include performance rating in the times given in the tables, so users need not calculate them.

4. They can be used to audit time studies for accuracy.

5. They are accepted as part of many union contracts.

Work Sampling

Work Sampling   As the name suggests, **work sampling** involves observing a portion or sample of the work activity. Then, based on the findings in this sample, statements can be made about the activity. For example, if we were to observe a fire department rescue squad 100 random times during the day and found it was involved in a rescue mission for 30 of the 100 times (en route, on site, or returning from a call), we would estimate that the rescue squad spends 30 percent of its time directly on rescue mission calls. (The time it takes to make an observation depends on what is being observed. Many times, only a glance is needed to determine the activity, and the majority of studies require only several seconds' observation.)

Observing an activity even 100 times may not, however, provide the accuracy desired in the estimate. To refine this estimate, three main issues must be decided. (These points are discussed later in this section, along with an example.)

1. What level of statistical confidence is desired in the results?

2. How many observations are necessary?

3. Precisely when should the observations be made?

The three primary applications for work sampling are

1. *Ratio delay* to determine the activity-time percentage for personnel or equipment. For example, management may be interested in the amount of time a machine is running or idle.

2. *Performance measurement* to develop a performance index for workers. When the amount of work time is related to the quantity of output, a measure of performance is developed. This is useful for periodic performance evaluation.

3. *Time standards* to obtain the standard time for a task. When work sampling is used for this purpose, however, the observer must be experienced because he or she must attach a performance rating to the observations.

The number of observations required in a work sampling study can be fairly large, ranging from several hundred to several thousand, depending on the activity and desired degree of accuracy. Although the number can be computed from formulas, the easiest way is to refer to a table such as Exhibit 11.12, which gives the number of observations needed for a 95 percent confidence level in terms of absolute error. Absolute error is the actual range of the observations. For example, if a clerk is idle 10 percent of the time and the designer of the study is satisfied with a 2.5 percent range (meaning that the true percentage lies between 7.5 and 12.5 percent), the number of observations required for the work sampling is 576. A 2 percent error (or an interval of 8 to 12 percent) would require 900 observations.

Five steps are involved in making a work sampling study.

1. Identify the specific activity or activities that are the main purpose for the study. For example, determine the percentage of time that equipment is working, idle, or under repair.

2. Estimate the proportion of time of the activity of interest to the total time (e.g., that the equipment is working 80 percent of the time). These estimates can be made from the analyst's knowledge, past data, reliable guesses from others, or a pilot work sampling study.

3. State the desired accuracy in the study results.

4. Determine the specific times when each observation is to be made.

5. At two or three intervals during the study period, recompute the required sample size by using the data collected thus far. Adjust the number of observations if appropriate.

The number of observations to be taken in a work sampling study is usually divided equally over the study period. Thus, if 500 observations are to be made over a 10-day period, observations are usually scheduled at 500/10, or 50 per day. Each day's observations are then assigned a specific time by using a random number table.

Work Sampling Applied to Nursing   There has been a long-standing argument that a large amount of nurses' hospital time is spent on nonnursing activities. This, the argument goes, creates an apparent shortage of well-trained nursing personnel, wastes talent, hinders efficiency, and increases hospital costs, because nurses' wages are the highest single cost in the operation of a hospital. Further, pressure is growing for hospitals and hospital administrators to contain costs. With that in mind, let us use work sampling to test the hypothesis that a large portion of nurses' time is spent on nonnursing duties.

Assume at the outset that we have made a list of all the activities that are part of nursing and will make our observations in only two categories; nursing and nonnursing activities.[5] (An expanded study could list all nursing activities to determine the portion

---

[5] Actually, there is much debate on what constitutes nursing activity. For instance, is talking to a patient a nursing duty?

	Exhibit 11.12	Percentage of Total Time Occupied by Activity or Delay, p	Absolute Error					
			±1.0%	±1.5%	±2.0%	±2.5%	±3.0%	±3.5%
Determining Number of Observations Required for a Given Absolute Error at Various Values of p, with 95 Percent Confidence Level		1 or 99	396	176	99	63	44	32
		2 or 98	784	348	196	125	87	64
		3 or 97	1,164	517	291	186	129	95
		4 or 96	1,536	683	384	246	171	125
		5 or 95	1,900	844	475	304	211	155
		6 or 94	2,256	1,003	564	361	251	184
		7 or 93	2,604	1,157	651	417	289	213
		8 or 92	2,944	1,308	736	471	327	240
		9 or 91	3,276	1,456	819	524	364	267
		10 or 90	3,600	1,600	900	576	400	294
		11 or 89	3,916	1,740	979	627	435	320
		12 or 88	4,224	1,877	1,056	676	469	344
		13 or 87	4,524	2,011	1,131	724	503	369
		14 or 86	4,816	2,140	1,204	771	535	393
		15 or 85	5,100	2,267	1,275	816	567	416
		16 or 84	5,376	2,389	1,344	860	597	439
		17 or 83	5,644	2,508	1,411	903	627	461
		18 or 82	5,904	2,624	1,476	945	656	482
		19 or 81	6,156	2,736	1,539	985	684	502
		20 or 80	6,400	2,844	1,600	1,024	711	522
		21 or 79	6,636	2,949	1,659	1,062	737	542
		22 or 78	6,864	3,050	1,716	1,098	763	560
		23 or 77	7,084	3,148	1,771	1,133	787	578
		24 or 76	7,296	3,243	1,824	1,167	811	596
		25 or 75	7,500	3,333	1,875	1,200	833	612
		26 or 74	7,696	3,420	1,924	1,231	855	628
		27 or 73	7,884	3,504	1,971	1,261	876	644
		28 or 72	8,064	3,584	2,016	1,290	896	658
		29 or 71	8,236	3,660	2,059	1,318	915	672
		30 or 70	8,400	3,733	2,100	1,344	933	686
		31 or 69	8,556	3,803	2,139	1,369	951	698
		32 or 68	8,704	3,868	2,176	1,393	967	710
		33 or 67	8,844	3,931	2,211	1,415	983	722
		34 or 66	8,976	3,989	2,244	1,436	997	733
		35 or 65	9,100	4,044	2,275	1,456	1,011	743
		36 or 64	9,216	4,096	2,304	1,475	1,024	753
		37 or 63	9,324	4,144	2,331	1,492	1,036	761
		38 or 62	9,424	4,188	2,356	1,508	1,047	769
		39 or 61	9,516	4,229	2,379	1,523	1,057	777
		40 or 60	9,600	4,266	2,400	1,536	1,067	784
		41 or 59	9,676	4,300	2,419	1,548	1,075	790
		42 or 58	9,744	4,330	2,436	1,559	1,083	795
		43 or 57	9,804	4,357	2,451	1,569	1,089	800
		44 or 56	9,856	4,380	2,464	1,577	1,095	804
		45 or 55	9,900	4,400	2,475	1,584	1,099	808
		46 or 54	9,936	4,416	2,484	1,590	1,104	811
		47 or 53	9,964	4,428	2,491	1,594	1,107	813
		48 or 52	9,984	4,437	2,496	1,597	1,109	815
		49 or 51	9,996	4,442	2,499	1,599	1,110	816
		50	10,000	4,444	2,500	1,600	1,111	816

Note: Number of observations is obtained from the formula $E = Z\sqrt{\dfrac{p(1-p)}{N}}$ and the required sample (N)

is $N = \dfrac{Z^2 p(1-p)}{E^2}$

where E = Absolute error

$\quad p$ = Percentage occurrence of activity or delay being measured

$\quad N$ = Number of random observations (sample size)

$\quad Z$ = Number of standard deviations to give desired confidence level (e.g., for 90 percent confidence, Z = 1.65; for 95 percent, Z = 1.96; for 99 percent, Z = 2.23). In this table Z = 2

of time spent in each.) Therefore, when we observe during the study and find the nurse performing one of the duties on the nursing list, we simply place a tally mark in the nursing column. If we observe anything besides nursing activities, we place a tally mark in the nonnursing column.

We can now proceed to plan the study. Assume that we (or the nursing supervisor) estimate that nurses spend 60 percent of their time in nursing activities. Assume that we would like to be 95 percent confident that findings of our study are within the absolute error range of ±3 percent; that is, that if our study shows nurses spend 60 percent of their time on nursing duties, we are 95 percent confident that the true percentage lies between 57 and 63 percent. From Exhibit 11.12, we find that 1,067 observations are required for 60 percent activity time and ±3 percent error. If our study is to take place over 10 days, we start with 107 observations per day.

To determine when each day's observations are to be made, we assign specific numbers to each minute and a random number table to set up a schedule. If the study extends over an eight-four shift, we can assign numbers to correspond to each consecutive minute.[6] Exhibit 11.13A shows the assignment of numbers to corresponding minutes. For simplicity, because each number corresponds to one minute, a three-number scheme is used, with the second and third numbers corresponding to the minute of the hour. A number of other schemes would also be appropriate.[7]

A.

Time	Assigned Numbers
7:00–7:59 AM	100–159
8:00–8:59 AM	200–259
9:00–9:59 AM	300–359
10:00–10:59 AM	400–459
11:00–11:59 AM	500–559
12:00–12:59 PM	600–659
1:00–1:59 PM	700–759
2:00–2:59 PM	800–859

B.

Random Number	Corresponding Time from the List in 11.13A
669	Nonexistent
831	2:31 PM
555	11:55 AM
470	Nonexistent
113	7:13 AM
080	Nonexistent
520	11:20 AM
204	8:04 AM
732	1:32 PM
420	10:20 AM

Exhibit 11.13

Sampling Plan for Nurses' Activities
A. Assignment of Numbers to Corresponding Minutes
B. Determination of Observation Times
C. Observation Schedule

C.

Observation	Schedule Time	Nursing Activity(✓)	Nonnursing Activity (✓)
1	7:13 AM		
2	8:04 AM		
3	10:20 AM		
4	11:20 AM		
5	11:55 AM		
6	1:32 PM		
7	2:31 PM		

[6] For this study, it is likely that the night shift (11:00 PM to 7:00 AM) would be run separately because the nature of nighttime nursing duties is considerably different from that of daytime duties.

[7] If a number of studies are planned, a computer program may be used to generate a randomized schedule for the observation times.

If we refer to a random number table and list three-digit numbers, we can assign each number to a time. The random numbers in Exhibit 11.13B demonstrate the procedure for seven observations.

This procedure is followed to generate 107 observation times, and the times are rearranged chronologically for ease in planning. Rearranging the times determined in Exhibit 11.13B give the total observations per day shown in Exhibit 11.13C (for our sample of seven).

To be perfectly random in this study, we should also "randomize" the nurse we observe each time. (The use of various nurses minimizes the effect of bias.) In the study, our first observation is made at 7:13 AM for Nurse X. We walk into the nurses area and, on seeing the nurse, check either a nursing or a nonnursing activity. Each observation need be only long enough to determine the class of activity—in most cases only a glance is needed. At 8:04 AM we observe Nurse Y. We continue in this way to the end of the day and the 107 observations. At the end of the second day (and 214 observations), we decide to check for the adequacy of our sample size.

Let us say we made 150 observations of nurses working and 64 of them not working, which gives 70.1 percent working. From Exhibit 11.12, this corresponds to 933 observations. Because we have already taken 214 observations, we need take only 719 over the next eight days, or 90 per day.

When the study is half over, another check should be made. For instance, if days 3, 4, and 5 showed 55, 59, and 64 working observations, the cumulative data would give 328 working observations of a total 484, or a 67.8 percent working activity. For a ±3% error, Exhibit 11.12 shows the sample size to be about 967, leaving 483 to be made—at 97 per day—for the following five days. Another computation should be made before the last day to see if another adjustment is required. If after the tenth day several more observations are indicated, these can be made on day 11.

If at the end of the study we find that 66 percent of nurses' time is involved with what has been defined as nursing activity, there should be an analysis to identify the remaining 34 percent. Approximately 12 to 15 percent is justifiable for coffee breaks and personal needs, which leaves 20 to 22 percent of the time that must be justified and compared to what the industry considers ideal levels of nursing activity. To identify the nonnursing activities, a more detailed breakdown could have been originally built into the sampling plan. Otherwise, a follow-up study may be in order.

Setting time standards using work sampling.   As mentioned earlier, work sampling can be used to set time standards. To do this, the analyst must record the subject's performance rate (or index) along with working observations. Exhibit 11.14 gives the additional data required and the formula for calculating standard time.

Work sampling compared to time study.   Work sampling offers several advantages:

1.   Several work sampling studies may be conducted simultaneously by one observer.
2.   The observer need not be a trained analyst unless the purpose of the study is to determine a time standard.
3.   No timing devices are required.
4.   Work of a long cycle time may be studied with a fewer observer hours.
5.   The duration of the study is longer, which minimizes effects of short-period variations.

Information	Source of Data	Data for One Day
Total time expended by operator (working time and idle time)	Computer Payroll System	480 min.
Number of parts produced	Inspection Department	420 pieces
Working time in percent	Work sampling	85%
Idle time in percent	Work sampling	15%
Average performance index	Work sampling	110%
Total allowances	Company time-study manual	15%

$$
\begin{array}{l}
\text{Standard time} \\
\text{per piece}
\end{array} = \frac{\left(\begin{array}{c}\text{Total time} \\ \text{in minutes}\end{array}\right) \times \left(\begin{array}{c}\text{Working time} \\ \text{proportion}\end{array}\right) \times \left(\begin{array}{c}\text{Performance} \\ \text{index}\end{array}\right)}{\text{Total number of pieces produced}} \times \frac{1}{1 - \text{Allowances}}
$$

$$
= \left(\frac{480 \times 0.85 \times 1.10}{420}\right) \times \left(\frac{1}{1 - 0.15}\right) = 1.26 \text{ minutes}
$$

Exhibit 11.14

Deriving a Time Standard Using Work Sampling

6. The study may be temporarily delayed at any time with little effect.
7. Because work sampling needs only instantaneous observations (made over a longer period), the operator has less chance to influence the findings by changing his or her work method.

When the cycle time is short, time study (or PMTS) is more appropriate than work sampling. One drawback of work sampling is that it does not provide as complete a breakdown of elements as time study. Another difficulty with work sampling is that observers, rather than following a random sequence of observations, tend to develop a repetitive route of travel. This may allow the time of the observations to be predictable and thus invalidate the findings. A third factor—a potential drawback—is that the basic assumption in work sampling is that all observations pertain to the same static system. If the system is in the process of change, work sampling may give misleading results.

FINANCIAL INCENTIVE PLANS

The third piece of the job design equation is the paycheck. In this section, we briefly review common methods for setting financial incentives.

Basic Compensation Systems

The main forms of basic compensation are hourly pay, straight salary, piece rate, and commissions. The first two are based on time spent on the job, with individual performance rewarded by an increase in the base rate. Piece rate plans reward on the basis of direct daily output. (A worker is paid $5 a unit; thus, by producing 10 units per day, the worker earns $50.) Sometimes a guaranteed base is included in a piece-rate plan; a worker would receive this base amount regardless of output, plus a piece-rate bonus. (For example, the worker's hourly base pay is $8, so this coupled with $50 piece-rate earnings gives the worker $114 for an eight-hour day.) Commissions may be thought of as sales-based piece rates and are calculated in the same general way.

Financial Incentive Plans

The two broad categories of **financial incentive plans** are individual or small-group incentive plans and organizationwide plans.

Individual and Small-Group Incentive Plans

Individual and work group plans traditionally have rewarded performance by using output (often defined by piece rates) and quality measures. Quality is accounted for by a quality adjustment factor, say a percentage of rework.[8] (For example: Incentive pay = Total output × [1 − Percent deduction for rework].) In recent years, skill development has also been rewarded. Sometimes called *pay for knowledge,* this means a worker is compensated for learning new tasks. This is particularly important in job shops using group technology, as well as in banking, where supervisors' jobs require knowledge of new types of financial instruments and selling approaches.

AT&T, for example, instituted incentive programs for its managers—an Individual Incentive Award (IIA) and a Management Team Incentive Award (MTIA). The IIA provides lump-sum bonuses to outstanding performers. These outstanding performers were determined by individual performance ratings accompanied by extensive documentation. The lump-sum bonus could range between 15 and 30 percent of base pay.

MTIAs are granted to members of specific divisions or units. Appropriate division or unit goals are established at the beginning of the year. The goals include department service objectives and interdepartmental goals. A typical MTIA could call for a standard amount equivalent to 1.5 percent of wages plus overtime for the next three years based on performance in the current year.

Organizationwide Plans

Profit Sharing

Profit sharing and gain sharing are the major types of organization-wide plans. **Profit sharing** is simply distributing a percentage of corporate profits across the workforce. In the United States, at least one-third of all organizations have profit sharing. In Japan, most major companies give profit-based bonuses twice a year to all employees. Such bonuses may range from 50 percent of salaries in good years, to nothing in bad years.

Gain Sharing

Gain sharing also involves giving organizationwide bonuses, but it differs from profit sharing in two important respects. First, it typically measures controllable costs or units of output, not profits, in calculating a bonus. Second, gain sharing is always combined with a participative approach to management. The original and best-known gainsharing plan is the Scanlon Plan.

Scanlon Plan   In the late 1930s, the Lapointe Machine and Tool Company was on the verge of bankruptcy, but through the efforts of union president Joseph Scanlon and company management, a plan was devised to save the company by reducing labor costs. In essence, this plan started with the normal labor cost within the firm. Workers as a group were rewarded for any reductions in labor cost below this base cost. The plan's success depended on committees of workers throughout the firm whose purpose was to search out areas for cost saving and to devise ways of improvement. There were many improvements, and the plan did, in fact, save the company.

---

[8] For a complete discussion of incentive plans including quality measures, see S. Globerson and R. Parsons, "Multi-Factor Incentive Systems: Current Practices," *Operations Management Review* 3, no. 2 (Winter 1985).

The basic elements of the Scanlon Plan are

1. *The ratio.* The ratio is the standard that serves as a measure for judging business performance. It can be expressed as

$$\text{Ratio} = \frac{\text{Total labor cost}}{\text{Sales value of production}}$$

2. *The bonus.* The amount of bonus depends on the reduction in costs below the preset ratio.
3. *The production committee.* The production committee is formed to encourage employee suggestions to increase productivity, improve quality, reduce waste, and so forth. The purpose of a production committee is similar to that of a QC circle.
4. *The screening committee.* The screening committee consists of top management and worker representatives who review monthly bonuses, discuss production problems, and consider improvement suggestions.

Gain-sharing plans are now used by more than a thousand firms in the United States and Europe, and are growing in popularity. One survey in the United States indicated that about 13 percent of all firms have them, and that more than 70 percent were started after 1982.[9] Though originally established in small companies such as Lapointe, Lincoln Electric Company, and Herman Miller, gain sharing has been installed by large firms such as TRW, General Electric, Motorola, and Firestone. These companies apply gain sharing to organizational units. Motorola, for example, has virtually all its plant employees covered by gain sharing. These plans are increasing because "they are more than just pay incentive plans; they are a participative approach to management and are often used as a way to install participative management."[10] A comparison of the typical applications of the plans is discussed, along with merit pay, in Exhibit 11.15.

Pay-for-Performance

Business Week magazine ran a survey of compensation for company presidents. Salaries ranged from $350,000 to $8 million. In every case there was an extra "kicker" (e.g., a healthy bonus for achievement of certain goals either in sales, profits, stock price, etc.). Despite gigantic salaries, every executive was offered an incentive bonus.

The following are more examples of recent incentive pay results:[11]

·   At Kaiser Aluminum, located in Jackson, Tennessee, the use of incentive pay contributed to an 80 percent productivity boost over five years. Poor quality costs decreased by 70 percent.

·   General Tire's 1,950-employee Mt. Vernon, Illinois, plant used a gain-sharing program to generate $30 million in savings over a five-year period,

---

[9] C. O'Dell, *People, Performance, and Pay* (Houston: American Productivity Center, 1987).

[10] E. E. Lawler III, "Paying for Organizational Performance," Report G 87-1 (92) (Los Angeles: Center for Effective Organizations, University of Southern California, 1987).

[11] These examples are from Woodruff Imberman, "Pay for Performance Boosts Quality Output," *Industrial Engineering,* October, 1996, p. 35.

| Exhibit 11.15 | Comparison of Common Reward/Incentive Plans |

Type of Plan	Application	Advantages	Disadvantages
Merit Pay	Individual	• Allows management to target specific behavior and to easily evolve criteria over time.	• Can be arbitrary and unbiased when incorrectly administered. • Often not clearly tied to business goals.
Profit Sharing	Group	• Ties business performance to employee reward.	• Often individual or group behavior is not correlated to business performance.
Gain-Sharing	Group	• Specific group performance directly tied to employee reward.	• Often focuses excessively on cost control. • More applicable for tactical improvements than strategic changes.
Lump-sum Bonuses and Individual Bonuses	Either	• Allows management to vary criteria and magnitude of reward; able to target specific actions and behavior.	• Often used for and seen as deferred compensation. • Not always a tie to business goals or performance.
Pay-for-knowledge	Individual	• Allows management to target specific types of skills and personal growth.	• May not impact business performance unless management targets correct skills and applies new skills effectively.
Piece Rate	Either	• Allows management to target specific output goals	• May lead to undesirable competition among workers • Standards must be kept up to date.

Source: Modified from Craig Giffi, A. Roth, and G. Seal, *Competing in World-Class Manufacturing, America's 21st Century Challenge* (Homewood, IL: Business One Irwin, 1990).

$20 million of which was paid out to workers in the form of bonuses. The company profited by $10 million.

• General Electric used a merit pay system to cut down its order-to-delivery time from 18 weeks to 5 weeks at its Louisville, Kentucky, appliance plant.

• Wrought Washer Manufacturing Company located in Milwaukee, Wisconsin, improved productivity by 39 percent with a gain-sharing program in 1993. The workforce earned $165,737 in extra bonuses and the company saved an additional $110,490.

• Whirlpool Corporation's Benton Harbor, Michigan, plant instituted a merit program in 1988. Since that time, the plant has shown productivity gains of about 19 percent annually, with each year building on the previous year. Quality improvements have been substantial, with the number of parts rejected sinking to 4 per million from 837 per million.

• Finally, Jostens, a company that makes quality class rings, instituted a piece-rate system based on the number of good rings produced by each employee. In 1990, the company was producing 16 good rings per employee (i.e., deducting rejects and rework). After the program began in 1993, employees began producing 25 (good) rings per employee—a 56 percent productivity boost—with a lead time of 10 calendar days from work order to shipping. In only a year, productivity increased further to 36 good rings per employee.

The results of these studies are overwhelming. Paying employees based on their performance does work. Many experts, including those at the American Productivity and Quality Center, predict that these systems will become a common part of the strategy that companies employ to improve their performance in the late 1990s and beyond.

In the supplement to this chapter, we will discuss learning curves, which are widely used in work measurement.

■ CONCLUSION

At the outset of this chapter we identified current trends in job design. What will the future hold? One thing is clear: Globalization and the successful application of sophisticated process technologies will make the human element even more important to operations competitiveness than before. Giffi, Roth, and Seal speculate that "the twenty-first century will be marked by the human resource renaissance." In their view, this renaissance will be characterized by companies actively cultivating their human resources through careful selection and training of the best and brightest employees, implementing innovative team-based employee involvement programs, developing genuinely participative management approaches, and continually retraining their employees.[12]

What is the future of the industrial engineering approaches also addressed in this chapter? In our opinion, they will always have application to analyzing work methods and, selectively, to setting work standards. The UPS (page 426) and the NUMMI (page 414) examples show how these classic tools are used quite differently, but effectively, by two very successful organizations.

FORMULA REVIEW

Standard time

$$ST = NT(1 + \text{Allowances})$$ (11.1)

$$ST = \frac{NT}{1 - \text{Allowances}}$$ (11.2)

SOLVED PROBLEMS

SOLVED PROBLEM 1

Brandon is very organized and wants to plan his day perfectly. To do this, he has his friend Kelly time his daily activities. Here are the results of her timing Brandon on polishing two pairs of black shoes using the snapback method of timing. What is the standard time for polishing

---

[12] C. Giffi, A. Roth, and G. M. Seal, *Competing in World-Class Manufacturing: America's 21st Century Challenge* (Homewood, IL. Richard D. Irwin, 1990), p. 299.

two pair? (Assume a 5 percent allowance factor for Brandon to put something mellow on the CD player. Account for noncyclically recurring elements by dividing their observed times by the total number of cycles observed.)

		Observed Times						
Element	1	2	3	4	ΣT	T	Performance Rating	NT
Get shoeshine kit	0.50						125%	
Polish shoes	0.94	0.85	0.80	0.81			110	
Put away kit				0.75			80	

Solution

	ST	$\bar{T}$	Performance Rating	NT
Get shoeshine kit	.50	.50/2 = .25	125%	.31
Polish shoes (2 pair)	3.40	3.40/2 = 1.70	110	1.87
Put away kit	.75	.75/2 = .375	80	.30
Normal time for one pair of shoes				2.48

Standard time for the pair = 2.48 × 1.05 = 2.60 minutes.

SOLVED PROBLEM 2

A total of 15 observations have been taken on a head baker for a school district. The numerical breakdown of the baker's activities is

Make Ready	Do	Clean Up	Idle
2	6	3	4

Based on this information, how many work sampling observations are required to determine how much of the baker's time is spent in "doing"? Assume a 5 percent desired absolute accuracy and 95 percent confidence level.

Solution

To calculate the number of observations, use the formula at the bottom of Exhibit 11.12, because the 95 percent confidence is required (i.e., $Z \cong 2$).

$$p = \text{"Doing"} = 6/15 = 40\%$$
$$E = 5\% \text{ (given)}$$
$$N = \frac{4p(1 - p)}{E^2} = \frac{4(.4)(1 - .4)}{(.05)(.05)} = \frac{.96}{.0025} = 384$$

REVIEW AND DISCUSSION QUESTIONS

1. Why might practicing managers and industrial engineers be skeptical about job enrichment and sociotechnical approaches to job design?

2. Chase, Aquilano, and Jacobs commonly complain to their families that book writing is hard work and that they should be excused from helping out with the housework so that they can rest. Which exhibit in this chapter should they never let their families see?

3. Is there an inconsistency when a company requires precise time standards and encourages job enlargement?

4. Match the following techniques to their most appropriate application:

MTM	Washing clothes at laundromat
SIMO chart	Tracing your steps in getting a parking permit
Worker–machine chart	Faculty office hours kept
Process chart	Development of a new word processor keyboard
Work sampling	Planning the assembly process for a new electronic device

5. You have timed your friend, Lefty, assembling widgets. His time averaged 12 minutes for the two cycles you timed. He was working very hard, and you believe that none of the nine other operators doing the same job can beat his time. Are you ready to put this time forth as the standard for making an order of 5,000 widgets? If not, what else should you do?

6. Comment on the following:
   a. "Work measurement is old hat. We have automated our office, and now we run every bill through our computer (after our 25 clerks have typed the data into our computer database)."
   b. "It's best that our workers don't know that they are being time studied. That way, they can't complain about us getting in the way when we set time standards."
   c. "Once we get everybody on an incentive plan, then we will start our work measurement program."
   d. "Rhythm is fine for dancing, but it has no place on the shop floor."

7. Organizationwide financial incentive plans cover all the workers. Some units or individuals may have contributed more to corporate profits than others. Does this detract from the effectiveness of the incentive plan system? How would your incentive scheme for a small software development firm compare to an established auto manufacturing firm?

PROBLEMS

1. Use the following form to evaluate a job you have held relative to the five principles of job design given in the chapter. Develop a numerical score by summing the numbers in parentheses.

	Poor (0)	Adequate (1)	Good (2)	Outstanding (3)
Task variety				
Skill variety				
Feedback				
Task identity				
Task autonomy				

1. Correspondence to the guidelines for job design is a pretty accurate predictor of the general level of subjective satisfaction.

   a. Compute the score for your job. Does the score match your subjective feelings about the job as a whole? Explain.
   b. Compare your score with the scores generated by your classmates. Is there one kind of job that everybody likes and one kind that everybody dislikes?

2. Examine the process chart in Exhibit 11.5. Can you recommend some improvements to cut down on delays and transportation? (Hint: The research laboratory can suggest changes in the requisition form.)

2. See SM.

✓ **3.** A time study was made of an existing job to develop new time standards. A worker was observed for 45 minutes. During that period, 30 units were produced. The analyst rated the worker as performing at a 90 percent performance rate. Allowances in the firm for rest and personal time are 12 percent.

3. *a.* 1.35 minutes.
   b. 1.51 minutes.
   c. ST = 1.53 minutes.
     The worker would not
     make the bonus.

4.   Observation
                  Times

   (045)   8:45
   (151)   9:51
   (152)   9:52
   (322)   11:22
   (331)   11:31

5. Standard time = .558
   minute.

6. ST = .078 min./donut.

7. *a.* NT = .9286 min./part. ✓
   b. ST = 1.0679 min./part.
   c. Daily output = 449.50
     Day's wages = $44.49.

8. *a.* NT = 11.7 min.
   b. ST = 13.455 min./
     portfolio.
   c. Daily output at
     standard = 35.67; 50
     portfolios, day's
     pay = $134.55.

a. What is the normal time for the task?

b. What is the standard time for the task?

c. If the worker produced 300 units in an eight-hour day, what would the day's pay be if the basic rate was $6 per hour and the premium payment system paid on a 100 percent basis?

4. The Bullington Company wants a time standard established on the painting operation of souvenir horseshoes for the local Pioneer Village. Work sampling is to be used. It is estimated that working time averages 95 percent of total time (working time plus idle time). A co-op student is available to do the work sampling between 8:00 AM and 12:00 noon. Sixty working days are to be used for the study. Use Exhibit 11.12 and an absolute error of 2.5 percent. Use the table of random numbers (Appendix B) to calculate the sampling schedule for the first day (i.e., show the times of day that an observation of working/idle should be made). Hint: Start random number selection with the first tour.

5. The final result of the study in Problem 4 estimated working time at 91.0 percent. In a 480-minute shift the best operator painted 1,000 horseshoes. The student's performance index was estimated to be 115 percent. Total allowances for fatigue, personal time, etc. are 10 percent. Calculate the standard time per piece.

6. Suppose you want to set a time standard for the baker making her specialty, square donuts. A work sampling study of her on "donut day" yielded the following results:

Time spent (working and idle)	32 minutes
Number of donuts produced	5,000
Working time	280 minutes
Performance rating	125%
Allowances	10%

What is the standard time per donut?

7. In an attempt to increase productivity and reduce costs, Rho Sigma Corporation is planning to install an incentive pay plan in its manufacturing plant. In developing standards for one operation, time-study analysts observed a worker for a 30-minute period. During that time the worker completed 42 parts. The analysts rated the worker as producing at 130 percent. The base wage rate of the worker is $5 per hour. The firm has established 15 percent as a fatigue and personal time allowance.

a. What is the normal time for the task?

b. What is the standard time for the task?

c. If the worker produced 500 units during an eight-hour day, what wages would the worker have earned?

8. Because new regulations will greatly change the products and services offered by savings and loan associations, time studies must be performed on tellers and other personnel to determine the number and types of personnel needed and incentive wage payment plans that might be installed.

As an example of the studies that the various tasks will undergo, consider the following problem and come up with appropriate answers.

A hypothetical case was set up in which the teller (to be retitled later as an *account adviser*) was required to examine a customer's portfolio and determine whether it was more beneficial for the customer to consolidate various CDs into a single issue currently offered, or to leave the portfolio unaltered. A time study made of the teller yielded the following findings:

Time of study	90 minutes
Number of portfolios examined	10 portfolios
Performance rating	130 percent
Rest for personal time	15 percent
Teller's proposed new pay rate	$12 per hour

  a. What is the normal time for the teller to do a portfolio analysis for the CDs?
  b. What is the standard time for the analysis?
  c. If the S&L decides to pay the new tellers on a 100 percent premium payment plan, how much would a teller earn for a day in which he analyzed 50 customer portfolios?

9. Based upon a manager's observations, a milling machine appears to be idle approximately 30 percent of the time. Develop a work sampling plan to determine the percentage of idle time accurate within a 3 percent error ($\pm 3\%$) with a 95 percent confidence level. Use the random numbers from Appendix B to derive the first day's sampling schedule (assume that the sample will take place over 60 days, and that an 8-hour shift is used from 8:00–12:00 and 1:00–5:00).

> 9. Sample size = 933. Approximately 16 observations per day. See IM for example of sampling schedule.

Case

Teamwork at Volvo

Volvo is trying to determine if the assembly line has become outdated as mass markets disappear. In 1974 the Swedish automaker dismantled the assembly line at its plant in Kalmar, Sweden. The line was replaced with a system in which cars are built by small, decentralized work teams that produce sections of cars. Volvo officials believe strongly that teams, and a return to craftsmanship, will improve quality and increase employees' pride in their work. In fact, Volvo believes so strongly in teamwork that this system is also being put into place at the company's new plant in Uddevalla, Sweden.

The Uddevalla plant was completed in 1990 to build the 740 and 940 models. By the end of 1991, the plant was producing about 22,000 cars annually; at full capacity, it will employ 1,000 workers and produce 40,000 cars annually. At the Uddevalla facility, self-managed teams of 8 to 10 members assemble complete cars from start to finish. Cars being assembled are not moved on a conveyor line from worker to worker but rather are assembled in a stationary position. A special device tilts the car as needed so that workers can perform their tasks. Each team has a high degree of autonomy and responsibility; they set their own break times and vacation schedules and reassign work when a team member is absent. Teams also participate in policy-making decisions and are responsible for a variety of tasks, including quality control, production planning, developing work procedures, servicing equipment, and ordering supplies.

Workers at the Uddevalla plant are paid for performance. In addition to wages, bonuses are paid for maintaining quality and productivity and for meeting weekly delivery targets. There are no supervisors and plant foremen; each of six "production workshops" houses 80 to 100 employees who are divided into assembly teams. Each assembly team has a coordinator (chosen on a rotating basis), who has direct contact with the managers. To make sure the system works, employees are provided with abundant information. Volvo also goes to great lengths to ensure that workers have an in-depth understanding of company history, tradition, and its strategy. The free flow of information is encouraged and workers have input on everything from assembly processes to new-product innovations.

The new system at Uddevalla isn't totally successful. Although morale is up and absenteeism is down, productivity is not as high as at Volvo's plant in Ghent, Belgium, where building a car on the assembly line takes about half the time. Lennert Ericson, president of the metal workers' union at the Uddevalla plant, thinks the approach there will work: "I am convinced that our ways [teams] will be successful and competitive. Our next goal is to be better than Kalmar, and when we get to that, our goal will be to get to Ghent."

Volvo has invested heavily in training workers at the Uddevalla plant. First, employees attend a 16-week initiation course as part of a 16-month training program in which workers learn about auto assembly. Workers are encouraged to share experiences with one another and exchange ideas.

Both union and management feel confident that the new system will improve the organization. But it will take time. The system puts numerous demands on everyone, and there has been some resistance. And like other automakers, Volvo hasn't escaped the current worldwide slump in car sales. But several experts pick Volvo as the company to invest in once the economy rebounds. Stock in the firm climbed from 35 in early 1991 to 60 about a year later, while shares of GM, Ford, and Chrysler were still down from their 1991 highs. Investment firm Bear Stearns thinks the Swedish automaker's profits will boom. In the meantime, striving to become the world's first truly global auto producer, Volvo has developed alliances with French automaker Renault and Japan's Mitsubishi.

Questions

1. What is the difference between teams at the Kalmar plant and self-managed teams at Uddevalla?

2. How important is empowerment in Volvo's Uddevalla facility?

3. Why do you think there is resistance to the team approach at Uddevalla? How can Volvo overcome this resistance?

4. The Uddevalla plant was closed in 1996. Why was it never able to produce cars as inexpensively as the Ghent plant? (Hint: remember that Uddevalla is in Sweden and Ghent is in Belgium.)

Source: J. M. Ivancevich, P. Lorenzi, and S. Skinner, *Management Quality and Competitiveness* (Homewood IL: Richard D. Irwin, 1994), pp. 279–80.

SELECTED BIBLIOGRAPHY

Barnes, Ralph M. *Motion and Time Study: Design and Measurement of Work.* 8th ed. New York: John Wiley & Sons, 1980.

Carlisle, Brian. "Job Design Implications for Operations Managers." *International Journal of Operations and Production Management* 3, no. 3 (1983), pp. 40–48.

Konz, Stephan. *Work Design: Industrial Ergonomics.* 2nd ed. New York: John Wiley & Sons, 1983.

Niebel, Benjamin W. *Motion and Time Study.* 9th ed. Homewood, IL: Richard D. Irwin, 1993.

Ramsey, Jr., George F. "Using Self-Administered Work Sampling in a State Agency." *Industrial Engineering,* February 1993, pp. 44–45.

Rutter, Rick, "Work Sampling: As a Win/Win Management Tool." *Industrial Engineering,* February 1994, pp. 30–31.

Sandberg, ëAke. *Enriching Production: Perspectives on Volvo's Uddevalla Plant as An Alternative to Lean Production.* Brookfield, VT: Avebury, 1995.

Sasser, W. Earl, and William E. Fulmer. "Creating Personalized Service Delivery Systems." In *Service Management Effectiveness,* ed. D. Bowen, R. Chase, and T. Cummings. San Francisco: Jossey-Bass, 1990, pp. 213–33.

Zandin, Kjell, *Most Work Measurement Systems.* New York: Marcel Dekker, 1990.

Zuboff, Shoshana. *In the Age of the Smart Machine: The Future of Work and Power.* New York: Basic Books, 1984.

Learning Curves

Supplement Outline

Application of Learning Curves, 446

Plotting Learning Curves, 447

    Logarithmic Analysis

    Learning Curve Tables

    Estimating the Learning Percentage

    How Long Does Learning Go On?

General Guidelines for Learning, 453

    Individual Learning

Organizational Learning, 454

Learning Curves Applied to Heart Transplant Mortality, 455

Key Terms

Learning Curve

Individual Learning

Organizational Learning

Learning Curve

A **learning curve** is a line displaying the relationship between unit production time and the cumulative number of units produced.

■ APPLICATION OF LEARNING CURVES

Learning (or experience) curve theory has a wide range of application in the business world. In manufacturing, it can be used to estimate the time for product design and production, as well as costs. Learning curves are important and are sometimes overlooked as one of the trade-offs in just-in-time (JIT) systems, where sequencing and short runs achieve lower inventories by forfeiting some advantages of experience benefits from long product runs. Learning curves are also an integral part in planning corporate strategy, such as decisions concerning pricing, capital investment, and operating costs based on experience curves.

Individual
Learning

Organizational
Learning

Learning curves can be applied to individuals or organizations. **Individual learning** is improvement that results when people repeat a process and gain skill or efficiency from their own experience. That is, "practice makes perfect." **Organizational learning** results from practice as well, but it also comes from changes in administration, equipment, and product design. In organizational settings, we expect to see both kinds of learning occurring simultaneously and often describe the combined effect with a single learning curve.

Learning curve theory is based on three assumptions:

1. The amount of time required to complete a given task or unit of a product will be less each time the task is undertaken.
2. The unit time will decrease at a decreasing rate.
3. The reduction in time will follow a predictable pattern.

Each of these assumptions was found to hold true in the airplane industry, where learning curves were first applied.[1] In this application, it was observed that, as output doubled, there was a 20 percent reduction in direct production worker-hours per unit between doubled units. Thus, if it took 100,000 hours for Plane 1, it would take 80,000 hours for Plane 2, 64,000 hours for Plane 4, and so forth. Because the 20 percent reduction meant that, say, Unit 4 took only 80 percent of the production time required for Unit 2, the line connecting the coordinates of output and time was referred to as an "80 percent learning curve." (By convention, the percentage learning rate is used to denote any given exponential learning curve.)

A learning curve may be developed from an arithmetic tabulation, by logarithms, or by some other curve-fitting method, depending on the amount and form of the available data.

There are two ways to think about the improved performance that comes with learning curves; that is, time per unit (as in Exhibit S11.1A) or as units of output per time period (as in S11.1B). *Time per unit* shows the decrease in time required for each successive unit. *Cumulative average time* shows the cumulative average performance times as the total number of units increases. Time per unit and cumulative average times are also called *progress curves* or *product learning,* and are useful for complex

---

[1] See the classic paper by T. P. Wright, "Factors Affecting the Cost of Airplanes," *Journal of the Aeronautical Sciences,* February 1936, pp. 122–28.

products or products with a longer cycle time. *Units of output per time period* is also called *industry learning* and is generally applied to high-volume production (short cycle time).

Note in Exhibit S11.1A that the cumulative average curve does not decrease as fast as the time per unit because the time is being averaged. For example, if the time for Units 1, 2, 3, and 4 were 100, 80, 70, and 64, they would be plotted that way on the time per unit graph, but would be plotted as 100, 90, 83.3, and 78.5 on the cumulative average time graph.

PLOTTING LEARNING CURVES

There are many ways to analyze past data to fit a useful trend line. We will use the simple exponential curve first as an arithmetic procedure and then by a logarithmic analysis. In an arithmetical tabulation approach, a column for units is created by doubling, row by row, as: 1, 2, 4, 8, 16. . . . The time for the first unit is multiplied by the learning percent to obtain the time for the second unit. The second unit is multiplied by the learning percent for the fourth unit, and so on. Thus, if we are developing an 80 percent learning curve, we would arrive at the figures listed in column 2 of Exhibit S11.2. Because it is often desirable for planning purposes to know the cumulative direct labor hours, column 4, which lists this information, is also

Learning Curves Plotted as Times and Numbers of Units

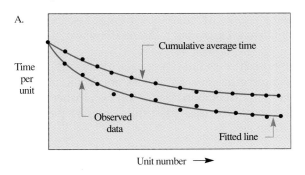

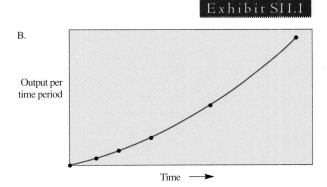

Unit, Cumulative, and Cumulative Average Direct Labor Worker-Hours Required for an **80** Percent Learning Curve

(1) Unit Number	(2) Unit Direct Labor Hours	(3) Cumulative Direct Labor Hours	(4) Cumulative Average Direct Labor Hours
1	100,000	100,000	100,000
2	80,000	180,000	90,000
4	64,000	314,210	78,553
8	51,200	534,591	66,824
16	40,960	892,014	55,751
32	32,768	1,467,862	45,871
64	26,214	2,392,453	37,382
128	20,972	3,874,395	30,269
256	16,777	6,247,318	24,404

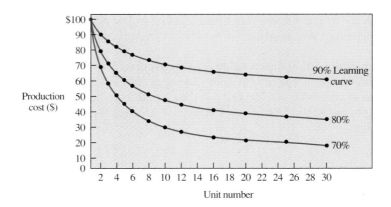

provided. The calculation of these figures is straightforward; for example, for Unit 4, cumulative average direct labor hours would be found by dividing cumulative direct labor hours by 4, yielding the figure given in column 4.

Exhibit S11.3 shows three curves with different learning rates: 90 percent, 80 percent, and 70 percent. Note that if the cost of the first unit was $100, the thirtieth unit would cost $59.63 at the 90 percent rate and $17.37 at the 70 percent rate. Differences in learning rates can have dramatic effects.

In practice, learning curves are plotted on log-log paper, with the results that the unit curves become linear throughout their entire range and the cumulative curve becomes linear after the first few units. The property of linearity is desirable because it facilitates extrapolation and permits a more accurate reading of the cumulative curve. Exhibit S11.4 shows the 80 percent unit cost curve and average cost curve on logarithmic paper. Note that the cumulative average cost is essentially linear after the eighth unit.

While the arithmetic tabulation approach is useful, direct logarithmic analysis of learning curve problems is generally more efficient since it does not require a complete enumeration of successive time-output combinations. Moreover, where such data are not available, an analytical model that uses logarithms may be the most convenient way of obtaining output estimates.

Logarithmic Analysis

The normal form of the learning curve equation is[2]:

$$Y_x = Kx^n$$

where

x = Unit number
Y_x = Number of direct labor hours required to produce the xth unit
K = Number of direct labor hours required to produce the first unit
n = $\log b / \log 2$ where b = Learning percentage

We can solve this mathematically or by using a table as shown in the next section. Mathematically, to find the labor-hour requirement for the eighth unit in our example (Exhibit S11.2), we would substitute as follows:

$$Y_8 = (100,000)(8)^n$$

---

[2] This equation says that the number of direct labor hours required for any given unit is reduced exponentially as more units are produced.

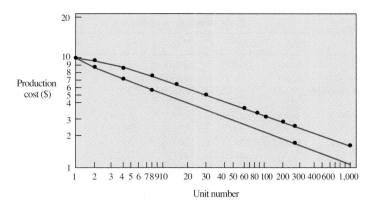

Exhibit S11.4

Logarithmic Plot of an
80 Percent Learning
Curve

Using logarithms:

$$Y_8 = 100,000(8)^{\log 0.8/\log 2}$$

$$= 100,000(8)^{-0.322} = \frac{100,000}{(8)^{0.322}}$$

$$= \frac{100,000}{1.9535} = 51,192$$

Therefore, it would take 51,192 hours to make the eighth unit.

Learning Curve Tables

When the learning percentage is known, Exhibits S11.5 and S11.6 can be easily used to calculate estimated labor hours for a specific unit or for cumulative groups of units. We need only multiply the initial unit labor hour figure by the appropriate tabled value.

To illustrate, suppose we want to double check the figures in Exhibit S11.2 for unit and cumulative labor hours for Unit 16. From Exhibit S11.5, the unit improvement factor for Unit 16 at 80 percent is .4096. This multiplied by 100,000 (the hours for Unit 1) gives 40,960, the same as in Exhibit S11.2. From Exhibit S11.6, the cumulative improvement factor for cumulative hours for the first 16 units is 8.920. When multiplied by 100,000, this gives 892,000, which is reasonably close to the exact value of 892,014 shown in Exhibit S11.2.

The following is a more involved example of the application of a learning curve to a production problem.

■ **example S11.1**   *Sample Learning Curve Problem*   Captain Nemo, owner of the Suboptimum Underwater Boat Company (SUB), is puzzled. He has a contract for 11 boats and has completed 4 of them. He has observed that his production manager, young Mr. Overick, has been reassigning more and more people to torpedo assembly after the construction of the first four boats. The first boat, for example, required 225 workers, each working a 40-hour week, while 45 fewer workers were required for the second boat. Overick has told them that "this is just the beginning" and that he will complete the last boat in the current contract with only 100 workers!

Overick is banking on the learning curve, but has he gone overboard?

solution   Because the second boat required 180 workers, and using a simple exponential curve, then the learning percentage is 80 percent (180 ÷ 225). To find

Improvement Curves:
Table of Unit Values

Unit Improvement Factor

Unit	60%	65%	70%	75%	80%	85%	90%	95%
1	1.0000	1.0000	1.0000	1.0000	1.0000	1.0000	1.0000	1.0000
2	.6000	.6500	.7000	.7500	.8000	.8500	.9000	.9500
3	.4450	.5052	.5682	.6338	.7021	.7729	.8462	.9219
4	.3600	.4225	.4900	.5625	.6400	.7225	.8100	.9025
5	.3054	.3678	.4368	.5127	.5956	.6857	.7830	.8877
6	.2670	.3284	.3977	.4754	.5617	.6570	.7616	.8758
7	.2383	.2984	.3674	.4459	.5345	.6337	.7439	.8659
8	.2160	.2746	.3430	.4219	.5120	.6141	.7290	.8574
9	.1980	.2552	.3228	.4017	.4930	.5974	.7161	.8499
10	.1832	.2391	.3058	.3846	.4765	.5828	.7047	.8433
12	.1602	.2135	.2784	.3565	.4493	.5584	.6854	.8320
14	.1430	.1940	.2572	.3344	.4276	.5386	.6696	.8226
16	.1290	.1785	.2401	.3164	.4096	.5220	.6561	.8145
18	.1188	.1659	.2260	.3013	.3944	.5078	.6445	.8074
20	.1099	.1554	.2141	.2884	.3812	.4954	.6342	.8012
22	.1025	.1465	.2038	.2772	.3697	.4844	.6251	.7955
24	.0961	.1387	.1949	.2674	.3595	.4747	.6169	.7904
25	.0933	.1353	.1908	.2629	.3548	.4701	.6131	.7880
30	.0815	.1208	.1737	.2437	.3346	.4505	.5963	.7775
35	.0728	.1097	.1605	.2286	.3184	.4345	.5825	.7687
40	.0660	.1010	.1498	.2163	.3050	.4211	.5708	.7611
45	.0605	.0939	.1410	.2060	.2936	.4096	.5607	.7545
50	.0560	.0879	.1336	.1972	.2838	.3996	.5518	.7486
60	.0489	.0785	.1216	.1828	.2676	.3829	.5367	.7386
70	.0437	.0713	.1123	.1715	.2547	.3693	.5243	.7302
80	.0396	.0657	.1049	.1622	.2440	.3579	.5137	.7231
90	.0363	.0610	.0987	.1545	.2349	.3482	.5046	.7168
100	.0336	.0572	.0935	.1479	.2271	.3397	.4966	.7112
120	.0294	.0510	.0851	.1371	.2141	.3255	.4830	.7017
140	.0262	.0464	.0786	.1287	.2038	.3139	.4718	.6937
160	.0237	.0427	.0734	.1217	.1952	.3042	.4623	.6869
180	.0218	.0397	.0691	.1159	.1879	.2959	.4541	.6809
200	.0201	.0371	.0655	.1109	.1816	.2887	.4469	.6757
250	.0171	.0323	.0584	.1011	.1691	.2740	.4320	.6646
300	.0149	.0289	.0531	.0937	.1594	.2625	.4202	.6557
350	.0133	.0262	.0491	.0879	.1517	.2532	.4105	.6482
400	.0121	.0241	.0458	.0832	.1453	.2454	.4022	.6419
450	.0111	.0224	.0431	.0792	.1399	.2387	.3951	.6363
500	.0103	.0210	.0408	.0758	.1352	.2329	.3888	.6314
600	.0090	.0188	.0372	.0703	.1275	.2232	.3782	.6229
700	.0080	.0171	.0344	.0659	.1214	.2152	.3694	.6158
800	.0073	.0157	.0321	.0624	.1163	.2086	.3620	.6098
900	.0067	.0146	.0302	.0594	.1119	.2029	.3556	.6045
1,000	.0062	.0137	.0286	.0569	.1082	.1980	.3499	.5998
1,200	.0054	.0122	.0260	.0527	.1020	.1897	.3404	.5918
1,400	.0048	.0111	.0240	.0495	.0971	.1830	.3325	.5850
1,600	.0044	.0102	.0225	.0468	.0930	.1773	.3258	.5793
1,800	.0040	.0095	.0211	.0446	.0895	.1725	.3200	.5743
2,000	.0037	.0089	.0200	.0427	.0866	.1683	.3149	.5698
2,500	.0031	.0077	.0178	.0389	.0806	.1597	.3044	.5605
3,000	.0027	.0069	.0162	.0360	.0760	.1530	.2961	.5530

Cumulative Improvement Factor

Improvement Curves:
Table of Cumulative
Values

Unit	60%	65%	70%	75%	80%	85%	90%	95%
1	1.000	1.000	1.000	1.000	1.000	1.000	1.000	1.000
2	1.600	1.650	1.700	1.750	1.800	1.850	1.900	1.950
3	2.045	2.155	2.268	2.384	2.502	2.623	2.746	2.872
4	2.405	2.578	2.758	2.946	3.142	3.345	3.556	3.774
5	2.710	2.946	3.195	3.459	3.738	4.031	4.339	4.662
6	2.977	3.274	3.593	3.934	4.299	4.688	5.101	5.538
7	3.216	3.572	3.960	4.380	4.834	5.322	5.845	6.404
8	3.432	3.847	4.303	4.802	5.346	5.936	6.574	7.261
9	3.630	4.102	4.626	5.204	5.839	6.533	7.290	8.111
10	3.813	4.341	4.931	5.589	6.315	7.116	7.994	8.955
12	4.144	4.780	5.501	6.315	7.227	8.244	9.374	10.62
14	4.438	5.177	6.026	6.994	8.092	9.331	10.72	12.27
16	4.704	5.541	6.514	7.635	8.920	10.38	12.04	13.91
18	4.946	5.879	6.972	8.245	9.716	11.41	13.33	15.52
20	5.171	6.195	7.407	8.828	10.48	12.40	14.61	17.13
22	5.379	6.492	7.819	9.388	11.23	13.38	15.86	18.72
24	5.574	6.773	8.213	9.928	11.95	14.33	17.10	20.31
25	5.668	6.909	8.404	10.19	12.31	14.80	17.71	21.10
30	6.097	7.540	9.305	11.45	14.02	17.09	20.73	25.00
35	6.478	8.109	10.13	12.72	15.64	19.29	23.67	28.86
40	6.821	8.631	10.90	13.72	17.19	21.43	26.54	32.68
45	7.134	9.114	11.62	14.77	18.68	23.50	29.37	36.47
50	7.422	9.565	12.31	15.78	20.12	25.51	32.14	40.22
60	7.941	10.39	13.57	17.67	22.87	29.41	37.57	47.65
70	8.401	11.13	14.74	19.43	25.47	33.17	42.87	54.99
80	8.814	11.82	15.82	21.09	27.96	36.80	48.05	62.25
90	9.191	12.45	16.83	22.67	30.35	40.32	53.14	69.45
100	9.539	13.03	17.79	24.18	32.65	43.75	58.14	76.59
120	10.16	14.11	19.57	27.02	37.05	50.39	67.93	90.71
140	10.72	15.08	21.20	29.67	41.22	56.78	77.46	104.7
160	11.21	15.97	22.72	32.17	45.20	62.95	86.80	118.5
180	11.67	16.79	24.14	34.54	49.03	68.95	95.96	132.1
200	12.09	17.55	25.48	36.80	52.72	74.79	105.0	145.7
250	13.01	19.28	28.56	42.05	61.47	88.83	126.9	179.2
300	13.81	20.81	31.34	46.94	69.66	102.2	148.2	212.2
350	14.51	22.18	33.89	51.48	77.43	115.1	169.0	244.8
400	15.14	23.44	36.26	55.75	84.85	127.6	189.3	277.0
450	15.72	24.60	38.48	59.80	91.97	139.7	209.2	309.0
500	16.26	25.68	40.58	63.68	98.85	151.5	228.8	340.6
600	17.21	27.67	44.47	70.97	112.0	174.2	267.1	403.3
700	18.06	29.45	48.04	77.77	124.4	196.1	304.5	465.3
800	18.82	31.09	51.36	84.18	136.3	217.3	341.0	526.5
900	19.51	32.60	54.46	90.26	147.7	237.9	376.9	587.2
1,000	20.15	31.01	57.40	96.07	158.7	257.9	412.2	647.4
1,200	21.30	36.59	62.85	107.0	179.7	296.6	481.2	766.6
1,400	22.32	38.92	67.85	117.2	199.6	333.9	548.4	884.2
1,600	23.23	41.04	72.49	126.8	218.6	369.9	614.2	1001.
1,800	24.06	43.00	76.85	135.9	236.8	404.9	678.8	1116.
2,000	24.83	44.84	80.96	144.7	254.4	438.9	742.3	1230.
2,500	26.53	48.97	90.39	165.0	296.1	520.8	897.0	1513.
3,000	27.99	52.62	98.90	183.7	335.2	598.9	1047.	1791.

out how many workers are required for the 11th boat, we look up unit 11 for an 80 percent improvement ratio in Exhibit S11.6 and multiply this value by the number required for the first sub. By interpolating between Unit 10 and Unit 12 we find the improvement ratio equal to 0.4629. This yields 104.15 workers (.4269 interpolated from table × 225). Thus, Overick's estimate missed the boat by 4 people.

SUB has produced the first unit of a new line of minisubs at a cost of $500,000—$200,000 for materials and $300,000 for labor. It has agreed to accept a 10 percent profit, based on cost, and it is willing to contract on the basis of a 70 percent learning curve. What will be the contract price for three minisubs?

Cost of first sub		$ 500,000
Cost of second sub		
Materials	$200,000	
Labor: $300,000 × .70	210,000	410,000
Cost of third sub		
Materials	200,000	
Labor: $300,000 × .5682	170,460	370,460
Total cost		1,280,460
Markup: $1,280,460 × .10		128,046
Selling price		$1,408,506

If the operation is interrupted, then some relearning must occur. How far to go back up the learning curve can be estimated in some cases. ■

Estimating the Learning Percentage

If production has been underway for some time, the learning percentage is easily obtained from production records. Generally speaking, the longer the production history, the more accurate the estimate. Because a variety of other problems can occur during the early stages of production, most companies do not begin to collect data for learning curve analysis until some units have been completed.

Statistical analysis should also be used. An exponential learning curve can be fitted to find out how well the curve fits past data. The data can also be plotted on log-log graph paper to check straight-line fit.

If production has not started, estimating the learning percentage becomes enlightened guesswork. In these cases the analyst has these options:

1. Assume that the learning percentage will be the same as it has been for previous applications within the same industry.
2. Assume that it will be the same as it has been for the same or similar products.
3. Analyze the similarities and differences between the proposed startup and previous startups and develop a revised learning percentage that appears best to fit the situation.

There are two reasons for disparities between a firm's learning rate and that of its industry. First, there are the inevitable differences in operating characteristics between any two firms, stemming from the equipment, methods, product design, plant organization, and so forth. Second, procedural differences are manifested in the development of the learning percentage itself, such as whether the industry rate is based on a single product or on a product line, and the manner in which the data were aggregated.

How Long Does Learning Go On?

Does output stabilize, or is there continual improvement? Some areas can be shown to improve continually even over decades—radios, computers, and other electronic devices; and, if we allow for the effects of inflation, also automobiles, washing machines, refrigerators, and most other manufactured goods. If the learning curve has been valid for several hundreds or thousands of units, it will probably be valid for several hundreds or thousands more. On the other hand, highly automated systems may have a near zero learning curve because, after installation, they quickly reach a constant volume.

◼ GENERAL GUIDELINES FOR LEARNING

In this section we offer guidelines for two categories of "learners": individuals and organizations.

Individual Learning

A number of factors affect an individual's performance and rate of learning. Remember that there are two elements involved: the rate of learning and the initial starting level. To explain this more clearly, compare the two learning curves in Exhibit S11.7. Suppose these were the times for two individuals who performed a simple mechanical test administered by the personnel department as part of their application for employment in the assembly area of manufacturing.

Which applicant would you hire? Applicant A had a much lower starting point but a slower learning rate. Applicant B, although starting at a much higher point, is clearly the better choice. This points out that performance times are important—not just the learning rate by itself.

Some general guidelines to improve individual performance based on learning curves include:

1. *Proper selection of workers.* A test should be administered to help choose the workers. These tests should be representative of the planned work: A dexterity test for assembly work, a mental ability test for mental work, tests for interaction with customers for front office work, and so on.

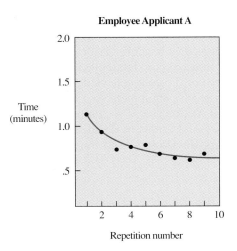
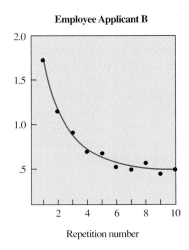

Test Results of Two Job Applicants

2. *Proper training.* The more effective the training, the faster the learning rate.

3. *Motivation.* Productivity gains based on learning curves are not achieved unless there is a reward. Rewards can be money (individual or group incentive plans) or nonmonetary (such as employee of the month, etc.).

4. *Work specialization.* As a general rule, the simpler the task, the faster the learning. Be careful that boredom doesn't interfere; if it does, redesign the task.

5. *Do one or very few jobs at a time.* Learning is faster on each job if completed one at a time, rather than working on all jobs simultaneously.

6. *Use tools or equipment that assists or supports performance.*

7. *Provide quick and easy access for help.* The benefits from training are realized and continue when assistance is available.

8. *Allow workers to help redesign their tasks.* Taking more performance factors into the scope of the learning curve can, in effect, shift the curve downward.

ORGANIZATIONAL LEARNING

Organizations learn as well. Its has been argued that organizational learning is critical to sustain a competitive advantage. For the individual, it is easy to conceptualize how knowledge is acquired and retained and how this results in an individual learning effect. Certainly, a main source of organizational learning is a result of the individual learning of the employees. An organization also acquires knowledge in its technology, its structure, documents that it retains, and standard operating procedures.[3] For example, as a manufacturing unit becomes experienced, knowledge is embedded in software and in tooling used for production. Knowledge can also be embedded in the organization's structure. For example, when an organization shifts its industrial engineering group from a functional organization centralized in one area to a decentralized organization where individuals are deployed to particular parts of the plant floor, knowledge about how to become more productive is embedded in the organization's structure.

Knowledge can depreciate if individuals leave the organization. When Lockheed had problems in the production of the L-1011 it was blamed on the fact that the company hired 2,000 inexperienced employees to quickly ramp up production. These employees were put through a four-week training program in aircraft construction. Initial costs rose rather than fell during the initial production of the plane due to the inexperienced workers.

Knowledge can also depreciate if technologies become inaccessible or difficult to use. An example of this is the difficulty in accessing data collected by Landsat, an earth surveillance program. Ninety percent of the data collected before 1979 is now inaccessible because the data were recorded by equipment that no longer exists or cannot be operated. Knowledge can also depreciate if a company's records and routine processes are lost. When Steinway Piano Company decided to put a discontinued piano back into production, the plant discovered it no longer had records or blueprints for the piano.

---

[3] See Linda Argote, "Organizational Learning Curves: Persistence, Transfer and Turnover," *International Journal of Technology Management* 11, no. 7, 8 (1996), pp. 759–69.

LEARNING CURVES APPLIED TO HEART TRANSPLANT MORTALITY

Learning curves provide an excellent means to examine performance. The best comparison for one's performance would be the learning rates for competitors in the industry. Even when a standard or expected level is unknown, much can still be learned by simply using and plotting data in a learning curve fashion. As an illustration of this ability to learn about one's performance, we present the experience of a heart transplant facility in a hospital.[4]

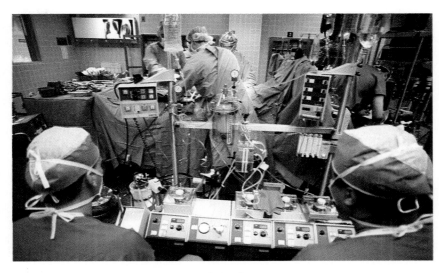

The learning curve model in the heart transplant analysis was of the form

$$Y_i = B_0 + B_1 x^{-B_2}$$

Y_i is the cumulative average resource consumption (the total number of deaths, costs, etc. divided by the number of transplants), B_0 is the asymptote (the minimum), B_1 is the maximum possible reduction (the difference between the first unit and minimum B_0), x is the total number of units produced, and B_2 is the rate of change for each successive unit as it moves toward the lower bound.

Exhibit S11.8 shows the coefficients that were obtained for the model. Exhibit S11.9 shows the cumulative death rate. This seems to follow an industrial learning curve with a rate just over 80 percent. Seven of the first 23 transplant patients died within a year after transplant surgery. Only 4 of the next 39 patients died within a year. For the cumulative average length of stay, shown in Exhibit S11.10, the reduction rate is approximately 9 percent.

The least sloping curve (the lowest learning rate) is the cost of heart transplants. Exhibit S11.11 shows that the initial costs were in the vicinity of $150,000. After 51 surviving patients (62 procedures, 11 died), the average cost was still close to $100,000. (A learning rate of 80 percent would result in an average cost of $40,000; a 90 percent rate would result in a cost of $80,000.)

	B_0 (Asymptote)	B_1 (Range)	B_2 (Rate)	Percent Decrease
Death rate	.2329	.8815	.2362	21.04%
Length of stay	28.26	23.76	.0943	9.00
Units of service	1,282.84	592.311	.0763	7.35
Adjusted charges	$96,465.90	$53,015.80	.0667	6.45

Exhibit S11.8

Consumption Coefficients for Heart Transplant Learning Model

---

[4] David B. Smith, and Jan L. Larsson, "The Impact of Learning on Cost: The Case of Heart Transplantation," *Hospital and Health Sciences Administration* 34, no. 1 (Spring 1989), pp. 85–97.

Death Rates, Less
than One Year
Survival

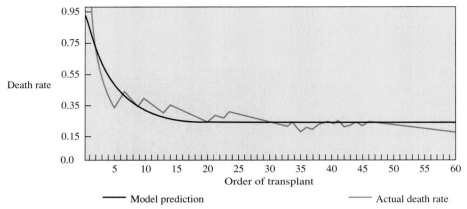

Source: David B. Smith and Jan L. Larsson, "The Impact of Learning on Cost: The Case of Heart Transplantation," *Hospital and Health Services Administration* 34, no. 1 (Spring 1989), p. 92.

Average Length of
Stay (ALOS) for Heart
Transplant Survivors

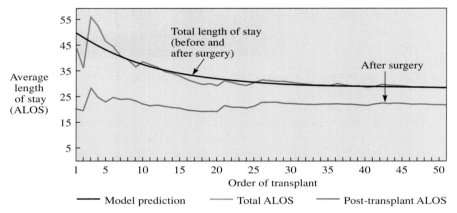

Note: For transplant admission only, actual costs are approximately 50 percent of charges.

Source: David B. Smith and Jan L. Larsson, "The Impact of Learning on Cost: The Case of Heart Transplantation," *Hospital and Health Services Administration* 34, no. 1 (Spring 1989), p. 93.

Cost for Heart
Transplant Survivors

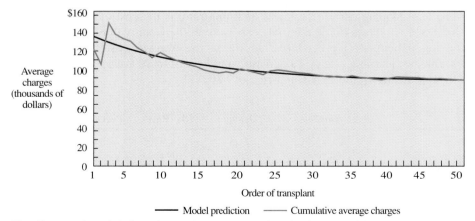

Note: For transplant admission only, actual costs are approximately 50 percent of charges.

Source: David B. Smith and Jan L. Larsson, "The Impact of Learning on Cost: The Case of Heart Implantation," *Hospital and Health Services Administration* 34, no. 1 (Spring 1989), p. 95.

Why are learning rates high in death rate reduction and low in average length of stay and the lowest rate in cost reduction? David Smith and Jan Larsson question whether the low learning rates may be related to conservatism in dealing with human lives. Or could it be due to the power and insulation of the heart transplant team from pressure to reduce cost? The importance and purpose of this study on learning curves was to make institutions and administrators aware of learning. Institutions need to behave in a learning curve logic—that is, in pricing as well as a motivation for continuous improvement.

FORMULA REVIEW

Logarithmic curve

$$Y_x = Kx^n \qquad\qquad (S11.1)$$

SOLVED PROBLEM

SOLVED PROBLEM 1

A job applicant is being tested for an assembly line position. Management feels that steady-state times have been approximately reached after 1,000 performances. Regular assembly line workers are expected to perform the task within four minutes.

    a. If the job applicant performed the first test operation in 10 minutes and the second one in 9 minutes, should this applicant be hired?

    b. What is the expected time that the job applicant would finish the tenth unit?

Solution

    a. Learning rate $= \dfrac{9 \text{ minutes}}{10 \text{ minutes}} = 90\%$

        From Exhibit S11.6, the time for the 1,000th unit is .3499 × 10 minutes = 3.499 minutes

        Yes, hire the person.

    b. From Exhibit S11.6, unit 10 at 90% is .7047. Therefore, time for tenth unit = .7047 × 10 = 7.047 minutes.

REVIEW AND DISCUSSION QUESTIONS

  1. If you kept any of your old exam grades from last semester, get them out and write down the grades. Use Exhibits S11.6 and S11.7 or use log-log graph paper to find whether the exponential curve fits showing that you experienced learning over the semester (insofar as your exam performance is concerned). If not, can you give some reasons why not?

  2. How might the following business specialists use learning curves: accountants, marketers, financial analysts, personnel managers, and computer programmers?

  3. As a manager, which learning percentage would you prefer (other things being equal), 110 percent or 60 percent? Explain.

  4. What difference does it make if a customer wants a 10,000 unit order produced and delivered all at one time or in 2,500 unit batches?

PROBLEMS

1. 100th = 0.18 hr.
   200th = 0.16 hr.
   400th = 0.15 hr.

2. *a.*
   1st 10 units = $2,500.00
   2nd 10 units = 1,750.00
   3rd 10 units = 1,420.50
   4th 10 units = 1,225.00
   5th 10 units = 1,092.00
   b. Between max. of
       $4,250 and min. of
       $2,645.50.

3. LR parts, 90%.   ✓
   Labor: 11,556 hours.
   Parts: $330,876

4. *a.* Labor, $570,150.
       Materials,
       1,356,750 plus
       something for profit.
   b. Need to consider
       forgetting and re-
       learning. Time and cost
       could be much higher.

5. *a.* From log-log plot,
       LR = 60%
   b. About 8,029 hours.
   c. 6.0 hours.

1. A time standard was set as .20 hour per unit after observing 50 cycles. If the task has a 90 percent learning curve, what would be the average time per unit after 100, 200, and 400 cycles?

2. You have just received 10 units of a special subassembly from an electronics manufacturer at a price of $250 per unit. A new order has also just come in for your company's product that uses these subassemblies, and you wish to purchase 40 more to be shipped in lots of 10 units each. (The subassemblies are bulky, and you need only 10 a month to fill your new order).

   a. Assuming a 70 percent learning curve by your supplier on a similar product last year, how much should you pay for each lot? Assume that the learning rate of 70 percent applies to each lot of 10 units, not per unit.

   b. Suppose you are the supplier and can produce 20 units now but cannot start production on the second 20 units for two months. What price would you try to negotiate?

3. Johnson Industries received a contract to develop and produce four high-intensity long-distance receiver/transmitters for cellular telephones. The first took 2,000 labor hours and $39,000 worth of purchased and manufactured parts, the second took 1,500 labor hours and $37,000 in parts, the third took 1,450 labor hours and $31,000 in parts, and the fourth took 1,270 labor hours and $31,000 in parts.

   Johnson was asked to bid on a follow-on contract for another dozen receiver/transmitter units. Ignoring any forgetting factor effects, what should Johnson estimate their time and parts costs to be for the dozen units? Estimate the learning curve using log-log paper. (Hint: There are two learning curves—one for labor and one for parts.)

4. Lambda Computer Products competed for and won a contract to produce two prototype units of a new type of computer that is based on optics using lasers rather than on electronic binary bits.

   The first unit produced by Lambda took 5,000 hours to produce and required $250,000 worth of material, equipment usage, and supplies. The second unit took 3,500 hours and used $200,000 worth of materials, equipment usage, and supplies. Labor is $30 per hour.

   a. You were asked by your customer to present a bid for 10 additional units as soon as the second unit was completed. Production would start immediately. What would your bid be?

   b. Suppose there was a significant delay between both contracts. During this time, personnel and equipment were reassigned to other projects. Explain how this would affect your subsequent bid.

5. You've just completed a pilot run of 10 units of a major product and found the processing time for each unit was as follows:

Unit Number	Time (hours)	Unit Number	Time (hours)
1	970	6	250
2	640	7	220
3	420	8	240
4	380	9	190
5	320	10	190

   a. According to the pilot run, what would you estimate the learning rate to be?

   b. Based on *a*, how much time would it take for the next 190 units, assuming no loss of learning?

   c. How much time would it take to make the 1,000th unit?

6. Lazer Technologies, Inc. (LTI) has produced a total of 20 high-power laser systems that could be used to destroy any approaching enemy missiles or aircraft. The 20 units have been produced, funded in part as private research within the research and development arm of LTI, but the bulk of the funding came from a contract with the U.S. Department of Defense (DOD).

Testing of the laser units has shown that they are effective defense weapons, and through redesign to add portability and easier field maintenance, the units could be truck-mounted.

DOD has asked LTI to submit a bid for 100 units.

The 20 units that LTI has built so far cost the following amounts and are listed in the order in which they were produced:

Unit Number	Cost ($ millions)	Unit Number	Cost ($ millions)	Unit Number	Cost ($ millions)	Unit Number	Cost ($ millions)
1	$ 12	6	$ 6	11	$ 3.9	16	$ 2.6
2	10	7	5	12	3.5	17	2.3
3	6	8	3.6	13	3.0	18	3.0
4	6.5	9	3.6	14	2.8	19	2.9
5	5.8	10	4.1	15	2.7	20	2.6

a. Based on past experience, what is the learning rate? (Hint: You may use log-log paper to plot the values and make estimates.)
b. What bid should LTI submit for the total order of 100 units, assuming that learning continues?
c. What is the cost expected to be for the last unit, under the learning rate you estimated?

✓ **7.** Jack Simpson, contract negotiator for Nebula Airframe Company, is currently involved in bidding on a follow-up government contract. In gathering cost data from the first three units, which Nebula produced under a research and development contract, he found that the first unit took 2,000 labor hours, the second took 1,800 labor hours, and the third took 1,692 hours.

In a contract for three more units, how many labor hours should Simpson plan for?

8. Honda Motor Company has discovered a problem in the exhaust system of one of its automobile lines and has voluntarily agreed to make the necessary modifications to conform with government safety requirements. Standard procedure is for the firm to pay a flat fee to dealers for each modification completed.

Honda is trying to establish a fair amount of compensation to pay dealers and has decided to choose a number of randomly selected mechanics and observe their performance and learning rate. Analysis demonstrated that the average learning rate was 90 percent, and Honda then decided to pay a $60 fee for each repair (3 hours × $20 per flat-rate hour).

Southwest Honda, Inc., has complained to Honda Motor Company about the fee. Six mechanics, working independently, have completed two modifications each. All took 9 hours on the average to do the first unit and 6.3 hours to do the second. Southwest refuses to do any more unless Honda allows at least $4^{1}/_{2}$ hours.

What is your opinion of Honda's allowed rate and the mechanics' performance?

9. United Research Associates (URA) had received a contract to produce two units of a new cruise missile guidance control. The first unit took 4,000 hours to complete and cost $30,000 in materials and equipment usage. The second took 3,200 hours and cost $21,000 in materials and equipment usage. Labor cost is charged at $18 per hour.

6. *a.* 70% (see SM for Exhibit 9).
b. $145,956,000.
c. Cost: .0851 × $12 = $1,021,200.

7. 4,710 hours.

8. Learning rate = 70%; unreasonable to ask for $4^{1}/_{2}$ hours. After 20 repetitions time is about 2 hours.

9. *a.* Cost of 22nd unit = $32,732.40.
b. 1,886 hours.
c. Average cost = $43,126.50.

The prime contractor has now approached URA and asked to submit a bid for the cost of producing *another* 20 guidance controls.

a. What will the last unit cost to build?

b. What will be the average time for the 20 missile guidance controls?

c. What will the average cost be for guidance control for the 20 in the contract?

10. *a.* If first unit is 100
minutes, the learn-
ing rate needs to be
75%, not 80%
$\left(\dfrac{80}{100}\right)$. Do not hire

b. See SM.

10. United Assembly Products (UAP) has a personnel screening process for job applicants to test their ability to perform at the department's long-term average rate. UAP has asked you to modify the test by incorporating learning theory. From the company's data, you discovered that if people can perform a given task in 30 minutes or less on the twentieth unit, they achieve the group long-run average. Obviously, all job applicants cannot be subjected to 20 performances of such a task, so you are to determine whether they will likely achieve the desired rate based only on two performances.

a. Suppose a person took 100 minutes on the first unit and 80 minutes on the second. Should this person be hired?

b. What procedure might you establish for hiring (i.e., how to evaluate the job applicant for his or her two performances)?

11. *a.* 3rd = 35.1 hrs. ✓
b. Average = 7.9
hrs. each; well
worth it.

11. A potentially large customer offered to subcontract assembly work which is profitable only if you can perform the operations at an average time of less than 20 hours each. The contract is for 1,000 units.

You run a test and do the first one in 50 hours and the second one in 40 hours.

a. How long would you expect it to take to do the third one?

b. Would you take the contract? Explain.

12. Interpolating;
11th 2.4476/.9 =
$2.7196 million
12th 2.3953/.9 =
$2.6615 million
$5.3811 million total

12. Western Turbine, Inc., has just completed the production of the tenth unit of a new high-efficiency turbine/generator. Its analysis showed that a learning rate of 85 percent existed over the production of the 10 units. If the tenth unit contained labor costs of $2.5 million, what price should Western Turbine charge for labor on the eleventh and twelfth units to make a profit of 10 percent of the selling price?

13. *a.* 42.165 minutes.
b. 35.56 minutes.

13. FES Auto has recently hired Jim the mechanic to specialize in front end alignments. Although he is a trained auto mechanic, he has not used their brand of equipment before taking this job. The standard time allocated for a front end alignment is 30 minutes. His first front end alignment took 50 minutes and his second 47.5 minutes.

a. What is the expected time for Jim on his tenth front end alignment?

b. What is the expected time for Jim on his one-hundredth front end alignment?

14. *a.* 70%
b. 501.5 minutes.
c. .78 minutes.

14. An initial pilot run of ten units produces the following times:

Unit Number	Time (Minutes)	Unit Number	Time (Minutes)
1	39	6	16
2	29	7	15
3	23	8	13
4	19	9	13
5	17	10	12

a. According to this pilot run, what is your estimate of the learning rate?

b. How much time will it take for the next 90 units?

c. How much time will it take to make the 2,000th unit?

SELECTED BIBLIOGRAPHY

Argote, Linda, and Dennis Epple. "Learning Curves in Manufacturing." *Science* 247 (February 1990), pp. 920–24.

Bailey, Charles D. "Forgetting and the Learning Curve: A Laboratory Study." *Management Science* 35, no. 3 (March 1989), pp. 340–52.

Globerson, Shlomo. "The Influence of Job-Related Variables on the Predictability Power of Three Learning Curve Models." *AIIE Transactions* 12, no. 1 (March 1980), pp. 64–69.

Irving, Robert. "A Convenient Method for Computing the Learning Curve." *Industrial Engineering* 14, no. 5 (May 1982), pp. 52–54.

Kopsco, David P., and William C. Nemitz. "Learning Curves and Lot Sizing for Independent and Dependent Demand." *Journal of Operations Management* 4, no. 1 (November 1983), pp. 73–83.

Kostiuk, Peter F., and Dean A. Follmann. "Learning Curves, Personal Characteristics, and Job Performance." *Journal of Labor Economics* 7, no. 2 (April 1989), pp. 129–46.

Logan, Gordon D. "Shapes of Reaction-Time Distribution and Shapes of Learning Curves." *Journal of Experimental Psychology: Learning, Memory, and Cognition* 18, no. 5 (Sept. 1992), pp. 883–915.

Smith, David B., and Jan L. Larsson. "The Impact of Learning on Cost: The Case of Heart Transplantation." *Hospital and Health Services Administration* 34, no. 1 (Spring 1989), pp. 85–97.

Smunt, Timothy L. "A Comparison of Learning Curve Analysis and Moving Average Ratio Analysis for Detailed Operational Planning." *Decision Sciences* 17, no. 4 (Fall 1986), pp. 475–95.

Towill, D. R. "The Use of Learning Curve Models for Prediction of Batch Production Performance." *International Journal of Operations and Production Management* 5, no. 2 (1985), pp. 13–24.

Yelle, Louie E. "The Learning Curves: Historical Review and Comprehensive Survey." *Decision Sciences* 10, no. 2 (April 1979), pp. 302–28.

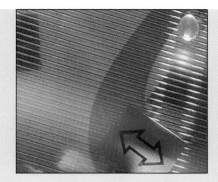

Section four

Managing the Supply Chain

12. Supply-Chain Management

13. Forecasting

14. Aggregate Planning

15. Inventory Systems for Independent Demand

16. Inventory Systems for Dependent Demand: MRP-Type Systems

Supplement 16 *SAP R/3*

17. Operations Scheduling

Supplement 17 *Simulation*

"WITHOUT SUPPLIES, NEITHER A GENERAL NOR A soldier is good for anything."

Clerchus of Sparta, in 401 BC, recognized the value of supply in his speech to the small Greek army he led in a civil war with Artaxerxes II. His army of 14,000 was 1,300 miles from Greece when the Battle of Cunaxa began. The survival of the Greek army depended not only upon its discipline, training, and morale but also upon its *supply chain*.

Today, the survival of most firms depends on intelligent supply chain decisions. Never has so much technology and brainpower been applied to improving supply chain performance. Point-of-sale scanners, electronic data interchange and the Internet let all stages of the supply chain hear the customer's voice and react to it.

This section starts with a chapter explaining the important new strategies for managing the supply chain for a firm. The following chapters on forecasting, inventory management, and scheduling detail many techniques that aid in the supply chain decision process. The supplement to Chapter 16 on SAP R/3 gives an overview of a leading software product that integrates virtually all of the techniques described in this book.

Chapter 12

Supply-Chain Management

Chapter Outline

Supply-Chain Management, 466

  Make or Buy

  Outsourcing

  Value Density

Purchasing, 472

  The Purchasing Organization

  The Firm as a Supplier

  Partnership Relationships: Buyer–Supplier

  Supplier Selection Using the Analytic
    Hierarchy Process

Just-in-Time Purchasing, 479

  Multiple Suppliers versus Few Suppliers

Global Sourcing, 482

  Purchasing in the International Marketplace

  International Distribution

Electronic Information Flow, 486

  Quick Response (QR)

  Efficient Consumer Response (ECR)

  Wal-Mart's Information System

Case: Thomas Manufacturing Company, 492

**Case: Ohio Tool Company (Vendor
Selection),** 493

Key Terms

Supply Chain

Outsourcing

Materials Management

Logistics

Make or Buy

Value Density

Strategic Partnership

Just-in-Time Purchasing

Quick Response (QR)

Efficient Consumer Response
(ECR)

www Links

Expert Choice (http://www.ahp.net)

Grant Thornton Consultants (http://www.gt.com)

National Association of Purchasing Management
(http://www.napm.org)

FedEx (http://fedex.com)

(A)T FIRST GLANCE, THE WORKFORCE AT VOLKSWAGEN'S truck and bus factory in Esende, Brazil, seems like any other, clad in unremarkable gray uniforms. But look at the pockets, and you will see the key to what Volkswagen executives call the factory of the future. The names stitched there are Rockwell, Cummins, Remon, and MWM. What are conspicuously scarce are Volkswagen workers.

In this new factory some 100 miles northwest of Rio de Janeiro, Volkswagen employs a mere 200 of the 1,000 workers, those responsible only for overall quality control, marketing, and research and design. The assembly work—from counting spark plugs to bolting down engines—is left to suppliers.

While truck makers and Japanese auto makers have long relied heavily on preassembled components, "We haven't heard of a completely supplier-run plant before," said Sean McAlinden of the University of Michigan Office for the Study of Automotive Transportation.

When it reaches capacity, the plant's two shifts are expected to produce 100 trucks a day, using only 800 assembly workers, compared with 2,500 in traditionally designed plants in Brazil. And Volkswagen is betting that with suppliers on hand to inspect each component before it becomes part of a vehicle, quality will be high. Volkswagen pays suppliers only when trucks are completed and pass inspection. If a component isn't up to quality, the supplier is not paid. ●

Source: Adapted from Diana Jean Shemo, *The New York Times Company,* November 19, 1996, and Laurie Goering, "Revolution at Plant X," *The Chicago Tribune,* April 13, 1997.

■ SUPPLY-CHAIN MANAGEMENT

Supply-chain management is one of the hot topics in business today. The idea is to apply a total systems approach to managing the entire flow of information, materials, and services from raw-materials suppliers through factories and warehouses to the end customer. The focus is on those core activities that a business must operate each day to meet demand. The other chapters of this section of the book cover the details of how the forecasting, aggregate planning, inventory management, and scheduling systems actually work. Many individuals in the field consider these activities the "bread and butter" of operations management. In this section, we give an overview of what supply-chain management is.

Supply Chain

The term **supply chain** comes from a picture of how organizations are linked together. If we begin with a purchasing department as a starting point and work down the supply side, it has a number of suppliers, each of which, in turn, has its own set of suppliers, and so on. The result is a supply network or series of chains. This is illustrated in Exhibit 12.1 for one purchasing department and three of its suppliers. These networks can quickly become very complex.

The goals of supply-chain management are to reduce uncertainty and risks in the supply chain, thereby positively affecting inventory levels, cycle time, processes, and, ultimately, end-customer service levels. The focus is on system optimization. The tools that can assist in optimizing the activities in the supply chain are the topics of the other chapters in this section (as noted above). These tools can be linked together in a hierarchical system as shown in Exhibit 12.2. Using a common database, we develop a forecast, which becomes the input to our aggregate plan. The aggregate plan sets constraints and guides the development of inventory plans, from which we can determine detailed workforce and equipment schedules.

The decisions that we make in one node of our supply chain impact the other nodes. For example, if we plan to assemble 1,000 automobiles this Friday in our plant, it is important that our supplier of tires have 4,000 tires at our plant in time for use on our assembly line. This does not happen automatically. It must be planned so that enough people, materials, and time are available to meet the requirements.

Outsourcing

In manufacturing, purchased items and services account for 60 to 70 percent of the cost of goods sold. **Outsourcing** is the term used to describe when a firm purchases material, assemblies, and other services that were initially done within the company, from sources outside the company. Outsourcing allows a firm to focus on activities that represent its core competencies. Thus, the company can create a competitive advantage while reducing cost. Possibly the most aggressive example of outsourcing is the new Volkswagen assembly plant, described in the opening vignette.

Materials Management Logistics

The coordination of outsourcing activities is typically handled by the materials management function within a company. The terms **materials management** and **logistics** are often used interchangeably. These terms refer to the grouping of management functions that support the complete cycle of material flow, from the purchase and internal control of production materials; to the planning and control of work-in-process; to the purchasing, shipping, and distribution of the finished product. The actual contracts with suppliers are handled in the purchasing department, which is a part of this function. In the rest of this chapter we discuss make-or-buy decisions, outsourcing, purchasing, selecting vendors, using the analytical hierarchy procedure, and electronic information flow.

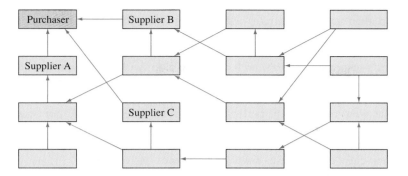

Source: Michiel R. Leenders and Harold E. Fearon, *Purchasing and Supply Management* (Burr Ridge, IL: Richard D. Irwin, 1997), p. 296.

Exhibit 12.1

The Complexity of Supplier Networks

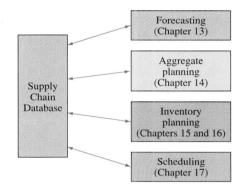

Exhibit 12.2

Hierarchical Set of Tools for Supply-Chain Integration

Make or Buy[1]

A critical strategic decision for any firm centers on the issue of **make or buy.** The whole character of the firm may be colored by its stance on this decision; it is one of vital importance to a firm's productivity and competitiveness. Managerial thinking on this issue has changed dramatically in the last few years, with increased global competition, pressures to reduce costs, downsizing, and focus on the firm's core competencies. The trend is now toward outsourcing or seeking outside suppliers for services or goods that had previously been provided in-house.

Traditionally, the make option tended to be favored by many large organizations, resulting in backward integration and ownership of a large range of manufacturing and subassembly facilities. Major purchases were largely confined to raw materials, which were then processed in-house. Current management trends favor flexibility, a focus on corporate strengths, closeness to the customer, and increased emphasis on productivity and competitiveness. This reinforces the idea of buying outside.

It would be very unusual if any one organization were superior to competition in all aspects of manufacturing or services. By buying outside, the management of the

Make or Buy

[1] This section is adapted from Michiel R. Leenders and Harold E. Fearson, *Purchasing and Supply Management* (Burr Ridge, IL: Richard D. Irwin, 1997), pp. 263–66.

purchasing firm can concentrate better on its main mission. This philosophy has already resulted in substantial downsizing and has created an expanded scope for purchasing in the process. With the world as a marketplace, it is the purchasing department's responsibility to search for or develop world-class suppliers suitable for the strategic needs of the firm.

A recent North American phenomenon has been the tendency to purchase services outside that were traditionally performed in-house. These include not only security, food services, and maintenance but also computer programming, training, engineering, accounting, legal, research, personnel, and even contract logistics and purchasing. Thus, a new class of purchases involving services has evolved.

The make-or-buy/outsource decision is an interesting one because of its many dimensions. Almost every organization is faced with it continually. For manufacturing companies, the make alternative may be a natural extension of activities already present or an opportunity for diversification. For nonmanufacturing concerns, it is normally a question of services rather than products. Should a hospital have its own laundry and operate its own dietary, security, and maintenance services, or should it

BREAKTHROUGH

Untapped Savings Abound

Two years ago, Microsoft Corp. decided it was time to rethink its entire production and distribution strategy for consumer products such as Encarta and Flight Simulator. The Redmond, Washington, software giant had always manufactured in and distributed through its own plants and distribution facilities in the Seattle area.

"We were having significant problems with inventory turns," says Wayne Hamilton, director of distribution-North America for Microsoft. "We needed to cut our inventories, and we needed to get product to market faster." Microsoft reengineered its manufacturing approach, as well as its logistics supply chain.

It improved manufacturing forecasting accuracy by installing a new demand-forecasting system that takes sales data by SKU (stock-keeping-unit) from distributors and combines that with on-hand inventory. The system allows the company to keep its production schedules open until one week before product is delivered and, in so doing, make what the market will consume.

Microsoft needed a manufacturer that could accommodate such short production leadtimes, so it outsourced consumer-products production to a turnkey software producer in Greeley, Colorado. "The software producer has excellent relationships with its raw-materials providers," notes Hamilton. As a result, the manufacturer was able to reduce cycle time for production and delivery to Microsoft's distribution center from five or six weeks to seven days.

Similarly, Microsoft's old logistics network was sluggish and unresponsive to customers, largely because of its location in the Northwest. "Most of our customers are in the Midwest and on the East Coast," Hamilton says. "But our distribution facility was in Seattle. This meant we had long leadtimes getting product to major markets."

Early in 1995 Microsoft decided to relocate its distribution facility to a 105,000-sq-ft high-speed flow-through distribution center in Indianapolis, and selected Interamerican Group, Chino, California, to operate the facility. That facility handles shipping responsibilities for 70 percent of Microsoft's consumer products, which represent between 15 percent and 30 percent of the company's business, depending on the time of year. From Indianapolis, Microsoft can reach 80 percent of its market within two days, Hamilton reports. That compares with former transit times of 7 to 10 days.

Source: Lisa Harrington, "Untapped Savings Abound," *Industry Week,* July 15, 1996, pp. 53–58. Reprinted with permission from Industry Week, 1996. Copyright Penton Publishing, Inc.

purchase from outside vendors? Becoming one's own supplier is an alternative that is a vital issue in every organization's procurement strategy.

What should be the attitude of an organization toward this make-or-buy issue? Many organizations do not have a consciously expressed policy but prefer to decide each issue as it arises. Moreover, it can be difficult to gather meaningful accounting data for economic analysis to support such decisions.

If it were possible to discuss the question in the aggregate for the individual firm, the problem should be formulated in the following manner: What should an organization's objective be in terms of how much supply value should be added in-house as a percentage of final product or service cost and in what form? A strong supply group would favor a buy tendency when other factors are not of overriding importance. For example, one corporation found its supply ability in international markets such a competitive asset that it deliberately divested itself of certain manufacturing facilities common to every competitor in the industry. A good example is given in the Breakthrough box of how Microsoft has outsourced its distribution services.

Outsourcing[2]

Outsourcing is a type of make-or-buy decision that has gained prominence in the 1990s. Organizations outsource when they decide to buy something they had been making in-house. Outsourcing is basically a reversal of a previous make decision. For example, a company whose employees clean the buildings may decide to hire an outside janitorial firm to provide this service. A huge wave of outsourcing and privatization (in the public sector) has hit almost all organizations during the last decade. In the urge to downsize, "right size," eliminate headquarters staff, and focus on value-added activities and core competencies in order to survive and prosper, public and private organizations have outsourced a broad range of functions and activities formerly performed in-house. Some activities, such as janitorial, food, and security services, have been outsourced for many years.

Information systems (IS) is one activity that has received much attention recently as a target for outsourcing. It has been estimated that worldwide outsourcing of the IS function was about $50 billion in the mid-1990s, and that number is growing rapidly. The contract logistics industry is expected to triple in size to $50 billion from its current $16–17 billion by the year 2000. Other popular outsourcing targets are mail   IS rooms, copy centers, and corporate travel departments.

An entire function may be outsourced, or some elements of an activity may be outsourced, with the rest kept in-house. For example, some of the elements of information technology may be strategic, some may be critical, and some may lend themselves to cheaper purchase and management by a third party. Identifying a function as a potential outsourcing target, and then breaking that function into its components, allows the decision makers to determine which activities are strategic or critical and should remain in-house and which can be outsourced on a commodity-like basis.

The growth in outsourcing in the logistics area is attributed to transportation deregulation, the focus on core competencies, reductions in inventories, and enhanced logistics management computer programs. Lean inventories mean there is less room

---

[2] Michiel R. Leenders and Harold E. Fearon, *Purchasing and Supply Management* (Burr Ridge, IL: Richard D. Irwin, 1997), pp. 268–69.

for error in deliveries, especially if the organization is operating in a just-in-time mode. Trucking companies such as Ryder have started adding the logistics aspect to their businesses—changing from merely moving goods from point A to point B, to managing all or part of all shipments over a longer period of time, typically three years, and replacing the shipper's employees with their own. Logistics companies now have complex computer tracking technology that reduces the risk in transportation and allows the logistics company to add more value to the firm than it could if the function were performed in-house. Third-party logistics providers track freight using electronic data interchange technology and a satellite system to tell customers exactly where its drivers are and when the delivery will be made. In a just-in-time environment, where the delivery window may be only 30 minutes, such technology is critical.

Federal Express has one of the most advanced systems available for tracking items being sent through their services. The system is available to all customers over the Internet. It tells the exact status of each item currently being carried by the company. Information on the exact time a package is picked up, when it is transferred between hubs in their network, and when it is delivered is available on the system. You can access this system at *http://www.fedex.com.* Select the "tracking" option on its opening page. Of course, you will need the actual "tracking number" for an item currently in the system to get information. Federal Express has integrated their tracking system with many of their customers' in-house information systems.

Another example of innovative outsourcing involves Hewlett-Packard. Hewlett-Packard turned over its inbound, raw materials warehousing in Vancouver, Washington, to Roadway Logistics.[3] Roadway's 140 employees operate the warehouse 24 hours a day, seven days a week, coordinating the delivery of parts to the warehouse and managing storage. Hewlett-Packard's 250 employees were transferred to other company activities. Hewlett-Packard reports savings of 10 percent in warehousing operating costs.

One of the drawbacks to outsourcing is the layoffs that often result. Even in cases where the service provider (third party) hires former employees, they are often hired back at lower wages with fewer benefits. Outsourcing is perceived by many unions as an effort to circumvent union contracts. The United Auto Workers Union has been particularly active in trying to prevent auto manufacturers from outsourcing fleet operations. Exhibit 12.3 lists some of the main reasons for outsourcing and some of the associated risks.

Purchasing's Role in Outsourcing   Research indicates that purchasing has had relatively moderate involvement in the outsourcing decisions made by many organizations. However, given the nature of the decision, purchasing should, by rights, be

---

[3] Jon Bigness, "In Today's Economy, There is Big Money to Be Made in Logistics," *The Wall Street Journal,* September 6, 1995, p. A1.

Exhibit 12.3

Reasons for, and Risks of, Outsourcing

Reasons for Outsourcing	Risks of Outsourcing
Cost reduction	Loss of control
Head-count reduction	Higher exit barriers
Focus on core competencies	Exposure to supplier risks: financial strength, loss of commitment to outsourcing, slow implementation, promised features not available, lack of responsiveness, poor daily quality
Acquire and deploy peripheral knowledge or process technology	
Minimize inventory, materials handling, and other non-value-added costs	
	Unexpected fees or "extra use" charges
Reduce development and production cycle times	Difficulty in quantifying economies
Improve efficiency	Conversion costs
Reaction to positive media reports	Supply restrictions
	Attention required by senior management
	Possibility of being tied to obsolete technology
	Concerns with long-term flexibility and meeting changing business requirements

heavily involved in outsourcing.[4] In fact, in some cases—such as information systems outsourcing, which has grown rapidly in the last few years—purchasing was not involved to any significant degree. Because outsourcing in the 1990s has focused primarily on services, and purchasing is typically not heavily involved in service acquisitions, it is logical that purchasing would not play a large role in the outsourcing decision. This may or may not change depending on the role of purchasing/supply in organizations in the future.

Value Density (Value per Unit of Weight)

Value Density

A common and important decision in purchasing is whether an item should be shipped by air or by ground transportation. While it may seem oversimplified, the value of an item per pound of weight—**value density**—is an important measure when deciding where items should be stocked geographically and how they should be shipped. In a classic Harvard case study, the Sorenson Research Company must decide whether to stock inventory for shipment at major warehouses, minor warehouses, or garage warehouses, and whether to ship by ground or air carrier.[5] Analysis shows that the time saved by shipping by air can be justified if the shipping cost is appropriate. The decision involves a trade-off: the savings of reduced transit time versus the higher cost to ship. Obviously, the solution involves a combination of methods.

We can approach the problem by examining a specific situation. Consider, for example, the cost of shipping from Boston to Tucson. Assume that the inventory cost is 30 percent per year of the product value (which includes cost of capital, insurance, decrease in warehouse costs, etc.), that regular UPS shipments take eight days, and

---

[4] Harold E. Fearon and Michiel R. Leenders, *Purchasing's Organizational Roles and Responsibilities* (Tempe, AZ: Center for Advanced Purchasing Studies/National Association of Purchasing Management, 1995), p. 23.

[5] W. Earl Sasser et al., *Cases in Operations Management* (Burr Ridge, IL: Richard D. Irwin, 1982), pp. 314–31.

that we are considering second-day air service with Federal Express. We can set up a comparison table as in Exhibit 12.4.

The problem then becomes comparing the additional cost of transportation to the savings of six days. Logically, we can make the general statement that expensive items can be sent by air from the factory warehouse, while lower-value items can be stocked at lower-level warehouses or shipped by a less expensive method.

$$\text{Shipping cost savings} = \text{Air shipping cost} - \text{Regular shipping cost}$$

At break-even, the cost savings is equal to inventory carrying cost.

$$\text{Cost savings} = \text{Inventory carrying cost} = \frac{\text{Item value} \times 0.30 \times 6 \text{ days}}{365 \text{ days per year}}$$

Solving for item value,

$$\text{Item value} = \frac{365 \times \text{Cost savings}}{0.30 \times 6}$$

The different cost savings in the fourth column of Exhibit 12.4 are substituted into the item value equation for each shipping weight. This gives the product value in the fifth column. Dividing by the package weight gives the break-even product value per pound in the last column. The exhibit indicates that any item whose value is greater than that amount should be sent by air. For example, a five-pound shipment of integrated circuits whose average value is $500 per pound should be shipped by Federal Express.

■ PURCHASING

Concerning the control of costs, purchasing is by far the most important area in the firm because two-thirds of the cost of goods sold are purchased items. We say elsewhere that design has the major impact on costs. But that is true only when the design,

Exhibit 12.4   Sorenson Research Company Shipping Cost Comparison

Shipping Weight (Pounds)	United Parcel Service (8 Days to Deliver)	Federal Express (2 Days to Deliver)	Cost Savings with UPS	Break-Even Product Value	Break-Even Product Value (per Pound)
1	$1.91	$11.50	$ 9.59	$1,944.64	$1,944.68
2	2.37	12.50	10.13	2,054.14	1,027.07
3	2.78	13.50	10.72	2,173.78	724.59
4	3.20	14.50	11.30	2,291.39	572.85
5	3.54	15.50	11.96	2,425.22	485.04
6	3.88	16.50	12.62	2,559.06	426.51
7	4.28	17.50	13.22	2,680.72	382.96
8	4.70	18.50	13.80	2,798.33	349.79
9	5.12	19.50	14.38	2,915.94	323.99
10	5.53	20.50	14.97	3,035.58	303.56

manufacturing, and purchasing relationships are not run correctly. It is purchasing's responsibility to know what is out there. Purchasing needs to know materials, performance, availability, and suppliers. It needs to know (as it should know) which features of purchased products are cosmetic and which features are functional. This directs its department to search for sources that support requirements. The National Association of Purchasing Managers (*http://www.napm.org*) is a widely recognized organization serving professional purchasers.

In the following sections we discuss the purchasing organization, the firm as its own internal supplier, single sourcing versus multiple sourcing, long-term manufacturer–supplier relationships, and some specific issues in just-in-time purchasing.

The Purchasing Organization

Eugene Muller conducted a survey that covered 1,541 persons employed in firms with a wide spectrum of sizes in eight sectors: manufacturing (U.S.), U.S. government/prime contractor, state/local government, institutional (primary education and hospitals), service (primarily utilities, transportation, communication, insurance, banking), retail (wholesale, retail-resale, retail-nonresale), food (primarily food manufacturers, restaurants, and food distributors), and manufacturing (Europe).[6]

The purposes of the survey were to compare purchasing managers' roles in various public and private sectors, and to update their duties. Here are some personal characteristics of the respondents:

Gender	Percentage
Male	74.7%
Female	26.3

Job Title	Percentage
Manager/Director	58.8%
Senior Buyer	23.3
Intermediate Buyer	12
Executive/VP	4
Junior Buyer	1.9

Education	Percentage
Bachelors degree	47.7%
Some college	30.4
Master's degree	14.4
High School	5.9
Law degree	.8
Doctorate	.5
Some high school	.3

Number of Personnel in Respondents Organization
Mean 28 Range 1–3,000

Number of Personnel Supervised by the Respondent
Mean 6.1 Range 0–326

Years in Present Position
Mean 5.2 Range 1–40

Years with Present Employer
Mean 10.7 Range 1–65

Years in Purchasing
Mean 13.3 Range 1–44

As a result of the survey, a list of 69 tasks was developed along with a description of the knowledge areas required by each task. Here is a summary of the areas where

---

[6] Eugene W. Muller, *Job Analysis: Identifying the Tasks of Purchasing* (Tempe, AZ: Center for Advanced Purchasing Studies, 1992), pp. 1–68.

purchasing managers were heavily involved; examples of the tasks are shown in parentheses:

· Procurement requests (review requests according to needs, budget, and vendor sources).
· Solicitation and evaluation of proposals (request quote).
· Supplier analysis (evaluate suppliers).
· Negotiation process (prepare strategies and negotiate product prices, delivery, etc.).
· Contract execution, implementation, and administration (prepare and follow contracts through).
· Forecasting and strategies (develop forecasts and purchasing strategies).
· Material flows (supervise and route incoming materials).
· Considerations for enhancing purchasing performance (find new sources of supply, make changes in policy, implement an MRP system).
· External and internal relationships (develop relationships with suppliers and other firms and agencies).
· Administrative aspects of the Purchasing Department (develop goals, budgets).
· Personnel issues (conduct hiring, supervision, evaluation).

Only about half of the respondents were involved with inventory management issues (such as organizing and storing materials, and reviewing inventory).

The Firm as a Supplier

As cartoon character Pogo might have said, "We have found our supplier, and it is us." Manufacturing firms usually view themselves as buyers; that is, they purchase components, parts, and materials, and then they produce products and services. But who buys the components, parts, products, and services the firm produces? Manufacturing firms rarely sell directly to the ultimate consumer. Some buyers are manufacturing firms that buy products and services and incorporate them into their own output. Other buyers are wholesalers, retailers, and distribution firms who buy the products and then distribute them further down the chain toward the ultimate consumers.

What difference does it make whether the firm acts as the buyer from suppliers or a supplier to other buyers? Buyers talk about such things as schedules, lot sizes, costs, lead times, and just-in-time delivery. We often take this as a given when finding suppliers who comply with our demands. As a supplier, however, the shoe is on the other foot. Schedules sent to us by our customers may not fit our schedules; the just-in-time deliveries that we demand from our vendors may not be compatible with, for example, our job-shop production.

 Randy Myer has made some interesting points concerning the need to understand the customer, to be able to evaluate the customer's costs, and even to decide whether the customer is worth keeping.[7] He reminds us that the balance of power in some areas is changing from the supplier to the buyer. In the retail business for example, average net return is 1 percent of sales. Suppliers average 4 percent net return! In the United

---

[7] Randy Myer, "Suppliers—Manage Your Customers," *Harvard Business Review*, November–December 1989, pp. 160–68.

Kingdom, the reverse is true in food retailing; retailers average 4 percent and suppliers 1 percent.

Myer suggests that firms should evaluate customers similarly as to how they calculate their own return on assets. Companies can measure the marketing, selling, and product development costs as well as asset investments in inventory and receivables that they can attribute to each customer. Further actions may then be indicated; these range from promoting greater efforts to further develop high-return customers to severing relationships with other customers.

Exhibit 12.5 shows interesting findings by a package goods company: Profitability is not a function of customer size; rather, profitability is a function of customer growth rate, though negatively. Fast-growing companies take advantage of their suppliers in pressuring for cost reductions, taking full advantage of return allowances, or demanding just-in-time deliveries, payment schedules, and so on. The result of this effort to evaluate customers is better understanding of the customer, of the customer's needs, of where lines should be drawn, and of what deviations are possible.

MARKETING
ACCOUNTING

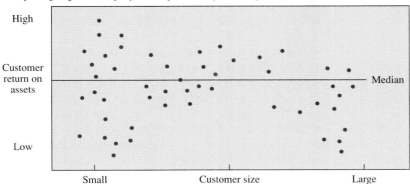

As a packaged-goods company found, profitability is usually not a function of customer size

Exhibit 12.5

Profitability from a Customer versus Customer Size and Customer Growth Rate

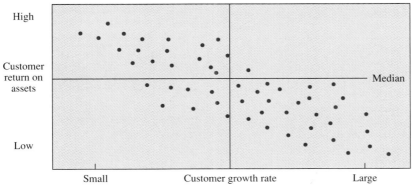

. . . but a function of customer growth rate

Note: Each dot represents one customer.

Source: Randy Myer, "Suppliers—Manage Your Customers," *Harvard Business Review,* November–December, 1989 p. 165.

Partnership Relationships: Buyer–Supplier

Strategic
Partnership

Vol. II "Supplier
Development
Outreach Program"

A **strategic partnership** between a buying firm and a supplying firm is defined as a continuing relationship involving a commitment over an extended time period, an exchange of information, and acknowledgment of the risks and rewards of the relationship.

In addition to cost, quality, and delivery reliability, supplier selection criteria includes factors such as management compatibility, goal congruence, and strategic direction of the supplier firm. While these measures are qualitative, the firms need to develop some sort of scale or weighting system for each factor. The Analytic Hierarchy Process (AHP) described next is a powerful technique to aid in this decision.

Supplier Selection Using the Analytic Hierarchy Process[8]

Assume that there are four criteria that are being used to evaluate suppliers (quality, price, service, and delivery). Further, assume that proposals from four suppliers (S1, S2, S3, and S4) are being considered. The measurement scale and hierarchy for this application are shown in Exhibit 12.6.

The buyer must now develop a set of pair-wise comparisons to define the importance of the criteria. If a buyer believes that quality is equally to moderately more important than price, a value of 2 expresses this judgment. If price is moderately more important than service, a value of 3 is appropriate. Assuming transitivity of judgments, quality is strongly to very strongly more important than service (i.e., a value of 6).

However, as previously mentioned, judgments are not always perfectly consistent. Suppose that, for example, quality is judged moderately to strongly more important than service, so a value of 4 is appropriate. Continuing with this process, the decision maker had decided that quality is moderately more important than delivery (i.e., a value of 2). These six judgments complete the pair-wise comparisons that are needed at this stage; this information is entered in a pair-wise comparison matrix shown in Exhibit 12.7. The other entries in the matrix are 1's along the diagonal and reciprocals of the six judgments as previously discussed.

Exhibit 12.6

AHP Measurement
Scale and Supplier
Hierarchy

Measurement Scale		Supplier Selection Hierarchy
Verbal Judgment or Preference	***Numerical Rating***	

Verbal Judgment or Preference	***Numerical Rating***
Extremely preferred	9
Very strongly preferred	7
Strongly preferred	5
Moderately preferred	3
Equally preferred	1

The intermediate values of 2, 4, 6, and 8 provide additional levels of discrimination

Reciprocals: If activity *i* has a specific numerical rating with respect to activity *j*, then *j* has the reciprocal value when compared to *i*.

Supplier Selection Hierarchy:

Select the best supplier

Quality	Price	Service	Delivery
S1	S1	S1	S1
S2	S2	S2	S2
S3	S3	S3	S3
S4	S4	S4	S4

---

[8] Adapted from a note written by Susan Svoboda, Manager of the University of Michigan Corporate Environmental Management Program (CEMP).

Pair-Wise Comparison Matrix and Computations: Evaluation Criteria

Exhibit 12.7

A. Original Matrix

	Quality	Price	Service	Delivery
Quality	1	2	4	3
Price	1/2	1	3	3
Service	1/4	1/3	1	2
Delivery	1/3	1/3	1/2	1
Column totals	25/12	11/3	17/2	9

B. Adjusted Matrix

	Quality	Price	Service	Delivery	Weights (Row Avg.)
Quality	12/25*	6/11	8/17	3/9	0.457
Price	6/25	3/11	6/17	3/9	0.300
Service	3/25	1/11	2/17	2/9	0.138
Delivery	4/25	1/11	1/17	1/9	0.105
				Total	1.000

* This entry is obtained by dividing the quality entry in the original matrix by the quality column total (25/12).

Supplier Comparisons

Exhibit 12.8

	S1	S2	S3	S4
A. With Respect to Quality				
S1	1	5	6	1/3
S2	1/5	1	2	1/6
S3	1/6	1/2	1	1/8
S4	3	6	8	1
Weights:	.297	.087	.053	.563
B. With Respect to Price				
S1	1	1/3	5	8
S2	3	1	7	9
S3	1/5	1/7	1	2
S4	1/8	1/9	1/2	1
Weights:	.303	.573	.078	.046

	S1	S2	S3	S4
C. With Respect to Service				
S1	1	5	4	8
S2	1/5	1	1/2	4
S3	1/4	2	1	5
S4	1/8	1/4	1/5	1
Weights:	.597	.140	.214	.050
D. With Respect to Delivery				
S1	1	3	1/5	1
S2	1/3	1	1/8	1/3
S3	5	8	1	5
S4	1	3	1/5	1
Weights:	.151	.060	.638	.151

	Quality		Price		Service		Delivery		Weights
S1	(.457)(.297)	+	(.300)(.303)	+	(.138)(.597)	+	(.105)(.151)	=	.325
S2	(.457)(.087)	+	(.300)(.573)	+	(.138)(.140)	+	(.105)(.060)	=	.237
S3	(.457)(.053)	+	(.300)(.078)	+	(.138)(.214)	+	(.105)(.638)	=	.144
S4	(.457)(.563)	+	(.300)(.046)	+	(.138)(.050)	+	(.105)(.151)	=	.294
							Total		1.000

Exhibit 12.9

Comparison of Supplier Alternatives

The data in the matrix can be used to generate a good estimate of the criteria weights. The weights provide a measure of the relative importance of each criterion. This is summarized in the following three steps:

1. Sum the elements in each column.
2. Divide each value by its column sum.
3. Compute row averages.

The computations are shown in Exhibit 12.7B. In this example, the final weights for quality, price, service, and delivery are 0.457, 0.300, 0.138, and 0.105, respectively. Therefore, quality is judged to be about one and one-half times (0.457/0.300) as important as price, about three and one-third times (0.457/0.138) as important as service, and four and one-third times (0.457/0.105) as important as delivery.

The AHP allows individuals to use their own personal psychometric scale for making the required pair-wise comparisons. Measuring the consistency of one's judgments allows a cross-check on how well that scale is being followed. As long as the scale is applied consistently by each individual, the AHP can correctly process their judgments.

Computations of the consistency ratio are somewhat more involved, but they are easily performed with a spreadsheet package such as Microsoft Excel. This type of analysis is also available in commercial software packages such as *Expert Choice* (see *http://www.ahp.net* for information about this software package and much additional information about the AHP). For the pair-wise comparison matrix given as Exhibit 12.7, it can be shown that the consistency is acceptable.

Next, the four suppliers must be compared pair-wise for each criterion. This process is virtually identical to the procedure that was used to develop the criteria comparison matrix. The only difference is that there is a supplier comparison matrix for each criterion. Therefore, the decision maker compares each pair of suppliers with respect to the quality criterion. This is repeated for the three other criteria. Assume that the buyer provided the four pair-wise comparison matrices given in Exhibit 12.8. The weights of the suppliers, for each criterion, are determined using the three-step procedure previously mentioned. These weights are also shown in Exhibit 12.8 for each matrix.

The final step of the AHP analysis is summarized in Exhibit 12.9. This table shows how the overall formulation scores are computed. This procedure can be explained as a simple weighted average technique. For a given supplier, four weights are computed, one for each of the four evaluation criteria (from Exhibit 12.9). These four weights are multiplied by the appropriate criteria weights in meeting the goal of the hierarchy (from Exhibit 12.7), and the results of the four multiplications are added together to compute the supplier score. Each supplier score represents the estimated total benefits to be obtained from selecting this supplier. In this example, supplier 1 (S1) with a score of 0.325 is judged to be best, S4 is second with a score of 0.294, followed by S2 (0.237) and S3 (0.144). Based on this simplified example, supplier 1 should be selected.

Use of the AHP approach offers a number of benefits. One important advantage is its simplicity. The AHP can also accommodate uncertain and subjective information, and allows the application of experience, insight, and intuition in a logical manner. Perhaps the most important advantage, however, is in developing the hierarchy itself. This forces buyers to seriously consider and justify the relevance of the criteria.

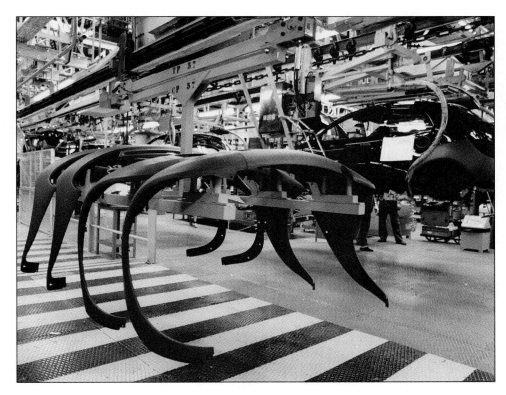

At Ford Motor Company's Valencia, Spain, plant more than 20 suppliers are located in an adjacent industrial park that feed parts, like these bumpers, JIT and in the right order directly to the assembly line.

JUST-IN-TIME PURCHASING

Just-in-time purchasing is a major element of just-in-time (JIT) systems, discussed in Chapter 8. The basic idea behind just-in-time purchasing is to establish agreements with vendors to deliver small quantities of materials just in time for production. This can mean daily, twice-daily, and sometimes hourly deliveries of purchased items. This approach contrasts with the traditional approach of bulk buying items that are delivered far in advance of production. The critical elements of JIT purchasing are

Just-in-Time Purchasing

· Reduced lot sizes.
· Frequent and reliable delivery schedules.
· Reduced and highly reliable lead times.
· Consistently high quality levels for purchased materials.

Each of these elements constitutes a major benefit to the purchasing firm, not the least of which is shortening the procurement cycle.

The ultimate objectives should be a single reliable source for each item and the consolidation of several items from each supplier. The result is far fewer suppliers in total. U.S. companies that have implemented JIT purchasing through fewer suppliers have obtained the following benefits:

1. *Consistent quality.* Involving suppliers during the early stages of product design can consistently provide high-quality products.

2. *Savings on resources.* Minimum investment and resources, such as buyer's time, travel, and engineering are needed when using a limited number of suppliers.

3. *Lower costs.* The overall volume of items purchased is higher, which eventually leads to lower costs.

4. *Special attention.* The suppliers are more inclined to pay special attention to the buyer's needs, since the buyer represents a large account.

5. *Saving on tooling.* Buyers often provide tools to their suppliers. Concentrating on only one supplier therefore saves a great deal of tooling costs.

6. *The establishment of long-term relationships.* Establishing long-term relationships with suppliers encourages loyalty and reduces the risk of an interrupted supply of parts to the buyer plant; this may be the most important benefit of all.

The most critical demands placed on the purchasing department to make JIT work are (1) reducing the number of suppliers and (2) locating suppliers who are nearby. (See Exhibit 12.10.) The strategy of single sourcing is to purchase all parts of a given kind from a single vendor. Nearby suppliers are obviously necessary to allow frequent, piece-by-piece delivery. How well purchasing handles these demands depends on the relationship the firm establishes with its suppliers. Suppliers should be seen as "outside partners" who can contribute to the long-run welfare of the buying firm instead of being seen as outside adversaries.[9]

JIT as an operating concept is a hot topic these days, but we must be careful not to become so captivated by the glamorous JIT single-source philosophy that we overlook the many occasions when multiple sourcing is justified. It is often advantageous to have suppliers compete for a firm's business. In addition to possible lower prices, interviewing and dealing with several vendors can give the buyer a lot of technical knowledge about the product—in many cases much more than from dealing with only one vendor. Also, many materials, parts, and suppliers are critical to a firm's continued operation, and any shutdown by a vendor—due to some sort of labor dispute or calamity such as a major fire or accident, for example—can significantly hurt. The U.S. Dept. of Defense must purchase military and critical supplies from more than one source. This is done, obviously, to reduce the risk of an enemy destroying the source of supply.

Multiple Suppliers versus Few Suppliers

Historically, the objective of purchasing and materials management has always been to have two or more suppliers. The thinking was that competition would drive down price and reduce the risk of supplies being cut off. JIT production, with its critical need for quality, and the new worldwide emphasis on quality products, is changing the buyer–supplier relationship.

In the early 1980s, U.S. auto manufacturers accepted materials, parts, and components with 1 to 3 percent defect rates. That amounts to 10,000 to 30,000 defects per million incoming parts! This defect rate is no longer acceptable.

---

[9] Chan K. Hahn, Peter A. Pinto, and Daniel J. Bragg, "Just-in-Time' Production and Purchasing," *Journal of Purchasing and Materials Management,* Fall 1983, p. 10.

Exhibit 12.10

Characteristics of JIT
Purchasing

Suppliers

Few suppliers

Nearby suppliers

Repeat business with same suppliers

Active use of analysis to enable desirable suppliers to become/stay price competitive

Clusters of remote suppliers

Competitive bidding mostly limited to new part numbers

Buyer plant resists vertical integration and subsequent wipeout of supplier business

Suppliers are encouraged to extend JIT buying to *their* suppliers

Quantities

Steady output rate (a desirable prerequisite)

Frequent deliveries in small lot quantities

Long-term contract agreements

Minimal release paperwork

Deliver quantities variable from release to release but fixed for whole contract term

Little or no permissible overage or underage of receipts

Suppliers encouraged to package in exact quantities

Suppliers encouraged to reduce their production lot sizes (or store unreleased material)

Quality

Minimal product specifications imposed on supplier

Help suppliers to meet quality requirements

Close relationships between buyers' and suppliers' quality ensurance people

Suppliers encouraged to use process control charts instead of lot sampling inspection

Shipping

Scheduling of inbound freight

Gain control by use of company-owned or contract shipping, contract warehousing, and trailers for freight consolidation/storage where possible instead of using common carriers

Source: Richard J. Schonberger and James P. Gilbert, "Just-in-Time Purchasing: A Challenge for U.S. Industry," *California Management Review,* Fall 1983, p. 58.

Xerox Corporation lost half of its worldwide market share in copiers from 1976 to 1982. Xerox had over 5,000 suppliers and spent 80 percent of manufacturing cost on purchased materials. To try to turn the company around, Xerox reduced its suppliers to just 400 and trained them in statistical process control, total quality control, and just-in-time manufacturing. As a result, product costs were greatly reduced, reject rates were reduced by 93 percent, and production lead time was reduced from 52 weeks to 18 weeks.

Working closely with fewer suppliers has many rewards. General Electric Company, for instance, publicizes the names of its best suppliers and awards them better contracts. GE's Appliance Division invites its 100 best suppliers to its annual Supplier Appreciation Day.

To compete effectively in world markets, a firm must have high-quality suppliers with acceptable costs and timely delivery. Chief purchasing officers (CPOs) should compile lists of approved suppliers and then create supplier development programs to improve suppliers' technical ability, quality, delivery, and cost. More than 70 percent of the companies in one survey had approved buyer lists.[10]

[10] Richard E. Plank and Valerie Kijewski, "The Use of Approved Supplier Lists," *International Journal of Purchasing and Materials Management,* Spring 1991, pp. 37–41.

The Western view is that single sourcing is a high risk for the buyer. Japan's single-sourcing tradition, however, may not be one of successful long-term sharing. It appears that the power is in the hands of the big buyers. John Ramsay states that power is so unbalanced in Japan's supplier network that suppliers are more like off-site workshops of the buyer.[11] The advantage to the buyer is that during economic down periods, the subcontracted work can be brought back into the buyer's plant. The buyer's firm can maintain stable employment while the supplier has a feast-or-famine existence.

In an attempt to improve their suppliers' quality, each year Pitney Bowes (PB) sends its purchasing personnel and quality engineers to visit vendors. They take along video cameras to tape operations on each supplier's shop floor. Back at PB, design and manufacturing engineers examine the tapes to learn which equipment the supplier uses and the line operator's performance in running that equipment. They also use the videos as excuses to talk with the supplier's workers to ascertain their attitude toward quality. As a result of these visits, some suppliers were removed from the vendor list. Suppliers are also brought to PB. During vendor days, suppliers see PB's operation and obtain a better understanding of their participation in PB's production process. Suppliers are also taught statistical process control if necessary. PB has found that suppliers make useful suggestions on materials, design, and so on.

Texas Instruments perceived quality as being so important that it instituted a 13-step certification program. Results proved the program to be very good.

Ford Motor Company issues long-term (three- to five-year) contracts to vendors. Practically every part is single sourced. Suppliers become involved during the design phase. Simultaneous engineering means that the design of a part depends on how it is to be made; that is, the process to be used to make a product influences its design. Early involvement of the supplier is important because suppliers are experts in their areas. They certainly know more about their processes than Ford so their knowledge influences Ford's designs.

One other interesting note on Ford's supplier relationship. In Supplement 11 we discussed learning curves. We stated that continuous production improves performance. Because Ford's long-term contracts allow the effects of learning to really take hold and be significant, Ford attached clauses to reduce prices each year. This cost reduction was recognized to be a side benefit of the relationship and should be shared by Ford as well.

■ GLOBAL SOURCING

We are in the middle of a major change in the global economy. Great opportunities are available because of the collapse of communism in the Eastern Bloc, the restructuring of countries such as Hungary and Czechoslovakia (now split into Slovakia and

---

[11] John Ramsay, "The Myth of the Cooperative Single Source," *Journal of Purchasing and Materials Management,* Winter 1990, pp. 2–5.

the Czech Republic), plus new markets in Turkey, India, South Africa, and so on. Already we are seeing results of agreements such as NAFTA (North American Free Trade Agreement) and GATT (General Agreement on Tariffs and Trade). China is a huge market and has now become a worthwhile trading partner.

Purchasing in the International Marketplace

There are a number of terms used interchangeably: *global purchasing, global sourcing, foreign sourcing, international sourcing, multinational sourcing,* and a variety of combinations of these.

Originally, purchasing on an international basis was an attempt to reduce production costs in the face of competition—primarily foreign competition. Global sourcing has now gone well beyond cost reduction motives to strategic ones to look at product availability, technology, and delivery lead times as well as labor availability and quality.

From a purchasing standpoint, what prompts firms to enter foreign markets? In a survey of 149 firms, Birou and Fawcett found that the two main reasons why firms begin purchasing globally were a lower price and accessibility to products unavailable in the United States. Exhibit 12.11 shows their complete list of responses. We usually think that the United States is superior in technology and product quality, but note items 4 and 5 in the exhibit: advanced technology and higher-quality products available from foreign sources.

Global sourcing is a standard procedure for over half of all firms with annual sales of more than $10 million. What stands out in the list of purchased items is the small percentage of companies that purchase services. Exhibit 12.12 shows that while foreign purchases of materials, parts, and equipment range from 69 percent to 81 percent, only 16 percent of the companies surveyed purchased foreign services.

Typically, evaluating foreign suppliers is more difficult and increased costs are relevant. Exhibit 12.12 shows cost elements for foreign sourcing. Naturally, most of these costs differ from domestic costs because of the expenses of dealing with foreign suppliers and exchange rates.

Rationale for International Sourcing	**Percentage of Firms**
1. Lower price available from foreign sources	74% of firms
2. Availability of foreign products that are not available domestically	49
3. Firm's worldwide operation and attitude	28
4. Advanced technology available from foreign sources	26
5. Higher-quality products available from foreign sources	25
6. Intensification of global competition	19
7. To help develop a foreign presence (precursor to global production or marketing)	17
8. To fulfill countertrade or local requirements	17
9. Better delivery or service available from foreign sources	8

Exhibit 12.11

Reasons for Beginning to Source Internationally

Source: Reprinted with permission from the publisher, the National Association of Purchasing Management, Inc. Laura M. Birou and Stanley E. Fawcett, "International Purchasing: Benefits, Requirements, and Challenges," *International Journal of Purchasing and Materials Management,* Spring 1993, p. 34.

Source: Joseph R. Carter and Ram Narasimhan, "Purchasing in the International Marketplace: Implications for Operations," *Journal of Purchasing and Materials Management*, Summer 1990, pp. 6, 8.

Exhibit 12.12

Foreign Sourcing Practices (Items Purchased Abroad)

Type of Purchases	Percentage of Respondents That Partially Source Abroad
Materials	76%
Machinery and equipment	69
Component parts	81
Services	16

Cost Elements to Evaluate

1. Unit price
2. Export taxes
3. International transportation costs
4. Insurance and tariffs
5. Brokerage costs
6. Letter of credit
7. Cost of money
8. Inland (domestic and foreign) freight cost
9. Risk of obsolescence
10. Cost of rejects
11. Damage in transit
12. Inventory holding costs
13. Technical support
14. Employee travel costs

MARKETING
PURCHASING

International sourcing is a competitive weapon if used correctly. International sourcing usually requires stable production, simpler designs, reduced numbers of components, and manufactured subassemblies as well as increased quality. It also promotes greater cooperation among manufacturing, marketing, and purchasing personnel.

In Chapter 6 on total quality management, we discussed certification of suppliers to ensure their performance in all aspects such as quality and delivery performance.

In the global market, service industries need logistic support as much as manufacturing industries do, whether it is sourcing materials, locating facilities, or monitoring flows of material, people, information, and ideas.

For international supply management, the specific organizational form is less important than having a clear, explicit assignment of responsibility and authority. Also important is the firm's reward structure; the firm's objectives must be clearly specified and appropriately rewarded. Otherwise, individuals may establish their own objectives, such as minimizing the cost of purchasing and transportation. While important, cost minimization should not be the sought-after goal. The ultimate goal is to choose suppliers who can become strategic partners that participate from the beginning of the product design stage.

International Distribution

How does a firm begin to develop foreign sources? Exhibit 12.13 shows both primary sources (firms that manufacture the products or produce the services) and intermediaries (middlemen who stand between the seller and the buyer). Unless a firm is quite

Exhibit 12.13   Forms of International Distribution Channels

	Advantage	Disadvantages
Source Intermediaries or "Middlemen"		
Distributors		
Buy and resell goods. Accept orders and payment. Assume warranty responsibility. May offer customer training.	Handle cultural, commercial, and technical problems. If delivery in United States, payment in dollars, standard terms. Simple handling of product defects.	Among the most costly sources; buyer pays both manufacturer's and distributor's profit and overhead. Probably foreign currency, L/C terms. (Letter of credit)
Manufacturer's Representatives		
Accept orders on behalf of a source; receive commission for the service. May provide technical and commercial support.	Handle cultural, commercial, and technical problems. Generally less expensive to use than a distributor.	Payment in foreign currency. L/C terms if a foreign rep. company. Bears no warranty liability; little use in dealing with defects.
Brokers		
Bring together parties to a transaction for a fee. Services very widely.	Least expensive intermediary. Wide range of services possible. May have wide contacts in the industry. Most willing to negotiate.	Least responsible for source or product performance, warranty. Probably little technical support. Foreign currency, L/C terms probable.
Trading Companies		
Broad scope of activities from brokering, representation, distribution, program management.	Worldwide contacts, broadest scope of sources. Experience and capability. Few cultural or language problems.	Generally a costly alternative. Most prefer to trade in existing markets or to make a market for new product, not to deal in isolated inquiries. Because of their scale, most buyers have little leverage.
Primary Sources		
Large Multinationals		
The majority of international business. May prefer new customers to buy through distribution or U.S. subsidiaries, which cannot be considered an offshore source.	Undisputed capability; possible benefits of economies of scale. Good support, training, warranty performance. Few cultural or language impediments.	Because of scale, few buyers have negotiating leverage. No benefit in purchases through U.S. subsidiary.
Midsize Manufacturers		
The vast majority of source opportunities. Public or private. Most already exporting. May have a U.S. presence in a liaison office.	Low costs at acceptable levels of risk. Opportunities for close, long-term relationships.	Some cultural and language barriers to overcome. Foreign currency, letter of credit.
Small Specialty Firms		
Usually individually or privately owned. Limited capability; usually one process or service.	Lowest cost. Probably most personalized, attentive service.	Most likely to present cultural and language problems. Buyer responsible for freight, duty of transaction. Foreign currency, letter of credit.
Captives		
Wholly owned subsidiaries or subcontractors controlled by larger firms through investment or predatory purchasing.	If accessible, may be very inexpensive and accustomed to quality, on-time performance.	Normally unwilling or precluded from accepting direct orders. Extra cost if accessed through the dominant company.

Source: Thomas K. Hickman and William M. Hickman, Jr., *Global Purchasing: How to Buy Goods and Services in Foreign Markets* (Homewood, IL: Business One Irwin, 1992), pp. 58–59. Reprinted with permission of the McGraw-Hill companies.

Campbell uses a system they call Continuous Product Replenishment. At the food retailer's warehouse, Campbell product arrives from the plant to replenish inventory at the same steady rate as the consumer takes it off the shelf. CPR is driven by an electronic ordering system managed by Campbell, freeing the retailer from this task. Steady production that meets predetermined inventory levels results in cost efficiencies across the entire supply chain.

experienced in direct purchases, dealing through an intermediary may be a good way to start in the international market. We will briefly comment on each of these sources.

A *distributor* usually carries a stock of a manufacturer's goods and has exclusive sales territorial rights. In underdeveloped countries these rights can vary widely. A *manufacturer's representative* does not carry a stock of goods but is a salesperson paid on commission. Generally, manufacturer's representatives have exclusive rights either to a territory or to a class of potential customers. A *broker's* primary purpose is to bring potential buyers and suppliers together, though many other supplementary services may be offered as well. *Trading companies* provide a wide variety of services—even financial and marketing if needed. They can also find technical help if needed by the buyer or supplier.

The *primary sources* are the actual manufacturers. If a firm has the experience in international purchasing, it is best to deal directly with the primary source rather than through an intermediary. Not only will it likely be cheaper, but chances of miscommunication are less when dealing directly. Of the primary sources (large multinationals, midsize manufacturers, small specialty firms, and captive firms), the small specialty firms are usually the best choice. The communication problems and the transactions and shipment are the areas that could become problems when dealing with small companies. Once a relationship is developed, it should be quite satisfactory.

ELECTRONIC INFORMATION FLOW

A supply chain links all of the stages together from raw materials through production to the consumer. While many operating systems (such as MRP-type systems) push the product out to the user, others pull it through (such as JIT systems where product is produced as needed). In all cases, however, the frequency and speed of communicating

BREAKTHROUGH

Trucks Keep Inventories Rolling Past Warehouses to Production Lines

It seems warehouses have grown wheels. Called "rolling inventories," trucks have become the place of choice for just-in-time stockpiles. Eighteen-wheelers pull up to factory loading docks to deliver parts that go almost immediately onto production lines, bypassing the warehouses.

"Companies now precisely plan their need of inventory so that [intermediate] warehouses aren't needed," says Don Schneider, president of trucking concern Schneider National Inc. and a member of the Chicago Federal Reserve Bank.

To be sure, just-in-time inventory methods aren't new. But as more companies come around to this approach, trucks and railcars have begun to function as warehouses for many producers—adding yet another anomaly to the economic recovery.

The construction of warehouse square footage tumbled nearly 18 percent in 1992 and 9 percent in 1993, even as the economy gained momentum and space in stores and shopping centers grew 6 percent and 12 percent, respectively.

For trucking companies, the trend means new business, but also more demanding customers. Many trucking companies say that in recent years, they've come under increasing pressure to deliver parts within a small window of time. "There are sometimes less than 10-minute lag times," says Larry Mulkey, president of Ryder Dedicated Logistics Inc., a Miami unit of transportation-services company Ryder Systems Inc.

Such use of trucks enables businesses to cut space costs, freeing up capital for investments such as equipment or new employees. "The back room decreases in size because you don't need it to store stockpiles and that means you have more floor space for selling," Mr. Mulkey says.

But a heavy reliance on trucks to keep inventories low isn't without its risks. The General Motors Corp., Toyota Motor Co. joint venture in Fremont, California, once had to shut down its production line because a just-in-time delivery truck broke down on the highway.

Ken Simonson, chief economist of the American Trucking Associations, says trucking for just-in-time orders generally works better in uncongested regions of the country.

But trucking companies have come a long way in eliminating delivery glitches. Mr. Schneider of Schneider National boasts that not one load was late because of the icy, wintry weather that hit much of the nation recently.

Technology enables trucking companies and their clients to track a load's progress from minute to minute. If a problem comes up, another truck can be dispatched immediately to pick up the load. Trucks also have become more reliable mechanically.

Source: Lucinda Harper, "Trucks Keep Inventories Rolling Past Warehouses to Production Lines," *The Wall Street Journal*, February 7, 1994, p. A7A. Reprinted by permission of *The Wall Street Journal* © 1994 Dow Jones & Co., Inc. All rights reserved worldwide.

information through the chain has a great effect on inventory levels, efficiencies, costs, and so on. An area that is growing rapidly to try to speed up this communication is electronic information flow.

The Grant Thornton LLP consulting company performs an annual survey of manufacturers. A recent survey indicated rapid growth in electronic data interchange (EDI).[12] Their survey indicates that 53 percent of midsize manufacturers share information electronically with their customers, most commonly to process product orders, invoices, and shipping instructions. In 55 percent of the cases, customers, initiate EDI links, although 23 percent say implementation occurs as a mutual agreement. Only 19 percent of midsize manufacturers suggested EDI to their customers. The majority

---

[12] The *Seventh Annual Grant Thornton Survey of American Manufacturers Report* (1996). Grant Thornton's Web site has much additional information related to supply chain management (*http://www.gt.com*).

(70 percent) concur that both sides benefit from increased "paperless" electronic communications.

In the following we review applications in the retail industry, such as department stores and supermarkets. There are many application areas for EDI. Terms such as quick response (QR) and efficient consumer response (ECR) have been adopted to describe the paperless communication between retailers and vendors. There have been significant improvements in communications through the use of open computer systems using Microsoft Windows software, but EDI, QR, and ECR go far beyond that.

Quick Response (QR)

Quick Response (QR)

Quick response (QR) programs have grown rapidly. A survey by Deloitte and Touche shows that 68 percent of retailers have either implemented or plan to implement QR within two years.[13] Quick response is based on bar code scanning and EDI. Its intent is to create a just-in-time replenishment system between vendors and retailers.

Virtually all medium and large stores use *Universal Product Code (UPC)* bar code scanning. *Point-of-sale (POS)* scanning at the register also uses *price-look-up (PLU)*, as reported by 90 percent of the respondents.

Efficient Consumer Response (ECR)

Efficient Consumer Response

Efficient consumer response is a variation of QR and EDI adopted by the supermarket industry as a business strategy where distributors, suppliers, and grocers work closely together to bring products to consumers. They can use bar code and EDI. Savings will come from reduced supply chain costs and reduced inventory.

A study by Kurt Salmon Associations estimates a potential savings of more than $30 billion.[14] In the dry grocery segment this could cut supply-chain inventory from 104 days to 61 days. In a study by McKinsey estimates were that dry grocery consumer prices could be reduced an average of 10.8 percent through industrywide adoption of ECR.[15]

Without ECR, manufacturers push products on the markets by offering low prices on large quantities: A few times a year the manufacturer offers the grocer a low price on a large quantity of product. This is forward buying. The manufacturer then works with the supermarket to offer coupons and incentives to entice customers to buy the product during a promotion. Products not sold during the promotion are stored in inventory to carry that supermarket until the next manufacturer's promotional deal.

ECR focuses on the customers to drive the system, not the manufacturers' deals. Customers pull goods through the store and through the pipeline by their purchases. This permits less inventory throughout the system.

Cooke cites a study that estimated that distributors purchase 80 percent of their merchandise during manufacturers' sales or "deals." They may buy four times per year and fill up their warehouses. Until the industry frees itself from this addiction to deal

---

[13] "Quick Response Grows," *Chain Store Age Executive,* May 1993, pp. 158–59.

[14] James Aaron Cooke, "The $30 Billion Promise," *Traffic Management,* December 1993, pp. 57–61.

[15] David B. Jenkins, "Jenkins Leads EDI Effort," *Chain Store Age Executive,* March 1993, p. 147.

buying, all the great replenishment techniques will be worthless.[16] Most experts predict that the grocery industry will implement ECR philosophy by the year 2000. All companies are preparing for it.

Wal-Mart's Information System

Wal-Mart has won awards for its Satellite Network, first installed in 1987. This network supports data, voice, and video and allows real-time sales and inventory information.

Wal-Mart's electronic data interchange, installed in 1990, issues electronic purchase orders and receives invoices from virtually all of Wal-Mart's vendors.

Wal-Mart's Retail Link, first installed in 1991, allows vendors to directly access in real-time *point-of-sale (POS)* data. This allows vendors to create better forecasts and better inventory management. The POS data come directly from store cash registers so they reflect activity in real time. E-mail capability is also included for corresponding within the supply system concerning scheduling, payments, and so on. Retail Link also includes the spreadsheet Microsoft Excel so the spreadsheet data can be accessed throughout the system.

Using Retail Link and point-of-sale data, arrangements have been made with some large suppliers to make their own decisions about Wal-Mart's purchases from them. They directly access point-of-sale data and create their own purchase orders. Wal-Mart is attempting to implement EDI internationally, but little progress has been made so far.[17]

■ CONCLUSION

In manufacturing, two-thirds of the costs of manufactured goods are purchased materials. Because of this, supply-chain management and the purchasing function have taken on high profiles and are being placed at high organizational levels.

In this chapter we have tried to show the many things that have changed in this area. Possibly the most significant changes are the move toward outsourcing and the use of global vendors. Vendors from around the world not only compete through their own marketing efforts but also are aggressively searched out by buyers looking for low-cost, reliable sources.

Managing the supply chain is being shifted, to a large extent, to the seller. Purchasing contracts are now tied to delivery schedules for the seller. We also covered a number of issues in JIT purchasing and delivery. The entry of electronic information flow has shifted routine activities to the vendor by allowing direct access to point-of-sales data and giving responsibility for forecasting and delivery of the vendor's product as needed. Such relationships tend to be long-term and make the selection of vendors even more important.

---

[16] Cooke, "$30 Billion," pp. 57–61.

[17] "Going Beyond EDI: Wal-Mart Cited for Vendor Links," *Chain Store Age Executive,* March 1993, pp. 150–51.

REVIEW AND DISCUSSION QUESTIONS

1. What recent changes have caused supply-chain management and purchasing to become much more important?
2. Using data from the text, give a simple profile of a purchasing manager and his/her job.
3. How are potential suppliers qualified by a firm?
4. Which characteristics of a supplier are most important to the buyer?
5. What is meant by a *strategic partnership* between a buyer and a supplier?
6. JIT suppliers have additional pressures that other suppliers do not have. What are they?
7. Small suppliers don't stand a chance competing against large suppliers for orders requiring JIT delivery. True or false? Comment.
8. With so much productive capacity and room for expansion in the United States, why would a company choose to purchase items from a foreign firm? Discuss the pros and cons.
9. What are the trade-offs in single-source versus multiple-source purchasing?
10. Which skills and training are most important for a purchasing agent?
11. Currently you are using multiple suppliers for each purchased item. How would you go about choosing one of them to be your long-term sole source?
12. As a supplier, which factors would you consider about a buyer (your potential customer) to be important in setting up a long-term relationship?
13. In electronic information flow, briefly define EDI, quick response (QR), efficient consumer response (ECR), and point of sale (POS). How have these helped industry?
14. "JIT purchasing is nothing more than a ploy to have vendors take over the burden of carrying inventory." Comment.
15. Distinguish between push and pull distribution systems. Give pros and cons of each.
16. For the value density example in Exhibit 12.4, what would the effect be if a competing firm offers you a similar service for 10 percent less than Federal Express's rates?

1. Supplier	Weight
S1	0.232
S2	0.314
S3	0.454

PROBLEMS

1. PCQ, Inc. has identified three criteria that they wish to use to select from among three potential suppliers. The criteria are performance, capability, and quality. Use the Analytic Hierarchy Process to determine the best supplier using the following matrices:

Pairwise Comparisions—Evaluation Criteria

	Performance	Capability	Quality
Performance	1	1/3	1/5
Capability	3	1	4
Quality	5	1/4	1

Supplier Comparision—Pairwise

Performance	S1	S2	S3
S1	1	3	4
S2	1/3	1	3
S3	1/4	1/3	1
Capability	**S1**	**S2**	**S3**
S1	1	2	1/5
S2	1/2	1	1/2
S3	5	2	1
Quality	**S1**	**S2**	**S3**
S1	1	1/5	1/4
S2	5	1	2
S3	4	1/2	1

2. CAQ, Inc. has decided to use the Analytic Hierarchy Process to select from three potential suppliers using the criteria of cost, availability, and quality. Use the following matrices to make this decision for CAQ.

2.	Supplier	Weight
	S1	0.294
	S2	0.509
	S3	0.197

Pairwise Comparisions-Evaluation Criteria

	Cost	Availability	Quality
Cost	1	1/3	0.2
Availability	3	1	1/3
Quality	5	3	1

Supplier Comparision-Pairwise

Cost	S1	S2	S3
S1	1		1/4
S2	2	1	3
S3	4		1

Availability	S1	S2	S3
S1	1	5	3
S2	1/5	1	2
S3	1/3	1/2	1

Quality	S1	S2	S3
S1	1	1/4	1
S2	4	1	3
S3	1	1/3	1

3. Calculate the break-even product value of using Express Mail (overnight delivery) versus Parcel Post (3-day delivery) for sending a package from Peoria, Illinois, to Memphis, Tennessee. The following table contains the appropriate costs. Assume that inventory carrying cost is 25 percent per year of the product value and that there are 365 days per year.

3.	Pounds	Break-Even Value per Pound
	2	$4,427.45
	3	3,384.77
	4	2,850.65
	5	2,547.70
	6	2,556.22
	7	2,271.34
	8	2,070.46
	9	1,905.30

Shipping cost: U.S. Postal Service; Peoria, IL, to Memphis, TN

Weight (Lbs.)	Cost (Overnight)	Cost (3-day)
2	$15.00	$2.87
3	17.25	3.34
4	19.40	3.78
5	21.55	4.10
6	25.40	4.39
7	26.45	4.67
8	27.60	4.91
9	28.65	5.16

Case

Thomas Manufacturing Company

"Delivery of our 412 casting is critical. We can't just stop production for this casting every time you have a minor pattern problem," said Mr. Litt, engineer for Thomas Manufacturing.

"I'm not interested in running rejects," answered Mr. James of A&B Foundry. "I cannot overextend my time on these castings when the other jobs are waiting."

"If you can't cast them properly and on time, I'll just have to take our pattern to another foundry that can," retorted Mr. Litt.

"Go ahead! It's all yours. I have other jobs with fewer headaches," replied Mr. James.

Mr. Litt returned to Thomas Manufacturing with the 412 casting pattern. (A pattern is used in making molds in which the gray iron is formed. After cooling, the mold is broken off, leaving the desired casting.) He remembered that Mr. Dunn, vice president of

manufacturing for Thomas (see Exhibit C12.1), had obtained a quote on his casting from Dawson, another gray iron foundry, several months before. It seemed that Dawson had the necessary capabilities to handle this casting.

To Mr. Litt's surprise, Mr. Dunn was not entirely happy to find the 412 pattern back in the plant. Mr. Dunn contacted personnel at Dawson Foundry, who said that they could not accept the job because of a major facilities conversion that would take six months. Locating another supplier would be difficult. Most foundries would undertake complex casting only if a number of orders for simple casting were placed at the same time.

Mr. Dunn knew that gray iron foundry capacity was tight. In general, foundries were specializing or closing down. Mr. Dunn had gathered some data on the gray iron industry located within a 500-mile radius of his

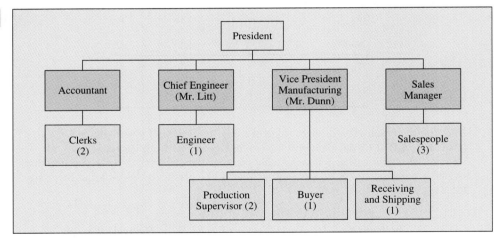

Exhibit C12.1

Organization Chart of Thomas Manufacturing Company

Exhibit C12.2

Foundry Data for Area within a 500-Mile Radius of the Thomas Plant

A. Shipments of Manufactured Goods

Gray Iron (Commercial Castings)	Quantity	Value
Previous year	280,000 tons	$65,000,000
Current year	243,000 tons	$54,000,000

B. Number of Establishments

									Current Year
140	133	131	134	137	134	134	128	126	116

10-Year History

plant (see Exhibit C12.2), which highlighted the problems his company was facing. There were three gray iron foundries within 60 miles of Thomas Manufacturing. Thomas had dealt with one foundry until it suffered a 12-month strike. Thomas then moved most of its casting needs to A&B Foundry, but Mr. Dunn had given the occasional order to Dawson and requested quotes quite regularly from them. In the past four years all had gone well with A&B Foundry. Mr. Dunn had planned to share his business with both foundries. A&B was comparable to Dawson on price and had done an excellent job until now.

A telephone call back to A&B Foundry indicated to Mr. Dunn that Mr. James was adamant in his refusal to take the pattern back.

The 412 Casting

Thomas Manufacturing Company was a portable generator manufacturer with sales above the $6 million level. Thomas employed approximately 160 people in a fairly modern plant. Many of its small portable generators were sold to clients all over North America.

The 412 casting was part of the most popular middle-of-the-line generator. The casting weighed 70 pounds and cost approximately $60; its pattern was worth $8,000. A run normally consisted of 100 castings, and Thomas usually received 100 castings every month. The 412 represented about 15 percent of Thomas's casting needs.

Normal lead time was at least eight weeks. When the supply problem arose, Thomas held six weeks' inventory.

Mr. Litt, an expert in pattern work, explained that the pattern was tricky, but once the difficulties were ironed out and the job set up, a hand molder could pour 50 castings in two days without any problems.

Questions

1. What alternatives are open to Mr. Dunn to prevent disruption of his company's most popular generator?

2. Was it appropriate for Mr. Litt to repossess the 412 pattern?

3. From the data given, does it appear that the Thomas Company has any leverage in dealing with the foundries?

Source: M. R. Leenders, H. E. Fearon, and W. B. England, *Purchasing and Materials Management*, 7th ed. (Homewood, IL: Richard D. Irwin, 1980), pp. 50–53.

Case

Ohio Tool Company (Vendor Selection)

The Ohio Tool Company designed a new machine, which it considered to be superior to anything else of its type on the market. Estimated sales were about $200,000 per year. The principal advantage of this machine over competition was a unique cam arrangement enabling the operator to adjust the unit quickly.

To achieve the advantages offered by the design, the cam—of which two were required per unit—had to be manufactured to very close tolerances. (See the accompanying sketch). Because of the difficulty of machining the several eccentric surfaces and the need for

an integral locating key in the center bore, the part could not readily be made from solid bar stock.

Possible methods of manufacture rapidly narrowed down to some type of casting. The materials under consideration were aluminum, zinc, and iron. Aluminum and iron sand castings were excluded because the close tolerances on the finished part would require precise, very difficult secondary machining operations. Aluminum and zinc die castings could not be used because draft or taper on the cam surfaces that is necessary in order to remove the part from the die, would also necessitate secondary machining operations to render the surfaces true again.

Another possibility for producing the part seemed to be through powder metallurgy, a process by which finely divided metal particles (in this case powdered iron) were formed to the desired shape by means of high pressure in a metal die, and then "sintered" at high temperature to form a solid metal piece. The Ohio Tool Company located three possible powdered-metal sources and sent parts drawings to each.

Supplier A, located about 1,000 miles away, was one of the leaders in the powder metallurgy field. The Ohio

Tool Company had purchased parts for another product from this supplier within the past year, and the supplier had failed to deliver on the agreed schedule. After many delivery promises via long-distance telephone and after a special trip to the plant by the purchasing manager, the parts arrived three months late. During this delay all other parts for the project had to be set aside and some workers laid off. In addition, the delay caused the Ohio Tool Company considerable loss of face with its customers because the product had been announced to the trade.

Supplier A submitted this quotation:

		Die cost—$1,968
5,000 pieces	$0.146 each	Delivery—Approximately
10,000 pieces	$0.145 each	10 weeks, depending on
20,000 pieces	$0.144 each	the production schedule at
		the time order is entered.

The quotation did not include incoming freight cost of $0.012 each. Further, it was based on furnishing a cam with a slight projection on one of the surfaces, which would require a machining operation by the Ohio Tool Company at an estimated cost of $0.05 each.

Supplier B, located 300 miles away, was a relative newcomer to the powdered-metal field. The manager of the shop had been with this firm only a short time but had gained his experience from one of the old-line companies. The Ohio Tool Company's experience with this company had been very satisfactory. It had undertaken the job at the same costs as Supplier A and had produced satisfactory parts in record time.

In reply to the request for a quotation, Supplier B suggested that, since it could not manufacture to specified tolerances, they be relaxed on several dimensions. However, the engineering department at Ohio Tool insisted that the critical function of this cam necessitated the tolerances as originally specified. When this information was passed along to Supplier B, it asked to be excused from quoting.

A third supplier, with whom the Ohio Tool Company had had no previous dealings, was asked to quote on the part. Supplier C was a subsidiary of one of the large automotive concerns and had an excellent technical reputation. It was understood, however, that the parent company was considering introducing several powdered-metal parts on its line of automobiles. The quotation of Supplier C was

5,000 pieces	$0.186 each	Die cost—$890
10,000 pieces	$0.185 each	Delivery—10 weeks
20,000 pieces	$0.183 each	

Supplier C was located 900 miles from the Ohio Tool Company plant, and incoming freight would cost $0.012

per unit. The drawing accompanying the quotation indicated a projection on one of the cam surfaces, which would have to be machined by the Ohio Tool Company for the proper functioning of the part. Although special machining techniques would be required in this case, the Ohio Tool Company estimator felt the company could machine off the projection for about $0.06 each in quantities of 5,000 or more.

Because of the past performance record of Supplier B, the purchasing manager decided that he should make an effort to obtain a quotation. He made a personal visit to the plant to discuss the problem, and learned that the plant could hold the tolerances on the center hole closer than the engineering department required, making the cumulative tolerances on the outside diameter of the cam surfaces almost within the tolerance specified. The engineering department agreed to change the drawing accordingly and grant additional latitude on the cam surfaces. On this basis, Supplier B entered the following quotation:

5,000 pieces	$0.50	each	
10,000 peices	$0.40	each	Die cost—$1,350
20,000 pieces	$0.32	each	Delivery—10 to 12 weeks
50,000 pieces	$0.275	each	

Freight in amounted to $0.005 each. The quotation was based on a part in exact accordance with the drawing, since the cost of secondary operations had been included in the quotation and would be performed by the supplier. By the time this quotation was received, manufacture of other parts of the product was ensured and final assembly was scheduled for 12 weeks from that date.

Upon reviewing all the quotations, the relatively high cost of Supplier B was readily apparent. The purchasing manager decided to call Supplier B and ask him to review his costs again. The quotation was revised:

5,000 pieces $0.45
10,000 pieces $0.37
No change in 20,000 and 50,000 price

Questions

1. Which vendor would you select for the job? Why?
2. Should a purchasing agent enter into negotiations with one vendor after bids from competitors have been examined?
3. With reference to Question 2, prepare a policy statement that would guide the future actions of the purchasing department.

SELECTED BIBLIOGRAPHY

Birou, Laura M., and Stanley E. Fawcett. "International Purchasing: Benefits, Requirements, and Challenges." *International Journal of Purchasing and Materials Management,* Spring 1993, pp. 28–37.

Burt, David N., and Michael F. Doyle. *The American Keiretsu: A Strategic Weapon for Global Competitiveness.* Homewood, IL: Business One Irwin, 1993.

Dumond, Ellen J. "Moving Toward Value-Based Purchasing." *International Journal of Purchasing and Materials Management,* Spring 1994, pp. 3–8.

Fearon, Harold E., Donald W. Dobler, and Kenneth H. Killen. *The Purchasing Handbook,* 5th ed. New York: McGraw-Hill, 1993.

Fearon, Harold E., and Michiel R. Leenders. *Purchasing's Organizational Roles and Responsibilities.* Tempe, AZ: Center for Advanced Studies/National Association of Purchasing Management, 1995.

Graw, LeRoy H., and Diedre M. Maples. *Service Purchasing: What Every Buyer Should Know.* New York: Van Nostrand Reinhold, 1994.

Hahn, Chan K., Charles A. Watts, and Kee Young Kim. "The Supplier Development Program." *Journal of Purchasing and Materials Management,* Spring 1990, pp. 2–7.

Hickman, Thomas K., and William M. Hickman, Jr. *Global Purchasing: How to Buy Goods and Services in Foreign Markets.* Homewood, IL: Business One Irwin, 1992.

Leenders, Michiel R., and Harold E. Fearon. *Purchasing and Supply Management,* 11th ed. Burr Ridge, IL: Richard D. Irwin, 1997.

Meger, Randy. "Suppliers—Manage Your Customers." *Harvard Business Review,* November–December 1989, pp. 160–68.

Muller, Eugene W. *Job Analysis: Identifying The Tasks of Purchasing.* Tempe, AZ: Center for Advanced Purchasing Studies, 1992.

Plank, Richard E., and Valerie Kijewski. "The Use of Approved Supplier Lists." *International Journal of Purchasing and Materials Management,* Spring 1991, pp. 3–41.

Poirier, Charles C., and Stephen E. Reiter. *Supply Chain Optimization: Building the Strongest Total Business Network.* San Francisco: Berrett-Koehler Publishers, 1996.

Ramsay, John. "The Myth of the Cooperative Single Source." *Journal of Purchasing and Materials Management,* Winter 1990, pp. 2–5.

Chapter 13

Forecasting

Chapter Outline

Demand Management, 498

Types of Forecasting, 500

Components of Demand, 500

Qualitative Techniques in Forecasting, 503

    Grass Roots

    Market Research

    Panel Consensus

    Historical Analogy

    Delphi Method

Time Series Analysis, 505

    Simple Moving Average

    Weighted Moving Average

    Exponential Smoothing

    Forecast Errors

    Sources of Error

    Measurement of Error

    Linear Regression Analysis

    Decomposition of a Time Series

Causal Relationship Forecasting, 526

    Multiple Regression Analysis

Choosing a Forecasting Method, 529

Focus Forecasting, 530

    Methodology of Focus Forecasting

    Developing a Focus Forecasting
       System

Computer Programs, 533

Key Terms

Dependent Demand

Independent Demand

Time Series Analysis

Grass Roots

Executive Judgment

Market Research

Panel Consensus

Delphi Method

Moving Averages

Exponential Smoothing

Smoothing Constants Alpha (α)
and Delta (δ)

Mean Absolute Deviation (MAD)

Tracking Signal

Linear Regression Forecasting

Trend Effect

Seasonal Factor

Deseasonalization of Demand

Causal Relationship

Focus Forecasting

www Links

Tech Web (http://www.techweb.com.)

a data base consultant in Boston

W AL-MART'S SIZE AND POWER IN THE RETAIL INDUS-
try is having a huge influence in the database industry. With more than seven terabytes
of data on two fast-growing NCR systems, Wal-Mart manages one of the world's
largest data warehouses. Now the retailer is about to squeeze even more value from
those systems with a new data-mining application that will help it replace inventories
in stores.

Wal-Mart's formula for success—getting the right product on the appropriate
shelf at the lowest price—owes much to the company's multi-million-dollar investment in data warehousing. "Wal-Mart can be more detailed than most of its competitors on what's going on by product, by store, by day—and act on it," says Richard
Winter, a database consultant in Boston. "That's a tremendously powerful thing."

Besides the two NCR Teradata databases, which handle most decision-
support applications, Wal-Mart has another 6 terabytes of data on IBM and Hitachi
mainframes and 500 Gbytes on hundreds of servers running Informix's OnLine
Dynamic Server database. Wal-Mart developed its own middleware to manage system
priorities. "We drive the warehouse right to 100 percent utilization all of the time,"
says Rick Dalzell, Wal-Mart's vice president of application development.

The systems house data on point of sale, inventory, products in transit, market
statistics, customer demographics, finance, product returns, and supplier performance. The data is used for three broad areas of decision support: analyzing trends,
managing inventory, and understanding customers. What emerges are "personality
traits" for each of Wal-Mart's 3,000 or so outlets, which Wal-Mart managers use to
determine product mix and presentation for each store.

Data mining is next. Wal-Mart is beginning to roll out a demand-forecasting
application, based on neural networking software and a 4,000-processor parallel
computer from Neo Vista Solutions Inc. in Cupertino, California. The application

"looks at individual items for individual stores to decide the seasonal sales profile" of each item, Dalzell says. The Neo Vista system keeps a year's worth of data on the sales of 100,000 products and predicts which items will be needed in each store.

Over the next six months, Wal-Mart plans to expand its use of market-basket analysis. Data will be collected on items that comprise a shopper's total purchase so that the company can analyze relationships and patterns in customer purchases. Dalzell says this collection of data could eventually triple the size of Wal-Mart's data warehouse.

In the spring, Wal-Mart will make its data warehouse available over the Web to its store managers and suppliers. Today, 3,500 users make 10,000 database queries a day. By the end of 1997, says Dalzell, those numbers could double.

"What Wal-Mart is doing is letting an army of people use the database to make tactical decisions," says consultant Winter.

"The cumulative impact is immense." ●

Source: John Foley, *Tech Web*, December 9, 1996. Tech Web is located at http://www.techweb.com

**FINANCE
ACCOUNTING
MARKETING**

Forecasts are vital to every business organization and for every significant management decision. Forecasting is the basis of corporate long-run planning. In the functional areas of finance and accounting, forecasts provide the basis for budgetary planning and cost control. Marketing relies on sales forecasting to plan new products, compensate sales personnel, and make other key decisions. Production and operations personnel use forecasts to make periodic decisions involving process selection, capacity planning, and facility layout, as well as for continual decisions about production planning, scheduling, and inventory.

Bear in mind that a perfect forecast is usually impossible. Too many factors in the business environment cannot be predicted with certainty. Therefore, rather than search for the perfect forecast, it is far more important to establish the practice of continual review of forecasts and to learn to live with inaccurate forecasts. This is not to say that we should not try to improve the forecasting model or methodology, but that we should try to find and use the best forecasting method available, *within reason.*

When forecasting, a good strategy is to use two or three methods and look at them for the commonsense view. Are there expected changes in the general economy that will affect the forecast? Are there changes in industrial and private consumer behaviors? Will there be a shortage of essential complementary items? Continual review and updating in light of new data are basic to successful forecasting. In this chapter we look at *qualitative* and *quantitative* forecasting and concentrate primarily on several quantitative time series techniques. We cover in some depth moving averages, linear regression, trends, seasonal ratios (including deseasonalization), and focused forecasting. We also discuss sources and measurements of errors.

■ DEMAND MANAGEMENT

The purpose of demand management is to coordinate and control all of the sources of demand so the productive system can be used efficiently and the product delivered on time.

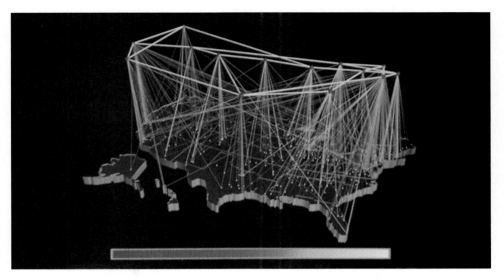

The National Science Foundation forecasts electronic traffic on the information highway measured in billions of bytes. Traffic volume range is depicted from zero bytes (purple) to 100 billion bytes (white). Such forecasts aid telecommunication companies in planning their product development as well as inventory and production levels.

Where does demand for a firm's product or service come from, and what can a firm do about it? There are two basic sources of demand: dependent demand and independent demand. **Dependent demand** is the demand for a product or service caused by the demand for other products or services. For example, if a firm sells 1,000 tricycles, then 1,000 front wheels and 2,000 rear wheels are needed. This type of internal demand does not need a forecast, simply a tabulation. As to how many tricycles the firm might sell, this is called **independent demand** because its demand cannot be derived directly from that of other products.[1] We discuss dependence and independence more fully in Chapters 15 and 16.

Dependent Demand

Independent Demand

There is not much a firm can do about dependent demand. It must be met (although the product or service can be purchased rather than produced internally). But there is a lot a firm can do about independent demand—if it wants to. The firm can

1. *Take an active role to influence demand.* The firm can apply pressure on its sales force, it can offer incentives both to customers and to its own personnel, it can wage campaigns to sell products, and it can cut prices. These actions can increase demand. Conversely, demand can be decreased through price increases or reduced sales efforts.

2. *Take a passive role and simply respond to demand.* There are several reasons a firm may not try to change demand but simply accept what happens. If a firm is running at full capacity, it may not want to do anything about demand. Other reasons are a firm may be powerless to change demand because of the expense to advertise; the market may be fixed in size and static; or demand is beyond its control (e.g., sole supplier). There are other competitive, legal, environmental, ethical, and moral reasons that market demand is passively accepted.

A great deal of coordination is required to manage these dependent and independent, and active and passive demands. These demands originate both internally and

---

[1] In addition to dependent and independent demands, other product relationships include complementary products and causal relationships where demand for one causes the demand for another.

externally in the form of new product sales from marketing, repair parts for previously sold products from product service, restocking from the factory warehouses, and supply items for manufacturing. In this chapter, our primary interest is in forecasting for independent items.

◼ TYPES OF FORECASTING

Time Series Analysis

Forecasting can be classified into four basic types: *qualitative, time series analysis, causal relationships,* and *simulation.*

Qualitative techniques are subjective or judgmental and are based on estimates and opinions. **Time series analysis,** the primary focus of this chapter, is based on the idea that data relating to past demand can be used to predict future demand. Past data may include several components, such as trend, seasonal, or cyclical influences, and is described in the following section. Causal forecasting, which we discuss using the linear regression technique, assumes that demand is related to some underlying factor or factors in the environment. Simulation models allow the forecaster to run through a range of assumptions about the condition of the forecast. Exhibit 13.1 describes a variety of the four basic types of forecasting models. In this chapter we discuss the first four time series analysis methods in the exhibit and the first of the causal techniques.

◼ COMPONENTS OF DEMAND

In most cases, demand for products or services can be broken down into six components: average demand for the period, a trend, seasonal element, cyclical elements, random variation, and autocorrelation. Exhibit 13.2 illustrates a demand over a four-year period, showing the average, trend, and seasonal components, and randomness around the smoothed demand curve.

Cyclical factors are more difficult to determine because the time span may be unknown or the cause of the cycle may not be considered. Cyclical influence on demand may come from such occurrences as political elections, war, economic conditions, or sociological pressures.

Random variations are caused by chance events. Statistically, when all the known causes for demand (average, trend, seasonal, cyclical, and autocorrelative) are subtracted from total demand, what remains is the unexplained portion of demand. If we cannot identify the cause of this remainder, it is assumed to be purely random chance.

Autocorrelation denotes the persistence of occurrence. More specifically, the value expected at any point is highly correlated with its own past values. In waiting line theory, the length of a waiting line is highly autocorrelated. That is, if a line is relatively long at one time, then shortly after that time, we would expect the line still to be long.

When demand is random, it may vary widely from one week to another. Where high autocorrelation exists, demand is not expected to change very much from one week to the next.

Trend lines are the usual starting point in developing a forecast. These trend lines are then adjusted for seasonal effects, cyclical, and any other expected events that may influence the final forecast. Exhibit 13.3 shows four of the most common types of

Forecasting Techniques and Common Models

Exhibit 13.1

I. Qualitative	Subjective; judgmental. Based on estimates and opinions.
Grass roots	Derives a forecast by compiling input from those at the end of the hierarchy who deal with what is being forecast. For example, an overall sales forecast may be derived by combining inputs from each salesperson, who is closest to his or her own territory.
Market research	Sets out to collect data in a variety of ways (surveys, interviews, etc.) to test hypotheses about the market. This is typically used to forecast long-range and new-product sales.
Panel consensus	Free open exchange at meetings. The idea is that discussion by the group will produce better forecasts than any one individual. Participants may be executives, salespeople, or customers.
Historical analogy	Ties what is being forecast to a similar item. Important in planning new products where a forecast may be derived by using the history of a similar product.
Delphi method	Group of experts responds to questionnaire. A moderator compiles results and formulates a new questionnaire which is submitted to the group. Thus, there is a learning process for the group as it receives new information and there is no influence of group pressure or dominating individual.
II. Time series analysis	Based on the idea that the history of occurrences over time can be used to predict the future.
Simple moving average	A time period containing a number of data points is averaged by dividing the sum of the point values by the number of points. Each, therefore, has equal influence.
Weighted moving average	Specific points may be weighted more or less than the others, as seen fit by experience.
Exponential smoothing	Recent data points are weighted more with weighting declining exponentially as data become older.
Regression analysis	Fits a straight line to past data generally relating the data value to time. Most common fitting technique is least squares.
Box Jenkins technique	Very complicated but apparently the most accurate statistical technique available. Relates a class of statistical models to data and fits the model to the time series by using Bayesian posterior distributions.
Shiskin time series	(Also called X-11). Developed by Julius Shiskin of the Census Bureau. An effective method to decompose a time series into seasonals, trends, and irregular. It needs at least three years of history. Very good in identifying turning points, for example, in company sales.
Trend projections	Fits a mathematical trend line to the data points and projects it into the future.
III. Causal	Tries to understand the system underlying and surrounding the item being forecast. For example, sales may be affected by advertising, quality, and competitors.
Regression analysis	Similar to least squares method in time series but may contain multiple variables. Basis is that forecast is caused by the occurrence of other events.
Econometric models	Attempts to describe some sector of the economy by a series of interdependent equations.
Input/output models	Focuses on sales of each industry to other firms and governments. Indicates the changes in sales that a producer industry might expect because of purchasing changes by another industry.
Leading indicators	Statistics that move in the same direction as the series being forecast but move before the series, such as an increase in the price of gasoline indicating a future drop in the sale of large cars.
IV. Simulation models	Dynamic models, usually computer-based, that allow the forecaster to make assumptions about the internal variables and external environment in the model. Depending on the variables in the model, the forecaster may ask such questions as: What would happen to my forecast if price increased by 10 percent? What effect would a mild national recession have on my forecast?

trends. A linear trend is obviously a straight continuous relationship. An S-curve is typical of a product growth and maturity cycle. The most important point in the S-curve is where the trend changes from a slow growth to a fast growth, or from fast to slow. An asymptotic trend starts with the highest demand growth at the beginning but then tapers off. Such a curve could happen when a firm enters an existing market with the objective of saturating and capturing a large share of the market. An

Exhibit 13.2

Historical Product
Demand Consisting of
a Growth Trend and
Seasonal Demand

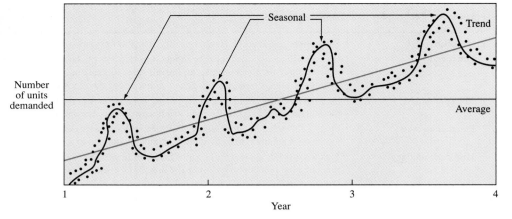

Exhibit 13.3

Common Types of
Trends

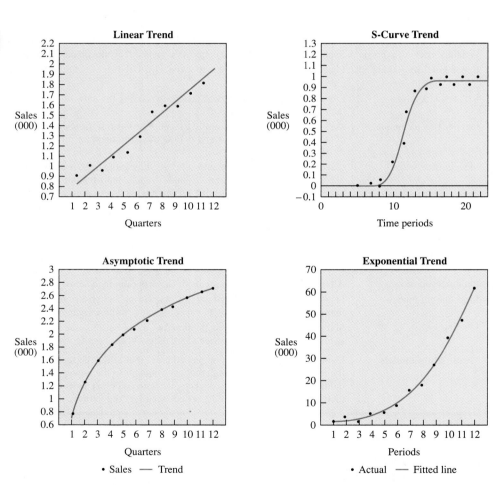

exponential curve is common in products with explosive growth. The exponential trend suggests that sales will continue to increase—an assumption that may not be safe to make.

A widely used forecasting method plots data and then searches for the standard distribution (such as linear, S-curve, asymptotic, or exponential) that fits best. The attractiveness of this method is that because the mathematics for the curve are known, solving for values for future time periods is easy.

Sometimes our data do not seem to fit any of the standard curves. This may be due to several causes essentially beating the data from several directions at the same time. For these cases, a simplistic but often effective forecast can be obtained by simply plotting data.

▇ QUALITATIVE TECHNIQUES IN FORECASTING

Grass Roots

Grass Roots

As stated in Exhibit 13.1, **grass roots** forecasting builds the forecast by adding successively from the bottom. The assumption here is that the person closest to the customer or end use of the product knows its future needs best. Though this is not always true, in many instances it is a valid assumption, and it is the basis for this method.

Forecasts at this bottom level are summed and given to the next higher level. This is usually a district warehouse, which then adds in safety stocks and any effects of ordering quantity sizes. This amount is then fed to the next level, which may be a regional warehouse. The procedure repeats until it becomes an input at the top level, which, in the case of a manufacturing firm, would be the input to the production system.

Market Research

Market Research

Firms often hire outside companies that specialize in **market research** to conduct this type of forecasting. You yourself may have been involved in market surveys through a marketing class. Certainly you have not escaped phone calls asking you about product preferences, your income, habits, and so on.

Market research is used mostly for product research in the sense of looking for new product ideas, likes and dislikes about existing products, which competitive products within a particular class are preferred, and so on. Again, the data collection methods are primarily surveys and interviews.

Panel Consensus

Panel Consensus

In a **panel consensus,** the idea that two heads are better than one is extrapolated to the idea that a panel of people from a variety of positions can develop a more reliable forecast than a narrower group. Panel forecasts are developed through open meetings with free exchange of ideas from all levels of management and individuals. The difficulty with this open style is that lower employee levels are intimidated by higher levels of management. For example, a salesperson in a particular product line may have a good estimate of future product demand but may not speak up to refute a much different estimate given by the vice president of marketing. The Delphi technique (which we discuss shortly) was developed to try to correct this impairment to free exchange.

When decisions in forecasting are at a broader and higher level (as when introducing a new product line or concerning strategic product decisions such as new marketing areas), the term **executive judgment** is generally used. The term is self-explanatory, because a higher level of management is involved.

**Executive
Judgment**

Historical Analogy

In trying to forecast demand for a new product, an ideal situation would be where an existing product or generic product could be used as a model. There are many ways to classify such analogies—for example, complementary products, substitutable or competitive products, and products as a function of income. Again, you have surely gotten a deluge of mail advertising products in a category similar to a product purchased via catalog or mail order. If you buy a CD through the mail, you will receive more mail about new CDs and CD players. A causal relationship (listed in Exhibit 13.1, Part III) would be that demand for compact discs is caused by demand for CD players. An analogy would be forecasting the demand for digital video disk players by analyzing the historic demand for stereo VCRs. The products are in the same general category of electronics and may be bought by consumers at similar rates. A simpler example would be toasters and coffee pots. A firm that already produces toasters and wants to produce coffee pots could use the toaster history as a likely growth model.

Delphi Method

Delphi Method

As we mentioned under panel consensus, a statement or opinion of a higher-level person will likely be weighted more than that of a lower-level person. The worst case is where lower-level people feel threatened and do not contribute their true beliefs. To prevent this problem, the **Delphi method** conceals the identity of the individuals participating in the study. Everyone has the same weight. Procedurally, a moderator creates a questionnaire and distributes it to participants. Their responses are summed and given back to the entire group along with a new set of questions.

The Delphi method was developed by the Rand Corporation in the 1950s. The step-by-step procedure is

1. Choose the experts to participate. There should be a variety of knowledgeable people in different areas.
2. Through a questionnaire (or E-mail), obtain forecasts (and any premises or qualifications for the forecasts) from all participants.
3. Summarize the results and redistribute them to the participants along with appropriate new questions.
4. Summarize again, refining forecasts and conditions, and again develop new questions.
5. Repeat Step 4 if necessary. Distribute the final results to all participants.

The Delphi technique can usually achieve satisfactory results in three rounds. The time required is a function of the number of participants, how much work is involved for them to develop their forecasts, and their speed in responding.

TIME SERIES ANALYSIS

Time series forecasting models try to predict the future based on past data. For example, sales figures collected for each of the past six weeks can be used to forecast sales for the seventh week. Quarterly sales figures collected for the past several years can be used to forecast future quarters. Even though both examples contain sales, different forecasting time series models would likely be used for forecasting.

Exhibit 13.4 shows the time series models and some of their characteristics. The simple moving average forecast is not shown in this table, but it would have the same characteristics as simple exponential smoothing. The weighted moving average can be more tricky if the forecaster includes seasonality or other cyclic influences. Its characteristics would lie somewhere between Holt's exponential smoothing and Winter's exponential smoothing. Though we do not cover the Holt and Winter models in detail, the reader may want to investigate these variations if exponential smoothing seems to apply to the data. Note that the models vary from simple to complex.

While recognizing that terms such as *short, medium,* and *long* are relative to the context in which they are used, in business forecasting *short-term* usually refers to under three months; *medium-term,* three months to two years; and *long-term,* greater than two years. In general, the short-term models compensate for random variation

A Guide to Selecting an Appropriate Forecasting Method

Exhibit 13.4

Forecasting Method	Amount of Historical Data	Data Pattern	Forecast Horizon	Preparation Time	Personnel Background
Simple exponential smoothing	5 to 10 observations to set the weight	Data should be stationary	Short	Short	Little sophistication
Holt's exponential smoothing	10 to 15 observations to set both weights	Trend but no seasonality	Short to medium	Short	Slight sophistication
Winter's exponential smoothing	At least 4 to 5 observations per season	Trend and seasonality	Short to medium	Short	Moderate sophistication
Regression trend models	10 to 20; for seasonality at least 5 per season	Trend and seasonality	Short to medium	Short	Moderate sophistication
Casual regression models	10 observations per independent variable	Can handle complex patterns	Short, medium, or long	Long development time, short time for implementation	Considerable sophistication
Time-series decomposition	Enough to see 2 peaks and troughs	Handles cyclical and seasonal patterns; may identify turning points	Short to medium	Short to moderate	Little sophistication
Box Jenkins	50 or more observations	Must be stationary or be transformed to stationarity	Short, medium, or long	Long	High sophistication

Source: J. Holton Wilson and Deborah Allison-Koerber, "Combining Subjective and Objective Forecasts Improves Results," *The Journal of Business Forecasting,* Fall 1992, p. 4.

and adjust for short-term changes (such as consumers' responses to a new product). Medium-term forecasts are useful for seasonal effects, and long-term models detect general trends and are especially useful in identifying major turning points.

Which forecasting model a firm should choose depends on

1. Time horizon to forecast.
2. Data availability.
3. Accuracy required.
4. Size of forecasting budget.
5. Availability of qualified personnel.

In selecting a forecasting model, there are other issues such as the firm's degree of flexibility. (The greater the ability to react quickly to changes the less accurate the forecast needs to be.) Another item is the consequence of a bad forecast. If a large capital investment decision is to be based on a forecast, it should be a good forecast.

Simple Moving Average

Moving Averages

When demand for a product is neither growing nor declining rapidly, and if it does not have seasonal characteristics, a moving average can be useful in removing the random fluctuations for forecasting. Although **moving averages** are frequently centered, it is more convenient to use past data to predict the following period directly. To illustrate, a centered five-month average of January, February, March, April, and May gives an average centered on March. However, all five months of data must already exist. If our objective is to forecast for June, we must project our moving average—by some means—from March to June. If the average is not centered but is at the forward end, we can forecast more easily, though we may lose some accuracy. Thus, if we want to forecast June with a five-month moving average, we can take the average of January, February, March, April, and May. When June passes, the forecast for July would be the average of February, March, April, May, and June. This is how Exhibits 13.5 and 13.6 were computed.

Although it is important to select the best period for the moving average, there are several conflicting effects of different period lengths: The longer the moving-average period, the greater the random elements are smoothed (which may be desirable in many cases). But if there is a trend in the data—either increasing or decreasing—the moving average has the adverse characteristic of lagging the trend. Therefore, while a shorter time span produces more oscillation, there is a closer following of the trend. Conversely, a longer time span gives a smoother response but lags the trend.

The formula for a simple moving average is

$$F_t = \frac{A_{t-1} + A_{t-2} + A_{t-3} + \cdots + A_{t-n}}{n} \tag{13.1}$$

where

$$F_t = \text{Forecast for the coming period}$$
$$n = \text{Number of periods to be averaged}$$
$$A_{t-1} = \text{Actual occurrence in the past period}$$
$$A_{t-2}, A_{t-3}, \text{ and } A_{t-n} = \text{Actual occurrences two periods ago, three periods ago,}$$
$$\text{and so on up to } n \text{ periods ago}$$

Week	Demand	3 Week	9 Week	Week	Demand	3 Week	9 Week
1	800			16	1,700	2,200	1,811
2	1,400			17	1,800	2,000	1,800
3	1,000			18	2,200	1,833	1,811
4	1,500	1,067		19	1,900	1,900	1,911
5	1,500	1,300		20	2,400	1,967	1,933
6	1,300	1,333		21	2,400	2,167	2,011
7	1,800	1,433		22	2,600	2,233	2,111
8	1,700	1,533		23	2,000	2,467	2,144
9	1,300	1,600		24	2,500	2,333	2,111
10	1,700	1,600	1,367	25	2,600	2,367	2,167
11	1,700	1,567	1,467	26	2,200	2,367	2,267
12	1,500	1,567	1,500	27	2,200	2,433	2,311
13	2,300	1,633	1,556	28	2,500	2,333	2,311
14	2,300	1,833	1,644	29	2,400	2,300	2,378
15	2,000	2,033	1,733	30	2,100	2,367	2,378

Exhibit 13.5

Forecast Demand Based on a Three- and a Nine-Week Simple Moving Average

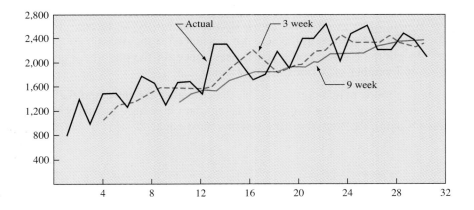

Exhibit 13.6

Moving Average Forecast of Three- and Nine-Week Periods versus Actual Demand

Exhibit 13.6, a plot of the data in Exhibit 13.5, shows the effects of various lengths of the period of a moving average. We see that the growth trend levels off at about the 23rd week. The three-week moving average responds better in following this change than the nine-week average, although overall, the nine-week average is smoother.

The main disadvantage in calculating a moving average is that all individual elements must be carried as data because a new forecast period involves adding new data and dropping the earliest data. For a three- or six-period moving average, this is not too severe. But plotting a 60-day moving average for the usage of each of 20,000 items in inventory would involve a significant amount of data.

Weighted Moving Average

Whereas the simple moving average gives equal weight to each component of the moving-average database, a weighted moving average allows any weights to be placed on each element, providing, of course, that the sum of all weights equals 1. For example, a department store may find that in a four-month period, the best forecast is derived by using 40 percent of the actual sales for the most recent month, 30 percent of two months ago, 20 percent of three months ago, and 10 percent of four months ago. If actual sales experience was

Month 1	Month 2	Month 3	Month 4	Month 5
100	90	105	95	?

the forecast for month 5 would be

$$F_5 = 0.40(95) + 0.30(105) + 0.20(90) + 0.10(100)$$
$$= 38 + 31.5 + 18 + 10$$
$$= 97.5$$

The formula for weighted moving average is

$$F_t = w_1 A_{t-1} + w_2 A_{t-2} + \cdots + w_n A_{t-n} \qquad (13.2)$$

where

w_1 = Weight to be given to the actual occurrence for the period $t - 1$
w_2 = Weight to be given to the actual occurrence for the period $t - 2$
w_n = Weight to be given to the actual occurrence for the period $t - n$
n = Total number of periods in the forecast

While many periods may be ignored (i.e., their weights are zero) and the weighting scheme may be in any order (e.g., more distant data may have greater weights than more recent data), the sum of all the weights must equal 1.

$$\sum_{i=1}^{n} w_i = 1$$

Suppose sales for month 5 actually turned out to be 110. Then the forecast for month 6 would be

$$F_6 = 0.40(110) + 0.30(95) + 0.20(105) + 0.10(90)$$
$$= 44 + 28.5 + 21 + 9$$
$$= 102.5$$

Choosing Weights   Experience and trial and error are the simplest ways to choose weights. As a general rule, the most recent past is the most important indicator of what to expect in the future, and therefore, it should get higher weighting. The past month's revenue or plant capacity, for example, would be a better estimate for the coming month than the revenue or plant capacity of several months ago.

However, if the data are seasonal, for example, weights should be established accordingly. Bathing suit sales in July of last year should be weighted more heavily than bathing suit sales in December (in the northern hemisphere).

The weighted moving average has a definite advantage over the simple moving average in being able to vary the effects of past data. However, it is more inconvenient and costly to use than the exponential smoothing method, which we will examine next.

Exponential Smoothing

In the previous methods of forecasting (simple and weighted moving average), the major drawback is the need to continually carry a large amount of historical data. (This is also true for regression analysis techniques, which we soon will cover.) As each new piece of data is added in these methods, the oldest observation is dropped, and the new forecast is calculated. In many applications (perhaps in most), the most recent occurrences are more indicative of the future than those in the more distant past. If this premise is valid—that the importance of data diminishes as the past becomes more distant—then **exponential smoothing** may be the most logical and easiest method to use.

Exponential Smoothing

The reason this is called exponential smoothing is because each increment in the past is decreased by $(1 - \alpha)$. If α is 0.05, for example, weights for various periods would be as follows (α is defined below):

	Weighting at $\alpha = 0.05$
Most recent weighting $= \alpha(1 - \alpha)^0$	0.0500
Data one time period older $= \alpha(1 - \alpha)^1$	0.0475
Data two time periods older $= \alpha(1 - \alpha)^2$	0.0451
Data three time periods older $= \alpha(1 - \alpha)^3$	0.0429

Therefore, the exponents 0, 1, 2, 3, . . . , and so on give it its name.

Exponential smoothing is the most used of all forecasting techniques. It is an integral part of virtually all computerized forecasting programs, and it is widely used in ordering inventory in retail firms, wholesale companies, and service agencies.

Exponential smoothing techniques have become well accepted for six major reasons:

1. Exponential models are surprisingly accurate.
2. Formulating an exponential model is relatively easy.
3. The user can understand how the model works.
4. Little computation is required to use the model.
5. Computer storage requirements are small because of the limited use of historical data.
6. Tests for accuracy as to how well the model is performing are easy to compute.

In the exponential smoothing method, only three pieces of data are needed to forecast the future: the most recent forecast, the actual demand that occurred for that forecast period, and a **smoothing constant alpha (α).** This smoothing constant determines the level of smoothing and the speed of reaction to differences between forecasts and actual occurrences. The value for the constant is determined both by the nature of the product and by the manager's sense of what constitutes a good response rate. For example, if a firm produced a standard item with relatively stable demand, the reaction rate to differences between actual and forecast demand would tend to be small, perhaps just 5 or 10 percentage points. However, if the firm were experiencing growth, it would be desirable to have a higher reaction rate, perhaps 15 to 30 percentage points, to give greater importance to recent growth experience. The more rapid the growth, the higher the reaction rate should be. Sometimes users of the

Smoothing Constant Alpha (α)

simple moving average switch to exponential smoothing but like to keep the forecasts about the same as the simple moving average. In this case, α is approximated by $2 \div (n + 1)$, where n is the number of time periods.

The equation for a single exponential smoothing forecast is simply

$$F_t = F_{t-1} + \alpha(A_{t-1} - F_{t-1}) \qquad (13.3)$$

where

F_t = The exponentially smoothed forecast for period t
F_{t-1} = The exponentially smoothed forecast made for the prior period
A_{t-1} = The actual demand in the prior period
α = The desired response rate, or smoothing constant

This equation states that the new forecast is equal to the old forecast plus a portion of the error (the difference between the previous forecast and what actually occurred).[2]

To demonstrate the method, assume that the long-run demand for the product under study is relatively stable and a smoothing constant (α) of 0.05 is considered appropriate. If the exponential method were used as a continuing policy, a forecast would have been made for last month.[3] Assume that last month's forecast (F_{t-1}) was 1,050 units. If 1,000 actually were demanded, rather than 1,050, the forecast for this month would be

$$F_t = F_{t-1} + \alpha(A_{t-1} - F_{t-1})$$
$$= 1,050 + 0.05(1,000 - 1,050)$$
$$= 1,050 + 0.05(-50)$$
$$= 1,047.5 \text{ units}$$

Because the smoothing coefficient is small, the reaction of the new forecast to an error of 50 units is to decrease the next month's forecast by only 2 ½ units.

Single exponential smoothing has the shortcoming of lagging changes in demand. Exhibit 13.7 presents actual data plotted as a smooth curve to show the lagging effects of the exponential forecasts. The forecast lags during an increase or decrease but overshoots when a change in the direction occurs. Note that the higher the value of alpha, the more closely the forecast follows the actual. To more closely track actual demand, a trend factor may be added. Adjusting the value of alpha also helps. This is termed *adaptive forecasting*. Both trend effects and adaptive forecasting are briefly explained in following sections.

Smoothing Constant Delta (δ)

Trend Effects in Exponential Smoothing   Remember that an upward or downward trend in data collected over a sequence of time periods causes the exponential forecast to always lag behind (be above or below) the actual occurrence. Exponentially smoothed forecasts can be corrected somewhat by adding in a trend adjustment. To correct the trend, we need two smoothing constants. Besides the smoothing constant α, the trend equation also uses a **smoothing constant delta (δ).** The delta reduces the impact of the error that occurs between the actual and the forecast. If both alpha and delta are not included, the trend would overreact to errors.

---

[2] Some writers prefer to call F_t a smoothed average.

[3] When exponential smoothing is first introduced, the initial forecast or starting point may be obtained by using a simple estimate or an average of preceding periods such as the average of the first two or three periods.

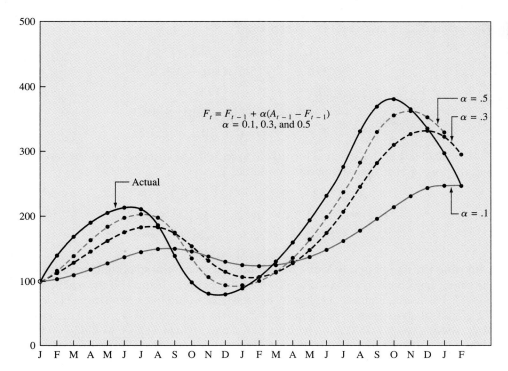

Exhibit 13.7

Exponential Forecasts
versus Actual
Demands for Units
of a Product over
Time Showing the
Forecast Lag

To get the trend equation going, the first time it is used the trend value must be entered manually. This initial trend value can be an educated guess or a computation based on observed past data.

The equation to compute the forecast including trend (FIT) is

$$\text{FIT}_t = F_t + T_t \tag{13.4}$$

$$F_t = \text{FIT}_{t-1} + \alpha(A_{t-1} - \text{FIT}_{t-1}) \tag{13.5}$$

$$T_t = T_{t-1} + \alpha\delta(A_{t-1} - \text{FIT}_{t-1}) \tag{13.6}$$

where

F_t = The exponentially smoothed forecast for period t
T_t = The exponentially smoothed trend for period t
FIT_t = The forecast including trend for period t
FIT_{t-1} = The forecast including trend made for the prior period
A_{t-1} = The actual demand for the prior period
α = Smoothing constant
δ = Smoothing constant

■ **example 13.1**   *Forecast Including Trend*   Assume an initial starting F_t of 100 units, a trend of 10 units, an alpha of .20, and a delta of .30. If actual demand turned out to be 115 rather than the forecast 100, calculate the forecast for the next period.

solution   Adding the starting forecast and the trend, we have

$$\text{FIT}_{t-1} = F_{t-1} + T_{t-1} = 100 + 10 = 110$$

The actual A_{t-1} is given as 115. Therefore,

$$F_t = \text{FIT}_{t-1} + \alpha(A_{t-1} - \text{FIT}_{t-1})$$
$$= 110 + .2(115 - 110) = 111.0$$
$$T_t = T_{t-1} + \alpha\delta(A_{t-1} - \text{FIT}_{t-1})$$
$$= 10 + (.2)(.3)(115 - 110) = 10.3$$
$$\text{FIT}_t = F_t + T_t = 111.0 + 10.3 = 121.3$$

If, instead of 121.3, the actual turned out to be 120, the sequence would be repeated and the forecast for the next period would be

$$F_{t+1} = 121.3 + .2(120 - 121.3) = 121.04$$
$$T_{t+1} = 10.3 + (.2)(.3)(120 - 121.3) = 10.22$$
$$\text{FIT}_{t+1} = 121.04 + 10.22 = 131.26 \qquad \blacksquare$$

Choosing the Appropriate Value for Alpha   Exponential smoothing requires that the smoothing constant alpha (α) be given a value between 0 and 1. If the real demand is stable (such as demand for electricity or food), we would like a small alpha to lessen the effects of short-term or random changes. If the real demand is rapidly increasing or decreasing (such as in fashion items or new small appliances), we would like a large alpha to try to keep up with the change. It would be ideal if we could predict which alpha we should use. Unfortunately, two things are going against us. First, it would take some passage of time to determine the alpha that would best fit our actual data. This would be tedious to follow and revise. Second, because demands do change, the alpha we pick this week may need to be revised in the near future. Therefore, we need some automatic method to track and change our alpha values.

Adaptive forecasting   There are two approaches to controlling the value of alpha. One uses various values of alpha. The other uses a tracking signal.

1. *Two or more predetermined values of alpha.* The amount of error between the forecast and the actual demand is measured. Depending on the degree of error, different values of alpha are used. If the error is large, alpha is 0.8; if the error is small, alpha is 0.2.
2. *Computed values for alpha.* A tracking alpha computes whether the forecast is keeping pace with genuine upward or downward changes in demand (as opposed to random changes). In this application, the tracking alpha is defined as the exponentially smoothed actual error divided by the exponentially smoothed absolute error. Alpha changes from period to period within the possible range of 0 to 1.

Forecast Errors

In using the word *error,* we are referring to the difference between the forecast value and what actually occurred. In statistics, these errors are called residuals. As long as the forecast value is within the confidence limits, as we discuss later in "Measurement of Error," this is not really an error. But common usage refers to the difference as an error.

Demand for a product is generated through the interaction of a number of factors too complex to describe accurately in a model. Therefore, all forecasts certainly contain some error. In discussing forecast errors, it is convenient to distinguish between *sources of error* and the *measurement of error.*

Sources of Error

Errors can come from a variety of sources. One common source that many forecasters are unaware of is projecting past trends into the future. For example, when we talk about statistical errors in regression analysis, we are referring to the deviations of observations from our regression line. It is common to attach a confidence band (i.e., statistical control limits) to the regression line to reduce the unexplained error. But when we then use this regression line as a forecasting device by projecting it into the future, the error may not be correctly defined by the projected confidence band. This is because the confidence interval is based on past data; it may or may not hold for projected data points and therefore cannot be used with the same confidence. In fact, experience has shown that the actual errors tend to be greater than those predicted from forecast models.

Errors can be classified as bias or random. *Bias errors* occur when a consistent mistake is made. Sources of bias include failing to include the right variables; using the wrong relationships among variables; employing the wrong trend line; mistakenly shifting the seasonal demand from where it normally occurs; and the existence of some undetected secular trend. *Random errors* can be defined as those that cannot be explained by the forecast model being used.

Measurement of Error

Several of the common terms used to describe the degree of error are *standard error, mean squared error* (or *variance*), and *mean absolute deviation*. In addition, tracking signals may be used to indicate any positive or negative bias in the forecast.

Standard error is discussed in the section on linear regression in this chapter. Because the standard error is the square root of a function, it is often more convenient to use the function itself. This is called the mean square error or variance.

The **mean absolute deviation (MAD)** was in vogue in the past but subsequently was ignored in favor of standard deviation and standard error measures. In recent years, MAD has made a comeback because of its simplicity and usefulness in obtaining tracking signals. MAD is the average error in the forecasts, using absolute values. It is valuable because MAD, like the standard deviation, measures the dispersion of some observed value from some expected value.

Mean Absolute Deviation (MAD)

MAD is computed using the differences between the actual demand and the forecast demand without regard to sign. It equals the sum of the absolute deviations divided by the number of data points, or, stated in equation form,

$$\text{MAD} = \frac{\sum_{i=1}^{n} |A_t - F_t|}{n} \tag{13.7}$$

where

t = Period number
A = Actual demand for the period
F = Forecast demand for the period
n = Total number of periods
$|\ |$ = A symbol used to indicate the absolute value disregarding positive and negative signs

When the errors that occur in the forecast are normally distributed (the usual case), the mean absolute deviation relates to the standard deviation as

$$1 \text{ standard deviation} = \sqrt{\frac{\pi}{2}} \times \text{MAD, or approximately 1.25 MAD.}$$

Conversely,

$$1 \text{ MAD} = 0.8 \text{ standard deviation}$$

The standard deviation is the larger measure. If the MAD of a set of points was found to be 60 units, then the standard deviation would be 75 units. In the usual statistical manner, if control limits were set at plus or minus 3 standard deviations (or ± 3.75 MADs), then 99.7 percent of the points would fall within these limits.

Tracking Signal

A **tracking signal** is a measurement that indicates whether the forecast average is keeping pace with any genuine upward or downward changes in demand. As used in forecasting, the tracking signal is the *number* of mean absolute deviations that the forecast value is above or below the actual occurrence. Exhibit 13.8 shows a normal distribution with a mean of zero and a MAD equal to 1. Thus, if we compute the tracking signal and find it equal to minus 2, we can see that the forecast model is providing forecasts that are quite a bit above the mean of the actual occurrences.

A tracking signal (TS) can be calculated using the arithmetic sum of forecast deviations divided by the mean absolute deviation:

$$\text{TS} = \frac{\text{RSFE}}{\text{MAD}} \tag{13.8}$$

where

RSFE is the running sum of forecast errors, considering the nature of the error. (For example, negative errors cancel positive errors and vice versa)

MAD is the average of all of the forecast errors (disregarding whether the deviations are positive or negative). It is the average of the absolute deviations

A Normal Distribution with Mean = 0 and MAD = 1

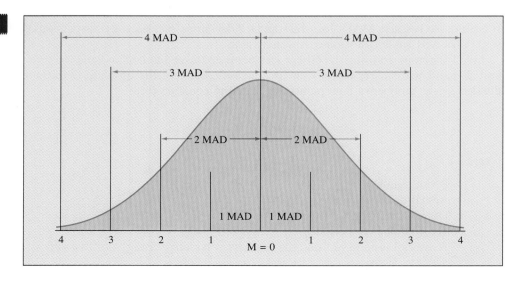

Exhibit 13.9 illustrates the procedure for computing MAD and the tracking signal for a six-month period where the forecast had been set at a constant 1,000 and the actual demands that occurred are as shown. In this example, the forecast, on the average, was off by 66.7 units and the tracking signal was equal to 3.3 mean absolute deviations.

We can get a better feel for what the MAD and tracking signal mean by plotting the points on a graph. Though this is not completely legitimate from a sample-size standpoint, we plotted each month in Exhibit 13.10 to show the drift of the tracking signal. Note that it drifted from minus 1 MAD to plus 3.3 MADs. This happened because actual demand was greater than the forecast in four of the six periods. If the actual demand does not fall below the forecast to offset the continual positive RSFE, the tracking signal would continue to rise and we would conclude that assuming a demand of 1,000 is a bad forecast.

Acceptable limits for the tracking signal depend on the size of the demand being forecast (high-volume or high-revenue items should be monitored frequently) and the amount of personnel time available (narrower acceptable limits cause more forecasts to be out of limits and therefore require more time to investigate). Exhibit 13.11 shows the area within the control limits for a range of one to four MADs.

Computing the Mean Absolute Deviation (MAD), the Running Sum of Forecast Errors (RSFE), and the Tracking Signal (TS) from Forecast and Actual Data

Exhibit 13.9

Month	Demand Forecast	Actual	Deviation	RSFE	Abs. Dev.	Sum of Abs. Dev.	MAD*	$TS = \dfrac{RSFE^{\dagger}}{MAD}$
1	1,000	950	−50	−50	50	50	50	−1
2	1,000	1,070	+70	+20	70	120	60	.33
3	1,000	1,100	+100	+120	100	220	73.3	1.64
4	1,000	960	−40	+80	40	260	65	1.2
5	1,000	1,090	+90	+170	90	350	70	2.4
6	1,000	1,050	+50	+220	50	400	66.7	3.3

* For Month 6, MAD = 400 ÷ 6 = 66.7.

† For Month 6, $TS = \dfrac{RSFE}{MAD} = \dfrac{220}{66.7} = 3.3$ MADs.

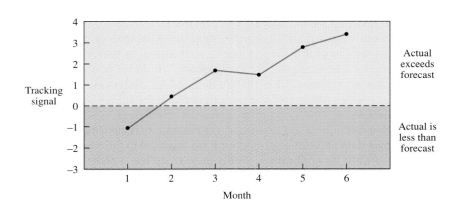

Exhibit 13.10

A Plot of the Tracking Signals Calculated in Exhibit 13.9

The Percentages of Points Included within the Control Limits for a Range of 1 to 4 MADs

	Control Limits		
Number of MADs	Related Number of Standard Deviations	Percentage of Points Lying within Control Limits
± 1	0.798	57.048
± 2	1.596	88.946
± 3	2.394	98.334
± 4	3.192	99.856

In a perfect forecasting model, the sum of the actual forecast errors would be zero; the errors that result in overestimates should be offset by errors that are underestimates. The tracking signal would then also be zero, indicating an unbiased model, neither leading nor lagging the actual demands.

Often, MAD is used to forecast errors. It might then be desirable to make the MAD more sensitive to recent data. A useful technique to do this is to compute an exponentially smoothed MAD as a forecast for the next period's error range. The procedure is similar to single exponential smoothing covered earlier in this chapter. The value of the MAD forecast is to provide a range of error. In the case of inventory control, this is useful in setting safety stock levels.

$$\text{MAD}_t = \alpha \left| A_{t-1} - F_{t-1} \right| + (1 - \alpha)\text{MAD}_{t-1}$$

where

MAD_t = Forecast MAD for the tth period
α = Smoothing constant (normally in the range of 0.05 to 0.20)
A_{t-1} = Actual demand in the period $t - 1$
F_{t-1} = Forecast demand for period $t - 1$

Linear Regression Analysis

Regression can be defined as a functional relationship between two or more correlated variables. It is used to predict one variable given the other. The relationship is usually developed from observed data. The data should be plotted first to see if they appear linear or if at least parts of the data are linear. Linear regression refers to the special class of regression where the relationship between variables forms a straight line.

The linear regression line is of the form $Y = a + bX$, where Y is the value of the dependent variable that we are solving for, a is the Y intercept, b is the slope, and X is the independent variable. (In time series analysis, X is units of time.)

Linear regression is useful for long-term forecasting of major occurrences and aggregate planning. For example, linear regression would be very useful to forecast demands for product families. Even though demand for individual products within a family may vary widely during a time period, demand for the total product family is surprisingly smooth.

Linear Regression Forecasting

The major restriction in using **linear regression forecasting** is, as the name implies, that past data and future projections are assumed to fall about a straight line. While this does limit its application, sometimes, if we use a shorter period of time, linear regression analysis can still be used. For example, there may be short segments of the longer period that are approximately linear.

Linear regression is used for both time series forecasting and for casual relationship forecasting. When the dependent variable (usually the vertical axis on a graph) changes as a result of time (plotted as the horizontal axis), it is time series analysis. If one variable changes because of the change in another variable, this is a casual relationship (such as the number of deaths from lung cancer increasing with the number of people who smoke).

We use the following example several times in this chapter to compare forecasting models and types of analysis. We use it for hand fitting a line, for the least squares analysis, and for a decomposition example.

■ **example 13.2**   *Hand Fitting a Trend Line*   A firm's sales for a product line during the 12 quarters of the past 3 years were as follows:

Quarter	Sales	Quarter	Sales
1	600	7	2,600
2	1,550	8	2,900
3	1,500	9	3,800
4	1,500	10	4,500
5	2,400	11	4,000
6	3,100	12	4,900

The firm wants to forecast each quarter of the fourth year, that is, quarters 13, 14, 15, and 16. In hand fitting a curve, we plot the data and use simple eyeballing or OHA (ocular heuristic approximation).

solution   The procedure is quite simple: Lay a straightedge (clear plastic rulers are nice) across the data points until the line seems to fit well, and draw the line. This is the regression line. The next step is to determine the intercept *a* and slope *b*.

Exhibit 13.12 shows a plot of the data and the straight line we drew through the points. The intercept *a*, where the line cuts the vertical axis, appears to be about 400. The slope *b* is the "rise" divided by the "run" (the change in the height of some portion of the line divided by the number of units in the horizontal axis). Any two points can

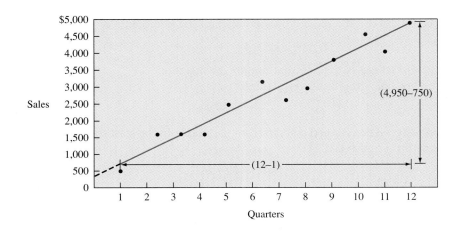

Exhibit 13.12

A Hand-Fitted Regression

be used, but two points some distance apart give the best accuracy because of the errors in reading values from the graph. We use values for the 1st and 12th quarters.

In Exhibit 13.12, by reading from the points on the line the Y values for quarter 1 and quarter 12 are about 750 and 4,950. Therefore,

$$b = (4,950 - 750)/(12 - 1) = 382$$

The hand-fit regression equation is therefore

$$Y = 400 + 382x$$

The forecasts for quarters 13 through 16 are

Quarter	Forecast
13	$400 + 382(13) = 5,366$
14	$400 + 382(14) = 5,748$
15	$400 + 382(15) = 6,130$
16	$400 + 382(16) = 6,512$

These forecasts are based on the line only and do not identify or adjust for elements such as seasonal or cyclical elements. ■

Least Squares Method   The least squares equation for linear regression is the same as we used in our hand-fit example:

$$Y = a + bx \tag{13.9}$$

where

Y = Dependent variable computed by the equation
y = The actual dependent variable data point
a = Y intercept
b = Slope of the line
x = Time period

The least squares method tries so fit the line to the data *that minimizes the sum of the squares of the vertical distance* between each data point and its corresponding point on the line. Exhibit 13.12 showed the 12 data points. If a straight line is drawn through the general area of the points, the difference between the point and the line is $y - Y$. Exhibit 13.13 shows these differences. The sum of the squares of the differences between the plotted data points and the line points is

$$(y_1 - Y_1)^2 + (y_2 - Y_2)^2 + \cdots + (y_{12} - Y_{12})^2$$

The best line to use is the one that minimizes this total.

As before, the straight line equation is

$$Y = a + bx$$

Previously we determined a and b from the graph. In the least squares method, the equations for a and b are

$$a = \bar{y} - b\bar{x} \tag{13.10}$$

$$b = \frac{\Sigma xy - n\bar{x} \cdot \bar{y}}{\Sigma x^2 - n\bar{x}^2} \tag{13.11}$$

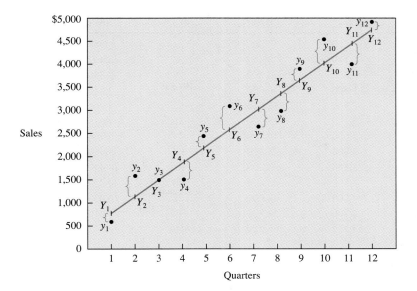

Exhibit 13.13

Least Squares
Regression Line

where

a = Y intercept
b = Slope of the line
$\bar{y}$ = Average of all ys
$\bar{x}$ = Average of all xs
x = x value at each data point
y = y value at each data point
n = Number of data points
Y = Value of the dependent variable computed with the regression equation

Exhibit 13.14 shows these computations carried out for the 12 data points in Exhibit 13.12 as part of example 13.2. Note that the final equation for Y shows an intercept of 441.6 and a slope of 359.6. The slope shows that for every unit change in X, that Y changes by 359.6.

Strictly based on the equation, forecasts for periods 13 through 16 would be

$$Y_{13} = 441.6 + 359.6(13) = 5,116.4$$
$$Y_{14} = 441.6 + 359.6(14) = 5,476.0$$
$$Y_{15} = 441.6 + 359.6(15) = 5,835.6$$
$$Y_{16} = 441.6 + 359.6(16) = 6,195.2$$

The standard error of estimate, or how well the line fits the data, is[4]

$$S_{yx} = \sqrt{\frac{\sum\limits_{i=1}^{n}(y_i - Y_i)^2}{n-2}} \qquad (13.12)$$

---

[4] An equation for the standard error that is often easier to compute is $S_{yx} = \sqrt{\dfrac{\sum y^2 - a\sum y - b\sum xy}{n-2}}$

Exhibit 13.14

Least Squares
Regression Analysis

(1) x	(2) y	(3) xy	(4) x^2	(5) y^2	(6) Y
1	600	600	1	360,000	801.3
2	1,550	3,100	4	2,402,500	1,160.9
3	1,500	4,500	9	2,250,000	1,520.5
4	1,500	6,000	16	2,250,000	1,880.1
5	2,400	12,000	25	5,760,000	2,239.7
6	3,100	18,600	36	9,610,000	2,599.4
7	2,600	18,200	49	6,760,000	2,959.0
8	2,900	23,200	64	8,410,000	3,318.6
9	3,800	34,200	81	14,440,000	3,678.2
10	4,500	45,000	100	20,250,000	4,037.8
11	4,000	44,000	121	16,000,000	4,397.4
12	4,900	58,800	144	24,010,000	4,757.1
78	33,350	268,200	650	112,502,500	

$\bar{x} = 6.5 \qquad b = 359.6153$

$\bar{y} = 2,779.17 \qquad a = 441.6666$

Therefore $Y = 441.66 + 359.6x$

$\qquad\qquad S_{yx} = 363.9$

The standard error of estimate is computed from the second and last columns of Exhibit 13.14;

$$S_{yx} = \sqrt{\frac{(600 - 801.3)^2 + (1,550 - 1,160.9)^2 + (1,500 - 1,520.5)^2 + \cdots + (4,900 - 4,757.1)^2}{10}}$$

$$= 363.9$$

We discuss the possible existence of seasonal components in the next section on decomposition of a time series.

Decomposition of a Time Series

A *time series* can be defined as chronologically ordered data that may contain one or more components of demand: trend, seasonal, cyclical, autocorrelation, and random. *Decomposition* of a time series means identifying and separating the time series data into these components. In practice, it is relatively easy to identify the trend (even without mathematical analysis, it is usually easy to plot and see the direction of movement) and the seasonal component (by comparing the same period year to year). It is considerably more difficult to identify the cycles (these may be many months or years long), autocorrelation, and random components. (The forecaster usually calls random anything left over that cannot be identified as another component.)

Trend Effects   When demand contains both seasonal and **trend effects** at the same time, the question is how they relate to each other. In this description, we examine two types of seasonal variation: *additive* and *multiplicative.*

Additive and Multiplicative Seasonal Variation Superimposed on Changing Trend

Exhibit 13.15

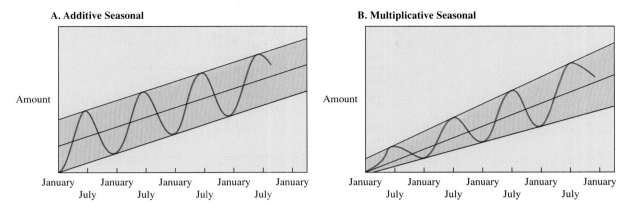

A. Additive Seasonal

B. Multiplicative Seasonal

Additive Seasonal Variation   Additive seasonal variation simply assumes that the seasonal amount is a constant no matter what the trend or average amount is.

Forecast including trend and seasonal = Trend + Seasonal

Exhibit 13.15A shows an example of increasing trend with constant seasonal amounts.

Multiplicative Seasonal Variation   In multiplicative seasonal variation, the trend is multiplied by the seasonal factors.

Forecast including trend and seasonal = Trend × Seasonal factor

Exhibit 13.15B shows the seasonal variation increasing as the trend increases because its size depends on the trend.

The multiplicative seasonal variation is the usual experience. Essentially, this says that the larger the basic amount projected, the larger the variation around this that we can expect.

Seasonal Factor (or Index)   A **seasonal factor** is the amount of correction needed in a time series to adjust for the season of the year.

Seasonal Factor

We usually associate *seasonal* with a period of the year characterized by some particular activity. We use the word *cyclical* to indicate other than annual recurrent periods of repetitive activity.

The following examples show where seasonal indexes are determined and used to forecast (1) a simple calculation based on past seasonal data and (2) the trend and seasonal index from a hand-fitted regression line. We follow this with a more formal procedure for the decomposition of data and forecasting using least squares regression.

■ example 13.3   *Simple Proportion*   Assume that in past years, a firm sold an average of 1,000 units of a particular product line each year. On the average, 200 units were sold in the spring, 350 in the summer, 300 in the fall, and 150 in the winter. The seasonal factor (or index) is the ratio of the amount sold during each season divided by the average for all seasons.

solution   In this example, the yearly amount divided equally over all seasons is $1,000 \div 4 = 250$. The seasonal factors therefore are

	Past Sales	Average Sales for Each Season (1,000/4)	Seasonal Factor
Spring	200	250	200/250 = 0.8
Summer	350	250	350/250 = 1.4
Fall	300	250	300/250 = 1.2
Winter	150	250	150/250 = 0.6
Total	1,000		

Using these factors, if we expected demand for next year to be 1,100 units, we would forecast the demand to occur as

	Expected Demand for Next Year	Average Sales for Each Season (1,100/4)		Seasonal Factor		Next Year's Seasonal Forecast
Spring		275	×	0.8	=	220
Summer		275	×	1.4	=	385
Fall		275	×	1.2	=	330
Winter		275	×	0.6	=	165
Total	1,100					

The seasonal factor may be periodically updated as new data are available. The following example shows the seasonal factor and multiplicative seasonal variation.

■ **example 13.4**   *Computing Trend and Seasonal Factor from a Hand-Fit Straight Line*   Here we must compute the trend as well as the seasonal factors.

solution   We solve this problem by simply hand fitting a straight line through the data points and measuring the trend and intercept from the graph. Assume the history of data is

Quarter	Amount	Quarter	Amount
I—1996	300	I—1997	520
II—1996	200	II—1997	420
III—1996	220	III—1997	400
IV—1996	530	IV—1997	700

First, we plot as in Exhibit 13.16 and then fit a straight line through the data simply by eyeballing. (Naturally, this line and the resulting equation are subject to variation.) The equation for the line is

$$\text{Trend}_t = 170 + 55t$$

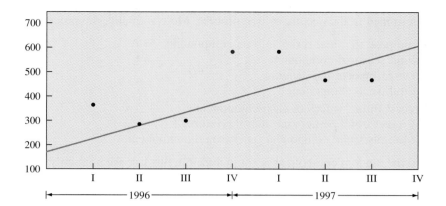

Exhibit 13.16

A Plot of Quarterly Demand History

Exhibit 13.17

Computing a Seasonal Factor from the Actual Data and Trend Line

Quarter	Actual Amount	From Trend Equation $T_t = 170 + 55t$	Ratio of Actual ÷ Trend	Seasonal Factor (Average of Same Quarters in Both Years)
1996				
I	300	225	1.33	I—1.25
II	200	280	.71	II—0.78
III	220	335	.66	III—0.69
IV	530	390	1.36	IV—1.25
1997				
I	520	445	1.17	
II	420	500	.84	
III	400	555	.72	
IV	700	610	1.15	

Our equation was derived from the intercept 170 plus a rise of $(610 - 170) \div 8$ periods. Next we can derive a seasonal index by comparing the actual data with the trend line as in Exhibit 13.17. The seasonal factor was developed by averaging the same quarters in each year.

We can compute the 1998 forecast including trend and seasonal factors (FITS) as follows:

$$FITS_t = Trend \times Seasonal$$
$$I—1998 \; FITS_9 = [170 + 55(9)]1.25 = 831$$
$$II—1998 \; FITS_{10} = [170 + 55(10)]0.78 = 562$$
$$III—1998 \; FITS_{11} = [170 + 55(11)]0.69 = 535$$
$$IV—1998 \; FITS_{12} = [170 + 55(12)]1.25 = 1,038$$

Decomposition Using Least Squares Regression   Decomposition of a time series means to find the series' basic components of trend, seasonal, and cyclical. Indexes are calculated for seasons and cycles. The forecasting procedure then reverses the process by projecting the trend and adjusting it by the seasonal and cyclical indices, which were determined in the decomposition process. More formally, the process is

1. Decompose the time series into its components.
   a. Find seasonal component.
   b. Deseasonalize the demand.
   c. Find trend component.
2. Forecast future values of each component.
   a. Project trend component into the future.
   b. Multiply trend component by seasonal component.

Note that the random component is not included in this list. We implicitly remove the random component from the time series when we average as in Step 1. It is pointless to attempt a projection of the random component in Step 2 unless we have information about some unusual event, such as a major labor dispute, that could adversely affect product demand (and this would not really be random).

Exhibit 13.18 shows the decomposition of a time series using least squares regression and the same basic data we used in our earlier examples. Each data point corresponds to using a single three-month quarter of the three-year (12-quarter) period. Our objective is to forecast demand for the four quarters of the fourth year.

Exhibit 13.18   Deseasonalized Demand

(1) Period (x)	(2) Quarter	(3) Actual Demand (y)	(4) Average of the Same Quarters of Each Year	(5) Seasonal Factor	(6) Deseasonalized Demand (y_d) Col (3) ÷ Col (5)	(7) x^2 (Col. 1)^2	(8) $x \times y_d$ Col (1) × Col (6)
1	I	600	(600 + 2,400 + 3,800)/3 = 2,266.7	0.82	735.7	1	735.7
2	II	1,550	(1,550 + 3,100 + 4,500)/3 = 3,050	1.10	1,412.4	4	2,824.7
3	III	1,500	(1,500 + 2,600 + 4,000)/3 = 2,700	0.97	1,544.0	9	4,631.9
4	IV	1,500	(1,500 + 2,900 + 4,900)/3 = 3,100	1.12	1,344.8	16	5,379.0
5	I	2,400		0.82	2,942.6	25	14,713.2
6	II	3,100		1.10	2,824.7	36	16,948.4
7	III	2,600		0.97	2,676.2	49	18,733.6
8	IV	2,900		1.12	2,599.9	64	20.798.9
9	I	3,800		0.82	4,659.2	81	41,932.7
10	II	4,500		1.10	4,100.4	100	41,004.1
11	III	4,000		0.97	4,117.3	121	45,290.1
12	IV	4,900		1.12	4,392.9	144	52,714.5
78		33,350		12.03	33,350.1*	650	265,706.9

$\bar{x} = \dfrac{78}{12} = 6.5$ $b = \dfrac{\Sigma xy_d - n\bar{x}\bar{y}_d}{\Sigma x^2 - n\bar{x}^2} = \dfrac{265,706.9 - 12(6.5)2,779.2}{650 - 12(6.5)^2} = 342.2$

$\bar{y}_d = 33,350/12 = 2,779.2$ $a = \bar{y}_d - b\bar{x} = 2,779.2 - 342.2(6.5) = 554.9$

Therefore $Y = a + bx = 554.9 + 342.2x$

*Column 3 and Column 6 totals should be equal at 33,350. Differences are due to rounding. Column 5 was rounded to two decimal places.

Step 1. Determine the seasonal factor (or index). Exhibit 13.18 summarizes all of the calculations needed. Column 4 develops an average for the same quarters in the three-year period. For example, the first quarters of the three years are added together and divided by three. A seasonal factor is then derived by dividing that average by the general average for all 12 quarters $\left(\dfrac{33{,}350}{12}\ \text{or}\ 2{,}779\right)$. These are entered in column 5. Note that the seasonal factors are identical for similar quarters in each year.

Step 2. Deseasonalize the original data. To remove the seasonal effect on the data, we divide the original data by the seasonal factor. This step is called the **deseasonalization of demand** and is shown in column 6 of Exhibit 13.18.

Deseasonalization of Demand

Step 3. Develop a least squares regression line for the deseasonalized data. The purpose here is to develop an equation for the trend line Y, which we then modify with the seasonal factor. The procedure is the same as we used before:

$$Y = a + bx$$

where

y_d = Deseasonalized demand
x = Quarter
Y = Demand computed using the regression equation $Y = a + bx$
a = Y intercept
b = Slope of the line

The least squares calculations using columns 1, 7, and 8 of Exhibit 13.18 are shown in the lower section of the exhibit. The final deseasonalized equation for our data is $Y = 554.9 + 342.2x$. This straight line is shown in Exhibit 13.19.

Step 4. Project the regression line through the period to be forecast. Our purpose is to forecast periods 13 through 16. We start by solving the equation for Y at each of these periods (shown in step 5, column 3).

Step 5. Create the final forecast by adjusting the regression line by the seasonal factor. Recall that the Y equation has been deseasonalized. We now reverse the procedure by multiplying the quarterly data we derived by the seasonal factor for that quarter:

Period	Quarter	Y from Regression Line	Seasonal Factor	Forecast (Y × Seasonal Factor)
13	1	5,003.5	0.82	4,102.87
14	2	5,345.7	1.10	5,880.27
15	3	5,687.9	0.97	5,517.26
16	4	6,030.1	1.12	6,753.71

Our forecast is now complete. The procedure is generally the same as what we did in the hand-fit previous example. In the present example, however, we followed a more formal procedure and computed the least squares regression line as well.

Error Range When a straight line is fitted through data points and then used for forecasting, errors can come from two sources. First, there are the usual errors similar to the standard deviation of any set of data. Second, there are errors that arise because the line is wrong. Exhibit 13.20 shows this error range. Instead of developing the

Exhibit 13.19

Straight Line Graph of
Deseasonalized
Equation

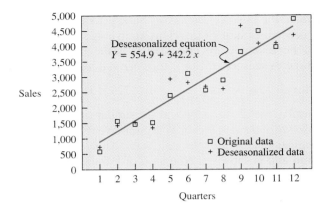

Exhibit 13.20

Prediction Intervals
for Linear Trend

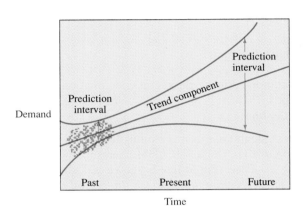

statistics here, we will briefly show why the range broadens. First, visualize that one line is drawn that has some error in that it slants too steeply upward. Standard errors are then calculated for this line. Now visualize another line that slants too steeply downward. It also has a standard error. The total error range, for this analysis, consists of errors resulting from both lines as well as all other possible lines. We included this exhibit to show how the error range widens as we go further into the future.

■ CAUSAL RELATIONSHIP FORECASTING

*Causal
Relationship*

To be of value for the purpose of forecasting, any independent variable must be a leading indicator. For example, we can expect that an extended period of rainy days will increase sales of umbrellas and raincoats. The rain causes the sale of rain gear. This is a **causal relationship,** where one occurrence causes another. If the causing element is far enough in advance, it can be used as a basis for forecasting.

The first step in causal relationship forecasting is to find those occurrences that are really the causes. Often, leading indicators are not causal relationships, but in some indirect way, they may suggest that some other things might happen. Other noncausal relationships just seem to exist as a coincidence. One study some years ago showed that the amount of alcohol sold in Sweden was directly proportional to teachers' salaries. Presumably this was a spurious (false) relationship. Following shows one example of a forecast using a causal relationship.

■ **example 13.5** *Forecasting Using a Causal Relationship* The Carpet City Store in Carpenteria has kept records of its sales (in square yards) each year, along with the number of permits for new houses in its area.

Year	Number of Housing Start Permits	Sales (in Sq. Yds.)
1989	18	13,000
1990	15	12,000
1991	12	11,000
1992	10	10,000
1993	20	14,000
1994	28	16,000
1995	35	19,000
1996	30	17,000
1997	20	13,000

Carpet City's operations manager believes forecasting sales is possible if housing starts are known for that year. First, the data are plotted in Exhibit 13.21, with

x = Number of housing start permits

y = Sales of carpeting

Because the points appear to be in a straight line, the manager decides to use the linear relationship $Y = a + bx$. We solve this problem by hand fitting a line. We could also solve for this equation using least squares regression as we did earlier.

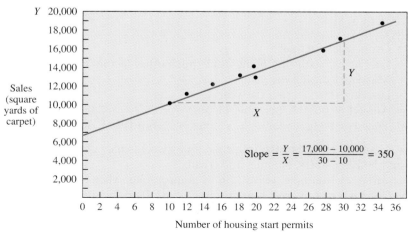

$$\text{Slope} = \frac{Y}{X} = \frac{17,000 - 10,000}{30 - 10} = 350$$

Exhibit 13.21

Causal Relationship: Sales to Housing Starts

s o l u t i o n   Projecting the hand fit line causes it to intercept the Y axis at about 7,000 yards. This could be interpreted as the demand when no new houses are built; that is, probably as replacement for old carpeting. To estimate the slope, two points are selected, such as

Year	x	y
1992	10	10,000
1996	30	17,000

From algebra the slope is calculated as

$$b = \frac{y(96) - y(92)}{x(96) - x(92)} = \frac{17,000 - 10,000}{30 - 10} = \frac{7,000}{20} = 350$$

The manager interprets the slope as the average number of square yards of carpet sold for each new house built in the area. The forecasting equation is therefore

$$Y = 7,000 + 350x$$

Now suppose that there are 25 permits for houses to be built in 1998. The 1998 sales forecast would therefore be

$$7,000 + 350(25) = 15,750 \text{ square yards}$$

In this problem, the lag between filing the permit with the appropriate agency and the new homeowner coming to Carpet City to buy carpet makes a causal relationship feasible for forecasting. ■

Multiple Regression Analysis

Another forecasting method is multiple regression analysis, in which a number of variables are considered, together with the effects of each on the item of interest. For example, in the home furnishings field, the effects of the number of marriages, housing starts, disposable income, and the trend can be expressed in a multiple regression equation, as

$$S = B + B_m(M) + B_h(H) + B_i(I) + B_t(T)$$

where

S = Gross sales for year
B = Base sales, a starting point from which other factors have influence
M = Marriages during the year
H = Housing starts during the year
I = Annual disposable personal income
T = Time trend (first year = 1, second = 2, third = 3, and so forth)

B_m, B_h, B_i, and B_t represent the influence on expected sales of the numbers of marriages and housing starts, income, and trend.

Forecasting by multiple regression is appropriate when a number of factors influence a variable of interest—in this case, sales. Its difficulty lies with the mathematical computation. Fortunately, standard computer programs for multiple regression analysis are available, relieving the need for tedious manual calculation.

■ CHOOSING A FORECASTING METHOD

The first question is, Do you need a forecasting system? The system can range from simple inexpensive tools (such as moving averages or exponential smoothing models implemented in a spreadsheet) to expensive programs requiring extensive commitments of resources and personnel.

A business uses forecasting in planning its inventory and production levels as well as for new product development, staffing, and budgets. At the product level, it is inexpensive to develop forecasts using simple moving average, weighted moving average, or exponential smoothing. These methods would apply to the large bulk of standard inventory items carried by a firm. The choice of which of these three methods to use is based on market conditions. Moving averages weight each period the same, exponential smoothing weights the recent past more, and weighted moving average allows the weights to be determined by the forecaster. Which is better? One test would be to use each method on sample data and measure the errors using the MAD and RSFE as previously discussed.

In any case, all forecasts should be passed on to the appropriate area to have someone familiar with the product adjust or modify the forecast. In using regression analysis, it is critical to assure that the data fit the model. If they do not, extrapolations will create serious errors.

A survey of users and uses of forecasting methods was performed by Herbig, Milewicz, and Golden.[5] There were 150 responses from manufacturing and service companies ranging in size from $10 million to over $500 million. Questionnaires were addressed to the "Forecasting/Marketing Managers," so the findings stated in Exhibit 13.22 have their biased views.

As expected, because of the marketing emphasis, we find executive opinion, sales force, and customer survey near the top of the list. Also, valuable forecast indicators are trends and market share.

In comparing manufacturing and service firms, manufacturing firms tend to be more thorough and provide more iterations in circulating and adjusting the forecast. The most important forecasts are by product lines and product life cycles. Manufacturers tend to use more quantitative techniques and are more satisfied with the forecasting process. They also tend to rate forecasting as well as the level of accuracy more important than service firms rate them.

Service firms tend to involve more people in forecasting and have a higher percentage of executive involvement. Service firms also tend to (1) view the weighted moving average as an important technique and (2) use subjective forecasting much more than manufacturers. Because of the different techniques each uses, service firms also reported that their forecasting process is more cumbersome than manufacturers'. Additionally, service firms are less satisfied with the forecast.

---

[5] Paul Herbig, John Milewicz, and James E. Golden, "Forecasting: Who, What, When and How," *The Journal of Business Forecasting,* Summer 1993, pp. 16–21.

A Survey of Forecasting Techniques

	Mentioned (%)[a]	Average Importance[b]	Rate of Usage[c]
Executive opinion	86%	6	2.9
Sales force	68	5	2.2
Customer survey	72	4.7	2.2
Trends	91	5.6	2.9
Market share	70	4.6	2.5
Regression	52	4.2	1.7
Econometric	52	4.2	1.4
Naive	41	2.0	1.1
Industry survey	45	3.2	1.4
Own computer model	68	5.2	2.2
Lead/lag	38	3	0.8
Simple correlation	42	3.6	1.2
Multiple correlation	34	1.8	0.6
Probabilistic	40	3.7	0.6
Time series	45	4.3	1.5
3 chart	28	1.4	1.45
Weighted moving	46	3.8	1.4
Exponential smoothing	36	2.8	0.9
Simple linear regression	38	4.0	1.3
Mult. linear regression	35	3.6	1.0
Mult. nonlinear regression	32	2.5	0.6
Product life cycle	47	3.0	1.3

[a] Percentage of respondents mentioned as using technique.

[b] Average importance rating based on 1 = Low, 4 = Average, 7 = Highest.

[c] Usage score based on 3 = Regularly used, 2 = Frequently used, 1 = Previously used, and 0 = Never used.

Source: Paul Herbig, John Milewicz, and James E. Golden, "Forecasting: Who, What, When and How," *The Journal of Business Forecasting,* Summer 1993, p. 20.

■ FOCUS FORECASTING

Focus forecasting is the creation of Bernie Smith.[6] Smith uses it primarily in finished-goods inventory management. Smith substantiates strong arguments that statistical approaches used in forecasting do not give the best results. He states that simple techniques that work well on past data also prove the best in forecasting the future.

Methodology of Focus Forecasting

Focus Forecasting

Focus forecasting simply tries several rules that seem logical and easy to understand to project past data into the future. Each of these rules is used in a computer simulation program to actually project demand and then measure how well that rule performed when compared to what actually happened. Therefore, the two components of the focus forecasting system are (1) several simple forecasting rules and (2) computer simulation of these rules on past data.

These are simple, commonsense rules made up and then tested to see whether they should be kept. Examples of simple forecasting rules could include

1.   Whatever we sold in the past three months is what we will probably sell in the next three months.

---

[6] Bernard T. Smith, *Focus Forecasting: Computer Techniques for Inventory Control* (Boston: CBI Publishing, 1984).

2. What we sold in the same three-month period last year, we will probably sell in that three-month period this year. (This would account for seasonal effects.)

3. We will probably sell 10 percent more in the next three months than we sold in the past three months.

4. We will probably sell 50 percent more over the next three months than we did for the same three months of last year.

5. Whatever percentage change we had for the past three months this year compared to the same three months last year will probably be the same percentage change that we will have for the next three months of this year.

These forecasting rules are not hard and fast. If a new rule seems to work well, it is added. If one has not been working well, it is deleted.

The second part of the process is computer simulation. To use the system, a data history should be available—for example, 18 to 24 months of data. The simulation process then uses each of the forecasting rules to predict some recent past data. The rule that did best in predicting the past is the rule used to predict the future. Example 13.6 is an exercise used by Smith.[7]

■ **example 13.6** *Demand in Units for a Broiler Pan* The following table shows unit demand for a broiler pan over an 18-month period. (Try to guess what demand might be for July, August, and September this year, and compare your guess to the actual data presented later.)

	Last Year	This Year		Last Year	This Year
January	6	72	July	167	
February	212	90	August	159	
March	378	108	September	201	
April	129	134	October	153	
May	163	92	November	76	
June	96	137	December	30	

solution For brevity, we will use only two rules to demonstrate the method: 1 and 5. In practice, they would all be used.

Using focus forecasting, we first try forecasting rule 1—whatever we sold in the past three months is what we will probably sell in the next three months. (We are using the terms *demand* and *sales* interchangeably, assuming that demands culminate in actual sales.) We first test this rule on the past three months:

$$\text{Forecast (April, May, June)} = \text{Demand (January + February + March)}$$
$$= 72 + 90 + 108 = 270$$

Because what actually occurred was 363 (134 + 92 + 137), the forecast was 270/363 = 74 percent. In other words, it was 26 percent low.

Let's try another, say rule 5—whatever percentage change we had over last year in the past three months will probably be our percentage change over last year in the next three months.

---

[7] We use this exercise because it is real data from the records of American Hardware Supply Company, where Smith was inventory manager. This forecasting exercise has been played by many people: buyers for American Hardware, inventory consultants, and numerous participants at national meetings of the American Production and Inventory Control Society. Further, data for the remainder of the year exist that allow for checking the results.

Forecast (April + May + June)

$$= \frac{\text{Demand (January + February + March) this year}}{\text{Demand (January + February + March) last year}}$$
$$\times \text{Demand (April + May + June) last year}$$

$$= \frac{72 + 90 + 108}{6 + 212 + 378} \times (129 + 163 + 96)$$

$$= \frac{270}{596}(388) = 175.77$$

What actually occurred during April, May, and June this year was 363 so the forecast was 175/363, or only 48 percent of the actual demand.

Because rule 1 was better in predicting the past three months, we use that rule in predicting July, August, and September of this year. Rule 1 says that whatever we sold in the past three months is what we will probably sell in the next three months.

Forecast (July + August + September) = Demand (April + May + June)

$$= 134 + 92 + 137 = 363$$

The actual demand for the period was 357, as seen in the table, which shows the completed demand history for this year and serves as a basis for comparison.

	Last Year	This Year		Last Year	This Year
January	6	72	July	167	120
February	212	90	August	159	151
March	378	108	September	201	86
April	129	134	October	153	113
May	163	92	November	76	97
June	96	137	December	30	40

Forecasts made using focus forecasting logic are then reviewed and modified (if necessary) by buyers or inventory control personnel who have responsibility over these items. When they see the forecasts made by the computer, they know which method was used and can either accept it or change the forecast if they do not agree. Smith says that about 8 percent of the forecasts are changed by the buyers because they know something that the computer does not (such as the cause of a previous large demand, or that the next forecast is too high because a competitor is introducing a competing product).

Smith states that in all the forecast simulations he has run using variations of exponential smoothing (including adaptive smoothing), focus forecasting gave significantly better results.

Developing a Focus Forecasting System

Here are suggestions for developing a focus forecasting system:

1. Don't try to add a seasonality index. Let the forecasting system find out seasonality by itself, especially with new items, because seasonality may not apply until the pipeline is filled and the system is stable. The forecasting rules can handle it.

2. When a forecast is unusually high or low (such as two or three times the previous period, or the previous year if there is seasonality), print out an indicator such as

the letter *R* telling the person affected by this demand to review it. Do not just disregard unusual demands because they may, in fact, be valid changes in the demand pattern.

3. Let the people who will be using the forecasts (such as buyers or inventory planners) participate in creating the rules. Smith plays his "can you outguess focus forecasting" game with all the company's buyers. Using two years of data and 2,000 items, focus forecasting makes forecasts for the past six months. Buyers are asked to forecast the past six months using any rule they prefer. If they are consistently better than the existing forecasting rules, their rules are added to the list.

4. Keep the rules simple. That way, they will be easily understood and trusted by users of the forecast.

In summary, it appears that focus forecasting has significant merit when demand is generated outside the system, such as in forecasting end-item demand, spare parts, and materials and suppliers used in a variety of products.

Computer time apparently is not very large since Smith forecasts 100,000 items every month using his focus forecasting rules.

COMPUTER PROGRAMS

Many commercial forecasting programs are available. Most are available for microcomputers and use shared network databases. Major companies, such as Wal-Mart are now using programs that work over the Internet. In the future, standards will be developed that offer a standardized way for manufacturers and merchants to work together on forecasts over the Internet.

All but the most sophisticated forecasting formulas are quite easy to understand. Anyone who can use a spreadsheet such as Microsoft Excel® can create a forecasting program on a PC. Depending on one's knowledge of the spreadsheet, a simple program can be written in anywhere from a few minutes to a couple of hours. How this forecast is to be used by the firm could be the bigger challenge. If demand for many items is to be forecast, this becomes a data-handling problem, not a problem in the forecasting logic.

Jack Yurkiewicz provides a list of 50 forecasting and statistical analysis programs for personal computer (PC) use.[8] Some are simple to use and others are advanced, with a large capacity for graphics and graphical interface. The Breakthrough box on the next page, "The Evolution of a Forecasting Department," (written by the director of sales forecasting at Warner-Lambert Company) discusses the development, methods, and benefits of his firm's forecasting system.

CONCLUSION

As shown in our "Breakthrough," developing a forecasting system is not easy. However, it must be done, because forecasting is fundamental to any planning effort. In the short run, a forecast is needed to predict the requirements for materials, products,

---

[8] Jack Yurkiewicz, "Forecasting Software Survey," *OR/MS Today,* December 1996, pp. 70–75.

BREAKTHROUGH

The Evolution of a Forecasting Department

At Warner-Lambert Company, the Consumer Health Product Group (CHPG) generated $732 million in 1992 sales. The products are divided into three main categories: oral care, upper respiratory, and women and skin care. The product line includes the mouth rinses, Listerine and Cool Mint Listerine, plus Benadryl cold and allergy products, Lubriderm skin lotion, and e.p.t home pregnancy test. Each of the businesses is highly promoted and subject to considerable seasonal swings, constituting a formidable challenge to the forecasting professional.

The CHPG Sales Forecasting Department was established in the late 1980s to improve forecast accuracy and customer service levels. However, the role of the forecaster, with no formal process or forecasting tools, was limited to attending forecast review meetings and performing ad-hoc analysis.

Though a step in the right direction, these efforts fell short of fulfilling the department's objectives and management's expectations. A project was initiated to identify and implement a forecasting system, tailored to our line of products and logistics needs. Key here was a robust tool set (i.e., seasonality decomposition, promotional analysis, and "what-if" capability) as well as the ability to integrate with the order processing and logistic systems.

After one year of developmental efforts, the main components of the system were "completed" and we began training the marketing staff. As we proceeded with the training and roll-out plan, it became increasingly evident that the system was overwhelming to the users. This was due to

1. The statistical and forecasting knowledge required to generate and interpret the models. The system provides eight "modified" trend analysis models, with a user override interface. Although designed to minimize the need for heavy statistics, the user must possess a good understanding of moving averages, trends, seasonal decomposition, random noise, and so on. However, marketing professionals are generalists and often lack statistical training.

2. Time investment by the marketing assistants. Although the system was designed to maximize productivity, it constituted a substantial investment of their time to properly generate the models. This was next to impossible, given their hectic schedules.

In the mean time, the forecast accuracy worsened and customer service was suffering. In addition, management's frustrations with the total forecasting process and the system's inability to deliver grew exponentially. We, therefore, focused our total efforts on the implementation process, redesigning and adding new features on the way.

How We Did It

We enlisted the assistance of Sales, Marketing, Manufacturing, MIS, forecasting consultants, and academia to develop a vision statement and strategic plan.

Our vision states that "We will be the best Sales Forecasting Department in the industry." To support it, the strategic plan calls for establishing a forecasting "center of excellence" consisting of professionals who (1) possess superior analytical and statistical skills, (2) have a solid understanding of our businesses and marketplace, and (3) possess solid communication and interpersonal skills. The plan further recommends the implementation of a forecast analyst program. In this scenario, each business category would have one forecast analyst totally dedicated to developing the sales forecast, conducting macro-economic analysis, developing customer specific models, and performing competitive benchmarks. The strategic plan and supporting ROI analysis were approved by management late in 1992.

In early 1993 we began to implement the plan with the Oral Care Category, since it is the most representative of our "flagship" brands. First, we embarked on identifying a qualified candidate for the analyst position. This was a challenging task since we were pursuing an analytical individual with strong interpersonal skills, a combination not easily found. Once on board, the analyst began a rigorous training program and, in

services, or other resources to respond to changes in demand. Forecasts permit adjusting schedules and varying labor and materials. In the long run, forecasting is required as a basis for strategic changes, such as developing new markets, developing new products or services, and expanding or creating new facilities.

For long-term forecasts that lead to heavy financial commitments, great care should be taken to derive the forecast. Several approaches should be used. Causal

May 1993, assumed full responsibility for the Oral Care forecasting process.

Two of the principal success factors underlining the new process are a solid understanding of the business and marketplace, and a strong relationship with the sales, marketing, finance and manufacturing organizations. At the same time, we must maintain a high degree of objectivity—a most difficult undertaking. The analysts work with the sales planning and marketing colleagues in every step of the forecasting process, incorporating their input in the models and conducting "what-if" scenarios.

Our Forecasting Process
Our forecasting cycle is monthly, culminating with a consensus forecast review meeting on the third workday of the month. After the review meeting, all changes are incorporated in the models and the final forecast is transmitted to manufacturing on the fifth workday. The models are continuously improved on throughout the month and, importantly, weekly customer service meetings are conducted to discuss the monthly forecast progress as well as any manufacturing or distribution issues.

The forecast is developed at the pack level (i.e., Listerine 32 oz) and is exploded to all component SKUs (open stock, floor displays, etc.). Currently in Oral Care alone there are close to 50 models, supporting 30 packs. For most packs, there are two models. One forecasts market consumption and the second trade demand. On an average, each model is comprised of 10 economic and event-specific variables.

How We Benefited from the System
Since the new process was implemented in May, we have realized benefits in two forms. First, forecast accuracy has improved substantially. Second, we have freed marketing resources from the arduous process of generating the forecast and can now focus on other value-added activities for business growth. And as we master the analytical process, we will reap a

by-product benefit in the form of "learning" that will help grow the business.

The forecast analyst program has been extended and is currently being implemented for the Upper Respiratory Category; we estimate assuming the forecasting responsibilities by early fourth quarter 1993. In addition, the role of the department is expanding.

We are currently spearheading several projects to improve Field Sales input, as well as the timing and execution of the forecast. We have also established forecasting relationships with key customers to work with them in developing their forecast. Additionally, we plan to redesign the forecasting data base to improve the regional and customer-specific analysis/forecasting tool set.

The forecasting process at Warner-Lambert's Consumer Products Division has experienced substantial successful evolution. It all started with a rudimentary process, evolving to the current "center of excellence" status, fully supported by a clear vision and strategic direction. Clearly, there are several morals to this evolution. First, the focus should be on the total forecasting process. It is paramount that the forecasting professionals have a solid knowledge of the business and marketplace, and that they translate this knowledge to the model development realm. It is equally critical that the forecasters are capable of making a smooth transition from the analytical to the business realm. You will certainly not build credibility if you talk "R-square" language to Sales and Marketing. Importantly, management's expectations should be managed carefully. It is necessary that all assumptions and payback analysis are documented and updated, as dictated by your "learning" and changing business conditions and priorities. Also, the forecasting professional must play the role of "salespeople," continuously marketing the "learning" and positive results to the organization.

Source: Luis Reyes, "The Evolution of a Forecasting Department," *The Journal of Business Forecasting*, Fall 1993, pp. 22–24.

methods such as regression analysis or multiple regression analysis are beneficial. These provide a basis for discussion. Economic factors, product trends, growth factors, and competition, as well as a myriad of other possible variables, need to be considered and the forecast adjusted to reflect the influence of each.

Short- and intermediate-term forecasting (such as required for inventory control as well as staffing and material scheduling) may be satisfied with simpler models, such as exponential smoothing with perhaps an adaptive feature or a seasonal index. In these applications, thousands of items are usually being forecast. The forecasting routine should therefore be simple and run quickly on a computer. The routines should also detect and respond rapidly to definite short-term changes in demand while at the same time ignoring the occasional spurious demands. Exponential smoothing, when monitored by management to control the value of alpha, is an effective technique.

Focus forecasting appears to offer a reasonable approach to short-term forecasting, say, monthly or quarterly but certainly less than a year. If there is one thing focus forecasting offers, it is close monitoring and rapid response.

In summary, forecasting is tough. A perfect forecast is like a hole in one in golf: great to get but we should be satisfied just to get close to the cup—or, to push the analogy, just to land on the green. The ideal philosophy is to create the best forecast that you reasonably can and then hedge by maintaining flexibility in the system to account for the inevitable forecast error.

FORMULA REVIEW

Simple moving average

$$F_t = \frac{A_{t-1} + A_{t-2} + A_{t-3} + \cdots + A_{t-n}}{n} \tag{13.1}$$

Weighted moving average

$$F_t = w_1 A_{t-1} + w_2 A_{t-2} + \cdots + w_n A_{t-n} \tag{13.2}$$

Single exponential smoothing

$$F_t = F_{t-1} + \alpha(A_{t-1} - F_{t-1}) \tag{13.3}$$

Exponential smoothing with trend

$$\text{FIT}_t = F_t + T_t \tag{13.4}$$
$$F_t = \text{FIT}_{t-1} + \alpha(A_{t-1} - \text{FIT}_{t-1}) \tag{13.5}$$
$$T_t = T_{t-1} + \alpha\delta(A_{t-1} - \text{FIT}_{t-1}) \tag{13.6}$$

Mean absolute deviation

$$\text{MAD} = \frac{\sum\limits_{t=1}^{n} |A_t - F_t|}{n} \tag{13.7}$$

Tracking signal

$$\text{TS} = \frac{\text{RSFE}}{\text{MAD}} \tag{13.8}$$

Least squares regression

$$Y = a + bx \tag{13.9}$$
$$a = \bar{y} - b\bar{x} \tag{13.10}$$
$$b = \frac{\Sigma xy - n\bar{x} \cdot \bar{y}}{\Sigma x^2 - n\bar{x}^2} \tag{13.11}$$

Standard error of estimate

$$S_{yx} = \sqrt{\frac{\sum\limits_{i=1}^{n} (y_i - Y_i)^2}{n - 2}}$$

(13.12)

SOLVED PROBLEMS

SOLVED PROBLEM 1

Sunrise Baking Company markets doughnuts through a chain of food stores. It has been experiencing over- and underproduction because of forecasting errors. The following data are its demand in dozens of doughnuts for the past four weeks. Donuts are made for the following day, such as Sunday's donut production is for Monday's sales, Monday's production for Tuesday's sales, and so forth. The bakery is closed Saturday, so Friday's production must satisfy demand for both Saturday and Sunday.

	4 Weeks Ago	3 Weeks Ago	2 Weeks Ago	Last Week
Monday	2,200	2,400	2,300	2,400
Tuesday	2,000	2,100	2,200	2,200
Wednesday	2,300	2,400	2,300	2,500
Thursday	1,800	1,900	1,800	2,000
Friday	1,900	1,800	2,100	2,000
Saturday				
Sunday	2,800	2,700	3,000	2,900

Make a forecast for this week on the following basis:

a. Daily, using a simple four-week moving average.
b. Daily, using a weighted average of 0.40, 0.30, 0.20, and 0.10 for the past four weeks.
c. Sunrise is also planning its purchases of ingredients for bread production. If bread demand had been forecast for last week at 22,000 loaves and only 21,000 loaves were actually demanded, what would Sunrise's forecast be for this week using exponential smoothing with $\alpha = 0.10$?
d. Supposing, with the forecast made in (*c*), this week's demand actually turns out to be 22,500. What would the new forecast be for the next week?

Solution

a. Simple moving average, four-week.

$$\text{Monday} \quad \frac{2,400 + 2,300 + 2,400 + 2,200}{4} = \frac{9,300}{4} = 2,325 \text{ doz.}$$

$$\text{Tuesday} \quad = \frac{8,500}{4} = 2,125 \text{ doz.}$$

$$\text{Wednesday} \quad = \frac{9,500}{4} = 2,375 \text{ doz.}$$

$$\text{Thursday} \quad = \frac{7,500}{4} = 1,875 \text{ doz.}$$

$$\text{Friday} \quad = \frac{7,800}{4} = 1,950 \text{ doz.}$$

$$\text{Saturday and Sunday} \quad = \frac{11,400}{4} = 2,850 \text{ doz.}$$

b. Weighted average with weights of .40, .30, .20, and .10.

	(.10)		(.20)		(.30)		(.40)		
Monday	220	+	480	+	690	+	960	=	2,350
Tuesday	200	+	420	+	660	+	880	=	2,160
Wednesday	230	+	480	+	690	+	1,000	=	2,400
Thursday	180	+	380	+	540	+	800	=	1,900
Friday	190	+	360	+	630	+	800	=	1,980
Saturday and Sunday	280	+	540	+	900	+	1,160	=	2,880
	1,300	+	2,660	+	4,110	+	5,600	=	13,670

c. Exponentially smoothed forecast for bread demand

$$F_t = F_{t-1} + \alpha(A_{t-1} - F_{t-1})$$
$$= 22,000 + 0.10(21,000 - 22,000)$$
$$= 22,000 - 100 = 21,900 \text{ loaves}$$

d. Exponentially smoothed forecast

$$F_{t+1} = 21,900 + .10(22,500 - 21,900)$$
$$= 21,900 + .10(600) = 21,960 \text{ loaves}$$

SOLVED PROBLEM 2

Here are the actual demands for a product for the past six quarters. Using Focus Forecasting rules 1 to 5, find the best rule to use in predicting the third quarter of this year.

	Quarter			
	I	**II**	**III**	**IV**
Last year	1,200	700	900	1,100
This year	1,400	1,000		

Solution

Rule 1: Next three months' demand = Last three months' demand.

Testing this on the last three months, $F_{II} = A_I$; therefore $F_{II} = 1,400$.

Actual demand was 1,000, so $\dfrac{1,000}{1,400} = 71.4\%$.

Rule 2: This quarter's demand equals demand in the same quarter last year.
The forecast for the second quarter this year will therefore be 700, the amount for that quarter last year.

Actual demand was 1,000, and $\dfrac{1,000}{700} = 142.9\%$.

Rule 3: 10 percent more than same quarter.

$$F_{II} = 1,400 \times 1.10 = 1,540$$

Actual was 1,000, and $\dfrac{1,000}{1,540} = 64.9\%$.

Rule 4: 50 percent more than same quarter last year.

$$F_{II} = 700 \times 1.50 = 1,050$$

Actual was 1,000, and $\dfrac{1,000}{1,050} = 95.2\%$.

Rule 5: Same rate of increase or decrease as last three months.

$$\frac{1,400}{1,200} = 1.167$$

$$F_{II} = 700 \times 1.167 = 816.7$$

Actual was 1,000, so $\frac{1,000}{816.7} = 122.4\%$.

Rule 4 was the closest in predicting the recent quarter—95.2 percent or just 4.8 percent under. Using this rule (50 percent more than the same quarter last year), we would forecast the third quarter this year as 50 percent more than the third quarter last year, or

This year $F_{III} = 1.50\ A_{III}$ (last year)

$$F_{III} = 1.50\ (900) = 1,350 \text{ units}$$

SOLVED PROBLEM 3

A specific forecasting model was used to forecast demand for a product. The forecasts and the corresponding demand that subsequently occurred are shown below. Use the MAD and tracking signal technique to evaluate the accuracy of the forecasting model.

	Actual	**Forecast**
October	700	660
November	760	840
December	780	750
January	790	835
February	850	910
March	950	890

Solution

Evaluate the forecasting model using MAD and tracking signal.

	Actual Demand	**Forecast Demand**	**Actual Deviation**	**Cumulative Deviation (RSFE)**	**Absolute Deviation**
October	700	660	40	40	40
November	760	840	−80	−40	80
December	780	750	30	−10	30
January	790	835	−45	−55	45
February	850	910	−60	−115	60
March	950	890	60	−55	60
				Total dev. =	315

$$\text{MAD} = \frac{315}{6} = 52.5$$

$$\text{Tracking signal} = \frac{-55}{52.5} = -1.05$$

Forecast model is well within the distribution.

SOLVED PROBLEM 4

Here are quarterly data for the past two years. From these data, prepare a forecast for the upcoming year using decomposition.

Period	Actual	Period	Actual
1	300	5	416
2	540	6	760
3	885	7	1191
4	580	8	760

Solution

(1) Period x	(2) Actual Y	(3) Period Average	(4) Seasonal Factor	(5) Deseasonalized Demand
1	300	358	0.527	568.99
2	540	650	0.957	564.09
3	885	1,038	1.529	578.92
4	580	670	0.987	587.79
5	416		0.527	789.01
6	760		0.957	793.91
7	1,191		1.529	779.08
8	760		0.987	770.21
Total	5,432	2,716	8.0	
Average	679	679	1	

Column 3 is seasonal average. For example, the first-quarter average is

$$\frac{300 + 416}{2} = 358$$

Column 4 is the quarter average (column 3) divided by the overall average (679). Column 5 is the actual data divided by the seasonal index.

To determine x^2 and xy we can construct a table as follows:

Period x	Deseasonalized Demand (y_d)	x^2	xy
1	568.99	1	569.0
2	564.09	4	1128.2
3	578.92	9	1736.7
4	587.79	16	2351.2
5	789.01	25	3945.0
6	793.91	36	4763.4
7	779.08	49	5453.6
8	770.21	64	6161.7
Sums	36	5,432	204	26,108.8
Average	4.5	679		

Now we calculate regression results for deseasonalized data.

$$b = \frac{(26108) - (8)(4.5)(679)}{(204) - (8)(4.5)^2} = 39.64$$

$$a = \bar{Y} - b\bar{x}$$

$$a = 679 - 39.64(4.5) = 500.6$$

Therefore, the deseasonalized regression results are

$$Y = 500.6 + 39.64x$$

Period	Trend Forecast		Seasonal Factor		Final Forecast
9	857.4	×	0.527	=	452.0
10	897.0	×	0.957	=	858.7
11	936.7	×	1.529	=	1431.9
12	976.3	×	0.987	=	963.4

REVIEW AND DISCUSSION QUESTIONS

1. What is the difference between dependent and independent demand?
2. Examine Exhibit 13.4 and suggest which model you might use for (1) bathing suit demand, (2) demand for new houses, (3) electrical power usage, (4) new plant expansion plans.
3. What is the logic in the least squares method of linear regression analysis?
4. Explain the procedure to create a forecast using the decomposition method of least squares regression.
5. Give some very simple rules you might use to manage demand for a firm's product. (An example is "limited to stock on hand.")
6. What strategies are used by supermarkets, airlines, hospitals, banks, and cereal manufacturers to influence demand?
7. All forecasting methods using exponential smoothing, adaptive smoothing, and exponential smoothing including trend require starting values to get the equations going. How would you select the starting value for, say, F_{t-1}?
8. From the choice of simple moving average, weighted moving average, exponential smoothing, and linear regression analysis, which forecasting technique would you consider the most accurate? Why?
9. Give some examples that you can think of that have a multiplicative seasonal trend relationship.
10. What is the main disadvantage of daily forecasting using regression analysis?
11. What are the main problems with using adaptive exponential smoothing in forecasting?
12. How is a seasonal index computed from a regression line analysis?
13. Discuss the basic differences between the mean absolute deviation and standard deviation.
14. What implications do forecast errors have for the search for ultrasophisticated statistical forecasting models?
15. What are the strongest selling points of focused forecasting?
16. Causal relationships are potentially useful for which component of a time series?

PROBLEMS

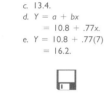

1. Demand for stereo headphones and CD players for joggers has caused Nina Industries to grow almost 50 percent over the past year. The number of joggers continues to expand, so Nina expects demand for headsets to also expand, because, as yet, no safety laws have been passed to prevent joggers from wearing them.
   Demand for the stereo units for last year were as follows:

	Demand (units)	Month	Demand (units)
January	4,200	July	5,300
February	4,300	August	4,900
March	4,000	September	5,400
April	4,400	October	5,700
May	5,000	November	6,300
June	4,700	December	6,000

   a. Using least squares regression analysis, what would you estimate demand to be for each month next year? Using a spreadsheet, follow the general format in Exhibit 13.14. Compare your results to those obtained by using the forecast spreadsheet function.
   b. To be reasonably confident of meeting demand, Nina decides to use three standard errors of estimate for safety. How many additional units should be held to meet this level of confidence?

2. Historical demand for a product is:

	Demand
January	12
February	11
March	15
April	12
May	16
June	15

   a. Using a weighted moving average with weights of 0.60, 0.30, and 0.10, find the July forecast.
   b. Using a simple three-month moving average, find the July forecast.
   c. Using single exponential smoothing with $\alpha = 0.2$ and a June forecast $= 13$, find the July forecast. Make whatever assumptions you wish.
   d. Using simple linear regression analysis, calculate the regression equation for the preceding demand data.
   e. Using the regression equation in (d), calculate the forecast for July.

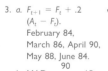

3. The following tabulations are actual sales of units for six months and a starting forecast in January.
   a. Calculate forecasts for the remaining five months using simple exponential smoothing with $\alpha = 0.2$.
   b. Calculate MAD for the forecasts.

	Actual	Forecast
January	100	80
February	94	
March	106	
April	80	
May	68	
June	94	

4. Zeus Computer Chips, Inc., used to have major contracts to produce the 386- and 486-type chips. The market has been declining during the past three years because of the pentium-type chips, which it cannot produce, so Zeus has the unpleasant task of forecasting next year. The task is unpleasant because the firm has not been able to find replacement chips for its product lines. Here is demand over the past 12 quarters:

4. See SM.

1995		1996		1997	
I	4,800	I	3,500	I	3,200
II	3,500	II	2,700	II	2,100
III	4,300	III	3,500	III	2,700
IV	3,000	IV	2,400	IV	1,700

Use the decomposition technique to forecast the four quarters of 1998.

5. Sales data for two years are as follows. Data are aggregated with two months of sales in each "period."

5. See SM.

Months	Sales	Months	Sales
January–February	109	January–February	115
March–April	104	March–April	112
May–June	150	May–June	159
July–August	170	July–August	182
September–October	120	September–October	126
November–December	100	November–December	106

a. Plot the data.
b. Fit a simple linear regression model to the sales data.
c. In addition to the regression model, determine multiplicative seasonal index factors. A full cycle is assumed to be a full year.
d. Using the results from parts (*b*) and (*c*) prepare a forecast for the next year.

6. The tracking signals computed using past demand history for three different products are as follows. Each product used the same forecasting technique.

6. TS 1: Rapid rise in trend. Will shortly be outside limits. Forecast model not good.
TS 2: Forecast OK. Within limits.
TS 3: Rapid rise. Outside limits. Forecast model not good.

	TS 1	TS 2	TS 3
1	−2.70	1.54	0.10
2	−2.32	−0.64	0.43
3	−1.70	2.05	1.08
4	−1.1	2.58	1.74
5	−0.87	−0.95	1.94
6	−0.05	−1.23	2.24
7	0.10	0.75	2.96
8	0.40	−1.59	3.02
9	1.50	0.47	3.54
10	2.20	2.74	3.75

Discuss the tracking signals for each and what the implications are.

✓ 7. The following is the past two years of quarterly sales information. Assume that there are both trend and seasonal factors and that the season cycle is one year. Use time series decomposition to forecast quarterly sales for the next year.

7. | Quarter | Forecast |
|---------|----------|
| 9 | 232 |
| 10 | 281 |
| 11 | 239 |
| 12 | 231 |

Quarter	Sales	Quarter	Sales
1	160	5	215
2	195	6	240
3	150	7	205
4	140	8	190

8. Tucson Machinery, Inc., manufactures numerically controlled machines, which sell for an average price of $0.5 million each. Sales for these NCMs for the past two years were as follows:

Quarter	Quantity (Units)	Quarter	Quantity (Units)
1996		**1997**	
I	12	I	16
II	18	II	24
III	26	III	28
IV	16	IV	18

a. Hand fit a line (or do a regression if your calculator has that feature).
b. Find the trend and seasonal factors.
c. Forecast sales for 1998.

9. Not all the items in your office supply store are evenly distributed as far as demand is concerned, so you decide to forecast demand to help plan your stock. Past data for legal-sized yellow tablets for the month of August are

Week 1	300
Week 2	400
Week 3	600
Week 4	700

a. Using a three-week moving average, what would you forecast the next week to be?
b. Using exponential smoothing with $\alpha = 0.20$, if the exponential forecast for week 3 was estimated as the average of the first two weeks $[(300 + 400)/2 = 350]$, what would you forecast week 5 to be?

10. Given the following history, use focus forecasting to forecast the third quarter of this year. Use three focus forecasting strategies.

	Jan	Feb	Mar	Apr	May	Jun	Jul	Aug	Sep	Oct	Nov	Dec
Last year	100	125	135	175	185	200	150	140	130	200	225	250
This year	125	135	135	190	200	190						

11. Here are the actual tabulated demands for an item for a nine-month period (January through September). Your supervisor wants to test two forecasting methods to see which method was better over this period.

Month	Actual	Month	Actual
January	110	June	180
February	130	July	140
March	150	August	130
April	170	September	140
May	160		

a. Forecast April through September using a three-month moving average.
b. Use simple exponential smoothing to estimate April through September.
c. Use MAD to decide which method produced the better forecast over the six-month period.

12. A particular forecasting model was used to forecast a six-month period. Here are the forecasts and actual demands that resulted.

	Forecast	Actual
April	250	200
May	325	250
June	400	325
July	350	300
August	375	325
September	450	400

Find the tracking signal and state whether you think the model being used is giving acceptable answers.

13. Harlen Industries has a simple forecasting model: Take the actual demand for the same month last year and divide that by the number of fractional weeks in that month. This gives the average weekly demand for that month. This weekly average is used as the weekly forecast for the same month this year. This technique was used to forecast the eight weeks for this year which are shown below along with the actual demand that occurred.

The following eight weeks shows the forecast (based on last year) and the demand that actually occurred.

Week	Forecast Demand	Actual Demand	Week	Forecast Demand	Actual Demand
1	140	137	5	140	180
2	140	133	6	150	170
3	140	150	7	150	185
4	140	160	8	150	205

   a. Compute the MAD of forecast errors.
   b. Using the RSFE, compute the tracking signal.
   c. Based on your answers to (*a*) and (*b*), comment on Harlen's method of forecasting.

14. The following table contains the demand from the last 10 months.

Month	Actual Demand
1	31
2	34
3	33
4	35
5	37
6	36
7	38
8	40
9	40
10	41

   a. Calculate the single exponential smoothing forecast for this data using an α of .30, and an initial forecast (F_1) of 31.
   b. Calculate the exponential smoothing with trend forecast for this data using an α of .30, a δ of .30, an initial trend forecast (T_1) of 1, and an initial exponentially smoothed forecast (F_1) of 30.
   c. Calculate the Mean Absolute Deviation (MAD) for each forecast, which is best?

13. *a.* MAD = 23.75.
    b. TS = 7.16.
    c. Tracking signal of 7.16 too large; model is poor.

14. *a.* See SM.
    b. See SM.
    c. Simple MAD = 2.90 With Trend MAD = 0.86 Exponential smoothing with trend is best

15. In this problem, you are to test the validity of your forecasting model. Here are the forecasts for a model you have been using and the actual demands that occurred.

Week	Forecast	Actual
1	800	900
2	850	1,000
3	950	1,050
4	950	900
5	1,000	900
6	975	1,100

Use the method stated in the text to compute the MAD and tracking signal. Then decide whether the forecasting model you have been using is giving reasonable results.

16. Assume that your stock of sales merchandise is maintained based on the forecast demand. If the distributor's sales personnel call on the first day of each month, compute your forecast sales by each of the three methods requested here.

	Actual
June	140
July	180
August	170

    a. Using a simple three-month moving average, what is the forecast for September?
    b. Using a weighted moving average, what is the forecast for September with weights of .20, .30, and .50 for June, July, and August, respectively?
    c. Using single exponential smoothing and assuming that the forecast for June had been 130, forecast sales for September with a smoothing constant alpha of .30.

17. Historical demand for a product is:

	Demand
April	60
May	55
June	75
July	60
August	80
September	75

    a. Using a simple fourth-month moving average, calculate a forecast for October.
    b. Using single exponential smoothing with $\alpha = 0.2$ and a September forecast = 65, calculate a forecast for October.
    c. Using simple linear regression, calculate the trend line for the historical data. Say the X axis is April = 1, May = 2, and so on, while the Y axis is demand.

$$n = 6 \qquad\qquad \Sigma x^2 = 91$$
$$\Sigma x = 21 \qquad\qquad \Sigma y^2 = 27,875$$
$$\Sigma y = 405 \qquad\qquad \Sigma xy = 1,485$$

    d. Calculate a forecast for October.

18. Sales by quarter for last year and the first three quarters of this year were as follows:

	Quarter			
	I	II	III	IV
Last year	23,000	27,000	18,000	9,000
This year	19,000	24,000	15,000	

Using the Focus Forecasting procedure described in the text, forecast expected sales for the fourth quarter of this year.

✓ **19.** The following table shows predicted product demand using your particular forecasting method along with the actual demand that occurred.

Forecast	Actual
1,500	1,550
1,400	1,500
1,700	1,600
1,750	1,650
1,800	1,700

a. Compute the tracking signal using the mean absolute deviation and running sum of forecast errors.
b. Discuss whether your forecasting method is giving good predictions.

20. Your manager is trying to determine what forecasting method to use. Based upon the following historical data, calculate the following forecast and specify what procedure you would utilize.

Month	Actual Demand	Month	Actual Demand
1	62	7	76
2	65	8	78
3	67	9	78
4	68	10	80
5	71	11	84
6	73	12	85

a. Calculate the simple 3-month moving average forecast for periods 4–12.
b. Calculate the weighted 3-month moving average using weights of 0.50, 0.30, and 0.20 for periods 4–12.
c. Calculate the single exponential smoothing forecast for periods 2-12 using an initial forecast (F_1) 61, and an α of 0.30.
d. Calculate the exponential smoothing with trend component forecast for periods 2-12 using an initial trend forecast (T_1) of 1.8, and initial exponential smoothing forecast (F_1) of 60, an α of 0.30, and a δ of 0.30.
e. Calculate the Mean Absolute Deviation (MAD) for the forecasts made by each technique in periods 4-12. Which forecasting method do you prefer?

21. Use regression analysis on deseasonalized demand to forecast demand in summer 1998, given the following historical demand data:

Year	Season	Actual Demand	Year	Season	Actual Demand
1996	Spring	205	1997	Spring	475
	Summer	140		Summer	275
	Fall	375		Fall	685
	Winter	575		Winter	965

19. *a.* MAD = 90;
 TS = −1.67.
b. Model okay because tracking is −1.67.

20. *a.* See SM.
b. See SM.
c. See SM.
d. See SM.
e. **Forecast   MAD**

Moving average 4.07
Weighted moving average 3.46
Single exponential smoothing 6.174
Exponential smoothing with trend 0.895
Select the exponential smoothing with trend forecast.

21. Forecast (Summer 1998)
= 209 + 55.8(10) = 767
767 × .45 (seasonal factor) = 345

22. Here are the data for the past 21 months for actual sales of a particular product.

	1996	1997		1996	1997
January	300	275	July	400	350
February	400	375	August	300	275
March	425	350	September	375	350
April	450	425	October	500	
May	400	400	November	550	
June	460	350	December	500	

Develop a forecast for the fourth quarter using three different focus forecasting rules. (Note that to correctly use this procedure, the rules are first tested on the third quarter; the best performing one is used to forecast the fourth quarter.) Do the problem using quarters, as opposed to forecasting separate months.

23. Actual demand for a product for the past three months was

Three months ago	400 units
Two months ago	350 units
Last month	325 units

a. Using a simple three-month moving average, make a forecast for this month.
b. If 300 units actually occurred this month, what would your forecast be for next month?
c. Using simple exponential smoothing, what would your forecast be for this month if the exponentially smoothed forecast for three months ago was 450 units and the smoothing constant was 0.20?

24. After using your forecasting model for six months, you decide to test it using MAD and a tracking signal. Here are the forecasted and actual demands for the six-month period:

Period	Forecast	Actual
May	450	500
June	500	550
July	550	400
August	600	500
September	650	675
October	700	600

a. Find the tracking signal.
b. Decide whether your forecasting routine is acceptable.

25. Goodyear Tire and Rubber Company is the world's largest rubber manufacturer, with automotive products accounting for 82 percent of sales. Cooper Tire and Rubber Company is the ninth largest tire manufacturer in the world, with tires accounting for about 80 percent of sales.

Here are earnings per share for each company by quarter from the first quarter of 1988 through the second quarter of 1991. Forecast earnings per share for the rest of 1991 and 1992. Use exponential smoothing to forecast the third period of 1991, and the time series decomposition method to forecast the last two quarters of 1991 and all four quarters of 1992. (It is much easier to solve this problem on a computer spreadsheet so you can see what is happening.)

Earnings per Share

	Quarter	Goodyear Tire	Cooper Tire		Quarter	Goodyear Tire	Cooper Tire
1988	I	$1.67	$0.17	1990	I	$ 0.29	$0.33
	II	2.35	0.24		II	−0.18 (loss)	0.40
	III	1.11	0.26		III	−0.97 (loss)	0.41
	IV	1.15	0.34		IV	0.20	0.47
1989	I	1.56	0.25	1991	I	−1.54 (loss)	0.30
	II	2.04	0.37		II	0.38	0.47
	III	1.14	0.36				
	IV	0.38	0.44				

   a. For the exponential smoothing method, choose the first quarter of 1988 as the beginning forecast. Make two forecasts: one with $\alpha = 0.10$ and one with $\alpha = 0.30$.

   b. Using the MAD method of testing the forecasting model's performance, plus actual data from 1988 through the second quarter of 1991, how well did the model perform?

   c. Using the decomposition of a time series method of forecasting, forecast earnings per share for the last two quarters of 1991 and all four quarters of 1992. Is there a seasonal factor in the earnings?

   d. Using your forecasts, comment on each company: Cooper Tire and Goodyear Tire.

26. Consolidated Edison Company of New York, Inc., sells electricity, gas, and steam to New York City and Westchester County. Here are sales revenues for 1981 through 1991. (The last four months of 1991 are estimated.) Forecast revenues for 1992 through 1995. Use your own judgment, intuition, or common sense concerning which model or method to use, as well as the period of data to include.

26. See SM.

	Revenue (millions)		Revenue (millions)
1981	$4,865.9	1987	$5,094.4
1982	5,067.4	1988	5,108.8
1983	5,515.6	1989	5,550.6
1984	5,728.8	1990	5,738.9
1985	5,497.7	1991	5,860.0
1986	5,197.7		

SELECTED BIBLIOGRAPHY

Bowerman, Bruce L., and Richard T. O'Connell. *Forecasting and Time Series: An Applied Approach,* 3rd ed. Belmont, CA: Duxbury Press, 1993.

Hudson, William J. *Executive Economics: Forecasting and Planning for the Real World of Business.* New York: John Wiley & Sons, 1993.

Jain, Chaman. "Developing Forecasts for Better Planning." *Long Range Planning* 26, no. 5 (October 1993), pp. 121–29.

The Journal of Business Forecasting. See various issues for interesting topics.

Niemira, Michael P. *Forecasting Financial and Economic Cycles.* New York: John Wiley & Sons, 1994.

Zarnowitz, Victor, *Business Cycles: Theory, History, Indicators, and Forecasting.* National Bureau of Economic Research Monograph. Chicago: University of Chicago Press, 1992.

Chapter 14

Aggregate Planning

Chapter Outline

Overview of Operations Planning Activities, 552
Hierarchical Production Planning, 554
Aggregate Production Planning, 555
    Production Planning Environment
    Relevant Costs
Aggregate Planning Techniques, 559
    A Cut-and-Try Example: The CA&J
    Company

Aggregate Planning Applied to Services:
    Tucson Parks and Recreation Department
    Level Scheduling
    Mathematical Techniques
Case: XYZ Brokerage Firm, 578

Key Terms

Aggregate Planning

Long-, Intermediate-, and
Short-Range Planning

Master Production Schedule (MPS)

Rough-Cut Capacity Planning

Capacity Requirements Planning

Order Scheduling

Production Rate

Workforce Level

Inventory on Hand

Demand Management

Production Planning Strategies

Pure Strategy

Mixed Strategy

www Links

National Association of Temporary and Staffing Services
(http://www.natss.com/staffing)

I NVENTORY IN THE GRANITE BUSINESS IS HARD TO MISS: we make tombstones—a custom product if there ever was one—and when quarry blocks, slabs, bases, and finished stones are hanging around, they're quite visible. It's also pretty dangerous when they pile up (literally) because stones have been known to topple over and fall on people.

It may not be immediately obvious, but tombstone manufacture is a seasonal business; in New England you can't "plant" anything in the winter, so there is a huge demand peak just before Memorial Day. Since quarrying can't be done in the winter either, quarry blocks have to be purchased in the Fall. Put this together with the fact that our dealers insist on consolidated shipments to various parts of the country given the weight of the finished product and you've got the makings of a whopping inventory position during the run-up to the end of May. Add the need for *lots* of overtime for highly skilled craftsmen, and an annual cash flow crisis is going to be part of your life.

My grandmother was president of J. O. Bilodeau & Company, manufacturers of *Paragon Memorials,* in the Granite Center of the World—Barre, Vermont. My uncle and my mother were vice presidents (Sales and Office Administration, respectively), my step-grandfather was general foreman and my other uncle was plant superinten-dent. (Our motto: If there's money to be made, for God's sake keep it in the family!) Lunch every day was a working meeting where children knew enough to be quiet; keeping one's mouth shut was a lot better than tangling with Grandma Pinard, so I was in high school before I figured out that "Goshdurninventory" was actually three separate words.

When I went off to MIT, grandma decided I should help pay back my tuition by reporting anything I found out which could help the family business. After hearing about some of systems theorist Jay Forrester's early work, I decided that grandma should know (and I was just the one to tell her!) that she didn't really have an *inventory* problem. It was just a matter of buying less raw stock so early, insisting that our customers place their Memorial Day orders before Christmas so we could do the work in slack periods and avoid overtime, and telling our dealers that they would just have to pay for more convenient (fewer consolidations) shipments. Fortunately for me, grandma spoke French-Canadian and hadn't permitted any of my generation to learn it very well, so I didn't fully understand her response. I did, however, grasp its general nature so got away as quickly as possible.

My mother, of course, took grandma's side and there was great hilarity about the wisdom being imparted at the great MIT. Grandma consoled herself with the thought that, in spite of its naive understanding of suppliers, customers, and dealers, MIT was probably giving me enough basic training in engineering that I would "learn a trade"—which would supplement the courses in sewing and tailoring she and my mother had put me through as backup in case MIT wasn't as great as its reputation.

Meanwhile, every year between early April and late May we had a Goshdurninventory problem, and for another month or so beyond that had a cash crisis of epic proportion—as did every other manufacturer in town, to the considerable delight of the local banks. Until the day she died, my grandmother found great humor in what MIT had to say about the Goshdurninventory problem. ●

Source: Professor Linda G. Sprague, University of New Hampshire.

Aggregate Planning

The problems of managing inventory and overtime discussed in the preceding vignette reflect one of the major areas addressed in aggregate planning. **Aggregate planning** involves translating annual and quarterly business plans into broad labor and output plans for the intermediate term (6 to 18 months). Its objective is to minimize the cost of resources required to meet demand over that period.

■ OVERVIEW OF OPERATIONS PLANNING ACTIVITIES

Long-Range Planning

Intermediate-Range Planning

Short-Range Planning

Exhibit 14.1 positions aggregate planning relative to other major operations planning activities presented in the text. The time dimension is shown as long, intermediate, and short range. **Long-range planning** is generally done annually, focusing on a horizon greater than one year. **Intermediate-range planning** usually covers a period from 6 to 18 months, with time increments that are monthly or sometimes quarterly. **Short-range planning** covers a period from one day or less to six months, with the time increment usually weekly.

Process planning deals with determining the specific technologies and procedures required to produce a product or service. (See Chapters 4 and 5.) Strategic capacity planning deals with determining the long-term capabilities (e.g., size and scope) of the production system. (See Chapter 7.) The aggregate planning process is essentially the same for services and manufacturing, the major exception being manufacturing's use of inventory buildups and cutbacks to smooth production (as we will discuss shortly). After the aggregate planning stage, manufacturing and service planning activities are generally quite different.

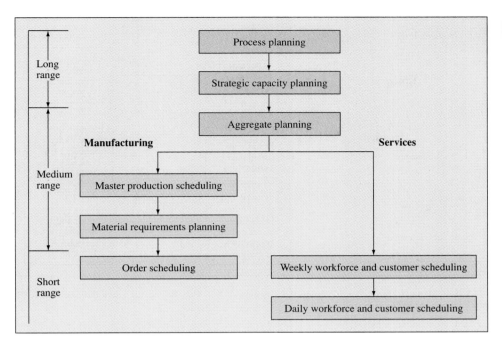

Exhibit 14.1

Overview of Major
Operations Planning
Activities

In manufacturing, the planning process can be summarized as follows: The production control group inputs existing or forecast orders into a **master production schedule (MPS).** The MPS generates the amounts and dates of specific items required for each order. **Rough-cut capacity planning** is then used to verify that production and warehouse facilities, equipment, and labor are available and that key vendors have allocated sufficient capacity to provide materials when needed. As Chapter 16 details, **material requirements planning (MRP)** takes the end product requirements from the MPS and breaks them down into their component parts and subassemblies to create a materials plan. This plan specifies when production and purchase orders must be placed for each part and subassembly to complete the products on schedule. Most MRP systems also allocate production capacity to each order. (This is called **capacity requirements planning.**) The final planning activity is daily or weekly **order scheduling** of jobs to specific machines, production lines, or work centers. (See Chapter 17 for details.)

In services, once the aggregate staffing level is determined, the focus is on workforce and customer scheduling during the week or even hour by hour during the day. Workforce schedules are a function of the hours the service is available to a customer, the particular skills needed at particular times over the relevant time period, and so on. Many service jobs have unique time and legal restrictions affecting scheduling that typical manufacturing work lacks. Airline flight crews are a good example of such constraints that make their scheduling far more complicated than scheduling manufacturing personnel. (Again, see Chapter 17.) Customer (or demand) scheduling deals with setting appointments and reservations for customers to use the service, and assigning priorities when they arrive at the service facility. These obviously range from formal reservation systems to simple sign-up sheets.

We now turn our attention back to manufacturing.

**Master Production
Schedule (MPS)**

**Rough-Cut
Capacity Planning**

**Material
Requirements
Planning (MRP)**

**Capacity
Requirements
Planning**

Order Scheduling

Vol. IV "Scheduling
Services—the
United Solution."

Exhibit 14.2

Hierarchical Planning
Process

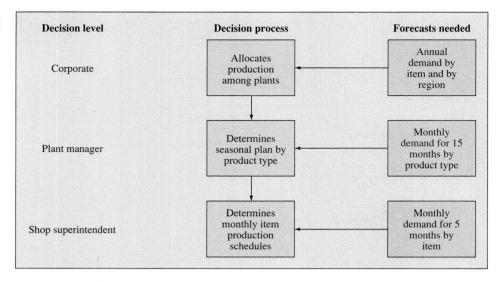

Decision level	Decision process	Forecasts needed
Corporate	Allocates production among plants	Annual demand by item and by region
Plant manager	Determines seasonal plan by product type	Monthly demand for 15 months by product type
Shop superintendent	Determines monthly item production schedules	Monthly demand for 5 months by item

Source: Harlan C. Meal, "Putting Production Decisions Where They Belong," *Harvard Business Review* 62, no. 2 (March–April 1984), p. 104.

HIERARCHICAL PRODUCTION PLANNING

We have looked at manufacturing planning activities within a framework of long range, medium range, and short range. If we were to overlay the organization chart of a firm onto Exhibit 14.1, we would note that higher levels within the organization deal with long-range planning and lower levels deal with short-range planning. In a more formal way, Harlan Meal uses the term *hierarchical production planning (HPP)* to tailor the planning structure to the organization.[1] As Exhibit 14.2 shows, higher levels of management would use aggregate data for top-level decisions, while shop-floor decisions would be made using detailed data. In the extreme case, HPP logically states that top management should not become involved in determining the production lot size at a machine center. By the same token, the production line supervisor should not become involved in planning new product lines.

Meal cites as an example a tire manufacturer with several plants. With a *conventional* approach, each plant would tend to build a stock of tires it was confident of selling. An unsatisfactory consequence was that slow-moving items were produced in small quantities during peak season when capacity was scarce.

By centralizing the decision, top managers expected that they could somehow decide which plants would produce which tires in what quantities. This became impossible; not only was the number of detailed variables much too large to review but also it took the decision-making power away from plant management, where it rightly belonged.

The hierarchical procedure divided the decision making, with top management allocating tire production among the plants on an annual basis. Plant management in

---

[1] Harlan C. Meal, "Putting Production Decisions Where They Belong," *Harvard Business Review* 62, no. 2 (March–April 1984), pp. 102–11.

Kawasaki Motors USA produces utility vehicles, motorcycles, all-terrain vehicles, and Jet Ski watercraft at its plant in Lincoln, Nebraska.

While the corporate plan would specify how many units in each product line, the aggregate plan would determine how to meet this requirement with available resources.

each of the plants would decide on seasonal effects, buildup of inventory, hiring, and so on. Shop management would perform the detailed scheduling of individual items. Shop supervisors, knowing the proportion of time they needed to spend on each product group, could then fill up available capacity.

An advantage of hierarchical planning is that each successive level has a smaller database and a simpler structure.

■ AGGREGATE PRODUCTION PLANNING

Again, aggregate production planning is concerned with setting production rates by product group or other broad categories for the intermediate term (6 to 18 months). Note again from Exhibit 14.1 that the aggregate plan precedes the master schedule. *The main purpose of the aggregate plan is to specify the optimal combination of production rate, the workforce level, and inventory on hand.* **Production rate** refers to the number of units completed per unit of time (such as per hour or per day). **Workforce level** is the number of workers needed for production. **Inventory on hand** is the balance of unused inventory carried over from the previous period.

Production Rate

Workforce Level

Inventory on Hand

Here is a formal statement of the aggregate planning problem: Given the demand forecast F_t for each period t in the planning horizon that extends over T periods, determine the production level P_t, inventory level I_t, and workforce level W_t for periods $t = 1, 2, \ldots , T$ that minimize the relevant costs over the planning horizon.

The form of the aggregate plan varies from company to company. In some firms, it is a formalized report containing planning objectives and the planning premises on which it is based. In other companies, particularly smaller ones, the owner may make simple calculations of workforce needs that reflect a general staffing strategy.

The process by which the plan itself is derived also varies. One common approach is to derive it from the corporate annual plan, as shown in Exhibit 14.1. A typical corporate plan contains a section on manufacturing that specifies how many units in each major product line need to be produced over the next 12 months to meet the sales forecast. The planner takes this information and attempts to determine how best to meet these requirements with available resources. Alternatively, some organizations combine output requirements into equivalent units and use this as the basis for aggregate planning. For example, a division of General Motors may be asked to produce a certain number of cars of all types at a particular facility. The production planner would then take the average labor hours required for all models as a basis for the overall aggregate plan. Refinements to this plan, specifically model types to be produced, would be reflected in shorter-term production plans.

Another approach is to develop the aggregate plan by simulating various master production schedules and calculating corresponding capacity requirements to see if adequate labor and equipment exist at each work center. If capacity is inadequate, additional requirements for overtime, subcontracting, extra workers, and so forth are specified for each product line and combined into a rough-cut plan. This plan is then modified by cut-and-try or mathematical methods to derive a final and (one hopes) lower-cost plan.

Production Planning Environment

Exhibit 14.3 illustrates the internal and external factors that constitute the production planning environment. In general, the external environment is outside the production planner's direct control, but in some firms, demand for the product can be managed as noted in Chapter 13. In general, there are two primary means for accomplishing **demand management:** (1) *pricing and promotion* and (2) *complementary products.*

Demand Management

MARKETING

Through close cooperation between marketing and operations, promotional activities and price cutting can be used to build demand during slow periods. Conversely, when demand is strong, promotional activities can be curtailed and prices raised to

Exhibit 14.3   Required Inputs to the Production Planning System

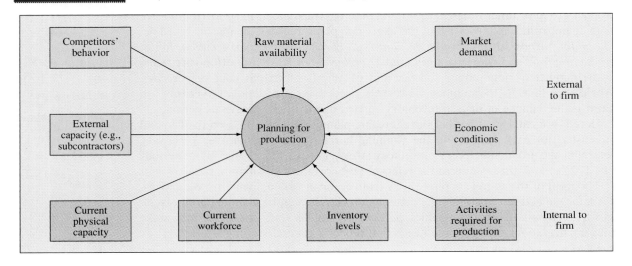

maximize the revenues from those products or services that the firm has the capacity to provide.

Complementary products may work for firms facing cyclical demand fluctuations. For instance, lawnmower manufacturers will have strong demand for spring and summer, but weak demand during fall and winter. Demands on the production system can be smoothed out by producing a complementary product with high demand during fall and winter, and low demand during spring and summer (for instance, snowmobiles, snowblowers, or leaf blowers). With services, cycles are more often measured in hours than months. Restaurants with strong demand during lunch and dinner will often add a breakfast menu to increase demand during the morning hours.

But even so, there are limits to how much demand can be controlled. Ultimately, the production planner must live with the sales projections and orders promised by the marketing function, leaving the internal factors as variables that can be manipulated in deriving a production plan. A new approach to facilitate managing these internal factors is termed *accurate response.* This entails refined measurement of historical demand patterns blended with expert judgment to determine when to begin production of particular items. The key element of the approach is clearly identifying those products for which demand is relatively predictable from those for which demand is relatively unpredictable.[2]

The internal factors themselves differ in their controllability. Current physical capacity (plant and equipment) is usually nearly fixed in the short run; union agreements often constrain what can be done in changing the workforce; physical capacity cannot always be increased; and top management may set limits on the amount of money that can be tied up in inventories. Still, there is always some flexibility in managing these factors, and production planners can implement one or a combination of the **production planning strategies** discussed here.

Production Planning Strategies

Production Planning Strategies   There are essentially three production planning strategies. These strategies involve trade-offs among the workforce size, work hours, inventory, and backlogs.

1. *Chase strategy.*[3] Match the production rate to the order rate by hiring and laying off employees as the order rate varies. The success of this strategy depends on having a pool of easily trained applicants to draw on as order volumes increase. There are obvious motivational impacts. When order backlogs are low, employees may feel compelled to slow down out of fear of being laid off as soon as existing orders are completed.

2. *Stable workforce—variable work hours.* Vary the output by varying the number of hours worked through flexible work schedules or overtime. By varying the number of work hours, you can match production quantities to orders. This strategy provides workforce continuity and avoids many of the emotional and tangible costs of hiring and firing associated with the chase strategy.

3. *Level strategy.* Maintain a stable workforce working at a constant output rate. Shortages and surpluses are absorbed by fluctuating inventory levels, order backlogs, and lost sales. Employees benefit from stable work hours at the costs of potentially decreased customer service levels and increased inventory costs. Another concern is the possibility of inventoried products becoming obsolete.

---

[2] Marshall L. Fisher, Janice H. Hammond, Walter R. Obermeyer, and Anath Raman, "Making Supply Meet Demand in an Uncertain World," *Harvard Business Review* 72, no. 3 (May–June 1994), p. 84.

[3] No relation to one of the authors of this text.

Pure Strategy

Mixed Strategy

When just one of these variables is used to absorb demand fluctuations, it is termed a **pure strategy;** two or more used in combination is a **mixed strategy.** As you might suspect, mixed strategies are more widely applied in industry.

Subcontracting   In addition to these strategies, managers may also choose to subcontract some portion of production. This strategy is similar to the chase strategy, but hiring and laying off are translated into subcontracting, and not subcontracting. Some level of subcontracting can be desirable to accommodate demand fluctuations. However, unless the relationship with the supplier is particularly strong, a manufacturer can lose some control over schedule and quality. For this reason, extensive subcontracting may be viewed as a high-risk strategy.

Relevant Costs

There are four costs relevant to aggregate production planning. These relate to the production cost itself as well as the cost to hold inventory and to have unfilled orders. More specifically, these are

1. *Basic production costs.* These are the fixed and variable costs incurred in producing a given product type in a given time period. Included are direct and indirect labor costs and regular as well as overtime compensation.

2. *Costs associated with changes in the production rate.* Typical costs in this category are those involved in hiring, training, and laying off personnel. Hiring temporary help is a way of avoiding these costs. See the Breakthrough box on page 561, "Worker Staffing Becomes a Hot Entrepreneurial Field."

3. *Inventory holding costs.* A major component is the cost of capital tied up in inventory. Other components are storing, insurance, taxes, spoilage, and obsolescence.

4. *Backordering costs.* Usually these are very hard to measure and include costs of expediting, loss of customer goodwill, and loss of sales revenues resulting from backordering.

Budgets   To receive funding, operations managers are generally required to submit annual, and sometimes quarterly, budget requests. Aggregate planning activities are key to the success of the budgeting process. Recall that the goal of aggregate planning is to minimize the total production-related costs over the planning horizon by determining the optimal combination of workforce levels and inventory levels. Thus, aggregate planning provides justification for the requested budget amount. Accurate medium-range planning increases the likelihood of (1) receiving the requested budget and (2) operating within the limits of the budget.

In the next section, we provide examples of medium-range planning in both manufacturing and service settings. These examples illustrate the trade-offs associated with different production planning strategies.[4]

---

[4] For an interesting application of aggregate planning in nonprofit humanitarian organizations, see Chwen Sheu and John G. Wacker, "A Planning and Control Framework for Non-profit Humanitarian Organizations," *International Journal of Operations and Production Management* 14, no. 4 (1994), pp. 64–77.

AGGREGATE PLANNING TECHNIQUES

Companies commonly use simple cut-and-try charting and graphic methods to develop aggregate plans. A cut-and-try approach involves costing out various production planning alternatives and selecting the one that is best. Elaborate spreadsheets are developed to facilitate the decision process. Sophisticated approaches involving linear programming and simulation are often incorporated into these spreadsheets. In the following, we demonstrate a spreadsheet approach to evaluate four strategies for meeting demand for the CA&J Company. Later, we discuss more sophisticated approaches using linear programming.

A Cut-and-Try Example: The CA&J Company

A firm with pronounced seasonal variation normally plans production for a full year to capture the extremes in demand during the busiest and slowest months. But we can illustrate the general principles involved with a shorter horizon. Suppose we wish to set up a production plan for the CA&J Company for the next six months. We are given the following information:

Demand and Working Days

	January	February	March	April	May	June	Totals
Demand forecast	1,800	1,500	1,100	900	1,100	1,600	8,000
Number of working days	22	19	21	21	22	20	125

Costs

Materials	$100.00/unit
Inventory holding cost	$1.50/unit/month
Marginal cost of stockout	$5.00/unit/month
Marginal cost of subcontracting	$20.00/unit ($120 subcontracting cost less $100 material savings)
Hiring and training cost	$200.00/worker
Layoff cost	$250.00/worker
Labor hours required	5/unit
Straight-line cost (first eight hours each day)	$4.00/hour
Overtime cost (time and a half)	$6.00/hour

Inventory

Beginning inventory	400 units
Safety stock	25% of month demand

In solving this problem, we can exclude the material costs. We could have included this $100 cost in all our calculations, but if we assume that a $100 cost is common to each demanded unit, then we need only to concern ourselves with the marginal costs. Because the subcontracting cost is $120, our true cost for subcontracting is just $20 because we save the materials.

Note that many costs are expressed in a different form than typically found in the accounting records of a firm. Therefore, do not expect to obtain all these costs directly from such records, but obtain them indirectly from management personnel, who can help interpret the data.

ACCOUNTING

Exhibit 14.4   Aggregate Production Planning Requirements

	January	February	March	April	May	June
Beginning inventory	400	450	375	275	225	275
Demand forecast	1,800	1,500	1,100	900	1,100	1,600
Safety stock (.25 × Demand forecast)	450	375	275	225	275	400
Production requirement (Demand forecast + Safety stock − Beginning inventory)	1,850	1,425	1,000	850	1,150	1,725
Ending inventory (Beginning inventory + Production requirement − Demand forecast)	450	375	275	225	275	400

Inventory at the beginning of the first period is 400 units. Because the demand forecast is imperfect, the CA&J Company has determined that a *safety stock* (buffer inventory) should be established to reduce the likelihood of stockouts. For this example, assume the safety stock should be one-quarter of the demand forecast. (Chapter 15 covers this topic in more depth.)

Before investigating alternative production plans, it is often useful to convert demand forecasts into *production requirements,* which take into account the safety stock estimates. In Exhibit 14.4, note that these requirements implicitly assume that the safety stock is never actually used, so that the ending inventory each month equals the safety stock for that month. For example, the January safety stock of 450 (25 percent of January demand of 1,800) becomes the inventory at the end of January. The production requirement for January is demand plus safety stock minus beginning inventory (1,800 + 450 − 400 = 1,850).

Now we must formulate alternative production plans for the CA&J Company. Using a spreadsheet, we investigate four different plans with the objective of finding the one with the lowest total cost.

Plan 1. Produce to exact monthly production requirements using a regular eight-hour day by varying workforce size.

Plan 2. Produce to meet expected average demand over the next six months by maintaining a constant workforce. This constant number of workers is calculated by finding the average number of workers required each day over the horizon. Take the total production requirements and multiply by the time required for each unit. Then, divide by the total time that one person works over the horizon [(8,000 units × 5 hours per unit) ÷ (125 days × 8 hours per day) = 40 workers]. Inventory is allowed to accumulate, with shortages filled from next month's production by back ordering. Notice that in this plan we use our safety stock in January, February, March, and June to meet expected demand.

Plan 3. Produce to meet the minimum expected demand (April) using a constant workforce on regular time. Subcontract to meet additional output requirements. The number of workers is calculated by locating the minimum monthly production requirement and determining how many workers would be needed for that month [(850 units × 5 hours per unit) ÷ (21 days × 8 hours per day) = 25 workers] and subcontracting any monthly difference between requirements and production.

Plan 4. Produce to meet expected demand for all but the first two months using a constant workforce on regular time. Use overtime to meet additional output requirements. The number of workers is more difficult to compute for this plan, but the goal is to finish June with an ending inventory as close as possible to the June safety stock.

BREAKTHROUGH

Worker Staffing Becomes a Hot Entrepreneurial Field

It isn't biotechnology, and it has nothing to do with the Internet. But the mundane staffing industry is emerging more clearly than ever as a hot entrepreneurial field. Revenues are soaring, and more companies are going public.

"We'll probably grow at least 50% again this year," says Ronald Bray, president of Simplified Employment Services Inc., Auburn Hills. Mich. The company, which saves other companies red tape by "leasing" employees to them, last week moved into a building three times as large as it had before.

Last year, *Inc.* magazine's list of 500 small closely held companies with exceptional growth rates included 38 staffing concerns, such as Simplified Employment Services, up from 29 staffing concerns in 1994 and 21 in 1992. A spot check shows that these companies are enjoying more rapid growth so far this year. Spurred by the outsourcing trend, the fastest growing concerns are typically in temporary employment and "employee leasing."

Bright Future

Employee-leasing companies see a particularly bright future. "This industry is growing around 30% a year, and we feel that rate can be sustained," says Milan P. Yager, executive vice president of the National Association of Professional Employer Organizations in Alexandria, Va. The association's member PEOs take responsibility for their client companies' services. They become the workforce's employer or co-employer and "lease" the employees, primarily permanent workers, back to the client company.

In handling all the red tape of employment for companies, the employee-leasing companies benefit from companies' growing desire to outsource as many functions as possible. Besides, the leasing concerns can often obtain health insurance and other benefits more cheaply than their clients, mainly small companies.

Temporary employment agencies are also profiting from the outsourcing trend. Hoping to keep their permanent staffs as lean as possible after downsizing, many companies rely on outside employment agencies to provide "temps" when they need extra help. The average daily employment of temporary employment services was 2,162,000 last year, nearly double the 1990 level, says the National Association of Temporary and Staffing Services of Alexandria, Va. *(http://www.natss.com/staffing)*

Source: Roger Ricklefs, "Work Staffing Becomes a Hot Entrepreneurial Field," *The Wall Street Journal*, June 4, 1996. Reprinted by permission of *The Wall Street Journal*. © 1996 Dow Jones & Company, Inc. All Rights Reserved Worldwide.

By trial and error it can be shown that a constant workforce of 38 workers is the closest approximation.

The next step is to calculate the cost of each plan. This requires the series of simple calculations shown in Exhibit 14.5. Note that the headings in each row are different for each plan because each is a different problem requiring its own data and calculations.

The final step is to tabulate and graph each plan and make a comparison of their costs. From Exhibit 14.6 we can see that making use of subcontracting resulted in the lowest cost (Plan 3). Exhibit 14.7 shows the effects of the four plans. This is a cumulative graph illustrating the expected results on the total production requirement.

Note that we have made one other assumption in this example: The plan can start with any number of workers with no hiring or layoff cost. This usually is the case, because an aggregate plan draws on existing personnel, and we can start the plan that way. However, in an actual application, the availability of existing personnel transferable from other areas of the firm may change the assumptions.

Each of these four plans focused on one particular cost, and the first three were simple pure strategies. Obviously, there are many other feasible plans, some of which would use a combination of workforce changes, overtime, and subcontracting. The problems at the end of this chapter include examples of such mixed strategies. In

Exhibit 14.5   Costs of Four Production Plans

Production Plan 1: Exact Production; Vary Workforce

	January	February	March	April	May	June	Total
Production requirement (from Exhibit 14.4)	1,850	1,425	1,000	850	1,150	1,725	
Production hours required (Production requirement × 5 hr./unit)	9,250	7,125	5,000	4,250	5,750	8,625	
Working days per month	22	19	21	21	22	20	
Hours per month per worker (Working days × 8 hrs./day)	176	152	168	168	176	160	
Workers required (Production hours required/hours per month per worker	53	47	30	25	33	54	
New workers hired (assuming opening workforce equal to first month's requirement of 53 workers)	0	0	0	0	8	21	
Hiring cost (New workers hired × $200)	$0	$0	$0	$0	$1,600	$4,200	$5,800
Workers laid off	0	6	17	5	0	0	
Layoff cost (Workers laid off × $250)	$0	$1,500	$4,250	$1,250	$0	$0	$7,000
Straight time cost (Production hours required × $4)	$37,000	$28,500	$20,000	$17,000	$23,000	$34,500	$160,000
						Total cost	$172,800

Production Plan 2: Constant Workforce; Vary Inventory and Stockout

	January	February	March	April	May	June	Total
Beginning inventory	400	8	−276	−32	412	720	
Working days per month	22	19	21	21	22	20	
Production hours available (Working days per month × 8 hr./Day × 40 workers)*	7,040	6,080	6,720	6,720	7,040	6,400	
Actual production (Production hours available/5 hr./unit)	1,408	1,216	1,344	1,344	1,408	1,280	
Demand forecast (from Exhibit 14.4)	1,800	1,500	1,100	900	1,100	1,600	
Ending inventory (Beginning inventory + Actual production − Demand forecast)	8	−276	−32	412	720	400	
Shortage cost (Units short × $5)	$0	$1,380	$160	$0	$0	$0	$1,540
Safety stock (from Exhibit 14.4)	450	375	275	225	275	400	
Units excess (Ending inventory − Safety stock) only if positive amount	0	0	0	187	445	0	
Inventory cost (Units excess × $1.50)	$0	$0	$0	$281	$668	$0	$948
Straight time cost (Production hours available × $4)	$28,160	$24,320	$26,880	$26,880	$28,160	$25,600	$160,000
						Total cost	$162,488

* (Sum of production requirement in Exhibit 14.4 × 5 hr./unit)/(Sum of production hours available × 8 hr./day) = (8,000 × 5)/(125 × 8) = 40.

Production Plan 3: Constant Low Workforce; Subcontract

	January	February	March	April	May	June	Total
Production requirement (from Exhibit 14.4)	1,850	1,425	1,000	850	1,150	1,725	
Working days per month	22	19	21	21	22	20	
Production hours available (Working days × 8 hrs./day × 25 workers)*	4,400	3,800	4,200	4,200	4,400	4,000	
Actual production (Production hours available/5 hr. per unit)	880	760	840	840	880	800	

Production Plan 3: Constant Low Workforce; Subcontract (continued)

	January	February	March	April	May	June	Total
Units subcontracted (Production requirement − Actual production)	970	665	160	10	270	925	
Subcontracting cost (Units subcontracted × $20)	$19,400	$13,300	$3,200	$200	$5,400	$18,500	$60,000
Straight time cost (Production hours available × $4)	$17,600	$15,200	$16,800	$16,800	$17,600	$16,000	$100,000
						Total cost	$160,000

*Minimum production requirement. In this example, April is minimum of 850 units. Number of workers required for April is $(850 \times 5)/(21 \times 8) = 25$.

Production Plan 4: Constant Workforce; Overtime

	January	February	March	April	May	June	Total
Beginning inventory	400	0	0	177	554	792	
Working days per month	22	19	21	21	22	20	
Production hours available (Working days × 8 hr./day × 38 workers)*	6,688	5,776	6,384	6,384	6,688	6,080	
Regular shift production (Production hours available/5 hrs. per unit)	1,338	1,155	1,277	1,277	1,338	1,216	
Demand forecast (from Exhibit 14.4)	1,800	1,500	1,100	900	1,100	1,600	
Units available before overtime (Beginning inventory + Regular shift production − Demand forecast). This number has been rounded to nearest integer.	−62	−345	177	554	792	408	
Units overtime	62	345	0	0	0	0	
Overtime cost (Units overtime × 5 hr./unit × $6/hr.)	$1,860	$10,350	$0	$0	$0	$0	$12,210
Safety stock (from Exhibit 14.4)	450	375	275	225	275	400	
Units excess (Units available before overtime − Safety stock) only if positive amount	0	0	0	329	517	8	
Inventory cost (Units excessive × $1.50)	$0	$0	$0	$494	$776	$12	$1,281
Straight time cost (Production hours available × $4)	$26,752	$23,104	$25,536	$25,536	$26,752	$24,320	$152,000
						Total cost	$165,491

*Workers determined by trial-and-error. See text for explanation.

Cost	Plan 1: Exact Production; Vary Workforce	Plan 2: Constant Workforce; Vary Inventory and Stockout	Plan 3: Constant Low Workforce; Subcontract	Plan 4: Constant Workforce; Overtime
Hiring	$ 5,800	$ 0	$ 0	$ 0
Layoff	7,000	0	0	0
Excess inventory	0	948	0	1,281
Shortage	0	1,540	0	0
Subcontract	0	0	60,000	0
Overtime	0	0	0	12,210
Straight time	160,000	160,000	100,000	152,000
	$172,800	$162,488	$160,000	$165,491

Exhibit 14.6

Comparison of Four Plans

Exhibit 14.7

Four Plans for
Satisfying a Production
Requirement over
the Number of
Production Days
Available

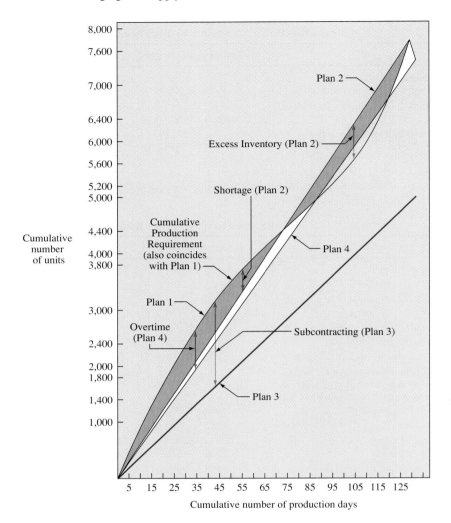

Cumulative number of production days

practice, the final plan chosen would come from searching a variety of alternatives and future projections beyond the six-month planning horizon we have used.

Keep in mind that the cut-and-try approach does not guarantee finding the minimum-cost solution. However, spreadsheet programs, such as Microsoft Excel, can perform cut-and-try cost estimates in seconds and have elevated this kind of what-if analysis to a fine art. More sophisticated programs can generate much better solutions without the user having to intercede, as in the cut-and-try method.

Aggregate Planning Applied to Services: Tucson Parks and Recreation Department

S Charting and graphic techniques are also very useful for aggregate planning in service applications. The following example shows how a city's parks and recreation department could use the alternatives of full-time employees, part-time employees, and subcontracting to meet its commitment to provide a service to the city.

Tucson Parks and Recreation Department has an operation and maintenance budget of $9,760,000. The department is responsible for developing and maintaining open space, all public recreational programs, adult sports leagues, golf courses, tennis courts, pools, and so forth. There are 336 full-time-equivalent employees (FTEs). Of these, 216 are full-time permanent personnel who provide the administration and year-round maintenance to all areas. The remaining 120 FTE positions are staffed with part-timers; about three-quarters of them are used during the summer and the remaining quarter in the fall, winter, and spring seasons. The three-fourths (or 90 FTE positions) show up as approximately 800 part-time summer jobs: lifeguards, baseball umpires, and instructors in summer programs for children. Eight hundred part-time jobs came from 90 FTEs because many last only for a month or two, while the FTEs are a year long.

Currently, the only parks and recreation work subcontracted amounts to less than $100,000. This is for the golf and tennis pros and for grounds maintenance at the libraries and veterans cemetery.

Because of the nature of city employment, the probable bad public image, and civil service rules, the option to hire and fire full-time help daily or weekly to meet seasonal demand is out of the question. However, temporary part-time help is authorized and traditional. Also, it is virtually impossible to have regular (full-time) staff for all the summer jobs. During the summer months, the approximately 800 part-time employees are staffing many programs that occur simultaneously, prohibiting level scheduling over a normal 40-hour week. Also, a wider variety of skills are required than can be expected from full-time employees (e.g., umpires, coaches, lifeguards, and teachers of ceramics, guitar, karate, belly dancing, and yoga).

Three options are open to the department in its aggregate planning.

1. The present method, which is to maintain a medium-level full-time staff and schedule work during off-seasons (such as rebuilding baseball fields during the winter months) and to use part-time help during peak demands.

2. Maintain a lower level of staff over the year and subcontract all additional work presently done by full-time staff (still using part-time help).

3. Maintain an administrative staff only and subcontract all work, including part-time help. (This would entail contracts to landscaping firms and pool-maintenance companies as well as to newly created private firms to employ and supply part-time help.)

The common unit of measure of work across all areas is full-time equivalent jobs or employees. For example, assume in the same week that 30 lifeguards worked 20 hours each, 40 instructors worked 15 hours each, and 35 baseball umpires worked 10 hours each. This is equivalent to $(30 \times 20) + (40 \times 15) + (35 \times 10) = 1{,}550 \div 40 = 38.75$ FTE positions for that week. Although a considerable amount of workload can be shifted to off-season, most of the work must be done when required.

Full-time employees consist of three groups: (1) the skeleton group of key department personnel coordinating with the city, setting policy, determining budgets, measuring performance, and so forth; (2) the administrative group of supervisory and office personnel who are responsible for or whose jobs are directly linked to the direct-labor workers; and (3) the direct-labor workforce of 116 full-time positions. These workers physically maintain the department's areas of responsibility, such as cleaning up, mowing golf greens and ballfields, trimming trees, and watering grass.

Cost information needed to determine the best alternative strategy is

Full-time direct-labor employees	
Average wage rate	$4.45 per hour
Fringe benefits	17% of wage rate
Administrative costs	20% of wage rate
Part-time employees	
Average wage rate	$4.03 per hour
Fringe benefits	11% of wage rate
Administrative costs	25% of wage rate
Subcontracting all full-time jobs	$1.6 million
Subcontracting all part-time jobs	$1.85 million

June and July are the peak demand seasons in Tucson. Exhibits 14.8 and 14.9 show the high requirements for June and July personnel. The part-time help reaches 576 full-time-equivalent positions (although in actual numbers, this is approximately 800 different employees). After a low fall and winter staffing level, the demand shown as

---

Exhibit 14.8   Actual Demand Requirement for Full-Time Direct Employees and Full-Time-Equivalent (FTE) Part-Time Employees

	Jan.	Feb.	Mar.	Apr.	May	June	July	Aug.	Sept.	Oct.	Nov.	Dec.	Total
Days	22	20	21	22	21	20	21	21	21	23	18	22	252
Full-time employees	66	28	130	90	195	290	325	92	45	32	29	60	
Full-time days*	1,452	560	2,730	1,980	4,095	5,800	6,825	1,932	945	736	522	1,320	28,897
Full-time-equivalent part-time employees	41	75	72	68	72	302	576	72	0	68	84	27	
FTE days	902	1,500	1,512	1,496	1,512	6,040	12,096	1,512	0	1,564	1,512	594	30,240

*Full-time days are derived by multiplying the number of days in each month by the number of workers.

Exhibit 14.9

Monthly Requirement for Full-Time Direct-Labor Employees (Other than Key Personnel) and Full-Time-Equivalent Part-Time Employees

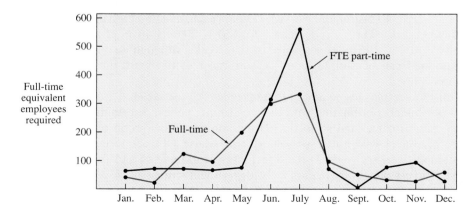

"full-time direct" reaches 130 in March (when grounds are reseeded and fertilized) and then increases to a high of 325 in July. The present method levels this uneven demand over the year to an average of 116 full-time year-round employees by early scheduling of work. As previously mentioned, no attempt is made to hire and lay off full-time workers to meet this uneven demand.

Exhibit 14.10 shows the cost calculations for all three alternatives. Exhibit 14.11 compares the total costs for each alternative. From this analysis, it appears that the department is already using the lowest-cost alternative (Alternative 1).

Three Possible Plans for the Parks and Recreation Department **Exhibit 14.10**

Alternative 1: Maintain 116 full-time regular direct workers. Schedule work during off-seasons to level workload throughout the year. Continue to use 120 full-time-equivalent (FTE) part-time employees to meet high demand periods.

Costs	Days per Year (Exhibit 14.8)	Hours (Employees × Days × 8 hours)	Wages (Full-time, $4.45; Part-time, $4.03)	Fringe Benefits (Full-time, 17%; Part-time, 11%)	Administrative Cost (Full-time, 20%; Part-time, 25%)
116 full-time regular employees	252	233,856	$ 1,040,659	$176,912	$208,132
120 part-time employees	252	241,920	974,938	107,243	243,735
Total cost = $2,751,619			$2,015,597	$284,155	$451,867

Alternative 2: Maintain 50 full-time regular direct workers and the present 120 FTE part-time employees. Subcontract jobs releasing 66 full-time regular employees. Subcontract cost, $1,100,000.

Cost	Days per Year (Exhibit 14.8)	Hours (Employees × Days × 8 hours)	Wages (Full-time, $4.45; Part-time, $4.03)	Fringe Benefits (Full-time, 17%; Part-time, 11%)	Administrative Cost (Full-time, 20%; Part-time, 25%)	Subcontract Cost
50 full-time employees	252	100,800	$ 448,560	$ 76,255	$ 89,712	$1,100,000
120 FTE part-time employees Subcontracting cost	252	241,920	974,938	107,243	243,735	
Total cost = $3,040,443			$1,423,498	$183,498	$333,447	$1,100,000

Alternative 3: Subcontract all jobs previously performed by 116 full-time regular employees. Subcontract cost $1,600,000. Subcontract all jobs previously performed by 120 full-time-equivalent part-time employees. Subcontract cost $1,850,000.

Cost	Subcontract Cost
0 full-time employees	
0 part-time employees	
Subcontract full-time jobs	$1,600,000
Subcontract part-time jobs	1,850,000
Total cost	$3,450,000

Exhibit 14.11   Comparison of Costs for All Three Alternatives

	Alternative 1: 116 Full-Time Direct Labor Employees, 120 Full-Time Equivalent Part-Time Employees	Alternative 2: 50 Full-Time Direct Labor Employees, 120 Full-Time Equivalent Part-Time Employees, Subcontracting	Alternative 3: Subcontracting Jobs Formerly Performed by 116 Direct Labor Full-Time Employees and 120 FTE Part-Time Employees
Wages	$2,015,597	$1,423,498	—
Fringe benefits	284,155	183,498	—
Administrative costs	451,867	333,447	—
Subcontracting, full-time jobs		1,100,000	$1,600,000
Subcontracting, part-time jobs			1,850,000
Total	$2,751,619	$3,040,443	$3,450,000

Level Scheduling

In this chapter we looked at four primary strategies for production planning: vary workforce size to meet demand, work overtime and undertime, vary inventory through excesses and shortages, and subcontract.

The just-in-time approach concentrates on keeping a *level production schedule.* A level schedule holds production constant over a period of time. It is something of a combination of the strategies we have mentioned here. For each period, it keeps the workforce constant and inventory low, and depends on demand to pull products through. Level production has a number of advantages:

1. The entire system can be planned to minimize inventory and work-in-process.
2. Product modifications are up-to-date because of the low amount of work-in-process.
3. There is a smooth flow throughout the production system.
4. Purchased items from vendors can be delivered when needed, and, in fact, often directly to the production line.

Toyota Motor Corporation, for example, creates a yearly production plan that shows the total number of cars to be made and sold. The aggregate production plan creates the system requirements to produce this total number with a level schedule. The secret to success in the Japanese level schedule is *production smoothing.* The aggregate plan is translated into monthly and daily schedules that *sequence* products through the production system. The procedure is essentially this: Two months in advance, the car types and quantities needed are established. This is converted to a detailed plan one month ahead. These quantities are given to subcontractors and vendors so that they can plan on meeting Toyota's needs. The monthly needs of various car types are then translated into daily schedules. For example, if 8,000 units of car type A are needed in one month, along with 6,000 type B, 4,000 type C, and 2,000 type D, and if we assume the line operates 20 days per month, then this would be translated to a daily output of 400, 300, 200, and 100, respectively. Further, this would be sequenced as four units of A, three of B, two of C, and one of D each 9.6 minutes of a two-shift day (960 minutes).

Each worker operates a number of machines, producing a sequence of products. To use this level scheduling technique,

1. Production should be repetitive (assembly-line format).
2. The system must contain excess capacity.
3. Output of the system must be fixed for a period of time (preferably a month).
4. There must be a smooth relationship among purchasing, marketing, and production.
5. The cost of carrying inventory must be high.
6. Equipment costs must be low.
7. The workforce must be multiskilled.

For more about level scheduling, see uniform plant loading in Chapter 8 on just-in-time production systems. Also see the discussion on mixed model line balancing in Chapter 10 on layout.

Mathematical Techniques

Linear Programming   Linear programming (LP) is appropriate to aggregate planning if the cost and variable relationships are linear and demand can be treated as deterministic. For the general case, the simplex method can be used. For the special case where hiring and firing are not considerations, the more easily formulated transportation method can be applied.

The application of an LP transportation matrix to aggregate planning is illustrated by the solved problem in Exhibit 14.12. This formulation is termed a *period model*

Production periods (sources)		Sales periods 1	2	3	4	Ending inventory	Unused inventory	Total capacity
Beginning inventory		50 [0]	[5]	[10]	[15]	[20]	[0]	50
1	Regular time	700 [50]	[55]	[60]	[65]	[70]	[0]	700
	Overtime	50 [75]	[80]	[85]	[90]	50 [95]	250 [0]	350
2	Regular time	X	700 [50]	[55]	[60]	[65]	[0]	700
	Overtime	X	100 [75]	[80]	[85]	150 [90]	[0]	250
3	Regular time	X	X	700 [50]	[55]	[60]	[0]	700
	Overtime	X	X	100 [75]	[80]	150 [85]	[0]	250
4	Regular time	X	X	X	700 [50]	[55]	[0]	700
	Overtime	X	X	X	100 [75]	150 [80]	[0]	250
Total requirements		800	800	800	800	500	250	3,950

Exhibit 14.12

Aggregate Planning by the Transportation Method of Linear Programming

Exhibit 14.13

Additional Factors
That Can Be Included
in the Transportation
Method for Aggregate
Planning

1. **Multiproduct production.** When more than one product shares common facilities, additional columns are included corresponding to each product. For each month, the number of columns will equal the number of products, and the cost entry in each cell will equal the cost for the corresponding product.

2. **Backordering.** The backorder time and the cost of backordering can be included by treating the assignments marked with an X in Exhibit 14.12 as feasible. If a product demanded in period 1 is delivered in period 2, this is equivalent to meeting period 1's demand with production in period 2. For, say, a $10 unit cost associated with such a backorder, the cost entry in the cell corresponding to period 2 regular time row and period 1 column will be $60 ($10 plus the $50 cost of regular-time production in period 2).

3. **Lost sales.** When stockouts are allowed and a part of the demand is not met, the firm incurs opportunity cost equal to the lost revenue. This can be included in the matrix by adding a "lost-sales" row for each period. The cost entry in the cell will be equal to lost revenue per unit.

4. **Perishability.** When perishability does not permit the sale of a product after it has been in stock for a certain period, the corresponding cells in the matrix are treated as infeasible. If the product in Exhibit 14.12 cannot be sold after it has been in stock for two periods, the cells occupying the intersection of period 1 rows and columns beyond period 3 will be infeasible.

5. **Subcontracting.** This can be included by adding a "subcontracting" row for each period. Cost values in each cell would be the unit cost to subcontract plus any inventory holding cost (incremented in the same fashion as regular time and overtime costs).

because it relates production demand to production capacity by periods.[5] In this case, there are four subperiods with demand forecast as 800 units in each. The total capacity available is 3,950 or an excess capacity of 750 (3,950 − 3,200). However, the bottom row of the matrix indicates a desire for 500 units in inventory at the end of the planning period, so unused capacity is reduced to 250. The left side of the matrix indicates the means by which production is made available over the planning period (that is, beginning inventory and regular and overtime work during each period). An X indicates a period where production cannot be backlogged. That is, you cannot produce in, say, Period 3 to meet demand in Period 2. (This is feasible if the situation allows back orders.) Finally, the costs in each cell are incremented by a holding cost of $5 for each period. Thus, if one produces on regular time in Period 1 to satisfy demand for Period 4, there will be a $15 holding cost. Overtime is, of course, more expensive to start with, but holding costs in this example are not affected by whether production is on regular time or overtime. The solution shown is an optimal one. The same allocation and evaluation methods (e.g., the stepping stone method) applied to the transportation problems in the Supplement to Chapter 7 can be applied to the period model.

The transportation matrix is remarkably versatile and can incorporate a variety of aggregate planning factors as described in Exhibit 14.13.

Observations on Linear Programming and Mathematical Techniques   Linear programming is appropriate when the cost and variable relationships are linear or can be cut into approximately linear segments. Regarding application of sophisticated aggregate planning techniques in industry (see Exhibit 14.14), only linear program-

---

[5] The analogy used here to the standard transportation problem is that (1) production periods are factories and sales periods are warehouses, (2) wages and holding costs are the transportation costs, and (3) ending inventory and unused capacity are dummy warehouses.

Summary Data on Aggregate Planning Methods

Methods	Assumptions	Techniques
1. Graphic and charting	None	Tests alternative plans through trial and error. Non-optimal, but simple to develop and easy to understand.
2. Simulation of aggregate plan	Existence of a computer-based production system	Tests aggregate plans developed by other methods.
3. Linear programming— transportation method	Linearity, constant workforce	Useful for the special case where hiring and firing costs are not a consideration. Gives optimal solution.
4. Linear programming— simplex method	Linearity	Can handle any number of variables but often is difficult to formulate. Gives optimal solution.
5. Linear decision rules*	Quadratic cost functions	Uses mathematically derived coefficients to specify production rates and workforce levels in a series of equations.
6. Management coefficients†	That managers are basically good decision makers	Uses statistical analysis of past decisions to make future decisions. Applies, therefore, to just one group of managers; non-optimal.
7. Search decision rules‡	Any type of cost structure	Uses pattern search procedure to find minimum points on total cost curves. Complicated to develop; non-optimal.

* Charles C. Holt et. al., *Planning Production, Inventories, and Work Force* (Englewood Cliffs, NJ: Prentice Hall, 1960).

† Edward H. Bowman and Robert B. Fetter, *Analysis for Production and Operations Management,* 3rd ed. (Homewood, IL: Richard D. Irwin, 1957).

‡ William H. Taubert, "A Search Decision Rule for the Aggregate Scheduling Problem," *Management Science,* February 1978, pp. B343–59.

ming has seen wide usage. Much of this is being done using the Solver Option in Microsoft Excel. The basic issue, in their view, is management's attitude toward models in general. Those companies where modeling is a way of life are likely to try the more sophisticated methods; in those where it is not, we would suspect that graphic and charting approaches would be used. Somewhere in the middle ground lie companies that have substantial experience in data processing and use the computer primarily for detailed scheduling. In these firms, we would expect to see experimentation with alternative cut-and-try plans in developing aggregate plans.

■ CONCLUSION

Remember that aggregate planning translates the corporate strategic and capacity plans into broad categories of workforce size, inventory quantity, and production levels. It does not do detailed planning. It is also useful to point out some practical considerations in aggregate planning:

First, demand variations are a fact of life so the planning system must include sufficient flexibility to cope with such variations. Flexibility can be achieved by developing alternative sources of supply, cross-training workers to handle a wide variety of orders, and engaging in more frequent replanning during high-demand periods.

Second, decision rules for production planning should be adhered to once they have been selected. However, they should be carefully analyzed prior to implementation by such checks as simulation of historical data to see what really would have happened if they had been in operation in the past.

SOLVED PROBLEM

Jason Enteprises (JE) is producing video telephones for the home market. Quality is not quite as good as it could be at this point, but the selling price is low and Jason can study market response while spending more time on R&D.

At this stage, however, JE needs to develop an aggregate production plan for the six months from January through June. As you can guess, you have been commissioned to create the plan. The following information should help you:

Demand and Working Days

	January	February	March	April	May	June	Totals
Demand forecast	500	600	650	800	900	800	4,250
Number of working days	22	19	21	21	22	20	125

Costs

Materials	$100.00/unit
Inventory holding cost	$10.00/unit/month
Marginal cost of stockout	$20.00/unit/month
Marginal cost of subcontracting	$100.00/unit ($200 subconstracting cost less $100 material savings)
Hiring and training cost	$50.00/worker
Layoff cost	$100.00/worker
Labor hours required	4/unit
Straight-line cost (first eight hours each day)	$12.50/hour
Overtime cost (time and a half)	$18.75/hour

Inventory

Beginning inventory	200 units
Safety stock required	0% of month demand

What is the cost of each of the following production strategies?
 a. Produce exactly to meet demand; vary workforce (assuming opening workforce equal to first month's requirements).
 b. Constant workforce; vary inventory and allow shortages only (assuming a starting workforce of 10).
 c. Constant workforce of 10; use subcontracting.

Solution

Aggregate Production Planning Requirements

	January	February	March	April	May	June	Total
Beginning inventory	200	0	0	0	0	0	
Demand forecast	500	600	650	800	900	800	
Safety stock (.25 × Demand forecast)	0	0	0	0	0	0	
Production requirement (Demand forecast + Safety stock − Beginning inventory)	300	600	650	800	900	800	
Ending inventory (Beginning inventory + Production requirement − Demand forecast)	0	0	0	0	0	0	

Production Plan 1: Exact Production; Vary Workforce

	January	February	March	April	May	June	Total
Production requirement	300	600	650	800	900	800	
Production hours required (Production requirement × 4 hr./unit)	1,200	2,400	2,600	3,200	3,600	3,200	
Working days per month	22	19	21	21	22	20	
Hours per month per worker (Working days × 8 hrs./day)	176	152	168	168	176	160	
Workers required (Production hours required/Hours per month per worker)	7	16	15	19	20	20	
New workers hired (assuming opening workforce equal to first month's requirement of 7 workers)	0	9	0	4	1	0	
Hiring cost (new workers hired × $50)	$0	$450	$0	$200	$50	$0	$700
Workers laid off	0	0	1	0	0	0	
Layoff cost (Workers laid off × $100)	$0	$0	$100	$0	$0	$0	$100
Straight time cost (Production hours required × $12.50)	$15,000	$30,000	$32,500	$40,000	$45,000	$40,000	$202,500

Total cost $203,300

Production Plan 2: Constant Workforce; Vary Inventory and Stockout

	January	February	March	April	May	June	Total
Beginning inventory	200	140	−80	−310	−690	−1150	
Working days per month	22	19	21	21	22	20	
Production hours available (Working days per month × 8 hr./day × 10 workers)*	1,760	1,520	1,680	1,680	1,760	1,600	
Actual production (Production hours available/4 hr./unit)	440	380	420	420	440	400	
Demand forecast	500	600	650	800	900	800	
Ending inventory (Beginning inventory + Actual production − Demand forecast)	140	−80	−310	−690	−1150	−1550	
Shortage cost (Units short × $20)	$0	$1,600	$6,200	$13,800	$23,000	$31,000	$75,600
Safety stock	0	0	0	0	0	0	
Units excess (Ending inventory − Safety stock; only if positive amount)	140	0	0	0	0	0	
Inventory cost (Units excess × $10)	$1,400	$0	$0	$0	$0	$0	$1,400
Straight time cost (Production hours available × $12.50)	$22,000	$19,000	$21,000	$21,000	$22,000	$20,000	$125,000

Total cost $202,000

*Assume a constant workforce of 10.

Production Plan 3: Constant Workforce; Subcontract

	January	February	March	April	May	June	Total
Production requirement	300	460[†]	650	800	900	800	
Working day per month	22	19	21	21	22	20	
Production hours available (Working day × 8 hrs./day × 10 workers)*	1,760	1,520	1,680	1,680	1,760	1,600	
Actual production (Production hours available/4 hr. per unit)	440	380	420	420	440	400	
Units subcontracted (Production requirements −Actual production)	0	220	230	380	460	400	
Subcontracting cost (Units subcontracted × $100)	$0	$8,000	$23,000	$38,000	$46,000	$40,000	$155,000
Straight time cost (Production hours available × $12.50)	$22,000	$19,000	$21,000	$21,000	$22,000	$20,000	$125,000

Total cost $280,000

*Assume a constant workforce of 10.

[†] 600−140 units of beginning inventory in February.

Summary

Plan Description	Hiring	Layoff	Sub-contract	Straight Time	Shortage	Excess Inventory	Total Cost
a. Exact production; vary workforce	$700	$100		$202,500			$203,300
b. Constant workforce; vary inventory and shortages				$125,000	$75,600	$1,400	$202,000
c. Constant workforce; subcontract			$155,000	$125,000			$280,000

REVIEW AND DISCUSSION QUESTIONS

1. What is the major difference between aggregate planning in manufacturing and aggregate planning in services?

2. What are the basic controllable variables of a production planning problem? What are the four major costs?

3. Distinguish between pure and mixed strategies in production planning.

4. Define level scheduling. How does it differ from the pure strategies in production planning?

5. Compare the best plans in the CA&J Company and the Tucson Parks and Recreation Department. What do they have in common?

6. Under which conditions would you have to use the general simplex method rather than the period model in aggregate planning?

7. How does forecast accuracy relate, in general, to the practical application of the aggregate planning models discussed in the chapter?

8. In which way does the time horizon chosen for an aggregate plan determine whether it is the best plan for the firm?

9. In the opening vignette, what did Dr. Sprague's mother and grandmother find so amusing about the wisdom being imparted about inventory "at the great MIT"?

PROBLEMS

1. For the Solved Problem, devise the least costly plan you can. You may choose your starting workforce level.

1. See SM.

2. Assume that Alan Industries has purchased Jason Enterprises (see the Solved Problem) and has instituted Japanese-style management in which workers are guaranteed a job for life (with no layoffs). Based on the data in Problem 1 (and additional information provided here), develop a production plan using the transportation method of linear programming. To keep things simple, plan for the first three months only and convert costs from hours to units in your model. Additional information: overtime is limited to 11 units per month per worker, and up to 5 units per month may be subcontracted at a cost of $100 per unit.

2. See SM for matrix.

✓ 3. Develop a production plan and calculate the annual cost for a firm whose demand forecast is fall, 10,000; winter, 8,000; spring, 7,000; summer, 12,000. Inventory at the beginning of fall is 500 units. At the beginning of fall you currently have 30 workers, but you plan to hire temporary workers at the beginning of summer and lay them off at the end of the summer. In addition, you have negotiated with the union an option to use the regular workforce on overtime during winter or spring if overtime is necessary to prevent stockouts at the end of those quarters. Overtime is *not* available during the fall. Relevant costs are: hiring $100 for each temp; layoff, $200 for each worker laid off; inventory holding, $5 per unit-quarter; back order, $10 per unit; straight time, $5 per hour; overtime, $8 per hour. Assume that the productivity is 0.5 units per worker hour, with eight hours per day and 60 days per season.

3. See SM. Total cost = $413,600.

4. Plan production for a four-month period: February through May. For February and March, you should produce to exact demand forecast. For April and May, you should use overtime and inventory with a stable workforce; *stable* means that the number of workers needed for March will be held constant through May. However, government constraints put a maximum of 5,000 hours of overtime labor per month in April and May (zero overtime in February and March). If demand exceeds supply, then back orders occur. There are 100 workers on January 1. You are given the following demand forecast: February, 80,000; March, 64,000; April, 100,000; May, 40,000. Productivity is four units per worker hour, eight hours per day, 20 days per month. Assume zero inventory on February 1. Costs are: hiring, $50 per new worker; layoff, $70 per worker laid off; inventory holding, $10 per unit-month; straight-time labor, $10 per hour; overtime, $15 per hour; back order, $20 per unit. Find the total cost of this plan.

4. See SM. Total cost = $1,158,000.

5. Plan production for the next year. The demand forecast is spring, 20,000; summer, 10,000; fall, 15,000; winter, 18,000. At the beginning of spring you have 70 workers and 1,000 units in inventory. The union contract specifies that you may layoff workers only once a year, at the beginning of summer. Also, you may hire new workers only at the end of summer to begin regular work in the fall. The number of workers laid off at the beginning of summer and the number hired at the end of summer should result in planned production levels for summer and fall that equal the demand forecasts for summer and fall, respectively. If demand exceeds supply, use overtime in spring only, which means that back orders could occur in winter. You are given these costs: hiring, $100 per new worker; layoff, $200 per worker laid off; holding, $20 per unit-quarter; back-order cost, $8 per unit; straight-time labor, $10 per hour; overtime, $15 per hour. Productivity is 0.5 units per worker hour, eight hours per day, 50 days per quarter. Find the total cost.

5. See SM. Total cost = $1,110,500.

✓ 6. DAT, Inc. needs to develop an aggregate plan for its product line. Relevant data are

6. *a.* Ending inventory = Safety stock.
b. Inventory cost includes forecast and safety stock.
c. Shortage cost is only based on the forecast. Total cost = $413,750.

Production time:	1 hour per unit	Beginning inventory:	500 units
Average labor cost:	$10 per hour	Safety stock:	One half month
Workweek:	5 days, 8 hours each day	Shortage cost:	$20 per unit per month
Days per month:	Assume 20 workdays per month	Carry cost:	$5 per unit per month

The forecast for 1998 is

Jan.	Feb.	Mar.	Apr.	May	June	July	Aug.	Sept.	Oct.	Nov.	Dec.
2,500	3,000	4,000	3,500	3,500	3,000	3,000	4,000	4,000	4,000	3,000	3,000

Management prefers to keep a constant workforce and production level, absorbing variations in demand through inventory excesses and shortages. Demand not met is carried over to the following month.

Develop an aggregate plan that will meet the demand and other conditions of the problem. Do not try to find the optimum; just find a good solution and state the procedure you might use to test for a better solution. Make any necessary assumptions.

7. See SM.

7. Old Pueblo Engineering Contractors creates six-month "rolling" schedules, which are recomputed monthly. For competitive reasons (they would need to divulge proprietary design criteria, methods, etc.), Old Pueblo does not subcontract. Therefore, its only options to meet customer requirements are (1) work on regular time; (2) work on overtime, which is limited to 30 percent of regular time; (3) do customers' work early, which would cost an additional $5 per hour per month; and (4) perform customers' work late, which would cost an additional $10 per hour per month penalty, as provided by their contract.

Old Pueblo has 25 engineers on its staff at an hourly rate of $30. Customers' hourly requirements for the six months from January to June are

January	February	March	April	May	June
5,000	4,000	6,000	6,000	5,000	4,000

Develop an aggregate plan using the transportation method of linear programming. Assume 20 working days in each month.

8. See SM.

8. Alan Industries is expanding its product line to include new models: Model A, Model B, and Model C. These are to be produced on the same productive equipment and the objective is to meet the demands for the three products using overtime where necessary. The demand forecast for the next four months, in required hours, is

Product	April	May	June	July
Model A	800	600	800	1,200
Model B	600	700	900	1,100
Model C	700	500	700	850

Because the products deteriorate rapidly, there is a high loss in quality and, consequently, a high carryover cost into subsequent periods. Each hour's production carried into future months costs $3 per productive hour of Model A, $4 for Model B, and $5 for Model C.

Production can take place during either regular working hours or during overtime. Regular time is paid at $4 when working on Model A, $5 for Model B, and $6 for Model C. Overtime premium is 50 percent.

The available production capacity for regular time and overtime is

	April	May	June	July
Regular time	1,500	1,300	1,800	1,700
Overtime	700	650	900	850

a. Set the problem up in matrix form and show appropriate costs.
b. Show a feasible solution.

9. Shoney Video Concepts produces a line of videodisc players to be linked to personal computers for video games. Videodiscs have much faster access time than tape. With such a computer/video link, the game becomes a very realistic experience. In a simple driving game where the joystick steers the vehicle, for example, rather than seeing computer graphics on the screen, the player is actually viewing a segment of a videodisc shot from a real moving vehicle. Depending on the action of the player (hitting a guard rail, for example), the disc moves virtually instantaneously to that segment and the player becomes part of an actual accident of real vehicles (staged, of course).

9. Many possible schedules exist. Monthly production (except July) = 580 units/month. Plan with 33 workers.

Shoney is trying to determine a production plan for the next 12 months. The main criterion for this plan is that the employment level is to be held constant over the period. Shoney is continuing in its R&D efforts to develop new applications and prefers not to cause any adverse feeling with the local workforce. For the same reasons, all employees should put in full workweeks, even if this is not the lowest-cost alternative. The forecast for the next 12 months is

Month	Forecast Demand	Month	Forecast Demand
January	600	July	200
February	800	August	200
March	900	September	300
April	600	October	700
May	400	November	800
June	300	December	900

Manufacturing cost is $200 per set, equally divided between materials and labor. Inventory storage cost is $5 per month. A shortage of sets results in lost sales and is estimated to cost an overall $20 per unit short.

The inventory on hand at the beginning of the planning period is 200 units. Ten labor hours are required per videodisc player. The workday is eight hours.

Develop an aggregate production schedule for the year using a constant workforce. For simplicity, assume 22 working days each month except July, when the plant closes down for three weeks' vacation (leaving seven working days). Make any assumptions you need.

10. Develop a production schedule to produce the exact production requirements by varying the workforce size for the following problem. Use the example in the chapter as a guide (Plan 1).

10. See SM.

The monthly forecast for Product X for January, February, and March is 1,000 1,500, and 1,200, respectively. Safety stock policy recommends that half of the forecast for that month be defined as safety stock. There are 22 working days in January, 19 in February, and 21 in March. Beginning inventory is 500 units.

Manufacturing cost is $200 per unit, storage cost is $3 per unit per month, standard pay rate is $6 per hour, overtime rate is $9 per hour, cost of stockout is $10 per unit per month, marginal cost of subcontracting is $10 per unit, hiring and training cost is $200 per worker, layoff cost is $300 per worker, and worker productivity is 0.1 units per hour. Assume that you start off with 50 workers and that they work 8 hours per day.

Case

XYZ Brokerage Firm

Consider the national operations group of the XYZ brokerage firm. The group, housed in an office building located in the Wall Street area, handles the transactions generated by registered representatives in more than 100 branch offices throughout the United States. As with all firms in the brokerage industry, XYZ's transactions must be settled within three trading days. This three-day period allows operations managers to smooth out the daily volume fluctuations.

Fundamental shifts in the stock market's volume and mix can occur overnight, so the operations manager must be prepared to handle extremely wide swings in volume. For example, on the strength of an international peace rumor, the number of transactions for XYZ rose from 5,600 one day to 12,200 the next.

Managers of XYZ, not unlike their counterparts in other firms, have trouble predicting volume. In fact, a random number generator can predict volume a week or even a month into the future almost as well as the managers can.

How do the operations managers in XYZ manage capacity when there are such wide swings? The answer differs according to the tasks and constraints facing each manager. Here's what two managers in the same firm might say:

Manager A: The capacity in our operation is currently 12,000 transactions per day. Of course, what we should gear up for is always a problem. For example, our volume this year ranged from 4,000 to 15,000 transactions per day. It's a good thing we have a high turnover rate; in periods of low volume, it helps us reduce our personnel without the morale problems caused by layoffs. [The labor turnover rate in this department is over 100 percent per year.]

Manager B: For any valid budgeting procedure, we need to estimate volume within 15 percent. Correlations between actual and expected volume in the brokerage industry have been so poor that I question the value of budgeting at all. I maintain our capacity at a level of 17,000 transactions per day.

Why the big difference in capacity management in the same firm? Manager A is in charge of the cashiering operation—the handling of certificates, checks, and cash. The personnel in cashiering are messengers, clerks, and supervisors. The equipment—file cabinets, vaults, calculators—is uncomplicated.

Manager B, however, is in charge of handling orders, an information processing function. The personnel are keypunch operators, EDP specialists, and systems analysts. The equipment is complex: computers, LANs, file servers, and communications devices that link national operations with the branches. The employees under B's control had performed their tasks manually until increased volume and a standardization of the information needs made it worthwhile to install computers.

Because the lead times required to increase the capacity of the information processing operation are long, however, and the incremental cost of the capacity to handle the last 5,000 transactions is low (only some extra peripheral equipment is needed), Manager B maintains the capacity to handle 17,000 transactions per day. He holds to this level even though the average number of daily transactions for any month has never been higher than 11,000 and the number of transactions for any one day has never been higher than 16,000.

Because a great deal of uncertainty about the future status of the stock certificate exists, the situation is completely different in cashiering. Attempts to automate the cashiering function to the degree reached by the order processing group have been thwarted because of the high risk of selecting a system not compatible with the future format of the stock certificate.

In other words, Manager A is tied to the "chase demand" strategy, and his counterpart, Manager B in the adjacent office, is locked into the "level capacity" strategy. However, each desires to incorporate more of the other's strategy into his own. A is developing a computerized system to handle the information processing requirements of cashiering; B is searching for some variable costs in the order processing operation that can be deleted in periods of low volume.

Questions

1. What appear to be the primary differences between the departments?

2. Do these differences eliminate certain strategy choices for either manager?

3. Which factors cause the current strategy to be desirable for each manager?

4. What are the mixed or subcontracting possibilities?

5. What are the problems associated with low standardization?

Source: W. E. Sasser, R. P. Olsen, and D. D. Wyckoff, *Management of Service Operations* © 1978, pp. 303–4. Reprinted by permission of Prentice Hall, Englewood Cliffs, New Jersey.

SELECTED BIBLIOGRAPHY

Fisher, Marshall L., Janice H. Hammond, Walter Obermeyer, and Anath Raman. "Making Supply Meet Demand in an Uncertain World." *Harvard Business Review* 72, no. 3 (May–June 1994) pp. 83–93.

Fisk, J. C., and J. P. Seagle. "Integration of Aggregate Planning with Resource Requirements Planning." *Production and Inventory Management,* 3rd quarter 1978, p. 87.

McLeavy, D., and S. Narasimhan. *Production Planning and Inventory Control.* Boston: Allyn & Bacon, 1985.

Monden, Yasuhiro. *Toyota Production System.* Atlanta, GA: Industrial Engineering and Management Press, 1983.

Plossl, G. W. *Production and Inventory Control: Principles and Techniques.* 2nd ed. Englewood Cliffs, NJ: Prentice Hall, 1985.

Silver, E. A., and R. Peterson. *Decision Systems for Inventory Management and Production Planning.* 2nd ed. New York: John Wiley & Sons, 1985.

Smith-Daniels, V., S. Scheweikhar, and D. Smith-Daniels. "Capacity Management in Health Care Services: Review and Future Research Directions." *Decision Sciences* 19 (1988), pp. 889–919.

Vollmann, T. E., W. L. Berry, and D. C. Whybark. *Manufacturing Planning and Control Systems.* 3rd ed. Homewood, IL: Richard D. Irwin, 1992.

Wight, Oliver W. *Production and Inventory Management in the Computer Age.* Boston: Cahners, 1974.

Chapter 15

Inventory Systems for Independent Demand

Chapter Outline

Definition of Inventory, 582

Purposes of Inventory, 583

Inventory Costs, 584

Independent versus Dependent Demand, 585

Inventory Systems, 585

    Classifying Models

Fixed-Order Quantity Models, 587

    Fixed-Order Quantity Model with Usage
      During Production Time

    Establishing Safety Stock Levels

    Fixed-Order Quantity Model with Specified
      Service Level

Fixed-Time Period Models, 599

    Fixed-Time Period Model with Specified
      Service Level

Special-Purpose Models, 601

Miscellaneous Systems and Issues, 605

    Three Simple Inventory Systems

    ABC Inventory Planning

    Inventory Accuracy and Cycle Counting

    Inventory Control in Services

Key Terms

Inventory

Raw Materials

Finished Products

Work in Process

Independent and Dependent
Demand

Fixed-Order Quantity Models
(Q Models)

Fixed-Time Period Models
(P Models)

Inventory Position

Safety Stock

Service Level

Price-Break Order Quantity

ABC Analysis

Optimal Replenishment System

Two-Bin System

One-Bin System

Inventory Accuracy

Cycle Counting

Stockkeeping Unit (SKU)

www Links

Ford Motor Company (http://ford.com)
General Motors (http://gm.com)

Wal-Mart (http://www.wal-mart.com)

GENERAL MOTORS CORP. IS OVERHAULING THE WAY IT gets vehicles to dealers in an effort to deliver the exact car that a customer wants in less than 24 hours.

Under the new program, which will affect all GM brands, large inventories of cars and light trucks will be kept in regional distribution centers across the U.S. rather than being parked on dealer lots, according to people close to the situation. That way, dealers who don't have a particular vehicle in stock will be able to receive it from a regional center in less than a day.

GM estimates that 35 percent of auto customers don't find the exact car they want on dealer lots and are forced to make a compromise; another 21 percent switch dealerships; and 11 percent end up going to a different automaker. The rest get the general kind of car they want.

The plan at GM is to greatly expand a program already under way at its Cadillac Division called Custom Xpress Delivery. GM used the Cadillac program—which began two years ago with a regional distribution center in Orlando, Florida—as a test to eliminate bugs from the system and make dealers comfortable with the changes. (*http://gm.com*)

Ford Motor Co. says it considered the regional distribution concept but chose instead to test a different concept that keeps its distribution system intact but changes its manufacturing system to reduce most special-order times to 15 to 20 days. Ford is testing the program with Mustangs and will expand it to other vehicles by the end of 1998. (*http://ford.com*) ●

Source: Gabriella Stern, "GM Expands Plan to Speed Cars to Buyers," *The Wall Street Journal,* October 21, 1996. Reprinted by permission of *The Wall Street Journal,* © 1996 Dow Jones & Company, Inc. All Rights Reserved Worldwide.

Question: Why would GM want to make this type of change in its distribution system? This is not an easy question to answer. It comes down to questions of service and cost. Which would be better, a bunch of little inventories scattered all over in different dealerships, or a few larger inventories from which customers can quickly receive cars? Mathematically, we can show that GM should be able to give better service and reduce its inventory investment with the distribution center approach. Are there other factors? Do customers want to see the different colors and options? Would customers rather go to a big dealership with a full variety of cars on the lot? It will be interesting to see if GM's approach works.

Consider this. The average cost of inventory across all manufacturing in the United States is 30 to 35 percent of its value. For example, if a firm carries an inventory of $20 million, it costs the firm more than $6 million per year. These costs are due to obsolescence, insurance, opportunity costs, and so forth. If the amount of inventory could be reduced to $10 million, for instance, the firm would save over $3 million, which goes directly to the bottom line. That is, the savings from reduced inventory shows as increased profit.

In this chapter, we present standard inventory models designed to help management keep the cost down while still meeting production and customer service requirements. Also included are special purpose models, such as price-break, as well as the ABC technique. In addition, we discuss inventory accuracy and show applications of the models in department stores and auto parts supply.

There are conflicting views concerning the teaching of classical inventory models. On one side, articles claim that economic order quantity (EOQ) models are invalid. The other side defends their use. We believe both sides are correct—from within their own arenas. While you must be careful in their application, there certainly are situations in manufacturing where EOQ models can be successfully used. Just-in-time manufacturing (JIT), for example, is based on the classical production-consumption inventory model discussed here. Classical models are quite valid for the many thousands of companies engaged in product and parts distribution.

Concerning JIT and safety stocks, recall that JIT does have safety stock! It shows up as the size of containers and the number of containers between each station in a production sequence. Further, all manufacturers that supply parts cannot have similar JIT schedules. A manufacturer using a JIT system utilizing twice-per-day deliveries by a supplier to the production line might be surprised that the supplier produces those supplies a month's worth at a time using an EOQ formula! How we compute inventory requirements depends on many factors—all methods are valid given the correct set of circumstances. Therefore, we should become familar with them all.

■ DEFINITION OF INVENTORY

Inventory

Vol. I "Manufacturing Inventory" and Vol. III "Washburn Guitar"

Raw Materials

Finished Products

Work in Process

Inventory is the stock of any item or resource used in an organization. An *inventory system* is the set of policies and controls that monitors levels of inventory and determines what levels should be maintained, when stock should be replenished, and how large orders should be.

By convention, manufacturing inventory generally refers to items that contribute to or become part of a firm's product output. Manufacturing inventory is typically classified into **raw materials, finished products, component parts, supplies,** and **work in process.** In services, inventory generally refers to the tangible goods to be sold and the supplies necessary to administer the service.

Inventory.
The longer it sits, the harder it is to move.

Despite what your balance sheet might tell you, inventory is no longer an asset. Today, big inventories can slow business and even bring it to a screeching halt. But you can keep your profits moving in the right direction by boosting productivity in your supply chain.

GE Information Services can help you shorten cycle times, improve inventory turns and eliminate out-of-stock occurrences. We'll show you how to link suppliers, manufacturers and distributors electronically so that your purchase orders and invoices are easily sent and tracked, auditing is greatly simplified and customer buying trends are instantly identified through point-of-sale data. For one large retailer, that meant reducing stock replenishment cycles from 3 days to 3 hours. Another one of our clients now gets spare parts to overseas distributors up to 10 days sooner.

You'd be surprised how much smoother your business will run after a tune-up by GE Information Services.
Productivity. It's All We Do.™

GE Information Services

For more information, please call 1-800-560-GEIS, or write GE Information Services, MC07F2, 401 N. Washington St., Rockville, MD 20850. Find us on the Internet at http://www.geis.com.

The basic purpose of inventory analysis in manufacturing and stockkeeping services is to specify (1) when items should be ordered and (2) how large the order should be. Many firms are tending to enter into longer-term relationships with vendors to supply their needs for perhaps the entire year. This changes the "when" and "how many to order" to "when" and "how many to deliver."

■ PURPOSES OF INVENTORY

All firms (including JIT operations) keep a supply of inventory for the following reasons:

1. To maintain independence of operations. A supply of materials at a work center allows that center flexibility in operations. For example, because there are costs for making each new production setup, this inventory allows management to reduce the number of setups.

Independence of workstations is desirable on assembly lines as well. The time that it takes to do identical operations will naturally vary from one unit to the next. Therefore, it is desirable to have a cushion of several parts within the workstation so that shorter performance times can compensate for longer performance times. This way the average output can be fairly stable.

2. To meet variation in product demand. If the demand for the product is known precisely, it may be possible (though not necessarily economical) to produce the product to exactly meet the demand. Usually, however, demand is not completely known, and a safety or buffer stock must be maintained to absorb variation.

3. To allow flexibility in production scheduling. A stock of inventory relieves the pressure on the production system to get the goods out. This causes longer lead times, which permit production planning for smoother flow and lower-cost operation through larger lot-size production. High setup costs, for example, favor the production of a larger number of units once the setup has been made.

4. To provide a safeguard for variation in raw material delivery time. When material is ordered from a vendor, delays can occur for a variety of reasons: a normal variation in shipping time, a shortage of material at the vendor's plant causing backlogs, an unexpected strike at the vendor's plant or at one of the shipping companies, a lost order, or a shipment of incorrect or defective material.

5. To take advantage of economic purchase-order size. There are costs to place an order: labor, phone calls, typing, postage, and so on. Therefore, the larger the size of each order, the fewer the number of orders that need be written. Also, shipping costs favor larger orders—the larger the shipment, the lower the per-unit cost.

For each of the preceding reasons (especially for items 3, 4, and 5), be aware that inventory is costly and large amounts are generally undesirable. Long cycle times are caused by large amounts of inventory and are undesirable as well.

■ INVENTORY COSTS

In making any decision that affects inventory size, the following costs must be considered.

1. Holding (or carrying) costs. This broad category includes the costs for storage facilities, handling, insurance, pilferage, breakage, obsolescence, depreciation, taxes, and the opportunity cost of capital. Obviously, high holding costs tend to favor low inventory levels and frequent replenishment.

2. Setup (or production change) costs. To make each different product involves obtaining the necessary materials, arranging specific equipment setups, filling out the required papers, appropriately charging time and materials, and moving out the previous stock of material.

If there were no costs or loss of time in changing from one product to another, many small lots would be produced. This would reduce inventory levels, with a resulting savings in cost. One challenge today is to try to reduce these setup costs to permit smaller lot sizes. (This is the goal of a JIT system.)

3. Ordering costs. These costs refer to the managerial and clerical costs to prepare the purchase or production order. Ordering costs include all the details, such as counting items and calculating order quantities. The costs associated with maintaining the system needed to track orders are also included in ordering costs.

4. Shortage costs. When the stock of an item is depleted, an order for that item must either wait until the stock is replenished or be canceled. There is a trade-off between carrying stock to satisfy demand and the costs resulting from stockout. This balance is sometimes difficult to obtain, because it may not be possible to estimate lost profits, the effects of lost customers, or lateness penalties. Frequently, the assumed shortage cost is little more than a guess, although it is usually possible to specify a range of such costs.

Establishing the correct quanity to order from vendors or the size of lots submitted to the firm's productive facilities involves a search for the minimum total cost resulting from the combined effects of four individual costs: holding costs, setup costs, ordering costs, and shortage costs. Of course, the timing of these orders is a critical factor that may impact inventory cost.

■ INDEPENDENT VERSUS DEPENDENT DEMAND

Independent and Dependent Demand

In inventory management, it is important to understand the difference between dependent and independent demand. The reason is that entire inventory systems are predicated on whether demand is derived from an end item or is related to the item itself.

Briefly, the distinction between **independent and dependent demand** is this: In independent demand, the demands for various items are unrelated to each other. For example, a workstation may produce many parts that are unrelated but meet some external demand requirement. In dependent demand, the need for any one item is a direct result of the need for some other item, usually a higher-level item of which it is part.

In concept, dependent demand is a relatively straightforward computational problem. Needed quantities of a dependent-demand item are simply computed, based on the number needed in each higher-level item in which it is used. For example, if an automobile company plans on producing 500 cars per day, then obviously it will need 2,000 wheels and tires (plus spares). The number of wheels and tires needed is *dependent* on the production levels and is not derived separately. The demand for cars, on the other hand, is *independent*—it comes from many sources external to the automobile firm and is not a part of other products; it is unrelated to the demand for other products.

To determine the quantities of independent items that must be produced, firms usually turn to their sales and market research departments. They use a variety of techniques, including customer surveys, forecasting techniques, and economic and sociological trends, as we discussed in Chapter 13 on forecasting. Because independent demand is uncertain, extra units must be carried in inventory. This chapter presents models to determine how many units need to be ordered, and how many extra units should be carried to provide a specified *service level* (percentage of independent demand) that the firm would like to satisfy immediately from stock on hand.

■ INVENTORY SYSTEMS

An inventory system provides the organizational structure and the operating policies for maintaining and controlling goods to be stocked. The system is responsible for ordering and receipt of goods: timing the order placement and keeping track of what has been ordered, how much, and from whom. The system must also follow up to answer such questions as: Has the supplier received the order? Has it been shipped? Are the dates correct? Are the procedures established for reordering or returning undesirable merchandise?

Classifying Models

There are two general types of inventory systems: **fixed-order quantity models** (also called the *economic order quantity,* EOQ, and **Q model**) and **fixed-time period models** (also referred to variously as the *periodic* system, *periodic review* system, *fixed-order interval* system, and **P model**).

The basic distinction is that fixed-order quantity models are "event triggered" and fixed-time period models are "time triggered." That is, a fixed-order quantity model initiates an order when the event of reaching a specified reorder level occurs. This event may take place at any time, depending on the demand for the items considered. In contrast, the fixed-time period model is limited to placing orders at the end of a predetermined time period; only the passage of time triggers the model.

To use the fixed-order quantity model (which places an order when the remaining inventory drops to a predetermined order point, R), the inventory remaining must be continually monitored. Thus, the fixed-order quantity model is a *perpetual* system, which requires that every time a withdrawal from inventory or an addition to inventory is made, records must be updated to ensure that the reorder point has or has not been reached. In a fixed-time period model counting takes place only at the review period. (We will discuss some variations of systems that combine features of both.)

Some additional differences that tend to influence the choice of systems are (also see Exhibit 15.1):

- The fixed-time period model has a larger average inventory because it must also protect against stockout during the review period, T; the fixed-quantity model has no review period.
- The fixed-order quantity model favors more expensive items because average inventory is lower.
- The fixed-order quantity model is more appropriate for important items such as critical repair parts because there is closer monitoring and therefore quicker response to potential stockout.
- The fixed-order quantity model requires more time to maintain because every addition or withdrawal is logged.

Exhibit 15.2 shows what occurs when each of the two models is put into use and becomes an operating system. As we can see, the fixed-order quantity system focuses

---

Exhibit 15.1   Fixed-Order Quantity and Fixed-Time Period Differences

Feature	*Q* **Fixed-Order Quantity Model**	*P* **Fixed-Time Period Model**
Order quantity	Q—constant (the same amount ordered each time)	q—variable (varies each time order is placed)
When to place order	R—when inventory position drops to the reorder level	T—when the review period arrives
Recordkeeping	Each time a withdrawal or addition is made	Counted only at review period
Size of inventory	Less than fixed-time period model	Larger than fixed-order quantity model
Time to maintain	Higher due to perpetual recordkeeping	
Type of items	Higher-priced, critical, or important items	

on order quantities and reorder points. Procedurally, each time a unit is taken out of stock, the withdrawal is logged and the amount remaining in inventory is immediately compared to the reorder point. If it has dropped to this point, an order for Q items is placed. If it has not, the system remains in an idle state until the next withdrawal.

In the fixed-time period system, a decision to place an order is made after the stock has been counted or reviewed. Whether an order is actually placed depends on the inventory position at that time.

FIXED-ORDER QUANTITY MODELS

Fixed-order quantity models attempt to determine the specific point, R, at which an order will be placed and the size of that order, Q. The order point, R, is always a specified number of units. An order of size Q is placed when the inventory available (currently in stock and on order) reaches the point R. **Inventory position** is defined as the on-hand plus on-order minus back ordered quantities. The solution to a fixed-order quantity model may stipulate something like this: When the inventory position drops to 36, place an order for 57 more units.

Inventory Position

The simplest models in this category occur when all aspects of the situation are known with certainty. If the annual demand for a product is 1,000 units, it is precisely 1,000—not 1,000 plus or minus 10 percent. The same is true for setup costs and

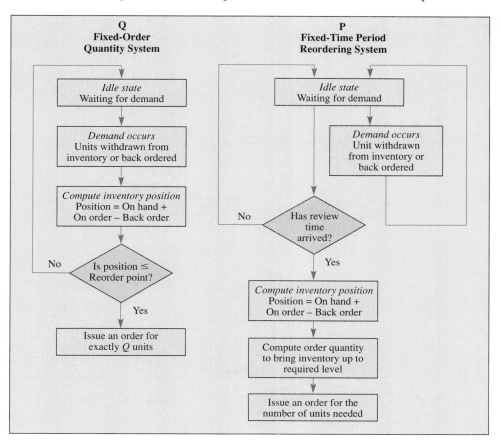

Exhibit 15.2

Comparison of Fixed-Order Quantity and Fixed-Time Period Reordering Inventory Systems holding costs. Although the assumption of complete certainty is rarely valid, it provides a good basis for our coverage of inventory models.

Exhibit 15.3 and the discussion about deriving the optimal order quantity are based on the following characteristics of the model. These assumptions are unrealistic, but they represent a starting point and allow us to use a simple example.

· Demand for the product is constant and uniform throughout the period.
· Lead time (time from ordering to receipt) is constant.
· Price per unit of product is constant.
· Inventory holding cost is based on average inventory.
· Ordering or setup costs are constant.
· All demands for the product will be satisfied. (No back orders are allowed.)

The "sawtooth effect" relating Q and R in Exhibit 15.3 shows that when the inventory position drops to point R, a reorder is placed. This order is received at the end of time period L, which does not vary in this model.

In constructing any inventory model, the first step is to develop a functional relationship between the variables of interest and the measure of effectiveness. In this case, because we are concerned with cost, the following equation pertains:

$$\begin{array}{ccccc} \text{Total} & = & \text{Annual} & + & \text{Annual} & + & \text{Annual} \\ \text{annual cost} & & \text{purchase cost} & & \text{ordering cost} & & \text{holding cost} \end{array}$$

or

$$TC = DC + \frac{D}{Q}S + \frac{Q}{2}H \tag{15.1}$$

Exhibit 15.3

Basic Fixed-Order Quantity Model

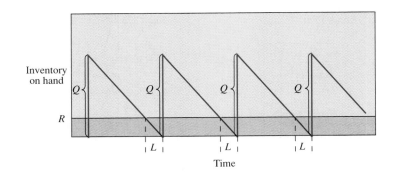

Exhibit 15.4

Annual Product Costs, Based on Size of the Order

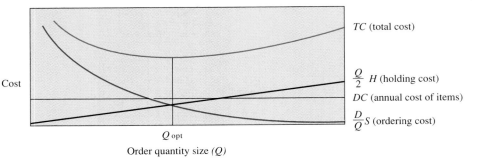

where

TC = Total annual cost
D = Demand (annual)
C = Cost per unit
Q = Quantity to be ordered (The optimum amount is termed the *economic order quantity*—EOQ—or $Q_{opt.}$)
S = Setup cost or cost of placing an order
R = Reorder point
L = Lead time
H = Annual holding and storage cost per unit of average inventory (Often, holding cost is taken as a percentage of the cost of the item, such as $H = iC$ where i is the percent carrying cost.)

On the right side of the equation, DC is the annual purchase cost for the units, $(D/Q)S$ is the annual ordering cost (the actual number of orders placed, D/Q, times the cost of each order, S), and $(Q/2)H$ is the annual holding cost (the average inventory, $Q/2$, times the cost per unit for holding and storage, H). These cost relationships are graphed in Exhibit 15.4.

The second step in model development is to find that order quantity Q_{opt}, at which total cost is a minimum. In Exhibit 15.4, the total cost is minimum at the point where the slope of the curve is zero. Using calculus, we take the derivative of total cost with respect to Q and set this equal to zero. For the basic model considered here, the calculations are

$$TC = DC + \frac{D}{Q}S + \frac{Q}{2}H$$

$$\frac{dTC}{dQ} = 0 + \left(\frac{-DS}{Q^2}\right) + \frac{H}{2} = 0$$

$$Q_{opt} = \sqrt{\frac{2DS}{H}} \qquad (15.2)$$

Because this simple model assumes constant demand and lead time, no safety stock is necessary, and the reorder point, R, is simply

$$R = \bar{d}L \qquad (15.3)$$

where

$\bar{d}$ = Average daily demand (constant)
L = Lead time in days (constant)

■ **example 15.1** *Economic Order Quantity and Reorder Point* Find the economic order quantity and the reorder point, given

Annual demand (D) = 1,000 units
Average daily demand (d) = 1,000/365
Ordering cost (S) = \$5 per order
Holding cost (H) = \$1.25 per unit per year
Lead time (L) = 5 days
Cost per unit (C) = \$12.50

What quantity should be ordered?

solution   The optimal order quantity is

$$Q_{opt} = \sqrt{\frac{2DS}{H}} = \sqrt{\frac{2(1,000)5}{1.25}} = \sqrt{8,000} = 89.4 \text{ units}$$

The reorder point is

$$R = \bar{d}L = \frac{1,000}{365}(5) = 13.7 \text{ units}$$

Rounding to the nearest unit, the inventory policy is as follows: When the inventory position drops to 14, place an order for 89 more.

The total annual cost will be

$$TC = DC + \frac{D}{Q}S + \frac{Q}{2}H$$

$$= 1,000(12.50) + \frac{1,000}{89}(5) + \frac{89}{2}(1.25)$$

$$= \$12,611.81$$

Note that in this example, the purchase cost of the units was not required to determine the order quantity and the reorder point because the cost was constant and unrelated to order size. ▪

Fixed-Order Quantity Model with Usage During Production Time

Equation 15.1 assumed that the quantity ordered would be received in one lot, but frequently this is not the case. In many situations, production of an inventory item and usage of that item take place simultaneously. This is particularly true where one part of a production system acts as a supplier to another part. For example, while aluminum extrusions are being made to fill an order for aluminum windows, the extrusions are cut and assembled before the entire extrusion order is completed. Also, companies are beginning to enter longer-term arrangements with suppliers. Under such contracts, a single order may cover product or material needs over a six-month or year period, with the vendor making deliveries weekly or sometimes even more frequently. If we let d denote a constant demand rate for some item going into production and let p be the production rate of that process that uses the item, we may develop the total cost equation[1]

$$TC = DC + \frac{D}{Q}S + \frac{(p-d)QH}{2p}$$

Again differentiating with respect to Q and setting the equation equal to zero, we obtain

$$Q_{opt} = \sqrt{\frac{2DS}{H} \cdot \frac{p}{(p-d)}} \tag{15.4}$$

This model is shown in Exhibit 15.5. We can see that the number of units on hand is always less than the order quantity, Q.

---

[1] Clearly, the production rate must exceed the rate of usage. Otherwise, Q would be infinite, resulting in continual production.

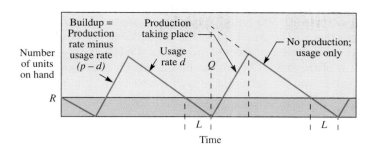

Exhibit 15.5

Fixed-Order Quantity
Model with Usage
during Production
Time

■ **example 15.2** *Optimal Lot Size* Product X is a standard item in a firm's inventory. Final assembly of the product is performed on an assembly line that is in operation every day. One component of product X (call it component X_1) is produced in another department. This department, when it produces X_1, does so at the rate of 100 units per day. The assembly line uses component X_1 at the rate of 40 units per day.

Given the following data, what is the optimal lot size for production of component X_1?

> Daily usage rate (d) = 40 units
> Annual demand (D) = 10,000 (40 units × 250 working days)
> Daily production (p) = 100 units
> Cost for production setup (S) = \$50
> Annual holding cost (H) = \$0.50 per unit
> Cost of component $X_1 (C)$ = \$7 each
> Lead time (L) = 7 days

solution The optimal order quantity and the reorder point are calculated as follows:

$$Q_{opt} = \sqrt{\frac{2DS}{H} \cdot \frac{p}{p-d}} = \sqrt{\frac{2(10,000)50}{0.50} \cdot \frac{100}{100-40}} = 1,826 \text{ units}$$

$$R = dL = 40(7) = 280 \text{ units}$$

This states that an order for 1,826 units of component X_1 should be placed when the stock drops to 280 units.

At 100 units per day, this run would take 18.26 days and provide a 45.65-day supply for the assembly line (1,826/40). Theoretically, the department would be occupied with other work for the 27.39 days when component X_1 is not being produced. ■

Establishing Safety Stock Levels

The previous model assumed that demand was constant and known. In the majority of cases, though, demand is not constant but varies from day to day. Safety stock must therefore be maintained to provide some level of protection against stockouts. **Safety stock** can be defined as the amount of inventory carried in addition to the expected demand. In a normal distribution, this would be the mean. For example, if our average monthly demand is 100 units and we expect next month to be the same, if we carry 120 units, then we have 20 units of safety stock.

The general literature on the subject of safety stocks contains two approaches relating to the demand for the inventory that is to be protected. First is the *probability* that demand will exceed some specified amount. For example, an objective may be something like "Set the safety stock level so that there will only be a 5 percent chance

Safety Stock

that demand will exceed 300 units." The second approach deals with the *expected number* of units that will be out of stock. For example, an objective might be to set the inventory level so that we can meet 95 percent of the orders for the unit (or be out of stock 5 percent of the time). Again, the first approach deals with the *probability* of exceeding a value, and the second approach is concerned the *how many* units were short.

The Probability Approach   Using the probability criterion to determine safety stock is pretty simple. With the models described in this chapter, we assume that the demand over a period of time is normally distributed with a mean and a standard deviation. *Again, remember that this approach only considers the probability of running out of stock, not how many units we are short.* To determine the probability of stocking out over the time period, we can simply plot a normal distribution for the expected demand and note where the amount we have on hand lies on the curve.

Let's take a few simple examples to illustrate this. Let's say we expect demand to be 100 units over the next month, and we know that the standard deviation is 20 units. If we go into the month with just 100 units, we know that our probability of stocking out is 50 percent. Half of the months we would expect demand to be greater than 100 units; half of the months, we would expect it to be less than 100 units. Taking this further, if we ordered a month's worth of inventory of 100 units at a time and received it at the beginning of the month, over the long run we would expect to run out of inventory in 6 months of the year.

If we found that running out this often was not acceptable, we would want to carry extra inventory to reduce this risk of stocking out. One idea might be to carry an extra 20 units of inventory for the item. In this case, we would still order a month's worth of inventory at a time, but we would schedule delivery to arrive when we still have 20 units remaining in inventory. This would give us that little cushion of safety stock to reduce the probability of stocking out. If the standard deviation associated with our demand were 20 units, we would then be carrying one standard deviation worth of safety stock. Looking at the Standard Normal Distribution (Appendix D), and moving one standard deviation to the right of the mean, gives a probability of .8413 (from the table we get .3413 and we need to add .5 to this). So, approximately 84 percent of the time we would not expect to stock out, and 16 percent of the time we would. Now if we order every month, we would expect to stock out approximately 2 months per year (.16 × 12 = 1.92).

It is common for companies using this approach to set the probability of not stocking out at 95 percent. This would mean that we would carry about 1.64 standard deviations of safety stock, or 33 units (1.64 × 20 = 32.8) for our example. Once again, keep in mind that this does not mean that we would order 33 units extra each month. Rather, it means that we would still order a month's worth each time, but we would schedule the receipt so that we could expect to have 33 units in inventory when the order arrives. In this case, we would expect to stock-out approximately .6 months per year, or that stock-outs would occur in 1 month of every 20 months.

The Service Level Approach   Using an analogy, we will convey the shortcomings in using the probability approach to determine safety stock. Suppose the weather forecaster predicts rain tomorrow. Are you satisfied with the yes/no (rain/no rain) prediction—or would you prefer to know if the prediction is for a light sprinkle or for heavy rains with possible flooding? If it happens to be winter, would you be satisfied with a simple forecast of snow (with an associated probability of being correct)? Wouldn't you rather know whether this is a light snow flurry or a heavy snowfall resulting in hazardous driving and, probably, closed airports? That is the same idea for our inventory model. We are interested not only in whether we will be out of stock (possibility of rain or snow) but also in how many units we will be short (how much total rain or snow).

We are now ready to define service level: **Service level** refers to the number of units demanded that can be supplied from stock currently on hand. For example, if annual demand for an item is 1,000 units, a 95 percent service level means that 950 can be supplied immediately from stock and 50 units are short. (This concept assumes that orders are small and randomly distributed—one or several at a time. This model would not apply, for example, where the entire annual demand might be sold to just a few customers since we need enough data points to approximate a normal distribution.)

Service Level

The discussion in this section on service levels is based on a statistical concept known as Expected z or $E(z)$. $E(z)$ is the expected number of units short during each lead time. Here, assume that the demand is normally distributed.

To compute service level, we need to know *how many* units are short. For example, assume that the average weekly demand for an item is 100 units with a standard deviation of 10 units. If we have 110 units at the beginning of a week, how many will we expect to be short? To do this, we need to summarize the probability that 111 are demanded (1 short), the probability that 112 are demanded (2 short), plus the probability that 113 are demanded (3 short), and so on. This summary would give us the number of units we would expect to be short by stocking 110 units.

While the concept is simple, the equations are impractical to solve by hand. Fortunately, Robert Brown has provided tables of expected values (Exhibit 15.6).

Exhibit 15.7 plots the numbers in Exhibit 15.6. This shows the expected number of units short each order cycle (whether it is a periodic model P or an order quantity model Q). Using our previous example, suppose the average demand for an item was 100 units and the standard deviation of that demand was 10 units. In Exhibit 15.7, we must multiply the vertical axis by 10 because the chart is based on a standard deviation of one unit. Reading from either the numbers in Exhibit 15.6 or the plot of these numbers in Exhibit 15.7, at $z = 1$, if we carry a safety stock of 10 units (one standard deviation), we should expect to be out of stock just .83 units total (.083 times 10 because the exhibits are based on a standard deviation of 1). Because normal demand during the period is 100 and we were only short .83 (less than one unit), our service level is 100 − .83, or 99.17 percent.

If in the same example we did not carry any safety stock (i.e., order just 100 units), we would be short 3.99 units (.399 times 10). Our service level would be 100 − 3.99, or 96.01 percent.

Again, from our same example, note that if we have a safety stock of minus one standard deviation, this just says to have 90 units at the beginning of the week rather than 100. At 90 units we would run short 10.83 units and our service level would be 89.17 percent. Carrying this further, if we have 80 units at the beginning of the week, we will be short 20.08 units; if we have 70 units, we will be short 30 units; and so on. Because these exhibits are based on a standard deviation of one unit, all we need to do is to multiply the figures by the actual data to be used. Another example, if demand was 550 units and the standard deviation was 36 units, then having 568 units would give a .5 standard deviation of safety stock with an expected number of units short of .198 × 36 = 7.128 units. The service level would therefore be (550 − 7.128)/550 = 98.7 percent.

Expected Number Out of Stock versus the Standard Deviation (This table is normalized to a standard deviation of 1.)

$E(z)$	z	$E(z)$	z	$E(z)$	z	$E(z)$	z
4.500	−4.50	2.205	−2.20	0.399	0.00	0.004	2.30
4.400	−4.40	2.106	−2.10	0.351	0.10	0.003	2.40
4.300	−4.30	2.008	−2.00	0.307	0.20	0.002	2.50
4.200	−4.20	1.911	−1.90	0.267	0.30	0.001	2.60
4.100	−4.10	1.814	−1.80	0.230	0.40	0.001	2.70
4.000	−4.00	1.718	−1.70	0.198	0.50	0.001	2.80
3.900	−3.90	1.623	−1.60	0.169	0.60	0.001	2.90
3.800	−3.80	1.529	−1.50	0.143	0.70	0.000	3.00
3.700	−3.70	1.437	−1.40	0.120	0.80	0.000	3.10
3.600	−3.60	1.346	−1.30	0.100	0.90	0.000	3.20
3.500	−3.50	1.256	−1.20	0.083	1.00	0.000	3.30
3.400	−3.40	1.169	−1.10	0.069	1.10	0.000	3.40
3.300	−3.30	1.083	−1.00	0.056	1.20	0.000	3.50
3.200	−3.20	1.000	−0.90	0.046	1.30	0.000	3.60
3.100	−3.10	0.920	−0.80	0.037	1.40	0.000	3.70
3.000	−3.00	0.843	−0.70	0.029	1.50	0.000	3.80
2.901	−2.90	0.769	−0.60	0.023	1.60	0.000	3.90
2.801	−2.80	0.698	−0.50	0.018	1.70	0.000	4.00
2.701	−2.70	0.630	−0.40	0.014	1.80	0.000	4.10
2.601	−2.60	0.567	−0.30	0.011	1.90	0.000	4.20
2.502	−2.50	0.507	−0.20	0.008	2.00	0.000	4.30
2.403	−2.40	0.451	−0.10	0.006	2.10	0.000	4.40
2.303	−2.30	0.399	0.00	0.005	2.20	0.000	4.50

z = Number of standard deviations of safety stock

$E(z)$ = Expected number of units short

Source: Revised from Robert G. Brown, *Decision Rules for Inventory Management* (New York: Holt, Rinehart & Winston, 1967), pp. 95–103.

Expected Numbers Out of Stock per Order Cycle

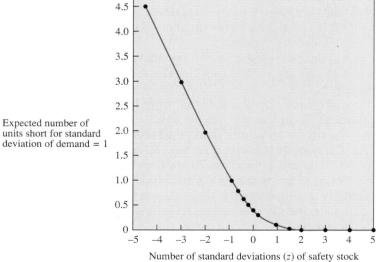

Expected number of units short for standard deviation of demand = 1

Number of standard deviations (z) of safety stock

To summarize the preceding discussion of the service level approach, what we did was simply convert the standard deviation associated with the demand to a base of one unit. Then, using Exhibit 15.6, we calculated the planned number of units short for a particular service level. In the case of the probability of stocking out approach, we just used the standard normal distribution directly (Appendix D) to determine the number of standard deviations of safety stock needed to reach our desired probability. The major advantage of the service level approach is that safety stock is determined based on the actual number of units we desire to deliver to our customers.

We will carry the explanations further within the context of two basic model types, the fixed-order quantity model and the fixed-time period model. We will cover important questions relating to how to design inventory control systems that provide reasonable levels of customer service while minimizing inventory investment. In our examples, we will demonstrate the service level approach to calculating safety stock. For those who prefer to use the probability of stockout approach, commonly used z values are 1.64 for 95 percent probability and 2.0 for 98 percent probability.

Fixed-Order Quantity Model with Specified Service Level

A fixed-order quantity system perpetually monitors the inventory level and places a new order when stock reaches some level, R. The danger of stockout in this model occurs only during the lead time, between the time an order is placed and the time it is received. As shown in Exhibit 15.8, an order is placed when the inventory position drops to the reorder point, R. During this lead time (L), a range of demands is possible. This range is determined either from an analysis of past demand data or from an estimate (if past data are not available).

The amount of safety stock depends on the service level desired, as previously discussed. The quantity to be ordered, Q, is calculated in the usual way considering the demand, shortage cost, ordering cost, holding cost, and so forth. A fixed-order quantity model can be used to compute Q such as the simple Q_{opt} model previously discussed. The reorder point is then set to cover the expected demand during the lead time plus a safety stock determined by the desired service level. Thus, *the key difference between a fixed-order quantity model, where demand is known and one where demand is uncertain is in computing the reorder point. The order quantity is the same in both cases.* The uncertainty element is taken into account in the safety stock.

The reorder point is

$$R = \bar{d}L + z\sigma_L \qquad (15.5)$$

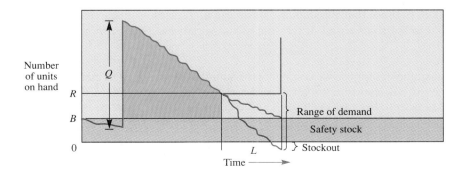

Exhibit 15.8

Fixed-Order Quantity Model

where

$\quad\quad R$ = Reorder point in units
$\quad\quad \bar{d}$ = Average daily demand
$\quad\quad L$ = Lead time in days (time between placing an order and receiving the items)
$\quad\quad z$ = Number of standard deviations for a specified service level
$\quad\quad \sigma_L$ = Standard deviation of usage during lead time

The term $z\sigma_L$ is the amount of safety stock. Note that if safety stock is positive, the effect is to place a reorder sooner. That is, R without safety stock is simply the average demand during the lead time. If lead time usage was expected to be 20, for example, and safety stock was computed to be 5 units, then the order would be placed sooner, when 25 units remained. The greater the safety stock, the sooner the order is placed.

Computing $\bar{d}$, σ_L and z   Demand during the lead time to receive a replenishment order is really an estimate or forecast of what is expected. It may be a single number (for example, if the lead time is a month, the demand may be taken as the previous year's demand divided by 12), or it may be a summation of expected demands over the lead time (such as the sum of daily demands over a 30-day lead time). For the daily demand situation, d can be a forecasted demand using any of the models in Chapter 13 on forecasting. For example, if a 30-day period was used to calculate d, then a simple average would be

$$\bar{d} = \frac{\sum\limits_{i=1}^{n} d_i}{n} \quad\quad\quad (15.6)$$

$$= \frac{\sum\limits_{i=1}^{30} d_i}{30}$$

where n is the number of days.

The standard deviation of the daily demand is:

$$\sigma_d = \sqrt{\frac{\sum\limits_{i=1}^{n} (d_i - \bar{d})^2}{n}} \quad\quad\quad (15.7)$$

$$= \sqrt{\frac{\sum\limits_{i=1}^{30} (d_i - \bar{d})^2}{30}}$$

Because σ_d refers to one day, if lead time extends over several days we can use the statistical premise that the standard deviation of a series of independent occurrences is equal to the square root of the sum of the variances. That is, in general,

$$\sigma_s = \sqrt{\sigma_1^2 + \sigma_2^2 + \cdots + \sigma_i^2} \quad\quad\quad (15.8)$$

For example, suppose we computed the standard deviation of demand to be 10 units per day. If our lead time to get an order is five days, the standard deviation for the five-day period, because each day can be considered independent, is

$$\sigma_L = \sqrt{(10)^2 + (10)^2 + (10)^2 + (10)^2 + (10)^2} = 22.36$$

Next, we need to compute z. We do this by computing $E(z)$, the number of units short that meets our desired service level, and then looking this up in Exhibit 15.6 for the appropriate z.

Suppose we wanted a service level of P. (For example, P might be .95.) In the course of a year we would be short $(1 - P)D$ units, or $0.05D$, where D is the annual demand. If we ordered Q units each time, we would be placing D/Q orders per year. Exhibit 15.6 is based on $\sigma_L = 1$. Therefore, any $E(z)$ that we read from the table needs to be multiplied by σ_L if it is other than 1. The expected number of units short per order, therefore, is $E(z)\sigma_L$. For the year, the expected number of units short is $E(z)\sigma_L D/Q$. Stated again, we have,

$$\begin{array}{ccccccc} \text{Percentage} & & \text{Annual} & & \text{Number short} & & \text{Number of} \\ \text{short} & \times & \text{demand} & = & \text{per order} & \times & \text{orders per year} \\[6pt] (1 - P) & \times & D & = & E(z)\sigma_L & \times & \dfrac{D}{Q} \end{array}$$

which simplifies to

$$E(z) = \frac{(1 - P)Q}{\sigma_L} \tag{15.9}$$

where

P = Service level desired (such as satisfying 95 percent expressed as the fraction .95 of demand from items in stock)

$(1 - P)$ = Fraction of demand unsatisfied

D = Annual demand

σ_L = Standard deviation of demand during lead time

Q = Economic order quantity calculated in the usual way (such as $Q = \sqrt{2DS/H}$)

$E(z)$ = Expected number of units short each order cycle from a normalized table where $\sigma = 1$

Note that D (annual demand) drops out of Equation 15.9. This is because $E(z)$ is the number short *each order cycle*. (There are D/Q cycles per year.)

We now compare two examples. The difference between them is that in the first, the variation in demand is stated in terms of standard deviation over the entire lead time, while in the second, it is stated in terms of standard deviation per day.

■ **example 15.3** *Economic Order Quantity*   Consider an economic order quantity case where annual demand $D = 1,000$ units, economic order quantity $Q = 200$ units, the desired service level $P = .95$, the standard deviation of demand during lead time $\sigma_L = 25$ units, and lead time $L = 15$ days. Determine the reorder point.

solution   In our example, $\bar{d} = 4$ (1,000 over a 250-workday year), and lead time is 15 days. We use the equation

$$R = \bar{d}\,L + z\sigma_L$$
$$= 4(15) + z(25)$$

To find z, we use equation 15.9 above for $E(z)$ and look this value up in the table. Our problem data gave us $Q = 200$, service level $P = .95$, and standard deviation of demand during lead time $= 25$. Therefore,

$$E(z) = \frac{(1 - P)Q}{\sigma_L} = \frac{(1 - .95)200}{25} = .4$$

From Exhibit 15.6 and $E(z) = .4$, we find $z = 0$. Completing the solution for R, we find

$$R = 4(15) + z(25) = 60 + 0(25) = 60 \text{ units}$$

This says that when the stock on hand gets down to 60 units, order 200 more.

Just to satisfy any skepticism, we can calculate the number of units demanded that are actually met per year to see if it really is 95 percent. $E(z)$ is the expected number short on each order based on a standard deviation of 1. The number short on each order for our problem is $E(z)\sigma_L = .4(25) = 10$. Because there are five orders per year $(1,000/200)$, this results in 50 units short. This verifies our achievement of a 95 percent service level, because 950 out of 1,000 demand were filled from stock. ■

■ **example I5.4**   *Order Quantity and Reorder Point*   Daily demand for a certain product is normally distributed with a mean of 60 and standard deviation of 7. The source of supply is reliable and maintains a constant lead time of six days. The cost of placing the order is $10 and annual holding costs are $0.50 per unit. There are no stockout costs, and unfilled orders are filled as soon as the order arrives. Assume sales occur over the entire year. Find the order quantity and reorder point to satisfy 95 percent of the customers from stock on hand.

solution   In this problem we need to calculate the order quantity Q as well as the reorder point R.

$$\bar{d} = 60 \qquad S = \$10$$
$$\sigma_d = 7 \qquad H = \$0.50$$
$$D = 60(365) \qquad L = 6$$

The optimal order quantity is

$$Q_{\text{opt}} = \sqrt{\frac{2DS}{H}} = \sqrt{\frac{2(60)365(10)}{0.50}} = \sqrt{876,000} = 936 \text{ units}$$

To compute the reorder point, we need to calculate the amount of product used during the lead time and add this to the safety stock.

The standard deviation of demand during the lead time of six days is calculated from the variance of the individual days. Because each day's demand is independent[2]

$$\sigma_L = \sqrt{\sum_{i=1}^{L} \sigma_{d_i}^2} = \sqrt{6(7)^2} = 17.2$$

Next we need to know how many standard deviations are needed for a specified service level. As previously defined,

$$E(z) = \frac{Q(1 - P)}{\sigma_L}$$

Therefore

$$E(z) = \frac{936(1 - .95)}{17.2} = 2.721$$

From Exhibit 15.6, interpolating at $E(z) = 2.721$, $z = -2.72$. The reorder point is

---

[2] As previously discussed, the standard deviation of a sum of independent variables equals the square root of the sum of the variances.

$$R = \bar{d}L + z\sigma_L = 60(6) + (-2.72)(17.2) = 313.2 \text{ units}$$

To summarize the policy derived in this example, an order for 936 units is placed whenever the number of units remaining in inventory drops to 313.

Note that in this case the safety stock $(z\sigma_L)$ turns out to be negative. This means that if we had ordered the order quantity ($Q = 936$) when our inventory position dropped to the expected demand during lead time ($\bar{d}L = 360$), we would have had a higher service level than we wanted. To get down to 95 percent service, we need to create more shortages by ordering at a slightly lower order point (313). While this may seem strange, it is nevertheless true. In this case, we actually do expect to stock out on each order cycle.

We can verify our service level in this example by noting that we would place 23.4 orders per year [60(365)/936]. Each period would experience 46.8 units out of stock (2.72 × 17.2). Thus, we would be out of stock 1,095 units per year (46.8 × 23.4). Service level, therefore, is 0.95 as we intended [(21,900 − 1,095)/21,900]. ■

As shown in these two examples, this technique of determining safety stock levels is relatively simple and straightforward. It allows us to control inventory to meet our desired service levels.

■ FIXED-TIME PERIOD MODELS

In a fixed-time period system, inventory is counted only at particular times, such as every week or every month. Counting inventory and placing orders on a periodic basis is desirable in situations such as when vendors make routine visits to customers and take orders for their complete line of products, or when buyers want to combine orders to save transportation costs. Other firms operate on a fixed-time period to facilitate planning their inventory count; for example, Distributor X calls every two weeks and employees know that all Distributor X's product must be counted.

Fixed-time period models generate order quantities that vary from period to period, depending on the usage rates. These generally require a higher level of safety stock than a fixed-order quantity system. The fixed-order quantity system assumes continual counting of inventory on hand, with an order immediately placed when the reorder point is reached. In contrast, the standard fixed-time period models assume that inventory is counted only at the time specified for review. It is possible that some large demand will draw the stock down to zero right after an order is placed. This condition could go unnoticed until the next review period. Then the new order, when placed, still takes time to arrive. Thus, it is possible to be out of stock throughout the entire review period, T, and order lead time, L. Safety stock, therefore, must protect us against stockouts during the review period itself as well as during the lead time from order placement to order receipt.

Fixed-Time Period Model with Specified Service Level

In a fixed-time period system, reorders are placed at the time of review (T), and the safety stock that must be reordered is

$$\text{Safety stock} = z\sigma_{T+L}$$

Exhibit 15.9 shows a fixed-time period system with a review cycle of T and a constant lead time of L. In this case, demand is randomly distributed about a mean $\bar{d}$.

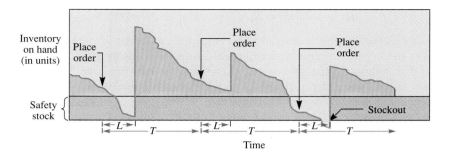

The quantity to order, q, is

$$\text{Order quantity} = \text{Average demand over the vulnerable period} + \text{Safety stock} - \text{Inventory currently on hand (plus on order, if any)} \qquad (15.10)$$

$$q = \bar{d}(T + L) + z\sigma_{T+L} - I$$

where

q = Quantity to be ordered
T = The number of days between reviews
L = Lead time in days (time between placing an order and receiving it)
$\bar{d}$ = Forecasted average daily demand
z = Number of standard deviations for a specified service level
σ_{T+L} = Standard deviation of demand over the review and lead time
I = Current inventory level (includes items on order)

Note: The demand, lead time, review period, and so forth can be any time units such as days, weeks, or years so long as it is consistent throughout the equation.

In this model, demand ($\bar{d}$) can be forecast and revised each review period if desired, or the yearly average may be used if appropriate. We assume that demand is normally distributed.

The value of z can be obtained by solving the following equation for $E(z)$ and reading the corresponding z value from Exhibit 15.6:

$$E(z) = \frac{\bar{d}T(1 - P)}{\sigma_{T+L}} \qquad (15.11)$$

where

$E(z)$ = Expected number units short from a normalized table where $\sigma = 1$
P = Service level desired expressed as a fraction (e.g., 95 percent as .95)
$\bar{d}T$ = Demand during the review period where $\bar{d}$ is daily demand and T is the number of days
σ_{T+L} = Standard deviation over the review period and lead time

■ **example 15.5**   *Quantity to Order*   Daily demand for a product is 10 units with a standard deviation of three units. The review period is 30 days, and lead time is 14 days. Management has set a policy of satisfying 98 percent of demand from items in stock. At the beginning of this review period, there are 150 units in inventory.
How many units should be ordered?

solution   The quantity to order is

$$q = \overline{d}(T + L) + z\sigma_{T+L} - I$$
$$= 10(30 + 14) + z\sigma_{T+L} - 150$$

Before we can complete the solution, we need to find σ_{T+L} and z. To find σ_{T+L}, we use the notion, as before, that the standard deviation of a sequence of independent random variables equals the square root of the sum of the variances. Therefore, the standard deviation during the period $T + L$ is the square root of the sum of the variances for each day:

$$\sigma_{T+L} = \sqrt{\sum_{i=1}^{T+L} \sigma_{d_1}^2} \qquad (15.12)$$

Because each day is independent and σ_d is constant,

$$\sigma_{T+L} = \sqrt{(T + L)\sigma_d^2} = \sqrt{(30 + 14)(3)^2} = 19.90$$

Now to find z, we first need to find $E(z)$ and look this value up in the table. In this case, demand during the review period is $\overline{d}\,T$, so

$$E(z) = \frac{\overline{d}\,T(1 - P)}{\sigma_{T+L}} = \frac{10(30)(1 - .98)}{19.90} = 0.302$$

From Exhibit 15.6 at $E(z) = 0.302$, by interpolation, $z = .21$.

The quantity to order, then, is

$$q = \overline{d}(T + L) + z\sigma_{T+L} - I = 10(30 + 14) + .21(19.90) - 150 = 294 \text{ units}$$

To satisfy 98 percent of the demand for units, order 294 at this review period. ∎

■ SPECIAL PURPOSE MODELS

The fixed-order quantity and the fixed-time period models presented thus far differed in their assumptions but had two characteristics in common: (1) The cost of units remained constant for any order size; and (2) the reordering process was continuous—that is, the items were ordered and stocked with the expectation that the need would continue.

This section presents two new models. The first illustrates the effect on order quantity when unit price changes with order size. The second is a single-period model (sometimes called a *static model*) in which ordering and stocking require a cost trade-off each time. This type of model is amenable to solution by marginal analysis.

Price-Break Models   Price-break models deal with the fact that, generally, the selling price of an item varies with the order size. This is a discrete or step change rather than a per-unit change. For example, wood screws may cost $0.02 each for 1 to 99 screws, $1.60 per 100, and $13.50 per 1,000. To determine the optimal quantity of any item to order, we simply solve for the economic order quantity for each price and at the point of price change. But not all of the economic order quantities determined by the formula are feasible. In the wood screw example, the Q_{opt} formula might tell us that the optimal decision at the price of 1.6 cents is to order 75 screws. This would be impossible, however, because 75 screws would cost 2 cents each.

Exhibit 15.10 Curves for Three Separate Order Quantity Models in a Three-Price-Break Situation (Blue line depicts feasible range of purchases.)

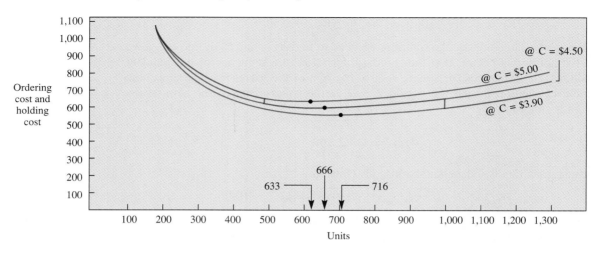

Price-Break Order Quantity

The total cost for each feasible economic order quantity and **price-break order quantity** is tabulated, and the Q that leads to the minimum cost is the optimal order size. If holding cost is based on a percentage of unit price, it may not be necessary to compute economic order quantities at each price. Procedurally, the largest order quantity (lowest unit price) is solved first; if the resulting Q is valid, that is the answer. If not, the next largest quantity (second lowest price) is derived. If that is feasible, the cost of this Q is compared to the cost of using the order quantity at the price break above, and the lowest cost determines the optimal Q.

Looking at Exhibit 15.10, we see that order quantities are solved from right to left, or from the lowest unit price to the highest, until a valid Q is obtained. Then the order quantity at each *price break* above this Q is used to find which order quantity has the least cost—the computed Q, or the Q at one of the price breaks.

■ **example 15.6** *Price-Break* Consider the following case, where

D = 10,000 units (annual demand)
S = \$20 to place each order
i = 20 percent of cost (annual carrying cost, storage, interest, obsolescence, etc.)
C = Cost per unit (according to the order size; orders of 0 to 499 units, \$5.00 per unit; 500 to 999, \$4.50 per unit; 1,000 and up, \$3.90 per unit)

What quantity should be ordered?

solution The appropriate equations from the basic fixed-quantity case are

$$TC = DC + \frac{D}{Q}S + \frac{Q}{2}iC$$

and

$$Q = \sqrt{\frac{2DS}{iC}} \qquad (15.13)$$

	$Q = 633$ where $C = \$5$	$Q = 666$ where $C = \$4.50$	$Q = 716$ where $C = \$3.90$	Price Break 1,000
Holding cost $\left(\dfrac{Q}{2}iC\right)$		$\dfrac{666}{2}(0.20)4.50$ $= \$299.70$		$\dfrac{1,000}{2}(0.20)3.90$ $= \$390$
Ordering cost $\left(\dfrac{D}{Q}S\right)$	Not feasible	$\dfrac{10,000(20)}{666}$ $= \$300$	Not feasible	$\dfrac{10,000(20)}{1,000}$ $= \$200$
Holding and ordering cost		\$599.70		\$590
Item cost (DC)		10,000(4.50)		10,000(3.90)
Total cost		\$45,599.70		\$39,590

Exhibit 15.11

Relevant Costs in a Three-Price-Break Model

Solving for the economic order size, we obtain

@ $C = \$3.90$, $Q = 716$ Not feasible
@ $C = \$4.50$, $Q = 666$ Feasible, Cost = \$45,599.70
Check $Q = 1,000$ Cost = \$39,590   Optimal solution

In Exhibit 15.10, which displays the cost relationship and order quantity range, note that most of the order quantity–cost relationships lie outside the feasible range and that only a single, continuous range results. This should be readily apparent because, for example, the first order quantity specifies buying 633 units at \$5.00 per unit. However, if 633 units are ordered, the price is \$4.50, not \$5.00. The same holds true for the third order quantity, which specifies an order of 716 units at \$3.90 each. This \$3.90 price is not available on orders of less than 1,000 units.

Exhibit 15.11 itemizes the total costs at the economic order quantities and at the price breaks. The optimal order quantity is shown to be 1,000 units. ∎

One practical consideration in price-break problems is that the price reduction from volume purchases frequently makes it seemingly economical to order amounts larger than the Q_{opt}. Thus, when applying the model, we must be particularly careful to obtain a valid estimate of product obsolescence and warehousing costs.

Single-Period Models   Some inventory situations involve placing orders to cover only one demand period or to cover short-lived items at frequent intervals. Sometimes called single-period or "newsboy" problems (for example, how many papers should a newsboy order each day), they are amenable to solution through the classic economic approach of marginal analysis. The optimal stocking decision, using marginal analysis, occurs at the point where the benefits derived from carrying the next unit are less than the costs for that unit. Of course, the selection of the specific benefits and costs depends on the problem. For example, we may be looking at costs of holding versus shortage costs or (as we develop further) marginal profit versus marginal loss.

When stocked items are sold, the optimal decision—using marginal analysis—is to stock that quantity where the profit from the sale or use of the last unit is equal to or greater than the losses if the last unit remains unsold. In symbolic terms, this is the condition where $MP \geq ML$, where

MP = Profit resulting from the nth unit if it is sold
ML = Loss resulting from the nth unit if it is not sold

Marginal analysis is also valid when we are dealing with probabilities of occurrence. In these situations, we are looking at expected profits and expected losses. By introducing probabilities, the marginal profit–marginal loss equation becomes

$$P(MP) \geq (1 - P)ML$$

where P is the probability of the unit's being sold and $1 - P$ is the probability of it not being sold, because one or the other must occur. (The unit is sold or is not sold.)[3]

Then, solving for P, we obtain

$$P \geq \frac{ML}{MP + ML} \qquad (15.14)$$

This equation states that we should continue to increase the size of the inventory so long as the probability of selling the last unit added is equal to or greater than the ratio $ML/(MP + ML)$.

Salvage value, or any other benefits derived from unsold goods, can easily be included in the problem. This simply reduces the marginal loss, as the following example shows.

■ **example 15.7** *Salvage Value*   A product is priced to sell at $100 per unit, and its cost is constant at $70 per unit. Each unsold unit has a salvage value of $20. Demand is expected to range between 35 and 40 units for the period; 35 units definitely can be sold and no units over 40 will be sold. The demand probabilities and the associated cumulative probability distribution (P) for this situation are shown in Exhibit 15.12.

The marginal profit if a unit is sold is the selling price less the cost, or $MP = \$100 - 70 = \$30$.

The marginal loss incurred if the unit is not sold is the cost of the unit less the salvage value, or $ML = \$70 - \$20 = \$50$.

How many units should be ordered?

solution   The optimal probability of the last unit being sold is

$$P \geq \frac{ML}{MP + ML} = \frac{50}{30 + 50} = 0.625$$

According to the cumulative probability table (the last column in Exhibit 15.12), the probability of selling the unit must be equal to or greater than 0.625, so 37 units should be stocked. The probability of selling the 37th unit is 0.75. The net benefit from stocking the 37th unit is the expected marginal profit minus the expected marginal loss.

$$
\begin{aligned}
\text{Net} &= P(MP) - (1 - P)(ML) \\
&= 0.75(\$100 - \$70) - (1 - 0.75)(\$70 - \$20) \\
&= \$22.50 - \$12.50 = \$10
\end{aligned}
$$

For the sake of illustration, Exhibit 15.13 shows all possible decisions. From the last column, we can confirm that the optimum decision is 37 units. ■

---

[3] P is actually a cumulative probability because the sale of the nth unit depends not only on exactly n being demanded but also on the demand for any number greater than n.

Number of Units Demanded	*(p)* Probability of This Demand	This Unit Is	*(P)* Probability of Selling
35	0.10	1 to 35	1.00
36	0.15	36	0.90
37	0.25	37	0.75
38	0.25	38	0.50
39	0.15	39	0.25
40	0.10	40	0.10
41	0	41 or more	0

Exhibit 15.12

Demand and Cumulative Probabilities

Marginal Inventory Analysis for Units Having Salvage Value

Exhibit 15.13

(N) Units of Demand	*(p)* Probability of Demand	*(P)* Probability of Selling *n*th Unit	*(MP)* Expected Marginal Profit of *n*th Unit $P(100 - 70)$	*(ML)* Expected Marginal Loss of *n*th Unit $(1 - P)(70 - 20)$	(Net) Net Profit of the *n*th Unit $(MP) - (ML)$
35	0.10	1.00	$30	$ 0	$30.00
36	0.15	0.90	27	5	22
37	0.25	0.75	22.50	12.50	10
38	0.25	0.50	15	25	−10
39	0.15	0.25	7.50	37.50	−30
40	0.10	0.10	3	45	
41	0	0			−42

Note: Expected marginal profit is the selling price of $100 less the unit cost of $70 times the probability the unit will be sold. Expected marginal loss is the unit cost of $70 less the salvage value of $20 times the probability the unit will not be sold.

■ MISCELLANEOUS SYSTEMS AND ISSUES

Obtaining actual order, setup, carrying, and shortage costs is difficult—sometimes impossible. Even the assumptions are sometimes unrealistic. For example, Exhibit 15.14 compares ordering costs that are assumed linear to the real case where every addition of a staff person causes a step increase in cost.

All inventory systems are plagued by two major problems: maintaining adequate control over each inventory item, and ensuring that accurate records of stock on hand are kept. In this section, we present three simple systems often used in practice (an optional replenishment system, a one-bin system, and a two-bin system), **ABC analysis** (a method for analyzing inventory based on value), and cycle counting (a technique for improving inventory record accuracy).

ABC Analysis

Three Simple Inventory Systems

Optional Replenishment System An **optional replenishment system** forces reviewing the inventory level at a fixed frequency (such as weekly) and ordering a replenishment supply if the level has dropped below some amount. In Exhibit 15.1,

Optional Replenishment System

Exhibit 15.14

Cost to Place Orders versus the Number of Orders Placed: Linear Assumption and Normal Reality

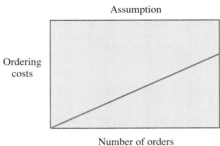

Assumption

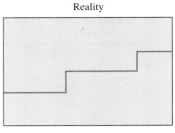

Reality

this is a *P* model. For example, the maximum inventory level (which we will call *M*) can be computed based on demand, ordering costs, and shortage costs. Because it takes time and costs money to place an order, a minimum order of size *Q* can be established. Then, whenever this item is reviewed, the inventory position (we will call it *I*) is subtracted from the replenishment level (*M*). If that number (call it *q*) is equal to or greater than *Q*, order *q*. Otherwise, forget it until the next review period. Stated formally,

$$q = M - I$$
$$\text{If } q \geq Q, \text{ order } q.$$

Otherwise, do not order any.

Two-Bin System

Two-Bin System   In a **two-bin system,** items are used from one bin, and the second bin provides an amount large enough to ensure that the stock can be replenished. In Exhibit 15.1, this is a Q model. Ideally, the second bin would contain an amount equal to the reorder point (*R*) calculated earlier. As soon as the second bin supply is brought to the first bin, an order is placed to replenish the second bin. Actually, these bins can be located together. In fact, there could be just one bin with a divider between. The key to a two-bin operation is to separate the inventory so that part of it is held in reserve until the rest is used first.

One-Bin System

One-Bin System   A **one-bin** inventory **system** involves periodic replenishment no matter how few are needed. At fixed periods (such as weekly), the inventory is brought up to its predetermined maximum level. The one bin is always replenished, and it therefore differs from the optional replenishment system, which only reorders when the inventory used is greater than some minimum amount. This is a P model in Exhibit 15.1.

ABC Inventory Planning

Maintaining inventory through counting, placing orders, receiving stock, and so on takes personnel time and costs money. When there are limits on these resources, the logical move is to try to use the available resources to control inventory in the best way. In other words, focus on the most important items in inventory.

In the nineteenth century, Villefredo Pareto, in a study of the distribution of wealth in Milan, found that 20 percent of the people controlled 80 percent of the wealth. This logic of the few having the greatest importance and the many having little importance has been broadened to include many situations and is termed the *Pareto principle*.[4]

---

[4] The Pareto principle is also widely applied in quality problems through the use of Pareto charts. (See Chapter 6.)

Item Number	Annual Dollar Usage	Percentage of Total Value
22	$ 95,000	40.8%
68	75,000	32.1
27	25,000	10.7
03	15,000	6.4
82	13,000	5.6
54	7,500	3.2
36	1,500	0.6
19	800	0.3
23	425	0.2
41	225	0.1
	$233,450	100.0%

Exhibit 15.15

Annual Usage of Inventory by Value

This is true in our everyday lives (most of our decisions are relatively unimportant, but a few shape our future) and is certainly true in inventory systems (where a few items account for the bulk of our investment).

Any inventory system must specify when an order is to be placed for an item and how many units to order. Most inventory control situations involve so many items that it is not practical to model and give thorough treatment to each item. To get around this problem, the ABC classification scheme divides inventory items into three groupings: high dollar volume (A), moderate dollar volume (B), and low dollar volume (C). Dollar volume is a measure of importance; an item low in cost but high in volume can be more important than a high-cost item with low volume.

ABC Classification   If the annual usage of items in inventory is listed according to dollar volume, generally, the list shows that a small number of items account for a large dollar volume and that a large number of items account for a small dollar volume. Exhibit 15.15 illustrates the relationship.

The ABC approach divides this list into three groupings by value: A items constitute roughly the top 15 percent of the items, B items the next 35 percent, and C items the last 50 percent. From observation, it appears that the list in Exhibit 15.15 may be meaningfully grouped with A including 20 percent (2 of the 10), B including 30 percent, and C including 50 percent. These points show clear delineations between sections. The result of this segmentation is shown in Exhibit 15.16 and plotted in Exhibit 15.17.

Segmentation may not always occur so neatly. The objective, though, is to try to separate the important from the unimportant. Where the lines actually break depends on the particular inventory under question and on how much personnel time is available. (With more time, a firm could define larger A or B categories.)

The purpose of classifying items into groups is to establish the appropriate degree of control over each item. On a periodic basis, for example, class A items may be more clearly controlled with weekly ordering, B items may be ordered biweekly, and C items may be ordered monthly or bimonthly. Note that the unit cost of items is not related to their classification. An A item may have a high dollar volume through a combination of either low cost and high usage or high cost and low usage. Similarly, C items may have a low dollar volume because of either low demand or low cost. In an automobile service station, gasoline would be an A item with daily or weekly replenishment; tires, batteries, oil, grease, and transmission fluid may be B items and ordered every two to four weeks; and C items would consist of valve stems, windshield

	Classification	Item Number	Annual Dollar Usage	Percentage of Total
Exhibit 15.16	A	22, 68	$170,000	72.9%
ABC Grouping of	B	27, 03, 82	53,000	22.7
Inventory Items	C	54, 36, 19, 23, 41	10,450	4.4
			$233,450	100.0%

Exhibit 15.17

ABC Inventory Classification (Inventory value for each group versus the group's portion of the total list)

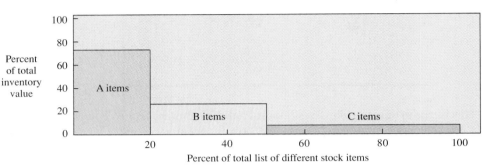

wiper blades, radiator caps, hoses, fan belts, oil and gas additives, car wax, and so forth. C items may be ordered every two or three months or even be allowed to run out before reordering because the penalty for stockout is not serious.

Sometimes, an item may be critical to a system if its absence creates a sizable loss. In this case, regardless of the item's classification, sufficiently large stocks should be kept on hand to prevent runout. One way to ensure closer control is to designate this item an A or a B, forcing it into the category even if its dollar volume does not warrant such inclusion.

Inventory Accuracy and Cycle Counting

Inventory Accuracy

Inventory records usually differ from the actual physical count; **inventory accuracy** refers to how well the two agree. Companies such as Wal-Mart (see Breakthrough Box) understand the importance of inventory accuracy and expend considerable effort ensuring it. The question is, How much error is acceptable? If the record shows a balance of 683 of part X and an actual count shows 652, is this within reason? Suppose the actual count shows 750, an excess of 67 over the record; is this any better?

Every production system must have agreement, within some specified range, between what the record says is in inventory and what actually is in inventory. There are many reasons why records and inventory may not agree. For example, an open stockroom area allows items to be removed for both legitimate and unauthorized purposes. The legitimate removal may have been done in a hurry and simply not recorded. Sometimes parts are misplaced, turning up months later. Parts are often stored in several locations, but records may be lost or the location recorded incorrectly. Sometimes stock replenishment orders are recorded as received, when in fact they never were. Occasionally, a group of parts is recorded as removed from inventory, but the customer order is canceled and the parts are replaced in inventory without canceling the record. To keep the production system flowing smoothly without parts shortages and efficiently without excess balances, records must be accurate.

How can a firm keep accurate, up-to-date records? The first general rule is to keep the storeroom locked. If only storeroom personnel have access, and one of their

BREAKTHROUGH

Inventory on a Grand Scale

Inventory at Wal-Mart is precision on a gargantuan scale, like a maneuver of the Atlantic Fleet or a dam project in the Yangtze River.

In his ruling on Wal-Mart's Tax Court case, Judge David Laro provided a behind-the-scenes look at the operation. Its effectiveness, he says, has led "many other companies, both domestic and foreign" to seek Wal-Mart's advice on inventory-taking.

Preparation alone takes four to six weeks. Forty-five days in advance, the chain's internal audit department sends a preparation kit to each store. It contains detailed instructions, including 13 schedules.

Involved in the inventory are a team of 18 to 40 independent counters and representatives of the company's operations division and departments of loss prevention and internal audit.

At randomly selected stores, employees of Ernst & Young, independent auditors for Wal-Mart, are present to test accuracy by recounting.

An inventory is taken between 8 AM and 6 PM, while the store—some of which are 24-hour operations—is open to customers. Immediately af-

ter the inventory is completed, the physical count team reconciles its findings with the book inventory. The results are reviewed later by the internal audit department.

Inventories are taken every 11 to 13 months, and most occur from March through September: inventory is never taken in November or December, when it would interfere with the Christmas season, or in the first week in January, when employees are recuperating and busy with exchanges and returns.

The job can be made no easier by the fact that Wal-Mart's inventory turns over 4.5 times a year (competitors average about 2.8 turns) and its stores carry between 60,000 and 90,000 specific types of merchandise.

Between physical counts, Wal-Mart employs the perpetual system that records, at the time of sale, the cost and quantity of goods sold. This "reveals the cost and/or quantity of goods sold since the beginning of the current period and . . . of goods that are on hand at any given time." (*http://wal.mart.com*)

Source: William Riggle. "Inventory on a Grand Scale," *Supermarket Business*, February 1997 p. 45. Reproduced with permission from Supermarket Business.

measures of performance when it comes time for personnel evaluation and merit increases is record accuracy, there is a strong motivation to comply. Every location of inventory storage, whether in a locked storeroom or on the production floor, should have a recordkeeping mechanism. A second way is to convey the importance of accurate records to all personnel and depend on them to assist in this effort. (What this all boils down to is: Put a fence that goes all the way to the ceiling around the storage area so that workers cannot climb over to get parts; put a lock on the gate and give one person the key. Nobody, but nobody, can pull parts without having the transaction authorized and recorded.)

Another way to ensure accuracy is to count inventory frequently and match this against records. A widely used method is called *cycle counting.*

Cycle counting is a physical inventory-taking technique in which inventory is counted on a frequent basis rather than once or twice a year. The key to effective cycle counting and, therefore, to accurate records lies in deciding which items are to be counted, when, and by whom.

Cycle Counting

Virtually all inventory systems these days are computerized. The computer can be programmed to produce a cycle count notice in the following cases:

1. When the record shows a low or zero balance on hand. (It is easier to count fewer items.)

2. When the record shows a positive balance but a backorder was written (indicating a discrepancy).

McKesson, a leading distributor of pharmaceuticals, uses technology effectively. The machine on the man's arm combines a scanner, computer, and two-way radio to keep track of inventory and speed order delivery.

3. After some specified level of activity.
4. To signal a review based on the importance of the item (as in the ABC system) such as in the following table:

Annual Dollar Usage	Review Period
$10,000 or more	30 days or less
$3,000–$10,000	45 days or less
$250–3,000	90 days or less
Less than $250	180 days or less

The easiest time for stock to be counted is when there is no activity in the stockroom or on the production floor. This means on the weekends or during the second or third shift, when the facility is less busy. If this is not possible, more careful logging and separation of items are required to do an inventory count while production is going on and transactions are occurring.

The counting cycle depends on the available personnel. Some firms schedule regular stockroom personnel to do the counting during lull times in the regular working day. Other companies contract out to private firms that come in and count inventory. Still other firms use full-time cycle counters who do nothing but count inventory and resolve differences with the records. While this last method sounds expensive, many firms believe that it is actually less costly than the usual hectic annual inventory count generally performed during the two- or three-week annual vacation shutdown.

The question of how much error is tolerable between physical inventory and records has been much debated. While some firms strive for 100 percent accuracy, others accept 1, 2, or 3 percent error. The accuracy level recommended by the American Production and Inventory Control Society (APICS) is ±0.2 percent for A items, ±1 percent for B items, and ±5 percent for C items. Regardless of the specific accuracy decided on, the important point is that the level be dependable so that safety stocks may be provided as a cushion. Accuracy is important for a smooth production process so that customer orders can be processed as scheduled and not held up because of the unavailability of parts.

Inventory Control in Services

To demonstrate how inventory conrol is conducted in service organizations, we have selected two areas to describe: a department store and an automobile service agency.

Department Store Inventory Policy   The common term used to identify an inventory item is the **stockkeeping unit (SKU).** The SKU identifies each item, its manufacturer, and its cost. The number of SKUs becomes large even for small departments. For example, if towels carried in a domestic items department are obtained from three manufacturers in three quality levels, three sizes (hand towel, face towel, and bath towel), and four colors, there are 108 different items ($3 \times 3 \times 3 \times 4$). Even if towels are sold only in sets of three pieces (hand towel, face towel, and bath towel), the number of SKUs needed to identify the towel sets is $3 \times 3 \times 1 \times 4 = 36$. Depending on the store, a housewares department may carry 3,000 to 4,000 SKUs, and a linen and domestic items department may carry 5,000 to 6,000.

Stockkeeping Unit (SKU)

Such large numbers mean that individual economic order quantities cannot be calculated for each item by hand. How, then, does a department keep tabs on its stock and place orders for replenishment? We answer this question in the context of an example dealing with a housewares department and an auto service department.

Generally, housewares are divided into staple and promotional items. Within these major divisions, further classifications are used, such as cookware and tableware. Also, items are frequently classified by price, as $5 items, $4, $3, and so forth.

The housewares department usually purchases from a distributor rather than directly from a manufacturer. The use of a distributor, who handles products from many manufacturers, has the advantage of fewer orders and faster shipping time (shorter lead time). Further, the distributor's sales personnel may visit the housewares department weekly and count all the items they supply to this department. Then, in line with the replenishment level that has been established by the buyer, the distributor's salesperson places orders for the buyer. This saves the department time in counting inventory and placing orders. The typical lead time for receipt of stock from a housewares distributor is two or three days. The safety stock, therefore, is quite low, and the buyer establishes the replenishment level so as to supply only enough items for the two- to three-day lead time, plus expected demand during the period until the distributor's salesperson's next visit.

Note that a formal method of estimating stockout and establishing safety stock levels is usually not followed because the number of items is too great. Instead, the total value of items in the department is monitored. Thus, replenishment levels are set by dollar allocation.

Through planning, each department has an established monthly value for inventory. By tabulating inventory balance, monthly sales, and items on order, an "open-to-buy" figure is determined. ("Open-to-buy" is the unspent portion of the budget.) This dollar amount is the sum available to the buyer for the following month. When an increase in demand is expected (Christmas, Mother's Day, and so forth), the allocation of funds to the department is increased, resulting in a larger open-to-buy position. Then the replenishment levels are raised in line with the class of goods, responding to the demand increases, thereby creating a higher stock of goods on hand.

In practice, the open-to-buy funds are largely spent during the first days of the month. However, the buyer tries to reserve some funds for special purchases or to restock fast-moving items. Promotional items in housewares are controlled individually (or by class) by the buyer.

Maintaining an Auto Replacement Parts Inventory   A firm in the automobile service business purchases most of its parts supplies from a small number of distributors. Franchised new-car dealers purchase the great bulk of their supplies from the auto manufacturer. A dealer's demand for auto parts originates primarily from the general public and other departments of the agency, such as the service department or body shop. The problem, in this case, is to determine the order quantities for the several thousand items carried.

A franchised auto agency of medium size may carry a parts inventory valued in the area of $500,000. Because of the nature of this industry, alternate uses of funds are plentiful, so opportunity costs are high. For example, dealers may lease cars, carry their own contracts, stock a larger new-car inventory, or open sidelines such as tire shops, trailer sales, or recreational vehicle sales—all with potentially high returns. This creates pressure to try to carry a low inventory level of parts and supplies while still meeting an acceptable service level.

While some dealers still perform their inventory ordering by hand, most use computers and software packages provided by car manufacturers. For both manual and computerized systems, an ABC classification works well. Expensive and high-turnover supplies are counted and ordered frequently; low-cost items are ordered in large quantities at infrequent intervals. A common drawback of frequent order placement is the extensive amount of time needed to physically put the items on the shelves and log them in. (However, this restocking procedure does not greatly add to an auto agency's cost because parts department personnel generally do this during slow periods.)

A great variety of computerized systems are currently in use. In a monthly reordering system, for example, the items to be ordered are counted and the number on hand is entered into the computer. By subtracting the number on hand from the previous month's inventory and adding the orders received during the month, the usage rate is determined. Some programs use exponential smoothing forecasts, while others use a weighted-average method. For the weighted-average method, the computer program stores the usage rate for, say, four previous months. Then, with the application of a set of weighting factors, a forecast is made in the same manner as described in Chapter 13. This works as follows: Suppose usage of a part during January, February, March, and April was 17, 19, 11, and 23, respectively, and the set of corresponding weights was 0.10, 0.20, 0.30, and 0.40. Thus, the forecast for May is 0.10(17) + 0.20(19) + 0.30(11) + 0.40(23), or 18 units. If safety stock were included and equal to one-month demand, then 36 units would be ordered (one-month demand plus one-month safety stock) less whatever is on hand at the time of order placement. This simple two-month rule allows for forecasted usage during the lead time plus the review period, with the balance providing the safety stock.

The computer output provides a useful reference file, identifying the item, cost, order size, and the number of units on hand. The output itself constitutes the purchase order and is sent to the distributor or factory supply house. The simplicity in this is attractive because, once the forecast weighting is selected, all that needs to be done is to input the number of units of each item on hand. Thus, negligible computation is involved, and very little preparation is needed to send the order out.

■ CONCLUSION

This chapter introduced the two main classes of demand: (1) independent demand referring to the external demand for a firm's end product and (2) dependent demand, usually referring—within the firm—to the demand for items created because of the demand for more complex items of which they are a part. Most industries have items in both classes. In manufacturing, for example, independent demand is common for finished products, service and repair parts, and operating supplies; and dependent demand is common for those parts and materials needed to produce the end product. In wholesale and retail sales of consumer goods, most demand is independent—each item is an end item, with the wholesaler or retailer doing no further assembly or fabrication.

Independent demand, the focus of this chapter, is based on statistics. In the fixed-order quantity and fixed-time period models, the influence of service level was shown on safety stock and reorder point determinations. Two special-purpose models—price-break and single-period—were also presented.

To distinguish among item categories for analysis and control, the ABC method was offered. The importance of inventory accuracy was also noted, and cycle counting was described. Finally, brief descriptions of inventory procedures in a department store and an auto parts shop illustrated some of the simpler ways nonmanufacturing firms carry out their inventory control functions.

In this chapter we also pointed out that inventory reduction requires a knowledge of the operating system. It is not simply a case of selecting an inventory model off the shelf and plugging in some numbers. In the first place, a model might not even be appropriate. In the second case, the numbers might be full of errors or even based on erroneous data. It is vital to understand that this is also not a trade-off compromise. Likewise, determining order quantities is often referred to as a trade-off problem; that is, trading off holding costs for setup costs. Note that companies really want to reduce both.

The simple fact is that firms have very large investments in inventory, and the cost to carry this inventory runs from 25 to 35 percent of the inventory's worth annually. Therefore, a major goal of most firms today is to reduce inventory.

A caution is in order, though. The formulas in this chapter try to minimize cost. Bear in mind that a firm's objective should be something like "making money" so be sure that reducing inventory cost does, in fact, support this. Usually, correctly reducing inventory lowers cost, improves quality and performance, and enhances profit.

FORMULA REVIEW

Q model. Total annual cost for an ordered Q, a per unit cost C, setup cost S, and per unit holding cost H.

$$TC = DC + \frac{D}{Q}S + \frac{Q}{2}H \tag{15.1}$$

Q model. Optimum (or economic) order quantity.

$$Q_{opt} = \sqrt{\frac{2DS}{H}} \tag{15.2}$$

Q model. Reorder point R based on average daily demand $\bar{d}$ and lead time L in days.

$$R = \bar{d}L \tag{15.3}$$

Q model (production-consumption model). Optimum order size when items are used at rate *d*, as they are produced at rate *p*.

$$Q_{\text{opt}} = \sqrt{\frac{2DS}{H} \cdot \frac{p}{(p-d)}} \qquad (15.4)$$

Q model. Reorder point providing a safety stock of $z\sigma_L$.

$$R = \bar{d}L + z\sigma_L \qquad (15.5)$$

Average daily demand over a period of *n* days.

$$\bar{d} = \frac{\sum\limits_{i=1}^{n} d_i}{n} \qquad (15.6)$$

Standard deviation of demand over a period of *n* days.

$$\sigma_d = \sqrt{\frac{\sum\limits_{i=1}^{n} (d_i - \bar{d})^2}{n}} \qquad (15.7)$$

Standard deviation of a series of independent demands.

$$\sigma_s = \sqrt{\sigma_1^2 + \sigma_2^2 + \cdots + \sigma_i^2} \qquad (15.8)$$

Q model. Expected number of units short in one order cycle for a service level *P* and optimum order quantity *Q*.

$$E(z) = \frac{(1-P)Q}{\sigma_L} \qquad (15.9)$$

P model. Optimum order quantity in a fixed period system with a review period of *T* days and lead time of *L* days.

$$q = \bar{d}(T + L) + z\sigma_{T+L} - I \qquad (15.10)$$

P model. Expected number of units short in one period of a fixed period system.

$$E(z) = \frac{\bar{d}T(1-P)}{\sigma_{T+L}} \qquad (15.11)$$

P model. Standard deviation of a series of independent demands over the review period *T* and lead time *L*.

$$\sigma_{T+L} = \sqrt{\sum\limits_{i=1}^{T+L} \sigma_{d_i}^2} \qquad (15.12)$$

Q model. Optimum order quantity based on an order cost *S*, holding cost as a percent (*i*) of the unit cost (*C*).

$$Q = \sqrt{\frac{2DS}{iC}} \qquad (15.13)$$

Single period model. Probability of selling the last unit as a ratio of marginal loss and marginal profit.

$$P \geq \frac{ML}{MP + ML} \qquad (15.14)$$

SOLVED PROBLEMS

SOLVED PROBLEM 1

Items purchased from a vendor cost $20 each, and the forecast for next year's demand is 1,000 units. If it costs $5 every time an order is placed for more units and the storage cost is $4 per unit per year, what quantity should be ordered each time?

    a. What is the total ordering cost for a year?
    b. What is the total storage cost for a year?

Solution
The quantity to be ordered each time is

$$Q = \sqrt{\frac{2DS}{H}} = \sqrt{\frac{2(1,000)5}{4}} = 50 \text{ units}$$

    a. The total ordering cost for a year is

$$\frac{D}{Q}S = \frac{1,000}{50}(\$5) = \$100$$

    b. The storage cost for a year is

$$\frac{Q}{2}H = \frac{50}{2}(\$4) = \$100$$

SOLVED PROBLEM 2

Daily demand for a product is 120 units, with a standard deviation of 30 units. The review period is 14 days and the lead time is 7 days. At the time of review there are 130 units in stock. If 99 percent of all demand is to be satisfied from items in stock, how many units should be ordered?

Solution

$$\sigma_{T+L} = \sqrt{(14 + 7)(30)^2} = \sqrt{18,900} = 137.5$$

$$E(z) = \frac{120(14)(1 - .99)}{137.5} = 0.122$$

From Exhibit 15.6, $z = .80$

$$q = \bar{d}(T + L) + z\sigma_{T+L} - I$$
$$= 120(14 + 7) + .80(137.5) - 130$$
$$= 2,500 \text{ units}$$

SOLVED PROBLEM 3

A company currently has 200 units of a product on hand that it orders every two weeks when the salesperson visits the premises. Demand for the product averages 20 units per day with a standard deviation of five units. Lead time for the product to arrive is seven days. Management has a goal of providing a 99 percent service level for this product.

The salesperson is due to come in late this afternoon when there are 180 units left in stock (assuming that 20 are sold today). How many units should be ordered?

Solution

Given $I = 180, T = 14, L = 7, \bar{d} = 20$

$$\sigma_{T+L} = \sqrt{21(5)^2} = 23$$

$$E(z) = \frac{\bar{d}T(1 - P)}{\sigma_{T+L}} = \frac{20(14)(1 - .99)}{23} = .1217$$

From Exhibit 15.6, $z = .80$

$$q = \bar{d}(T + L) + z\sigma_{T+L} - I$$
$$= 20(14 + 7) + .80(23) - 180$$
$$q = 258.4 \text{ units}$$

REVIEW AND DISCUSSION QUESTIONS

1. Distinguish between dependent and independent demand in a McDonald's, in an integrated manufacturer of personal copies, and in a pharmaceutical supply house.
2. Distinguish between in-process inventory, safety stock inventory, and seasonal inventory.
3. Discuss the nature of the costs that affect inventory size.
4. Under which conditions would a plant manager elect to use a fixed-order quantity model as opposed to a fixed-time period model? What are the disadvantages of using a fixed-time period ordering system?
5. Discuss the general procedure for determining the order quantity when price breaks are involved. Would there be any differences in procedure if holding cost were a fixed percentage of price rather than a constant amount?
6. What two basic questions must be answered by an inventory-control decision rule?
7. Discuss the assumptions that are inherent in production setup cost, ordering cost, and carrying costs. How valid are they?
8. "The nice thing about inventory models is that you can pull one off the shelf and apply it so long as your cost estimates are accurate." Comment.
9. Which type of inventory system would you use in the following situations?
   a. Supplying your kitchen with fresh food.
   b. Obtaining a daily newspaper.
   c. Buying gas for your car.
   To which of these items do you impute the highest stockout cost?
10. Why is it desirable to classify items into groups, as the ABC classification does?
11. What kind of policy or procedure would you recommend to improve the inventory operation in a department store? What advantages and disadvantages does your system have a vis-à-vis the department store inventory operation described in this chapter?

PROBLEMS

1. Order 22.

1. Ray's Satellite Emporium wishes to determine the best order size for their best-selling satellite dish (model TS111). Ray has estimated the annual demand for this model at 1,000 units. His cost to carry one unit is $100 per year per unit, and he has estimated that each order cost $25 to place. Using the EOQ model, how many should Ray order each time he places an order?

2. Jim's Knives manufactures knives for a certain retail store. His skilled worker can produce 10 knives a day of their best-selling knife (a Bowie knife). Their retail store sells an average of 5 knives per day. Jim's workers prefer to work on only one type of knife at any given time for efficiency reasons. They have estimated that changing from one type of knife to another cost $100. Inventory cost for this knife has been estimated at $10 per year per knife. Jim's Knives operate both their factory and retail store 250 days per year. What batch size for the production of Bowie knives would you recommend to Jim?

✓ **3.** Dunstreet's Department Store would like to develop an inventory ordering policy to satisfy 95 percent of its customers' demands for products directly from inventory stock on hand. To illustrate your recommended procedure, use as an example the ordering policy for white percale sheets.

Demand for white percale sheets is 5,000 per year. The store is open 365 days per year. Every two weeks (14 days) an inventory count is made and a new order is placed. It takes 10 days for the sheets to be delivered. Standard deviation of demand for the sheets is five per day. There are currently 150 sheets on hand.

How many sheets should you order?

4. Charlie's Pizza orders all of its pepperoni, olives, anchovies, and mozzarella cheese to be shipped directly from Italy. An American distributor stops by every four weeks to take orders. Because the orders are shipped directly from Italy, it takes three weeks to arrive.

Charlie's Pizza uses an average of 150 pounds of pepperoni each week, with a standard deviation of 30 pounds. Since Charlie's prides itself on offering only the best-quality ingredients and a high level of service, it wants to ensure that it can satisfy 99 percent of the customers who demand pepperoni on their pizza.

Assume that the sales representative just walked in the door and there is currently 500 pounds of pepperoni in the walk-in cooler. How many pounds of pepperoni would you order?

5. Given the following information, formulate an inventory management system. The item is demanded 50 weeks a year.

Item cost	$10.00	Standard deviation of weekly	
Order cost	$250.00	demand	25 per week
Annual holding cost (%)	33% of item cost	Lead time	1 week
Annual demand	25,750	Service level	95%
Average demand	515 per week		

 a. State the order quantity and reorder point.
 b. Determine the annual holding and order costs.
 c. How many units per order cycle would you expect to be short?
 d. If a price break of $50 per order was offered for purchase quantities of over 2,000, would you take advantage of it? How much would you save on an annual basis?

6. Lieutenant Commander Data is planning to make his monthly (every 30 days) trek to Gamma Hydra City to pick up a supply of isolinear chips. The trip will take Data about two days. Before he leaves, he calls in the order to the GHC Supply Store. He uses chips at an average rate of five per day (seven days per week) with a standard deviation of demand of one per day. He needs a 99 percent service level. If he currently has 35 chips in inventory, how many should he order? What is the most he will ever have to order?

✓ **7.** Jill's Job Shop buys two parts (Tegdiws and Widgets) for use in its production system from two different suppliers. The parts are needed throughout the entire 52-week year. Tegdiws are used at a relatively constant rate and are ordered whenever the remaining quantity drops to the reorder level. Widgets are ordered from a supplier who stops by every three weeks. Data for both products are as follows:

---

2. $Q_{opt} = 224$ knives.

3. $E(z) = .39147 \Rightarrow z$
 $= .0156$ (by interpolation).
 $q = 179.148$.

4. $q = 634$ pounds.

5. *a.* $Q = 1975$,
 $R = 416$.
 b. Holding cost
 $= \$3,258.75$.
 Ordering cost $=$
 $\$3,259.49$.
 c. 98.75.
 d. $643.

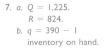

6. First question, 127 chips. Second question, 162 chips.

7. *a.* $Q = 1,225$.
 $R = 824$.
 b. $q = 390 - I$
 inventory on hand.

Item	Tegdiw	Widget
Annual demand	10,000	5,000
Holding cost (% of item cost)	20%	20%
Setup or order cost	$150.00	$25.00
Lead time	4 weeks	1 week
Safety stock	55 units	5 units
Item cost	$10.00	$2.00

   a. What is the inventory control system for Tegdiws; that is, what is the reorder quantity and what is the reorder point?

   b. What is the inventory control system for Widgets?

8. Demand for an item is 1,000 units per year. Each order placed costs $10; the annual cost to carry items in inventory is $2 each.

   a. In what quantities should the item be ordered?

   b. Supposing a $100 discount on each order is given if orders are placed in quantities of 500 or more. Should orders be placed in quantities of 500, or should you stick to the decision you made in *a*?

9. The annual demand for a product is 15,600 units. The weekly demand is 300 units with a standard deviation of 90 units. The cost to place an order is $31.20, and the time from ordering to receipt is four weeks. The annual inventory carrying cost is $0.10 per unit. Find the reorder point necessary to provide a 99 percent service level.

   Suppose the production manager is ordered to reduce the safety stock of this item by 50 percent. If he does so, what will the new service level be?

10. Daily demand for a product is 100 units, with a standard deviation of 25 units. The review period is 10 days and the lead time is 6 days. At the time of review there are 50 units in stock. If 98 percent of all demand is to be satisfied from items in stock, how many units should be ordered?

11. Item X is a standard item stocked in a company's inventory of component parts. Each year, the firm, on a random basis, uses about 2,000 of item X, which costs $25 each. Storage costs, which include insurance and cost of capital, amount to $5 per unit of average inventory. Every time an order is placed for more item X, it costs $10.

   a. Whenever item X is ordered, what should the order size be?

   b. What is the annual cost for ordering item X?

   c. What is the annual cost for storing item X?

12. Annual demand for a product is 13,000 units; weekly demand is 250 units with a standard deviation of 40 units. The cost of placing an order is $100, and the time from ordering to receipt is four weeks. The annual inventory carrying cost is $0.65 per unit. To provide a 99 percent service level, what must the reorder point be?

   Suppose the production manager is told to reduce the safety stock of this item by 10 units. If this is done, what will the new service level be?

13. A particular raw material is available to a company at three different prices, depending on the size of the order:

Less than 100 pounds	$20 per pound
100 pounds to 999 pounds	$19 per pound
More than 1,000 pounds	$18 per pound

The cost to place an order is $40. Annual demand is 3,000 units. Holding (or carrying) cost is 25 percent of the material price.

What is the economic order quantity to buy each time?

14. In the past, Taylor Industries has used a fixed-time period inventory system that involved taking a complete inventory count of all items each month. However, increasing labor costs are forcing Taylor Industries to examine alternate ways to reduce

<!-- margin answers -->
8. *a.* $Q = 100$ units.

  b. Order 100 each time.

9. $Q = 3,120$,

  $R = 1,305$,

  Service level = 98.3%.

10. $z = .49$ (by interpolation), $q = 1599$.

11. *a.* $Q = 89.44$. ✓

  b. $223.61.

  c. $223.61

12. $Q = 2,000$.

  $R = 1,028$.

  Service level = 98.8%.

13. $TC = 56,370$; 1,000 at a time.

✓

the amount of labor involved in inventory stockrooms, yet without increasing other costs, such as shortage costs. Here is a random sample of 20 of Taylor's items.

Item Number	Annual Usage	Item Number	Annual Usage
1	$ 1,500	11	$13,000
2	12,000	12	600
3	2,200	13	42,000
4	50,000	14	9,900
5	9,600	15	1,200
6	750	16	10,200
7	2,000	17	4,000
8	11,000	18	61,000
9	800	19	3,500
10	15,000	20	2,900

a. What would you recommend Taylor do to cut back its labor cost? (Illustrate using an ABC plan.)

b. Item 15 is critical to continued operations. How would you recommend it be classified?

15. Gentle Ben's Bar and Restaurant uses 5,000 quart bottles of an imported wine each year. The effervescent wine costs $3 per bottle and is served in whole bottles only since it loses its bubbles quickly. Ben figures that it costs $10 each time an order is placed, and holding costs are 20 percent of the purchase price. It takes three weeks for an order to arrive. Weekly demand is 100 bottles (closed two weeks per year) with a standard deviation of 30 bottles.

Ben would like to use an inventory system that minimizes inventory cost and will satisfy 95 percent of his customers who order this wine.

a. What is the economic order quantity for Ben to order?

b. At what inventory level should he place an order?

c. How many bottles of wine will be short during each order cycle?

16. Retailers Warehouse (RW) is an independent supplier of household items to department stores. RW attempts to stock enough items to satisfy 98 percent of the requests from its customers.

A stainless steel knife set is one item it stocks. Demand (2,400 sets per year) is relatively stable over the entire year. Whenever new stock is ordered, a buyer must assure that numbers are correct for stock on hand and then phone in a new order. The total cost involved to place an order is about $5. RW figures that to hold inventory in stock and to pay for interest on borrowed capital, insurance, and so on adds up to about $4 holding cost per unit per year.

Analysis of the past data shows that the standard deviation of demand from retailers is about four units per day for a 365-day year. Lead time to get the order once placed is seven days.

a. What is the economic order quantity?

b. What is the reorder point?

✓ **17.** Daily demand for a product is 60 units with a standard deviation of 10 units. The review period is 10 days, and lead time is 2 days. At the time of review there are 100 units in stock. If 98 percent of all demand is to be satisfied from items in stock, how many units should be ordered?

18. University Drug Phamaceuticals orders its antibiotics every two weeks (14 days) when a salesperson visits from one of the pharmaceutical companies. Tetracycline is one of its most prescribed antibiotics, with average daily demand of 2,000 capsules. The standard deviation of daily demand was derived from examining prescriptions filled over the past three months and was found to be 800 capsules. It takes five days for the order to arrive. University Drug would like to satisfy 99 percent of the prescriptions. The salesperson just arrived, and there are currently 25,000 capsules in stock. How many capsules should be ordered?

19. Produce 600 T-shirts.

19. Sally's Silk Screening produces specialty T-shirts that are primarily sold at special events. She is trying to decide how many to produce for an upcoming event. During the event itself, which lasts one day, Sally can sell T-shirts for $20 apiece. However, when the event ends, any unsold T-shirts are sold for $4 apiece. It costs Sally $8 to make a specialty T-shirt. Using Sally's estimate of demand that follows, how many T-shirts should she produce for the upcoming event?

Demand	Probability
300	.05
400	.10
500	.40
600	.30
700	.10
800	.05

20. *a.* 1,414 units.
    b. 14.1 orders.
    c. 1,000.
    d. 1,300.

20. Magnetron, Inc., manufactures microwave ovens for the commercial market. Currently, Magnetron is producing part 2104 in its fabrication shop for use in the adjacent unit assembly area. Next year's requirement for part 2104 is estimated at 20,000 units. Part 2104 is valued at $50 per unit, and the combined storage and handling cost is $8 per unit per year. The cost of preparing the order and making the production setup is $200. The plant operates 250 days per year. The assembly area operates every working day, completing 80 units, and the fabrication shop produces 160 units per day when it is producing part 2104.
a. Compute the economic order quantity.
b. How many orders will be placed each year?
c. If part 2104 could be purchased from another firm with the same costs as described, what would the order quantity be? (The order is received all at once.)
d. If the average lead time to order from another firm is 10 working days and a safety stock level is set at 500 units, what is the reorder point?

21. *Q* = 7,500 blades. ✓

21. Garrett Corporation, turbine manufacturer, works an 18-hour day, 300 days a year. Titanium blades can be produced on its turbine blade machine number 1, TBM1, at a rate of 500 per hour, and the average usage rate is 5,000 per day. The blades cost $15 apiece, and storage costs $0.10 per day per blade because of insurance, interest on investments, and space allocation. TBM1 costs $250 to set up for each run. Lead time requires production to begin after stock drops to 500 blades. What is the optimal production run for TBM1?

22. *a.* Similar to Exhibit
        15.13
    b. 2,400 dozen.
    c. ∴ *P* = .50

22. Famous Albert prides himself on being the Cookie King of the West. Small, freshly baked cookies are the specialty of his shop. Famous Albert has asked for help to determine the number of cookies he should make each day. From an analysis of past demand he estimates demand for cookies as

Demand	Probability of Demand
1,800 dozen	0.05
2,000	0.10
2,200	0.20
2,400	0.30
2,600	0.20
2,800	0.10
3,000	0.05

Each dozen sells for $.69 and costs $.49, which includes handling and transportation. Cookies that are not sold at the end of the day are reduced to $0.29 and sold the following day as day-old merchandise.

a. Construct a table showing the profits or losses for each possible quantity.

b. What is the optimal number of cookies to make?

c. Solve this problem by using marginal analysis.

23. Mike's Muffler shop has one standard muffler that fits a large variety of cars. They wish to establish a reorder point system to manage their inventory of this standard muffler. Use the following information to determine the best order size, and the reorder point.

23. $Q_{opt} = 216.02 \sim 216$.
$R = 26.17 \sim 27$.

Annual demand	3,500 mufflers	Ordering cost	$50 per order
Standard deviation of daily demand	6 mufflers per working day	Service level	99%
Item cost	$30 per muffler	Lead time	2 working days
Annual holding cost	25% of item value	Working days	300 per year

24. Alpha Products, Inc., is having a problem trying to control inventory. There is insufficient time to devote to all its items equally. Here is a sample of some items stocked, along with the annual usage of each item expressed in dollar volume.

24. *a.* ABC.
b. A items (f, k, q); B items (c, e, g, n, r, t); C items (remainder).

Item	Annual Dollar Usage	Item	Annual Dollar Usage
a	$ 7,000	k	$80,000
b	1,000	l	400
c	14,000	m	1,100
d	2,000	n	30,000
e	24,000	o	1,900
f	68,000	p	800
g	17,000	q	90,000
h	900	r	12,000
i	1,700	s	3,000
j	2,300	t	32,000

a. Can you suggest a system for allocating control time?

b. Specify where each item from the list would be placed.

✓ 25. After graduation, you decide to go into a partnership in an office supply store that has existed for a number of years. Walking through the store and stockrooms, you find a great discrepancy in service levels. Some spaces and bins for items are completely empty; others have supplies that are covered with dust and have obviously been there a long time. You decide to take on the project of establishing consistent levels of inventory to meet customer demands. Most of your supplies are purchased from just a few distributors that call on your store once every two weeks.

25. $\bar{d} = \dfrac{5,000}{365}$,
$q = 208$.

You choose, as your first item for study, computer printer paper. You examine the sales records and purchase orders and find that demand for the past 12 months was 5,000 boxes. Using your calculator you sample some days' demands and estimate that the standard deviation of daily demand is 10 boxes. You also search out these figures:

Cost per box of paper: $11.

Desired service level: 98 percent.

Store is open every day.

Salesperson visits every two weeks.

Delivery time following visit is three days.

Using your procedure, how many boxes of paper would be ordered if, on the day the salesperson calls, there are 60 boxes on hand?

26. *a.* $Q_{opt} = 31.62 \sim 32$
    units.
    b. $18.83 \sim 19$ units.

26. A distributor of large appliances needs to determine the order quantities and reorder points for the various products it carries. The following data refer to a specific refrigerator in its product line:

Cost to place an order	$100
Holding cost	20 percent of product cost per year
Cost of refrigerator	$500 each
Annual demand	500 refrigerators
Standard deviation during lead time	10 refrigerators
Lead time	7 days

Consider an even daily demand and a 365-day year.
a. What is the economic order quantity?
b. If the distributor wants to satisfy 97 percent of its demand, what reorder point, *R*, should be used?

27. *a.* $Q_{opt} = 75.59 \sim 76$
    units.
    b. $E(z) = 0.253 \Rightarrow$
    $z = 0.34$.
    $R = 12.76 \sim 13$ units.

27. It is your responsibility, as the new head of the automotive section of Nichols Department Store, to ensure that reorder quantities for the various items have been correctly established. You decide to test one of the items and choose Michelin tires, XW size 185 × 14 BSW. A perpetual inventory system has been used so you examine this as well as other records and come up with the following data:

Cost per tire	$35 each
Holding cost	20 percent of tire cost per year
Demand	1,000 per year
Ordering cost	$20 per order
Standard deviation of daily demand	3 tires
Delivery lead time	4 days

Because customers generally do not wait for tires but go elsewhere, you decide on a service level of 98 percent.
a. Determine the order quantity.
b. Determine the reorder point.

28. 590 hamburgers.

28. UA Hamburger Hamlet (UAHH) places an order, for its high-volume items daily (hamburger patties, buns, milk, etc.). UAHH counts its current inventory on hand once per day and phones in its order for delivery 24 hours later. Determine the number of hamburgers UAHH should order for the following conditions:

Average daily demand	600
Standard deviation of demand	100
Desired service level	99%
Hamburger inventory	800

29. 5,000 pounds. ✓

29. CU, Incorporated (CUI), produces copper contacts that it uses in switches and relays. CUI needs to determine the order quantity, *Q*, to meet the annual demand at the lowest cost. The price of copper depends on the quantity ordered. Here are price-break data and other data for the problem:

Price of copper: $0.82 per pound up to 2,499 pounds
$0.81 per pound for orders between 2,500 and 4,999 pounds
$0.80 per pound for orders greater than 5,000 pounds
Annual demand: 50,000 pounds per year
Holding cost: 20 percent per unit per year of the price of the copper
Ordering cost: $30

Which quantity should be ordered?

30. A items (5, 3);
    B items (4, 7, 9);
    C items (remainder).

30. DAT, Inc., produces digital audiotapes to be used in the consumer audio division. DAT lacks sufficient personnel in its inventory supply section to closely control each item stocked, so it has asked you to determine an ABC classification. Here is a sample from the inventory records:

Item	Average Monthly Demand	Price per Unit
1	700	$ 6.00
2	200	4.00
3	2,000	12.00
4	1,100	20.00
5	4,000	21.00
6	100	10.00
7	3,000	2.00
8	2,500	1.00
9	500	10.00
10	1,000	2.00

Develop an ABC classification for these 10 items.

31. A local service station is open 7 days per week, 365 days per year. Sales of 10W40 grade premium oil average 20 cans per day. Inventory holding costs are $0.50 per can per year. Ordering costs are $10 per order. Lead time is two weeks. Back orders are not practical—the motorist drives away.

    a. Based on this data, choose the appropriate inventory model and calculate the economic order quantity and reorder point. Describe in a sentence how the plan would work. Hint: Assume demand is deterministic.

    b. The boss is concerned about this model because demand really varies. The standard deviation of demand was determined from a data sample to be 6.15 cans per day. The manager wants to satisfy 99.5 percent of his customers (practically all) when they ask for oil. Determine a new inventory plan based on this new information and the data in (*a*). Use Q_{opt} from (*a*).

31. a. Q = 540 cans.
R = 280.
b. R = 299.

32. Dave's Auto Supply custom mixes paint for their customers. They perform an inventory count of the main colors that are used for mixing paint on a weekly basis. Determine the amount of white paint that should be ordered using the following information:

32. q = 23.41 ∼ 24.

Average weekly demand	20 gallons
Standard deviation of demand	5 gallons/week
Desired service level	98%
Current inventory	25 gallons
Lead time	1 week

SELECTED BIBLIOGRAPHY

Brooks, Roger B., and Larry W. Wilson. *Inventory Record Accuracy: Unleashing the Power of Cycle Counting.* Essex Junction, VT: Oliver Wight, 1993.

Fogarty, Donald W., John H. Blackstone, and Thomas R. Hoffmann. *Production and Inventory Management.* 2nd ed. Cincinnati, OH: South-Western, 1991.

Graves, Steven C., A. H. G. Rinnoy Kan, and Paul H. Zipkin. *Logistics of Production and Inventory.* New York: North-Holland, 1993.

Silver, E., D. Pyke, and R. Peterson. *Decision Systems for Inventory Management and Production Planning and Control.* 3rd ed. New York: Wiley, 1997.

Sipper, Daniel and Robert L. Bulfin, Jr. *Production Planning, Control, and Integration.* New York: McGraw-Hill, 1997.

Tersine, Richard J. *Principles of Inventory and Materials Management.* 4th ed. New York: North-Holland, 1994.

Vollmann, T. E., W. L. Berry, and D. C. Whybark. *Manufacturing Planning and Control Systems.* 4th ed. Burr Ridge, IL: Richard D. Irwin, 1997.

Young, Jan B. *Modern Inventory Operations: Methods for Accuracy and Productivity.* New York: Van Nostrand Reinhold, 1991.

Chapter 16

Inventory Systems for Dependent Demand MRP-Type Systems

Chapter Outline

Where MRP Can Be Used, 627

A Simple MRP Example, 627

Master Production Schedule, 629

    Time Fences

Material Requirements Planning (MRP) Systems, 631

    Purposes of MRP

    Advantages of MRP

    Disadvantages of MRP

Material Requirements Planning System Structure, 633

    Demand for Products

    Bill of Materials File

    Inventory Records File

    MRP Computer Program

    Output Reports

    Net Change Systems

An Example Using MRP, 639

    Forecasting Demand

    Developing a Master Schedule

    Bill of Material (Product Structure) File

    Inventory Records (Item Master) File

    Running the MRP Program

Improvements in the MRP System, 644

    Computing Work Center Load

    Closed-Loop MRP

    MRP II (Manufacturing Resource Planning)

Embedding JIT into MRP, 647

Lot Sizing in MRP Systems, 648

    Lot-for-Lot

    Economic Order Quantity

    Least Total Cost

    Least Unit Cost

    Choosing the Best Lot Size

Advanced MRP-Type Systems, 653

    SAP AG's R/3

Case: Nichols Company, 665

Key Terms

Material Requirements Planning (MRP)

Manufacturing Resource Planning (MRP II)

Master Production Schedule (MPS)

Bill of Materials (BOM)

Inventory Records File

Net Change System

Closed-Loop MRP

Lot-For-Lot (L4L)

Enterprise Resource Planning (ERP)

SAP/R3

www Links

SAP/R3 (http://www.sap.com)

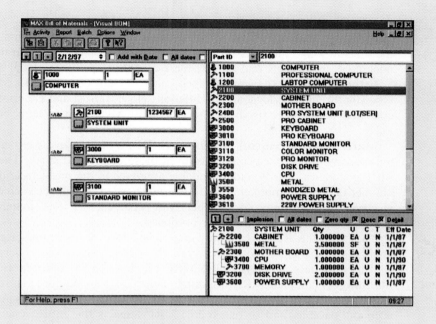

IN THE PAST, MRP AND MRP II WERE ASSOCIATED exclusively with mainframes and minicomputers. This perspective has been changing. Today's software options include those supporting Windows platforms and a host of different network operating systems. For years, small manufacturers didn't have a system available to them—primarily because of cost, says Carol A. Ptak, president of Eagle Enterprises and author of *MRP and Beyond.*

Many manufacturers of all sizes are using PC solutions because they are just as robust as midrange products. Sheldon Needle, president of CTS, publishers of *The Guide to PC Manufacturing Software,* believes PC-based software is more practical for manufacturers because it typically embraces the latest development tools, interfaces to third-party software, and industry-standard database architectures.

The limited time it takes to do an MRP calculation in modern PC computing applications also means that users have the opportunity to be more experimental. Ptak agrees that production planners used to be limited by, and plan the week around, the amount of time it took to run MRP. As recent as 10 years ago, it could take a mainframe hours or days to run the same MRP calculation that today would take only minutes on a PC.

The relatively new client/server networking architecture allows part of the application to run on the client and part on the server. Because of this "split," less data needs to be transferred back and forth between the two, greatly enhancing network performance and, ultimately, the performance of the application.

The Internet and World Wide Web are also having a profound impact on these applications. New Internet technology has allowed real-time collaboration. As users communicate and share what they have learned, companies are able to expand their knowledge base and accumulated learning. The results of this, says Ptak, are better decision-making and planning processes. ●

Source: Adapted from James Diamond, "Production and Inventory Control: The Move to the PC," *IIE Solutions,* January 1997, pp. 18–22.

**Material
Requirements
Planning (MRP)**

FINANCE
ACCOUNTING

**Manufacturing
Resource Planning
(MRP II)**

As Virginia Slims ads used to say, "You've come a long way, baby." So has material requirements planning (MRP) come a long way. From humble beginnings computing the schedules and amounts of materials required, MRP has grown to become fully integrated, interactive, real time systems capable of multisite global applications.

In this chapter we go back to the beginning and introduce the basic MRP system and take you through the logic and calculations of scheduling and materials ordering. We conclude the chapter by discussing the latest MRP-type systems being developed today.

Material requirements planning (MRP) systems have been installed almost universally in manufacturing firms, even those considered small. The reason is that MRP is a logical, easily understandable approach to the problem of determining the number of parts, components, and materials needed to produce each end item. MRP also provides the time schedule specifying when each of these materials, parts, and components should be ordered or produced.

The original MRP planned only materials. However, as computer power grew and applications expanded, so did the breadth of MRP. Soon it considered resources as well as materials and was called **MRP II,** standing for **manufacturing resource planning.** A complete MRP program included 20 or so modules controlling the entire system from order entry through scheduling, inventory control, finance, accounting, accounts payable, and so on. Today, MRP impacts the entire system and includes just-in-time, kanban, and computer-integrated manufacturing (CIM).

All firms maintain a bill of materials file (BOM) which is simply the sequence of everything that goes into the final product. It can be called a *product structure tree,* a *schematic,* or a *flow diagram,* which shows the order of creating the item. Also maintained by all firms is an inventory file. This database contains specifications about each item, where it is purchased or produced, and how long it takes. MRP in its basic form is a computer program determining how much of each item is needed and when it is needed to complete a specified number of units in a specific time period. MRP does this by reaching into the bill of materials file and inventory records file to create a time schedule and the number of units needed at each step in the process.

MRP is based on dependent demand. Dependent demand is that demand caused by the demand for a higher-level item. Tires, wheels, and engines are dependent demand items that depend on the demand for automobiles.

Determining the number of dependent demand items needed is essentially a straightforward multiplication process. If one Part A takes five parts of B to make, then five parts of A require 25 parts of B. The basic difference in independent demand covered in the previous chapter and dependent demand covered in this chapter is as follows: If Part A is sold outside of the firm, the amount of Part A that we sell is uncertain. We need to create a forecast using past data or do something like a market analysis. Part A is an independent item. However, Part B is a dependent part and its use depends on Part A. The number of B needed is simply the number of A times five. As a result of this type of multiplication, the requirements of other dependent demand items tend to become more and more lumpy as we go farther down into the product creation sequence. Lumpiness means that the requirements tend to bunch or lump rather than having an even disbursement. This is also caused by the way manufacturing is done. When manufacturing occurs in lots, items needed to produce the lot are withdrawn from inventory in quantities (perhaps all at once) rather than one at a time.

The main purpose of this chapter is to explain MRP more thoroughly and to demonstrate its use. We show that just-in-time (JIT) systems and MRP are not necessarily competing ways for production but can work effectively together. Finally we discuss advanced MRP-type systems including enterprisewide and industrywide modules and data requirements.

WHERE MRP CAN BE USED

MRP is being used in a variety of industries with a job-shop environment (meaning that a number of products are made in batches using the same productive equipment). The list in Exhibit 16.1 includes process industries, but note that the processes mentioned are confined to job runs that alternate output product and do not include continuous processes such as petroleum or steel.

As you can see in the exhibit, MRP is most valuable to companies involved in assembly operations and least valuable to those in fabrication.

One more point to note: MRP does not work well in companies that produce a low number of units annually. Especially for companies producing complex expensive products requiring advanced research and design, experience has shown that lead times tend to be too long and too uncertain, and the product configuration too complex for MRP to handle. Such companies need the control features that network scheduling techniques offer; they would be better off using project scheduling methods (covered previously in Chapter 3).

A SIMPLE MRP EXAMPLE

Before discussing details of an MRP system, we briefly explain how quantities are calculated, lead times are offset, and order releases and receipts are established.

Industry Type	Examples	Expected Benefits	
Assemble-to-stock	Combines multiple component parts into a finished product, which is then stocked in inventory to satisfy customer demand. Examples: watches, tools, appliances.	High	**Exhibit 16.1** Industry Applications and Expected Benefits of MRP
Fabricate-to-stock	Items are manufactured by machine rather than assembled from parts. These are standard stock items carried in anticipation of customer demand. Examples: piston rings, electrical switches.	Low	
Assemble-to-order	A final assembly is made from standard options that the customer chooses. Examples: trucks, generators, motors.	High	
Fabricate-to-order	Items manufactured by machine to customer order. These are generally industrial orders. Examples: bearings, gears, fasteners.	Low	
Manufacture-to-order	Items fabricated or assembled completely to customer specification. Examples: turbine generators, heavy machine tools.	High	
Process	Industries such as foundries, rubber and plastics, specialty paper, chemicals, paint, drug, food processors.	Medium	

Suppose that we are to produce Product T, which is made of two parts U and three parts V. Part U, in turn, is made of one part W and two parts X. Part V is made of two parts W and two parts Y. Exhibit 16.2 shows the product structure tree of Product T. By simple computation, we calculate that if 100 units of T are required, we need

Part U:	$2 \times$ number of Ts $=$	2×100	$= 200$
Part V:	$3 \times$ number of Ts $=$	3×100	$= 300$
Part W:	$\begin{cases} 1 \times \text{ number of Us } = \\ +2 \times \text{ number of Vs } = \end{cases}$	$\begin{matrix} 1 \times 200 \\ +2 \times 300 \end{matrix} \Big\}$	$= 800$
Part X:	$2 \times$ number of Us $=$	2×200	$= 400$
Part Y:	$2 \times$ number of Vs $=$	2×300	$= 600$

Now, consider the time needed to obtain these items, either to produce the part internally or to obtain it from an outside vendor. Assume, now, that T takes one week to make; U, 2 weeks; V, 2 weeks; W, 3 weeks; X, 1 week; and Y, 1 week. If we know when Product T is required, we can create a time schedule chart specifying when all materials must be ordered and received to meet the demand for T. Exhibit 16.3 shows which items are needed and when. We have thus created a material requirements plan

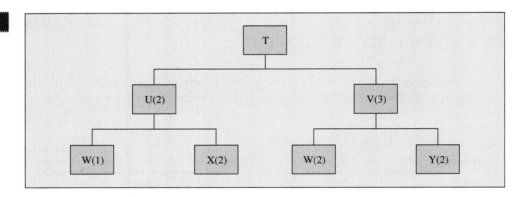

		Week							
		1	2	3	4	5	6	7	
T	Required date							100	T Lead time = 1 week
	Order placement						100		
U	Required date						200		U Lead time = 2 weeks
	Order placement				200				
V	Required date						300		V Lead time = 2 weeks
	Order placement			300					
W	Required date				800				W lead time = 3 weeks
	Order placement	800							
X	Required date				400				X Lead time = 1 week
	Order placement			400					
Y	Required date				600				Y Lead time = 1 week
	Order placement			600					

based on the demand for Product T and the knowledge of how T is made and the time needed to obtain each part.

From this simple illustration, it is apparent that developing a material requirements plan manually for thousands or even hundreds of items would be impractical—a great deal of computation is needed, and a tremendous amount of data must be available about the inventory status (number of units on hand, on order, and so forth) and about the product structure (how the product is made and how many units of each material are required). Because we are compelled to use a computer, our emphasis from here on in this chapter is to discuss the files needed for a computer program and the general makeup of the system. However, the basic logic of the program is essentially the same as that for our simple example.

MASTER PRODUCTION SCHEDULE

Generally, the master schedule deals with end items. If the end item is quite large or quite expensive, however, the master schedule may schedule major subassemblies or components instead.

All production systems have limited capacity and limited resources. This presents a challenging job for the master scheduler. While the aggregate plan provides the general range of operation, the master scheduler must specify exactly what is to be produced. These decisions are made while responding to pressures from various functional areas, such as the sales department (meet the customer's promised due date), finance (minimize inventory), management (maximize productivity and customer service, minimize resource needs), and manufacturing (have level schedules and minimize setup time).

To determine an acceptable feasible schedule to be released to the shop, trial master production schedules are run through the MRP program. The resulting planned order releases (the detailed production schedules) are checked to make sure that resources are available and that the completion times are reasonable. What appears to be a feasible master schedule may turn out to require excessive resources once the product explosion has taken place and materials, parts, and components from lower levels are determined. If this does happen (the usual case), the master production schedule is then modified with these limitations and the MRP program is run again. To ensure good master scheduling, the master scheduler (the human being) must

Include all demands from product sales, warehouse replenishment, spares, and interplant requirements.

Never lose sight of the aggregate plan.

Be involved with customer order promising.

Be visible to all levels of management.

Objectively trade off manufacturing, marketing, and engineering conflicts.

Identify and communicate all problems.

MARKETING
SALES
ENGINEERING

The upper portion of Exhibit 16.4 shows an aggregate plan for the total number of mattresses planned per month, without regard for mattress type. The lower portion shows a master production schedule specifying the exact type of mattress and the quantity planned for production by week. The next level down (not shown) would be the MRP program that develops detailed schedules showing when cotton batting, springs, and hardwood are needed to make the mattresses. If carried further, this

Exhibit 16.4

The Aggregate Plan
and the Master
Production Schedule
for Mattresses

Aggregate Production
Plan for Mattresses

Month	1	2
Mattress production	900	950

Master Production
Schedule for
Mattress Models

	1	2	3	4	5	6	7	8
Model 327	200			400		200	100	
Model 538		100	100		150		100	
Model 749			100			200		200

mattress example would look like Exhibit 16.16, which shows parts and subassemblies for electrical meters.

To again summarize the planning sequence, the aggregate production plan, discussed in Chapter 14, specifies product groups. It does not specify exact items. The next level down in the planning process is the master production schedule. The **master production schedule (MPS)** is the time-phased plan specifying how many and when the firm plans to build each end item. For example, the aggregate plan for a furniture company may specify the total volume of mattresses it plans to produce over the next month or next quarter. The MPS goes the next step down and identifies the exact size mattresses and their qualities and styles. All of the mattresses sold by the company would be specified by the MPS. The MPS also states period by period (usually weekly) how many and when each of these mattress types is needed.

Master Production Schedule (MPS)

Still further down the disaggregation process is the MRP program, which calculates and schedules all raw materials, parts, and supplies needed to make the mattress specified by the MPS.

Time Fences

The question of flexibility within a master production schedule depends on several factors: production lead time, commitment of parts and components to a specific end item, relationship between the customer and vendor, amount of excess capacity, and the reluctance or willingness of management to make changes.

The purpose of time fences is to maintain a reasonably controlled flow through the production system. Unless some operating rules are established and adhered to, the system could be chaotic and filled with overdue orders and constant expediting.

Exhibit 16.5 shows an example of a master production schedule time fence. Management defines *time fences* as periods of time having some specified level of opportunity for the customer to make changes. (The customer may be the firm's own marketing department, which may be considering product promotions, broadening variety, etc.) Note in the exhibit that for the next eight weeks, this particular master schedule is frozen. Each firm has its own time fences and operating rules. Under these rules, *frozen* could be defined as anything from absolutely no changes in one company to only the most minor of changes in another. *Moderately firm* may allow changes in specific products within a product group so long as parts are available. *Flexible* may allow almost any variations in products, with the provision that capacity remains about the same and that there are no long lead time items involved.

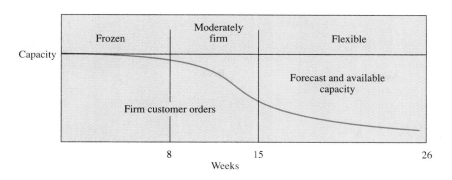

Exhibit 16.5

Master Production
Schedule Time Fences

■ MATERIAL REQUIREMENTS PLANNING (MRP) SYSTEMS

As we stated previously, based on a *master schedule* derived from a *production plan,* a *material requirements planning (MRP) system* creates schedules identifying the specific parts and materials required to produce end items, the exact numbers needed, and the dates when orders for these materials should be released and be received or completed within the production cycle. MRP systems use a computer program to carry out these operations. Most firms have used computerized inventory systems for years, but they were independent of the scheduling system; MRP links them together.

Purposes of MRP

The main purposes of a basic MRP system are to control inventory levels, assign operating priorities for items, and plan capacity to load the production system. These may be briefly expanded as follows:

Inventory

Order the right part.

Order in the right quantity.

Order at the right time.

Priorities

Order with the right due date.

Keep the due date valid.

Capacity

Plan for a complete load.

Plan an accurate load.

Plan for an adequate time to view future load.

The *theme* of MRP is "getting the right materials to the right place at the right time."

The *objectives* of inventory management under an MRP system are the same as under any inventory management system: to improve customer service, minimize inventory investment, and maximize production operating efficiency.

The *philosophy* of material requirements planning is that materials should be expedited (hurried) when their lack would delay the overall production schedule, and de-expedited (delayed) when the schedule falls behind and postpones their need. Traditionally, and perhaps still typically, when an order is behind schedule, significant effort is spent trying to get it back on schedule. However, the opposite is not always true; when an order, for whatever reason, has its completion date delayed, the appropriate adjustments are not made in the schedule. This results in a one-sided effort—later orders are hurried, but early orders are not rescheduled for later. Aside from perhaps using scarce capacity, it is preferable not to have raw materials and work-in-process before the actual need because inventories tie up finances, clutter up stockrooms, prohibit design changes, and prevent the cancellation or delay of orders.

Advantages of MRP

In past years, when firms switched from existing manual or computerized systems to an MRP system, they realized many benefits:

Ability to price more competitively.

Reduced sales price.

Reduced inventory.

Better customer service.

Better response to market demands.

Ability to change the master schedule.

Reduced setup and tear-down costs.

Reduced idle time.

In addition, the MRP system:

Gives advance notice so that managers can see the planned schedule before actual release orders.

Tells when to de-expedite as well as expedite.

Delays or cancels orders.

Changes order quantities.

Advances or delays order due dates.

Aids capacity planning.

During their conversions to MRP systems, many firms claimed as much as 40 percent reductions in inventory investment.

Disadvantages of MRP

MRP is very well developed technically, and implementation of an MRP system should be pretty straightforward. Yet there are many problems with the MRP systems and many "failures" in trying to install them. Why do such problems and outright failures occur with a "proven" system?

The answer partially lies with organizational and behavioral factors. Three major causes have been identified: the lack of top management commitment, the failure to recognize that MRP is only a software tool that needs to be used correctly, and the integration of MRP and JIT.

Part of the blame for the lack of top management's commitment may be MRP's image. It sounds like a manufacturing system rather than a business plan. However, an MRP system is used to plan resources and develop schedules. Also, a well-functioning schedule can use the firm's assets effectively, thus increasing profit. MRP should be accepted by top management as a planning tool with specific reference to profit results. Intensive executive education is needed, emphasizing the importance of MRP as a closed-loop, integrated, strategic planning tool.

The second cause of the problem concerns the MRP proponents that overdid themselves in selling the concept. MRP was presented and perceived as a complete and stand-alone system to run a firm, rather than as part of the total system. The third issue, which we discuss later in this chapter, is how MRP can be made to function with JIT.

MRP also needs a high degree of accuracy for operation, which often requires (1) changing how the firm operates and (2) updating files. For example, many firms have had open access to inventory stores. This causes differences between recorded inventory and actual inventory on hand. Also, many engineering drawings and bills of materials become outdated, and MRP requires accuracy to function correctly.

Perhaps one of the biggest complaints by users is that MRP is too rigid. When MRP develops a schedule, it is quite difficult to veer away from the schedule if need arises.

■ MATERIAL REQUIREMENTS PLANNING SYSTEM STRUCTURE

The material requirements planning portion of manufacturing activities most closely interacts with the master schedule, bill of materials file, inventory records file, and the output reports. Exhibit 16.6 shows a different perspective of Exhibit 14.1 in Chapter 14 with several additions. Note that capacity is not considered in this exhibit, nor are there any feedback loops to higher levels. We discuss these elements later in this chapter under MRP II and capacity requirements planning.

Each facet of Exhibit 16.6 is detailed in the following sections, but essentially, the MRP system works as follows: Orders for products are used to create a master

Overall View of the
Inputs to a Standard
Material Requirements
Planning Program
and the Reports
Generated by the
Program

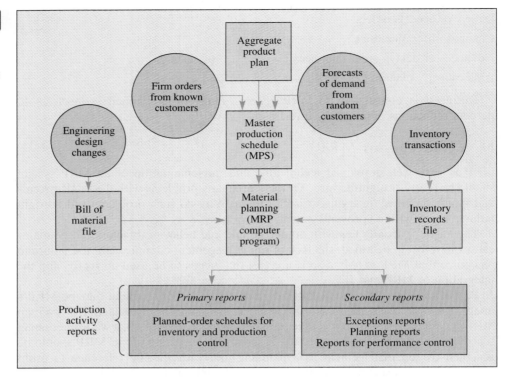

production schedule, which states the number of items to be produced during specific time periods. A bill of materials file identifies the specific materials used to make each item and the correct quantities of each. The inventory records file contains data such as the number of units on hand and on order. These three sources—master production schedule, bill of materials file, and inventory records file—become the data sources for the material requirements program, which expands the production schedule into a detailed order scheduling plan for the entire production sequence.

Demand for Products

Product demand for end items comes primarily from two main sources. The first is known customers who have placed specific orders, such as those generated by sales personnel, or from interdepartment transactions. These orders usually carry promised delivery dates. There is no forecasting involved in these orders—simply add them up. The second source is forecast demand. These are the normal independent-demand orders; the forecasting models presented in Chapter 13 can be used to predict the quantities. The demand from the known customers and the forecast demand are combined and become the input for the master production schedule.

In addition to the demand for end products, customers also order specific parts and components either as spares, or for service and repair. These demands for items less complex than the end product are not usually part of the master production schedule; instead, they are fed directly into the material requirements planning program at the appropriate levels. That is, they are added in as a gross requirement for that part or component.

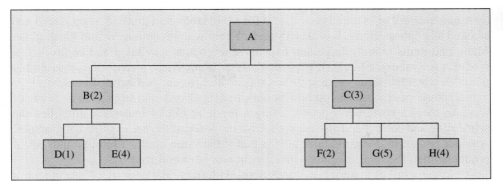

Exhibit 16.7

Bill of Materials (Product Structure Tree) for Product A

Indented Parts List	Single-Level Parts List
A	A
B(2)	B(2)
D(1)	C(3)
E(4)	B
C(3)	D(1)
F(2)	E(4)
G(5)	C
H(4)	F(2)
	G(5)
	H(4)

Exhibit 16.8

Parts List in an Indented Format and in a Single-Level List

Bill of Materials File

The **bill of materials (BOM)** file contains the complete product description, listing not only the materials, parts, and components but also the sequence in which the product is created. This BOM file is one of the three main inputs to the MRP program. (The other two are the master schedule and the inventory records file.)

The BOM file is often called the *product structure file* or *product tree* because it shows how a product is put together. It contains the information to identify each item and the quantity used per unit of the item of which it is a part. To illustrate this, consider Product A shown in Exhibit 16.7. Product A is made of two units of Part B and three units of Part C. Part B is made of one unit of Part D and four units of Part E. Part C is made of two units of Part F, five units of Part G, and four units of Part H.

In the past, bill of materials files have often listed parts as an indented file. This clearly identifies each item and the manner in which it is assembled because each indentation signifies the components of the item. A comparison of the indented parts in Exhibit 16.8 with the item structure in Exhibit 16.7 shows the ease of relating the two displays. From a computer standpoint, however, storing items in indented parts lists is very inefficient. To compute the amount of each item needed at the lower levels, each item would need to be expanded ("exploded") and summed. A more efficient procedure is to store parts data in a single-level explosion. That is, each item and component is listed showing only its parent and the number of units needed per unit of its parent. This avoids duplication because it includes each assembly only once. Exhibit 16.8 shows both the indented parts list and the single-level parts list for Product A.

Bill of Materials (BOM)

Vol. IV "Production Tour of Vision Light System at Federal Signal."

A *modular* bill of materials is the term for a buildable item that can be produced and stocked as a subassembly. It is also a standard item with no options within the module. Many end items that are large and expensive are better scheduled and controlled as modules (or subassemblies). It is particularly advantageous to schedule subassembly modules when the same subassemblies appear in different end items. For example, a manufacturer of cranes can combine booms, transmissions, and engines in a variety of ways to meet a customer's needs. Using a modular bill of materials simplifies the scheduling and control and also makes it easier to forecast the use of different modules. Another benefit in using modular bills is that if the same item is used in a number of products, then the total inventory investment can be minimized.

A *planning* bill of materials includes items with fractional options. (A planning bill can specify, for example, 0.3 of a part. What that means is that 30 percent of the units produced contain that part and 70 percent do not.)

Low-Level Coding   If all identical parts occur at the same level for each end product, the total number of parts and materials needed for a product can be computed easily. Consider Product L shown in Exhibit 16.9a. Notice that Item N, for example, occurs both as an input to L and as an input to M. Item N, therefore, needs to be lowered to level 2 (Exhibit 16.9b) to bring all Ns to the same level. If all identical items are placed at the same level, it becomes a simple matter for the computer to scan across each level and summarize the number of units of each item required.

Inventory Records File

Inventory Records File

The **inventory records file** under a computerized system can be quite lengthy. Each item in inventory is carried as a separate file and the range of details carried about an item is almost limitless. Exhibit 16.10 shows the variety of information contained in the inventory records files. The MRP program accesses the *status* segment of the file according to specific time periods (called *time buckets* in MRP slang). These files are accessed as needed during the program run.

The MRP program performs its analysis from the top of the product structure downward, exploding requirements level by level. There are times, however, when it is desirable to identify the parent item that caused the material requirement. The MRP

Exhibit 16.9   Product L Hierarchy in (a) Expanded to the Lowest Level of Each Item in (b)

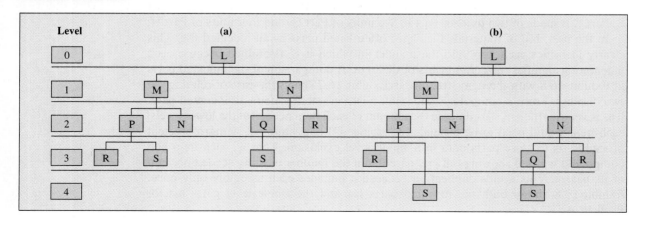

program allows the creation of a *peg record* file either separately or as part of the inventory record file. Pegging requirements allows us to retrace a material requirement upward in the product structure through each level, identifying each parent item that created the demand.

Inventory Transactions File The inventory status file is kept up to date by posting inventory transactions as they occur. These changes occur because of stock receipts and disbursements, scrap losses, wrong parts, canceled orders, and so forth.

MRP Computer Program

The material requirements planning program operates on the inventory file, the master schedule, and the bill of materials file. It works in this way: A list of end items needed by time periods (as in the discussion of master scheduling in this chapter) is specified by the master schedule. A description of the materials and parts needed to make each item is specified in the bill of materials file. The number of units of each item and material currently on hand and on order are contained in the inventory file. The MRP program "works" on the inventory file (which is segmented into time periods) while continually referring to the bill of materials file to compute the quantities of each item needed. The number of units of each item required is then corrected for on-hand amounts, and the net requirement is "offset" (set back in time) to allow for the lead time needed to obtain the material.

(One obstacle that many potential users of an MRP program have found is that their current bill of materials files and inventory records files are not adequate to provide data in the format required by the program. Thus, they must modify these files before installing an MRP system. We discuss other problems as well later in the chapter.)

If the MRP program being used does not consider capacity constraints, the master scheduler must do some capacity balancing by hand. Through an iterative process, the master scheduler feeds a tentative master schedule into the MRP system (along with

Exhibit 16.10

The Inventory Status Record for an Item in Inventory

<table>
<tr><td rowspan="3">Item master data segment</td><td>Part No.</td><td>Description</td><td>Lead time</td><td>Std. cost</td><td>Safety stock</td></tr>
<tr><td>Order quantity</td><td>Setup</td><td>Cycle</td><td>Last year's usage</td><td>Class</td></tr>
<tr><td>Scrap allowance</td><td>Cutting data</td><td>Pointers</td><td colspan="2">Etc.</td></tr>
<tr><td rowspan="5">Inventory status segment</td><td>Allocated</td><td>Control balance</td><td colspan="2">Period 1 2 3 4 5 6 7 8</td><td>Totals</td></tr>
<tr><td>Gross requirements</td><td></td><td colspan="2"></td><td></td></tr>
<tr><td>Scheduled receipts</td><td></td><td colspan="2"></td><td></td></tr>
<tr><td>On hand</td><td></td><td colspan="2"></td><td></td></tr>
<tr><td>Planned-order releases</td><td></td><td colspan="2"></td><td></td></tr>
<tr><td rowspan="4">Subsidiary data segment</td><td>Order details</td><td colspan="4"></td></tr>
<tr><td>Pending action</td><td colspan="4"></td></tr>
<tr><td>Counters</td><td colspan="4"></td></tr>
<tr><td>Keeping track</td><td colspan="4"></td></tr>
</table>

other items requiring the same resources), and the output is examined for production feasibility. The master schedule is adjusted to try to correct any imbalances, and the program is executed again. This process is repeated until the output is acceptable. Although it would seem to be a simple matter to have the computer simulate some schedules that consider resource limitations, in reality, this can be a time-consuming problem.

To further complicate the problem today, there is not simply one master scheduler; there are a number of them. Often, firms divide the scheduling work among the schedulers by assigning one master scheduler for each major product line. The result of this is competition: Each master scheduler competes for limited resources for his or her own product line. As a group, however, they are trying to balance resource usage and due dates for the production system as a whole.

Output Reports

Because the MRP program has access to the bill of materials file, the master production schedule, and the inventory records file, outputs can take on an almost unlimited range of format and content. These reports are usually classified as *primary* and *secondary* reports. (With the expansion of MRP into MRP II and later versions, many additional reports are available.)

Primary Reports   Primary reports are the main or normal reports used for inventory and production control. These reports consist of

1. *Planned orders* to be released at a future time.
2. *Order release notices* to execute the planned orders.
3. *Changes in due dates* of open orders due to rescheduling.
4. *Cancellations or suspensions* of open orders due to cancellation or suspension of orders on the master production schedule.
5. *Inventory status data.*

Secondary Reports   Additional reports, which are optional under the MRP system, fall into three main categories:

1. *Planning reports* to be used, for example, in forecasting inventory and specifying requirements over some future time horizon.
2. *Performance reports* for purposes of pointing out inactive items and determining the agreement between actual and programmed item lead times and between actual and programmed quantity usage and costs.
3. *Exceptions reports* that point out serious discrepancies, such as errors, out-of-range situations, late or overdue orders, excessive scrap, or nonexistent parts.

Net Change Systems

Ordinarily an MRP system is initiated from a master schedule every week or two. This results in the complete explosion of items and the generation of the normal and exception reports. Many MRP programs, however, offer the option of generating intermediate schedules, called *net change* schedules. Net change systems are "activity" driven. Only if a transaction is processed against a particular item would that item be reviewed in a **net change system.** However, net change systems can be modified to respond only to unplanned or exception occurrences. Rather than being buried in paperwork output from an MRP system (which can easily happen), management may elect not to have the expected occurrences reported, but only deviations that should be noted. For example, if orders are received on time, a report is not produced. On the other hand, if the quantity delivered differs significantly from the order, this item is included in the net change report. Other reasons to include an item in a net change run might be to note a lost shipment, scrap losses, lead time changes, or a counting error in inventory. Based on these changes, new reports are generated.

Net Change System

AN EXAMPLE USING MRP

Ampere, Inc., produces a line of electric meters installed in residential buildings by electric utility companies to measure power consumption. Meters used on single-family homes are of two basic types for different voltage and amperage ranges. In addition to complete meters, some parts and subassemblies are sold separately for repair or for changeovers to a different voltage or power load. The problem for the MRP system is to determine a production schedule that would identify each item, the period it is needed, and the appropriate quantities. This schedule is then checked for feasibility, and the schedule is modified if necessary.

Forecasting Demand

Demand for the meters and components originates from two sources: regular customers that place firm orders, and unidentified customers that make the normal random demands for these items. The random requirements were forecast using one of the usual techniques described in Chapter 13 and past demand data. Exhibit 16.11 shows the requirement for Meters A and B, Subassembly D, and Part E for a six-month period (months three through eight).

Developing a Master Production Schedule

For the meter and component requirements specified in Exhibit 16.11, assume that the quantities to satisfy the known demands are to be delivered according to cus-

	Meter A		Meter B		Subassembly D		Part E	
Month	Known	Random	Known	Random	Known	Random	Known	Random
3	1,000	250	400	60	200	70	300	80
4	600	250	300	60	180	70	350	80
5	300	250	500	60	250	70	300	80
6	700	250	400	60	200	70	250	80
7	600	250	300	60	150	70	200	80
8	700	250	700	60	160	70	200	80

Exhibit 16.11

Future Requirements for Meters A and B, Subassembly D, and Part E stemming from Specific Customer Orders and from Random Sources

tomers' delivery schedules throughout the month, but that the items to satisfy random demands must be available during the first week of the month.

Our schedule assumes that *all* items are to be available the first week of the month. This assumption trial is reasonable because management (in our example) prefers to produce meters in one single lot each month rather than a number of lots throughout the month.

Exhibit 16.12 shows the trial master schedule that we use under these conditions, with demands for months 3 and 4 listed in the first week of each month, or as weeks 9 and 13. For brevity, we will work only with these two demand periods. The schedule we develop should be examined for resource availability, capacity availability, and so on, and then revised and run again. We will stop with our example at the end of this one schedule, however.

Bill of Materials (Product Structure) File

The product structure for Meters A and B is shown in Exhibit 16.13 in the typical way using low-level coding, in which each item is placed at the lowest level at which it appears in the structure hierarchy. Meters A and B consist of two subassemblies, C and D, and two parts, E and F. Quantities in parentheses indicate the number of units required per unit of the parent item.

Exhibit 16.12

A Master Schedule to Satisfy Demand Requirements as Specified in Exhibit 16.11

	Week								
	9	10	11	12	13	14	15	16	17
Meter A	1,250				850				550
Meter B	460				360				560
Subassembly D	270				250				320
Part E	380				430				380

Exhibit 16.13   Product Structure for Meters A and B

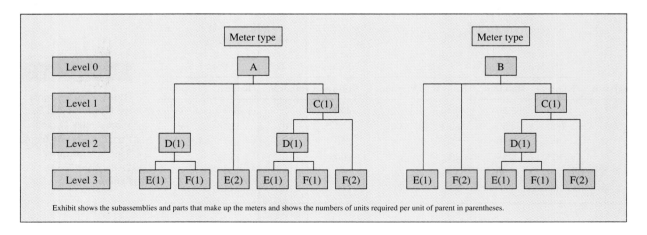

Exhibit shows the subassemblies and parts that make up the meters and shows the numbers of units required per unit of parent in parentheses.

Exhibit 16.14 shows an indented parts list for the structure of Meters A and B. As mentioned earlier in the chapter, the BOM file carries all items without indentation for computational ease, but the indented printout clearly shows the manner of product assembly.

Inventory Records (Item Master) File

The inventory records file would be similar to the one shown in Exhibit 16.10. The difference, as we saw earlier in this chapter, is that the inventory records file also contains much additional data, such as vendor identity, cost, and lead times. For this example, the pertinent data contained in the inventory records file are the on-hand inventory at the start of the program run and the lead times. Taken from the inventory records file, these data are shown in Exhibit 16.15.

Running the MRP Program

The correct conditions are now set to run the MRP computer program: End-item requirements have been established through the master production schedule, while the status of inventory and the order lead times are contained in the inventory item master file, and the bill of materials file contains the product structure data. The MRP program now explodes the item requirements according to the BOM file, level by level, in conjunction with the inventory records file. A release data for the net requirements order is offset to an earlier time period to account for the lead time. Orders for parts and subassemblies are added through the inventory file, bypassing the master production schedule, which, ordinarily, does not schedule at a low enough level to include spares and repair parts.

Meter A				Meter B		
A				B		
	D(1)				E(1)	
		E(1)			F(2)	
		F(1)			C(1)	
	E(2)					D(1)
	C(1)					E(1)
		D(1)				F(1)
			E(1)		F(2)	
			F(1)			
		F(2)				

Item	On-Hand Inventory	Lead Time (Weeks)
A	50	2
B	60	2
C	40	1
D	30	1
E	30	1
F	40	1

Exhibit 16.16 shows the planned order release dates for this particular run. The following analysis explains the program logic. (We will confine our analysis to the problem of meeting the gross requirements for 1,250 units of Meter A, 460 units of Meter B, 270 units of Subassembly D, and 380 units of Part E, all in Week 9.)

The 50 units of A on hand results in a net requirement of 1,200 units of A. To receive Meter A in Week 9, the order must be placed in Week 7 to account for the two-week lead time. The same procedure follows for Item B, resulting in a planned 400-unit order released in Period 7.

The rationale for these steps is that for an item to be released for processing, all of its components must be available. The planned order release date for the parent item therefore becomes the same gross requirement period for the subitems.

Exhibit 16.16   Material Requirements Planning Schedule for Meters A and B, Subassemblies C and D, and Parts E and F

Item		4	5	6	7	8	9	10	11	12	13
A	Gross requirements						1,250				850
	On hand 50						50				
	Net requirements						1,200				
(LT = 2)	Planned-order receipt						1,200				
	Planned-order release				1,200						
B	Gross requirements						460				360
	On hand 60						60				
	Net requirements						400				
(LT = 2)	Planned-order receipt						400				
	Planned-order release				400						
C	Gross requirements				400						
	On hand 40				1,200						
	Net requirements				40						
(LT = 1)	Planned-order receipt				1,560						
	Planned-order release			1,560	1,560						
D	Gross requirements			1,560	1,200		270				250
	On hand 30			30	0		0				
	Net requirements			1,530	1,200		270				
(LT = 1)	Planned-order receipt			1,530	1,200		270				
	Planned-order release		1,530	1,200		270					
E	Gross requirements		1,530	1,200	2,400	270	380				430
					400						
	On hand 30		30	0	0	0	0				
	Net requirements		1,500	1,200	2,800	270	380				
(LT = 1)	Planned-order receipt		1,500	1,200	2,800	270	380				
	Planned-order release	1,500	1,200	2,800	270	380					
F	Gross requirements		1,530	3,120	800	270					
				1,200							
	On hand 40		40	0	0	0					
	Net requirements		1,490	4,320	800	270					
(LT = 1)	Planned-order receipt		1,490	4,320	800	270					
	Planned-order release	1,490	4,320	800	270						

Referring to Exhibit 16.13, level 1, one unit of C is required for each A and each B. Therefore, the gross requirements for C in Week 7 are 1,600 units (1,200 for A and 400 for B.) Taking into account the 40 units on hand and the one-week lead time, 1,560 units of C must be ordered in Week 6.

Level 2 of Exhibit 16.13 shows that one unit of D is required for each A and each C. The 1,200 units of D required for A are gross requirements in Week 7, and the 1,560 units of D for item C are the gross requirements for Week 6. Using the on-hand inventory first and the one-week lead time results in the planned order releases for 1,530 units in Week 5 and 1,200 units in Week 6.

Level 3 contains Items E and F. Because E and F are each used in several places, Exhibit 16.17 is presented to identify more clearly the parent item, the number of units required for each parent item, and the week in which it is required. Two units of Item E are used in each Item A. The 1,200-unit planned order release for A in Period 7 becomes the gross requirement for 2,400 units of E in the same period. One unit of E is used in each B, so the planned order release for 400 units of B in Period 7 becomes the gross requirement for 400 units of E in week 7. Item E is also used in Item D at the rate of one per unit. The 1,530-unit planned order release for D in Period 5 becomes the gross requirement for 1,530 units of E in Period 5 and a 1,500-unit planned order release in Period 4 after accounting for the 30 units on hand and the one-week lead time. The 1,200-unit planned order release for D in Period 6 results in gross requirements for 1,200 units of E in Week 6 and a planned order release for 1,200 units in Week 5.

Item F is used in B, C, and D. The planned order releases for B, C, and D become the gross requirements for F for the same week, except that the planned order release for 400 units of B and 1,560 of C become gross requirements for 800 and 3,120 units of F, because the usage rate is two per unit.

The independent order for 270 units of subassembly D in Week 9 is handled as an input to D's gross requirements for that week. This is then exploded into the derived requirements for 270 units of E and F. The 380-unit requirement for Part E to meet an independent repair part demand is fed directly into the gross requirements for Part E.

The independent demands for Week 13 have not been expanded as yet.

The bottom line of each item in Exhibit 16.16 is taken as a proposed load on the productive system. The final production schedule is developed manually or with the

Item	Parent	Number of Units per Parent	Resultant Gross Requirement	Gross Requirement Week
C	A	1	1,200	7
C	B	1	400	7
D	A	1	1,200	7
D	C	1	1,560	6
E	A	2	2,400	7
E	B	1	400	7
E	D	1	1,530	5
E	D	1	1,200	6
F	B	2	800	7
F	C	2	3,120	6
F	D	1	1,200	6
F	D	1	1,530	5

Exhibit 16.17

The Identification of the Parent of Items C, D, E, and F and Item Gross Requirements Stated by Specific Weeks

firm's computerized production package. If the schedule is infeasible or the loading unacceptable, the master production schedule is revised and the MRP package is run again with the new master schedule.

■ IMPROVEMENTS IN THE MRP SYSTEM

MRP, as it was originally introduced and as we have discussed it so far in this chapter, considered only materials. Revising the schedule because of capacity considerations was done external to the MRP software program. The schedule was revised because of the capacity constraints and the MRP program was run again. (The Nichols case at the end of this chapter requires that the schedule be revised manually in Question 2 of the case.) The response to all other elements and resource requirements were not part of the system. Later refinements included the capacity of the work centers as part of the software program. Feedback of information was also being introduced. We will give an example of capacity planning at a work center and a closed-loop system. Following that we will discuss MRP II systems and advanced versions of MRP.

Computing Work Center Load

The place to start in computing capacity requirements is right from the routing sheets for the jobs scheduled to be processed. Exhibit 4.14 in Chapter 4 shows the routing sheet for a plug assembly. Note that the routing sheet specifies where a job is to be sent, the particular operations involved, and the standard setup time and run time per piece. These are the types of figures used to compute the total work at each work center.

While the routing sheet is a "job view" that follows a particular job around the productive facility, a work center file is the view seen from a work center. Each work center is generally a functionally defined center so that jobs routed to it require the same type of work and the same equipment. From the work center view, if there is adequate capacity, the issue is just sequencing because all jobs will be done on time.

	Week	Job No.	Units	Setup Time	Run Time per Unit	Total Job Time	Total for Week
Exhibit 16.18	10	145	100	3.5	.23	26.5	
		167	160	2.4	.26	44.0	
Workload for Work Center A		158	70	1.2	.13	10.3	
		193	300	6.0	.17	57.0	137.8
	11	132	80	5.0	.36	33.8	
		126	150	3.0	.22	36.0	
		180	180	2.5	.30	56.5	
		178	120	4.0	.50	64.0	190.3
	12	147	90	3.0	.18	19.2	
		156	200	3.5	.14	31.5	
		198	250	1.5	.16	41.5	
		172	100	2.0	.12	14.0	
		139	120	2.2	.17	22.6	128.8

Computing Work Center Capacity

The available capacity in standard hours is 161.5 hours per five-day week, calculated as (2 machines) × (2 shifts) (10 hours/shift) (85% machine utilization) (95% efficiency).

(We discuss priority scheduling rules in Chapter 17). If there is insufficient capacity, however, the problem must be resolved because some jobs will be late unless the schedule is adjusted.

Exhibit 16.18 shows a work center that has various jobs assigned to it. Note that the capacity per week was computed at the bottom of the exhibit at 161.5 hours. The jobs scheduled for the three weeks result in two weeks planned under work center capacity, and one week over capacity.

Exhibit 16.18 uses the terms *utilization* and *efficiency*. Both of these terms have been defined and used in a variety of ways, some conflicting. In this exhibit, utilization refers to the actual time that the machines are used. Efficiency refers to how well the machine is performing while it is being used. Efficiency is usually defined as a comparison to a defined standard output or an engineering design rate. For instance, a machine used for six hours of an eight-hour shift was utilized 6/8, or 75 percent. If the standard output for that machine is defined as 200 parts per hour and an average of 250 parts were made, then efficiency is 125 percent. Note that in these definitions, efficiency can be more than 100 percent, but utilization cannot.

Exhibit 16.19 shows a loading representation of Work Center A for the three weeks. The scheduled work exceeds capacity for Week 11. There are several options available:

1. Work overtime.
2. Select an alternate work center that could perform the task.
3. Subcontract to an outside shop.
4. Try to schedule part of the work of Week 11 earlier into Week 10, and delay part of the work into Week 12.
5. Renegotiate the due date and reschedule.

An MRP program with a capacity requirements planning module allows rescheduling to try to level capacity. Two techniques used are backward scheduling and forward scheduling—the fourth option on the preceding list. The objective of the master scheduler is to try to spread the load in Exhibit 16.19 more evenly to remain within the available capacity.

Closed-Loop MRP

When the material requirements planning (MRP) system has information feedback from its module outputs, this is termed **closed-loop MRP.** The American Production and Inventory Control Society defines closed-loop MRP as

Closed-Loop MRP

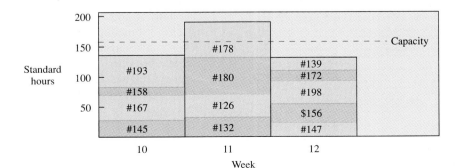

Exhibit 16.19

Scheduled Workload
for Work Center A

A system built around material requirements that includes the additional planning functions of sales and operations (production planning, master production scheduling, and capacity requirements planning). Once this planning phase is complete and the plans have been accepted as realistic and attainable, the execution functions come into play. These include the manufacturing control functions of input-output (capacity) measurement, detailed scheduling and dispatching, as well as anticipated delay reports from both the plant and suppliers, supplier scheduling, etc. The term "closed-loop" implies that not only is each of these elements included in the overall system, but also that feedback is provided by the execution functions so that the planning can be kept valid at all times.[1]

Exhibit 16.20 shows a closed-loop MRP system. The closed loop means that questions and output data are looped back up the system for verification and, if necessary, modification. Recognize that the input to the MRP system is the master production schedule, as was stated earlier in the chapter. The MRP program does an explosion of all the parts, components, and other resources needed to meet this schedule. The capacity requirements planning module then checks the MRP output to see if sufficient capacity exists. If it does not, feedback to the MRP module indicates that the schedule needs to be modified. Continuing through the MRP system, orders are released to the production system by executing the capacity and material plans. From that point on, it is a matter of monitoring, data collection, completing the order, and evaluating results. Any changes in production, capacity, or material are fed back into the system.

Vol. I "Lean Production"

MRP II (Manufacturing Resource Planning)

An expansion of the material requirements planning system to include other portions of the productive system was natural and to be expected. One of the first to be included was the purchasing function. At the same time, there was a more detailed inclusion of the production system itself—on the shop floor, in dispatching, and in the detailed scheduling control. MRP had already included work center capacity limitations, so it was obvious that the name *material requirements planning* was no longer adequate to describe the expanded system. Someone (probably Ollie Wight) introduced the name *manufacturing resource planning (MRP II)* to reflect the idea that more and more of the firm was becoming involved in the program. To quote Wight,

---

[1] Dictionary definitions are reprinted with the permission of APICS, Inc., *APICS Dictionary*, 8th ed., 1995.

Exhibit 16.20   Closed-Loop MRP System Showing Feedback

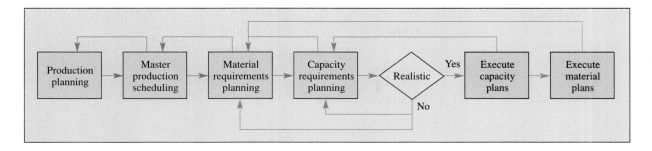

The fundamental manufacturing equation is:
   What are we going to make?
   What does it take to make it?
   What do we have?
   What do we have to get?[2]

The initial intent for MRP II was to plan and monitor all of the resources of a manufacturing firm—manufacturing, marketing, finance, and engineering—through a closed-loop system generating financial figures. The second important intent of the MRP II concept was that it simulate the manufacturing system.

■ EMBEDDING JIT INTO MRP

MRP and JIT each have benefits. The question is: Can they work together successfully, and how would one go about combining them? As stated earlier in the chapter, most major manufacturing firms use MRP. Of the firms using MRP, many in repetitive manufacturing also use JIT techniques. Although JIT is best suited to repetitive manufacturing, MRP is used in everything from custom job shops to assembly-line production. A challenge arises in integrating the shop-floor improvement approaches of JIT with an MRP-based planning and control system. The MRP/JIT combination creates what might be considered a hybrid manufacturing system.

Exhibit 16.21 shows a master production schedule with an MRP system on the left. MRP systems can help create the master production schedule. From that point on, it stays as a pure MRP system. Scheduling resources such as inventory are continuously controlled and monitored.

The right side of Exhibit 16.21 shows a master production schedule at the top feeding a JIT system. Computer control has been severed and the JIT portion operates as its own separate pull method drawing from preceding stages. MRP may well be used to help create the master production schedule, but MRP's involvement stops there.

Exhibit 16.22 shows a hybrid MRP/JIT system. The top half shows a conventional MRP system with its standard inputs such as forecasted demand, inventory status, and

---

[2] Oliver Wight, *The Executive's Guide to Successful MRP II* (Williston, VT: Oliver Wight, 1982), pp. 6, 17.

Controlling
Production Processes
with MRP Alone and
MRP/JIT Combined

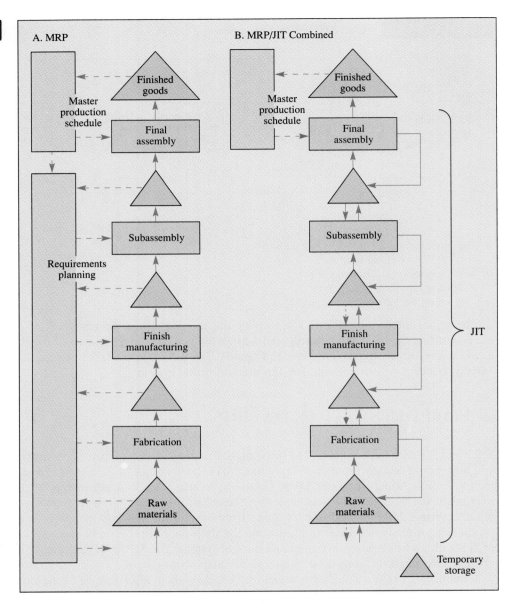

bills of materials. It produces a plan. The system in the bottom of the exhibit, in a JIT manner, controls when vendors should deliver material, when product is to be produced, and when completed product is to be distributed. The middle section—the shop schedule and kanban system—is the interface coupling the MRP and JIT systems along with the capacity control and group technology planning.

LOT SIZING IN MRP SYSTEMS

The determination of lot sizes in an MRP system is a complicated and difficult problem. Lot sizes are the part quantities issued in the planned order receipt and planned order release sections of an MRP schedule. For parts produced in-house, lot

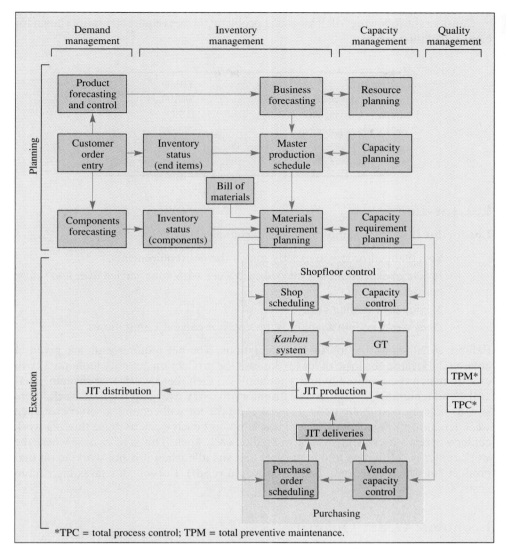

Source: Choong Y. Lee, "A Recent Development of the Integrated Manufacturing System: A Hybrid of MRP and JIT," *International Journal of Operations and Production Management* 13, no. 4 (1993), p. 9.

sizes are the production quantities of batch sizes. For purchased parts, these are the quantities ordered from the supplier. Lot sizes generally meet part requirements for one or more periods.

Most lot-sizing techniques deal with how to balance the setup or order costs and holding costs associated with meeting the net requirements generated by the MRP planning process. Many MRP systems have options for computing lot sizes based on some of the more commonly used techniques. It should be obvious, though, that the use of lot-sizing techniques increases the complexity in generating MRP schedules. When fully exploded, the numbers of parts scheduled can be enormous.

Next, we explain four lot-sizing techniques using a common example. The lot-sizing techniques presented are lot-for-lot (L4L), economic order quantity (EOQ), least total cost (LTC), and least unit cost (LUC).

Consider the following MRP lot-sizing problem; the net requirements are shown for eight scheduling weeks:

Cost per item	$10.00
Order or setup cost	$47.00
Inventory carrying cost/week	0.5%

Weekly net requirements:

1	2	3	4	5	6	7	8
50	60	70	60	95	75	60	55

Lot-for-Lot

Lot-for-Lot (L4L)

Lot-for-lot (L4L) is the most common technique. It

- Sets planned orders to exactly match the net requirements.
- Produces exactly what is needed each week with none carried over into future periods.
- Minimizes carrying cost.
- Does not take into account setup costs or capacity limitations.

Exhibit 16.23 shows the lot-for-lot calculations. The net requirements are given in column 2. Because the logic of lot-for-lot says the production quantity (column 3) will exactly match the required quantity (column 2), then there will be no inventory left at the end (column 4). Without any inventory to carry over into the next week, there is zero holding cost (column 5). However, lot-for-lot will require a setup cost each week (column 6). Incidentally, there is a setup cost each week because this is a work center where a variety of items are worked on each week. This is not a case where the work center is committed to one product and sits idle when it is not working on that product (in which case, only one setup would result). Lot-for-lot causes high setup costs.

Economic Order Quantity

In Chapter 15 we already discussed the EOQ model that explicitly balances setup and holding costs. In an EOQ model, either fairly constant demand must exist or safety

---

Exhibit 16.23   Lot-for-Lot Run Size for an MRP Schedule

(1) Week	(2) Net Requirements	(3) Production Quantity	(4) Ending Inventory	(5) Holding Cost	(6) Setup Cost	(7) Total Cost
1	50	50	0	$0.00	$47.00	$ 47.00
2	60	60	0	0.00	47.00	94.00
3	70	70	0	0.00	47.00	141.00
4	60	60	0	0.00	47.00	188.00
5	95	95	0	0.00	47.00	235.00
6	75	75	0	0.00	47.00	282.00
7	60	60	0	0.00	47.00	329.00
8	55	55	0	0.00	47.00	376.00

stock must be kept to provide for demand variability. The EOQ model uses an estimate of total annual demand, the setup or order cost, and the annual holding cost. EOQ was not designed for a system with discrete time periods such as MRP. The lot-sizing techniques used for MRP assume that part requirements are satisfied at the start of the period. Holding costs are then charged only to the ending inventory for the period, not to the average inventory as in case for the EOQ model. EOQ assumes that parts are used on a continuous basis during the period. The lot sizes generated by EOQ do not always cover the entire number of periods. For example, the EOQ might provide the requirements for 4.6 periods. Using the same data as in lot-for-lot example, the economic order quantity is calculated as follows:

$$\text{Annual demand based on the 8 weeks} = D = \frac{525}{8} \times 52 = 3{,}412.5 \text{ units}$$

$$\text{Annual holding cost} = H = 0.5\% \times \$10 \times 52 \text{ weeks} = \$2.60 \text{ per unit}$$

$$\text{Setup cost} = S = \$47 \text{ (given)}$$

$$\therefore \text{EOQ} = \sqrt{\frac{2DS}{H}} = \sqrt{\frac{2(3{,}412.5)(\$47)}{\$2.60}} = 351 \text{ units}$$

Exhibit 16.24 shows the MRP schedule using an EOQ of 351 units. The EOQ lot size in Week 1 is enough to meet requirements for Weeks 1 through 5 and a portion of Week 6. Then, in Week 6 another EOQ lot is planned to meet the requirements for Weeks 6 through 8. Notice that the EOQ plan leaves some inventory at the end of Week 8 to carry forward into Week 9.

Least Total Cost

The least total cost method (LTC) is a dynamic lot-sizing technique that calculates the order quantity by comparing the carrying cost and the setup (or ordering) costs for various lot sizes and then selects the lot in which these are most nearly equal.

The top half of Exhibit 16.25 shows the least cost lot size results. The procedure to compute least total cost lot sizes is to compare order costs and holding costs for various numbers of weeks. For example, costs are compared for producing in Week 1 to cover the requirements for Week 1; producing in Week 1 for Weeks 1 and 2; producing in Week 1 to cover Weeks 1, 2, and 3, and so on. The correct selection is the lot size where the ordering costs and holding costs are approximately equal. In Exhibit 16.25 the best lot size is 335 because a $38 carrying cost and a $47 ordering

Economic OrderQuantity Run Size for an MRP Schedule   **Exhibit 16.24**

Week	Net Requirements	Production Quantity	Ending Inventory	Holding Cost	Setup Cost	Total Cost
1	50	351	301	$15.05	$47.00	$ 62.05
2	60	0	241	12.05	0.00	74.10
3	70	0	171	8.55	0.00	82.65
4	60	0	111	5.55	0.00	88.20
5	95	0	16	0.80	0.00	89.00
6	75	351	292	14.60	47.00	150.60
7	60	0	232	11.60	0.00	162.20
8	55	0	177	8.85	0.00	171.05

Exhibit 16.25	Least Total Cost Run Size for an MRP Schedule

Weeks	Quantity Ordered	Carrying Cost	Order Cost	Total Cost	
1	50	$ 0.00	$47.00	$ 47.00	
1–2	110	3.00	47.00	50.00	
1–3	180	10.00	47.00	57.00	
1–4	240	19.00	47.00	66.00	
1–5	335	38.00	47.00	85.00	← Least total cost
1–6	410	56.75	47.00	103.75	
1–7	470	74.75	47.00	121.75	
1–8	525	94.00	47.00	141.00	
6	75	0.00	47.00	47.00	
6–7	135	3.00	47.00	50.00	
6–8	190	8.50	47.00	55.50	← Least total cost

Weeks	Net Requirements	Production Quantity	Ending Inventory	Holding Cost	Setup Cost	Total Cost
1	50	335	285	$14.25	$47.00	$ 61.25
2	60	0	225	11.25	0.00	72.50
3	70	0	155	7.75	0.00	80.25
4	60	0	95	4.75	0.00	85.00
5	95	0	0	0.00	0.00	85.00
6	75	190	115	5.75	47.00	137.75
7	60	0	55	2.75	0.00	140.50
8	55	0	0	0.00	0.00	140.05

cost are closer than $56.25 and $47 ($9 versus $9.25). This lot size covers requirements for Weeks 1 through 5. Unlike EOQ, the lot size covers only whole numbers of periods.

Based on the Week 1 decision to place an order to cover five weeks, we are now located in Week 6, and our problem is to determine how many weeks into the future we can provide for from here. Exhibit 16.25 shows that holding and ordering costs are closest in the quantity that covers requirements for Weeks 6 through 8. Notice that the holding and ordering costs here are far apart. This is because our example extends only to Week 8. If the planning horizon were longer, the lot size planned for Week 6 would likely cover more weeks into the future beyond Week 8. This brings up one of the limitations of both LTC and LUC (discussed below). Both techniques are influenced by the length of the planning horizon. The bottom half of Exhibit 16.25 shows the final run size and total cost.

Least Unit Cost

The least unit cost method is a dynamic lot-sizing technique that adds ordering and inventory carrying cost for each trial lot size and divides by the number of units in each lot size, picking the lot size with the lowest unit cost. The top half of Exhibit 16.26 calculates the unit cost for ordering lots to meet the needs of Weeks 1 through 8. Note that the minimum occurred when the quantity 410, ordered in Week 1, was sufficient to cover Weeks 1 through 6. The lot size planned for Week 7 covers through the end of the planning horizon.

The least unit cost run size and total cost are shown in the bottom half of Exhibit 16.26.

Least Unit Cost Run Size for an MRP Schedule

Exhibit 16.26

Weeks	Quantity Ordered	Carrying Cost	Order Cost	Total Cost	Unit Cost
1	50	$ 0.00	$47.00	$ 47.00	$0.9400
1–2	110	3.00	47.00	50.00	0.4545
1–3	180	10.00	47.00	57.00	0.3167
1–4	240	19.00	47.00	66.00	0.2750
1–5	335	38.00	47.00	85.00	0.2537
1–6	410	56.75	47.00	103.75	0.2530 ← Least unit cost
1–7	470	74.75	47.00	121.75	0.2590
1–8	525	94.00	47.00	141.00	0.2686
7	60	0.00	47.00	47.00	0.7833
7–8	115	2.75	47.00	49.75	0.4326 ← Least unit cost

Week	Net Requirements	Production Quantity	Ending Inventory	Holding Cost	Setup Cost	Total Cost
1	50	410	360	$18.00	$47.00	$ 65.00
2	60	0	300	15.00	0.00	80.00
3	70	0	230	11.50	0.00	91.50
4	60	0	170	8.50	0.00	100.00
5	95	0	75	3.75	0.00	103.75
6	75	0	0	0	0	103.75
7	60	115	55	2.75	47.00	153.50
8	55	0	0	0	0	$153.50

Choosing the Best Lot Size

Using the lot-for-lot method, the total cost for the eight weeks is $376; the EOQ total cost is $171.05; the least total cost method is $140.50; and the least unit cost is $153.50. The lowest cost was obtained using the least total cost method of $140.50. If there were more than eight weeks, the lowest cost could differ.

The advantage of the least unit cost method is that it is a more complete analysis and would take into account ordering or setup costs that might change as the order size increases. If the ordering or setup costs remain constant, the lowest total cost method is more attractive because it is simpler and easier to compute; yet it would be just as accurate under that restriction.

■ ADVANCED MRP-TYPE SYSTEMS

For more than two decades, MRP systems were the first choice for firms that focused at the plant production level. MRP took as its input the product demands, inventory levels, and resource availability and produced production schedules as well as inventory ordering quantities. During this time the world was changing, with new global competition, multiplant international sites, wide global product demand, international subcontracting, and varying political environments and currency markets. Existing MRP software programs in their standard form could not handle these widened applications.

In today's environment, MRP users want instant access to information on customers' needs, which plants can meet these needs, and companywide inventory levels and available capacity.

What has been the response to these needs? There are more than 300 vendors for MRP systems. While most of these were involved with MRP systems from years ago and are still selling and maintaining their existing systems, many others are changing their systems to accommodate the new requirements; other firms are at the state of the art in developing new advanced systems based on MRP logic.

Enterprise Resource Planning (ERP)

Various names have been given to this new generation of MRP. The Gartner Group called the new MRP **Enterprise Resource Planning (ERP).** To fully operate in an enterprise sense, there needs to be distributed applications for planning, scheduling, costing, and so on to the multiple layers of the organization: work centers, sites, divisions, corporate. Multiple languages and currencies are also being included for global applications.

Advanced MRP systems (also called next-generation MRP II) include

Client/server architecture.

Relational database with SQL query and report generation.

Windows graphic user interface.

Distributed database support.

Front-end systems for decision support.

Automated EDI.

Interoperability with multiple platforms (Windows NT and Unix).

Standard application programming interfaces.

World Wide Web data interchange is often included for better communication with customers and suppliers.

SAP AG's R/3

SAP AG'S R/3

FINANCE
ACCOUNTING
MARKETING
MANAGEMENT

SAP AG, a German firm, is the world leader in providing ERP software. Its flagship product is known as R/3. Many of the world's largest companies use the software, including, in the U.S., Baxter Healthcare, Exxon, and even the software giant Microsoft. The software consists of four major modules, Financial Accounting, Human Resources, Manufacturing and Logistics, and Sales and Distribution.

The software is designed to operate in a three-tier client/server configuration. As shown in Exhibit 16.27, the core of the system is a high-speed network of database servers. These database servers are special computers designed to efficiently handle a large database of information. The applications, which consist of the modules listed above, can be run on separate computers. The applications are networked around the database cluster and have independent access to it. Users communicate with the applications through the front-end servers, which typically are PCs running Microsoft Windows NT.

The R/3 applications are fully integrated so that data is shared between all applications. If, for example, an employee posts a shipping transaction in the Sales and Distribution module, the transaction is immediately seen by Accounts Payable in the

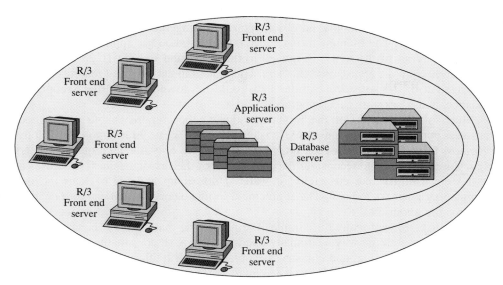

Sources: Jonathon Blain, *Using SAP R/3* (Indianapolis, IN: Que, 1996), p. 42; and Nancy H. Bancroft, *Implementing SAP R/3: How to Introduce a Large System into a Large Organization* (Greenwich, CT: Manning Publications, 1996).

Exhibit 16.27

Triple Client Server Configuration

SAP Application	Program	Chapter in Book
Cross application (CA)	Business Process Technology (CA-BPT) CAD Integration (CA-CAD)	Chapters 4, S4, and 19
Project system (PS)	Project Planning (PS-PLN) Project Execution/Integration (PS-EXE)	Chapter 3
Logistics general (LO)	Logistics Information System (LO-LIS) Master Data (LO-MD)	Chapter 9
Human resources (HR)	Workforce Planning (PD-WFP)	Chapters 14 and 17
Personnel administration (HR-PA)	Time Management (PA-TIM) Incentive Wages (PA-INW)	Chapter 11
Production planning (PP)	Sales and Operations Planning (PP-SOP) Master Planning (PP-MP) Capacity Requirements Planning (PP-CRP) Material Requirements Planning (PP-MRP) Kanban/Just-in-Time Production (PP-KAB) Repetitive Manufacturing (PP-REM) Assembly Orders (PP-ATO) Production Planning for Process Industries (PP-PI) Plant Data Collection (PP-PDC)	Chapters 8, 14, 16, and 17
Materials management (MM)	Material Requirements Planning (MM-MRP) Purchasing (MM-PUR) Inventory Management (MM-IM) Warehouse Management (MM-WM) Electronic Data Interchange (MM-EDI)	Chapters 12, 13, and 15
Quality management (QM)	Planning Tools (QM-PT) Inspection Processing (QM-IM) Quality Control (QM-QC) Quality Certificates (QM-CA)	Chapters 6 and S6

Exhibit 16.28

SAP R/3 and the Applications that Implement Topics Discussed in This Book

Financial Accounting module, and by Inventory Management in the Materials Management module. The Manufacturing and Logistics module has applications that support virtually all of the topics discussed in this book and Exhibit 16.28 maps these applications into the appropriate chapters. This is an impressive list of features that are packaged with the software. Similar lists could be developed for the Accounting, Finance, and Marketing functional areas.

Much of the success of the product is due to the comprehensive coverage of business applications. In a sense, SAP has changed the face of information technology. We now have the enterprisewide integrated system we only dreamed of a few years ago. Companies can now consider the automation of their basic business processes as if it were a utility like electricity or water. Hook it up and get back to the real challenging business at hand. The supplement to this chapter provides more detailed information about SAP R/3.

Of course, it is not really this simple. The problem is that many of the applications do not line up with the way a company operates. The SAP consultants argue that the modules are designed around industry "best practices." But this, in many cases, means that a firm wishing to use SAP needs to change its practices to those implemented by the SAP programmers. This can be a painful and time-consuming process. We must remember that software such as SAP R/3 is merely in its infancy. It will be exciting to see how this develops in the future.

You can contact SAP AG at http://www.sap.com.

Furniture Maker Uses MRP II to Cut Lead Time

For a manufacturer like Harpers, Inc., it was the ultimate in good news/bad news: The company's sales kept going up, but its profits kept going down.

That was January 1988. By March, Harpers' plant in Torrance, California, experienced the manufacturing equivalent of a nervous breakdown. It was accustomed to a 12-week raw-material-to-market cycle (also known as lead time) to make its freestanding office furniture.

Meanwhile, its competitors—Herman Miller, Inc., Steelcase, Inc., and Haworth, Inc., all in Michigan and all nationwide suppliers—were taking just six weeks to convert raw plastic and metal into modular "systems furniture," the pastel, rat-maze furniture that was becoming popular.

"We were forced to either become a 'systems furniture' manufacturer or sell the company to other manufacturers," says Joe Wisniewski, executive vice president and general manager at Harpers. "We chose systems."

Executives and managers at Harpers did something many faltering firms only talk about doing: "We actually had a strategic planning meeting and

determined a number of critical success factors," Wisniewski says.

The first success factor was the most predictable. Harpers decided to cut manufacturing costs by 15 percent. One way to do that was to reduce lead time to three weeks or less versus the new industry standard of six weeks.

Second, the firm decided to cut product design and development lead time—a critical phase for a company bent on being responsive to its marketplace—to six months instead of the three *years* Harpers had previously enjoyed.

It wasn't going to be easy.

For one thing, Harpers' material requirements processing (formerly known as MRP I, or "little" MRP) system was homemade with no forecasting, "no real integration between order processing and accounting and no inventory location system in the plant," Wisniewski says.

Wisniewski and his managers drew up a detailed plan of objectives to complement Harpers' lofty goals of reducing manufacturing costs and lead times.

First was a marketing objective. The company decided it would carve out a niche for "custom

CONCLUSION

Since the 1970s, MRP has grown from its purpose of determining simple time schedules, to its present advanced types that tie together all major functions of an organization. During its growth and its application, MRP's disadvantages as a scheduling mechanism have been well recognized. This is largely because MRP tries to do too much in light of the dynamic, often jumpy system in which it is trying to operate.

MRP is recognized, however, for its excellent databases and linkages within the firm. MRP also does a good job in helping to produce master schedules. Many firms in repetitive manufacturing are installing JIT systems to link with the MRP system. JIT takes the master production schedule as its pulling force but does not use MRP's generated schedule. Results indicate that this is working very well.

Many newer MRP-type software programs have been developed since the early 1990s. Several others are currently in the development stage. These allow more open exchange of data than the earlier systems, embrace a larger part of the firm's operation (such as multiple sites, global customers, languages, and currency rates), and operate in real time.

MRP's service applications have not fared well, even though it seems that they should have. The MRP approach would appear to be valuable in producing services

solutions," which would appeal to companies that were, for example, converting their engineering staff from drawing boards to computers. Such projects often demand products that are not of a standard size. Wisniewski decided on a design lead time of two weeks, with custom furniture "shippable in no more than four weeks."

The second objective was to acquire "flexible manufacturing" machinery. The system would be able to increase or decrease the number of features a particular furniture system offered at the customer's whim.

But what would make the whole system work was a manufacturing resource planning (MRP II, or "big" MRP) system that would "integrate our engineering, marketing, manufacturing, and accounting efforts and simultaneously engineer and deliver those custom products," Wisniewski says.

Harpers took a look at its hardware requirements, narrowed the possibilities down to Digital Equipment Corp. and IBM, determined that more solutions were available on the IBM platform, and selected IBM's Application System/400, which was new at the time.

Finding MRP II software became a contest between IBM, Systems Software Associates, Inc. in Chicago, Andersen Consulting in Chicago, and Pansophic Systems, Inc., now a subsidiary of Computer Associates International, Inc., in Lisle, Illinois. Andersen Consulting's Mac-Pac won, partly because it included an expert system, Expert Configurator, that was developed to improve order accuracy and response time.

By October 1990, the system was installed and running.

Harpers has not yet met its goal of a three-week manufacturing lead time, but 20 percent of its furniture is out within two weeks, with the remainder clocking in at four weeks.

Harpers, which was bought by Jasper, Indiana–based Kimball International last January, now makes modular furniture at the rate of $60 million a year. Wisniewski says the company accomplishes that with only 350 factory employees, compared with an output of $50 million in 1988 with 580 employees.

Source: Robert M. Knight, "Furniture Maker Uses MRP II to Cut Lead Time," *Computerworld*, June 8, 1992, p. 80. Copyright 1992 by Computerworld, Inc., Framingham, MA 01701.

because service scheduling consists of identifying the final service and then tracing back to the resources needed, such as equipment, space, and personnel. Consider, for example, a hospital operating room planning an open-heart surgery. The master schedule can establish a time for the surgery (or surgeries, if several are scheduled). The BOM could specify all required equipment and personnel—MDs, nurses, anesthesiologist, operating room, heart/lung machine, defibrillator, and so forth. The inventory status file would show the availability of the resources and commit them to the project. The MRP program could then produce a schedule showing when various parts of the operation are to be started, expected completion time, required materials, and so forth. Checking this schedule would allow "capacity planning" in answering such questions as "Are all the materials and personnel available?" and "Does the system produce a feasible schedule?"

We still believe that MRP systems will eventually find their way into service applications. But after a number of years of believing this, we still have not seen development and implementation. One reason is that even service managers who are aware of it believe that MRP is just a manufacturing tool. Also, service managers tend to be people-oriented and skeptical of tools from outside their industry.

SOLVED PROBLEMS

SOLVED PROBLEM 1

Product X is made of two units of Y and three of Z. Y is made of one unit of A and two units of B. Z is made of two units of A and four units of C.

Lead time for X is one week; Y, two weeks; Z, three weeks; A, two weeks; B, one week; and C, three weeks.

a. Draw the bill of materials (product structure tree).

b. If 100 units of X are needed in week 10, develop a planning schedule showing when each item should be ordered and in what quantity.

Solution

a.

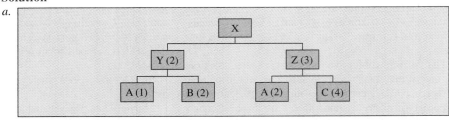

b.

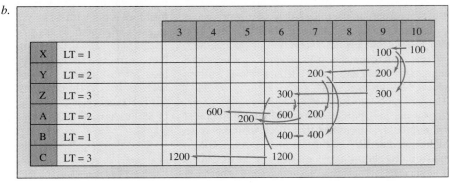

		3	4	5	6	7	8	9	10
X	LT = 1							100	100
Y	LT = 2					200		200	
Z	LT = 3				300			300	
A	LT = 2			600	200	600	200		
B	LT = 1					400	400		
C	LT = 3	1200			1200				

SOLVED PROBLEM 2

Product M is made of two units of N and three of P. N is made of two units of R and four units of S. R is made of one unit of S and three units of T. P is made of two units of T and four units of U.

a. Show the bill of materials (product structure tree).

b. If 100 M are required, how many units of each component are needed?

c. Show both a single-level parts list and an indented parts list.

Solution

a.

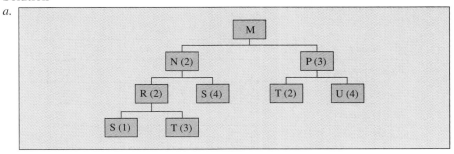

b. M = 100   S = 800 + 400 = 1,200
   N = 200   T = 600 + 1,200 = 1,800
   P = 300   U = 1,200
   R = 400

c.

Single-Level Parts List		Indented Parts List			
M		M			
	N (2)		N (2)		
	P (3)			R (2)	
N					S (1)
	R (2)				T (3)
	S (4)			S (4)	
R			P (3)		
	S (1)			T (2)	
	T (3)			U (4)	
P					
	T (2)				
	U (4)				

REVIEW AND DISCUSSION QUESTIONS

1. Discuss the meaning of MRP terms such as *planned order release* and *scheduled order receipts.*

2. Many practitioners currently update MRP weekly or biweekly. Would it be more valuable if it were updated daily? Discuss.

3. What is the role of safety stock in an MRP system?

4. How does MRP relate to CIM? (See the supplement to Chapter 4.)

5. Contrast the significance of the term *lead time* in the traditional EOQ context and in an MRP system.

6. Discuss the importance of the master production schedule in an MRP system.

7. "MRP just prepares shopping lists. It does not do the shopping or cook the dinner." Comment.

8. What are the sources of demand in an MRP system? Are these dependent or independent, and how are they used as inputs to the system?

9. State the types of data that would be carried in the bill of materials file and the inventory record file.

10. How do the advanced versions of MRP differ from the basic system?

PROBLEMS

1. See table.

1. In the following MRP planning schedule for Item J, indicate the correct net requirements, planned order receipts, and planned order releases to meet the gross requirements. Lead time is one week.

			Week Number			
Item J	0	1	2	3	4	5
Gross requirements			75		50	70
On hand 40			40		0	0
Net requirements			35		50	70
Planned order receipt			35		50	70
Planned order release		35		50	70	

2. See SM.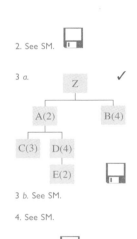

2. Repeat Solved Problem 1 using current on-hand inventories of 20 X, 40 Y, 30 Z, 50 A, 100 B, and 900 C.

3 a. ✓

3 b. See SM.

4. See SM.

3. Assume that Product Z is made of two units of A and four units of B. A is made of three units of C and four D. D is made of two units of E.

Lead times for purchase or fabrication of each unit to final assembly are: Z takes two weeks; A, B, C, and D take one week each; and E takes three weeks.

Fifty units are required in Period 10. (Assume that there is currently no inventory on hand of any of these items.)

a. Show the bill of materials (product structure tree).

b. Develop an MRP planning schedule showing gross and net requirements, order release and order receipt dates.

4. *Note:* For Problems 4 through 9, to simplify data handling to include the receipt of orders that have actually been placed in previous periods, the following six-level scheme can be used. (There are a number of different techniques used in practice, but the important issue is to keep track of what is on hand, what is expected to arrive, what is needed, and what size orders should be placed). One way to calculate the numbers is as follows:

				Week					
Gross requirements									
Scheduled receipts									
On hand from prior period									
Net requirements									
Planned order receipt									
Planned order release									

One unit of A is made of three units of B, one unit of C, and two units of D. B is composed of two units of E and one unit of D. C is made of one unit of B and two units of E. E is made of one unit of F.

Items B, C, E, and F have one-week lead times; A and D have lead times of two weeks.

Assume that lot-for-lot (L4L) lot sizing is used for items A, B, and F; lots of size 50, 50, and 200 are used for items C, D, and E, respectively. Items C, E, and F have on-hand (beginning) inventories of 10, 50 and 150, respectively; all other items have zero beginning inventory. We are scheduled to receive 10 units of A in Week 2, 50 units of E in Week 1, and also 50 units of F in Week 1. There are no other scheduled receipts. If 30 units of A are required in Week 8, use the low-level-coded bill of materials to find the necessary planned order releases for all components.

5. One unit of A is made of two units of B, three units of C, and two units of D. B is composed of one unit of E and two units of F. C is made of two units of F and one unit of D. E is made of two units of D. Items A, C, D, and F have one-week lead times; B and E have lead times of two weeks. Lot-for-lot (L4L) lot sizing is used for Items A, B, C, and D; lots of size 50 and 180 are used for items E and F, respectively. Item C has an on-hand (beginning) inventory of 15; D has an on-hand inventory of 50; all other items have zero beginning inventory. We are scheduled to receive 20 units of Item E in week 2; there are no other scheduled receipts.

Construct simple and low-level-coded bills of materials (product structure tree) and indented and summarized parts list.

If 20 units of A are required in Week 8, use the low-level-coded bill of materials to find the necessary planned order releases for all components. (See note in Problem 4.)

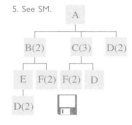

6. One unit of A is made of one unit of B and one unit of C. B is made of four units of C and one unit of E and F. C is made of two units of D and one unit of E. E is made of three units of F. Item C has a lead time of one week; Items A, B, E, and F have two-week lead times; and Item D has a lead time of three weeks. Lot-for-lot lot sizing is used for Items A, D, and E; lots of size 50, 100, and 50 are used for Items B, C, and F, respectively. Items A, C, D, and E have on-hand (beginning) inventories of 20, 50, 100, and 10, respectively; all other items have zero beginning inventory. We are scheduled to receive 10 units of A in week 1, 100 units of C in Week 1, and 100 units of D in Week 3; there are no other scheduled receipts. If 50 units of A are required in Week 10, use the low-level-coded bill of materials (product structure tree) to find the necessary planned order releases for all components. (See note in Problem 4.)

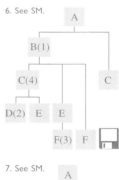

7. One unit of A is made of two units of B and one unit of C. B is made of three units of D and one unit of F. C is composed of three units of B, one unit of D, and four units of E. D is made of one unit of E. Item C has a lead time of one week; Items A, B, E, and F have two-week lead times; and Item D has a lead time of three weeks. Lot-for-lot lot sizing is used for Items C, E, and F; lots of size 20, 40, and 160 are used for items A, B, and D, respectively. Items A, B, D, and E have on-hand (beginning) inventories of 5, 10, 100, and 100, respectively; all other items have zero beginning inventories. We are scheduled to receive 10 units of A in Week 3, 20 units of B in Week 7, 40 units of F in week 5, and 60 units of E in Week 2; there are no other schedule receipts. If 20 units of A are required in Week 10, use the low-level-coded bill of materials (product structure tree) to find the necessary planned order releases for all components. (See note in Problem 4.)

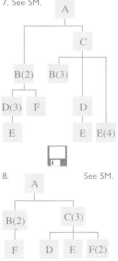

8. One unit of A is composed of 2 units of B and three units of C. Each B is composed of one unit of F. C is made of one unit of D, one unit of E, and two units of F. Items A, B, C, and D have 20, 50, 30, and 25 units of on-hand inventory. Items A, B, and C use lot-for-lot (L4L) as their lot sizing technique, while D, E, and F require multiples of 50, 100, and 100, respectively, to be purchased. B has scheduled receipts of 30 units in period 1. No other scheduled receipts exist. Lead times are one period for items A, B, and D, and two periods for items C, E, and F. Gross requirements for A are 20 units in period 1, 20 units in period 2, 60 units in period 6, and 50 units in period 8. Find the planned order releases for all items.

9. See SM.

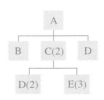

9. Each unit of A is composed of one unit of B, two units of C, and one unit of D. C is composed of two units of D, and three units of E. Items A, C, D, and E have on-hand inventories of 20, 10, 20, and 10 units, respectively. Item B has a scheduled receipt of 10 units in period one, and C has a scheduled receipt of 50 units in period one. Lot-for-lot (L4L) is used for items A and B. Item C requires a minimum lot size of 50 units. D and E are required to be purchased in multiples of 100 and 50, respectively. Lead time are 1 period for items A, B, and C, and 2 periods for items D and E. The gross requirements for A are 30 in period 2, 30 in period 5, and 40 in period 8. Find the planned order releases for all items.

10. Using least total cost ✓ method, order 250 units. The least unit cost method indicates order of 450 units.

10. The MRP gross requirements for Item A are shown here for the next 10 weeks. Lead time for A is three weeks and setup cost is $10 per setup. There is a carrying cost of $0.01 per unit per week. Beginning inventory is 90 units.

	Week									
	1	**2**	**3**	**4**	**5**	**6**	**7**	**8**	**9**	**10**
Gross requirements	30	50	10	20	70	80	20	60	200	50

Use the least total cost or the least unit cost lot-sizing method to determine when and for what quantity the first order should be released.

11. See SM.

11. (This problem is intended as a very simple exercise to go from the aggregate plan to the master schedule to the MRP.) Gigamemory Storage Devices, Inc., produces CD ROMs (read only memory) and WORMs (write once read many) for the computer market. Aggregate demand for the WORMs for the next two quarters are 2,100 units and 2,700 units. Assume that demand is distributed evenly for each month of the quarter.

There are two models of the WORM: an internal model and an external model. The drive assemblies in both are the same but the electronics and housing are different. Demand is higher for the external model and currently is 70 percent of aggregate demand.

The bill of materials and the lead times follow. One drive assembly and one electronic and housing unit go into each WORM.

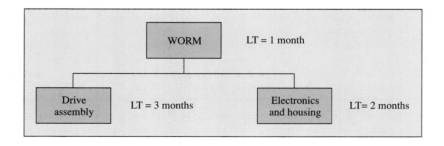

The MRP system is run monthly. Currently, 200 external WORMs and 100 internal WORMs are in stock. Also in stock are 250 drive assemblies, 50 internal electronic and housing units, and 125 external electronic and housing units.

Problem: Show the aggregate plan, the master production schedule, and the full MRP with the gross and net requirements and planned order releases.

12.

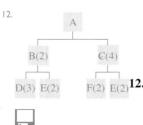

12. Product A is an end item and is made from two units of B and four of C. B is made of three units of D and two of E. C is made of two units of F and two of E.

A has a lead time of one week. B, C, and E have lead times of two weeks, and D and F have lead times of three weeks.

a. Show the bill of materials (product structure tree).
b. If 100 units of A are required in week 10, develop the MRP planning schedule, specifying when items are to be ordered and received. There are currently no units of inventory on hand.

✓ 13. Product A consists of two units of subassembly B, three units of C, and one unit of D. B is composed of four units of E and three units of F. C is made of two units of H and three units of D. H is made of five units of E and two units of G.
   a. Construct a simple bill of materials (product structure tree).
   b. Construct a product structure tree using low-level coding.
   c. Construct an indented parts list.
   d. To produce 100 units of A, determine the numbers of units of B, C, D, E, F, G, and H required.

13. See SM.

14. The MRP gross requirements for Item X are shown here for the next 10 weeks. Lead time for A is two weeks, and setup cost is $9 per setup. There is a carrying cost of $0.02 per unit per week. Beginning inventory is 70 units.

14. Using least total cost method, order 180 units. Using least unit cost method, order either 180 units or 220 units.

					Week					
	1	**2**	**3**	**4**	**5**	**6**	**7**	**8**	**9**	**10**
Gross requirements	20	10	15	45	10	30	100	20	40	150

Use the least total cost or the least unit cost lot-sizing method to determine when and for what quantity the first order should be released.

15. Audio Products, Inc., produces two AM/FM/CD players for cars. The radio/CD units are identical, but the mounting hardware and finish trim differ. The standard model fits intermediate and full-size cars, and the sports model fits small sports cars.

15. See SM.

Audio Products handles the production in the following way. The chassis (radio/CD unit) is assembled in Mexico and has a manufacturing lead time of two weeks. The mounting hardware is purchased from a sheet steel company and has a three-week lead time. The finish trim is purchased form a Taiwan electronics company with offices in Los Angeles as prepackaged units consisting of knobs and various trim pieces. Trim packages have a two-week lead time. Final assembly time may be disregarded because adding the trim package and mounting are performed by the customer.

Audio Products supplies wholesalers and retailers, who place specific orders for both models up to eight weeks in advance. These orders, together with enough additional units to satisfy the small number of individual sales, are summarized in the following demand schedule:

				Week			
	1	**2**	**3**	**4**	**5**	**6**	**7**	**8**
Standard model				300				400
Sports model					200			100

There are currently 50 radio/CD units on hand but no trim packages or mounting hardware.

Prepare a material requirements plan to meet the demand schedule exactly. Specify the gross and net requirements, on-hand amounts, and the planned order release and receipt periods for the radio/CD chassis, the standard trim and sports car model trim, and the standard mounting hardware and the sports car mounting hardware.

16. An item has a set-up cost of $100 and a weekly holding cost of $0.50 per unit. Given the following net requirements, what should the lot sizes be using lot-for-lot (L4L), economic order quantity (EOQ), and least total cost (LTC)? Also, what is the total cost associated with each lot sizing technique?

16. L4L: place 8 orders equal to net requirements, total cost $800. EOQ: place 3 orders of size 110 in periods 1, 5, & 8, total cost $550. LTC: place an order of size 100 in week 1, and an order of size 140 in week 5, total cost $415.

Week	Net Requirements
1	10
2	30
3	10
4	50
5	20
6	40
7	50
8	30

17. See SM.

17. Brown and Brown Electronics manufactures a line of digital audiotape (DAT) players. While there are differences among the various products, there are a number of common parts within each player. The bill of materials, showing the number of each item required, lead times, and the current inventory on hand for the parts and components, follows:

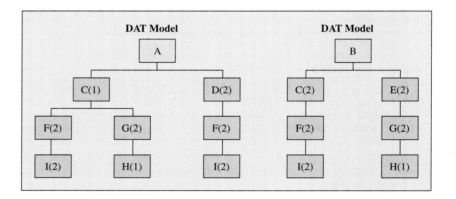

	Number Currently in Stock	Lead Time (Weeks)
DAT Model A	30	1
DAT Model B	50	2
Subassembly C	75	1
Subassembly D	80	2
Subassembly E	100	1
Part F	150	1
Part G	40	1
Raw material H	200	2
Raw material I	300	2

Brown and Brown created a forecast that it plans to use as its master production schedule, producing exactly to schedule. Part of the MPS shows a demand for 700 units of Model A and 1,200 units of Model B in Week 10.

Develop an MRP schedule to meet the demand.

Case

Nichols Company

This particular December day seemed bleak to Joe Williams, president of Nichols Company (NCO). He sat in his office watching the dying embers in his fireplace, hoping to clear his mind. Suddenly there came a tapping by someone gently rapping, rapping at his office door. "Another headache," he muttered, "tapping at my office door. Only that and nothing more."*

The intruder was Barney Thompson, director of marketing. "A major account has just canceled a large purchase of A units because we are back ordered on tubing. This can't continue. My sales force is out beating the bushes for customers, and our production manager can't provide the product."

For the past several months, operations at NCO have been unsteady. Inventory levels have been high, while at the same time, there have been stockouts. This has resulted in late deliveries, complaints, and cancellations. To compound the problem, overtime has been excessive.

History

Nichols Company was started by Joe Williams and Peter Schaap, both with MBAs from the University of Arizona. Much has happened since Williams and Schaap formed the company. Schaap has left the company and is working in real estate development in Queensland, Australia. Under the direction of Williams, NCO has diversified to include a number of other products.

NCO currently has 355 full-time employees directly involved in manufacturing the three primary products: A, B, and C. Final assembly takes place in a converted warehouse adjacent to NCO's main plant.

The Meeting

Williams called a meeting the next day to get input on the problems facing NCO and to lay the groundwork for some solutions. Attending the meeting, besides himself and Barney Thompson, were Phil Bright of production and inventory control, Trevor Hansen of purchasing, and Steve Clark of accounting.

The meeting lasted all morning. Participation was vocal and intense.

Bright said, "The forecasts that marketing sends us are always way off. We are constantly having to expedite one product or another to meet current demand. This runs up our overtime."

Thompson said, "Production tries to run too lean. We need a large inventory of finished goods. If I had the merchandise, my salespeople could sell 20 percent more product."

Clark said, "No way! Our inventory is already uncomfortably high. We can't afford the holding costs, not to mention how fast technology changes around here causing even more inventory, much of it obsolete."

Bright said, "The only way I can meet our stringent cost requirement is to buy in volume."

At the end of the meeting, Williams had lots of input but no specific plan. What do you think he should do? Use Exhibits C16.1 through C16.4 showing relevant data to answer the specific questions at the end of the case.

Questions

Use Microsoft Excel to solve the Nichols Company case. (Note that if you start from scratch, it will take several hours to answer question 1, about the same for Question 2, and perhaps double that for question 3. Two spreadsheets are included on the CD included with this book to help with this problem.)

Simplifying assumption: To get the program started, some time is needed at the beginning because MRP backloads the system. For simplicity, assume that the forecasts (and therefore demands) are zero for Periods 1 through 3. Also assume that the starting inventory specified in Exhibit C16.3 is available from Week 1. For the master production schedule, use only End Items A, B, and C.

To modify production quantities, adjust only Products A, B, and C. Do not adjust the quantities of D,

---

* With apologies to E. A. P. (Edgar Allen Poe).

Product A			Product B		Product C			
.A			.B		.C			**Bills of Materials for**
	.D(4)			.F(2)		.G(2)		**Products A, B, and C**
		.I(3)		.G(3)			.I(2)	
	.E(1)				.I(2)	.H(1)		
	.F(4)							

Exhibit C16.1

Exhibit CI6.2   Work Center Routings for Products and Components

Item	Work Center Number	Standard Time (Hours per Unit)	Item	Work Center Number	Standard Time (Hours per Unit)
Product A	1	0.20	Compnent E	2	0.15
	4	0.10		4	0.05
Product B	2	0.30	Compnent F	2	0.15
	4	0.08		3	0.20
Product C	3	0.10	Compnent G	1	0.30
	4	0.05		2	0.10
Component D	1	0.15	Compnent H	1	0.05
	4	0.10		3	0.10

Exhibit CI6.3

Inventory Levels and Lead Times for Each Item on the Bill of Materials at the Beginning of Week 1

Product/Component	On Hand (Units)	Lead Time (Weeks)
Product A	100	1
Product B	200	1
Product C	175	1
Component D	200	1
Component E	195	1
Component F	120	1
Component G	200	1
Component H	200	1
I (Raw material)	300	1

Exhibit CI6.4

Forecasted Demand for Weeks 4 to 27

Week	Product A	Product B	Product C	Week	Product A	Product B	Product C
1				15	1,900	1,900	1,500
2				16	2,200	2,300	2,300
3				17	2,000	2,300	2,300
4	1,500	2,200	1,200	18	1,700	2,100	2,000
5	1,700	2,100	1,400	19	1,600	1,900	1,700
6	1,150	1,900	1,000	20	1,400	1,800	1,800
7	1,100	1,800	1,500	21	1,100	1,800	2,200
8	1,000	1,800	1,400	22	1,000	1,900	1,900
9	1,100	1,600	1,100	23	1,400	1,700	2,400
10	1,400	1,600	1,800	24	1,400	1,700	2,400
11	1,400	1,700	1,700	25	1,500	1,700	2,600
12	1,700	1,700	1,300	26	1,600	1,800	2,400
13	1,700	1,700	1,700	27	1,500	1,900	2,500
14	1,800	1,700	1,700				

E, F, G, H, and I. These should be linked so that changes in A, B, and C automatically adjust them.

1. Disregarding machine-center limitations, develop an MRP schedule and also capacity profiles for the four machine centers.

2. Work center capacities and costs follow. Repeat (1) creating a *feasible* schedule (within the capacities of the machine centers) and compute the relevant costs. Do this by adjusting the MPS only. Try to minimize the total cost of operation for the 27 weeks.

3. Suppose end items had to be ordered in multiples of 100 units, components in multiples of 500 units, and raw materials in multiples of 1,000 units. How would this change your schedule?

	Capacity	Cost
Work center 1	6,000 hours available	$20 per hour
Work center 2	4,500 hours available	$25 per hour
Work center 3	2,400 hours available	$35 per hour
Work center 4	1,200 hours available	$65 per hour
Inventory carrying cost		
End items A, B, and C	$2.00 per unit	
Components D, E, F, G, and H	$1.50 per unit	
Raw material I	$1.00 per unit	
Back order cost		
End items A, B, and C	$20 per unit	
Components D, E, F, G, and H	$14 per unit	
Raw material I	$8 per unit	

SELECTED BIBLIOGRAPHY

Bancroft, Nancy H. *Implementing SAP R/3: How to Introduce a Large System into a Large Organization.* Greenwich, CT: Manning Publications, 1996.

Blain, Jonathan. *Using SAP R/3.* Indianapolis, IN: Que, 1996.

Lee, Choong Y. "A Recent Development of the Integrated Manufacturing System: A Hybrid of MRP and JIT." *International Journal of Operations and Production Management* 13, no. 4 (1993), pp. 3–17.

Orlicky, Joseph. *Materials Requirements Planning.* New York: McGraw-Hill, 1975. (This is the classic book on MRP.)

Sipper, Daniel, and Robert Bulfin. *Production: Planning, Control, and Integration.* New York: McGraw-Hill, 1997.

Turbide, David A. *MRP+: The Adaptation, Enhancement, and Application of MRP.* New York: Industrial Press, 1993.

Vollmann, Thomas E.; William L. Berry; and D. Clay Whybark. *Manufacturing Planning and Control Systems,* 4th ed. Burr Ridge, IL: Richard D. Irwin, 1997.

Wallace, Thomas F. "MRP II & JIT Work Together in Plan and Practice." *Automation,* March 1990, pp. 40–42.

_____. *MRP II: Making It Happen.* 2nd ed. Essex Junction, VT: Oliver Wight, 1990.

Wight, Oliver. *The Executive Guide to Successful MRP II.* Williston, VT: Oliver Wight, 1982.

SAP R/3

Supplement Outline

R/3 History, 670
    R/3 before 1994
    R/3 in 1995
    R/3 in 1996
    R/3 in 1997
    R/3 beyond 1997

Details of the Functional Components, 672
    Financial Accounting
    Human Resources
    Manufacturing and Logistics
    Sales and Distribution
Implementing SAP R/3, 676

Key Terms

Enterprise Resource Planning
  (ERP)

Data Warehouse

Complimentary Software Partner

Application Link Enabling (ALE)

Application Modules
  Financial Accounting
  Human Resources
  Manufacturing and Logistics
  Sales and Distribution

Rapid Implementation

www Links

SAP America (http://www.sap.com)
APICS Software Buyers Guide (http://lionhrtpub.com)

There is widespread agreement that SAP has set new standards in the information technology market with R/3, its client/server application software system. Since the system was launched in 1992, the number of workplaces using R/3 applications has soared to over 100,000 worldwide. Leading high-tech companies, major producers of consumer goods, prominent chemicals groups, and numerous small and medium-sized firms have adopted this innovative software suite.

SAP AG had sales of over DM 3.7 billion (over U.S.$2 billion) during 1996, 75 percent of which were generated in international markets. SAP is headquartered in Walldorf, Germany, and has over 10,350 employees. The company has major development centers in Germany, the United States, and Japan. The company added 2,000 jobs in 1996 and 1997.

The purpose of this chapter is to provide an overview of the software package, showing how the package has developed over time and describing the comprehensive set of applications that are included. We believe that the SAP R/3 package represents a significant new class of **enterprise resource planning (ERP)** software that takes advantage of new distributed client/server computer technology. As indicated in Exhibit S16.1, there are many companies that offer alternatives to the R/3 package. Our purpose is not to endorse the SAP R/3 product as the only software product that a firm should consider; rather, it is a good benchmark for comparing other competing products.

Enterprise Resource Planning (ERP)

In a sense, it can be argued that SAP AG was in the right place at the right time. In the early 1990s, many large companies realized that it was time to update their existing information systems to take advantage of new technologies. Programs written in programming languages such as Cobol, PL1, RPG, and assembler were becoming increasingly expensive to maintain. Further, the mainframe computer technology was not cost effective compared to the ever more powerful and inexpensive microprocessor-based computers. Change was inevitable, and SAP offered a comprehensive solution.

Vendor	Special Software Features	Web Site
AIM Computer Solutions	Comprehensive selection of software.	*http://www.aimcom.com*
American Software	Comprehensive selection; focus on supply chain management.	*http://www.amsoftware.com*
The Baan Company	Baan IV client/server; dynamic enterprise modeling.	*http://www.baan.com*
Chesapeake Software Systems	Optimized manufacturing scheduling.	*http://www.chessie.com*
Manugistics	Optimization of logistics functions.	*http://www.manugistics.com*
PeopleSoft	Comprehensive selection; client/server products.	*http://www.peoplesoft.com*
Red Pepper Software (a division of PeopleSoft)	Real-time planning and control.	*http://www.pepper.com*

Exhibit S16.1

Major Developers of Enterprise Resource Planning Software

Note: For a comprehensive list of suppliers of business software, see the annual *APICS Software Buyers Guide* available at http://lionhrtpub.com

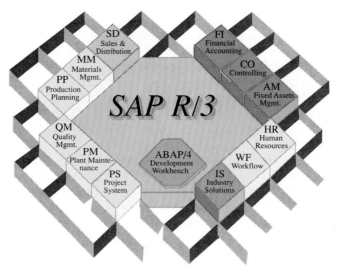

Source: Copyright by SAP AG. Used with permission.

■ R/3 HISTORY

R/3 is built around a comprehensive set of application modules that can be used either alone or in combination. Exhibit S16.2 shows the major modules of R/3. The modules can be used to support processes that span different functional areas in the firm. Because the modules are integrated and use a common database, transactions processed in one area immediately update all other areas. For example, if an order is received from a customer via the Internet Web page, accounting, production scheduling, and purchasing immediately know about the order and the impact it has on their area.

The following is a quick chronological review of the major technical developments in the package.[1]

R/3 before 1994

Since its inception in 1992, R/3 has always used a common, integrated database with shared application modules. Interactive interfacing with R/3 originally required that all computers in the network be physically connected using a communications mechanism unique to the software. Quickly, SAP adopted the industry standard communications mechanism, known as TCP/IP, used by the Internet. SAP also supports the IBM SNA protocol.

Data Warehouse

Another feature that has been incorporated into the software from the start is the use of a **data warehouse.** See the Breakthrough box titled "R/3s Open Information Warehouse" for an example of how this works.

---

[1] Based on information contained in "R/3 System—The Business Framework," from the SAP, AG Web Site (*http://www.sap.com*), May 22, 1997.

BREAKTHROUGH

R/3s Open Information Warehouse

Any modern database will let you easily formulate an SQL query like "What sales did my company have in Italy in 1997?" A report generated in response to such a query could look like that shown below:

Region	Q1	Q2	Q3	Q4	Total
Umbria	1000	1200	800	2000	5000
Toscana	2000	2600	1600	2800	9000
Calabria	400	300	150	450	1300
Total	3400	4100	2550	5250	15300

But things get more complex if, for instance, we then want to take this answer as the basis for *drilling down* to look at the sales for different quarters and sales representatives in the various regions. Drilling down means descending through an existing hierarchy to bring out more and more detail.

In the following example, we drill down through the sales hierarchy (sales representatives in Toscana). Signore Corleone's sales do not appear to have been affected by the holiday season in the third quarter.

Source: This example was taken from Claus Heinrich and Martin Hofmann, "Decision Support from the SAP Open Information Warehouse," SAP WEB site, May 23, 1997, p. 4.

Sales	Q1	Q2	Q3	Q4	Total
S. Paolo	500	600	300	500	1900
S. Vialli	700	600	200	700	2200
S. Ferrari	600	700	400	700	2400
S. Corleone	200	700	700	900	2500
Total	2000	2600	1600	2800	9000

At this point, you can switch to another dimension—for instance, from sales representative to product sold. This is often referred to as *slice and dice.*

Product	Q1	Q2	Q3	Q4	Total
X-11	2000	2500	1500	3550	9550
Z-12	1400	1600	1050	1700	5750
Total	3400	4100	2550	5250	15300

From the standpoint of a data analyst, it can now be useful to check sales of particular products in each region. SAP R/3 allows the end user to do this easily using the data warehouse approach implemented within the system.

Early in the development of the software, it was felt that being able to interface with other software was very important. The **Complementary Software Partner** (CSP) program gave software developers outside the company the information needed to integrate with the R/3 system. Systems such as Computer Aided Design, Geographical Information, Shop Floor Control, and Process Control could be interfaced with R/3 through this program. R/3 is written in a unique computer language known as ABAP/4. The system can be extended with custom applications using the ABAP/4 Development Workbench module.

Complementary Software Partner

R/3 in 1995

R/3 version 3.0 represented a major breakthrough in the support of distributed, customer defined, and flexible business processes. **Application link enabling** (ALE) introduced the ability to distribute functions to physically separate computer systems. ALE handles the synchronization of separate R/3 system databases. In addition, the application software modules can also be run on separate computers. This is important because it allows the computer workload to be shared, thus increasing the capacity of the system. Version 3.0 of the software also formalized the SAP Business Object

Application Link Enabling

model that allowed programmers to work at a high level of abstraction over the underlying data.

R/3 in 1996

Version 3.1 of R/3, delivered in 1996, placed a new emphasis on the optimization of logistics processes within the system. External optimization products from such vendors as Chesapeake, Numetrix, Red Pepper, and Manugistics were integrated into R/3. In addition, an Internet component has been developed that allows direct interfacing with World Wide Web applications.

R/3 in 1997

The new version 4.0 of R/3 allows the Human Resources, Financial, and Logistics modules to be implemented stand-alone. The modules then can be incrementally expanded upon with additional R/3 modules or third-party software. This may sound like a step backward, but from a practical standpoint, it solves some problems. This allows third-party applications to be interfaced more easily. In addition, each of these applications can be implemented separately, thus simplifying this process. This should also result in significant performance improvements due to the smaller scope of each application.

R/3 beyond 1997

The separation of the core financial and core logistics system will allow for the best of both with respect to centralized and/or decentralized deployment of the system. SAP indicates that users will have the option of using a single centralized database. A second option allows decentralized deployment of the system with decentralized databases. Each system can be run with separate maintenance cycles. A third option will allow the decentralized deployment of the system, with a single centralized database. The idea is to allow integration options that best fit the firm.

■ DETAILS OF THE FUNCTIONAL COMPONENTS[2]

MIS
ACCOUNTING
HUMAN RESOURCES
SALES

In our review of the application modules that make up R/3 (see Exhibit 16.2), the emphasis is placed on what these modules actually do, not on the technical aspects of how they communicate with one another. The technical aspects of how SAP has implemented this software is interesting, particularly if you are a student in the information systems area. Much information on the technical aspects of the software is available from the SAP Web page located at *http://www.sap.com.*

SAP organizes the R/3 modules in a variety of ways in its documents. In general, there are four major elements to the organization: financial accounting, human resources, manufacturing and logistics, and sales and distribution. We describe these four elements in terms of functionality, but these descriptions are by no means complete. SAP indicates that modules are updated twice a year, based upon changes

---

[2] Jonathon Blain, *Using SAP R/3* (Indianapolis, IN: Que, 1996), pp. 26–30.

in business practices, technological advances, and the changing requirements of their customers.

Financial Accounting

The **financial accounting** segment of R/3 is defined as including three major categories of functionality needed to run the financial accounts for a company—financials (FI), controlling (CO), and asset management (AM). FI includes accounts payable, accounts receivable, general ledger, and capital investments. Also included in the FI category are the procedures to post accounts; close the books for the month and year; prepare financial statements, including the balance sheet; and planning functions. Naturally, the system provides the capability to document processes, prepare reports, archive certain data, and make additions and changes to the financial data as necessary.

As with all the modules in the R/3 system, the user will find all information current and integrated. Thus, an individual manufacturing plant or sales organization will be able to run a profit-and-loss report at any time during the month and be shown the most up-to-date information. This, of course, depends upon having set up the company hierarchy in such a way that the plant or sales group is designated as a profit-and-loss center.

The controlling category includes costing; cost center, profit center, and enterprise accounting and planning; internal orders; open item management; posting and allocation; profitability analysis; and a variety of reporting functions. It also includes a project system to track activity and costs related to major corporate projects, such as the implementation of an R/3 system. This is not the same thing as a project management system, which can be found in the manufacturing modules.

Also included is a module to add activity-based costing (ABC) to other types of costing approaches. ABC is recognized as an effective approach to model the flow of costs between cost objects. Activity costs can then be allocated to business processes.

The asset management category includes the ability to manage all types of corporate assets, including fixed assets, leased assets, and real estate. It also includes the capital investment management module, which provides the ability to manage, measure, and oversee capital investment programs. Treasury capabilities are offered, including the ability to manage cash and funds belonging to the corporation.

Financial Accounting

Human Resources (HR)

The **human resources** (HR) segment contains the full set of capabilities needed to manage, schedule, pay, and hire the people who make the company run. It includes payroll, benefits administration, applicant data administration, personnel development planning, workforce planning, schedule and shift planning, time management, and travel expense accounting.

Because the structure of most companies shifts frequently, one of the functions in the human resources category provides the ability to represent organizational charts, including organizational units, jobs, positions, workplaces, and tasks. Thus, the user can represent and plan matrix organization, split responsibilities, and temporary project groups.

Capturing data from the human resources module, the SAP Business Workflow (WF) system provides management with the ability to define and manage the flow of

Human Resources

work required in a cross-functional business process. Process owners find this useful for monitoring activities that have deadlines either by individual or by position.

Manufacturing and Logistics

Manufacturing and Logistics

The **manufacturing and logistics** segment is the largest and most complex of the module categories. It can be divided into five major components. They are materials management (MM), plant maintenance (PM), quality management (QM), production planning and control (PP), and a project management system (PS). Each component is divided into a number of subcomponents. Materials management covers all tasks within the supply chain, including consumption-based planning, purchasing, vendor evaluation, and invoice verification. It also includes inventory and warehouse management to manage stock until usage dictates the cycle should begin again. Electronic kanban/just-in-time delivery is supported.

Plant maintenance supports the activities associated with planning and performing repairs and preventive maintenance. Completion and cost reports are available. Maintenance activities can be managed and measured.

The quality management capability plans and implements procedures for inspection and quality assurance. It is built on the ISO 9001 standard for quality management. It is integrated with the procurement and production processes so that the user can identify inspection points both for incoming materials and for products during the manufacturing process.

Production planning and control supports both discrete and process manufacturing processes. Repetitive and configure-to-order approaches are provided. This set of modules supports all phases of manufacturing, providing capacity leveling and requirements planning, material requirements planning, product costing, bills of material explosion and implosion, CAD dialog interface, and engineering change management. The system allows users to link rework orders to production schedules. Orders can be generated from internal sales orders or from links to a World Wide Web site.

The project management system provides the user the capability to setup, manage, and evaluate large, complex projects. While the financial costing project system focuses on costs, the manufacturing project system is used for planning and monitoring dates and resources. The system walks the user through the typical project steps—concept, rough-cut planning, detailed planning, approval, execution, and closing. It manages a sequence of activities, each with its interrelationships to the others. Activities are defined as tasks that take time, are processed without interruption, require resources, and incur costs. Projects are measured based on projected and actual dates and results. The system provides one the capability to manage availability, budget, capacity and cost planning, project status, and time scheduling.

Sales and Distribution (SD)

Sales and Distribution

The **sales and distribution** (SD) set of modules provides prospective customers and customer management, sales order management, configuration management, distribution, export controls, shipping, and transportation management, as well as billing, invoicing, and rebate processing. Because this, like the other modules, can be implemented on a global basis, the user can manage the sales process globally. For example, an order may be received in Hong Kong. If the products are not available locally, they may be internally procured from warehouses in other parts of the world and shipped to arrive together at the Hong Kong customer's site.

In sales and distribution, products or services are sold to customers. In implementing the SD module (as in other modules), the company structure must be represented in the system so that, for example, R/3 knows where and when to recognize revenue. It is possible to represent the structure of the firm from the point of view of accounting, materials management, or sales and distribution. These structures can also be combined.

When a sales order is entered, it automatically includes the correct information on pricing, promotions, availability, and shipping options. Batch order processing is available for specialized industries such as food, pharmaceutical, or chemical. Users have the ability to reserve inventory for specific customers, request production of subassemblies, or enter orders that are assemble-to-order, build-to-order, or engineer-to-order as well as special customized orders. Exhibit S16.3 depicts the complex data linkages between modules needed to integrate information managed by the system.

The modules included with the R/3 system are built on what SAP considers best practices. SAP has a research and development group that continually looks for better ways to carry out a particular process or subprocess. System upgrades are designed to reflect the newest best practices.

In addition to the set of standard modules, SAP also has special add-on modules called Industry Solutions (IS) tailored to specific industries. Included in the current set are modules for the following industries: chemical/petrochemical, oil and gas, public sector, hospital, retailing, printing and publishing, insurance, and banking. These modules add special features that are needed in each industry. SAP expects to develop many more of these types of modules in the future.

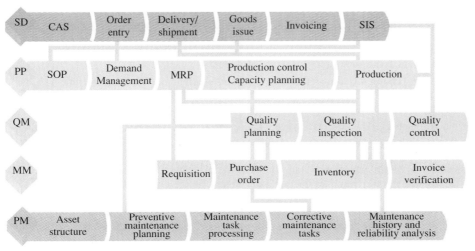

Exhibit SI6.3

Logistics Integration Overview

Source: Copyright SAP AG. Used with permission.

IMPLEMENTING SAP R/3

Implementing R/3 has proven to be a challenge for many companies. Implementation of the system requires that the company change its business processes to conform to the approaches implemented in the R/3 software logic. These processes can be significantly different from those currently implemented within the company. To say the least, adapting a company to a software program is a radical departure from a conventional approach.

To give an example of the problems, Applied Materials, Inc., had originally thought that deploying R/3 to 2,200 users would take approximately a year. In reality, performance problems, complexity, and lack of SAP expertise caused delays of more than two years. The project had consumed over $23 million and still was not complete. The company, though, was still committed to the project.[3]

Rapid Implementation

More recently, Pioneer New Media, the industrial products division of Pioneer Electronics, went live with four SAP modules in just five months—and right on budget.[4] Pioneer used a new **rapid implementation** methodology that boiled the process down into clearly defined, specifically ordered phases. The idea is to bring the business up on the software as quickly as possible by implementing just those modules or portions of the modules that are absolutely critical to operations. Later, usually in a preplanned second phase, the additional modules are added.

Consultants and experienced users are now learning how to successfully implement this software. This is all part of the learning curve that is inherent in using any new technology. Keep in mind that SAP R/3 represents a new class of software. The software is designed around the capabilities now available through distributed hardware systems. It will be exciting to see how these new software platforms develop in the future.

REVIEW AND DISCUSSION QUESTIONS

1. What are the key technological features of SAP R/3 that set it apart from conventional business accounting/planning/control software?

2. SAP R/3 version 4.0 allows the human resources, financial accounting, and manufacturing and logistics modules to be implemented separately. How would this change impact the implementation process?

3. A feature that many companies are considering is the taking of customer orders via World Wide Web sites. Put yourself in the place of the person at Ford Motor Company considering this approach to taking customer orders for the Ford Explorer sport utility vehicle. What information would you need to collect from the customer? What information would you give the customer regarding the order? How would the information be used within Ford Motor Company? What major problems would you anticipate need solving prior to implementing the system? If this project is successful—that is, customers find ordering their Explorer over the Web preferable to negotiating with a dealer—what are the long-term implications to Ford Motor Company?

---

[3] Jeff Moad, "R/3: Little Material Gain for Applied," *PC Week*, May 20, 1996, p. 1.

[4] Erin Callaway, "On Time, On Budget," *PC Week,* May 19, 1997, pp. 135–36.

SELECTED BIBLIOGRAPHY

ASAP World Consultancy, et al. *Using SAP R/3.* Indianapolis, IN: Que, 1996.

Bancroft, Nancy. *Implementing SAP R/3: How to Introduce a Large System into a Large Organization.* Greenwich, CT: Manning, 1996.

Curran, Thomas; Gerhard Keller, and Andrew Ladd. *Business Blueprint: Understanding SAP's R/3 Reference Model.* Upper Saddle River, NJ: Prentice Hall PTR, 1998.

Hernâandez, Josâe Antonio. *The SAP R/3 Handbook.* New York: McGraw-Hill, 1997.

Kretschmer, Rèudiger, and Wolfgang Weiss. *Developing SAP's R/3 Applications with ABAP/4.* San Francisco: Sybex, 1996.

Sams Development Group. *SAP R/3 Unleashed.* Indianpolis, IN: Sams Publishing, 1996.

Sharpe, Simon. *10 Minute Guide to SAP R/3.* Indianapolis, IN: Que, 1997.

Chapter 17

Operations Scheduling

Chapter Outline

The Nature and Importance of Work Centers, 680

    Typical Scheduling and Control Functions

    Objectives of Work-Center Scheduling

    Job Sequencing

Priority Rules and Techniques, 684

    Scheduling n Jobs on One Machine

    Comparison of Priority Rules

    Scheduling n Jobs on Two Machines

    Scheduling a Set Number of Jobs on the Same Number of Machines

    Scheduling n Jobs on m Machines

Shop-Floor Control, 692

    Gantt Charts

    Tools of Shop-Floor Control

    Input/Output Control

    Data Integrity

Example of a Shop Floor Control System, 696

    Principles of Work Center Scheduling

Improving Shop Performance, 697

Personnel Scheduling in Services, 698

    Scheduling Consecutive Days Off

    Scheduling Daily Work Times

    Scheduling Hourly Work Times

Case: Keep Patients Waiting? Not in My Office, 708

Case: McCall Diesel Motor Works, 710

Key Terms

Work Center

Infinite Loading

Finite Loading

Forward Scheduling

Backward Scheduling

Machine-Limited Process

Labor-Limited Process

Dispatching

Sequencing

Priority Rules

Johnson's Rule

Assignment Method

Shop-Floor Control

Input/Output (I/O) Control

First-Hour Principle

www Links

i2 Technologies (http://www.i2.com)

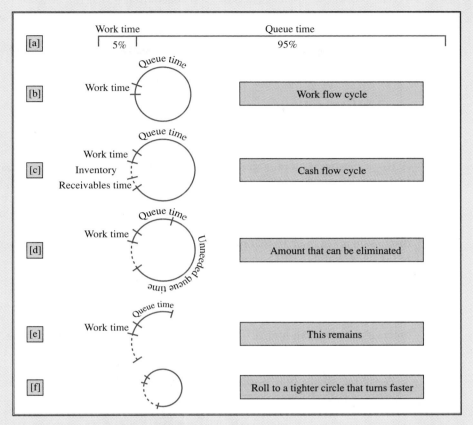

Source: Modified from William E. Sandman with J. P. Hayes, *How to Win Productivity in Manufacturing* (Dresher, PA: Yellow Book of Pennsylvania, 1980), p. 57.

WHY SHOULD ACCOUNTING AND FINANCE TYPES worry about the nitty gritty problems of scheduling, such as long queue times? Answer: Workflow equals cash flow, and workflow is driven by the schedule!

Consider the figure above. In poorly scheduled job shops, it is not at all uncommon for jobs to wait for 95 percent of their total production cycle (a). This results in a long workflow cycle (b). Add inventory time and receivables collection time to this and you get a long cash flow cycle (c). But if you can do a good job of scheduling, you can eliminate, say, 75 percent of the queue time (d,e) and cut your cash flow cycle by the same amount of time. ●

Vol. III "Washburn Guitars"

Again, workflow equals cash flow, and scheduling lies at the heart of the process. A schedule is a timetable for performing activities, utilizing resources, or allocating facilities. In this chapter, we discuss short-run scheduling and control of orders with an emphasis on work centers. We also introduce some basic approaches to short-term scheduling of workers in services.

■ THE NATURE AND IMPORTANCE OF WORK CENTERS

Work Center

A **work center** is an area in a business in which productive resources are organized and work is completed. The work center may be a single machine, a group of machines, or an area where a particular type of work is done. These work centers can be organized according to function in a job-shop configuration; or by product in a flow, assembly line, or group technology-cell (GT-cell) configuration. Recall from the discussion in Chapter 10 that many firms have moved from the job-shop configuration to GT cells. Exhibit 10.15 showed an example of job-shop and GT-cell configurations from Rockwell Telecommunications Division.

In the case of the job shop, jobs need to be routed between functionally organized work centers to complete the work. When a job arrives at a work center—for example, the drilling department in a factory that makes custom printed circuit boards—it enters a queue to wait for a drilling machine that can be used to drill the required holes. Scheduling, in this case, involves determining the order for running the jobs, and also assigning a machine that can be used to make the holes.

A characteristic that distinguishes one scheduling system from another is how capacity is considered in determining the schedule. Scheduling systems can use either

This work center at Dana Corporation's Warner Electric facility in Chihuahua, Mexico, manufactures cruise control motors for Ford Motor Company. The facility uses the latest in welding and machining technology and reported less than six defects per million units delivered.

infinite or finite loading. **Infinite loading** occurs when work is assigned to a work center simply based on what is needed over time. No consideration is given directly to whether there is sufficient capacity at the resources required to complete the work, nor is the actual sequence of the work as done by each resource in the work center considered. Often, a simple check is made of key resources to see if they are overloaded in an aggregate sense, as demonstrated in Chapter 16 in Exhibit 16.19. This is done by calculating the amount of work required over a period (usually a week) using setup and runtime standards for each order. When using an infinite loading system, lead time is estimated by taking a multiple of the expected operation time (setup and run time) plus an expected queuing delay caused by material movement and waiting for the order to be worked on.

Infinite Loading

A **finite loading** approach actually schedules in detail each resource using the setup and run time required for each order. In essence, the system determines exactly what will be done by each resource at every moment during the working day. In the case in which an operation is delayed due to a part(s) shortage, the order will sit in queue and wait until the part is available from a preceding operation. Theoretically, all schedules are feasible when finite loading is used.

Finite Loading

Another characteristic that distinguishes scheduling systems is whether the scheduled is generated forward or backward in time. For this forward–backward dimension, the most common is forward scheduling. **Forward scheduling** refers to the situation in which the system takes an order and then schedules each operation that must be completed forward in time. A system that forward schedules can tell the earliest date that an order can be completed. Conversely, **backward scheduling** starts from some date in the future (possibly a due date) and schedules the required operations in reverse sequence. The backward schedule tells when an order must be started in order to be done by a specific date.

Forward Scheduling

Backward Scheduling

A material requirement planning (MRP) system is an example of an infinite, backward scheduling system for materials. With simple MRP, each order has a due date sometime in the future. In this case, the system calculates parts needs by backward scheduling the time that the operations will be run to complete the orders. The time required to make each part (or batch of parts) is estimated based on historical data. The scheduling systems addressed in this chapter are intended for the processes required to actually make those parts and subassemblies.

Thus far, the term "resources" has been used in a generic sense. In practice, we need to decide what we are going to actually schedule. Commonly, processes are referred to as either machine limited or labor limited. In a **machine-limited** process, equipment is the critical resource that is scheduled. Similarly, in a **labor-limited** process, people are the key resource that is scheduled. Most actual processes are either labor limited or machine limited but, luckily, not both.

Machine-Limited Process

Labor-Limited Process

Exhibit 17.1 describes the scheduling approaches typically used for different manufacturing processes. Whether capacity is considered is dependent on the actual process. Available computer technology allows for the generation of very detailed schedules, such as scheduling each job on each machine and assigning a specific worker to the machine at a specific point in time. Systems that capture the exact state of each job and each resource are also available. Using bar-coding technology, these systems can efficiently capture all of this detailed information. The Breakthrough box on the Optimax system on page 684 is typical of the innovative new scheduling systems that are being developed to interface with enterprise resource planning software such as SAP (see the Supplement to Chapter 16).

Exhibit 17.1

Types of
Manufacturing
Processes and
Scheduling
Approaches

Type	Product	Characteristics	Typical Scheduling Approach
Pure process	Chemicals, steel, wire and cables, liquids (beer, soda), canned goods	Full automation, low labor content in product costs, facilities dedicated to one product	Finite forward scheduling of the process; machine limited
High-volume manufacturing	Automobiles, telephones, fasteners, textiles, motors, household fixtures	Automated equipment, partial automated handing, moving assembly lines, most equipment in line	Finite forward scheduling of the line (a production rate is typical); machine limited. Parts are pulled to the line using just-in-time (kanban) system
Mid-volume manufacturing	Industrial parts suppliers, high-end consumer products	GT cells, focused mini-factories	Infinite forward scheduling typical; priority control; typically labor limited, but often machine limited; often responding to just-in-time orders from customers or MRP due dates.
Low-volume job shops	Custom or prototype equipment, specialized instruments, low-volume Industrial products	Machining centers organized by manufacturing function (not in line), high labor content in product cost, general-purpose machinery with significant changeover time, little automation of material handling, large variety of product	Infinite, forward scheduling of jobs; usually labor limited, but certain functions may be machine limited (a heat-treating process or a precision machining center, for example); priorities determined by MRP due dates

Typical Scheduling and Control Functions

The following functions must be performed in scheduling and controlling an operation:

1. Allocating orders, equipment, and personnel to work centers or other specified locations. Essentially, this is short-run capacity planning.

2. Determining the sequence of order performance (that is, establishing job priorities).

Dispatching

3. Initiating performance of the scheduled work. This is commonly termed **dispatching** of orders.

4. Shop-floor control (or production activity control) involving
    a. Reviewing the status and controlling the progress of orders as they are being worked on.
    b. Expediting late and critical orders.[1]

---

[1] Despite the fact that expediting is frowned on by production control specialists, it is nevertheless a reality of life. In fact, a very typical entry-level job in production control is that of expeditor or "stock chaser." In some companies, a good expeditor—one who can negotiate a critical job through the system or can scrounge up materials that nobody thought were available—is a prized possession.

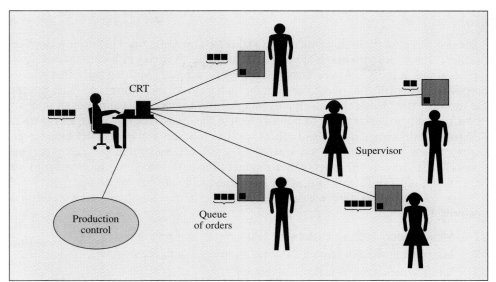

Exhibit 17.2

Typical Scheduling
Process

A simple work-center scheduling process is shown in Exhibit 17.2. At the start of the day, the scheduler (in this case, a production control person assigned to this department) selects and sequences available jobs to be run at individual workstations. The scheduler's decisions would be based on the operations and routing requirements of each job, the status of existing jobs at each work center, the queue of work before each work center, job priorities, material availability, anticipated job orders to be released later in the day, and work-center resource capabilities (labor and/or machines).

To help organize the schedule, the scheduler would draw on job status information from the previous day, external information provided by central production control, process engineering, and so on. The scheduler would also confer with the supervisor of the department about the feasibility of the schedule, especially workforce considerations and potential bottlenecks. The details of the schedule are communicated to workers via dispatch lists shown on computer terminals, in hard-copy printouts, or by posting a list of what should be worked on in central areas. The use of visible schedule boards such as depicted in the picture above of Bernard Welding are highly effective ways to communicate the priority and current status of work.

Objectives of Work-Center Scheduling

The objectives of work-center scheduling are (1) to meet due dates, (2) to minimize lead time, (3) to minimize setup time or cost, (4) to minimize work-in-process inventory, and (5) to maximize machine or labor utilization. (The last objective is controversial because simply keeping all equipment and/or employees busy may not be the most effective way to manage flow through the process.)

Job Sequencing

Sequencing

Priority Rules

The process of determining which job to start first on some machine or in some work center is know as **sequencing** or priority sequencing. **Priority rules** are the rules used in obtaining a job sequence. These can be very simple, requiring only that jobs be sequenced according to one piece of data, such as processing time, due date, or order of arrival. Other rules, though equally simple, may require several pieces of information, typically to derive an index number such as the least-slack rule and the critical-ratio rule (both defined later). Still others, such as Johnson's rule (also discussed later), apply to job scheduling on a sequence of machines and require a computational procedure to specify the order of performance. Ten of the more common priority rules are shown in "Ten Priority Rules for Job Sequencing" on the next page.

The following standard measures of schedule performance are used to evaluate priority rules:

1. Meeting due dates of customers or downstream operations.

2. Minimizing the flow time (the time a job spends in the process).

3. Minimizing work-in-process inventory.

4. Minimizing idle time of machines or workers.

▪ PRIORITY RULES AND TECHNIQUES

Scheduling *n* Jobs on One Machine

Let's look at some of the 10 priority rules compared in a static scheduling situation involving 4 jobs on 1 machine. (In scheduling terminology, this class of problems is referred to as an "*n* job—one-machine problem" or simply "*n*/1"). The theoretical

BREAKTHROUGH

Optimax Intelligent Scheduling and Planning

One of the newer wrinkles in the scheduling arena is "order promising," observes Jeff Herrman, president and CEO of Optimax Systems Corp., a Cambridge, Massachusetts, provider of intelligent scheduling and planning systems. Optimax offers real-time available-to-promise (ATP) functionality in its latest offering, OptiFlex ATP, which it began offering in early 1997. "It doesn't simply match orders to preplanned production slots, but actually determines the factory's ability to fulfill an order by checking detailed constraints such as machine capacity, material availability, labor, and logistics," Herrman says. "It does this in real time, while the customer is on the line. I like to call it 'The customer schedules the factory.'" The approach: A user connects to a Web page, then clicks on order entry, then order configuration, and requests a shipment date—and receives an "instant" reply as to whether the order can be fulfilled by the requested date.

More likely, the analysis of the factory's ability to produce and ship an order by a given date would occur in response to a query from a dealer or a salesman in the field, he notes. "But ultimately, the customer could bypass sales," Herrman predicts. "For routine orders, this is very possible."

While the OptiMax product is designed to supplement ERP systems (it will work with SAP), some vendors of broad-based packages are talking about offering sophisticated Internet-compatible scheduling systems as integral parts of the ERP software.

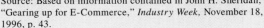

Note: The latest scheduling software is featured on the i2 Technologies Web site at http://www.i2.com.
Source: Based on information contained in John H. Sheridan, "Gearing up for E-Commerce," *Industry Week,* November 18, 1996, p. 43.

difficulty of scheduling problems increases as more machines are considered rather than as more jobs must be processed; therefore, the only restriction on *n* is that it be a specified, finite number. Consider the following example.

■ **example 17.1** *n Jobs on One Machine* Mike Morales is the supervisor of Legal Copy-Express, which provides copy services for downtown Los Angeles law firms. Five customers submitted their orders at the beginning of the week. Specific scheduling data are as follows:

Job (in Order of Arrival)	Processing Time (Days)	Due Date (Days Hence)
A	3	5
B	4	6
C	2	7
D	6	9
E	1	2

All orders require the use of the only color copy machine available; Morales must decide on the processing sequence for the five orders. The evaluation criterion is minimum flow time. Suppose that Morales decides to use the FCFS rule in an attempt to make Legal Copy-Express appear fair to its customers.

Ten Priority Rules for Job Sequencing

1. **FCFS** (first-come, first-served). Orders are run in the order they arrive in the department.

2. **SOT** (shortest operating time). Run the job with the shortest completion time first, next shortest second, and so on. This is identical to SPT (shortest processing time).

3. **Due date**—earliest due date first; run the job with the earliest due date first. DDate—when referring to the entire job; OPNDD—when referring to the next operation.

4. **Start date**—due date minus normal lead time. (Run the job with the earliest start date first.)

5. **STR** (slack time remaining). This is calculated as the difference between the time remaining before the due date minus the processing time remaining. Orders with the shortest STR are run first.

6. **STR/OP** (slack time remaining per operation). Orders with shortest STR/OP are run first. STR/OP is calculated as follows:

$$STR/OP = \frac{\text{Time remaining before due date} - \text{Remaining processing time}}{\text{Number of remaining operations}}$$

7. **CR** (critical ratio). This is calculated as the difference between the due date and the current date divided by the number of work days remaining. Orders with the smallest CR are run first.

8. **QR** (queue ratio). This is calculated as the slack time remaining in the schedule divided by the planned remaining queue time. Orders with the smallest QR are run first.

9. **LCFS** (last-come, first-served). This rule occurs frequently by default. As orders arrive they are placed on the top of the stack; the operator usually picks up the order on top to run first.

10. **Random order or whim**. The supervisors or the operators usually select whichever job they feel like running.

Source: List modified from Donald W. Fogarty, John H. Blackstone, Jr., and Thomas R. Hoffmann, *Production and Inventory Management* (Cincinnati: South-Western Publishing, 1991), pp. 452–53.

solution FCFS RULE: The FCFS rule results in the following flow times:

FCFS Schedule

Job Sequence	Processing Time (Days)	Due Date (Days Hence)	Flow Time (Days)
A	3	5	$0 + 3 = 3$
B	4	6	$3 + 4 = 7$
C	2	7	$7 + 2 = 9$
D	6	9	$9 + 6 = 15$
E	1	2	$15 + 1 = 16$

Total flow time $= 3 + 7 + 9 + 15 + 16 = 50$ days

Mean flow time $= \dfrac{50}{5} = 10$ days

Comparing the due date of each job with its flow time, we observe that only Job A will be on time. Jobs B, C, D, and E will be late by 1, 2, 6, and 14 days, respectively. On the average, a job will be late by $(0 + 1 + 2 + 6 + 14)/5 = 4.6$ days. ■

solution SOT RULE: Let's now consider the SOT rule. Here, Morales gives the highest priority to the order that has the shortest processing time. The resulting flow times are

SOT Schedule

Job Sequence	Processing Time (Days)	Due Date (Days Hence)	Flow Time (Days)
E	1	2	$0 + 1 = 1$
C	2	7	$1 + 2 = 3$
A	3	5	$3 + 3 = 6$
B	4	6	$6 + 4 = 10$
D	6	9	$10 + 6 = 16$

Total flow time $= 1 + 3 + 6 + 10 + 16 = 36$ days

Mean flow time $= \dfrac{36}{5} = 7.2$ days

SOT results in a lower average flow time than the FCFS rule. In addition, Jobs E and C will be ready before the due date, and Job A is late by only one day. On the average a job will be late by $(0 + 0 + 1 + 4 + 7)/5 = 2.4$ days. ■

solution DDATE RULE: If Morales decides to use the DDate rule, the resulting schedule is

DDate Schedule

Job Sequence	Processing Time (Days)	Due Date (Days Hence)	Flow Time (Days)
E	1	2	$0 + 1 = 1$
A	3	5	$1 + 3 = 4$
B	4	6	$4 + 4 = 8$
C	2	7	$8 + 2 = 10$
D	6	9	$10 + 6 = 16$

Total completion time $= 1 + 4 + 8 + 10 + 16 = 39$ days

Mean flow time $= 7.8$ days

In this case Jobs B, C, and D will be late. On the average, a job will be late by $(0 + 0 + 2 + 3 + 7)/5 = 2.4$ days. ■

solutions LCFS, RANDOM, and STR RULES: Here are the resulting flow times of the LCFS, random, and STR rules:

Job Sequence	Processing Time (Days)	Due Date (Days Hence)	Flow Time (Days)
LCFS schedule			
E	1	2	$0 + 1 = 1$
D	6	9	$1 + 6 = 7$
C	2	7	$7 + 2 = 9$
B	4	6	$9 + 4 = 13$
A	3	5	$13 + 3 = 16$

Total flow time = 46 days
Mean flow time = 9.2 days
Average lateness = 4.0 days

Random Schedule			
D	6	9	$0 + 6 = 6$
C	2	7	$6 + 2 = 8$
A	3	5	$8 + 3 = 11$
E	1	2	$11 + 1 = 12$
B	4	6	$12 + 4 = 16$

Total flow time = 53 days
Mean flow time = 10.6 days
Average lateness = 5.4 days

STR Schedule			
E	1	2	$0 + 1 = 1$
A	3	5	$1 + 3 = 4$
B	4	6	$4 + 4 = 8$
D	6	9	$8 + 6 = 14$
C	2	7	$14 + 2 = 16$

Total flow time = 43 days
Mean flow time = 8.6 days
Average lateness = 3.2 days

■

Comparison of Priority Rules

Here are some of the results summarized for the rules that Morales examined:

Rule	Total Completion Time (Days)	Average Completion Time (Days)	Average Lateness (Days)
FCFS	50	10	4.6
SOT	36	7.2	2.4
DDate	39	7.8	2.4
LCFS	46	9.2	4.0
Random	53	10.6	5.4
STR	43	8.6	3.2

Obviously, here SOT is better than the rest of the rules, but is this always the case? The answer is yes. Moreover, it can be shown mathematically that the SOT rule yields an optimum solution for the $n/1$ case in such other evaluation criteria as mean waiting time and mean completion time. In fact, so powerful is this simple rule that it has been termed "the most important concept in the entire subject of sequencing."[2]

Scheduling *n* Jobs on Two Machines

Johnson's Rule

The next step up in complexity is the $n/2$ flow-shop case, where two or more jobs must be processed on two machines in a common sequence. As in the $n/1$ case, there is an approach that leads to an optimal solution according to certain criteria. The objective of this approach, termed **Johnson's rule** or *method* (after its developer), is to minimize the flow time, from the beginning of the first job until the finish of the last. Johnson's rule consists of the following steps:

1. List the operation time for each job on both machines.
2. Select the shortest operation time.
3. If the shortest time is for the first machine, do the job first; if it is for the second machine, do the job last.
4. Repeat Steps 2 and 3 for each remaining job until the schedule is complete.

■ **example 17.2**   *n Jobs on Two Machines*   We can illustrate this procedure by scheduling four jobs through two machines.

solution   *Step 1:* List operation times.

Job	Operation Time on Machine 1	Operation Time on Machine 2
A	3	2
B	6	8
C	5	6
D	7	4

Steps 2 and 3: Select the shortest operation time and assign. Job A is shortest on Machine 2 and is assigned first and performed last. (Once assigned, Job A is no longer available to be scheduled.)

Step 4: Repeat Steps 2 and 3 until completion of schedule. Select the shortest operation time among the remaining jobs. Job D is second shortest on Machine 2, so it is performed second to last. (Remember, Job A is last.) Now Jobs A and D are not available anymore for scheduling. Job C is the shortest on Machine 1 among the remaining jobs. Job C is performed first. Now only Job B is left with the shortest operation time on Machine 1. Thus, according to Step 3, it is performed first among the remaining, or second overall. (Job C was already scheduled first.)

In summary, the solution sequence is C → B → D → A, and the flow time is 25 days, which is a minimum. Also minimized are total idle time and mean idle time. The final schedule appears in Exhibit 17.3.

These steps result in scheduling the jobs having the shortest time in the beginning and ending of the schedule. As a result, the concurrent operating time for the two machines is maximized, thus minimizing the total operating time required to complete the jobs. ■

---

[2] R. W. Conway, William L. Maxwell, and Louis W. Miller, *Theory of Scheduling* (Reading, MA: Addison-Wesley, 1967), p. 26. A classic book on the subject.

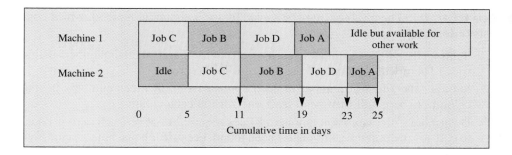

Exhibit 17.3

Optimal Schedule of
Jobs Using Johnson's
Rule

| | Machine | | | | |
Job	**A**	**B**	**C**	**D**	**E**
I	$5	$6	$4	$8	$3
II	6	4	9	8	5
III	4	3	2	5	4
IV	7	2	4	5	3
V	3	6	4	5	5

Exhibit 17.4

Assignment Matrix
Showing Machine
Processing Costs for
Each Job

Johnson's method has been extended to yield an optimal solution for the $n/3$ case. When flow-shop scheduling problems larger than $n/3$ arise (and they generally do), analytical solution procedures leading to optimality are not available. The reason for this is that even though the jobs may arrive in static fashion at the first machine, the scheduling problem becomes dynamic, and series of waiting lines start to form in front of machines downstream.

Scheduling a Set Number of Jobs on the Same Number of Machines

Some job shops have enough of the right kinds of machines to start all jobs at the same time. Here the problem is not which job to do first, but rather which particular assignment of individual jobs to individual machines will result in the best overall schedule. In such cases, we can use the assignment method.

The **assignment method** is a special case of the transportation method of linear programming. It can be applied to situations where there are n supply sources and n demand uses (e.g., five jobs on five machines) and the objective is to minimize or maximize some measure of effectiveness. This technique is convenient in applications involving allocation of jobs to work centers, people to jobs, and so on. The assignment method is appropriate in solving problems that have the following characteristics:

Assignment Method

1. There are n "things" to be distributed to n "destinations."
2. Each thing must be assigned to one and only one destination.
3. Only one criterion can be used (minimum cost, maximum profit, or minimum completion time, for example).

■ **example** 17.3 *Assignment Method* Suppose that a scheduler has five jobs that can be performed on any of five machines ($n = 5$). The cost of completing each job–machine combination is shown in Exhibit 17.4. The scheduler would like to devise a minimum-cost assignment. (There are 5!, or 120, possible assignments.)

solution   This problem may be solved by the assignment method, which consists of four steps:

1.   Subtract the smallest number in each *row* from itself and all other numbers in that row. (There will then be at least one zero in each row.)
2.   Subtract the smallest number in each *column* from all other numbers in that column. (There will then be at least one zero in each column.)
3.   Determine if the *minimum* number of lines required to cover each zero is equal to *n*. If so, an optimum solution has been found, because job machine assignments must be made at the zero entries, and this test proves that this is possible. If the minimum number of lines required is less than *n*, go to Step 4.
4.   Draw the least possible number of lines through all the zeros. (These may be the same lines used in Step 3.) Subtract the smallest number not covered by lines from itself and all other uncovered numbers, and add it to the number at each intersection of lines. Repeat Step 3.

Exhibit 17.5

Procedure to Solve an Assignment Matrix

Step 1: Row reduction—the smallest number is subtracted from each row.

Job	Machine				
	A	B	C	D	E
I	2	3	1	5	0
II	2	0	5	4	1
III	2	1	0	3	2
IV	5	0	2	3	1
V	0	3	1	2	2

Step 2: Column reduction—the smallest number is subtracted from each column.

Job	Machine				
	A	B	C	D	E
I	2	3	1	3	0
II	2	0	5	2	1
III	2	1	0	1	2
IV	5	0	2	1	1
V	0	3	1	0	2

Step 3: Apply line test—the number of lines to cover all zeros is 4; because 5 are required, go to step 4.

Job	Machine				
	A	B	C	D	E
I	2	3	1	3	0
II	2	0	5	2	1
III	2	1	0	1	2
IV	5	0	2	1	1
V	0	3	1	0	2

Step 4: Subtract smallest uncovered number and add to intersection of lines—using lines drawn in Step 3, smallest uncovered number is 1.

Job	Machine				
	A	B	C	D	E
I	1	3	0	2	0
II	1	0	4	1	1
III	2	2	0	1	3
IV	4	0	1	0	1
V	0	4	1	0	3

Optimum solution—by "line test."

Job	Machine				
	A	B	C	D	E
I	1	3	0	2	0
II	1	0	4	1	1
III	2	2	0	1	3
IV	4	0	1	0	1
V	0	4	1	0	3

Optimum assignments and their costs.

Job I to Machine E	$ 3
Job II to Machine B	4
Job III to Machine C	2
Job IV to Machine D	5
Job V to Machine A	3
Total cost	$17

For the example problem, the steps listed in Exhibit 17.5 would be followed.

Note that even though there are two zeros in three rows and three columns, the solution shown in Exhibit 17.5 is the only one possible for this problem because Job III must be assigned to machine C to meet the "assign to zero" requirement. Other problems may have more than one optimum solution, depending, of course, on the costs involved. ■

The nonmathematical rationale of the assignment method is one of minimizing opportunity costs.[3] For example, if we decided to assign Job I to machine A instead of to machine E, we would be sacrificing the opportunity to save $2($5 − $3). The assignment algorithm in effect performs such comparisons for the entire set of alternative assignments by means of row and column reduction, as described in Steps 1 and 2. It makes similar comparisons in Step 4. Obviously, if assignments are made to zero cells, no opportunity cost, with respect to the entire matrix occurs.

Scheduling *n* Jobs on *m* Machines

Complex job shops are characterized by multiple machine centers processing a variety of different jobs arriving at the machine centers in an intermittent fashion throughout the day. If there are *n* jobs to be processed on *m* machines and all jobs are processed on all machines, then there are $(n!)^m$ alternative schedules for this job set. Because of the large number of schedules that exist for even small job shops, computer simulation (see the supplement to this chapter) is the only practical way to determine the relative merits of different priority rules in such situations. As in the case of *n* jobs on one machine, the 10 priority rules (and more) have been compared relative to their performance on the evaluation criteria previously mentioned. By way of example, John Kanet and Jack Hayya focused on due date-oriented priority rules to see which one was best. Their simulation of a complex job shop led to the finding that total job competition rules of "DDATE, STR, and CR were outperformed by their 'operation' counterparts OPNDD, STR/OP, and OPCR" for all seven of the performance criteria used.[4]

Which Priority Rule Should Be Used?   We believe that the needs of most manufacturers are reasonably satisfied by a relatively simple priority scheme that embodies the following principles:

1.   It should be dynamic, that is, computed frequently during the course of a job to reflect changing conditions.

2.   It should be based in one way or another on slack (the difference between the work remaining to be done on a job and the time remaining to do it). This embodies the due-date features suggested by Kanet and Hayya.

---

[3] The underlying rationale of the procedure of adding and subtracting the smallest cell values is as follows: Additional zeros are entered into the matrix by subtracting an amount equal to one of the cells from all cells. Negative numbers, which are not permissible, occur in the matrix. To get rid of the negative numbers, an amount equal to the maximum negative number must be added to each element of the row or column in which it occurs. This results in adding this amount twice to any cell that lies at the intersection of a row and a column that were both changed. The net result is that the lined rows and columns revert to their original amounts, and the intersections increase by the amount subtracted from the uncovered cells. (The reader may wish to prove this by solving the example without using lines.)

[4] John K. Kanet and Jack C. Hayya, "Priority Dispatching with Operation Due Dates in a Job Shop," *Journal of Operations Management* 2, no. 3 (May 1982), p. 170.

Newer approaches combine simulation with human schedulers to create schedules on standard PCs. See the box below, "Interactive Scheduling Using the JOB System."

■ SHOP-FLOOR CONTROL

Shop-Floor Control

Scheduling job priorities is just one aspect of **shop-floor control** (now often called *production activity control*). The *APICS Dictionary* defines a *shop-floor control system* as

> A system for utilizing data from the shop floor as well as data processing files to maintain and communicate status information on shop orders and work centers.

The major functions of shop-floor control are:

1. Assigning priority of each shop order.
2. Maintaining work-in-process quantity information.
3. Conveying shop-order status information to the office.
4. Providing actual output data for capacity control purposes.
5. Providing quantity by location by shop order for WIP inventory and accounting purposes.
6. Providing measurement of efficiency, utilization, and productivity of manpower and machines.

Interactive Scheduling Using the JOB System

The JOB system developed by Pruett and Schartner uses a simulation model that allows for human interaction in scheduling jobs and balancing workloads across machine centers. It involves three scheduling approaches: successive, interactive, and semi-interactive.

The *successive approach* is characterized by the computer scheduling work orders automatically according to a priority rule (e.g., earliest due date), ignoring load balancing considerations. The *interactive approach* is characterized by a human scheduling one work order at a time. The schedule is developed interactively through JOB by the scheduler who simultaneously considers both work order scheduling needs and machine group load capacities. The *semi-interactive approach* is a combination of the interactive and successive approaches.

Work orders are automatically scheduled using the successive approach criteria, but with prespecified machine group load thresholds (usually set at 100 percent). When a machine group load threshold is exceeded, the algorithm pauses and human intervention (interactive approach) is required to rectify the overload. Once the loading problem for that one work order is corrected, the algorithm (successive approach) is allowed to resume the scheduling process.

The interactive process entails the use of computer generated bar chart schedules shown on the computer screen. The system is menu driven and provides such statistics as average work in process, average cycle time, overloaded and underloaded machine groups, and late and early work orders.

Source: James M. Pruett and Andreas Schartner, "JOB: An Instructive Job Shop Scheduling Environment," *International Journal of Operations & Production Management* 13, no. 11, 1993, pp. 4–34.

Gantt Chart

Exhibit 17.6

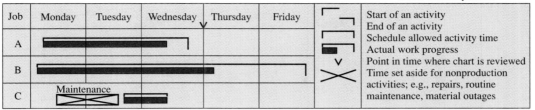

Gantt Chart Symbols

Job	Monday	Tuesday	Wednesday	Thursday	Friday
A					
B					
C	Maintenance				

Symbol	Meaning
⌐	Start of an activity
¬	End of an activity
⌐——¬	Schedule allowed activity time
▬	Actual work progress
∨	Point in time where chart is reviewed
✕	Time set aside for nonproduction activities; e.g., repairs, routine maintenance, material outages

Gantt Charts

Smaller job shops and individual departments of large ones employ the venerable Gantt chart to help plan and track jobs. As described in Chapter 3 the Gantt Chart is a type of bar chart that plots tasks against time. Gantt charts are used for project planning as well as to coordinate a number of scheduled activities. The example in Exhibit 17.6 indicates that job A is behind schedule by about four hours, Job B is ahead of schedule, and Job C has been completed, after a delayed start for equipment maintenance. Note that whether the job is ahead of schedule or behind schedule is based on where it stands compared to where we are now. In Exhibit 17.6 we are at the end of Wednesday, and Job A should have been completed. Job B has already had some of Thursday's work completed.

Tools of Shop-Floor Control

The basic tools of shop-floor control are

1. The *daily dispatch list,* tells the supervisor which jobs are to be run, their priority, and how long each will take. (See Exhibit 17.7a).
2. Various *status and exception reports,* including
   a. The anticipated delay report, made out by the shop planner once or twice a week and reviewed by the chief shop planner to see if there are any serious delays that could affect the master schedule. (See Exhibit 17.7b).
   b. Scrap reports.
   c. Rework reports.
   d. Performance summary reports giving the number and percentage of orders completed on schedule, lateness of unfilled orders, volume of output, and so on.
   e. Shortage list.
3. An *input/output control report,* which is used by the supervisor to monitor the workload–capacity relationship for each workstation. (see Exhibit 17.7c.)

Input/Output Control

Input/output (I/O) control is a major feature of a manufacturing planning and control system. Its major precept is that the planned work input to a work center should never exceed the planned work output. When the input exceeds the output, backlogs build up at the work center, which in turn increases the lead-time estimates for jobs upstream. Moreover, when jobs pile up at the work center, congestion occurs,

Input/Output (I/O) Control

Exhibit 17.7

Some Basic Tools of
Shop-Floor Control

A. Dispatch List

Work center 1501—Day 205

Start date	Job #	Description	Run time
201	15131	Shaft	11.4
203	15143	Stud	20.6
205	15145	Spindle	4.3
205	15712	Spindle	8.6
207	15340	Metering rod	6.5
208	15312	Shaft	4.6

B. Anticipated Delay Report

Dept. 24 April 8

Part #	Sched. date	New date	Cause of delay	Action
17125	4/10	4/15	Fixture broke	Toolroom will return on 4/15
13044	4/11	5/1	Out for plating—plater on strike	New lot started
17653	4/11	4/14	New part-holes don't align	Engineering laying out new jig

C. Input/Output Control Report

Work center 0162

Week ending	505	512	519	526
Planned input	210	210	210	210
Actual input	110	150	140	130
Cumulative deviation	−100	−160	−230	−310
Planned output	210	210	210	210
Actual output	140	120	160	120
Cumulative deviation	−70	−160	−210	−300

processing becomes inefficient, and the flow of work to downstream work centers becomes sporadic. (The water flow analogy to shop capacity control in Exhibit 17.8 illustrates the general phenomenon.) Exhibit 17.7c shows an I/O report for a downstream work center. Looking first at the lower or output half of the report, we see that output is far below plan. It would seem that a serious capacity problem exists for this work center. However, looking at the input part of the plan, it becomes apparent that the serious capacity problem exists at an upstream work center feeding this work center. The control process would entail finding the cause of upstream problems and adjusting capacity and inputs accordingly. The basic solution is simple: Either increase capacity at the bottleneck station, or reduce the input to it. (Input reduction at bottleneck work centers, incidentally, is usually the first step recommended by production control consultants when job shops get into trouble.)

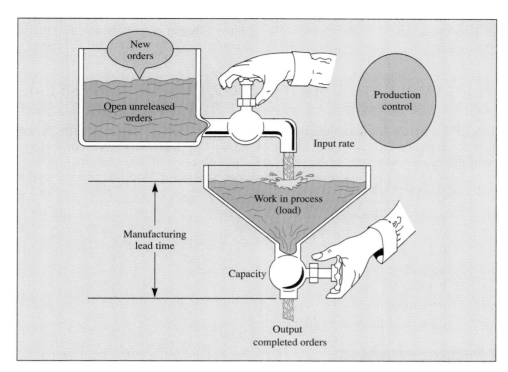

Exhibit 17.8

Shop Capacity
Control Load Flow

Source: "Training Aid—Shop Floor Control," undated. Reprinted with permission of APICS—The Educational Society for Resource Management, Falls Church, VA.

Data Integrity

Shop-floor control systems in most modern plants are now computerized, with job status information entered directly into a computer as the job enters and leaves a work center. Many plants have gone heavily into bar coding and optical scanners to speed up the reporting process and to cut down on data-entry errors.[5] As you might guess, the key problems in shop-floor control are data inaccuracy and lack of timeliness. When these occur, data fed back to the overall planning system are wrong, and incorrect production decisions are made. Typical results are excess inventory, stock-out problems, or both; missed due dates, and inaccuracies in job costing.

Of course, maintaining data integrity requires that a sound data-gathering system be in place; but more important, it requires adherence to the system by everybody interacting with it. Most firms recognize this, but maintaining what is variously referred to as *shop discipline, data integrity,* or *data responsibility* is not always easy. And despite periodic drives to publicize the importance of careful shop-floor reporting by creating data-integrity task forces, inaccuracies can still creep into the system in many ways: A line worker drops a part under the workbench and pulls a replacement from stock without recording either transaction. An inventory clerk makes an error in a cycle count. A manufacturing engineer fails to note a change in the routing of a part.

---

[5] Some companies also use "smartshelves" (inventory bins with weight sensors beneath each shelf). When an item is removed from inventory, a signal is sent to a central computer that notes the time, date, quantity, and location of the transaction.

A department supervisor decides to work jobs in a different order than specified in the dispatch list.

■ EXAMPLE OF A SHOP FLOOR CONTROL SYSTEM

Hewlett-Packard's Manufacturing Management II (MMII) program illustrates the features available for shop-floor control. MMII is a fully integrated system interacting with the various functions within the firm and with external customers.[6]

Exhibit 17.9 shows the logic of the Shop Floor Scheduling Model that addresses the following areas:

- Routings and workcenters.
- Work-in-process (WIP) control.
- Work-order scheduling.
- Shop-floor dispatching.
- Work-order tracking.
- Input/output analysis.
- Labor collection and reporting.

The capacity requirements planning features of MMII interact with this shop-floor model to assure that scheduling is within the capacity limits of the facility.

The routings to work centers have on-line entry through terminals and various screen views available on a CRT as shown on the left. There are a number of different screens that can be reviewed covering various conditions for shop floor control. A screen called PARTROUTINGS, for example, shows all the parts, operation numbers, routings, labor, alternate workstations, parallel sequences, common parts routings, available capacity at each work center, and exception or repair steps in routings.

For production scheduling, the orders scheduling function calculates start and completion times for each production sequence. For on-line use, screens to review the tentative order routing (REVTENT ROUTING) allow a production scheduler to review a work order's scheduled dates and times.

There are other screens, such as shop-floor dispatching and STEP COMPLETION, which show a continuous picture of the status and location of each work order. From the screen, any information shown can be updated manually or by using barcoded data-entry methods.

Principles of Work-Center Scheduling

Much of our discussion of work-center scheduling systems can be summarized in the following principles:

[6] From Hewlett-Packard, *Manufacturing Management II Sales Guide 1993.*

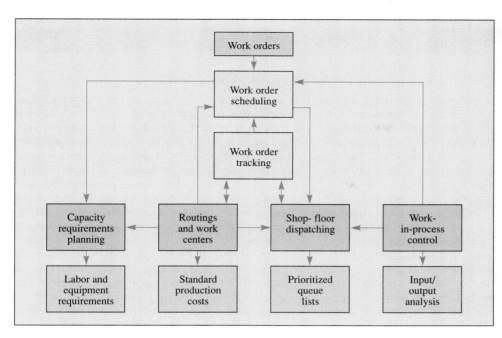

Exhibit 17.9

Hewlett-Packard's
Shop-Floor Control
System

Source: Adapted from Hewlett-Packard, *Manufacturing Management II Sales Guide 1993.*

1. There is a direct equivalence between work flow and cash flow.
2. The effectiveness of any shop should be measured by speed of flow through the shop.
3. Schedule jobs as a string, with process steps back to back.
4. Once started, a job should not be interrupted.
5. Speed of flow is most efficiently achieved by focusing on bottleneck work centers and jobs.
6. Reschedule every day.
7. Obtain feedback each day on jobs that are not completed at each work center.
8. Match work-center input information to what the worker can actually do.
9. When seeking improvement in output, look for incompatibility between engineering design and process execution.
10. Certainty of standards, routings, and so forth is not possible in a shop, but always work towards achieving it.

■ IMPROVING SHOP PERFORMANCE

Managing a shop is more than just priorities and systems—it requires an integrative philosophy of production management, and communication of that philosophy to the managers and workers. The Breakthrough box "Improving Shop Performance at Schlumberger" shown on the next page, provides an example of what this entails, with particular emphasis on the evils of batching.

Improving Shop Performance at Schlumberger

The HDS (Houston Downhole Sensors) Division of Schlumberger builds electromechanical sensors (logging tools) that collect and process geological data for oil and gas exploration. The division operates under all the demands facing the classic job shop. Its Houston factory turns out 200 different products with 30,000 line items in inventory. Engineering changes—sometimes major changes—are an inescapable fact of life. Logging tools must be customized to reflect the kind of drilling they are used for, the underground formations they operate in, and other geological, climatic, and performance factors. Monthly output of each product ranges from 1 to 20 units; prices range from $5,000 to $15,000. Monthly sales volume has ranged from $15 million to less than $1 million, a reflection of the cyclical nature of the oil and gas business.

In the summer of 1985, HDS was struggling. Operations were costly, chaotic, and falling short of acceptable standards. Customers were dissatisfied. About 15 percent of the logging tools failed on final acceptance test. Most products were built to schedules established far in advance, but on-time delivery was no better than 70 percent. The average lead times exceeded 12 months.

Senior management was also dissatisfied. Cost of sales was unacceptably high (as exemplified by the nearly two-to-one ratio of overhead to direct labor), and the plant was bulging with inventories. WIP alone averaged five months of output.

Most job shop managers will instantly recognize these troubled conditions; the situation at HDS has been the rule for job shops, not the exception. In our experience, on-time delivery for master-scheduled items seldom exceeds 75 percent and can be as low as 20 percent. Lead times have grown insidiously over the past decade, and most job shops cannot respond effectively to swings in the business cycle. Backlogs (and lead times) shrink during recessions but soar during periods of robust economic growth—a phenomenon that managers explain away with the slogan, "Backlogs always grow in expansionary periods."

What explains the chronic and intractable problems afflicting job shops? At HDS, most products were batched for final assembly and tested in lots that usually represented two to three months' requirements. Therefore, lead times on orders were at least two to three months—and in reality much longer—even though many logging tools could be assembled and tested in two weeks.

So why batch? Because management wanted to be as efficient as possible—with efficiency defined as minimizing direct labor charges. Batching generated short-term savings in virtually every phase of the production process. Batching, in effect, allowed all the factory's workers to be busy all the time.

In the long term, however, batching becomes a big obstacle to the very efficiencies it seeks to achieve. The long lead-time, large-lot, long-queue philosophy invariably results in split lots, broken setups, lost and defective parts, late deliveries, and large WIP. The results are visible in job shops everywhere: the monthly shipments hockey stick, where a large

■ PERSONNEL SCHEDULING IN SERVICES

Vol. IV "Scheduling Services—the United Solution"

The scheduling problem in most service organizations revolves around setting weekly, daily, and hourly personnel schedules. In this section, we present simple analytical approaches for developing such schedules.

Scheduling Consecutive Days Off

A practical problem encountered in many services is setting schedules so that employees can have two consecutive days off. The importance of the problem stems from the fact that the Fair Labor Standards Act requires overtime for any work hours (by hourly workers) in excess of 40 hours per week. Obviously, if two consecutive days off cannot be scheduled each week for each employee, the likelihood of unnecessary overtime is quite high. In addition, most people probably prefer two consecutive days

volume of product leaves the factory at the end of each measurement period, relaxation of quality standards under pressure to make quotas; secret high-rework jobs hidden in WIP; everchanging production priorities; and daily crises on the shop floor.

We believe the real solution lies in eliminating batching, smoothing, and artificial economies of scale, and organizing a job shop that can quickly and efficiently "change over" from one product to another without incurring large delays and cost penalties.

HDS adopted just such a production philosophy. It emphasizes shorter lead times (down from an average of three months under the batching system to two weeks today), small to nonexistent queues, low inventories, and quick recognition and correction of defects. The factory is now more responsive to external changes in product mix and volumes. It is also more manageable. The number of work orders open at any particular time is small, so their status is easier to monitor. Likewise, the number of problem orders is modest, so they can, and are, handled with greater urgency.

Getting control over the shop floor has allowed us to slash overhead. In the summer of 1985, 520 of the division's 830 employees were salaried or indirect personnel. The overhead count now stands at 220 employees. The largest reductions came from three departments—quality control; shipping, receiving, and warehousing; and production control (expediters, dispatchers)—whose roles diminish as quality and on-time performance improves.

The specific directives and actions HDS followed to implement its philosophy included

- *Making quality mandatory.* Quality was defined to include both product defects and late and partial shipments.
- *Making the schedule, every time.* On-schedule was defined as having every job start and complete on schedule. An accompanying policy was to never start jobs early.
- *Capacity should not be sacrificed for cost.* This required that managers plan for realistic manpower requirements rather than for ideal productivity levels.
- *Reduce setup times.* This involved extensive worker cross-training, simplification of manufacturing instructions, and JIT layouts.
- *Focus on making parts rather than running machines.* Machine utilization was taken out of the shop performance measures.
- *Make performance visible.* All workers were made aware of the progress of each job, speed of correction of defects, and current and anticipated parts shortages.
- *Improve feeder shop and vendor responsiveness.* All supplying operations were made aware of the master schedule and aggressively pursued reductions in planned lead times for their operations.

Source: Reprinted by permission of the *Harvard Business Review.* An excerpt "Time to Reform Job Shop Manufacturing," by James E. Ashton and Frank X. Cook, Jr., (March/April 1989). Copyright 1989 by the President and Fellows of Harvard College; All Rights Reserved.

off per week. The following heuristic procedure was modified from that developed by James Browne and Rajen Tibrewala to deal with this problem.[7]

Objective   Find the schedule that minimizes the number of five-day workers with two consecutive days off, subject to the demands of the daily staffing schedule.

Procedure   Starting with the total number of workers required for each day of the week, create a schedule by adding one worker at a time. This is a two-step procedure:

Step 1. Assign the first worker to all of the days that require staffing. Do this by simply recopying the total requirements for each day. (This gives us an easy way to keep track of the number of workers needed each day.) A positive number means that the worker has been assigned to work that day.

---

[7] James J. Browne and Rajen K. Tibrewala, "Manpower Scheduling," *Industrial Engineering* 7, no. 8 (August 1975), pp. 22–23.

Since the first worker may have been assigned to all seven days, circle the two consecutive days with the lowest numbers. These will be considered for days off. The lowest pair is the one where the highest number in the pair is equal to or lower than the highest number in any other pair. This ensures that the days with the highest requirements are covered by staff. (Monday and Sunday may be chosen even though they are at opposite ends of the array of days.) In case of ties, choose the days-off pair with the lowest requirement on an adjacent day. This day may be before or after the pair. If a tie still remains, choose the first of the available tied pairs. (Do not bother using further tie-breaking rules, such as second lowest adjacent days.)

Step 2. For worker 2, subtract 1 from each of the days not circled with positive numbers and enter this in the worker 2 row. This indicates that one less worker is required on these days because the first worker has just been assigned to them.

The two steps are repeated for the second worker, the third worker, and so forth, until no more workers are required to satisfy the schedule.

■ **example 17.4**   *Scheduling Days Off*

Number of Workers Required

	M	Tu	W	Th	F	S	Su
	4	**3**	**4**	**2**	**3**	**1**	**2**
Worker 1	4	3	4	2	3	①	②
Worker 2	3	2	3	1	②	①	2
Worker 3	2	1	2	0	2	①	①
Worker 4	1	⓪	①	0	1	1	1
Worker 5	0	0	1	0	0	0	0

solution   This solution consists of five workers covering 19 worker days, although slightly different assignments may be equally satisfactory.

The schedule is Worker 1 assigned S–Su off, Worker 2 F–S off, Worker 3 S–Su off, Worker 4 Tu–W off, and Worker 5 works only on Wednesday because there are no further requirements for the other days. Note that workers 3 and 4 are also off on Thursday. ■

Scheduling Daily Work Times

The example below shows how bank clearinghouses and back-office operations of large bank branches establish daily work times. Basically, management wants to derive a staffing plan that (1) requires the least number of workers to accomplish the daily workload and (2) minimizes the variance between actual output and planned output.

In structuring the problem, bank management defines inputs (checks, statements, investment documents, and so forth), as *products,* which are routed through different processes or *functions* (receiving, sorting, encoding, and so forth).

To solve the problem, a daily demand forecast is made by product for each function. This is converted to labor hours required per function, which in turn is converted to workers required per function. These figures are then tabled, summed, and adjusted by an absence and vacation factor to give planned hours. Then they are divided by the number of hours in the workday to yield the number of workers required. This yields the daily staff hours required. (See Exhibit 17.10.) This becomes the basis for a departmental staffing plan that lists the workers required, workers available, variance, and managerial action in light of variance. (See Exhibit 17.11.)

Daily Staff Hours Required to Schedule Daily Work Times

Exhibit 17.10

Product	Daily Volume	Receive P/H	Receive H_{std}	Preprocess P/H	Preprocess H_{std}	Microfilm P/H	Microfilm H_{std}	Verify P/H	Verify H_{std}	Totals H_{std}
		Function								
Checks	2,000	1,000	2.0	600	3.3	240	8.3	640	3.1	16.7
Statements	1,000	—	—	600	1.7	250	4.0	150	6.7	12.4
Notes	200	30	6.7	15	13.3		—			20.0
Investments	400	100	4.0	50	8.0	200	2.0	150	2.7	16.7
Collections	500	300	1.7			300	1.7	60	8.4	11.8
Total hours required			14.4		26.3		16.0		20.9	77.6
Times 1.25 (absences and vacations)			18.0		32.9		20.0		26.1	
Divided by 8 hours equals staff required			2.3		4.1		2.5		3.3	12.2

Note: P/H indicates production rate per hour; H_{std} indicates required hours.

Function	Staff Required	Staff Available	Variance (±)	Management Actions
Receive	2.3	2.0	−0.3	Use overtime.
Preprocess	4.1	4.0	−0.1	Use overtime.
Microfilm	2.5	3.0	+0.5	Use excess to verify.
Verify	3.3	3.0	−0.3	Get 0.3 from microfilm.

Exhibit 17.11

Staffing Plan

Scheduling Hourly Work Times

Services such as restaurants face changing requirements from hour to hour. More workers are needed for peak hours, and fewer are needed in between. Management must continuously adjust to this changing requirement. This kind of personnel scheduling situation can be approached by applying a simple rule, the **"first-hour" principle.**[8] This procedure can be best explained using the following example. Assume that each worker works continuously for an eight-hour shift. The first-hour rule says that for the first hour, we will assign a number of workers equal to the requirement in that period. For each subsequent period, assign the exact number of additional workers to meet the requirements. When in a period one or more workers come to the end of their shifts, add more workers only if they are needed to meet the requirement. The following table shows the worker requirements for the first 12 hours in a 24-hour restaurant:

First-Hour Principle

	10AM	11AM	Noon	1PM	2PM	3PM	4PM	5PM	6PM	7PM	8PM	9PM
	Period											
Requirement	4	6	8	8	6	4	4	6	8	10	10	6

[8] Ibid. Also, see the Nanda and Browne text on employee scheduling listed in the Bibliography for a discussion of this as well as many other techniques and software.

The schedule shows that four workers are assigned at 10 AM, and two are added at 11 AM, and another two are added at noon to meet the requirement. From noon to 5 PM, we have eight workers on duty. Note the overstaffing between 2 PM and 6 PM. The four workers assigned at 10 AM finish their eight-hour shifts by 6 PM, and four more workers are added to start their shifts. The two workers starting at 11 AM leave by 7 PM, and the number of workers available drops to six. Therefore, four new workers are assigned at 7 PM. At 9 PM, there are 10 workers on duty, which is more than the requirement, so no worker is added. This procedure continues as new requirements are given.

	Period											
	10AM	**11AM**	**Noon**	**1PM**	**2PM**	**3PM**	**4PM**	**5PM**	**6PM**	**7PM**	**8PM**	**9PM**
Requirement	4	6	8	8	6	4	4	6	8	10	10	6
Assigned	4	2	2	0	0	0	0	0	4	4	2	0
On duty	4	6	8	8	8	8	8	8	8	10	10	10

Another option is splitting shifts. For example, the worker can come in, work for four hours, then come back two hours later for another four hours. The impact of this option in scheduling is essentially similar to that of changing lot size in production. When workers start working, they have to log in, change uniforms, and probably get necessary information from workers in the previous shift. This preparation can be considered as the "setup cost" in a production scenario. Splitting shifts is like having smaller production lot sizes and thus more preparation (more setups). This problem can be solved by linear programming methods described in the Nanda and Browne bibliographic reference.

■ CONCLUSION

In manufacturing job shops, scheduling now relies heavily on simulation to estimate the flow of work through the system to determine bottlenecks and adjust job priorities. Various software packages are available to do this. In services, the focus is typically on employee scheduling using mathematical tools that can be used to set work schedules in light of expected customer demand. No matter what the scheduling situation is, it is important to avoid suboptimization—a schedule that works well for one part of the organization but creates problems for other parts or, most importantly, for the customer.

SOLVED PROBLEM

Joe's Auto Seat Cover and Paint Shop is bidding on a contract to do all the custom work for Smiling Ed's used car dealership. One of the main requirements in obtaining this contract is rapid delivery time, because Ed—for reasons we shall not go into here—wants the cars facelifted and back on his lot in a hurry. Ed has said that if Joe can refit and repaint five cars that Ed has just received (from an unnamed source) in 24 hours or less, the contract will be his. Following is the time (in hours) required in the refitting shop and the paint shop for each of the five cars. Assuming that cars go through the refitting operations before they are repainted, can Joe meet the time requirements and get the contract?

Car	Refitting Time (Hours)	Repainting Time (Hours)
A	6	3
B	0	4
C	5	2
D	8	6
E	2	1

Solution

This problem can be viewed as a two-machine flow shop and can be easily solved using "Johnson's method." The final schedule is B-D-A-C-E.

	Original Data			Johnson Method	
Car	Refitting Time (Hours)	Repainting Time (Hours)		Order of Selection	Position in Sequence
A	6	3		4th	3d
B	0	4		1st	1st
C	5	2		3d	4th
D	8	6		5th	2d
E	2	1		2d	5th

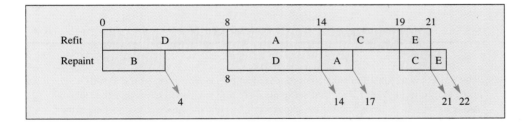

REVIEW AND DISCUSSION QUESTIONS

1. What are the objectives of work-center scheduling?

2. Distinguish between a job shop, a GT cell, and a flow shop.

3. What practical considerations are deterrents to using the SOT rule?

4. What priority rule do you use in scheduling your study time for midterm examinations? If you have five exams to study for, how many alternative schedules exist?

5. The SOT rule provides an optimal solution in a number of evaluation criteria. Should the manager of a bank use the SOT rule as a priority rule? Why?

6. Data integrity is a big deal in industry. Why?

7. Why does batching cause so much trouble in job shops? (Hint: See the Breakthrough box on Schlumberger (page 698).)

8. What job characteristics would lead you to schedule jobs according to "longest processing time first"?

9. Why is managing bottlenecks so important in job-shop scheduling?

10. Under what conditions is the assignment method appropriate?

11. How might planning for a special customer affect the personnel schedule in a service?

PROBLEMS

1. Car	Priority
C	First
A	Tie for second
B	Tie for second

1. Joe has three cars that must be overhauled by his ace mechanic, Jim. Given the following data about the cars, use least slack per remaining operation to determine Jim's scheduling priority for each.

Car	Customer Pick-Up Time (Hours Hence)	Remaining Overhaul Time (Hours)	Remaining Operations
A	10	4	Painting
B	17	5	Wheel alignment, painting
C	15	1	Chrome plating, painting, seat repair

2. See table.

2. A hotel has to schedule its receptionists according to hourly loads. Management has identified the number of receptionists needed to meet the hourly requirement, which changes from day to day. Assume each receptionist works a four-hour shift. Given the following staffing requirement in a certain day, use the first-hour principle to find the personnel schedule.

	Period											
	8AM	9AM	10AM	11AM	Noon	1PM	2PM	3PM	4PM	5PM	6PM	7PM
Requirement	2	3	5	8	8	6	5	8	8	6	4	3
Assigned	2	1	2	3	2			6	2			1
On duty	2	3	5	8	8	7	5	8	8	8	8	3

3. Job order

5
6
7
3
1
2
4

✓

3. There are seven jobs that must be processed in two operations: A and B. All seven jobs must go through A and B in that sequence—A first, then B. Determine the optimal order in which the jobs should be sequenced through the process using these times:

Job	Process A Time	Process B Time
1	9	6
2	8	5
3	7	7
4	6	3
5	1	2
6	2	6
7	4	7

4. 4 workers: 2—TuW,
1—SuM, 1—WTh,
answer may vary

4. Jumbo's Restaurant is trying to create a consecutive days off schedule that uses the fewest workers. Use the following information to create a consecutive days off schedule:

Day	M	Tu	W	Th	F	S	Su
Requirements	2	2	1	3	3	4	2

5. The following list of jobs in a critical department includes estimates of their required times:

Job	Required Time (Days)	Days to Delivery Promise	Slack
A	8	12	4
B	3	9	6
C	7	8	1
D	1	11	10
E	10	−10	—
F	6	10	4
G	5	−8	—
H	4	6	2

a. Use the shortest operation time rule to schedule these jobs.
What is the schedule?
What is the mean flow time?

b. The boss does not like the schedule in (*a*). Jobs E and G must be done first, for obvious reasons. (They are already late.) Reschedule and do the best you can while scheduling Jobs E and G first and second, respectively.
What is the new schedule?
What is the new mean flow time?

✓ 6. The following matrix shows the costs in thousands of dollars for assigning individuals A, B, C, and D to do jobs 1, 2, 3, and 4. Solve the problem showing your final assignments in order to minimize cost.

		Jobs		
	1	**2**	**3**	**4**
A	7	9	3	5
B	3	11	7	6
C	4	5	6	2
D	5	9	10	12

(Individuals — rows A–D)

✓ 7. A manufacturing facility has five jobs to be scheduled into production. The following table gives the processing times plus the necessary wait times and other necessary delays for each of the jobs. Assume that today is April 3 and the jobs are due on the dates shown:

Job	Days of Actual Processing Time Required	Days of Necessary Delay Time	Total Time Required	Date Job Due
1	2	12	14	April 30
2	5	8	13	April 21
3	9	15	24	April 28
4	7	9	16	April 29
5	4	22	28	April 27

Determine *two* schedules, stating the order in which the jobs are to be done. Use the critical ratio priority rule for one. You may use any other rule for the second schedule as long as you state what it is.

8. An accounting firm, Debits 'R Us, would like to keep its auditing staff to a maximum of five people and still satisfy the staffing needs and the policy of two days off per week. Given the following requirements, is this possible? What should the schedule be?
Requirements (Monday through Sunday): 3, 2, 3, 5, 4, 3, 4.

9. Johnson's method;
    E
    A
    B
    D
    C

9. Jobs A, B, C, D, and E must go through Processes I and II in that sequence (i.e., Process I first, then Process II). Use Johnson's rule to determine the optimal sequence to schedule the jobs to minimize the total required time.

Job	Required Processing Time on A	Required Processing Time on B
A	4	5
B	16	14
C	8	7
D	12	11
E	3	9

10. See SM.

10. In a job shop operation, six machinists were uniquely qualified to operate any one of the five machines in the shop. The job shop had considerable backlog and all five machines were kept busy at all times. The one machinist not operating a machine was usually occupied doing clerical or routine maintenance work. Given the value schedule below for each machinist on each of the five machines, develop an optimal assignment. (Hint: Add a dummy column with zero cost values, and solve using the assignment method.)

	Machine				
Machinist	1	2	3	4	5
A	65	50	60	55	80
B	30	75	125	50	40
C	75	35	85	95	45
D	60	40	115	130	110
E	90	85	40	80	95
F	145	60	55	45	85

11. **Area**   **Cost**
    BB 3 $ 700
    DD 1   600
    BFN 4   500
    TD 2   1,800
          $ 3,600

11. Joe has achieved a position of some power in the institution in which he currently resides and works. In fact, things have gone so well that he has decided to divide the day-to-day operations of his business activities among four trusted subordinates: Big Bob, Dirty Dave, Baby Face Nick, and Tricky Dick. The question is how he should do this in order to take advantage of his associates' unique skills and to minimize the costs from running all areas for the next year. The following matrix summarizes the costs that arise under each possible combination of men and areas.

	Area			
	1	2	3	4
Big Bob	$1,400	$1,800	$ 700	$1,000
Dirty Dave	600	2,200	1,500	1,300
Baby Face Nick	800	1,100	1,200	500
Tricky Dick	1,000	1,800	2,100	1,500

12. Order of performance:
    8, 9, 5, 7, 3, 1, 2, 6,
    10, 4.

12. Joe has now been released from his government job. Based on his excellent performance, he was able to land a job as production scheduler in a brand-new custom refinishing auto service shop located near the border. Techniques have improved in the several years he was out of circulation, so processing times are considerably faster. This system is capable of handling 10 cars per day. The sequence now is customizing first, followed by repainting.

Car	Customizing Time (Hours)	Painting (Hours)	Car	Customizing Time (Hours)	Painting (Hours)
1	3.0	1.2	6	2.1	0.8
2	2.0	0.9	7	3.2	1.4
3	2.5	1.3	8	0.6	1.8
4	0.7	0.5	9	1.1	1.5
5	1.6	1.7	10	1.8	0.7

In what sequence should Joe schedule the cars?

13. The following table contains information regarding jobs that are to be scheduled through one machine.

Job	Processing Time (Days)	Due Date
A	4	20
B	12	30
C	2	15
D	11	16
E	10	18
F	3	5
G	6	9

a. What is the First Come, First Served (FCFS) schedule?
b. What is the Shortest Operating Time (SOT) schedule?
c. What is the Slack Time Remaining (STR) schedule?
d. What is the earliest Due Date (DD) schedule?
e. What are the mean flow times for each of the schedules above?

13. *a.* A, B, C, D, E, F, G.
b. C, F, A, G, E, D, B.
c. F, G, D, E, C, A, B.
d. F, G, C, D, E, A, B.
e. FCFS 28.0; SOT 20.0; STR 25.4; DD 23.0 days.

14. Schedule the following six jobs through two machines in sequence to minimize the flow time using Johnson's Rule.

14. C, B, D, F, E, A.

Job	Operations Time Machine 1	Machine 2
A	5	2
B	16	15
C	1	9
D	13	11
E	17	3
F	18	7

15. Larry's Bar and Grill wishes to create a consecutive days off schedule for their waitering staff. Even though their business is heaviest on Friday and Saturday, part-time workers are difficult to find in his area. Create a consecutive days off schedule using the fewest workers possible given the following wait staff requirements for each day of the week.

15. 9 workers: 5—TW, 3—SuM, 1—WTh.

	Day						
	M	Tu	W	Th	F	S	Su
Requirements	5	2	3	4	8	9	3

16. The following requirements are needed for the wait staff at a restaurant. Use the first-hour principle to generate a personnel schedule. Assume a four-hour shift.

16. See table.

							Period				
	11AM	**Noon**	**1PM**	**2PM**	**3PM**	**4PM**	**5PM**	**6PM**	**7PM**	**8PM**	**9PM**
Requirements	4	8	5	3	2	3	5	7	5	4	2
Assigned	4	4				3	2	2			
On-duty	4	8	8	8	4	3	5	7	7	4	2

17. A to 4
    B to 3
    C to 2
    D to 5
    E to 1
    Cost is $41

17. The following matrix contains the costs (in dollars) associated with assigning jobs A, B, C, D, and E to machines 1, 2, 3, 4, and 5. Assign jobs to machines to minimize costs.

Machines	**1**	**2**	**3**	**4**	**5**
Jobs					
A	6	11	12	3	10
B	5	12	10	7	9
C	7	14	13	8	12
D	4	15	16	7	9
E	5	13	17	11	12

Case

Keep Patients Waiting? Not in My Office

Good doctor-patient relations begin with both parties being punctual for appointments. This is particularly important in my specialty—pediatrics. Mothers whose children have only minor problems don't like them to sit in the waiting room with really sick ones, and the sick kids become fussy if they have to wait long.

But lateness—no matter who's responsible for it—can cause problems in any practice. Once you've fallen more than slightly behind, it may be impossible to catch up that day. And although it's unfair to keep someone waiting who may have other appointments, the average office patient cools his heels for almost 20 minutes, according to one recent survey. Patients may tolerate this, but they don't like it.

I don't tolerate that in my office, and I don't believe you have to in yours. I see patients *exactly* at the appointed hour more than 99 times out of 100. So there are many GPs (grateful patients) in my busy solo practice. Parents often remark to me, "We really appreciate your being on time. Why can't other doctors do that too?" My answer is "I don't know, but I'm willing to tell them how I do it."

Booking Appointments Realistically

The key to successful scheduling is to allot the proper amount of time for each visit, depending on the services required, and then stick to it. This means that the physician must pace himself carefully, receptionists must be corrected if they stray from the plan, and patients must be taught to respect their appointment times.

By actually timing a number of patient visits, I found that they break down into several categories. We allow half an hour for any new patient, 15 minutes for a well-baby checkup or an important illness, and either 5 or 10 minutes for a recheck on an illness or injury, an immunization, or a minor problem like warts. You can, of course, work out your own time allocations, geared to the way you practice.

When appointments are made, every patient is given a specific time, such as 10:30 or 2:40. It's an absolute no-no for anyone in my office to say to a patient, "Come in 10 minutes" or "Come in a half-hour." People often interpret such instructions differently, and nobody knows just when they'll arrive.

There are three examining rooms that I use routinely, a fourth that I reserve for teenagers, and a fifth for emergencies. With that many rooms, I don't waste time waiting for patients, and they rarely have to sit in the reception area. In fact, some of the younger children complain that they don't get time to play with the toys and puzzles in the waiting room before being examined, and their mothers have to let them play awhile on the way out.

On a light day I see 20 to 30 patients between 9 AM and 5 PM. But our appointment system is flexible enough to let me see 40 to 50 patients in the same number of hours if I have to. Here's how we tighten the schedule:

My two assistants (three on the busiest days) have standing orders to keep a number of slots open throughout each day for patients with acute illnesses. We try to reserve more such openings in the winter months and on the days following weekends and holidays, when we're busier than usual.

Initial visits, for which we allow 30 minutes, are always scheduled on the hour or the half-hour. If I finish such a visit sooner than planned, we may be able to squeeze in a patient who needs to be seen immediately. And, if necessary, we can book two or three visits in 15 minutes between well checks. With these cushions to fall back on, I'm free to spend an extra 10 minutes or so on a serious case, knowing that the lost time can be made up quickly.

Parents of new patients are asked to arrive in the office a few minutes before they're scheduled in order to get the preliminary paperwork done. At that time the receptionist informs them, "The doctor always keeps an accurate appointment schedule." Some already know this and have chosen me for that very reason. Others, however, don't even know that there *are* doctors who honor appointment times, so we feel that it's best to warn them on the first visit.

Fitting in Emergencies

Emergencies are the excuse doctors most often give for failing to stick to their appointment schedules. Well, when a child comes in with a broken arm or the hospital calls with an emergency Caesarean section, naturally I drop everything else. If the interruption is brief, I may just scramble to catch up. If it's likely to be longer, the next few patients are given the choice of waiting or making new appointments. Occasionally my assistants have to reschedule all appointments for the next hour or two. Most such interruptions, though, take no more than 10 to 20 minutes, and the patients usually choose to wait. I then try to fit them into the spaces we've reserved for acute cases that require last-minute appointments.

The important thing is that emergencies are never allowed to spoil my schedule for the whole day. Once a delay has been adjusted for, I'm on time for all later appointments. The only situation I can imagine that would really wreck my schedule is simulatenous emergencies in the office and at the hospital—but that has never occurred.

When I return to the patient I've left, I say, "Sorry to have kept you waiting, I had an emergency—a bad cut" (or whatever). A typical reply from the parent: "No problem, Doctor. In all the years I've been coming here, you've never made me wait before. And I'd surely want you to leave the room if *my* kid were hurt."

Emergencies aside, I get few walk-ins, because it's generally known in the community that I see patients only by appointment except in urgent circumstances. A non-emergency walk-in is handled as a phone call would be. The receptionist asks whether the visitor wants advice or an appointment. If the latter, he or she is offered the earliest time available for non-acute cases.

Taming the Telephone

Phone calls from patients can sabotage an appointment schedule if you let them. I don't. Unlike some pediatricians, I don't have a regular telephone hour, but my assistants will handle calls from parents at any time during office hours. If the question is a simple one, such as "How much aspirin do you give a one-year-old?" the assistant will answer it. If the question requires an answer from me, the assistant writes it in the patient's chart and brings it to me while I'm seeing another child. I write the answer in—or she enters it in the chart. Then she relays it to the caller.

What if the caller insists on talking with me directly? The standard reply is "Doctor will talk with you personally if it won't take more than one minute. Otherwise you'll have to make an appointment and come in." I'm rarely called to the phone in such cases, but if the mother is very upset, I prefer to talk with her. I don't always limit her to one minute; I may let the conversation run two or three. But the caller knows I've left a patient to talk with her, so she tends to keep it brief.

Dealing with Latecomers

Some people are habitually late; others have legitimate reasons for occasional tardiness, such as a flat tire or "He threw up on me." Either way, I'm hard-nosed enough not to see them immediately if they arrive at my office more than 10 minutes behind schedule, because to do so would delay patients who arrived on time. Anyone who is less than 10 minutes late is seen right away, but is reminded of what the appointment time was.

When it's exactly 10 minutes past the time reserved for a patient and he hasn't appeared at the office, a receptionist phones his home to arrange a later appointment. If there's no answer and the patient arrives at the office a few minutes later, the receptionist says pleasantly, "Hey, we were looking for you. The doctor's had to go ahead with his other appointments, but we'll squeeze you in as soon as we can." A note is then made in the patient's chart showing the date, how late he was, and whether he was seen that day or given another appointment. This helps us identify the rare chronic offender and take stronger measures if necessary.

Most people appear not to mind waiting if they know they themselves have caused the delay. And I'd rather incur the anger of the rare person who *does* mind than risk the ill will of the many patients who would otherwise have to wait after coming in on schedule. Although I'm prepared to be firm with parents, this is rarely necessary. My office in no way resembles an army camp. On the contrary, most people are happy with the way we run it, and tell us so frequently.

Coping with No-Shows

What about the patient who has an appointment, doesn't turn up at all, and can't be reached by telephone? Those facts, too, are noted in the chart. Usually there's a simple explanation, such as being out of town and forgetting about the appointment. If it happens a second time, we follow the same procedure. A third-time offender, though, receives a letter reminding him that time was set aside for him and he failed to keep three appointments. In the future, he's told, he'll be billed for such wasted time.

That's about as tough as we ever get with the few people who foul up our scheduling. I've never dropped a patient for doing so. In fact, I can't recall actually billing a no-show; the letter threatening to do so seems to cure

them. And when they come back—as nearly all of them do—they enjoy the same respect and convenience as my other patients.

Questions

1. What features of the appointment scheduling system were crucial in capturing "many grateful patients"?

2. What procedures were followed to keep the appointment system flexible enough to accommodate the emergency cases, and yet be able to keep up with the other patients' appointments?

3. How were the special cases such as latecomers and no-shows handled?

Source: W. B. Schafer, "Keep Patients Waiting? Not in My Office," *Medical Economics,* May 12, 1986, pp. 137–141. Copyright © 1986 and published by Medical Economics Company, Inc., Oradell, NJ 07649. Reprinted by permission.

Case

McCall Diesel Motor Works (Need for a Complete System of Production Control)

McCall Diesel Motor Works has been a pioneer in the manufacture of a particular internal combustion engine. The plant is located on tidewater in the state of New Jersey because the company originally built engines for the marine field, chiefly fishing boats and pleasure craft. Subsequently, its activities were extended to the stationary type of engines used primarily for production of power in small communities, in manufacturing plants, or on farms.

During the earlier years of the company's operation, its engines were largely special-order jobs. Even at the present time about 60 percent of the output is made to order. There has been in recent years, however, a trend toward standardization of component parts and reduction in the variety of engines produced. The Engineering Department has followed the principle of simplification and standardization in the case of minor parts, such as studs, bolts, and springs, giving a degree of interchangeability of these components among the various sizes and types of engines. Sizes of marine engines have been standardized to some extent, although customer requirements still necessitate some different designs. In the small engines for agricultural use there has been a genuine effort to concentrate sales on a standard line of engines of three sizes: 20, 40, and 60 HP.

The company has always been advanced in its engineering development and design. The production phase, on the other hand, has not been progressive. The

heritage of jobshop operation persists, and despite the definite trend toward standardization, manufacturing continues largely on a made-to-order basis. The increasing popularity of diesel engines has brought many new producing companies into the field, with a consequent tightening of the competitive situation.

High manufacturing costs and poor service have been reflected in the loss of orders. Customer complaints, together with pressure from the Sales Department, prompted management to call in a consulting engineer to make a survey of the Manufacturing department and recommend a plan of action.

The report of the engineer showed the following:

1. *Manufacturing methods,* while still largely of the job-shop character, are in the main good, and no wholesale change should be made. As production is still 60 percent special orders, a complete shift to line manufacture or departmentalization by product is not feasible.

2. *Machinery and equipment* are, for the most part, general-purpose in line with manufacturing requirements. Some machine tools are approaching obsolescence, and for certain operations high-production, single-purpose machines would be advisable. Extensive replacement of machine tools is not a pressing need, but an increased use of jigs and fixtures should be undertaken immediately. There are

many bottlenecks existing in the plant, but contrary to the belief of foreman and other shop executives, there is no serious lack of productive equipment. The trouble lies in the improper utilization of the machine time available.

3. *Production control* is the major element of operating weakness, and improvement is imperative. The lack of proper control over production shows up in many ways:

   a. High in-process inventory, as indicated by piles of partially completed parts over the entire manufacturing floor areas.

   b. Absence of any record concerning the whereabouts of orders in the process from their initiation to delivery at assembly.

   c. Inordinate number of rush orders, particularly in assembly but also in parts manufacture.

   d. Too many parts chasers who force orders through the shops by pressure methods.

   e. Piecemeal manufacture—a lot of 20 parts usually is broken up into four or five lots before it is finished. Not infrequently, the last sublot remains on the shop floor for months and, in a number of instances, is lost as far as records are concerned. Subsequent orders for the same part are issued and new lots pass through to completion while the remains of the old lot lie in partially fabricated condition.

   f. Excessive setup costs resulting from the piecemeal methods mentioned in *(e),* as well as failure to use proper lot sizes, even when lots are not broken up during manufacture.

   g. Failure of all necessary component parts to reach assembly at approximately the same time. The floor of the assembly department is cluttered with piles of parts awaiting receipt of one or more components before engines can be assembled.

   h. Lack of definite sequence of manufacturing operations for a given part. Responsibility for the exact way by which a part is to be made rests entirely on the various department foremen; these men are able machinists, but burdened with detail, their memories cannot be relied on to ensure that parts will always be manufactured in the best, or even the same, sequence of operations. Moreover, they have the responsibility for determining the department to which a lot of parts should be sent when it has been completed in their department.

   i. In the case of certain small standard parts, shop orders have been issued as many as six or eight times in a single month.
   Information is lacking from which to estimate, with any degree of close approximation, the overall manufacturing time for an engine. The result is failure to meet delivery promises or high production cost due to rush or overtime work.

   j. Parts in process or in stores, and destined for imminent assembly, are frequently taken by the Service Department to supply an emergency repair order. The question here is not the academic determination of priority between the customer whose boat may be lying idle because of a broken part and the customer who has not yet received an engine; the question is why there should be any habitual difficulty in rendering adequate repair service and at the same time meeting delivery promises.

   k. Virtually all basic manufacturing data reside in the heads of the superintendent, department foreman, assistant foremen, and setup men.

   l. Delivery dates are set by the Sales Department and generally are dates that customers arbitrarily stipulate.

   m. The general superintendent shows little enthusiasm for the idea of a system of production control; in fact, he is opposed to such an installation. He is of the opinion that reasonably satisfactory results are now being obtained by placing responsibility on the foremen and maintaining contact between them and the parts chasers, who in turn are held responsible for meeting delivery promises. He believes that no system can be substituted for the foremen's knowledge of the ability of the workers. He feels that operation of a production control system requires time studies of all jobs. Time study, he points out, is difficult because of the many operations involved, the high degree of special work, the probable resistance of the workers, and the cost. He further protests that emergencies and rush orders would upset any rigid scheduling of work through the plant. Finally, he is convinced that any system of production control involves an excessive amount of clerical detail to which the foremen, who are practical shop men, object.

The state of affairs the consultant found had, he realized, two main causes:

1. The strong influence of the original job-shop character of manufacture and the very slow evolution to large-scale operation.

2. The fact that the top management of the company was essentially sales minded.

His recommendations, therefore, had to be a simple, straightforward program that would provide adequate control over production and could be instituted gradually and logically.

Questions

1. Outline the essential features of a production control system for this company, giving sufficient detail to make clear how the system will function.

2. Indicate which part of your procedure should be centralized and which part decentralized. What functions should be handled by a central production control office and what functions should be carried out in the various production and assembly departments?

3. What data must be compiled before your system can become fully effective?

4. Enumerate the benefits the company will derive when your production control system is in operation.

5. Set forth in proper order the steps that should be taken and the departments that should be involved in the determination of delivery promises to customers.

6. What arguments would you advance in answer to the general superintendent's objections, as presented in paragraph *m* of the consultant's report?

7. Generally speaking, what is the foremen's place in the scheme of things when a fully developed production control system is in operation and when a production control department has been established?

SELECTED BIBLIOGRAPHY

Ashton, James E., and Frank X. Cook, Jr. "Time to Reform Job Shop Manufacturing." *Harvard Business Review,* March–April 1989, pp. 106–111.

Baker, K. R. "The Effects of Input Control in a Simple Scheduling Model." *Journal of Operations Management* 4, no. 2 (February 1984), pp. 99–112.

Berry, W. L., R. Penlesky, and T. E. Vollmann. "Critical Ratio Scheduling: Dynamic Due-Date Procedures under Demand Uncertainty." *IIE Transactions* 16, no. 1 (March 1984), pp. 81–89.

Conway, R. W., William L. Maxwell, and Louis W. Miller. *Theory of Scheduling.* Reading, MA: Addison-Wesley, 1967.

Gershkoff, I. "Optimizing Flight Crew Schedules." *Interfaces* 19, no. 4 (July–August 1989), pp. 29–43.

Goldratt, E. M., and J. Cox. *The Goal: A Process of Ongoing Improvement.* Great Barrington, MA: North River Press, 1992.

Johnson, S. M. "Optimal Two Stage and Three Stage Production Schedules with Setup Time Included." *Naval Logistics Quarterly* 1, no. 1 (March 1954), pp. 61–68.

Moody, P. E. *Strategic Manufacturing: Dynamic New Directions for the 1990s.* Homewood, IL: Richard D. Irwin, 1990.

Nanda, Ravinder, and Jim Browne. *Introduction to Employee Scheduling.* New York: Van Nostrand Reinhold, 1992.

Richter, H. "Thirty Years of Airline Operations Research." *Interfaces* 19, no. 4 (July–August 1989), pp. 3–9.

Sandman, W. E., with J. P. Hayes. *How to Win Productivity in Manufacturing.* Dresher, PA: Yellow Book of Pennsylvania, 1980.

Sule, Dileep R. *Industrial Scheduling.* Boston: PWS Publishing Company, 1997.

Wild, Ray. *International Handbook of Production and Operations Management.* London, England: Cassell Educational Ltd., 1989.

Simulation

Supplement Outline

Definition of Simulation, 715

Simulation Methodology, 715

    Problem Definition

    Constructing a Simulation Model

    Specifying Values of Variables and
      Parameters

    Evaluating Results

    Validation

    Proposing a New Experiment

    Computerization

Simulating Waiting Lines, 721

    Example: A Two-Stage Assembly Line

Spreadsheet Simulation, 725

Simulation Programs and Languages, 726

    Desirable Features of Simulation
      Software

**Advantages and Disadvantages of
Simulation,** 730

Key Terms

Parameters

Variables

Decision Rules

Probability Distributions

Time Incrementing

Run Length (Run Time)

Computer Model

www Links

Palisade Corporation-@RISK
(http://www.palisade.com)

Systems Modeling Corporation
(http://www.sm.com)

Improving
Efficiency in the
Operating Room

Challenge. To effectively utilize both staff and facilities in the operating room of a small, primary care hospital.

Strategy. Use simulation software to mimic the surgical environment and the complexities involved with staffing the facility.

Results. The engineering group was able to determine the optimum use of staff and facilities and can make adjustments as the hospital's needs change.

St. Francis Hospital is a small, primary care facility located in Escanaba, Michigan. The hospital is part of the OSF Healthcare System, a Catholic corporation comprised of seven hospitals, two nursing homes, a subsidiary for home health and physician offices, an HMO, and a PPO.

Surgeons at St. Francis were frustrated with the turnover time of their surgery suites—the time that elapsed between operations or "from close to cut." The staff believed that there were several causes for the long turnover time—from overutilized surgery professional staff to the lack of suite cleaning staff. One surgeon commented that he and his colleague performed five cases with a total of 3.5 hours of elapsed operating time over a work period of nine hours. He suspected that their idle time was caused by a single staff member who was busy cleaning suites and transporting patients while everyone else waited. The situation was obviously unacceptable.

Two solutions had been suggested by the doctors and staff. One solution involved leveling the daily surgery case load by limiting the daily cases to 10, two-hour case units. When this 10-unit threshold was reached, the operating rooms would be closed, except for emergency surgeries. Unfortunately, this solution could produce a woefully inadequate schedule. What happens to utilization levels if five or six of these case units really lasted only one hour or less?

Another solution involved adding surgical staff. However, the director of surgery wouldn't consider this option because the ratio of workload (cases or surgery hours to staff hours worked) was already too low. Increasing staff would have further lowered this ratio, increasing the hospital's overhead.

An internal operations analysis group attacked the problem with simulation. The simulation model showed that surgeon turnover time is critically affected by the number of surgery teams. Using the simulation, they found that having one more surgery team than operating suites allowed the doctors to leapfrog from one case to the next. This improves the turnover time. A doctor can finish surgery and go quickly to the next-scheduled operating room. Three surgery teams working two suites alleviated the concerns of surgeon turnover time. This situation continues to be monitored and evaluated at the hospital.

Source: Pritsker Corp. press release, "Improving Efficiency in the Operating Room," *Industrial Engineering Solutions,* January 1997, pp. 52–53. Reprinted with permission of the Institute of Industrial Engineers, 25 Technology Park, Norcross, GA 30092, 770-449-0461. Copyright © 1997.

Simulation has become a standard tool in business. In manufacturing, simulation is used to determine production schedules, inventory levels, and maintenance procedures; to do capacity planning, resource requirements planning, and process planning; and more. In services, it is widely used to analyze waiting-lines and scheduling operations such as discussed in the opening vignette. Often, when a mathematical technique fails, we turn to simulation to save us.

■ DEFINITION OF SIMULATION

While the term *simulation* can have various meanings depending on its application, in business, it generally refers to using a digital computer to perform experiments on a model of a real system.[1] These experiments may be undertaken before the real system is operational, to aid in its design, to see how the system might react to changes in its operating rules, or to evaluate the system's response to changes in its structure. Simulation is particularly appropriate to situations in which the size or complexity of the problem makes the use of optimizing techniques difficult or impossible. Thus, job shops, which are characterized by complex queuing problems, have been studied extensively via simulation, as have certain types of inventory, layout, and maintenance problems (to name but a few). Simulation can also be used in conjunction with traditional statistical and management science techniques.

In addition, simulation is useful in training managers and workers in how the real system operates, in demonstrating the effects of changes in system variables, in real-time control, and in developing new ideas about how to run the business.

■ SIMULATION METHODOLOGY

Exhibit S17.1 is a flowchart of the major phases in a simulation study. In this section, we develop each phase with particular reference to the key factors noted at the right of the chart.

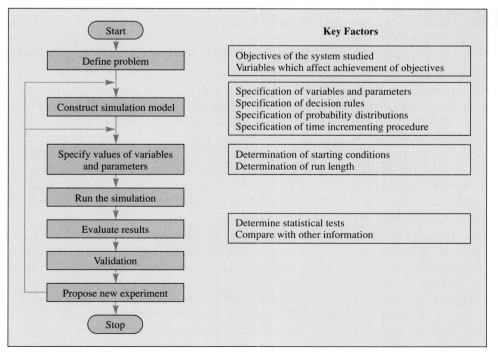

Exhibit S17.1

Major Phases in a Simulation Study

---

[1] Examples of other types of simulation are airplane flight simulators, video games, and virtual reality animation.

Problem Definition

Problem definition for purposes of simulation differs little from problem definition for any other tool of analysis. Essentially, it entails specifying the objectives and identifying the relevant controllable and uncontrollable variables of the system to be studied. Consider the example of a fish market. The objective of the market's owner is maximizing the profit on sales of fish. The relevant controllable variable (i.e., under the control of the decision maker) is the ordering rule; the relevant uncontrollable variables are the daily demand levels for fish and the amount of fish sold. Other possible objectives could also be specified, such as to maximize profit from the sale of lobsters or to maximize sales revenue.

Constructing a Simulation Model

A feature that distinguishes simulation from techniques such as linear programming or queuing theory is the fact that a simulation model must be custom built for each problem situation. (A linear programming model, in contrast, can be used in a variety of situations with only a restatement of the values for the objective function and constraint equations.) There are simulation languages that make the model building easier, however. We discuss this subject later in the chapter. The unique nature of each simulation model means that the procedures discussed later for building and executing a model represent a synthesis of various approaches to simulation and are guidelines rather than rigid rules.

Parameters

Variables

Specification of Variables and Parameters   The first step in constructing a simulation model is determining which properties of the real system should be fixed (called **parameters**) and which should be allowed to vary throughout the simulation run (called **variables**). In a fish market, the variables are the amount of fish ordered, the amount demanded, and the amount sold; the parameters are the cost of the fish and the selling price of the fish. In most simulations, the focus is on the status of the variables at different points in time, such as the number of pounds of fish demanded and sold each day.

Decision Rules

Specification of Decision Rules   **Decision rules** (or operating rules) are sets of conditions under which the behavior of the simulation model is observed. These rules are either directly or indirectly the focus of most simulation studies. In many simulations, decision rules are priority rules (for example, which customer to serve first, which job to process first). In certain situations these can be quite involved, taking into account a large number of variables in the system. For example, an inventory ordering rule could be stated in such a way that the amount to order would depend on the amount in inventory, the amount previously ordered but not received, the amount back ordered, and the desired safety stock.

Distributions

Specification of Probability Distributions   Two categories of **distributions** can be used for simulation: empirical frequency distributions, and standard mathematical distributions. An empirical distribution is one derived from observing the relative frequencies of some event such as arrivals in a line or demand for a product. In other words, it is a custom-built demand distribution that is relevant only to a particular situation. It might appear like the one shown on the left side of Exhibit S17.2. Such distributions have to be determined by direct observation or detailed analysis of records. (We will show how to use these later in the waiting line simulation example.) But often demand, for example, can reasonably be assumed to closely approximate a standard mathematical distribution such as the normal or Poisson. This greatly simplifies data collection and computerization.

Actual Distribution of Demand and Normal Distribution with the Same Mean

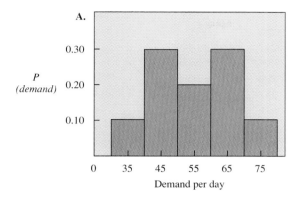
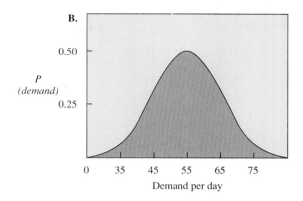

■ **example SI7.I**   *Relating Random Numbers to a Standard Distribution*   To illustrate how to relate random numbers to a standard distribution, let us suppose that daily demand for newspapers from a vending machine is normally distributed with a mean of 55 and standard deviation of 10. (This distribution is shown on the right side of Exhibit S17.2.) Under this assumption, the generation of daily demand would employ a table of randomly distributed normal numbers (or deviates) in conjunction with the statistical formula $D_n = \bar{x} + Z_n\sigma$ (terms defined later), derived from the Z transform used to enter a standard normal table.[2] The specific steps are

solution

1. Draw a five- or six-digit number from Exhibit S17.3. The entries in this table are randomly developed deviate values that pertain to a normal distribution having a mean of zero and a standard deviation of 1. The term *deviate* refers to the number of standard deviations some value is from the mean and, in this case, represents the number of standard deviations that any day's demand is from the mean demand. In the preceding formula for D_n, it would be the value for Z on day n. If we are simulating Day 1 and using the first entry in Exhibit S17.3, then $Z_1 = 1.23481$. A negative deviate value means simply that the particular level of demand to be found by using it will be less than the mean, not that demand will be a negative value.

2. Substitute the value of Z_1, along with the predetermined values for x and σ, into the formula

$$D_n = \bar{x} + Z_n\sigma$$

where

  D_n = Demand on day n
  $\bar{x}$ = Mean demand (55 in this example)
  σ = Estimated standard deviation (10 in this example)
  Z_n = Number of standard deviations from the mean on day n

Thus $D_n = 55 + (1.23481)(10)$.

---

[2] The basis formula is $Z = \dfrac{x - \mu}{\sigma}$, which when restated in terms of x, appears as $x = \mu + Z\sigma$. We then substituted D_n for x and $\bar{x}$ for μ to relate the method more directly to the sample problem.

1.23481	−1.66161	1.49673	−.26990	−.23812	.34506
1.54221	.02629	1.22318	.52304	.18124	.20790
.19126	1.18250	1.00826	.24826	−1.35882	.70691
−.54929	−.87214	−2.75470	−1.19941	−1.45402	.16760
1.14463	−.23153	1.11241	1.08497	−.28185	−.17022
−.63248	−.04776	−.55806	.04496	1.16515	2.24938
−.29988	.31052	−.49094	−.00926	−.28278	−.95339
−.32855	−.93166	−.04187	−.94171	1.64410	−.96893
.35331	.56176	−.98726	.82752	.32468	.36915
.72576					
.04406					

Exhibit SI7.3

Randomly Distributed Normal Numbers

3. Solve for D_n:

$$D_n = 55 + 12.3481$$

$$D_n = 67.3481$$

4. Repeat Steps 1 to 3, using different normal deviates from the table until the desired number of days have been simulated. ■

Time Incrementing

Specification of Time-Incrementing Procedure   In a simulation model, time can be advanced by one of two methods: (1) fixed-time increments or (2) variable-time increments. Under both methods of **time incrementing,** the concept of a simulated clock is important. In the fixed-time increment method, uniform clock-time increments (e.g., minutes, hours, days) are specified, and the simulation proceeds by fixed intervals from one time period to the next. At each point in clock time, the system is scanned to determine if any events are to occur. If they are, the events are simulated, and time is advanced; if they are not, time is still advanced by one unit.

In the variable-time increment method, clock time is advanced by the amount required to initiate the next event.

Which method is most appropriate? Experience suggests that the fixed-time increment is desirable when events of interest occur with regularity or when the number of events is large, with several commonly occurring in the same time period. The variable-time increment method is generally desirable, taking less computer run time when there are relatively few events occurring within a considerable amount of time.[3]

Specifying Values of Variables and Parameters

A variable, by definition, changes in value as the simulation progresses, but it must be given an initial starting value. The value of a parameter, remember, stays constant; however, it may be changed as different alternatives are studied in other simulations.

Determining Starting Conditions   Determining starting conditions for variables is a major tactical decision in simulation. This is because the model is biased by the set of initial starting values until the model has settled down to a steady state. To cope with this problem, analysts have followed various approaches, such as (1) discarding

---

[3] It ignores time intervals where nothing happens and immediately advances to the next point when some event does take place.

data generated during the early parts of the run, (2) selecting starting conditions that reduce the duration of the warm-up period, or (3) selecting starting conditions that eliminate bias. To employ any of these alternatives, however, the analyst must have some idea of the range of output data expected. Therefore, in one sense, the analyst biases results. On the other hand, one of the unique features of simulation is that it allows judgment to enter into the design and analysis of the simulation; so if the analyst has some information that bears on the problem, it should be included.

Determining Run Length   The length of the simulation run (**run length** or **run time**) depends on the purpose of the simulation. Perhaps the most common approach is to continue the simulation until it has achieved an equilibrium condition. In the fish market example, this would mean that simulated fish sales correspond to their historical relative frequencies. Another approach is to run the simulation for a set period, such as a month, a year, or a decade, and see if the conditions at the end of the period appear reasonable. A third approach is to set run length so that a sufficiently large sample is gathered for purposes of statistical hypothesis testing. This alternative is considered further in the next section.

Run Length (Run Time)

Evaluating Results

The types of conclusions that can be drawn from a simulation depend, of course, on the degree to which the model reflects the real system, but they also depend on the design of the simulation in a statistical sense. Indeed, many analysts view simulation as a form of hypothesis testing, with each simulation run providing one or more pieces of sample data that are amenable to formal analysis through inferential statistical methods.[4]

In most situations, the analyst has other information available with which to compare the simulation results: past operating data from the real system, operating data from the performance of similar systems, and the analyst's own intuitive understanding of the real system's operation. Admittedly, however, information obtained from these sources is probably not sufficient to validate the conclusions derived from the simulation. Thus, the only true test of a simulation is how well the real system performs after the results of the study have been implemented.

Validation

In this context, *validation* refers to testing the computer program to ensure that the simulation is correct. Specifically, it is a check to see whether the computer code is a valid translation of the flowchart model and whether the simulation adequately represents the real system. Errors may arise in the program from mistakes in the coding or from mistakes in logic. Mistakes in coding are usually easily found because the program is most likely not executed by the computer. Mistakes in logic, however, present more of a challenge. In these cases, the program runs, but it fails to yield correct results.

To deal with this problem, the analyst has three alternatives: (1) have the program print out all calculations and verify these calculations by separate computation,

---

[4] Statistical procedures commonly used in evaluating simulation results include analysis of variance, regression analysis, and *t* tests.

(2) simulate present conditions and compare the results with the existing system, or (3) pick some point in the simulation run and compare its output to the answer obtained from solving a relevant mathematical model of the situation at that point. Even though the first two approaches have obvious drawbacks, they are more likely to be employed than the third, because if we had a relevant mathematical model in mind, we would probably be able to solve the problem without the aid of simulation.

Proposing a New Experiment

Based on the simulation results, a new simulation experiment may be in order. We might like to change many of the factors: parameters, variables, decision rules, starting conditions, and run length. As for parameters, we might be interested in replicating the simulation with several different costs or prices of a product to see what changes would occur. Trying different decision rules would obviously be in order if the initial rules led to poor results or if these runs yielded new insights into the problem. (The procedure of using the same stream of random numbers is a good general approach in that it sharpens the differences among alternatives and permits shorter runs.) Also, the values from the previous experiment may be useful starting conditions for subsequent simulations.

Finally, whether trying different run lengths constitutes a new experiment rather than a replication of a previous experiment depends on the types of events that occur in the system operation over time. It might happen, for example, that the system has more than one stable level of operation and that reaching the second level is time dependent. Thus, while the first series of runs of, say, 100 periods shows stable conditions, doubling the length of the series may provide new and distinctly different but equally stable conditions. In this case, running the simulation over 200 time periods could be thought of as a new experiment.

Computerization

Computer Model

When using a **computer model,** we reduce the system to be studied to a symbolic representation to be run on a computer. Although it is beyond this book's scope to detail the technical aspects of computer modeling, some that bear directly on simulation are

1.   Computer language selection.
2.   Flowcharting.
3.   Coding.
4.   Data generation.
5.   Output reports.
6.   Validation.

We will say more about simulation programs and languages at the end of this supplement.

Output Reports   General-purpose languages permit the analyst to specify any type of output report (or data) desired, providing one is willing to pay the price in programming effort. Special-purpose languages have standard routines that can be activated by one or two program statements to print out such data as means, variances, and standard deviations. Regardless of language, however, our experience has been that too much data from a simulation can be as dysfunctional to problem solving as too little data; both situations tend to obscure important, truly meaningful information about the system under study.

◾ SIMULATING WAITING LINES

Waiting lines that occur in series and parallel (such as in assembly lines and job shops) usually cannot be solved mathematically. However, because waiting lines are often easily simulated on a computer, we have chosen a two-stage assembly line as our second simulation example.

Example: A Two-Stage Assembly Line

Consider an assembly line which assembles a product of significant physical size, such as a refrigerator, stove, car, boat, TV, or furniture. Exhibit S17.4 shows two workstations on such a line.

The size of the product is an important consideration in assembly-line analysis and design because the number of products that can exist at each workstation affects worker performance. If the product is large, then the workstations are dependent on each other. Exhibit S17.4, for example, shows Bob and Ray working on a two-stage line where Bob's output in Station 1 is fed to Ray in Station 2. If the workstations are adjacent so that there is no room for items in-between, then Bob, by working slowly, would cause Ray to wait. Conversely, if Bob completes a product quickly (or if Ray takes longer to finish the task), then Bob must wait for Ray.

In this simulation, assume that Bob, the first worker on the line, can pull over a new item to work on whenever needed. We will concentrate our analysis on the interaction between Bob and Ray.

Objective of the Study   There are a number of questions we would like to have answered about the assembly line from this study. A partial list would be

- What is the average performance time of each worker?
- What is the output rate of product through this line?
- How much time does Bob wait for Ray?

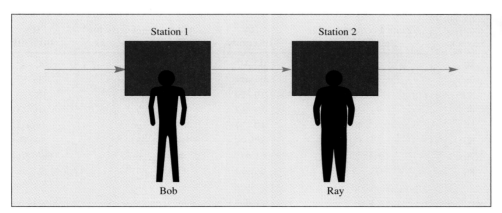

Exhibit S17.4

Two Workstations on an Assembly Line

Station 1   Station 2

Bob   Ray

· How much time does Ray wait for Bob?
· If the space between the two stations were increased so that items could be stored there and give workers some independence, how would this affect output rates, wait times, and so on?

Data Collection   To simulate this system, we need the performance times of Bob and Ray. One way to collect this data is to divide the range of performance times into segments, and then observe each worker. A simple check or tally mark in each of these segments results in a useful histogram of data.

Exhibit S17.5 shows the data collection form used to observe the performances of Bob and Ray. To simplify the procedure, performance time was divided into 10-second intervals. Bob was observed for 100 repetitions of the work task, and Ray was observed just 50 times. The number of observations does not have to be the same, but the more there are and the smaller the size of the time segments, the more accurate the study will be. The trade-off is that more observations and smaller segments take more time and more people (as well as more time to program and run a simulation).

Exhibit S17.6 contains the random number intervals assigned that correspond to the same ratio as the actual observed data. For example, Bob had 4 out of 100 times at 10 seconds. Therefore, if we used 100 numbers, we would assign 4 of those numbers as corresponding to 10 seconds. We could have assigned any four numbers, for example, 42, 18, 12, and 93. However, these would be a nuisance to search for so we assign consecutive numbers, such as 00, 01, 02, and 03.

Exhibit S17.5

Data Collection Form for Worker Observation

Seconds	Bob	Totals	Ray	Totals
5–14.99	||||	4	||||	4
15–24.99	⊞ |	6	⊞	5
25–34.99	⊞ ⊞	10	⊞ |	6
35–44.99	⊞ ⊞ ⊞ ⊞	20	⊞ ||	7
45–54.99	⊞ ⊞ ⊞ ⊞ ⊞ ⊞ ⊞ ⊞	40	⊞ ⊞	10
55–64.99	⊞ ⊞ |	11	⊞ |||	8
65–74.99	⊞	5	⊞ |	6
75–84.99	||||	4	||||	4
		100		50

Exhibit S17.6

Random Number Intervals for Bob and Ray

Seconds	Time Frequencies for Bob (Operation 1)	RN Intervals	Time Frequencies for Ray (Operation 2)	RN Intervals
10	4	00–03	4	00–07
20	6	04–09	5	08–17
30	10	10–19	6	18–29
40	20	20–39	7	30–43
50	40	40–79	10	44–63
60	11	80–90	8	64–79
70	5	91–95	6	80–91
80	4	96–99	4	92–99
	100		50	

There were 50 observations of Ray. There are two ways we could assign random numbers. First, we could use just 50 numbers (say 00–49) and ignore and numbers over that. However, this is wasteful because we would discard 50 percent of all the numbers from the list. Another choice would be to double the frequency number. For example, rather than assign, say, numbers 0–03 to account for the 4 observations out of 50 that took 10 seconds, we could assign numbers 00–07 to represent 8 observations out of 100, which is double the observed number but the same frequency. Actually, for this example and the speed of computers, the savings of time by doubling is insignificant.

Exhibit S17.7 shows a hand simulation of 10 items processed by Bob and Ray. The random numbers used were from Appendix B, starting at the first column of two numbers and working downward.

Assume that we start out at time 00 and run it in continuous seconds (not bothering to convert this to hours and minutes). The first random number is 56 and corresponds to Bob's performance at 50 seconds on the first item. The item is passed to Ray, who starts at 50 seconds. Relating the next random number 83 to Exhibit S17.6 we find that Ray takes 70 seconds to complete the item. In the meantime, Bob starts on the next item at time 50 and takes 50 seconds (random number 55), finishing at time 100. However, Bob cannot start on the third item until Ray gets through with the first item at time 120. Bob, therefore, has a wait time of 20 seconds. (If there was storage space between Bob and Ray, this item could have been moved out of Bob's workstation and Bob could have started the next item at time 100.) The remainder of the exhibit was calculated following the same pattern: obtaining a random number, finding the corresponding processing time, noting the wait time (if any), and computing the finish time. Note that with no storage space between Bob and Ray, there was considerable waiting time for both workers.

We can now answer some questions and make some statements about the system. For example,

The output time averages 60 seconds per unit (the complete time 600 for Ray divided by 10 units).

Simulation of Bob and Ray—Two-Stage Assembly Line

Exhibit S17.7

Item Number	Bob					Storage Space	Ray				
	Random Number	Start Time	Performance Time	Finish Time	Wait Time		Random Number	Start Time	Performance Time	Finish Time	Wait Time
1	56	00	50	50		0	83	50	70	120	50
2	55	50	50	100	20	0	47	120	50	170	
3	84	120	60	180		0	08	180	20	200	10
4	36	180	40	220		0	05	220	10	230	20
5	26	220	40	260		0	42	260	40	300	30
6	95	260	70	330		0	95	330	80	410	30
7	66	330	50	380	30	0	17	410	20	430	
8	03	410	10	420	10	0	21	430	30	460	
9	57	430	50	480		0	31	480	40	520	20
10	69	480	50	530		0	90	530	70	600	10
			470		60				430		170

Utilization of Bob is $^{470}/_{530}$ = 88.7 percent.

Utilization of Ray is $^{430}/_{550}$ = 78.2 percent (disregarding the initial startup wait for the first item of 50 seconds).

The average performance time for Bob is $^{470}/_{10}$ = 47 seconds.

The average performance time for Ray is $^{430}/_{10}$ = 43 seconds.

We have demonstrated how this problem would be solved in a simple manual simulation. A sample of 10 is really too small to place much confidence in, so this problem should be run on a computer for several thousand iterations. (We extend this same problem further in the next section of this supplement).

It is also vital to study the effect of item storage space between workers. The problem would be run to see what the throughput time and worker utilization times

---

Exhibit S17.8   Bob and Ray Two-Stage Assembly Line on Microsoft Excel

		Bob					Ray						Average
Item	RN	Start Time	Perf. Time	Finish Time	Wait Time	RN	Start Time	Perf. Time	Finish Time	Wait Time	Average Time/Unit	Total Time	Time in System
1	93	0	70	70	0	0	70	10	80	70	80.0	80	80.0
2	52	70	50	120	0	44	120	50	170	40	85.0	100	90.0
3	15	120	30	150	20	72	170	60	230	0	76.7	110	96.7
4	64	170	50	220	10	35	230	40	270	0	67.5	100	97.5
5	86	230	60	290	0	2	290	10	300	20	60.0	70	92.0
6	20	290	40	330	0	82	330	70	400	30	66.7	110	95.0
7	83	330	60	390	10	31	400	40	440	0	62.9	110	97.1
8	89	400	60	460	0	13	460	20	480	20	60.0	80	95.0
9	69	460	50	510	0	53	510	50	560	30	62.2	100	95.6
10	41	510	50	560	0	48	560	50	610	0	61.0	100	96.0
11	32	560	40	600	10	13	610	20	630	0	57.3	70	93.6
12	1	610	10	620	10	67	630	60	690	0	57.5	80	92.5
13	11	630	30	660	30	91	690	70	760	0	58.5	130	95.4
14	2	690	10	700	60	76	760	60	820	0	58.6	130	97.9
15	11	760	30	790	30	41	820	40	860	0	57.3	100	98.0
16	55	820	50	870	0	34	870	40	910	10	56.9	90	97.5
17	18	870	30	900	10	28	910	30	940	0	55.3	70	95.9
18	39	910	40	950	0	53	950	50	1000	10	55.6	90	95.6
19	13	950	30	980	20	41	1000	40	1040	0	54.7	90	95.3
20	7	1000	20	1020	20	21	1040	30	1070	0	53.5	70	94.0
21	29	1040	40	1080	0	54	1080	50	1130	10	53.8	90	93.8
22	58	1080	50	1130	0	39	1130	40	1170	0	53.2	90	93.6
23	95	1130	70	1200	0	70	1200	60	1260	30	54.8	130	95.2
24	27	1200	40	1240	20	60	1260	50	1310	0	54.6	110	95.8
25	59	1260	50	1310	0	93	1310	80	1390	0	55.6	130	97.2
26	85	1310	60	1370	20	51	1390	50	1440	0	55.4	130	98.5
27	12	1390	30	1420	20	35	1440	40	1480	0	54.8	90	98.1
28	34	1440	40	1480	0	51	1480	50	1530	0	54.6	90	97.9
29	60	1480	50	1530	0	87	1530	70	1600	0	55.2	120	98.6
30	97	1530	80	1610	0	29	1610	30	1640	10	54.7	110	99.0

are with no storage space between workers. A second run should increase this storage space to one unit, with the corresponding changes noted. Repeating the runs for two, three, four, and so on offers management a chance to compute the additional cost of space compared with the increased use. Such increased space between workers may require a larger building, more materials and parts in the system, material handling equipment, transfer machine, plus added heat, light, building maintenance, and so on.

This would also be useful data for management to see what changes in the system would occur if one of the worker positions was automated. The assembly line could be simulated using data from the automated process to see if such a change would be cost justified.

SPREADSHEET SIMULATION

As we have stated throughout this book, spreadsheets such as Microsoft Excel are very useful for a variety of problems. Exhibit S17.8 shows Bob and Ray's two-stage assembly line on an Excel spreadsheet. The procedure follows the same pattern as our manual display in Exhibit S17.8.

The total simulation on Excel passed through 1,200 iterations (shown in Exhibits S17.10 and S17.11); that is, 1,200 parts were finished by Ray. Simulation, as an analytic tool, has an advantage over quantitative methods in that it is a dynamic simulation, whereas analytic methods show long-run average performance. As you can see in Exhibits S17.9 and S17.10, there is an unmistakable startup (or transient) phase. We could even raise some questions about the long-term operation of the line because it does not seem to have settled to a constant (steady state) value, even after the 1,200 items. Exhibit S17.9 shows 100 items that pass through the Bob and Ray two-stage system. Notice the wide variation in time for the first units completed. These figures are the average time that units take. It is a cumulative number; that is, the first unit takes the time generated by the random numbers. The average time for two units is the average time of the sum of the first and second units. The average time for three units is the average time for the sum of the first three units, and so on. This display could have almost any starting shape, not necessarily what we have shown. It all depends on the stream of random numbers. What we can be sure of is that the times do oscillate for awhile until they settle down as units are finished and smooth the average.

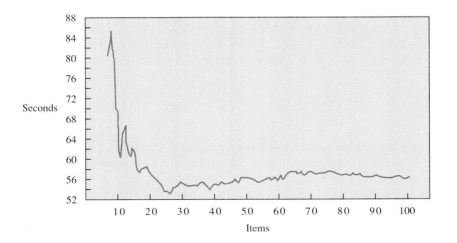

Exhibit S17.9

Average Time per Unit of Output (Finish time/number of units)

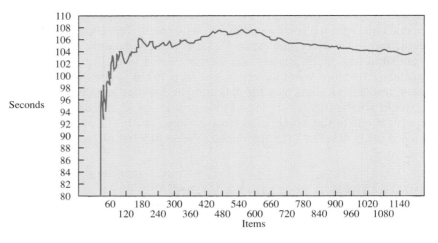

	Bob	**Ray**	**Unit**
Utilization	0.81	0.85	
Average wait time	10.02	9.63	
Average performance time	46.48	46.88	
Average time per unit			57.65
Average time in system			103.38

Exhibit S17.10 shows the average time that parts spend in the system. At the start, the display shows an increasing amount of time in the system. This can be expected because the system started empty and there are no interruptions for parts passing from Bob to Ray. Often, parts enter the system and may have to wait between stages as work-in-process; this causes delays for subsequent parts and adds to the waiting time. As time goes on, however, stability should occur unless the capacity of the second stage is less than the first stage's. In our present case, we did not allow space between them. Therefore, if Bob finished first, he had to wait for Ray. If Ray finished first, he had to wait for Bob.

Exhibit S17.11 shows the results of simulating Bob and Ray completing 1,200 units of product. Compare these figures to those that we obtained simulating 10 items by hand. Not too bad, is it! The average performance time for Bob is shown as 46.48 seconds. This is close to the weighted average of what you would expect in the long run. For Bob it is $(10 \times 4 + 20 \times 6 + 30 \times 10$ etc.$)/100 = 45.9$ seconds. Ray's expected time is $(10 \times 4 + 20 \times 5 + 30 \times 6$ etc.$)/50 = 46.4$ seconds.

■ SIMULATION PROGRAMS AND LANGUAGES

Simulation models can be classified as *continuous* or *discrete*. Continuous models are based on mathematical equations and therefore are continuous, with values for all points in time. In contrast, discrete simulation occurs only at specific points. For example, customers arriving at a bank teller's window would be discrete simulation. The simulation jumps from point to point; the arrival of a customer, the start of a service, the ending of service, the arrival of the next customer, and so on. Discrete

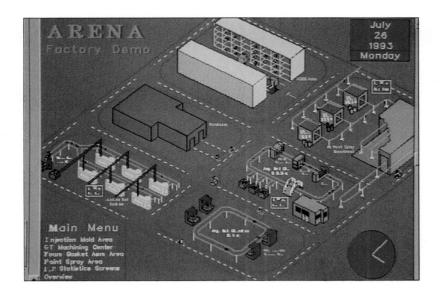

Systems Modeling
Corporation makes
simulation software for
systems from manu-
facturing operations to fast
food restaurants. Models
developed with their
products, SIMAN/
Cinema V and Arena, can
be used to help engineers
and managers look for
bottlenecks and problems
in an existing system or
gauge the capacity flow of
a proposed system such as
the factory shown here.

(http://www.sm.com)

simulation can also be triggered to run by units of time (daily, hourly, minute by minute). This is called *event simulation;* points in between either have no value to our simulation or cannot be computed because of the lack of some sort of mathematical relationships to link the succeeding events. Operations management applications almost exclusively use discrete (event) simulation.

Simulation programs also can be categorized as general-purpose and special-purpose. General-purpose software is really language that allows programmers to build their own models. Examples are SLAM II, SIMSCRIPT II.5, SIMAN, GPSS/H, GPSS/PC, PC-MODEL, and RESQ. Special-purpose software simulation programs are specially built to simulate specific applications, such as MAP/1, and SIMFAC-TORY. In a specialized simulation for manufacturing, for example, provisions in the model allow for specifying the number of work centers, their description, arrival rates, processing time, batch sizes, quantities of work in process, available resources including labor, sequences, and so on. Additionally, the program may allow the observer to watch the animated operation and see the quantities and flows throughout the system as the simulation is running. Data are collected, analyzed, and presented in a form most suitable for that type of application.

There are many software simulation programs available to use on computers, from micros to mainframes. How, then, do you choose a program from a long list?

The first step is to understand the different types of simulation. Then it becomes a matter of reviewing programs on the market to find one that fits your specific needs. (See the Breakthrough box on the next page "Hospital Overcrowding Solutions Are Found with Simulation" for a successful application of a commercial program.) Even if a program does exist, however, sometimes it is still easier to create a special-purpose one. It may be better suited and less troublesome to use.

As a last comment on simulation programs, do not rule out spreadsheets for simulation. As you noticed, we simulated Bob and Ray on a spreadsheet in the preceding section. Spreadsheets are becoming quite user-friendly and are adding

BREAKTHROUGH

Hospital Overcrowding Solutions Are Found with Simulation

Thanks to increased life expectancy through improved health care coupled with shifting population demographics, hospitals everywhere are becoming increasingly overcrowded. Limited health care budgets are forcing hospitals to explore creative solutions. But creative solutions can be risky, so they need to be carefully evaluated. From the standpoint of cost, the earlier a solution can be evaluated and either accepted or rejected, the better.

Along these lines, the Outpatient Laboratory at Bay Medical Center was experiencing serious capacity constraints. Adding to their difficulties, a renovation designed to improve efficiency actually added to the overcrowding problem. In early 1992, Dave Nall, a Management Engineer for Bay Medical Center, ran a study to evaluate several alternatives and make recommendations designed at reducing bottlenecks and improving patient flow through the Outpatient Laboratory. The objective of this study was to develop and evaluate alternative ways of reducing overcrowding at the Outpatient Laboratory.

Solution

The key technology employed by Dave in conducting this analysis was computer simulation. Dave had used

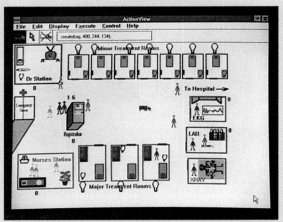

computer simulation numerous times in the past and had found that it was an efficient way to both gain insight into the problem as well as evaluate the solutions.

Through discussions with managers responsible for the Outpatient Laboratory, Dave built a network

---

many features, such as allowing random number generation and asking what-if questions. The simplicity in using a spreadsheet for simulation may well compensate for any needed reduction in the complexity of the problem in order to use the spreadsheet.

@RISK is an add-in program that works with Microsoft Excel. The program adds many useful simulation-related functions to the spreadsheet. Using @RISK automates the process of taking random values from a specified distribution function, automates the recalculation of the spreadsheet with the new random values, and captures output values and statistics. @RISK simplifies the process of building and running spreadsheet simulations.[5]

Desirable Features of Simulation Software

Simulation software takes awhile to learn to use. Once a specific software is learned, the tendency is to stay with it for a long time, so be careful when making the choice. Simulation software should

1. Be capable of being used interactively as well as allowing complete runs.
2. Be user-friendly and easy to understand.

---

[5] See Wayne L. Winston, *Simulation Modeling Using @RISK* (Belmont, CA: Wadsworth Publishing Company, 1996). @RISK is a product of Palisade Corporation (http://www.palisade.com).

describing the patient's flow through the Laboratory as it was currently configured. Then, data were collected on the times required for patients to receive the various services they might need as well as the travel time between rooms where the service was provided. From this information, Dave constructed a computer simulation of the baseline Laboratory configuration.

Dave then modified the computer simulation and used it to study issues relating to three categories of solutions to Outpatient Laboratory overcrowding; 1) changing staff, including both medical and administrative staff, 2) utilizing another clinic as an overflow laboratory, and 3) possible redesign of the laboratory facility itself.

With respect to staffing, the computer simulation verified that the medical staff currently employed was indeed the optimal number. However, Dave found that the administrative staff, if anything, was overstaffed and that a staff reduction could take place with no appreciable reduction in patient service. Staffing was not the key problem. With respect to the option of utilizing another laboratory as an overflow, there were significant opportunities for improving throughput if other patients could be enticed to use the another laboratory. While the simulation did not tell him how to

get the patients to use an alternative laboratory, it did allow Dave to quantify the benefits of implementing policies that would increase alternative laboratory usage by 5%, 10%, etc. With respect to redesign of the existing outpatient laboratory, Dave determined that, with a relatively minor redesign of the facility and a procedural change, the laboratory would become significantly more productive. Increased productivity would, of course, lead to increased patient service.

Benefits
Individually, no one could have accurately guessed the impact of the different ways of addressing overcrowding at the Outpatient Laboratory at Bay Medical Center. Through the results of the simulation analysis and the insights gained. Dave was able to assess the relative merits of each alternative as well as predict their impact. With a small investment in Dave's time, Bay Medical Center was able to make informed decisions with an understanding of both costs and benefits. As a result, the right decisions were made, money was saved, and patients were better served.

Source: Micro Analysis and Design Simulation Software, Inc., Boulder, CO.

3. Allow modules to be built and then connected. In this way models can be worked on separately without affecting the rest of the system.

4. Allow users to write and incorporate their own routines; no simulation program can provide for all needs.

5. Have building blocks that contain built-in commands (such as statistical analysis or decision rules of where to go next).

6. Have macro capability, such as the ability to develop machining cells.

7. Have material-flow capability. Operations involve the movement of material and people; the program should have the ability to model trucks, cranes, conveyers, and so on.

8. Output standard statistics such as cycle times, utilizations, and wait times.

9. Allow a variety of data analysis alternatives for both input and output data.

10. Have animation capabilities to display graphically the product flow through the system.

11. Permit interactive debugging of the model so the user can trace flows through the model and more easily find errors.[6]

---

[6] S. Wali Haider and Jerry Banks, "Simulation Software Products for Analyzing Manufacturing Systems," *Industrial Engineering* 18, no. 7 (July 1986), pp. 98–103.

ADVANTAGES AND DISADVANTAGES OF SIMULATION

The following is not intended as a comprehensive list of reasons why one should elect to use or not use simulation as a technique. Rather, we state some of the generally accepted advantages and disadvantages.

Advantages

1. Developing the model of a system often leads to a better understanding of the real system.
2. Time can be compressed in simulation; years of experience in the real system can be compressed into seconds or minutes.
3. Simulation does not disrupt ongoing activities of the real system.
4. Simulation is far more general than mathematical models and can be used where conditions are not suitable for standard mathematical analysis.
5. Simulation can be used as a game for training experience.
6. Simulation provides a more realistic replication of a system than mathematical analysis.
7. Simulation can be used to analyze transient conditions, whereas mathematical techniques usually cannot.
8. Many standard packaged models, covering a wide range of topics, are available commercially.
9. Simulation answers what-if questions.

Disadvantages

1. While a great deal of time and effort may be spent to develop a model for simulation, there is no guarantee that the model will, in fact, provide good answers.
2. There is no way to prove that a simulation model's performance is completely reliable. Simulation involves numerous repetitions of sequences that are based on randomly generated occurrences. An apparently stable system can, with the right combination of events—however unlikely—explode.
3. Depending on the system to be simulated, building a simulation model can take anywhere from an hour to 100 worker years. Complicated systems can be very costly and take a long time.
4. Simulation may be less accurate than mathematical analysis because it is randomly based. If a given system can be represented by a mathematical model, it may be better to use than simulation.
5. A significant amount of computer time may be needed to run complex models.
6. The technique of simulation, while making progress, still lacks a standardized approach. Therefore, models of the same system built by different individuals may differ widely.

CONCLUSION

We could make the statement that anything that can be done mathematically can be done with simulation. However, simulation is not always the best choice. Mathematical analysis, when appropriate to a specific problem, is usually faster and less expensive. Also, it is usually provable as far as the technique is concerned, and the only real question is whether the system is adequately represented by the mathematical model.

Simulation, however, has nothing fixed; there are no boundaries to building a model or making assumptions about the system. Expanding computer power and memory have pushed out the limits of what can be simulated. Further, the continued development of simulation languages and programs—both general-purpose programs (SIMAN, SLAM) and special-purpose programs (MAP/1, SIMFACTORY, Optima!)—promises to make the entire process of creating simulation models much easier.

SOLVED PROBLEMS

SOLVED PROBLEM 1

To use an old statistical example for simulation, if an urn contains 100 balls, of which 10 percent are green, 40 percent are red, and 50 percent are spotted, develop a simulation model of the process of drawing balls at random from the urn. Each time a ball is drawn and its color noted, it is replaced. Use the following random numbers as you desire.

Simulate drawing 10 balls from the urn. Show which numbers you have used.

26768	66954	83125	08021
42613	17457	55503	36458
95457	03704	47019	05752
95276	56970	84828	05752

Solution

Assign random numbers to the balls to correspond to the percentage present in the urn.

	Random Number
10 green balls	00–09
40 red balls	10–49
50 spotted balls	50–99

Many possible answers exist, depending on how the random numbers were assigned and which numbers were used from the list provided in the problem.

For the random number sequence above and using the first two numbers of those given, we obtain

RN	Color	RN	Color
26	Red	17	Red
42	Red	3	Green
95	Spotted	56	Spotted
95	Spotted	83	Spotted
66	Spotted	55	Spotted

For the 10 there were 1 green, 3 red, and 6 spotted balls—a good estimate based on a sample of only 10!

SOLVED PROBLEM 2

A rural clinic receives a delivery of fresh plasma once each week from a central blood bank. The supply varies according to demand from other clinics and hospitals in the region but ranges between four and nine pints of the most widely used blood type, type O. The number of patients per week requiring this blood varies from zero to four, and each patient may need from one to four pints. Given the following delivery quantities, patient distribution, and demand per patient, what would be the number of pints in excess or short for a six-week period? Use simulation to derive your answer. Consider that plasma is storable and there is currently none on hand.

Patient Distribution

Delivery Quantities		Patients per Week Requiring Blood		Demand per Patient	
Pints per Week	**Probability**		**Probability**	**Pints**	**Probability**
4	0.15	0	0.25	1	0.40
5	0.20	1	0.25	2	0.30
6	0.25	2	0.30	3	0.20
7	0.15	3	0.15	4	0.10
8	0.15	4	0.05		
9	0.10				

Solution

First, develop random number sequence; then, simulate.

Delivery			Number of Patients			Patient Demand		
Pints	**Probability**	**Random Number**	**Blood**	**Probability**	**Random Number**	**Pints**	**Random Probability**	**Number**
4	.15	00–14	0	.25	00–24	1	.40	00–39
5	.20	15–34	1	.25	25–49	2	.30	40–69
6	.25	35–59	2	.30	50–79	3	.20	70–89
7	.15	60–74	3	.15	80–94	4	.10	90–99
8	.15	75–89	4	.05	95–99			
9	.10	90–99						

Week No.	Beginning Inventory	Quantity Delivered		Total Blood on Hand	Patients Needing Blood		Quantity Needed			Number of Pints Remaining
		RN	**Pints**		**RN**	**Patients**	**Patient**	**RN**	**Pints**	
1	0	74	7	7	85	3	First	21	1	6
							Second	06	1	5
							Third	71	3	2
2	2	31	5	7	28	1		96	4	3
3	3	02	4	7	72	2	First	12	1	6
							Second	67	2	4
4	4	53	6	10	44	1		23	1	9
5	9	16	5	14	16	0				14
6	14	40	6	20	83	3	First	65	2	18
							Second	34	1	17
							Third	82	3	14
7	14									

At the end of six weeks, there were 14 pints on hand.

REVIEW AND DISCUSSION QUESTIONS

1. Why is simulation often called a technique of last resort?
2. What roles do statistical hypothesis testing play in simulation?
3. What determines whether a simulation model is valid?

4. Must you use a computer to get good information from a simulation? Explain.

5. What methods are used to increment time in a simulation model? How do they work?

6. What are the pros and cons of starting a simulation with the system empty? With the system in equilibrium?

7. Distinguish between known mathematical distributions and empirical distributions. What information is needed to simulate using a known mathematical distribution?

8. What is the importance of run length in simulation? Is a run of 100 observations twice as valid as a run of 50? Explain.

PROBLEMS

1. CLASSROOM SIMULATION: FISH FORWARDERS

1. See SM.

This is a competitive exercise designed to test players' skills at setting inventory ordering rules over a 10-week planning horizon. Maximum profit at the end determines the winner.

Fish Forwarders supplies fresh shrimp to a variety of customers in the New Orleans area. It places orders for cases of shrimp from fleet representatives at the beginning of each week to meet a demand from its customers at the middle of the week. Shrimp are subsequently delivered to Fish Forwarders and then, at the end of the week, to its customers.

Both the supply of shrimp and the demand for shrimp are uncertain. The supply may vary as much as ±10 percent from the amount ordered, and by contract, Fish Forwarders must purchase this supply. The probability associated with this variation is −10 percent, 30 percent of the time; 0 percent, 50 percent of the time; and +10 percent, 20 percent of the time. Weekly demand for shrimp is normally distributed with a mean of 800 cases and standard deviation of 100 cases.

A case of shrimp costs Fish Forwarders $30 and sells for $50. Any shrimp not sold at the end of the week are sold to a cat-food company at $4 per case. Fish Forwarders may, if it chooses, order the shrimp flash-frozen by the supplier at dockside, but this raises the cost of a case by $4 and, hence, costs Fish Forwarders $34 per case.

Procedure for play. The game requires that each week a decision be made as to how many cases to order of regular shrimp and of flash-frozen shrimp. The number ordered may be any amount. The instructor plays the role of referee and supplies the random numbers. The steps in playing the game are as follows:

a. Decide on the order amount of regular shrimp or flash-frozen shrimp and enter the figures in column 3 of the worksheet. (See Exhibit S17.12 on the next page.) Assume that there is no opening inventory of flash-frozen shrimp.

b. Determine the amount that arrives and enter it under "Orders received." To accomplish this, the referee draws a random number from a uniform random number table (such as that in Appendix B) and finds its associated level of variation from the following random number intervals: 00 to 29 = −10 percent, 30 to 70 = 0 percent, and 80 to 99 = +10 percent. If the random number is, say, 13, the amount of variation will be −10 percent. Thus if you decide to order 1,000 regular cases of shrimp and 100 flash-frozen cases, the amount you would actually receive would be 1,000 − 0.10(1,000), or 900 regular cases, and 100 − 0.10(100), or 90 flash-frozen cases. (Note that the variation is the same for both regular and flash-frozen shrimp.) These amounts are then entered in column 4.

c. Add the amount of flash-frozen shrimp in inventory (if any) to the quantity of regular and flash-frozen shrimp just received and enter this amount in column 5. This would be 990, using the figures provided earlier.

Exhibit S17.12 Simulation Worksheet

(1)	(2)	(3) Orders placed		(4) Orders received		(5) Available (regular and flash-frozen)	(6) Demand (800 + 100Z)	(7) Sales (minimum of demand or available)	(8) Excess		(9) Shortages
Week	Flash-frozen inventory	Regular	Flash-frozen	Regular	Flash-frozen				Regular	Flash	
1											
2											
3											
4											
5											
6											
7		MARDI GRAS					*				
8											
9											
10											
Total											

*Flash-frozen only.

d. Determine the demand for shrimp. To accomplish this, the referee draws a random normal deviate value from Exhibit S17.3 or Appendix C and enters it into the equation at the top of column 6. Thus if the deviate value is -1.76, demand for the week is $800 + 100(-1.76)$, or 624.

e. Determine the amount sold. This will be the lesser of the amount demanded (column 6) and the amount available (column 5). Thus, if a player has received 990 and demand is 624, the quantity entered will be 624 (with $990 - 624$, or 366 left over).

f. Determine the excess. The amount of excess is simply that quantity remaining after demand for a given week is filled. Always assume that regular shrimp are sold before the flash-frozen. Thus if we use the 366 figure obtained in (e), the excess would include all the original 90 cases of flash-frozen shrimp.

g. Determine shortages. This is simply the amount of unsatisfied demand each period, and it occurs only when demand is greater than sales. (Because all customers use the shrimp within the week in which they are delivered, back orders are not relevant.) The amount of shortage (in cases of shrimp) is entered in column 9.

Profit determination. Exhibit S17.13 is provided for determining the profit achieved at the end of play. The values to be entered in the table are obtained by summing the relevant columns of Exhibit S17.12 and making the calculations.

Exhibit S17.13

Profit from Fish Forwarders' Operations

Revenue from sales ($50 × Col. 7)	$ _____	
Revenue from salvage ($4 × Col. 8 reg.)	$ _____	
Total revenue		$ _____
Cost of regular purchases ($30 × Col. 4 reg.)	$ _____	
Cost of flash-frozen purchases ($34 × Col. 4 flash)	$ _____	
Cost of holding flash-frozen shrimp ($2 × Col. 8 flash)	$ _____	
Cost of shortages ($20 × Col. 9)	$ _____	
Total cost		$ _____
Profit		$ _____

Assignment. Simulate operations for a total of 10 weeks. It is suggested that a 10-minute break be taken at the end of Week 5, allowing the players to evaluate how they may improve their performance. They might also wish to plan an ordering strategy for the week of Mardi Gras, when no shrimp will be supplied.

✓ **2.** The manager of a small post office is concerned that the growing township is overloading the one-window service being offered. Sample data are collected on 100 individuals who arrive for service:

2. Average customer waiting time = 1/6 min. Average teller idle time = 4/6 min.

Time between Arrivals (Minutes)	Frequency	Service Time (Minutes)	Frequency
1	8	1.0	12
2	35	1.5	21
3	34	2.0	36
4	17	2.5	19
5	6	3.0	7
	100	3.5	5
			100

Using the following random number sequence, simulate six arrivals; estimate the average customer waiting time and the average idle time for clerks.

RN: 08, 74, 24, 34, 45, 86, 31, 32, 45, 21, 10, 67, 60, 17, 60, 87, 74, 96

3. Thomas Magnus, a private investigator, has been contacted by a potential client in Kamalo, Molokai. The call came just in time because Magnus is down to his last $10. Employment, however, is conditional on Magnus meeting the client at Kamalo within eight hours. Magnus, presently at the Masters' residence in Kipahulu, Maui, has three alternative ways to get to Kamalo. Magnus may

  a. Drive to the native village of Honokahua and take an outrigger to Kamalo.
  b. Drive to Honokahua and swim the 10 miles across Pailolo Channel to Kamalo.
  c. Drive to Hana and ask his friend T. C. to fly him by helicopter to Kamalo.

3. Option *a*:

Total Pay	Total Time
$6	7
$9	7

Option *b*:	Total Time
	6.5
	7.5

Option *c*.	Total Time
	5
	4

Average trip time:
Option *a* = 7
Option *b* = 7
Option *c* = 4.5

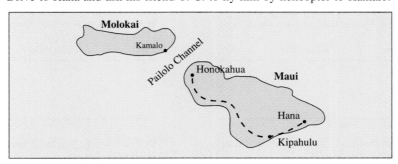

If option *a* is chosen, driving times to Honokahua are given in Distribution 1. Once at Honokahua, Magnus must negotiate with the friendly Tai natives. Negotiations always include a few Mai Tais, so if Magnus begins to negotiate, swimming becomes impossible. Negotiations center on how much each of the three outrigger crew members will be paid. Negotiation time, crew pay, and outrigger travel time are in Distributions 3, 4, and 5, respectively. You may assume each crew member is paid the same amount. If crew pay totals more than $10, Magnus is out of luck—trip time may then be taken to be infinity.

If option *b* is chosen, driving times to Honokahua and swimming times are given in Distributions 1 and 6.

If option *c* is chosen, driving times to Hana are given in Distribution 2. T. C., however, is at the airport only 10 percent of the time. If T. C. is not at the airport,

Magnus will wait for him to arrive. Magnus's waiting time is given by Distribution 8. T. C. may refuse to fly for the $10 Magnus has available; Magnus puts the probability of T. C. refusing to fly for $10 at 30 percent. You may assume negotiation time is zero. If T. C. refuses, Magnus will drive to Honokahua via Kipahulu and swim to Kamalo. Helicopter flying times are given in Distribution 7.

Simulate each of the three alternative transportation plans *twice* and, based on your simulation results, calculate the average trip time for each plan. Use the following random numbers in the order they appear; do not skip any random numbers.

RN: 7, 3, 0, 4, 0, 5, 3, 5, 6, 1, 6, 6, 4, 8, 4, 9, 0, 7, 7, 1, 7, 0, 6, 8, 8, 7, 9, 0, 1, 2, 9, 7, 3, 2, 3, 8, 6, 0, 6, 0, 5, 9, 7, 9, 6, 4, 7, 2, 8, 7, 8, 1, 7, 0, 5

Distribution 1: Time to drive from Kipahulu to Honokahua (hours)

Time	Probability	RN
1	.2	0–1
1.5	.6	2–7
2	.2	8–9

Distribution 2: Time to drive from Kipahulu to Hana and vice versa (hours)

Time	Probability	RN
.5	.2	0–1
1	.7	2–8
1.5	.1	9

Distribution 3: Negotiation time (hours)

Time	Probability	RN
1	.2	0–1
1.5	.3	2–4
2	.3	5–7
2.5	.2	8–9

Distribution 4: Outrigger pay per crew member

Pay	Probability	RN
$2	.3	0–2
3	.3	3–5
4	.4	6–9

Distribution 5: Outrigger travel time from Honokahua to Kamalo (hours)

Time	Probability	RN
3	.1	0
4	.5	1–5
5	.4	6–9

Distribution 6: Time to swim from Honokahua to Kamalo (hours)

Time	Probability	RN
5	.2	0–1
6	.6	2–7
7	.2	8–9

Distribution 7: Time to fly from Hana to Kamalo (hours)

Time	Probability	RN
1	.1	0
1.5	.7	1–7
2	.2	8–9

Distribution 8: Magnus's waiting time at airport (hours)

Time	Probability	RN
1	.1	0
2	.2	1–2
3	.4	3–6
4	.3	7–9

4. Average downtime = 14.5/5, or 2.9 hours.

4. A bank of machines in a manufacturing shop breaks down according to the following interarrival-time distribution. The time it takes one repairperson to complete the repair of a machine is given in the service-time distribution:

Interarrival Time (Hours)	P(X)	RN	Service Time (Hours)	P(X)	RN
.5	.30	0–29	.5	.25	0–24
1.0	.22	30–51	1.0	.20	25–44
1.5	.16	52–67	2.0	.25	45–69
2.0	.10	68–77	3.0	.15	70–84
3.0	.14	78–91	4.0	.10	85–94
4.0	.08	92–99	5.0	.05	95–99
	1.00			1.00	

Simulate the breakdown of five machines. Calculate the average machine downtime using two repairpersons and the following random number sequence. (Both repairpersons cannot work on the same machine.)

RN: 30, 81, 02, 91, 51, 08, 28, 44, 86, 84, 29, 08, 37, 34, 99

5. Jennifer Jones owns a small candy store she operates herself. A study was made observing the time between customers coming into the store, and the time that Ms. Jones took to serve them. The following data were collected from 100 customers observed:

5. See SM.

Interarrival Time (Minutes)	Number of Observations	Service Time (Minutes)	Number of Observations
1	5	1	10
2	10	2	15
3	10	3	15
4	15	4	20
5	15	5	15
6	20	6	10
7	10	7	8
8	8	8	4
9	5	9	2
10	2	10	1

Simulate the system (all of the arrivals and services) until 10 customers pass through the system and are serviced by Ms. Jones.

How long does the average customer spend in the system? Use Appendix B to obtain random numbers.

6. A professional football coach has six running backs on his squad. He wants to evaluate how injuries might affect his stock of running backs. A minor injury causes a player to be removed from the game and miss only the next game. A major injury puts the player out of action for the rest of the season. The probability of a major injury in a game is 0.05. There is at most one major injury per game. The probability distribution of minor injuries per game is

6. See SM.

Number of Injuries	Probability
0	.2
1	.5
2	.22
3	.05
4	.025
5	.005
	1.000

Injuries seem to happen in a completely random manner, with no discernible pattern over the season. A season is 10 games.

Using the following random numbers, simulate the fluctuations in the coach's stock of running backs over the season. Assume that he hires no additional running backs during the season.

RN: 044, 392, 898, 615, 986, 959, 558, 353, 577, 866, 305, 813, 024, 189, 878, 023, 285, 442, 862, 848, 060, 131, 963, 874, 805, 105, 452

✓ **7.** At Tucson Mills, minor breakdowns of machines occur frequently. The occurrence of breakdowns and the service time to fix the machines are randomly distributed. Management is concerned with minimizing the cost of breakdowns. The cost per hour for the machines to be down is $40. The cost of service repairpersons is $12 per hour. A preliminary study has produced the following data on times between successive breakdowns and their service times:

Relative Frequency of Breakdowns

Time between breakdowns (in minutes)	4	5	6	7	8	9
Relative frequency	.10	.30	.25	.20	.10	.05

Relative Frequency of Service Times

Service time (in minutes)	4	5	6	7	8	9
Relative frequency	.10	.40	.20	.15	.10	.05

Perform a simulation of 30 breakdowns under two conditions: with one service repairperson and with two service repairpersons.

Use the following random number sequence to determine time between breakdowns:

RN: 85, 16, 65, 76, 93, 99, 65, 70, 58, 44, 02, 85, 01, 97, 63, 52, 53, 11, 62, 28, 84, 82, 27, 20, 39, 70, 26, 21, 41, 81

Use the following random number sequence to determine service times:

RN: 68, 26, 85, 11, 16, 26, 95, 67, 97, 73, 75, 64, 26, 45, 01, 87, 20, 01, 19, 36, 69, 89, 81, 81, 02, 05, 10, 51, 24, 36

a. Using the results of the simulations, calculate
   (1) The total idle time for the service repairpersons under each condition.
   (2) The total delay caused by waiting for a service repairperson to begin working on a breakdown.

b. Determine the lowest-cost approach.

8. Jethro's service station has one gasoline pump. Because everyone in Kornfield County drives big cars, there is room at the station for only three cars, including the car at the pump. Cars arriving when there are already three cars at the station drive on to another station. Use the following probability distributions to simulate the arrival of four cars to Jethro's station:

Interarrival Time (Minutes)	P(X)	RN		Service Time (Minutes)	P(X)	RN
10	.40	0–39		5	.45	0–44
20	.35	40–74		10	.30	45–74
30	.20	75–94		15	.20	75–94
40	.05	95–99		20	.05	95–99

Use the following random numbers sequence:
RN: 99, 00, 73, 09, 38, 53, 72, 91

Margin answers:

7. Condition 1   **Condition 2**

a. (1) Idle 18 min.   76 + 134
                              = 210 min.
   (2) Delay 87 min.   0 min.
b. Cost of repairperson
      $ 38.80 $ 77.20
   Cost of machine down
      175.33   117.33
      $214.13 $194.53
   Lowest cost is Condition 2.

8. Avg. time in system is 35/4 or 8.75 minutes.

How many cars go to another station?

What is the average time a car spends at the station?

9. You have been hired as a consultant by a supermarket chain to provide an answer to the basic question: How many items per customer should be permitted in the fast checkout line? This is no trivial question for the chain's management; your findings will be the basis for corporate policy for all 2,000 stores. The vice president of operations has given you one month to do the study and two assistants to help you gather the data.

9. See SM.

In starting this study, you decide to avoid queuing theory as the tool for analysis (because of your concern about the reliability of its assumptions) and instead opt for simulation. Given the following data, explain in detail how you would go about your analysis stating (1) the criteria you would use in making your recommendation, (2) what additional data you would need to set up your simulation, (3) how you would gather the preliminary data, (4) how you would set up the problem for simulation, and (5) which factors would affect the applicability of your findings to all of the stores.

Store locations: The United States and Canada

Hours of operation: 16 per day

Average store size: 9 checkout stands including fast checkout

Available checkers: 7 to 10 (Some engage in stocking activities when not at a checkout stand.)

10. The saga of Joe from Chapter 17 continues. Joe has the opportunity to do a big repair job for a local motorcycle club. (Their cycles were accidentally run over by a garbage truck.) The compensation for the job is good, but it is vital that the total repair time for the five cycles be less than 40 hours. (The leader of the club has stated that he would be very distressed if the cycles were not available for a planned rally.) Joe knows from experience that repairs of this type often entail several trips between processes for a given cycle, so estimates of time are difficult to provide. Still, Joe has the following historical data about the probability that a job will start in each process, processing time in each process, and transitional probabilities between each pair of processes:

10. See SM.
Joe can finish the job in 15 hours according to the simulation and schedule.

Process	Probability of Job Starting in Process	Processing Time Probability (hours)			Probability of Going from Process to Other Processes or Completion (out)			
		1	2	3	Frame	Engine Work	Painting	Out
Frame repair	0.5	0.2	0.4	0.4	—	0.4	0.4	0.2
Engine work	0.3	0.6	0.1	0.3	0.3	—	0.4	0.3
Painting	0.2	0.3	0.3	0.4	0.1	0.1	—	0.8

Given this information, use simulation to determine the repair times for each cycle. Display your results on a Gantt chart showing an FCFS schedule. (Assume that only one cycle can be worked on at a time in each process.) Based on your simulation, what do you recommend Joe do next?

11. "Eat at Joe's" has decided to add a drive-up window to their restaurant. Due to limited capital, there is only enough space for 2 cars in the drive-up window lane (one being served and one waiting). Joe would like to know how many customers are by-passing his restaurant due to the limited space in the drive-up window lane. Simulate 10 cars as they attempt to use the drive-up window using the following distributions and random numbers.

11. One car by-passes.

Time between Arrivals (Minutes)	Probability	Service Time (Minutes)	Probability
1	0.40	1	0.20
2	0.30	2	0.40
3	0.15	3	0.40
4	0.15		

Use the following two-digit random numbers for this problem:
Arrivals: 37, 60, 79, 21, 85, 71, 48, 39, 31, 35
Service: 66, 74, 90, 95, 29, 72, 17, 55, 15, 36

12. See SM.

12. Jane's Auto World has a policy on their most popular model of placing an order for 27 automobiles whenever their inventory reaches 20. Lead time on delivery is 2 weeks and they currently have 25 automobiles on hand. Simulate 15 weeks worth of sales using the following probabilities that were derived from historical information.

Sales per Week	Probability
5	.05
6	.05
7	.10
8	.10
9	.10
10	.20
11	.20
12	.10
13	.05
14	.05

Use the following random numbers for sales: 23, 59, 82, 83, 61, 00, 48, 33, 06, 32, 82, 51, 54, 66, 55.

Does this policy appear to be appropriate? Explain.

SELECTED BIBLIOGRAPHY

Conway, R., W. L. Maxwell, J. D. McClain, and S. L. Worona. *XCELL & Factory Modeling System Release 4.0,* 3rd ed. San Francisco: Scientific Press, 1990.

Haider, S. Wali, and Jerry Banks. "Simulation Software Products for Analyzing Manufacturing Systems." *Industrial Engineering* 18, no.7 (July 1986), pp. 98–103.

MicroAnalysis and Design Software Inc., "Hospital Overcrowding Solutions are Found with Simulation," *Industrial Engineering,* December 1993, p. 557.

Law, Averill M., and W. David Kelton. *Simulation Modeling and Analysis.* 2nd ed. New York: McGraw-Hill, 1991.

Payne, James A. *Introduction to Simulation.* New York: McGraw-Hill, 1982.

Solomon, Susan L. *Simulation of Waiting Lines.* Englewood Cliffs, NJ: Prentice-Hall, 1983.

Swedish, Julian. "Simulation Brings Productivity Enhancements to the Social Security Administration." *Industrial Engineering* (May 1993), pp. 28–30.

Winston, Wayne L. *Simulation Modeling Using @RISK.* Belmont, CA: Wadsworth Publishing Company, 1996.

Woolsey, G. "Whatever Happened to Simple Simulation? A Question and Answer." *Interfaces* 9, no.4 (August 1979), pp. 9–11.

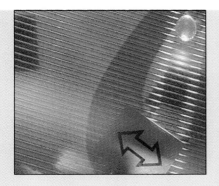

Section five

Revising the System

18 Operations Consulting

19 Business Process
Reengineering

20 Synchronous Manufacturing
and Theory of Constraints

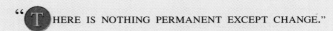

"THERE IS NOTHING PERMANENT EXCEPT CHANGE."

Greek philosopher Heraclitus, 500 B.C.

"If it ain't broke, don't fix it" is a questionable maxim in the business world of today. If a company is not improving its operations, its managers just aren't doing their jobs. The reality is that competing companies are improving. To keep up with improved business practices, improved technology, and better products, change is inevitable.

In this section, we describe three major forces that are driving change. Chapter 18 describes the work of consulting firms with major practices in operations management. Chapter 19 covers the controversial business process reengineering topic. Many of the recent changes made by firms have been under the guise of reengineering projects. Finally, Chapter 20 covers some of the innovative "Theory of Contraints" ideas of Dr. Eliyahu M. Goldratt. Dr. Goldratt's ideas have forced both practitioners and academics to rethink many conventional business and engineering practices.

Chapter 18

Operations Consulting

Chapter Outline

What Is Operations Consulting? 744

The Nature of the Management Consulting Industry, 745

Economics of Consulting Firms, 747

When Operations Consulting Is Needed, 748

When Are Operations Consultants Needed?

The Operations Consulting Process, 750

Operations Consulting Tool Kit, 752

Problem Definition Tools

Data Gathering

Data Analysis and Solution Development

Cost Impact and Payoff Analysis

Implementation

Conclusion: Example of a Consulting Project—"Creating a Service Advantage at a Cellular Telephone Service Provider," 759

Key Terms

"Finders"

"Minders"

"Grinders"

Brain Surgery Projects

Gray Hair Projects

Procedures Projects

www Links

Andersen Consulting (http://www.ac.com)

Management Consultant Network International (http://www.mcninet.com)

Institute of Management Consultants (http://www.imcusa.org)

Fast Company magazine (http://www.fastcompany.com)

Consultants News (http://www.kennedypub.com)

McKinsey & Co. (http://www.mckinsey.com)

Booz-Allen & Hamilton (http://www.bah.com)

Ernst & Young's Ernie (http://ernie.ey.com)

MARK THOMAS, WHO IS A PRINCIPAL OF A UK FIRM called Performance Dynamics, argues energetically that people in support functions—such as finance, human resource, information technology, and procurement—should strive to become internal consultants.

At one time it was common for major companies to have internal consultancy resources available for deployment wherever they might be needed. Did subsidiary A have a manufacturing problem or division B a distribution problem calling for mathematical analysis? Today, although some firms have their experts in "change"—and myriad cross-functional teams are at work on projects of every kind— the consultants have all but disappeared. In the enthusiasm for downsizing and outsourcing, they have been tossed overboard. After all, there are plenty of management consulting firms out there, eager for the call.

Michael Goold of Ashridge Strategic Management Centre accepts that internal resources of this somewhat rarefied nature are wholly justified: "where you have a more cost-effective and skillful group than could be obtained from any outside source." Nevertheless, he argues, "the basic logic for putting work out to third parties is fairly strong. . . . If anything, people are tending to outsource more than they used to do."

There are signs that a countertrend may be developing. In New York, Bristol Myers Squibb has recently set up a management consulting and innovation group. Led by a recruit from McKinsey, this group undertakes the usual range of logistical, marketing, organizational, and strategic tasks, sometimes in association with external consulting firms. ●

Source: Adapted from "Where It's an Inside Job," *Management Today,* October 1996, pp. 13–16.

Reengineering and restructuring have increased the demand for consulting services, such as those advertised here by Andersen Consulting, that promotes their ability to help big organizations become more agile.

This Andersen Consulting ad emphasizes the need for modern companies to be nimble, especially today, when agility and flexibility are prerequisites for remaining competitive. Consulting is one of the fastest growing areas of employment for individuals with operations expertise.

The purpose of this chapter is to discuss some of the specifics of how one goes about consulting for operations, and to discuss the nature of the consulting business, which itself has a major operations component. Our basic assumption is that the reader is familiar with the particular techniques and tools of process analysis, TQM, capacity analysis, queuing methods, and the other standard subject areas of OM. (That is, you've read the book!) As the opening vignette indicates, some companies still find a need for internal consultants. Even if you are not interested in working for a consulting firm, this chapter is important for you since you may be an internal consultant or interacting with consultants.

◼ WHAT IS OPERATIONS CONSULTING?[1]

Operations consulting deals with assisting clients in developing operations strategies and improving production processes. In strategy development, the focus is on analyzing the capabilities of operations in light of the firm's competitive strategy. By way of example, Treacy and Wiersema suggest that market leadership can be attained in one

---

[1] Thanks to Jeb Horton of Arthur Andersen for his help in preparing this chapter.

of three ways: through product leadership, through operational excellence, or through customer intimacy.[2] Each of these strategies may well call for different operations capabilities and focus. The operations consultant must be able to assist management in understanding these differences and be able to define the most effective combination of technology and systems to execute the strategy. In process improvement, the focus is on employing analytical tools and methods to help operating managers enhance performance of their departments. Deloitte & Touche Consulting lists the actions to improve processes as follows: refine/revise processes, revise activities, reconfigure flows, revise policies/procedures, change outputs, and realign structure. We will have more to say about both strategy issues and tools later. Regardless of where one focuses, *an effective job of operations consulting results in an alignment between strategy and process dimensions in a way that enhances the business performance of the client.*

■ THE NATURE OF THE MANAGEMENT CONSULTING INDUSTRY

Fredrick W. Taylor, "the father of scientific management," is also credited as "the father of management consulting." Taylor, a young engineer, devised a philosophy and system of production management at the turn of the century. His book, *The Principles of Scientific Management,* converted what had been an art into a systematic, teachable approach to the study of work. Since Taylor's time, management consulting has reached far beyond the shop floor. Today, management consulting is booming, as can be seen by the revenue figures given in Exhibit 18.1. The reasons for this boom include the following: market pressures on clients to reengineer their core processes and eliminate their non-core processes; globalization requiring companies to seek expert advice on entering foreign markets and defending local ones against new competitors; and the need to better manage information technology, including systems integration and packaged software solutions.

The management consulting industry can be categorized in three ways: by size, by specialization, and by in-house and external consultants. Most consulting firms are small, generating less than $500,000 in annual billings. But as David J. Collis notes in his article, "The Management Consulting Industry," the typical consultant works for a large firm, with three-quarters working for firms employing more than 100 professionals.[3] Relative to specialization, while all large firms provide a variety of services, they may also specialize by function, such as process/operations management, or by industry, such as financial services (see Exhibit 18.2 for other specializations). Most large consulting companies are built on information technology (IT) and accounting work. The third basis for segmentation, in-house versus external, refers to whether a company maintains its own consulting organization or buys consulting services from the outside. Collis observes that internal consulting arms are common in large companies and are often affiliated with planning departments.

ACCOUNTING
MIS

Consulting firms are also frequently characterized according to whether their primary skill is in strategic planning or in tactical analysis and implementation.

---

[2] M. Treacy and F. Wiersema, *The Discipline of Market Leaders* (Reading, MA: Addison Wesley, 1997).

[3] David J. Collis, "The Management Consulting Industry," *Internet Class Notes,* Harvard Business School, 1996.

Exhibit 18.1

Top 25 U.S.–Based
Management
Consulting Firms,
1996

	Management Consulting Revenues*, $m		Consultants Worldwide no.	Revenues per Consultant $000
	World	United States		
Andersen Consulting	3,115	1,590	43,808	71
McKinsey & Co	2,100	800	3,944	532
Ernst & Young[†]	2,100	1,400	11,200	188
Coopers & Lybrand Consulting[‡]	1,918	1,005	9,000	213
KPMG Peat Marwick[‡]	1,380	770	10,764	128
Arthur Andersen[§]	1,380	766	15,000	92
Deloitte & Touche[Δ]	1,303	821	10,000	130
Mercer Consulting Group	1,159	707	9,241	125
Towers Perrin	903	659	6,262	144
A.T. Kearney	870	530	2,300	378
Price Waterhouse**	840	481	6,230	135
IBM Consulting Group	730	530	3,970	184
Booz-Allen & Hamilton[††]	720	540	5,685	127
Watson Wyatt Worldwide	656	417	3,730	176
The Boston Consulting Group	600	180	1,550	387
Gemini Consulting	600	218	1,470	408
Arthur D. Little	574	299	1,939	296
Hewitt Associates[‡]	568	538	3,807	149
Aon Consulting	473	318	4,370	108
Bain & Company	450	240	1,350	333
American Management Systems	440	300	2,960	149
Woodrow Milliman	350	188	1,150	304
Grant Thornton[‡‡]	306	66	886	345
Sedgwick Noble Lowndes	262	78	3,142	83
The Hay Group	259	119	1,035	250

*Less reimbursed expenses   Year ending: [†]Oct 1996   [‡]Sept 1996   [§]Aug 1996   [Δ]May 1996   **June 1996
[††]March 1997 projected   [‡‡]July 1996 for US, various for worldwide

Source: *Consultants News,* cited in the *Economist,* March 22, 1997, p. 5.

Exhibit 18.2   Services Offered

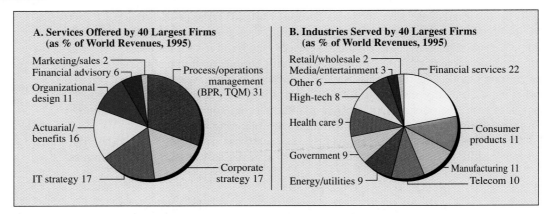

A. Services Offered by 40 Largest Firms (as % of World Revenues, 1995)

Marketing/sales 2
Financial advisory 6
Organizational design 11
Actuarial/benefits 16
IT strategy 17
Corporate strategy 17
Process/operations management (BPR, TQM) 31

B. Industries Served by 40 Largest Firms (as % of World Revenues, 1995)

Retail/wholesale 2
Media/entertainment 3
Other 6
High-tech 8
Health care 9
Government 9
Energy/utilities 9
Financial services 22
Consumer products 11
Manufacturing 11
Telecom 10

Source: *Consultants News,* cited in the *Economist,* March 22, 1997, p. 40.

McKinsey and Company and the Boston Consulting Group are standard examples of strategy-type companies, while Gemini Consulting and the Hay Group focus rather extensively on tactical and implementation projects. The big accounting firms and Andersen Consulting are known for providing a wide range of services. The major new players in the consulting business are the large, information technology firms such as Computer Sciences Corporation (CSC), Electronic Data Systems (EDS), and IBM. Consultancies are faced with problems similar to those of their clients: the need to provide a global presence, the need to computerize to coordinate activities, and the need to continually recruit and train their workers. This has led consultancies to make the hard choice of being very large or being a boutique firm. Being in the middle creates problems of lack of scale economies on the one hand and lack of focus and flexibility on the other.

The hierarchy of the typical consulting firm can be viewed as a pyramid. At the top of the pyramid are the partners or seniors, whose primary function is sales and client relations. In the middle are managers, who manage consulting projects or "engagements." At the bottom are juniors, who carry out the consulting work as part of a consulting team. There are gradations in rank within each of these categories (e.g., senior partners). The three categories are frequently referred to colloquially as the **"finders"** (of new business), the **"minders"** (or managers) of the project teams, and the **"grinders"** (the consultants who do the work). Consulting firms typically work in project teams, selected according to needs of the client and the preferences of the project managers and the first-line consultants themselves. Getting oneself assigned to interesting, high-visibility projects with good coworkers is an important career strategy of most junior consultants. Being in demand for team membership and obtaining quality consulting experiences are critical for achieving long-term success with a consulting firm (or being attractive to another firm within or outside of consulting).

"Finders"
"Minders"
"Grinders"

◼ ECONOMICS OF CONSULTING FIRMS

The economics of consulting firms has been written about extensively by David H. Maister. In his classic article, "Balancing the Professional Service Firm,"[4] he draws the analogy of the consulting firm as a job shop, where the right kinds of "machines" (professional staff) must be correctly allocated to the right kinds of jobs (consulting projects). As in any job shop, the degree of job customization and attendant complexity is critical. The most complex projects, which Maister calls **"brain surgery"** projects, require innovations and creativity. Next comes **"gray hair"** projects, which require a great deal of experience but little in the way of innovation. A third type of project is the **"procedures"** project, where the general nature of the problem is well known and the activities necessary to complete it are similar to those performed on other projects.

"Brain Surgery"
"Gray Hair"

"Procedures"

Because consulting firms are typically partnerships, the goal is to maximize profits for the partners. This, in turn, is achieved by leveraging the skills of the partners through the effective use of middle level and junior consultants. This is often presented as a ratio of partners to middle level to junior consultants for the average

---

[4] David H. Maister, "Balancing the Professional Service Firm," *Sloan Management Review* 24, no. 1 (Fall 1982), pp. 15–29.

Exhibit 18.3   The Economics of Guru Associates

Level	No.	Target Utilization	Target Billable Hours @ 2,000 Hours per Person per Year	Billing Rate	Fees	Salary per Individual	Total Salaries
Partner (Senior)	4	75%	6,000	$200	$1,200,000	(see calculations below)	
Middle	8	75%	12,000	$100	$1,200,000	$75,000	$600,000
Junior	20	90%	36,000	$50	$1,800,000	$32,000	$640,000
Totals					$4,200,000		$1,240,000

Fees	$4,200,000
Salaries	(1,240,000)
Contributions	$2,960,000
Overhead*	$1,280,000
Partner profits	$1,680,000
Per partner	$ 420,000

*Assume overhead costs of $40,000 per professional.

Source: David H. Maister, *Managing the Professional Service Firm* (New York: The Free Press, 1993), p. 11.

project. (See Exhibit 18.3 for a numerical example of how profitability is calculated for a hypothetical consulting firm, Guru Associates.) Because most consulting firms are engaged in multiple projects simultaneously, the percentage of billable employee hours assigned to all projects (target utilization) will be less than 100 percent. A practice that specializes in cutting-edge, high-client risk (brain surgery) work must be staffed with a high partner-to-junior ratio, because lower level people will not be able to deliver the quality of services required. In contrast, practices that deal with more procedural, low-risk work will be inefficient if they do not have a lower ratio of partners to juniors because high-priced staff should not be doing low-value tasks.

The most common method for improving efficiency is the use of uniform approaches to each aspect of a consulting job. Andersen Consulting, the company most famous for this approach, sends its new consultants through a boot camp at its St. Charles, Illinois, training facility. At this boot camp, it provides highly refined, standardized methods for such common operations work as systems design, process reengineering, and continuous improvement, and for the project management and reporting procedures by which such work is carried out. Of course, other large consulting firms have their own training methods and step-by-step procedures for selling, designing, and executing consulting projects.

WHEN OPERATIONS CONSULTING IS NEEDED

The following are some of the major strategic and tactical areas where companies typically seek operations consulting. Looking first at manufacturing consulting areas (grouped under the 5 Ps of production) we have:

- *Plant:* Adding and locating new plants, expanding, contracting, or refocusing existing facilities.

- *People:* Quality improvement, setting/revising work standards, learning curve analysis.
- *Parts:* Make or buy decisions, vendor selection decisions.
- *Processes:* Technology evaluation, process improvement, reengineering.
- *Planning and control systems:* Supply chain management, MRP, shop floor control, warehousing, and distribution.

Obviously, many of these issues are interrelated, calling for systemwide solutions. Examples of common themes reflecting this are: developing manufacturing strategy, designing and implementing JIT systems, implementing MRP or proprietary software such as SAP and Baan IV, and systems integration involving client server technology. Typical questions addressed are: "How can the client cut lead times? How can inventory be reduced? How can better control be maintained over the shop floor?" Among the hot areas of manufacturing strategy consulting are: developing factory focus, the factory of the future (although much of this requires engineering expertise), supply chain management, and of course, global manufacturing networks. At the tactical level, there is a huge market for consulting in ISO 9000 quality certification, TQM training, and designing and implementing decentralized production control systems.

Turning to services, while consulting firms in manufacturing may have broad specialties in process industries on the one hand and assembly or discrete product manufacture on the other, service operations consulting typically has a strong industry or sector focus. A common consulting portfolio of specialties in services (and areas of consulting need) would include the following:

Financial services (staffing, automation, and quality studies).

Health care (staffing, billing, office procedures, phone answering, layout).

Transportation (route scheduling and shipping logistics for goods haulers, reservation systems and baggage handling for airlines).

Hospitality (reservations, staffing, cost containment, and quality programs).

Without question, however, the major area of operations consulting emphasis in most service industries is reengineering (discussed in Chapter 19).

When Are Operations Consultants Needed?

Companies typically seek out operations consultants when they are faced with major investment decisions or when they believe that they are not getting maximum effectiveness from their productive capacity. As an example of the first type of situation, consider the following:

A national pie restaurant chain retained consultants to determine if a major addition to their freezer storage capacity was needed at their pie making plant. Their lease had run out on a nearby freezer warehouse so they had to make a decision rather quickly. The pie plant manager wanted a $500,000 increase in capacity. After analysis of the demand for various types of pies, the distribution system, and the contractual arrangement with the shipper, the consultant concluded that management could avoid all but a $30,000 investment in capacity if they did the following: Run a mixed model production schedule for pies according to a forecast for each of 10 kinds of pies (e.g., 20 percent strawberry, 30 percent cherry, 30 percent apple, and 20 percent other pies each two-day pie production cycle). To do this, more timely information of pie demand at each of the chain

restaurants had to obtained. This in turn required that information links for pie requirements go directly to the factory. (Previously, the distributor bought the pies and resold
them to the restaurants). Finally, the company renegotiated pick-up times from the pie
plant to enable just-in-time delivery at the restaurants. The company was in a much
stronger bargaining situation than they were five years previously and the distributor was
willing to make reasonable adjustments.

The lesson to be learned from this is that few investment decisions in operations are
all or nothing, and that good solutions can be obtained by simply applying standard
OM concepts of production planning, forecasting, and scheduling. The solution recognized that the problem must be viewed at a systemwide level to see how better planning
and distribution could be used to substitute for brick and mortar capacity.

■ THE OPERATIONS CONSULTING PROCESS

The broad steps in the operations consulting process are roughly the same as for any
type of management consulting. The major differences exist in the nature of the
problem to be analyzed and the kinds of analytical methods to be employed. Like
general management consulting, operations consulting may focus on the strategic
level or tactical level, and the process itself generally requires extensive interviewing
of employees, managers, and, frequently, customers. If there is one major difference,
it is that operations consulting leads to changes in physical or information processes
whose results are measurable immediately. General management consulting usually
calls for changes in attitudes and culture, which take a longer period of time to yield
measurable results. The roles in which consultants find themselves range from an
expert, to a *pair of hands,* to a *collaborative or process consultant.* Generally, the
collaborative or process consultation role is most effective in most operations management consulting projects.

While having skills in modeling, communication, human relations, and writing are
expected attributes of the operations consultant, one skill that is often overlooked is
what we might term the "Columbo factor," after the rumpled TV police detective who
is able to deduce "who done it" from the smallest of clues. The sources of such clues
often lie in such innocuous documents as the "parts short report" compiled at shop-
floor work stations. Tracing through such lists inevitably provides clues as to why the
parts are missing, and the root source of the problem.

 The steps in the typical operations consulting process are summarized in Exhibit 18.4 and are developed in more detail as follows:

1. **Sales and Proposal Development**
    There is a good deal of interaction between the client and the consulting firm,
    especially when the client is a new one.
    A. Obtain a client data package including such items as annual reports, organiza-
    tion charts, process charts, customer complaint letters, employee surveys, and
    product literature.
    B. Perform background research, including the following:
    · Industry analysis (trends/technology).
    · Client position in the industry.
    · Analysis of past and on-going projects.
    C. Develop a shared understanding of the real versus perceived client need using
    an organizational systems view. This underlies the proposal.

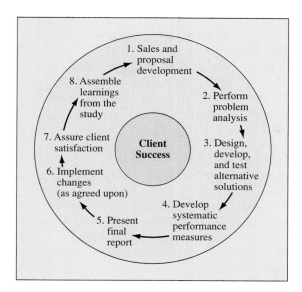

Exhibit 18.4

Stages in the
Operations Consulting
Process

D. Develop proposal letter including the following:
- · Situation faced by client.
- · Desired client outcomes.
- · Planning premises (including possible complications).
- · Specific problem statement.
- · Initial hypotheses.
- · Work plan, including approach to be followed, client involvement, and data needs from the client (including identification of contact person(s).
- · Scope of project, identifying specific phase and deliverables from each phase. (Hint: *Be very explicit in bounding the depth and breadth of project.*)
- · Identification of project team members and support capabilities.
- · Fee structure and payment schedule.
- · Specification of the precise features of a service guarantee (if used).

2. Perform Problem Analysis
- **A.** Develop data-gathering strategy.
- **B.** Gather data from multiple sources.
- **C.** Perform target analysis, simplifying as much as possible.
- **D.** Design and develop alternative solutions built on fact-based analysis.
- **E.** Apply appropriate tools and methods, simulate and refine solutions.

3. Design, Develop and Test Alternative Solutions
- **A.** Check for reasonableness.
- **B.** Check for consistency and synergy among recommendations.
- **C.** Pilot test and debug further.
- **D.** Prioritize recommendations (some consulting firms recommend implementing some pilot solutions at this stage to get early buy-in from client).

4. Develop Systematic Performance Measures
- **A.** Develop a family of measures that clearly link the success of the engagement to client business success (refine earlier cost, quality, time measures).
- **B.** Measures should evaluate performance on processes and outputs.
  Good output performance measures are

· Aligned with corporate missions and goals.
· Focused on end customer wants.
· Designed to promote continuous improvement.
· Balanced with respect to cost, quality, and time.
· Few in number.
Good process measures are
· Clearly understandable.
· Process, not people, oriented.
· Developed by people doing the job.

5. **Present Final Report to the Client**
   A. Prepare a final report.
   Typical format: executive summary, company and industry background, analysis, recommendations (grouped by priority), time-phased implementation plan and contingencies, and appendix (Hints: *Clearly explain each calculation in the exhibits, and get a preliminary read from your client before the formal presentation.*)

6. **Implement Changes (as agreed upon)**
   A. Leave the client with capabilities to perform major changes.
   B. Develop a communications plan with management to assure that all stakeholders are aware of what is happening.

7. **Assure Client Satisfaction**
   A. Continue your relationship management. Stay in contact with the client after the engagement to assure that everything is done to the client's satisfaction.
   B. Follow-up all engagements with a mailed client feedback questionnaire. According to Maister, there is no substitute for a mailed questionnaire to each and every contact at the end of every client project. The advantage of this is that it is more systematic than occasional managing partner visits, team debriefings, and so forth. An example of such a questionnaire is given on pages 85 and 86 of Maister's book, *Managing the Professional Firm* (cited in the chapter bibliography).

8. **Assemble Learnings from the Study**
   Consulting companies are on the leading edge of knowledge management and knowledge sharing systems. Arthur Andersen, for example, prides itself on being able to bring to bear all of its information resources to a consulting team working anywhere in the world.
   A. Add notes from the engagement to the consulting company's database.
   B. Formalize/standardize good ideas for future projects.

■ OPERATIONS CONSULTING TOOL KIT

MARKETING
MIS

Operations consulting tools can be categorized as tools for *problem definition, data gathering, data analysis and solution development, cost impact and payoff analysis,* and *implementation.* These—along with some tools from strategic management, marketing, and information systems that are commonly used in OM consulting—are noted in Exhibit 18.5 and are described below. (Note that several of these tools are used in more than one stage of a project.)

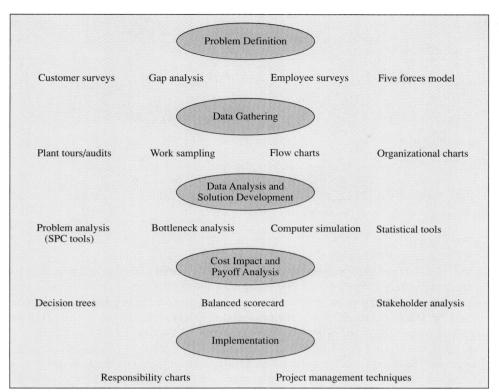

Exhibit 18.5

Operations Consulting
Tool Kit

Problem Definition Tools

Customer Surveys   Frequently OM consultants are called in to address problems identified by customer surveys performed by marketing consultants or marketing staffs. Often, however, these are out of date or are in a form that does not separate process issues from advertising or other marketing concerns. Even if the surveys are in good form, calling customers and soliciting their experience with the company is a good way to get a feel for process performance. A key use of customer surveys is *customer loyalty analysis* although in reality, customers are not so much "loyal" (your dog Spot is loyal) as "earned" through effective performance. Nevertheless, the term loyalty captures the flavor of how well an organization is performing according to three critical market measures: customer retention, share of wallet, and price sensitivity relative to competitors. Having such information available helps the OM consultant drill down into the organization to find what operational factors are directly linked to customer retention. While loyalty studies are usually performed by marketing groups, OM consultants should be aware of their importance.

MARKETING

Gap Analysis   Gap analysis is used to assess the client's performance relative to the expectations of its customers, or relative to the performance of its competitors. An example is shown in Exhibit 18.6.

Exhibit 18.6

Gap Analysis

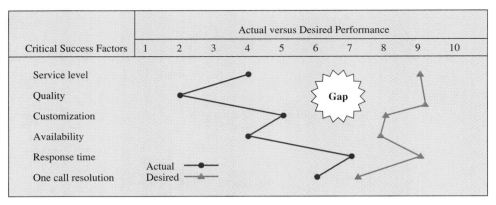

Source: Deloitte & Touche Consulting Group.

Another form of gap analysis is benchmarking particular client company processes against exemplars in the process and measuring the differences. For example, if one is interested in billing process accuracy and problem resolution, American Express would be the benchmark; for timeliness and efficiency in railway transportation, Japanese Railways, or for order entry in catalogue sales, it would be L.L. Bean.

Employee Surveys   Such surveys range from employee satisfaction surveys to suggestion surveys. A key point to remember is if the consultant requests employee suggestions, such information must be carefully evaluated and acted upon by management. A few years ago, Singapore Airlines distributed a questionnaire to its flight personnel, but made the mistake of not following through to address their concerns. As a result, the employees were more critical of the company than if the survey had not been taken, and to this day the company does not use this form of evaluation.

Five Forces Model   This is one of the better-known approaches to evaluating a company's competitive position in light of the structure of its industry. The five forces are: buyer power, potential entrants, suppliers, substitute products, and industry rivals. The consultant applies the model by developing a list of factors that fit under each of these headings. Some examples of where a client's competitive position might be strong are: when buyers have limited information, there are major barriers to potential entrants, there are many alternative suppliers, there are few substitute products (or services), and there are few industry rivals.

Often used with the five forces model is the *value chain,* such as shown in Exhibit 18.7. The value chain provides a structure to capture the linkage of organizational activities that create value for the customer and profit for the firm. It is particularly useful to get across the notion that operations and the other activities must work cross-functionally for optimal organizational performance (and avoid the dreaded "functional silo" syndrome).

A tool similar to the five forces model is *SWOT analysis.* This is a somewhat more general method of evaluating an organization, and has the advantage of being easy to remember: *S*trengths of the client, *W*eaknesses of the client, *O*pportunities for the client in the industry, and *T*hreats from competitors or the economic and market environment.

Exhibit 18.7

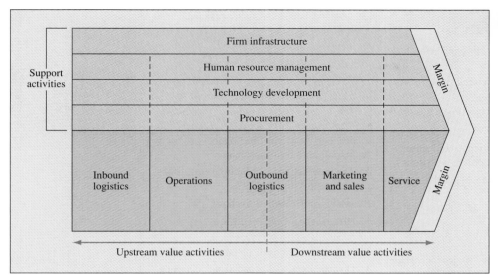

Source: Michael E. Porter, *Competition in Global Industries* (Boston, MA: Harvard Business School Press, 1986), p. 24.

Data Gathering

Plant Tours/Audits   These can be classified as manufacturing tours/audits and service facility tours/audits. Full manufacturing audits are a major undertaking, entailing measurement of all aspects of the production facility and processes, as well as support activities such as maintenance and inventory stock keeping. Frequently, these require several weeks, utilizing checklists developed explicitly for the client's industry. Plant tours, on the other hand, are usually much less detailed and can be done in a half day. The purpose of the tour is to get a general understanding of the manufacturing process before focusing on a particular problem area. Tours use generic checklists or general questions such as given in the box "Field Guide to Plants" developed for our classes.[5] (See the next page.)

Complete service facility audits are also a major undertaking, but they differ from manufacturing audits in that, when properly done, they focus on the customer's experience as much as on the utilization of resources. Typical questions in a service audit address time to get service, the cleanliness of the facility, staff sizing, and customer satisfaction. A service facility tour or walk-through can often be done as a mystery shopper, where the consultant actually partakes of the service and records his or her experiences. (In consulting with the Peninsula Hotel in Beverly Hills 90210, one of the authors went through the grueling ordeal of staying the night in a $2,500-per-night villa and reporting back to management on the quality of the experience.)

Work Sampling   Work sampling entails random sampling observations of work activities, designed to give a statistically valid picture of how time is being spent by a worker or the utilization of equipment. Diary studies are another way to collect activity data. These are used by consultants to get an understanding of very specific

---

[5] For further discussion of plant tours, see D. Upton and S. Macadam, "Why (and How) to Take a Plant Tour," *Harvard Business Review* 75, no. 3 (May–June 1997), pp. 97–106.

Plant

1. What is the overall capacity of the plant? ($ or units)
2. What are the bottleneck resource(s) in the plant?
3. How do they measure productivity?

People

1. Is there clear evidence of employee involvement and a positive attitude?
2. Is this a good place to work? (incentives, bonuses)
3. Are the employees well-informed and knowledgeable?

Parts

1. Do you see any major inventory buildup? (raw mtls., WIP, finished goods)
2. Are parts storage areas isolated with limited access?

3. Are defects (scraps, rework) clearly identified and quarantined?

Processes

1. What is their process flow? (job shop, batch, assembly line, continuous flow)
2. What are the major processing departments of the plant? Sketch the process flow for the major products manufactured at the plant.
3. Are they active at reducing setup times and improving quality?

Planning and Control Systems

1. How do they plan operations? (make to order, make to forecast)
2. Are they using pull or push systems?
3. Do they measure on-time delivery, inventory turns, backorder, backlog, etc?

tasks being performed by the workforce. In these, the employee simply writes down the activities he or she performs during the week as they occur. This avoids the problem of having analysts look over a worker's shoulder to gather data. Examples of where these studies are used include library front desks, nursing, and knowledge work.

 Flow Charts   Flow charts can be used in both manufacturing and service to track materials, information, and people flows. Workflow software, such as Optima! and BPR Capture, are widely used for process analysis. In addition to providing capabilities for defining a process, most workflow software provides four other basic functions: work assignment and routing, scheduling, work list management, and automatic status and process metrics. Flow charts used in services—service blueprints— are basically the same thing, but add the important distinction of the line of visibility to clearly differentiate activities that take place with the customer versus those that are behind the scenes. In our opinion, the service blueprint is not used to its full potential by consulting firms, perhaps because relatively few consultants are exposed to them in their training.

Organization Charts   Organization charts are often subject to change, so care must be taken to see who really reports to whom. Some companies are loath to share organization charts externally. Several years ago a senior manager from a large electronics firm told us that a detailed organization chart gives free information to the competition.

Data Analysis and Solution Development

Problem Analysis (SPC Tools)   Pareto analysis, fishbone diagrams, run charts, scatter diagrams, and control charts are fundamental tools in virtually every continuous improvement project. *Pareto analysis* as applied to inventory management under the heading of ABC analysis. Such ABC analysis is still the standard starting point of production control consultants when examining inventory management problems. *Fishbone diagrams* (or cause-and-effect diagrams) are a great way to organize one's first cut at a consulting problem (and they make a great impression when used to analyze, for example, a case study as part of the employment selection process for a consulting firm). *Run charts, scatter diagrams,* and *control charts* are tools that one is simply expected to know when doing operations consulting.

Bottleneck Analysis Resource bottlenecks appear in most OM consulting projects. In such cases the consultant has to specify how available capacity is related to required capacity for some product or service in order to identify and eliminate the bottleneck. This isn't always evident, and abstracting the relationships calls for the same kind of logical analysis used in the classic "word problems" you loved in high school algebra.

Computer Simulation Computer simulation analysis has become a very common tool in OM consulting. For example, Arthur Andersen supplies Optima!, a process charting package with simulation capability, in the CD-ROM packages they supply to their analysts. Other general purpose simulation packages used by consultants, as well as in many business schools, are Extend and Crystal Ball. SimFactory and ProModel (manufacturing systems), MedModel (hospital simulation), and ServiceModel are examples of specialized packages. For smaller and less complex simulations, consultants often use Excel.

Some of the new simulation packages include causal loop diagrams. These are a form of systems diagrams which are particularly useful when modeling the factors that enhance or degrade system performance. Causal loops are of two types, reinforcing loops and balancing loops. Reinforcing loops generate exponential growth and collapse, in which the growth or collapse continues at an ever-increasing rate. Balancing loops reflect the mechanisms which counter reinforcing loops, thereby driving the system toward an equilibrium. By way of example, with reference to Exhibit 18.8, suppose you have a quality goal which is reflected in a quality standard. The reinforcing loop (R) indicates that the standard, if left unmodified, would yield an ever-increasing (or decreasing) level of actual quality. In reality, what happens is that the balancing loop (B) comes into play. Effective time required to meet the standard determines time pressure (on the workers) which, in turn, modifies the actual quality achieved and ultimately achievement of the quality standard itelf. An obvious use of

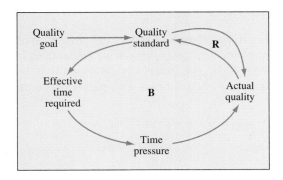

Exhibit 18.8

Causal Loop Analysis

the system shown here would be to hypothesize the consequences of raising the quality goal, or raising or lowering the values of the other variables in the system. In addition to its use in problem analysis, consultants often use causal loop analysis simulations to help client companies become more effective learning organizations.[6]

Statistical Tools   *Correlation analysis* and *regression analysis* are expected skills for consulting in OM. The good news is that these types of analyses are easily performed with spreadsheets. *Hypothesis testing* is mentioned frequently in the consulting firm methodology manuals, and one should certainly be able to perform Chi-square and t-tests in analyzing data. Two other widely used tools that use statistical analysis are *queuing theory* and *forecasting*. Consultants frequently use queuing theory to investigate how many service channels are needed to handle customers in person or on the phone. Forecasting problems likewise arise continually in OM consulting (e.g., forecasting the incoming calls to a call center).

A newly emerging tool (not shown on our exhibit) is *data envelopment analysis*. DEA is a linear programming technique used to measure the relative performance of branches of multisite service organizations such as banks, franchise outlets, and public agencies. A DEA model compares each branch with all other branches and computes an efficiency rating based on the ratio of resource inputs to product or service outputs. The key feature of the approach is that it permits using multiple inputs such as materials and labor hours, and multiple outputs such as products sold and repeat customers, to get an efficiency ratio. This feature provides a more comprehensive and reliable measure of efficiency than a set of operating ratios or profit measures.[7]

Cost Impact and Payoff Analysis

Decision Trees   Decision trees represent a fundamental tool from the broad area of risk analysis. They are widely used in examining plant and equipment investments and R&D projects. Decision trees are built into various software packages such as @ Risk (*Risk Analysis for Spreadsheets,* Palisade Publications, 1995), which in addition to tree-type analysis has simulation capability.

Stakeholder Analysis   Most consulting projects impact in some way each of five types of stakeholders: customers, stockholders, employees, suppliers, and the community. The importance of considering the interest of all stakeholders is reflected in the mission statements of virtually all major corporations and, as such, provides guidance for consultants in formulating their recommendations.

Balanced Scorecard   In an attempt to reflect the particular needs of each stakeholder group in a performance measurement system, accountants have developed what is termed a *balanced scorecard*. (Balance refers to the fact that the scorecard looks at more than just the bottom line or one or two other performance measures.) Atkinson,

---

[6] See Peter Senge, *The Fifth Discipline: The Art and Practice of the Learning Organization* (New York: Doubleday Currency, 1990).

[7] J. Fitzsimmons and M. Fitzsimmons, *Service Management for Competitive Advantage* (New York: McGraw-Hill, 1994), p. 319–20.

et al. note how the Bank of Montreal has used the balanced scorecard notion in setting specific goals and measures for customer service, employee relations, return to owners, and community relations. A key feature of their system is that it is tailored to what senior management and branch level management can control.[8]

Implementation

Responsibility Charts A responsibility chart is used in planning the task responsibilities for a project. It usually takes the form of a matrix with tasks listed across the top and project team members down the side. The goal is to make sure that a checkmark exists in each cell to assure that a person is assigned to each task.

Project Management Techniques Consulting firms use the project management techniques of CPM/PERT and Gantt charts to plan and monitor both the entire portfolio of consulting engagements of the firm, as well as individual consulting projects. Microsoft Project and Primavera Project Planner are examples of commonly used software to automate such tools. It should be emphasized that these planning tools are very much secondary to the people management skills needed to successfully execute a consulting project. This admonition is likewise true for all of the tools we have discussed in this section.

■ CONCLUSION: EXAMPLE OF A CONSULTING PROJECT—"CREATING A SERVICE ADVANTAGE AT A CELLULAR TELEPHONE SERVICE PROVIDER"

We conclude this chapter with the following description of an actual consulting project provided by the MAC Consulting Group (now named Gemini Consulting). As you read the study, consider how the MAC team identified the project issues to focus on, how they gathered and analyzed data (including OM tools used), how they moved between solution and implementation, and the level of benefits achieved for the client.

Background

In October 1989, MAC completed the development of a marketing strategy for a leading cellular telephone service provider (the client). As a result, the client redirected resources to target the productivity-minded segment and focused improvement efforts on issues most important to that segment:

- Cellular system performance (e.g., transmission quality, call disconnect rate, call completion rate); and
- Customer service.

Six key pilot programs formed the core of strategy implementation. MAC planned and helped implement four of the six:

- Customer service upgrade (piloted in the Dallas market).[9]
- Benefits-based advertising (marketing cellular telephones as productivity tools).
- Salesforce compensation (new emphasis on retaining customers).
- Key customer/lifecycle programs (targeted toward heavy users to provide better proactive service).

This discussion outlines the customer service upgrade project, which began in February 1990 and concluded December 1990.

Pilot Objective

The Dallas market was selected for the pilot because it

---

[8] A. Atkinson, R. Banker, R. Kaplan, and M. Young, *Management Accounting* (Englewood Cliffs, NJ: Prentice Hall, 1995), p. 446.

[9] Cities have been disguised to maintain the anonymity of the client.

had a history of providing the worst customer service in the organization. The pilot's main goal was to create "Customer Service Utopia," accomplishing four primary objectives in the process:

1. Answer the question: "How do our customers define quality service?"
2. Identify barriers to providing what customers define as quality service.
3. Implement new programs, policies, procedures, and structures to remove those barriers, adapting them along the way as necessary.
4. Plan and facilitate a companywide "customer service summit" to roll out the results of all customer-service-related pilots and hold working group sessions on topics critical to improving customer satisfaction.

Activities

How do our customers define quality service, and what barriers prevent us from delivering that service?

To answer these questions, MAC used the following: information collected during the market segmentation study; data already existing with the client; 30 customer interviews in the Dallas market; Customer Service/Operations employee and management interviews in three markets (Dallas, New York, Little Rock); and Customer Service Representative (CSR) observations (sitting with CSRs and listening to their conversations with customers).

Using the information gathered, we (MAC and the client) determined that customers wanted "Customer Service Utopia," which meant:

- A one-stop shop.
  - The customer calls once and speaks with one person to solve his problem.
  - The customer receives an answer before he hangs up.
  - The customer is "guaranteed" that his problem has been solved.
- Empowered CSRs.
  - They make decisions, appropriately and accurately, to satisfy the customer.
  - They have the necessary knowledge, authority, and tools.
- Professional CSRs.
  - The CSRs are interested and friendly.
  - They help customers forget they ever had a problem.
- CSR ownership and accountability.
  - The CSR removes all responsibility from the customer.
  - The CSR sees the problems through to resolution.
  - The CSR calls back, if necessary, to confirm resolution.

- The CSR is responsive if future problems arise.
- High overall product quality.
  - Postcards are sent following calls to confirm action.
  - Low customer hold time.
  - Other, more subtle, indicators of excellence, such as an on-hold message or music.

Of the myriad barriers preventing the client from delivering Utopia, we selected six key areas to address:

1. Outdated customer service organization—structure, policies, and procedures.
2. Poor inter- and intradepartmental communication and relations.
3. Insufficient (or nonexistent) training.
4. Substandard customer satisfaction measurement programs.
5. Unsophisticated methods to determine staffing levels (one-CSR-for-every-2,500-customers rule).
6. Ill-defined career path for CSRs, compounded by a confusing compensation system and no formal reward/recognition program.

Barrier 1: *Outdated Customer Service Organization*

The road to Utopia began with a new organization. We created three teams—two retail teams and one major accounts team. Retail teams took all incoming calls, while the major accounts team focused on corporate accounts and heavy users.

Besides reorganizing the department, the client changed the way customer service did business. These changes included the following:

- Committed to a 24-hour turnaround on all customer inquiries/problems for those calls not able to be handled within the one-stop shop. Internally, all departments in the organization committed to a 24-hour turnaround on interdepartmental requests for research and/or information when related to customer inquiries/problems.
- Gave total decision-making authority to front-line CSRs on all customer-related issues. All dollar limits on credits and adjustments—previously $25 in Dallas and as low as $18 in other markets—were removed. No increase in the amount of money CSRs credited back to the customer occurred.
- Required documentation of all customer credits and adjustments on screen (in the computer system), but eliminated the need for paper documentation of any credit/adjustment under $100. Previously CSRs were required to provide paper backup on everything including 10¢ airtime adjustments. The cost of that documentation included copying costs, materials, and research time spent by the rep away from the phone, thus making him/her unavailable for incoming calls.

· For any remaining research required, we designed a new research process. Each week, one or two CSRs from each team would act as the research rep for their team. A system utilizing red (immediate research required) and white (research required before the end of the day) flags was implemented to make the process more efficient. Research positions rotated weekly.

· Set staffing levels using a staffing model based on queueing theory rather than the client's standard one-CSR-for-every-2,500-customers rule (see Barrier 5).

Barrier 2: *Poor Inter- and Intradepartmental Communication and Relations*

As in many organizations, we found a "we/they" adversarial relationship among CSRs and management; among CSRs and CSRs; and among all departments. To improve relations, we took steps designed to build lines of communication and involve all groups in those decision-making processes that affected them. This involved creating a cross-functional customer satisfaction improvement team (CSIT).

The CSIT's purpose is to improve customer satisfaction by providing a forum to do the following:

· Eliminate cross-functional barriers to excellent service.

· Facilitate information flow among departments.

· Generate, test, and implement ideas, solutions, and changes that affect more than one department.

· Build interdepartmental cooperation and communication.

· Give the front line (those dealing most directly with the customer) a voice in decisions.

Barrier 3: *Insufficient to Nonexistent Training*

Early in the project, we held a two-day training brainstorming session that included management and front-line personnel from all seven markets. The group assessed current training materials, agreed to a modular training format, and created an outline of each module, which included both the topics to be covered and when each module should be taught in the course of a CSR's career.

Following this session, the corporate human resources director hired a PhD training materials design specialist to create the new modular "Exceptional Customer Service Training Program." From that point on, MAC's role consisted of overseeing the specialist and ensuring that all of the markets continued to have input into the training program.

Barrier 4: *Substandard Customer Satisfaction Measurement Program*

Working with the client and Burke Marketing Research, MAC designed a three-pronged approach to measuring customer satisfaction:

1. A revised general telephone survey designed to produce actionable results in all areas measured. All markets participated.

2. A customer service mail survey sent to customers within 48 hours of having contacted customer service. The survey uses benefit/deficiency analysis to correlate specific attributes with customer satisfaction. A per-rep analysis can be done on a point-in-time basis (depending on per-rep sample size). This survey measured quality, providing balance to quantitative measurements (hold time, productivity) available through the ACD (phone) system. All markets participated. The following are two examples of the survey's output:

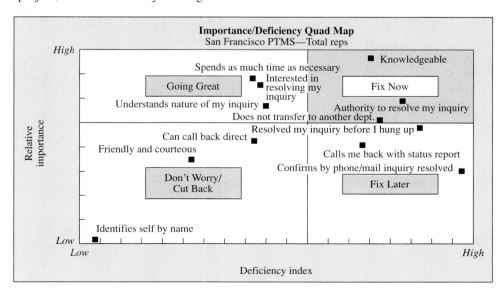

Importance/Deficiency Quad Map
San Francisco PTMS—Total reps

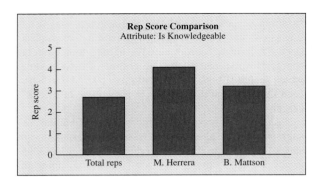

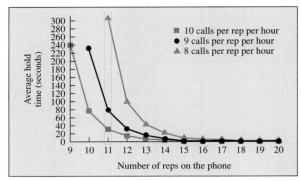

3. A disconnect study to poll customers who have recently moved to the competitor or disconnected their cellular service. The study is designed to help the client prioritize problems (identified in the above surveys). This study is currently being piloted in the New York and Dallas markets.

The three studies are designed to work together, surveying real customers, producing actionable results prioritized for the most immediate impact to improve customer satisfaction.

Barrier 5: *Unsophisticated Means to Determine Staffing Levels*

Each market, no matter what unique characteristics it might have, used the standard one-CSR-for-every-2,500-customers-rule when determining staffing levels. MAC had two key responsibilities relating to staffing:

1. Educate the client as to the importance of staffing and why the standard rule was insufficient.

2. Build a staffing model utilizing queueing theory that could take into consideration each market's unique characteristics.

Two factors that affect staffing were found:

1. Number of phone reps required at any one time, determined by:
   · Rep productivity.
   · Incoming-call rate.

2. Total headcount, determined by:
   · Number of phone reps required.
   · Overall organizational structure (e.g., number of supervisors, administrative staff, vacation days, etc.).

Both productivity and incoming call rates varied depending on numerous factors, including commitment to one-stop shop, rep authorization levels, size of customer base, timing of the billing cycle, and so forth. A small slip in productivity could lead to a giant setback in performance.

As the above figure shows, a 20 percent decrease in productivity from ten calls per hour to eight calls per hour can lead to a tenfold increase in hold time.

Underestimating incoming call rates guaranteed unacceptable hold times. For example, as the figure below shows, a 25 percent increase in the incoming-call rate from 100 to 125 can lead to an 800 percent increase in hold time.

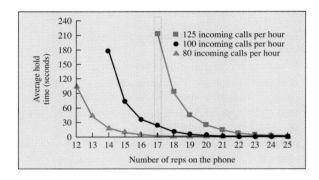

We found that hold times and abandonment rates were highly correlated: The rate of abandoned calls increases dramatically as hold times increase. (See the figure below.)

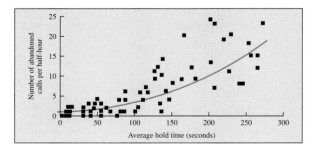

Source: MAC Group analysis of ACD data from Dallas for three days in May 1990 (heavy, medium, and light call volume).

Note: Each point on the graph represents the average hold time and the number of abandoned calls during a half-hour period.

Very conservative estimates demonstrated that abandoned calls were expensive, with the client losing at least $1,427,343 due to abandoned calls in Dallas alone. Consider the following:

· Current hold times lead to an average of 90 abandoned calls per day.[10]
· Assuming 200 business days per year, 18,000 calls are abandoned each year.
· In the first six months of 1990 alone, *7,050* customers in the Dallas market have disconnected.

Assuming that only 5 percent of these disconnects are due to not being able to get through to customer service:

· For every 25 abandoned calls, one customer will disconnect service.
· 705 Dallas customers will disconnect in 1990 due to abandonment.[11]
· Average revenue per customer is $1,524.60 per year.[12]
· Selling costs to replace these customers equals $352,500.[13]

However, eliminating hold times completely was not cost-effective, but as the following figure shows, achieving desirable hold time is.

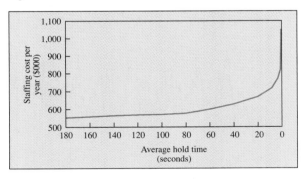

Having identified the importance of staffing, the MAC team needed to convince the client to abandon the standard one-for-every-2,500-customers rule in favor of the staffing (queueing) model that took each market's unique attributes into account.

As noted in the following figures, daily calls per 1,000 customers varied across markets, leading to widely different performance in the percentage of calls answered and average hold times.

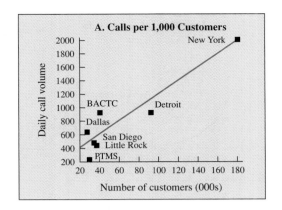

Using the staffing model, the MAC team looked at each market to determine its individual staffing requirements (assuming the current environment with no changes in operating procedures, productivity, etc.).

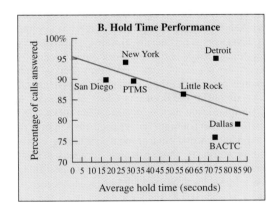

Characteristics of the Dallas Market

· Peak incoming-call rate of 100 calls per hour.
· Call-handling rate of 8 calls per rep per hour.

As the next figure shows, Dallas needs 14 reps on the phones to achieve an average hold time of 30 seconds.

---

[10] Dallas averaged 655 calls per day and an abandonment rate of 90 calls per day in November 1990.

[11] 7,050 in 6 months extrapolates to 14,100 per year. 5% of 14,100 = 705.

[12] Based on MAC Group analysis, monthly average revenue per customer is $127.05.

[13] Selling costs are $500 a customer × 705 customers.

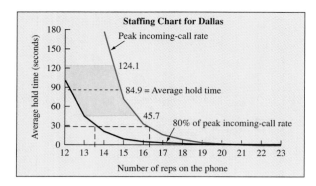

Source: ACD statistics for Dallas, August 1990.

Note: The shaded area represents a band of one standard deviation around the average hold time (indicated by the dotted line). This means that nearly 70 percent of incoming calls will encounter a hold time within the range of the shaded band.

Barrier 6: *Ill-Defined Career Path for CSRs Compounded by a Confusing Compensation System and no Formal Reward/Recognition Process*

A survey of excellent customer service companies was undertaken to benchmark several issues: compensation (entry level versus advanced), training, reward/recognition systems, career path, and work environment.

The survey's results indicated that excellent service companies paid higher than average salaries to get entry-level personnel in the door. As CSRs progressed, however, compensation as a motivator was replaced by career path, formal training, recognition/reward programs, and a positive work environment (including extensive front-line authority, demonstrated companywide commitment to customer satisfaction, etc.). In addition, the cap on salaries for CSRs who did not wish to enter management was $10,000 higher than that of the client, which led to lower turnover and a more experienced staff in general. From the survey, it was concluded that, in terms of compensation, the client offered salaries in line with those offered by the excellent service companies. However, in the other four areas, the client's offerings were well below those of the excellent service companies. All of these issues were addressed during the Dallas pilot and/or at a Customer Service Summit.

Results

This project yielded two sets of results:

1. Measurable improvements on several service dimensions as a result of the Dallas pilot.
2. An agreement on satisfaction strategy, the establishment of firmwide goals, and a transfer of knowledge gained during pilots to other divisions through the Customer Service Summit.

Toward the end of the Dallas pilot, while MAC was still involved, the client realized important improvement both quantitatively and qualitatively. The new Customer Satisfaction Survey confirmed the improvement in Dallas.

The ACD statistics indicated improvement as well. For although call volumes continued their erratic trend as shown below, the percentage of calls answered was consistently higher and hold times were trending downward (as shown in the first two figures on the next page).

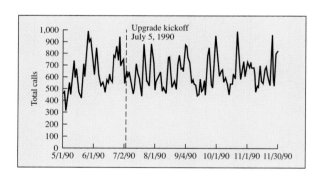

Customer Satisfaction Survey, October 1990

	Dallas							
	Sept.	**Oct.**	**BA**	**LR**	**DS**	**NY**	**PS**	**D**
Overall satisfaction	7.3	8.3	8.0	8.0	7.7	7.8	8.1	8.3
Satisfaction with customer service	8.1	8.9	8.8	8.8	8.4	8.3	8.2	8.6
Satisfaction with billing	8.2	8.6	8.4	8.8	8.3	8.4	8.0	8.2

Note: Based on a scale of 1 to 10. Number of respondents ranges from 71 to 101.

Source: Burke telephone survey.

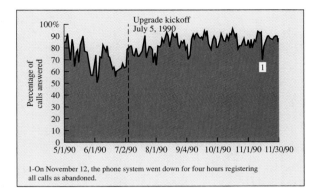

1-On November 12, the phone system went down for four hours registering all calls as abandoned.

Most importantly, these improvements occurred while successfully resolving all customer inquiries and problems within 24 hours. (See figure below.)

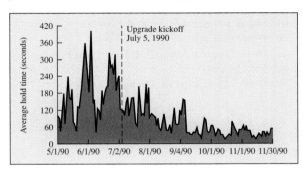

On average, phone reps were handling more customers each day. (See figures below.)

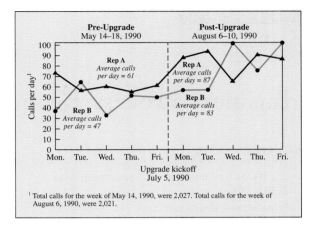

But best of all were the nonquantifiable signs of improvement:

· Gifts and flowers received by CSRs—previously a rare occurrence.

· Quotes from customers and agents:
"I wanted to let you know that Customer Service has really turned around in the last two months. They have a great attitude, and I haven't had any complaints. Thank you. I can really tell the difference."

REVIEW AND DISCUSSION QUESTIONS

1. Check out the Web sites of the consulting companies listed in the chapter outline. Which ones impressed you most as a potential client and as a potential employee?
2. What does it take to be a good consultant? Is this the career for you?

PROBLEMS

1. How did the MAC team in the Conclusion decide which issues to focus on? How did they gather data, and what OM tools did they use? How did they move between solution and implementation? What benefits did the client receive?
2. You have been asked to bid on a consulting job to increase profitability of a golf course company. It owns three courses in Cleveland, Ohio. Prepare a proposal to find out why other companies are more profitable and what to do about it.
3. Find two other students and develop a two-page prospectus describing the particular features of an OM consulting practice you would start after graduation. (Hint: Identify a target market and unique skills your team possesses that fit that market.)

SELECTED BIBLIOGRAPHY

Greiner, Larry, and Richard Savich. *Consulting to Management*. New York: Prentice-Hall, 1998.
Maister, David H. *Managing the Professional Service Firm.* The Free Press, 1993.

Upton, David, and Stephen Macadam. "Why (and How) to Take a Plant Tour." *Harvard Business Review,* May–June 1997, pp. 97–106.

Chapter 19

Business Process Reengineering

Chapter Outline

The Nature of Business Process Reengineering (BPR), 768
Principles of Reengineering, 768
The Reengineering Process, 771
    State a Case for Action
    Identify the Process
    Evaluate Enablers
    Understanding the Current Process
    Create a New Process Design
    Implement the Reengineered Process

Process Redesign Techniques and Tools, 776
Reengineering and Total Quality Management, 779
Integrating Reengineering and Process Improvement, 780
Case: A California Auto Club Reengineers Customer Service, 782
Case: Deborah Phelps of Showtime, 784

Key Terms

Reengineering

Vision Statement

Value-Adding Work

Non-Value Adding Work

Waste

Process Redesign

Total Quality Management

Continuous Improvement

www Links

U.S. Department of Defense Process Design
Methodology (http://www.dtic.dla.mil/dodim/)

"IT WAS A GUT FEELING I HAD," RECALLS JOE COL-
WIN. "We were profitable, but not as profitable as I knew we should be." He was talking about Mid-States Aluminum Corp., a 30-year-old manufacturer of customized aluminum extrusions that he bought in 1984. Located in Fond du Lac, Wisconsin, the company has increased its sales 20 percent a year since 1984—a cumulative leap of some 500 percent. But the bottom line was not increasing at anywhere near that rate.

Colwin could not understand it. He had invested heavily in workforce training, new equipment, and total quality management. Yet the bottom line remained flat. "My gut said that our 'soft costs' were eating up money that should have gone to profits," Colwin says. These costs are created by processes and tasks that often involve redundant signoffs and duplicated work—steps that produce no customer value and for which customers are not willing to pay.

Reengineering has proceeded incrementally at Mid-States since 1991, when Colwin became convinced that his company was "sick." For example, it was applied to the critical routine of producing job estimates and quotes. Analysis showed that sales personnel spent $156,526 each year to prepare estimates and quotes for customers. But only 8 percent of these quotes were converted into actual orders. A significant amount of effort and money was being spent in activity that generated no revenue. Mid-States is now redesigning its estimating process so that accurate and consistent information generated by different departments can be funneled into a single, reliable source for people creating quotes. The company has also started to produce less complex price quotes tailored to help customers make quicker decisions. Moreover, these quotes are being prepared by clerical staff, allowing sales personnel to spend more of their time selling.

"We have more focus on the customer by more people . . . the whole company is getting closer to the customer," Colwin says. ●

Source: Ronald E. Yates, "The New Fix for Corporate America's Organizational Ills? Reengineering." *Chicago Tribune*, October 17, 1993. Copyrighted Chicago Tribune Company. All rights reserved. Used with permission.

Change is the only constant in today's business environment. In fact, the 1990s have developed into the decade of radical change as businesses in the United States and around the world begin to realize that they are "entering the twenty-first century with companies designed during the nineteenth century to work well in the twentieth."[1] Organizations are now addressing the need to remain or become competitive through dramatic improvements in quality, costs, time-to-market, and customer service. They are doing this by attempting to reinvent themselves by organizing work around processes. The "de-Adam-Smithizing" of business has begun. The focus is shifting away from functional silos toward a holistic view of organizations. Such change is being made through process and organizational innovation as well as through creative application of information technology.

In this chapter we discuss business process reengineering, a management concept that many consider to be the essence of the current business revolution.

THE NATURE OF BUSINESS PROCESS REENGINEERING (BPR)

Reengineering

Vol. III
"Reengineering at
Caterpillar"

Michael Hammer, the management expert who heads the reengineering movement, defines **reengineering** as "the fundamental rethinking and radical redesign of business processes to achieve dramatic improvements in critical, contemporary measures of performance, such as cost, quality, service, and speed."[2]

The concept of reengineering has been around for nearly two decades and was implemented in a piecemeal fashion in organizations. Production organizations have been in the vanguard without knowing it. They have undertaken reengineering by implementing concurrent engineering, lean production, cellular manufacturing, group technology, and pull-type production systems. These represent fundamental rethinking of the manufacturing process. Manufacturers generally made significant improvements in their internal operations during the 1980s. But excellence in manufacturing has not always translated to superior sustainable results in the marketplace. More recently, the focus appears to have shifted out of the manufacturing process to other interfunctional and interorganizational and customer-based processes. Rapid advances in information technology and its applications have been a major enabler of business process reengineering in services.

Global interest in business process reengineering has grown rapidly. Though Japanese companies do not typically use the term *reengineering* to describe radical process change, they are very interested in developing new processes using information technology. In Korea and Singapore, one of the authors spoke with several banks that are engaged in reengineering initiatives.

PRINCIPLES OF REENGINEERING

Reengineering is about achieving a significant improvement in processes so that contemporary customer requirements of quality, speed, innovation, customization, and service are met. This entails seven new rules of doing work proposed by Hammer,

---

[1] Michael Hammer and James Champy, *Reengineering the Corporation: A Manifesto for Business Revolution* (New York: Harper Business, 1993), p. 30.

[2] Ibid., p. 32.

Reengineering has been underway at Stamford, Connecticut–based GTE Corp., the communications company that last year chalked up $2.3 billion in revenues—four-fifths from its telephone operations. Confronted by smaller, more nimble competitors, GTE has used reengineering programs to get closer to its customers. Marketing executives determined that customers wanted "one-stop shopping"—one telephone number that they can dial to solve any problem.

In early 1993, when it analyzed its customer service division, GTE found that a customer's problems were solved only once every 200 calls while the customer was still on the phone. By creating specially trained "front-end technicians" who have testing and switching equipment at the same desk where they take customers' calls, customers' problems were solved quickly, usually with "one stop." GTE now has linked sales and billing to repair via a menu of touchtone options that will let customers connect to any service they wish. The first step was to "grow" GTE operators' jobs. That was done when they were given software that allows them to access corporate databases that were once off-limits so they can now deal with just about any customer problem. These projects have so far shown a 20 to 30 percent increase in productivity.

GTE's rewired customer-contact process displays most of the salient traits of reengineering. It is occurring in a dramatically altered competitive landscape; it is a major change, with big results; it cuts across departmental lines; it requires hefty investment in training and information technology; and layoffs result. Says Michael Hammer, reengineering's John the Baptist, "To succeed at reengineering, you have to be a visionary, a motivator, and a leg breaker."

Source: Excerpted from Thomas A. Stewart, "Reengineering: The Hot New Managing Tool," *Fortune,* August 23, 1993, pp. 41–42; and Ronald E. Yates, "The New Fix for Corporate America's Organizational Ills? Reengineering," *Chicago Tribune,* October 17, 1993. Revised based on company information in May, 1997.

---

relating to who does the work, where and when it is done, and information gathering and integration.[3]

Rule 1. Organize Around Outcomes, Not Tasks   Several specialized tasks previously performed by different people should be combined into a single job. This could be performed by an individual "case worker" or by a "case team." The new job created should involve all the steps in a process that creates a well-defined outcome. Organizing around outcomes eliminates the need for handoffs, resulting in greater speed, productivity, and customer responsiveness. It also provides a single knowledgeable point of contact for the customer. GTE's "front-end technician" position described in the box above "The New GTE: Dreaming and Doing" illustrates this principle.

Rule 2. Have Those Who Use the Output of the Process Perform the Process   In other words, work should be carried out where it is makes the most sense to do it. This results in people closest to the process actually performing the work, which shifts work across traditional intra- and interorganizational boundaries. For instance, employees can make some of their own purchases without going through purchasing, customers can perform simple repairs themselves, and suppliers can be asked to

---

[3] Michael Hammer, "Reengineer Work: Don't Automate, Obliterate," *Harvard Business Review* 90, no. 4 (July–August 1990), pp. 104–12.

This team of maintenance and operating workers at Union Carbide's factory in Taft, Louisiana, tore up their old process map, created a new one, and found savings worth more than $20 million—50 percent more than what management expected.

manage parts inventory. Relocating work in this fashion eliminates the need to coordinate the performers and users of a process.

Rule 3. Merge Information-Processing Work into the Real Work that Produces the Information   This means that people who collect information should also be responsible for processing it. It minimizes the need for another group to reconcile and process that information, and greatly reduces errors by cutting the number of external contact points for a process. A typical accounts payable department that reconciles purchase orders, receiving notices, and supplier invoices is a case in point. By eliminating the need for invoices by processing orders and receiving information on-line, much of the work done in the traditional accounts payable function becomes unnecessary.

Rule 4. Treat Geographically Dispersed Resources as Though They Were Centralized   Information technology now makes the concept of hybrid centralized/decentralized operations a reality. It facilitates the parallel processing of work by separate organizational units that perform the same job, while improving the company's overall control. For instance, centralized databases and telecommunication networks now allow companies to link with separate units or individual field personnel, providing them with economies of scale while maintaining their individual flexibility and responsiveness to customers.

Rule 5. Link Parallel Activities Instead of Integrating Their Results   The concept of only integrating the outcomes of parallel activities that must eventually come together is the primary cause for rework, high costs, and delays in the final outcome of the overall process. Such parallel activities should be linked continually and coordinated during the process.

Rule 6. Put the Decision Point Where the Work Is Performed, and Build Control into the Process   Decision making should be made part of the work performed. This is possible today with a more educated and knowledgeable workforce plus decision-aiding technology. Controls are now made part of the process. The vertical compression that results produces flatter, more responsive organizations.

Rule 7. Capture Information Once—at the Source   Information should be collected and captured in the company's on-line information system only once—at the source where it was created. This approach avoids erroneous data entries and costly reentries.

The principles of business process reengineering just enumerated are based on a common platform of the innovative use of information technology. But creating a new process and sustaining the improvement requires more than a creative application of information technology.

No matter how well designed a process is, it's the people who make it work. As Marv Levy, head coach of the Buffalo Bills professional football team, has said, "Game plans don't win football games. Players do." "The only thing that distinguishes us is our people and what's in their heads and hearts," says Richard Chandler, CEO of Sunrise Medical of Torrance, California. "Your most important investment is anything that educates them and puts more in their heads or gives more motivation in their hearts."[4]

Bartlett's and Ghoshal's study of employee culture at companies successful with reengineering indicates that these companies have established employee cultures with four characteristics: discipline, support, trust, and stretch. Discipline encourages all employees to strive voluntarily to meet and exceed their own commitments. These companies have implemented support structures characterized by coaching, helping, and guiding. Trust is most easily recognized in transparent, open management processes that give employees equity and involvement. Trust is perhaps the most vital component of a management context for renewal because it is essential for risk taking. Finally, in a company in which people feel stretched, they are constantly encouraged to see themselves and the organization not in terms of its past or present constraints but in terms of its future possibilities.[5]

■ THE REENGINEERING PROCESS

Process reengineering requires innovation. (See Exhibit 19.1 for examples of what manufacturers are doing.) What is still essential is a disciplined approach to the effort. Here is a six-step plan for process reengineering:

Step 1. State a case for action.

Step 2. Identify the process for reengineering.

Step 3. Evaluate enablers of reengineering.

Step 4. Understand the current process.

Step 5. Create a new process design.

Step 6. Implement the reengineered process.

---

[4] Michael Hammer, *Beyond Reengineering* (New York: Harper Collins, 1996), p. 117.

[5] Source: Christopher A. Bartlett and Sumantra Ghoshal, "Rebuilding Behavioral Context: Turn Process Reengineering into People Rejuvenation," *Sloan Management Review*, Fall 1995, pp. 11–23.

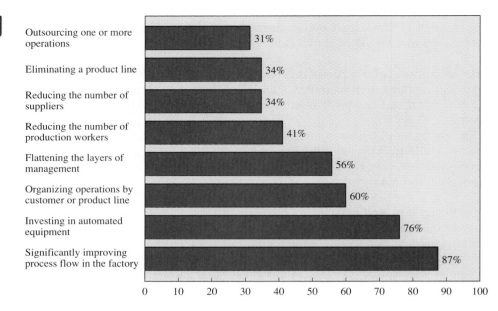

Source: Grant Thorton Survey of American Manufacturers Annual Report, p. 23. © 1993 Grant Thorton.

State a Case for Action

The need for change should be effectively communicated to company employees through educational and communication campaigns. Two key messages should be articulated: (1) a need for action ("Here is where we are as a company, and this is why we can't stay here.") and (2) a vision statement ("This is what we as a company need to become."). Exhibit 19.2 is the Harley-Davidson Motor Company vision statement as printed on the back of employee business cards.[6]

Vision Statement

The objectives for reengineering must be in the form of a qualitative and quantitative **vision statement.** These objectives can include goals for cost reduction, time-to-market, quality and customer satisfaction levels, and financial indicators. The objectives can be used to measure progress and to constantly spur ongoing action. The vision statement presented by Federal Express in its infancy is a classic example: "We will deliver the package by 10:30 the next morning." This statement provided measurable operational objectives that redefined an industry.

The company's leader is responsible for communicating these important messages, first to senior management and then to the rest of the firm. This represents the first step in communication, an activity that must be continued consistently over the duration of the reengineering project. A senior management steering committee that includes the top executive typically champions the change process, sets goals, assigns resources, and expedites progress. Redesign and implementation are typically the responsibility of a cross-functional process evaluation team.

Identify the Process

All major processes in an organization should be initially identified. However, not all major processes should be reengineered at the same time. The following questions

---

[6] Hammer and Champy, *Reengineering the Corporation*, p. 149.

CORPORATE VISION

HARLEY-DAVIDSON MOTOR COMPANY IS AN ACTION-ORIENTED COMPANY. A LEADER IN ITS COMMITMENT TO CONTINUOUSLY IMPROVE THE QUALITY OF PROFITABLE RELATIONSHIPS WITH STAKEHOLDERS (CUSTOMERS, EMPLOYEES, SUPPLIERS, SHAREHOLDERS, GOVERNMENT AND SOCIETY). HARLEY-DAVIDSON BELIEVES THE KEY TO SUCCESS IS TO BALANCE STAKEHOLDERS INTERESTS THROUGH THE EMPOWERMENT OF ALL ITS EMPLOYEES TO FOCUS ON VALUE-ADDED ACTIVITIES.

Exhibit 19.2

The Harley-Davidson Motor Company Corporate Vision

Source: The back of Anthony Reese's business card. Mr. Reese is an assembly engineer at Harley-Davidson.

define the criteria for selecting processes for reengineering:

Which processes are currently most problematic?

Which processes are critical to accomplishing company strategy and have the greatest impact on the company's customer?

Which processes are most likely to be successfully redesigned?

What is the project scope, and what are the costs involved?

What is the strength of the reengineering team, and the commitment of process owners and sponsors?

Can continuous improvement deliver the required improvements?

Is the process antiquated or is the technology used outdated?

Responses to these questions can be weighted in accordance with the company's need for improvement. The selected process should have a manageable reengineering project scope with well-defined process boundaries. Though all processes in organizations are interrelated, the limits of the current change effort must be identified.

Evaluate Enablers

Information technology and human/organizational issues act as enablers of the reengineering process. Technology evaluation has now become a core competency required of all companies. Companies should develop the ability to evaluate current and emerging information technology, and identify creative applications to redesign their existing processes. Exhibit 19.3 identifies categories in which information technology supports process reengineering. The Breakthrough box, "Mellon Trust Reengineers Workflow Management System for 401(k) Plan" on page 776, demonstrates the importance of information technology to BPR.

MIS

The current organizational culture should also be evaluated in light of the impending change to be brought about by reengineering. Participative and customer-oriented cultures that have evolved from the quality revolution of the 1980s provide a suitable environment for further change. But the magnitude of change created by process redesign makes the management of change a necessity. Issues of measurement and compensation, career paths, work enrichment, and new skills training should be addressed. The appropriate design of these factors will have significant impact on the successful implementation of the reengineered process.

Source: Reprinted by permission of Harvard Business School Press from *Process Innovation: Reengineering Work Through Information Technology* by Thomas H. Davenport. Boston: 1993, p. 51. Copyright 1993 by The President and Fellows of Harvard College, all rights reserved.

Exhibit 19.3	Impact	Explanation
The Impact of Information Technology on Process Innovation	Automational	Eliminating human labor from a process
	Informational	Capturing process information for purposes of understanding
	Sequential	Changing process sequence or enabling parallelism
	Tracking	Closely monitoring process status and objects
	Analytical	Improving analysis of information and decision making
	Geographical	Coordinating processes across distances
	Integrative	Coordination between tasks and processes
	Intellectual	Capturing and distributing intellectual assets
	Disintermediating	Eliminating intermediaries from a process

Understanding the Current Process

The current process must be diagnosed as a means to understand it and its relationship to other processes. Process evaluation techniques such as flow charts, fishbone diagrams, and quality function deployment are used. Because the purpose is not to fix the old process but to create a new, radically better, process, there is no need for detailed time and motion studies.

The current process must be studied to understand the activities which are essential to completion. We need to introduce some terminology to describe component activities to aid our analysis.[7] All work activities can be classified into three types:

Value-Adding Work

Non-Value-Adding Work

Waste

- **Value-adding work,** or work for which the customer is willing to pay.
- **Non-value-adding work,** which creates no value for the customer but is required in order to get the value-adding work done.
- **Waste,** or work that neither adds nor enables value.

Value-adding work is easy to identify. It consists of all of the activities that create the goods and services that customers want. If a customer wants an order filled, value-adding activities include inventory allocation, picking, packing, route planning, and shipping. Value-adding work can rarely be eliminated from a process, although it can be improved.

Waste work is pointless work whose absence would, by definition, not be noticed by the customer. Producing reports that no one reads, doing work erroneously so that it needs to be redone, and redundant checking activities are all waste work. Waste work needs to be eliminated.

Non-value-adding work is the glue that binds together the value-adding work in conventional processes. It is mainly administrative overhead—the reporting, checking, supervising, controlling, reviewing, and coordinating. It is work that is needed to make conventional processes function, but it is also the source of errors, delay, inflexibility, and rigidity. Michael Hammer argues that it is necessary to design non-value-adding work out by reorganizing the value-adding tasks into a new and more efficient process.

---

[7] Adapted from Hammer, *Beyond Reengineering*, p. 33.

Create a New Process Design

Process redesign requires beginning with a clean sheet of paper. The creative nature of innovation makes it nonalgorithmic and nonroutine. Reengineers should suspend current rules, procedures, and values so as to create new process designs. They also need to utilize the principles of reengineering that have been discerned.

Process Redesign

The first emphasis in reengineering a process is to eliminate all waste work. Waste work can often be eliminated immediately during the reengineering effort. Next, the focus is on the elimination of non-value-adding work. Hammer has found in his work that it is not at all uncommon to find less than 10 percent of the activities in a process to be value-adding! The next section on Process Redesign Techniques and Tools discusses some important methods and tools applied in the process redesign phase of reengineering.

The consequences of redesigning processes to reduce non-value-adding work are significant. A major outcome is that jobs become bigger and more complex. To understand why this happens, consider that when work is broken into small and simple tasks, one needs complex processes full of non-value-adding glue—reviews, managerial audits, checks, approvals, transfers, and so forth—to put them back together. The way to avoid using so much glue is to start with bigger fragments—in other words, bigger jobs.

The experience at GTE (see the box on page 769) in reengineering their system for responding to customer electricity outages is typical. At GTE, responding to a customer's report of an outage involves three value-adding tasks: (1) getting the information from the customer, (2) checking GTE's own equipment and lines, and (3) if necessary, dispatching a repair person. Formerly performed by three specialists, all three tasks are now performed by one person, a customer care advocate. When three people are involved, there is a need for coordination, communication, and checking; this is not the case when only one person is involved.

Much of this book is focused on how best to organize and perform the value-adding activities; thus, in this section, we will not discuss any of these specific activities. Once waste and non-value-added activities are eliminated, the task of determining the best method for performing the new job can be challenging. The task involves the selection of the appropriate technology and may require specialized training to prepare the worker for the new job.

Implement the Reengineered Process

Leadership is critical, not just to the implementation process, but to the entire reengineering effort. The extent of change necessitates the direct and continued engagement on the part of the senior executive and the senior management steering committee. Process engineering teams are typically responsible for implementing the new designs. However, support and buy-in from line managers are crucial to success because implementation changes accountabilities of line managers while expecting them to deliver on the improvements. Training employees in additional skills needed to perform in the new environment is also essential. The reengineered process design forms the basis for a pilot project that is followed by phased introduction. Postimplementation assessment is usually made in relation to the objectives defined at the beginning of the reengineering project.

BREAKTHROUGH

Mellon Trust Reengineers Workflow Management System for 401(k) Plan

Fraught with change, the defined-contribution business presents opportunities only for those financial institutions that can meet the challenge of radically escalated customer expectations. Mellon Bank Corp.'s Master Trust Services is meeting this challenge by transforming the way it conducts business, using sophisticated technology to reengineer its information systems and workflow management.

Valuing 401(k) plans daily requires the latest in record-keeping and voice-response technology, which helps provide plan participants with 24-hour access to up-to-date investment information. With this data, participants can make informed decisions, tracking their holdings and transferring funds should their investment objectives require it.

Previously, the Mellon Trust defined-contribution department operated on a defined-benefit philosophy, revolving around monthly processing. But even with the monthly lead time, the operational components of cash management, reconciling Mellon record keeping with client payroll, and working in an automated manner with outside fund managers presented challenges to outmoded technology and workflow management. Up to 50 percent of a trust employee's time had been consumed by non-value-added activities, such as typing, photocopying and coordinating information that is not universally disseminated.

With this old system, trust employees were forced to concentrate on the process rather than the customer. Up to six copies of a document had to be produced and distributed between several different floors in two separate buildings. This constant passing of data back and forth not only took up valuable time, but created a propensity for potential errors. And these procedures were also less responsive.

Mellon Trust's Workflow Management System

Enlisting the expertise of an outside consultant enabled Mellon Trust to verify its BPR concepts as sound and determine that the concepts were economically feasible, says Barber. The consultant also developed a demonstration system for Mellon employees "like a little lab room," Barber adds. This system simulation was not only an excellent tool for orienting employees but for marketing as well. Potential clients were shown the system to exhibit Mellon's dedication to improving service quality.

Mellon describes the new workflow management system as an "intelligent" system that automatically, electronically manages and coordinates information associated with each step of the 401(k) process and each related department. Based on architecture consisting of an image server, PC workstations and local area networks (LAN), the system uses digital imaging to capture and display on workstations images of physical documents such as letters, forms and faxes. The system allows processing to be done at individual workstations while providing access to multiple mainframe systems and databases, and it is designed to facilitate report management by replacing paper or microfiche reports with computerized output to laser disk.

With this new system, each department captures and stores incoming client faxes directly into the system via fax modem. Documents received through the mail will be scanned into the system manually. A plan administrator reviews each image at his or her workstation to determine what action the account requires, entering the appropriate process codes and related information. The system then creates an electronic file "folder" and routes it to the appropriate departments via the LAN for further processing. The system audits each electronic file folder, and if any information is missing or incorrect, the system allows the plan administrator to write a brief note that is either automatically faxed back to the client or input into an automatic "call back" reminder. Once one activity in the service process is complete, the person responsible for the next step sees it queued on his or her workstation along with processing instructions. Each workstation automatically interfaces with all

■ PROCESS REDESIGN TECHNIQUES AND TOOLS

 Inductive Thinking   This involves recognizing potential solutions and then seeking and recognizing obvious or latent problems that may be solved. This approach is required in the creative application of information technology to reengineer processes.

mainframe systems so that it eliminates the effort of logging-on and accessing multiple systems, as well as the need to constantly re-enter data such as account name and number.

The Company expects this new system to yield benefits in four areas:

Quality—The new system should:
- reduce errors due to a lack of information;
- immediately detect processing difficulties;
- facilitate employee training in how to avoid errors;
- eliminate re-entry of data into multiple systems;
- automatically track and report service quality measures;
- build in work rules and error detection; and
- decrease risks associated with missed steps or misinterpretations of data.

Service—The new system should:
- easily accommodate customized service requests;
- produce accurate client status reports instantaneously;
- make management reports customized, more timely, and more accurate;
- foster teamwork and client interaction;
- provide on-line responses to customer inquiries without delay;
- archive all documents and back-up notes in an electronic file folder; and
- automatically log all service inquiries.

Speed—The new system should:
- eliminate delays due to missing reminders or lack of follow-up;
- reduce work cycles with parallel processing;
- enable easier, quicker reallocation of staff resources to avoid backlogs;
- keep routine work flowing by eliminating time-consuming meetings and memos;

- implement revisions to processing requirements; and
- eliminate delays due to manual copying, logging and retrieving of files.

Control—The new system should:
- help enforce standard procedures:
- ensure that work files are accurate and up-to-date via a common workflow database;
- improve accountability by clearly defining which person is responsible for every step;
- automatically generate operating statistics for management review;
- automatically generate reminders and system checks;
- electronically create and seal audit trials; and
- guard against inadvertent or unwanted system disruptions through security control.

From Transactions to Relationships

The new workflow management system will be rolled out over the next nine months. In this period, the BPR team will reclassify jobs and train staff on the new operating environment, as well as bring new clients onto the new system.

Once the new system is in place, employees will receive technical training. Barber estimates that a telephone rep might need a week or two of training; client services people might require two to four half-day sessions. Even though the system has a user-friendly, icon-driven, Windows-like environment, it will require "a significant amount of training, even for casual users," Barber says. "You can have the best system in the world, but the people have to know how to use it to its potential."

Source: Reprinted with permission from *Industrial Engineering Magazine,* May 1994. Copyright 1994, Institute of Industrial Engineers, 25 Technology Park, Norcross, Georgia 30092, 770-449-0461.

For instance, the use of teleconferencing is not to eliminate business travel entirely but to be able to get more individuals working together.

Flowcharting   Though mentioned previously under "Understanding the Current Process" on page 774, flow charts or blueprints are the fundamental tool when initiating BPR. The flow chart may be the only tool that is used in 100 percent of the applications of BPR. They can be simple, such as boxes and arrows placed on a huge roll of brown paper that is then rolled out along a wall. (This was used by consultants studying BellSouth telephone company to help categorize 81 processes into the 13 most important "process streams" of the business.[8]) Or, flow charts can be made using sophisticated proprietary charting software packages.

Creative Process Redesign   Applying the principles of reengineering discussed in the beginning of this chapter is an approach to creative process redesign. Questioning the assumptions that underlie current business practices leads to new methods. Many successes in process reengineering are in the areas of purchasing and procurement. These have arisen because of challenging long-held beliefs. Eliminating the rule that the supplier is a business adversary has led to sharing operational information to improve the combined performance of both supplier and buyer. The need for invoices as a prerequisite for payment has been altered. Reengineered firms now pay on receipt of goods, thus eliminating the need for invoices.

Process Benchmarking   Benchmarking is usually considered a continuous improvement tool, but it can also be used to gain information regarding a company's relative position in key business processes and core competencies. During the initial stages of a reengineering program, benchmarking can help create an industry context for the goals being set. Benchmarking will also provide a firm with examples of best practices in terms of new processes and the approach to their implementation. Benchmarking's value is not just to imitate another company's processes. Practitioners report that benchmarking's most important value in the reengineering process is that a team's imagination is stimulated when it sees creative solutions implemented by the companies being benchmarked. In some cases there may be no external standard for comparison.

Simulation   Discrete-event computer simulation and animation can be very useful in understanding processes. The simulations could be used to visualize and evaluate the redesigned processes. This can be accomplished even before the pilot project stage, providing reengineers with an appropriate tool for evaluating new processes.

Reengineering Software   There is adequate software available to help draw detailed process maps, and software tools for understanding existing processes and designing new ones are being developed on the basis of the U.S. Dept. of Defense process design methodology called Integrated Definition (IDEF). For details about IDEF, see the Web site at http://www.dtic.dla.mil/dodiml. Texas Instruments' Business Design Facility and Meta Software's Design/IDEF are two such tools that facilitate modeling and evaluation of business processes.[9] The availability of such software tools and methodologies aids the redesign phase of process reengineering. The ultimate exercise, however, is an overall migration plan to move the organization from the current state to a vastly improved future state. Reengineering software tools should be utilized within this framework.

---

[8] Connie Brittain, "Reengineering Complements BellSouth's Major Business Strategies," *Industrial Engineering,* February 1994, pp. 34–36.

[9] "The Role of IT in Business Reengineering," *I/S Analyzer* 31, no. 8 (August 1993), pp. 11–14.

■ REENGINEERING AND TOTAL QUALITY MANAGEMENT

The ideas developed in this chapter have emerged since the early 1990s. **Total quality management** (TQM), a topic covered in-depth in Chapter 6, is often compared to reengineering. Some people have said that the two are, in fact, the same, while others have even argued that they are incompatible. Michael Hammer argues that the two concepts are compatible and actually compliment one another. Both concepts are centered on a customer focus. The concepts of teamwork, worker participation and empowerment, cross-functionality, process analysis and measurement, supplier involvement, and benchmarking are significant contributions from quality management. In addition, the need for a "total" view of the organization has been reemphasized by quality management in an era of extensive functionalization of business. Quality management has also influenced company culture and values by exposing organizations to the need for change.

Quality management has emphasized **continuous** and incremental **improvement** of processes that are in control. Reengineering, on the other hand is about radical discontinuous change through process innovation. Exhibit 19.4 illustrates how TQM and reengineering fit together over time in the life of a process. First, the process is enhanced until its useful lifetime is over, at which point it is reengineered. Then, enhancement is resumed and the entire cycle starts again. Hammer points out that this is not a once-in-a-lifetime endeavor. As business circumstances change in major ways, so must process designs.

Exhibit 19.5 contains a list of some similarities and differences between TQM/Continuous Improvement and reengineering. The dissimilarities that have been identified may create an impression that reengineering is outside the realm of quality management. The reengineering guru Hammer, together with quality gurus such as Deming and Juran, all agree that innovation and breakthroughs in processes are an essential part of quality management. TQM assumes that the design of the process is sound and that all it needs is some enhancement. But if the world has changed dramatically since the process was first (or most recently) designed, the current design may be fundamentally flawed and incapable of delivering the required performance. Reengineering is then necessary.

Total Quality Management

Continuous Improvement

Exhibit 19.4

Illustration of How TQM and Reengineering Fit Together over the Life of a Process

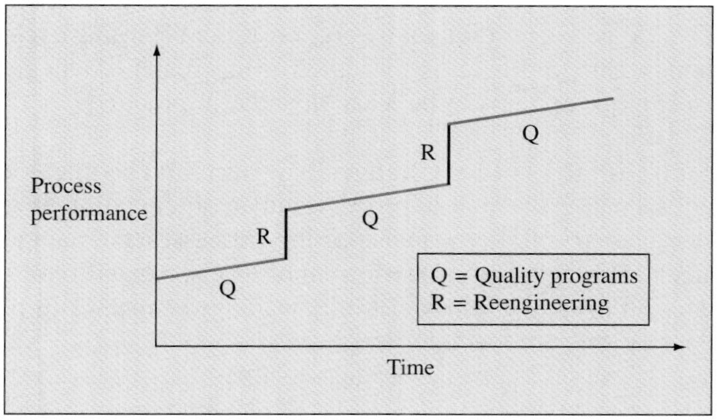

Source: Michael Hammer, *Beyond Reengineering* (New York: Harper Collins, 1996), p. 83.

	Reengineering	TQM/Continuous Improvement
Similarities		
Basis of analysis	Processes	Processes
Performance measurement	Rigorous	Rigorous
Organizational change	Significant	Significant
Behavioral change	Significant	Significant
Time investment	Substantial	Substantial
Differences		
Level of change	Radical	Incremental
Starting point	Clean slate	Existing process
Participation	Top-down	Bottom-up
Typical scope	Broad, cross-functional	Narrow, within functions
Risk	High	Moderate
Primary enabler	Information technology	Statistical control
Type of change	Cultural and structural	Cultural

Reprinted by permission of Harvard Business School Press from *Process Innovation: Reengineering Work Through Information Technology* by Thomas H. Davenport. Boston: 1993, p. 11. Copyright 1993 by the President and Fellows of Harvard College.

◼ INTEGRATING REENGINEERING AND PROCESS IMPROVEMENT

Organizations must develop a framework for placing reengineering activity in the context of other change initiatives they may undertake. It should not be considered the once and for all "big fix." Integrating will help keep the different change initiatives' expectations, methods, and results distinct from each other, thereby minimizing the confusion and cynicism that usually result from undertaking an assortment of management initiatives. Four approaches to integrating process improvement and reengineering activities in organizations are discussed next.[10]

Sequencing Change Initiatives   This approach suggests cycling through process stabilization, process reengineering, and continuous improvement. The disadvantage for such an initiative is that it may take at least five years to go through one cycle of change, which would be longer than many organizational learning cycles and product life cycles. Though this approach is discussed to a greater extent in management literature, the technique appears to be least valuable in practice.

Creating a Portfolio of Process Change Programs   This method involves the categorization of all processes and subprocesses in an organization on the basis of the type of change necessary. Criteria for selecting processes for reengineering could include relevance to strategy, current performance levels, capability of sponsor, available investment, and history of change. Many leading companies in process reengineering are adopting this approach to integration.

---

[10] Thomas H. Davenport, "Need Radical Innovation and Continuous Improvement? Integrate Process Reengineering and TQM," *Planning Review,* May–June 1993, pp. 6–12.

Limiting the Scope of Work Design   In this approach, high-level processes are designed by the responsible reengineering teams. But employees who perform the jobs design the detail work processes involved within the specifications decided by the reengineering team. This is an attempt to combine the participative nature of continuous improvement with the top-down approach common to process reengineering.

Undertaking Improvement through Innovation   This approach combines short-term improvement methods and long-term reengineering in the same process-change effort. Improvement methods such as value analysis can be used to obtain quick benefits, which are then invested in the longer-term reengineering effort. The improvement projects may also be a means to move the current process forward to a stage where radical process change is possible.

The different approaches to process change are complementary. Organizations need to determine how and when they need to apply the appropriate methods to their different processes. While it is important to have an integrated approach to operational change, it is far more important to effect that change.

◼ CONCLUSION

Although we have presented reengineering in a positive light, it is not a panacea. Like any other management approach, how you apply it makes a difference.[11] Nevertheless, it appears that reengineering will eventually affect most organizations. The revolution in computer technology that is a central feature of reengineering virtually guarantees this happening.

Operations management resides at the very heart of reengineering. This text tries to convey the understanding and the management of processes by which goods and services are created. Reengineering involves integrating all of the operations concepts to come up with a new, more intelligent way of running the organization.

REVIEW AND DISCUSSION QUESTIONS

1. Think about the registration process at your university. Develop a flow chart to understand it. How would you radically redesign this process?
2. Have you driven any car lately? Try not to think of the insurance claims settlement process while you drive! How would you reengineer your insurance company's claims process?
3. Identify the typical processes in manufacturing firms. Discuss how the new product development process interacts with the traditional functions in the firm.
4. An order management process is at the heart of a company's operations. It begins with the customer placing an order with the company and continues through to the customer's receipt of that order and the firm's receipt of payment. Draw a flowchart describing this process. Identify organizational and information technology enablers that would help you innovate the order management process.

---

[11] An example of misapplication is Greyhound Lines, Inc.'s poorly designed and implemented Trips reservation system that according to *The Wall Street Journal* (October 20, 1994, pp. A1, A10) still can't assure a passenger a seat on a given bus.

5. Sketch a typical materials procurement process that exists in functional organizations. Using reengineering principles, challenge the status quo and redesign this process.

6. An equipment manufacturer has the following steps in its order entry process:
   a. Sales representative takes order and faxes to Order Entry.
   b. Enter order into system (10 percent unclear or incorrect).
   c. Check stock availability (stock not available for 15 percent of orders).
   d. Perform customer credit check. (Ten percent of orders have credit questions.)
   e. Send bill of materials to warehouse.

   The order-receipt to warehouse cycle time is typically 48 hours, 80 percent of the orders are handled without error, and order handling costs are 6 percent of order revenue. Should you reengineer this process, or is continuous improvement the appropriate approach? If you choose to reengineer, how would you go about it?

Case

A California Auto Club Reengineers Customer Service

For the 3 million members who count on its services, the California State Automobile Association (CSAA) often seems like a trusted member of the family.

Yet CSAA is no mom-and-pop operation. Were it a publicly traded corporation, CSAA, with its $3.2 billion in assets, would rank on the *Fortune* 500 list of America's largest diversified financial companies. Its 5,700 employees operate in a network of 72 district offices throughout its membership territory in Northern California and Nevada. CSAA's diversified operations range from tour books and emergency road services to airline ticketing, auto and homeowners insurance, and travelers checks.

Two years ago CSAA embarked on a long-term reengineering effort. From an operations center on the 23rd floor of its San Francisco headquarters, teams of employees have been putting every business process under a microscope. They are seeking ways to make operations better and more efficient, while rekindling the close relationship with members that had been CSAA's trademark.

"It was obvious that the old ways of doing business wouldn't work in the future, and that we needed to make some fundamental changes," says Gregory A. Smith, vice president and general manager of insurance operations. The goals are to improve customer service threefold; to reduce baseline expenses by as much as 20 percent; and to enrich jobs and enhance career growth for employees. For the daily transactions that are the bread and butter of the organization, the targeted process time reductions are also ambitious: 2 days to renew an automobile policy instead of 25; 2 days for a new homeowners policy instead of 21; 7 minutes for hotel reservations instead of 13.

A Reengineered Job

Through its reengineering effort, CSAA has designed a new system for serving customers centering around a new position called "member service consultant." The people serving in this job will be capable of handling 80 percent of a member's needs, from renting a car to making an insurance claim. Specialists will field the remaining calls or visits that require additional expertise.

Supporting the service consultant will be a new information system that links data that currently resides in three separate systems. This technology will enable a service consultant to respond to most members on the spot.

Business reengineering at CSAA is very much a work in progress, with pilot programs and tests scheduled for rollout through 1993. Before the reengineering effort was launched in February 1991, however, a preliminary phase was designed to find "quick hits"—immediate, tangible steps to streamline operations.

Three Quickies

One quick hit was to authorize field offices to give insured members a proof of coverage form that previously had to be routed through CSAA headquarters. Another streamlining step was to expand the expiration time for membership cards to two years instead of one, resulting in savings of about $500,000. Average turnaround time for processing new business applications was reduced from six days to three days; and the proportion of new auto policies that had to be "reworked" (processed more than once) dropped from 50 percent to 16 percent. In total, the quick hits resulted in estimated savings of nearly $4 million.

A Comprehensive Survey

Four employee teams, reflecting the range of CSAA's operations—sales and underwriting, claims, service delivery (representing the main functional areas)—were formed along with a strategic marketing team to focus on broader issues. These teams undertook the most comprehensive survey of CSAA members and employees in the organization's history. Members were asked about CSAA services and products in focus groups and during visits to district offices. Employees were asked a range of questions about their work including, "What would you do if you were president of CSAA for a day?"

The surveys showed remarkable coherence between the issues cited by members and employees. Most of the frustrations for both groups concerned the highly segmented way that CSAA's services were provided. A member visiting a typical office had to go to one window for an insurance claim, another for a road map, and still others for registration renewals, travelers checks, and additional services. As James P. Molinelli, executive vice president described it, "That's not service—that's a pinball effect." If a member phoned in for help, the CSAA staffer answering questions about underwriting couldn't handle a question about travel or claims, and had to refer callers to another phone number.

Telephone Gridlock

The whole issue of telephone service emerged as a headache for members and employees alike. Members spoke of confusing recorded messages and long waiting periods in limbo while on hold. By one estimate, up to 30 percent of callers were hanging up before being helped. Rather than battle the telephone log jam, some members were making personal visits to district offices for their transactions. However, increasing personnel at the offices was not only expensive, it didn't solve the long-term problem.

Furthermore, members and employees alike said that CSAA's activities had become so varied that it was difficult to understand the range of services. For example, many holders of automobile insurance policies said they were unaware that CSAA also offered homeowners insurance.

In addition to the internal issues, the reengineering effort also had to address an operating environment that was increasingly difficult and complex. New competition is entering every arena of CSAA's business, from car manufacturers offering their own emergency road services to companies providing computer systems that let travelers book airline flights from their homes.

Get Crazy

The reengineering teams are tackling these and other issues in a series of meetings that the service-delivery team describes as "Get Smart—Get Crazy—Get Serious —Get Going."

"The ground rules for the meetings were—no hidden agendas, be open and honest, and have a sense of urgency," says Phyllis M. Love, manager of mail and records processing, who serves on the teams. "At meetings there's a lot of back and forth, negotiation, and compromise."

The central issue that emerged was the fragmented way that CSAA services were dispensed—insurance underwriting here, travel services there. The member service consultant was a key innovation, but making it work required intensive cross-training for employees on the range of CSAA services, and a computer system that would pull all the vital information together and make it readily available. In the fall of 1991, three employees from field offices went to headquarters for an intensive, three-week cross-training program. They also helped design, develop, and test a prototype system that would support the new service consultant.

The acid test for the new business model came when the group began acting out scenarios simulating work in the CSAA office of the future. "Members" played by employees would interact with an employee playing the role of the service consultant. Needed modifications in the business model were identified, and within two months simulations were being conducted for senior CSAA management.

Meanwhile, the teams adhered to a policy of "communicate, communicate, communicate" to the entire CSAA workforce. Workshops and meetings in the field, posters and newsletters, and a series of videotapes called *New Directions* explained the rationale for the program, and helped prepare the workforce for the transition.

Sell with Scenarios

The powerful new information system will liberate the service consultants from a paper-intensive, error-prone work environment. On-screen prompts will announce changes in regulations and procedures, replacing stacks of thumbtacked memos that now fill up bulletin boards. The system will also allow the running of rapid "what-if" scenarios for a member who wants to know, for example, how changing the deductible will affect her insurance premium.

The reengineering effort is now being carried forward by five interdisciplinary teams whose focus includes workforce retraining, reward and performance measurement, and information technology.

"We're trying to create a learning environment for the future, for all levels of employees from clerical to management," says John Clark, a regional claims manager who has served on two reengineering teams.

A One Stop Shop

There's a "back to the future" aspect to the reengineering effort. "In the past, when district offices were smaller, a member could walk in and talk to anybody on the staff about any problem. Everyone in the office had to know something about everything, and members could get complete service with just one stop," says James P. Molinelli, executive vice president. Now, CSAA's best practices of the past are about to re-emerge with a distinctly contemporary look.

Questions

1. Describe the customer service process at CSAA and discuss the different phases of the reengineering effort.

2. Discuss process enablers' role developing the new design.

Source: Reprinted from Robert S. Buday, "Reengineering One Firm's Product Development and Another's Service Delivery," *Planning Review,* March–April 1993, pp. 17–19. Reprinted with permission from The Planning Forum, the International Society for Strategic Management and Planning.

Case

Deborah Phelps of Showtime

In 1991, Showtime Networks decided that it had to reinvent its billing and collection processes. The old system was costing Viacom Inc., the owner of the Movie Channel, Showtime, and other premium cable TV channels, $10 million a year in direct write-offs and even more in lost sales.

In the cable TV industry, operators of local cable systems buy programming from companies like Showtime. The contracts generally call for the cable operator to pay a fee for each customer who uses a particular service. The cable operators keep tallies of subscribers and calculate the monthly payments. Showtime's audit department checked the subscriber tallies and payments, but it got around to only about one-third of its clients each year, so errors could drag on and compound themselves over as many as three years. A $15,000 mistake could grow to more than half a million dollars over 36 months. As a result, it wasn't unusual for Showtime's financial department to phone customers and tell them that they owed several hundred thousand dollars in back fees. Naturally, this led to disputes, and Showtime often settled these conflicts by writing off some of the charges—to the tune of about $10 million a year, or 2 percent of its revenue.

But the $10 million a year was only a small fraction of the true cost of Showtime's poor billing practices. Because angry clients weren't eager to buy new services, sales representatives wasted time smoothing ruffled feathers and straightening out misunderstandings when they should have been out selling more services. Something had to be done.

Before Showtime's transformation, Deborah Phelps was a collection representative in the credit department. Today, she is a financial service representative, leading a process team that handles everything from writing

contracts to collecting payments to answering customers questions.

Before, I handled a portfolio of regional accounts. I kept track of whether customers were paying us on time. If there were problems, I'd call them. But if they said they didn't owe anything, I'd do the paperwork and have it signed off by my supervisor, who had it signed off by the director, who had it signed off by the vice president.

If it wasn't the right amount, I didn't worry about that. I was just concerned about whether it was on time. In fact, I didn't even know if it was the right amount; I didn't have enough information to know that. I just knew whether we got a check for January's license payments. That was all I did.

The accounts receivable department worried about whether it was correct. It would come to their attention when their data-entry clerks entered the payment. If something came up on the screen that looked inappropriate, the data-entry clerk would take it to his or her supervisor, who would take it to the manager, to the director, and on and on. There was no group of people who actively understood what the contracts and deals entailed, or who could speak with affiliates to correct the situation.

It was a very hierarchical system—very rigid and very traditional. I had a manager; I reported to him. He reported to the director, and the director reported to the vice president. At no point would anyone speak to anyone else unless they were directly above them. You really had to follow the chain of command. For the first year, I didn't think my department head knew who I was because we never spoke. It was the classic organization where you didn't cross any lines and you spoke only to the person you reported to.

Other people in my area also did collections, but we had no interaction. They didn't work on my accounts, and I didn't work on theirs. I might go to them to find out how to process a certain form, but they had no knowledge of the specifics of my accounts. It was just me and my boss.

Then, in June of 1992, Showtime's chief financial officer, Jerry Cooper, and the CEO, Tony Cox, held a town meeting about how the company was hurting itself with some of its business procedures. They focused on how our system of auditing payments often resulted in arguments with the clients and in settlements that essentially threw money out the window. They also pointed out how we irritated clients when they called us by transferring them all over the place. That was true. I only did one function, so if someone got my name because I was helpful, I couldn't help with anything else because I didn't know what was going on.

The executives did a presentation on these problems and on how we had to improve the relationship between our own financial department and the sales staff so we could become more customer-service oriented. At that point, they introduced the concept of reengineering. I'd worked for another organization that operated in team mode, and I remembered how rewarding it was. I thought it was wonderful that they were going to do it here. Then, I was lucky enough to be selected to work on the pilot project.

It couldn't have come at a better time for me. Before that, I was pretty bored and thinking about leaving Showtime. It's a really creative company, but it was rigid. I felt like I was in a box.

My team was myself, someone from accounts receivable, and a couple of people from audit. We moved from the accounting area to another part of the building. There was a real team sense to it. It wasn't like, "This is my job and I'm not interacting with other people." When I think back on all my work experience at Showtime, this was probably the most exciting time for me.

The first thing we did was to cross-train each other. I had to learn how to interpret our contracts, how we billed customers, and how they paid. I learned that it wasn't enough for a customer to send us a check; I had to understand whether the payment was correct. That was a big piece. Until that point, I didn't understand the deals and contracts. I also had to understand a little about what our auditors do. And I had to have a more global sense of our business, which I didn't have until then.

We also had liaisons with field sales. They met with us and talked about contracts and about what they did.

The biggest piece of our work was to identify what happened in our different work areas, then figure out how to make it work better. We looked at the whole audit process—accounts receivable, collection, credit, and billings—and we tried to figure out how a team of four or five people could handle all those functions and eliminate the handoffs. Our goal was to make it one-stop shopping for our field sales people as well as for our customers.

The team was very participatory, not at all like the old hierarchical system. I felt that what I thought counted and that our leader rolled up his shirtsleeves to work with us. In a hierarchy, you're not party to a lot of what's going on because it's behind the scenes. In this environment, pretty much everything was on the table.

Within the team it took us a while to figure out how we were going to work. We were told there were no rules and to

be as creative as we could. Maybe for the first week or two, I thought, "Do they really mean that?" Then, I just went for it, as did some other people. I felt we'd been given this golden opportunity. But some people held back.

After about six months we took the pilot program department-wide. There was a town meeting led by the chief financial officer and the new head of the financial services department, Tom Hayden. At that session, Tom answered questions about what would be happening with everyone's job. He also set a time to meet with every person in the department for a half-hour talk about their concerns and what they'd like to do in the organization.

When we introduced the new plan, some people thought it was really exciting and challenging. But others never quite understood it and were resistant. The implementation phase has been difficult for a lot of people. Some weren't able to adapt and had to leave the company.

When the program was first rolled out, I applied to be a team leader. But I wasn't chosen, so I became one of four financial account specialists on a team that was based in New York, but with a leader in Denver. Because the leader wasn't in the same office, it called for a lot of initiative from the team members. I ended up assuming a leadership position because I took more initiative than anyone else on the team.

If a problem came up, I suggested we get together as a team and purpose a solution rather than just calling Denver and asking for one. I think I was pretty instrumental in pulling the team together for meetings on a regular basis. There were also a lot of meetings among the leadership team—all the team leaders. Since our leader was in Denver, I was always called in to represent my team. This gave me a lot of information firsthand that I shared with the rest of my team. I tried to solicit input and opinions from everyone as often as possible.

There's been a lot of reshuffling of the teams since we first put them together. Eventually, it was decided that the team leaders had to be in the same location as the teams. I was promoted to be a team leader, and I moved to Chicago, which was the area we serviced. Normally, the team does the hiring of new members. But in this instance, I was the only one left on the team, so I basically hired the two new people. I looked for people with high energy and experience in the industry. The two people I eventually hired came with impeccable references from the Chicago office. I thought it would be a real ace in the hole if I could come in with people who already had contacts and had proven themselves in Chicago.

At a recent training session in New York, we did some teambuilding exercises and talked about our goals. We looked at the department's vision statement and wrote a vision statement for our team. I think people are starting to feel that the company's goals and objectives are theirs rather than something that was just handed down. We've also looked at areas we thought we need to work on.

On my team last year, one difficult issue was taking initiative and taking full ownership of the work. When we went through our organizational shake-up, a number of people were asked to leave. Most of them had been with the company for a long time. I think they'd become comfortable and weren't used to going the extra mile. They were told they had to take more initiative and participate more. That's not a problem on our team now; there's a lot of initiative and risk taking.

Another important thing about teams is that your work really affects the other members. So we have had to learn to give feedback and deal with each other. It's really difficult to try to change behavior, but it can be done. One person on our team didn't respond until her teammates started giving her direct feedback. She hadn't paid much attention when she'd been getting direction from her boss because she figured that the supervisor "doesn't know what I do anyway." But when she heard the same thing from four members of her team, she really took it to heart. She was offered assistance in getting up to speed, and she took it. People would say, "What do you need? What gets in the way of your following through?" And she'd work on learning.

For example, she wasn't very well trained in the accounts receivable process, so our expert sat down with her and went through the whole system while she took notes and asked questions. I think she came as far as she did because she had a real desire to be with the company, and although she was struggling, she saw the benefits of the new work style. I think there were people who didn't care and didn't see any benefit in trying to change.

Under the team system, there's no place to hide and eventually everything becomes apparent. In New York, there was this really nice person that everyone liked, but we were finding all these mistakes. After a while, other members of the team got frustrated at the work that wasn't getting done right and the extra time they had to put in. It caught up with him. When we did a reevaluation of the organization, we were told to look at performance, not personality. People were really honest, and he came up short.

Another thing that's changed in our new, flatter organization is that you have to look at the whole concept of promotions differently. It's no longer about achieving the next level, it's about increasing your skills set and getting compensated for it. In my current position, I want to develop sales skills so I can interface better with our affiliates. We're selling an idea to them in addition to just performing a service. Regional directors in the sales organization have some skills that I don't have, like contract negotiation.

There's a lot of room for growth and movement. I could move from being a regional team leader to being the team leader of a national accounts group team. It's a larger portfolio of accounts—more subscribers, greater revenue.

At one time, if you were a bean counter, you were always a bean counter. Today, we have people who moved from financial services into the sales organization, and other people who moved from sales into financial services. There's more room for movement within the organization.

One of the really nice things since reengineering is that my relationships with customers have changed. With the team approach, all the customers in our region know who we are, and we stay in touch on a regular basis. We don't just call because they didn't pay their bill right or owe us money. Sometimes we call just to see how things are going.

We also get out of the office and talk to clients. We try to find out from them how we can provide better services. That's the kind of contact we never had before. It makes my job a lot more fun.

Within the company, I've been able to contribute more and to learn more. I learn from team members and other leaders and share my knowledge and experience. I think there's more respect all around.

Also, management is much more open with us. That's really important. Now you know things almost as soon as they happen. I received a copy of my team's budget in today's interoffice mail with last year's forecast, the year-to-date actuals, to what degree we're over or under. In the old days, it was unheard-of to know the real numbers.

I don't know that I'll stay at Showtime forever. But whatever moves I make, I could never go back to the old kind of organization. I'm really challenged and stimulated by the work.

Questions

1. How has Deborah Phelps' job changed in terms of the task(s) she performs?

2. How has the way Deborah is evaluated changed?

3. How has the way Deborah organizes her work changed? Who tells Deborah what to do?

Source: Michael Hammer, *Beyond Reengineering* 1996, pp. 19–26. Reprinted by permission of Harper Collins Publishers.

SELECTED BIBLIOGRAPHY

Bartlett, Christopher A., and Sumantra Ghoshal. "Rebuilding Behavioral Context: Turn Process Reengineering into People Rejuvenation." *Sloan Management Review,* Fall 1995, pp. 11–23.

Davenport, Thomas H. *Process Innovation: Reengineering Work through Information Technology.* Boston: Harvard Business School Press, 1993.

Davenport, Thomas H., and James E. Short. "The New Industrial Engineering: Information Technology and Business Process Redesign." *Sloan Management Review* 31, no. 4 (Summer 1990), pp. 11–27.

Davidson, William H. "Beyond Re-Engineering: The Three Phases of Business Transformation." *IBM Systems Journal* 32, no. 1 (1993) pp. 65–79.

Hall, Gene, Jim Rosenthal, and Judy Wade. "How to Make Reengineering Really Work." *Harvard Business Review* 93, no. 6 (November–December 1993), pp. 119–31.

Hammer, Michael. *Beyond Reengineering.* New York: Harper Collins Publishers, 1996.

————. "Reengineering Work: Don't Automate, Obliterate." *Harvard Business Review* 90, no. 4 (July–August 1990), pp. 104–12.

Hammer, Michael, and James Champy. *Reengineering the Corporation: A Manifesto for Business Revolution.* New York: Harper Business, 1993.

Heygate, Richard, and Gresh Brebach. "Corporate Reengineering." *The McKinsey Quarterly,* Spring 1991, pp. 44–55.

Pine II, B. Joseph. *Mass Customization: The New Frontier in Business Competition.* Boston: Harvard Business School Press, 1992.

Reengineering Handbook. Indianapolis: AT&T Quality Steering Committee, February 1992.

Rohleder, Thomas R., and Edward A. Silver. "A Tutorial on Business Process Improvement." *Journal of Operations Management*, forthcoming.

Chapter 20

Synchronous Manufacturing and Theory of Constraints

Chapter Outline

Hockey-Stick Phenomenon, 792

Goal of the Firm, 793

Performance Measurements, 793

    Financial Measurements

    Operational Measurements

    Productivity

Unbalanced Capacity, 795

    Dependent Events and Statistical
      Fluctuations

**Bottlenecks and Capacity-Constrained
Resources,** 798

Basic Manufacturing Building Blocks, 799

Methods for Control, 800

    Time Components

    Finding the Bottleneck

    Saving Time

Avoid Changing a Nonbottleneck into a
    Bottleneck

Drum, Buffer, Rope

Importance of Quality

Batch Sizes

How to Treat Inventory

**Comparing Synchronous Manufacturing to
MRP and JIT,** 810

VAT Classification of Firms, 810

    "V" Plant

    "A" Plant

    "T" Plant

Relationship with Other Functional Areas, 815

    Accounting's Influence

    Marketing and Production

Key Terms

Synchronous Manufacturing

Hockey-Stick Phenomenon

Throughput

Inventory

Operating Expense

Productivity

Unbalanced Capacity

Bottleneck, Nonbottleneck

Capacity-Constrained Resource (CCR)

Drum, Buffer, Rope

Time Buffer

Process and Transfer Batch

Dollar Days

Backward/Forward Scheduling

VAT Classification

www Links

Avraham Y. Goldratt Institute (http://www.rogo.com)   Software Technology Limited (http://www.stg.co.uk)

SCENE: ALEX ROGO IS THE PLANT MANAGER AT THE Barrington Plant of UniWare, a Division of UniCo. He has had a lot of trouble with his plant in keeping schedules, reducing inventory, improving quality, and cutting costs, among other problems. Bill Peach, division vice president, just visited him and gave him three months to improve, or else the plant will be closed.

Alex's son Dave and his Boy Scout troop are taking a 20-mile overnight hike (10 miles to Devil's Gulch where they will camp for the night, returning the following morning). Alex had been coaxed by his wife and son to accompany the troop. They are now on the hike and way behind schedule. The line of scouts is spread way out with the fastest kids in front; Herbie, the slowest, lags way behind in the rear. Alex is trying to figure out how he can make the Boy Scouts stay together and move faster.

Up front, you've got Andy, who wants to set a speed record. And here you are stuck behind Fat Herbie, the slowest kid in the woods. After an hour, the kid in front—if he's really moving at three miles per hour—is going to be two miles ahead—which means you're going to have to run two miles to catch up with him.

Alex is thinking, "If this were my plant, Peach wouldn't even give me three months. I'd already be on the street by now. The demand was for us to cover 10 miles in five hours, and we've only done half of that. Inventory is racing out of sight. The carrying costs on that inventory would be rising. We'd be ruining the company."

"Okay," I say. "Everybody join hands."

They all look at each other.

"Come on! Just do it!" I tell them. "And don't let go."

Then I take Herbie by the hand and, as if I'm dragging a chain, I go up the trail, snaking past the entire line. Hand in hand, the rest of the troop follows. I pass Andy and keep walking. When I'm twice the distance of the lineup, I stop. What I've done is turn the entire troop around so that the boys have exactly the opposite order they had before.

"Now listen up!" I say. "This is the order you're going to stay in until we reach where we're going. Understood? Nobody passes anybody.

"The idea of this hike is not to see who can get there the fastest. The idea is to get there together. We're not a bunch of individuals out here. We're a team."

So we start off again. And it works. No kidding. Everybody stays together behind Herbie. I've gone to the back of the line so I can keep tabs, and I keep waiting for the gaps to appear, but they don't.

"Mr. Rogo, can't we put somebody faster up front?" asks a kid ahead of me.

"Listen, if you guys want to go faster, then you have to figure out a way to let Herbie go faster," I tell them.

One of the kids in the rear says, "Hey, Herbie, what have you got in your pack?"

Herbie stops and turns around. I tell him to come to the back of the line and take off his pack. As he does, I take the pack from him—and nearly drop it.

"Herbie, this thing weighs a ton," I say. "What have you got in here?"

"Nothing much," says Herbie.

I open it up and reach in. Out comes a six-pack of soda. Next are some cans of spaghetti. Then come a box of candy bars, a jar of pickles, and two cans of tuna fish. Beneath a rain coat and rubber boots and a bag of tent stakes, I pull out a large iron skillet.

"Herbie, look, you've done a great job of lugging this stuff so far. But we have to make you able to move faster," I say. "If we take some of the load off you, you'll be able to do a better job at the front of the line."

Herbie finally seems to understand.

Again we start walking. But this time, Herbie can really move. Relieved of most of the weight in his pack, it's as if he's walking on air. We're flying now, doing twice the speed as a troop that we did before. And we still stay together. Inventory is down. Throughput is up.

Dave and I share the same tent that night. We're lying inside it, both of us tired. Dave is quiet for a while. Then he speaks up.

He says, "You know, Dad, I was really proud of you today."

"You were? How come?"

"The way you figured out what was going on and kept everyone together, and put Herbie in front."

"Thanks," I tell him. "Actually, I learned a lot of things today."

"You did?"

"Yeah, stuff that I think is going to help me straighten out the plant," I say.

"Really? Like what?"

"Are you sure you want to hear about it?"

"Sure I am," he claims.

This is the beginning of Alex's successful turnaround of his plant—applying simple principles to the plant's operation. ●

Source: Eliyahu M. Goldratt and Jeff Cox, *The Goal: A Process of Ongoing Improvement*, 2nd rev. ed. (Great Barrington, MA: North River Press, 1992), pp. 114–18.

The story of Herbie is an analogy to the problems facing plant manager Alex Rogo and comes from a best selling novel *The Goal*, by Dr. Eli Goldratt.[1] Around 1980, Goldratt contended that manufacturers were not doing a good job in scheduling and in controlling their resources and inventories. To solve this problem, Goldratt and his associates at a company named Creative Output developed software that scheduled jobs through manufacturing processes, taking into account limited facilities, machines, personnel, tools, materials, and any other constraints that would affect a firm's ability to adhere to a schedule.

This was called *optimized production technology (OPT)*. The schedules were feasible and accurate, and could be run on a computer in a fraction of the time needed by an MRP system. This was because the scheduling logic was based on the separation of bottleneck and nonbottleneck operations. To help understand the principles behind the OPT scheduling logic, Goldratt described nine production scheduling rules (See Exhibit 20.1). After approximately 100 large firms had installed this software, Goldratt went on to promote the logic of the approach rather than the software. The software is still being developed and sold by Software Technology Limited *(http://www.stg.co.uk)*.

In broadening his scope, Goldratt has developed his "Theory of Constraints" (TOC), which has become popular as a problem-solving approach that can be applied to many business areas (see Exhibit 20.2). His Goldratt Institute teaches courses in

---

1. Do not balance capacity—balance the flow.
2. The level of utilization of a nonbottleneck resource is not determined by its own potential but by some other constraint in the system.
3. Utilization and activation of a resource are not the same.
4. An hour lost at a bottleneck is an hour lost for the entire system.
5. An hour saved at a nonbottleneck is a mirage.
6. Bottlenecks govern both throughput and inventory in the system.
7. Transfer batch may not and many times should not be equal to the process batch.
8. A process batch should be variable both along its route and in time.
9. Priorities can be set only by examining the system's constraints. Lead time is a derivative of the schedule.

Exhibit 20.1

Goldratt's Rules of Production Scheduling

---

1. Identify the system constraints. (No improvement is possible unless the constraint or weakest link is found.)
2. Decide how to exploit the system constraints. (Make the constraints as effective as possible.)
3. Subordinate everything else to that decision. (Align every other part of the system to support the constraints even if this reduces the efficiency of nonconstraint resources.)
4. Elevate the system constraints. (If output is still inadequate, acquire more of this resource so it no longer is a constraint.)
5. If, in the previous steps, the constraints have been broken, go back to Step 1, but do not let inertia become the system constraint. (After this constraint problem is solved, go back to the beginning and start over. This is a continuous process of improvement: identifying constraints, breaking them, and then identifying the new ones that result.)

Exhibit 20.2

Goldratt's Theory of Constraints (TOC)

---

[1] Most of this chapter is based on the writings and teaching of Dr. Eliyahu M. Goldratt. Dr. Goldratt founded the Avraham Y. Goldratt Institute. The Institute's Web site is at *http://www.rogo.com*. We thank Dr. Goldratt for his permission to freely use his concepts, definitions, and other material.

improving production, distribution, and project management. The common thread through all of these courses is Goldratt's TOC concepts.

In this chapter, we focus on Goldratt's approach to manufacturing. To correctly treat the topic, we decided to approach it in the same way that Goldratt did; that is, first defining some basic issues about firms—purposes, goals, and performance measures—and then dealing with scheduling, providing buffer inventories, the influences of quality, the interactions with marketing, and accounting.

Synchronous Manufacturing

In this chapter we discuss **synchronous manufacturing,** which refers to the entire production process working together in harmony to achieve the goals of the firm. Synchronous manufacturing logic attempts to coordinate all resources so that they work together and are in harmony or are *synchronized*. In such a synchronous state, emphasis is on total system performance, not on localized performance measures such as labor or machine utilization.

■ HOCKEY-STICK PHENOMENON

Hockey-Stick Phenomenon

Just about every company faces a problem called the **hockey-stick phenomenon**—rushing to meet quotas at the end of the time period. If the time period is a month, then this is an end-of-the-month-syndrome; if the period is a quarter, it is an end-of-the-quarter syndrome (see Exhibit 20.3). This problem is described as a hockey stick because it looks like a hockey stick—with a relatively flat bottom and a long, rapid rise like a handle. The reason that this is a problem is primarily because of the chaos that occurs at the end of the month. The system never runs smoothly; everyone works under pressure during the early flat part of the cycle as well as during the end of the cycle. The cause of the problem is that two sets of measurements are being employed:

Hockey-Stick Phenomenon (The end-of-the-period rush)

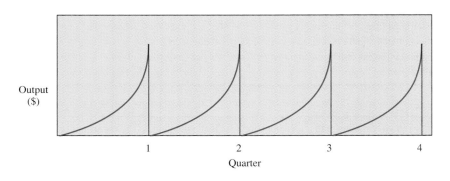

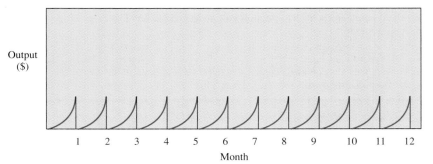

At the beginning of the period, cost accounting *efficiency* measurements are used. These are local measurements. This encourages minimizing setups through large batches. As the end of the month approaches, however, pressure mounts to meet a different set of measurements, one that relates to financial *performance.* They are stated in terms such as dollars of output shipped. On the financial statements, these measurements are expressed as net profit, return on investment, and cash flow. As soon as the end of the month passes (with its daily overtime, weekend work, constant expediting, and frequent setups aimed toward getting the product out), pressure decreases and everyone again looks at the cost accounting measurements of standards and utilization—and so the cycle repeats.

To emphasize the value of techniques such as synchronous manufacturing, Goldratt tells two stories of what can happen. One is about a firm that did not need the third shift because of a slump in the market. The workers were highly skilled and, because the company expected the market to rebound in three months, it decided to keep the workers. With a weekly payroll of $25,000, the company allocated $300,000 to carry the workers for three months, within which time they expected renewed market demand. To the surprise of management, however, these workers consumed $400,000 worth of inventory during the first week and another $400,000 during the second week, so the workers were laid off. There was so much pressure to keep the workers busy that they were not allowed to just be idle (nor would the workers feel right just sitting around waiting). Two months later, market demand increased, but not for the products that the workers had been producing.

The second story is about a plant whose demand went down because the overall market had deteriorated. Because the company was having cash flow problems, it decided to cut expenses. Noticing that the setup workers were the highest paid in the plant, management decided to double all the batch sizes (which meant only half the setups were needed) and lay off half the setup workers. The result put the plant out of business! With double batch sizes, the increase in work in process drained all the company's cash so that it could no longer operate.

■ GOAL OF THE FIRM

Although many people disagree with him, Goldratt has a very straightforward idea of the goal of a firm:

THE GOAL OF A FIRM IS TO MAKE MONEY

Goldratt argues that while an organization may have many purposes—providing jobs, consuming raw materials, increasing sales, increasing share of the market, developing technology, or producing high-quality products—these do not guarantee long-term survival of the firm. They are means to achieve the goal, not the goal itself. If the firm makes money—and only then—it will prosper. When a firm has money, then it can place more emphasis on other objectives.

■ PERFORMANCE MEASUREMENTS

To adequately measure a firm's performance, two sets of measurements must be used: one from the financial point of view and the other from the operations point of view.

FINANCE
ACCOUNTING

Financial Measurements

We have three measures of the firm's ability to make money:

1. *Net profit*—an absolute measurement in dollars
2. *Return on investment*—a relative measure based on investment.
3. *Cash flow*—a survival measurement.

All three measurements must be used together. For example, a *net profit* of $10 million is important as one measurement, but it has no real meaning until we know how much investment it took to generate that $10 million. If the investment was $100 million, this is a 10 percent *return on investment. Cash flow* is important because cash is necessary to pay bills for day-to-day operations; without cash, a firm can go bankrupt even though it is very sound in normal accounting terms. A firm can have a high profit and a high return on investment but still be short on cash if, for example, profit is invested in new equipment or tied up in inventory.

Operational Measurements

Financial measurements work well at the higher level, but they cannot be used at the operational level. We need another set of measurements that will give us guidance:

Throughput

Inventory

Operating Expenses

1. **Throughput**—the rate at which money is generated by the system through sales.
2. **Inventory**—all the money that the system has invested in purchasing things it intends to sell.
3. **Operating expenses**—all the money that the system spends to turn inventory into throughput.

Throughput is specifically defined as goods *sold*. An inventory of finished goods is not throughput, but inventory. Actual sales must occur. It is specifically defined this way to prevent the system from continuing to produce under the illusion that the goods *might* be sold. Such action simply increases costs, builds inventory, and consumes cash. Inventory that is carried (whether work in process or finished goods) is valued only at the cost of the materials it contains. Labor cost and machine hours are ignored. (In traditional accounting terms, money spent is called *value added*.)

While this is often an arguable point, using only the raw material cost is a conservative view. When using the value-added method (which includes all costs of production), inventory is inflated and presents some serious income and balance sheet problems. Consider, for example, work-in-process or finished-goods inventory that has become obsolete, or for which a contract was canceled. It is a difficult management decision to declare large amounts of inventory as scrap because it is often carried on the books as assets even though it may really have no value. Using just raw-materials cost also avoids the problem of determining which costs are direct and which are indirect.

Operating expenses include production costs (such as direct labor, indirect labor, inventory carrying costs, equipment depreciation, and materials and supplies used in production) and administrative costs. The key difference here is that there is no need to separate direct and indirect labor.

As shown in Exhibit 20.4, the objective of a firm is to treat all three measurements simultaneously and continually; this achieves the goal of making money.

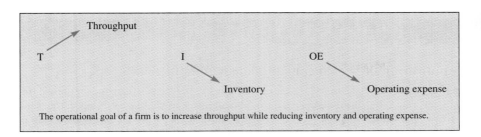

Exhibit 20.4

Operational Goal

Throughput

T

I   OE

Inventory   Operating expense

The operational goal of a firm is to increase throughput while reducing inventory and operating expense.

From an operations standpoint, the goal of the firm is to

INCREASE THROUGHPUT WHILE SIMULTANEOUSLY REDUCING
INVENTORY AND REDUCING OPERATING EXPENSE.

Productivity

Typically, **productivity** is measured in terms of output per labor hour. However, this
measurement does not ensure that the firm will make money (for example, when extra
output is not sold but accumulates as inventory). To test whether productivity has
increased, we should ask these questions: Has the action taken increased throughout?
Has it decreased inventory? Has it decreased operational expense? This leads us to a
new definition:

PRODUCTIVITY IS ALL THE ACTIONS THAT BRING A COMPANY
CLOSER TO ITS GOALS.

The Breakthrough box titled "Application of the Theory of Constraints in Banks" on
the next page shows how these items can be applied to a service company.

Productivity

■ UNBALANCED CAPACITY

Unbalanced
Capacity

Historically (and still typically in most firms); manufacturers have tried to balance
capacity across a sequence of processes in an attempt to match capacity with market
demand. However, this is the wrong thing to do—**unbalanced capacity** is better. The
vignette at the beginning of this chapter is an example of unbalanced capacity. Some
Boy Scouts were fast walkers, while Herbie was very slow. The challenge is to use this
difference advantageously.

Consider a simple process line with several stations, for example. Once the output
rate of the line has been established, production people try to make the capacities of
all stations the same. This is done by adjusting machines or equipment used,
workloads, skill and type of labor assigned, tools used, overtime budgeted, and so on.

In synchronous manufacturing thinking, however, making all capacities the same
is viewed as a bad decision. Such a balance would be possible only if the output times
of all stations were constant or had a very narrow distribution. A normal variation in
output times causes downstream stations to have idle time when upstream stations
take longer to process. Conversely, when upstream stations process in a shorter time,
inventory builds up between the stations. The effect of the statistical variation is
cumulative. The only way that this variation can be smoothed is by increasing work

BREAKTHROUGH

Application of the Theory of Constraints in Banks

The three operational performance measures we have defined are interpreted by Bramorski, Madan, and Motwani in terms applicable to banking.

- *Throughput* is the rate at which a banking system generates revenue for services provided in a way consistent with its goal. Throughput in banks can be generated by investing in such markets as customer lending, institutional lending, real estate, and investment firms. Moreover, banks generate money by offering a variety of services such as wire transfers, foreign exchange, and cashier's checks.
- *Operating expenses* include all the money the bank spends in the process of generating throughput. These expenses include all direct and indirect expenses except for the cost of obtaining money in the market.
- *Inventory investment* is the amount of money spent by a bank to raise capital necessary to generate throughput. Inventory investment consists of the principal amount and the interest paid on deposits.

It should be noted that in the banking business, both the primary input—inventory—and output consist entirely of money. Banks use the money obtained from depositors and invest in ventures varying in the degree of risk. In contrast with manufacturing, banks do not need to convert physical inventory of products into money through sales. Hence, the length of the process of generating throughput in banks is much shorter than in manufacturing.

A bank located in the midwest region of the U.S. has successfully implemented the principles of TOC. The bank identified its weakest link as the mortgage department. It took the bank too long to process individual home mortgage applications, and it wanted to reduce the average processing time to three weeks. In order to achieve the goal, the management of the bank decided to use the five-step TOC focusing process (Exhibit 20.2). First, it formed a cross-functional group of eight people, who were selected to form the mortgage improvement team (MIT). People from different functional levels within the branch and other branches made up the team.

The team used flow charting as a tool to analyze processes. An early indication of the complexity of improvement was that it took too long to verify

in process to absorb the variation (a bad choice because we should be trying to reduce work in process), or increasing capacities downstream to be able to make up for the longer upstream times. The rule here is that capacities within the process sequence should not be balanced to the same levels. Rather, attempts should be made to balance the flow of product through the system. When flow is balanced, capacities are unbalanced. This idea is further explained in the next section.

Dependent Events and Statistical Fluctuations

The term *dependent events* refers to a process sequence. If a process flows from A to B to C to D, and each process must be completed before passing on to the next step, then B, C, and D are dependent events. The ability to do the next process is dependent on the preceding one.

Statistical fluctuation refers to the normal variation about a mean or average. When statistical fluctuations occur in a dependent sequence without any inventory between workstations, there is no opportunity to achieve the average output. When one process takes longer than the average, the next process cannot make up the time. We follow through an example of this to show what could happen.

Suppose that we wanted to process five items that could come from the two distributions in Exhibit 20.5. The processing sequence is from A to B with no space for inventory in between. Process A has a mean of 10 hours and a standard deviation of 2 hours. This means that we would expect 95.5 percent of the processing time to

employment and to conduct the appraisal and the survey. After further analysis and discussions, it was agreed that because all of the forgoing activities were independent of each other, they should be immediately addressed. This was a crucial turning point in the life of the MIT. In addition, the first TOC step of focusing and identifying the weakest links was accomplished.

The second step in the TOC process is to exploit the constraint. In other words, how can the time taken for verification of employment and for conducting the appraisal and surveys be reduced? The team learned through data collection that there were several different methods for shortening this time. As an example, to reduce the two weeks to verify employment status, the loan officer now requested the applicant to bring in the last two years' W-2 forms and the last month's pay stub. Similar solutions were found for reducing time to conduct surveys and appraisals.

This example not only illustrates how the bank exploited the constraint but also how it had personnel subordinate their actions so that the constraint could perform at a higher level of performance. The subordination is the third step of TOC, meaning that everyone supports the first two steps of identifying and exploiting the constraint. Furthermore, these actions caused operating expense and inventory to decrease, and throughput to increase.

The fourth step of TOC is taken when the exploitation and subordination steps as related to the constraint have been exhausted and the demand is so great that additional time for verification can be justified.

The fifth step is that once the first four steps have been completed, inertia is not permitted to become the system's constraint. In other words, the bank should look for new constraints and start the process over without becoming complacent regarding its accomplishments.

Source: Adapted from Tom Bramorski, Manu S. Madan, and Jaideep Motwani, "Application of the Theory of Constraints in Banks," *The Bankers Magazine,* January/February 1997, pp. 53–59.

Processing and Completion Times, Process A to Process B

Exhibit 20.5

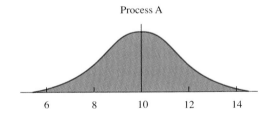

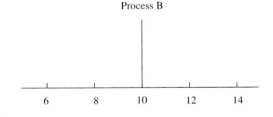

Item Number	Start Time	Processing Time	Finish Time
1	0 hrs	14 hrs	14 hrs
2	14	12	26
3	26	10	36
4	36	8	44
5	44	6	50
	Average = 10 hours		

Item Number	Start Time	Processing Time	Finish Time
1	14 hrs	10 hrs	24 hrs
2	26	10	36
3	36	10	46
4	46	10	56
5	56	10	66
	Average = 10 hours		

Here the flow is from Process A to Process B. Process A has a mean of 10 hours and a standard deviation of 2 hours; Process B has a constant 10-hour processing time.

Processing and Completion Times, Process B to Process A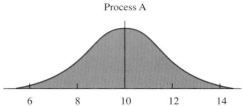

Item Number	Start Time	Processing Time	Finish Time
1	0 hrs	10 hrs	10 hrs
2	10	10	20
3	20	10	30
4	30	10	40
5	40	10	50
		Average = 10 hours	

Item Number	Start Time	Processing Time	Finish Time
1	10 hrs	6 hrs	16 hrs
2	20	8	28
3	30	10	40
4	40	12	52
5	52	14	66
		Average = 10 hours	

This is similar to Exhibit 20.5. However, the processing sequence has been reversed as well as the order of Process A's times.

be between 6 hours and 14 hours (plus or minus 2 sigma). Process B has a constant processing time of 10 hours.

We see that the last item was completed in 66 hours, for an average of 13.2 hours per item, although the expected time of completion was 60, for an average of 12 hours per item (taking into account the waiting time for the first unit by process B).

Suppose we reverse the process—B feeds A. To illustrate the possible delays, we also reverse A's performance times. (See Exhibit 20.6.) Again, the completion time of the last item is greater than the average (13.2 hours rather than 12 hours). Process A and process B have the same average performance time of 10 hours, and yet performance is late. In neither case could we achieve the expected output average rate. Why? Because the time lost when the second process is idle cannot be made up.

This example is intended to challenge the theory that capacities should be balanced to an average time. *Rather than balancing capacities, the flow of product through the system should be balanced.*

■ BOTTLENECKS AND CAPACITY-CONSTRAINED RESOURCES

Bottleneck

A **bottleneck** is defined as any resource whose capacity is less than the demand placed upon it. A bottleneck is a constraint within the system that limits throughput. It is that point in the manufacturing process where flow thins to a narrow stream. A bottleneck may be a machine, scarce or highly skilled labor, or a specialized tool. Observations in industry have shown that most plants have very few bottleneck operations.

If there is no bottleneck, then excess capacity exists and the system should be changed to create a bottleneck (such as more setups or reduced capacity), which we will discuss later.

Capacity is defined as the available time for production. This excludes maintenance and other downtime. A **nonbottleneck** is any resource whose capacity is greater than

Nonbottleneck

the demand placed on it. A nonbottleneck, therefore, should not be working constantly because it can produce more than is needed. A nonbottleneck contains idle time.

A **capacity-constrained resource (CCR)** is one whose utilization is close to capacity and could be a bottleneck if it is not scheduled carefully. For example, a CCR may be receiving work in a job-shop environment from several sources. If these sources schedule their flow in a way that causes occasional idle time for the CCR in excess of its unused capacity time, the CCR becomes a bottleneck. This can happen if batch sizes are changed or if one of the upstream operations is not working for some reason and does not feed enough work to the CCR.

Capacity-
Constrained
Resource (CCR)

■ BASIC MANUFACTURING BUILDING BLOCKS

All manufacturing processes and flows can be simplified to four basic configurations, as shown in Exhibit 20.7. In Exhibit 20.7A, product that flows through process X feeds into process Y. In section B, Y is feeding X. In section C, process X and process Y are creating subassemblies, which are then combined, say to feed the market demand. In section D, process X and process Y are independent of each other and are supplying their own markets. The last column in the exhibit shows possible sequences of nonbottleneck resources, which can be grouped and displayed as Y to simplify the representation.

The value in using these basic building blocks is that a production process can be greatly simplified for analysis and control. Rather than track and schedule all of the steps in a production sequence through nonbottleneck operations, for example, attention can be placed at the beginning and end points of the building block groupings.

The Basic Building Blocks of Manufacturing Derived by Grouping Process Flows   Exhibit 20.9

Description	Basic Building Blocks Simplified by Grouping Nonbottlenecks	Original Representation
A. Bottleneck feeding nonbottleneck	X ⟶ Y ⟶ Market	Y ⏞ X ⟶ A ⟶ B ⟶ C ⟶ D ⟶ Market
B. Nonbottleneck feeding bottleneck	Y ⟶ X ⟶ Market	Y ⏞ A ⟶ B ⟶ C ⟶ D ⟶ X ⟶ Market
C. Output of bottleneck and nonbottleneck assembled into a product	X ↘ Final Assembly ⟶ Market Y ↗	X ↘ Final Assembly ⟶ Market Y A ⟶ B ⟶ C ⟶ D ↗
D. Bottleneck and nonbottleneck have independent markets for their output	X ↗ Market Y ↘ Market	Y A ⟶ B ⟶ C ⟶ D ↗ X ↗ Market ↘ Market

X is a bottleneck
Y is a nonbottleneck (has excess capacity).

■ METHODS FOR CONTROL

Exhibit 20.8 shows how bottleneck and nonbottleneck resources should be managed.

Resource X and Resource Y are work centers that can produce a variety of products. Each of these work centers has 200 hours available per month. For simplicity, assume that we are dealing with only one product and we will alter the conditions and makeup for four different situations. Each unit of X takes one hour of production time and the market demand is 200 units per month. Each unit of Y takes 45 minutes of production time and the market demand is also 200 units per month.

Situation A in Exhibit 20.8 is a bottleneck feeding a nonbottleneck. Product flows from work center X to work center Y. X is the bottleneck since it has a capacity of 200 units (200 hours/1 hour per unit) and Y has a capacity of 267 units (200 hours/45 minutes per unit). Since Y has to wait for X and Y has a higher capacity than X, no extra product accumulates in the system. It all flows through to the market.

Situation B is the reverse of A, with Y feeding X. This is a nonbottleneck feeding a bottleneck. Since Y has a capacity of 267 units and X has a capacity of only 200 units, we should only produce 200 units of Y (75 percent of capacity) or else work in process will accumulate in front of X.

Situation C is one in which the products produced by X and Y are assembled and then sold to the market. Since one unit from X and one unit from Y form an assembly, X is the bottleneck with 200 units of capacity and, therefore, Y should not work more than 75 percent or else extra parts will accumulate.

Situation D is one where equal quantities of product from X and Y are demanded by the market. In this case we can call these products "finished goods" since they face independent demands. Here Y has access to material independent of X and, with a

Exhibit 20.8

Product Flow through Bottlenecks and Nonbottlenecks

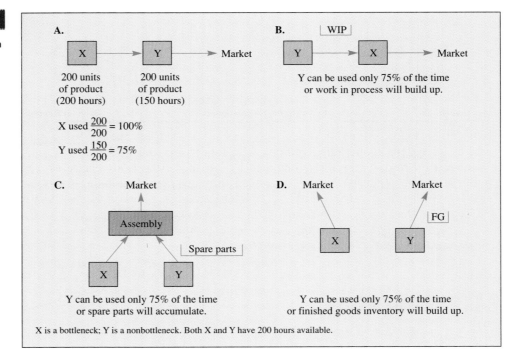

higher capacity than needed to satisfy the market, it can produce more product than the market will take. However, this would create an inventory of unneeded finished goods.

The four situations just discussed demonstrate bottleneck and nonbottleneck resources and their relationship to production and market demand. They show that the industry practice of using resource utilization as a measure of performance can encourage the overuse of nonbottlenecks and result in excess inventories.

Time Components

The following various kinds of time make up production cycle time:

1. *Setup time*—the time that a part spends waiting for a resource to be set up to work on this same part.
2. *Process time*—the time that the part is being processed.
3. *Queue time*—the time that a part waits for a resource while the resource is busy with something else.
4. *Wait time*—the time that a part waits not for a resource but for another part so that they can be assembled together.
5. *Idle time*—the unused time; that is, the cycle time less the sum of the setup time, processing time, queue time, and wait time.

For a part waiting to go through a bottleneck, queue time is the greatest. As we discuss later in this chapter, this is because the bottleneck has a fairly large amount of work to do in front of it (to make sure that it is always working). For a nonbottleneck, wait time is the greatest. The part is just sitting there waiting for the arrival of other parts so that an assembly can take place.

Schedulers are tempted to save setup times. Suppose that the batch sizes are doubled to save half the setup times. Then, with a double batch size, all of the other times (processing time, queue time, and wait time) increase twofold. Because these times are doubled while saving only half of the setup time, the net result is that the work in process is approximately doubled, as is the investment in inventory.

Finding the Bottleneck

There are two ways to find the bottleneck (or bottlenecks) in a system. One is to run a capacity resource profile; the other is to use our knowledge of the particular plant, look at the system in operation, and talk with supervisors and workers.

A capacity resource profile is obtained by looking at the loads placed on each resource by the products that are scheduled through them. In running a capacity profile, we assume that the data are reasonably accurate, although not necessarily perfect. As an example, consider that products have been routed through resources M1 through M5. Suppose that our first computation of the resource loads on each resource caused by these products shows the following:

M1	130 percent of capacity	M4	95 percent of capacity
M2	120 percent of capacity	M5	85 percent of capacity
M3	105 percent of capacity		

For this first analysis, we can disregard any resources at lower percentages because they are nonbottlenecks and should not be a problem. With this list in hand, we should physically go to the facility and check all five operations. Note that M1, M2, and M3 are overloaded; that is, they are scheduled above their capacities. We would expect to see large quantities of inventory in front of M1. If this is not the case, errors must exist somewhere—perhaps in the bill of materials or in the routing sheets. Let's say that our observations and discussions with shop personnel showed that there were errors in M1, M2, M3, and M4. We tracked them down, made the appropriate corrections, and ran the capacity profile again:

M2	115 percent of capacity	M4	90 percent of capacity
M1	110 percent of capacity	M5	85 percent of capacity
M3	105 percent of capacity		

M1, M2, and M3 are still showing a lack of sufficient capacity, but M2 is the most serious. If we now have confidence in our numbers, we use M2 as our bottleneck.

If the data contain too many errors to do a reliable data analysis, it may not be worth spending time (it could take months) making all the corrections. Instead, it would be quicker to use our knowledge about the VAT classification scheme (covered later in this chapter) to give us guidance. Defining the plant as V, A, or T helps direct us to where the bottlenecks would most likely be. To find a bottleneck, use the VAT scheme and then go and look and listen. From talking with workers and supervisors in the plant, we would expect to hear comments such as "We're always waiting for parts from the NC machine" or "They're feeding me more work than I can possibly do and I can't keep up." These are clues to be followed.

Saving Time

Recall that a bottleneck is a resource whose capacity is less than the demand placed on it. Because we focus on bottlenecks as restricting *throughput* (defined as *sales*), a bottleneck's capacity is less than the market demand. There are a number of ways we can save time on a bottleneck (better tooling, higher-quality labor, larger batch sizes, reducing setup times, and so forth), but how valuable is the extra time? Very, very valuable!

> AN HOUR SAVED AT THE BOTTLENECK ADDS AN EXTRA HOUR
> TO THE ENTIRE PRODUCTION SYSTEM.

How about time saved on a nonbottleneck resource?

> AN HOUR SAVED AT A NONBOTTLENECK IS A MIRAGE AND
> ONLY ADDS AN HOUR TO ITS IDLE TIME.

Because a nonbottleneck has more capacity than the system needs for its current throughput, it already contains idle time. Implementing any measures to save more time does not increase throughput but only serves to increase its idle time.

Avoid Changing a Nonbottleneck into a Bottleneck

When nonbottleneck resources are scheduled with larger batch sizes, this action could create a bottleneck that we certainly would want to avoid. Consider the case in Exhibit 20.9, where Y_1, Y_2, and Y_3 are nonbottleneck resources. Y_1 currently produces part A, which is routed to Y_3, and part B is routed to Y_2. To produce part A, Y_1 has a 200-minute setup time and a processing time of 1 minute per part. Part A is

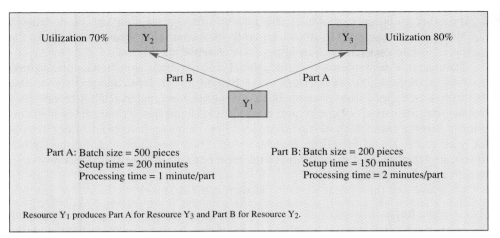

Exhibit 20.9

Nonbottleneck
Resources

Utilization 70% Y_2 Y_3 Utilization 80%

Part B   Part A

Y_1

Part A: Batch size = 500 pieces
Setup time = 200 minutes
Processing time = 1 minute/part

Part B: Batch size = 200 pieces
Setup time = 150 minutes
Processing time = 2 minutes/part

Resource Y_1 produces Part A for Resource Y_3 and Part B for Resource Y_2.

currently produced in batches of 500 units. To produce part B, Y_1 has a setup time of 150 minutes and 2 minutes' processing time per part. Part B is currently produced in batches of 200 units. With this sequence, Y_2 is utilized 70 percent of the time and Y_3 is utilized 80 percent of the time.

Because setup time is 200 minutes for Y_1 on part A, both worker and supervisor mistakenly believe that more production can be gained if fewer setups are made. Let's assume that the batch size is increased to 1,500 units and see what happens. The illusion is that we have saved 400 minutes of setup. (Instead of three setups taking 600 minutes to produce three batches of 500 units each, there is just one setup with a 1,500-unit batch.)

The problem is that the 400 minutes saved served no purpose, but this delay did interfere with the production of part B because Y_1 produces part B for Y_2. The sequence before any changes were made was part A (700 minutes), part B (550 minutes), part A (700 minutes), part B (550 minutes), and so on. Now, however, when the part A batch is increased to 1,500 units (1,700 minutes), Y_2 and Y_3 could well be starved for work and have to wait more time than they have available (30 percent idle time for Y_2 and 20 percent for Y_3). The new sequence would be part A (1,700 minutes), part B (1,350 minutes), and so on. Such an extended wait for Y_2 and Y_3 could be disruptive. Y_2 and Y_3 could become temporary bottlenecks and lose throughput for the system.

Drum, Buffer, Rope

Every production system needs some control point or points to control the flow of product through the system. If the system contains a bottleneck, the bottleneck is the best place for control. This control point is called the **drum,** because it strikes the beat that the rest of the system (or those parts that it influences) uses to function. Recall that a *bottleneck* is defined as a resource that does not have the capacity to meet demand. Therefore, a bottleneck is working all the time, and one reason for using it as a control point is to make sure that the operations upstream do not overproduce and build up excess work-in-process inventory that the bottleneck cannot handle.

If there is no bottleneck, the next best place to set the drum would be a capacity-constrained resource (CCR). A capacity-constrained resource, remember, is one that is operating near capacity but, on the average, has adequate capability as long as it is not incorrectly scheduled (for example, with too many setups, causing it to run short of capacity, or producing too large a lot size, thereby starving downstream operations).

Drum

If neither a bottleneck nor a CCR is present, the control point can be designated anywhere. The best position would generally be at some divergent point where the output of the resource is used in several downstream operations.

Dealing with the bottleneck is most critical, and our discussion focuses on ensuring that the bottleneck always has work to do. Exhibit 20.10 shows a simple linear flow A through G. Suppose that resource D, which is a machine center, is a bottleneck. This means that the capacities are greater both upstream and downstream from it. If this sequence is not controlled, we would expect to see a large amount of inventory in front of work center D and very little anywhere else. There would be little finished-goods inventory because (by the definition of the term *bottleneck*) all the product produced would be taken by the market.

There are two things that we must do with this bottleneck:

Buffer

1. Keep a **buffer** inventory in front of it to make sure that it always has something to work on. Because it is a bottleneck, its output determines the throughput of the system.

Rope

2. Communicate back upstream to A what D has produced so that A provides only that amount. This keeps inventory from building up. This communication is called the **rope.** It can be formal (such as a schedule) or informal (such as daily discussion).

Time Buffer

The buffer inventory in front of a bottleneck operation is a **time buffer.** We want to make sure that work center D always has work to do, and it does not matter which of the scheduled products are worked on. We might, for example, provide 96 hours of inventory in the buffer as shown in the sequence A through P in Exhibit 20.11. Jobs A through about half of E are scheduled during the 24 hours of day 1; jobs E through

---

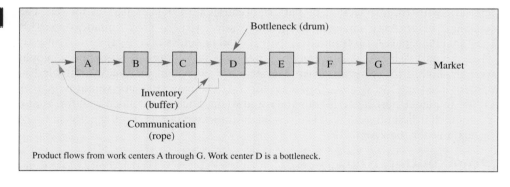

Product flows from work centers A through G. Work center D is a bottleneck.

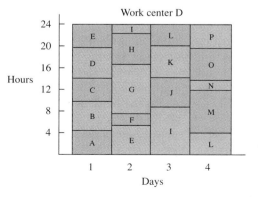

a portion of job I are scheduled during the second 24-hour day; jobs I through part of L are scheduled during the third 24-hour day; and jobs L through P are scheduled during the fourth 24-hour day, for a total of 96 hours. This means that through normal variation, or if something happens upstream and the output has been temporarily stalled, D can work for another 96 hours protecting the throughput. (The 96 hours of work, incidentally, includes setups and processing times contained in the job sheets, which usually are based on engineering standard times.)

We might ask, How large should the time buffer be? The answer: as large as it needs to be to ensure that the bottleneck continues to work. By examining the variation of each operation, we can make a guess. Theoretically, the size of the buffer can be computed statistically by examining past performance data, or the sequence can be simulated. In any event, precision is not critical. We could start with an estimate of the time buffer as one-fourth of the total lead time of the system. Say the sequence A to G in our example (Exhibit 20.10) took a total of 16 days. We could start with a buffer of four days in front of D. If during the next few days or weeks the buffer runs out, we need to increase the buffer size. We do this by releasing extra material to the first operation, A. On the other hand, if we find that our buffer never drops below three days, we might want to hold back releases to A and reduce the time buffer to three days. Experience is the best determination of the final buffer size.

If the drum is not a bottleneck but a CCR (and thus it can have a small amount of idle time), we might want to create two buffer inventories—one in front of the CCR and the second at the end as finished goods. (See Exhibit 20.12.) The finished-goods inventory protects the market, and the time buffer in front of the CCR protects throughput. For this CCR case, the market cannot take all that we can produce so we want to ensure that finished goods are available when the market does decide to purchase.

We need two ropes in this case: (1) a rope communicating from finished-goods inventory back to the drum to increase or decrease output, and (2) a rope from the drum back to the material release point, specifying how much material is needed.

Exhibit 20.13 is a more detailed network flow showing one bottleneck. Inventory is provided not only in front of that bottleneck but also after the nonbottleneck assembly to which it is assembled. This ensures that the flow of product after it leaves the bottleneck is not slowed down by having to wait.

Importance of Quality

An MRP system allows for rejects by building a larger batch than actually needed. A JIT system cannot tolerate poor quality because JIT success is based on a balanced

Exhibit 20.12

Linear Flow of Product with a Capacity-Constrained Resource

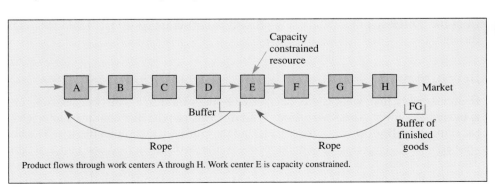

Product flows through work centers A through H. Work center E is capacity constrained.

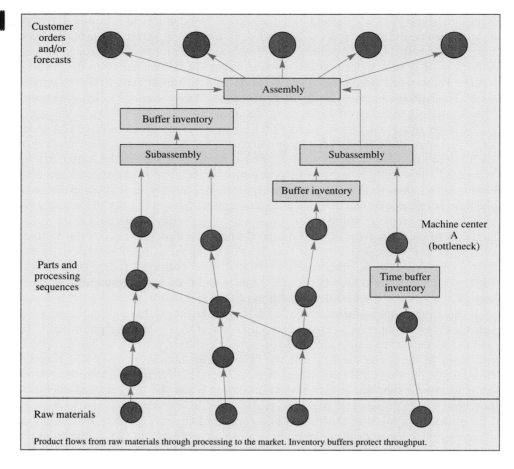

Exhibit 20.13

Network Flow with
One Bottleneck

Product flows from raw materials through processing to the market. Inventory buffers protect throughput.

capacity. A defective part or component can cause a JIT system to shut down, thereby losing throughput of the total system. Synchronous manufacturing, however, has excess capacity throughout the system, except for the bottleneck. If a bad part is produced upstream of the bottleneck, the result is that there is a loss of material only. Because of the excess capacity, there is still time to do another operation to replace the one just scrapped. For the bottleneck, however, extra time does not exist, so there should be a quality control inspection just prior to the bottleneck to ensure that the bottleneck works only on good product. Also, there needs to be assurance downstream from the bottleneck that the passing product is not scrapped—that would mean lost throughput.

 Batch Sizes

In an assembly line, what is the batch size? Some would say "one" because one unit is moved at a time; others would say "infinity" because the line continues to produce the same item. Both answers are correct, but they differ in their point of view. The first answer, "one," in an assembly line focuses on the *part* transferred one unit at a time. The second focuses on the *process*. From the point of view of the resource, the process batch is infinity because it is continuing to run the same units. Thus, in an assembly

Effect of Changing the Process Batch Sizes on Production Lead Time for a Job Order of 1,000 Units

Exhibit 20.14

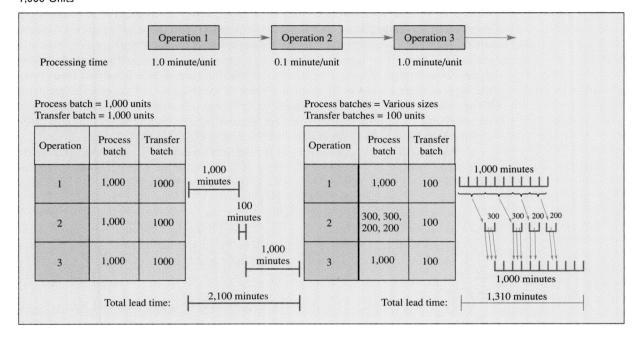

line, we have a **process batch** of infinity (or all the units until we change to another process setup) and a **transfer batch** of one unit.

Process Batch
Transfer Batch

Setup costs and carrying costs were treated in depth in Chapter 15 ("Inventory Systems for Independent Demand"). In the present context, setup costs relate to the process batch and carrying costs relate to the transfer batch.

A process batch is of a size large enough or small enough to be processed in a particular length of time. From the point of view of a resource, two times are involved: setup time and processing run time (ignoring downtime for maintenance or repair). Larger process batch sizes require fewer setups and therefore can generate more processing time and more output. For bottleneck resources, larger batch sizes are desirable. For nonbottleneck resources, smaller process batch sizes are desirable (by using up the existing idle time), thereby reducing work-in-process inventory.

Transfer batches refer to the movement of part of the process batch. Rather than wait for the entire batch to be finished, work that has been completed by that operation can be moved to the next downstream workstation so that it can begin working on that batch. A transfer batch can be equal to a process batch, but it cannot be larger.[2]

The advantage of using transfer batches that are smaller than the process batch quantity is that the total production time is shorter so the amount of work in process is smaller. Exhibit 20.14 shows a situation where the total production lead time was reduced from 2,100 to 1,310 minutes by using a transfer batch size of 100 rather than 1,000, and reducing the process batch sizes of operation 2.

---

[2] It would not be logical to have a transfer batch larger than the process batch. This could only occur if a completed process batch was held until sometime later when a second batch was processed. If this later time was acceptable in the beginning, then both jobs should be combined and processed together at the later time.

How to Determine Process Batch and Transfer Batch Sizes   Logic would suggest that the master production schedule (however it was developed) be analyzed as to its effect on various work centers. In an MRP system, this means that the master production schedule should be run through the MRP and the CRP (capacity requirements planning program) to generate a detailed load on each work center. Srikanth states that from his experience, there are too many errors in the manufacturing database to do this.[3] He suggests using the alternative procedures of first identifying the type of plant (V, A, or T, described later in this chapter) to suggest the probable CCRs and bottlenecks. There should be only one (or a few), and they should be reviewed by managers so that they understand which resources are actually controlling their plant. These resources set the drumbeat.

Rather than try to adjust the master production schedule to change resource loads, it is more practical to control the flow at each bottleneck or CCR to bring the capacities in line. The process batch sizes and transfer batch sizes are changed after comparing past performances in meeting due dates.

Smaller transfer batches give lower work-in-process inventory but faster product flow (and consequently shorter lead time). More material handling is required, however. Larger transfer batches give longer lead times and higher inventories, but there is less material handling. Therefore, the transfer batch size is determined by a trade-off of production lead times, inventory reduction benefits, and costs of material movement.

When trying to control the flow at CCRs and bottlenecks, there are four possible situations:

1.   A bottleneck (no idle time) with no setup required when changing from one product to another.
2.   A bottleneck with setup times required to change from one product to another.
3.   A capacity-constrained resource (CCR with a small amount of idle time) with no setup required to change from one product to another.
4.   A CCR with setup time required when changing from one product to another.

In the first case (a bottleneck with no setup time to change products), jobs should be processed in the order of the schedule so that delivery is on time. Without setups, only the sequence is important. In the second case, when setups are required, larger batch sizes combine separate similar jobs in the sequence. This means reaching ahead into future time periods. Some jobs will therefore be done early. Because this is a bottleneck resource, larger batches save setups and thereby increase throughput. (The setup time saved is used for processing.) The larger process batches may cause the early scheduled jobs to be late. Therefore, frequent small-sized transfer batches are necessary to try to shorten the lead time.

Situations 3 and 4 include a CCR without a setup and a CCR with setup time requirements. Handling the CCR would be similar to handling a nonbottleneck, though more carefully. That is, a CCR has some idle time. It would be appropriate here to cut the size of some of the process batches so that there can be more frequent changes of product. This would decrease lead time and jobs would be more likely to be done on time. In a make-to-stock situation cutting process batch sizes has a

---

[3] Mokshagundam L. Srikanth, *The Drum–Buffer–Rope System of Material Control* (New Haven, CT: Spectrum Management Group, 1987), pp. 25–37.

much more profound effect than increasing the number of transfer batches. This is because the resulting product mix is much greater, leading to reduced WIP and production lead time.

How to Treat Inventory

The traditional view of inventory is that its only negative impact on a firm's performance is its carrying cost. We now realize inventory's negative impact also comes from lengthening lead times and creating problems with engineering changes. (When an engineering change on a product comes through, which commonly occurs, product still within the production system often must be modified to include the changes. Therefore, less work in process reduces the number of engineering changes to be made.)

Fox and Goldratt propose to treat inventory as a loan given to the manufacturing unit. The value of the loan is based only on the purchased items that are part of the inventory. As we stated earlier, inventory is treated in this chapter as material cost only, and without any accounting-type value added from production. If inventory is carried as a loan to manufacturing, we need a way to measure how long the loan is carried. One measurement is dollar days.

Dollar Days   A useful performance measurement is the concept of **dollar days,** a measurement of the value of inventory and the time it stays within an area. To use this measure, we could simply multiply the total value of inventory by the number of days inventory spends within a department.

Dollar Days

Suppose department X carries an average inventory of $40,000, and, on the average, the inventory stays within the department five days. In dollar days then, department X is charged with $40,000 times five days, or $200,000 dollar days of inventory. At this point, we cannot say the $200,000 is high or low, but it does show where the inventory is located. Management can then see where it should focus attention and determine acceptable levels. Techniques can be instituted to try to reduce the number of dollar days while being careful that such a measure does not become a local objective (i.e., minimizing dollar days) and hurt the global objectives (such as increasing ROI, cash flow, and net profit).

Dollar days could be beneficial in a variety of ways. Consider the current practice of using efficiencies or equipment utilization as a performance measurement. To get high utilizations, large amounts of inventory are held to keep everything working. However, high inventories would result in a high number of dollar days, which would discourage high levels of work in process. Dollar day measurements could also be used in other areas:

MARKETING
PURCHASING

- Marketing, to discourage holding large amounts of finished-goods inventory. The net result would be to encourage sale of finished products.
- Purchasing, to discourage placing large purchase orders that on the surface appear to take advantage of quantity discounts. This would encourage just-in-time purchasing.
- Manufacturing, to discourage large work in process and producing earlier than needed. This would promote rapid flow of material within the plant.
- Project management, to quantify a project's limited resource investments as a function of time. This promotes the proper allocation of resources to competing projects.

■ COMPARING SYNCHRONOUS MANUFACTURING TO MRP AND JIT

Backward Scheduling

MRP uses **backward scheduling** after having been fed a master production schedule. MRP schedules production through a bill of materials explosion in a backward manner—working backward in time from the desired completion date. As a secondary procedure, MRP, through its capacity resource planning module, develops capacity utilization profiles of work centers. When work centers are overloaded, either the master production schedule must be adjusted or enough slack capacity must be left unscheduled in the system so that work can be smoothed at the local level (by work center supervisors or the workers themselves). Trying to smooth capacity using MRP is so difficult and would require so many computer runs that capacity overloads and underloads are best left to local decisions, such as at the machine centers. An MRP schedule becomes invalid just days after it was created.

Forward Scheduling

The synchronous manufacturing approach uses **forward scheduling** because it focuses on the critical resources. These are scheduled forward in time, ensuring that loads placed on them are within capacity. The noncritical (or nonbottleneck) resources are then scheduled to support the critical resources. (This can be done backward to minimize the length of time that inventories are held.) This procedure ensures a feasible schedule. To help reduce lead time and work in process, in synchronous manufacturing the process batch size and transfer batch size are varied—a procedure that MRP is not able to do. (We say more on this later.)

Comparing JIT to synchronous manufacturing, JIT does an excellent job in reducing lead times and work in process, but it has several drawbacks:

1. JIT is limited to repetitive manufacturing.
2. JIT requires a stable production level (usually about a month long).
3. JIT does not allow very much flexibility in the products produced. (Products must be similar with a limited number of options.)
4. JIT still requires work in process when used with kanban so that there is "something to pull." This means that completed work must be stored on the downstream side of each workstation to be pulled by the next workstation.
5. Vendors need to be located nearby because the system depends on smaller, more frequent deliveries.

Because synchronous manufacturing uses a schedule to assign work to each workstation, there is no need for more work in process other than that being worked on. The exception is for inventory specifically placed in front of a bottleneck to ensure continual work, or at specific points downstream from a bottleneck to ensure flow of product.

Concerning continual improvements on the system, JIT is a trial-and-error procedure applied to a real system. In synchronous manufacturing, the system can be programmed and simulated on a computer because the schedules are realistic (can be accomplished) and computer run time is short.

■ VAT CLASSIFICATION OF FIRMS

All manufacturing firms can be classified into one or a combination of three types designated V, A, and T, depending on the products and processes. Exhibit 20.15

VAT Classification of Firms

Exhibit 20.15

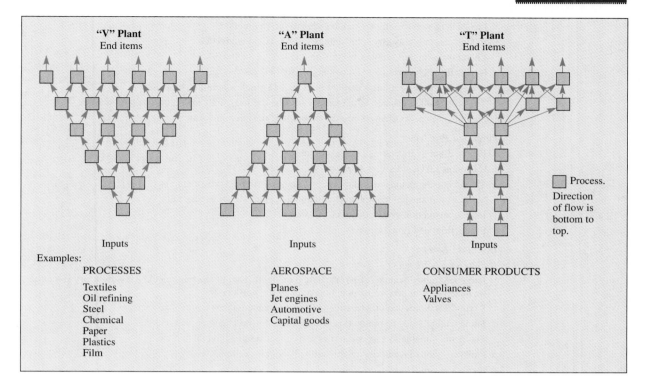

"V" Plant
End items

"A" Plant
End items

"T" Plant
End items

☐ Process.
Direction
of flow is
bottom to
top.

Inputs

Inputs

Inputs

Examples:

PROCESSES

AEROSPACE

CONSUMER PRODUCTS

Textiles
Oil refining
Steel
Chemical
Paper
Plastics
Film

Planes
Jet engines
Automotive
Capital goods

Appliances
Valves

shows all three types. The reason for using the **VAT classification** is obvious when we note the actual appearance of the product flow through the system. In a "V" plant, there are few raw materials and they are transformed through a relatively standard process into a much larger number of end products. Consider a steel plant, for example: A few raw materials are converted into a large number of types of sheet steel, beams, rods, wire, and so forth.

VAT Classification

An "A" plant is the opposite. In an "A" plant, many raw materials, components, and parts are converted into few end products. Examples in aerospace would be making jet engines, airplanes, and missiles. In a "T" plant, the final product is assembled in many different ways out of similar parts and components. There are two stages in the production process: First, the basic parts and components are manufactured in a relatively straightforward way (the lower portion of the T) and are stored. Second, assembly takes place, combining these common parts into the many possible options to create the final product.

"V" Plant

Exhibit 20.16 shows the characteristics of a "V" plant. Problems that occur in a "V" plant show up as poor customer service, poor delivery, and high inventories of finished goods. The basic cause is generally a zealous effort to achieve high utilization levels, which instigates overly large process batch sizes.

Exhibit 20.16

"V" Plant

Characteristics

- There are a large number of end items, compared to the number of raw materials.
- Products use essentially the same sequence and processes.
- Equipment is generally capital-intensive and specialized.
- There are a limited number of routings.
- Generally, each part crosses a resource only once.
- It tends to produce a large number of parts in a small amount of time.
- The total available space in the facility may be the only limit to inventory accumulation.
- Significant process changes require substantial resource investment.

Perceived Problems

- Finished-goods inventories are too large.
- Customer service/delivery is poor.
- Manufacturing managers complain that demand is constantly changing.
- Marketing managers complain that manufacturing is slow to respond.
- Interdepartmental conflicts are common.
- Production lead time becomes unpredictable.

Inventory Levels

If there is a bottleneck:

- Large inventory (usually of wrong items) exists in front of the bottleneck. This inventory is caused by misallocation and overproduction prior to the bottleneck.
- Beyond the bottleneck there are small queues since there is excess capacity.
- Management tends to blame this wrong inventory on changing demand.
- The firm is unable to respond to the market because of large inventory.
- Finished-goods inventories of the wrong products accumulate.

If there is no bottleneck:

There are large finished-goods inventories of the wrong products.

Causes

- Batch sizes are too large because the plant is capital-intensive and the setup times are large.
- To achieve high levels of utilization, material is released to production too early.
- Supervisors are measured on utilizations of labor and equipment.
- Jobs are combined for larger batches, and product families are grouped together.
- Considerable expediting is done at the bottleneck.

Correct Course of Action

- Reduce batch size.
- Reduce production lead times. This improves forecast accuracy and the ability to react to changes in demand.
- Increase customer service with
  - Reliable promise dates.
  - Reduced production lead times.
- Reduce production costs by
  - Selling more product.
  - Reducing inventory.
  - Focusing on quality improvements.

"A" Plant

Exhibit 20.17 shows the characteristics of an "A" plant. In an "A" plant, management areas of concern are low equipment utilization, high unplanned overtime, parts shortages, and lack of control of the production process. When the flow is controlled correctly, there is a better utilization of resources, overtime is reduced or eliminated, and inventory levels are greatly decreased.

Exhibit 20.17

"A" Plant

Characteristics

- Assembly feature is dominant.
- Machines tend to be general-purpose rather than specialized.
- Assembly time tends to be long.
- Resources are shared within and across routings.
- Resource efficiencies are less than 100 percent, but there is still overtime.
- Large completed-parts inventory exists, but severe shortage exists for other parts.
- Process time typically is less than production lead time.
- Wandering bottlenecks occur.
- Fabrication complains that demand is changing, leading to plant chaos and poor vendor performance.
- Operating expenses (particularly unplanned overtime) is a sore point.
- Problem parts are most likely not common to many assemblies.
- Relatively few parts cross the bottleneck (capacity constraint).
- Lack of control is voiced as the key problem.
- Assembly complains of shortages and mismatches.
- Production is designated early in the process (the opposite of a "V" plant).
- People perceive the problem as a lack of parts.
- Routings can vary widely; one part may require 50 operations, while another for the same assembly may require only a few.
- The same machine may be used several times on the same part during its routing.
- Parts are unique to specific end items (unlike a "V" or "T" plant); jet engine blades, for example, are only for particular engines.
- There is little opportunity for misallocation of parts because they are peculiar to end items.

Conventional Tactics for Corrective Action

Reduce unit cost by

- Strict control of overtime. (Management perceives abuse of overtime; restriction of use aggravates problem.)
- Automation of processes. (This makes matters worse since flexibility is lost through the automation.)
- Better planning of labor needs. (The illusion is that there are too many workers.)

Improve control by

- Integrated production system. (The problem here is that different parts of the plant operate differently so a single system is unlikely to satisfy all needs.)

Actual Causes

Too-large batch sizes and too-early release of material causing

- Moving bottlenecks.
- Low utilizations.
- Frequent use of overtime.
- All parts needed for assembly not being there at the same time; assembly operations constantly being short the parts needed to assemble the product.
- Frequent expediting to rush through missing parts.

Solution

- Reduce batch size.
- Use drum–buffer–rope for control.

Exhibit 20.18

"T" Plant

Characteristics

- Two distinctive processes and flows:
  - Fabrication.
  - Assembly.
- Due-date performance is very poor; there is a split between very early and very late (e.g., 40 percent early, 20 percent on time, 40 percent late).
- Overtime and expediting in fabrication are random and frequent.
- A very high degree of commonality of parts is dominant.
- The assignment of parts (even subassemblies) to orders occurs very late in the process.
- Fabrication is done in huge batches.
- There is a large amount of inventory at the stocking level between fabrication and assembly.

Causes of Problems

- Improvement in due-date performance is attempted by heavy reliance on inventory of both finished and semifinished goods, and in volume and variety.
- The drive to attain efficiencies and dollars shipped
  - Undermines assembly activity objectives of due-date performance and assemble-to-order.
  - Undermines fabrication activity objective of purchase and fabricate to forecast.
  - Causes intentional misallocation of parts and cannibalization at assembly and subassembly areas.

Core Problem

- Due-date performance is bad and management cannot seem to do anything about it.

Solution

- Reduce batch sizes in fabrication.
- Use drum-buffer-rope in fabrication to control flow.
- Stop the "stealing" of parts and components in assembly.

"T" Plant

The main characteristic of a "T" plant is that the parts and components are common to many end items. The assembly of end products in a "T" plant is a combinatorial problem, with customers placing orders for different colors, features, or sizes, thus creating many possibilities. The lead time, as far as the customer is concerned, is the height of the cross bar of the T. This means that a customer's order is assembled from the standard parts and components that are stocked. Typically, management erroneously perceives the problem as a need for better forecasting, improved inventory control in warehouses, and reduced unit cost by controlling overtime and setups and by introducing automation and simplified designs. Exhibit 20.18 summarizes "T" plant characteristics. The correct approach using synchronous manufacturing is to improve due-date delivery performance and to reduce operating expenses by

1. Controlling the flow through the fabrication portion of the process.

2. Reducing batch sizes to eliminate the wavelike motion.

3. Stopping the "stealing" of parts and components at assembly.

The vertical part of the T is the fabrication process that needs to be controlled using smaller batches. These parts are then stored below the crossbar. Final assembly is done in the crossbar.

Stealing parts is caused by the pressure from each supervisor in the assembly process to maintain high utilizations. When supervisors and workers are caught up on orders that are currently due, or when they cannot assemble a product because parts

Exhibit 20.19

Summary of VAT
Plant Characteristics
and Perceived
Problems

Summary

"V" Plant	Capital-intensive
	Highly mechanized
	Dedicated
	Inflexible
	Specialization within the flow process
"A" Plant	Less capital-intensive
	Versatile
	Flexible machines
	Can work at different levels of product flow
"T" Plant	Has fabrication and assembly areas
	Fabrication:
	Short routing
	Versatile machines
	Assembly area:
	Assembly is the predominant activity.
	Assembly lead time (days) is short.

Management-Perceived Problems

"V" Plant	Cost is the focus.
"A" Plant	There is a need for control (constantly expediting, overtime, material availability, no idea of problem, wandering bottleneck).
"T" Plant	Due-date performance is usually bad, but management cannot seem to change it.

are missing, they reach ahead and assemble products for future orders. The result is that some other products in the assembly area are short those items and are therefore late.

In conclusion, the VAT classification can lead us quickly and directly to the source of the problem. Exhibit 20.19 summarized plant characteristics and perceived problems. In a "V" plant, we would look for large inventories. In an "A" plant, we would expect to find moving bottlenecks. In a "T" plant, we would suspect that people are stealing parts to build ahead.

■ RELATIONSHIP WITH OTHER FUNCTIONAL AREAS

The production system must work closely with the other functional areas to achieve the best operating system. This section briefly discusses accounting and marketing—areas where conflicts can occur—and where cooperation and joint planning should occur.

ACCOUNTING
MARKETING

Accounting's Influence

Sometimes we are led into making decisions to suit the measurement system rather than to follow the firm's goals. Consider the following example: Suppose that two old machines are currently being used to produce a product. The processing time for each is 20 minutes per part and, because each has the capacity of three parts per hour, they have the combined capacity of six per hour, which exactly meets the market demand of six parts per hour. Suppose that engineering finds a new machine that produces parts in 12 minutes rather than 20. However, the capacity of this one machine is only five per hour, which does not meet the market demand. Logic would seem to dictate that the supervisor should use an old machine to make up the lacking one unit per hour. However, the system does not allow this. The standard has been changed from the 20 minutes each to 12 minutes each and performance would look very bad on paper because the variance would be 67 percent high $[20 - 12)/12]$ for units made on the old machines. The supervisor, therefore, would work the new machine on overtime.

Problems in Cost Accounting Measurements   Cost accounting is used for performance measurement, cost determinations, investment justification, and inventory valuation. Two sets of accounting performance measurements are used for evaluation: (1) global measurements, which are financial statements, showing net profit, return on investment, and cash flow (with which we agree); and (2) local cost accounting measurements showing efficiencies (as variances from standard) or utilization rate (hours worked/hours present).

From the cost accounting (local measurement) viewpoint, then, performance has traditionally been based on cost and full utilization. This logic forces supervisors to activate their workers all the time, which leads to excessive inventory. The cost accounting measurement system can also instigate other problems. For example, attempting to use the idle time to increase utilization can create a bottleneck, as we discussed earlier in this chapter. Any measurement system should support the objectives of the firm and not stand in the way. Fortunately, the cost accounting measurement philosophy is changing.

Marketing and Production

Marketing and production should communicate and conduct their activities in close harmony. In practice, however, they act very independently. There are many reasons for this. The difficulties range from differences in personalities and cultures to unlike systems of merits and rewards in the two functions. Marketing people are judged on the growth of the company in terms of sales, market share, and new products introduced. Marketing is sales oriented. Manufacturing people are evaluated on cost and utilization. Therefore, marketing wants a variety of products to increase the company's position, while manufacturing is trying to reduce cost.

Data used for evaluating marketing and manufacturing are also quite different. Marketing data are "soft" (qualitative); manufacturing data are "hard" (quantitative). The orientation and experiences of marketing and production people also differ. Those in marketing management have likely come up through sales and a close association with customers. Top manufacturing managers have likely progressed through production operations and therefore have plant performance as a top objective.

Cultural differences can also be important in contrasting marketing and manufacturing personnel. Top managers in each can live quite differently because they have different motivations, goals, and hobbies as well. Marketing people tend to have a greater ego drive and are more outgoing. Manufacturing personnel tend to be more meticulous and perhaps more introverted (at least less extroverted than their marketing counterparts).

The solution to coping with these differences is to develop an equitable set of measurements to evaluate performance in each area, and to promote strong lines of communications so that they both contribute to reaching the firm's goals.

We now present two examples to show that different objectives and measurement criteria can lead to the wrong decisions. These examples also show that, even though you may have all the data required, you still may not be able to solve the problem—unless you know how!

■ **example 20.1** *What to Produce?* In this first example, three products (A, B, and C) are sold in the market at $50, $75, and $60 per unit, respectively. The market will take all that can be supplied.

Three work centers (X, Y, and Z) process the three products as shown in Exhibit 20.20. Processing times for each work center are also shown. Note that each work center works on all three products. Raw materials, parts, and components are added at each work center to produce each product. The per unit cost of these materials is shown as RM.

Which product or products should be produced?

solution Three different objectives could exist that lead to different conclusions:

1. Maximize sales revenue since marketing personnel are paid commissions based on total revenue.
2. Maximize per unit gross profit.
3. Maximize total gross profit.

In this example we use gross profit as selling price less materials. We could also include other expenses such as operating expenses, but we left them out for simplicity. (We include operating expenses in our next example.)

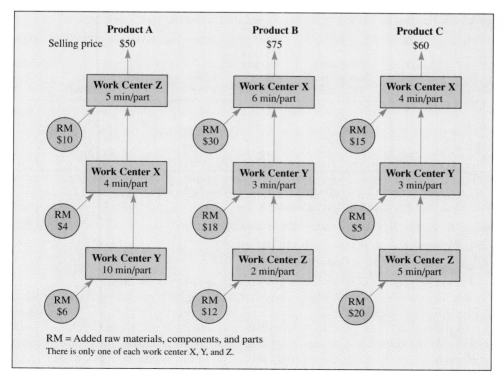

Exhibit 20.20

Prices and Production Requirements for Three Products and Three Work Centers

Objective 1: Maximize sales commission. Sales personnel in this case are unaware of the processing time required so, therefore, they will try to sell only B at $75 per unit and none of A or C. Maximum revenue is determined by the limiting resource as follows:

Product	Limiting Resource	Time Required	Number Produced per Hour	Selling Price	Sales Revenue per Hour
A	Y	10 min	6	$50	$300
B	X	6 min	10	75	750
C	Z	5 min	12	60	720

Objective 2: Maximize per unit gross profit.

	(1)	(2)	(3)	(4)
	Product	Selling Price	Raw Material Cost	Gross Profit per Unit (2) − (3)
	A	$50	$20	$30
	B	$75	$60	$15
	C	$60	$40	$20

The decision would be to sell only product A, which has a $30 per unit gross profit.

Objective 3: Maximize total gross profit. We can solve this problem by finding either total gross profit for the period or the rate at which profit is generated. We use rate to solve the problem both because it is easier and because it is a more appropriate measure. We use profit per hour as the rate.

Note that each product has a different work center which limits its output. The rate at which the product is made is then based on this bottleneck work center.

(1)	(2)	(3)	(4)	(5)	(6)	(7)	(8)
Product	Limiting Work Center	Processing Time per Unit (Minutes)	Product Output Rate (per Hour)	Selling Price	Raw Material Cost	Profit per Unit	Profit per Hour (4) × (7)
A	Y	10	6	$50	$20	$30	$180
B	X	6	10	75	60	15	150
C	Z	5	12	60	40	20	240

From our calculations, product C provides the highest profit of $240 per hour. Note that we get three different answers:

1. We choose B to maximize sales revenue.
2. We choose A to maximize profit per unit.
3. We choose C to maximize total profit.

Choosing product C is obviously the correct answer for the firm.

In this example, all work centers were required for each product and each product had a different work center as a constraint. We did this to simplify the problem and to ensure that only one product would surface as the answer. If there were more work centers or the same work center constraint in different products, the problem could still easily be solved using linear programming (as in the Supplement to Chapter 7). ■

■ **example 20.2** *How Much to Produce?* In this example, shown in Exhibit 20.21, there are two workers producing four products. The plant works three shifts. The market demand is unlimited and takes all the products that the workers can produce. The only stipulation is that the ratio of products sold cannot exceed 10 to 1 between the maximum sold of any one product and the minimum of another. For example, if the maximum number sold of any one of the products is 100 units, the minimum of any other cannot be fewer than 10 units. Workers 1 and 2, on each shift, are not cross-trained and can only work on their own operations. The time and raw material (RM) costs are shown in the exhibit, and a summary of the costs and times involved is on the lower portion of the exhibit. Weekly operating expenses are $3,000.

What quantities of A, B, C, and D should be produced?

solution As in the previous example, there are three answers to this question, depending on each of the following objectives:

1. Maximizing revenue for sales personnel who are paid on commission.
2. Maximizing per unit gross profit.
3. Maximizing the utilization of the bottleneck resource (leading to maximum gross profit).

Objective 1: Maximizing sales commission on sales revenue. Sales personnel prefer to sell B and D (selling price $32) rather than A and C (selling price $30). Weekly operating expenses are $3,000.

Production Requirements and Selling Price for Four Products

Exhibit 20.21

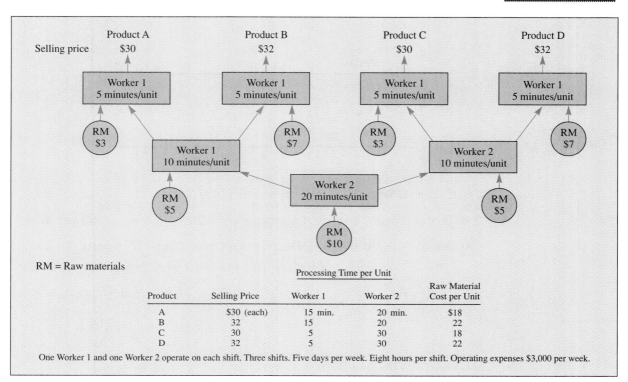

One Worker 1 and one Worker 2 operate on each shift. Three shifts. Five days per week. Eight hours per shift. Operating expenses $3,000 per week.

Product	Selling Price	Worker 1	Worker 2	Raw Material Cost per Unit
A	$30 (each)	15 min.	20 min.	$18
B	32	15	20	22
C	30	5	30	18
D	32	5	30	22

The ratio of units sold will be: 1A : 10B : 1C : 10D.

Worker 2 on each shift is the bottleneck and therefore determines the output.[4]

$$5 \text{ days per week} \times 3 \text{ shifts} \times 8 \text{ hours} \times 60 \text{ minutes} = \frac{7{,}200 \text{ minutes per}}{\text{week available}}$$

Worker 2 spends these times on each unit:

A   20 minutes   B   20 minutes   C   30 minutes   D   30 minutes

The ratio of output units is 1 : 10 : 1 : 10. Therefore

$$1x(20) + 10x(20) + 1x(30) + 10x(30) = 7{,}200$$
$$550x = 7{,}200$$
$$x = 13.09$$

Therefore, the numbers of units produced are

A = 13   B = 131   C = 13   D = 131

Total revenue is

$$13(30) + 131(32) + 13(30) + 131(32) = \$9{,}164 \text{ per week}$$

For comparison with objectives 2 and 3, we will compute gross profit per week.

Gross profit per week (selling price less raw material less weekly expenses) is

$$13(30 - 18) + 131(32 - 22) + 13(30 - 18) + 131(32 - 22) - 3{,}000$$
$$= 156 + 1{,}310 + 156 + 1{,}310 - 3{,}000$$
$$= (\$68) \text{ loss.}$$

Objective 2: Maximizing per unit gross profit.

	Gross Profit	=	Selling Price	−	Raw Material Cost
A	12	=	30	−	18
B	10	=	32	−	22
C	12	=	30	−	18
D	10	=	32	−	22

A and C have the maximum gross profit so the ratio will be 10 : 1 : 10 : 1 for A, B, C, and D. Worker 2 is the constraint and has

$$5 \text{ days} \times 3 \text{ shifts} \times 8 \text{ hours} \times 60 \text{ minutes} = 7{,}200 \text{ minutes available per week}$$

As before, A and B take 20 minutes, while C and D take 30 minutes. Thus

$$10x(20) + 1x(20) + 10x(30) + 1x(30) = 7{,}200$$
$$550x = 7{,}200$$
$$x = 13$$

---

[4] Note that if this truly is a bottleneck with an unlimited market demand, this should be a seven-day-per-week operation, not just a five-day workweek.

Therefore, the number of units produced is

$$A = 131 \quad B = 13 \quad C = 31 \quad D = 13$$

Gross profit (selling price less raw materials less $3,000 weekly expense) is

$$131(30 - 18) + 13(32 - 22) + 131(30 - 18) + 13(32 - 22) - 3,000$$
$$= 1,572 + 130 + 1,572 + 130 - 3,000$$
$$= \$404 \text{ profit}$$

Objective 3: Maximizing the use of the bottleneck resource, worker 2. For every hour worker 2 works, the following number of products and gross profit result

(1) Product	(2) Production Time	(3) Units Produced per Hour	(4) Selling Price Each	(5) Raw Material Cost per Unit	(6) Gross Profit per Hour (3) × [(4) − (5)]
A	20 minutes	3	$30	$18	$36
B	20	3	32	22	30
C	30	2	30	18	24
D	30	2	32	22	20

Product A generates the greatest gross profit per hour of worker 2 time, so the ratio is 10 : 1 : 1 : 1 for A, B, C, and D.

Available time for worker 2 is the same as before:

$$3 \text{ shifts} \times 5 \text{ days} \times 8 \text{ hours} \times 60 \text{ minutes} = 7,200 \text{ minutes}$$

Worker 2 should produce 10 As for every 1 B, 1 C, and 1 D. Worker 2's average production rate is

$$10x(20) + 1x(20) + 1x(30) + 1x(30) = 7,200$$
$$280x = 7,200$$
$$x = 25.7$$

Therefore, the number of units that should be produced is

$$A = 257 \quad B = 25.7 \quad C = 25.7 \quad D = 25.7$$

Gross profit (price less raw materials less $3,000 weekly expenses) is

$$257(30 - 18) + 25.7(32 - 22) + 25.7(30 - 18) + 25.7(32 - 22) - 3,000$$
$$= 3,084 + 257 + 308.4 + 257 - 3,000$$
$$= \$906.40$$

In summary, using three different objectives to decide how many of each product to make gave us three different results:

1. Maximizing sales commission resulted in a $68 loss in gross profit.
2. Maximizing gross profit gave us a profit of $404.
3. Maximizing the use of the capacity-constrained worker gave us the best gross profit, $906.40. ∎

BREAKTHROUGH

The Trane Company

The Trane Company is a large industrial organization headquartered in LaCrosse, Wisconsin. The Trane Company's Commercial Systems factory in Macon, Georgia, produces the company's line of large self-contained air conditioner units for buildings. In 1987 the self-contained unit production was transferred from a sister factory to the Macon plant. The plant was originally configured in 1988 as a balanced assembly line to accept the self-contained unit production. The Macon factory operates on an eight-hour-per-day, five-days-per-week basis. Total plant employment is about 150 employees. There are about 90 direct-labor employees. All permanent Macon employees are salaried. Temporary employees are hired on a daily basis from a local employment agency. The number of temporary employees varies with the production rate from 0 to 25 percent of the permanent direct-labor employees. At the time of this writing, about 20 percent of the 90 direct-labor employees were temporaries. The factory had 1990 sales of about $25 million and was profitable under generally accepted accounting standards criteria.

The production planning and control system used at the Macon factory is a combination of MRP, JIT, and TOC.* An MRP system was purchased in early 1989. The software package is identified as CONTROL produced by Cincom, Inc. The decision to purchase the MRP software was based on a survey of factory user requirements that compared several different MRP systems. The MRP system consists of several generic modules linked by customized interfaces. Currently, the Macon factory uses the master production scheduling module, the MRP calculation module, the accounting module, and the bill-of-materials module. A separate purchasing system was selected and implemented together with the MRP system in 1989. The shop-floor control module that was available as part of the CONTROL software package was not implemented. The factory's decision not to implement the shop-floor control module was based on the desire to use TOC and JIT methods. Management believes that the MRP system provided a framework for the TOC and JIT methods.

The company employed an outside consultant in 1988 to improve aspects of the production process using the JIT approach. The Macon factory uses a leveled master production schedule, production schedule linearity, scheduled preventive maintenance, multiskilled employees, and plant layout revisions to accommodate JIT. Kanban triggers are also used for replenishing subassemblies into the final assembly area. Suppliers use triggering methods to replenish hardware and other purchased finished components. The factory is organized into five work teams, called cells, and all cell supervisors have been trained on JIT methods. Production decisions, such as the scheduling of overtime, are made by consensus of the cell employees.

The factory implemented TOC in 1989. The performance measurement aspects of throughput, inventory, and operating expense are used for internal management decisions. The shop floor is controlled by the drum–buffer–rope and buffer management methods. Management has been trained in the use of TOC techniques and the underlying performance measurement methods. The OPT software is not used at the factory. The bottleneck operation was identified and a "constraint" buffer was used as well as a "space" buffer after the bottleneck operation.

Inventory management is a shared responsibility between the cell supervisors and support employees. Manufacturing lead time is two to five days. Raw material is 70 percent of the total inventory and has a current turnover of about six times per year. Work-in-process inventory is about 10 percent of the total inventory investment and has a turnover of 100 times per year. Finished goods are about 20 percent of the total inventory and have a turnover of about 10 times per year. Factory management has 1992 turnover targets for raw material inventory of 12 times per year, work-in-process inventory at 250 times per year, and finished goods at 15 times per year.

---

* TOC (Theory of Constraints). See Exhibit 20.2, page 791.

When first begun, the balanced assembly line used the kanban pull system and produced an average of three units per day. When drum–buffer–rope and buffer management techniques were implemented, the assembly line average increased to six units per day with the same workforce. Management attributes the increase in productivity to TOC and believes that the dramatic reduction in lead time significantly contributes to the competitiveness of its product lines in the marketplace.

New Product Introduction

In 1991, The Trane Company was faced with a decision concerning whether to introduce two new products into the marketplace. The first product was a refrigerant cleaning service unit that measured approximately $5 \times 4 \times 3$ feet. The second product was a refrigerant evacuation unit that was smaller than the cleaning service unit. The company could have built the units in a factory in Pennsylvania. However, traditional cost-accounting–based calculations indicated that the expected price of the products would not be sufficient to generate a profit at that factory. The company then had to consider the abandonment of the two product lines. The self-contained air conditioner units assembled at the Macon factory measure about $7 \times 5 \times 10$ feet. Because of the much larger size, the Macon factory was not initially considered for the assembly of the two new product lines. The Macon factory undertook its own implementation study based on the TOC performance measurement methods. As a result of the study, both products were assigned to be manufactured at the Macon factory, and the product lines were introduced into the market in 1992. Traditional cost accounting valuation methods led the company to abandon two product lines that have proved to be profitable under TOC calculation.

The Macon factory determined that enough space had been made available through the use of TOC and JIT methods in what had been the finished stores area that both product lines could be assembled in the factory. Further, because neither of the product lines used the existing self-contained unit assembly line, the bottleneck operation would not be jeopardized by the introduction of the two products. Because factory space already existed, there would be no capital outlay except for the required assembly tools, considered an addition to operating expenses. Under TOC costing, only raw material costs are included in the inventory figure for each. All labor and overheads are part of operating expense and are controlled at the factory level rather than being assigned to a specific product. Therefore, the expected selling price of both product lines exceeded the raw material inventory cost for the product lines. Operating expense at the plant level was determined to increase less than the total amount of throughput for each product line. The net profit from each product line was equal to total throughput minus the additional operating expense. Return on investment in the new product lines equaled the net profit from the new product lines divided by the added investment needed to support the new product lines. Therefore, the Macon factory readily accepted the introduction of the two product lines, while other factories could not justify the introduction using traditional cost accounting methods.

Two Accounting Systems

The Macon factory uses a dual accounting system. External reports are generated by the accounting module of the MRP system. The external reports are sent to Trane headquarters using traditional accounting methods (allocation of overheads is based on direct-labor hours). The factory is measured on profit-and-loss calculations based on standard accounting practices. Internal factory management reports use TOC methods based on throughput, inventory, and operating-expense calculations. To a degree the decision made by Trane headquarters to assign the two product lines to Macon indicates an acceptance of TOC calculations even though traditional performance measures are used in the formal external reporting system.

Source: M. S. Spencer, "Economic Theory, Cost Accounting, and Theory of Constraints: An Examination of Relationships and Problems," *International Journal of Production Research* 32, no. 2 (1994), pp. 304–7.

Both examples demonstrate that production and marketing need to interact. Marketing should sell the most profitable use of available capacity. However, to plan capacity, production needs to know from marketing what products could be sold.

■ CONCLUSION

The measurement system within a firm should encourage the increase of net profits, return on investment, and cash flow. The firm can accomplish this if, at the operations level, it rewards performance based on the amount of throughput, inventory, and operating expense created. This is essential for a firm's success.

To control throughput, inventory, and operating expense, the system must be analyzed to find bottlenecks and capacity-constrained resources. Only then can the company proceed to define a drum for control, buffers to ensure throughput, and ropes for communicating the correct information to the correct locations, while minimizing work in process everywhere else. Without this focus, problems are not correctly diagnosed and solution procedures are impossible.

Goldratt defined nine rules (Exhibit 20.1) to help guide the logic of an operating system and to identify the important points. These are basic to any operating system and were originally called the Nine Rules of OPT.

The underlying philosophy presented in this chapter—the vital importance of concentrating on system limitations imposed by capacity-constrained resources—has led Goldratt to broaden his view of the importance of system limitations and to develop his five-step "general theory of constraints."[5] (See Exhibit 20.2.)

While the terms *bottleneck* and *constraint* can mean essentially the same thing, Goldratt uses *constraint* in the broadest sense to mean anything that limits the performance of a system and slows or prevents it from continuing to move toward its goal.

This general theory of constraints directs companies to find what is stopping them from moving toward their goals and finding ways to get around this limitation. If, in a manufacturing environment, the limitation is insufficient capacity, then ways to break the constraint might be overtime, specialized tools, supporting equipment, exceptionally skilled workers, subcontracting, redesigning product or process, alternate routings, and so on. Point 5 (Exhibit 20.2) warns against letting biases in thinking prevent the search for further exploitation of constraints. For example, if a search and exploitation of a constraint has been conducted under the limitation of cost, make sure that this cost measure is not carried into the next search. Start clean each time.

MARKETING
FINANCE
ENGINEERING

One last comment in summary of this chapter: The firm should operate as a synchronized system, with all parts in harmony and supporting each other. Marketing, finance, production, and engineering (as well as all the other functional staff and administrative entities) are all necessary parts of the system and are all seeking to achieve the common goals of the firm.

SOLVED PROBLEM

SOLVED PROBLEM

Here is the process flow for products A, B, and C. Products A, B, and C sell for $20, $25, and $30, respectively. There is only one resource X and one resource Y, which are used to produce

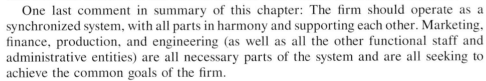

---

[5] Eliyahu M. Goldratt, *The General Theory of Constraints* (New Haven, CT: Abraham Y. Goldratt Institute, 1989).

A, B, and C for the numbers of minutes stated on the diagram. Raw materials are needed at the process steps as shown, with the costs in dollars per unit of raw material. (One unit is used for each product.)

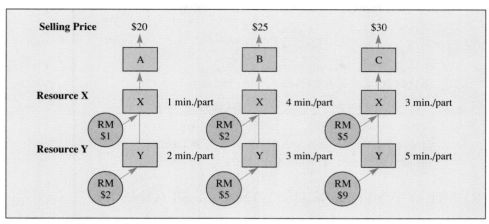

The market will take all that you can produce.

    a. Which product would you produce to maximize gross margin per unit?

    b. If sales personnel are paid on commission, which product or products would they sell and how many could they sell?

    c. Which and how many product or products should you produce to maximize gross profit for a one-week period?

    d. From (c), how much gross profit would there be for the week?

Solution

    a. Maximizing gross margin per unit

	Gross Margin	**=**	**Selling Price**	**−**	**Raw Material Cost**
A	17	=	20	−	3
B	18	=	25	−	7
C	16	=	30	−	14

        Product B will be produced.

    b. Maximizing sales commission. Sales personnel would sell the highest-priced product, C (unless they knew the market and capacity limitations). If we assume the market will take all that we can make, then we would work 7 days/week, 8 hours/day. Y is the constraint in producing C. The number of C we can make in a week is

$$C = \frac{8 \text{ hours/day} \times 7 \text{ days/week} \times 60 \text{ minutes/hour}}{5 \text{ minutes/part}} = 672 \text{ units}$$

    c. To maximize profit, we need to compare profits per hour for each product.

(1)	(2)	(3)	(4)	(5)	(6)	(7)
Product	**Constraint Resource**	**Production Time on Resource**	**Number of Units Output per Hour**	**Selling Price ($)**	**RM Cost ($)**	**Gross Profit per Hour (4) × (5 − 6)**
A	Y	2	30	20	3	$510
B	X	4	15	25	7	270
C	Y	5	12	30	14	192

If the constraining resource were the same for all three products, our problem would be solved and the answer would be to produce just A, and as many as possible. However, X is the constraint for B, so the answer could be a combination of A and B. To test this, we can see that the value of each hour of Y while producing B is

$$\frac{60 \text{ minutes/hour}}{3 \text{ minutes/unit}} \times (\$25 - 7) = \$360/\text{hour}$$

Since this is less than the $510 per hour producing A, we would produce only A. The number of units of A produced during the week is

$$\frac{60 \text{ minutes/hour} \times 24 \text{ hours/day} \times 7 \text{ days/week}}{2 \text{ minutes/unit}} = 5,040$$

d. Gross profit for the week is $5,040 \times \$17 = \$85,680$.

Solved using profit per hour: $\$510 \times 24 \times 7 = \$85,680$.

REVIEW AND DISCUSSION QUESTIONS

1. State the global performance measurements and operational performance measurements and briefly define each of them. How do these differ from traditional accounting measurements?

2. Discuss process batch and transfer batches. How might you determine what the sizes should be?

3. Compare and contrast JIT, MRP, and synchronized manufacturing, stating their main features, such as where each is or might be used, amounts of raw materials and work-in-process inventories, production lead times and cycle times, and methods for control.

4. Compare and contrast VAT-type plants, bringing in such points as where they are best applied, the main features of each (such as product flow and equipment type), major problems of each, likely source of the problems, and likely solution to the problems.

5. Compare the importance and relevance of quality control in JIT, MRP, and synchronous manufacturing.

6. Discuss what is meant by forward loading and backward loading.

7. Define and explain the cause or causes of a moving bottleneck.

8. Explain how a nonbottleneck can become a bottleneck.

9. What are the functions of inventory in MRP, JIT, and synchronous manufacturing scheduling?

10. Define process batch and transfer batch and their meaning in each of these applications: MRP, JIT, and bottleneck or constrained resource logic.

11. Discuss how a production system is scheduled using MRP logic, JIT logic, and synchronous manufacturing logic.

12. Discuss the concept of "drum–buffer–rope."

13. From the standpoint of the scheduling process, how are resource limitations treated in an MRP application and how are they treated in a synchronous manufacturing application?

14. What are operations people's primary complaints against the accounting procedures used in most firms? Explain how such procedures can cause poor decisions for the total company.

15. Most manufacturing firms try to balance capacity for their production sequences. Some believe that this is an invalid strategy. Explain why balancing capacity does not work.

16. Discuss why transfer batches and process batches many times may not and should not be equal.

PROBLEMS

✓ **1.** For the four basic configurations that follow, assume that the market is demanding product that must be processed by both resource X and resource Y for cases I, II, and III. For case IV, both resources supply separate but dependent markets; that is, the number of units of output from both X and Y must be equal.

   Plans are being made to produce a product that requires 40 minutes on resource X and 30 minutes on resource Y. Assume that there is only one of each of these resources, and that market demand is 1,400 units per month.

   How, would you schedule X and Y? What would happen otherwise in each case?

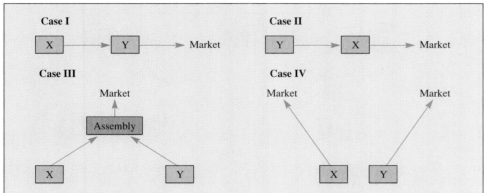

1. Case I:
   X used = 933.3 hours
   Y used = 700 hours
Case II:
   Y = 700 hrs.
   X = 933.3 hrs.
Case III:
   X = 933.3 hrs.
   Y = 700 hrs.
Case IV:
   X = 933.3 hrs.
   Y = 700 hrs.
Otherwise:
Case I NO problem
Case II Excess work-in-process
Case III Excess spare parts
Case IV Excess finished goods

2. Following are the process flow sequences for three products: A, B, and C. There are two bottleneck operations—on the first leg and fourth leg—marked with an X. Boxes represent processes, which may be either machine or manual. Suggest the location of the drum, buffer, and ropes.

2. See SM.

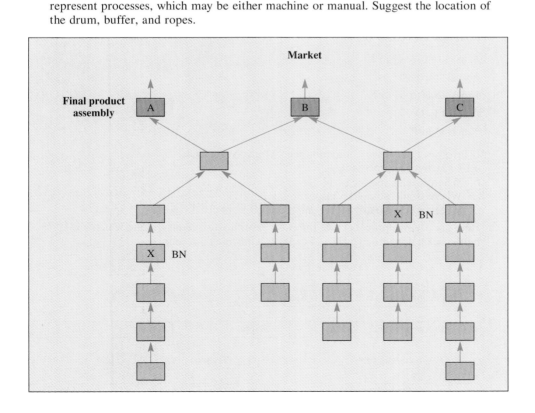

3. The accompanying figure shows a production network model with the parts and processing sequences. State clearly on the figure (1) where you would place inventory; (2) where you would perform inspection; and (3) where you would emphasize high-quality output. (Note: Operations may be shown either as rectangles in Problem 2 or as circles in Problem 3.)

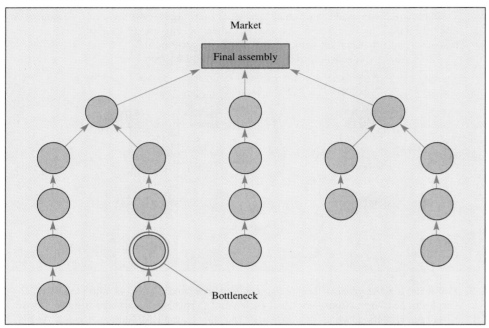

4. The following production flow shows parts, E, I, and N; subassembly O; and final assembly for product P.

A to B to C to D to E

F to G to H to I

J to K to L to M to N

E and I to O

N and O to P

B involves a bottleneck operation, and M involves a CCR.
a. Draw out the process flow.
b. Where would you locate buffer inventories?
c. Where would you place inspection points?
d. Where would you stress the importance of quality production?

5. Here are average process cycle times for several work centers. State which are bottlenecks, nonbottlenecks, and capacity-constrained resources.

Processing time		Setup time

Processing time	Setup	Idle

Processing time	Setup	Idle

Processing time	Setup	Idle

Processing time	Setup	Idle

6. The following diagram shows the flow process, raw material costs, and machine processing time for three products: A, B, and C. There are three machines (W, X, and Y) used in the production of these products; the times shown are in required minutes of production per unit. Raw material costs are shown in cost per unit of product. The market will take all that can be produced.

6. *a.* Product C
  b. Product B at $15.
  c. Product A
     $200/hour.

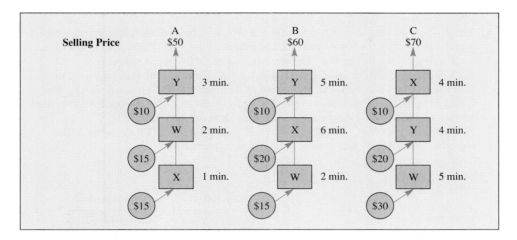

a. Assuming that sales personnel are paid on a commission basis, which product should they sell?

b. On the basis of maximizing gross profit per unit, which product should be sold?

c. To maximize total profit for the firm, which product should be sold?

7. Willard Lock Company is losing market share because of horrendous due-date performance and long delivery lead times. The company's inventory level is high and includes a good deal of finished goods that do not match the short-term orders. Material control analysis shows that purchasing has ordered on time, the vendors have delivered on time, and the scrap/rework rates have been as expected. However, the buildable mix of components and subassemblies does not generally match the

7. See SM.

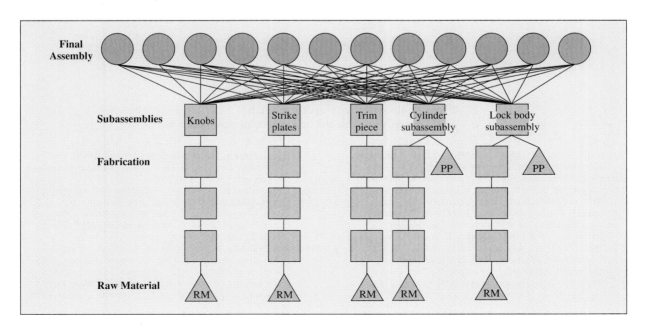

short-term and past-due requirements at final assembly. End-of-month expediting and overtime is the rule, even though there is idle time early in the month. Overall efficiency figures are around 70 percent for the month. These figures are regarded as too low.

You have just been hired as a consultant and must come up with recommendations. Help the firm understand its problems. Specifically state some actions that it should take.

8. The M–N plant manufactures two different products: M and N. Selling prices and weekly market demands are shown in the following diagram. Each product uses raw materials with costs as shown. The plant has three different machines: A, B, and C. Each performs different tasks and can work on only one unit of material at a time.

Process times for each task are shown in the diagram. Each machine is available 2,400 minutes per week. There are no "Murphys" (major opportunities for the system to foul up). Setup and transfer times are zero. Demand is constant.

Operating expenses (including labor) total a constant $12,000 per week. Raw materials are not included in weekly operating expenses.

8. *a.* Machine B ✓
   b. All of M and as many of N as possible.
   c. $600.

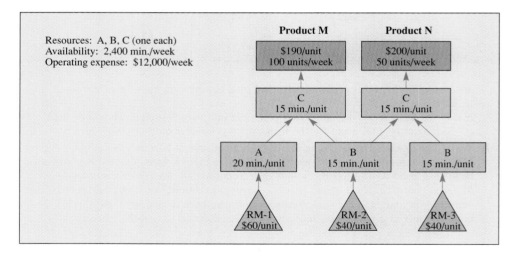

a. Where is the constraint in this plant?
b. What product mix provides the highest profit?
c. What is the maximim weekly profit this plant can earn?

SELECTED BIBLIOGRAPHY

Aggarwal, S. "MRP, JIT, OPT, FMS?" *Harvard Business Review,* September-October 1985, pp. 8–16.

Bramorski, Tom, Manu S. Madan, and Jaideep Motwani. "Application of the Theory of Constraints in Banks." *Bankers Magazine,* January/February 1997, pp. 53–59.

Dettmer, H. William. *Goldratt's Theory of Constraints: A Systems Approach to Continuous Improvement.* Milwaukee, WI: ASQC Quality Press, 1997.

Gardiner, Stanley C., and John H. Blackstone, Jr. "The 'Theory of Constraints' and the Make-or-Buy Decision." *International Journal of Purchasing and Materials Management* 27, no. 3 (Summer 1991), pp. 38–43.

Goldratt, Eliyahu. The *Haystack Syndrome: Sifting Information Out of the Data Ocean.* Croton-on-Hudson, NY: North River Press, 1990.

———. *What Is This Thing Called the Theory of Constraints and How Should It Be Implemented.* Croton-on-Hudson, NY: North River Press, 1990.

———. *Critical Chain.* Croton-on-Hudson, NY: North River Press, 1997.

Goldratt, Eliyahu M., and Jeff Cox. *The Goal: Excellence in Manufacturing.* 2nd rev. ed. Croton-on-Hudson, NY: North River Press, 1992.

Goldratt, Eliyahu M., and Robert E. Fox. *The Race for a Competitive Edge.* Milford, CT: Creative Output, 1986.

Kaplan, Robert S. "Yesterday's Accounting Undermines Production." *Harvard Business Review,* July–August 1984, pp. 95–102.

Neely, A. D., and M. D. Byrne. "A Simulation Study of Bottleneck Scheduling." *International Journal of Production Economics* 26, no. 1–3 (1992), pp. 187–92.

Plossl, George W. "Managing by the Numbers—But Which Numbers." *APICS, Conference Proceedings* (Falls Church, VA: APICS, 1987). pp. 499–503.

Spencer, Michael S. "Economic Theory, Cost Accounting, and Theory of Constraints: An Examination of Relationships and Problems." *International Journal of Production Research* 32, no. 2 (1994), pp. 299–308.

Spencer, Michael S., and James F. Cox III. "Master Production Scheduling Development in a Theory of Constraints Environment." *Production and Inventory Management Journal,* first quarter 1995, pp. 8–14.

Srikanth, Mokshagundam L., and Harold E. Cavallaro, Jr. *Regaining Competitiveness: Putting the Goal to Work.* New Haven, CT: Spectrum, 1987.

Umble, M. Michael, and M. L. Srikanth, *Synchronous Manufacturing: Principles for World Class Excellence.* Cincinnati Ohio: Southwestern, 1990.

Appendixes

Outline

A. Financial Analysis of Operations, 834

Concepts and Definitions
Activity-Based Costing
The Effects of Taxes
Choosing Among Investment Proposals
Determining the Cost-of-Capital
Interest Rate Effects
Methods of Ranking Investments
Sample Problems: Investment Decisions

B. Uniformly Distributed Random Digits, 855

C. Normally Distributed Random Digits, 856

D. Areas of the Standard Normal Distribution, 857

E. Areas of the Cumulative Standard Normal Distribution, 858

F. Negative Exponential Distribution: Values of e^{-x}, 860

G. Interest Tables, 862

Compound Sum of $1
Sum of an Annuity of $1 for N Years
Present Value of $1
Present Value of an Annuity of $1

H. Answers to Selected Problems, 866

Appendix A

Financial Analysis of Operations

FINANCE
ACCOUNTING

In this appendix we review basic concepts and tools of financial analysis for OM. These include the types of cost (fixed, variable, sunk, opportunity, avoidable), risk and expected value, and depreciation (straight line, sum-of-the-years'-digits, declining balance, double-declining balance, and depreciation-by-use). We also discuss activity-based costing and cost-of-capital calculations. Our focus is on capital investment decisions.

■ CONCEPTS AND DEFINITIONS

We will begin with some basic definitions.

Fixed Costs

A **fixed cost** is any expense that remains constant regardless of the level of output. Although no cost is truly fixed, many types of expense are virtually fixed over a wide range of output. Examples are rent, property taxes, most types of depreciation, insurance payments, and salaries of top management.

Variable Costs

Variable costs are expenses that fluctuate directly with changes in the level of output. For example, each additional unit of sheet steel produced by USX requires a specific amount of material and labor. The incremental cost of this additional material and labor can be isolated and assigned to each unit of sheet steel produced. Many overhead expenses are also variable because utility bills, maintenance expense, and so forth vary with the production level.

Exhibit A.1 illustrates the fixed and variable cost components of total cost. Note that total cost increases at the same rate as variable costs because fixed costs are constant.

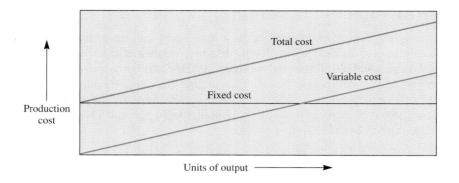

Sunk Costs

Sunk costs are past expenses or investments that have no salvage value and therefore should not be taken into account in considering investment alternatives. Sunk costs could also be current costs that are essentially fixed, such as rent on a building. For example, suppose an ice cream manufacturing firm occupies a rented building and is considering making sherbet in the same building. If the company enters sherbet production, its cost accountant will assign some of the rental expense to the sherbet operation. However, the building rent remains unchanged and therefore is not a relevant expense to be considered in making the decision. The rent is *sunk;* that is, it continues to exist and does not change in amount regardless of the decision.

Opportunity Costs

Opportunity cost is the benefit *forgone,* or advantage *lost,* that results from choosing one action over the *best-known alternative* course of action.

Suppose a firm has $100,000 to invest, and two alternatives of comparable risk present themselves, each requiring a $100,000 investment. Investment A will net $25,000; investment B will net $23,000. Investment A is clearly the better choice, with a $25,000 net return. If the decision is made to invest in B instead of A, the opportunity cost of B is $2,000, which is the benefit forgone.

Avoidable Costs

Avoidable costs include any expense that is *not* incurred if an investment is made but that *must* be incurred if the investment is *not* made. Suppose a company owns a metal lathe that is not in working condition but is needed for the firm's operations. Because the lathe must be repaired or replaced, the repair costs are avoidable if a new lathe is purchased. Avoidable costs reduce the cost of a new investment because they are not incurred if the investment is made. Avoidable costs are an example of how it is possible to "save" money by spending money.

Expected Value

Risk is inherent in any investment because the future can never by predicted with absolute certainty. To deal with this uncertainty, mathematical techniques such as expected value can help. **Expected value** is the expected outcome multiplied by the probability of its occurrence. Recall that in the preceding example the expected outcome of alternative A was $25,000 and B, $23,000. Suppose the probability of A's actual outcome is 80 percent while B's probability is 90 percent. The expected values of the alternatives are determined as follows:

$$\begin{array}{c} \text{Expected} \\ \text{outcome} \end{array} \times \begin{array}{c} \text{Probability that actual} \\ \text{outcome will be the} \\ \text{expected outcome} \end{array} = \begin{array}{c} \text{Expected} \\ \text{value} \end{array}$$

Investment A: $25,000 \times 0.80 = $20,000

Investment B: $23,000 \times 0.90 = $20,700

Investment B is now seen to be the better choice, with a net advantage over A of $700.

Economic Life and Obsolescence

When a firm invests in an income-producing asset, the productive life of the asset is estimated. For accounting purposes, the asset is depreciated over this period. It is assumed that the asset will perform its function during this time and then be considered **obsolete** or worn out, and replacement will be required. This view of asset life rarely coincides with reality.

Assume that a machine expected to have a productive life of 10 years is purchased. If at any time during the ensuing 10 years a new machine is developed that can perform the same task more efficiently or economically, the old machine has become obsolete. Whether or not it is "worn out" is irrelevant.

The *economic life* of a machine is the period over which it provides the best method for performing its task. When a superior method is developed, the machine has become obsolete. Thus, the stated *book value* of a machine can be a meaningless figure.

Depreciation

Depreciation is a method for allocating costs of capital equipment. The value of any capital asset—buildings, machinery, and so forth—decreases as its useful life is expended. *Amortization* and *depreciation* are often used interchangeably. Through convention, however, *depreciation* refers to the allocation of cost due to the physical or functional deterioration of *tangible* (physical) assets, such as buildings or equipment, while *amortization* refers to the allocation of cost over the useful life of *intangible* assets, such as patents, leases, franchises, and goodwill.

Depreciation procedures may not reflect an asset's true value at any point in its life because obsolescence may at any time cause a large difference between true value and book value. Also, because depreciation rates significantly affect taxes, a firm may choose a particular method from the several alternatives with more consideration for its effect on taxes than its ability to make the book value of an asset reflect the true resale value.

Next we describe five commonly used methods of depreciation.

Straight-Line Method   Under this method, an asset's value is reduced in uniform annual amounts over its estimated useful life. The general formula is

$$\text{Annual amount to be depreciated} = \frac{\text{Cost} - \text{Salvage value}}{\text{Estimated useful life}}$$

A machine costing $10,000, with an estimated salvage value of $0 and an estimated life of 10 years, would be depreciated at the rate of $1,000 per year for each of the 10 years. If its estimated salvage value at the end of the 10 years is $1,000, the annual depreciation charge is

$$\frac{\$10,000 - \$1,000}{10} = \$900$$

Sum-of-the-Years'-Digits (SYD) Method   The purpose of the SYD method is to reduce the book value of an asset rapidly in early years and at a lower rate in the later years of its life.

Suppose that the estimated useful life is five years. The numbers add up to 15: $1 + 2 + 3 + 4 + 5 = 15$. Therefore, we depreciate the asset by $5 \div 15$ after the first year, $4 \div 15$ after the second year, and so on, down to $1 \div 15$ in the last year.

Declining-Balance Method   This method also achieves an accelerated depreciation. The asset's value is decreased by reducing its book value by a constant percentage each year. The percentage rate selected is often the one that just reduces book value to salvage value at the end of the asset's estimated life. In any case, the asset should never be reduced below estimated salvage value. Use of the declining-balance method and allowable rates are controlled by Internal Revenue Service regulations. As a simplified illustration, the preceding example is used in the next table with an arbitrarily selected rate of 40 percent. Note that depreciation is based on full cost, *not* cost minus salvage value.

Year	Depreciation Rate	Beginning Book Value	Depreciation Charge	Accumulated Depreciation	Ending Book Value
1	0.40	$17,000	$6,800	$ 6,800	$10,200
2	0.40	10,200	4,080	10,880	6,120
3	0.40	6,120	2,448	13,328	3,672
4	0.40	3,672	1,469	14,797	2,203
5		2,203	203	15,000	2,000

In the fifth year, reducing book value by 40 percent would have caused it to drop below salvage value. Consequently, the asset was depreciated by only $203, which decreased book value to salvage value.

Double-Declining-Balance Method   Again, for tax advantages, the double-declining-balance method offers higher depreciation early in the life span. This method uses a percentage twice the straight line for the life span of the item but applies this rate to the undepreciated original cost. The method is the same as the declining-balance method, but the term *double-declining balance* means double the straight-line rate. Thus, equipment with a 10-year life span would have a straight-line depreciation rate of 10 percent per year, and a double-declining-balance rate (applied to the undepreciated amount) of 20 percent per year.

Depreciation-by-Use Method   The purpose of this method is to depreciate a capital investment in proportion to its use. It is applicable, for example, to a machine that performs the same operation many times. The life of the machine is not estimated in years but rather in the total number of operations it may reasonably be expected to perform before wearing out. Suppose that a metal-stamping press has an estimated life of 1 million stamps and costs $100,000. The charge for depreciation per stamp is then $100,000 ÷ 1,000,000 or $0.10. Assuming a $0 salvage value, the depreciation charges are as shown in the accompanying table.

Year	Total Yearly Stamps	Cost per Stamp	Yearly Depreciation Charge	Accumulated Depreciation	Ending Book Value
1	150,000	0.10	$15,000	$ 15,000	$85,000
2	300,000	0.10	30,000	45,000	55,000
3	200,000	0.10	20,000	65,000	35,000
4	200,000	0.10	20,000	85,000	15,000
5	100,000	0.10	10,000	95,000	5,000
6	50,000	0.10	5,000	100,000	0

The depreciation-by-use method is an attempt to gear depreciation charges to actual use and thereby coordinate expense charges with productive output more accurately. Also, because a machine's resale value is related to its remaining productive life, it is hoped that book value will approximate resale value. The danger, of course, is that technological improvements will render the machine obsolete, in which case book value will not reflect true value.

■ ACTIVITY-BASED COSTING

ACCOUNTING
FINANCE

To know how much it costs to make a certain product or deliver a service, some method of allocating overhead costs to production activities must be applied. The traditional approach is to allocate overhead costs to products on the basis of direct labor dollars or hours. By dividing the total estimated overhead costs by total budgeted direct labor hours, an overhead rate can be established. The problem with this approach is that direct labor as a percentage of total costs has fallen dramatically over the past decade. For example, introduction of advanced manufacturing technology and other productivity improvements has driven direct labor to as low as 7 to 10 percent of total manufacturing costs in many industries. As a result, overhead rates of 600 percent or even 1,000 percent are found in some highly automated plants.[1]

This traditional accounting practice of allocating overhead to direct labor can lead to questionable investment decisions; for example, automated processes may be chosen over labor-intensive processes based on a comparison of projected costs. Unfortunately, overhead does not disappear when the equipment is installed, and overall costs

---

[1] Matthew J. Libertore, *Selection and Evaluation of Advanced Manufacturing Technologies* (New York: Springer-Verlag, 1990), pp. 231–56.

may actually be lower with the labor-intensive process. It can also lead to wasted effort because an inordinate amount of time is spent tracking direct labor hours. For example, one plant spent 65 percent of computer costs tracking information about direct labor transactions even though direct labor accounted for only 4 percent of total production costs.[2]

Activity-based costing techniques have been developed to alleviate these problems by refining the overhead allocation process to more directly reflect actual proportions of overhead consumed by the production activity. Causal factors, known as cost drivers, are identified and used as the means for allocating overhead. These factors might include machine hours, beds occupied, computer time, flight hours, or miles driven. The accuracy of overhead allocation, of course, depends on the selection of appropriate cost drivers.

Activity-based costing involves a two-stage allocation process, with the first stage assigning overhead costs to cost activity pools. These pools represent activities such as performing machine setups, issuing purchase orders, and inspecting parts. In the second stage, costs are assigned from these pools to activities based on the number or amount of pool-related activity required in their completion. Exhibit A.2 shows a comparison of traditional cost accounting and activity-based costing.

Consider the example of activity-based costing in Exhibit A.3. Two products, A and B, are produced using the same number of direct labor hours. The same number of direct labor hours produces 5,000 units of Product A and 20,000 units of Product B. Applying traditional costing, identical overhead costs would be charged to each product. By applying activity-based costing, traceable costs are assigned to specific activities. Because each product required a different amount of transactions, different overhead amounts are allocated to these products from the pools.

As stated earlier, activity-based costing overcomes the problem of cost distortion by creating a cost pool for each activity or transaction that can be identified as a cost driver, and by assigning overhead cost to products or jobs on a basis of the number of separate activities required for their completion. Thus, in the previous situation, the low-volume product would be assigned the bulk of the costs for machine setup, purchase orders, and quality inspections, thereby showing it to have high unit costs compared to the other product.

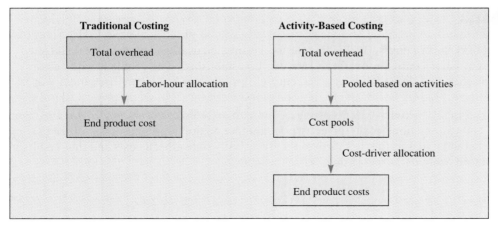

Exhibit A.2

Traditional and Activity-Based Costing

[2] Thomas Johnson and Robert Kaplan, *Relevance Lost: The Rise and Fall of Management Accounting* (Boston: Harvard Business School Press, 1987), p. 188.

Overhead Allocations
by an Activity
Approach

Basic Data

Activity	Traceable Costs	Events of Transactions		
		Total	Product A	Product B
Machine setups	$230,000	5,000	3,000	2,000
Quality inspections	160,000	8,000	5,000	3,000
Production orders	81,000	600	200	400
Machine-hours worked	314,000	40,000	12,000	28,000
Material receipts	90,000	750	150	600
Number of units produced		25,000	5,000	20,000
	$875,000			

Overhead Rates by Activity

Activity	*(a)* Traceable Costs	*(b)* Total Events or Transactions	*(a)* ÷ *(b)* Rate per Event or Transaction
Machine setups	$230,000	5,000	$46/setup
Quality inspections	160,000	8,000	$20/inspection
Production orders	81,000	600	$135/order
Machine-hours worked	314,000	40,000	$7.85/hour
Material receipts	90,000	750	$120/receipt

Overhead Cost per Unit of Product

	Product A		Product B	
	Events or Transactions	Amount	Events or Transactions	Amount
Machine setups, at $46/setup	3,000	$138,000	2,000	$ 92,000
Quality inspections, at $20/inspection	5,000	100,000	3,000	60,000
Product orders, at $135/order	200	27,000	400	54,000
Machine-hours worked, at $7.85/hour	12,000	94,200	28,000	219,800
Material receipts, at $120/receipt	150	18,000	600	72,000
Total overhead cost assigned		$377,200		$497,800
Number of units produced		5,000		20,000
Overhead cost per unit, $\frac{\text{Total overhead}}{\text{No. of units}}$		$75.44		$24.89

Source: Ray Garrison, *Managerial Accounting,* 6th ed. (Homewood, IL: Richard D. Irwin, 1991), p. 94.

Finally, activity-based costing is sometimes referred to as *transactions costing.* This transactions focus gives rise to another major advantage over other costing methods; that is, that it improves the traceability of overhead costs and thus results in more accurate *unit* cost data for management.

◼ THE EFFECTS OF TAXES

Tax rates and the methods of applying them occasionally change. When analysts evaluate investment proposals, tax considerations often prove to be the deciding factor because depreciation expenses directly affect taxable income and therefore profit. The ability to write off depreciation in early years provides an added source of funds for investment. Before 1986, firms could employ an *investment tax credit,* which allowed a direct reduction in tax liability. But tax laws change, so it is crucial to stay on top of current tax laws and try to predict future changes that may affect current investments and accounting procedures.

◼ CHOOSING AMONG INVESTMENT PROPOSALS

The capital investment decision has become highly rationalized, as evidenced by the variety of techniques available for its solution. In contrast to pricing or marketing decisions, the capital investment decision can usually be made with a higher degree of confidence because the variables affecting the decision are relatively well known and can be quantified with fair accuracy.

Investment decisions may be grouped into six general categories:

1. Purchase of new equipment and/or facilities.
2. Replacement of existing equipment or facilities.
3. Make-or-buy decisions.
4. Lease-or-buy decisions.
5. Temporary shutdowns or plant-abandonment decisions.
6. Addition or elimination of a product or product line.

Investment decisions are made with regard to the *lowest acceptable rate of return* on investment. As a starting point, the lowest acceptable rate of return may be considered to be the cost of investment capital needed to underwrite the expenditure. Certainly an investment will not be made if it does not return at least the cost of capital.

Investments are generally ranked according to the return they yield in excess of their cost of capital. In this way, a business with only limited investment funds can select investment alternatives that yield the highest *net* returns. (*Net return* is the earnings an investment yields after gross earnings have been reduced by the cost of the funds used to finance the investment.) In general, investments should not be made unless the return in funds exceeds the *marginal* cost of investment capital. (*Marginal cost* is the incremental cost of each new acquisition of funds from outside sources.)

◼ DETERMINING THE COST OF CAPITAL

The **cost of capital** is calculated from a weighted average of debt and equity security costs. This average will vary depending on the financing strategy employed by the company.[3] The most common sources of financing are short-term debt, long-term debt, and equity securities. A bank loan is an example of short-term debt. Bonds normally provide long-term debt. Finally, stock is a common form of equity financing. In the following, we will give a short example of each form of financing, and then show how they are combined to find the weighted average cost of capital.

The cost of **short-term debt** depends on the interest rate on the loan and whether the loan is discounted or not. Remember that interest is a tax-deductible expense for a company.

$$\text{Cost of short-term debt} = \frac{\text{Interest paid}}{\text{Proceeds received}}$$

If a bank discounts a loan, interest is deducted from the face of the loan to get the proceeds. When a compensating balance is required (that is, a percent of the face value of the load is held by the bank as collateral), proceeds are also reduced. In either case, the effective or real interest rate on the loan is higher than the face interest rate owing to the proceeds received from the loan being less than the amount (face value) of the loan.

Example of Short-Term Debt   A company takes a $150,000, one-year, 13 percent loan. The loan is discounted, and a 10 percent compensating balance is required. The effective interest rate is computed as follows:

$$\frac{13\% \times \$150,000}{\$115,500} = \frac{\$19,500}{\$115,000} = 16.89\%$$

Proceeds received equals

Face of loan	$150,000
Less interest	(19,500)
Compensating balance (10% × $150,000)	(15,000)
Proceeds	$115,500

Notice how the effective cost of the loan is significantly greater than the stated interest rate.

Long-term debt is normally provided through the sale of corporate bonds. The real cost of bonds is obtained by computing two types of yield: simple (face) yield and yield to maturity (effective interest rate). The first involves an easy approximation, but the second is more accurate. The nominal interest rate equals the interest paid on the face (maturity value) of the bond and is always stated on a per-annum basis. Bonds are generally issued in $1,000 denominations and may be sold above face value (at a premium) or below (at a discount, termed original issue discount, or OID). A bond is sold at a discount when the interest rate is below the going market rate. In this case, the yield will be higher than the nominal interest rate. The opposite holds for bonds issued at a premium.

The issue price of a bond is the par (or face value) times the premium (or discount).

---

[3] A recent survey indicated that the average discount rate applied to constant-dollar cash flows was 12.2 percent. This is higher than standard cost-of-capital analysis would suggest. See James M. Poterba and Lawrence H. Summers, "A CEO Survey of U.S. Companies' Time Horizons and Hurdle Rates," *Sloan Management Review,* Fall 1995, pp. 43–53.

$$\text{Simple yield} = \frac{\text{Nominal interest}}{\text{Issue price of bond}}$$

$$\text{Yield to maturity} = \frac{\text{Nominal interest} + \dfrac{\text{Discount (or premium)}}{\text{Years}}}{\dfrac{\text{Issue price} + \text{Maturity value}}{2}}$$

Example of Long-Term Debt   A company issues a $400,000, 12 percent, 10-year bond for 97% of face value. Yield computations are as follows:

$$
\begin{aligned}
\text{Nominal annual payment} &= 12\% \times \$400,000 \\
&= \$48,000 \\
\text{Bond proceeds} &= 97\% \times \$400,000 \\
&= \$388,000 \\
\text{Bond discount} &= 3\% \times \$400,000 \\
&= \$12,000 \\
\text{Simple yield} &= \frac{12\% \times \$400,000}{97\% \times \$400,000} = \frac{\$48,000}{\$388,000} = 12.4\% \\[2em]
\text{Yield to maturity} &= \frac{\$48,000 + \dfrac{\$12,000}{10}}{\dfrac{\$388,000 + \$400,000}{2}} = \frac{\$48,000 + \$1,200}{\$394,000} = 12.5\%
\end{aligned}
$$

Note that because the bonds were sold at a discount, the yield exceeds the nominal interest rate (12 percent). Bond interest is tax deductible to the corporation.

The actual **cost of equity securities (stocks)** comes in the form of dividends, which are not tax deductible to the corporation.

$$\text{Cost of common stock} = \frac{\text{Dividends per share}}{\text{Value per share}} + \text{Growth rate of dividends}$$

where the value per share equals the Market price per share − flotation costs (that is, cost of issuing securities, such as brokerage fees and, printing costs). It should be noted that this valuation does not consider what the investor expects in market price appreciation. This expectation is based on the expected growth in earnings per share and the relative risk taking by purchasing the stock. The capital asset pricing model (CAPM) can be used to capture this impact.[4]

Example of the Cost of Common Stock   A company's dividend per share is $10, net value is $70 per share, and the dividend growth rate is 5 percent.

$$\text{Cost of the stock} = \frac{\$10}{\$70} + 0.05 = 19.3\%$$

To compute the **weighted average cost of capital,** we consider the percent of the total capital that is being provided by each financing alternative. We then calculate the

---

[4] A description of capital asset pricing is included in many finance textbooks; see, for example, Zvi Bodie, Alex Kane, and Alan Marcus, *Investments,* 3rd ed. (Burr Ridge, IL: Richard D. Irwin, 1996), pp. 236–65.

after-tax cost of each financing alternative. Finally, we weight these costs in proportion to their use.

Example of Calculating the Weighted Average Cost of Capital   Consider a company that shows the following figures in its financial statements:

Short-term bank loan (13%)	$ 1 million
Bonds payable (16%)	$ 4 million
Common stock (10%)	$ 5 million

For our example, assume that each of the percentages given above represents the cost of the source of capital. In addition, to the above we need to consider the tax rate of the firm, since the interest paid on the bonds and on the short-term loan is tax deductible. Assume a corporate tax rate of 40 percent.

	Percent	After-Tax Cost	Weighted Average Cost
Short-term bank loan	10%	13% × 60% = 7.8%	.78%
Bonds payable	40%	16% × 60% = 9.6%	3.84%
Common stock	50%	10%	5%
Total	100%		9.62%

Keep in mind that in developing this section we have made many assumptions in these calculations. When applying these ideas to a specific company many of these assumptions may change. The basic concepts, though, are the same and keep in mind that the goal is to simply calculate the after tax cost of the capital used by the company. We have shown the cost of capital for the entire company, though often only the capital employed for a specific project, is used in the calculation.

■ INTEREST RATE EFFECTS

There are two basic ways to account for the effects of interest accumulation. One is to compute the total amount created over the time period into the future as the *compound value.* The other is to remove the interest rate effect over time by reducing all future sums to present-day dollars, or the *present value.*

Compound Value of a Single Amount

Albert Einstein was quoted as saying that compound interest is the eighth wonder of the world. After reviewing this section showing compound interest's dramatic growth effects over a long time, you might wish to propose a new government regulation: On the birth of a child, the parents must put, say, $1,000 into a retirement fund for that child available at age 65. This might reduce the pressure on Social Security and other state and federal pension plans. While inflation would decrease the value significantly, there would still be a lot left over. At 14 percent return on investment, our $1,000 would increase to $500,000 after subtracting the $4.5 million for inflation. That is still

Hopefully, you are all doing these calculations using a spreadsheet program. Even though the computer makes these calculations simple, it is very important that you understand what the computer is actually doing. Further, you should check your calculations manually to make sure that you have the formulas set up correctly in your spreadsheet. There are many stories of the terrible consequences of making a wrong decision based on a spreadsheet with errors!

For your quick reference, the following are the financial functions you will find most useful. These are from the Microsoft Excel help screens.

PV(rate, nper, pmt)—Returns the present value of an investment. The present value is the total amount that a series of future payments is worth now. For example, when you borrow money, the loan amount is the present value to the lender. Rate is the interest rate per period. For example, if you obtain an automobile loan at a 10 percent annual interest rate and make monthly payments, your interest rate per month is 10%/12, or .83%. You would enter 10%/12, or .83%, or .0083, in the formula as the rate. Nper is the total number of payment periods in an annuity. For example, if you get a four-year car loan and make monthly payments, your loan has 4*12 (or 48) periods. You would enter 48 into the formula for nper. Pmt is the payment made each period and cannot change over the life of the annuity. Typically, this includes principal and interest but no other fees or taxes. For example, the monthly payment on a $10,000, four-year car loan at 12 percent is $263.33. You would enter 263.33 into the formula as pmt.

FV(rate, nper, pmt)—Returns the future value of an investment based on periodic, constant payment and a constant interest rate. Rate is the interest rate per period. Nper is the total number of payment periods in an annuity. Pmt is the payment made each period; it cannot change over the life of the annuity. Typically, pmt contains principal and interest but no other fees or taxes.

NPV(rate, value1, value2, . . .)—Returns the net present value of an investment based on a series of periodic cash flows and a discount rate. The net present value of an investment is today's value of a series of future payments (negative values) and income (positive values). Rate is the rate of discount over the length of one period. Value1, value2, . . . must be equally spaced in time and occur at the end of each period.

IRR(values)—Returns the internal rate of return for a series of cash flows represented by the numbers in values. (Values is defined below.) These cash flows do not have to be even, as they would be for an annuity. The internal rate of return is the interest rate received for an investment consisting of payments (negative values) and income (positive values) that occur at regular periods. Values is an array or a reference to cells that contain numbers for which you want to calculate the internal rate of return. Values must contain at least one positive value and one negative value to calculate the internal rate of return. IRR uses the order of values to interpret the order of cash flows. Be sure to enter your payment and income values in the sequence you want.

Using a Spreadsheet

Source: Microsoft Excel, Version 7, help screen for financial functions.

a 500-fold increase. (Many mutual funds today have long-term performances in excess of 14 percent per year.)

Spreadsheets and calculators make such computation easy. The Excel information box above shows the most useful financial functions. However, many people still refer to tables for compound values. Using Appendix F, Table F.1 (compound sum of $1), for example, we see that the value of $1 at 10 percent interest after three years is $1.331. Multiplying this figure by $10 gives $13.31, as computed previously.

Compound Value of an Annuity

An *annuity* is the receipt of a constant sum each year for a specified number of years. Usually an annuity is received at the end of a period and does not earn interest during that period. Therefore, an annuity of $10 for three years would bring in $10 at the end of the first year (allowing the $10 to earn interest if invested for the remaining two years), $10 at the end of the second year (allowing the $10 to earn interest for the remaining one year), and $10 at the end of the third year (with no time to earn interest). If the annuity receipts were placed in a bank savings account at 5 percent interest, the total or compound value of the $10 at 5 percent for the three years would be

Year	Receipt at End of Year		Compound Interest Factor $(1 + i)^n$		Value at End of Third Year
1	$10.00	×	$(1 + 0.05)^2$	=	$11.02
2	10.00	×	$(1 + 0.05)^1$	=	10.50
3	10.00	×	$(1 + 0.50)^0$	=	10.00
					$31.52

The general formula for finding the compound value of an annuity is

$$S_n = R[(1 + i)^{n-1} + (1 + i)^{n-2} + \cdots + (1 + i)^1 + 1]$$

where

$S_n =$ Compound value of an annuity
$R =$ Periodic receipts in dollars
$n =$ Length of the annuity in years

Applying this formula to the preceding example, we get

$$S_n = R[(1 + i)^2 + (1 + i) + 1]$$
$$= \$10[(1 + 0.05)^2 + (1 + 0.05) + 1] = \$31.52$$

In Appendix G, Table G.2 lists the compound value factor of $1 for 5 percent after three years as 3.152. Multiplying this factor by $10 yields $31.52.

In a fashion similar to our previous retirement investment example, consider the beneficial effects of investing $2,000 each year, just starting at the age of 21. Assume investments in AAA-rated bonds are available today yielding 9 percent. From Table G.2 in Appendix G, after 30 years (at age 51) the investment is worth 136.3 times $2,000, or $272,600. Fourteen years later (at age 65) this would be worth $963,044 (using a hand calculator, because the table only goes up to 30 years, and assuming the $2,000 is deposited at the end of each year)! But what 21-year-old thinks about retirement?

Present Value of a Future Single Payment

Compound values are used to determine future value after a specific period has elapsed; present value (PV) procedures accomplish just the reverse. They are used to determine the current value of a sum or stream of receipts expected to be received in the future. Most investment decision techniques use present value concepts rather than compound values. Because decisions affecting the future are made in the present, it is better to convert future returns into their present value at the time the decision is being made. In this way, investment alternatives are placed in better perspective in terms of current dollars.

An example makes this more apparent. If a rich uncle offers to make you a gift of $100 today or $250 after 10 years, which should you choose? You must determine whether the $250 in 10 years will be worth more than the $100 now. Suppose that you base your decision on the rate of inflation in the economy and believe that inflation averages 10 percent per year. By deflating the $250, you can compare its relative purchasing power with $100 received today. Procedurally, this is accomplished by solving the compound formula for the present sum, P, where V is the future amount of $250 in 10 years at 10 percent. The compound value formula is

$$V = P(1 + i)^n$$

Dividing both sides by $(1 + i)^n$ gives

$$P = \frac{V}{(1 + I)^n}$$

$$= \frac{250}{(1 + 0.10)^{10}} = \$96.39$$

This shows that, at a 10 percent inflation rate, $250 in 10 years will be worth $96.39 today. The rational choice, then, is to take the $100 now.

The use of tables is also standard practice in solving present value problems. With reference to Appendix G, Table G.3, the present value factor for $1 received 10 years hence is 0.386. Multiplying this factor by $250 yields $96.50.

Present Value of an Annuity

The present value of an annuity is the value of an annual amount to be received over a future period expressed in terms of the present. To find the value of an annuity of $100 for three years at 10 percent, find the factor in the present value table that applies to 10 percent in *each* of the three years in which the amount is received and multiply each receipt by this factor. Then sum the resulting figures. Remember that annuities are usually received at the end of each period.

Year	Amount Received at End of Year		Present Value Factor at 10%		Present Value
1	$100	×	0.909	=	$ 90.90
2	100	×	0.826	=	82.60
3	100	×	0.751	=	75.10
Total receipts	$300		Total present value =		$248.60

The general formula used to derive the present value of an annuity is

$$A_n = R\left[\frac{1}{(1 + i)} + \frac{1}{(1 + i)^2} + \cdots + \frac{1}{(1 + i)^n}\right]$$

where

A_n = Present value of an annuity of n years
R = Periodic receipts
n = Length of the annuity in years

Applying the formula to the preceding example gives

$$A_n = \$100\left[\frac{1}{(1 + 0.10)} + \frac{1}{(1 + 0.10)^2} + \frac{1}{(1 + 0.10)^3}\right]$$
$$= \$100(2.487) = \$248.70$$

In Appendix G, Table G.4 contains present values of an annuity for varying maturities. The present value factor for an annuity of $1 for three years at 10 percent (from Appendix G, Table G.4) is 2.487. Given that our sum is $100 rather than $1, we multiply this factor by $100 to arrive at $248.70.

When the stream of future receipts is uneven, the present value of each annual receipt must be calculated. The present values of the receipts for all years are then summed to arrive at total present value. This process can sometimes be tedious, but it is unavoidable.

Discounted Cash Flow

The term **discounted cash flow** refers to the total stream of payments that an asset will generate in the future discounted to the present time. This is simply present value analysis that includes all flows: single payments, annuities, and all others.

■ METHODS OF RANKING INVESTMENTS

Net Present Value

The net present value method is commonly used in business. With this method, decisions are based on the amount by which the present value of a projected income stream exceeds the cost of an investment.

A firm is considering two alternative investments. The first costs $30,000 and the second, $50,000. The expected yearly cash income streams are shown in the next table.

	Cash Inflow	
Year	Alternative A	Alternative B
1	$10,000	$15,000
2	10,000	15,000
3	10,000	15,000
4	10,000	15,000
5	10,000	15,000

To choose between alternatives A and B, find which has the highest net present value. Assume an 8 percent cost of capital.

Alternative A

3.993 (PV factor)
   × $10,000   = $39,930
Less cost of investment =   30,000
Net present value   = $ 9,930

Alternative B

3.993 (PV factor)
   × $15,000   = $59,895
Less cost of investment =   50,000
Net present value   = $ 9,895

Investment A is the better alternative. Its net present value exceeds that of investment B by $35 ($9,930 − $9,895 = $35).

Payback Period

The **payback method** ranks investments according to the time required for each investment to return earnings equal to the cost of the investment. The rationale is that the sooner the investment capital can be recovered, the sooner it can be reinvested in new revenue-producing projects. Thus, supposedly, a firm will be able to get the most benefit from its available investment funds.

Consider two alternatives requiring a $1,000 investment each. The first will earn $200 per year for six years; the second will earn $300 per year for the first three years and $100 per year for the next three years.

If the first alternative is selected, the initial investment of $1,000 will be recovered at the end of the fifth year. The income produced by the second alternative will total $1,000 after only four years. The second alternative will permit reinvestment of the full $1,000 in new revenue-producing projects one year sooner than the first.

Though the payback method is declining in popularity as the sole measure in investment decisions, it is still frequently used in conjunction with other methods to indicate the time commitment of funds. The major problems with payback are that it does not consider income beyond the payback period and it ignores the time value of money. A method that ignores the time value of money must be considered questionable.

Internal Rate of Return

The **internal rate of return** may be defined as the interest rate that equates the present value of an income stream with the cost of an investment. There is no procedure or formula that may be used directly to compute the internal rate of return—it must be found by interpolation or iterative calculation.

Suppose we wish to find the internal rate of return for an investment costing $12,000 that will yield a cash inflow of $4,000 per year for four years. We see that the present value factor sought is

$$\frac{\$12,000}{\$4,000} = 3.000$$

and we seek the interest rate that will provide this factor over a four-year period. The interest rate must lie between 12 and 14 percent because 3.000 lies between 3.037 and 2.914 (in the fourth row of Appendix G, Table G.4). Linear interpolation between these values, according to the equation

$$I = 12 + (14 - 12)\frac{(3.037 - 3.000)}{(3.037 - 2.914)}$$

$$= 12 + 0.602 = 12.602\%$$

gives a good approximation to the actual internal rate of return.

When the income stream is discounted at 12.6 percent, the resulting present value closely approximates the cost of investment. Thus the internal rate of return for this investment is 12.6 percent. The cost of capital can be compared with the internal rate of return to determine the net rate of return on the investment. If, in this example, the cost of capital were 8 percent, the net rate of return on the investment would be 4.6 percent.

The net present value and internal rate of return methods involve procedures that are essentially the same. They differ in that the net present value method enables investment alternatives to be compared in terms of the dollar value in excess of cost, whereas the internal rate of return method permits comparison of rates of return on alternative investments. Moreover, the internal rate of return method occasionally encounters problems in calculation, as multiple rates frequently appear in the computation.

Ranking Investments with Uneven Lives

When proposed investments have the same life expectancy, comparison among them, using the preceding methods, will give a reasonable picture of their relative value. When lives are unequal, however, there is the question of how to relate the two different time periods. Should replacements be considered the same as the original? Should productivity for the shorter-term unit that will be replaced earlier be considered to have higher productivity? How should the cost of future units be estimated?

No estimate dealing with investments unforeseen at the time of decision can be expected to reflect a high degree of accuracy. Still, the problem must be dealt with, and some assumptions must be made in order to determine a ranking.

■ SAMPLE PROBLEMS: INVESTMENT DECISIONS

■ **example A.I**   *An Expansion Decision*   William J. Wilson Ceramic Products, Inc., leases plant facilities in which firebrick is manufactured. Because of rising demand, Wilson could increase sales by investing in new equipment to expand output. The selling price of $10 per brick will remain unchanged if output and sales increase. Based on engineering and cost estimates, the accounting department provides management with the following cost estimates based on an annual increased output of 100,000 bricks.

Cost of new equipment having an expected life of five years	$500,000
Equipment installation cost	20,000
Expected salvage value	0
New operation's share of annual lease expense	40,000
Annual increase in utility expenses	40,000
Annual increase in labor costs	160,000
Annual additional cost for raw materials	400,000

The sum-of-the-years'-digits method of depreciation will be used, and taxes are paid at a rate of 40 percent. Wilson's policy is not to invest capital in projects earning less than a 20 percent rate of return. Should the proposed expansion be undertaken?

solution   Compute cost of investment:

Acquisition cost of equipment	$500,000
Equipment installation costs	20,000
Total cost of investment	$520,000

Determine yearly cash flows throughout the life of the investment.

The lease expense is a sunk cost. It will be incurred whether or not the investment is made and is therefore irrelevant to the decision and should be disregarded. Annual production expenses to be considered are utility, labor, and raw materials. These total $600,000 per year.

Annual sales revenue is $10 \times 100,000$ units of output, which totals $1,000,000. Yearly income before depreciation and taxes is thus $1,000,000 gross revenue, less $600,000 expenses, or $400,000.

Next, determine the depreciation charges to be deducted from the $400,000 income each year using the SYD method (sum-of-years' digits $= 1 + 2 + 3 + 4 + 5 = 15$):

Year	Proportion of $500,000 to Be Depreciated		Depreciation Charge
1	5/15 × $500,000	=	$166,667
2	4/15 × 500,000	=	133,333
3	3/15 × 500,000	=	100,000
4	2/15 × 500,000	=	66,667
5	1/15 × 500,000	=	33,333
	Accumulated depreciation		$500,000

Find each year's cash flow when taxes are 40 percent. Cash flow for only the first year is illustrated:

Earnings before depreciation and taxes		$400,000
Deduct: Taxes at 40%	$160,000	
(40% × 400,000) Tax benefit of depreciation expense (0.4 × 166,667)	66,667	93,333
Cash flow (1st year)		$306,667

Determine the present value of the cash flow. Since Wilson demands at least a 20 percent rate of return on investments, multiply the cash flows by the 20 percent present value factor for each year. The factor for each respective year must be used because the cash flows are not an annuity.

Year	Present Value Factor		Cash Flow		Present Value
1	0.833	×	$306,667	=	$255,454
2	0.694	×	293,333	=	203,573
3	0.579	×	280,000	=	162,120
4	0.482	×	266,667	=	128,533
5	0.402	×	253,334	=	101,840
	Total present value of cash flows (discounted at 20%) =				$851,520

Now find whether net present value is positive or negative:

Total present value of cash flows	$851,520
Total cost of investment	520,000
Net present value	$331,520

Net present value is positive when returns are discounted at 20 percent. Wilson will earn an amount in excess of 20 percent on the investment. The proposed expansion should be undertaken. ■

■ **example A.2**   *A Replacement Decision*   For five years Bennie's Brewery has been using a machine that attaches labels to bottles. The machine was purchased for $4,000 and is being depreciated over 10 years to a $0 salvage value using straight-line depreciation. The machine can be sold now for $2,000. Bennie can buy a new labeling machine for $6,000 that will have a useful life of five years and cut labor costs by $1,200 annually. The old machine will require a major overhaul in the next few months at an estimated cost of $300. If purchased, the new machine will be depreciated over five years to a $500 salvage value using the straight-line method. The company will invest in any project earning more than the 12 percent cost of capital. The tax rate is 40 percent. Should Bennie's Brewery invest in the new machine?

solution   Determine the cost of investment:

Price of the new machine		$6,000
Less: Sale of old machine	$2,000	
Avoidable overhaul costs	300	2,300
Effective cost of investment		$3,700

Determine the increase in cash flow resulting from investment in the new machine.

Yearly cost savings = $1,200
Differential depreciation
  Annual depreciation on old machine:
$$\frac{Cost - Salvage}{Expected\ life} = \frac{\$4,000 - \$0}{10} = \$400$$
  Annual depreciation on new machine:
$$\frac{Cost - Salvage}{Expected\ life} = \frac{\$6,000 - \$500}{5} = \$1,100$$
  Differential depreciation = $1,100 − $400 = $700
    Yearly net increase in cash flow into the firm:

Cost savings		$1,200
Deduct: Taxes at 40%	$480	
Add: advantage of increase in depreciation (0.4 × $700)	280	200
Yearly increase in cash flow		$1,000

Determine total present value of the investment:
The five-year cash flow of $1,000 per year is an annuity.
Discounted at 12 percent, the cost of capital, the present value is
  3.605 × $1,000 = $3,605
The present value of the new machine, if sold at its salvage value of $500 at the end of the fifth year, is
  0.567 × $500 = $284
Total present value of the expected cash flows is
  $3,605 + $284 = $3,889

Determine whether net present value is positive:

Total present value	$3,889
Cost of investment	3,700
Net present value	$ 189

Bennie's Brewery should make the purchase because the investment will return slightly more than the cost of capital.

Note: The importance of depreciation has been shown in this example. The present value of the yearly cash flow resulting from operations is

$$(\text{Cost savings} - \text{Taxes}) \times (\text{Present value factor})$$
$$(\$1,200 - \$480) \quad \times \quad (3.605) \quad = \$2,596$$

This figure is $1,104 less than the $3,700 cost of the investment. Only a very large depreciation advantage makes this investment worthwhile. The total present value of the advantage is $1,009:

$$(\text{Tax rate} \times \text{Differential depreciation}) \times (\text{PV factor})$$
$$(0.4 \times \$700) \quad \times \quad (3.605) \quad = \$1,009 \quad \blacksquare$$

■ **example A.3**   *A Make-or-Buy Decision*   The Triple X Company manufactures and sells refrigerators. It makes some of the parts for the refrigerators and purchases others. The engineering department believes it might be possible to cut costs by manufacturing one of the parts currently being purchased for $8.25 each. The firm uses 100,000 of these parts each year. The accounting department compiles the following list of costs based on engineering estimates:

Fixed costs will increase by $50,000.

Labor costs will increase by $125,000.

Factory overhead, currently running $500,000 per year, may be expected to increase 12 percent.

Raw materials used to make the part will cost $600,000.

Given the preceding estimates, should Triple X make the part or continue to buy it?

solution   Find total cost incurred if the part were manufactured:

Additional fixed costs	$ 50,000
Additional labor costs	125,000
Raw materials cost	600,000
Additional overhead costs = 0.12 × $500,000	60,000
Total cost to manufacturer	$835,000

Find the cost per unit to manufacture:

$$\frac{\$835,000}{100,000} = \$8.35 \text{ per unit}$$

Triple X should continue to buy the part. Manufacturing costs exceed the present cost to purchase by $0.10 per unit.   ■

SELECTED BIBLIOGRAPHY

Bodie, Zri, Alex Kane, and Alan Marcus. *Investments*, 3rd ed. Burr Ridge, IL: Richard D. Irwin, 1996.

Brigham, Eugene F. *Fundamentals of Financial Management*. New York: Dryden Press, 1986.

Gitman, Lawrence J. *Principles of Managerial Finance*. 4th ed. New York: Harper & Row, 1985.

Gup, Benton E. *Principles of Financial Management*, 2nd ed. New York: John Wiley & Sons, 1987.

Hodder, James E., and Henry E. Riggs. "Pitfalls in Evaluating Risky Projects." *Harvard Business Review,* January–February 1985, pp. 128–35.

Poterba, James M., and Lawrence H. Summers. "A CEO Survey of U.S. Companies' Time Horizons and Hurdle Rates." *Sloan Management Review,* Fall 1995, pp. 43–53.

Pringle, John J., and Robert S. Harris. *Essentials of Managerial Finance.* Glenview, IL: Scott, Foresman, 1984.

Soloman, Eyra, and John J. Pringle. *An Introduction to Financial Management.* Santa Monica, CA: Goodyear, 1980.

Van Horne, James C. *Financial Management and Policy.* 7th ed. Englewood Cliffs, NJ: Prentice Hall, 1986.

———. *Fundamentals of Financial Managment.* 6th ed. Englewood Cliffs, NJ: Prentice Hall, 1986.

Welsch, Glenn A., and Robert N. Anthony. *Fundamentals of Financial Accounting.* Homewood, IL: Richard D. Irwin, 1984.

Uniformly Distributed Random Digits

56970	10799	52098	04184	54967	72938	50834	23777	08392
83125	85077	60490	44369	66130	72936	69848	59973	08144
55503	21383	02464	26141	68779	66388	75242	82690	74099
47019	06683	33203	29603	54553	25971	69573	83854	24715
84828	61152	79526	29554	84580	37859	28504	61980	34997
08021	31331	79227	05748	51276	57143	31926	00915	45821
36458	28285	30424	98420	72925	40729	22337	48293	86847
05752	96045	36847	87729	81679	59126	59437	33225	31280
26768	02513	58454	56958	20575	76746	40878	06846	32828
42613	72456	43030	58085	06766	60227	96414	32671	45587
95457	12176	65482	25596	02678	54592	63607	82096	21913
95276	67524	63564	95958	39750	64379	46059	51666	10433
66954	53574	64776	92345	95110	59448	77249	54044	67942
17457	44151	14113	02462	02798	54977	48340	66738	60184
03704	23322	83214	59337	01695	60666	97410	55064	17427
21538	16997	33210	60337	27976	70661	08250	69509	60264
57178	16730	08310	70348	11317	71623	55510	64750	87759
31048	40058	94953	55866	96283	40620	52087	80817	74533
69799	83300	16498	80733	96422	58078	99643	39847	96884
90595	65017	59231	17772	67831	33317	00520	90401	41700
33570	34761	08039	78784	09977	29398	93896	78227	90110
15340	82760	57477	13898	48431	72936	78160	87240	52710
64079	07733	36512	56186	99098	48850	72527	08486	10951
63491	84886	67118	62063	74958	20946	28147	39338	32109
92003	76568	41034	28260	79708	00770	88643	21188	01850
52360	46658	66511	04172	73085	11795	52594	13287	82531
74622	12142	68355	65635	21828	39539	18988	53609	04001
04157	50070	61343	64315	70836	82857	35335	87900	36194
86003	60070	66241	32836	27573	11479	94114	81641	00496
41208	80187	20351	09630	84668	42486	71303	19512	50277
06433	80674	24520	18222	10610	05794	37515	48619	62866
39298	47829	72648	37414	75755	04717	29899	78817	03509
89884	59651	67533	68123	17730	95862	08034	19473	63971
61512	32155	51906	61662	64430	16688	37275	51262	11569
99653	47635	12506	88535	36553	23757	34209	55803	96275
95913	11085	13772	76638	48423	25018	99041	77529	81360
55804	44004	13122	44115	01601	50541	00147	77685	58788
35334	82410	91601	40617	72876	33967	73830	15405	96554
57729	88646	76487	11622	96297	24160	09903	14047	22917
86648	89317	63677	70119	94739	25875	38829	68377	43918
30574	06039	07967	32422	76791	30725	53711	93385	13421
81307	13114	83580	79974	45929	85113	72268	09858	52104
02410	96385	79067	54939	21410	86980	91772	93307	34116
18969	87444	52233	62319	08598	09066	95288	04794	01534
87863	80514	66860	62297	80198	19347	73234	86265	49096
08397	10538	15438	62311	72844	60203	46412	65943	79232
28520	45247	58729	10854	99058	18260	38765	90038	94209
44285	09452	15867	70418	57012	72122	36634	97283	95943
86299	22510	33571	23309	57040	29285	67870	21913	72958
84842	05748	90894	61658	15001	94005	36308	41161	37341

Normally Distributed Random Digits

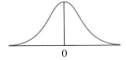

0

An entry in the table is the value z from a normal distribution with a mean of 0 and a standard deviation of 1.

1.98677	1.23481	−.28360	.99217	−.87919	−.21600
−.59341	1.54221	−.65806	1.08372	1.68560	1.14899
.11340	.19126	−.65084	.12188	.02338	−.61545
.89783	−.54929	−.03663	−1.89506	.15158	−.20061
−.50790	1.14463	1.30917	1.26528	.09459	.16423
−1.63968	−.63248	.21482	−1.16241	−.60015	−.55233
1.14081	−.29988	−.48053	−1.21397	−.34391	−1.84881
−.43354	−.32855	.67115	.52289	−1.42796	−.14181
.05707	.35331	.20470	.01847	1.71086	−1.44738
.77153	.72576	−.29833	.26139	1.25845	−.35468
−1.38286	.04406	−.75499	.61068	.61903	−.96845
1.60166	−1.66161	.70886	−.20302	−.28373	2.07219
−.48781	.02629	−.34306	2.00746	−1.12059	.07943
−1.10632	1.18250	−.60065	.09737	.63297	1.00659
.77000	−.87214	−.63584	−.39546	−.72776	.45594
−.56882	−.23153	−2.03852	−.28101	.30384	−.14246
.27721	−.04776	.11740	−.17211	1.63483	1.34221
−.40251	−.31052	−1.04834	−.23243	−1.52224	.85903
1.27086	−.93166	−.03766	1.21016	.13451	.81941
1.14464	.56176	.89824	1.54670	1.48411	.14422
.04172	1.49672	−.15490	.77084	−.29064	2.87643
−.36795	1.22318	−1.05084	−1.05409	.82052	.09670
1.94110	1.00826	−.85411	−1.31341	−1.85921	.74578
.14946	−2.75470	−.10830	1.02845	.69291	−.78579

Areas of the Standard Normal Distribution

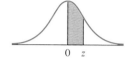

0   z

An entry in the table is the proportion under the entire curve which is between $z = 0$ and a positive value of z. Areas for negative values of z are obtained by symmetry.

z	.00	.01	.02	.03	.04	.05	.06	.07	.08	.09
0.0	.0000	.0040	.0080	.0120	.0160	.0199	.0239	.0279	.0319	.0359
0.1	.0398	.0438	.0478	.0517	.0557	.0596	.0636	.0675	.0714	.0753
0.2	.0793	.0832	.0871	.0910	.0948	.0987	.1026	.1064	.1103	.1141
0.3	.1179	.1217	.1255	.1293	.1331	.1368	.1406	.1443	.1480	.1517
0.4	.1554	.1591	.1628	.1664	.1700	.1736	.1772	.1808	.1844	.1879
0.5	.1915	.1950	.1985	.2019	.2054	.2088	.2123	.2157	.2190	.2224
0.6	.2257	.2291	.2324	.2357	.2389	.2422	.2454	.2486	.2517	.2549
0.7	.2580	.2611	.2642	.2673	.2703	.2734	.2764	.2794	.2823	.2852
0.8	.2881	.2910	.2939	.2967	.2995	.3023	.3051	.3078	.3106	.3133
0.9	.3159	.3186	.3212	.3238	.3264	.3289	.3315	.3340	.3365	.3389
1.0	.3413	.3438	.3461	.3485	.3508	.3531	.3554	.3577	.3599	.3621
1.1	.3643	.3665	.3686	.3708	.3729	.3749	.3770	.3790	.3810	.3830
1.2	.3849	.3869	.3888	.3907	.3925	.3944	.3962	.3980	.3997	.4015
1.3	.4032	.4049	.4066	.4082	.4099	.4115	.4131	.4147	.4162	.4177
1.4	.4192	.4207	.4222	.4236	.4251	.4265	.4279	.4292	.4306	.4319
1.5	.4332	.4345	.4357	.4370	.4382	.4394	.4406	.4418	.4429	.4441
1.6	.4452	.4463	.4474	.4484	.4495	.4505	.4515	.4525	.4535	.4545
1.7	.4554	.4564	.4573	.4582	.4591	.4599	.4608	.4616	.4625	.4633
1.8	.4641	.4649	.4656	.4664	.4671	.4678	.4686	.4693	.4699	.4706
1.9	.4713	.4719	.4726	.4732	.4738	.4744	.4750	.4756	.4761	.4767
2.0	.4772	.4778	.4783	.4788	.4793	.4798	.4803	.4808	.4812	.4817
2.1	.4821	.4826	.4830	.4834	.4838	.4842	.4846	.4850	.4854	.4857
2.2	.4861	.4864	.4868	.4871	.4875	.4878	.4881	.4884	.4887	.4890
2.3	.4893	.4896	.4898	.4901	.4904	.4906	.4909	.4911	.4913	.4916
2.4	.4918	.4920	.4922	.4925	.4927	.4929	.4931	.4932	.4934	.4936
2.5	.4938	.4940	.4941	.4943	.4945	.4946	.4948	.4949	.4951	.4952
2.6	.4953	.4955	.4956	.4957	.4959	.4960	.4961	.4962	.4963	.4964
2.7	.4965	.4966	.4967	.4968	.4969	.4970	.4971	.4972	.4973	.4974
2.8	.4974	.4975	.4976	.4977	.4977	.4978	.4979	.4979	.4980	.4981
2.9	.4981	.4982	.4982	.4983	.4984	.4984	.4985	.4985	.4986	.4986
3.0	.4987	.4987	.4987	.4988	.4988	.4989	.4989	.4989	.4990	.4990

Areas of the Cumulative Standard Normal Distribution

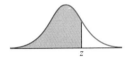

An entry in the table is the proportion under the curve cumulated from the negative tail.

z	G(z)	z	G(z)	z	G(z)
−4.00	0.00003	−1.30	0.09680	1.40	0.91924
−3.95	0.00004	−1.25	0.10565	1.45	0.92647
−3.90	0.00005	−1.20	0.11507	1.50	0.93319
−3.85	0.00006	−1.15	0.12507	1.55	0.93943
−3.80	0.00007	−1.10	0.13567	1.60	0.94520
−3.75	0.00009	−1.05	0.14686	1.65	0.95053
−3.70	0.00011	−1.00	0.15866	1.70	0.95543
−3.65	0.00013	−0.95	0.17106	1.75	0.95994
−3.60	0.00016	−0.90	0.18406	1.80	0.96407
−3.55	0.00019	−0.85	0.19766	1.85	0.96784
−3.50	0.00023	−0.80	0.21186	1.90	0.97128
−3.45	0.00028	−0.75	0.22663	1.95	0.97441
−3.40	0.00034	−0.70	0.24196	2.00	0.97725
−3.35	0.00040	−0.65	0.25785	2.05	0.97982
−3.30	0.00048	−0.60	0.27425	2.10	0.98214
−3.25	0.00058	−0.55	0.29116	2.15	0.98422
−3.20	0.00069	−0.50	0.30854	2.20	0.98610
−3.15	0.00082	−0.45	0.32636	2.25	0.98778
−3.10	0.00097	−0.40	0.34458	2.30	0.98928
−3.05	0.00114	−0.35	0.36317	2.35	0.99061
−3.00	0.00135	−0.30	0.38209	2.40	0.99180
−2.95	0.00159	−0.25	0.40129	2.45	0.99286
−2.90	0.00187	−0.20	0.42074	2.50	0.99379
−2.85	0.00219	−0.15	0.44038	2.55	0.99461
−2.80	0.00256	−0.10	0.46017	2.60	0.99534
−2.75	0.00298	−0.05	0.48006	2.65	0.99598
−2.70	0.00347	0.00	0.50000	2.70	0.99653
−2.65	0.00402	0.05	0.51994	2.75	0.99702
−2.60	0.00466	0.10	0.53983	2.80	0.99744
−2.55	0.00539	0.15	0.55962	2.85	0.99781
−2.50	0.00621	0.20	0.57926	2.90	0.99813
−2.45	0.00714	0.25	0.59871	2.95	0.99841
−2.40	0.00820	0.30	0.61791	3.00	0.99865
−2.35	0.00939	0.35	0.63683	3.05	0.99886
−2.30	0.01072	0.40	0.65542	3.10	0.99903
−2.25	0.01222	0.45	0.67364	3.15	0.99918
−2.20	0.01390	0.50	0.69146	3.20	0.99931
−2.15	0.01578	0.55	0.70884	3.25	0.99942
−2.10	0.01786	0.60	0.72575	3.30	0.99952
−2.05	0.02018	0.65	0.74215	3.35	0.99960

z	$G(z)$	z	$G(z)$	z	$G(z)$
−2.00	0.02275	0.70	0.75804	3.40	0.99966
−1.95	0.02559	0.75	0.77337	3.45	0.99972
−1.90	0.02872	0.80	0.78814	3.50	0.99977
−1.85	0.03216	0.85	0.80234	3.55	0.99981
−1.80	0.03593	0.90	0.81594	3.60	0.99984
−1.75	0.04006	0.95	0.82894	3.65	0.99987
−1.70	0.04457	1.00	0.84134	3.70	0.99989
−1.65	0.04947	1.05	0.85314	3.75	0.99991
−1.60	0.05480	1.10	0.86433	3.80	0.99993
−1.55	0.06057	1.15	0.87493	3.85	0.99994
−1.50	0.06681	1.20	0.88493	3.90	0.99995
−1.45	0.07353	1.25	0.89435	3.95	0.99996
−1.40	0.08076	1.30	0.90320	4.00	0.99997
−1.35	0.08851	1.35	0.91149		

Negative Exponential Distribution: Values of e^{-x}

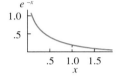

x	e^{-x} (value)	x	e^{-x} (value)	x	e^{-x} (value)	x	e^{-x} (value)
0.00	1.00000	0.50	0.60653	1.00	0.36788	1.50	0.22313
0.01	0.99005	0.51	.60050	1.01	.36422	1.51	.22091
0.02	.98020	0.52	.59452	1.02	.36060	1.52	.21871
0.03	.97045	0.53	.58860	1.03	.35701	1.53	.21654
0.04	.96079	0.54	.58275	1.04	.35345	1.54	.21438
0.05	.95123	0.55	.57695	1.05	.34994	1.55	.21225
0.06	.94176	0.56	.57121	1.06	.34646	1.56	.21014
0.07	.93239	0.57	.56553	1.07	.34301	1.57	.20805
0.08	.92312	0.58	.55990	1.08	.33960	1.58	.20598
0.09	.91393	0.59	.55433	1.09	.33622	1.59	.20393
0.10	.90484	0.60	.54881	1.10	.33287	1.60	.20190
0.11	.89583	0.61	.54335	1.11	.32956	1.61	.19989
0.12	.88692	0.62	.53794	1.12	.32628	1.62	.19790
0.13	.87809	0.63	.53259	1.13	.32303	1.63	.19593
0.14	.86936	0.64	.52729	1.14	.31982	1.64	.19398
0.15	.86071	0.65	.52205	1.15	.31664	1.65	.19205
0.16	.87514	0.66	.51685	1.16	.31349	1.66	.19014
0.17	.84366	0.67	.51171	1.17	.31037	1.67	.18825
0.18	.83527	0.68	.50662	1.18	.30728	1.68	.18637
0.19	.82696	0.69	.50158	1.19	.30422	1.69	.18452
0.20	.81873	0.70	.49659	1.20	.30119	1.70	.18268
0.21	.81058	0.71	.49164	1.21	.29820	1.71	.18087
0.22	.80252	0.72	.48675	1.22	.29523	1.72	.17907
0.23	.79453	0.73	.48191	1.23	.29229	1.73	.17728
0.24	.78663	0.74	.47711	1.24	.28938	1.74	.17552
0.25	.77880	0.75	.47237	1.25	.28650	1.75	.17377
0.26	.77105	0.76	.46767	1.26	.28365	1.76	.17204
0.27	.76338	0.77	.46301	1.27	.28083	1.77	.17033
0.28	.75578	0.78	.45841	1.28	.27804	1.78	.16864
0.29	.74826	0.79	.45384	1.29	.27527	1.79	.16696
0.30	.74082	0.80	.44933	1.30	.27253	1.80	.16530
0.31	.73345	0.81	.44486	1.31	.26982	1.81	.16365
0.32	.72615	0.82	.44043	1.32	.26714	1.82	.16203
0.33	.71892	0.83	.43605	1.33	.26448	1.83	.16041
0.34	.71177	0.84	.43171	1.34	.26185	1.84	.15882
0.35	.70469	0.85	.42741	1.35	.25924	1.85	.15724
0.36	.69768	0.86	.42316	1.36	.25666	1.86	.15567
0.37	.69073	0.87	.41895	1.37	.25411	1.87	.15412
0.38	.68386	0.88	.41478	1.38	.25158	1.88	.15259
0.39	.67706	0.89	.41066	1.39	.24908	1.89	.15107

x	e^{-x} (value)	x	e^{-x} (value)	x	e^{-x} (value)	x	e^{-x} (value)
0.40	.67032	0.90	.40657	1.40	.24660	1.90	.14957
0.41	.66365	0.91	.40252	1.41	.24414	1.91	.14808
0.42	.65705	0.92	.39852	1.42	.24171	1.92	.14661
0.43	.65051	0.93	.39455	1.43	.23931	1.93	.14515
0.44	.64404	0.94	.39063	1.44	.23693	1.94	.14370
0.45	.63763	0.95	.38674	1.45	.23457	1.95	.14227
0.46	.63128	0.96	.38289	1.46	.23224	1.96	.14086
0.47	.62500	0.97	.37908	1.47	.22993	1.97	.13946
0.48	.61878	0.98	.37531	1.48	.22764	1.98	.13807
0.49	.61263	0.99	.37158	1.49	.22537	1.99	.13670
0.50	.60653	1.00	.36788	1.50	.22313	2.00	.13534

Interest Tables

Table G.I   Compound Sum of $1

Year	1%	2%	3%	4%	5%	6%	7%	8%	9%
1	1.010	1.020	1.030	1.040	1.050	1.060	1.070	1.080	1.090
2	1.020	1.040	1.061	1.082	1.102	1.124	1.145	1.166	1.188
3	1.030	1.061	1.093	1.125	1.158	1.191	1.225	1.260	1.295
4	1.041	1.082	1.126	1.170	1.216	1.262	1.311	1.360	1.412
5	1.051	1.104	1.159	1.217	1.276	1.338	1.403	1.469	1.539
6	1.062	1.126	1.194	1.265	1.340	1.419	1.501	1.587	1.677
7	1.072	1.149	1.230	1.316	1.407	1.504	1.606	1.714	1.828
8	1.083	1.172	1.267	1.369	1.477	1.594	1.718	1.851	1.993
9	1.094	1.195	1.305	1.423	1.551	1.689	1.838	1.999	2.172
10	1.105	1.219	1.344	1.480	1.629	1.791	1.967	2.159	2.367
11	1.116	1.243	1.384	1.539	1.710	1.898	2.105	2.332	2.580
12	1.127	1.268	1.426	1.601	1.796	2.012	2.252	2.518	2.813
13	1.138	1.294	1.469	1.665	1.886	2.133	2.410	2.720	3.066
14	1.149	1.319	1.513	1.732	1.980	2.261	2.579	2.937	3.342
15	1.161	1.346	1.558	1.801	2.079	2.397	2.759	3.172	3.642
16	1.173	1.373	1.605	1.873	2.183	2.540	2.952	3.426	3.970
17	1.184	1.400	1.653	1.948	2.292	2.693	3.159	3.700	4.328
18	1.196	1.428	1.702	2.026	2.407	2.854	3.380	3.996	4.717
19	1.208	1.457	1.754	2.107	2.527	3.026	3.617	4.316	5.142
20	1.220	1.486	1.806	2.191	2.653	3.207	3.870	4.661	5.604
25	1.282	1.641	2.094	2.666	3.386	4.292	5.427	6.848	8.623
30	1.348	1.811	2.427	3.243	4.322	5.743	7.612	10.063	13.268

Year	10%	12%	14%	15%	16%	18%	20%	24%	28%
1	1.100	1.120	1.140	1.150	1.160	1.180	1.200	1.240	1.280
2	1.210	1.254	1.300	1.322	1.346	1.392	1.440	1.538	1.638
3	1.331	1.405	1.482	1.521	1.561	1.643	1.728	1.907	2.067
4	1.464	1.574	1.689	1.749	1.811	1.939	2.074	2.364	2.684
5	1.611	1.762	1.925	2.011	2.100	2.288	2.488	2.932	3.436
6	1.772	1.974	2.195	2.313	2.436	2.700	2.986	3.635	4.398
7	1.949	2.211	2.502	2.660	2.826	3.185	3.583	4.508	5.629
8	2.144	2.476	2.853	3.059	3.278	3.759	4.300	5.590	7.206
9	2.358	2.773	3.252	3.518	3.803	4.435	5.160	6.931	9.223
10	2.594	3.106	3.707	4.046	4.411	5.234	6.192	8.594	11.806
11	2.853	3.479	4.226	4.652	5.117	6.176	7.430	10.657	15.112
12	3.138	3.896	4.818	5.350	5.936	7.288	8.916	13.216	19.343
13	3.452	4.363	5.492	6.153	6.886	8.599	10.699	16.386	24.759
14	3.797	4.887	6.261	7.076	7.988	10.147	12.839	20.319	31.691
15	4.177	5.474	7.138	8.137	9.266	11.974	15.407	25.196	40.565
16	4.595	6.130	8.137	9.358	10.748	14.129	18.488	31.243	51.923
17	5.054	6.866	9.276	10.761	12.468	16.672	22.186	38.741	66.461
18	5.560	7.690	10.575	12.375	14.463	19.673	26.623	48.039	85.071
19	6.116	8.613	12.056	14.232	16.777	23.214	31.948	59.568	108.89
20	6.728	9.646	13.743	16.367	19.461	27.393	38.338	73.864	139.38
25	10.835	17.000	26.462	32.919	40.874	62.669	95.396	216.542	478.90
30	17.449	29.960	50.950	66.212	85.850	143.371	237.376	634.820	1645.5

Table G.2   Sum of an Annuity of $1 for N Years

Year	1%	2%	3%	4%	5%	6%	7%	8%
1	1.000	1.000	1.000	1.000	1.000	1.000	1.000	1.000
2	2.010	2.020	2.030	2.040	2.050	2.060	2.070	2.080
3	2.030	3.060	3.019	3.122	3.152	3.184	3.215	3.246
4	4.060	4.122	4.184	4.246	4.310	4.375	4.440	4.506
5	5.101	5.204	5.309	5.416	5.526	5.637	5.751	5.867
6	6.152	6.308	6.468	6.633	6.802	6.975	7.153	7.336
7	7.214	7.434	7.662	7.898	8.142	8.394	8.654	8.923
8	8.286	8.583	8.892	9.214	9.549	9.897	10.260	10.637
9	9.369	9.755	10.159	10.583	11.027	11.491	11.978	12.488
10	10.462	10.950	11.464	12.006	12.578	13.181	13.816	14.487
11	11.567	12.169	12.808	13.486	14.207	14.972	15.784	16.645
12	12.683	13.412	14.192	15.026	15.917	16.870	17.888	18.977
13	13.809	14.680	15.618	16.627	17.713	18.882	20.141	21.495
14	14.947	15.974	17.086	18.292	19.599	21.051	22.550	24.215
15	16.097	17.293	18.599	20.024	21.579	23.276	25.129	27.152
16	17.258	18.639	20.157	21.825	23.657	25.673	27.888	30.324
17	18.430	20.012	21.762	23.698	25.840	28.213	30.840	33.750
18	19.615	21.412	23.414	25.645	28.132	30.906	33.999	37.450
19	20.811	22.841	25.117	27.671	30.539	33.760	37.379	41.446
20	22.019	24.297	26.870	29.778	33.066	36.786	40.995	45.762
25	28.243	32.030	36.459	41.646	47.727	54.865	63.249	73.106
30	34.785	40.568	47.575	56.085	66.439	79.058	94.461	113.283

Year	9%	10%	12%	14%	16%	18%	20%	24%
1	1.000	1.000	1.000	1.000	1.000	1.000	1.000	1.000
2	2.090	2.100	2.120	2.140	2.160	2.180	2.200	2.240
3	3.278	3.310	3.374	3.440	3.506	3.572	3.640	3.778
4	4.573	4.641	4.770	4.921	5.066	5.215	5.368	5.684
5	5.985	6.105	6.353	6.610	6.877	7.154	7.442	8.048
6	7.523	7.716	8.115	8.536	8.977	9.442	9.930	10.980
7	9.200	9.487	10.089	10.730	11.414	12.142	12.916	14.615
8	11.028	11.436	12.300	13.233	14.240	15.327	16.499	19.123
9	13.021	13.579	14.776	16.085	17.518	19.086	20.799	24.712
10	15.193	15.937	17.549	19.337	21.321	23.521	25.959	31.643
11	17.560	18.531	20.655	23.044	25.733	28.755	32.150	40.238
12	20.141	21.384	24.133	27.271	30.850	34.931	39.580	50.985
13	22.953	24.523	28.029	32.089	36.786	42.219	48.497	64.110
14	26.019	27.975	32.393	37.581	43.672	50.818	59.196	80.496
15	29.361	31.772	37.280	43.842	51.660	60.965	72.035	100.815
16	33.003	35.950	42.753	50.980	60.925	72.939	87.442	126.011
17	36.974	40.545	48.884	59.118	71.673	87.068	105.931	157.253
18	41.301	45.599	55.750	68.394	84.141	103.740	128.117	195.994
19	46.018	51.159	63.440	78.969	98.603	123.414	154.740	244.033
20	51.160	57.275	72.052	91.025	115.380	146.628	186.688	303.601
25	84.701	93.347	133.334	181.871	249.214	342.603	471.981	898.092
30	136.308	164.494	241.333	356.787	530.312	790.948	1181.882	2640.916

Table G.3   Present Value of $1

Year	1%	2%	3%	4%	5%	6%	7%	8%	9%	10%	12%	14%	15%
1	.990	.980	.971	.962	.952	.943	.935	.926	.917	.909	.893	.877	.870
2	.980	.961	.943	.925	.907	.890	.873	.857	.842	.826	.797	.769	.756
3	.971	.942	.915	.889	.864	.840	.816	.794	.772	.751	.712	.675	.658
4	.961	.924	.889	.855	.823	.792	.763	.735	.708	.683	.636	.592	.572
5	.951	.906	.863	.822	.784	.747	.713	.681	.650	.621	.567	.519	.497
6	.942	.888	.838	.790	.746	.705	.666	.630	.596	.564	.507	.456	.432
7	.933	.871	.813	.760	.711	.665	.623	.583	.547	.513	.452	.400	.376
8	.923	.853	.789	.731	.677	.627	.582	.540	.502	.467	.404	.351	.327
9	.914	.837	.766	.703	.645	.592	.544	.500	.460	.424	.361	.308	.284
10	.905	.820	.744	.676	.614	.558	.508	.463	.422	.386	.322	.270	.247
11	.896	.804	.722	.650	.585	.527	.475	.429	.388	.350	.287	.237	.215
12	.887	.788	.701	.625	.557	.497	.444	.397	.356	.319	.257	.208	.187
13	.879	.773	.681	.601	.530	.469	.415	.368	.326	.290	.229	.182	.163
14	.870	.758	.661	.577	.505	.442	.388	.340	.299	.263	.205	.160	.141
15	.861	.743	.642	.555	.481	.417	.362	.315	.275	.239	.183	.140	.123
16	.853	.728	.623	.534	.458	.394	.339	.292	.252	.218	.163	.123	.107
17	.844	.714	.605	.513	.436	.371	.317	.270	.231	.198	.146	.108	.093
18	.836	.700	.587	.494	.416	.350	.296	.250	.212	.180	.130	.095	.081
19	.828	.686	.570	.475	.396	.331	.276	.232	.194	.164	.116	.083	.070
20	.820	.673	.554	.456	.377	.312	.258	.215	.178	.149	.104	.073	.061
25	.780	.610	.478	.375	.295	.233	.184	.146	.116	.092	.059	.038	.030
30	.742	.552	.412	.308	.231	.174	.131	.099	.075	.057	.033	.020	.015

Year	16%	18%	20%	24%	28%	32%	36%	40%	50%	60%	70%	80%	90%
1	.862	.847	.833	.806	.781	.758	.735	.714	.667	.625	.588	.556	.526
2	.743	.718	.694	.650	.610	.574	.541	.510	.444	.391	.346	.309	.277
3	.641	.609	.579	.524	.477	.435	.398	.364	.296	.244	.204	.171	.146
4	.552	.516	.482	.423	.373	.329	.292	.260	.198	.153	.120	.095	.077
5	.476	.437	.402	.341	.291	.250	.215	.186	.132	.095	.070	.053	.040
6	.410	.370	.335	.275	.227	.189	.158	.133	.088	.060	.041	.029	.021
7	.354	.314	.279	.222	.178	.143	.116	.095	.059	.037	.024	.016	.011
8	.305	.266	.233	.179	.139	.108	.085	.068	.039	.023	.014	.009	.006
9	.263	.226	.194	.144	.108	.082	.063	.048	.026	.015	.008	.005	.003
10	.227	.191	.162	.116	.085	.062	.046	.035	.017	.009	.005	.003	.002
11	.195	.162	.135	.094	.066	.047	.034	.025	.012	.006	.003	.002	.001
12	.168	.137	.112	.076	.052	.036	.025	.018	.008	.004	.002	.001	.001
13	.145	.116	.093	.061	.040	.027	.018	.013	.005	.002	.001	.001	.000
14	.125	.099	.078	.049	.032	.021	.014	.009	.003	.001	.001	.000	.000
15	.108	.084	.065	.040	.025	.016	.010	.006	.002	.001	.000	.000	.000
16	.093	.071	.054	.032	.019	.012	.007	.005	.002	.001	.000	.000	
17	.080	.060	.045	.026	.015	.009	.005	.003	.001	.000	.000		
18	.069	.051	.038	.021	.012	.007	.004	.002	.001	.000	.000		
19	.060	.043	.031	.017	.009	.005	.003	.002	.000	.000			
20	.051	.037	.026	.014	.007	.004	.002	.001	.000	.000			
25	.024	.016	.010	.005	.002	.001	.000	.000					
30	.012	.007	.004	.002	.001	.000	.000						

Table G.4   Present Value of an Annuity of $1

Year	1%	2%	3%	4%	5%	6%	7%	8%	9%	10%
1	0.990	0.980	0.971	0.962	0.952	0.943	0.935	0.926	0.917	0.909
2	1.970	1.942	1.913	1.886	1.859	1.833	1.808	1.783	1.759	1.736
3	2.941	2.884	2.829	2.775	2.723	2.673	2.624	2.577	2.531	2.487
4	3.902	3.808	3.717	3.630	3.546	3.465	3.387	3.312	3.240	3.170
5	4.853	4.713	4.580	4.452	4.329	4.212	4.100	3.993	3.890	3.791
6	5.795	5.601	5.417	5.242	5.076	4.917	4.766	4.623	4.486	4.355
7	6.728	6.472	6.230	6.002	5.786	5.582	5.389	5.206	5.033	4.868
8	7.652	7.325	7.020	6.733	6.463	6.210	6.971	5.747	5.535	5.335
9	8.566	8.162	7.786	7.435	7.108	6.802	6.515	6.247	5.985	5.759
10	9.471	8.983	8.530	8.111	7.722	7.360	7.024	6.710	6.418	6.145
11	10.368	9.787	9.253	8.760	8.306	7.887	7.449	7.139	6.805	6.495
12	11.255	10.575	9.954	9.385	8.863	8.384	7.943	7.536	7.161	6.814
13	12.134	11.348	10.635	9.986	9.394	8.853	8.358	7.904	7.487	7.103
14	13.004	12.106	11.296	10.563	9.899	9.295	8.745	8.244	7.786	7.367
15	13.865	12.849	11.938	11.118	10.380	9.712	9.108	8.559	8.060	7.606
16	14.718	13.578	12.561	11.652	10.838	10.106	9.447	8.851	8.312	7.824
17	15.562	14.292	13.166	12.166	11.274	10.477	9.763	9.122	8.544	8.022
18	16.398	14.992	13.754	12.659	11.690	10.828	10.059	9.372	8.756	8.201
19	17.226	15.678	14.324	13.134	12.085	11.158	10.336	9.604	8.950	8.365
20	18.046	16.351	14.877	13.590	12.462	11.470	10.594	9.818	9.128	8.514
25	22.023	19.523	17.413	15.622	14.094	12.783	11.654	10.675	9.823	9.077
30	25.808	22.397	19.600	17.292	15.373	13.765	12.409	11.258	10.274	9.427

Year	12%	14%	16%	18%	20%	24%	28%	32%	36%
1	0.893	0.877	0.862	0.847	0.833	0.806	0.781	0.758	0.735
2	1.690	1.647	1.605	1.566	1.528	1.457	1.392	1.332	1.276
3	2.402	2.322	2.246	2.174	2.106	1.981	1.868	1.766	1.674
4	3.037	2.914	2.798	2.690	2.589	2.404	2.241	2.096	1.966
5	3.605	3.433	3.274	3.127	2.991	2.745	2.532	2.345	2.181
6	4.111	3.889	3.685	3.498	3.326	3.020	2.759	2.534	2.339
7	4.564	4.288	4.039	3.812	3.605	3.242	2.937	2.678	2.455
8	4.968	4.639	4.344	4.078	3.837	3.421	3.076	2.786	2.540
9	5.328	4.946	4.607	4.303	4.031	3.566	3.184	2.868	2.603
10	5.650	5.216	4.833	4.494	4.193	3.682	3.269	2.930	2.650
11	5.988	5.453	5.029	4.656	4.327	3.776	3.335	2.978	2.683
12	6.194	5.660	5.197	4.793	4.439	3.851	3.387	3.013	2.708
13	6.424	5.842	5.342	4.910	4.533	3.912	3.427	3.040	2.727
14	6.628	6.002	5.468	5.008	4.611	3.962	3.459	3.061	2.740
15	6.811	6.142	5.575	5.092	4.675	4.001	3.483	3.076	2.750
16	6.974	6.265	5.669	5.162	4.730	4.033	3.503	3.088	2.758
17	7.120	6.373	5.749	5.222	4.775	4.059	3.518	3.097	2.763
18	7.250	6.467	5.818	5.273	4.812	4.080	3.529	3.104	2.767
19	7.366	6.550	5.877	5.316	4.844	4.097	3.539	3.109	2.770
20	7.469	6.623	5.929	5.353	4.870	4.110	3.546	3.113	2.772
25	7.843	6.873	6.097	5.467	4.948	4.147	3.564	3.122	2.776
30	8.055	7.003	6.177	5.517	4.979	4.160	3.569	3.124	2.778

Answers to Selected Problems

Chapter 2

1. Productivity (hours)
   Deluxe   0.20
   Limited   0.20
   Productivity (dollars)
   Deluxe   133.33
   Limited   135.71

Chapter 3

3. *b.* A-C-F-G-I and A-D-F-G-I.
   c. C: 2 weeks;
       D: 2 weeks;
       G: 2 weeks.
   d. Three paths: A-B-E-I; A-C-F-G-I; and
       A-D-F-G-I; 14 weeks.

6. *a.* Critical path is A-E-G-C-D.
   b. 26 weeks.
   c. No difference in completion date.

8. *a.* Critical path is A-C-D-F-G.
   b.

Day	Cost	Activity
First	$1,000	A
Second	1,200	B
Third	1,500	D (or F)
Fourth	1,500	F (or D)

Supplement 5

5. l_s = 4.125 minutes.
   $\bar{n}_l$ = 4.05 cars.
   $\bar{n}_s$ = 4.95 cars.

9. *a.* L = .22 waiting.
   b. W = .466 hours.
   c. D = .362

10. *a.* 2 people.
    b. 6 minutes.
    c. .2964

d. 67%.
e. .03375 hour.

Supplement 6

1. *a.* Not inspecting cost = $20/hr. Cost to
       inspect = $9/hr. Therefore, inspect.
   b. $.18 each.
   c. $.22 per unit.

6. $\bar{\bar{X}}$ = 999.1
   $UCL_{\bar{x}}$ = 1014.965
   $LCL_{\bar{x}}$ = 983.235
   $\bar{R}$ = 21.773
   UCL_R = 49.551
   LCL_R = 0
   Process is "in-control".

9. *a.* n = 31.3 (round sample size n up).
   b. Random sample 32; reject if more than 8 are
       defective.

13. *a.* $2.73 per unit.
    b. Loss per unit will increase.
    c. $1.54 per unit.

Chapter 7

3. No. Must consider demand in fourth year.

Supplement 7

2. Optimum combination is B = 10 and A = 15.

6. *a.*

	D	E	F	G
A	0	0	25	25
B	40	0	0	0
C	10	60	0	5
Total cost = $1,000				

10. *a.* $x = 60$, $Y = 0$, $Z = 90$, $S_1 = 0$, $S_2 = 0$, $S_3 = 40$

b.

	Would You Buy?	At What Price?	How Many?
S_1	Yes	<2	15
S_2	Yes	<3	45
S_3	Yes	<0	∞

	Would You Sell?	At What Price?	How Many?
S_1	Yes	>2	30
S_2	Yes	>3	20
S_3	Yes	>0	40

Chapter 8

1. 5 Kanban card sets.

Chapter 9

1. $C_X = 176.7$
   $C_Y = 241.5$

2. *a.* Store #2 first;
   Store #3 second;
   b. Store #4 third.

Chapter 10

7. *b.* 90 seconds.
   c. 4.55
   d. 5 stations.
   e. 91%.
   f. Reduce cycle time to 85 seconds and work 17.6 minutes overtime.

Chapter 11

3. *a.* 1.35 minutes.
   b. 1.51 minutes.
   c. ST = 1.53 minutes. The worker would not make the bonus.

7. *a.* NT = .9286 minute/part.
   b. ST = 1.0679 minutes/part.
   c. Daily output = 449.50
   Day's wages = $44.49

Supplement 11

3. *LR* labor, 80%.
   LR parts, 90%.
   Labor = 11,556 hours.
   Parts = $330,876

7. 4,710 hours.

11. *a.* 3rd = 35.1 hours.
    b. Average = 7.9 hours each; well worth it.

Chapter 13

3. *a.* February 84
   March 86
   April 90
   May 88
   June 84
   b. MAD = 15

7.

Quarter	Forecast
9	232
10	281
11	239
12	231

11. *a.* April to September = 130, 150, 160, 170, 160, 150
    b. April to September = 136, 146, 150, 159, 153, 146
    c. Exponential smoothing performed better.

15. MAD = 104
    TS = 3.1
    Model is acceptable, but could be better.

19. *a.* MAD = 90
    TS = -1.67
    b. Model okay since tracking is -1.67

Chapter 14

3. Total cost = $413,600

6. *a.* Ending inventory = Safety stock.
   b. Inventory cost includes forecast and safety stock.
   c. Shortage cost is only based on the forecast.
   Total cost = $413,750

Chapter 15

3. $q = 179.148$

7. *a.* $Q = 1,225$
   $R = 824$
   b. $q = 390 -$ Inventory on hand.

11. *a.* $Q = 89.44$
    b. $223.61
    c. $223.61

14. *a.* A (4, 13, 18);
    B (2, 5, 8, 10, 11, 14, 16);
    C (remainder).
    b. Classify as A.

17. ~624

21. 7,500 blades.

25. 208 boxes.

29. 5,000 pounds.

Chapter 16

3.

10. Least total cost method: Order 250 units in period one for periods 1–8;

 Least unit cost method: Order 450 units in period one for periods 1–9.

13. *c.* .A

    .B(2)

        .E(4)

        .F(3)

    .C(3)

        .D(3)

        .H(2)

            .E(5)

            .G(2)

    .D(1)

d. Level 0   100 units of A

 Level 1   200 units of B

             300 units of C

 Level 2   600 units of F

             600 units of H

             1000 units of D

 Level 3   3800 units of E

             1200 units of G

Chapter 17

3. Job order: 5, 6, 7, 3, 1, 2, 4

6. A to 3, B to 1, C to 4, D to 2; Cost = $17

7. Critical ratio schedule: 5, 3, 2, 4, 1

 Earliest due date, job priority: 2, 5, 3, 4, 1

 Shortest processing time (including delay time): 2, 1, 4, 3, 5

Supplement 17

2. Average customer waiting time = 1/6 minute.
 Average teller idle time = 4/6 minute.

7. *a.*

	Condition 1	Condition 2
1)	Idle 18 min.	76 + 134 = 210 min.
2)	Delay 87 min.	0 min.

 b.

	Condition 1	Condition 2
Cost of repairman	$ 38.80	$ 77.20
Cost of machine down	175.33	$117.33
	$214.13	$194.53

Chapter 20

1. Case I: X used = 9333.3 hours.
              Y used = 700 hours.

 Case II: Y = 700 hours.
            X = 933.3 hours.

 Case III: X = 933.3 hours.
            Y = 700 hours.

 Case IV: X = 933.3 hours.
            Y = 700 hours.

 Otherwise:

 Case I: No problem.

 Case II: Excess WIP.

 Case III: Excess spare parts.

 Case IV: Excess finished goods.

8. *a.* Machine B is the constraint.

 b. All of M; as many N as possible.

 c. $600

Photo Credits

Name Index

A

Abernathy, William, 17
Adler, Paul S., 117, 413n, 414
Aggarwal, S., 830
Aksoy, Yasemin, 765
Albrecht, Karl, 142n, 144
Albright, S. Christian, 197, 321
Allison-Koerber, Deborah, 505
Anderson, C., 45
Andrea, David, J., 96, 348
Andrews, Sean, 371-73
Ansari, A., 349
Anthony, Robert N., 854
Apte, Uday, 21
Aquilano, Nicholas J., 15, 79
Araki, Ryuji, 96
Ardalan, Alireza, 290, 363, 363n
Argote, Linda, 454n, 461
Arter, Dennis R., 222
Ashton, James E., 699, 712
Aslup, Fred, 259
Atkinson, A., 758, 759n
Avishai, Bernard, 139
Azani, Hossein, 360n

B

Bachman, Timothy A., 410
Bailey, Charles D., 461
Baker, K. R., 712
Bakke, Nils Arne, 290
Ballard, Mark, 166
Ballou, Ronald H., 373
Bancroft, Nancy H., 655, 667, 677
Banker, R., 759n
Banks, Jerry, 729n, 740
Bardi, Edward J., 373
Barieau, Becky, 164
Barnes, Ralph M., 444
Bartlett, Christopher A., 771, 771n, 786
Bartness, Andrew D., 373
Bary, William L., 667
Bedricky, Alec, 323
Benson, Randall J., 340n

Bergh, Peter A., 223n, 225, 226, 234
Berkley, Blair J., 129n
Bernstein, A., 45
Berry, W. L., 579, 623, 712
Bigness, Jon, 470n
Birch, David, 247, 247n
Birou, Laura M., 483, 495
Bitner, Mary Jo, 397, 397n, 410
Bitran, Gabriel R., 167
Black, J. T., 125, 139
Blackburn, Joseph D., 45, 349, 373
Blackstone, John H., Jr., 623, 685, 830
Blain, Jonathon, 655, 667, 672
Bodie, Zvi, 843n, 853
Bohutinsky, Catherine H., 765
Bonett, Doulgas G., 410
Boothroyd, Geoffrey, 93n, 116, 117
Bowen, D., 444
Bowerman, Bruce L., 549
Bowman, Edward H., 15, 571
Bragg, Denial J., 480n
Bramorski, Tom, 796-97, 830
Bray, Ronald, 561
Brebach, Gresh, 787
Bremner, B., 45
Brigham, Eugene F., 853
Bright, Phil, 665-66
Brittain, Connie, 778n
Brooks, Roger B., 623
Brown, Don W., 259
Brown, Robert G., 593, 594
Browne, James J., 699, 699n, 701n, 702, 712
Buday, Robert S., 784
Buffa, Elwood, 15
Bulfin, Robert L., Jr., 623, 667
Burt, David N., 495
Busby, J. S., 139
Byrne, M. D., 831

C

Callaway, Rin, 676
Camp, Robert C., 45
Carley, William M., 199

Carlisle, Brian, 444
Carroll, Thomas M., 357
Carter, Joseph R., 484
Carton, Barbara, 122
Castellano, Joseph F., 118
Cavallaro, Harold E., Jr., 831
Cedergren, Christopher, 96
Chambers, Stuart, 290
Champy, James, 768n, 772n, 787
Chandler, Richard, 771
Chase, Richard B., 9, 10, 15, 21, 155n, 167, 197, 444
Cho, Fujio, 325-26
Choobineh, F., 410
Chowdhury, Subir, 234
Christensen, Clayton M., 765
Clark, John, 783
Clark, Kim B., 17, 22, 45, 52, 85, 110, 118
Clark, Steve, 665-66
Clausing, Don, 91
Cleland, David I., 79
Clemson, Barry A., 293
Cohen, Morris A., 167
Cohen, Stephen S., 45
Cole, Robert E., 22
Colley, John L., 167
Collier, D. A., 167
Collins, Phil, 765
Collis, David J., 745, 745n, 746, 765
Colwin, Joe, 767
Conway, R. W., 688, 712, 740
Cook, Fran X., Jr., 699, 712
Cooke, James Aaron, 488, 488n, 489n
Cooley, Ross, 394
Cooper, Jerry, 785
Cooper, Robert B., 197
Coupe, Henry, 410
Cox, James F., III, 831
Cox, Jeff, 712, 790, 830
Cox, Tony, 785
Coyle, John J., 373
Coyne, Kevin, 150, 151n
Cozzette, Dave, 114-15
Creculius, Kathy, 370

Creech, Bill, 234
Crosby, Philip B., 206-207, 210n, 226, 227, 234
Cummings, T., 444
Curran, Thomas, 677
Cusack, Marjorie, 426

D

Dalzell, Rick, 497-98
Dantzig, George B., 13
Davenport, Thomas H., 774, 780, 780n, 786
Davidow, W. H., 21
Davidson, William H., 786
Davis, Mark M., 197
Dean, Robert D., 357
Dell, Michael, 114-15
Deming, W. Edwards, 13, 18, 22, 202, 206-207, 209, 234, 324, 425, 779
Dettmer, H. William, 830
Dewhurst, Peter, 93n, 117
Diamond, James, 625
DiCiara, Robert, 47-48
Dickson, W. J., 15
Dixon, Lance, 343
Dobler, Donald W., 495
Dodge, H. G., 13, 239n
Donoghue, J. A., 88
Doyle, Michael F., 495
Dreifus, Shirley B., 273
Drezner, Zvi, 373
Drucker, Peter F., 22, 117
Dumaine, Brian, 213n
Dumond, Ellen J., 495
Durand, Ian G., 234

E

Edmonson, Harold E., 117
Einstein, Albert, 844
Elshennawy, Ahmad, 167
Engelberger, Gay, 120
England, W. B., 493
Eppen, G. D., 321
Epple, Dennis, 461
Ericson, Lennert, 443
Evans, Mac, 229-30

F

Farnham, Alan, 83
Farsad, Behshid, 167
Fawcett, Stanley E., 483, 495
Fearon, Harold E., 467, 469n, 471n, 493, 495
Feigenbaum, A. V., 234, 259
Fetter, Robert B., 571
Finsthal, Timothy, 167
Fisher, Edward L., 383n
Fisher, Marshall, 557n, 579

Fisk, J. C., 579
Fitzsimmons, James A., 167, 197, 362n, 758
Fitzsimmons, M. J., 197, 758
Flaig, L. Scott, 139
Flint, Jerry, 167
Fogarty, Donald W., 623, 685
Foley, John, 498
Follmann, Dean A., 461
Ford, Henry, 13, 14n, 130, 324
Fourer, Robert, 765
Fox, R. E., 712, 809, 830
Francis, R. L., 373, 380n, 410
Freeman, John, 424
Frosch, Robert A., 123
Fucini, Joseph J., 349
Fucini, Suzy, 349
Fulmer, William E., 444

G

Gagnon, Roger, 410
Gantt, Henry L., 14
Gardiner, Stanley C., 830
Garrison, Ray, 840
Garvin, David A., 9, 10, 21
Gates, William H., 22
Gaynor, Gerard H., 40n, 139
George, Stephen, 234
Gershkoff, I., 712
Ghosh, Soumen, 410
Ghoshal, Sumantra, 771, 771n, 786
Gibbs, Curt, 323
Giffi, Craig A., 22, 45, 234, 290, 438, 439, 439n
Gilbert, James P., 481
Gilbert, Paul, 765
Gilbreth, Frank, 13, 14, 422
Gilbreth, Lillian, 13, 14, 422
Gitlow, Howard S., 234
Gitman, Lawrence J., 853
Giunipero, Larry C., 349
Globerson, Shlomo, 158, 158n, 436n, 461
Golden, James, E., 529, 530, 530n
Goldratt, Eliyahu M., 13, 712, 741, 790-93, 791n, 809, 824, 824n, 830
Goold, Michael, 743
Gould, F. J., 321
Gozinto, Zepartzat, 103
Graham, Alan, 234
Grant, E. L., 244, 244n
Graves, Steven C., 623
Graw, LeRoy H., 495
Green, Timothy J., 411
Greenberg, H. J., 321
Greenblatt, Sherwin, 343
Greenwald, John, 351
Greiner, Larry, 765
Grover, V., 45
Gryna, F. M., 234, 259

Gumbel, Peter, 264
Gummesson, Evert, 21
Gunther, R. E., 411
Gup, Benton E., 853
Gupta, A., 129n

H

Hackett, Gregory P., 167
Hahn, Chan K., 480n, 495
Haider, S. Wali, 729n, 740
Hall, Gene, 786
Hall, Robert, 339n, 340, 340n, 349, 390
Hamilton, Wayne, 468
Hamler, Mark, 229
Hammer, Michael, 13, 18, 22, 117, 121, 121n, 768, 768n, 769, 769n, 771n, 772n, 774n, 775, 779, 784, 786, 787
Hammesfahr, R. D. Jack, 290
Hammond, Janice H., 557n, 579
Hansen, Trevor, 665
Hardesky, John L., 259
Harland, Christine, 290
Harper, Lucinda, 487
Harrington, Lisa, 468
Harris, Ford Whitman, 13
Harris, Robert S., 854
Harrison, Alan, 290
Hart, Christopher W. L., 45, 161n, 167, 270, 290, 373
Harwood, John, 743
Hauser, John R., 91
Hayden, Tom, 783
Hayes, J. P., 679, 712
Hayes, Robert H., 17, 22, 45, 97, 99, 117
Haywood-Farmer, John, 280, 280n, 281, 290
Heinrich, Claus, 671
Hendricks, Kevin B., 234
Heragu, Sunderesh, 411
Herbig, Paul, 529, 530, 530n
Hernâandez, Jose Antonio, 677
Herrman, Jeff, 684
Heskett, James L., 45, 147, 147n, 167, 290, 373
Heuslein, William, 167
Heygate, Richard, 785
Heymann, Nicholas, 88
Hickman, Thomas K., 485, 495
Hickman, William M., Jr., 485, 495
Hill, Terry J., 25, 25n, 29, 45, 117
Hillier, Frederick S., 197
Hodder, James E., 854
Hodges, Richard M., 206n, 234
Hoech, Johannes, 167
Hoel, Paul G., 857
Hoffherr, Glen D., 234
Hoffmann, Tomas R., 623, 685
Hofmann, Martin, 671
Holt, Charles C., 571
Hopp, Wallace, 45

Horowitz, Ira, 293n
Horton, Jeb, 744n
Hout, Thomas M., 22
Howard, Keith, 334n
Hudson, William J., 549
Huthwaite, Bart, 117
Hyer, Nancy Lea, 411

I

Imai, Masaaki, 233
Irman, R. Anthony, 342
Irving, Robert, 461
Ishikawa, Kaoru, 234
Ivancevich, J. M., 444
Ivey, M., 45

J

Jacobs, Derya A., 293
Jain, Charman, 549
Jenkins, David B., 488n
Johnson, G. D., 411
Johnson, Richard S., 234
Johnson, Roger, 381n, 411
Johnson, S. M., 712
Johnson, Thomas, 839n
Johnson, Thomas W., 22
Johnston, Robert, 290
Jones, Daniel T., 22, 38n, 45, 324n, 349
Juran, Joseph M., 13, 18, 206-207, 209, 234, 259, 324, 779

K

Kan, A. H. G. Rinnoy, 623
Kane, Alex, 843n, 853
Kanet, John K., 691, 691n
Kano, Noriak, 216
Kaplan, Robert S., 135, 135n, 759n, 831, 839n
Katz, K. L., 171, 197
Keller, Gerhard, 677
Kelly, J. E., 54
Kelton, W. David, 740
Kernan, Jerome B., 397, 397n
Kerzner, Harold, 79
Khorramshahgol, Reza, 360n
Kijewski, Valerie, 482n, 495
Killen, Kenneth H., 495
Kim, Jay S., 28n
Kim, Kee Young, 495
Kimes, Sheryl E., 362n
King, William R., 79
Klein, Donald, 118
Kleiner, Art, 765
Klipstine, Tom, 348
Knight, Robert M., 657
Knight, Winston, 93n, 117
Kolb, Hank, 229-31
Konz, Stephan, 444

Kopsco, David P., 461
Koronacki, Jacek, 259
Kostiuk, Peter F., 461
Kotha, Surech, 17, 22
Kretschmer, Rudiger, 677

L

Labon, Peter, 765
Ladd, Andrew, 677
Lalli, Karen, 375
Lamprecht, James L., 234
Laro, David, 609
Larson, B. M., 171, 197
Larson, Richard C., 170, 171, 197
Larsson, Jan L., 455n, 456, 457, 470
Law, Averill M., 740
Lawler, Edward E., III, 234, 417n, 437n
Leader, Charles, 215n
Leavenworth, R., 244, 244n
Lee, Choong Y., 649, 667
Lee, Hau L., 167
Leenders, Michael R., 467, 469n, 471n, 493, 495
Leonard, Frank S., 231
Leonard, Stu, 398
LeVitt, Richard, 218-19
Levitt, Theodore, 157n, 157-58
Levy, Marv, 771
Lewis, Bill, 266-67
Libertore, Matthew J., 838n
Lillrank, Paul, 216
Linde, Claas Vander, 20n, 22
Little, Charles H., 21
Llewellyn, John, 321
Logan, Gordon D., 461
Long, Scott, 159
Lorenzi, M. P., 444
Losee, Stephanie, 115
Lotfi, Vahid, 383, 383n
Love, John F., 411
Love, Phyliis M., 783
Lovelock, C. H., 158, 158n
Lu, David J., 234

M

Mabert, V. A., 87
Macadam, S., 755n, 765
McCarthy, Daniel J., 371
McClain, J. D., 740
McGraw, Dan, 395
Machalaba, Daniel, 426
McKinzie, Gordon, 88
McLeavy, D., 579
McManus, Jim, 765
McMillan, Charles J., 14n, 22
Madan, Manu S., 796-97, 830
Maggard, M. J., 158, 158n, 197
Mahoney, Francis X., 234
Maister, David H., 747, 747n, 748, 765

Malhotra, M. K., 45
Malorie, M. S., 22
Mandelbaum, Avi, 117
Manglesdorf, Martha E., 346
Manley, Bruce R., 293n
Maples, Diedre M., 495
Marcus, Alan, 843n, 853
Marquardt, Donald W., 234
Marshall, Paul W., 105
Martin, Hugh F., 290
Marucheck, A., 45
Mason, Mark, 355
Maxwell, W. L., 688, 712, 740
Mayo, Elton, 13, 15
Meal, Harlan C., 554, 554n
Meger, Randy, 495
Mehra, Satish, 342
Melnyk, Steven A., 139
Meyer, Christopher, 84, 84n, 118, 290
Milewicz, John, 529, 530, 530n
Miller, Louis, W., 688, 712
Mito, Setsuo, 349
Mitra, G., 321
Moad, Jeff, 676
Modarress, B., 349
Moffat, Susan, 17, 22
Mohrman, Susan Albers, 234
Mokshagundam, L. Srikanth, 808
Molinelli, James P., 783-84
Monden, Yasuhiro, 349, 391, 392n, 411, 579
Moody, Patricia E., 712
Morey, Russell, 45
Morgan, Michael S., 283
Moriarty, Rowland T., 167
Morita, Akio, 35
Motwani, Jaideep, 12n, 22, 796-97, 830
Mulkey, Larry, 487
Muller, Euguene W., 473, 473n, 495
Mumford, Enid, 418n
Murray, Chuck, 120
Muther, Richard, 382n
Myer, Randy, 474, 474n, 475

N

Nadler, Gerald, 234
Nadworny, Milton J., 14n, 22
Nagel, S., 321
Naisbitt, John, 130
Nall, Dave, 730-31
Nanda, Ravinder, 701n, 702, 712
Narasimhan, Ram, 139, 484
Narasimhan, S., 579
Narisetti, Raju, 83
Nasar, Sylvia, 37
Needle, Sheldon, 625
Neely, A. D., 831
Negroponte, Nicholas, 139
Nemitz, William C., 461
Neuborne, Ellen, 141

Nguyen, Vin, 117
Nicholas, John M., 79
Niebel, Benjamin W., 428, 429, 444
Niemira, Michael P., 549
Nolle, Henry, 14
Nollet, Jean, 280, 280n, 290
Noori, Hamid, 139
Nordstrom, Bruce, 141
Nordstrom, John, 159
Norman, Richard, 400n, 411

O

Obermeyer, Walter R., 557n, 579
O'Connell, Richard T., 549
Odell, Annie, 164–65
O'Dell, C., 437n
O'Halloran, David O., 215n
Ohno, Tai-ichi, 13, 324, 349
Oliver, S., 290
Olsen, R. Paul, 281, 281n, 284, 284n, 410, 578
O'Neil, Paul H., 375
Orfalea, Paul, 164
Orlicky, Joseph, 13, 16, 667
O'Rourke, J. Tracy, 139
Osborn, D., 22
Ostle, Bernard, 857
Ottinger, L. V., 125

P

Pannesi, A. R., 45
Pareto, Vilfredo, 606
Park, Sung, 345
Parsons, R., 436n
Payne, James A., 740
Peach, Bill, 789
Peach, Robert W., 234
Pegels, C. Carl, 383, 383n
Penlesky, R., 712
Peters, Tom, 53, 141, 142, 159, 159n
Peterson, P., 79
Peterson, R., 579, 623
Peterson, R. S., 411
Petroski, Henry, 118
Petzinger, Thomas, Jr., 166n
Phelps, Deborah, 784–86
Pine, B. Joseph, II, 19n, 22, 290, 495, 787
Pinto, Peter A., 480n
Pisano, Gary P., 45
Plank, Richard E., 482n, 495
Plossl, George W., 579, 831
Poirier, Charles C., 495
Polise, Joseph, 426
Pope, James A., 290
Port, Otis, 116
Porter, Michael E., 20n, 22, 356n
Porter, Michael L., 765
Poterba, James M., 842n, 854
Prentis, Eric L., 22

Pringle, John J., 854
Pruett, James M., 692
Ptak, Carol A., 625
Puffer, Sheila M., 371
Pyle, James C., 234
Pyzdek, Thomas, 167

Q

Quinn, James Brian, 22

R

Rabbitt, John T., 223n, 225, 226, 234
Radford, Russell, 139
Raia, Ernest, 323
Raman, Anath, 557n, 579
Ramsay, John, 482, 482n, 495
Ramsey, George F., Jr., 444
Rangan, V. Kasturi, 167
Read, Jerry, 122
Reagan, Ronald, 201
Reardon, Ann, 371–73
Reinertsen, Donald G., 38
Reiter, Stephen E., 495
Relnersen, Donald, 38
Renschler, Andreas, 366
Reyes, Luis, 535
Richter, H., 712
Ricklefs, Roger, 561
Riggle, William, 609
Riggs, Henry E., 117, 854
Robinson, Alan, 156n, 217n, 234
Roehm, Harper A., 118
Roethlisberger, F. J., 15
Rogers, Tom, 79
Rogo, Alex, 789–91
Rohleder, Thomas R., 787
Romig, H. G., 13, 239n
Roos, Daniel, 22, 324n, 349
Rosenthal, Jim, 786
Ross, David, 45
Ross, Elliot B., 167
Roth, Aleda, 22, 40, 40n, 41, 45, 234, 290, 438, 439, 439n
Rothery, Brian, 234
Ruestman, Arlen, 122
Rutter, Rick, 444

S

Sadowski, Randall P., 411
Sakai, Kuniyasu, 117, 118
Sandberg, Ake, 444
Sandberg, Jared, 166n
Sanders, Betsy, 159
Sandman, William E., 679, 712
Sandvig, J. C., 87
Sasser, W. Earl, Jr., 45, 167, 281, 281n, 284, 284n, 290, 373, 410, 444, 471, 578
Savich, Richard, 765

Savoie, Michael, 12n, 22
Scanlon, Joseph, 436
Schaap, Peter, 665
Schafer, W. B., 710
Schartner, Andreas, 692
Scheving, Eberhard E., 21
Schmidt (steelworker); *see* Nolle, Henry
Schneider, Don, 487
Schonberger, Richard J., 22, 272, 339, 349, 393, 411, 481
Schroeder, Dean, 156n
Schweikhar, S., 579
Schwerer, Elizabeth, 117
Seagle, J. P., 579
Seal, Gregory M., 22, 234, 290, 438, 439, 439n
Senge, Peter, 758, 765
Sewell, G., 340
Shapiro, Benson P., 167
Sharda, Ramesh, 321
Sharpe, Simon, 677
Shemo, Diana Jean, 465
Sheridan, John H., 684
Sheu, Chwen, 558n
Shewhart, Walter, 13
Shiba, Shoji, 234
Shingo, Shigeo, 216–17, 234, 340
Shiskin, Julius, 501
Short, James E., 786
Shouldice, Dr., 288–89
Shunk, Dan L., 118
Shycon, Harvey N., 373
Silan, Murat N., 293
Silver, E. A., 579, 785
Silver, E. D., 623
Simmonds, Peter J., 371
Simmons, Wayne, 229–30
Simonson, Ken, 487
Singhal, Vinod R., 234
Sink, D. Scott, 45
Sipper, Daniel, 623, 667
Skinner, C. Wickham, 17, 25, 27, 27n, 31, 31n, 45, 271, 271n, 373
Skinner, S., 444
Slack, Nigel, 32, 45, 290
Smalley, Harold E., 424
Smith, Adam, 768
Smith, Bernard T., 530n, 530–33, 531n
Smith, David B., 455n, 456, 457, 461
Smith, Gregory A., 782–83
Smith, Jack, 142
Smith, Preston G., 38
Smith-Daniels, Dwight E., 79, 579
Smith-Daniels, Vickie L., 79, 579
Smunt, Timothy L., 461
Sohal, Amrik, 334n
Solo, S., 45
Soloman, Eyra, 854
Solomon, Susan L., 740
Sommers, Montrose S., 397, 397n

Sonnenberg, Frank K., 167
Souvlaki, Soteriou, 408, 409
Sower, Victor, 12n, 22
Spann, Mary S., 118
Spearman, Mark, 45
Spencer, M. S., 823, 831
Spizizen, G., 270
Sprague, Linda G., 552
Sprague, William R., 116
Srikanth, Mokshagundam L., 808, 808n, 831
Stalk, George, Jr., 22, 45
Starr, Martin K., 45
Steel, D. C., 45
Stein, Martin M., 343
Stewart, Dale, 372-73
Stewart, Douglas M., 155n, 167, 409
Stewart, Thomas A., 769
Sule, D. R., 373, 411, 712
Sullivan, R. S., 167
Sumanth, David J., 39, 40
Summers, Lawrence H., 842n, 854
Suzaki, Kiyoshi, 326n, 349
Svoboda, Susan, 476
Swaim, Jeffery C., 45
Swamidass, Paul M., 268
Swedish, Julian, 740
Swink, Morgan L., 87

T

Taguchi, Genichi, 234, 248, 259
Taha, Hamdy A., 321
Tang, Kitty, 39, 40
Taormina, Tom, 90, 234
Tatikonda, Mohan V., 341
Taubert, William H., 571
Taylor, Frederick W., 13-15, 413, 422, 425, 745
Taylor, George, 351
Templeman, John, 367
Tersine, Richard J., 623
Thomas, D. R., 45
Thomas, Mark, 743
Thompson, Barney, 665-67
Thompson, James R., 259
Thor, Carl G., 234
Threadgill, John A., 293n

Tibrewala, Rajen K., 699, 699n, 701n
Tidd, Joseph, 139
Tippett, L. H. C., 13
Tompkins, James A., 373
Towill, D. R., 461
Toyoda, Tatsuro, 346
Treacy, M., 744, 745n
Turbide, David A., 667
Turner, Joseph, 248n
Turner, Richard, 264

U

Umble, M. Michael, 831
Upton, D., 755, 765

V

Van Horne, James C., 854
Vargas, Gustavo A., 22
Varol, John, 114
Vollmann, T. E., 579, 623, 667, 712

W

Wacker, John G., 558n
Wade, Judy, 786
Wald, Matthew L., 47n
Waldman, David, 234
Walker, M. R., 54
Wallace, Thomas F., 667
Walleck, Steven, 215n
Wantuck, Kenneth A., 324, 325n, 334, 349
Watson, Ricky M., 259
Watts, Charles A., 495
Webster, William, 293n
Weimershirch, Arnold, 234
Weir, Mary, 418n
Weiss, Wolfgang, 677
Welch, John F., 199
Welsch, Glenn A., 854
Werner, Helmut, 366
Wetherill, G. Barrie, 259
Wheeler, John D., 382n
Wheelwright, Steven C., 17, 22, 45, 52, 85, 97, 99, 110, 117, 118
White, John A., 373n, 380n, 410
White, Richard E., 333n, 349

Whybark, D. C., 579, 623, 667
Wiersema, F., 744, 744n
Wild, Ray, 712
Williams, Joe, 665-66
Williams, Michael, 346
Williams, Paul B., 48, 49, 79
Wilson, J. Holton, 505
Wilson, Larry W., 623
Windsor, Wallis, 164-65
Winston, Wayne L., 197, 321, 728, 740
Winter, Richard, 497
Wisniewski, Joe, 656-57
Womack, James P., 22, 37, 38, 38n, 45, 324n, 349
Woodruff, David, 367
Woolsey, G., 740
Woolsey, Robert E. D., 410
Worona, S. L., 740
Wright, T. P., 446
Wyckoff, D. Daryl, 270, 281, 281n, 284, 284n, 410, 578

Y

Yager, Milan P., 561
Yates, Ronald E., 767, 769
Yelle, Louie E., 461
Yorkmark, John, 132
Young, Jan B., 623
Young, M., 759n
Young, R. F., 158, 158n
Yurkiewicz, Jack, 533, 533n

Z

Zandin, Kjell, 444
Zappe, Christopher, 293n
Zarnfaller, Erich, 370
Zarnowitz, Victor, 549
Zemke, Ron, 142n, 144
Ziemke, M. Carl, 118
Zimmer, Ken, 234
Zipkin, Paul H., 349, 623
Zuboff, Shoshana, 444
Zurawski, Chuck, 348
Zysman, John, 45

Subject Index

A

"A" plants, 812-13
ABC inventory systems, 605-608
Absolute error, 431, 432
Acceptable quality level (AQL), 237-39
Acceptance sampling, 236-40
Accountants/Accounting, 4, 341, 815-16
Accurate response production planning, 557
Activity-based costing, 838-40
Adaptive forecasting, 512
Additive seasonal variation, 521
Aggregate planning, 550-79
    budgets, 558
    case study, 578
    costs, 558, 560-64
    cut-and-try technique, 559-64
    demand management, 55
    hierarchical production (HPP), 554-55
    level scheduling, 568-69
    linear programming, 569-71
    mathematical techniques, 569-71
    MRP, 629-30
    operations planning overview, 552-53
    production, 555-58
    costs, 558, 560-64
    smoothing, 568
    services, 564-68
    techniques, 559-71
Alcoa, 375-76
Allen-Bradley Co., 632
Allocations in transportation method, 309-11
Aluminum Company of America, 375
Ambient conditions, retail service facility
    layout, 397-98
America Online (AOL), 166-67
American Red Cross (ARC), 292
American Society of Mechanical Engineers
    (ASME), 103
Amortization, 836
Ampere, Inc., 639-44
AM/PM International, 365

*Analysis for Production and Operations
    Management* (Bowman and Fetter), 15
Analytic Delphi Model, 360-61
Analytic Hierarchy Process, 361
    selection of suppliers using, 476-78
Anderson Consulting, 744, 746-48
Annuities, 846-48
    table, 863
Application link enabling (ALE), 671-72
ARCH (Automated Restaurant Crew Helper),
    120-21
Archer Daniels Midland (ADM), 352
ARCO Corporation, 365
Ardalan heuristic method, 363
Arrival phenomena, 170-75
Arrival rate, 172
Arvin North American Automotive (NAA),
    334-35
Arvin Total Quality Production System
    (ATQPS), 333, 334
Ashridge Strategic Management Centre, 743
Assembly charts, 102, 103
Assembly drawings, 102-103
Assembly lines, 97-99, 383, 385-92
    balancing, 385-87
    two-stage, simulation, 721-25
Assembly processes, 97
Assignment method, job shop scheduling,
    689-91
AT&T, 436
Attribute measurements in process control,
    240-41
Audits, 755-56
Autocorrelation, 500
Automated systems
    ARCH (Automated Restaurant Crew
        Helper), 120-21
    factory automation, 13, 17, 129, 327
    guidance vehicles (AGVs), 124, 127
    for inspection, 327
    manufacturing planning and control
        systems (MP&CS), 128-29

Automated systems—*Cont.*
    materials handling (AMH) systems, 124,
        127, 128
    office automation, 129-30
    storage and retrieval (AS/RS), 124
Automobile replacement parts inventory, 612

B

Backflush measurement, 339
Backlogs/backlogging
    costs, 558
    production planning, 557
Backordering, 570
Backward scheduling, 681, 810
Balanced scorecard, 758-59
Baldrige National Quality Award; *see* Malcolm
    Baldrige National Quality Award
Batch manufacturing, 97
Batch sizes, 806-809
Bay Medical Center, 728-29
Benchmarking, 205
    for continuous improvement (CI), 213,
        215
    process, 778
"Bermuda triangle" of operational complexity,
    284
Bernard Welding Co., 683
Best operating level, 267
Bill of materials (BOM), 626, 635-36, 640-41
Boeing, 55, 88
Bonuses; *see* Financial incentive plans
Boothroyd Dewhurst Inc., 116
Boston Consulting Group, 747
Bottleneck analysis, 757
Bottlenecks, 798, 801-806
Bottom-round management, 333
Box-Jenkins forecasting, 501, 505
"Brain surgery" projects, 747
Break-even analysis, 100-102
Brokers, 486
Budgets, aggregate production planning, 558
Buffer stock; *see* Safety stock

Business climate, 353-354
Business process reengineering (BPR), 4, 13, 18, 121, 766-787
approach, 771-775
benchmarking, 778
candidate identification, 772
case study, 782-86
continuous improvement and, 779
creativity, 778
current process diagnosis, 774
enablers and, 773-74
flowcharting, 777-78
implementation, 775
inductive thinking, 776-77
innovation, 781
nature of, 768
outcomes, 769
principles, 768-71
process improvement and, 780-81
process redesign, 775-78
scope limiting, 781
simulation, 778
software for, 778
technology evaluation, 773-74
total quality management and, 779
type of change categorization, 780
vision statement, 772

C

CAD (computer-aided design), 13, 93, 128, 133
CAE (computer-aided engineering), 128
California State Automobile Association (CSAA), 782-84
CAM (computer-aided manufacturing), 13, 129, 133
Campbells, 486
Capability index, 246-47
Capacity, 106-107, 146, 264-67
Capacity constrained resources (CCR), 799, 803-805
Capacity cushions, 274
Capacity focus, 271
Capacity planning, 262-321
case study, 288-90
concepts, 267-72
decision tree analysis, 276-79
defined, 264-67
dependent events, 794
economies of scale, 268-69, 271
experience curves, 269-71
external sources of, 273-74
flexibility in, 271-72
focused factory, 271
increases to capacity, 272-74
linear programming; *see* Linear programming (LP)
multisite growth stages, 281-84
operating levels, 267

Capacity planning—*Cont.*
plant-within-a-plant (PWP), 271
quality and, 280-281
requirements analysis, 274-75, 553
rough-cut, 553
service industry, 279-84
in service organizations, 146-47
time horizons for, 265
unbalanced, 795-98
utilization rate, 267-68
Capacity resource profile, 801
CAPP (computer-aided process planning), 128
Case studies
aggregate production planning, 578
business process reengineering (BPR), 782-86
capacity planning, 288-90
facilities
layout, 408-410
location, 370-73
JIT production, 345-48
MRP, 665-67
scheduling, 708-712
supply-chain management, 492-94
total quality management (TQM), 229-33
work measurement and standards, 443-44
Cash flow, 794
Causal forecasting, 500, 501, 504, 505, 526-28
Causal loop analysis, 757
Cause and effect diagrams, 214, 231, 232
Cellular manufacturing, 325-26, 376, 392-95
Center of gravity method, facilities location, 358-60
Charting, 571
Chase production planning strategy, 557
Chrysler Corporation, 271
CIM (computer-integrated manufacturing), 4, 10, 13, 17, 31, 129, 137-38
Cincinnati Milacron facility, 127, 128
Client/server systems, 132
Closed-loop MRP systems, 645-46
Common stock, 843
Compaq Computer, 43-44, 392, 394-95
Compensation systems, 435-39
Competitive advantage, facilities location and, 356
Competitive priorities, 28-29
Competitiveness, U.S., operations strategy, 36-38
Complementary products, 556
Complementary Software Partner (CSP), 671
Complex job shops, 691
Component parts, 582
Compound value, 844-46
table, 862
Computer applications
CAD (computer-aided design), 13, 93, 128, 133

Computer applications—*Cont.*
CAE (computer-aided engineering), 128
CAM (computer-aided manufacturing), 13, 129, 133
CAPP (computer-aided process planning), 128
CIM (computer-integrated manufacturing), 4, 10, 13, 17, 31, 129, 137-38
forecasting, 500, 501, 530-33
graphics, 128
information processing, 770
job shop scheduling, 692
languages, 728-31
linear programming (LP) output, 305-307
local area networks (LANs), 132
Manufacturing Management II, 696
models; *see* Simulation
MRP systems, 637-38, 653-56
process layout, 380-81
product layout, 384
programs: *see* software *below*
project management, 67
shop-floor control, 696
simulation; *see* Simulation
software, 728-29
business process reengineering (BPR), 778
facilities layout, 384
FactoryFLOW, 384
MRP, 637-38, 653-56
project management, 67
R/3 software, 654-56, 668-77
simulation; *see* Simulation
superservers, 132
systems, networked, 132
waiting line management, 189-90
Computer Sciences Corporation (CSC), 747
Computer simulation, 757-58
Computerized line balancing, 389
Computerized Relative Allocation of Facilities Technique (CRAFT), 380-81
Concurrent engineering (CE), 87-88, 147
Conformance quality, 208
Consecutive days off, scheduling, 698-99
Constraint equations, 295
Constraints; *see also* Synchronized production
Consulting; *see* Operations consulting
Continuous flow manufacturing, 99; *see also* Assembly lines
Continuous improvement (CI), 415-16
Baldrige criteria, 212-16
benchmarking, 205, 213, 215
kaisen, 213
tools and procedures, 213
business process reengineering (BPR), 779
Continuous simulation, 726

Control
  process; *see* Process control
  project; *see* Project planning/control
Control charts, 214, 756
Control limits, 240–42
Control methods, synchronous
  manufacturing, 800–809
Conversion processes, 96
Conveyors, 124
Core capabilities, 30–32
Core enterprise, 30
Core services, 10
Corporate strategy, 5, 24, 33
Correlation analysis, 758
Cost(s)
  accounting, 341, 816
  activity-based, 838–40
  aggregate production planning, 558,
    560–64
  analysis, 107–108
  avoidable, 835
  backlogging, 558
  basic production, 558
  of capital, 841–44
  direct, 63–66
  distribution, 134
  of equity securities (stocks), 843
  fixed, 834
  indirect, 63–66
  inspection, justified, 237
  inventory, 134, 558, 584–85
  labor, 133, 340, 341
  least total (LTC), 651–52
  least unit (LUC), 652–53
  material, 133–34
  operating, 794–95
  as operations strategy, 25–27
  opportunity, 835
  process layout, 377–79
  process selection, 101–102
  product variability, 248–51
  production rate change, 558
  project management, 63–66
  purchasing and, 472
  of quality (COQ), 134, 209–11
  reductions in, from technology, 133–34
  SAP R/3 software, 673
  sunk, 833
  time-cost models, 63–66
  total, 354, 651–52
  transportation, 134
  variable, 834–35
  waiting line economics, 169
Cost effectiveness balance, 169
CPM (critical path method); *see* Project
  planning/control
CRAFT method, 380–81
Creativity, business process reengineering
  (BPR), 778

Critical path method (CPM); *see* Project
  Management
Cross-training, 414
CTS, 625
Cumulative average time, 446
Custom Clothing Technology Corporation
  (CCTC), 345
Custom manufacturing, 130
Customer(s), 143
  arrivals, 170–75
  contact, 144–45
  focus, 204
  product design and, 84, 89–92, 208
  proximity to, 279–80, 352–53, 361–67
  quality function deployment (QFD) and,
    90–92
  of service organizations, 143–45
Customer surveys, 753
Customs (import), 355
Cut-and-try production planning, 559–64
Cycle counting, 609–10
Cycle times, 385
  manufacturing, 135, 328–29
  time-to-market, 19, 38, 110
Cycles (forecasting), 500

D

Daily work times, 700–701
Dana Corporation, 680
Data envelopment analysis (DEA), 758
Data integrity, scheduling, 695–96
Data warehouse, 670
Decision rules, simulation, 716
Decision support systems, 132, 138
Decision trees, 276–79, 758
Declining-balance depreciation, 837
Defects, 217
Degeneracy, 315
Delivery
  reliability of, 26
  speed of, 25–26
Delivery systems, service organization, 147
Dell Computer, 114–15
Deloitte & Touche Consulting, 745
Delphi method, 501, 503–504
  Analytic Model, 360–61
Demand for products
  demand-pull scheduling, 336, 343–44
  dependent, 499, 585
  forecasting; *see* Forecasting (demand)
  independent, 499, 585
  management of, 498–500, 556
  MRP; *see* Material requirements planning
    (MRP)
Deming Prize, 200, 202–203
Deming wheel, 213, 214
Department store inventory, 611–12

Dependent demand, 499, 585
Dependent events, 796
Depreciation, 836–38
Deseasonalization of demand, 524, 525
Design for manufacturing and assembly
  (DFMA), 93–96
Design quality, 207–208
DFM (design for manufacturability), 116, 147
Digital Equipment Corporation, 10
Direct costs, 63–66
Discounted cash flow, 848
Discrete simulation, 726–27
Disney, 263–64
  theme park, 176
Dispatch lists, daily, 693
Dispatching, 682
Distributed processing, 132
Distribution costs, 134
Distributors, 486
Dollar days inventory, 809
Double-declining-balance depreciation,
  837–38
Drums, Synchronized production, 803–805

E

Eagle Enterprises, 625
Early start schedule, CPM, 58–59
Eastman Kodak, 418
Econometric forecasting, 501
Economic life, 836
Economic order quantity (EOQ), 586, 589–90,
  597–98
  in MRP systems, 650–51
Economic purchase-order size, 584
Economics
  of operations consulting, 747–48
  of waiting line problem, 169–70
Economies of scale, 268–69, 271
Economies of scope, 272
Efficiency, 645
Efficient consumer response (ECR), 488–89
EG&G, Inc., 370
Eldora Company (EDC), 371–73
Electronic data interchange (EDI), 131,
  487–88
Electronic Data Systems (EDS), 747
Electronic enterprise, 13, 18
Elemental standard-time data, 428
Employee(s)
  availability, 275
  Baldrige criteria and, 204
  costs
    JIT production and, 340, 341
    reduced, 133
  development, 204
  flexibility, 272
  interacting with equipment, 422–23
  interacting with other workers, 423–24

Employee(s)—*Cont.*
  leasing, 561
  levels of, 555
  management of, 20, 557-58
    production planning, 562-63
  meaningful employment, 415
  quality, 354
  respect for, 332-333
  scheduling, 698-700
  specialization, 415-16
  temporary, 415, 561
Employee involvement (EI) teams, 417
Employee surveys, 754
Enterprise resource planning (ERP), 654,
  669
Entrepreneurial stage, multisite service
  growth, 281-82
Entrepreneurs, 4
Environmental issues, 20, 136-37, 356
Equipment
  availability of, 275
  selection of, 100-101, 275
  worker interaction with, 422-23
Ergonomics, 418
Errors
  absolute, 431, 432
  design, 217
  forecasting, 512-16, 525-26
Euro Disney, 263-64
Event simulation, 727
Excel for Windows, 305-307, 478, 489, 533,
  571, 725, 757
Exceptions reports, 638, 693
Executive judgment forecasting, 504
Expansion example, financial analysis,
  850-51
Expected value, risk and, 836
Experience curves, 260-71
Expert systems, 132
Exponential distribution of arrivals, 173
Exponential smoothing, 501, 505, 509-512
Express package services, 342

F

Fabrication processes, 97
Facilities
  layout of, 374-411
    ambient conditions, 397-98
    assembly lines, 383, 385-92
    case studies, 408-410
    computerized techniques, 380
    cost considerations, 379
    CRAFT, 380-81
    fixed-position, 377, 395-96
    flexible line layouts, 389, 390
    flow-shop; *see* product based, *below*
    group technology (cellular), 376,
      392-95
    guidelines, 400-401

Facilities—*Cont.*
  layout of—*Cont.*
    in Japan, 401
    of offices, 400
    process based, 376-83
    product based, 376, 383-92
    production formats, 376-77
    retail service, 397-400
    servicescapes, 397
    signs, symbols, and artifacts, 399-400
    software for, 383
    spatial layout and functionality,
      398-99
    systematic planning (SLP), 381-83
    task splitting, 387-88
  locating, 350-373
    business climate and, 353-54
    case studies, 370-73
    center of gravity method, 358-60
    competitive advantage, 356
    costs, 354
    customer proximity, 352-53
    Delphi method, 360-61
    environmental regulation, 356
    factor-rating system methods,
      356-58
    formula review, 367
    free trade zones, 354
    government barriers, 354
    host community, 356
    infrastructure, 354
    issues, 352-356
    labor quality, 354
    linear programming for, 358
    methods, 356-61
    other facilities and, 354
    political risk, 354
    service facilities, 361-67
    suppliers, 354
    trading blocs, 354, 356
  services and, 143, 361-67, 392-400
Factor-rating methods, 356-58
Factories
  automation of, 13, 17, 129
  Factory FLOW software, 384
  focused, 27, 271
  of the future (FOF), 17, 129
  virtual, 100
Factory Planning Software Cimetechnologies
  Corp., 384
Fail-safe procedures; *see* Poka-yokes
Fail-safing
  of service(s), 154-56
  Shingo system, 216-17
Feasibility, area of, linear programming and,
  295
Federal Express, 26, 212-13, 470, 472
Feedback (job design), 418
Field-based services, 143

Field support, 10
Financial analysis, 834-54
  activity-based costing, 838-40
  alternate investments, 841
  amortization, 836
  annuities, 846-848
    table, 863
  avoidable costs, 835
  compound value, 844-46
    table, 862
  depreciation, 836-38
  discounted cash flow (DCF), 848
  economic life, 836
  examples, 850-53
  expansion example, 850-51
  expected value, risk and, 836
  fixed costs, 834
  interest rate effects, 844-48
  internal rate of return, 849-50
  make-or-buy example, 853
  negative exponential distribution table,
    860-61
  net present value, 848-49
  obsolescence, 836
  opportunity costs, 835
  payback period, 849
  present value, 846-48
    tables, 864-65
  random digit tables, 855-56
  ranking investments, 848-50
  replacement example, 852-53
  risk and expected value, 836
  standard distribution tables, 857-59
  sunk costs, 835
  taxes, 840-41
  uneven lives of investments, 850
  variable costs, 834-35
Financial incentive plans, 435-39
Financial managers, 4
Financial measurements, 794
"Finders," 747
Finished-goods inventory, 530
Finished products, 582
Finite loading, 681
Finite population, waiting line management,
  172, 187-89
Firm(s)
  goals of, 793-95
  as supplier, 474-76
  VAT classifications, 811-15
First-hour principle, 701
Fishbone diagrams, 756
Five forces model, 754
Five P's of operations management (OM), 7,
  17
5W2H quality method, 213, 215
Fixed-order quantity inventory; *see* Inventory,
  fixed-order quantity
Fixed-position layout, 377, 395-96

Fixed-time period inventory; *see* Inventory, fixed-time period
Flat-rate pricing, 166
Flexibility
  in capacity planning, 271–72
  FMS (flexible manufacturing systems), 13, 17, 19, 100, 126, 127, 138
  in line layouts, 389, 390
  as operations strategy, 26–28
  in production scheduling, 584
Flow in process analysis, 105–108
Flowcharts, 756
  business process reengineering (BPR), 777–78
  service businesses, 154–55
Flow diagrams (BOM); *see* Bill of materials (BOM)
Flow shop(s), layout of, 376, 383–92
FMS (flexible manufacturing system), 13, 17, 19, 117, 127
Focus forecasting, 530–33
Ford Motor Company, 14, 479, 482, 581
Forecasting (demand), 496–549, 758; *see also* Material requirements planning (MRP)
  autocorrelation, 500
  Box-Jenkins technique, 501, 505
  capacity planning example, 274–75
  causal relationships, 500, 501, 504, 505, 526–28
  computer simulation, 530–33
  cyclical elements, 500
  Delphi method, 501, 503–504
  demand management, 498–500
  dependent demand, 499
  econometric models, 501
  executive judgment, 504
  focus, 530–33
  formula review, 536–37
  grass roots, 501, 503
  historical analogy, 501, 504
  Holt's exponential smoothing, 505
  independent demand, 499
  input/output models, 501
  leading indicators, 501
  market research, 501, 503
  method selection, 529–30
  MRP example, 639
  multiple regression analysis, 528
  panel consensus, 501, 503–504
  periods, 500
  qualitative, 500, 501, 503–504
  random variation, 500
  seasonal elements, 501, 521–25
  Shiskin time series, 501
  simulation models, 500, 501
  time series analysis, 500, 501, 505–526
    adaptive, 512
    Box-Jenkins technique, 501

Forecasting (demand)—*Cont.*
  time series analysis—*Cont.*
    decomposition, 505, 520–26
    errors, 512–516, 525–26
    exponential smoothing, 501, 505, 509–512
    hand fitting, 517–18, 522–23
    least squares method, 518–20, 523–25
    linear regression analysis, 516–20
    mean absolute deviation (MAD), 513–16
    moving averages, 501, 505–508
    seasonal variations, 521–25
    Shiskin, 501
    simple moving average, 501, 505–507
    simple proportion, 521–22
    smoothing constants
      alpha (α), 509–512
      delta (δ), 510–511
    tracking signals, 514–16
    weighted moving average, 501, 507–508
  trend effects, 500–503, 520
  types of, 500
  at Warner-Lambert Company, 534–35
  Winters' exponential smoothing, 505
Formula reviews
  facilities location, 367
  forecasting, 536–37
  inventory systems, independent demand, 613–15
  logarithmic curve, 457
  process control, 252
  standard time, 439
  waiting line management, 190–91
Forward scheduling, 681, 810
Franchises, 281–84
Free trade zones, 354
Freeze windows, 339
Functionality, spatial layout and, 398–99
Functional projects, 52, 53

G

Gain sharing bonus plans, 436–38
Gantt charts, 50, 51, 56, 66
  scheduling, 693
Gap analysis, 753–54
Gemini Consulting; *see* MAC Consulting Group
General Electric Co., 199–200, 389, 391, 438, 481, 583
General Motors, 38, 98, 142, 348, 581–82
General Tire, 437–48
Geographical Information Systems (GIS), 361
Glenn-Mark Auto Agency, 184–87
Global joint venture, 108–109

Global-positioning-satellite (GPS) technology, 122–23
Global product design strategy, 109
Global production networks, 19
Global sourcing, 482–86
  international distribution, 484–85
Governmental issues
  barriers to facilities location, 354
  regulations, 20, 354
Grant Thorton LLP consulting company, 487
Graphical linear programming, 294–97
Graphing, 571
Grass roots forecasting, 501, 503
"Gray hair" projects, 747
"Grinders," 747
Group technology (GT), 326, 680
  layouts, 376, 392–95
GTE, 769, 775

H

Hackers Computer Store, 276–79
Hand fitting, linear regression analysis, 517–18, 522–23
Hardware technologies, 124–28
Harley-Davidson Motor Company, 772, 773
Harper's Furniture, 656–57
Harvard Business School, 13, 15, 17
Hawthorne studies, 13, 15
Hay Group, 747
HDS (Houston Downhole Sensors) Division, 698–99
Heart transplants, learning curve example, 455–57
Hewlett-Packard, 10, 38, 88, 89, 218, 237–38, 389, 470, 696–97
Hierarchical production planning (HPP), 554–55
Histograms, 214
Historical analogy forecasting, 501, 504
Hockey-stick phenomenon, 792–93
Holding costs, 584
Holt's exponential smoothing, 505
Host community, facilities location and, 356
Hourly work times, scheduling, 701–702
House of quality matrix, 91–92
Housewares department inventory, 611
Human factors in job design, 418
Human resources; *see* Employee(s)
Hypothesis testing, 758

I

IBM, 13, 38, 141, 747
Image processing systems, 130–31
Improvement curves, 450–51
In Search of Excellence (Peters), 141
Independent demand, 499, 585
Indirect costs, 63–66

Individual bonuses, 438
Individual financial incentive plans, 436
Individual learning, 446, 453-54
Inductive thinking, 776-77
Industrial design, 89
Industrial engineering (IE), 5
Industrial robots, 124-26
Industry learning, 447
Infinite loading, 681
Infinite population, waiting line management, 172
Information
 "informating" workers, 415
 as value-added service of manufacturing, 10
Information processing, 770; *see also* Computer applications
Information systems (IS), 469
Infrastructure, facilities location and, 354
Input/output control, 693-94
Input/output forecasting, 501
Interest rate effects, financial analysis, 844-48
Intermediate range planning, 265, 552
Internal rate of return, 849-50
International Organization for Standardization, 13, 18
Internet, 13, 18, 21
Inventory, 794
 ABC type, 605-608
 accuracy, 608-611
 costs, 134, 558, 584-85
 cycle counting, 609-610
 defined, 582-83
 economic order quantity (EOQ); *see* Economic order quantity
 fixed order quantity, 586-99
  basic, 586-90
  optimal lot size, 591
  service levels and, 592-99
  with usage, 590-91
 fixed-time period, 586, 599-601
  order quantity, 600-601
 formula review, 613-15
 on hand, 555
 material requirements planning (MRP); *see* Material requirements planning
 models, 586-605
 one-bin system, 606
 optional replenishment, 605-606
 planning strategy, 557
 price-break model, 601-603
 production planning, 557
 purposes of, 583-84
 records file, 636-37, 641
 reorder points, 588-90, 595-96, 598-99
 safety stock, 560, 591-99, 804-805
 salvage value, 604

Inventory—*Cont.*
 sawtooth model, 588-89
 service business, 611-12
 service levels, 593-99
 single-period, 603-605
 special purpose, 601-605
 synchronized production, 794, 809
 systems, 580-623
 two-bin, 606
 types, 587-605
Inventory investments, 796
Inventory position, 587
Inventory transactions file, 637
Investment evaluation of technology, 132-37
Investments, financial analysis of; *see* Financial analysis
Ireland, 353
ISO 9000 standards, 13, 18, 200, 217-26
 applicability example, 223-25
 Baldrige criteria and, 225
 certification under, 221, 223
 consulting for, 749
 elements in, 221, 222
 guidelines for, 219-21

J

J. O. Bilodeau & Company, 551-52
Japanese industry, 16-17, 24, 29
 aggregate production planning, 568
 barriers to entry, 354, 355
 bottom-round management, 333
 Deming Prize, 202-203
 employee involvement (EI) teams, 417
 employees, respect for, 332-33
 group technology (GT), 326
 information technology and, 136-37
 JIT production, 325-33
 kaisen, 213
 kanban production control, 329-32
 keiretsu, 38
 office layout, 401
 product development and, 117
 productivity approach, 325-33
 quality at the source, 326-27
 quality circles, 333
 setup times, minimized, 332
 Shingo system, 216-17
 small group improvement activities (SGIA), 333
 suppliers and, 482
 uniform plant loading, 328-29
 waste elimination, 325-32
JIT; *see* Just-in-time (JIT) production
Job(s)
 design of, 412-44
 behavioral considerations, 415-18
 decisions, 414-15
 enlargement, 414

Job(s)—*Cont.*
 enrichment, 416-17
 equipment interaction, 422-23
 feedback, 418
 fixed workplace, 422
 labor specialization, 415-16
 methods analysis, 418-24
 motion studies, 422
 physical considerations, 418
 production process, 419-21
 skill variety, 417
 sociotechnical systems, 417-18
 specialization of labor, 415-16
 tasks, 417, 418
 work measurement and standards; *see* Work measurement and standards
 work methods, 418-24
 work physiology, 418
 worker interactions, 423-24
Job shops, 97, 337-38, 627, 680; *see also* Schedules/Scheduling
 labor-limited, 681
JOB systems, 692
Joint ventures, global, 108-109
Jostens, 438-39
Just-in-time (JIT) production, 4, 13, 16-17, 31, 322-49
 backflush measurement, 339
 bottom-round management, 333
 case studies, 345-48
 cost accounting, 341
 defined, 327-28
 express package service and, 342
 freeze windows, 339
 group technology (GT), 326
 implementation requirements, 334-40
 Japan, 325-33
 job shops, 337-38
 kanban production control, 329-32
 labor costs, 340, 341
 layouts and design flows, 335-37
 level scheduling, 338, 568-69
 line flow applications, 336-37
 logic of, 324-25
 MRP and, 633, 647-48
 preventive maintenance, 335
 purchasing; *see* Just-in-time purchasing
 quality at the source, 326-27
 quality circles, 333, 340
 in services, 340-44
 setup times, minimized, 332
 small group improvement activities (SGIA), 333
 stable schedules, 338-39
 suppliers and, 339-40, 344-45
 synchronous production and, 810-811
 total quality control (TQC), 338

Just-in-time (JIT)—*Cont.*
    uniform plant loading, 328-29
    U.S. modifications, 333-34
    waste elimination, 325-32
Just-in-time purchasing, 479-82
    multiple vs. few suppliers, 480-81

K

Kaisen, 213
Kaiser Aluminum, 437
Kanban production control, 329-32
Kanaban pull system, 329
Kawasaki Motors, 97, 555
Keiretsu, 38
Kinko's Copier Stores, 164-66
Korea, 269

L

Labor; *see* Employees
Labor costs, 133, 340, 341
Labor-limited process, 681
Lapointe Machine and Tool Co., 436-37
La Quinta Motor Inns, 362-63
Late start schedule, 59
Layouts
    facility; *see* Facilities
    JIT production, 335-37
Lead time, 656
Leadership, Baldrige criteria, 204
Leading indicators, 501
Learning curve(s), 445-61
    application, 446-47
    guidelines, 453-54
    heart transplant example, 455-57
    individual, 446, 453-54
    length of, 453
    logarithmic analysis, 448-49
    organizational, 446, 454
    percentage, 452
    plotting, 447-53
    tables, 449-52
Least-cost allocation method, 310
Least squares method, 518-20, 523-25
Least total cost (LTC), 651-52
Least unit cost (LUC), 652-53
Level production planning, 338, 557, 568-69
Leveraging, 747
Lexus, 90
Life cycle(s)
    process, 99
    product, 99
    production systems, 11-12
Limited, The, 10
Line flow applications, 336-37
Linear programming (LP), 291-321
    aggregate production planning, 569-71
    applications, 292
    conditions for use, 293

Linear programming (LP)—*Cont.*
    constraint equations, 295
    degeneracy, 315
    Excel and, 305-307
    facility location and, 358
    graphical, 294-97
    initial allocations, 309-11
    matrix set up, 308-309
    maximization, 297-304
    minimization, 303
    model, 294
    optimal solution, 312-15
    optimum points, 296-97
    pivot method, 300-301
    ranging, 304
    search path of, 303-304
    sensitivity analysis, 305
    shadow prices, 305
    simplex method, 292, 297-307
    six-step solution procedure, 297-303
    slack variables, 297-98
    spreadsheets, 305-307
    stepping stone evaluation method,
        312-14
    transportation method, 292, 307-315,
        358
Linear regression, 516-20
Local area networks (LANs), 132
Location dependence of services, 279-80
Logarithmic analysis, 448-49
Logistics, defined, 466
Long-range debt, 842-43
Long-range planning, 265, 552
Loose Knit textile mill, 187-89
Los Angeles Toy Company (LATC), 44-45
Lost sales, 570
Lot size
    in MRP, 648-53
    optimal, 591
    setup costs and, 335-36
    statistical quality control, 240
Lot tolerance percent defective (LTPD),
    237-39
Low-level parts coding, 636
Lump-sum bonuses, 438

M

MAC Consulting Group, 759-65
McCall Diesel Motor Works, 710-12
McDonald's, 13, 18, 120-21, 156-58, 411
McDonnell Douglas, 330
Machine-limited process, 681
Machining centers, 124, 125, 128
McKinsey & Co., 743, 746-47
McKinsey Global Institute, 266-67
Maintenance, preventive, 335
Make-or-buy decisions, 31, 467-69
    example, 853

Malcolm Baldrige National Quality Award, 13,
    18, 159, 200-207, 226
    benchmarking, 205, 213, 215
    benefits, 205-206
    criteria, 203-204
    eligibility, 203
    ISO 9000 standards and, 225
    winners, 203
        characteristics, 206, 213, 215
Management and the Worker
    (Roethlisberger and Dickson), 15
Management coefficients, 571
Management science (MS), 5-6, 15; *see also*
    Operations research
Manufacturability, product design and, 116,
    147
Manufacturer's representatives, 486
Manufacturing, 84
    facilities; *see* Facilities
    global, 108-109
    materials management; *see* Purchasing
    operations, 10, 12; *see also* Operations
        management
    process planning; *see* Process planning
    strategy; *see* Operations strategy
    synchronized; *see* Synchronized
        production
Manufacturing cells, 127
Manufacturing Futures Survey, 28, 29
Manufacturing Strategy Paradigm, 13, 17-18
Manufacturing technology, 123-29
Marketing, 84
    product development, 84, 149-51
    specialists, 4
    strategies, 149-51
    synchronized production and, 816
Market research, 501, 503
Market risks of technology, 136-37
Marriott, 151
Mass customization, 16, 19, 136
Master production schedules (MPS); *see*
    Schedules/Scheduling
Material(s)
    costs, 133-34
    flows, 97-99
    handling, automated (AMH), 124, 127,
        128
    management, 466
        logistics, defined,
        purchasing; *see* Purchasing
    shipping charges, 471-72
    value density, 471-72
Material requirements planning (MRP), 13,
    16, 553, 624-67, 681
    advanced, 653-56
    advantages, 632-33
    bill of materials (BOM) file, 626, 635-36,
        640-41
    case study, 665-67

Material requirements planning (MRP)—*Cont.*
  closed-loop, 645-46
  computer programs, 637-38, 653-56
  defined, 626
  demand for products, 634
  disadvantages, 633
  economic order quantity (EOQ), 650-51
  EDI (electronic data interface),
  Enterprise Resource Planning (ERP), 654
  example, 627-29, 639-44
  improvements to, 644-47
  inventory records file, 636-37, 641
  JIT production, 633, 647-48
  least total cots (LTC), 651-52
  least unit cost (LUC), 652-53
  lot-for-lot, 650
  lot sizing in, 648-53
  master production schedules, 629-30,
    639-40
  MRP II (manufacturing resource planning,
    626, 646-47
  net change systems, 638-39
  output reports, 638
  purposes of, 631-32
  R/3 software, 654-56
  running the program, 641-44
  SAP AG, 654
  software, 637-38, 653-56
  structure, 633-39
  synchronous production and, 808-809
  systems, 631-33
  time fences, 630
  uses, 627
  work center loading, 644-45
Matrix projects, 52, 54
Maturity stage, multisite service growth, 284
Maximization, 297-304
Mean absolute deviation (MAD), 513-16
Mean charts, 242-46
Megatrends (Naisbitt), 130
Mellon Bank, 774-75
Mercedes-Benz, 336-37
Merit Pay, 438
Methods time measurement (MTM), 429
Microsoft Corporation, 13, 19, 468
Microsoft Excel for Widows, 305-307, 478,
    489, 533, 571, 725
Mid-States Aluminum Corp., 765
Milestones, 48, 49, 51, 52
Milacron, 126-28
Miller Brewing Company, 97
"Minders," 747
Minimization, 303
Minimum-cost scheduling, 63-66
MIS specialists, 4
MIT Commission on Industrial Productivity,
    36
Mixed-model assembly line balancing, 389-92
Mixed strategy, 558

Model construction, simulation, 716-18
Modern Production Management (Buffa), 15
Modular bill of materials (BOM), 636
Most work measurement systems (MOST),
    429
Motion studies, 422
Motorola, 136, 245, 247
Moving assembly lines, 13-15
Moving averages, 501, 505-508
MRP; *see* Material requirements planning
Multifactor productivity measures, 39
Multiple regression analysis, 528
Multiplicative seasonal variation, 521
Multiproduct production, 570
Multisite service growth, 281-84

N

National Bicycle Industrial Company (NBIC),
    16-17
National Science Foundation, 499
Navistar International,
NCR Corp., 116, 497
Negative exponential distribution table,
    858-59
Neo Vista Solutions, Inc., 497-98
Net change systems, 638-39
Net present value, 846-47
Net profit, 792
Netscape Communications, 13, 19
Networked computer systems, 132
New United Motor Manufacturing Inc.
    (NUMMI), 414, 425
Nichols Company (NCO), 665-67
Nintendo, 335
Nonbottlenecks, 796-97, 800-801
Non-value-adding work, 772
Nordstrom, 141, 158-59
Normal time, 426-28
Northwest-corner allocation method, 310
Numerically controlled (NC) machines, 124
Nursing, work sampling application, 431,
    433-34

O

Objective functions, linear programming and,
    294-96
Obsolescence, 834
Office automation, 129-130
Office layout, 400
Ohio Tool Co., 493-94
One-bin inventory system, 606
Operating characteristic (OC) curves, 238-39
Operating expenses, 792-94
Operating levels, 267
Operation and route sheets, 103, 104
Operational measurements, 792-93
Operational risk, 136

Operations charts, 422
Operations capabilities, 30
Operations consulting, 742-65
  defined, 744
  economics of, 747-48
  example, 759-65
  management of, 744-47
  need for, 748-50
  process, 750-52
  tool kit, 752-59
    cost impact and payoff analysis,
      758-59
    data analysis and solution
      development, 756-58
    data gathering, 755-56
    implementation, 759
    problem definition, 753-54
Operations focus, 27
Operations priorities, 25-29
Operations management (OM), 1-22
  business specialties, 4
  capacity planning; *see* Capacity planning
  current issues, 19-20
  defined, 4, 5
  field of, 5-9, 15
  five P's of, 7, 17
  historical development, 12-19
  linear programming; *see* Linear
    programming
  nature and context, 3-20
  in organizational chart, 8, 9
  production systems, 7
  queues; *see* Waiting line management
  studying, 4
  waiting lines; *see* Waiting line
    management
Operations planning
  aggregate; *see* Aggregate planning
  capacity; *see* Capacity planning
  overview, 552-53
  processes; *see* Process planning
  project; *see* Project planning/control
Operations research (OR), 5-6, 15
Operations scheduling; *see*
  Schedules/Scheduling
Operations strategy, 5, 22-45
  comparative industry approach,
  competitiveness, 36-38
  concept-to-production,
  core capabilities, 30-32
  costs and, 25, 27
  defined, 24
  developing, 31-32
  flexibility as, 26-27
  framework for, 30-32
  paradigm; *see* Manufacturing Strategy
    Paradigm
  priorities, 25-29
  product quality as, 25, 135

Operations strategy—*Cont.*
    productivity measurement, 39–40
    in services, 33–36
    Strategic Service Vision, 147
    target markets, 30
    types, 25–27
    U.S. competitiveness, 36–38
Operations technology, 119–39
Optimax Systems Corp., 684
Optimization, 296–97, 789
    linear programming method; *see* Linear
        programming,
    lot size, 591
    optimal solutions, 312–15
Optimized production technology (OPT), 791
Optimum points, 296–97
Optional replenishment inventory, 605–606
Order qualifiers, 29
Order scheduling, 553
Order winners, 29
Ordering costs, 584
Organization charts, 8, 9, 756
Organizational learning, 446, 454
Organizational risks of technology, 136
Organizational structures, project planning
    and control, 52–54
Oshkosh B'Gosh, 420
Output reports
    linear programming (LP), 305–307
    MRP, 638
    simulation, 720–21
Outsourcing, 466, 469–71
Overhead costs, 340, 341

P

P model; *see* Inventory, fixed-time period
Panasonic Individual Customer System (PICS),
    16–17
Panel consensus forecasting, 501, 503–504
Parameters, simulation, 716, 718–19
Pareto analysis, 214, 606, 756
Partial productivity measures, 39
Partnership relationships, 343
    purchasing, 476
Pay for knowledge, 436, 438
Pay-for-performance, 437–39
Payback period, 847
PDCA (plan-do-act) cycle, 213–14
Peg records (MRP), 637
Performance, measurement of, 431, 791–93
Performance dynamics, 743
Performance ratings, 426–27
Performance reports, 638
Periodic inventory system; *see* Inventory,
    fixed-time period,
Perishability, 570
Perpetual inventory systems; *see* Inventory,
    fixed-order quantity

Personal attention approach to service
    delivery, 158–61
Personnel; *see* Employee(s)
Personnel specialists, 4
PERT (program evaluation and review
    technique), 13, 54–56, 63, 66–69
Physical considerations in job design, 418
Piece rate incentives, 438
Pitney Bowes (PB), 482
Pivot method, 300–301
Planning
    aggregate; *see* Aggregate planning
    capacity; *see* Capacity planning
    intermediate range, 265, 552
    long-range, 265, 552
    process; *see* Process planning
    project; *see* Project planning/control
    short range, 265, 552
Planning bill of materials (BOM), 636
Planning reports, 638
Plants, 7, 268; *see also* Facilities
    tours of, 755
Plant-within-a-plant (PWP), 27, 33, 271
Plotting, learning curves, 447–53
Point-of-sale (POS) systems, 488, 489
Poisson distribution of arrivals, 173–74
Poka-yokes, 217, 220
    services and, 155–56
Political risk, facilities location and, 354
Precedence diagrams, 386
Precedence relationship, 385
Predetermined motion-time data systems
    (PMTS), 428–30
Present value, 844–46
    tables, 862–63
Preventive maintenance, 335
Prices/Pricing, 556
    flat-rate, 166
Price-break inventory model, 601–603
Price-look-up (PLU), 488
Principles of Scientific Management (Taylor),
    14, 744
Priority rules, job shop, 684–92
Pritsker Corp.,
Probability distributions, simulation, 716
Problem analysis, 756
Problem definition, simulation, 716
Problem solving, 10
"Procedures" project, 747
Process(es), 7
    batch, 805–807
    layout of, 376–83
    manufacturing, scheduling tools for, 682
    quality of, as operations strategy, 25
Process analysis, 105–108
Process capability, 245–47
Process control, 240–47
    attribute measurements, 240–41
    control limits, 240–42

Process control—*Cont.*
    formula review, 252
    mean and range charts, 242–46
    process capability, 245–47
        index, 246–47
    range charts, 241–45
    samples attributes, 240–41
    six-sigma limits, 245–47
    Taguchi methods, 248–51
    variability, 248–51
    variable measurements, 241–45
Process flow charts, 214
Process flow design, 102–104
Process flow structures, 97–99
    assembly lines, 97–99
    batch, 97
    continuous flow, 99
    job shop, 97
Process planning, 552; *see also* Process
    selection
    capacity analysis, 106–107
    computer-aided (CAPP), 128
    flow, 341
    manufacturing, 96–111
    process selection contrasted with, 96
Process redesign, 773–76
Process reengineering (BPR); *see* Business
    process reengineering
Process selection, 96–102; *see also* Process
    planning
    break-even analysis, 100–102
    contrasted with process planning, 96
    equipment selection, 100–101
    flow structures, 97–99
    product-process matrix, 99–100
    types of, 96–97
    virtual factories, 100
Proctor & Gamble, 19
Procurement, defined; *see* Purchasing
Product(s)
    cycle times, 135, 328–29
    design, 82–96
        concurrent engineering, 87–88
        customers and, 84, 89–92, 208
        global, 108–109
        manufacturability and, 116
        for manufacture and assembly,
            92–96
        process selection and, 140–67
    development, 83–89, 117
        marketing and, 149–51
        measuring, 109–110
        phases of, 85–87
        time-to-market, 19, 38, 110
    features, 135
    layout, 376, 383–92
    quality, 25, 135
    time-to-market, 19, 38, 110
    variety, 134–135

Product-process matrix, 99-100
Product structure tree, 626, 628
Production
    activity control, 692-96
    aggregate planning; *see* Aggregate
        planning
    formats, facilities layout, 376-77
    goods vs. services, 8
    management; *see* Operations management
        (OM)
    multiproduct, 570
    planning; *see* Aggregate planning
    rate, 555
    scheduling; *see* Schedules/Scheduling
    smoothing, 568
    synchronized; *see* Synchronized
        production
Production line approach, 157-58
Production planning strategies, 557
Production process, job design, 419-22
Production systems, 7
Productivity, 414, 793
    Japanese approach to, 325-333
    measurement of, 39-40, 110
    MIT Commission on, 36
    service quality and, 13, 18
Profit sharing, 436, 438
Profitability, purchasing and, 475
Progress curves, 446
Project management, 46-79
    control aspects, 50-52
    CPM (critical path method), 13, 54-69
        criticisms, 66-69
        early start schedule, 58-59
        late start schedule, 59
        single time estimate, 56-59
        three activity time estimates, 59-63
        time-cost models, 63-66
    defined, 48-49
    functional projects, 52, 53
    Gantt charts, 50, 51, 56, 66
    information systems, 67
    matrix projects, 52, 54
    milestone charts, 51, 52
    ongoing schedule maintenance, 63
    organizational structures, 52-54
    PERT (program evaluation and review
        technique), 13, 54-56, 63, 66-69
    progress tracking, 66
    pure projects, 52, 53
    reporting mechanisms, 50-52
    resource management, 66
    techniques, 759
    time-cost models, 63-66
    time-oriented techniques, 55-63
    work breakdown structure (WBDS),
        49-50
Project management information systems
    (PMIS), 67

Promotion, 556
Purchasing, 472-82
    brokers, 486
    cost control and, 472
    distributors, 486
    economic order size, 584
    efficient consumer response (ECR),
        488-89
    electronic information flow, 486-89
    firm as supplier, 474-76
    global sourcing, 482-86
        international distribution, 484-85
        international marketplace, 483-84
    international distribution and,
        multiple vs. few, 480-81
        strategic, 108-109
    just-in-time (JIT), 479-82
    manufacturer's representatives, 486
    organization, 473-74
    partnership relationships, 476
    profitability and, 475
    quick response (QR), 488
    role of, in outsourcing, 470-71
    suppliers; *see also* Suppliers
    trading companies, 486
Pure projects, 52, 53
Pure strategy, 558

Q

Qualitative analysis, 500, 501, 503-504
Quality; *see also* Total quality management
    conformance, 208
    design, 207
    cost of (COQ), 134, 209-11
    dimensions of, 208
    as operations strategy, 25
    service, and productivity, 13, 18
    at the source, 208, 326-27, 414
Quality certification; *see* ISO 9000 standards
Quality circles, 333, 340
Quality control, statistical; *see* Statistical
    quality control
Quality functions deployment (QFD), 90-92,
    201
Quality Parts Company, 347-48
Quality specifications, 207-209
Queues, 169; *see also* Waiting line
    management
Queuing phenomenon, 170-79
Queuing theory, 758
Quick response (QR) programs, 488

R

R/3 MRP software; *see* SAP R/3 software
Rand Corporation, 504
Random numbers, 718-19, 722-23
    tables of, 853-54

Random variations in forecasting, 500
Range charts, 241-45
Ranging, 304-305
Rapid implementation, 676
Rath and Strong Consulting, 161
Ratio delay, 430
Rationalization stage, multisite service
    growth, 282-83
Raw materials, 582
Recycling, 121
    automobile, 123
Reengineering; *see* Business process
    reengineering
Regression analysis, 501, 505, 758
    linear, 516-20
    multiple, 528
Regression model, 363
Reorder points, 588-90, 595-96,
    598-99
Repair parts, 634
Replacement example, financial analysis,
    850-51
Resource management, 66
Responsibility charts, 759
Results evaluation, simulation, 719-20
Retail service facility layout, 397-400
Return on investment, 792
Rinaldi Co., 372
Risk
    environmental or market, 136-37
    expected value and, 834
    operational, 136
    organizational, 136
    political, 354
    technology and, 135-37
Ritz-Carlton, 158-60
Robot Company, The, 183-84
Robots, industrial, 124-26
Ropes, synchronized production,
    802-803
Rothfos Corp., 114
Rough-cut capacity planning, 553
Rubbermaid, 83-84
Run charts, 214, 756
Run length simulation, 719
Russia, 370
Ryder Systems, Inc., 323, 487

S

Safety stock, 560, 591-99, 802-803
Sales, lost, 570
Sales support, 10
Salvage value, 604
Sampling
    acceptance, 236-40
    work, 430-35
SAP AG, 654, 669

SAP R/3 software, 132, 654-56, 668-77
  functional components of, 672-75
    financial accounting, 673
    human resources, 673-74
    manufacturing and logistics, 674
    sales and distribution, 674-75
  history of, 670-72
  implementation of, 676
Saturn Corporation, 323
Sawtooth model, 588-89
Scanlon bonus plan, 436-37
Scatter diagrams, 214, 756
Schedules/Scheduling, 678-712
  assignment method, 689-691
  backward, 681
  case studies, 708-12
  complex, 691
  consecutive days off, 698-99
  daily work times, 700-701
  data integrity, 695-96
  early start, 58-59
  evaluation of, 684
  forward, 681
  Gantt charts, 693
  hourly work times, 701-702
  improving, 697
  input/output control, 693-94
  JOB system, 692
  late start, 59
  Manufacturing Management II, 696
  master production (MPS), 553, 629-30,
      639-40
    flexibility, 584
  minimum-cost, 63-66
  of personnel, 698-700
  priority rules, 684-92
  production activity control, 692-96
  schedule evaluation, 684
  sequencing, 684
  in services, 698-700
  shop-floor control, 692-96
  stable, 338-39
  tools, 693
  work centers, 680-84
    functions of, 682-83
    objectives of, 683
Schematic (product), 626
Schlumberger, 698-99
Schneider National, Inc., 487
Scientific management, 13-14
Search decision rules, 571
Seasonal elements in forecasting, 501,
    521-25
Secret of Saving Lost Motion, The (Taylor),
    14
Self-service approach, 158
Sensitivity analysis, 305
Sequencing, job shop, 684
Servers (computers), 132

Service(s), 10, 140-63
  aggregate production planning, 564-68
  blueprinting, 154-56
  businesses defined, 143
  capacity planning/analysis, 146-47,
      280-84
  classification of, operational, 144-46
  customers, 143-45
  delivery of, 156-61
  facility location, 279-80, 361-67
  fail-safing, 154-56
  flowcharts and, 154-55
  focus on, 147-48
  growth matrix, 282
  guarantees, 161-62
  internal, 143
  inventory control in, 611-12
  JIT production for, 340-44
  Kinko's copier example, 164-66
  levels (inventory), 592-99
  location, of facilities, 279-80, 361-67
  management, 143-44, 150
  marketing, operations and, 149-51
  multisite growth stages, 281-84
  nature of, 142-44
  operating focus, 147-48
  operations strategy, 33-36
  organization design, 146-51
  performance dimensions, 33, 34
  personal attention delivery approach,
      158-61
  poka-yokes, 155-56
  product design/process selection, 140-67
  production line delivery approach,
      157-58
  productivity and, 13, 18
  quality programs, 280-81
  retail, facility layout, 397-400
  scheduling, 698-700
  sector, growth in the U.S., 35-36
  self-service delivery approach, 158
  Strategic Service Vision, 147
  strategy, 147-51
  system, characteristics of, 162
  technologies in, 129-32, 342
  Three T's and, 156
  time dependence of, 279
  value-added, 10
Service package, 143
Service-system design matrix, 151-53
Servicescapes, 397
Setup cost, 335-36, 584, 805
Setup time, 332, 799
7-Eleven, 136-37
Shadow prices, 305
Shift splitting, 702
Shingo system, 216-17
Shiskin time series forecasting, 501
Shop-floor control, 692-96

Short range planning, 265, 552
Short-term debt, 840
Shortage costs, 584-85
Shouldice Hospital Corp., 288-90
Showtime Networks, 782-84
Signs/Symbols, retail facility layout, 399-400
Silo effect, 19
Simple moving average, 501, 505-507
Simple proportion forecasting, 521-22
Simplex method; *see* Linear programming (LP)
Simulation, 189-90, 500, 501, 713-40
  advantages, 730
  assembly line, two-stage, 721-25
  business process reengineering (BPR),
      776
  computer, 757-58
    modeling aspects, 720
  decision rules, 716
  definition of, 715
  disadvantages of, 730
  example of, 717-18, 721-25, 728-29
  hospital overcrowding example of,
      728-29
  languages, 726-29
  methodology, 715-21
  model construction, 716-18
  new experiments based on, 720
  operating room efficiency, 714
  output reports, 720-21
  probability distributions, 716
  problem definition, 716
  programs, 726-29
  random numbers in, 718-19, 722-23,
      853-54
  results evaluation, 719-20
  run length, 719
  software features, 728-29
  spreadsheets, 725-26
  starting conditions, 718-19
  time-incrementing procedure, 718
  two-stage assembly line, 721-25
  validation, 719-20
  variable and parameters, 716, 718-19
  waiting line example of, 721-25
Single-period inventory model, 603-605
Single time estimate CPM, 56-59
Six-sigma limits in process control, 245-47
Six-step solution, simplex LP method,
    297-303
Skill variety, 417
Skunk works; *see* Pure projects
Slack variables, 297-98
Small-group financial incentive plans, 436
Smoothing constants
  alpha (α), 509-512
  delta (δ), 510-11
Sociotechnical systems of job design, 417-18
Software; *see also* Computer applications
  technologies, 124, 128-29

Solver, 305, 571
Sorenson Research Company, 471
Sourcing; *see* Purchasing
Soviet Union, 370
Spatial layout and functionality, 398-99
Specialization of labor, 416-17
Specifications limits, 245
Speed of delivery, 25-27
Spreadsheets, 130, 848
    linear programming (LP), 305-307
    simulation, 725-26
Stable workforce planning strategy, 557
Stakeholder analysis, 758
Standard deviation
    inventory models and, 593-601
    in process control, 242-45
Standard distributions
    in forecasting, 503
    simulation example of, 717-718
    tables, 855-57
Standard time, 427-28
Standardized Industrial Code Classification
    (SIC), 268-69
Standards, ISO 9000; *see* ISO 900 standards
Starting conditions, simulation, 718-19
Statement of work (SOW), 48
Statistical process control (SPC), 201, 207,
    211, 213, 214, 217, 231, 236
    tools, 756
Statistical quality control (SQC), 201, 212,
    235-54
    acceptance sampling, 236-40
    costs to justify inspection, 237-38
    lot size effects, 240
    operating characteristic (OC) curves,
        238-39
    process control; *see* Process control
Statistical tools, 758
Status reports, 693
Status segments (MRP), 636
Stepping stone evaluation method, 312-14
Stewart Co., 274-75
Stockkeeping units (SKU), 611
Stocks, 841
Storage in process analysis, 105-108
Straight-line depreciation, 835
Strategic capacity planning; *see* Capacity
    planning
Strategic partnership, 476
Strategic suppliers, 108-109
Strategy, operations; *see* Operations strategy
Subcontracting, 558, 570
Subtasks (project subdivision), 48
Sum-of-the-year's digits (SYD) depreciation, 835
Superservers (computers), 132
Suppliers
    electronic information flow, 486-89
    firm as, 474-75
    in JIT production, 339-340, 344-45

Supplies—*Cont.*
    multiple vs. few, 480-81
    plant location and, 354
    selection of, 476-78
Supplies, 582
Supply-chain management, 13, 19, 463-95
    cases, 492-94
    defined, 466
    make or buy decision, 466-69
    outsourcing, 466, 469-71
    purchasing; *see* Purchasing
    value density, 471-72
SWOT analysis, 754
Synchronized production, 786-829
    accounting and, 813-14
    batch sizes, 804-807
    bottlenecks, 796, 799-804
    building blocks, 797, 798
    capacity, unbalanced, 793-96
    capacity constrained resources (CCR),
        797, 801-803
    cash flow, 792
    control methods, 798-807
    dependent events, 794
    dollar days inventory, 807
    drums, 801-803
    examples, 815-22
    financial measurements, 792
    functional area coordination and, 813-22
    goal of the firm, 791
    hockey-stick phenomenon, 790-91
    inventory, 792, 807
    JIT and, 808-809
    marketing and, 814
    MRP and, 808-809
    net profit, 792
    nonbottlenecks, 796-97, 800-801
    operating expenses, 792-94
    operational measurements, 792-93
    performance measurements, 791-93
    productivity, 793
    quality, 803-804
    resources, constrained, 797, 801-803
    return on investment, 792
    ropes, 802-803
    statistical fluctuations, 794-96
    throughput, 792, 794
    time buffers, 802-803
    time components, 799
    unbalanced capacity, 793-96
    VAT classification of firms, 808-13
Systematic layout planning (SLP), 381-83
Systems Modeling Corporation, 727

T

"T" plants, 812-13
Taco Bell, 397
Taguchi methods, 248-51

Target markets, 30, 147
Task(s), 48, 417-418
    in process analysis, 105-108
    splitting, 387-88
Task autonomy, 418
Task identity, 418
Task variety, 417
Taxes, 838-839
Teams, 83, 88, 91
Technology(ies)
    automated systems; *see* Automated
        systems
    benefits, 133-35
    computer applications; *see* Computer
        applications
    cost reductions and, 133-34
    decision support systems, 132, 138
    electronic data interchange (EDI), 131
    evaluation, business process
        reengineering (BPR), 771-72
    expert systems, 132
    flexible manufacturing systems (FMS),
        126, 127, 138
    group (GT); *see* Group technology (GT)
    hardware, 124-28
    image processing systems, 130-31
    industrial robots, 124-26
    information, 121
    investment evaluation, 132-37
    machining centers, 124, 125, 128
    manufacturing, 123-29
    materials, 121
    networked computer systems, 132
    numerically controlled (NC) machines,
        124
    office automation, 129-30
    operations, 119-39
    risk and, 135-37
    in services, 129-32, 342
    software, 124, 128-29
Tektronix, 9
Temporary employment, 415, 561
Testing processes, 97
Texas Instruments, 482
Therbligs, 422
Thomas Manufacturing Co., 492-93
Three T's, services and, 156
Throughput, 792, 794
Time per unit, 446
Time buckets (MRP), 636
Time buffers, 802-803
Time components, synchronized production,
    799
Time-cost models, 63-66
Time dependence of services, 279
Time fences, 630
Time-incrementing, simulation, 718
Time measurement units (TMUs), 429
Time-oriented project management, 55-63

Time series analysis; *see* Forecasting (demand)
Time standards, 431, 434
Time studies; *see* Work measurement and standards
Time-to-market, 19, 38, 110
Tolerance limits, 245
Toshiba, 19
Total factor productivity measure, 39
Total factory automation, 129
Total quality control (TQC), 13, 17
    JIT production and, 338
Total quality management (TQM), 4, 13, 17, 18, 20, 31, 198-233, 344, 414-15; *see also* Quality
    business process reengineering (BPR), 777
    case studies, 229-33
    consulting in, 749
    continuous improvement (CI), 212-16
    cost of quality (COQ), 209-11
    Deming wheel, 213, 214
    elements, 201
    5W2H method, 213, 215
    house of quality matrix, 91-92
    ISO 9000 standards, 217-25
    Malcolm Baldrige National Quality Award;
        see Malcolm Baldrige National Quality Award
    PDCA (plan-do-act) cycle, 213-14
    quality function deployment (QFD), 90-92
    quality specifications, 207-209
    Shingo system, 216-17
    specifications and costs of quality, 207-12
    tools, 211-12
    value analysis/value engineering (VA/VE), 92
Toyota, 13, 20, 96, 346, 351, 391, 568
Toys "R" Us, 355
Tracking signals, 514-16
Trading blocs, 354, 356
Trading companies, 486
Trane Co., 820-21
Transfer batch, 805-807
Transformation processes, 7
Transportation costs, 134
Transportation method; *see* Linear programming
Trend effects in forecasting, 500-503, 520
Tucson Parks and Recreation Department, 564-68
Two-bin inventory system, 606

U

Unbalanced capacity, 793-96
Uniform plant loading, 328-29
Union Carbide, 768

Unions, 14
United Auto Workers Union, 470
United Parcel Service (UPS), 425, 426
Universal product code (UPC), 488
UniWare, 787
U.S. competitiveness, 36-38
Usage in fixed-order quantity inventory model, 590-91
USSR (former), 370
Utilization, 645
Utilization rate, capacity, 267-68

V

"V" plants, 809-810
Validation, simulation, 719-20
Value-added services, 10
Value-adding work, 772
Value analysis/value engineering (VA/VE), 92
Value chain, 754, 755
Value density, 471-72
Variability in process control, 248-51
Variable measurements in process control, 241-45
Variable work hours planning strategy, 557
Variables, simulation, 716, 718-19
VAT classification, 808-813
Vendor(s); *see* Suppliers
Virtual factories, 100
Vision statements, 770
Vogel's approximation allocation method (VAM), 310-11
Volkswagen, 465, 466
Volume considerations in process flow, 99-100
Volvo, 100, 443-44

W

Waiting line management, 168-97
    computer simulation, 189-90, 721-25
    customer(s)
        arrivals, 170-75
            distribution, 172-74
            model, 180-89
            patterns, 174
            rates, 172-74
        in line, 180, 182-183
    economics, 169-70
    equipment selection, 183-84
    finite population, 172, 187-89
    formula review, 190-91
    infinite population, 172
    models, 180-89
    queuing systems, 175-79
        line structures, 177-78
        mixed, 179
        multichannel, 178-79
        number of lines, 176

Waiting line management—*Cont.*
    queuing systems—*Cont.*
        queue discipline, 176-77
        queue length, 175-76
        service rate, 177
        service time distribution, 177
        single channel, 178
        waiting lines, 175
    servers, number of, 184-87
    simulation, 189-90, 721-25
    suggestions for, 171
Wal-Mart, 489, 497-98, 533, 608, 609
Warner-Lambert Company, 534-35
Waste
    elimination of, in production, 325-332
    reengineering, 772
Weighted average cost of capital, 841-42
Weighted moving average, 501, 507-508
Western National Bank, 180, 182-83
Whirlpool Corporation, 438
Winters' exponential smoothing, 505
Work, job design; *see* Job, design of
Work breakdown structure (WBDS), 49-50
Work centers, 680-84
Work factor measurement systems, 429
Work hours, production planning,
Work in process, 582
Work measurement and standards, 424-35
    case studies, 443-44
    elemental standard-time data, 428
    financial incentive plans, 435-39
    learning curves; *see* Learning curves
    methods time measurement (MTM), 429
    most work measurement systems (MOST), 429
    normal time, 426-28
    performance ratings, 426-427
    predetermined motion-time data systems (PMTS), 428-30
    reasons for, 424-25
    standard time, 427-28
    techniques, 425-35
    time measurement units (TMUs), 429
    time standards, 431, 434
    time study, 425-28
    work sampling compared, 434-35
    work factor measurement systems, 429
    work sampling, 430-35
        error in, 431, 432
        nursing application, 431, 433-34
        steps, 431
        time standards from, 434
        time study compared, 434-35
Work methods, 418-24
Work package, 48
Work physiology, 418
Work sampling, 430-35, 755-56
Workers; *see* Employee(s)

World-class manufacturers, 28
World Wide Web, 13, 18, 121
Wrought Washer Manufacturing Company,
    438

X

Xerox, 126, 270, 481

Y

Yoplait, 141

Z

Zero-changeover time, 271
Zero defects, 208